The CRB Commodity Yearbook 2015

Commodity Research Bureau

www.crbyearbook.com

For general information on our other products and services or for technical support, please contact our Customer Support Department within the United States at (800) 621-5271, outside the United States at (312) 554-8456 or fax (312) 939-4135.

ISBN 978-0-910418-93-5

Printed in the United States of America

10   9   8   7   6   5   4   3   2   1

Commodity Research Bureau
209 W. Jackson Blvd, 2nd Floor
Chicago, Illinois 60606
800.621.5271 or +1.312.554.8456
Fax: +1.312.939.4135
Website: www.crbyearbook.com
Email: info@crbyearbook.com

Table of Contents

The Commodity Price Trend

The Continuous Commodity Index (CCI) showed a small recovery rally in early 2014 but then plunged during the remainder of the year to post a new 5-year low and close -11.9% lower for 2014. The CCI index has now plunged by a total of -39% from the record high posted in April 2011, giving back more of the 278% rally seen during the 2001-11 bull market, which was the largest rally in post-war history. The CCI index moved lower in 2014 due to (1) weak commodity demand tied to the soft global economy, (2) the sharp rally in the dollar index seen in late 2014, (3) the general disinflationary trend seen in the developed world, and (4) the Federal Reserve's move in October 2014 to end its third quantitative easing program.

Four of the six CCI futures sub-sectors closed lower in 2014 while two sectors closed higher. The ranked returns in 2014 were as follows: Softs +12.3%, Meats +8.3%, Grains -10.3%, Metals -11.0%, Industrials -22.8%, and Energy -41.5%. These sub-sector changes are calculated by taking the average of the percentage changes of the constituents in each sub-sector.

Energy

The CCI Energy sub-sector, which is composed of Crude Oil, Heating Oil, and Natural Gas, accounts for 18% of the overall CCI Index. The constituents in the Energy sub-sector in 2014 closed down -41.5%, breaking the string of five consecutive annual gains. On a nearest-futures basis, crude oil in 2014 closed down -45.9%, gasoline closed down -48.5%, heating oil closed down -40.0%, and natural gas closed down -31.7%. Crude oil prices plunged in 2014 after Saudi Arabia refused to cut production to battle the world's oil oversupply and instead said that it would protect its market share regardless of how far oil prices might fall. Natural gas prices during 2014 closed sharply lower on adequate supplies.

Grains

The CCI Grains and Oilseeds sub-sector, which is composed of Corn, Soybeans, and Wheat, accounts for 18% of the overall CCI Index. The constituents in the Grains and Oilseeds sub-sector closed down -10.3% in 2014, adding to the -23.1% sell-off seen in 2013. On a nearest-futures basis, corn in 2014 fell -5.9%, soybeans fell -22.3%, and wheat fell -2.6%. Corn, soybeans and wheat prices were weak again in 2014 with another year of bumper crops and sharply higher ending stocks for corn and soybeans.

Industrials

The CCI Industrials sub-sector, which is composed of Copper and Cotton, accounts for 12% of the overall Index. The constituents in the Industrials sub-sector showed a -22.8% decline in 2014. Cotton in 2014 closed down -28.8% in 2014 after the moderate recovery rally of +12.6% seen in 2013. Copper fell by -17.8% in 2014 due to the strong dollar and weak demand tied to slow global economic growth and especially to slower growth in China.

Livestock

The CCI Livestock sub-sector, which is composed of Live Cattle and Lean Hogs, accounts for 12% of the CCI Index. The constituents in the Livestock sub-sector closed up +8.3% in 2014, which was the sixth consecutive annual gain. On a nearest-futures basis, live cattle in 2014 closed up +21.5% on tight supply conditions, but hog prices fell -4.9%.

Precious Metals

The CCI Precious Metals sub-sector, which is composed of Gold, Platinum, and Silver, accounts for 17% of the overall Index. The constituents in the Precious Metals sub-sector closed down -11.0% in 2014, adding to the sharp -25.0% sell-off seen in 2013. Gold fell -1.5%, silver fell -19.5%, and platinum fell -11.8%. Precious metals prices showed continued weakness in 2014 due to the sharp rally in the dollar, weak global economic growth, and world disinflation.

Softs

The CCI Softs sub-sector, which is composed of Cocoa, Coffee, Orange Juice, and Sugar #11, accounts for 23% of the CCI Index. The constituents in the Softs sub-sector in 2014 closed up +12.3% following its unchanged performance in 2013. Softs markets closing higher included: coffee +50.5%, cocoa +7.4%, and orange juice +2.6%. Sugar, however, closed 2014 down -11.5%.

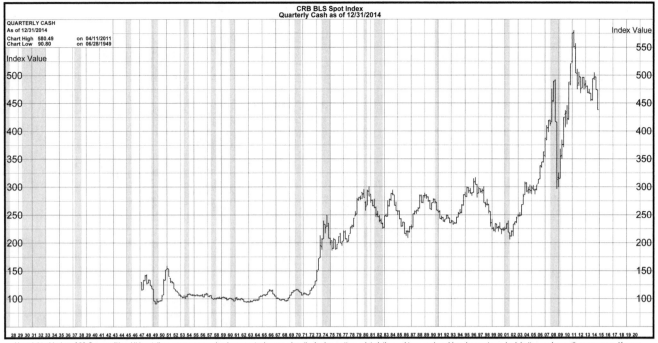

CRB BLS Spot Index
Quarterly Cash as of 12/31/2014

QUARTERLY CASH
As of 12/31/2014

Chart High 580.49   on 04/11/2011
Chart Low   90.80   on 06/28/1949

Unweighted Index of 23 Commodities: Hides, tallow, copper scrap, lead scrap, steel scrap, zinc, tin, burlap, cotton, print cloth, wool tops, rosin, rubber, hogs, steers, lard, butter, soybean oil, cocoa, corn, Kansas City wheat, Minneapolis wheat, and sugar.   Shaded areas indicate US recessions.

CRB BLS Spot Index
Weekly Cash as of 01/02/2015

WEEKLY CASH
As of 01/02/2015

Chart High 580.49   on 04/11/2011
Chart Low   286.50   on 08/15/2005

Unweighted Index of 23 Commodities.   Shaded areas indicate US recessions.

CRB Spot Sub-Index   (1967=100)

Year	Jan.	Feb.	Mar.	Apr.	May	June	July	Aug.	Sept.	Oct.	Nov.	Dec.	Average
2005	291.19	290.08	298.13	299.24	297.73	298.26	292.80	290.63	293.94	297.75	297.48	301.05	295.69
2006	308.31	311.58	310.86	319.47	330.81	332.19	337.82	341.11	341.85	347.18	354.58	359.35	332.93
2007	358.84	366.47	381.36	388.90	396.79	405.08	410.71	405.97	410.96	414.11	412.79	413.88	397.16
2008	424.32	449.73	464.01	470.41	476.34	475.87	478.60	456.61	428.42	367.61	318.88	303.90	426.23
2009	320.03	312.26	305.91	326.11	347.44	359.84	358.67	374.28	378.72	381.73	403.44	416.74	357.10
2010	428.27	417.21	433.51	441.48	431.40	420.89	425.03	449.12	473.29	489.05	491.25	507.30	450.65
2011	538.09	562.60	566.40	575.61	559.14	557.32	553.30	543.59	527.83	506.85	496.08	480.93	538.98
2012	488.60	498.90	501.77	490.93	480.92	474.62	480.69	488.41	493.34	486.07	477.98	484.25	487.21
2013	485.62	481.97	481.13	477.55	474.67	474.05	469.75	471.23	470.60	462.25	458.57	459.56	472.25
2014	457.25	465.09	487.18	497.58	500.90	495.60	491.20	484.78	479.78	465.82	455.62	445.75	477.21

Average.   *Source: Commodity Research Bureau*

CRB INDICIES

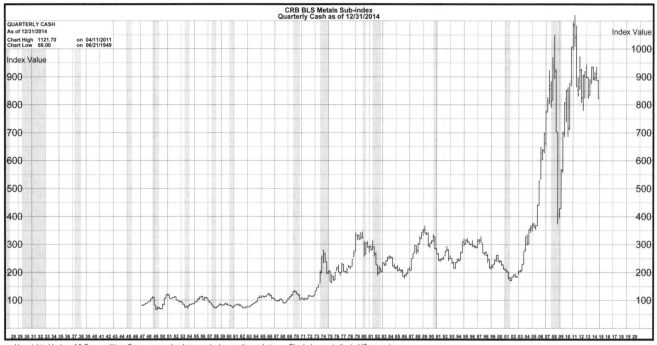

Unweighted Index of 5 Commodities: Copper scrap, lead scrap, steel scrap, tin, and zinc. Shaded areas indicate US recessions.

Unweighted Index of 5 Commodities. Shaded areas indicate US recessions.

CRB Spot Metals Sub-Index   (1967=100)

Year	Jan.	Feb.	Mar.	Apr.	May	June	July	Aug.	Sept.	Oct.	Nov.	Dec.	Average
2005	355.95	364.50	371.99	371.31	365.83	369.32	361.39	363.75	364.70	369.68	370.47	425.84	371.23
2006	458.64	485.21	504.91	571.37	623.28	616.35	621.31	617.86	623.05	660.11	681.87	693.51	596.46
2007	668.94	691.71	761.81	798.96	798.65	803.29	834.00	840.13	835.06	868.19	828.50	812.12	795.11
2008	843.66	883.22	947.21	1,011.63	1,006.52	914.50	901.61	837.56	728.05	545.95	404.38	400.04	785.36
2009	409.17	416.80	421.44	455.21	410.21	552.61	591.59	651.17	688.67	704.55	716.43	767.81	565.47
2010	830.98	773.24	833.04	850.73	765.47	717.04	728.15	804.22	853.40	896.08	905.01	971.85	827.43
2011	1,029.49	1,085.28	1,066.15	1,096.80	1,033.85	1,023.86	1,063.60	994.80	942.14	874.77	868.19	849.37	994.03
2012	903.04	949.99	931.85	908.47	878.62	843.33	800.76	828.46	883.07	862.76	859.31	910.40	880.01
2013	929.61	930.76	908.99	870.31	850.59	841.39	838.54	875.10	881.56	883.73	891.08	919.04	885.06
2014	925.99	920.45	900.88	905.67	908.51	897.46	921.84	922.59	903.65	876.01	856.97	836.99	898.08

Average.   *Source: Commodity Research Bureau*

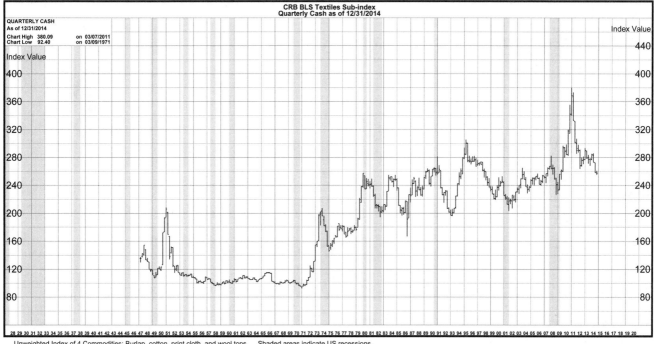

CRB BLS Textiles Sub-index
Quarterly Cash as of 12/31/2014

QUARTERLY CASH
As of 12/31/2014

Chart High 380.09 on 03/07/2011
Chart Low 92.40 on 03/09/1971

Unweighted Index of 4 Commodities: Burlap, cotton, print cloth, and wool tops.   Shaded areas indicate US recessions.

CRB BLS Textiles Sub-index
Weekly Cash as of 01/02/2015

WEEKLY CASH
As of 01/02/2015

Chart High 380.09 on 03/07/2011
Chart Low 226.60 on 11/12/2008

Unweighted Index of 4 Commodities.   Shaded areas indicate US recessions.

CRB Spot Textiles Sub-Index   (1967=100)

Year	Jan.	Feb.	Mar.	Apr.	May	June	July	Aug.	Sept.	Oct.	Nov.	Dec.	Average
2005	239.93	240.36	247.12	247.73	246.60	244.69	247.21	243.08	246.64	251.24	248.96	250.83	246.20
2006	255.02	255.52	251.74	248.26	244.26	244.16	242.03	243.89	245.78	244.89	246.37	251.15	247.76
2007	252.50	251.35	251.91	248.99	245.40	250.72	260.09	256.51	261.58	264.79	265.79	265.28	256.24
2008	267.18	269.60	271.76	267.02	264.71	262.29	263.92	261.98	255.47	241.15	231.28	235.84	257.68
2009	241.13	237.01	229.83	240.05	252.00	253.03	258.94	253.52	257.42	265.67	280.85	293.96	255.28
2010	290.62	287.34	291.16	294.69	292.22	290.03	284.28	295.19	310.18	329.04	341.31	344.99	304.25
2011	347.26	365.82	372.19	365.44	352.18	344.70	319.66	310.92	310.19	303.37	299.19	289.50	331.70
2012	294.47	293.94	289.55	288.47	276.62	269.11	268.88	274.55	277.06	276.65	272.43	276.20	279.83
2013	279.44	283.14	289.79	286.96	286.20	283.33	278.59	278.23	275.03	274.73	269.70	275.78	280.08
2014	278.29	278.84	283.25	283.66	283.35	277.98	268.12	262.53	262.02	259.07	257.53	258.34	271.08

Average.   *Source: Commodity Research Bureau*

CRB INDICIES

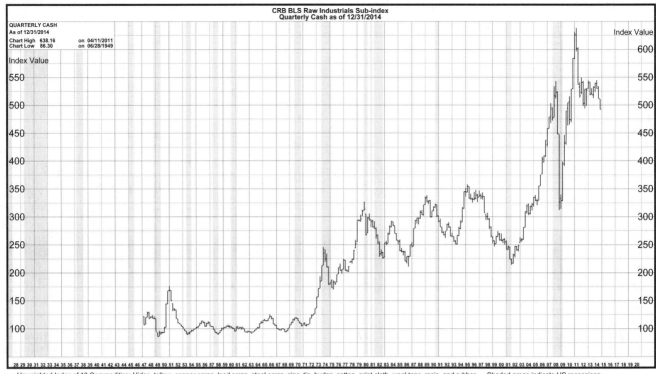

CRB BLS Raw Industrials Sub-index
Quarterly Cash as of 12/31/2014

QUARTERLY CASH
As of 12/31/2014

Chart High 638.16   on 04/11/2011
Chart Low   86.30   on 06/28/1949

Unweighted Index of 13 Commodities: Hides, tallow, copper scrap, lead scrap, steel scrap, zinc, tin, burlap, cotton, print cloth, wool tops, rosin, and rubber.   Shaded areas indicate US recessions.

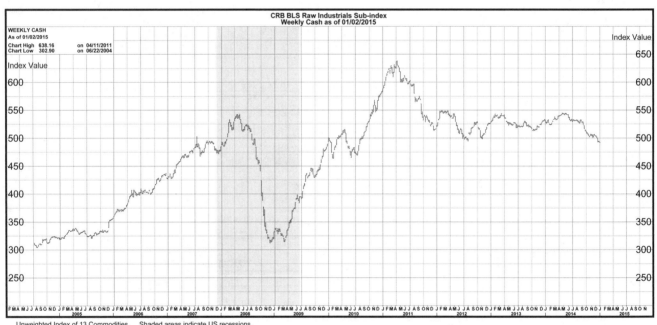

CRB BLS Raw Industrials Sub-index
Weekly Cash as of 01/02/2015

WEEKLY CASH
As of 01/02/2015

Chart High 638.16   on 04/11/2011
Chart Low   302.90   on 06/22/2004

Unweighted Index of 13 Commodities.   Shaded areas indicate US recessions.

CRB Spot Raw Industrials Sub-Index   (1967=100)

Year	Jan.	Feb.	Mar.	Apr.	May	June	July	Aug.	Sept.	Oct.	Nov.	Dec.	Average
2005	320.94	324.57	333.31	336.68	331.99	331.88	325.29	324.52	329.36	332.79	332.83	349.53	331.14
2006	363.05	371.00	372.08	385.69	400.62	399.97	403.50	403.90	403.19	415.76	426.67	434.25	398.31
2007	430.87	434.54	452.81	465.37	468.44	475.75	485.36	478.47	483.09	492.43	486.68	475.95	469.15
2008	487.92	502.29	522.98	534.29	532.30	517.02	517.29	495.17	460.96	392.49	329.86	317.83	467.53
2009	335.09	331.50	321.35	343.49	370.17	391.18	403.99	431.59	439.72	435.97	455.27	480.02	394.95
2010	492.93	476.13	499.63	510.22	489.56	476.07	474.97	498.86	518.04	539.43	555.01	574.70	508.80
2011	595.51	619.22	621.89	628.72	606.29	602.99	596.81	573.01	559.74	536.77	528.95	519.49	582.45
2012	531.91	546.88	544.73	538.46	526.82	510.28	500.22	510.14	524.29	515.30	506.62	523.72	523.28
2013	534.06	538.69	539.87	532.46	524.75	523.74	520.86	525.30	521.20	514.92	519.98	529.58	527.12
2014	528.48	527.92	535.44	541.50	542.77	534.33	532.02	529.81	520.65	506.18	504.60	497.80	525.13

Average.   *Source: Commodity Research Bureau*

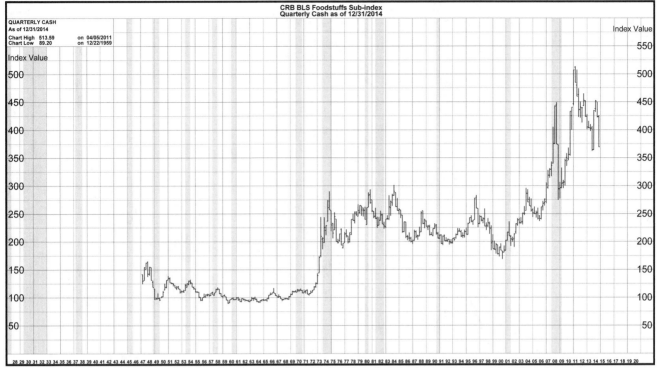

Unweighted Index of 10 Commodities: Hogs, steers, lard, butter, soybean oil, cocoa, corn, Kansas City wheat, Minneapolis wheat, and sugar.   Shaded areas indicate US recessions.

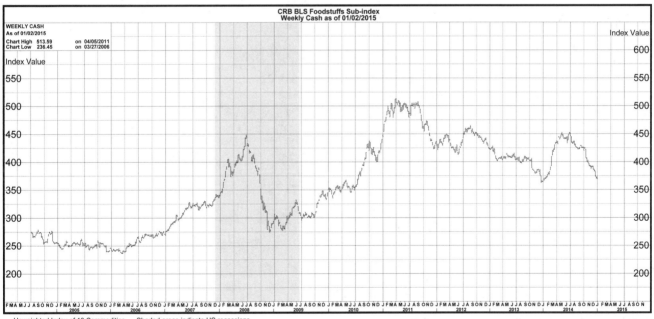

Unweighted Index of 10 Commodities.   Shaded areas indicate US recessions.

CRB Spot Foodstuffs Sub-Index   (1967=100)

Year	Jan.	Feb.	Mar.	Apr.	May	June	July	Aug.	Sept.	Oct.	Nov.	Dec.	Average
2005	252.84	246.44	253.58	252.19	254.21	255.43	251.31	247.65	249.22	253.37	252.74	242.54	250.96
2006	243.31	241.95	239.60	243.17	250.70	253.86	261.17	267.04	269.14	267.52	271.19	273.16	256.82
2007	275.31	286.30	297.37	299.85	311.98	320.79	322.44	319.95	325.01	322.19	325.40	337.97	312.05
2008	346.56	383.11	390.10	391.07	405.44	421.87	427.47	405.89	385.15	334.27	303.48	284.65	373.26
2009	299.83	286.21	284.71	302.35	316.81	318.81	301.83	304.44	305.01	314.86	338.56	339.54	309.41
2010	349.28	344.48	352.89	357.94	359.11	352.01	361.74	385.62	415.09	424.20	411.58	423.33	378.11
2011	464.45	489.47	494.49	506.33	497.04	497.00	495.67	503.38	484.57	466.21	451.87	429.91	481.70
2012	431.88	436.61	445.29	429.26	421.32	427.19	453.49	458.33	451.49	446.42	439.14	432.15	439.38
2013	422.99	410.14	407.07	407.78	410.33	410.17	404.33	402.51	405.75	395.29	382.14	374.23	402.73
2014	370.69	387.03	424.76	440.01	445.70	444.24	437.38	426.08	426.02	412.87	392.84	379.75	415.61

Average.   *Source: Commodity Research Bureau*

CRB INDICIES

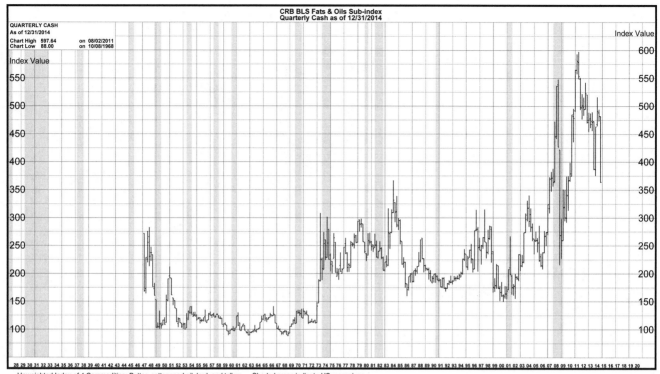

CRB BLS Fats & Oils Sub-index
Quarterly Cash as of 12/31/2014

QUARTERLY CASH
As of 12/31/2014

Chart High 597.64 on 08/02/2011
Chart Low 88.00 on 10/08/1968

Unweighted Index of 4 Commodities: Butter, cottonseed oil, lard, and tallow.   Shaded areas indicate US recessions.

CRB BLS Fats & Oils Sub-index
Weekly Cash as of 01/02/2015

WEEKLY CASH
As of 01/02/2015

Chart High 597.64 on 08/02/2011
Chart Low 208.14 on 04/17/2006

Unweighted Index of 4 Commodities.   Shaded areas indicate US recessions.

CRB Spot Fats and Oils Sub-Index   (1967=100)

Year	Jan.	Feb.	Mar.	Apr.	May	June	July	Aug.	Sept.	Oct.	Nov.	Dec.	Average
2005	248.45	238.13	252.70	263.98	262.93	266.01	245.81	243.51	259.50	268.43	269.77	231.17	254.20
2006	231.10	221.46	217.14	214.75	222.03	221.97	247.09	271.97	267.18	257.29	264.75	270.94	242.31
2007	274.74	274.35	300.01	313.08	339.65	366.31	376.09	357.79	365.74	365.51	381.69	364.06	339.92
2008	381.95	418.92	459.52	457.65	467.23	498.89	526.26	467.08	443.38	366.91	283.76	238.42	417.50
2009	283.42	254.79	243.41	285.09	321.74	335.76	308.54	340.28	324.64	298.33	343.85	344.85	307.06
2010	337.27	329.26	366.69	378.35	381.68	374.59	379.27	399.57	444.83	471.40	463.11	458.65	398.72
2011	536.41	542.91	553.67	561.25	569.84	588.10	587.94	578.55	567.28	536.83	502.49	499.60	552.07
2012	488.60	489.04	512.32	501.11	495.37	490.44	506.48	516.93	532.05	501.87	478.36	474.48	498.92
2013	478.78	463.85	472.83	480.48	466.32	473.86	473.76	463.55	484.31	435.85	427.75	414.70	461.34
2014	383.34	388.71	444.35	482.96	511.46	492.95	483.40	482.99	488.24	444.49	416.67	383.76	450.28

Average.   *Source: Commodity Research Bureau*

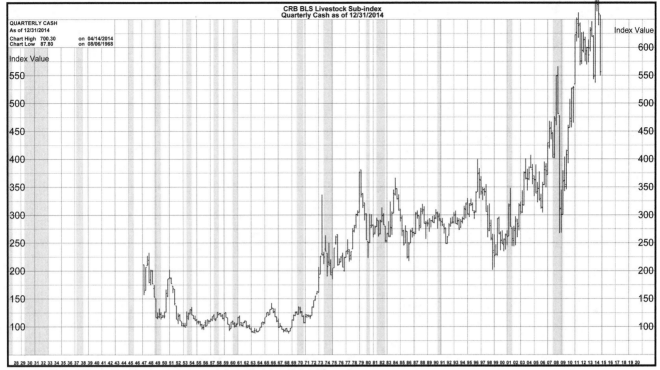

CRB BLS Livestock Sub-index
Quarterly Cash as of 12/31/2014

QUARTERLY CASH
As of 12/31/2014

Chart High 700.30 on 04/14/2014
Chart Low 87.80 on 08/06/1968

Unweighted Index of 5 Commodities: Hides, hogs, lard, steers, and tallow.   Shaded areas indicate US recessions.

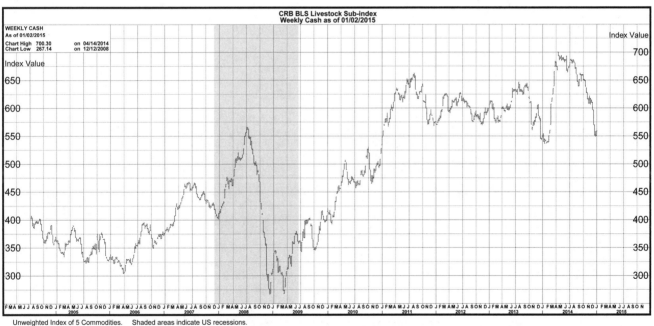

CRB BLS Livestock Sub-index
Weekly Cash as of 01/02/2015

WEEKLY CASH
As of 01/02/2015

Chart High 700.30 on 04/14/2014
Chart Low 267.14 on 12/12/2008

Unweighted Index of 5 Commodities.   Shaded areas indicate US recessions.

CRB Spot Livestock Sub-Index   (1967=100)

Year	Jan.	Feb.	Mar.	Apr.	May	June	July	Aug.	Sept.	Oct.	Nov.	Dec.	Average
2005	359.25	341.74	353.05	373.63	377.41	361.10	330.39	331.75	349.24	358.04	369.98	337.97	353.63
2006	331.93	328.72	320.09	314.72	327.28	340.29	359.18	388.13	384.78	366.35	364.05	372.08	349.80
2007	379.93	388.03	407.19	425.25	449.92	462.39	459.18	445.81	444.91	434.88	425.72	412.45	427.97
2008	417.36	451.42	468.41	483.09	510.01	522.82	556.10	526.98	492.24	426.75	342.41	288.42	457.17
2009	333.60	310.58	288.18	321.58	347.01	368.85	362.91	393.37	389.53	350.90	386.75	403.06	354.69
2010	411.55	408.71	450.01	478.92	488.46	470.53	465.13	475.55	498.82	495.89	485.02	505.23	469.49
2011	561.16	577.76	601.55	629.36	618.46	635.68	646.41	644.21	626.64	618.26	580.65	580.02	610.01
2012	575.19	598.32	620.12	600.69	612.10	619.49	613.35	601.44	582.23	585.33	577.18	594.91	598.36
2013	606.27	584.54	580.26	598.17	601.26	626.31	634.54	630.72	637.72	591.03	583.70	571.43	603.83
2014	543.02	557.63	645.13	685.62	689.00	676.46	683.71	661.15	656.18	639.12	613.66	573.26	635.33

Average.   *Source: Commodity Research Bureau*

CRB INDICIES

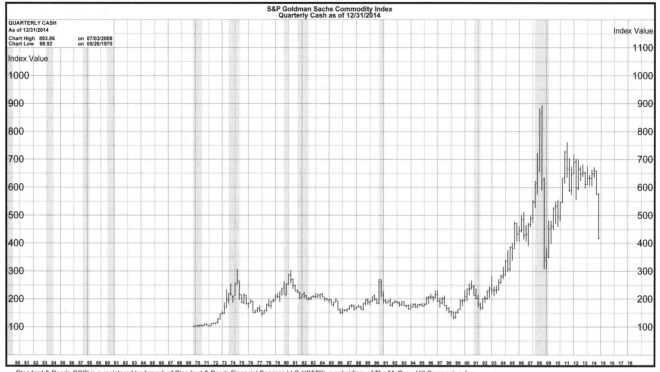

Standard & Poor's GSCI is a registered trademark of Standard & Poor's Financial Services LLC ("S&P"), a subsidiary of The McGraw-Hill Companies, Inc.
Currently the S&P GSCI includes 24 commodity nearby futures contracts.   Shaded areas indicate US recessions.

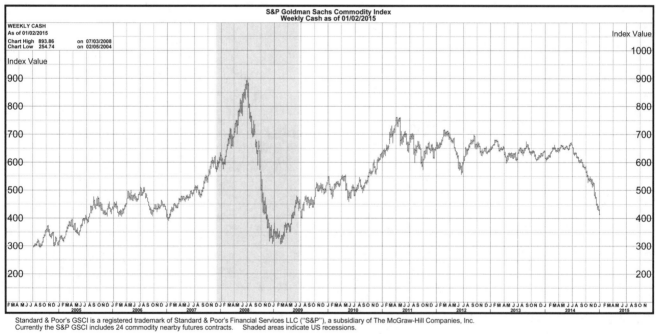

Standard & Poor's GSCI is a registered trademark of Standard & Poor's Financial Services LLC ("S&P"), a subsidiary of The McGraw-Hill Companies, Inc.
Currently the S&P GSCI includes 24 commodity nearby futures contracts.   Shaded areas indicate US recessions.

S&P Goldman Sachs Commodity Index (GSCI)   (12/31/1969=100)

Year	Jan.	Feb.	Mar.	Apr.	May	June	July	Aug.	Sept.	Oct.	Nov.	Dec.	Average
2005	324.47	332.80	374.05	371.68	350.65	382.96	396.64	431.85	455.28	444.90	418.56	435.45	393.27
2006	442.12	422.49	427.47	469.73	477.93	471.65	490.32	485.65	434.56	431.13	442.05	444.62	453.31
2007	406.98	435.26	446.69	469.60	470.72	485.26	504.65	490.16	528.83	559.36	600.37	593.12	499.25
2008	606.71	638.88	689.26	717.94	778.15	832.31	818.90	716.84	644.00	496.05	405.96	338.27	640.27
2009	346.03	327.48	350.86	367.12	410.82	458.22	429.21	466.68	453.77	492.51	509.71	505.07	426.46
2010	520.05	503.83	523.07	543.90	499.87	497.00	503.57	517.41	526.98	561.66	579.86	614.79	532.67
2011	634.64	661.44	707.87	744.48	695.62	679.91	689.47	651.63	638.94	625.65	653.51	642.72	668.82
2012	661.12	685.83	701.92	681.61	637.66	579.93	627.42	661.68	670.25	654.57	639.84	640.09	653.49
2013	658.10	669.41	648.20	624.14	627.04	622.56	639.34	645.98	645.31	633.40	614.88	631.12	638.29
2014	617.20	640.25	645.88	653.19	652.42	657.64	636.14	609.55	588.76	548.78	521.86	449.57	601.77

Average.   *Source: CME Group; Chicago Mercantile Ezchange*

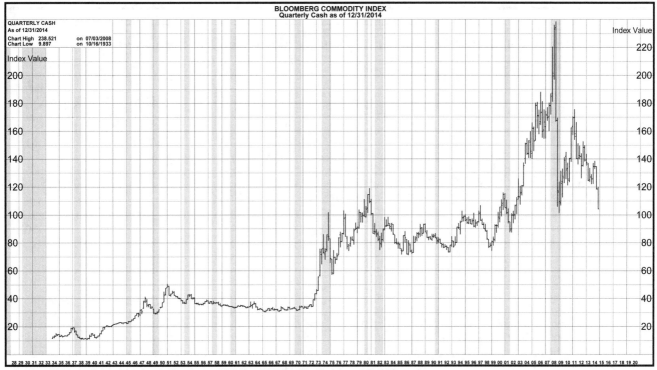

Dow Jones-UBS Commodity Index is a trademark of Dow Jones and UBS AG.   12/31/1990=100   Shaded areas indicate US recessions.

Dow Jones-UBS Commodity Index is a trademark of Dow Jones and UBS AG.   12/31/1990=100   Shaded areas indicate US recessions.

Bloomberg Commodity Index   (12/31/1990=100)

Year	Jan.	Feb.	Mar.	Apr.	May	June	July	Aug.	Sept.	Oct.	Nov.	Dec.	Average
2005	145.78	147.75	160.62	156.52	149.46	155.99	157.72	164.37	171.95	173.78	165.65	173.56	160.26
2006	169.96	165.06	162.42	172.83	179.22	170.50	174.84	173.39	161.59	164.26	169.68	168.39	169.35
2007	160.36	167.86	168.37	172.74	172.50	172.41	171.57	165.81	173.32	177.90	182.03	180.86	172.14
2008	188.93	202.02	210.29	209.98	214.57	225.51	218.94	192.70	176.00	141.46	125.23	112.57	184.85
2009	114.17	107.49	107.93	111.21	119.75	125.98	119.71	128.50	125.34	132.15	134.35	135.93	121.88
2010	137.76	131.70	132.79	134.85	127.45	125.94	127.89	132.81	137.28	144.46	148.49	156.14	136.46
2011	160.80	163.41	165.87	171.91	163.23	161.47	162.81	159.01	154.26	145.52	146.73	141.41	158.04
2012	143.34	146.45	144.63	139.84	134.79	129.46	141.40	143.91	147.64	146.02	142.06	140.45	141.67
2013	140.01	139.55	137.44	132.99	132.04	129.38	127.65	128.32	128.98	127.48	123.20	126.25	131.11
2014	125.24	130.97	134.71	136.56	135.81	134.75	130.44	126.39	121.57	117.97	116.95	109.39	126.73

Average.   *Source: CME Group; Chicago Board of Trade*

COMMODITY PRICES SINK ON WEAK DEMAND AND STRONG SUPPLY

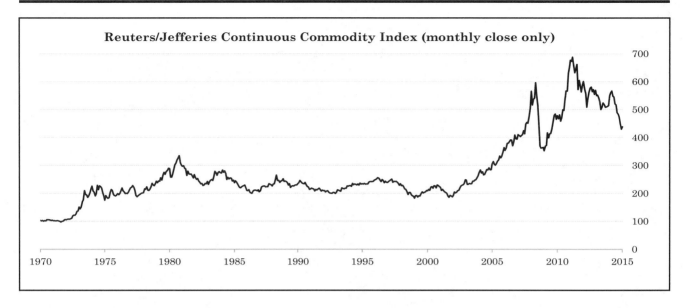

Reuters/Jefferies Continuous Commodity Index (monthly close only)

The Continuous Commodity Index (CCI) saw another weak year in 2014. The CCI index since 2011 has now plunged by a total of -39% and posted a 5-year low in January 2015.

The CCI index continues to move lower after the extraordinary rally that began in 2001 reached a record high in April 2011 of 691.09. That decade-long rally of +278% is by far the largest commodity bull market in post-war history, exceeding even the rallies seen in the 1970s. The 1971-74 and 1977-80 commodity bull markets were separated by two years of consolidation in 1975-76. Even if those two rallies are counted as one large bull market, that bull market of 250% is less than the 2001-2011 bull market of 278%.

The 2001-11 commodity bull market was driven mainly by strong commodity demand from fast-growing emerging countries such as China, India, Brazil, and others. The fact that the rally was driven by demand, as opposed to a temporary supply disruption, accounts for its size and longevity. The commodity rallies in the 1970s, by contrast, were driven mainly by supply disruptions and inflation, not by demand. A rally caused by demand is typically much more durable.

Along with strong demand, the weak dollar was an important driver of the commodity bull market from 2001 through 2008. During that time frame, the dollar plunged and provided a powerful bullish factor for commodity prices. As the value of the dollar falls, the price of hard assets tends to rise to account for the lower value of the currency in which the hard assets are priced. From 2008 through mid-2014, however, the dollar had less impact on commodity prices because the dollar was in a sideways consolidation mode.

The commodity bull market received a new head of steam in 2009-2011 in the aftermath of the 2008-09 global financial crisis. Commodity prices were driven higher during 2009-11 by extra liquidity from the Fed's extraordinarily easy monetary policy and by safe-haven buying of commodities as protection in the event that the Fed's extraordinarily easy monetary policy might eventually cause hyperinflation and a plunge in the dollar.

However, commodity prices topped out in early 2011 and have since been on a downward track. Commodity prices have been driven lower in the past four years by weak physical demand for commodities due to below-par global economic growth. In addition, many investors have been forced to give up on any imminent arrival of hyperinflation stemming from the Fed's extraordinarily easy monetary policy. Indeed, the U.S. and global economies are still feeling deflationary pressures during the current post-crisis recovery period. The latest reading of +1.3% y/y for the Fed's preferred inflation measure, the core PCE deflator, is only +0.4 points above the record low of +0.9% posted in July 2012. It is remarkable that core inflation is currently near a post-war low despite nearly six years of economic recovery and the Fed's injection of $3.6 trillion of excess liquidity into the financial system.

Commodity Bull Markets Ranked by Percentage Gain of Continuous Commodity Index (CCI) (1960-2014[1])							
	-------- Low --------		-------- High --------		Percent Rally	Rally Duration Months	Avg CPI (yr-yr%)
2001-11	Oct-01	182.83	Apr-11	691.09	278.0%	114	2.4%
1971-74	Oct-71	96.40	Feb-74	237.80	146.7%	28	4.9%
1977-80	Aug-77	184.70	Nov-80	337.60	82.8%	39	10.2%
1986-88	Jul-86	196.16	Jun-88	272.19	38.8%	23	3.2%
1992-96	Aug-92	198.17	Apr-96	263.79	33.1%	44	2.8%

[1] Data as of February 2015.   *Source: Commodity Research Bureau*

Commodity prices over the past four years have also been hurt by heavy long liquidation pressures after the long 2001-2011 bull market. The long liquidation pressure was particularly heavy in the precious metals markets. The amount of gold held in exchange-traded products plunged by -39% to 51.3 million troy ounces by January 2015 from the record high of 84.6 million ounces posted in December 2012.

Commodity prices have also been pressured by the Fed's move in October 2014 to end its third quantitative easing program (QE3). The Fed still has a massive $3.6 trillion of excess liquidity in the system but the Fed has at least halted its balance sheet expansion. The end of the Fed's QE programs means there is less fuel for the commodities markets and a reduced risk of eventual hyperinflation.

Commodity prices weakened during 2013-14 as growth slowed in China and the emerging countries. Chinese GDP in 2013-14 weakened to the mid 7% area, which was the weakest growth rate in 2-1/2 decades. Most observers believe the days of double-digit GDP growth in China are long gone. China's economy is going through a difficult transition to an economic model based more on consumer consumption than on the decades-long economic model based mainly on investment and exports.

Commodity prices starting in mid-2014 also saw weakness due to the +21% surge in the dollar index through January 2015 to an 11-1/2 year high. The surge in the dollar index undercut the price of commodities in terms of appreciated dollars.

The plunge in oil prices that started in late 2014 was a big contributor to the sharp sell-off in the commodity indexes. In addition, petroleum-based fuel is a big cost component for the production of many commodities, meaning the plunge in petroleum prices is also putting some downward pressure on the prices of other commodities. The plunge in crude oil prices was mainly due to a global oversupply of crude oil. However, the plunge in oil prices was also due to weak global demand, the sharp rally in the dollar index, and deflationary global conditions, which are all factors that hurt commodity prices in general.

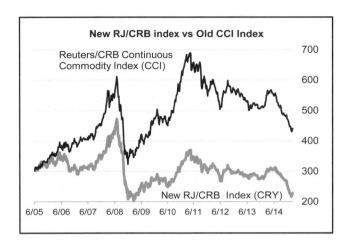

Yet commodity prices over the longer term will eventually find a bottom and start to recover once the world economy regains its balance and once strong commodity demand reemerges from the developing world. The need in the developing world continues to be enormous for food, shelter and infrastructure, which are all sectors that utilize raw commodities. According to the World Bank's Development Indicators, 80% of the world's population lives on less than $10 per day. As these people are slowly integrated into the global economy in the coming years and decades, their food, shelter and transportation needs will expand and they will use more commodities. Commodity demand will also be driven higher over the long term by population growth. The United Nations forecasts that there will be a net 2.2 billion more people on earth by 2050, bringing the world's population to 9.0 billion from its current level near 6.8 billion.

The world economy has been through a harrowing experience since 2007 and has yet to get fully back onto its feet. Yet as the world economy slowly normalizes, commodities should find a bottom and start to slowly recover.

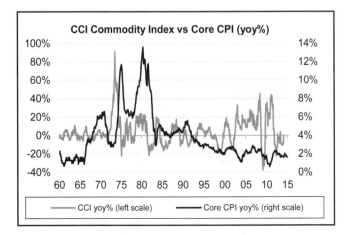

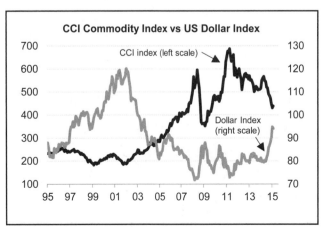

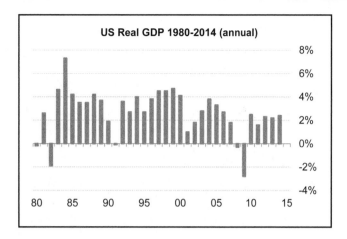

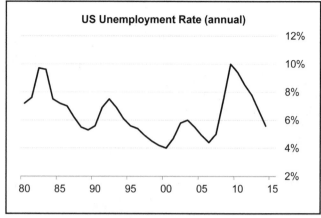

The U.S. economy in 2014 finally kicked into a higher gear after nearly five years of a disappointing recovery from the Great Recession that lasted from December 2007 through June 2009. U.S. GDP growth in Q1-2014 fell by -2.1% due to very bad winter weather. However, U.S. GDP then came roaring back with growth of +4.6% in Q2-2014, +5.0% in Q3-2014, and +2.2% in Q4-2014.

Looking ahead, the market consensus is for U.S. GDP to stabilize near +3.0% in 2015 and beyond. That would be slightly weaker than the post-war average of +3.3% but much better than the very poor 10-year average of +1.7%.

Optimism about the U.S. economy stems in part from the strong improvement in the U.S. labor market. U.S. payroll growth showed an average monthly increase of +260,000 in 2014, which was much better than even the pre-recession (2004-06) average of +184,000. The U.S. economy has now produced a net 11.2 million jobs from the payroll trough in February 2010 and has more than exceeded the jobs lost during the Great Recession.

Moreover, the U.S. unemployment rate has fallen much more sharply than the Fed or economists had expected. The U.S. unemployment rate by February 2015 fell to a 6-3/4 year low of 5.5%. That unemployment rate of 5.5% was only +0.4 points above the Fed's forecast that the U.S. unemployment rate will stabilize and move sideways near 5.1% in 2016 and 2017. The unemployment rate therefore does not need to fall much farther before it reaches a more acceptable level for the Fed.

Meanwhile, U.S. consumer spending continues to chug along at a decent pace and is helping to support the overall economy. Personal consumption in Q4-2014 strengthened to a 9-year high of +4.2%. U.S. consumers are now in much better shape due to lower debt levels and an improving labor market, although wage growth remains tepid. The plunge in gasoline prices has also provided a big boost for consumers by reducing their fuel costs and providing more disposable income.

The U.S. housing market continues to provide support for the overall U.S. economy. U.S. existing home sales were at 5.04 million units in December 2014, which was only 6% below the 5-year high of 5.38 million units posted in July 2013. U.S. housing starts in January 2015 were at 1.065 million units, which was only 4% below the 7-year high of 1.105 million units posted in November 2013. Meanwhile, the U.S. home price index from the Federal Home Financing Agency has risen by +19% from the 2011 trough and has posted a new 7-year high.

The U.S. manufacturing sector is also contributing to a stronger U.S. economy with U.S. industrial production rising by a very strong +4.9% y/y in December 2014. However, manufacturing confidence faded a bit in late 2014 due to (1) concern about U.S. export demand with the sharp rally in the dollar, and (2) the plunge in crude oil prices which decimated petroleum industry investment and caused some businesses to delay new manufacturing orders as they await lower prices.

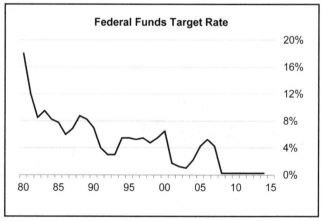

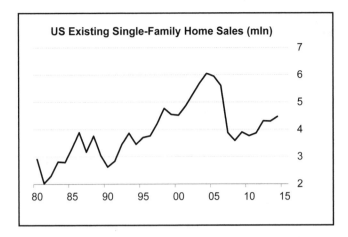

US Existing Single-Family Home Sales (mln)

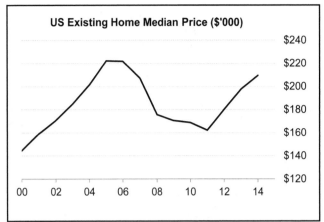

US Existing Home Median Price ($'000)

The current obstacles for the U.S. economy stem mainly from overseas factors. The Eurozone economy is barely keeping its head above water with a market consensus for weak 2015 GDP growth of +1.2% after +0.8% growth in 2014. Moreover, Chinese GDP growth is headed slowly lower, also reducing demand for U.S. products.

There are a host of other threats for the U.S. economy such as concern that the Russian-proxy war in Ukraine could cause the U.S. and Europe to tighten sanctions even further on Russia, thus potentially causing an implosion of the Russian financial system. There is also the threat of renewed Eurozone systemic problems with Greece threatening to renege on its bailout conditions. The Iran nuclear negotiations have yet to produce an agreement and there is still the threat of U.S. and/or Israeli military action against Iran at some point in the future. The threat of terrorist attacks in the U.S. and Europe have grown with the rise of ISIS and Islamic extremism.

Despite these threats, the U.S. economy continues to see support from the Federal Reserve, which is expected to maintain its zero interest rate monetary policy at least through mid-2015. The Fed has stopped its QE programs but has not made any move as yet to reduce the $3.6 trillion of excess liquidity that it has in the financial system.

The 10-year T-note yield in 2014 fell sharply from 3.00% at the end of 2013 to a 2-year low of 1.64% by early 2015. The sharp drop in the 10-year T-note yield was driven by (1) the plunge in inflation expectations caused by the overall 60% drop in crude oil prices, (2) the outlook for continued weak global economic growth in 2015, and (3) safe-haven demand for Treasury securities driven by various hot spots including Greece, Russia-Ukraine, Iran, and the Middle East in general. Even though the Fed ended QE3 in October 2014, the T-note market continued to see support from expectations that the Fed will not start raising interest rates until mid to late 2015 and that the Fed after that will move very slowly with any rate hike program.

The S&P 500 index rallied steadily again in 2014 and progressively posted new record highs. The S&P 500 index closed +11% higher in 2014, adding to the 30% rally seen in 2013. The U.S. stock market during 2014 received support from the Fed's continued stimulative monetary policy, the stronger U.S. economy, and a solid improvement in the U.S. labor market. The stock market also received a boost from another year of respectable earnings growth of +8% y/y for the S&P 500 companies.

The stock market has now rallied for more than three years without a major downside correction. That rally has been driven by respectable U.S. economic growth combined with a steady rise in U.S. earnings growth. However, U.S. earnings growth in 2015 is expected to show very weak growth of only +2% due to the sharp rally in the dollar and continued slow overseas growth. Expectations for weak earnings growth in 2015 means that further gains in the stock market may be more grudging.

S&P 500 Index

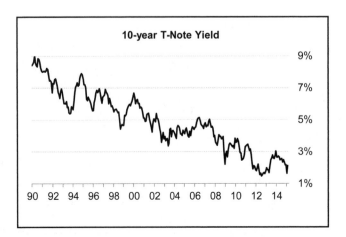

10-year T-Note Yield

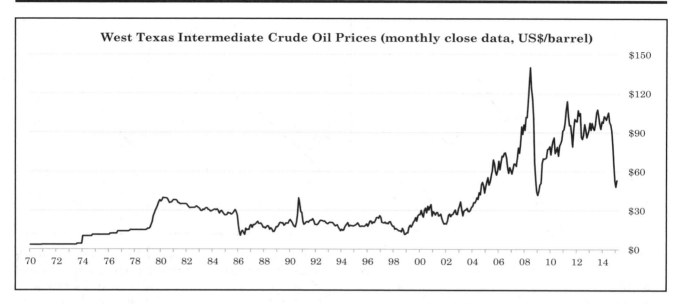

West Texas Intermediate Crude Oil Prices (monthly close data, US$/barrel)

CME West Texas Intermediate (WTI) crude oil futures prices in the second half of 2014 plunged by a total of -$64 per barrel (-60%) from a 1-1/2 year high of $107.68 in June 2014 to a 6-year low of $43.58 in January 2015. Crude oil prices then recovered modestly in the first half of February 2015 to the $52 per barrel area.

The main trigger for the plunge in oil prices was Saudi Arabia's announcement that it would not cut production in response to world oil oversupply and would instead maintain its current market share regardless of how far crude oil prices might drop. Saudi Arabia finally gave up on its role as the swing producer for OPEC and indeed the world where it would previously fine-tune its production to keep oil prices within desired ranges. Instead, Saudi Arabia and its Persian Gulf partners declared war on high-cost oil producers the world over.

Saudi Arabia enjoys some of the lowest extraction costs in the world at less than $15 per barrel. That means that Saudi Arabia will be the last one standing in the oil price war. Saudi Arabia's goal is to force global oil companies to slash their exploration and drilling activities and for high-cost producers to shut down existing oil production.

The plunge in oil prices has been driven mainly by an

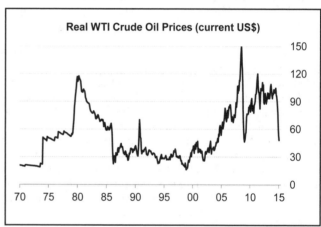

Real WTI Crude Oil Prices (current US$)

oversupply of oil considering that demand has been mostly steady. The only way for oil prices to stabilize and recover is a cut in supply. Demand in the oil markets is relatively inelastic, which means that demand will not increase much in response to lower prices.

Yet even four months into the oil price free-fall, there has not been a significant drop in world oil production. U.S. oil companies by February 2015 slashed the number of U.S. oil wells by -687 wells (-43%) to a 4-year low of 922

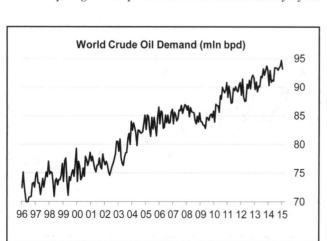

World Crude Oil Demand (mln bpd)

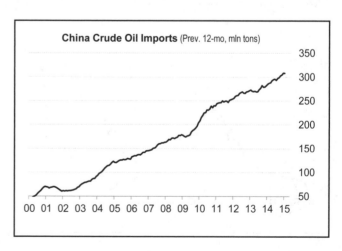

China Crude Oil Imports (Prev. 12-mo, mln tons)

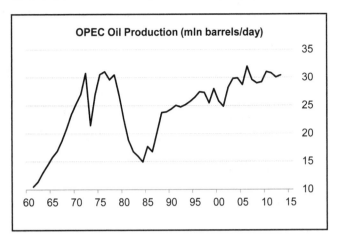

OPEC Oil Production (mln barrels/day)

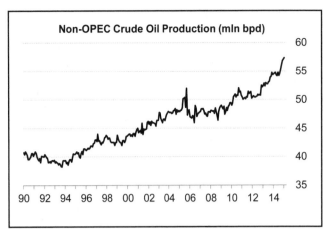

Non-OPEC Crude Oil Production (mln bpd)

wells from the record high of 1,609 wells in October 2014. However, U.S. oil companies closed marginal wells and boosted production at the remaining wells. Thus, even with fewer U.S. oil wells, U.S. oil production reached a new 41-year high of 9.3 million barrels per day in February 2015.

U.S. oil production has surged by 65% since the end of 2010 thanks to new horizontal drilling and fracking technology that has allowed the U.S. to exploit reserves that were previously uneconomical. In addition, there are plenty of other U.S. oil reserves that can be tapped if oil prices recover. The Lower Monterey Shale and Santos oil fields in California together contain more than three times as much recoverable oil as the Bakken field in North Dakota. In fact, the International Energy Agency forecasts that within five years the U.S. will surpass Saudi Arabia as the world's largest oil producer. The IEA also says that the U.S. will become self-sufficient in oil in about two decades.

The surge in U.S. oil production has produced a record high in U.S. crude oil inventories. Moreover, crude oil inventories at the Cushing, Oklahoma hub, which is where CME WTI crude oil futures prices are set, soared by +138% from August 2014 to post a new 1-1/2 year high of 42.6 million barrels in early February 2015. This Cushing oil glut is putting downward pressure on WTI oil prices.

Despite the plunge in oil prices, OPEC in January 2015 actually boosted its production by +1.6% m/m to 30.905 million barrels per day (bpd). Saudi Arabia in January 2015 pumped 9.50 million bpd of oil, which was

just slightly below the 12-month average of 9.67 million bpd.

There is little appetite within the rest of OPEC to cut production. Most countries in OPEC are in one type of trouble or another and need to pump as much oil as possible to maximize their revenues. In addition, Iraqi oil production in 2014 rose by +14% to post a new 14-1/2 year high of 3.52 million bpd as the post-war Iraqi oil industry attracts global petroleum investment and expands oil fields and drilling activity.

The emergence of the new oil extraction technologies that caused the surge in U.S. oil production have been a game-changer for the world oil markets. There is still the possibility of temporary upward oil spikes from supply disruptions caused by storms or wars. However, the long-term outlook is now for low to moderate oil prices for at least the next decade. Oil prices cannot trade at higher levels for long because that would attract higher-cost producers back into the market, thus boosting supply and pushing prices back down. OPEC has lost its grip on the world oil markets.

The surge in U.S. oil production and the plunge in oil prices is providing a major benefit for the U.S. economy since cheap energy gives U.S. industry a major competitive advantage relative to overseas competitors. In addition, the decline in U.S. oil imports and the increase in U.S. refined petroleum exports should also lead to a sustained decline in the U.S. trade deficit, which should be a major supportive factor for the dollar.

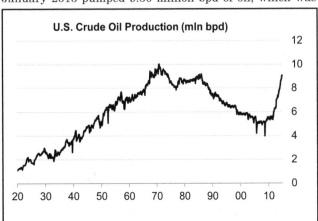

U.S. Crude Oil Production (mln bpd)

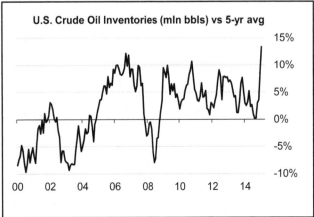

U.S. Crude Oil Inventories (mln bbls) vs 5-yr avg

US Current Account as % GDP vs. Dollar Index

US Current Account as % of GDP (left scale)

Dollar Index (right scale)

US Ex-Petroleum Trade Deficit (US$ bln)

US Trade Deficit Ex-Petroleum

US Trade Deficit

The U.S. dollar index starting in May 2014 rallied sharply by +21% to post a new 11-1/2 year of 95.48 by January 2015. The dollar index finally broke out of the sideways range seen during 2009-2013. Before 2008, the dollar index took a huge -41% hit during the 2002-07 bear market when the dollar plunged on the Fed's easy monetary policy and the sharp widening of America's trade deficit.

The dollar index rallied sharply in the latter half of 2014 because of the relative strength of the U.S. economy and because the Fed finally ended its string of quantitative easing programs and is expected to start raising interest rates much sooner than Europe or Japan.

U.S. GDP growth in 2014 was rather lackluster at +2.4%. Still, the U.S. GDP performance was much better than the Eurozone's GDP growth rate of +0.8% in 2014 and Japan's zero growth rate. In addition, the U.S. economy is expected to outperform again in 2015 with growth of +3.1%, much better than the consensus for Eurozone GDP to improve to only +1.2% in 2015 and for Japan GDP to improve to just +1.0%.

The dollar rallied sharply in the latter half of 2014 when it became clear that the Fed would follow through on expectations for it to end its quantitative easing programs. The FOMC at its Oct 28-29 meeting announced a final cut to zero in its third quantitative easing program (QE3), finalizing the tapering process that began in Dec 2013. The Fed's QE3 program, which lasted from Sep 2012 to Oct 2014, involved the purchase of $1.7 trillion of Treasury

securities and mortgage-backed securities. That was larger than the QE2 program of $600 billion and the QE1 program of $1.425 trillion.

When QE3 ended in Dec 2014, the Fed's balance sheet totaled $4.5 trillion and the Fed had injected a net $3.6 trillion of excess liquidity into the U.S. financial system. In normal times, a central bank that engages in such a bond-buying program risks causing hyperinflation and a plunge in its currency. However, the Fed has been able to get away with this liquidity injection so far because (1) there are still heavy deflationary pressures that are bearing down on the U.S. and global economies, (2) other major central banks have also engaged in QE programs, and (3) global investors remain willing to hold dollars for safe-haven purposes.

The dollar has also rallied sharply because the markets are expecting the Fed to start raising interest rates much sooner than the European Central Bank (ECB) or the Bank of Japan (BOJ). A rate hike is not even on the radar for the ECB or the BOJ while the markets are expecting the Fed to announce its first 25 basis point rate hike by mid to late 2015. Higher interest rates are supportive for a currency because those higher rates are anti-inflationary and attract money flows from global investors

The dollar is also still getting support from safe-haven demand. Global investors remain traumatized by the 2008/09 global financial crisis and the subsequent Eurozone sovereign debt crisis. Moreover, there is the potential for new global problems with slowing Chinese GDP growth

Euro ($USD/euro)

Dollar/yen (yen per USD)

US Export Growth (yoy%)

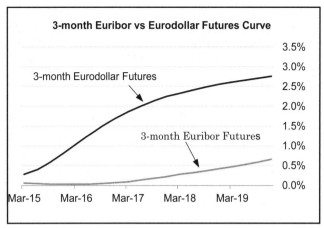

3-month Euribor vs Eurodollar Futures Curve

3-month Eurodollar Futures

3-month Euribor Futures

and various geopolitical hot spots such as Ukraine, Iran, and the Middle East in general. The dollar is the world's reserve currency and has the greatest depth of investment opportunities. The dollar is therefore perceived to be the best place to park assets during times of stress.

The large U.S. current account deficit continues to be a major bearish factor for the dollar. The U.S. current account deficit, which is the broadest measure of U.S. trade, was most recently reported at -$100.3 billion in Q3-2014. That means that a net $1.1 billion worth of dollars are flowing out of the U.S. each calendar day to pay for goods and services. That net dollar outflow puts downward pressure on the dollar since the recipients of those dollars sell them into the foreign exchange market if they do not want to hold them and invest them in dollar-denominated investments.

In terms of GDP, however, the U.S. trade position has improved substantially in the past several years. The U.S. current account deficit peaked at -6.2% of GDP in Q4-2005 and has since narrowed sharply to -2.3% of GDP. That means the U.S. trade deficit is now much less of a bearish factor for the dollar than it was during the 2000-07 period.

Moreover, the prospects look good for a steady narrowing of the U.S. current account deficit in coming years as U.S. oil production surges and reduces the need for the U.S. to import oil. In addition, the U.S. is already a net exporter of refined petroleum products and that will only grow in coming years as U.S. oil production expands.

The continued crisis situation in Europe continues to be a major bearish factor for the euro (EUR/USD) and a bullish factor for the dollar index. The ECB in January 2015 announced a major quantitative easing (QE) program involving the purchase of some 60 billion euros per month of sovereign bonds of the Eurozone nations and other securities. That followed the ECB's two rate cuts in 2014, which brought the ECB's refinancing rate down to a negligible 0.05% by September 2014. The ECB was forced to cut rates and implement a QE program in response to the weak Eurozone economy and increased deflation risks. ECB's highly expansionary monetary policy was a major bearish factor for the euro during 2014 and early 2015.

Meanwhile, the dollar has rallied sharply against the yen over the last three years. USD/JPY has rallied by 60% from a record low of 76.03 yen in Feb 2012 to a 7-1/2 year high of 121.84 yen by December 2014. The yen has been driven lower against the dollar by the Bank of Japan's highly stimulative monetary policy and its explicit attempt to push inflation higher. This has been part of Prime Minister Shinzo Abe's pursuit of extraordinarily aggressive policies to boost the Japanese economy and shock the nation out of more than 15 years of deflation. The BOJ has been pursuing a massive QE program designed to push inflation higher and has had its policy interest rate pegged near zero since 2008. The BOJ has had to combat a variety of ills including a recession in the middle part of 2014 (Q2 GDP -7.3%, Q3 -1.6%) caused by the hike in the country's sales tax to 8% from 5% in April 2014.

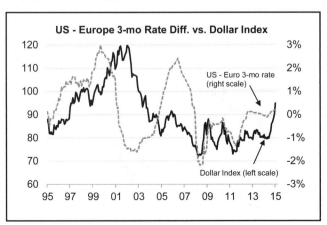

US - Europe 3-mo Rate Diff. vs. Dollar Index

US - Euro 3-mo rate (right scale)

Dollar Index (left scale)

US - Japan 3-mo Rate Diff. vs. Dollar Index

Dollar Index (left scale)

US - Japan 3-mo rate (right scale)

The Federal Reserve is still engaged in a massively stimulative monetary policy even though it has now been eight years since the U.S. housing bubble started deflating in 2006 and nearly six years since the U.S. 2007/09 recession officially ended in June 2009.

The Fed kept its federal funds rate target near zero all during 2014. However, the Fed in October 2014 announced the end of its third quantitative easing program (QE3) that began in September 2012 at $85 billion per month. The Fed starting in December 2013 cut its QE3 program by $10 billion per month at each successive FOMC meeting, making the final $15 billion cut at its Oct 28-29, 2014 meeting.

The QE3 program ended up totaling $1.7 trillion and left the Fed's balance sheet at $4.5 trillion, representing $3.6 trillion of excess liquidity compared with where the Fed's balance sheet was before the financial crisis began. The Fed is currently maintaining its balance sheet asset level at about $4.5 trillion by rolling over maturing securities. If the Fed did not roll over maturing securities, then its balance sheet would slowly decline, representing a small back-door tightening of monetary policy.

The Fed responded very aggressively to the financial crisis in 2008 with a wide range of measures. The Fed started cutting its federal funds rate target in October 2007 from 5.25% when the housing crisis started. By early 2009 the Fed had cut the funds rate to the current range of zero to 0.25%.

After the financial crisis erupted into global proportions in September 2008 with the bankruptcy of Lehman Brothers, the Fed began a broad range of liquidity programs to lend money not only to banks but also to securities firms and directly into the commercial paper and mortgage markets. The Fed began its first quantitative easing move (QE1) in March 2008, which eventually involved the purchase of $1.425 trillion of securities by the time it ended in March 2010.

When the economy continued to struggle in the first half of 2010, the Fed launched its QE2 program of buying $600 billion worth of Treasury securities from November 2010 through June 2011. The U.S. economy in the first half of 2011, however, started to falter again due to a confluence of negative events that included high gasoline prices, the Japanese earthquake/tsunami in March 2011, and the U.S. debt ceiling debacle in early summer 2011. In addition, the European debt crisis flared up in 2011 and the European banking system was near an all-out systemic crisis.

The Fed in September 2011 therefore began a new program dubbed "Operation Twist" in which the Fed sold shorter-term Treasury securities from its portfolio and used the proceeds to buy longer-term securities. The purpose of this program was to keep long-term Treasury yields low, which in turn keeps other key rates low such as mortgage rates and corporate bond yields.

The U.S. economy remained weak through 2012 as the European debt crisis continued to rage and as U.S. domestic demand remained weak. The Fed in September 2012 therefore began its QE3 program, which initially involved the open-ended purchase of $40 billion per month of mortgage securities. The Fed in December 2012 then announced that it would expand QE3 to $85 billion per month involving the purchase of $45 billion of longer-term Treasury securities and $40 billion of mortgage securities. The Fed's QE3 program lasted until October 2014.

The wisdom of the Fed's quantitative easing programs remains open to debate. The Fed's goals with its QE programs included (1) keeping banks fully supplied with excess reserves to reduce the chance of any liquidity squeeze and to provide plenty of reserves as a base for expanded lending, (2) keeping long-term Treasury yields relatively low in order to hold down private rates such as corporate bond yields and mortgage rates, and (3) providing a boost to asset prices and the stock market to increase household confidence and wealth. The Fed's QE measures were intended to prevent the U.S. economy from slipping into a deflationary trap such as the one seen in Japan for the past two decades.

Only time will tell whether the Fed made a huge mistake with its QE programs. The Fed has now permanently injected a massive $3.6 trillion of liquidity into the U.S. financial system with its QE programs, which

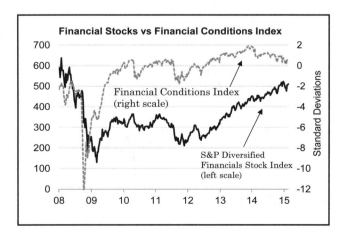

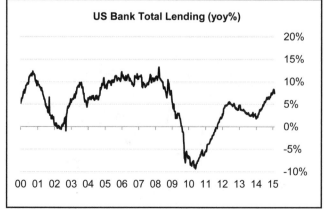

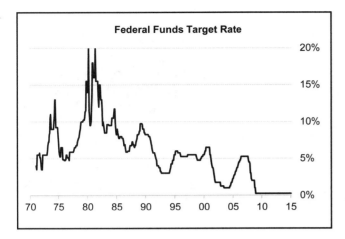

Federal Funds Target Rate

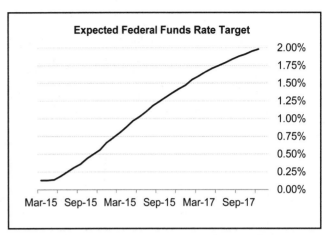

Expected Federal Funds Rate Target

is equal to about 15% of U.S. GDP. In normal times, this high-powered liquidity could cause hyper-inflation.

Yet the U.S. economy continues to experience deflationary pressures as seen by the fact that the Fed's preferred inflation measure, the core PCE deflator, was at only +1.3% y/y in December 2014, far below the Fed's 2.0% inflation target. In fact, the core PCE deflator of +1.3% was only 0.4 points above the record low of +0.9% posted in December 2010. U.S. inflation is currently close to the lowest level in post-war history even though the Fed has about $3.6 trillion of excess liquidity in the banking system.

The question is what will happen when the U.S. economy finally normalizes and banks start putting that high-powered money to work. The Fed claims that it has an exit plan whereby it will be able to drain those excess reserves out of the banking system over a number of years. However, there is the very real possibility that bond market investors may panic at some point about an inflation outbreak and push long-term Treasury yields sharply higher. That would then force the Fed to raise its federal funds rate target sharply to curb inflation fears, producing a U.S. recession.

The Fed's exit strategy includes slowly raising interest rates, halting its bond rollovers to allow its balance sheet asset level to slowly decline, and conducting large reserve draining operations to mop up excess reserves.

The markets as of early 2015 were actively discussing the June 2015 FOMC meeting as the most likely date

for the Fed's first 25 basis point rate hike. However, the federal funds futures market is not fully discounting the Fed's first 25 bp rate hike to 0.50% until November 2015.

After the first hike in the federal funds rate to 0.50% by November 2015, the federal funds futures market is then expecting three 25 bp rate hikes in 2016 to bring the federal funds rate to 1.25% by September 2016. The market is then expecting another three rate hikes in 2017 to bring the funds rate to 2.00% by late 2017. The expected funds rate of 2.00% at the end of 2017 would still be 325 bp below the 5.25% funds rate that prevailed before the housing bust and the Great Recession began.

The markets expect the Fed to move very slowly in returning to a more normal monetary policy. The U.S. and world economies are still feeling major negative effects from the Great Recession. Moreover, the world is still feeling disinflationary pressures. The Fed does not want to start raising interest rates only to cause a new U.S. recession. Instead, the Fed wants to wait until it believes that the U.S. economy has enough momentum to continue growing even as interest rates rise.

The Fed will face a very tricky task over the next few years in trying to exit from its monetary largesse. If the Fed tightens too quickly, it will cause a recession. If the Fed tightens too slowly, it will risk causing an inflation panic that would result in a big upward spike in interest rates, also causing a recession. The Fed's exit path could easily end up causing some major volatility for the economy and the markets over the next few years.

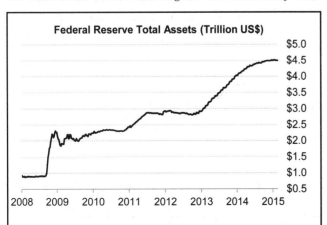

Federal Reserve Total Assets (Trillion US$)

U.S. 10-year Inflation Expectations

10-yr T-note minus TIPS

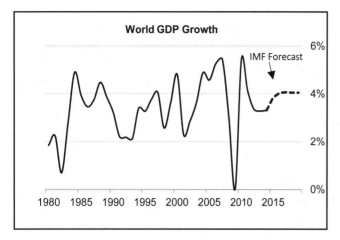

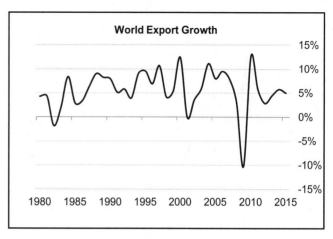

The global economy in 2014 continued to struggle. World GDP growth in 2014 of +3.3% was little changed from the two previous years, according to the IMF, well below the average GDP rate of +4.1% seen in the 1990-2007 period before the world financial crisis emerged in 2008. However, the IMF is forecasting that world GDP growth will improve to +3.8% in 2015 and then stabilize near +4.0% during 2016 through 2019.

The global economy in 2014 was hurt by weak growth in both developed and emerging countries. U.S. real GDP in 2014 improved just slightly to +2.4% from the +2.25% average seen in 2012-13. The U.S. economy in Q1-2014 took a hit from bad winter weather but then recovered nicely in the last three quarters of 2014. The market consensus is for U.S. GDP to improve to +3.1% in 2015 but then fade back to the +2.8% area in 2016-17.

The Eurozone economy in 2014 finally emerged from two years of recession but showed only paltry growth of +0.8% in 2014. The Eurozone in 2014 was able to largely move past the sovereign debt crisis but the economy continued to be weighed down by weak demand, tight fiscal conditions, a weak banking sector, and concern about deflation. However, the market consensus is for Eurozone GDP to slowly improve to +1.2% in 2015 and +1.6% in 2016.

Japan's GDP in 2014 showed zero growth largely because of the April 2014 hike in the sales tax to 8% from 5%, which caused a steep recession in Q2 (-6.7%) and Q3

(-2.3%). The market is expecting Japan's GDP to remain weak at +1.1% in 2015 and +1.4% in 2016.

The Chinese economy continued to struggle in 2014 with GDP slowing to a 24-year low of +7.4%. The market consensus is for China's GDP to slow to +7.0% in 2015, +6.75% in 2016, and +6.5% in 2017. The days of double-digit Chinese economic growth are long gone as the Chinese economy faces a difficult transition period to an economy based more on consumer consumption than on exports and investment.

Two other BRIC countries had a tough year during 2014. Brazil's GDP slowed to +0.1% in 2014 from +2.5% in 2013 and is expected to show no growth in 2015, finally improving to only +1.6% in 2016. Russia's GDP slowed to +0.6% in 2014 and is expected to experience a deep recession of -4.0% in 2015 due to weak crude oil prices and Western sanctions over Ukraine. India's economy was one of the world's few bright spots with GDP growth in 2014 of about +5.2%. The market is looking for India's growth rate to improve to +5.5% in 2015 and +6.25% in 2016.

Looking ahead, the global economy should slowly gain some traction in 2015 since global monetary policy remains very stimulative. However, there are still plenty of risks that could derail the global economy such as an unexpected meltdown in China, an implosion of the Russian banking system on sanctions, a revival of the Eurozone debt crisis, or increased tensions with Iran over its nuclear program.

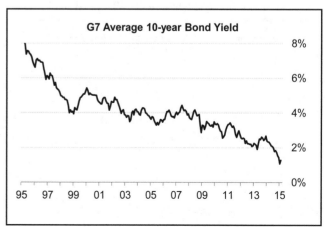

EUROZONE DEBT CRISIS RECEDES WITH EXTRAORDINARY DROP IN YIELDS

The Eurozone in 2014 largely moved past its sovereign debt crisis and the Eurozone economy showed at least a tepid recovery. After showing negative GDP growth rates of -0.7% in 2012 and -0.4% in 2013, Eurozone GDP finally achieved a positive growth rate of +0.8% in 2014. However, the Eurozone recovery remains tepid with GDP growth expected to improve only to +1.2% in 2015 and +1.6% in 2016.

The European Central Bank (ECB) in September 2012 was finally able to largely snuff out the Eurozone debt crisis that raged in the previous three years by declaring its "Outright Monetary Transactions" (OMT). Under the OMT program, the ECB can provide unlimited short-term 1-3 year liquidity to troubled countries while the European Stability Mechanism (ESM) can provide longer-term direct financing to troubled countries with debt maturities beyond 3 years.

The ECB with its OMT program greatly expanded the capacity of the Eurozone's bailout facilities, which had previously been too small to handle bailouts if they became necessary for both Spain and Italy. The OMT program has yet to be used but is ready in the event that it is needed. The ECB's OMT program finally convinced the markets that the ECB was serious about using its unlimited balance sheet to snuff out the crisis.

Greece, however, began causing problems again in early 2015 after Greek citizens voted the anti-austerity Syriza party into power. The Syriza party promised to reject bailout austerity conditions and renegotiate Greece's bailout program. In February 2015, Greece and the EU came to an agreement to extend its bailout program for four months to allow more time to negotiate a new long-term bailout program. There is still the outside possibility that Greece could end up exiting the Eurozone, but the markets in early 2015 showed only minor concern about the Greek situation and there was no major contagion for other Eurozone countries.

The ECB in 2014 and early 2015 was forced to adopt additional stimulus measures to combat weak Eurozone economic growth and the very real possibility of deflation. The Eurozone CPI in January 2015 fell -0.6% y/y due in large part to the plunge in oil prices. Meanwhile, the Eurozone core CPI in January 2015 fell to a record low of +0.6% y/y, which was far below the ECB's inflation target of just under +2.0%.

The ECB in 2014 cut its refinancing rate twice, once in June 2014 by 10 bp to 0.15% and again in September by another 10 bp to 0.05%. The ECB also took the rather drastic step of cutting its deposit rate to the negative level of -0.20% in September. The negative deposit rate means that banks have to pay 0.20% to leave funds on deposit with the ECB, thus encouraging them to withdraw those deposits and put them to work in the real economy.

The ECB in January 2015 also announced a major quantitative easing (QE) program involving the purchase of 60 billion euros per month of sovereign bonds and other securities. The ECB said it intends for the program to last from March 2015 through September 2016 and for the program to total at least 1.1 trillion euros. That program marked the first time that the ECB engaged in QE since the global financial crisis began in 2008. The fact that the ECB finally engaged in QE was a testament to the weak position of the Eurozone economy and the threat of deflation.

The Eurozone's troubles were highlighted in 2014 with an extraordinary drop in bond yields. The German 10-year bund yield fell from 1.93% at the beginning of 2014 to a record low of 0.30% by early 2015. The French 10-year bond yield fell to 0.54% by early 2015.

Moreover, the bond yields of troubled Eurozone countries also fell sharply during 2014, illustrating that concern about the Eurozone debt crisis had substantially receded. By early 2015, the 10-year bond yields fell to 1.50% for Spain and 1.57% for Italy. By early 2015, 10-year bond yields also fell to 2.21% for Portugal and 1.09% for Ireland, which were near or below the U.S. 10-year T-note yield of 2.11% at the time.

While the Eurozone economy continues to face major obstacles before any type of victory can be declared, the chances for an eventual Eurozone recovery improved substantially in 2014 as the ECB took much more aggressive stimulus measures and as investor trust slowly improved for Eurozone sovereign countries and banks.

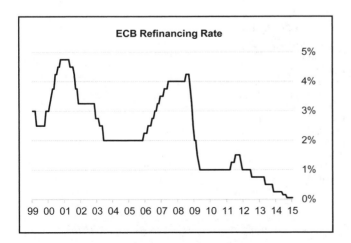

ECB Refinancing Rate

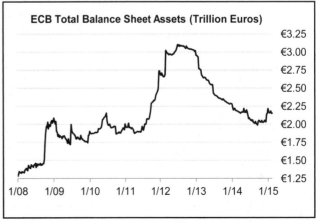

ECB Total Balance Sheet Assets (Trillion Euros)

Volume - U.S.

U.S. Futures Volume Highlights
2013 in Comparison with 2012

2013 Rank	Top 50 Contracts Traded in 2013	2013 Contracts	%	2012 Contracts	%	2012 Rank
1	Eurodollars (3-month), CME	517,250,183	18.71%	426,438,437	15.42%	2
2	E-Mini S&P 500 Index, CME	452,291,450	16.36%	474,278,939	17.15%	1
3	T-Notes (10-year), CBT	325,928,194	11.79%	264,997,089	9.58%	3
4	T-Notes (5-year), CBT	175,328,163	6.34%	133,342,429	4.82%	5
5	Crude Oil, NYMEX	147,690,593	5.34%	140,531,588	5.08%	4
6	T-Bonds (30-year), CBT	97,963,266	3.54%	91,745,232	3.32%	7
7	Natural Gas, NYMEX	84,282,495	3.05%	94,799,542	3.43%	6
8	Corn, CBT	64,322,600	2.33%	73,184,337	2.65%	8
9	Euro FX, CME	61,285,617	2.22%	67,407,741	2.44%	9
10	E-Mini NASDAQ 100, CME	59,393,053	2.15%	63,530,758	2.30%	10
11	T-Notes (2-year), CBT	57,815,900	2.09%	55,108,651	1.99%	11
12	COMEX Gold (100 oz.), NYMEX	47,294,551	1.71%	43,893,311	1.59%	13
13	Soybeans, CBT	46,721,081	1.69%	52,041,615	1.88%	12
14	Japanese Yen, CME	42,762,257	1.55%	23,520,562	0.85%	24
15	CBOE Volatility Index, CFE	39,944,022	1.44%	23,785,831	0.86%	23
16	Mini ($5) Dow Jones Industrial Index, CBT	35,448,824	1.28%	30,902,047	1.12%	18
17	Gasoline, RBOB, NYMEX	34,470,288	1.25%	36,603,841	1.32%	14
18	Heating Oil #2, NYMEX	32,749,553	1.18%	36,087,707	1.31%	15
19	Sugar #11, ICE	29,813,680	1.08%	27,126,728	0.98%	21
20	British Pound, CME	29,237,763	1.06%	26,166,290	0.95%	22
21	E-Mini Russell 2000 Index, ICE	28,837,712	1.04%	33,044,716	1.20%	16
22	Australian Dollar, CME	26,332,299	0.95%	32,727,390	1.18%	17
23	Wheat, CBT	24,993,158	0.90%	27,379,403	0.99%	20
24	Soybean Oil, CBT	23,805,912	0.86%	27,627,590	1.00%	19
25	Ultra T-Bond, CBT	21,149,865	0.76%	16,560,093	0.60%	28
26	Soybean Meal, CBT	20,237,181	0.73%	18,187,433	0.66%	26
27	Canadian Dollar, CME	17,427,832	0.63%	22,799,446	0.82%	25
28	High Grade Copper, NYMEX	17,127,383	0.62%	16,158,815	0.58%	29
29	COMEX Silver (5,000 oz.), NYMEX	14,475,593	0.52%	13,315,679	0.48%	31
30	Live Cattle, CME	12,463,043	0.45%	13,985,374	0.51%	30
31	Nikkei 225 Index (JPY), CME	11,792,392	0.43%	5,738,629	0.21%	43
32	Henry Hub Swap, NYMEX	11,457,837	0.41%	18,156,113	0.66%	27
33	Lean Hogs, CME	11,277,038	0.41%	11,461,892	0.41%	33
34	Mexican Peso, CME	10,374,701	0.38%	11,482,886	0.42%	32
35	Brent Crude Oil, Last Day (BZ)	9,214,951	0.33%	1,161,113	0.04%	
36	Swiss Franc, CME	9,061,770	0.33%	9,911,325	0.36%	34
37	US Dollar Index, ICE	8,050,966	0.29%	6,321,418	0.23%	39
38	Coffee "C", ICE	7,124,029	0.26%	6,125,484	0.22%	41
39	Cocoa, ICE	6,583,746	0.24%	5,999,813	0.22%	42
40	Natural Gas Penultimate Swap, NYMEX	6,418,797	0.23%	7,945,695	0.29%	36
41	Cotton #2, ICE	6,155,024	0.22%	6,130,352	0.22%	40
42	MSCI EM	6,102,827	0.22%	3,044,608	0.11%	47
43	E-mini S&P MidCap 400 Index, CME	5,601,547	0.20%	6,536,907	0.24%	37
44	Wheat, KCBT	5,452,437	0.20%	5,302,197	0.19%	44
45	Nikkei 225 Index (USD)	4,680,898	0.17%	1,690,244	0.06%	
46	Federal Funds (30-day), CBT	4,649,878	0.17%	6,425,956	0.23%	38
47	S&P 500 Index, CME	4,156,499	0.15%	5,032,650	0.18%	45
48	New Zealand Dollar	3,618,319	0.13%	3,655,690	0.13%	46
49	Platinum	3,262,775	0.12%	2,621,704	0.09%	48
50	PJM Western Hub Real-Time Off-Peak (N9)	3,098,831	0.11%	1,290,881	0.05%	
	Top 50 Contracts	2,209,728,590	69.72%	2,106,875,734	78.33%	
	Contracts Below the Top 50	959,748,352	30.28%	582,885,084	21.67%	
	TOTAL	**3,169,476,942**	**100.00%**	**2,689,760,818**	**100.00%**	

* For 2012 Top 50 contracts totaled 2,541,258,774 including 3 contracts that are not among 2013's Top 50.

U.S. Futures Volume Highlights
2013 in Comparison with 2012

2013 Rank	EXCHANGE	2013 Contracts	%	2012 Contracts	%	2012 Rank
1	Chicago Mercantile Exchange (CME Group)	1,290,230,093	40.71%	1,215,594,457	45.19%	1
2	Chicago Board of Trade (CME Group)	901,909,220	28.46%	800,706,309	29.77%	2
3	ICE Futures U.S.	465,833,636	14.70%	180,757,780	6.72%	4
4	New York Mercantile Exchange (CME Group)	441,373,921	13.93%	435,672,648	16.20%	3
5	CBOE Futures Exchange	40,193,447	1.27%	23,892,203	0.89%	5
6	NYSE Liffe U.S.	13,504,571	0.43%	18,822,300	0.70%	6
7	OneChicago	9,515,194	0.30%	6,432,217	0.24%	7
8	Kansas City Board of Trade	5,452,437	0.17%	5,302,197	0.20%	8
9	Minneapolis Grain Exchange	1,460,651	0.05%	1,223,584	0.05%	9
10	ELX Futures	3,772	0.00%	818,664	0.03%	10
	NASDAQ OMX Futures Exchange			518,360	0.02%	11
	Chicago Climate Exchange			20,099	0.00%	12
	Total Futures	**3,169,476,942**	**100.00%**	**2,689,760,818**	**100.00%**	

CBOE Futures Exchange (CFE)

FUTURE	2013	2012	2011	2010	2009
CBOE Volatility Index (VIX)	39,944,022	23,785,831	12,031,528	4,392,796	1,144,858
CBOE Mini-Volatility Index (VM)	18,198	17,057	8,388	9,429	9,268
CBOE Nasdaq 100 Volatility Index (VXN)	6,576	2,316			
CBOE Emerging Market ETF Volatility Index	24,751	55,388			
CBOE Gold ETF-Volatility Index (GVZ)	15,960	6,378	129		
CBOE Brazil ETF Volume Index Securities Futures	8,490	7,262			
CBOE Oil ETF Volatility Index Securities Futures	8,285	11,215			
Russell 2000 Volatility Index (RVX)	758				670
S&P Variance (IIK)	166,287	6,550			
CBOE Radar Logic 28-Day Real Estate Index (RPX)	120	170			
Total Futures	**40,193,447**	**23,892,203**	**12,040,074**	**4,402,616**	**1,155,969**

Chicago Board of Trade (CBT), division of the CME Group

FUTURE	2013	2012	2011	2010	2009
Wheat	24,993,158	27,379,403	24,283,331	23,090,255	17,677,547
Mini Wheat	125,944	95,600	149,102	91,560	61,355
Corn	64,322,600	73,184,337	79,004,801	69,841,420	50,948,804
Mini Corn	206,491	267,428	363,832	237,394	203,474
Oats	254,958	279,570	349,316	344,587	314,305
Soybeans	46,721,081	52,041,615	45,143,755	36,933,960	35,758,855
Mini Soybeans	299,308	359,324	394,119	412,732	466,367
Soybean Oil	23,805,912	27,627,590	24,156,509	20,791,164	17,132,082
Soybean Meal	20,237,181	18,187,433	16,920,194	14,052,845	12,880,767
Grain Bais Swap	41,280	241,054	235,642	57,423	7,918
Rough Rice	280,048	388,936	555,854	448,724	277,065
Fertilizer Products	10,436	4,175	360		
T-Bonds (30-year)	97,963,266	91,745,232	92,338,638	83,509,754	62,232,671
Ultra T-Bond	21,149,865	16,560,093	15,461,984	7,713,395	
T-Notes (10-year)	325,928,194	264,997,089	317,402,598	293,718,907	189,852,019
T-Notes (5-year)	175,328,163	133,342,429	170,563,052	132,149,948	98,391,120
T-Notes (2-year)	57,815,900	55,108,651	72,178,803	66,977,168	48,158,948
Interest Rate Swap (30-year)	207	1,552	13,966	31,564	55,228
Interest Rate Swap (10-year)	126,450	224,486	316,847	444,751	871,074
Interest Rate Swap (5-year)	79,356	274,251	658,376	1,039,064	1,331,017
30-year Swap rate	89,144	1,816			
10-year Swap rate	681,577	12,246			
5-year Swap rate	516,179	8,570			
2-year Swap rate	75,017	4,475			
30-Day Federal Funds	4,649,878	6,425,956	12,306,131	12,753,228	10,349,071
Ethanol	298,718	330,913	238,946	162,725	67,168
OTC Ethanol Forward Swap	44,452	355,943	632,211	636,444	270,596
Dow Jones Industrial Index ($25)	100	32	224	1,907	3,867
Dow Jones Industrial Index ($10)	166,905	202,771	286,697	188,109	395,584
Mini Dow Jones Industrial Index ($5)	35,448,824	30,902,047	32,496,922	34,059,544	39,889,836
DJ US Real Estate	52,486	14,081	6		
Dow-UBS Commodity Index	192,673	132,339	140,479	84,314	97,223
Dow-UBS Commodity Index Swap	1,682	678		1,592	
Dow-UBS Roll Select Commodity Index	1,787				
Total Futures	**800,706,309**	**906,707,754**	**799,926,808**	**587,984,965**	**825,257,796**

Chicago Mercantile Exchange (CME), division of the CME Group

FUTURE	2013	2012	2011	2010	2009
Live Cattle	12,463,043	13,985,374	13,532,554	11,332,739	8,797,033
Feeder Cattle	1,669,284	1,796,592	1,580,387	1,330,421	1,059,109
Lean Hogs	11,277,038	11,461,892	9,969,961	8,076,535	6,819,061
Class III Milk	293,941	294,497	368,614	277,860	280,636
Class IV Milk	20,115	2,755	10,744	968	332
Nonfat Dry Milk	12,015	5,355	6,372	5,696	1,480
Butter	3,191	1,050		1	59
Cash Butter	24,758	16,509	16,939	14,197	16,983
Cash Settled Cheese	35,800	30,164	15,990	3,189	
Dry Whey	11,457	11,904	10,601	7,490	5,246
Malaysian Palm Oil Calendar Swap	14,980				
USD Crude Palm Oil	1,080	318	1,016	572	
Wood Pulp	19,271	19,595	686	1,263	3,364
Random Lumber	224,351	304,928	319,333	311,902	317,227
One Month LIBOR	11,440	110,823	187,511	385,821	452,340
Eurodollar (3-month)	517,250,183	426,438,437	564,086,746	510,955,113	437,585,193
Euroyen	1	210	10,388	22,833	40,879
Euro Bonds	40	8,661	4,568		
Australian Dollar	26,332,299	32,727,390	30,751,538	25,903,355	16,732,682
British Pound	29,237,763	26,166,290	29,028,755	30,220,239	24,853,787
Brazilian Real	353,333	168,852	260,730	50,020	30,398
Canadian Dollar	17,427,832	22,799,446	22,416,680	22,083,807	15,481,166
Czech Koruna	5,708	112	219	727	224

Chicago Mercantile Exchange (CME), division of the CME Group (continued)

FUTURE	2013	2012	2011	2010	2009
Euro FX	61,285,617	67,407,741	84,236,825	86,232,358	54,393,644
E-Mini Euro FX	1,039,366	1,010,884	1,426,462	1,245,374	664,350
Hungarian Forint	15,645	792	2,117	2,080	975
Indian Rupee	166,114				
Israeli Shekel	9,681	9,350	5,599	6,329	7,495
Japanese Yen	42,762,257	23,520,562	28,369,147	31,862,793	22,749,569
E-Mini Japanese Yen	334,137	123,064	129,518	67,354	28,906
Korean Won	5,246	8,144	3,939	5,271	1,411
Mexican Peso	10,374,701	11,482,886	9,203,730	6,763,808	4,298,939
New Zealand Dollar	3,618,319	3,655,690	2,077,277	2,235,390	1,220,227
Norwegian Krone	13,963	8,206	13,082	11,241	11,652
Polish Zloty	19,594	22,312	38,951	20,318	19,848
Russian Ruble	244,995	313,867	687,845	238,490	162,314
South African Rand	141,518	164,012	143,544	138,144	77,848
Swedish Krona	13,438	4,306	3,217	6,972	5,396
Swiss Franc	9,061,770	9,911,325	10,238,684	12,011,173	10,618,630
Turkish Lira	45,418	39,286	13,729	26,521	12,011
Australian Dollar / Canadian Dollar	1,179	1,503	1,694	4,079	3,582
Australian Dollar / Japanese Yen	31,712	24,811	26,857	26,094	3,493
Australian Dollar / New Zealand Dollar	672	532	438	167	281
British Pound / Japanese Yen	31,209	31,925	36,105	28,977	6,395
British Pound / Swiss Franc	3,240	22,380	10,610	8,762	2,610
Canadian Dollar / Japanese Yen	1,205	1,591	624	838	301
Chinese Renimibi / US Dollar	18,981	4,101	7,563	4,937	7,024
Chinese Renimibi / Euro	6				
Swiss Franc / Japanese Yen	1,960	3,944	8,337	3,323	302
Euro / Australian Dollar	12,193	9,527	4,816	9,290	531
Euro / British Pound	739,215	461,063	341,899	275,335	125,657
Euro / Canadian Dollar	9,508	8,502	4,049	1,213	277
Euro / Czech Koruna	9,301	6		177	90
Euro / Hungarian Forint	19,771	7		450	189
Euro / Japanese Yen	904,294	368,161	369,522	295,766	219,109
Euro / Norwegian Krone	2,118	3,275	1,386	104	356
Euro / Polish Zloty	44,416	41,911	31,006	46,514	35,455
Euro / Swedish Krona	3,579	3,602	1,110	174	110
Euro / Swiss Franc	446,215	332,729	351,429	152,038	85,059
Euro / Turkish Lira	27,706	30,188	10,825	39,549	22,280
Micro JPY/USD	177,033	46,755	68,499	29	
Micro CHF/USD	61,530	45,582	59,900	78	
Micro CAD/USD	59,749	45,460	24,582	13	
E-micro EUR/USD	2,014,893	1,653,362	1,532,755	1,063,133	424,726
E-micro GBP/USD	388,124	364,989	206,527	240,081	170,411
E-micro USD/CAD	20	1,365	12,898	48,573	39,809
E-micro USD/JPY	98	10,595	29,465	34,453	94,508
E-micro AUD/USD	393,937	239,396	240,406	89,358	65,031
FCXRX	434				
Euro Quarterly Variance (VEQ)	556				
S&P 500 Index	4,156,499	5,032,650	7,220,582	7,689,961	10,435,912
E-mini S&P 500 Index	452,291,450	474,278,939	620,368,790	555,328,670	556,314,143
E-mini S&P SmallCap 600 Index	353	1,752	13,422	32,168	66,471
E-mini S&P MidCap 400 Index	5,601,547	6,536,907	7,689,306	7,657,372	9,133,223
S&P MidCap 400 Index	20,744	24,182	42,724	38,467	59,360
E-micro S&P CNX Nifty Index	47	2,936	44,757	143,753	
S&P Citigroup Growth	689	522	554	1,463	1,351
S&P Citigroup Value	733	522	697	4,971	5,437
E-Mini NASDAQ 100 Index	59,393,053	63,530,758	75,165,277	79,637,745	77,972,143
NASDAQ 100 Index	234,032	332,288	472,587	507,824	756,919
Nikkei 225 Index (USD)	4,680,898	1,690,244	2,766,559	2,951,246	2,935,616
Nikkei 225 Index (JPY)	11,792,392	5,738,629	7,670,282	5,108,015	4,167,340
E-mini S&P Financial Sector	49,872	24,455	10,000		
E-mini S&P Consumer Discretionary Sector	21,625	15,881	5,570		
E-mini S&P Consumer Staples Sector	43,185	25,599	7,766		
E-mini S&P Energy Sector	82,626	25,266	17,788		
E-mini S&P Health Sector	45,818	25,476	6,810		
E-mini S&P Industrial Sector	23,630	27,956	15,953		
E-mini S&P Materials Sector	22,769	20,928	16,133		
E-mini S&P Technology Sector	40,270	24,833	6,581		
E-mini S&P Utilities Sector	50,600	25,018	8,197		
Ibovespa Index	28,968	3,397			
HDD Weather	23,636	14,843	28,491	64,388	70,619
HDD Seasonal Weather Strips	600	1,350	3,975	6,257	3,550
CDD Weather	15,924	16,305	22,856	57,993	53,398
CDD Seasonal Weather Strips	3,550	2,121	3,150	250	2,900
Euro HDD Weather	3,800	5,675	4,664	8,275	16,950
Euro CAT Weather	3,550		1,650	1,025	775

Chicago Mercantile Exchange (CME), division of the CME Group (continued)

FUTURE	2013	2012	2011	2010	2009
Euro HDD Seasonal Strip Weather	1,000	2,050	1,028	5,435	300
Euro CAT Seasonal Strip Weather	50			100	150
Weekly Average Temperature	10,100	4,250	50		1,850
CSI Housing Index	230	357	195	88	295
Goldman Sachs Commodity Index	305,187	291,520	328,281	521,886	520,462
GSCI Excess Return Index	12,057	16,680	92,046	16,085	55,178
S&P GSCI Enhanced Excess Return Swap	18,548	4,732			
OTC SP GSCI ER Swap	4,505	26,409	4,708	12,216	
Total Futures	**1,290,230,093**	**1,215,594,457**	**1,535,793,841**	**1,418,240,658**	**1,276,264,462**

ELX Futures Exchange (ELX)

FUTURE	2013	2012	2011	2010	2009
2-Year Treasury Note (ZTE)	10	27,025	2,443,559	3,424,750	1,075,171
5-Year Treasury Note (ZFE)	454	134,639	3,599,102	3,565,576	2,012,132
10-Year Treasury Note (ZNE)	2,310	175,254	2,970,234	3,600,261	1,322,429
Ultra Long-Term US T-Bond (ZUE)	14	37,589	70,943	20,989	
30-Year Treasury Bond (ZBE)	77	258,447	3,785,858	1,243,715	594,251
Eurodollar (GEE)	907	185,710	3,888,256	1,287,250	
Total Futures	**3,772**	**818,664**	**16,757,952**	**13,142,541**	**5,003,983**

ERIS Exchange

FUTURE	2013
2-Year Standards	96,619
5-Year Standards	54,020
7-Year Standards	10,122
10-Year Standards	79,027
30-Year Standards	2,400
Flexes	61,892
Total Futures	**304,080**

ICE Futures U.S. (ICE)

FUTURE	2013	2012	2011	2010	2009
Coffee 'C'	7,124,029	6,125,484	5,174,538	5,488,196	4,235,349
Cocoa	6,583,746	5,999,813	4,948,052	3,797,679	3,086,966
Cotton #2	6,155,024	6,130,352	5,288,454	5,732,906	3,574,995
Orange Juice, Frozen Concentrate	505,019	586,775	627,610	691,583	656,995
Sugar #11	29,813,680	27,126,728	24,629,369	29,052,539	27,300,259
Sugar #16	76,117	76,565	74,876	99,049	66,719
U.S. Corn	103,000	153,577			
U.S. Soybeans	52,204	154,453			
U.S. Soybean Meal	5,324	29,874			
U.S. Soybean Oil	9,071	46,442			
U.S. Wheat	75,295	79,809			
Australian Dollar / Canadian Dollar	8,389	15,043	18,411	18,378	6,671
Australian Dollar / Japanese Yen	7,229	10,439	19,346	16,593	17,871
Australian Dolar / New Zealand Dollar	12,791	13,485	17,688	18,768	9,326
Australian Dollar / US Dollar (KAU)	3,579	2,303	4,219		
British Pound / Australian Dollar	9,552	12,649	19,111	18,216	6,271
British Pound / Canadian Dollar	9,330	14,563	14,099	12,598	1,033
British Pound / Japanese Yen	20,751	33,868	82,549	48,674	25,686
British Pound / New Zealand Dollar	5,423	5,595	7,019	6,535	2,245
British Pound / Norwegian Krone	11,937	13,579	17,952	10,717	383
British Pound / South Africa Rand	1,240				4
British Pound / Swedish Krona	410	2			4
British Pound / Swiss franc	19,391	19,249	15,076	13,911	16,317
Canadian Dollar / Japanese Yen	7,847	13,362	17,562	16,147	6,719
Canadian Dollar / US Dollar (KSV)	14	844	178		
Euro / Australian Dollar (KRA)	31,443	53,939	28,941		
Euro / British Pound (KGB)	63,612	114,160	30,679		
Euro / Canadian Dollar (KEP)	11,969	16,097	5,609		
Euro / Czech Koruna	23,423	22,692	34,069	39,172	25,233
Euro / Hungarian Forint	35,207	54,051	42,289	49,112	40,094
Euro / Japanese Yen (KEJ)	118,255	98,906	31,351		
Euro / Norwegian (KOL)	47,570	61,363	17,743		
Euro / South African Rand	1,329	393	183	113	117
Euro / Swedish Krona (KRK)	45,792	38,806	11,268		
Euro / Swiss Franc (KRZ)	24,120	16,871	3,934		
Euro / US Dollar (KEO)	113,818	101,583	79,547		
Indian Rupee / US Dollar	77				
Japanese Yen / US Dollar (KSN)	12	857	371		
Mexican Peso / US Dollar	20				
Million Euro / US Dollar	1,150	1,450	3,752	1,198	3,062
Million US Dollar / Japanese Yen	50		36		4,780
New Zealand Dollar / Japanese Yen	11,497	12,176	12,900	19,141	2,461
New Zealand Dollar / US Dollar (KZX)	6	364	191		

VOLUME - U.S.

ICE Futures U.S. (ICE) (continued)

FUTURE	2013	2012	2011	2010	2009
Norwegian Krone / Japanese Yen	2,174	708	176	83	1,333
Norwegian Krone / Swedish Koruna	20,590	22,715	17,044	22,460	29,257
Small British Pound / US Dollar	5,513	6,426	20,833	12,402	31,175
Swedish Krona / Japanese Yen	1,554				
Swiss Franc / Japanese Yen (KZY)	7,820	5,188	1,820		
Swiss Franc / US Dollar (KMF)	52	262	137		
US Dollar / Czech Koruna (Half Size)	19,142	20,729	32,584	17,901	31,581
US Dollar / Hungarian Forint (Half Size)	23,307	28,895	39,723	18,500	21,426
US Dollar / Norwegian Krone (Half Size)	52,755	59,163	80,993	58,091	30,359
US Dollar / South African Rand	117,262	94,907	102,942	123,105	149,046
US Dollar / Swedish Krona (Half Size)	65,457	84,331	70,409	35,785	42,749
Russian Ruble / US Dollar (KRU)	19,549	6,595			
US Dollar Index	8,050,966	6,321,418	7,751,270	6,369,517	2,523,927
Markit CDX Investment Grade WI	695				
Russell 1000 Mini Index	315,793	362,590	414,079	326,645	445,752
Russell 1000 Growth Index Mini	190,268	72,078	120,758	35,031	
Russell 1000 Value Index Mini	138,772	109,958	129,021	31,506	
Russell 2000 Growth Index Mini	54				
Russell 2000 Value Index Mini	1,050				
Russell 2000 Mini Index	28,837,712	33,044,716	43,594,169	39,747,503	38,686,673
North American Natural Gas	239,612,322	60,193,117			
North American Power	137,201,064	33,064,337			
Reuters-CRB Futures Index (CCI)	23	980	2,787	9,500	15,973
Total Futures	**465,833,636**	**180,757,780**	**94,106,767**	**92,520,026**	**81,715,275**

Kansas City Board of Trade (KCBT)

FUTURE	2013	2012	2011	2010	2009
Wheat	5,452,437	5,302,197	6,342,782	5,549,842	3,660,343
Total Futures	**5,452,437**	**5,302,197**	**6,342,782**	**5,549,842**	**3,660,343**

Minneapolis Grain Exchange (MGE)

FUTURE	2013	2012	2011	2010	2009
Spring Wheat	1,460,147	1,223,457	1,732,331	1,687,228	1,198,013
Apple Juice Concentrate	504	127			
Total Futures	**1,460,651**	**1,223,584**	**1,732,331**	**1,690,207**	**1,206,824**

New York Mercantile Exchange (NYMEX), division of the CME Group

FUTURE	2013	2012	2011	2010	2009
Gold (GC)	47,294,551	43,893,311	49,175,593	44,730,345	35,139,541
Platinum (PL)	3,262,775	2,621,704	1,993,263	1,486,507	802,884
Palladium (PA)	1,486,016	1,118,480	1,139,529	901,584	400,821
Silver (SI)	14,475,593	13,315,679	19,608,557	12,826,666	7,990,528
Silver (1,000) (SIL)	56,864				
Gold, miNY (QO)	97,252	111,323	192,575	105,236	59,900
E-micro Gold (MGC)	372,280	260,447	474,444	23,534	
Silver, E-mini (6Q)	9	7	15	1,975	660
Silver, miNY (QI)	19,153	26,842	106,576	24,722	13,367
Copper (HG)	17,127,383	16,158,815	12,491,517	10,305,670	6,398,967
Copper, miNY (QC)	18,025	20,717	23,655	10,566	5,987
Hot-Rolled Steel (HR)	53,793	43,867	31,738	21,613	13,494
Australian Coke Coal (ALW)	168	31	102		
Copper (HGS)	1,761	289			
Aluminum MW US Transaction Premium Platts	139				
Iron Ore 62% Fe, CFR North China (Platts) (PIO)	60	75			
NYMEX Iron Ore (TIO)	22,302	7,032	1,854	80	
U.S. Midwest #1 Busheling Ferrous Scrap (AMM)	1,567	506			
Steel Billet, FOB Black Sea (Platts) Swap (SSF)	219	1,065			
Uranium (UX)	6,515	8,113	22,598	26,097	6,149
Crude Oil, Physical (CL)	147,690,593	140,531,588	175,036,216	168,652,141	137,428,494
Crude Oil (WS)	306,513	406,087	313,463	453,557	1,139,308
Crude Oil, miNY (QM)	1,764,795	2,097,040	3,000,140	3,157,814	3,368,983
Brent Crude Oil, Last Day (BZ)	9,214,951	1,161,113	787,768	144,625	31,708
No. 2 Heating Oil, NY (HO)	32,749,553	36,087,707	31,838,626	26,970,106	21,426,015
Heating Oil Financial (BH)	48,452	40,449	44,784	50,834	91,152
Heating Oil, miNY (QH)	167	205	289	411	415
NY Harbor RBOB Gasoline (RB)	34,470,288	36,603,841	31,129,256	27,898,698	21,159,516
RBOB Gasoline, miNY (QU)	50	52	49	205	84
Natural Gas (HP)	217,114	81,777	27,786		
LTD Natural Gas (HH)	2,389,724	922,816	63,980	1,540	
Natural Gas, miNY (QG)	318,694	435,591	547,462	670,266	1,030,118
PJM Financially Settled Monthly - Peak (JM)	35,503	154,039	215,741	115,132	126,778
Natural Gas (NG)	84,282,495	94,799,542	76,864,334	64,323,068	47,951,353
RBOB Gas (RT)	89,192	74,124	45,008	48,088	9,800
3.5% Fuel Oil (Platts) CIF MED Swap (7D)	132	30	29	34	278
3.5% Fuel Oil CIF MED (Platts) BALMO (8D)	2				

New York Mercantile Exchange (NYMEX), division of the CME Group (continued)

FUTURE	2013	2012	2011	2010	2009
AER-Dayton Hub Daily (VD)	142	100		260	
AER-Dayton Hub Monthly - Peak (VM)	5,944	16,960	20,332	5,718	4,000
AER Dayton Hub Monthly - Off-Peak (VP)	3,782	14,921	17,979	5,892	11,716
Algonquin City - Gates Natural Gas Index Swap (N7)	527		5,839	3,454	
Algonquin City - Gates Natural Gas Basis Swap (B4)	6,126	10,705	9,891	3,243	1,924
ANR - Louisiana Basis Swap (ND)	183	2,122	5,140	15,887	46,530
ANR - Oklahoma Basis (NE)	2,842	3,065	20,157	28,380	70,712
Central Appalachian Coal (QL)	84,710	81,015	95,330	162,020	139,732
Argus LLS vs WTI (Arg) T (E5)	93,158	43,898	35,595	7,187	843
Argus Propane Far East Index Swap (7E)	3,344	5,079	5,952	4,583	2,220
Argus Propane (Saudi Aramco) Swap (9N)	11,231	10,737	8,313	2,792	433
Brent (ICE) Crude Oil BALMO Swap (J9)	4,560	7,385	2,363	3,145	4,619
Brent (ICE) Calendar Swap (CY)	113,912	223,213	221,197	157,237	313,572
Brent CFD (Platts) vs Front Month Swap (1C)	255	64	3,685	7,639	12,357
Brent (CFD) Swap (6W)	1,395	6,070	7,753	25,585	61,632
Brent Bullet Swap (BB)	239,036	343,578	241,343	176,357	276,532
Canadian Light Sweet Oil (CIL)	45				
Carbon EUA Emissions Euro (RC)	600				
Centerpoint Basis Swap (PW)	4,521	12,988	19,409	79,471	188,819
Chicago Basis Swap (NB)	120	836	480	428	73,011
Chicago Ethanol Swap (CU)	789,683	358,041	227,267	55,779	15,169
Chicago ULSD (Platts) Swap (4C)	20	60			
Chicago ULSD PL vs HO SPR (5C)	4,810	1,437	971	110	
Chicago Unleaded Gasoline vs RBOB Spread Swap	1,220	425	61		300
CIG Basis Swap (CI)	4,900	7,467	21,569	28,833	42,065
Cinergy Hub Off-Peak LMP Swap (EJ)	1,642	6,270	5,840	12,348	32,146
Cinergy Hub LMP Swap-Peak (EM)	1,148	7,972	12,722	23,962	43,856
Cinergy Hub 5mw Day Ahead Off-Peak (K2)	331,736	263,776	571,672	680,344	604,840
Cinergy Hub 5mw Day Ahead Peak (H5)	20,886	12,089	44,471	42,043	46,939
Cinergy Hub 5mw Real-Time Off-Peak (H4)	924,760	392,008	171,600	185,328	236,576
Cinergy Hub 5mw Real-Time Peak (H3)	53,842	20,636	25,243	19,088	15,321
Coal (API 5) fob Newcastle (argus/McCloskey) Swap	280				
SSI - Coal (API 8) cfr South China (Argus/McCloskey)	10,225	845			
Columbia Gulf Mainline Basis Swap (5Z)	1,774	5,682	21,690	71,361	99,036
Conway Natural Gas (OPIS) Swap (8L)	115	1,341	3,890	1,575	220
Conway Normal Butane (OPIS) Swap (8M)	1,049	752	2,523	490	362
Conway Propane 5 decimals Swap (8K)	8,648	18,089	13,514	18,067	4,129
Crude Oil Last Day Financial Futures (26)	120		531	347	130
Crude Oil Outrights	4,833	3,339	3,001	1,883	
Dated to Frontline Brent BALMO Swap (FE)	775	2,190	2,792		
Canadian Heavy Crude Oil (Net Energy) Index (WCC)	68,497	46,461	18,615	2,040	
Argus Sour Crude Index vs WTI Diff Spread Calendar	150	309	800		
RME Biodiesel (Argus) FOB Rdam vs ICE Gasoil	290	12,766	15,858	4,850	
Fame 0 Biodiesel FOB Rdam vs ICE Gasoil Spread	375	33,553	27,945	5,170	
Daily European Union Allowance (EUL)	2,560		1,450	2,200	
PJM AEP Dayton Hub Real-Time Off-Peak Calendar-	6,720				
PJM AEP Dayton Hub Day-Ahead Peak Calendar-	226				
PJM Daily Load Forecast (PDJ)	257				
Dated Brent (Platts) Daily Swap (7G)	1,262	8,865	11,816	35,626	1,802
Dated-to-Frontline Brent Swap (FY)	28,215	37,723	44,615	48,303	141,760
Diesel 10ppm Barge FOB Rdam vs ICE Gasoil	155	124	389	335	254
Diesel 10ppm Barge FOB Rdam BALMO Swap (U7)	5		1		
Dominion Natural Gas Index Swap (IH)	360	1,304	25,127	2,816	46,703
Dominion Basis Swap (PG)	21,471	25,964	28,072	46,950	102,937
Dubai Crude Oil BALMO Swap (BI)	200	1,150	1,975	6,847	3,774
Dubai Crude Oil Calendar Swap (DC)	22,614	123,003	207,050	413,157	923,539
Eastern Rail CSX Coal Swap (QX)	115,418	72,557	66,795	40,325	29,060
East-West Fuel Oil Spread Swap (EW)	15,338	43,339	20,056	13,850	18,589
EIA Flat Tax On-Highway Diesel Swap (A5)	7,221	5,317	3,929	4,986	6,974
ERCOT West Zone MCPE 5mw Peak Swap (N1)	11,395	19,117		210	
Ercot West 345 kV Hub M5mw Off-Peak Swap (O1)	296,125	478,848			
Electric MISO Peak (4L)	6,552	2,360	6,968	8,225	800
Electric MISO Peak (55)	767				
Electric NYISO Off-Peak (4M)	75,963	28,080	122,528	117,598	15,520
Electric NYISO Off-Peak (58)	14,008				
ERCOT Daily Load Forecast (EMC)	9,307				
Certified Emission Reduction Plus (CERplusSM)	817	750			
ERCOT North ZMCPE 5mw Off-Peak (I6)	268,480	185,685			
ERCOT North ZMCPE 5mw Peak (I5)	16,530	19,933	4,233	745	4,285
Ethanol T2 FOB Rdam Incl Duty Swap (Z1)	19,555	9,327	6,149	2,338	300
European 1% Fuel Oil BALMO Swap (KX)	690	597	258	532	1,886
European 3.5% Fuel Oil Rdam BALMO Swap (KR)	5,898	4,813	1,790	2,295	5,121
European 3.5% Fuel Oil Spread Swap (FK)	2,895	1,940	1,295	1,540	740
Brent (Euro Denominated) Financial (IBE)	60	144			
Mini 3.5% Fuel Oil Barges FOB Rdam (Platts) (Euro	20				

New York Mercantile Exchange (NYMEX), division of the CME Group (continued)

FUTURE	2013	2012	2011	2010	2009
European Gasoil 10ppm Rdam Barges Swap (GT)	398	87	508	379	42
European Gasoil 10ppm Rdam Barges vs Gasoil (ET)	4,357	3,740	4,848	6,228	4,789
Europe 1% Fuel Oil Calendar Swap (UF)	5,100	9,471	12,576	18,943	24,162
Europe 1% Fuel Oil Rdam Calendar Swap (UH)	680	521	2,092	4,517	9,115
European 6.5% Fuel Oil MED Calendar Swap (UI)	410	898	175	541	533
Europe 3.5% Fuel Oil Rotterdam Calendar Swap (UV)	103,960	178,569	89,321	76,245	126,496
European Gasoil (ICE) (7F)	58,540	44,956	17,317	5,871	1,644
European Naptha BALMO Swap (KZ)	2,649	2,594	1,423	1,804	936
European Naptha Crack Spread (EN)	102,003	125,320	99,444	126,917	110,560
European Dated Brent Crude Oil Calendar Swap	13,324	41,226	45,517	94,187	91,481
European Jet Kero NWE Calendar Swap (UJ)	516	629	430	969	782
European Naptha Calendar Swap (UN)	30,109	34,187	27,807	30,006	25,031
European Propane CIF ARA Swap (PS)	8,481	11,214	12,819	6,016	3,555
Freight Route TD3 (Baltic) Forward (FT3)	40		30	65	
Freight Route TC6 (Baltic) (TC6)	60				
3.5% Fuel Oil Rdam Crack Swap (FO)	192,036	311,707	130,348	80,788	78,398
1% Fuel Oil NWE Crack Spread Swap (FI)	11,938	28,195	15,426	3,469	9,042
Fuel Oil (Platts) CAR CM (1W)	257	401	875	116	785
1% Fuel Oil (Platts) Cargoes CIF NEW Swap (1X)	203	385	579	856	210
High-Low Sulfur Fuel Oil Spread Swap (FS)	15,683	37,853	20,067	7,328	21,931
Gas EuroBob OXY NWE Barges (7H)	99,668	92,156	73,570	70,147	12,549
Gas EuroBob OXY NWE Barges Crack (7K)	248,729	218,455	140,943	78,732	15,321
Gasoil 0.1 Barges FOB Rdam vs ICE Gasoil BALMO	75	43	60	134	137
Gasoil 0.1 Cargoes CIF NEW Swap (TW)	50	24	79	195	104
Gasoil 0.1 CIF MED vs ICE Gasoil Swap (Z5)	821	943	1,043	1,589	3,233
Gasoil 0.1 Cargoes CIF NWE vs ICE Gasoil Swap	176	71	93	609	1,294
Gasoil 0.1 CIF MED vs ICE Gasoil BALMO Swap	13	104	89	197	230
Gasoil 0.1 Cargoes NWE vs ICE Gasoil BALMO Swap	15	30	14	75	59
Gasoil 0.1 Barges FOB Rdam vs ICE Gasoil Swap	3,561	5,403	10,455	4,111	14,180
Gasoil 0.1 Barges FOB Rdam Swap (VL)	51	212	517	3,790	1,833
Gasoil 10ppm Cargoes CIF NEW vs ICE Gasoil	113	425	347	491	495
Gasoil 10ppm Cargoes CIF NWE Swap (TY)	36	148	805	599	351
Gasoil 10ppm Cargoes CIF NWE vs ICE Gasoil Swap	2,990	3,598	7,439	6,895	9,233
Gasoil (ICE) Calendar Swap (GX)	1,643	5,217	10,202	17,272	14,669
Gasoil Crack Spread Swap (GZ)	96,363	91,366	97,917	76,952	257,528
Gasoil (ICE) Mini Calendar Swap (QA)	1,673	3,441	14,106	22,064	
Gasoline Up-Down (Argus) Swap (UZ)	1,708	3,550	3,227	3,946	2,992
Gasoline Up-Down BALMO Swap (1K)	6,332	5,520	4,234	3,547	697
Gulf Coast ULSD vs Gulf Coast Jet Spread (VV)	300				
Group Three ULSD (Platts) Swap (A7)	180	8,676			
Group Three (Platts) vs Heating Oil Spread Swap	55,817	19,799	3,671	217	
Group Three Unlead Gas (Platts) vs RBOB Gas	3,287	11,935	1,695	124	
Gulf Coast 3.0% Fuel Oil BALMO Swap (VZ)	20,130	23,044	32,679	22,229	16,852
Gulf Coast Gasoline Calendar Swap (GS)	1,378	1,885	1,042	8,130	3,473
Gulf Coast Jet Fuel Calendar Swap (GE)	12,881	16,248	870	522	410
Gulf Coast Jet vs NY Harbor No 2 HO Spread Swap	497,944	169,807	114,056	113,926	97,772
Gulf Coast No 6 Fuel Oil 3.0% Sulfur Swap (MF)	755,088	714,705	854,111	644,907	683,433
Gulf Coast No 6 Fuel Oil Crack Swap (MG)	38,427	32,740	66,893	139,544	75,852
Gulf Coast ULSD Calendar Swap (LY)	10,021	46,558	9,143	8,729	7,538
Gulf Coast ULSD Crack Spread Swap (GY)	36,317	44,656	17,900	4,155	106
Heating Oil BALMO Calendar Swap (1G)	680	43	62	139	
Heating Oil Crack Spread BALMO Swap (1H)	28				
Heating Oil vs ICE Gasoil (HA)	82,627	52,815	28,587	33,564	72,340
Henry Hub Basis Swap (HB)	115,810	60,564	66,870	98,290	309,092
Henry Hub Index Swap (IN)	106,126	62,518	48,277	65,144	187,879
Henry Hub Swap (NN)	11,457,837	18,156,113	20,825,660	20,417,178	25,670,240
Henry Hub Swing Swap (SN)	1,200	1,704	4,074	8,055	19,156
Houston Ship Channel Basis Swap (NH)	1,716	20,162	33,836	184,062	595,698
Houston Ship Channel Index Swap (IP)	200	643	2,139	23,394	69,071
ICE Brent-Dubai Swap (DB)	16,689	28,014	51,835	72,518	207,977
ICE Gasoil BALMO Swap (U9)	1	338	138	101	40
In Delivery Month EUA (6T)	402,555	158,501	14,167	47,267	9,029
MISO Indiana Hub 5mw Off-Peak Calendar Month	23,400	6,528	4,704		
MISO Indiana Hub Real-Time Off-Peak Calendar-	1,776				
MISO Indiana Hub 5mw Off-Peak Calendar Month	138,775	23,570	575,856		
MISO Indiana Hub 5mw Peak Calendar Month Day-	1,899	321	1,530		
MISO Indiana Hub Real-Time Peak Calendar-Day 5	114				
MISO Indiana Hub 5mw Peak Calendar Month Real	4,683	5,295	27,443		
Indonesian Coal (MCC)	7,190	1,450	195		
ISO New England Off-Peak (KI)	6,498	18,126	16,802	18,038	27,468
ISO New England LMP Swap Peak (NI)	2,954	25,314	24,342	19,322	38,225
Japan C&F Naptha Crack Spread Swap (JB)	270	1,997			30
Japan C&F Naptha Swap (JA)	23,502	29,467	24,965	40,120	32,132
Japan Naptha BALMO Swap (E6)	958	565	312	500	201
Jet AV Fuel (P) Car FM ICE Gas Swap (1V)	141	117	42	39	290

New York Mercantile Exchange (NYMEX), division of the CME Group (continued)

FUTURE	2013	2012	2011	2010	2009
European Jet Rotterdam Barges vs Gasoil Swap (JR)	74	64	145	392	384
European Jet CIF NWE vs Gasoil Swap (JC)	2,451	3,980	6,428	9,156	17,561
Jet Fuel Barges FOB Rdam vs ICE Gasoil BALMO	18	5	12	4	5
Jet Fuel Cargoes CIF NEW vs ICE Gasoil BALMO	55	88	504	397	941
Jet Fuel Up-Down BALMO CL (1M)	14,185	2,952	2,908	1,703	75
Los Angeles CARB Diesel (OPIS) Outright Swap (LX)	378	586	291	550	259
Los Angeles CARB Diesel (OPIS) Spread Swap (KL)	15,548	17,185	22,688	19,997	13,142
Los Angeles CARBOB (OPIS) Spread Swap (JL)	12,660	4,770	20,325	21,024	4,075
Los Angeles Jet Fuel vs NYH #2 Heating Oil Spread	2,776	900	1,260	1,100	162
Los Angeles Jet (OPIS) Spread Swap (JS)	10,985	11,450	21,548	28,818	33,572
LLS (Argus) Calendar Swap (XA)	5,485	1,010	100		
LLS (Argus) vs WTI Spread Calendar Swap (WJ)	211,157	33,463	36,158	13,250	2,135
Mars (Argus) vs WTI Spread Calendar Swap (YX)	25,015	1,790	2,202	3,180	1,500
Mars (Argus) vs WTI Spread Trade Month Swap (YV)	1,560	6,826	3,699	2,035	3,720
Coal (API2) cis ARA (Argus/McCloskey) Swap (MTF)	989,486	260,219	2,592	24	
Coal (API4) fob Richards Bay (Argus/McCloskey)	278,396	64,790	1,140	24	
Mini Gasoil 0.1 (Platts) Cargoes CIF NEW vs Gasoil	24	10			
Mini ULSD 10ppm (Platts) Cargoes CIF NEW vs	673	268			
MichCon Natural Gas Index Swap (Y8)	2,080		2,322	5,994	5,413
MichCon Basis Swap (NF)	2,950	6,482	11,495	73,658	173,256
Midwest Michigan Hub 5 MW Off-Peak Calendar-	102,840				
Midwest ISO Michigan Hub 5mw Peak Calendar-	6,932	640			
Mini Gasoline Euro–bob Oxy NWE Barges (Argus)	337				
Mini RBOB Gasoline vs. Euro–bob Oxy NWE Barges	93				
Mini RBOB Gasoline vs. Euro–bob Oxy NWE Barges	130				
Mini European Jet Kero (Platts) Cargoes CIF NEW vs	984	916	672		
Mini European Naptha CIF NEW Swap (MNC)	33,522	4,870	2,369	78	
Mont Belvieu Ethane 5 Decimals (OPIS0 Swap (C0)	18,578	21,193			
Mont Belvieu Ethane (OPIS) BALMO (8C)	35	1,105	920	2,938	126
Mont Belvieu LDH Propane 5 Decimal (OPIS) Swap	115,047	139,722	114,417	210,632	66,945
Mont Belvieu LDH Propane (OPIS) BALMO Swap	3,676	3,155	5,009	6,389	1,059
Mont Belvieu Natural Gas 5 Decimal (OPIS) Swap	26,436	37,653	58,523	54,771	15,257
Mont Belvieu Natural Gas (OPIS) BALMO Swap (R0)	2,161	697	1,677	939	355
Mont Belvieu Normal Butane 5 Decimal (OPIS) Swap	92,711	58,873	46,202	56,408	28,214
Mont Belvieu Normal Butane (OPIS) BALMO Swap	4,232	2,891	2,477	3,002	148
Transco Zone 6 Non-N.Y. Natural Gas (Platts IFERC)	8,978				
Transco Zone 6 Non New York Natural Gas (Platts	806				
Natural Gas Penultimate Swap (NP)	6,418,797	7,945,695	7,384,147	8,995,324	11,038,692
NEPOOL CNCTCT Day Ahead Off-Peak (P3)	14,175	1,440	159,019	461,528	1,194,942
NEPOOL CONECTIC 5mw Day Ahead Peak (P2)	720	1,317	12,271	27,569	66,666
NEPOOL INTR HUB 5mw Day Ahead Off-Peak (H2)	419,727	541,375	851,583	1,021,109	2,433,442
NEPOOL INTR HUB 5mw Day Ahead Peak (U6)	29,060	35,662	42,914	67,190	140,169
NE Maine HUB 5mw Day Ahead Off-Peak (W2)	2,751	21,805	89,376	46,848	75,404
NE Maine HUB 5mw Day Ahead Peak (P9)	149	1,180	7,520	5,928	4,415
NEPOOL New Hamp 5mw Day Ahead Peak (U2)	512		3,058	7,073	
NEPOOL New Hamp 5mw Day Ahead Off-Peak (U3)	9,328		56,460	129,365	
NEPOOL Rhode Island 5mw Day Ahead Peak (U4)	3,825	1,017	15,934	255	
NEPOOL Rhode Island 5mw Day Ahead Off-Peak	69,830	18,990	294,247		
NEPOOL W CNTR Mass 5mw Day Ahead Off-Peak	42,240	137,618	74,173	82,358	277,045
NEPOOL W CNTR Mass 5mw Day Ahead Peak (R6)	2,310	8,554	5,290	4,961	17,055
New York 0.3% Fuel Oil HiPr (Platts) Swap (8N)	500	700	2,897	7,973	3,850
New York Ethanol Swap (EZ)	10,789	8,424	11,158	16,371	8,215
New York Hub Zone G Peak Swap (GN)	319	260	840	100	320
NYISO Zone J Day-Ahead Peak Calendar-Day 5 MW	119				
NGPL Mid-Continent Basis Swap (NL)	5,584	34,039	21,895	116,520	275,602
NGPL Mid-Continent Natural Gas Index Swap (IW)	60		542	3,965	14,420
NGPL TEX/OK Basis Swap (PD)	4,420	24,645	43,928	184,279	430,388
Northern Illinois Hub Daily Futures Peak (UD)	300				
Northern Illinois Hub Monthly Peak (UM)	3,560	11,247	16,542	12,508	38,455
No 2 Heating Oil Up-Down Spread Calendar Swap	12,943	12,191	14,564	29,118	20,285
Northern Natural Gas Ventura Basis Swap (PF)	1,763	11,827	36,903	71,867	259,500
Northern Illinois Hub Monthly Off-Peak (UO)	2,892	16,620	18,323	5,383	29,433
Northwest Rockies Basis Swap (NR)	5,349	16,953	23,587	88,194	293,089
Rockies Natural Gas (Platts IFERC) Fixed Price	270				
New York 1% Fuel Oil vs Gulf Coast 3% Fuel Oil Swap	77,742	81,710	70,946	103,093	42,976
New York 3.0% Fuel Oil Swap (H1)	3,452	2,492	4,653	3,904	2,293
NY Harbor Fuel Oil 1.0% Sulfur BALMO Swap (VK)	4,451	3,294	7,927	8,425	5,375
NY Harbor Heating Oil Calendar Swap (MP)	64,489	138,224	93,313	157,545	141,753
NY Harbor Residual Fuel 1.0% Sulfur Swap (MM)	142,479	172,096	141,667	209,696	189,772
NY Harbor Residual Fuel Oil Crack Swap (ML)	1,160	335	1,070	14,622	6,672
NY Harbor No 2 Crack Spread Calendar Swap (HK)	66,551	26,098	63,503	102,877	148,936
New York Heating Oil (Platts) vs NYMEX Heating Oil	9,347		2,962	1,981	1,895
NYISO Zone A LBMP Swap Peak (KA)	16,929	10,952	9,728	8,401	12,687
NYISO Zone A LBMP Swap Off-Peak (KB)	5,364	4,146	4,982	4,164	5,600
NYISO NYC In-City Capacity Calendar Month Swap	648	408	125		

New York Mercantile Exchange (NYMEX), division of the CME Group (continued)

FUTURE	2013	2012	2011	2010	2009
NYISO Rest of the State Capacity Calendar Month	790	1,007	56		
NYISO Zone G LBMP Swap Peak (KG)	9,474	9,570	7,814	8,224	10,459
NYISO Zone G LBMP Swap Off-Peak (KH)	9,437	4,490	3,608	3,780	10,050
NYISO Zone J LBMP Swap Peak (KJ)	5,988	6,701	5,680	7,361	8,221
NYISO Zone J LBMP Swap Off-Peak (KK)	1,066	3,036	2,264	2,834	2,660
NYISO Zone A 5mw Day Ahead Off-Peak (K4)	1,345,805	375,201	267,274	129,788	284,962
NYISO Zone A 5mw Day Ahead Peak (K3)	118,501	21,858	12,809	12,994	18,320
NYISO Zone C 5mw Day Ahead Off-Peak (A3)	67,986	387,833	118,395	82,560	108,840
NYISO Zone C 5mw Day Ahead Peak (Q5)	6,839	21,404	6,454	4,780	8,555
NYISO Zone G 5mw Day Ahead Off-Peak (D2)	1,137,172	259,269	213,204	57,833	154,380
NYISO Zone G 5mw Day Ahead Peak (T3)	98,468	25,734	26,581	21,407	11,162
NYISO Zone J 5mw Day Ahead Off-Peak (D4)	453,830	63,441	73,623	93,738	37,768
NYISO Zone J 5mw Day Ahead Peak (D3)	42,122	12,843	10,947	8,287	7,512
NY Jet Fuel (Argus) vs Heating Oil Swap (5U)	100	150	350	50	50
NY Jet Fuel (Platts) vs Heating Oil Swap (1U)	11,550	4,200	4,850	350	1,150
NYISO Zone A LBMP Daily Peak Swap (AN)	70	100		180	
NY ULSD (Argus) vs Heating Oil Spread Swap (7Y)	20,560	32,776	4,653	6,068	530
OneOk, OK Basis Swap (8X)	1,570	2,625	6,739	11,179	21,659
Ontario Off-Peak Calendar Day Swap (OFD)	1,120	5,040	2,480		
Ontario Off-Peak Calendar Month Swap (OFM)	186,534	74,114	122,410		
Ontario Peak Calendar Day Swap (OPD)	885	630	965		
Ontario Peak Calendar Month Swap (OPM)	46,135	812	4,103		
Panhandle Basis Swap (PH)	22,481	35,642	121,303	417,511	1,277,176
Panhandle Index Swap (IV)	488	2,876	2,899	11,966	24,002
Panhandle Pipe Swap (XH)	135				
El Paso Natural Gas Permian Basin Basis Swap (PM)	1,327	6,359	31,758	68,883	152,858
Argus Propane Far East Index BALMO Swap (22)	462	460	637	262	
European Propane CIF ARA (Argus) BALMO Swap	2,075	964	1,063	299	
Mont Belvieu LDH Propane (OPIS) vs European CIF	10	271	42		
Mont Belvieu Mini LDH Propane (81)	40	481	1,905	380	
Mont Belvieu Iso-Butane (8I)	5,414	1,780	3,761	2,735	90
Argus Propane Far East Index vs European Propane	899	942	325		
HDPE High Density Polyethylene In-Well (HPE)	360	1,028	546	8	
LNG Japan/Korea Marker (Platts) (JKM)	1	1			
Mini Argus Propane Far East Index (MAE)	10				
Mini Argus Propane (Saudi Aramco) (MAS)	110				
Mont Belvieu Spot Ethylene In-Well (MBE)	10,280	6,436	7,020	880	
Mont Belvieu Normal Butane LDH (OPIS) Swap	19,859	23,594	10,871	10	
Singapore Fuel Oil 380 cst (Platts) 6.35 Dubai Crack	63	721			
Singapore Fuel Oil 180 cst (Platts) 6.35 Brent Crack	4,020	448			
Singapore Fuel Oil 180 cst (Platts) 6.35 Dubai Crack	5,623	4,364	750		
Gulf Coast CBOB Gasoline A1 (Platts) vs RBOB	150	500	500		
Gulf Coast CBOB Gasoline A2 (Platts) vs RBOB	1,221	1,297	187		
RBOB Gasoline vs Eurobob Oxy (Argus) NEW Barges	15,778	13,791	1,051		
NY 3% Fuel Oil vs GC #6 Fuel Oil 3% (Platts) Swap	4,576	3,985	637		
Gulf Coast #6 Fuel Oil 3% (Platts) vs Brent Crack	8,015	13,107	5,006		
Gulf Coast #6 Fuel Oil 3% vs European 3.5% Fuel Oil	183,614	171,446	159,564		
Gulf Coast #6 Fuel Oil (Platts) Crack Spread BALMO	1,263	1,027	695		
Heating Oil vs Brent Crack Spread Swap (HOB)	7,643	11,237	1,345		
Singapore Jet Kerosene (Platts) Dubai Crack Spread	1,700	700			
NY 1% Fuel Oil (Platts) vs Gulf Coast 3% Fuel Oil	895	686	1,917		
NY 1% Fuel Oil vs European 1% Fuel Oil Cargoes	11,435	23,750	21,103		
NY 0.3% Fuel Oil HiPr (Platts) vs NY Fuel Oil 1.0%	125				
RBOB Gasoline vs Brent Crack Spread Swap (RBB)	128,250	144,282	68,379		
Gulf Coast Unleaded 87 Gasoline MD (Platts) vs	2,415	1,700	4,490		
Singapore Mogas 92 Unleaded (Platts) Brent Crack	24,989	5,758	260		
Singapore Mogas 92 Unleaded (Platts) Dubai (Platts)	50				
Petro European Naptha Crack Spread BALMO Swap	2,433	2,812	3,739	4,688	
RME Biodiesel (Argus) FOB Rdam (RED Compliant)	9,150	5,574			
3.5% Fuel Oil (Platts) Barges FOB Crack Spread Swap	7,847	1,665	452	53	
Argus Gasoline Eurobob Oxy Barges NWE Crack	34		30	15	
European Propane CIF ARA (Argus) vs Naptha CIF	2,859	3,475	1,659		
Singapore Fuel Oil 380 cst (Platts) vs. European 3.5%	1,743				
FAME 0 Biodiesel (Argus) FOB Rdam (RED	16,067	6,827			
1.0% Fuel Oil (Platts) Cargoes FOB NEW Crack	487	36			
Gulf Coast #5 Fuel Oil 3% vs Euro 3.5% Fuel Oil	475	978	1,162		
Gasoil (ICE) Crack Spread Swap (GOC)	1,632	1,139	820	23	
Gasoil 50ppm (Platts) Barges FOB Rdam vs ICE	26	40	40		
Gasoil 50ppm (Platts) Barges FOB Rdam vs ICE	35	110	320		
Mini Gasoil 0.1 Barges FOB Rdam (Platts) vs Gasoil	54	31			
Mini European Diesel 10ppm Barges FOB Rdam	658	744			
Naptha (Platts) Cargoes CIF NEW Crack Spread	36	6			
Naptha Cargoes CIF NEW vs Gasoil Swap (NOB)	1,373	1,036	136	101	
Singapore Fuel Oil 180 Crack Spread Swap (SFC)	105	5,483	214	240	
D4 Biodiesel RINS (Argus) 2013 (D43)	105				

New York Mercantile Exchange (NYMEX), division of the CME Group (continued)

FUTURE	2013	2012	2011	2010	2009
D4 Biodiesel RINS (Argus) 2014 Futures (D44)	50				
D5 Advanced Biofuel RINS (Argus) 2013 (D53)	180				
D6 Ethanol RINS (Argus) 2012 (D62)	70				
D6 Ethanol RINS (Argus) 2013 (D63)	1,299				
D6 Ethanol RINS (Argus) 2014 (D64)	272				
East-West Fuel Oil Spread (Platts) BALMO (EWB)	75				
East-West Gasoline Spread (Platts-Argus) Swap	126				
Tokyo Bay Gasoline (RIM) Swap (RMG)	420	340			
Tokyo Bay Kerosene (RIM) Swap (RMK)	1,740	230			
Mini Japan Naptha (Platts) BALMO Swap (E6M)	1,178	148			
Mini Japan C&F Naptha (Platts) Swap (MJN)	23,703	2,018	226		
Mini European 1% Fuel Oil (Platts) Cargoes FOB	1,257	124	60		
Mini European 1% Fuel Oil (Platts) Cargoes FOB	70				
Mini European 3.5% Fuel Oil Barges FOB Rdam	38,764	27,053	28,573	4,940	
Mini European 3.5% Fuel Oil Barges FOB Rdam	712	24			
Mini Singapore Fuel Oil 180 cst (Platts) SWAP (0F)	15,698	1,886	811		
Jet Aviation Fuel (Platts) Cargoes FOB MED Swap	78	19	15		
1% Fuel Oil Rdam vs 1% Fuel Oil NWE (Platts) Swap	1,421	3,154	2,212	144	
Brent CFD (Platts) vs Brent Third Month (Platts)	1,134	2,276			
Mini Singapore Fuel Oil 180 cst (Platts) BALMO	1,345				
3.5% Fuel Oil Rdam vs 3.5% FOB MED Spread Balmo	1,101	322	742	133	
European 1% Fuel Oil (Platts) Barges FOB Rdam	25	9	8		
Gasoil EuroBob Oxy NWE Barges Crack Spread	2,929	2,013	1,996	2,115	
EuroBob Gasoline 10ppm (Platts) Barges FOB Rdam	15	6	19	39	
Gasoil EuroBob Oxy NWE Barges BALMO Swap (7R)	7,602	6,260	3,615	4,976	3
Northwest Europe Fuel oil High-Low Sulfur Spread	118	391		5	
Conway Normal Butane (OPIS) BALMO Swap (CBB)	20	76	75		
Gulf Coast CBOB Gasoline A1 (Platts) Crack Spread	270	243	229	265	
European 3.5% Fuel Oil Cargoes FOB MED BALMO	22	112		50	
European 1% Fuel Oil Cargoes FOB MED Swap	450	1,097	173	20	
Euro 1% Fuel Oil Cargoes FOB MED vs Euro 1% Fuel	1,038	730	100	20	
East-West Naptha Japan C&F vs Cargoes CIF NEW	171	20			
FAME 0 Biodiesel FOB Rdam (Argus) (RED	70	200			
Mont Belvieu Ethylene (PCW) Financial Swap (MBN)	5,553	2,036	942	1,023	
RME Biodiesel FOB Rdam (Argus) (RED Compliant)	1,060	110			
Mini European 1% Fuel Oil Barges FOB Rdam Swap	213	202	804	28	
NY ULSD (Argus) vs Heating Oil Spread BALMO	4,345	1,225			
Singapore Mogas 95 Unleaded Swap (V0)	2,635	850	750	275	
Singapore Mogas 95 Unleaded (Platts) BALMO Swap	175	230	15		
Singapore Mogas 95 Unleaded (Platts) Swap (X0)	468	50	516		
Dated Brent (Platts) BALMO Swap (DBB)	1,046	1,205			
3.5% Fuel Oil (Platts) Barges FOB Rdam Crack	1,857	1,976			
Steel Billet FOB Black Sea (Platts) (FOB)	20				
1% Fuel Oil (Platts) Cargoes FOB MED BALMO	10	44			
Gasoline 10ppm FOB MED (Platts) Crack Spread	233	50			
EIA Flat Tax U.S. Retail Gasoline Swap (JE)	30	174			
Mont Belvieu LDH Iso-butane (OPIS) Swap (MBL)	1,424	4,880			
Mini European Naptha (Platts) BALMO Swap (MEN)	3,561	228			
Mini Gasoline Euro-bob Oxy (Argus) NEW Barges	78,260	5,323			
Mini 1% Fuel Oil Cargoes FOB MED (Platts) Swap	224	169			
Mini 1% Fuel Oil Cargoes FOB MED (Platts) Swap	310	773			
New York 0.3% Fuel Oil HiPr (Platts) BALMO Swap	125	200	75		
New York 3% Fuel Oil (Platts) BALMO Swap (NYT)	519	739	558		
Euro bob OXY NWE Barges (ARGUS) (XER)	900				
PJM AD Hub 5mw Real-Time Off-Peak (V3)	2,056,995	789,550	853,031	430,142	72,498
PJM AD Hub 5mw Real-Time Peak (Z9)	99,141	28,646	51,695	14,608	9,962
PJM AECO Day Ahead Off-Peak (X1)	70,320	243,904		87,350	3,920
PJM AECO Day Ahead Peak (Y1)	3,825	13,436		6,095	308
PJM APS Zone Day Ahead Off-Peak (W4)	42,144		60,680	33,886	
PJM APS Zone Day Ahead Peak (S4)	2,298		3,805	1,876	
PJM BGE Day Ahead Off-Peak (R3)	32,840	32,816	246,229	305,027	823,697
PJM BGE Day Ahead Peak (E3)	1,780	5,854	10,928	21,080	49,163
PJM ComEd 5mw Day Ahead Off-Peak (D9)	123,585	119,279	155,803	4,648	149,456
PJM ComEd 5mw Day Ahead Peak (D8)	6,490	7,048	8,559	515	10,144
PJM Financially Settled Daily Peak (JD)	330	1,416	860	3,220	350
PJM Dayton Day Ahead Off-Peak (R7)	246,892	508,893	640,076	287,026	269,270
PJM Dayton Day Ahead Peak (D7)	17,071	37,046	45,571	17,026	38,051
PJM JCPL Zone Hub Off-Peak Cal-Mth Day Ahead	23,400	19,440	141,238	329,176	653,460
PJM JCPL Zone Hub Peak Cal-Mth Day Ahead LMP	1,275	4,895	9,896	23,322	44,379
PJM Northern IL Hub 5mw Real-Time Off-Peak (B3)	80,710	35,494	65,570	26,815	32,478
PJM Northern IL Hub 5mw Real-Time Peak (B6)	1,187,306	880,993	1,619,448	440,021	465,914
PJM Northern IL Hub Day Ahead Off-Peak (L3)	408,282	400,759	1,057,271	402,357	1,683,800
PJM Northern IL Hub Day Ahead Peak (N3)	25,056	38,589	58,068	27,594	91,606
PJM Off-Peak LMP Swap (JP)	70,952	35,702	41,402	32,744	61,397
PJM PPL Day Ahead Off-Peak (F5)	55,976	35,234	203,108	608,959	332,772

VOLUME - U.S.

New York Mercantile Exchange (NYMEX), division of the CME Group (continued)

FUTURE	2013	2012	2011	2010	2009
PJM PPL Day Ahead Peak (L5)	3,597	1,540	10,729	41,097	37,398
PJM PSEG Day Ahead Off-Peak (W6)	4,696	322,642	789,728	1,249,809	2,801,488
PJM PSEG Day Ahead Peak (L6)	254	19,591	48,385	82,035	203,264
PJM Western Hub Day Ahead Off-Peak (E4)	758,040	783,668	1,671,911	4,913,517	6,810,613
PJM Western Hub Day Ahead Peak (J4)	33,946	57,013	115,898	317,505	531,995
PJM Western Hub Real-Time Off-Peak (N9)	3,098,831	1,290,881	2,248,985	1,565,616	1,727,213
PJM Western Hub Real-Time Peak (L1)	145,354	56,375	83,776	78,894	98,311
PGP Polymer Grade Propylene (PCW) Calendar Swap	4,135	3,797	1,722		
Polypropylene (PCW) Calendar Swap (PPP)	66	86	227	336	
High Density Polyethylene (P6)	14	282	815	806	
Premium Unld Gasoline 10ppm FOB MED (3G)	5,376	5,756	2,987	1,736	1,234
Premium Unld Gasoline 10ppm FOB (8G)	1,890	909	527	442	280
Premium Unld Gasoline 10ppm Rdam FOB BALMO	45	23	52	94	60
Premium Unld Gasoline 10ppm FOB Swap (7L)	616	1,418	467	121	234
Propane Non-LDH Mt Belvieu (OPIS) BALMO Swap	817	1,670	399	28	315
Propane Non-LDH Mt Belvieu (OPIS) Swap (1R)	6,854	4,132	4,905	1,986	3,390
RBOB Calendar Swap (RL)	95,844	123,922	151,780	156,852	112,652
RBOB Crack Spread Swap (RM)	18,780	7,335	37,893	144,319	151,414
RBOB Crack Spread BALMO Swap (1E)	26	44		1,010	
RBOB Gasoline BALMO Swap (1D)	12,816	14,522	4,891	6,262	3,274
RBOB vs NYMEX RBOB Gasoline Spread Swap (RI)	697	11,400		1,500	
RBOB Up-Down Calendar Swap (RV)	107,547	103,909	114,851	97,772	93,703
RBOB vs Heating Oil Swap (RH)	300	14,286	13,450	14,707	2,860
San Juan Basis Swap (NJ)	1,332	6,979	13,109	28,434	93,864
Singapore Fuel Oil 180cst BALMO Swap (BS)	1,852	1,506	2,718	3,478	5,762
Singapore Fuel Oil 380cst BALMO Swap (BT)	1,144	997	901	1,169	929
Singapore Fuel Oil 380cst Calendar Swap (SE)	46,652	21,239	17,417	16,529	5,982
Singapore Fuel Oil 180cst Calendar Swap (UA)	98,722	99,854	105,335	121,756	133,362
Singapore Fuel Oil Spread Swap (SD)	17,584	16,427	10,611	11,980	11,276
Mini Singapore Fuel Oil 380 cst (Platts) BALMO	784	78	55		
Mini Singapore Fuel Oil 380 cst (Platts) Swap (MTS)	20,476	1,569	401		
Singapore Gasoil 10ppm BALMO Swap (STL)	150		75		
Singapore Gasoil 10ppm vs 0.5% Sulfur Spread	2,250	8,810	8,730		
Singapore Gasoil BALMO Swap (VU)	7,035	13,807	19,196	23,926	28,166
Mini Singapore Gasoil (Platts) Futures (MSG)	80				
Singapore Gasoil Calendar Swap (SG)	144,385	143,251	192,079	260,561	321,662
Singapore Gasoil vs Rdam Gasoil Swap (GA)	52,945	76,211	35,079	33,009	69,019
Singapore Jet Kerosene BALMO Swap (BX)	1,028	2,057	1,921	3,567	7,740
Singapore Jet Kerosene vs Gasoil Spread Swap (RK)	27,884	54,044	31,603	35,730	64,490
Singapore Jet Kerosene Swap (KS)	74,257	67,208	48,422	66,582	81,705
Singapore Jet Kero vs Gasoil BALMO Swap (Z0)	2,885	2,200	1,775	2,690	255
Singapore Mogas 92 Unleaded BALMO (1P)	7,368	7,918	3,438	1,236	425
Singapore Mogas 92 Unleaded Swap (1N)	136,999	113,468	105,150	31,649	11,224
Singapore Naptha Swap (SP)	2,757	2,562	3,504	9,286	13,887
Singapore Fuel Oil 180cst vs 380cst Spread (Platts)	210	45			
SoCal Pipe Swap (XN)	114	364	15,768		
Southern Star TX,OK,KS Natural Gas Basis Swap	2,390	4,647	12,698	19,049	4,304
Sumas Basis Swap (NK)	3,419	6,841	7,049	6,102	6,652
TC2 Rotterdam to USAC 37K (TM)	730	920	435	2,135	395
TC5 Ras Tanura to Yokohama Freight (TH)	1,119	2,410	2,566	3,275	5,256
TCO Basis Swap (TC)	2,146	1,348	11,872	34,315	110,615
TD3 Middle Eastern Gulf to Japan 250K MT (TL)	320	5,281	1,292	2,505	651
Tennessee 800 Leg Natural Gas Index Swap (L4)	6,939	5,774	35,017		
Tennesse 500 Leg Natural Gas Swing Swap (T7)	78				
Tennessee 800 Basis Swap (6Z)	6,457	4,472	47,179	4,560	6,426
Tennessee Zone 0 Basis Swap (NQ)	1,406	2,488	5,448	11,083	12,040
TETCO South Texas Basis Swap (TX)	96	1,628	4,528	5,334	12,289
Texas Eastern Zone M-3 Basis Swap (NX)	23,212	2,856	28,924	94,942	232,939
Texas Gas Zone 1 Basis Swap (9F)	2,420		492	6,391	11,113
Texas Gas Zone SL Basis Swap (TB)	1,666	1,832	3,476	18,023	81,101
Transco Zone 3 Basis Swap (CZ)	7,300				
Transco Zone 4 Basis Swap (TR)	3,890	2,957	4,761	34,684	70,159
Transco Zone 4 Natural Gas Index (B2)	720	58	5,000	14,467	1,611
Transco Zone 6 Basis Swap (NZ)	2,696	3,912	8,324	32,080	94,997
Transco Zone 6 Index (IT)	112				
Mini ULSD 10 ppm Cargos CIF MED (Platts) vs.	256				
ULSD 10ppm Cargoes CIF MED BALMO Swap (X7)	9	6	13		
ULSD 10ppm CIF MED Swap (Z6)	18	120	325	238	146
ULSD 10ppm CIF MED vs ICE Gasoil Swap (Z7)	1,331	2,278	4,018	4,725	3,057
ULSD 10ppm CIF NW BALMO Swap (B1)	5		12		4
ULSD 10ppm CIF MED vs ICE Gasoil BALMO Swap	70	231	507	193	334
ULSD Up-Down BALMO Swap (1L)	30,520	26,059	20,681	9,483	1,206
Up Down GC ULSD vs NYMEX Heating Oil Spread	660,461	550,191	556,663	525,152	228,195
US Gulf Coast Unleaded 87 Crack Spread Calendar	6,785	3,170	7,500	7,805	8,045
WAHA Basis Swap (NW)	3,694	41,141	41,601	149,767	425,807

New York Mercantile Exchange (NYMEX), division of the CME Group (continued)

FUTURE	2013	2012	2011	2010	2009
Western Rail Powder River Basin Coal Swap (QP)	74,721	74,015	19,145	17,580	24,085
WTI Brent (ICE) Bullet Swap (BY)	18,544	2,590	4,200		
WTI-Brent (ICE) Calendar Swap (BK)	348,918	83,466	99,413	70,919	107,192
WTI Crude Oil Calendar Swap (CS)	417,936	459,044	879,489	1,216,576	1,057,843
WTS (Argus) vs WTI Spread Calendar Swap (FF)	14,664	300	576		3,600
WTS (Argus) vs WTI Spread Trade Month Swap (FH)	11,113	2,826	7,414	2,646	1,460
Daily European Naphtha CIF NWE (Platts) (NCP)	20				
NYMEX Cocoa (CJ)	197	384	1,608	1,338	1,318
NYMEX Coffee (KT)	332	356	1,077	1,847	1,335
NYMEX Cotton (TT)	572	365	2,949	4,964	1,764
NYMEX Sugar #11 (YO)	793	1,030	3,516	9,244	7,197
Total Futures	**441,373,921**	**435,672,648**	**458,412,470**	**419,914,148**	**362,428,100**

NYSE LIFFE U.S.

FUTURE	2013	2012	2011	2010	2009
100 oz Gold	5,705	17,905	103,864	471,446	1,467,450
Mini New York Gold	1,065,347	1,105,993	1,955,899	2,090,555	2,122,569
5,000 oz Silver	2,795	7,065	45,694	108,114	107,941
Mini New York Silver	485,998	668,178	1,550,088	1,060,631	647,314
Eurodollar	1,801,716	8,193,209	11,752,482		
2-Year Treasury Note	212,512	621,888	477,387		
5-Year Treasury Note	189,615	1,126,649	1,094,298		
10-Year Treasury Note	278,746	1,328,464	1,484,004		
US Bond	109,983	487,614	343,038		
Ultra Bond	1,690	16,972	24,215		
Agency GCF	310	3,520			
Mortgage GCF	24,714	15,012			
Treasury GCF	1,024,704	386,275			
NYSE Arca Gold Miners Index (GDF)	44				
MSCI EAFE	2,078,265	1,745,910	860,513	194,080	75,697
MSCI EM	6,102,827	3,044,608	1,148,430	139,613	49,373
MSCI Europe Growth	21				
MSCI Europe Value	21				
MSCI Euro	10,481				
MSCI USA	100	7		335	4,390
MSCI Canada	527	623			
MSCI EM Latin America	4,716	2,808			
MSCI World	24,424	656			
MSCI Pan Euro	79,310	48,937	51,297		
Total Futures	**13,504,571**	**18,822,300**	**20,896,432**	**4,064,780**	**4,474,734**

ONECHICAGO

FUTURE	2013	2012	2011	2010	2009
Single Stock Futures	6,742,536	5,150,363	3,599,917	4,758,640	2,624,496
Exchange Traded Funds	2,772,658	1,281,854	42,157	44,842	101,660
Total Futures	**9,515,194**	**6,432,217**	**3,679,484**	**4,971,160**	**2,983,148**

Total Futures Volume

	2013	2012	2011	2010	2009
Total Futures	**3,169,781,022**	**2,689,760,818**	**3,056,541,757**	**2,764,784,436**	**2,328,123,926**
Precent Change	**17.85%**	**-12.00%**	**10.55%**	**18.76%**	**-19.84%**

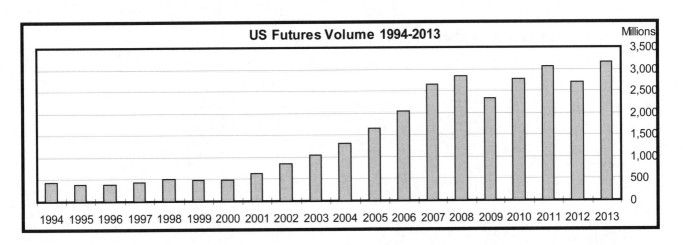

US Futures Volume 1994-2013

Options Traded on U.S. Futures Exchanges Volume Highlights
2013 in Comparison with 2012

2013 Rank	EXCHANGE	2013 Contracts	%	2012 Contracts	%	2012 Rank
1	Chicago Mercantile Exchange (CME Group)	261,572,433	44.54%	214,258,946	46.19%	1
2	Chicago Board of Trade (CME Group)	182,915,946	31.15%	143,010,967	30.83%	2
3	New York Mercantile Exchange (CME Group)	77,848,760	13.26%	80,793,179	17.42%	3
4	ICE Futures U.S.	64,736,820	11.02%	25,680,667	5.54%	4
5	Kansas City Board of Trade	171,828	0.03%	102,044	0.02%	5
6	Minneapolis Grain Exchange	23,006	0.00%	16,157	0.00%	6
	Chicago Climate Futures Exchange			1,559	0.00%	7
	NYSE Liffe U.S.			93	0.00%	8
	Total Options	**587,268,793**	**100.00%**	**463,863,612**	**100.00%**	

Chicago Board of Trade (CBT), division of the CME Group

OPTION	2013	2012	2011	2010	2009
Wheat	4,603,551	5,278,947	4,680,418	4,495,955	3,635,792
Corn	23,534,308	26,599,756	28,650,380	20,810,260	14,435,687
Oats	31,378	22,546	19,727	18,312	20,830
Soybeans	14,760,704	18,402,208	13,236,367	10,046,345	9,555,840
Soybean Crush	3,224	1,260	1,016	3,044	3,254
Soybean Oil	1,428,088	2,212,857	2,360,836	1,843,307	1,255,304
Soybean Meal	2,044,056	1,675,979	946,723	1,021,831	891,551
Rough Rice	17,245	14,180	37,222	38,317	15,674
Corn Nearby + 2 Calendar Spread	157,010	70,606	41,790	5,946	186
Soybean Nearby + 2 Calendar Spread	10,319	865	18,973	5,106	603
Wheat Nearby + 2 Calendar Spread	34,528	46,068	43,257	2,618	510
Soy Meal Nearby + 2 Calendar Spread	115		70	300	
Wheat - Corn ICSO	1,778	195	1,109	90	
Soy Oil Nearby + 2 Calendar Spread	2,129	3,236	4,380	2,470	
May-Nov Soybean Calendar Spread	80				
July-Nov Soybean Calendar Spread	59,922	95,742	104,727	78,669	20,799
Aug-Nov Soybean Calendar Spread	363	1,831	530		
Nov-Nov Soybean Calendar Spread	587	52	16,105		
Nov-July Soybean Calendar Spread	50	1,106	9,607	1	
July-Dec Soy Oil Calendar Spread	460	60	585	625	
Mar-Dec Corn Calendar Spread	510				
July-Dec Corn Calendar Spread	93,045	104,046	64,105	21,673	50
Dec-July Corn Calendar Spread	562	2,478	400	80	
Dec-Dec Corn Calendar Spread	2,239	4,933	1,926	7,340	
July-July Wheat Calendar Spread	675	2,540	5,934	5,254	451
July-Dec Wheat Calendar Spread	7,351	5,756	1,375	669	320
Mar-July Wheat Calendar Spread	185				
Treasury Bonds (30-year)	19,125,728	17,668,681	12,849,585	14,447,974	11,142,149
Treasury Notes (10-year)	90,401,169	56,070,376	50,797,081	55,280,257	40,206,023
Treasury Notes (5-year)	24,336,555	10,291,773	10,849,707	6,064,380	4,803,364
Treasury Notes (2-year)	1,928,675	3,182,052	2,686,449	2,400,459	2,397,210
Federal Funds (30-Day)	54,120	1,062,855	3,272,313	6,666,619	4,217,906
Ultra T-Bond	88,106	64,775	185,581	51,022	
Flexible Treasury Notes (10-year)	400	1,150	5,050	45,404	7,550
Dow Jones Industrial Index	4,472	1,325	1,948	3,188	22,718
Mini ($5) Dow Jones Industrial Index	182,259	97,994	107,389	85,425	85,934
Total Options	**182,915,946**	**143,010,967**	**131,039,321**	**123,666,496**	**92,848,854**

Chicago Mercantile Exchange (CME), division of the CME Group

OPTION	2013	2012	2011	2010	2009
Live Cattle	2,737,051	3,006,744	3,012,718	2,089,701	1,355,251
Live Cattle Calendar ISO	856	2,778	135	94	
Feeder Cattle	215,072	219,142	153,216	119,382	74,777
Lean Hogs	1,596,454	1,596,423	1,070,098	653,785	651,731
Lean Hogs CSO	122	630	20		
Class III Milk	260,071	273,517	304,232	172,384	153,513
Class IV Milk	24,943	3,201	4,667	48	
Nonfat Dry Milk	6,400	3,078	177	2	59
Mini BFP Milk	1,125	1,719	2,365	1,057	562
Cash Settled Cheese	26,471	14,557	1,368	25	
Dry Whey	3,526	1,429	974	468	862
Cash Butter	15,145	5,839	2,310	758	223
Random Lumber	15,605	8,111	7,226	8,840	13,883
Eurodollar (3-month)	27,821,432	48,279,896	100,855,181	106,893,369	117,553,569
Eurodollar Mid-Curve	122,159,718	91,189,258	92,429,741	76,490,147	43,369,605

Chicago Mercantile Exchange (CME), division of the CME Group (continued)

OPTION	2013	2012	2011	2010	2009
Australian Dollar	1,737,747	1,203,772	946,663	551,060	273,516
British Pound	1,841,943	659,792	735,630	1,208,577	465,413
Canadian Dollar	1,103,543	789,900	782,225	889,708	465,264
Euro FX	6,462,404	6,083,870	5,684,036	6,651,318	2,207,616
Japanese Yen	3,684,829	1,540,799	1,292,246	1,366,149	758,564
Mexican Peso	2,843	750		43	158
New Zealand Dollar	62	10			
Russian Ruble	1,186	1,186	15,600	750	
Swiss Franc	175,718	67,608	306,134	174,320	112,861
Euro FX European	72,293	56,306	69,717	107,476	94,244
Euro FX / Japanese Yen	2,502				
Euro FX / Swiss Franc	779	6,392	1,000	1,440	400
Australian Dollar European	14,277	2,850	1,966	1,682	3,800
British Pound European	29,267	9,139	6,845	23,463	61,434
Canadian Dollar European	14,524	27,890	14,484	21,403	26,775
Japanese Yen European	33,371	4,267	6,654	14,468	40,178
Swiss Franc European	5,291	2,165	3,479	10,226	20,423
S&P 500 Index	6,985,661	6,966,596	11,718,229	10,719,451	10,350,127
E-Mini S&P 500 Index	56,641,470	35,726,356	36,130,942	22,778,255	18,142,915
EOM S&P 500 Index	839,407	797,394	1,521,319	1,859,912	1,470,660
EOM E-Mini S&P 500 Index	7,594,221	5,096,141	3,793,860	1,872,924	845,519
EOW1 S&P 500 Index	339,834	83,907	212,794	287,033	153,184
EOW1 E-mini S&P 500 Index	5,930,560	2,908,629	1,885,408	769,266	88,404
EOW2 S&P 500 Index	540,683	197,960	382,127	287,542	114,594
EOW2 E-mini S&P 500 Index	5,800,851	3,517,143	1,961,040	708,912	82,869
EOW4 E-mini S&P 500 Index	5,837,467	2,988,624	1,973,286	404,518	
E-Mini S&P MidCap 400 Index	1,436	457	581	3,534	5,272
NASDAQ 100 Index	379	277	13,005	607	1,535
E-Mini NASDAQ 100 Index	889,508	758,987	923,266	514,551	440,634
CDD Weather	6,950	10,785	7,875	61,325	27,050
HDD Weather	5,366	12,750	27,220	40,215	40,250
HDD Seasonal Weather Strip	38,260	48,720	83,086	99,150	115,300
CDD Seasonal Weather Strip	39,060	35,800	67,600	84,000	98,950
HDD Weather European	1,500	1,000	20,000	4,500	3,500
Euro HDD Seasonal Strip Weather	11,000	28,500	9,000	21,300	3,000
Euro CAT Seasonal Strip Weather	1,500		500		7,500
Binary Seasonal Hurricane	750	4,000	2,950	3,000	
Total Options	**261,572,433**	**214,258,946**	**268,518,626**	**238,175,073**	**199,818,941**

ICE Futures U.S. (ICE)

OPTION	2013	2012	2011	2010	2009
Coffee 'C'	1,691,629	2,498,884	2,624,667	2,292,800	1,427,032
Coffee Calendar Spread	21,635	36,265	5,463	3,428	
Coffee 'C' Weekly Options	706	2,658			
Cotton #2	2,452,654	2,366,598	2,794,411	2,911,509	1,709,004
Cotton #2 1-month	3,707	1,335			
Cotton #2 2-month	1,885	3,481			
Orange Juice Frozen Concentrate	130,160	184,931	153,176	237,790	243,741
Sugar #11	4,930,254	5,063,067	6,667,573	8,448,556	7,280,380
Sugar #11 1-month	73,296	41,105			
Sugar #11 2-month	2,840	8,465			
Cocoa	733,129	579,668	652,080	322,121	318,805
U.S. Wheat	250	2,600			
U.S. Soybeans	200	4,896			
US Dollar Index	41,915	19,608	41,793	22,248	55,822
Russell 2000 Index Mini	65,132	67,774	155,824	206,624	157,126
North American Natural Gas and Power	54,587,428	14,789,230			
Total Options	**64,736,820**	**25,680,667**	**13,180,700**	**14,654,805**	**11,309,749**

Kansas City Board of Trade (KCBT)

OPTION	2013	2012	2011	2010	2009
Wheat	171,820	102,044	239,891	148,032	108,317
Short Dated New Crop Wheat	8				
Total Options	**171,828**	**102,044**	**239,891**	**148,032**	**108,317**

Minneapolis Grain Exchange (MGE)

OPTION	2013	2012	2011	2010	2009
American Spring Wheat	18,971	16,157	43,315	27,354	24,937
Apple Juice Concentrate	4,035				
Total Options	**23,006**	**16,157**	**43,315**	**32,290**	**25,137**

VOLUME - U.S.

New York Mercantile Exchange (NYMEX), division of the CME Group

OPTION	2013	2012	2011	2010	2009
COMEX Copper (HX)	36,172	5,689	6,897	17,509	18,568
COMEX Gold (OG)	10,587,160	9,454,650	10,080,754	7,730,488	4,755,427
COMEX Silver (SO)	2,043,988	1,741,080	2,124,108	1,640,232	1,066,721
NYMEX Platinum (PO)	183,818	98,351	84,927	10,643	20
Palladium (PAO)	134,120	66,307	37,389	12,214	
Short Term Gold (L04)	25		147		
Short Term Gold (L06)	22		2		
Short Term Gold (L08)	100		27		
Short Term Gold (L29)	70		6,114		
Short Term Gold (L30)	96	12	150		
Iron Ore China (ICT)	5,896	24,599	6,633		
NYMEX Hot Rolled Steel (HRO)	8,420	1,800			
Appalachian Coal (6K)	1,000	1,955	1,815	1,200	
Brent 1-month Calendar Spread (AA)	566	2,050			
Brent Crude Oil Average Price (BA)	350,250	617,716	566,278	139,273	137,549
Brent Crude Oil Last Day - European (BE)	129,920	309,727	516,740	79,143	18,562
Brent Crude Oil Last Day - American (OS)	269,125	171,509	139,652	29,880	2,410
Cinergy Hub Peak Month (OY)	2,140	13,440	27,080	94,552	142,190
Coal (API 2) CIF ARA (Argus/McCloskey) Option on	485	160			
Coal (API 2) CIF ARA (Argus/McCloskey) Swap (CQA)	175	200			
Coal (API 4) FOB Richards Bay (Argus/McCloskey)	75				
CSX Coal (Platts OTC Broker Index) Swap (CPF)	265	90			
Powder River Basin Coal (Platts OTC Broker Index)	4,200	740			
Crude Oil 1-month CSO (WA)	2,281,455	2,873,842	2,886,427	2,049,582	719,802
Crude Oil APO (AO)	742,805	1,549,657	2,488,882	4,621,556	3,203,460
Crude Oil Calendar Strip (6F)	50	25		775	
Dubai Crude Oil Average Price (AH)	10,038	25,800	3,104	100	
Dated Brent (Platts) Average Price (DBP)	5,040	6,180	4,200		
Crude Oil Physical (CD)	16,675	47,170	113,280	130,902	86,932
Crude Oil European Style (LC)	196,720	312,533	860,949	1,195,827	1,507,042
Crude Oil (LO)	31,478,060	32,525,624	36,716,805	32,785,267	28,551,730
Daily Crude Oil (DNM)	14,600	100	3,350		
PJM Northern Illinois Hub Peak 50 MW Calendar-	2				
PJM 50MW Calendar Month LMP Swap (PML)	2,983	12,920	34,087		
Ethanol Swap (CVR)	31,900	9,238	2,135		
Gulf Coast Jet Fuel (Platts) APO (GVR)	40,861	900			
European 1% Fuel Oil Barges FOB Rdam (Platts)	570				
European Naptha (Platts) Calendar Swap (NWE)	70	542			
European Jet Kerosene NEW APO (30)	193	117	312	344	10
Gasoil Crack Spread APO (3U)	1,800	2,511	2,550		
Heating Oil Physical - European (LB)	8,810	4,218	3,201	6,261	11,479
Heating Oil (OH)	564,974	755,394	889,524	884,849	686,270
Henry Hub Financial Last Day (E7)	64,590	17,292	27,294	28,775	16,892
Heating Oil 1-month CSO (FA)	12,875	31,075	25,785	10,350	16,345
In Delivery Month EUA (6U)	3,000	2,500	2,000	16,000	1,250
ISO New England Calendar-Month LMP Swap (OE)	2,360	12,270	49,790	7,186	17,410
Coal (API 2) CIF ARA (Argus/McCloskey) Swap (MTO)	10,775	2,685			
Coal (API 4) FOB Richards Bay (Argus/McCloskey)	2,730	1,500			
Natural Gas 1-month CSO Financial (G4)	836,761	379,022	303,810	258,719	15,874
Natural Gas 1-month CSO Financial (IA)	600	1,000	7,400	37,875	43,290
Natural Gas 2-month CSO Financial (G2)	3,400	5,800	7,800	1,650	
Natural Gas 3-month CSO Financial (G3)	262,605	683,351	567,772	338,267	52,855
Natural Gas 5-month CSO Financial (G5)	5,000	500		850	
Natural Gas 6-month CSO Financial (G6)	95,038	198,550	109,575		
Natural Gas Calendar Strip (6J)	18,636	27,585	98,055	11,801	3,240
Natural Gas Physical (KD)	264,701	483,564	466,319	369,439	213,170
Natural Gas Physical - European (LN)	21,053,064	24,260,726	23,773,183	23,957,725	25,309,214
Natural Gas Physical (ON)	3,480,049	2,778,387	2,064,055	1,360,225	1,135,135
Natural Gas Summer Strip (4D)	460	2,700	3,300	400	1,000
Natural Gas Winter Strip (6I)	200		1,600	5,800	
Northern Rockies Pipe (ZR)	4,744	13,227	20,506	51,800	87,840
NY Harbor Heating Oil Swap (AT)	220,389	331,398	423,583	858,571	661,036
NYMEX European Gasoil APO (F7)	916	2,813	12,826	32,369	9,957
Panhandle Pipe Swap (PU)	500	3,004	5,508	65,996	105,368
Petrochemicals (4H)	23,746	17,080	7,318	9,035	645
Petrochemicals - Mt Bel Ethane (OPIS) APO (4J)	15,410	17,105	6,540	4,735	
Petrochemicals - Mt Bel Normal Butane (OPIS) APO	6,500	1,800	267	735	
Conway Propane (OPIS) APO (CPR)	588	119	300		
Singapore Fuel Oil 380 cst (Platts) APO (8H)	2,773	522	18		
PJM Calendar Strip (6O)	15,950	47,340	82,040	13,484	
PJM Monthly Financially Settled Electricity (JO)	2,600	5,762	107,834	707,300	528,316
RBOB 1-Month CSO (ZA)	5,925	5,820	18,830	30,517	32,381
RBOB 6-Month CSO (ZM)	300				
RBOB Calendar Swap (RA)	87,514	58,290	28,167	90,392	57,384
RBOB Gasoline (OB)	520,529	502,982	470,606	546,878	680,635

New York Mercantile Exchange (NYMEX), division of the CME Group (continued)

OPTION	2013	2012	2011	2010	2009
RBOB Gasoline European style (RF)	6,645	1,599	165	10,016	21,007
Rotterdam 3.5% Fuel Oil CL (Q6)	13,818	15,487	12,047	6,857	1,881
San Juan Pipe (PJ)	3,600	5,244	6,216	5,652	22,118
Short Term Natural Gas (U11)	3,550	475	100		
Short Term Natural Gas (U12)	4,600	2,625	200		
Short Term Natural Gas (U13)	4,525	1,750			
Short Term Natural Gas (U14)	4,600	2,700	50		
Short Term Natural Gas (U15)	1,780	1,700	75		
Short Term Natural Gas (U22)	3,750	950	400		
Short Term Natural Gas (U23)	1,450	625			
Short Term Natural Gas (U24)	825	800			
Short Term Natural Gas (U25)	1,275	305	500		
Short Term Natural Gas (U26)	955	500			
Light Sweet Crude Oil (C03)	300	1	10		
Light Sweet Crude Oil (C16)	875	125	1		
Short Term Natural Gas (U01)	1,850	1,375	50		
Short Term Natural Gas (U02)	600	1,100	100		
Short Term Natural Gas (U03)	5,875	1,575	275		
Short Term Natural Gas (U04)	3,200	500	50		
Short Term Natural Gas (U05)	2,400	1,675			
Short Term Natural Gas (U06)	2,435	1,175	25		
Short Term Natural Gas (U07)	3,675	450	200		
Short Term Natural Gas (U08)	875	700			
Short Term Natural Gas (U09)	2,750	1,900	750		
Short Term Natural Gas (U10)	3,225	1,250			
Short Term Natural Gas (U16)	2,015	975			
Short Term Natural Gas (U17)	1,525	300	175		
Short Term Natural Gas (U18)	2,500	900			
Short Term Natural Gas (U19)	3,300	1,150	250		
Short Term Natural Gas (U20)	1,300	1,500			
Short Term Natural Gas (U21)	5,150	1,000			
Short Term Natural Gas (U27)	2,175	325	100		
Short Term Natural Gas (U28)	1,625	200			
Short Term Natural Gas (U29)	400	950			
Short Term Natural Gas (U30)	3,300	1,275			
Short Term Natural Gas (U31)	2,200	625	100		
Singapore Fuel Oil 180 CST (C5)	805	3,404	3,305	1,157	318
Singapore Gasoil APO (M2)	200	9,882	1,200	150	
Singapore Jet Fuel Calendar (N2)	17,588	30,352	6,060	2,395	3,023
SoCal Pipe Swap (ZN)	300	9,744	53,688	46,172	119,320
WTI Crude Oil 12-month CSO (WZ)	15,150	10,500	15,575	42,570	20,675
WTI Crude Oil 6-month CSO (WM)	2,050	100	1,000	6,100	
WTI-Brent Bullet Swap (BV)	700,183	52,079	24,943	1,000	
Crude Oil Financial Calendar Spread (1-month) (7A)	826,639	81,250	21,350	33,450	5,370
Total Options	**77,848,760**	**80,793,179**	**86,514,666**	**80,574,639**	**70,210,423**

Total Volume

	2013	2012	2011	2010	2009
Total Options	587,268,793	463,863,612	499,550,971	457,337,022	374,457,084
Percent Change	26.60%	-7.14%	9.23%	22.13%	-27.84%

Options Traded on U.S. Securities Exchanges Volume Highlights
2013 in Comparison with 2012

2013 Rank	EXCHANGE	2013 Contracts	%	2012 Contracts	%	2012 Rank
1	Chicago Board of Options Exchange	1,070,865,472	26.25%	1,059,404,089	26.46%	1
2	Nasdaq OMX PHLX	681,995,742	16.72%	791,443,344	19.77%	2
3	International Securities Exchange	606,765,206	14.87%	631,827,834	15.78%	3
4	NYSE-AMEX	549,050,523	13.46%	564,814,869	14.11%	5
5	NYSE-ARCA	451,427,061	11.07%	411,936,938	10.29%	4
6	Nasdaq Options Market	326,388,360	8.00%	203,505,324	5.08%	6
7	BATS Exchange	151,814,889	3.72%	130,624,660	3.26%	8
8	Boston Options Exchange	89,546,651	2.20%	144,987,873	3.62%	7
9	C2 Exchange	76,583,750	1.88%	51,020,411	1.27%	9
10	Miami International Securities Exchange	39,430,903	0.97%	27,934	0.00%	11
11	NASDAQ OMX BX Exchange	35,334,377	0.87%	14,278,032	0.36%	10
	Total Options	**4,079,202,934**	**100.00%**	**4,003,871,308**	**100.00%**	

Volume - Worldwide

Athens Derivatives Exchange S.A. (ADEX), Greece

	2013	2012	2011	2010	2009
FTSE/Athex 20	2,322,341	2,903,594	2,482,713	2,987,458	2,371,733
FTSE/Athex-CSE Banking Index	1,886	962	2,100	4,964	
All Futures on Individual Equities	6,666,992	24,861,696	7,553,643	4,767,973	5,037,065
Total Futures	**8,991,219**	**27,766,252**	**10,038,456**	**7,760,395**	**7,408,798**
FTSE/Athex 20	194,455	429,874	328,391	615,122	383,555
All Options on Individual Equities	18,481	65,098	64,238	105,764	67,590
Total Options	**212,936**	**494,972**	**392,629**	**720,886**	**451,154**

Australian Stock Exchange (ASX), Australia

	2013	2012	2011	2010	2009
S&P/ASX Index	257,098	258,989	270,236	370,800	396,723
All Futures on Individual Equities	6,117,166	5,407,123	3,460,934	543,676	777,732
Total Futures	**6,374,264**	**5,666,112**	**3,731,170**	**914,476**	**1,174,455**
S&P / ASX Index	9,224,326	11,501,735	10,321,625	5,274,603	3,486,914
All Options on Individual Equities	124,300,972	140,439,020	108,860,114	15,455,208	14,465,066
Total Futures	**133,525,298**	**151,940,755**	**119,181,739**	**20,729,811**	**17,951,980**

Bolsa de Mercadorias & Futuros (BM&F), Brazil

	2013	2012	2011	2010	2009
Arabica Coffee	147,301	237,663	450,802	640,754	596,435
Arabica Coffee Rollover	9,858	9,656	8,002	33,252	48,764
Live Cattle	863,127	758,720	975,362	1,153,778	834,304
Ethanol	43,030	66,610	81,725	20,925	1
Corn Cash Settled	738,812	683,881	464,387	364,045	259,610
Cross Listing Mini-Sized Soybeans CME	32,465	22			
Crystal Sugar Settled	40				224
Soybean Cash Settled	56,913	52,034	37,465		
Gold Forward	5,683	1,811	14,147	1,195	176
Gold	180			80	640
Gold Spot (250g)	11,682	10,258	23,579	9,567	12,403
Pound Sterling	58,972	16,236	42,771	46,600	
Australian Dollar	73,569	111,648	138,216	49,090	
Canadian Dollar	37,047	116,360	74,623	7,725	
Chilean Peso	3,515	872			
Chinese Yuan	120	135			
New Zealand Dollar	1,245	1,955	260		
Mexican Peso	88,008	123,482	58,419	31,650	
South African Rand	9,765	1,412	600		
Swiss Franc	29,977	19,487	6,468		
Turkish Lira	1,825	1,270	2,032		
Japanese Yen	143,934	21,887	30,303	7,140	
E-mini S&P 500	243,120	51,848			
E-mini S&P 500 Rollover	19,576				
Bovespa Stock Index Futures	20,443,962	22,328,572	21,650,138	18,039,345	16,350,493
Bovespa Rollover	4,639,339	3,142,382	3,075,094	1,943,040	1,382,060
Bovespa Mini Index	49,215,793	38,951,711	26,234,515	16,705,118	12,374,969
One Day Inter-Bank Deposit	394,055,420	340,800,485	320,821,062	293,065,417	151,958,184
One Day Repurchase Agreement	382,475				
SELIC x US Dollar Spread	10				
SELIC x US Dollar FRA	20				
SELIC x US Dollar Swap with Reset	48,645				
Interest Rate Swap	179,626	263,945	161,230	144,440	71,545
Interest Rate x Exchange Rate Swap	158,613	461,109	193,759	449,476	368,853
Interest Rate x Price Index Swap (formerly Inflation)	1,148,801	1,238,285	1,646,628	1,303,131	655,582
Exchange Rate Swap	11,441	21,913	32,571	138,165	27,883
Forward Exchange Rate	9,841		2,205	79	
ID x US Dollar Spread Futures	1,521,459	1,124,566	1,685,441	1,045,712	738,389
FRA on ID x US Dollar Spread	36,458,503	34,986,267	33,933,356	21,075,685	17,487,272
ID x IPCA Spread	23,725	4,495	4,425	39,485	6,240
Global 2020	755	1,943	2,460		
Global 2040	220	300	1,020	2,070	3,409
US T-Note	31,637	15,221	30,065	13,563	26,291
US Dollar	83,426,499	84,049,097	86,167,955	82,453,621	66,776,180
US Dollar Rollover	25,400,303	23,236,158	20,145,632	19,223,570	15,280,530
Mini US Dollar	2,393,580	1,821,820	2,259,014	1,969,427	573,839
US Dollar forward points	3,072,885	2,553,745	3,303,276	4,337,700	3,157,515
Euro	348,861	656,707	552,481	390,295	75,265
Mini Euro	75				
Total Futures	**625,592,252**	**557,948,335**	**524,392,180**	**464,830,782**	**289,549,270**
Gold on Actuals	56,724	316,816	710,184	361,960	369,564
US $ Denominated Arabica Coffee	6,108	8,878	4,009	17,453	8,459
Corn Cash Settled	58,746	110,337	88,833	114,619	17,364
Soybean Cash Settled	2,715	13,664	33,174		

Bolsa de Mercadorias & Futuros (BM&F), Brazil (continued)

	2013	2012	2011	2010	2009
Live Cattle	200,723	270,098	172,660	166,319	46,001
Hydrous Ethanol	350	3,094	9,556	1,305	
Bovespa Stock	2,353,368	8,658,743	5,586,998	1,995,760	1,714,845
Interest Rate	13,540,084	17,185,582	9,361,846	12,477,540	4,545,435
Interest Rate (volatility)	59,235	359,215	3,637,180	3,148,715	1,455,990
Interest Rate (IDI)	40,626,100	107,961,438	95,790,772	88,014,027	40,174,869
IDI Index (volatility)	404,500	908,045	7,156,160	12,415,185	5,894,010
Flexible Spot Interest Rate Index	615,515	2,125	53,402	35,192	159,582
Flexible Bovespa Stock Index	68,150	154,236	191,537	358,446	622,374
US Dollar on Actuals	8,609,024	9,422,497	11,136,468	24,170,975	21,631,255
US Dollar Volatility	357,155	331,030	597,785	1,395,970	1,485,170
Flexible Currency	155,764	70,150	514,642	732,042	357,381
Total Options	**67,114,261**	**146,139,337**	**135,084,822**	**153,803,010**	**83,836,882**

Bolsa de Valores de Colombia (BCV), Colombia

	2013	2012	2011	2010	2009
COLCAP Index	851	611	563		
10-year Treasury Bond	25,879	27,955	24,293	14,017	
5-year Treasury Bond	75,019	61,881	54,774	12,723	
2-year Treasury Bond	73,744	47,896	95,196	24,002	
Other Treasury Bonds	51,570				
IBR	256	161			
Consumer Price Index	248	391			
US Dollar	218,756	272,587	389,693	116,311	
Mini US Dollar	125,757	165,149	198,216	25,785	
All Futures on Individual Equities	113,053	53,959	32,563	94,654	
Total Futures	**685,133**	**630,590**	**795,298**	**287,492**	

Bombay Stock Exchange, India

	2013	2012	2011	2010	2009
Mankex Index (BKX)	10	223,252			
BSETECK Index (TEC)	22				
BSE 100 Index (BSI)	1,201,058	406,970			
Sensex Index (BSX)	914,349	8,326,789	2,467,231		
All Futures on Individual Equities	1,640,045	170,421	156,842		
Total Futures	**3,755,484**	**9,142,734**	**2,624,073**		
S&P BSE 100 Index (BSI)	141,727,404	86,243,943			
S&P Sensex Index (BSX)	108,612,615	148,314,519			
All Options on Individual Equities	750,426	45,908			
Total Futures	**251,090,445**	**234,614,523**			

BOVESPA, Brazil

	2013	2012	2011	2010	2009
Ibovespa Index	982,688	1,045,256	623,103	281,815	199,147
Exchange Traded Funds	597,500	1,540,039	2,018,403	959,093	242,863
All Options on Individual Equities	909,313,950	929,284,637	838,325,495	802,229,293	546,547,550
Total Options	**910,894,138**	**931,869,932**	**840,967,001**	**803,470,201**	**546,989,560**

Budapest Stock Exchange (BSE), Hungary

	2013	2012	2011	2010	2009
Feed Corn	2,911	3,165	3,352	3,476	5,068
Mill Wheat	200	408	298	7	
Euro Wheat	439	112	203	1,021	874
Feed Barley	239	83	135	290	391
Sunflower Seed	946	366	872	1,070	1,874
Rapeseed	178	352	377	750	1,785
Budapest Stock Index (BUX)	402,264	799,939	1,881,620	3,635,407	2,881,483
CAD/HUF	1,010	1,440	500		
CHF/HUF	110,200	200,085	1,322,258	254,925	101,249
CZK/HUF	150			4,930	2,430
EUR/HUF	3,282,205	2,128,821	1,894,259	2,764,599	3,426,699
GBP/HUF	210,272	137,950	16,350	24,080	14,700
JPY/HUF	16,440	9,350	17,900	29,300	17,780
NOK/HUF	3,660	4,800	400		
PLN/HUF	2,845	1,300	120	4,320	7,040
TRY/HUF	42,200	27,620	37,775	3,300	20,400
USD/HUF	1,056,745	755,858	1,086,439	1,046,731	700,606
AUD/CAD	4,600	2,500	850	200	
AUD/CHF	600		1,200	400	
AUD/JPY	2,700	600	2,600	1,800	5,550
AUD/USD	21,500	43,860	14,180	27,700	29,400
CAD/JPY	100		200	500	1,000
CHF/PLN	1,000		600	200	
GBP/AUD	6,900	400	1,400	4,200	
GBP/CAD	5,800	700	2,600	600	

Budapest Stock Exchange (BSE), Hungary (continued)

	2013	2012	2011	2010	2009
GBP/CHF	1,000	300	4,250	11,300	35,200
GBP/JPY	5,300	4,400	8,300	17,800	116,050
GBP/PLN	2,000		100		
GBP/SEK	200	800	800	6,200	15,500
GBP/USD	46,960	11,200	12,300	56,900	103,010
EURO/AUD	7,650	9,370	1,000		
EURO/CAD	1,200	3,520	100		
EURO/CHF	138,370	100,150	196,790	124,600	44,300
EURO/CZK	2,800	200	1,200	600	1,900
EURO/GBP	11,400	7,870	5,650	29,300	17,650
EURO/JPY	98,295	26,450	69,400	199,170	241,440
EURO/NOK	14,650	100	3,700	3,300	23,600
EURO/PLN	5,100	5,150	26,000	23,050	51,400
EURO/RON	900	4,200	4,675	17,300	35,750
EURO/RUB	3,050	400	200		400
EURO/SEK	1,300	800		3,100	27,000
EURO/TRY	141,220	45,300	126,835	26,625	99,385
EURO/USD	611,104	340,190	365,652	582,380	416,160
USD/CAD	4,040	8,000	5,600	12,840	34,120
USD/CHF	20,600	3,300	33,000	23,300	20,400
USD/CZK	500	100		117,500	400
USD/JPY	171,910	49,440	99,300	106,500	64,900
USD/NOK	1,200				2,200
USD/PLN	8,200	2,800	2,000	21,400	7,800
USD/SEK	1,100				1,400
USD/TRY	49,850	21,250	12,750	7,400	21,625
EUR (1 week)	33,000	48,600	43,700	367,650	493,066
GBP (1 week)	21,500	18,400	3,500	23,900	56,830
USD (1 week)	25,300	71,650	49,500	91,800	140,290
AUD/CAD (1 week)	200	200	3,500	800	
AUD/CHF (1 week)	1,800		2,600	600	
AUD/JPY (1 week)	12,000	800	200		
AUD/USD (1 week)	9,000	28,800	27,200	27,200	12,800
CAD/CHF (1 week)	1,200	800	100		
CHF/PLN (1 week)	1,800	1,200	1,600	600	
EUR/AUD (1 week)	1,200				
EUR/CAD (1 week)	1,200	200	400		
EUR/CHF (1 week)	3,500	1,400	16,600	2,100	
EUR/JPY (1 week)	26,600	17,400	15,000	158,000	110,550
EUR/USD (1 week)	115,400	208,100	424,150	561,303	429,700
GBP/AUD (1 week)	19,000	2,600	7,700	1,200	
GBP/CAD (1 week)	18,100	2,400	9,800	2,300	
GBP/CHF (1 week)	3,200	200	7,200	23,600	33,773
GBP/JPY (1 week)	12,950	3,500	2,200	42,550	189,750
GBP/PLN (1 week)	3,800	1,000	800		
GBP/USD (1 week)	31,300	16,000	25,500	90,100	106,100
USD/CAD (1 week)	3,800	9,100	16,900	36,900	40,850
USD/CHF (1 week)	6,400	800	7,600	40,800	51,600
USD/JPY (1 week)	2,500	400	4,400	59,150	45,000
USD/PLN (1 week)	11,000	12,000	7,200	8,600	
All Futures on Individual Equities	686,028	609,797	806,061	1,033,190	1,204,849
Total Futures	**7,577,781**	**5,821,356**	**8,750,083**	**11,780,544**	**11,570,661**
US Dollar	7,000	16,900	2,000	500	4,750
EUR	10,100	16,060	12,775	20,750	155,350
EUR/CHF	5,750	8,590	1,300		
EUR/JPY	800				
EUR/TRY	7,850	1,200	1,700		
EUR/USD	200	1,600	1,000	8,000	6,600
USD/JPY	600		750		
USD/TRY	2,500	1,800	3,900		225
Total Options	**34,800**	**58,300**	**36,697**	**29,750**	**224,345**

China Financial Futures Exchange (CFFE)

	2013	2012	2011	2010	2009
CSI 300 Index	193,220,516	105,061,825	50,411,860	45,873,295	
5-year Treasury Bond	328,795				
Total Futures	**193,549,311**	**105,061,825**	**50,411,860**	**45,873,295**	

Dubai Mercantile Exchange (DME)

	2013	2012	2011	2010	2009
Oman Crude Oil	1,600,918	1,176,056	883,359	744,727	553,888
Total Futures	**1,600,918**	**1,176,056**	**883,359**	**744,727**	**553,888**

Dalian Commodity Exchange (DCE), China

	2013	2012	2011	2010	2009
Corn	13,313,633	37,824,356	26,849,738	35,999,573	16,744,088
Egg	1,951,323				
No 1 Soybeans	10,993,500	45,475,425	25,239,532	37,393,600	42,507,076
No 2 Soybeans	7,236	10,400	10,662	14,709	32,048
Palm Oil	82,495,230	43,310,013	22,593,961	41,799,813	44,426,498
Soybean Oil	96,334,673	68,858,554	58,012,550	91,406,238	94,836,881
Soybean Meal	265,357,592	325,876,653	50,170,334	125,581,888	155,404,029
Iron Ore	2,189,215				
Block Board	1,988,112				
Fibre Board	2,374,759				
Linear Low Density Polyethylene (LLDPE)	72,142,084	71,871,537	95,219,058	62,488,306	44,752,979
Coke	115,306,637	32,915,885	1,512,734		
Hard Coking Coal	34,259,550				
Polyvinyl Cloride (PVC)	1,787,233	6,900,153	9,438,431	8,483,624	18,078,662
Total Futures	**700,500,777**	**633,042,976**	**289,047,000**	**403,167,751**	**416,782,261**

EUREX, Frankfurt, Germany

	2013	2012	2011	2010	2009
DAX	28,417,740	37,409,537	44,990,070	40,994,689	40,101,438
DivDAX	18,418	23,090	3,948	3,409	1,803
Euro Stoxx 50 ex Financials Index	611	1,005			
Euro Stoxx 50	268,495,189	315,179,597	408,860,002	372,229,766	333,407,299
Euro Stoxx Select Dividend 30 Index	98,978	95,555	92,084	73,762	132,793
Euro Stoxx	30,389	24,457	2,663	190	
Euro Stoxx Large	5,376	6,701	2,735	186	
Euro Stoxx Mid	16,744	17,185	9,699	3,737	
Euro Stoxx Small	48,792	50,057	22,009	5,921	
MDAX	214,848	310,476	422,382	404,815	297,724
MSCI AC Asia Pacific ex Japan	537				
MSCI Emerging Markets	8,151				
MSCI Emerging Markets Latin America	14				
MSCI Europe	115,939				
MSCI India	40				
MSCI Japan Index	10,372	32,123	1,112	892	426
MSCI Malaysia	35				
MSCI Mexico	84				
MSCI Philippines	20				
MSCI Russia	824				
MSCI Russia Index	46,581	76,144	41,514		
MSCI Thailand	100				
MSCI World	24,952				
OMX-Helsinki 25	66,326	134,950	255,060	250,475	148,333
RDXxt USD Index	698,674	233,968			
Swiss Leader index (SLI)	14,413	11,313	21,384	9,007	43,871
Swiss Market Index Mid-Cap (SMIM)	156,740	216,059	181,654	100,531	80,081
Swiss Market Index (SMI)	8,243,441	8,942,315	13,482,706	11,626,179	12,135,437
Stoxx Europe 50 Index	914,717	1,050,022	1,330,841	1,417,882	1,300,945
Stoxx Europe 600	2,490,175	1,272,689	1,247,960	93,633	
Stoxx Europe Large 200	50,194	53,037	75,207	7,657	
Stoxx Europe Mid 200	258,243	400,450	490,301	57,847	
Stoxx Europe Small 200	284,290	278,232	428,524	38,155	
TecDAX	80,485	90,248	203,962	232,025	245,270
Euro Stoxx Automobiles	56,758	111,429	58,072	54,507	84,664
Euro Stoxx Banks	10,074,089	9,565,474	5,229,347	1,156,447	437,131
Euro Stoxx Basic Resources	28,293	33,644	32,098	44,913	30,634
Euro Stoxx Chemicals	11,844	21,950	29,076	65,913	36,940
Euro Stoxx Construction & Materials	44,408	41,537	39,676	38,599	44,989
Euro Stoxx Financial Services	7,765	15,467	8,502	10,227	22,295
Euro Stoxx Food and Beverage	42,175	32,292	24,402	25,563	22,160
Euro Stoxx Healthcare	22,372	52,490	49,145	42,894	36,312
Euro Stoxx Industrial Goods & Services	33,284	30,660	24,727	46,383	35,546
Euro Stoxx Insurance	288,511	378,492	220,847	204,346	192,823
Euro Stoxx Media	22,705	25,771	25,575	42,233	34,959
Euro Stoxx Oil & Gas	242,109	123,732	67,219	148,169	85,545
Euro Stoxx Personal & Household Goods	13,002	24,088	15,058	18,442	21,120
Euro Stoxx Real Estate	2,072	4,670	4,706	3,508	2,413
Euro Stoxx Retail	12,986	12,440	41,504	17,663	28,668
Euro Stoxx Technology	27,856	51,724	44,757	51,565	89,955
Euro Stoxx Telecom	299,547	182,580	125,229	127,420	143,714
Euro Stoxx Travel & Leisure	12,053	34,628	19,914	19,712	32,092
Euro Stoxx Utilities	168,313	131,201	89,787	131,250	109,173
Euro Stoxx 600 Automobiles & Parts	334,787	320,017	303,586	151,258	145,939
Euro Stoxx 600 Banks	1,355,558	1,852,717	2,456,184	1,727,129	1,178,604
Euro Stoxx 600 Basic Resources	774,499	765,336	707,868	490,447	491,332
Euro Stoxx 600 Chemicals	69,926	82,899	114,697	74,946	75,880

EUREX, Frankfurt, Germany (continued)

	2013	2012	2011	2010	2009
Euro Stoxx 600 Construction & Materials	76,901	100,264	130,865	67,965	69,729
Euro Stoxx 600 Financial Services	35,442	30,022	38,373	22,647	28,542
Euro Stoxx 600 Food & Beverage	250,561	245,242	268,565	189,505	212,780
Euro Stoxx 600 Healthcare	220,028	267,426	411,857	372,362	366,782
Euro Stoxx 600 Industrial Goods & Services	282,456	420,605	577,074	452,187	306,558
Euro Stoxx 600 Insurance	323,586	454,975	757,845	412,506	333,646
Euro Stoxx 600 Media	128,112	153,951	254,493	271,169	201,928
Euro Stoxx 600 Oil & Gas	387,800	349,893	645,483	425,478	490,611
Euro Stoxx 600 Personal & Household Goods	57,732	84,122	116,613	104,779	101,473
Euro Stoxx 600 Real Estate	39,066	13,942	24,520	32,431	34,407
Euro Stoxx 600 Retail	65,943	61,431	148,710	114,683	164,015
Euro Stoxx 600 Technology	101,429	147,659	172,508	177,025	124,442
Euro Stoxx 600 Telecom	359,203	439,407	346,960	414,900	396,821
Euro Stoxx 600 Travel & Leisure	94,692	62,227	138,866	207,146	158,307
Euro Stoxx 600 Utilities	250,923	270,383	361,392	290,852	229,079
Euro Stoxx 50 Index Dividend	3,676,120	3,543,392	4,232,260	3,585,955	2,534,348
Euro Stoxx Banks Index Dividend	7,370	1,000			
Euro Stoxx Insurance Index Dividend	500	1,500			
Euro Stoxx Oil Gas Index Dividend	525				
Euro Stoxx Utilities Index Dividend	150	1,050			
SMI Index Dividend	4,464	10,544	14,375	13,691	2,576
Mini-Futures auf VStoxx	5,324,708	3,901,530	1,889,492	431,669	14,576
Swiss Government Bond (CONF)	141,272	150,484	181,740	205,109	279,720
Euro-BTP	9,285,418	4,870,645	2,386,768	1,396,953	327,914
Euro-BOBL	129,530,977	107,645,238	142,309,151	133,851,275	105,820,542
Euro-BUND	190,299,482	184,338,704	236,188,831	231,484,529	180,755,004
Euro-BUXL	3,987,038	2,465,158	1,806,195	1,360,503	925,627
Euro-OAT	11,734,475	4,342,912			
Euro-SCHATZ	95,505,726	93,840,656	165,798,952	140,923,898	125,607,110
Mid-term Euro-OAT	350,965				
Short-term Euro-BTP	1,961,926	814,408	575,349	131,195	
Mid-term Euro-BTP	9	3,581	10,156		
3-Month Euribor	275,098	66,360	125,557	267,985	403,243
CER MidDec	70	1,548	252	175	23
European Carbon	91,695	81,777	36,624	735	
European Whey Powder	118	17			
Butter	1,887	691	510	10	
European Processing Potatoes	53,947	50,382	52,918	49,336	15,575
Hogs	902	1,814	2,009	2,215	1,367
Piglets	143	309	258	579	289
Skimmed Milk Powder	392	200	7	16	
DJ UBS Agriculture Sub-Index	2,683	1,126	6,481	10,298	5,552
DJ UBS Commodity Index	64,036	61,544	54,974	57,255	14,177
DJ UBS Energy Sub-Index	7,965	2,248	2,898	5,148	2,238
DJ UBS Grains Sub-Index	892	2,712	2,214	214	
DJ UBS Industrial Metals Sub-Index	3,758	3,637	4,771	3,528	308
DJ UBS Livestock Sub-Index	2	1,044	937		
DJ UBS Petroleum Sub-Index	867	1,333	2,337	1,263	
DJ UBS Precious Metals Sub-Index	21,891	19,674	8,649	3,241	
DJ UBS Softs Sub-Index	84	2,305	2,125	843	
Euro Inflation	1	3			
IPD UK Annual All Property Index	13,171	9,913	3,337	1,652	547
Gold	835	1,433	2,105	777	4,154
Xetra-Gold	3	292	668	135	
Silver	198	385	948	474	81
Exchange Traded Funds	305,552	14	5		30
Single Stock Dividend	2,330,137	2,078,118	938,950	779,542	
All Futures on Individual Equities	179,424,059	196,072,416	174,271,102	202,195,229	116,771,129
Total Futures	**961,842,729**	**987,389,647**	**1,217,288,593**	**1,153,170,392**	**928,766,700**
DAX	42,288,248	51,558,088	67,616,997	75,123,356	95,926,938
DAX 1st Friday Weekly	974,314	571,327	603,610	529,697	180,486
DAX 2nd Friday Weekly	835,862	537,235	542,074	500,470	117,787
DAX 4th Friday Weekly	910,077	621,495	654,937	539,207	193,299
DAX 5th Friday Weekly	343,615	191,218	144,953	251,562	68,591
DivDAX	10,990	760			
Euro STOXX 50 Index	225,105,846	280,610,954	369,241,952	284,707,318	300,208,574
Euro STOXX 50 Index - 1st Friday	3,593,745	1,750,970	792,380	227,729	72,606
Euro STOXX 50 Index - 2nd Friday	2,744,799	1,531,056	527,710	223,769	78,701
Euro STOXX 50 Index - 4th Friday	3,360,601	2,169,215	855,663	248,929	73,304
Euro STOXX 50 Index - 5th Friday	1,543,774	615,003	299,572	95,331	38,518
MDAX	10,145	6,066	44,866	78,895	60,560
MSCI Emerging Markets	21,681				
MSCI Europe	130,178				
MSCI Europe Growth	4,000				
MSCI World	16,154				

EUREX, Frankfurt, Germany (continued)

	2013	2012	2011	2010	2009
HEX 25	215	2,516	911	1,333	755
RDX USD Index	1,081,541	542,989			
Swiss Leader Index (SLI)	24,672	40,452	53,573	53,685	48,110
Swiss Market Index Mid-Cap (SMIM)	25,690	20,107	33,981	74,286	54,287
Swiss Market Index (SMI)	4,101,925	4,287,524	5,679,053	4,236,899	4,094,103
Stoxx Europe 50 Index	8,038	87,381	41,866	15,701	52,816
Stoxx Europe 600 Index	16,337	9,160	5,367	529	16,113
Stoxx Europe Mid 200	51,696	52,941	105,985	520	
TecDAX	3,577	4,474	16,566	23,590	53,753
Euro Stoxx Automobiles & Parts	14,074	11,159	14,662	4,790	
Euro Stoxx Banks	8,618,864	3,922,934	1,888,904	389,123	32,571
Euro Stoxx Basic Resources	736		694	120	21
Euro Stoxx Chemicals	230		3,620	6,950	12,317
Euro Stoxx Construction & Materials	719		132	80	
Euro Stoxx Financial Services	590		191		1,511
Euro Stoxx Food and Beverage	1,000	900	2,581	8	1,200
Euro Stoxx Healthcare	1,187	975	281	157	74
Euro Stoxx Industrial Goods & Services	3,537	800	24		
Euro Stoxx Insurance	15,585	2,014	21,056	34,497	5,430
Euro Stoxx Oil & Gas	26,137	7,440	2,406	1,109	1,652
Euro Stoxx Personal & Household Goods	2,400		868	5,200	10
Euro Stoxx Telecom	23,910	24,562	12,189	5,043	9,741
Euro Stoxx Travel & Leisure	151		577		75
Euro Stoxx Utilities	27,879	5,978	2,383	7,362	15,989
Euro Stoxx 600 Automobiles & Parts	129,041	146,946	33,677	21,211	8,580
Euro Stoxx 600 Banks	132,340	316,343	916,728	642,558	245,012
Euro Stoxx 600 Basic Resources	431,342	252,566	313,369	180,572	95,564
Euro Stoxx 600 Chemicals	4,332	7,755	15,389	6,395	2,221
Euro Stoxx 600 Construction & Materials	60,879	177,681	9,535	4,550	1,018
Euro Stoxx 600 Financial Services	673		259	741	1,246
Euro Stoxx 600 Food & Beverage	5,363	10,028	8,070	1,462	1,384
Euro Stoxx 600 Healthcare	18,904	6,850	23,403	19,709	28,654
Euro Stoxx 600 Industrial Goods & Services	11,644	32,400	104,553	68,363	57,026
Euro Stoxx 600 Insurance	25,501	13,223	72,791	121,461	147,459
Euro Stoxx 600 Media	12,253		3,196	15,260	5,990
Euro Stoxx 600 Oil & Gas	73,256	24,659	163,125	69,994	39,455
Euro Stoxx 600 Personal & Household Goods	570	40	11,365	1,714	706
Euro Stoxx 600 Real Estate	960	895			
Euro Stoxx 600 Retail	16,933	3,726	12,747	11,685	19,958
Euro Stoxx 600 Technology	910	30	323	382	1,550
Euro Stoxx 600 Telecom	25,048	24,996	15,088	6,941	76,903
Euro Stoxx 600 Travel & Leisure	6,545	16,476	559	40,610	9,208
Euro Stoxx 600 Utilities	11,129	19,540	14,372	11,804	38,748
Euro Stoxx 50 Index Dividend	1,125,677	1,290,153	804,612	144,620	
KOPSI 200 Index	20,498,732	32,402,451	17,442,744	166,170	
Stoxx	2,010,663	1,437,759	553,463	562,745	
Euro-Bobl	14,790,234	11,378,443	16,188,346	7,803,983	6,955,457
Euro-Bund	35,220,103	39,924,387	38,154,098	39,301,301	28,392,790
Euro-OAT	18,605				
Euro-Schatz	16,343,935	20,570,946	26,531,383	17,712,470	16,215,924
December Mid-Curve	1,250				
March Mid-Curve	4,000				
September Mid-Curve	27,000				
3-Month Euribor	89,500		100,003	371,000	
Gold	9,311	13,664	14,543	10,799	13,181
Xetra-Gold	518	650	1,488	142	
Silver	540	810	747	426	106
All Options on Exchange Traded Funds	1,016	66,321	62,623	141,718	5,515
All Options on Austrian Equities	382,695	255,359	559,998	308,428	188,289
All Options on Belgian Equities	497,785	454,324	309,027	244,081	104,865
All Options on Dutch Equities	7,033,679	5,150,348	6,552,069	5,646,218	6,813,332
All Options on Scandinavian Equities	24,308,008	18,161,501	24,569,269	28,816,601	19,342,143
All Options on French Equities	21,861,783	19,255,843	17,081,302	13,138,701	10,539,983
All Options on German Equities	99,551,563	119,585,110	156,521,894	178,639,023	186,930,541
All Options on Great Britain Equities	224,736	107,168	121,109	85,034	
All Options on Ireland Equities	5,580	5,580			
All Options on Italian Equities	2,857,908	2,077,547	2,439,964	1,457,602	1,394,120
All Options on Russian Equities	69,585	90,211	44,789	18,119	59,885
All Options on Spanish Equities	4,681,837	4,958,061	2,160,580	1,794,803	1,202,642
All Options on Swedish Equities	714	827	1,500	121,600	
All Options on Individual Swiss Equities	41,338,189	44,817,876	64,969,435	78,588,478	77,977,503
Total Options	**589,867,488**	**672,248,125**	**826,127,000**	**743,746,006**	**758,392,598**

VOLUME - WORLDWIDE

Hong Kong Futures Exchange (HKFE), Hong Kong

	2013	2012	2011	2010	2009
Hang Seng Index	19,580,330	20,353,069	23,085,833	21,031,085	20,728,034
Mini Hang Seng Index	7,853,800	8,545,847	10,294,537	8,300,654	9,279,877
H-Shares Index	20,871,257	15,923,813	15,003,870	12,429,800	12,394,116
Mini H-Shares Index	2,252,621	1,560,515	1,845,116	992,224	799,894
HSI Dividend Point Index	11,214	20,793	11,196	2,123	
HSCEI Dividend Point Index	156,496	184,786	53,054	4,667	
HIS Volatility Index	978	1,526			
CES China 120 Index	50,213				
1-Month HIBOR	20	10	245	14	204
3-Month HIBOR	2	150	414	1,055	2,573
3-Year Exchange Fund Note	25				
USD/CNH	138,708	20,277			
All Futures on Individual Equities	459,190	322,715	444,014	239,259	271,766
Total Futures	**51,374,854**	**46,933,708**	**50,741,995**	**43,006,523**	**43,483,237**
Hang Seng Index	8,601,509	9,230,145	10,667,426	8,515,049	5,367,403
Mini Hang Seng Index	1,157,266	1,230,997	954,414	482,691	286,591
Flexible Hang Seng Index	9,197	14,183	9,260	11,222	
H-Shares Index	8,027,274	6,300,889	3,771,799	2,910,713	1,961,131
Flexible H-Shares Index	30,789	11,171	23,510	2,532	
All Options on Individual Equities	60,827,975	56,081,545	74,325,068	61,125,647	47,439,896
Total Options	**78,654,010**	**72,868,930**	**89,751,477**	**73,047,854**	**55,055,021**

Hong Kong Mercantile Exchange (HKMEx), Hong Kong

	2013	2012	2011	2010	2009
USD Gold (32 Troy Ounce)	145,223	1,245,473	663,953		
USD Silver (1,000 Troy Ounce)	11,128	197,232	137,574		
Total Futures	**156,351**	**1,442,705**	**801,527**		

ICE Futures Canada (ICE), Canada

	2013	2012	2011	2010	2009
Canola (Rapeseed)	5,491,687	4,870,261	4,653,153	4,118,428	3,351,793
Durum Wheat	5	234			
Milling Wheat	5	713			
Barley	70	1,157			
Total Futures	**5,491,767**	**4,872,500**	**4,653,582**	**4,121,060**	**3,406,632**
Canola	194,733	166,660	68,375	87,818	85,115
Canola 1-Month CSO	1,795				
Total Options	**196,528**	**166,660**	**68,375**	**87,818**	**85,115**

ICE Futures Europe (ICE), United Kingdom

	2013	2012	2011	2010	2009
Brent Crude Oil (Monthly)	159,093,303	147,385,858	132,045,563	100,022,169	74,137,750
Brent Crude Oil (Quarters)	2,334	4,350	1,947		
Brent Crude Oil (Calendars)	756	33,120	8,940		
Brent NX Crude Oil (Monthly)	286	8,105	150		
WTI Crude (Monthly)	36,106,788	33,142,089	51,097,818	52,586,415	46,393,671
WTI Crude (Quarters)	3,465	1,179	1,206		
WTI Crude (Calendars)	660	32,016	6,540		
Gas Oil (Monthly)	63,964,827	63,503,591	65,774,151	52,296,582	36,038,870
Gas Oil (Quarters)	300	2,754	1,503		
LS Gas Oil (Monthly)	33,789	105,932	1,149		
Heating Oil (Monthly)	4,147,790	2,571,293	876,937	118,863	135,265
NYH (RBOB) Gasoline (Monthly)	4,094,627	2,100,786	664,784	2,257	4,965
UK Natural Gas Monthly (NBP)	3,057,320	3,114,820	2,788,240	2,105,730	1,629,980
UK Natural Gas (Quarters)	683,880	864,090	651,180	423,585	255,435
UK Natural Gas (Seasons)	2,276,010	3,096,300	2,604,150	1,638,720	907,470
UK Natural Gas (Calendars)	11,460	44,640			
UK Natural Gas (Daily)	50				
Dutch TTF Gas (Monthly)	138,890	74,210	21,040	10,860	
Dutch TTF Gas (Quarter)	90,810	105,750	14,040	4,800	
Dutch TTF Gas (Seasons)	100,560	131,460	9,600	25,860	
Dutch TTF Gas (Calendars)	15,000	38,520	21,360	41,040	
Dutch TTF Gas Base Load (Monthly)	60,201				
Dutch TTF Gas Base Load (Quarters)	79,377				
Dutch TTF Gas Base Load (Seasons)	18,150				
Dutch TTF Gas Base Load (Calendar)	8,544				
ICE UK Base Electricity (Monthly)	4,875	3,600	3,315	1,020	895
ICE UK Base Electricity (Quarters)	345	2,940	1,395	255	1,140
ICE UK Base Electricity (Seasons)	3,630	11,670	16,470	18,180	16,830
ICE UK Power Baseload (Gregorian)(Seasons)	366				
ICE UK Peak Electricity (Monthly)	1,700				
ECX EUA (Monthly)	7,260,390	6,465,262	5,444,050	4,263,655	3,775,621
ECX EUA (Daily)	43,115	265	5,855	194,981	38,214
ECX CER (Monthly)	463,503	1,572,020	1,272,128	864,089	766,349
ECX CER (Daily)	6,458				

ICE Futures Europe (ICE), United Kingdom (continued)

	2013	2012	2011	2010	2009
ECX ERU (Monthly)	114,206	411,393	61,119	3,045	
ICE Rotterdam Coal (Monthly)	34,342	64,101	40,976	39,901	28,735
ICE Rotterdam Coal (Quarters)	292,260	263,892	266,238	216,516	135,240
ICE Rotterdam Coal (Seasons)	834	2,124	5,238	5,790	2,190
ICE Rotterdam Coal (Calendar)	401,064	492,048	529,464	357,336	255,420
ICE Richards Bay Coal (Monthly)	15,793	29,299	30,281	33,601	14,225
ICE Richards Bay Coal (Quarters)	48,348	72,186	88,221	102,915	44,265
ICE Richards Bay Coal (Calendar)	56,568	73,524	91,200	159,564	91,680
gCNewcastle Coal (Monthly)	17,726	13,217	10,634	8,295	4,625
gCNewcastle Coal (Quarters)	86,109	64,839	66,669	52,050	18,210
gCNewcastle Coal (Calendars)	61,296	34,704	33,996	62,880	39,240
Central Appalachian Coal (Quarters)	360	60	630		
CSX Coal (Monthly)	2,865	15			
CSX Coal (Quarters)	11,085	75			
CSX Coal (Calendars)	9,540				
FOB Indo sub-mit Coal (Calendars)	120				
ECX EUAA (Monthly)	1,450	230			
CFR South China Coal (Monthly)	80				
CFR South China Coal (Quarters)	480				
CFR South China Coal (Calendars)	240				
Belgian Power Base Load (Monthly)	125				
Belgian Power Base Load (Quarters)	1,620				
Belgian Power Base Load (Calendars)	1,968				
Dutch Power Base Load (Monthly)	819				
Dutch Power Peak Load (8-20)(Monthly)	403				
Dutch Power Base Load (Quarters)	3,159				
Dutch Power Peak Load (8-20)(Quarters)	1,224				
Dutch Power Base Load (Calendars)	10,776				
Dutch Power Peak Load (8-20)(Calendars)	4,320				
ICE Global Oil Products	15,218,162	2,727,003			
Total Futures	**298,170,901**	**268,666,188**	**264,580,563**	**215,679,470**	**164,741,409**
Brent Crude Oil	9,675,876	8,908,862	2,191,733	165,286	212,341
WTI Crude Oil	3,535,888	1,959,493	829,972	198,245	18,200
Gasoil	617,993	568,594	407,827	259,499	213,884
Heating Oil	225				
UK Natural Gas	543,665	530,090	204,195		
Dutch TTF Gas	13,560	3,600			
Dutch TTF Gas Base Load	3,780				
ECX EUA	499,001	735,351	700,929	740,889	416,567
Rotterdam Coal	11,484	24,084	1,560		
Rotterdam Coal Quarter 1x	97,242	2,160			
Rotterdam Coal Calendar 1x	89,196	8,220			
Richards Bay Coal Quarter 1x	10,389	300			
Richards Bay Coal Calendar 1x	8,400	600			
gC Newcastle Coal Quarter 1x	3,750				
gC Newcastle Coal Calendar 1x	10,944				
ICE Global Oil Products	2,191,790	623,323			
Total Options	**17,313,183**	**13,454,527**	**4,423,220**	**1,441,303**	**952,122**

JSE Securities Exchange of South Africa, Africa

	2013	2012	2011	2010	2009
White Maize 100 Ton (WMAZ)	787,282	914,850	863,992	773,177	687,472
Yellow Maize 100 Ton (YMAZ)	447,925	391,819	376,723	313,899	311,589
White Maize 10 Ton (WNCI)	754				
Yellow Maize 10 Ton (YNCI)	2				
White Maize Can-Do (XWMS)	430				
Yellow Maize Can-Do (XYMS)	400				
Wheat Can-Do (XWHT)	4,000				
Corn	116,247	120,953	132,886	63,997	15,016
Wheat (WEAT)	498,644	544,570	449,532	441,738	379,365
Sunflower Seeds (SUNS)	123,504	105,338	156,785	89,194	127,807
Mini Soybean (SOYA)	361,721	368,061	218,111	136,802	116,530
Soya (50t)	12,489				
Sorghum (SOTG)	374	490	218	274	
CBOT Soybeans	6,515	4,696	795	190	
CBOT Soybean Meal	1,160	13	28	173	
CBOT Soybean Oil	494	7	2	1	
CBOT Wheat	7,711	12,224	3,784		
KCBT Wheat	2,147	4,330			
Cape Wheat	297	938			
Quantro Coffee (QCFF)	367				
Quantro Corn (QCRN)	58				
Quantro Cotton (QCTN)	56,933				
Quantro Sugar (QSUG)	402				
Copper	4,073	810	480	317	

JSE Securities Exchange of South Africa, Africa (continued)

	2013	2012	2011	2010	2009
Quantro Copper (QCOP)	499	30			
Gold	11,587	16,958	21,285	3,838	1,725
Quantro Gold (QGLD)	2,627	215			
Silver	1,154	1,041	3,743	395	
Quantro Silver (QSIL)	197	9			
Platinum	11,071	15,163	7,240	1,745	1,596
Quantro Platinum (QPLT)	2,334	25			
Quantro Palladium (QPLD)	174				
Brent Crude Oil	10				
Crude Oil	17,514	30,070	25,313	3,002	742
Quantro Crude Oil (QBRN)	466	153			
Quantro Natural Gas (QNAT)	64				
FTSE/JSE Top 40 Index (ALSI)	11,718,018	11,807,337	13,214,316	11,782,186	12,145,844
FTSE/JSE Top 40 Index - Mini (ALMI)	407,581	243,878	146,690	29,253	10,876
FTSE/JSE African Banks Index (J835)	330	4,327	1,386	754	56
FTSE/JSE 25 Index (INDI)	59,067	71,045	20,741	1,379	3,058
FTSE/JSE General Retailers Index (GERE)	501	828	84	200	
FTSE/JSE FINI 15 Index (FINI)	70,032	5,376	2,520	4,471	17,826
FTSE/JSE FNDI 30 Index (FNDI)	19,003	41,841	105,506	131,351	183,311
FTSE/JSE Capped Top 40 Index (CTOP)	152	636	4,600	7,585	11,420
FTSE/JSE Shareholder Weighted Top 40 Index (DTOP)	4,142,588	3,565,051	4,742,391	4,603,466	4,361,957
FTSE/JSE Equally Weighted Top 40 (ETOP)	2,004				
FTSE/JSE Mid Cap Index (MIDI)	250				
MSCI South African Index (MXZA)	27,013				
FTSE/JSE RESI 20 Index	5,512	11,082	994	360	780
Can-Do	13,918,352	2,663,021	1,347,604	9,304,664	10,619,562
Dollar / Rand	16,348,258	8,516,917	9,052,270	5,243,573	5,604,875
Euro / Rand	1,493,161	861,757	675,946	321,554	370,297
British Pound / Rand	846,122	873,172	630,975	434,603	328,838
ZAAD / Rand	512,467	222,656	283,494	178,492	873,552
Japanese Yen / Rand	168,233	250,352	86,378	18,093	
Canadian Dollar / Rand	5,519	556	11,425	9,525	
Swiss Franc / Rand	16,179	346,396	15,893	1,897	
Chinese Renminbi / Rand	200				
New Zealand Dollar / Rand	134,600	8,000			
Maxi Dollar / Rand	2,177,000	1,941,700	916,400	210	
Any-Day Expiry Dollar/Rand	2,555,860	1,267,946	1,163,137		
Quantro Euro / Dollar	865				
Currency Can-Do	1,786,079	1,053,585	398,349		
Dividend Futures	18,872,537	16,643,159	20,305,731	15,266,618	16,364,671
IDX Futures	45,920,079	31,602,019	22,287,098	15,475,728	4,321,081
IDX Dividend Futures	40,118,014	26,774,209	19,365,740	6,764,568	172,914
eCFD	230,083				
All Futures on Individual Equities	26,288,569	28,806,202	50,769,051	78,620,861	88,791,925
Total Futures	**190,325,854**	**140,116,164**	**147,812,806**	**150,037,770**	**145,845,620**
White Maize (WMAZ)	166,507	318,872	234,436	191,223	182,400
Yellow Maize (YMAZ)	58,484	75,394	46,162	39,934	41,635
Corn	2,754	2,132	10,421	26,304	61
Wheat (WEAT)	15,734	31,991	57,962	47,078	28,620
Sunflower Seeds (SUNS)	4,387	4,689	6,860	12,343	7,108
Soybeans (SOYA)	23,245	29,774	26,061	10,922	6,914
Soya (50t)	3,562				
Sorghum (SORG)	6	3	19	14	
Gold	11	24			
Platinum	136	1,033			
Crude Oil	534	2,854	302		
FTSE/JSE Top 40 Index (ALSI)	2,710,866	2,974,782	3,291,168	3,483,237	5,691,546
FTSE/JSE Top 40 Index - Mini (ALMI)	1,952	75	21		
FTSE/JSE FNDI 30 Index (FNDI)	14	8,971		25,463	71,950
FTSE/JSE Shareholder Weighted Top 40 Index (DTOP)	1,439,012	1,239,480	1,318,751	1,808,511	4,975,451
Can-Do	40,851,087	723,964	567,128	645,553	1,247,761
RESI	890	2,334			
Dollar / Rand	3,822,600	1,223,422	993,499	1,136,585	578,442
Euro / Rand	1,321,170	244,114	193,736	112,417	68,919
British Pound / Rand	26,358	218,797	76,726	7,824	87,924
ZAAD / Rand	1,707			200	
Maxi Dollar/Rand	100,000	94,700	20,600		
Any-Day Expiry Dollar/Rand	2,969,268	1,793,865	186,694		
All Options on Individual Equities	10,667,955	9,783,374	11,327,943	12,313,211	15,670,869
Total Options	**64,188,239**	**18,794,716**	**18,384,846**	**19,860,839**	**28,659,600**

Korea Futures Exchange (KFE), Korea

	2013	2012	2011	2010	2009
3-Year Treasury Bond	29,291,859	29,728,075	34,140,210	26,922,414	20,050,788
5-Year Treasury Bond	15				
10-Year Treasury Bond	11,992,729	13,045,101	3,503,677	33,054	
KOPSI 200*	49,970,933	62,430,640	87,274,461	86,214,025	83,117,030
Lean Hogs	68	11	5,981	13,943	13,703
Mini Gold	34,858	22,644	182,278		
US Dollar	51,814,466	53,549,300	70,212,467	64,256,678	41,161,819
Japanese Yen	907,501	862,806	803,734	411,117	272,531
Euro	306,023	93,939	205,395	388,294	310,540
All Futures on Individual Equities	95,870,157	100,490,960	59,966,166	44,711,133	36,971,510
Total Futures	**240,188,609**	**260,223,478**	**256,294,408**	**222,950,753**	**181,900,142**
*KOPSI 200 Index	580,460,364	1,575,394,249	3,671,662,258	3,525,898,562	2,920,990,655
US Dollar	**15,648**			**484**	
Total Options	**580,476,012**	**1,575,394,249**	**3,671,662,258**	**3,525,910,648**	**2,920,991,635**

London Metal Exchange (LME), United Kingdom

	2013	2012	2011	2010	2009
High Grade Primary Aluminium	63,767,903	59,123,583	59,558,330	46,537,180	46,988,069
Aluminium Alloy	521,980	606,102	610,935	466,206	427,452
North American Special Aluminium Alloy	573,770	603,378	699,863	588,269	920,336
Copper - Grade A	40,486,017	35,874,789	34,537,310	29,949,765	24,922,949
Standard Lead	12,931,067	14,248,937	10,921,882	7,744,747	5,983,323
Primary Nickel	13,678,490	11,164,449	8,056,421	7,325,219	6,717,299
Special High Grade Zinc	30,270,370	29,559,338	21,984,302	18,065,641	15,901,774
Mediterranean Steel (MS)	71,752	144,724	219,163	191,179	30,764
Tin	2,061,899	1,846,814	1,891,633	1,554,269	4,567,915
Cobalt	13,827	13,291	6,578	6,812	
Molybdenum	512	461	513	510	
Primary Aluminium LMEswap	5,565	15,079			
Copper LMEswap	331	30			
Lead LMEswap	123				
Nickel LMEswap	74	94			
Tin LMEswap	26				
Zinc LMWswap	815	308			
Total Futures	**164,384,521**	**153,201,377**	**138,487,658**	**112,439,117**	**106,463,839**
High Grade Primary Aluminium	2,681,694	2,424,466	3,218,299	3,479,888	2,505,499
North American Special Aluminium Alloy	370	1,175	4,178	17,428	4,333
Copper - Grade A	2,408,984	2,605,512	3,371,191	3,111,996	1,624,350
Primary Nickel	285,039	178,844	233,837	172,075	142,168
Special High Grade Zinc	826,821	952,958	913,771	732,279	712,526
Tin	13,227	14,014	26,114	26,009	33,562
Primary Aluminium TAPOS	140,542	45,361	44,196	38,299	55,149
Copper Grade A TAPOS	50,219	16,649	24,309	21,532	15,212
Lead TAPOS	6,920	4,764	6,806	1,622	3,065
Nickel TAPOS	7,250	3,157	2,091	2,547	3,541
Special High Grade Zinc TAPOS	64,234	11,239	74,938	9,648	5,335
Total Options	**6,485,300**	**6,518,404**	**8,109,887**	**7,819,002**	**5,466,989**

Bursa Malaysia Derivatives Berhad (BMD), Malaysia

	2013	2012	2011	2010	2009
Crude Palm Oil (FCPO)	7,966,096	7,443,143	5,871,587	4,064,361	4,008,882
Gold	24,253				
3-Month KLIBOR (FKB3)	16,791	50,946	101,979	95,477	126,690
KLSE Composite Index (FKLI)	2,607,429	2,096,493	2,489,204	1,994,907	1,997,955
Total Futures	**10,614,569**	**9,590,582**	**8,462,770**	**6,154,745**	**6,137,827**
Crude Palm Oil (OCPO)	2,020	821			
KLSE Composite Index (OKLI)	5,040	5,493	16		
Total Options	**7,060**	**6,314**	**16**		

MEFF Renta Variable (RV), Spain

	2013	2012	2011	2010	2009
IBEX 35 Plus Index	5,578,607	4,745,067	5,281,218	6,280,999	5,436,989
Mini IBEX 35 Index	1,987,362	2,424,766	3,099,647	3,579,263	3,148,292
Ibex Dividends	3,520	2,162	3,154		
Stock Dividend	66,650	25,000			
10-Year Notional Bond (NEW)	13,667	45,238			
All Futures on Individual Equities	14,927,659	21,220,876	27,578,789	19,684,108	44,586,779
Total Futures	**22,577,465**	**28,463,109**	**35,962,808**	**29,544,370**	**53,172,060**
IBEX 35 Plus Index	5,172,426	4,206,058	2,198,967	3,072,418	4,357,260
All Options on Individual Equities	26,944,611	34,507,360	29,410,340	37,607,374	35,527,914
Total Options	**32,117,037**	**38,713,418**	**31,609,307**	**40,679,792**	**39,885,174**

Mexican Derivatives Exchange (MEXDER), Mexico

	2013	2012	2011	2010	2009
US Dollar	13,535,162	9,827,086	7,189,846	5,662,462	1,587,858
Euro FX	24,919	14,411	24,397	36,168	64,327
IPC Stock Index	952,165	1,060,760	1,231,048	1,321,686	1,130,528
CETE 91	466,000	1,697,650	4,990,595	3,802,874	4,877,430
TIIE 28	9,609,597	25,408,966	26,906,390	26,208,542	37,545,841
M3 Bond	317,000	272,824	197,623	1,051,818	216,150
M5 Bond	2,621	31,917	50,575		
M10 Bond	383,867	1,686,335	2,917,800	2,281,187	2,613,021
M20 Bond	983,644	1,335,787	2,241,045	1,377,266	269,904
M30 Bond	229,480	327,252	396,078		
28-day Interbank Equilibrium Interest Rate (TIIE) Swap	3,104				
10-Year Interest Rate Swap (Centrally Cleared)	3,200	3,860	6,434	5,226	
2-Year Interest Rate Swap (Centrally Cleared)	700	14,496	19,580	14,571	
All Futures on Individual Equities	66,870	35,839	63,711	12,044	
Total Futures	**26,578,329**	**41,717,187**	**46,246,427**	**41,827,321**	**48,394,113**
MXN / USD	18,075	1,673	422	963	145
IPC Stock Index	54,853	42,653	65,631	147,411	40,723
Exchange Traded Funds	5,599	391,580	2	10	
All Options on Individual Equities	701,376	477,565	446,547	619,870	345,718
Total Options	**779,903**	**913,471**	**512,602**	**768,254**	**386,586**

Montreal Exchange (ME), Canada

	2013	2012	2011	2010	2009
3-Month Bankers Acceptance (BAX)	22,578,143	20,804,167	20,865,769	13,698,870	7,668,781
2-Year Canadian Gov't Bond (CGZ)	79,349	71,699	59,650	611	
5 Year Canadian Gov't Bond (CGF)	276,610	153,598	105,580		12,055
10-Year Canadian Gov't Bond (CGB)	13,824,451	9,951,321	7,788,218	6,405,525	5,310,537
S&P Canada 60 Index (SXF)	3,994,992	3,826,976	4,228,938	4,070,604	4,157,917
S&P/TSX Composite Index Mini (SCF)	406	539	232	261	1,151
S&P/TSX 60 Index Mini (SXM)	100,194	132,549	100,554		
Total Futures	**40,854,145**	**34,940,999**	**33,148,941**	**24,176,031**	**17,150,708**
3-Month Bankers Acceptance (OBX)	588,279	493,047	635,046	349,675	234,861
10-Year Canadian Gov't Bond (OGB)	4,669	4,767	8,775	9,742	12,531
US Dollar (USX)	6,931	5,235	16,947	17,705	29,902
S&P Canada 60 Index (SXO) (incl LEAPS)	511,384	314,631	93,151	77,820	34,056
ETFs	2,905,949	4,405,451			
All Options on Individual Equities	21,335,465	24,200,766	24,211,857	16,353,284	14,507,261
Total Options	**25,352,677**	**29,423,897**	**28,832,465**	**20,120,876**	**17,602,373**

Moscow Interbank Currency Exchange (MICEX), Russia

	2013	2012	2011	2010	2009
Sugar (Deliverable - SU)	218,722	256,163	184	2,071	12,602
AUD/USD	2,138,081	883,238	1,228,766	73,446	
EUR/USD	66,436,523	33,632,175	45,657,240	39,476,420	13,658,237
EUR/RUB	8,210,577	1,980,420	1,736,514	1,298,081	479,084
GBP/USD	4,370,140	471,425	1,361,481	124,956	
USD/RUB	373,466,315	373,108,731	206,820,695	81,122,195	8,468,200
USD/CHF	336,814				
USD/JPY	1,471,045				
USD/UAH	2,950				
Ruble 3 Monthly Credit Interbank Mkt Moscow MosPrime	42,743	16,927	141,858	123,375	17,861
Ruble Overnight Index Average (RUONIA)	2,705				
2-Year Federal Bond issued by Russian Federation	1,629,490	3,978,269	2,530,693		
4-Year Federal Bond issued by Russian Federation	2,668,125	6,326,067	4,645,995		
6-Year Federal Bond issued by Russian Federation	2,152,683	10,741,890	159,000		
10-Year Federal Bond issued by Russian Federation	6,535,538	192,374			
15-Year Federal Bond issued by Russian Federation	4,382,830				
RTS Consumer & Retail Index	69	234	8,380	1,265	1,246
RTS Index	266,131,127	321,031,540	377,845,640	224,696,733	150,019,917
RTS Oil & Gas Index	5,963	58,060	48,882	7,289	29,798
RTS Standard Index	136,796	709,342	1,197,521	2,327,517	
FTSE/JSE Top 40	158	346			
Hang Seng Index	651	3,899			
IBOVESPA	1,312	8,317			
MICEX Index	1,511,962	1,045,857	663,411		
Russian Volatility Index	3,641	12,719	47,244		
SENSEX Index	37	10			
Brent Oil	18,170,809	11,952,101	18,707,384	11,127,254	7,471,665
Urals Oil	4	104	284	785	28,070
Copper	68,722	68,869	118,593	18,912	
Gold	15,892,846	8,156,949	13,018,359	5,562,423	2,903,120
Palladium	6,988	18,224	10,871	1,982	391
Platinum	144,356	211,431	379,285	275,555	34,570
Refined Silver	1,833,579	1,359,708	3,923,342	714,645	104,531

Moscow Interbank Currency Exchange (MICEX), Russia (continued)

	2013	2012	2011	2010	2009
All Futures on Individual Equities	302,635,507	242,630,281	355,374,012	226,711,751	249,278,962
Total Futures	**1,080,609,808**	**1,019,741,152**	**1,054,106,253**	**632,209,693**	**473,773,814**
RTS Index	42,233,069	33,915,936	35,389,828	13,179,587	5,062,653
MICEX Index	78,664	41,425	6,195		
US Dollar	522,116	1,051,410	853,367	1,280,316	1,863,930
EUR/USD	32,742	43,041	24,332	17,522	
EUR/RUB	28,721	750			
USD/RUB	3,348,701	904,498			
Gold	149,251	156,569	139,284	98,002	84,164
Platinum	5,003	34,139	20,453	13,420	
Refined Silver	17,091	47,559	40,481	21,784	1,336
Brent Crude Oil	37,901	33,971	45,911	12,251	
All Options on Individual Equities	7,414,191	5,865,454	8,411,748	9,153,070	12,962,387
Total Options	**53,867,450**	**42,094,752**	**44,931,599**	**23,775,952**	**19,974,470**

MCX-SX, India

	2013	2012	2011	2010	2009
US Dollar/Indian Rupee	496,230,881	551,326,121	807,559,846	821,254,927	224,273,548
EUR/Indian Rupee	14,409,559	10,496,445	29,403,759	46,411,303	
GBP/Indian Rupee	9,027,201	4,414,631	7,305,618	9,889,564	
JPY/Indian Rupee	9,706,316	4,624,969	5,859,837	7,051,048	
Total Futures	**529,373,957**	**570,862,166**	**850,129,060**	**884,606,842**	**224,273,548**

National Stock Exchange of India

	2013	2012	2011	2010	2009
US Dollar/Indian Rupee	566,399,936	620,215,043	697,825,411	699,042,420	226,362,368
EUR/Indian Rupee	16,984,993	5,770,205	18,065,186	17,326,787	
GBP/Indian Rupee	10,259,534	2,591,566	5,569,204	1,488,555	
JPY/Indian Rupee	9,715,049	2,689,841	5,411,351	1,491,520	
Bank Nifty Index	26,253,848	21,741,473	17,131,900	13,732,237	
CNX INFRA	144	389	1,072		
CNX IT Index	63,462	43,015	71,672	67,577	
CNX PSE	277	230	984		
DJIA Index	195,252	408,998	230,828		
FTSE 100	22,939	302,162			
Mini S&P CNX Nifty Index	248,422	9,471,381	14,994,257	14,154,716	
Nifty Midcap 50 Index	19,449	5,723	2,935	4,117	
S&P CNX Nifty Index	74,863,943	80,061,861	123,144,880	128,392,858	195,759,414
S&P 500 Index	81,970	257,093	135,323		
All Futures on Individual Equities	157,885,578	153,122,207	160,878,260	175,674,069	161,053,345
Total Futures	**862,994,796**	**896,681,187**	**1,043,463,263**	**1,051,374,856**	**583,175,127**
US Dollar/Indian Rupee	252,398,423	237,062,966	252,807,126	6,277,165	
Bank Nifty Index	55,120,938	15,369,585	1,867,147	777,136	
CNX INFRA	7	55	3,779		
CNX IT Index	735	834	873	640	
FTSE 100	52	126,763			
Mini S&P CNX Nifty Index	95,734	931,336	309,211	147,415	
Nifty Midcap 50 Index	4	11	23,639	18,445	
S&P CNX Nifty Index	874,835,809	803,086,926	868,684,582	528,831,609	321,265,217
S&P 500 Index	479	12,815	31,023		
All Options on Individual Equities	90,190,480	57,221,005	33,172,963	28,363,426	14,066,778
Total Options	**1,272,642,661**	**1,113,812,300**	**1,156,903,387**	**564,415,836**	**335,331,995**

NYSE-LIFFE European Derivatives Market

	2013	2012	2011	2010	2009
3-Month Eonia	15	904	15,110	85,181	135,594
3-Month Euribor	238,493,786	178,762,097	241,950,875	248,504,960	192,859,090
3-Month Euroswiss	6,579,896	6,428,995	8,233,176	7,179,251	4,768,825
3-Month Short Sterling	144,279,092	114,915,025	115,586,702	112,944,490	104,073,092
Long Gilt	42,299,274	37,777,306	34,362,932	28,525,983	23,977,779
Medium Gilt	40,030	43,146	36,307	166,521	11,455
Short Gilt	107,137	268,635	432,744	365,824	30,680
Japanese Government Bond	5,472	6,899	40,614	49,610	50,953
10-Year Swapnote EUR	124,012	150,409	77,825	78,536	76,200
5-Year Swapnote EUR	371,687	283,872	220,966	254,717	251,078
2-Year Swapnote EUR	433,411	376,091	357,849	392,976	452,362
Euro/US Dollar	1,421	1,210	2,949	5,206	6,588
AEX Stock Index	9,038,280	10,476,310	12,602,311	11,958,934	10,524,741
AEX Mini	4,157				
AMX Index	297	1,336			
Bel 20 Index	35,837	58,094	106,922	158,047	296,543
CAC 40 Stock Index 10 Euro	37,211,714	38,092,777	43,403,809	44,559,669	41,940,487
CAC 40 Dividend Index	15,700	13,382	20,643	82,139	322
CAC 40 Mini	1,491				
FTSE 100 Index	33,529,120	32,619,662	39,283,942	37,627,230	38,515,933

NYSE-LIFFE European Derivatives Market (continued)

	2013	2012	2011	2010	2009
FTSE 100 Dividend Index	941,252	692,288	447,151	910,456	667,052
FTSE Mid 250 Index	46,872	57,439	81,345	101,194	91,362
FTSE EPRA Eurozone	2,552	5,820	9,859	13,592	28,659
FTSE EPRA Europe	56,784	82,456	79,618	78,147	87,274
FTSE Eurotop 100 Index	253	96	233	737	9,882
FTSEurofirst 100	138	105	239	407	122
FTSEurofirst 80	47,891	51,577	52,345	107,837	186,634
MSCI Europe Net Total Return Index	111,878	131,237			
PSI-20 Index	112,489	66,279	77,939	126,127	61,225
Index F Other Bclear	1,512,449	1,653,292	1,032,135	550,503	95,287
All Futures on Individual Equities	120,239,502	246,541,679	250,441,783	289,334,111	199,044,957
Cocoa #7	5,125,146	4,106,182	4,079,975	3,519,409	3,218,726
Corn	497,114	574,067	402,397	240,028	149,008
Malted Barley	7,492	22,253	25,009	6,200	
Rapeseed	1,864,450	1,973,468	1,908,310	1,202,153	812,779
Robusta Coffee - 10 Tonne	4,075,212	3,104,053	3,502,508	2,789,953	2,514,457
Wheat	117,266	135,037	162,683	147,684	114,133
Wheat #2	6,471,781	7,472,845	5,687,888	4,374,323	1,925,916
White Sugar	2,049,442	1,852,267	1,497,216	1,854,156	1,852,702
Total Futures	**655,851,792**	**688,798,810**	**766,265,296**	**798,511,326**	**629,257,336**
3-Month Euribor	50,888,649	70,671,111	126,535,338	121,077,679	121,612,383
3-Month Euribor 2-Year Mid-curve	24,345,916	8,445,744	131,056	134,920	30,402
3-Month Euribor 3-Year Mid-curve	13,409,662	3,089,075			
3-Month Euribor 4-Year Mid-curve	481,211	150,040			
3-Month Euribor Mid Curve	29,825,751	10,504,341	16,617,712	20,425,277	18,498,853
3-Month Short Sterling	9,916,727	8,982,932	21,575,685	26,157,563	37,876,416
3-Month Sterling 2-Year Mid-curve	7,064,627	4,441,041	94,370	45,000	10,550
3-Month Sterling 3-Year Mid-curve	480,911	33,800			
3-Month Sterling Mid-curve	5,541,772	5,381,200	11,784,839	20,766,671	12,109,210
Euro / US Dollar (EDX)	188,100	181,873	170,392	266,086	388,488
AEX Stock Index (AEX)	12,774,623	15,490,211	25,079,752	26,158,523	24,660,898
AMX Index	460	1,854			
Bel 20 (E10) Index	675	707	149	20	
CAC 40 Index, 10 EUR	4,400,084	4,996,392	5,281,378	6,329,140	6,126,542
FTSE 100 Index (ESX)	23,427,928	17,146,155	20,341,926	23,440,064	30,155,112
Other Bclear	867,614	949,265	578,002	1,246,316	2,400,296
All Options on Individual Equities	98,697,280	112,840,693	150,562,241	175,228,607	170,870,365
Cocoa	1,048,269	783,694	79,238	730,027	556,860
Corn	57,348	38,789	43,794	20,245	5,720
Rapeseed	290,353	443,698	408,554	271,993	79,385
Robusta Coffee - 10 Tonne	877,076	770,343	898,109	482,483	192,398
Wheat	884	1,025	1,363	873	656
Wheat	1,363,852	1,646,903	1,298,748	1,016,600	655,099
White Sugar	1,672	11,824	17,624	22,482	50,195
Total Options	**285,951,444**	**267,003,410**	**381,519,447**	**424,045,446**	**426,754,760**

New Zealand Futures Exchange (NZFOE), New Zealand

	2013	2012	2011	2010	2009
10-Year Government Stock	11,940	1,780	260	1,742	4,329
NZ 30-Day OCR Interbank	50	552	1,780	400	20
90-Day Bank Bill	1,121,995	1,307,096	2,018,667	1,426,513	1,484,030
ASX NZ Base Load Calendar Month Electricity	2				
NZ Electricity (Otahuhu)	3,163	3,064	537	195	6
NZ Electricity (Benmore)	3,816	4,143	816	272	52
Total Futures	**1,140,966**	**1,316,635**	**2,022,060**	**1,430,222**	**1,490,947**

NASDAQ OMX Oslo, Norway

	2013	2012	2011	2010	2009
Carbon CER	178	5,120	9,119		
Carbon EUA	7,029	38,514	41,567	40	
Carbon EUA Spot	115	1,243	1,122	9,818	
Carbon EUA Deferred Settlement	130	4,634	7,307	16,732	40,850
El Cert EUA Deferred Settlement	297				
El Cert EUR Deferred Settlement	30				
UK Power Base NPC Other	147				
UK Power Base (Quarter)	51	805			
UK Power Base (Month)	1,145	9,250			
UK Power Base (Week)	96	11,235			
UK Power Base (Season)	146	2,375			
German Power Base (Year)	3,738	1,897	2,161	1,826	2,710
German Power Base (Quarter)	1,888	278	303	554	1,002
German Power Base (Month)	4,551	2,178	287	706	449
German Power Base (Week)	2,930	4,525	125	235	100
German Power Base (Day)	825				

NASDAQ OMX Oslo, Norway (continued)

	2013	2012	2011	2010	2009
Nordic Power Base (Year)	73,920	79,248	79,667	82,382	118,404
Nordic Power Base (Quarter)	303,083	289,245	287,396	408,218	307,694
Nordic Power Base (Month)	157,775	185,802	163,672	192,260	136,195
Nordic Power Base (Week + Day)	119,733	140,401	133,201	140,954	214,819
Nordic Power Base (Day)	111,863	47,249	57,766	52,380	
Nordic Power Base (CfD Year)	10,215	9,214	11,428	11,561	50,148
Nordic Power Base (CfD Month)	19,438	18,926	22,930	27,198	
Nordic Power Base (CfD Quarter)	17,372	15,282	20,864	22,729	
Nordic Power Peak (Month)	160	49	1	20	
Total Futures	**836,855**	**868,344**	**841,012**	**972,685**	**877,992**
Nordic Power Base (Year)	3,100	3,272	7,642	10,531	28,104
Nordic Power Base (Quarter)	8,710	8,226	9,210	20,978	
Total Options	**11,810**	**11,498**	**16,852**	**31,509**	**28,104**

OMX Exchanges, Swedish, Finnish, Danish & Icelandic Exchanges

	2013	2012	2011	2010	2009
3-Month STIBOR	15,394,749	19,118,953	19,872,815	15,640,119	12,923,736
NIBOR-FRA	342,500	511,600	638,600		
CIBOR	11,000	87,002	15,016		
Mortgage Bond Future (20MBFH)	150				
Mortgage Bond Future (3MBFH)	2,100				
Mortgage Bond Future (20MBFU)	2,500				
Mortgage Bond Future (3MBFU)	8,625				
Mortgage Bond Future (3YMBF)	5,700				
Mortgage Bond Short (MBFS)	7,500	15,100	29,250		
Mortgage Bond Futures 20 Year in Danish Kronor	900				
3% Danish Mortgage Bond (3MBF)	6,300	8,475			
Danish Mortgage Bond Futures (20MBFZ)	2,950				
Danish Mortgage Bond Futures (3MBFZ)	9,700				
Danish Mortgage Bond Futures (3YMBFZ)	5,900				
Mortgage Bond Future (3YMBFH)	400				
Policy Rate (RIBA)	5,348,960	6,495,914	4,680,389	2,114,300	1,040,006
2-Year Swedish Gov't Bond Forward (R2)	1,842,401	1,752,451	2,303,865	2,950,624	2,096,471
5-Year Swedish Gov't Bond Forward (R5)	1,480,964	1,161,729	1,445,999	1,511,946	1,179,563
10-Year Swedish Gov't Bond Forward (R10)	1,331,975	1,536,138	1,339,726	1,063,189	885,565
30-Year Swedish Gov't Bond Forward (R30)	900				
2-Year Nordea Hypotek Bond Forward (NBHYP2)	188,646	218,544	175,208	340,514	345,156
5-Year Nordea Hypotek Bond Forward (NBHYP5)	124,877	99,917	216,357	290,635	202,314
2-Year Spintab Bond Forward (SPA2)	168,729	217,141	252,565	310	176,791
5-Year Spintab Bond Forward (SPA5)	195,582	228,715	250,373	477,440	240,372
2-Year Stadshypotek Bond Forward (ST2)	527,279	575,566	275,194	385,412	257,681
5-Year Stadshypotek Bond Forward (ST5)	402,211	356,112	298,374	352,728	331,842
OMX Index	30,898,519	32,637,547	37,462,177	32,427,696	33,700,054
All Futures on Individual Equities	3,613,984	1,979,581	4,012,218	2,468,839	6,718,987
Total Futures	**61,926,001**	**67,008,230**	**73,420,598**	**60,056,299**	**60,099,788**
Interest Rate	888,000	707,500	1,312,800	2,043,400	1,170,505
NIBOR-FRA	61,000	28,000	32,500		
2-Year Sewdish Government Bond Forward (R2)	29,000	24,000	14,700		
5-Year Sewdish Government Bond Forward (R5)	17,500	2,750	4,250		
10-Year Sewdish Government Bond Forward (R10)	2,750	7,800	50		
OMX Index	7,987,697	9,625,030	12,485,788	13,761,881	14,225,611
All Options on Individual Equities	27,476,014	27,500,926	29,836,598	32,753,859	28,775,091
All Options on Individual Equities	**36,461,961**	**37,896,006**	**43,686,686**	**48,559,140**	**44,171,207**

Osaka Securities Exchange (OSE), Japan

	2013	2012	2011	2010	2009
Nikkei 225 Index	30,907,691	19,523,347	19,294,064	22,483,722	25,368,919
Nikkei 225 Mini	233,860,478	130,443,680	117,905,210	125,113,769	104,738,309
Nikkei VI Index	38,496	12,959			
Nikkei 300 Index	250		16	148	405
DJIA	26,816	19,154			
US Dollar/Japanese Yen	2,549,202	1,328,936	2,906,939	1,813,592	243,611
Euro/Japanese Yen	1,135,263	1,906,365	2,438,817	929,577	108,118
British Pound/Japanese Yen	282,828	448,515	1,056,471	390,457	51,086
Australian Dollar/Japanese Yen	679,488	1,393,231	2,652,305	1,002,638	52,858
Swiss Franc/Japanese Yen	136,787	122,877	229,941	27,224	4,953
Canadian Dollar/Japanese Yen	88,022	116,458	111,099	46,340	13,069
New Zealand/Japanese Yen	168,062	217,237	312,812	118,211	7,567
South African Rand/Japanese Yen	398,581	275,521	76,872		
Euro/US Dollar	98,954	308,364	582,463	218,219	71,516
British Pound/US Dollar	28,121	35,286	85,917	24,566	30,241

Osaka Securities Exchange (OSE), Japan (continued)

	2013	2012	2011	2010	2009
Australian Dollar/US Dollar	92,771	93,970	98,760		
Total Futures	**270,491,810**	**156,245,900**	**147,751,686**	**152,168,463**	**130,690,652**
Nikkei 225 Index	57,269,727	48,763,723	45,192,519	43,791,011	34,986,005
All Options on Individual Equities	22,978	120,545	1,231,796	390,805	408,752
Total Options	**57,292,705**	**48,884,268**	**46,424,315**	**44,181,816**	**35,394,757**

Oslo Stock Exchange (OSE), Norway

	2013	2012	2011	2010	2009
OBX Index	3,505,641	5,017,556	6,468,392	8,001,664	9,041,941
Single Stock Forwards	3,685,393	1,645,446	2,279,603	1,460,982	1,173,476
Total Futures	**7,191,034**	**6,663,002**	**8,747,995**	**9,462,646**	**10,215,417**
OBX	864,097	802,028	711,566	734,458	746,589
All Options on Individual Equities	3,638,828	3,361,910	4,131,235	3,363,236	2,549,240
Total Options	**4,502,925**	**4,163,938**	**4,842,801**	**4,097,694**	**3,295,829**

Rosario Futures Exchange (ROFEX), Argentina

	2013	2012	2011	2010	2009
Wheat	4,551	5,881	3,074	1,654	267
Corn	7,616	4,663	4,635	2,622	88
Soybeans	119,325	83,430	68,583	72,183	26,047
Chicago Soybeans	140,041	73,192	4,698		
Chicago Corn	76,601	16,324			
Rosafe Soybean Index (ISR)	125,746	212,783	227,596	154,872	133,712
Gold	68,023	63,891	139,207	20,869	
TVPP	72,535	21,045			
WTI Crude Oil	18,198	18,664	9,928		
US Dollar (DLR)	50,360,076	50,359,614	54,373,381	61,729,396	51,107,696
Euro (EC)	122,714	112,087	132,020	30,023	11,974
Total Futures	**51,115,426**	**50,971,574**	**54,967,681**	**62,011,935**	**51,286,802**
Chicago Soybeans	7,192	2,366			
Chicago Corn	4,318				
Rosafe Soybean Index (ISR)	31,582	29,489	25,755	23,273	53,114
Gold	2,000	51,504	2,444		
US Dollar (DLR)	16,032	10,872	4,048	4,353	128,362
Total Options	**61,124**	**99,653**	**32,360**	**34,885**	**196,627**

Shanghai Metal Exchange, China

	2013	2012	2011	2010	2009
Copper	64,295,856	57,284,835	48,961,130	50,788,568	81,217,436
Aluminum	3,305,575	3,942,680	9,953,918	17,261,995	20,530,548
Lead	172,759	68,646	293,280		
Zinc	12,083,166	21,100,924	53,663,483	146,589,373	32,253,386
Steel Rebar	293,728,929	180,562,480	81,884,789	225,612,417	161,574,521
Wire Rod	3,862	2,717	3,242	151,702	1,092,016
Gold	20,087,824	5,916,745	7,221,758	3,397,044	3,406,233
Silver	173,222,611	21,264,954			
Rubber	72,438,058	75,176,266	104,286,399	167,414,912	89,035,959
Bitumen	3,134,301				
Fuel Oil	1,039	9,132	1,971,141	10,682,204	45,753,969
Total Futures	**642,473,980**	**365,329,379**	**308,239,140**	**621,898,215**	**434,864,068**

Singapore Exchange (SGX), Singapore

	2013	2012	2011	2010	2009
RSS3	17,267	13,196	22,454	35,712	20,027
TSR20 (FOB)	328,994	242,619	205,439	191,160	48,544
Euroyen TIBOR	10,221	25,826	59,250	85,840	161,492
Mini Japanese Gov't Bond	862,112	1,025,937	759,703	741,764	694,655
Nikkei 225 Index	39,087,816	27,994,913	29,022,284	28,785,870	25,353,225
Nikkei 225 Index (USD)	3,601	1,341	2,695	3,010	666
Mini Nikkei 225 Index	12,080	6,124	68,298	134,449	1,857
Nikkei Stock Average Dividend Point Index	159,223	152,554	62,653	21,216	
Straits Times Index	253	570	229	436	2,916
Euro Stoxx 50 Index	76	5,748	5,139	200	
FTSE/China A50 Index	21,906,479	10,022,496	3,071,428	531,865	1
S&P CNX Nifty Index	16,079,671	14,719,166	14,678,520	10,479,168	7,115,255
MSCI India Index	82				
MSCI Indonesia Index	344,691	59,947			
MSCI PSE Philippines Index	123				
MSCI Singapore Index	3,732,386	4,027,281	4,358,862	3,718,450	3,947,690
MSCI Taiwan Index	18,357,967	17,183,604	17,624,091	15,576,877	15,718,096
MSCI Thailand Index	1,266				
SGX AUD/JPY	1,803				
SGX AUD/USD	1,202				
SGX INR/USD	5,819				
SGX KRW/JPY	4				

Singapore Exchange (SGX), Singapore (continued)

	2013	2012	2011	2010	2009
SGX KRW/USD	102				
SGX USD/SGD	2,184				
LME-SGX Aluminum	10	310	16,751		
LME-SGX Zinc	32	517	33,155		
Total Futures	**100,915,464**	**75,482,509**	**70,028,574**	**60,961,099**	**53,065,083**
MSCI Taiwan Index	26,167	9,352	10,695	5,400	9,901
SGX S&P CNX Nifty Index	290,588	323,217			
Nikkei 225 Index	10,184,676	4,393,629	2,070,984	610,630	102,142
Total Options	**10,501,431**	**4,728,108**	**2,091,076**	**632,983**	**114,671**

Sydney Futures Exchange (SFE), Australia

	2013	2012	2011	2010	2009
SPI 200	10,239,412	10,025,717	12,130,237	10,061,779	9,538,554
S&P/ASX 200 Volatility Index	57				
S&P/ASX 200 Financials-x-A-REIT Index	1,286				
S&P/ASX 200 Resources Index	806				
30-Day Interbank Cash Rate	4,913,943	4,499,015	6,296,489	5,214,205	2,315,374
90-Day Bank Bills	29,020,415	21,382,203	22,391,055	17,910,061	14,435,474
3-Month Overnight Index Swap	5,624	12,006			
3-Year Treasury Bonds	48,978,355	44,003,411	41,662,349	34,482,136	24,197,537
3-Year Interest Rate Swaps	101	8,142	1,980		
10-Year Treasury Bonds	23,926,468	18,469,473	15,954,349	13,454,773	10,072,494
10-Year Interest Rate Swaps	40	1,620	2,650	4,799	6,001
d-cypha NSW Base Load Electricity	34,962	47,572	64,143	52,543	42,330
d-cypha QLD Base Load Electricity	27,587	31,722	49,345	38,211	28,811
d-cypha SA Base Load Electricity	4,916	4,398	4,530	2,733	1,751
d-cypha VIC Base Load Electricity	29,294	26,393	42,174	49,574	34,867
d-cypha NSW Peak Period Electricity	4,914	7,862	7,668	2,883	1,501
d-cypha QLD Peak Period Electricity	1,865	3,223	1,819	2,130	1,436
d-cypha SA Peak Period Electricity	203	457	319	28	105
d-cypha VIC Peak Period Electricity	3,886	2,641	5,476	2,831	1,774
d-cypha NSW Base $300 CAP	11,181	9,761	12,051	12,378	1,728
d-cypha QLD Base $300 CAP	4,781	5,811	5,729	4,537	2,734
d-cypha SA Base $300 CAP	2,402	1,871	1,185	768	232
d-cypha VIC Base $300 CAP	10,281	10,150	9,837	12,401	3,085
VIC Gas	10				
d-cypha ASX NSW Monthly Base Load Electricity	5				
d-cypha ASX QLD Monthly Base Load Electricity	355				
d-cypha ASX VIC Monthly Base Load Electricity	25				
Greasy Wool	48	1,410	6,996	6,377	9,971
WA Wheat	16,580	18,582	12,283		
NSW Wheat	178,357	322,372	93,940		
Eastern Australian Feed Barley	28,490	49,128	8,558		
Australian Sorghum	9,530	12,467	1,690		
Eastern Australia Canola	80	50			
Total Futures	**117,456,259**	**98,957,493**	**98,767,181**	**81,315,280**	**60,696,359**
SPI 200	388,450	441,838	423,390	382,378	319,735
90-Day Bank Bills	3,750	6,788	53,602	40,840	33,146
3-Year Treasury Bond	423,077	526,889	509,638	205,816	446,182
Overnight 3-Year Treasury Bond	1,890,929	1,301,374	1,433,184	1,740,511	1,136,306
3-Year Bonds Intra-Day	1,711,088	1,096,285	1,249,257	1,049,240	430,590
10-Year Treasury Bonds	12,731	11,706	2,052	5,475	9,335
Overnight 10-Year Treasury Bond	1,000	550	2,250	2,150	2,250
NSW Wheat	1,250	14,930	160		
Eastern Feed Barley	1,500	1,210			
d-cypha ASX NSW Monthly Base Load Electricity	175				
d-cypha ASX QLD Monthly Base Load Electricity	372				
d-cypha ASX VIC Monthly Base Load Electricity	740				
d-cypha ASX SA Monthly Base Load Electricity	15				
Total Options	**4,435,077**	**3,401,670**	**3,673,533**	**3,426,510**	**2,377,784**

Taiwan Futures Exchange, Taiwan

	2013	2012	2011	2010	2009
TAIEX (TX)	22,693,270	24,642,382	30,611,932	25,332,827	24,625,062
Mini TAIEX (MTX)	13,093,325	15,980,510	19,128,802	13,893,559	13,926,904
Taiwan 50 Index	231	445	2,503	618	888
Taiwan Stock Exchange Electronic Sector Index	931,196	1,036,915	1,552,291	1,092,763	1,166,622
Taiwan Stock Exchange Bank & Insurance Sector Index	1,042,597	1,256,952	2,287,601	1,257,861	1,482,264
GreTai Securities Weighted Stock Index (GTF)	4,634	18,695	30,478	43,335	66,610
Taiwan Stock Exch NonFin/NonElec SubIndex (XIF)	108,487	100,024	181,233	106,768	157,613
30-Day Commercial Paper Interest Rate (CPF)	8	14	27	2	13,149
Gold (GDF)	7	36	383	677	205
NT Dollar Gold (TGF)	67,341	62,418	105,458	75,218	3,342,838
All Futures on Individual Equities	5,448,554	4,670,750	2,471,605	724,375	
Total Futures	**43,389,650**	**47,769,142**	**56,372,485**	**42,529,023**	**44,886,570**

Taiwan Futures Exchange, Taiwan (continued)

	2013	2012	2011	2010	2009
TAIEX	109,311,515	108,458,103	125,767,624	95,666,916	72,082,548
TSE Electronic Sector Index	113,279	105,009	187,576	382,747	786,132
TSE Financial Sector Index	245,997	209,689	352,241	797,910	761,886
GreTai Securities Weighted Stock Index (GTO)	4	109	36,595	123,537	688,481
Taiwan Stock Exch NonFin/NonElec SubIndex (XIO)	979	801	46,334	118,565	741,908
DTB-demoninated Gold (TGO)	85,176	75,925	101,708	76,873	5,821,638
All Options on Individual Equities	78,638	113,134	130,558	70,272	8,240,390
Total Options	**109,835,588**	**108,962,770**	**126,622,686**	**97,263,868**	**90,239,125**

Tel-Aviv Stock Exchange (TASE), Israel

	2013	2012	2011	2010	2009
TA-25 Index	60,237	48,172	35,429	24,484	43,025
TA-Banks Index	1,174	22,861	19,496	21,524	8,435
Total Futures	**61,411**	**92,186**	**188,734**	**407,506**	**106,666**
TA-25 Index	48,764,430	57,396,506	87,133,824	70,573,392	62,271,157
TA-Banks Index	13,926	27,102	22,489	75,248	73,937
Shekel-Dollar Rate	9,957,286	8,683,705	10,400,167	7,927,235	8,067,320
Shekel-Euro Rate	638,681	499,774	392,139	484,415	73,937
All Options on Individual Equities	1,078,697	480,087	827,357	973,129	321,228
Total Options	**60,453,020**	**67,087,609**	**98,776,425**	**80,033,419**	**70,807,579**

Thailand Futures Exchange, Thailand

	2013	2012	2011	2010	2009
SET 50	5,688,404	4,034,460	4,316,437	2,362,845	2,522,465
Gold, 50 Baht	551,887	1,045,370	1,817,483	792,960	311,591
Gold, 10 Baht	1,655,381	2,597,235	2,171,795	178,463	
Silver	1,237	14,590	31,567		
Brent Crude Oil	46,496	147,823	3,320		
U.S. Dollar	239,345	396,138			
All Futures on Individual Equities	7,915,967	2,168,037	1,578,092	804,156	142,837
Total Futures	**16,098,717**	**10,403,871**	**9,919,123**	**4,138,465**	**2,976,893**
SET 50	65,409	54,057	107,993	107,317	95,504
Total Options	**65,409**	**54,057**	**107,993**	**107,317**	**95,504**

Tokyo Commodity Exchange (TOCOM), Japan

	2013	2012	2011	2010	2009
Gold	12,224,611	11,895,357	16,075,145	12,198,340	11,913,502
Gold Mini	2,475,797	2,814,289	3,312,107	2,477,688	5,010,476
Silver	96,374	120,436	373,445	236,296	111,775
Platinum	4,278,478	3,489,874	3,455,529	4,390,452	3,617,988
Platinum Mini	420,524	314,882	287,322	308,711	413,310
Palladium	79,352	59,934	110,163	156,946	107,829
Gasoline	2,257,935	2,390,679	2,462,261	2,509,734	2,732,376
Kerosene	925,421	746,163	900,700	1,196,729	1,026,529
Chukyo Gasoline	33,409	61,919	65,225	7,800	
Chukyo Kerosene	14,607	38,232	52,213	3,856	
Gas Oil	4,644	9,787	11,314	4,366	
Crude Oil	1,166,495	1,285,388	1,297,512	943,450	624,307
Red Beans	24,764				
Corn	325,518				
Rubber	2,329,414	2,251,817	3,259,984	3,130,073	3,320,088
Raw Sugar	1,199				
Soybeans	187,170				
Total Futures	**26,845,712**	**25,479,111**	**31,670,031**	**27,636,367**	**28,881,948**

Tokyo International Financial Futures Exchange (TIFFE), Japan

	2013	2012	2011	2010	2009
3-Month Euroyen	5,044,236	4,734,503	7,201,901	11,274,925	13,066,020
Nikkei 225 Margin	5,153,821	1,609,751	812,346	62,000	
DAX Margin	88,219	83,266	100,509	3,616	
FTSE 100 Margin	39,709	21,353	80,189	1,857	
FTSE China 25 Margin	6,252	5,712	13,112	218	
US Dollar / Japanese Yen	20,120,943	9,212,876	31,441,164	27,551,634	20,198,781
Euro / Japanese Yen	11,291,735	16,927,476	26,769,174	19,921,565	9,961,673
British pound / Japanese Yen	3,387,074	3,969,313	11,782,185	17,108,444	16,266,521
Australian Dollar / Japanese Yen	10,256,158	16,500,368	41,589,199	34,272,436	17,793,787
Swiss Franc / Japanese Yen	337,848	489,095	1,631,739	368,567	183,224
Canadian Dollar / Japanese Yen	303,776	397,062	1,156,599	927,926	467,812
New Zealand Dollar / Japanese Yen	2,369,064	3,337,884	5,781,332	2,196,138	2,097,853
South African Rand / Japanese Yen	2,650,993	2,191,285	2,138,750	1,185,379	860,162
Norway Krone / Japanese Yen	86,320	68,347	80,369	36,144	27,956
Hong Kong Dollar / Japanese Yen	29,498	12,764	42,391	53,830	21,825
Sweden Krona / Japanese Yen	72,398	40,082	56,304	21,591	15,926
Paland Zloty / Japanese Yen	700,069	709,891	259,632	152,485	217,530
Chinese Yuan / Japanese Yen	31,279	29,426	31,992		

Tokyo International Financial Futures Exchange (TIFFE), Japan (continued)

	2013	2012	2011	2010	2009
Korean Won / Japanese Yen	55,023	86,094	90,877		
Indian Rupee / Japanese Yen	121,444	123,411	90,019		
Euro / US Dollar	1,083,008	3,628,083	8,246,516	3,674,987	1,116,564
British Pound / US Dollar	281,851	288,047	772,999	555,891	426,937
British Pound / Swiss Franc	56,602	56,633	186,041	79,909	27,895
US Dollar / Swiss Franc	75,880	144,767	497,869	145,093	75,115
US Dollar / Canadian Dollar	61,444	68,262	178,483	111,927	45,869
Australian Dollar / US Dollar	799,275	1,216,523	2,369,321	1,003,682	542,598
Euro / Swiss Franc	67,457	80,461	522,352	82,892	20,485
Euro / British Pound	55,076	49,537	157,660	100,441	88,194
New Zealand Dollar / US Dollar	204,479	150,176	195,778	94,114	38,640
Euro / Australian Dollar	470,198	526,204	355,969	208,708	24,891
British Pound / Australian Dollar	226,661	154,758	233,642	81,296	59,698
Total Futures	**65,527,790**	**66,924,393**	**144,866,413**	**121,277,695**	**83,645,956**

Tokyo Grain Exchange (TGE), Japan

	2013	2012	2011	2010	2009
American Soybeans	36,569	635,794	1,199,496	1,147,425	2,320,782
Arabic Coffee	191	2,627	22,938	50,526	46,281
Azuki (Red Beans)	2,828	87,888	114,724	180,591	243,415
Corn	59,217	794,146	1,131,856	1,084,049	1,867,864
Rice	4,529	56,270	52,304		
Raw Sugar	3,911	25,688	133,953	365,267	157,102
Total Futures	**107,245**	**1,603,076**	**2,660,753**	**2,866,588**	**4,829,183**

Tokyo Stock Exchange (TSE), Japan

	2013	2012	2011	2010	2009
10-Year Government Yen Bond	9,053,623	8,769,717	6,802,032	7,914,448	6,765,074
Mini 10-Year Government Yen Bond	17,831	32,065	7,734		46
REIT Index	74,612	60,388	51,457	46,696	52,799
TOPIX Stock Index	22,714,121	15,192,439	14,608,165	14,541,751	15,190,781
Mini TOPIX Stock Index	3,156,452	2,148,039	621,569	1,044,343	681,248
Bank Index	16,398	3,500		5,808	
TOPIX Core 30 Index	8,383	10,150	91,715	242,105	362,882
Nikkei 225 Dividend Index	111,644	123,512	61,050	19,553	
Total Futures	**35,153,064**	**26,339,810**	**22,243,722**	**23,814,704**	**23,052,830**
TOPIX	386,231	22,683	21,342	120,040	52,523
10-Year Government Yen Bond	1,692,752	2,283,839	1,853,672	1,999,282	2,433,217
All Options on Individual Equities	1,129,358	433,602	601,156	834,941	662,813
Total Options	**3,208,341**	**2,740,124**	**2,476,170**	**2,954,263**	**3,148,553**

Borsa Istanbul, Turkey

(formerly TurkDEX)	2013	2012	2011	2010	2009
Gold	26,567	48,941	165,729	144,965	118,347
US Dollar/Ounce Gold	1,710,574	1,347,200	595,495	2,523	
Base Load Electricity	152	928	32		
ISE-100 Index	5,325	5,910	9,788	8,066	6,654
ISE-30 Index	40,433,038	48,757,352	54,612,000	56,508,907	65,393,094
ISE 30 - 100 Index Spread	1,107	2,508	5,576	2,331	
US Dollar	8,927,709	10,503,364	16,028,342	7,095,340	13,687,292
Euro	861,744	468,524	1,416,367	171,375	225,314
Euro/US Dollar Cross Currency	1,127,698	1,339,713	1,453,964	12,906	
All Futures on Individual Equities	24,073	6,291			
Total Futures	**53,117,987**	**62,480,755**	**74,287,630**	**63,952,147**	**79,431,323**
BIST 30 Index	8,572				
All Options on Individual Equities	45,806	2,710			
Total Options	**54,378**	**2,710**			

Turquoise Derivatives, London

(Formerly EDX)	2013	2012	2011	2010	2009
FTSE Russia IOB Index	3,051	29,361	27,843	10,244	32
FTSE SLQ Index	31,089				
OBX Index	995,644	1,027,366	1,456,874	2,015,356	
IOB DR Stock Dividend	56,720	183,894	212,705		
Norwegian Futures on Individual Equities	428,969	410,351	170,000	372	
ION DR Futures on Individual Equities	272,227	104,757	648,800		
Total Futures	**1,755,963**	**2,520,530**	**2,025,972**	**4,032**	
FTSE Russia IOB Index	2,031	90,273	103,946	92,416	38,441
FTSE 100 Index	2,341	16,316	15,518		
OBX Index	269,462	212,804	206,763	239,687	
Norwegian Options on Individual Equities	874,146	1,203,051	1,551,337	1,273,411	
ION DR Options on Individual Equities	14,948,193	28,351,903	34,060,682	40,612,119	34,865,057
Total Options	**16,096,173**	**29,874,347**	**35,938,246**	**42,217,633**	**34,903,498**

VOLUME - WORLDWIDE

United Stock Exchange of India, India

	2013	2012	2011	2010	2009
US Dollar / Indian Rupee	11,878,194	6,872,015	340,576,642	124,766,134	
EUR / Indian Rupee	1,215,402	576,630	2,297,323	187,331	
GBP / Indian Rupee	830,664	437,678	827,136	195,808	
JPY / Indian Rupee	1,249,399	546,456	898,837	205,594	
Total Futures	**15,173,659**	**8,432,779**	**344,599,938**	**125,354,867**	
US Dollar / Indian Rupee	29,757,433	431,783	7,718,412	6,025	
Total Options	**29,757,433**	**431,783**	**7,718,412**	**6,025**	

Warsaw Stock Exchange, Poland

	2013	2012	2011	2010	2009
WIG 20 Index	8,259,066	9,077,040	13,642,282	13,481,633	12,766,415
WIG 40 Index	81,468	14,048	29,439	32,998	30,182
CHFPLN	95,672	28,343	73,155	7,673	9,418
EURPLN	215,902	110,832	21,885	22,625	59,438
USDPLN	2,538,358	821,760	104,450	88,777	93,382
1-Month WIBOR	208				
3-Month WIBOR	1,200				
Long Term Bond	610				
Medium Term Bond	723				
Short Term Bond	206				
All Futures on Individual Equities	613,563	540,330	737,742	375,496	465,757
Total Futures	**11,806,976**	**10,592,353**	**14,608,953**	**14,009,202**	**13,424,593**
WIG20 Index	808,360	715,364	897,801	675,112	396,208
Total Options	**808,360**	**715,364**	**897,801**	**675,112**	**396,208**

Wiener Borse - Derivatives Market of Vienna, Austria

	2013	2012	2011	2010	2009
ATF Index	50,205	32,799	42,764	42,254	34,664
ATX Index	300,324	328,923	284,229	266,786	219,038
CeCe (5 Eastern European Indices)	8,029	9,916	15,109	22,167	13,362
All Futures on Individual Equities	16	215	4,430	4,575	6,053
Total Futures	**358,574**	**371,853**	**346,592**	**335,782**	**273,117**
ATF Index	3,598	4,843	4,994	7,588	3,993
ATX Index	11,278	20,044	23,338	26,005	14,821
All Options on Individual Equities	120,767	313,682	499,139	469,216	474,697
Total Options	**135,643**	**338,569**	**527,471**	**503,129**	**493,511**

Zhengzhou Commodity Exchange (ZCE), China

	2013	2012	2011	2010	2009
Cotton #1 (CF)	7,452,748	21,033,646	139,044,152	86,955,310	8,534,688
Early Rice (ER)	358,249	3,838,605	5,925,454	26,854,086	1,950,083
Early Rice (RI)	515,471	1,287			
Japonica Rice (JR)	40,480				
Methanol (ME)	3,497,720	3,797,412	316,107		
Common Wheat (PM)	1,894	6,262			
Rapeseed (RS)	1,174,626	137,084			
Rapeseed Meal (RM)	160,100,378	421,207			
Rapeseed Oil (RO)	855,411	6,255,398	4,320,115	9,527,915	10,956,863
Rapeseed Oil (OI)	11,853,858	2,021			
White Sugar (SR)	69,794,046	148,290,190	128,193,356	305,303,131	146,063,344
Strong Gluten Wheat (WS)	1,035,689	25,796,425	7,909,755	5,804,642	13,735,956
Strong Gluten Wheat (WH)	1,871,991	10,262			
Thermal Coal (TC)	4,357,384				
Flat Glass (FG)	186,105,091	16,136,920			
PTA (TA)	76,283,987	121,263,913	120,528,824	61,424,805	45,851,417
Total Futures	**525,299,023**	**347,091,533**	**406,390,664**	**495,904,984**	**227,112,521**

Total Worldwide Volume

	2013	2012	2011	2010	2009
Total Futures	**8,522,767,018**	**8,036,856,094**	**8,695,599,403**	**8,043,244,801**	**5,632,779,850**
Percent Change	**6.05%**	**-7.58%**	**8.11%**	**42.79%**	**7.86%**
Total Options	**4,726,796,145**	**5,648,591,935**	**7,759,707,692**	**6,772,701,767**	**5,569,496,199**
Percent Change	**-16.32%**	**-27.21%**	**14.57%**	**21.60%**	**5.89%**
Total Futures and Options	**13,249,563,163**	**13,685,448,029**	**16,455,307,095**	**14,815,946,568**	**11,202,276,049**
Percent Change	**-3.19%**	**-16.83%**	**11.06%**	**32.26%**	**6.87%**

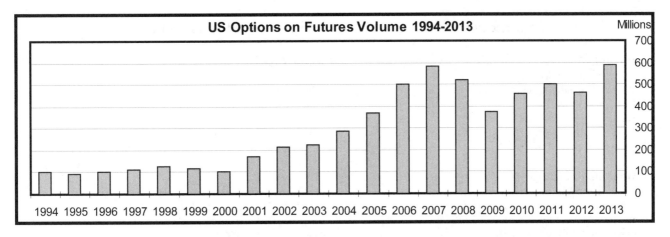

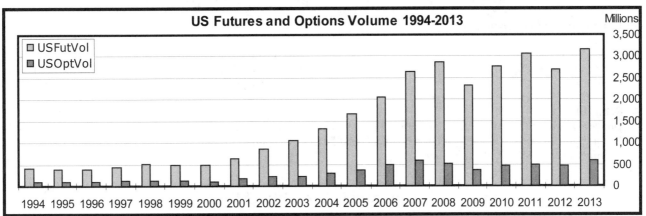

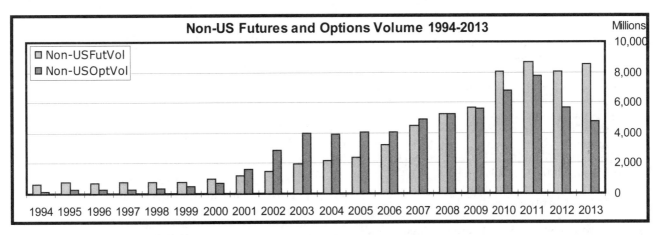

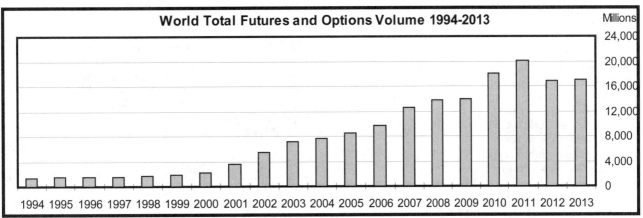

Conversion Factors

Commonly Used Agricultural Weights and Measurements

Bushel Weights:
Corn, Sorghum and Rye = 56 lbs.
Wheat and Soybeans = 60 lbs.
Canola = 50 lbs.
Barley Grain = 48 lbs.
Barley Malt = 34 lbs.
Oats = 32 lbs.

Bushels to tonnes:
Corn, Sorghum and Rye = bushels x 0.0254
Wheat and Soybeans = bushels x 0.027216
Barley Grain = bushels x 0.021772
Oats = bushels x 0.014515

1 tonne (metric ton) equals:
2204.622 lbs.
1,000 kilograms
22.046 hundredweight
10 quintals

Ethanol
1 bushel Corn = 2.75 gallons Ethanol = 18 lbs Dried Distillers Grain
1 tonne Corn = 101.0 gallons Ethanol = 661 lbs Dried Distillers Grain
1 tonne Sugar = 149.3 gallons Ethanol

1 tonne (metric ton) equals:
39.3679 bushels of Corn, Sorghum or Rye
36.7437 bushels of Wheat or Soybeans
22.046 hundredweight
45.9296 bushels of Barley Grain
68.8944 bushels of Oats
4.5929 Cotton bales (the statistical bale used by the USDA and ICAC contains a net weight of 480 pounds of lint)

Area Measurements:
1 acre = 43,560 square feet = 0.040694 hectare
1 hectare = 2.4710 acres = 10,000 square meters
640 acres = 1 square mile = 259 hectares

Yields:
Rye, Corn: bushels per acre x 0.6277 = quintals per hectare
Wheat: bushels per acre x 0.6725 = quintals per hectare
Barley Grain: bushels per acre x 0.538 = quintals per hectare
Oats: bushels per acre x 0.3587 = quintals per hectare

Commonly Used Weights

The troy, avoirdupois and apothecaries' grains are identical in U.S. and British weight systems, equal to 0.0648 gram in the metric system. One avoirdupois ounce equals 437.5 grains. The troy and apothecaries' ounces equal 480 grains, and their pounds contain 12 ounces.

Troy weights and conversions:
24 grains = 1 pennyweigh
20 pennyweights = 1 ounce
12 ounces = 1 pound
1 troy ounce = 31.103 grams
1 troy ounce = 0.0311033 kilogram
1 troy pound = 0.37224 kilogram
1 kilogram = 32.1507 troy ounces
1 tonne = 32,151 troy ounces

Avoirdupois weights and conversions:
27 11/32 grains = 1 dram
16 drams = 1 ounce
16 ounces = 1 lb.
1 lb. = 7,000 grains
14 lbs. = 1 stone (British)
100 lbs. = 1 hundredweight (U.S.)
112 lbs. = 8 stone = 1 hundredweight (British)
2,000 lbs. = 1 short ton (U.S. ton)
2,240 lbs. = 1 long ton (British ton)
160 stone = 1 long ton
20 hundredweight = 1 ton
1 lb. = 0.4536 kilogram
1 hundredweight (cwt.) = 45.359 kilograms
1 short ton = 907.18 kilograms
1 long ton = 1,016.05 kilograms

Metric weights and conversions:
1,000 grams = 1 kilogram
100 kilograms = 1 quintal
1 tonne = 1,000 kilograms = 10 quintals
1 kilogram = 2.204622 lbs.
1 quintal = 220.462 lbs.
1 tonne = 2204.6 lbs.
1 tonne = 1.102 short tons
1 tonne = 0.9842 long ton

U.S. dry volumes and conversions:
1 pint = 33.6 cubic inches = 0.5506 liter
2 pints = 1 quart = 1.1012 liters
8 quarts = 1 peck = 8.8098 liters
4 pecks = 1 bushel = 35.2391 liters
1 cubic foot = 28.3169 liters

U.S. liquid volumes and conversions:
1 ounce = 1.8047 cubic inches = 29.6 milliliters
1 cup = 8 ounces = 0.24 liter = 237 milliliters
1 pint = 16 ounces = 0.48 liter = 473 milliliters
1 quart = 2 pints = 0.946 liter = 946 milliliters
1 gallon = 4 quarts = 231 cubic inches = 3.785 liters
1 milliliter = 0.033815 fluid ounce
1 liter = 1.0567 quarts = 1,000 milliliters
1 liter = 33.815 fluid ounces
1 imperial gallon = 277.42 cubic inches = 1.2 U.S. gallons = 4.546 liters

Energy Conversion Factors

U.S. Crude OIl (average gravity)
1 U.S. barrel = 42 U.S. gallons
1 short ton = 6.65 barrels
1 tonne = 7.33 barrels

Barrels per tonne for various origins

Abu Dhabi	7.624
Algeria	7.661
Angola	7.206
Australia	7.775
Bahrain	7.335
Brunei	7.334
Canada	7.428
Dubai	7.295
Ecuador	7.580
Gabon	7.245
Indonesia	7.348
Iran	7.370
Iraq	7.453
Kuwait	7.261
Libya	7.615
Mexico	7.104
Neutral Zone	6.825
Nigeria	7.410
Norway	7.444
Oman	7.390
Qatar	7.573
Romania	7.453
Saudi Arabia	7.338
Trinidad	6.989
Tunisia	7.709
United Arab Emirates	7.522
United Kingdom	7.279
United States	7.418
Former Soviet Union	7.350
Venezuela	7.005
Zaire	7.206

Barrels per tonne of refined products:

aviation gasoline	8.90
motor gasoline	8.50
kerosene	7.75
jet fuel	8.00
distillate, including diesel	7.46

(continued above)

residual fuel oil	6.45
lubricating oil	7.00
grease	6.30
white spirits	8.50
paraffin oil	7.14
paraffin wax	7.87
petrolatum	7.87
asphalt and road oil	6.06
petroleum coke	5.50
bitumen	6.06
LPG	11.6

Approximate heat content of refined products:

(Million Btu per barrel, 1 British thermal unit is the amount of heat required to raise the temperature of 1 pound of water 1 degree F.)

Petroleum Product	Heat Content
asphalt	6.636
aviation gasoline	5.048
butane	4.326
distillate fuel oil	5.825
ethane	3.082
isobutane	3.974
jet fuel, kerosene	5.670
jet fuel, naptha	5.355
kerosene	5.670
lubricants	6.065
motor gasoline	5.253
natural gasoline	4.620
pentanes plus	4.620

Petrochemical feedstocks:

naptha less than 401*F	5.248
other oils equal to or greater than 401*F	5.825
still gas	6.000
petroleum coke	6.024
plant condensate	5.418
propane	3.836
residual fuel oil	6.287
special napthas	5.248
unfinished oils	5.825
unfractionated steam	5.418
waxes	5.537

Source: U.S. Department of Energy

Natural Gas Conversions

Although there are approximately 1,031 Btu in a cubic foot of gas, for most applications, the following conversions are sufficient:

Cubic Feet			MMBtu		
1,000	(one thousand cubic feet)	=	1 Mcf	=	1
1,000,000	(one million cubic feet)	=	1 MMcf	=	1,000
10,000,000	(ten million cubic feet)	=	10 MMcf	=	10,000
1,000,000,000	(one billion cubic feet)	=	1 Bcf	=	1,000,000
1,000,000,000,000	(one trillion cubic feet)	=	1 Tcf	=	1,000,000,000

Acknowledgments

The editors wish to thank the following for source material:

Agricultural Marketing Service (AMS)

Agricultural Research Service (ARS)

American Bureau of Metal Statistics, Inc. (ABMS)

American Iron and Steel Institute (AISI)

American Metal Market (AMM)

Bureau of the Census

Bureau of Economic Analysis (BEA)

Bureau of Labor Statistics (BLS)

Chicago Board of Trade (CBT)

Chicago Mercantile Exchange (CME / IMM / IOM)

Commodity Credit Corporation (CCC)

Commodity Futures Trading Commision (CFTC)

The Conference Board

Economic Research Service (ERS)

Edison Electric Institute (EEI)

Farm Service Agency (FSA)

Federal Reserve Bank of St. Louis

Food and Agriculture Organization of the United Nations (FAO)

Foreign Agricultural Service (FAS)

Futures Industry Association (FIA)

ICE Futures U.S, Canada, Europe (ICE)

International Cotton Advisory Committee (ICAC)

International Cocoa Organization (ICCO)

Johnson Matthey

Kansas City Board of Trade (KCBT)

Leather Industries of America

Minneapolis Grain Exchange (MGEX)

National Agricultural Statistics Service (NASS)

New York Mercantile Exchange (NYMEX)

Oil World

The Organisation for Economic Co-Operation and Development (OECD)

The Silver Institute

The Society of the Plastics Industry, Inc. (SPI)

United Nations (UN)

United States Department of Agriculture (USDA)

Wall Street Journal (WSJ)

Aluminum

Aluminum (symbol Al) is a silvery, lightweight metal that is the most abundant metallic element in the earth's crust. Aluminum was first isolated in 1825 by a Danish chemist, Hans Christian Oersted, using a chemical process involving a potassium amalgam. A German chemist, Friedrich Woehler, improved Oersted's process by using metallic potassium in 1827. He was the first to show aluminum's lightness. In France, Henri Sainte-Claire Deville isolated the metal by reducing aluminum chloride with sodium and established a large-scale experimental plant in 1854. He displayed pure aluminum at the Paris Exposition of 1855. In 1886, Charles Martin Hall in the U.S. and Paul L.T. Heroult in France simultaneously discovered the first practical method for producing aluminum through electrolytic reduction, which is still the primary method of aluminum production today.

By volume, aluminum weighs less than a third as much as steel. This high strength-to-weight ratio makes aluminum a good choice for construction of aircraft, railroad cars, and automobiles. Aluminum is used in cooking utensils and the pistons of internal-combustion engines because of its high heat conductivity. Aluminum foil, siding, and storm windows make excellent insulators. Because it absorbs relatively few neutrons, aluminum is used in low-temperature nuclear reactors. Aluminum is also useful in boat hulls and various marine devices due to its resistance to corrosion in salt water.

Futures and options on Primary Aluminum and Aluminum Alloy are traded on the London Metal Exchange (LME). Aluminum futures are traded on the Multi Commodity Exchange of India (MCX), the Singapore Exchange (SGX), and the Shanghai Futures Exchange (SHFE). The London Metals Exchange aluminum futures contracts are priced in terms of dollars per metric ton.

Prices – The London Metals Exchange 3-month forward aluminum contract reached a record high of $3,380 per metric ton in early 2008 but then plunged to $1,279 by early 2009 due to the global financial crisis. Aluminum prices recovered to $2,803 by mid-2011 but then fell sharply and have since been moving largely sideways. Aluminum closed 2014 up +2.9% at $1,852.50 per metric ton.

Supply – World production of aluminum in 2014 rose by +3.6% to a new record high of 49.300 million metric tons. The world's largest producers of aluminum are China with 47.3% of world production in 2014, Russia (7.1%), Canada (6.0%), U.S. (3.5%), and Australia (3.4%). U.S. production of primary aluminum in 2014 fell -12.1% yr/yr to 1.710 million metric tons.

Demand – U.S. consumption of aluminum in 2014 rose +12.4% yr/yr to 5.090 million metric tons, up from the three decade low of 3.320 million metric tons in 2009.

Trade – U.S. exports in 2014 fell -3.8% yr/yr to 3.260 million metric tons, below last year's record high of 3.390 million metric tons. U.S. imports of aluminum in 2014 fell 0.2% yr/yr to 4.150 million metric tons, down from the 2005 record high of 4.850 million metric tons. The U.S. was a net importer in 2014 and relied on imports for 33% of its consumption.

World Production of Primary Aluminum   In Thousands of Metric Tons

Year	Australia	Brazil	Canada	China	France	Germany	Norway	Russia	Spain	United Kingdom	United States	Vene-zuela	World Total
2005	1,903	1,499	2,894	7,800	442	648	1,372	3,647	394	369	2,481	615	31,900
2006	1,932	1,605	3,051	9,360	442	516	1,331	3,718	349	360	2,284	610	33,900
2007	1,957	1,655	3,083	12,600	428	551	1,357	3,955	408	365	2,554	610	37,900
2008	1,974	1,661	3,120	13,200	389	606	1,358	4,190	408	326	2,658	608	39,700
2009	1,943	1,536	3,030	12,900	345	292	1,139	3,815	360	253	1,727	561	37,200
2010	1,928	1,536	2,963	16,200	356	402	1,109	3,947	340	186	1,726	335	41,200
2011	1,945	1,440	2,988	18,100	334	432	1,122	3,993	365	213	1,986	380	44,400
2012	1,864	1,436	2,781	20,300	349	410	1,145	3,924	230	60	2,070	200	45,800
2013[1]	1,778	1,330	2,967	22,100	346	492	1,100	3,724	235	44	1,946	160	47,600
2014[2]	1,680	960	2,940	23,300		500	1,200	3,500			1,720		49,300

[1] Preliminary.   [2] Estimate.   *Source: U.S. Geological Survey (USGS)*

Production of Primary Aluminum (Domestic and Foreign Ores) in the U.S.   In Thousands of Metric Tons

Year	Jan.	Feb.	Mar.	Apr.	May	June	July	Aug.	Sept.	Oct.	Nov.	Dec.	Total
2005	209	191	214	211	214	206	210	208	199	207	204	208	2,481
2006	197	179	198	190	197	189	192	185	183	190	188	197	2,285
2007	202	185	217	209	210	209	219	220	216	224	220	225	2,556
2008	233	219	234	228	236	224	225	222	214	217	202	204	2,658
2009	193	149	154	145	147	132	135	133	129	137	133	140	1,727
2010	142	130	146	142	148	141	146	146	143	148	144	148	1,724
2011	152	140	162	162	170	167	171	172	169	175	171	177	1,988
2012	178	167	179	174	179	173	177	171	164	170	166	171	2,069
2013	171	155	172	167	171	165	168	163	157	154	149	154	1,946
2014[1]	153	139	153	143	147	140	143	143	136	137	134		1,711

[1] Preliminary.   *Source: U.S. Geological Survey (USGS)*

ALUMINUM

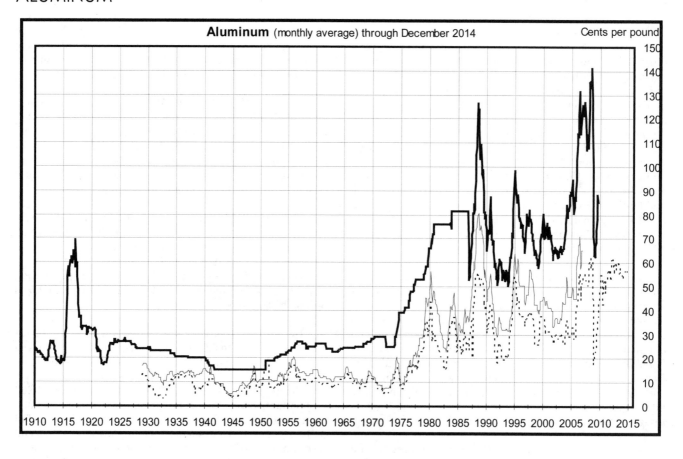

Aluminum (monthly average) through December 2014   Cents per pound

Salient Statistics of Aluminum in the United States   In Thousands of Metric Tons

Year	Net Import Reliance as a % of Apparent Consumption	Production Primary	Secondary	Primary Shipments	Recovery from Scrap Old	New	Apparent Consumption	Plate, Sheet, Foil	Wrought Products Rolled Structural Shapes[3]	Extruded Shapes[4]	All	Permanent Mold	Castings Die	Sand	All	Total All Net Shipments
2004	39	2,516	3,030	10,400	1,160	1,870	6,570	4,750	579	1,810	7,140	735	1,250	221	2,370	9,510
2005	41	2,481	3,030	10,461	1,080	1,950	6,530	5,330	1,080	2,090	8,500	785	1,110	289	2,290	10,790
2006	31	2,284	3,540	10,500	1,580	2,800	5,700	4,690	608	192	5,490	754	1,170	335	2,310	7,800
2007	18	2,554	4,120	9,730	1,660	2,450	5,170	5,000	888	1,580	7,468	615	1,260	315	2,230	9,698
2008	E	2,658	3,630	8,570	1,500	2,130	3,940	4,770	789	1,380	6,939	570	1,030	255	1,900	8,839
2009	10	1,727	2,820	6,810	1,260	1,570	3,320	4,050	632	1,070	5,752	377	691	160	1,230	6,982
2010	14	1,726	2,790	7,720	1,250	1,540	3,460	4,450	703	1,530	6,683	475	949	147	1,580	8,263
2011	3	1,986	3,120	8,520	1,470	1,640	3,570	4,000	537	1,700	6,237	494	1,010	178	1,690	7,927
2012	11	2,070	3,270	9,080	1,440	1,830	3,950	4,100	579	1,840	6,519	589	1,110	127	1,860	8,379
2013[1]	21	1,946	3,480	9,260	1,630	1,850	4,530	4,080	572	1,880	6,532	604	1,240	132	2,000	8,532

[1] Preliminary.   [2] To domestic industry.   [3] Also rod, bar & wire.   [4] Also rod, bar, tube, blooms & tubing.   [5] Consists of total shipments less shipments to other mills for further fabrication.   *Source: U.S. Geological Survey (USGS)*

Supply and Distribution of Aluminum in the United States   In Thousands of Metric Tons

Year	Apparent Consumption	Production Primary	From Old Scrap	Imports	Exports	Inventories - December 31 - Private	Government[2]	Year	Apparent Consumption	Production Primary	From Old Scrap	Imports	Exports	Inventories - December 31 - Private	Government[2]
2003	7,120	2,703	1,070	4,130	1,540	1,400	----	2009	3,320	1,727	1,260	3,680	2,710	937	----
2004	6,570	2,516	1,160	4,720	1,820	1,470	----	2010	3,460	1,726	1,250	3,610	3,040	1,010	----
2005	6,530	2,481	1,080	4,850	2,370	1,430	----	2011	3,570	1,986	1,470	3,710	3,420	1,060	----
2006	5,700	2,284	1,580	4,660	2,820	1,410	----	2012	3,950	2,070	1,440	3,760	3,480	1,140	----
2007	5,170	2,554	1,660	4,020	2,840	1,400	----	2013[1]	4,530	1,946	1,630	4,160	3,390	1,130	----
2008	3,940	2,658	1,500	3,710	3,280	1,220	----	2014[2]	5,090	1,720	1,700	4,150	3,260	1,100	----

[1] Preliminary.   [2] Estimate.   [3] National Defense Stockpile.   *Source: U.S. Geological Survey (USGS)*

Aluminum Products Distribution of End-Use Shipments in the United States   In Thousands of Metric Tons

Year	Building & Construction	Consumer Durables	Containers and Packaging	Electrical	Exports	Machinery and Equipment	Trans-portation	Other	Total
2004	1,680	713	2,310	720	930	730	3,860	416	11,400
2005	1,671	708	2,320	746	1,125	741	3,939	336	11,586
2006	1,650	746	2,320	774	1,270	762	3,930	330	11,800
2007	1,410	664	2,230	762	1,450	736	3,580	359	11,200
2008	1,180	607	2,240	700	1,490	688	2,830	334	10,100
2009	964	458	2,150	593	1,280	475	1,910	254	8,090
2010	1,030	547	2,200	668	1,460	564	2,390	318	9,180
2011	1,110	631	2,160	798	1,700	682	2,820	322	10,200
2012	1,180	672	2,110	861	1,690	696	3,220	343	10,800
2013[1]	1,190	699	2,080	865	1,720	725	3,370	331	11,000

[1] Preliminary.   Source: U.S. Geological Survey (USGS)

World Consumption of Primary Aluminum   In Thousands of Metric Tons

Year	Brazil	Canada	China	France	Germany	India	Italy	Japan	Korea, South	Russia	United Kingdom	United States	World Total
1992	377.1	420.4	1,253.8	730.5	1,457.1	414.3	660.0	2,271.6	397.0	1,242.0	550.0	4,616.9	18,529.5
1993	378.9	492.5	1,339.9	667.2	1,150.7	475.3	554.0	2,138.3	524.8	657.0	540.0	4,877.1	18,122.6
1994	414.1	559.0	1,500.1	736.3	1,370.3	475.0	660.0	2,344.8	603.9	470.0	570.0	5,407.1	19,670.8
1995	500.6	611.9	1,941.6	743.8	1,491.3	581.0	665.4	2,335.6	675.4	476.0	620.0	5,054.8	20,480.9
1996	497.0	619.9	2,135.3	671.7	1,355.4	584.8	585.1	2,392.6	674.3	443.8	571.0	5,348.0	20,596.4
1997	478.6	628.2	2,260.3	724.2	1,558.4	553.4	671.0	2,434.3	666.3	469.2	583.0	5,390.0	21,721.8
1998	521.4	720.6	2,425.4	733.8	1,519.0	566.5	675.4	2,082.0	505.7	489.2	579.0	5,813.6	21,797.2
1999	463.1	777.2	2,925.9	774.2	1,438.6	569.5	735.3	2,112.3	814.0	562.8	496.8	6,203.3	23,323.0
2000	513.8	798.7	3,499.1	780.4	1,490.3	602.4	780.3	2,224.9	822.6	748.4	575.5	6,079.5	24,811.4
2001[1]	550.8	759.6	3,545.4	772.9	1,590.9	558.0	770.4	2,014.0	849.6	786.2	433.3	5,117.0	23,612.8

[1] Preliminary.   Source: American Metal Market (AMM)

Salient Statistics of Recycling Aluminum in the United States

Year	Percent Recycled	New Scrap[1]	Old Scrap[2]	Recycled Metal[3]	Apparent Supply	New Scrap[1]	Old Scrap[2]	Recycled Metal[3]	Apparent Supply
		---------------- In Thousands of Metric Tons ----------------				-------------------- Value in Millions of Dollars --------------------			
2003	32	1,750	1,070	2,820	8,870	2,620	1,610	4,230	13,300
2004	33	1,870	1,160	3,030	9,080	3,460	2,140	5,600	16,800
2005	33	1,950	1,080	3,030	9,220	3,910	2,160	6,070	18,500
2006	52	2,800	1,580	4,380	8,500	7,490	4,220	11,700	22,700
2007	56	2,450	1,660	4,120	7,320	6,610	4,480	11,100	19,700
2008	60	2,130	1,500	3,630	6,070	5,660	3,970	9,640	16,100
2009	58	1,570	1,260	2,820	4,890	2,740	2,200	4,940	8,550
2010	56	1,540	1,250	2,790	5,000	3,550	2,880	6,430	11,500
2011	60	1,640	1,470	3,120	5,210	4,200	3,770	7,980	13,300
2012	57	1,830	1,440	3,270	5,780	4,080	3,210	7,290	12,900

[1] Scrap that results from the manufacturing process.   [2] Scrap that results from consumer products.   [3] Metal recovered from new plus old scrap.
Source: U.S. Geological Survey (USGS)

Producer Prices for Aluminum Used Beverage Can Scrap   In Cents Per Pound

Year	Jan.	Feb.	Mar.	Apr.	May	June	July	Aug.	Sept.	Oct.	Nov.	Dec.	Average
2005	64.80	65.79	71.91	71.40	64.75	62.23	60.05	62.96	60.40	61.76	65.25	72.90	65.35
2006	81.03	85.76	85.13	91.08	99.41	83.50	83.40	82.74	80.70	79.66	83.90	85.00	85.11
2007	89.05	89.58	90.18	93.14	93.16	87.86	85.90	80.39	76.37	79.57	82.98	79.68	85.66
2008	82.81	90.35	100.19	100.09	97.52	98.88	98.75	88.83	79.38	63.43	55.67	46.33	83.52
2009	43.70	41.42	41.91	44.00	46.80	50.64	54.27	61.62	58.00	61.43	64.42	71.16	53.28
2010	73.95	68.05	75.48	78.77	69.10	65.77	67.43	72.45	74.76	82.57	79.38	82.26	74.16
2011	86.78	89.11	90.98	96.08	94.72	940.50	90.95	86.54	83.69	78.07	75.25	73.18	157.15
2012	77.30	79.83	79.87	75.67	74.27	69.76	70.81	70.35	77.82	75.72	74.33	80.09	75.49
2013	79.03	79.19	75.69	76.25	75.18	73.08	71.02	72.27	68.95	69.74	68.16	68.76	73.11
2014	73.24	76.75	77.52	82.43	79.62	80.41	83.80	85.33	85.93	85.92	91.17	88.64	82.56

Source: American Metal Market (AMM)

ALUMINUM

Average Price of Cast Aluminum Scrap (Crank Cases) in Chicago[1]   In Cents Per Pound

Year	Jan.	Feb.	Mar.	Apr.	May	June	July	Aug.	Sept.	Oct.	Nov.	Dec.	Average
2005	29.00	29.00	31.61	33.00	31.33	28.00	28.00	28.00	28.00	28.00	28.00	39.71	30.14
2006	42.50	42.50	43.80	47.50	47.50	55.91	46.48	45.46	44.50	46.45	51.15	51.10	47.07
2007	52.50	52.50	54.00	55.50	55.50	53.07	52.50	52.50	51.34	50.50	50.50	50.50	52.58
2008	50.50	52.00	58.50	62.09	60.12	57.50	60.00	60.60	53.69	35.76	26.94	18.45	49.68
2009	17.50	17.50	22.27	22.50	22.50	22.50	24.55	27.50	37.50	37.50	37.50	42.24	27.63
2010	45.39	47.50	48.80	55.23	51.50	43.41	42.50	47.27	47.50	51.31	52.50	47.50	48.37
2011	48.75	52.50	52.50	52.50	52.50	56.00	57.50	56.93	54.50	54.70	52.45	53.61
2012	55.05	59.60	61.50	60.93	59.23	55.93	55.50	55.50	58.55	59.50	57.00	58.67	58.08
2013	60.50	60.45	59.50	59.00	58.50	58.35	55.50	56.00	55.90	55.54	55.55	54.50	57.44
2014	54.50	53.50	53.50	55.00	56.50	56.50	56.50	56.55	57.40	56.50	56.50	55.45	55.70

[1] Dealer buying prices.   Source: American Metal Market (AMM)

Aluminum Exports of Crude Metal and Alloys from the United States   In Thousands of Metric Tons

Year	Jan.	Feb.	Mar.	Apr.	May	June	July	Aug.	Sept.	Oct.	Nov.	Dec.	Total
2005	26.5	23.4	24.3	27.0	28.9	29.6	25.9	33.1	27.2	29.5	29.6	23.9	328.9
2006	40.0	26.0	30.5	29.4	38.8	25.3	23.7	32.0	26.1	25.8	27.0	22.0	346.6
2007	32.1	27.1	27.0	28.6	33.8	31.1	26.4	30.3	28.5	29.9	29.6	24.5	348.9
2008	30.8	26.8	26.4	30.4	28.4	27.6	25.9	26.4	27.4	25.3	17.3	15.6	308.3
2009	15.9	15.9	12.7	14.8	24.7	24.9	24.6	24.7	24.4	28.0	26.4	25.1	262.1
2010	20.2	22.0	22.4	16.8	20.5	25.6	22.8	24.5	35.2	24.4	26.0	23.5	283.9
2011	25.5	24.2	30.2	34.6	26.1	23.1	25.7	23.2	23.2	24.3	29.5	24.4	314.0
2012	30.8	29.5	32.0	29.9	31.0	30.6	31.6	32.2	24.3	24.3	33.0	24.5	353.7
2013	27.5	29.4	31.1	32.9	30.0	29.8	26.5	33.7	31.0	32.3	32.3	25.9	362.4
2014[1]	31.1	25.6	30.5	30.7	33.0	31.0	28.7	31.5	30.0	33.7	26.9		362.9

[1] Preliminary.   Source: U.S. Geological Survey (USGS)

Aluminum General Imports of Crude Metal and Alloys into the United States   In Thousands of Metric Tons

Year	Jan.	Feb.	Mar.	Apr.	May	June	July	Aug.	Sept.	Oct.	Nov.	Dec.	Total
2005	334.0	289.0	262.0	372.0	372.0	324.0	324.0	264.0	282.0	298.0	240.0	299.0	3,660.0
2006	348.0	247.0	289.0	353.0	315.0	298.0	249.0	315.0	289.0	259.0	233.0	241.0	3,436.0
2007	251.0	258.0	238.0	259.0	220.0	254.0	236.0	266.0	268.0	244.0	238.0	215.0	2,947.0
2008	240.0	208.0	247.0	238.0	237.0	263.0	227.0	204.0	229.0	249.0	219.0	233.0	2,794.0
2009	270.0	204.0	333.0	233.0	292.0	200.0	299.0	216.0	212.0	207.0	211.0	217.0	2,894.0
2010	238.0	209.0	230.0	257.0	233.0	232.0	223.0	207.0	224.0	203.0	209.0	179.0	2,644.0
2011	211.0	212.0	232.0	220.0	285.0	263.0	220.0	241.0	263.0	243.0	192.0	245.0	2,827.0
2012	281.0	284.0	248.0	231.0	293.0	240.0	233.0	234.0	214.0	204.0	196.0	244.0	2,902.0
2013	248.0	220.0	283.0	457.0	314.0	267.0	273.0	271.0	242.0	219.0	299.0	220.0	3,313.0
2014[1]	253.0	221.0	439.0	291.0	290.0	294.0	237.0	270.0	253.0	271.0	213.0		3,307.6

[1] Preliminary.   Source: U.S. Geological Survey (USGS)

Average Open Interest of Aluminum Futures in New York   In Contracts

Year	Jan.	Feb.	Mar.	Apr.	May	June	July	Aug.	Sept.	Oct.	Nov.	Dec.
2002	3,277	2,744	2,738	2,250	2,397	2,902	3,903	4,618	4,643	5,139	8,057	10,479
2003	9,573	9,163	6,960	7,190	7,686	8,529	8,402	8,445	7,655	7,283	8,434	9,427
2004	8,815	7,384	9,666	10,575	10,363	10,370	9,626	10,287	10,292	10,035	9,706	8,879
2005	8,183	8,487	7,464	6,612	5,654	5,061	4,359	3,223	3,225	2,676	2,232	1,670
2006	1,066	708	482	1,110	948	816	1,068	1,125	1,116	865	994	950
2007	608	614	491	450	415	368	329	276	237	194	156	132
2008	0	0	0	0	0	0	0	0	0	0	0	0

Source: CME Group; New York Mercantile Exchange (NYMEX)

Volume of Trading of Aluminum Futures in New York   In Contracts

Year	Jan.	Feb.	Mar.	Apr.	May	June	July	Aug.	Sept.	Oct.	Nov.	Dec.	Total
2002	2,774	4,635	4,924	2,593	5,388	5,389	8,953	4,194	2,571	7,328	16,185	9,066	74,000
2003	12,565	9,625	8,163	5,440	10,567	8,463	11,797	9,451	5,119	6,222	8,536	11,542	107,490
2004	9,425	9,621	9,548	9,770	5,438	5,453	5,280	2,063	5,533	4,822	2,525	2,691	72,169
2005	5,294	2,829	3,244	2,627	2,613	1,832	1,247	902	1,625	623	3,135	2,520	28,491
2006	633	245	1,343	1,558	210	471	1,046	1,546	662	323	842	270	9,149
2007	94	332	82	28	2	56	84	19	25	0	1	0	723
2008	0	0	0	0	0	0	0	0	0	0	0	0	

Source: CME Group; New York Mercantile Exchange (NYMEX)

Antimony

Antimony (atomic symbol Sb) is a lustrous, extremely brittle and hard crystalline semi-metal that is silvery white in its most common allotropic form. Antimony is a poor conductor of heat and electricity. In nature, antimony has a strong affinity for sulfur and for such metals as lead, silver, and copper. Antimony is primarily a byproduct of the mining, smelting and refining of lead, silver, and copper ores. There is no longer any mine production of antimony in the U.S.

The most common use of antimony is in antimony trioxide, a chemical that is used as a flame retardant in textiles, plastics, adhesives and building materials. Antimony trioxide is also used in battery components, ceramics, bearings, chemicals, glass, and ammunition.

Prices – Antimony prices in 2014 fell by -8.7% to 428.42 cents per pound, remaining well below the 2011 record high of 671.10 cents per pound. However, antimony prices in 2014 were far above the 35-year low price of 66.05 cents per pound posted in 1999.

Supply – World mine production of antimony in 2014 rose +3.9% yr/yr to 160,000 metric tons, below the 2008 record high of 182,000 metric tons. China accounted for 78.1% of world antimony production in 2014. After China, the only significant producers were Russia (4.4% of world production) and Bolivia (3.1%). U.S. secondary production of antimony in 2013 (latest data available) fell by -6.2% yr/yr to 3,500 metric tons.

Demand – U.S. industrial consumption of antimony in 2012 (latest data available) remained unchanged yr/yr at 10,200 metric tons. Of the consumption in the U.S. in 2012, 37% was used for non-metal products, 35% was used for flame-retardants, and 29% was used for metal products.

Trade –The total U.S. gross weight of imports of antimony ore in 2012 (latest data available) rose +24.5% to 523 metric tons. The antimony content of that ore rose by +31.9% to 380 metric tons. The gross weight of U.S. imports of antimony oxide in 2012 fell by -5.5% to 20,700 metric tons. U.S. exports of antimony oxide in 2012 rose by +7.9% to 4,660 metric tons.

World Mine Production of Antimony (Content of Ore)   In Metric Tons

Year	Australia	Bolivia	Canada	China[2]	Kyrgyzstan	Russia	South Africa	Tajikistan	Turkey	World Total
2011	1,577	3,947	10,000	150,000	1,500	6,348	4,700	2,000	3,400	183,000
2012	2,481	4,000	7,000	145,000	1,500	6,500	3,800	2,000	1,900	174,000
2013[1]		5,000		120,000		7,000	3,100	4,700		154,000
2014[2]		5,000		125,000		7,000	3,100	4,700		160,000

[1] Preliminary.   [2] Estimate.   [3] Includes antimony content of miscellaneous smelter products.   [4] Recoverable.
Source: U.S. Geological Survey (USGS)

Salient Statistics of Antimony in the United States   In Metric Tons

Year	Avg. Price Cents/lb. C.i.f. U.S. Ports	Primary[2] Mine	Primary[2] Smelter	Secondary (Alloys)[2]	Ore Gross Weight	Ore Antimony Content	Oxide (Gross Weight)	Exports (Oxide)	Metallic	Oxide	Sulfide	Other	Total
2010	401.19	----	W	3,520	308	181	24,900	2,540	124	1,060	W	372	1,560
2011	650.30	----	W	3,230	420	288	21,900	4,170	183	840	W	408	1,430
2012[1]	564.51	----	W	3,730	523	380	20,700	4,710	116	886	W	431	1,430
2013[2]	462.63	----	W	3,500		342		3,980					1,470

[1] Preliminary.   [2] Estimate.   [3] Antimony content.   [4] Including primary antimony residues & slag.   W = Withheld proprietary data.
Source: U.S. Geological Survey (USGS)

Industrial Consumption of Primary Antimony in the United States   In Metric Tons (Antimony Content)

Year	Ammunition	Antimonial Lead[3]	Sheet & Pipe[4]	Bearing Metal & Bearings	Solder	Products	Flame Retardants Plastics	Flame Retardants Total	Ceramics & Glass	Pigments	Plastics	Total	Grand Total
2009	W	W	W	14	44	2,000	1,820	2,330	W	403	W	2,430	6,770
2010	W	W	W	26	34	2,130	2,610	3,190	W	399	W	3,540	8,860
2011	W	W	W	20	34	3,040	3,000	3,430	W	393	W	3,720	10,200
2012[1]	W	W	W	13	40	3,650	2,690	3,000	W	371	W	3,530	10,200

[1] Preliminary.   [2] Estimated coverage based on 77% of the industry.   W = Withheld proprietary data.   *Source: U.S. Geological Survey (USGS)*

Average Price of Antimony[1] in the United States   In Cents Per Pound

Year	Jan.	Feb.	Mar.	Apr.	May	June	July	Aug.	Sept.	Oct.	Nov.	Dec.	Average
2011	609.29	651.09	712.14	765.95	718.79	696.68	635.94	635.04	683.64	700.48	652.50	591.71	671.10
2012	558.83	581.28	585.96	585.68	634.62	626.94	602.20	568.77	567.71	572.22	560.42	544.57	582.43
2013	511.16	501.22	501.22	480.61	471.23	460.51	427.00	450.50	474.58	476.77	450.55	427.04	469.37
2014	439.77	445.66	442.85	434.58	434.27	437.72	434.94	425.73	419.04	415.53	409.75	401.22	428.42

[1] Prices are for antimony metal (99.65%) merchants, minimum 18-ton containers, c.i.f. U.S. Ports.   *Source: American Metal Market (AMM)*

Apples

The apple tree is the common name of trees from the rose family, Rosaceae, and the fruit that comes from them. The apple tree is a deciduous plant and grows mainly in the temperate areas of the world. The apple tree is believed to have originated in the Caspian and Black Sea area. Apples were the favorite fruit of the ancient Greeks and Romans. The early settlers brought apple seeds with them and introduced them to America. John Champman, also known as Johnny Appleseed, was responsible for extensive planting of apple trees in the Midwestern United States.

Prices – The average monthly price of apples received by growers in the U.S. in 2014, the last full reporting year, fell by -12.0% yr/yr to 37.6 cents per pound.

Supply – World apple production in the 2014-15 marketing year fell -1.1% yr/yr to 70.833 million metric tons. The world's largest apple producers in 2014-15 were China (with 53% of world production), the European Union (19%), the U.S. (6.9%), and Turkey (3.2%). U.S. apple production in 2014-15 rose +3.9% to 4.877, a new 16-year high and far above the 2-decade low of 3.798 million metric tons posted in 2002-03.

Demand – The utilization breakdown of the 2011 (latest data available) apple crop showed that 67.6% of apples were for fresh consumption, 13.7% for juice and cider, 12.2% for canning, 2.7% for frozen apples, and 1.7% for dried apples. U.S. per capita apple consumption in 2009 (latest data available) was 16.4 pounds.

World Production of Apples[3], Fresh (Dessert & Cooking)   In Thousands of Metric Tons

Year	Argen-tina	Brazil	Chile	China	European Union	India	Japan	Russia	South Africa	Turkey	Ukraine	United States	World Total
2007-08	980	1,124	1,350	24,800	10,335	2,001	911	1,300	749	2,458	719	4,103	53,087
2008-09	933	1,223	1,280	29,800	12,703	1,985	846	1,115	747	2,600	853	4,324	60,769
2009-10	830	1,279	1,370	31,681	12,096	1,777	787	1,230	781	2,750	897	4,280	62,057
2010-11	1,060	1,339	1,431	33,263	10,981	2,891	655	910	767	2,500	954	4,175	63,334
2011-12	860	1,336	1,360	35,985	12,338	2,203	794	1,124	813	2,700	1,127	4,231	67,273
2012-13	860	1,335	1,420	38,500	12,207	2,200	793	1,264	907	2,900	1,120	4,049	69,637
2013-14[1]	630	1,335	1,310	39,680	11,974	2,200	800	1,416	900	2,900	1,120	4,693	71,589
2014-15[2]	860	1,335	1,410	37,800	13,300	2,200	800	1,550	910	2,250	1,120	4,877	70,833

[1] Preliminary.   [2] Estimate.   NA = Not available.   *Source: Foreign Agricultural Service, U.S. Department of Agriculture (FAS-USDA)*

Salient Statistics of Apples[2] in the United States

Year	-- Production -- Total	Utilized	- Growers Prices - Fresh Cents/lb.	Pro-cessing $/ton	---------- Utilization of Quantities Sold ------------ Fresh	Canned	--------------- Processed[5] --------------- Dried	Frozen	Juice & Cider	Other[3]	Avg. Fram Price Cents/lb.	Farm Value Million $	----- Foreign Trade[4] ------ --- Domestic --- Exports Fresh	Dried[5]	Imports Fresh & Dried[5]	Fresh Per Capita Con-sump-tion Lbs.
2006	9,823	9,730	31.6	129.0	6,309	1,167	253	272	1,550	61	22.7	2,213.2	652.8	32.9	255.3	17.7
2007	9,089	9,045	38.3	190.0	6,077	1,091	204	258	1,257	60	28.8	2,608.2	680.6	31.7	238.3	16.4
2008	9,633	9,540	30.1	198.0	6,274	1,253	213	211	1,349	112	23.2	2,599.5	811.0	26.8	206.7	15.9
2009	9,705	9,453	31.4	132.0	6,314	1,158	161	236	1,389	55	23.1	2,187.0	748.1	22.1	225.7	16.3
2010	9,292	9,213	32.6	187.0	6,257	1,083	176	206	1,266	74	25.1	2,313.6	817.0	26.8	184.5	15.3
2011	9,425	9,318	39.4	226.0	6,302	1,124	184	191	1,208	71	30.3	2,823.4	840.9		172.8	15.4
2012	8,981	8,917	45.3	281.0	6,585	NA	NA	NA	NA	NA	37.1	3,307.6	889.3		195.6	16.0
2013[1]	10,442	10,347	40.7	203.0	6,887						30.5	3,154.7				

[1] Preliminary.   [2] Commercial crop.   [3] Mostly crushed for vinegar, jam, etc.   [4] Year beginning July.   [5] Fresh weight basis.
NA = Not available.   Source: Economic Research Service, U.S. Department of Agriculture (ERS-USDA)

Price of Apples Received by Growers (for Fresh Use) in the United States   In Cents Per Pound

Year	Jan.	Feb.	Mar.	Apr.	May	June	July	Aug.	Sept.	Oct.	Nov.	Dec.	Average
2007	29.9	29.7	29.2	28.1	26.9	29.6	30.6	34.4	40.2	37.9	40.3	35.0	32.7
2008	35.5	34.8	34.4	33.8	36.2	41.2	44.6	53.7	50.6	42.5	36.0	29.3	39.4
2009	27.2	23.7	21.5	20.4	18.7	18.1	17.2	23.8	35.7	31.2	33.3	27.5	24.9
2010	29.0	28.9	29.5	29.7	30.9	30.8	29.9	29.1	36.5	35.7	35.3	29.3	31.2
2011	30.0	28.0	28.2	26.6	25.6	26.3	35.8	45.8	42.1	43.1	34.4	30.2	33.0
2012	32.0	30.6	33.2	30.0	30.0	38.4	41.9	52.9	61.6	53.5	47.9	47.4	41.6
2013	44.2	43.5	40.4	NQ	NQ	NQ	NQ	NQ	NQ	NQ	NQ	NQ	42.7
2014[1]	NQ	NQ	NQ	39.6	34.9	35.2	34.1	37.5	48.3	43.6	32.9	32.4	37.6

[1] Preliminary.   NQ = No quote.   *Source: Economic Research Service, U.S. Department of Agriculture (ERS-USDA)*

Arsenic

Arsenic (atomic symbol As) is a silver-gray, extremely poisonous, semi-metallic element. Arsenic, which is odorless and flavorless, has been known since ancient times, but it wasn't until the Middle Ages that its poisonous characteristics first became known. Metallic arsenic was first produced in the 17th century by heating arsenic with potash and soap. Arsenic is rarely found in nature in its elemental form and is generally recovered as a by-product of ore processing. Recently, small doses of arsenic have been found to put some forms of cancer into remission. It can also help thin blood. Homoeopathists have successfully used undetectable amounts of arsenic to cure stomach cramps.

The U.S. does not produce any arsenic and instead imports all its consumption needs for arsenic metals and compounds. More than 95 percent of the arsenic consumed in the U.S. is in compound form, mostly as arsenic trioxide, which in turn is converted into arsenic acid. Production of chromated copper arsenate, a wood preservative, accounts for about 90% of the domestic consumption of arsenic trioxide. Three companies in the U.S. manufacture chromate copper arsenate. Another company used arsenic acid to produce an arsenical herbicide. Arsenic metal is used to produce nonferrous alloys, primarily for lead-acid batteries.

One area where there is increased consumption of arsenic is in the semiconductor industry. Very high-purity arsenic is used in the production of gallium arsenide. High-speed and high-frequency integrated circuits that use gallium arsenide have better signal reception and lower power consumption. An estimated 30 metric tons per year of high-purity arsenic is used in the production of semiconductor materials.

In the early 2000's, as much as 88% of U.S. arsenic production was used for wood preservative treatments, so the demand for arsenic was closely tied to new home construction, home renovation, and deck construction. However, the total demand for arsenic in 2004 dropped by 69% from 2003, and due to arsenic's toxicity and tighter environmental regulation; only 65% of that much smaller amount was used for wood preservative treatments. Since then the specific percentage used for wood preservative treatments is no longer available.

Supply –World production of white arsenic (arsenic trioxide) in 2014 rose by +1.8% to 46,000 metric tons. The world's largest producer is China with about 54% of world production, followed by Chile with 22% of world production, Russia with 3%, and Belgium with 2%. China's production of arsenic use to be fairly constant at about 40,000 metric tons per year but that has dropped to about 25,000 to 30,000 in the last eight years. The U.S. supply of arsenic in 2013 (latest data) rose by +3.0% to 6,824 metric tons.

Demand – U.S. demand for arsenic in 2012 (latest data) rose by +25.9% to 6,180 metric tons. The use for arsenic is no longer available but in 2004 (latest data) about 65% was for wood preservatives, 10% was for non-ferrous alloys and electric usage, 10% was for glass, and 3% was for other uses.

Trade – U.S. imports of trioxide arsenic in 2012 (latest data available) rose by +14.9% to 7,550 metric tons, above the 2010 record low of 5,920 metric tons. U.S. exports of trioxide arsenic in 2014 rose +96.3% 3,200 metric tons, just below the record high of 3,270 metric tons in 2005.

World Production of White Arsenic (Arsenic Trioxide)   In Metric Tons

Year	Belgium	Bolivia	Chile	China	Japan	Mexico	Morocco	Peru	Morocco	Peru	Portugal	Russia	World Total
2007	1,000	----	11,400	25,000	40	1,600	8,950	4,321	15	1,500	53,900	1,500	60,900
2008	1,000	74	10,000	25,000	40	513	8,800	4,822	15	1,500	50,500	1,500	53,900
2009	1,000	115	11,000	25,000	40	500	8,655	301	15	1,500	47,600	1,500	50,500
2010	1,000	155	11,000	25,000	40	----	13,731	----	15	1,500	52,400	1,500	47,600
2011	1,000	99	10,000	25,000	40	----	8,154	----	15	1,500	45,800	1,500	52,400
2012	1,000	100	10,000	26,000	40	----	8,000	----	15	1,500	46,700	1,500	45,800
2013[1]	1,000		10,000	25,000			7,500	----		1,500	45,200	1,500	46,700
2014[2]	1,000		10,000	25,000			8,000			1,500	46,000	1,500	45,000

[1] Preliminary. [2] Estimate. [3] Output of Tsumeb Corp. Ltd. only. [4] Includes low-grade dusts that were exported to the U.S. for further refining.
Source: U.S. Geological Survey (USGS)

Salient Statistics of Arsenic in the United States   (In Metric Tons -- Arsenic Content)

	------ Supply ------			--- Distribution ---			---- Estimated Demand Pattern ----						- Average Price -			
	---- Imports ----		Industry			Industry	Agricultural		Wood	Non-Ferrous			Trioxide	Metal		
Year	Metal	Compounds	Stocks Jan. 1	Total	Apparent Demand	Stocks Dec. 31	Chemicals	Glass	Preservatives	Alloys & Electric	Other	Total	Mexican Cents/Pound	Chinese Cents/Pound	Imports Trioxide[3]	Exports
2007	759	7,010	----	7,769	5,280	----	----	----	----	----	----	5,280	----	122	9,220	2,490
2008	376	4,810	----	5,186	4,130	----	----	----	----	----	----	4,130	----	125	6,320	1,050
2009	438	4,660	----	5,098	4,740	----	----	----	----	----	----	4,740	----	121	6,130	354
2010	769	4,530	----	5,299	4,820	----	----	----	----	----	----	4,820	----	72	5,920	481
2011	628	4,990	----	5,618	4,910	----	----	----	----	----	----	4,910	----	74	6,570	705
2012	883	5,740	----	6,623	6,180	----	----	----	----	----	----	6,180	----	75	7,550	439
2013[1]	514	6,310	----	6,824		----	----	----	----	----			----	73		1,630
2014[2]	650	5,300														3,200

[1] Preliminary. [2] Estimate. [3] For Consumption. *Source: U.S. Geological Survey (USGS)*

Barley

Barley is the common name for the genus of cereal grass and is native to Asia and Ethiopia. Barley is an ancient crop and was grown by the Egyptians, Greek, Romans and Chinese. Barley is now the world's fourth largest grain crop, after wheat, rice, and corn. Barley is planted in the spring in most of Europe, Canada and the United States. The U.S. barley crop year begins June 1. It is planted in the autumn in parts of California, Arizona and along the Mediterranean Sea. Barley is hardy and drought resistant and can be grown on marginal cropland. Salt-resistant strains are being developed for use in coastal regions. Barley grain, along with hay, straw, and several by-products are used for animal feed. Barley is used for malt beverages and in cooking. Barley, like other cereals, contains a large proportion of carbohydrate (67%) and protein (12.8%).

Barley futures and options are traded on the Mercado a Termino de Buenos Aires (MTBA), the NYSE LIFFE European Derivatives Market and the Sydney Futures Exchange (SFE). Barley futures are traded on the Budapest Stock Exchange (BSE), ICE Futures Canada, the Multi Commodity Exchange of India (MCX), and the National Commodity & Derivatives Exchange (NCDEX).

Prices – The monthly average price for all barley received by U.S. farmers in the 2014-15 marketing year fell by -9.3% yr/yr to $5.89 per bushel.

Supply – World barley production in the 2014-15 marketing year fell by -3.9% yr/yr to 139.739 million metric

tons. The world's largest barley crop of 179.038 million metric tons occurred in 1990-91. The world's largest barley producers are the European Union with 42.9% of world production in 2014-15, Russia (14%), Ukraine (6.7%), Australia (5.4%), Canada (5.1%), and Turkey (2.9%).

U.S. barley production in the 2014-15 marketing year fell by -18.4% yr/yr to 176.764 million bushels and that is less than 50% of the record U.S. barley crop of 608.532 million bushels seen in 1986-87. U.S. farmers harvested -19.6% yr/yr more acres in 2014-15 at 2.443 million acres, less than the 2006-07 level of 2.951 million acres which was the lowest acreage since 1885. Barley yield in 2014-15 rose +1.5% yr/yr to 72.4 bushels per acre, down from the 2010-11 record high yield of 73.1 bushels per acre. Ending stocks for the 2014-15 marketing year remained unchanged at 82.20 million bushels.

Demand – U.S. total barley disappearance in 2014-15 fell -9.0% yr/yr to 211.9 million bushels. About 69% of barley is used for food and alcoholic beverages, 24% for animal feed, and 3% for seed.

Trade – World exports of barley in 2014-15 rose +3.1% yr/yr to 23.618 million metric tons. The largest world exporters of barley in 2014-15 were Australia with 19.0% of world exports, the European Union with 28.3%, Canada with 5.1%, and the U.S. with only 1.0%. The single largest importer of barley is Saudi Arabia with 8.000 million metric tons of imports in 2014-15, which is about 34% of total world imports.

World Barley Supply and Demand   In Thousands of Metric Tons

Year	Exports Australia	Canada	European Union	Total Non-US	United States	World Total	Imports Saudi Arabia	Unaccounted	World Total	Utilization Russia	United States	World Total	Ending Stocks Canada	United States	World Total
2005-06	5,267	2,232	3,257	17,600	606	18,206	7,100	660	17,498	15,500	4,570	140,285	3,289	2,350	28,333
2006-07	1,851	1,232	3,394	14,913	441	15,354	6,800	350	15,076	16,400	4,596	143,540	1,491	1,500	21,477
2007-08	3,386	3,046	3,760	14,531	902	15,433	7,400	455	15,681	15,050	4,324	134,102	1,568	1,485	20,583
2008-09	3,234	1,483	3,569	19,710	288	19,998	7,200	----	19,320	17,100	5,102	143,323	2,964	1,932	31,592
2009-10	3,915	1,309	1,123	17,017	123	17,140	7,300	----	16,834	16,650	4,589	144,897	2,502	2,515	37,444
2010-11	4,664	1,207	4,873	15,751	165	15,916	5,500	----	14,161	9,500	4,536	134,464	1,502	1,945	24,347
2011-12	5,376	1,299	3,008	20,199	193	20,392	8,700	----	20,638	14,300	4,170	135,464	1,195	1,306	22,651
2012-13	4,482	1,434	4,939	19,414	193	19,607	8,500	----	20,136	12,100	4,638	132,210	983	1,750	20,777
2013-14[1]	6,216	1,559	5,741	22,602	311	22,913	9,500	----	23,579	12,600	4,775	141,770	1,924	1,791	25,032
2014-15[2]	4,500	1,200	6,700	23,400	218	23,618	8,000	----	23,597	14,300	4,394	140,783	1,149	1,790	23,967

[1] Preliminary.   [2] Estimate.   *Source: Foreign Agricutural Service, U.S. Department of Agriculture (FAS-USDA)*

World Production of Barley   In Thousands of Metric Tons

Year	Australia	Belarus	Canada	China	European Union	India	Iran	Kazakhstan	Russia	Turkey	Ukraine	United States	World Total
2005-06	9,483	1,864	11,678	3,444	54,902	1,200	2,857	1,528	15,791	7,600	8,975	4,613	136,228
2006-07	4,257	1,831	9,573	3,130	56,430	1,220	2,956	1,953	18,155	7,500	11,341	3,923	136,962
2007-08	7,159	1,911	10,910	2,785	57,765	1,330	3,104	2,441	15,663	6,000	5,981	4,575	132,960
2008-09	7,996	2,212	11,786	2,823	65,759	1,200	1,547	2,059	23,148	5,700	12,612	5,205	155,010
2009-10	7,865	2,123	9,528	2,318	62,393	1,690	3,446	2,519	17,881	6,500	11,833	4,934	151,055
2010-11	7,995	1,966	7,627	1,972	53,691	1,350	3,580	1,313	8,350	5,900	8,484	3,924	123,122
2011-12	8,221	1,979	7,892	1,637	51,883	1,660	2,900	2,593	16,938	7,000	9,098	3,370	133,522
2012-13	7,472	1,917	8,012	1,626	54,875	1,620	3,400	1,500	13,952	5,500	6,935	4,768	129,807
2013-14[1]	9,539	1,674	10,237	1,500	59,639	1,750	3,200	2,539	15,389	7,300	7,561	4,719	145,359
2014-15[2]	7,600	2,100	7,120	1,550	59,927	1,810	3,200	2,500	19,500	4,000	9,400	3,849	139,739

[1] Preliminary.   [2] Estimate.   *Source: Foreign Agricutural Service, U.S. Department of Agriculture (FAS-USDA)*

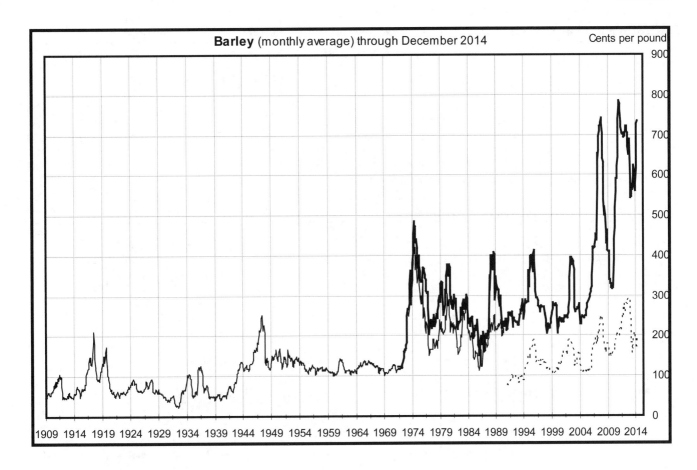

Barley (monthly average) through December 2014 — Cents per pound

Barley Acreage and Prices in the United States

Crop Year Beginning June 1	Acreage 1,000 Acres Planted	Acreage 1,000 Acres Harvested for Gain	Yield Per Harvested Acre Bushels	Seasonal Prices Received by Farmers[3] All	Feed[4]	Malting[4]	Portland No. 2 Western	National Average Loan Rate	Target Price	Put Under Support (mil. Bu.)	Percent of Production
				Dollars per Bushel							
2007-08	4,018	3,502	60.0	4.14	4.42	4.00	5.71	1.85	2.24	4.4	2.1
2008-09	4,246	3,779	63.6	5.23	3.61	5.56	5.29	1.85	2.24	6.7	2.8
2009-10	3,567	3,113	73.0	4.58	2.62	4.95	----	1.85	2.24	12.7	5.6
2010-11	2,872	2,465	73.1	3.90	3.40	4.06	----	1.95	2.63	6.4	3.6
2011-12	2,559	2,239	69.6	5.37	4.88	5.46	----	1.95	2.63	2.8	1.8
2012-13	3,660	3,274	66.9	6.36	5.62	6.50	----	1.95	2.63	3.1	1.4
2013-14[1]	3,528	3,040	71.3	6.07	4.21	6.50	----	1.95	2.63		
2014-15[2]	2,975	2,443	72.4	5.32	3.30	5.84	----				

[1] Preliminary.   [2] Estimate.   [3] Excludes support payments.   *Source: Economic Research Service, U.S. Department of Agriculture (ERS-USDA)*

Salient Statistics of Barley in the United States   In Millions of Bushels

Crop Year Beginning June 1	Supply Beginning Stocks	Production	Imports	Total Supply	Disappearance Domestic Use Food & Alcohol Beverage	Seed	Feed & Residual	Total	Exports	Total Disappearance	Ending Stocks Gov't Owned	Privately Owned	Total Stocks
2007-08	68.9	210.1	29.2	308.2	161.6	7.0	30.0	198.6	41.4	240.0	0	68.2	68.2
2008-09	68.2	240.2	29.0	337.4	163.0	5.9	66.6	235.5	13.2	248.7	0	88.7	88.7
2009-10	88.7	227.3	16.6	332.7	158.7	5.0	47.8	211.5	5.7	217.2	0	115.5	115.5
2010-11	115.5	180.3	9.5	305.2	153.7	4.8	49.8	208.3	7.6	215.9	0	89.4	89.4
2011-12	89.4	155.8	16.3	260.4	149.0	6.0	36.6	191.6	8.8	200.4	0	60.0	60.0
2012-13	60.0	219.0	23.3	302.3	141.0	5.8	66.2	213.0	8.9	221.9	0	80.4	80.4
2013-14[1]	80.4	216.7	18.7	315.9	148.3	6.3	64.7	219.4	14.3	233.6	0	82.3	82.3
2014-15[2]	82.3	176.8	25.0	284.0	145.9	6.0	45.0	196.9	10.0	206.9	0	77.2	77.2

[1] Preliminary.   [2] Estimate.   [3] Uncommitted inventory.   [4] Includes quantity under loan & farmer-owned reserve.   [5] Included in Food & Alcohol.
Source: Economic Research Service, U.S. Department of Agriculture (ERS-USDA)

BARLEY

Average Price Received by Farmers for All Barley in the United States   In Dollars Per Bushel

Year	June	July	Aug.	Sept.	Oct.	Nov.	Dec.	Jan.	Feb.	Mar.	Apr.	May	Average
2007-08	3.30	3.46	3.55	4.05	4.53	4.31	4.44	4.35	4.38	4.18	4.56	4.52	4.14
2008-09	4.78	5.12	5.46	5.97	5.73	5.44	5.49	5.34	4.99	5.03	4.84	4.59	5.23
2009-10	4.70	5.09	5.17	4.78	4.41	4.46	4.54	4.68	4.53	4.22	4.08	4.25	4.58
2010-11	3.64	3.79	3.69	3.61	3.73	3.86	3.86	3.86	3.95	4.29	4.41	4.15	3.90
2011-12	4.65	5.07	5.27	5.45	5.51	5.44	5.46	5.44	5.41	5.34	5.69	5.72	5.37
2012-13	5.52	6.25	6.54	6.42	6.49	6.49	6.44	6.41	6.48	6.49	6.30	6.45	6.36
2013-14	6.35	6.38	6.15	5.88	5.94	6.20	6.11	6.04	5.90	5.97	5.93	5.94	6.07
2014-15[1]	6.08	5.62	5.60	5.22	4.95	5.12	5.15	4.82					5.32

[1] Preliminary.   *Source: National Agricultural Statistical Service, U.S. Department of Agriculture (NASS-USDA)*

Average Price Received by Farmers for Feed Barley in the United States   In Dollars Per Bushel

Year	June	July	Aug.	Sept.	Oct.	Nov.	Dec.	Jan.	Feb.	Mar.	Apr.	May	Average
2007-08	3.50	3.27	3.60	4.47	4.89	5.05	4.79	4.89	4.67	4.29	4.67	4.99	4.42
2008-09	5.49	4.72	4.54	4.46	3.82	3.43	3.00	2.90	2.63	2.73	2.65	2.99	3.61
2009-10	3.16	2.94	2.49	2.14	2.29	2.50	2.63	2.63	3.11	2.66	2.40	2.49	2.62
2010-11	2.24	2.40	2.39	2.89	3.38	3.34	3.40	3.46	3.56	4.26	4.89	4.61	3.40
2011-12	4.74	5.04	4.91	5.07	4.76	4.85	4.88	4.81	4.74	4.76	5.10	4.89	4.88
2012-13	5.46	5.53	5.61	5.58	5.72	5.67	5.53	5.60	5.91	5.61	5.55	5.68	5.62
2013-14	5.75	5.17	4.42	4.25	4.10	3.63	3.65	4.21	3.77	3.78	3.65	4.15	4.21
2014-15[1]	4.53	3.85	3.32	2.99	2.94	2.83	2.99	2.98					3.30

[1] Preliminary.   *Source: National Agricultural Statistical Service, U.S. Department of Agriculture (NASS-USDA)*

Average Price Received by Farmers for Malting Barley in the United States   In Dollars Per Bushel

Year	June	July	Aug.	Sept.	Oct.	Nov.	Dec.	Jan.	Feb.	Mar.	Apr.	May	Average
2007-08	3.25	3.49	3.52	3.74	4.16	4.10	4.28	4.09	4.29	4.14	4.51	4.38	4.00
2008-09	4.51	5.23	5.67	6.40	6.20	5.63	5.91	5.62	5.54	5.50	5.33	5.17	5.56
2009-10	5.38	5.48	5.47	5.32	4.94	4.88	4.84	4.87	4.70	4.43	4.55	4.51	4.95
2010-11	4.24	4.14	3.94	3.96	3.88	3.98	3.97	3.97	4.06	4.29	4.22	4.04	4.06
2011-12	4.60	5.09	5.31	5.57	5.69	5.57	5.55	5.54	5.50	5.43	5.87	5.84	5.46
2012-13	5.54	6.43	6.68	6.70	6.65	6.65	6.57	6.49	6.56	6.64	6.48	6.55	6.50
2013-14	6.68	6.56	6.56	6.44	6.49	6.61	6.52	6.52	6.42	6.35	6.45	6.37	6.50
2014-15[1]	6.30	5.90	6.11	5.81	5.80	5.69	5.64	5.46					5.84

[1] Preliminary.   *Source: National Agricultural Statistical Service, U.S. Department of Agriculture (NASS-USDA)*

Stocks of Barley in the United States   In Thousands of Bushels

Year	On Farms Mar. 1	On Farms June 1	On Farms Sept. 1	On Farms Dec. 1	Off Farms Mar. 1	Off Farms June 1	Off Farms Sept. 1	Off Farms Dec. 1	Total Stocks Mar. 1	Total Stocks June 1	Total Stocks Sept. 1	Total Stocks Dec. 1
2007	38,310	14,580	105,600	62,050	78,756	54,300	83,095	73,728	117,066	68,880	188,695	135,778
2008	28,270	9,950	127,750	77,050	82,154	58,273	81,669	95,766	110,424	68,223	209,419	172,816
2009	44,310	27,010	154,050	114,630	84,791	61,723	85,414	91,759	129,101	88,733	239,464	206,389
2010	67,370	40,440	125,070	91,660	89,985	75,059	98,818	88,720	157,355	115,499	223,888	180,380
2011	57,700	26,040	93,050	55,320	80,424	63,311	82,007	83,621	138,124	89,351	175,057	138,941
2012	26,480	9,670	111,550	72,580	67,248	50,317	85,226	85,473	93,728	59,987	196,776	158,053
2013	35,180	15,840	105,620	81,340	81,897	64,557	90,470	88,063	117,077	80,397	196,090	169,403
2014[1]	43,830	19,110	97,820	74,410	77,734	63,145	81,997	83,308	121,564	82,255	179,817	157,718

[1] Preliminary.   *Source: National Agricultural Statistics Service, U.S. Department of Agriculture (NASS-USDA)*

Production of Barley in the United States, by State   In Thousands of Bushels

Year	Arizona	California	Colorado	Idaho	Minnesota	Montana	North Dakota	Oregon	Pennsylvania	Virginia	Washington	Wyoming	U.S. Total
2007	3,410	2,560	6,960	42,900	5,940	31,680	77,840	2,809	3,066	2,130	13,950	4,505	210,110
2008	4,800	3,300	8,640	49,880	7,150	37,740	86,240	2,100	4,125	3,060	11,115	6,900	240,193
2009	5,175	2,970	10,395	48,450	4,880	41,040	79,100	1,920	3,375	3,182	6,208	6,720	227,323
2010	5,500	4,350	8,379	43,240	4,340	38,440	43,550	2,960	3,375	3,216	5,832	6,076	180,268
2011	8,000	4,725	7,938	46,500	3,060	31,000	16,450	2,400	3,575	6,160	8,510	6,111	155,780
2012	4,935	4,400	6,710	54,000	6,270	40,290	60,600	3,816	3,604	2,870	12,425	6,141	218,990
2013	8,142	3,150	7,714	57,660	5,175	43,160	46,080	3,500	4,080	3,608	14,040	6,052	216,745
2014[1]	4,000	1,825	6,696	47,940	3,120	44,660	35,845	1,500	3,550	2,212	6,300	6,741	176,794

[1] Preliminary.   *Source: National Agricultural Statistics Service, U.S. Department of Agriculture (NASS-USDA)*

Bauxite

Bauxite is a naturally occurring, heterogeneous material comprised of one or more aluminum hydroxide minerals plus various mixtures of silica, iron oxide, titanium, alumina-silicates, and other impurities in trace amounts. Bauxite is an important ore of aluminum and forms by the rapid weathering of granite rocks in warm, humid climates. It is easily purified and can be converted directly into either alum or metallic aluminum. It is a soft mineral with hardness varying from 1 to 3, and specific gravity from 2 to 2.55. Bauxite is dull in appearance and may vary in color from white to brown. It usually occurs in aggregates in pea-sized lumps.

Bauxite is the only raw material used in the production of alumina on a commercial scale in the United States. Bauxite is classified according to the intended commercial application, such as abrasive, cement, chemical, metallurgical, and refractory. Of all the bauxite mined, about 95 percent is converted to alumina for the production of aluminum metal with some smaller amounts going to nonmetal uses as various forms of specialty alumina. Small amounts are used in non-metallurgical bauxite applications. Bauxite is also used to produce aluminum chemicals and is used in the steel industry.

Supply – World production of bauxite in 2014 fell -17.3% yr/yr to 234.000 million metric tons. The world's largest producer of bauxite is Australia with 34.6% of the world's production in 2014, followed by China (20.1%), Brazil (13.9%), Guinea (8.3%), India (8.1%), and Jamaica (4.2%). Chinese production of bauxite has almost quadrupled in the past 10 years. India's bauxite production has also risen rapidly and is about triple the amount seen 15 years ago.

Demand – U.S. consumption of bauxite in 2012 (latest data) rose by +8.4% yr/yr to 9.560 million metric tons but still well below the record high of 15.962 million metric tons seen in 1980. The alumina industry took almost 98% of bauxite production in 2012, or 9.330 million metric tons. According to 2004 data (the latest data available) the refractory industry usually takes about 1.4% of the U.S. bauxite supply, the abrasive industry takes about 0.2%, and the chemical industry takes the rest.

Trade – The U.S. relies on imports for almost 100% of its consumption needs. Domestic ore, which provides less than 1 percent of the U.S. requirement for bauxite, is mined by one company from surface mines in the states of Alabama and Georgia. U.S. imports of bauxite rose +8.0% yr/yr to 10.300 million metric tons in 2012, which was still well below the record of 14.976 million metric tons seen in 1974. U.S. exports of bauxite in 2012 were negligible at 11,000 metric tons and down -52.7% yr/yr.

World Production of Bauxite   In Thousands of Metric Tons

Year	Australia	Brazil	China	Greece	Guinea	Guyana[3]	Hungary	India	Jamaica[3]	Russia[3]	Sierra Leone	Suriname	World Total
2005	59,959	22,034	22,000	2,495	16,817	1,694	535	12,385	14,116	5,000	----	4,757	178,000
2006	61,780	23,236	27,000	2,163	18,784	1,479	538	13,940	14,865	6,300	1,071	4,924	193,000
2007	62,398	25,461	30,000	2,126	18,519	2,239	546	20,343	14,568	5,775	1,169	5,054	221,000
2008	64,038	28,098	35,000	2,176	16,000	2,109	511	21,210	14,636	5,675	954	5,333	227,000
2009	65,231	26,074	40,000	1,935	13,600	1,485	267	16,000	7,817	5,775	757	3,388	210,000
2010	68,414	32,028	44,000	1,902	15,300	1,083	307	18,000	8,540	5,690	1,089	3,104	238,000
2011	69,976	33,695	45,000	1,900	15,300	1,818	278	19,000	10,189	5,943	1,300	3,236	259,000
2012	76,282	34,000	47,000	2,100	17,823	2,214	250	19,000	9,339	5,700	776	3,400	258,000
2013[1]	81,100	32,500	46,000	2,100	18,800	1,710		15,400	9,440	5,320		2,700	283,000
2014[2]	81,000	32,500	47,000	2,100	19,300	1,800		19,000	9,800	5,300		2,700	234,000

[1] Preliminary.   [2] Estimate.   [3] Dry Bauxite equivalent of ore processed.   *Source: U.S. Geological Survey (USGS)*

Salient Statistics of Bauxite in the United States   In Thousands of Metric Tons

Year	Net Import Reliance as a % of Apparent Consump	Average Price F.O.B. Mine $ per Ton	Consumtion by Industry Total	Alumina	Abrasive	Chemical	Re-fractoty	Dry Equivalent Imports[4]	Exports[3]	Con-sumption	Stocks, December 31 Producers & Consumers	Gov't Owned	Total
2004	100	22	13,600	12,500	53	W	260	9,640	42	13,600	3,120	----	3,120
2005	100	26	12,400	11,900	W	W	W	11,800	34	12,400	W	----	W
2006	100	28	12,300	11,800	W	W	W	11,600	20	12,300	W	----	W
2007	100	31	10,200	9,830	W	W	W	9,840	15	10,200	W	----	W
2008	100	26	9,550	9,310	W	W	W	10,500	14	9,550	W	----	W
2009	100	30	5,490	5,330	W	W	W	6,970	9	4,960	W	----	W
2010	100	29	8,180	8,050	W	W	W	8,120	21	8,180	W	----	W
2011	100	39	8,820	8,670	----	----	----	9,540	22	8,820	W	----	W
2012[1]	100	36	9,560	9,330	----	----	----	10,300	11	9,560	W	----	W
2013[2]	100			----	----	----	----	9,830	4		W	----	W

[1] Preliminary.   [2] Estimate.   [3] Including concentrates.   [4] For consumption.   W = Withheld.   *Source: U.S. Geological Survey (USGS)*

Bismuth

Bismuth (symbol Bi) is a rare metallic element with a pinkish tinge. Bismuth has been known since ancient times, but it was confused with lead, tin, and zinc until the middle of the 18th century. Among the elements in the earth's crust, bismuth is ranked about 73rd in natural abundance. This makes bismuth about as rare as silver. Most industrial bismuth is obtained as a by-product of ore extraction.

Bismuth is useful for castings because of the unusual way that it expands after solidifying. Some of bismuth's alloys have unusually low melting points. Bismuth is one of the most difficult of all substances to magnetize. It tends to turn at right angles to a magnetic field. Because of this property, it is used in instruments for measuring the strength of magnetic fields.

Bismuth finds a wide variety of uses such as pharmaceutical compounds, ceramic glazes, crystal ware, and chemicals and pigments. Bismuth is found in household pharmaceuticals and is used to treat stomach ulcers. Bismuth is opaque to X-rays and can be used in fluoroscopy. Bismuth has also found new use as a nontoxic substitute for lead in various applications such as brass plumbing fixtures, crystal ware, lubricating greases, pigments, and solders. There has been environmental interest in the use of bismuth as a replacement for lead used in shot for waterfowl hunting and in fishing sinkers. Another use has been for galvanizing to improve drainage characteristics of galvanizing alloys. Zinc-bismuth alloys have the same drainage properties as zinc-lead without being as hazardous.

Prices – The average price of bismuth (99.99% pure) in the U.S. in 2014 rose by +30.1% to $11.39 per pound, below the 2007 record high of $13.32 per pound. Up until 2007, bismuth prices were much lower in the range of $3.00 to $5.00 per pound.

Supply – World mine production of bismuth in 2014 rose +1.2% to 8,500 metric tons, a new record high. The world's largest producer in 2014 was China with 89.4% of world production, followed by Mexico with 9.7%, and Canada far behind with 0.4%. Regarding production of the refined metal in 2012 (latest data), China had 87.5% of production, Mexico had 5.0%, Japan had 3.0%, and Kazakhstan had 0.9%. The U.S. does not have any significant domestic refinery production of bismuth.

Demand – U.S. consumption of bismuth in 2014 rose by +16.3% to 900 metric tons, but still below the record high of 2,420 metric tons in 2004. In 2012 (latest data) the consumed uses of bismuth were 67.1% for chemicals, 31% for metallurgical additives, 8.1% for fusible alloys, and 0.5% for other alloy uses.

Trade – U.S. imports of bismuth in 2014 rose +22.8% to 2,100 metric tons, well below the 2007 record high of 3,070 metric tons. Of U.S. imports in 2013 (latest data), 22.8% came from Belgium. U.S. exports of bismuth and alloys in 2014 fell 26.5% yr/yr to 600 metric tons, well below the 2010 record high of 1,040 metric tons.

World Production of Bismuth — In Metric Tons (Mine Output=Metal Content)

	Mine Output, Metal Content						Refined Metal						
Year	Canada	China	Japan	Mexico	Peru	World Total	Belgium	China	Japan	Kazak-hastan[3]	Mexico	Peru	World Total
2008	71	5,000	----	1,132	1,061	7,500	----	13,100	480	----	1,132	1,061	16,000
2009	86	6,000	----	854	423	7,500	----	12,300	423	90	854	423	14,000
2010	91	6,500	----	952	----	7,700	----	14,000	454	150	982	----	16,000
2011	92	7,000	----	935	----	8,100	----	15,000	460	150	935	----	17,000
2012	121	6,000	----	800	----	7,000	----	14,000	470	150	800	----	16,000
2013[1]	35	7,500	----	824	----	8,400							
2014[2]	35	7,600		824		8,500							

[1] Preliminary. [2] Estimate. *Source U.S. Geological Survey (USGS)*

Salient Statistics of Bismuth in the United States — In Metric Tons

	Bismuth Consumed, By Uses						Exports	Imports from				Dealer Price
Year	Metal-lurgical Additives	Other Alloys & Uses	Fusible Alloys	Chem-icals[3]	Total Consumption	Consumer Stocks Dec. 31	of Metal & Alloys	Belgium	Mexico	Preu	Total	$ Per Pound
2007	1,130	45	709	744	2,630	139	421	1,020.0	420.0	3.7	3,070	14.07
2008	375	38	75	597	1,210	228	375	509.0	40.0	55.7	1,930	12.73
2009	232	2	58	528	812	134	397	450.0	59.4	29.4	1,250	7.84
2010	231	4	62	589	636	133	1,040	674.0	0.4	0.5	1,620	8.76
2011	W	W	68	492	696	138	628	713.0	0.1	----	1,750	11.47
2012[1]	W	W	52	434	647	134	764	505.0	----	----	1,700	10.10
2013[2]				774		50	816	389.0	----	----	1,710	8.71

[1] Preliminary. [2] Estimate. [3] Includes pharmaceuticals. *Source: U.S. Geological Survey (USGS)*

Average Price of Bismuth (99.99%) in the United States — In Dollars Per Pound

Year	Jan.	Feb.	Mar.	Apr.	May	June	July	Aug.	Sept.	Oct.	Nov.	Dec.	Average
2011	9.18	9.46	10.21	11.06	11.41	11.45	11.45	11.45	12.83	12.88	12.31	10.75	11.20
2012	10.58	10.86	10.74	10.45	10.59	10.39	10.21	9.59	9.36	9.78	9.20	8.64	10.03
2013	8.73	8.81	9.12	9.16	8.92	8.75	8.12	7.86	8.42	8.89	9.03	8.99	8.73
2014	9.25	9.99	10.50	10.45	10.45	10.50	10.65	11.51	12.39	12.41	11.96	11.03	10.92

Source: American Metal Market (AMM)

Broilers

Broiler chickens are raised for meat rather than for eggs. The broiler industry was started in the late 1950's when chickens were selectively bred for meat production. Broiler chickens are housed in massive flocks mainly between 20,000 and 50,000 birds, with some flocks reaching over 100,000 birds. Broiler chicken farmers usually rear five or six batches of chickens per year.

After just six or seven weeks, broiler chickens are slaughtered (a chicken's natural lifespan is around seven years). Chickens marketed as pouissons, or spring chickens, are slaughtered after four weeks. A few are kept longer than seven weeks to be sold as the larger roasting chickens.

Prices – The average monthly price received by farmers for broilers (live weight) rose in 2014 by +6.9% yr/yr to 64.4 cents per pound. The average monthly price for wholesale broilers (ready-to-cook) in 2014 rose +5.2% to 104.88 cents per pound, a new record high.

Supply – Total production of broilers in 2014 rose +2.0% yr/yr to 38.586 billion pounds. The number of broilers raised for commercial production in 2013 was up +0.7% yr/yr to 8.524 billion birds, down from the 2008 record high of 9.009 billion birds. The average live-weight per bird rose +1.2% to 5.94 pounds, which was a new record high and was about 50% heavier than the average bird weight of 3.62 pounds seen in 1970, attesting to the increased efficiency of the industry.

Demand – U.S. per capita consumption of broilers in 2014 rose by +1.8% to 83.4 pounds (ready-to-cook) per person per year, down very slightly from the 2006 record high of 86.5. U.S. consumption of chicken has nearly doubled in the past two decades, up from 47.0 pounds in 1980, as consumers have increased their consumption of chicken because of the focus on low-carb diets and because chicken is a leaner and healthier meat than either beef or pork.

Broiler Supply and Prices in the United States

Years and Quarters	Number (Million)	Average Weight (Pounds)	Liveweight Pounds (Mil. Lbs.)	Certified RTC[3] Weight (Mil. Lbs.)	Total Production RTC[3] (Mil. Lbs.)	Per Capita Consumption RTC[3] Basis (Mil. Lbs.)	Farm	Georgia Dock[4]
							Cents per Pound	
2009	8,519	5.59	47,604	35,505	35,511	79.6	45.17	84.97
2010	8,649	5.70	49,313	36,909	36,911	82.3	49.08	85.25
2011	8,532	5.80	49,520	37,178	37,201	82.9	46.67	86.37
2012	8,429	5.86	49,349	37,035	37,039	80.4	51.42	93.60
2013[1]	8,505	5.92	50,353	37,826	37,830	81.9	60.25	103.26
2014[2]	8,522	6.01	50,839	38,271	38,586	83.4	64.42	109.71
I	2,058	6.00	12,339	9,283	9,283	20.2	59.33	104.30
II	2,136	5.98	12,780	9,618	9,618	20.9	71.33	109.64
III	2,185	5.97	13,048	9,835	9,835	21.1	64.33	112.01
IV	2,144	6.08	12,671	9,535	9,850	21.2	62.67	112.88

[1] Preliminary. [2] Estimate. [3] Total production equals federal inspected slaughter plus other slaughter minus cut-up & further processing condemnation.
[4] Ready-to-cook basis. *Source: Economic Research Service, U.S. Department of Agriculture (ERS-USDA)*

Salient Statistics of Broilers in the United States

Year	Commercial Production Number (Mil. Lbs.)	Commercial Production Liveweight (Mil. Lbs.)	Average Liveweight Per Bird (Mil. Lbs.)	Average Price (cents Lb.)	Value of Production (Mil. $)	Production Federally Inspected	Production Other Chickens	Total	Storage Stocks January 1	Exports	Broiler Feed Ratio (pounds)	Consumption Total (Mil. Lbs.)	Consumption Per Capita[4] (Pounds)
						In Millions of Pounds							
2007	8,907	49,331	5.54	43.6	21,514	36,159	387	36,546	732	5,904	5.1	29,961	85.31
2008	9,009	50,442	5.60	45.8	23,203	36,906	395	37,301	719	6,961	3.7	29,619	83.54
2009	8,550	47,752	5.58	45.2	21,823	35,511	380	35,891	745	6,818	4.1	28,540	79.79
2010	8,624	49,153	5.70	49.1	23,692	36,910	395	37,305	616	6,762	4.5	29,703	82.36
2011	8,608	50,082	5.82	46.7	22,988	37,202	398	37,601	773	6,968	3.1	30,126	82.92
2012[1]	8,463	49,656	5.87	51.4	24,828	37,039	396	37,435	590	7,274	3.1	29,419	80.39
2013[2]	8,525	50,627	5.94	60.3	30,680						3.7		81.80

Preliminary. [2] Estimate. [3] Ready-to-cook. [4] Retail weight basis. Source: Economic Research Service, U.S. Department of Agriculture (ERS-USDA)

Average Wholesale Broiler[2] Prices RTC (Ready-to-Cook)   In Cents Per Pound

Year	Jan.	Feb.	Mar.	Apr.	May	June	July	Aug.	Sept.	Oct.	Nov.	Dec.	Average
2008	75.91	78.79	79.51	77.84	81.58	82.48	84.60	79.34	77.98	77.65	78.51	82.01	79.68
2009	81.90	80.17	77.01	76.39	82.96	86.22	82.95	74.50	72.81	71.00	71.76	73.56	77.60
2010	81.57	81.07	84.00	82.12	86.35	86.63	86.12	83.25	84.04	80.42	81.12	78.38	82.92
2011	76.28	75.43	81.97	82.12	83.38	82.44	79.97	80.89	75.42	73.71	76.46	80.28	79.03
2012	81.76	86.59	93.23	85.01	87.26	85.41	82.62	84.40	82.68	84.05	95.42	97.81	87.19
2013	101.48	101.80	107.27	107.10	110.40	108.28	99.04	91.12	91.51	90.02	93.72	94.60	99.70
2014[1]	96.45	92.45	106.26	110.11	117.59	113.40	107.16	99.69	107.05	106.68	103.68	98.07	104.88

[1] Preliminary. [2] 12-city composite wholesale price. *Source: Economic Research Service, U.S. Department of Agriculture (ERS-USDA)*

Butter

Butter is a dairy product produced by churning the fat from milk, usually cow's milk, until it solidifies. In some parts of the world, butter is also made from the milk of goats, sheep, and even horses. Butter has been in use since at least 2,000 BC. Today butter is used principally as a food item, but in ancient times it was used more as an ointment, medicine, or illuminating oil. Butter was first churned in skin pouches thrown back and forth over the backs of trotting horses.

It takes about 10 quarts of milk to produce 1 pound of butter. The manufacture of butter is the third largest use of milk in the U.S. California is generally the largest producing state, followed closely by Wisconsin, with Washington as a distant third. Commercially finished butter is comprised of milk fat (80% to 85%), water (12% to 16%), and salt (about 2%). Although the price of butter is highly correlated with the price of milk, it also has its own supply and demand dynamics.

The consumption of butter has dropped in recent decades because pure butter has a high level of animal fat and cholesterol that have been linked to obesity and heart disease. The primary substitute for butter is margarine, which is produced from vegetable oil rather than milk fat. U.S. per capita consumption of margarine has risen from 2.6 pounds in 1930 to recent levels near 8.3 pounds, much higher than U.S. butter consumption.

Futures on butter are traded at the Chicago Mercantile Exchange (CME). The CME's butter futures contract calls for the delivery of 40,000 pounds of Grade AA butter and is priced in cents per pound.

Prices – The average monthly price of butter at the CME in 2014 rose +39.1% yr/yr to 216.43 cents/pound, a new record high.

Supply – World production of butter in 2015 is expected to rise +3.4% yr/yr to 9.760 million metric tons, a new record high. The world's largest producers of butter will be India with 51.6% of the world production in 2015, the European Union with 23.3%, the United States with 9.2%, New Zealand with 5.9%, and Russia with 2.5%. Production of creamery butter by U.S. factories in 2014 fell -1.7% yr/yr to 1.831 billion pounds, below last year's record high of 1.863 billion pounds.

Demand – Total commercial use of creamery butter in the U.S fell by -0.7% yr/yr to 1.725 million pounds in 2014, just below the 2013 record high. That is about one-third higher that the commercial use of butter back in the 1950's. Cold storage stocks of creamery butter in the U.S. on December 1, 2014 fell -17.0% yr/yr to 100.899 million pounds.

Trade – World imports of butter are expected to fall -4.0% yr/yr to 290,000 metric tons in 2015. U.S. imports of butter are expected to fall by -11.1% yr/yr to 16,000 metric tons in 2015. World exports of butter in 2015 are expected to rise by +0.4% yr/yr to 865,000 metric tons. U.S exports in 2015 are expected to fall -20.3% yr/yr to 55,000 metric tons, which would still be well below the 1993 record high of 145,000 metric tons.

Supply and Distribution of Butter in the United States   In Millions of Pounds

| | Supply | | | | Distribution | | | | | | 93 Score | |
| | | Cold Storage | | | Domestic Disappearance | | | Department of Agriculture | | | AA Wholesale Price | |
Year	Pro-duction	Stocks[3] Jan. 1	Imports	Total Supply	Total	Per Capita (Pounds)	Exports	Stocks[4] Jan. 1	Stocks[4] Dec 31	Removed by USDA Programs	Total Use	$ per Pound
2006	1,448	59	41.887	1,550	1,418	4.7	24	----	----	----	1,442	---- 1.2364
2007	1,533	109	39.683	1,680	1,437	4.7	88	----	----	----	1,526	---- 1.3682
2008	1,645	154	35.274	1,834	1,519	5.0	196	----	----	----	1,715	---- 1.4631
2009	1,572	119	37.478	1,728	1,530	5.0	66	----	----	----	1,596	---- 1.2427
2010	1,563	132	22.046	1,717	1,506	4.9	130	----	----	----	1,636	---- 1.7280
2011	1,810	82	26.455	1,918	1,669	5.4	143	----	----	----	1,812	---- 1.9618
2012	1,858	106	39.683	2,004	1,748	5.5	104	----	----	----	1,852	---- 1.6029
2013[1]	1,863	152	26.455	2,041	1,724		205	----	----	----	1,929	----
2014[2]	1,885	112	26.455	2,024	1,737		187				1,925	

[1] Preliminary.   [2] Estimates.   [3] Includes butter-equivalent.   [4] Includes butteroil.   [5] Includes stocks held by USDA.
Source: Economic Research Service, U.S. Department of Agriculture (ERS-USDA)

Quarterly Commercial Disappearance of Creamery Butter in the United States   In Millions of Pounds

Year	First Quarter	Second Quarter	Third Quarter	Fourth Quarter	Total	Year	First Quarter	Second Quarter	Third Quarter	Fourth Quarter	Total
2003	305.1	264.3	315.0	408.7	1,293.1	2009	371.0	352.3	343.2	457.9	1,524.6
2004	283.8	296.3	335.5	410.3	1,325.9	2010	362.6	353.0	365.1	443.5	1,524.1
2005	283.8	300.0	347.7	414.2	1,345.7	2011	387.0	372.0	426.3	494.5	1,679.7
2006	294.5	288.5	356.5	459.8	1,399.4	2012	402.5	403.6	435.6	491.3	1,733.0
2007	337.8	284.3	349.2	459.2	1,430.5	2013	412.3	372.2	434.2	517.8	1,736.5
2008	350.1	321.4	369.0	477.0	1,517.5	2014[1]	389.1	431.3	421.7	483.0	1,725.1

[1] Preliminary.   *Source: Economic Research Service, U.S. Department of Agriculture (ERS-USDA)*

World Production of Butter[3]   In Thousands of Metric Tons

Year	Australia	Brazil	Canada	Egypt	European Union	India	Japan	Mexico	New Zealand	Russia	Ukraine	United States	World Total
2008	111	84	85	----	2,040	3,690	72	180	413	305	85	746	7,872
2009	118	76	86	----	2,030	3,910	81	171	482	246	75	713	8,039
2010	132	78	80	----	1,980	4,162	74	182	441	207	79	709	8,179
2011	121	79	85	----	2,055	4,330	63	187	487	217	76	821	8,584
2012	119	81	98	----	2,100	4,525	69	190	527	216	88	843	8,914
2013	117	83	95	----	2,100	4,745	68	190	535	219	93	845	9,150
2014[1]	117	93	85	----	2,195	4,887	60	190	570	235	115	835	9,440
2015[2]	115	95	90	----	2,275	5,035	65	195	580	240	110	900	9,760

[1] Preliminary.   [2] Forecast.   [3] Factory (including creameries and dairies) & farm.   NA = Not available.
Source: Foreign Agricultural Service, U.S. Department of Agriculture (FAS-USDA)

Production of Creamery Butter in Factories in the United States   In Millions of Pounds

Year	Jan.	Feb.	Mar.	Apr.	May	June	July	Aug.	Sept.	Oct.	Nov.	Dec.	Total
2007	150.6	134.0	138.4	133.0	124.0	110.0	116.5	110.9	112.9	130.4	130.8	141.5	1,532.9
2008	168.8	146.8	151.9	150.1	142.6	119.8	114.2	115.7	121.0	130.0	133.7	156.3	1,651.1
2009	176.7	147.2	147.0	141.7	139.2	125.3	114.4	101.0	94.7	113.1	120.9	151.3	1,572.5
2010	162.4	140.2	139.3	133.1	131.9	117.1	111.2	101.5	113.8	122.2	133.5	157.8	1,564.0
2011	167.1	150.1	165.4	158.7	155.9	141.3	135.5	133.7	137.9	145.7	152.8	165.9	1,809.8
2012	181.6	170.6	176.3	169.9	164.1	137.0	133.6	129.5	136.3	144.5	142.9	173.1	1,859.6
2013	188.1	173.8	181.4	166.7	163.8	140.1	132.7	134.4	132.2	145.9	142.2	161.7	1,863.0
2014[1]	182.4	163.9	165.4	165.8	164.5	140.4	137.0	128.6	130.2	143.8	142.2	167.0	1,831.2

[1] Preliminary.   *Source: Economic Research Service, U.S. Department of Agriculture (ERS-USDA)*

Cold Storage Holdings of Creamery Butter in the United States, on First of Month   In Millions of Pounds

Year	Jan.	Feb.	Mar.	Apr.	May	June	July	Aug.	Sept.	Oct.	Nov.	Dec.
2007	108.6	148.7	185.4	193.1	245.9	270.2	273.0	271.5	260.9	240.3	196.6	143.2
2008	155.2	188.1	210.4	224.8	251.5	269.5	258.4	246.1	213.7	186.9	149.4	119.9
2009	119.0	176.5	204.9	212.5	240.0	253.3	262.9	262.8	259.6	227.9	190.6	142.7
2010	133.0	168.1	202.9	195.9	206.3	212.5	197.6	193.5	155.3	130.0	108.8	69.9
2011	81.7	118.8	138.7	144.2	141.7	170.1	190.3	187.8	165.7	151.0	130.7	93.5
2012	106.9	170.3	205.2	208.3	254.2	261.6	243.2	234.4	201.1	195.8	145.1	127.3
2013	153.0	207.1	238.3	255.0	309.7	322.0	318.9	295.8	263.9	233.0	181.8	121.6
2014[1]	112.5	143.9	171.8	191.8	186.9	209.4	199.2	180.8	172.8	152.4	148.0	107.6

[1] Preliminary.   *Source: Agricultural Statistics Board, U.S. Department of Agriculture (ASB-USDA)*

Average Price of Butter at Chicago Mercantile Exchange   In Cents Per Pound

Year	Jan.	Feb.	Mar.	Apr.	May	June	July	Aug.	Sept.	Oct.	Nov.	Dec.	Average
2007	122.5	121.9	132.2	137.3	148.3	150.2	149.1	144.6	137.8	130.2	135.9	131.9	136.8
2008	122.5	120.9	134.5	139.1	147.5	150.0	153.9	162.8	169.7	173.2	161.7	120.1	146.3
2009	111.0	111.0	117.7	120.4	125.3	122.4	123.5	120.1	122.0	128.3	150.1	139.7	124.3
2010	139.5	135.6	146.4	154.6	159.0	163.8	177.9	199.0	222.6	219.0	193.0	163.3	172.8
2011	203.5	206.2	208.6	199.7	207.2	210.8	204.4	208.8	187.2	183.0	173.6	161.2	196.2
2012	158.3	142.7	149.0	141.4	135.3	147.7	158.3	176.9	188.0	190.9	179.1	155.9	160.3
2013	149.3	157.1	164.2	172.0	160.0	151.1	147.5	140.1	152.3	152.7	161.3	159.6	155.6
2014	177.6	180.5	191.5	193.6	217.1	226.3	246.2	259.1	297.4	231.8	199.7	176.3	216.4

Source: Economic Research Service, U.S. Department of Agriculture (ERS-USDA)

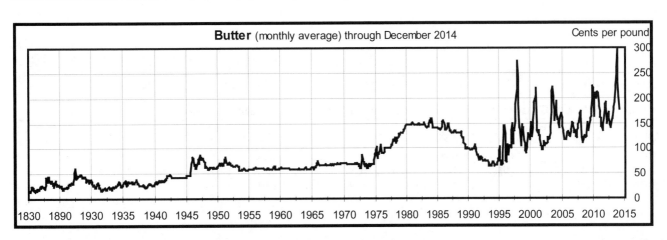

Butter (monthly average) through December 2014 — Cents per pound

Cadmium

Cadmium (atomic symbol Cd) is a soft, bluish-white, metallic element that can easily be shaped and cut with a knife. Cadmium melts at 321 degrees Celsius and boils at 765 degrees Celsius. Cadmium burns brightly in air when heated, forming the oxide CdO. In 1871, the German chemist Friedrich Stromeyer discovered cadmium in incrustations in zinc furnaces.

Rare greenockite is the only mineral bearing cadmium. Cadmium occurs most often in small quantities associated with zinc ores, such as sphalerite. Electrolysis or fractional distillation is used to separate the cadmium and zinc. About 80% of world cadmium output is a by-product from zinc refining. The remaining 20% comes from secondary sources and recycling of cadmium products. Cadmium recycling is practical only from nickel-cadmium batteries and from some alloys and dust from electric-arc furnaces.

Cadmium is used primarily for metal plating and coating operations in transportation equipment, machinery, baking enamels, photography, and television phosphors. It is also used in solar modules, pigments and lasers, and in nickel-cadmium and solar batteries.

Prices – Cadmium prices for the 8 years up through 2004 were at severely depressed levels, reflecting the decreased demand for the substance. However, cadmium prices then rallied sharply during 2005-07 and posted a record high of $334.28 per pound in 2007. Cadmium prices have since trended lower. In 2014, cadmium prices closed the year down -10.9% at $81.76 per pound.

Supply – World cadmium production in 2014 rose by +0.9% yr/yr to a new record high of 22,200 metric tons. The largest producer was China with 32.9% of total world production followed by Republic of Korea with 18.4%, Japan with 8.1%, and Canada with 5.7%. U.S. production in 2010 (latest data) fell by -0.6% to 637 metric tons, which was just above the 2009 record low of 633 metric tons.

Demand – U.S. cadmium consumption in 2010 (latest available data) rose by +139.7% yr/yr to 477 metric tons. Of the total apparent consumption, generally about 75% is used for batteries, 12% for pigments, 8% for coatings and plating, 4% for nonferrous alloys, and 1% for other uses.

Trade – The U.S. has been a net exporter of cadmium since 2004. In 2014 the U.S. imported 110 metric tons which was down -71.7% from 2013. U.S. exports of cadmium in 2014 fell -42.3% yr/yr to 240 metric tons, way below the 2009 17-year high of 661 metric tons.

World Refinery Production of Cadmium   In Metric Tons

Year	Australia	Canada	China	Germany	India	Japan	Kazakh-stan	Korea, South	Mexico	Nether-lands	Russia	United States[3]	World Total
2007	351	1,388	4,210	475	580	1,939	1,300	2,846	1,617	495	810	735	18,700
2008	350	1,409	6,960	420	599	2,126	1,100	3,090	1,550	530	800	777	21,600
2009	370	1,299	7,050	278	627	1,824	1,300	2,500	1,510	490	700	633	20,300
2010	350	1,357	7,360	290	632	2,053	1,400	4,166	1,464	560	700	637	22,700
2011	390	1,203	7,000	300	616	1,755	1,300	3,005	1,485	570	700	W	20,400
2012	380	1,100	7,300	300	620	1,800	1,300	3,000	1,624	560	700	W	20,900
2013[1]	380	1,400	7,000		450	1,830	1,200	4,000	1,490	560	1,200	W	22,000
2014[2]	380	1,270	7,300		450	1,790	1,200	4,090	1,440	570	1,200	W	22,200

[1] Preliminary.   [2] Estimate.   [3] Primary and secondary metal.   *Source: U.S. Geological Survey (USGS)*

Salient Statistics of Cadmium in the United States   In Metric Tons of Contained Cadmium

Year	Net import Reliance As a % of Apparent Consumption	Production (Metal)	Producer Shipments	Cadmium Sulfide Production	Production Other Compounds	Imports of Cadmium Metal[3]	Exports[4]	Apparent Consumption	Industry Stocks Dec. 31[5]	New York Dealer Price $ Per Lb.
2008	E	777	774	----	----	153	421	528	1,460	2.69
2009	E	633	737	----	----	117	661	199	1,450	1.30
2010	9	637	563	----	----	221	306	703	W	1.77
2011	E	W	W	----	----	211	271	W	W	1.25
2012	E	W	W	----	----	192	631	W	W	.92
2013[1]	E	W	W	----	----	388	417	W	W	.87
2014[2]	E	W	W	----	----	110	240	W	W	.88

[1] Preliminary.   [2] Estimate.   [3] For consumption.   [4] Cadmium metal, alloys, dross, flue dust.   [5] Metallic, Compounds, Distributors.   [6] Sticks & Balls in 1 to 5 short ton lots of metal (99.95%).   E = Net exporter.   *Source: U.S. Geological Survey (USGS)*

Average Price of Cadmium (99.95%) in the United States   In Dollars Per Pound

Year	Jan.	Feb.	Mar.	Apr.	May	June	July	Aug.	Sept.	Oct.	Nov.	Dec.	Average
2010	173.42	193.16	238.91	225.34	212.88	203.41	197.50	187.27	185.00	185.00	185.00	180.00	197.24
2011	161.38	144.61	140.00	140.00	140.00	140.00	140.00	140.00	125.71	125.00	121.63	116.18	136.21
2012	104.00	91.75	91.25	87.50	87.50	85.95	84.05	80.22	80.00	84.78	86.13	85.00	87.34
2013	85.54	88.68	89.43	94.77	103.41	101.50	94.21	88.87	88.50	90.00	90.00	86.26	91.76
2014	82.98	82.50	80.71	80.00	80.00	80.00	80.00	81.90	85.00	85.00	83.06	80.00	81.76

Source: American Metal Market (AMM)

Canola (Rapeseed)

Canola is a genetic variation of rapeseed that was developed by Canadian plant breeders specifically for its nutritional qualities and its low level of saturated fat. The term Canola is a contraction of "Canadian oil." The history of canola oil begins with the rapeseed plant, a member of the mustard family. The rape plant is grown both as feed for livestock and birdfeed. For 4,000 years, the oil from the rapeseed was used in China and India for cooking and as lamp oil. During World War II, rapeseed oil was used as a marine and industrial lubricant. After the war, the market for rapeseed oil plummeted. Rapeseed growers needed other uses for their crop, and that stimulated the research that led to the development of canola. In 1974, Canadian plant breeders from the University of Manitoba produced canola by genetically altering rapeseed. Each canola plant produces yellow flowers, which then produce pods. The tiny round seeds within each pod are crushed to produce canola oil. Each canola seed contains approximately 40% oil. Canola oil is the world's third largest source of vegetable oil accounting for 13% of world vegetable oils, following soybean oil at 32%, and palm oil at 28%. The rest of the seed is processed into canola meal, which is used as high protein livestock feed.

The climate in Canada is especially suitable for canola plant growth. Today, over 13 million acres of Canadian soil are dedicated to canola production. Canola oil is Canada's leading vegetable oil. Due to strong demand from the U.S. for canola oil, approximately 70% of Canada's canola oil is exported to the U.S. Canola oil is used as a salad oil, cooking oil, and for margarine as well as in the manufacture of inks, biodegradable greases, pharmaceuticals, fuel, soap, and cosmetics.

Canola futures and options are traded at ICE Futures Canada. The futures contract calls for the delivery of 20 metric tons of canola and 5 contracts are together called a "1 board lot." The futures contract is priced in Canadian dollars per metric ton.

Prices – Winnipeg canola prices on the nearest-futures chart (Barchart.com symbol code RS) in 2014 moved mostly sideways in 2014 after the sell-off seen in 2013. Canola prices posted a 4-1/2 year low in Sep 2014 but then rebounded late in the year to close 2014 up +2.8% at CD$452.30 per metric ton.

The average monthly wholesale price of canola oil in the Midwest in 2014 fell -25.3% yr/yr to 18.43 cents per pound. The average monthly wholesale price of canola meal (delivery Pacific Northwest) in the 2013-14 crop year fell -8.5% to $329.03 per short ton.

Supply – World canola production in the 2014-15 marketing year rose +11.2% yr/yr to 71.940 million metric tons, a new record high. The world's largest canola producers were the European Union with 33.5% of world production in 2014-15, Canada (21.6%), China (20.4%), and India (10.4%). U.S. production of canola and canola oil in 2014-15 rose by +32.4% yr/yr to 1.329 million metric tons. Regarding canola products, world production of canola oil in 2014-15 rose +1.4% to 26.459 million metric tons, a new record high. U.S. production of canola oil in 2014-15 rose +9.7% to 811,000 metric tons, which is a new record high. World production of canola meal in 2014-15 rose +1.0% to 39.060 million metric tons, a new record high.

Demand – World crush demand for canola in 2014-15 rose +1.3% yr/yr to 66.285 million metric tons, a new record high. World consumption of canola oil in 2014-15 rose +5.3% yr/yr to 26.375 million metric tons, a new record high. World consumption of canola meal in 2014-15 rose by +0.3% to 38.591 million metric tons, a new record high.

Trade – World canola exports in 2014-15 fell -12.3% to 13.270 million metric tons, world canola oil exports rose +10.5% to 4.173 million metric tons, and world canola meal exports fell -5.5% yr/yr to 5.687 million metric tons. World canola imports in 2014-15 fell -12.7% to 12.736 million metric tons, world canola oil imports rose +8.6% to 4.173 million metric tons, and world canola meal imports fell -10.0% to 5.320 million metric tons. Regarding U.S. canola trade, U.S. canola imports in 2014-15 fell -3.5% to 900,000 metric tons and U.S. exports rose +13.9% to 180,000 metric tons.

World Production of Canola (Rapeseed)   In Thousands of Metric Tons

Year	Australia	Bangla-desh	Belarus	Canada	China	European Union	India	Pakistan	Romania	Russia	Ukraine	United States	World Total
2005-06	1,419	191	150	9,483	13,052	15,564	7,000	181	----	303	285	718	48,596
2006-07	573	189	115	9,000	10,966	16,112	5,800	221	----	523	606	633	45,024
2007-08	1,214	228	240	9,611	10,573	18,397	5,450	185	----	630	1,047	650	48,604
2008-09	1,844	203	514	12,644	12,102	19,062	6,700	199	----	752	2,873	656	57,861
2009-10	1,907	223	611	12,898	13,657	21,633	6,400	162	----	667	1,873	665	60,989
2010-11	2,359	246	374	12,789	13,082	20,782	7,100	192	----	670	1,470	1,112	60,558
2011-12	3,427	262	379	14,608	13,426	19,240	6,200	330	----	1,050	1,437	694	61,573
2012-13[1]	4,142	294	705	13,869	14,007	19,631	6,800	350	----	1,035	1,300	1,087	63,762
2013-14[2]	3,761	230	676	17,966	14,458	21,102	7,300	320	----	1,393	2,352	1,004	71,146
2014-15[3]	3,300	230	700	15,555	14,700	24,077	7,500	300	----	1,500	2,200	1,140	71,940

[1] Preliminary.   [2] Estimate.   [3] Forecast.   *Source: Economic Research Service, U.S. Department of Agriculture (ERS-USDA); The Oil World*

CANOLA

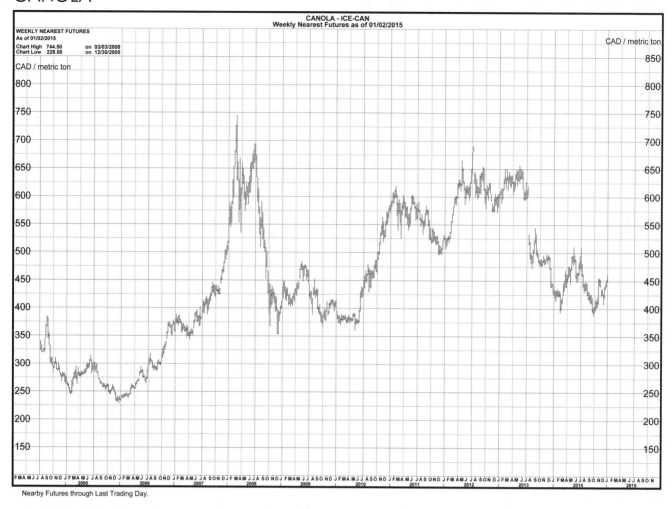

Nearby Futures through Last Trading Day.

Volume of Trading of Canola Futures in Winnipeg   In 20 Metric Ton Units

Year	Jan.	Feb.	Mar.	Apr.	May	June	July	Aug.	Sept.	Oct.	Nov.	Dec.	Total
2005	116,678	207,198	141,717	124,636	102,424	178,001	87,724	121,749	138,701	200,004	145,231	258,922	1,822,985
2006	195,189	240,070	237,537	229,470	211,688	238,967	129,433	145,133	212,164	284,033	191,676	291,994	2,607,354
2007	204,893	309,278	198,589	273,755	281,240	321,022	160,846	181,145	212,288	396,852	268,743	360,531	3,169,182
2008	368,963	388,180	307,536	318,641	209,631	290,152	172,089	170,596	220,479	293,978	126,273	265,670	3,132,188
2009	265,415	345,108	267,276	358,030	286,069	326,924	161,569	188,651	268,629	340,368	211,160	332,594	3,351,793
2010	239,347	349,512	283,156	415,932	232,711	534,781	200,250	277,736	351,663	500,943	284,703	447,694	4,118,428
2011	345,505	483,744	342,887	417,453	326,805	436,050	268,144	331,289	490,065	443,909	361,250	406,052	4,653,153
2012	375,738	588,006	536,743	535,291	367,014	399,329	299,775	279,962	332,661	487,242	279,767	388,733	4,870,261
2013	413,545	558,269	295,056	489,741	355,341	347,609	276,608	381,094	523,431	654,471	479,983	716,539	5,491,687
2014	536,669	570,465	454,015	552,959	369,170	424,087	331,748	298,308	486,457	615,158	346,000	568,304	5,553,340

Contract size = 20 tonnes.   *Source: ICE Futures Canada (ICE)*

Average Open Interest of Canola Futures in Winnipeg   In 20 Metric Ton Units

Year	Jan.	Feb.	Mar.	Apr.	May	June	July	Aug.	Sept.	Oct.	Nov.	Dec.
2005	64,147	75,090	65,205	63,514	54,341	53,390	57,706	56,305	65,700	68,186	66,117	87,246
2006	82,651	88,576	84,828	88,970	84,710	81,561	81,243	77,356	81,597	80,800	90,694	102,651
2007	103,317	103,250	94,001	102,050	114,244	124,321	117,967	111,470	121,589	122,965	146,879	156,698
2008	164,326	172,229	165,282	135,226	111,687	102,353	91,891	82,272	90,075	90,062	91,459	88,373
2009	88,487	100,072	97,016	104,423	111,922	109,921	94,574	104,426	95,168	99,968	93,108	99,736
2010	112,406	125,895	122,112	133,172	134,768	159,949	154,881	150,209	155,712	181,660	199,487	193,948
2011	204,715	207,186	188,138	176,678	166,554	166,105	150,624	166,066	188,592	166,852	160,276	140,345
2012	151,192	181,837	200,941	228,092	242,231	224,287	220,919	224,646	233,085	198,147	157,664	147,883
2013	155,134	189,913	178,763	164,200	143,013	129,283	118,115	145,257	186,811	177,248	200,975	226,220
2014	230,796	224,847	230,852	219,844	168,705	165,651	147,462	165,501	173,282	159,986	142,371	139,732

Contract size = 20 tonnes.   *Source: ICE Futures Canada (ICE)*

World Supply and Distribution of Canola and Products   In Thousands of Metric Tons

	Canola					Canola Meal					Canola oil				
Year	Pro-duction	Exports	Imports	Crush	Ending Stocks	Pro-duction	Exports	Imports	Con-sumption	Ending Stocks	Pro-duction	Exports	Imports	Con-sumption	Ending Stocks
2007-08	48,604	8,163	7,535	46,678	3,951	27,582	3,685	3,552	27,435	302	18,523	1,900	2,025	18,302	882
2008-09	57,861	12,126	12,114	52,024	7,284	30,687	3,579	3,577	30,734	253	20,610	2,441	2,442	20,370	1,123
2009-10	60,989	10,842	10,744	56,638	8,892	33,414	3,484	3,622	33,354	451	22,549	2,755	2,923	22,625	1,215
2010-11	60,558	10,867	10,099	58,864	7,400	34,599	5,099	4,973	34,415	509	23,470	3,423	3,332	23,462	1,132
2011-12	61,573	12,915	13,182	60,514	5,648	35,649	5,396	5,094	35,291	565	24,117	3,970	4,011	23,666	1,624
2012-13[1]	63,762	12,452	12,660	62,476	4,029	36,945	5,319	5,195	37,065	321	24,983	3,936	3,873	23,617	2,927
2013-14[2]	71,146	15,124	14,584	65,442	6,246	38,669	6,016	5,913	38,488	399	26,087	3,778	3,732	25,048	3,920
2014-15[3]	71,940	13,270	12,736	66,285	6,828	39,060	5,687	5,320	38,591	501	26,459	4,173	4,053	26,375	3,884

[1] Preliminary.   [2] Estimate.   [3] Forecast.   *Source: Economic Research Service, U.S. Department of Agriculture (ERS-USDA); The Oil World*

Salient Statistics of Canola and Canola Oil in the United States   In Thousands of Metric Tons

	Canola							Canola Oil						
	Supply				Disappearance			Supply				Disappearance		
Year	Stocks June 1	Pro-duction	Imports	Total Supply	Crush	Exports	Total[3]	Stocks Oct. 1	Pro-duction	Imports	Total Supply	Domestic	Exports	Total
2007-08	135	650	874	1,659	1,050	423	1,659	68	460	1,016	1,544	1,326	158	1,544
2008-09	158	656	825	1,639	1,218	191	1,639	60	501	1,050	1,611	1,284	249	1,611
2009-10	203	669	568	1,440	1,116	177	1,440	78	490	1,067	1,635	1,296	251	1,635
2010-11	122	1,113	482	1,717	1,304	294	1,717	88	524	1,421	2,033	1,665	232	2,033
2011-12	91	699	622	1,412	1,203	153	1,412	136	507	1,492	2,135	1,749	301	2,135
2012-13	29	1,112	394	1,535	1,251	177	1,535	85	576	1,252	1,913	1,634	215	1,913
2013-14[1]	80	1,004	933	2,017	1,700	158	2,017	64	739	1,495	2,298	2,037	136	2,298
2014-15[2]	124	1,329	900	2,353	1,928	180	2,353	125	811	1,550	2,486	2,202	210	2,486

[1] Preliminary.   [2] Forecast.   [3] Includes planting seed and residual.   *Source: Economic Research Service, U.S. Department of Agriculture (ERS-USDA)*

Wholesale Price of Canola Oil in Midwest   In Cents Per Pound

Year	Jan.	Feb.	Mar.	Apr.	May	June	July	Aug.	Sept.	Oct.	Nov.	Dec.	Average
2007	38.56	40.06	38.95	38.44	40.44	42.56	45.00	44.25	48.00	50.38	57.30	61.50	45.45
2008	64.94	71.80	70.56	71.38	73.05	76.69	74.13	61.05	54.88	42.85	39.81	37.19	61.53
2009	38.80	35.66	35.38	39.75	41.50	42.38	39.80	42.00	39.31	41.55	44.38	42.90	40.28
2010	40.56	41.88	42.50	42.20	40.00	40.00	44.00	47.19	47.38	51.45	53.63	58.25	45.75
2011	59.50	60.13	60.25	62.05	60.19	59.56	60.70	60.00	58.45	56.81	56.13	55.40	59.10
2012	55.06	56.94	59.10	60.94	55.88	54.10	57.44	58.75	59.75	57.50	58.20	57.13	57.57
2013	57.19	59.38	58.95	60.44	60.45	57.50	53.25	48.05	46.00	44.88	45.05	42.63	52.81
2014[1]	39.75	42.56	45.75	47.63	47.50	46.00	43.63	40.10	38.94	39.45	38.94	39.25	42.46

[1] Preliminary.   *Source: Economic Research Service, U.S. Department of Agriculture (ERS-USDA)*

Average Price of Canola in Vancouver   In Canadian Dollars Per Metric Ton

Year	Jan.	Feb.	Mar.	Apr.	May	June	July	Aug.	Sept.	Oct.	Nov.	Dec.	Average
2007	354.09	357.65	350.26	348.36	357.87	368.11	372.55	380.70	401.35	402.61	417.23	453.82	380.38
2008	519.88	608.92	618.85	594.74	578.47	616.27	601.79	517.00	457.86	391.62	399.41	371.48	523.02
2009	413.77	416.13	409.67	428.95	459.08	461.29	422.69	429.38	394.03	377.19	377.74	389.42	414.95
2010	376.26	373.42	374.40	377.22	372.83	400.29	439.34	443.06	453.22	481.16	514.84	542.25	429.02
2011	567.16	577.71	558.19	569.44	555.48	574.44	563.30	547.52	528.64	509.52	513.06	502.88	547.28
2012	512.75	539.92	591.55	626.52	624.60	629.57	657.26	632.65	644.75	627.09	594.75	601.67	606.92
2013	613.04	636.36	635.99	641.70	643.47	626.04	571.91	513.54	473.76	457.25	461.44	418.96	557.79
2014	386.37	380.71	412.23	435.66	459.42	453.37	446.33	430.27	397.71	404.23	423.82	419.92	420.84

Source: ICE Futures Canada (ICE)

Average Wholesale Price of Canola Meal, 36% Pacific Northwest   In Dollars Per Short Ton

Year	Oct.	Nov.	Dec.	Jan.	Feb.	Mar.	Apr.	May	June	July	Aug.	Sept.	Average
2007-08	167.24	192.25	226.30	276.78	285.83	276.85	268.14	258.75	293.20	310.19	239.88	220.42	251.32
2008-09	192.55	217.99	228.62	279.23	243.30	217.02	230.06	287.99	325.48	261.55	277.30	224.74	248.82
2009-10	220.90	177.69	NA	248.63	218.18	214.11	226.95	222.28	224.56	245.18	244.44	231.20	224.92
2010-11	251.03	257.73	265.54	275.80	261.20	260.32	254.68	267.82	263.45	277.55	271.04	257.34	263.63
2011-12	238.70	235.20	NA	253.98	257.63	277.83	313.38	333.69	335.26	378.86	388.13	370.79	307.59
2012-13	354.49	334.46	349.55	347.22	359.23	356.74	340.42	362.51	376.19	374.89	340.44	354.55	354.22
2013-14	334.95	342.86	373.60	365.48	384.21	383.68	398.39	407.14	387.65	317.81	303.74	316.94	359.70
2014-15[1]	301.75	356.31	349.31	311.56									329.73

[1] Preliminary.   *Source: Economic Research Service, U.S. Department of Agriculture (ERS-USDA)*

Cattle and Calves

The beef cycle begins with the cow-calf operation, which breeds the new calves. Most ranchers breed their herds of cows in summer, thus producing the new crop of calves in spring (the gestation period is about nine months). This allows the calves to be born during the milder weather of spring and provides the calves with ample forage through the summer and early autumn. The calves are weaned from the mother after 6-8 months and most are then moved into the "stocker" operation. The calves usually spend 6-10 months in the stocker operation, growing to near full-sized by foraging for summer grass or winter wheat. When the cattle reach 600-800 pounds, they are typically sent to a feedlot and become "feeder cattle." In the feedlot, the cattle are fed a special food mix to encourage rapid weight gain. The mix includes grain (corn, milo, or wheat), a protein supplement (soybean, cottonseed, or linseed meal), and roughage (alfalfa, silage, prairie hay, or an agricultural by-product such as sugar beet pulp). The animal is considered "finished" when it reaches full weight and is ready for slaughter, typically at around 1,200 pounds, which produces a dressed carcass of around 745 pounds. After reaching full weight, the cattle are sold for slaughter to a meat packing plant. Futures and options on live cattle and feeder cattle are traded at the CME Group. Both the live and feeder cattle futures contracts trade in terms of cents per pound.

Prices – CME live cattle futures prices (Barchart.com electronic symbol LE) began 2014 at a then-record high of $1.34500 per pound and continued higher to post a new record $1.53000 a pound in Feb 2014 as cattle supplies remained tight. The USDA's semiannual cattle inventory report released on Jan 31, 2014 showed that the U.S. cattle herd shrank by 1.8% yr/yr as of Jan 1, 2014 to a 63-year low of 87.7 million head. The USDA estimated that U.S. 2014 beef output would fall 5.3% yr/yr to 24.43 billion pounds, the lowest since 1994, as cattle supplies were still reeling from the 2012 drought in the Great Plains that prompted cattle ranchers to cull their herds. Cattle prices then fell back to the low for the year of $1.35400 in May 2014 as record-high retail beef prices decimated domestic beef consumption. The sell-off in cattle prices was short-lived, however, as beef supplies remained tight and cattle prices rallied into Oct 2014 and posted a record high $1.71975 a pound, the highest since cattle futures trading began in 1964. Fewer cattle were coming to market, which kept beef supplies low, as the Sep 2014 Cattle on Feed report showed feedlot cattle sales, or marketings, totaled 1.69 million head as of August 31, 2014, down -9.6% yr/yr and the lowest for an August since data began in 1996. Domestic beef demand was sharply curtailed due to record high prices and cattle prices fell back the rest of the year and finished 2014 up +23.2% yr/yr at $1.65700 a pound.

Supply – The world's number of cattle as of January 1, 2014 rose +3.8% to 1.029 million head. As of January 1, 2014 the number of cattle and calves on farms in the U.S. fell -0.9% to 88.526 million, which was the lowest level since the 1952 figure of 88.072. World production of beef and veal in 2014 rose by +0.3% to 59.598 million metric tons (carcass weight equivalent). The USDA is forecasting that world production in 2015 will fall by -0.1% to 18.739 million metric tons in 2014. U.S. commercial production of beef in 2015 is predicted to fall -1.7% to 23.830 billion pounds.

Demand – World consumption of beef and veal in 2014 rose +0.2% to 57.834 million metric tons. The USDA is forecasting a -0.2% decline in world consumption of beef and veal in 2015 to 56.884 million metric tons. U.S. consumption of beef and veal in 2014 fell -3.4% to 11.215 million metric tons. The USDA is forecasting a drop in U.S. consumption of beef and veal of -2.4% in 2015 to 10.944 million metric tons.

Trade – U.S. imports of live cattle in 2014 rose +11.8% to 2.272 million head. U.S. exports of live cattle in 2014 fell -35.0% yr/yr to 107,172 head, below the 2011 record high of 194,108 head. By weight, U.S. imports of beef in 2015 are projected to fall -5.2% to 2.700 billion pounds. U.S. exports of beef in 2015 are projected to fall -2.3% to 2.525 billion pounds, just below the 2011 record high of 2.779 billion pounds.

World Cattle and Buffalo Numbers as of January 1   In Thousands of Head

Year	Argentina	Australia	Brazil	Canada	China	European Union	India	Mexico	Russia	South Africa	Ukraine	United States	World Total (Mil. Head)
2006	54,266	28,183	172,111	14,655	109,908	90,364	293,000	23,669	21,625	13,790	6,514	96,342	1,024.2
2007	55,664	28,393	173,830	14,135	104,651	89,329	298,000	23,316	21,562	13,934	6,175	96,573	1,023.1
2008	55,662	28,037	175,437	13,755	105,948	89,899	304,418	22,850	21,546	14,082	5,491	96,035	1,025.3
2009	54,260	27,321	179,540	13,030	105,760	90,408	306,000	22,666	21,040	14,195	5,079	94,721	1,017.2
2010	49,057	27,906	185,159	12,670	107,265	89,829	304,500	22,192	20,677	----	4,827	94,081	998.1
2011	48,156	27,550	190,925	12,155	106,264	87,831	302,500	21,456	19,970	----	4,494	92,887	991.0
2012	49,597	28,506	197,550	12,245	103,605	87,054	300,000	20,090	20,134	----	4,426	91,160	989.2
2013	51,095	29,000	203,273	12,305	103,434	87,106	299,606	18,521	19,930	----	4,646	90,095	991.9
2014[1]	51,545	29,290	207,960	12,220	103,000	87,645	300,600	17,760	19,564	----	4,534	87,730	1,029.3
2015[2]	51,695	27,600	212,700	11,950	102,950	88,050	301,100	17,175	19,000	----	4,100	87,750	

[1] Preliminary.   [2] Forecast.   *Source: Foreign Agricultural Service, U.S. Department of Agriculture (FAS-USDA)*

Cattle Supply and Distribution in the United States   In Thousands of Head

Year	Cattle & Calves on Farms Jan. 1	Imports	Calves Born	Total Supply	Federally Inspected	Other[3]	All Commercial	Farm	Total Slaughter	Deaths on Farms	Exports	Total Disappearance
2005	95,438	1,816	37,575	134,829	32,549	573	33,122	189	33,311	4,052	22	37,385
2006	96,342	2,289	37,016	135,646	33,844	566	34,410	187	34,597	4,167	50	38,813
2007	96,573	2,495	36,759	135,827	34,465	557	35,022	187	35,209	4,251	66	39,526
2008	96,035	2,284	36,153	134,471	34,747	574	35,322	186	35,507	4,074	107	39,688
2009	94,521	2,002	35,939	132,462	33,696	587	34,283	185	34,468	4,064	58	38,590
2010	93,881	2,284	35,695	131,860	34,566	561	35,128	197	35,325	4,001	91	39,417
2011	92,682	2,107	35,313	130,103	34,394	546	34,939	169	35,108	4,017	194	39,319
2012	90,769	2,285	34,279	127,333	33,185	538	33,723	151	33,874	3,881	192	37,947
2013[1]	89,300	2,032	33,730	125,062	32,698	523	33,221				165	
2014[2]	88,526	2,360	33,900	124,786	30,242						108	

[1] Preliminary.   [2] Estimate.   [3] Wholesale and retail.   *Source: Economic Research Service, U.S. Department of Agriculture (ERS-USDA)*

Beef Supply and Utilization in the United States

Years and Quarters	Beginning Stocks	Commercial	Total	Imports	Total Supply	Exports	Ending Stocks	Total Disappearance	Carcass Weight	Retail Weight Total
2011	----	26,195	26,195	2,057	28,252	2,785	----	----	----	57.3
I	----	6,410	6,410	461	6,871	633	----	----	----	14.1
II	----	6,559	6,559	593	7,152	702	----	----	----	14.6
III	----	6,736	6,736	548	7,284	766	----	----	----	14.7
IV	----	6,490	6,490	454	6,944	683	----	----	----	14.0
2012	----	25,913	25,913	2,220	28,133	2,452	----	----	----	57.4
I	----	6,282	6,282	582	6,864	558	----	----	----	14.0
II	----	6,473	6,473	669	7,142	624	----	----	----	14.7
III	----	6,586	6,586	516	7,102	650	----	----	----	14.5
IV	----	6,572	6,572	453	7,025	620	----	----	----	14.2
2013	----	25,720	25,720	2,250	27,970	2,590	----	----	----	56.3
I	----	6,175	6,175	590	6,765	557	----	----	----	13.7
II	----	6,513	6,513	629	7,142	637	----	----	----	14.5
III	----	6,609	6,609	515	7,124	716	----	----	----	14.3
IV	----	6,423	6,423	516	6,939	680	----	----	----	13.9
2014[1]	----	24,249	24,249	2,848	27,097	2,584	----	----	----	54.3
I	----	5,868	5,868	596	6,464	583	----	----	----	13.1
II	----	6,183	6,183	768	6,951	667	----	----	----	14.0
III	----	6,178	6,178	764	6,942	679	----	----	----	13.7
IV	----	6,020	6,020	720	6,740	655	----	----	----	13.5
2015[2]	----	23,830	23,830	2,700	26,530	2,525	----	----	----	52.7
I	----	5,685	5,685	645	6,330	575	----	----	----	12.8
II	----	6,225	6,225	725	6,950	650	----	----	----	13.8
III	----	5,955	5,955	725	6,680	675	----	----	----	13.1
IV	----	5,965	5,965		5,965	625	----	----	----	13.1

[1] Preliminary.   [2] Forecast.   *Source: Economic Research Service, U.S. Department of Agriculture (ERS-USDA)*

United States Cattle on Feed in 13 States   In Thousands of Head

Year	Number on Feed[3]	Placed on Feed	Marketings	Other Disappearance	Year	Number on Feed[3]	Placed on Feed	Marketings	Other Disappearance
2011	11,513	23,812	22,577	887	2013[1]	11,172	21,860	21,618	849
I	11,513	5,470	5,555	171	I	11,172	5,191	5,219	220
II	11,257	5,290	5,901	213	II	10,924	5,326	5,643	232
III	10,433	6,850	5,784	217	III	10,375	5,444	5,533	176
IV	11,282	6,202	5,337	286	IV	10,110	5,899	5,223	221
2012	11,861	22,254	22,028	915	2014[2]	10,523	21,445	20,464	903
I	11,861	5,353	5,489	243	I	10,523	5,472	4,997	207
II	11,482	5,269	5,797	244	II	10,873	5,003	5,490	259
III	10,710	5,933	5,466	188	III	10,127	5,287	5,162	194
IV	10,989	5,699	5,276	240	IV	10,058	5,683	4,815	243

[1] Preliminary.   [2] Estimate.   [3] Beginning of period.   *Source: Economic Research Service, U.S. Department of Agriculture (ERS-USDA)*

CATTLE AND CALVES

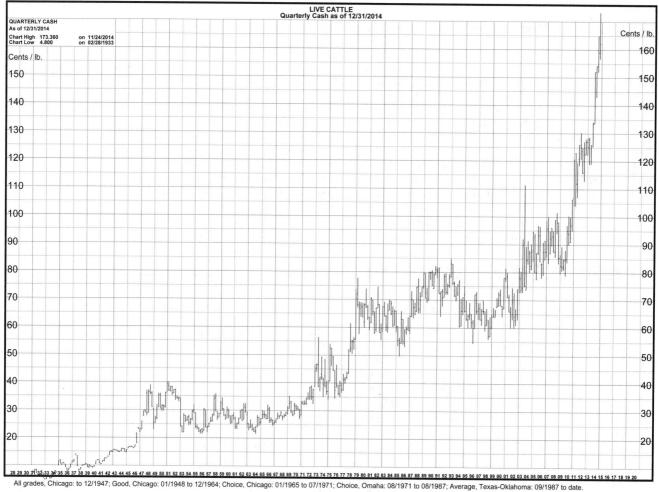

All grades, Chicago: to 12/1947; Good, Chicago: 01/1948 to 12/1964; Choice, Chicago: 01/1965 to 07/1971; Choice, Omaha: 08/1971 to 08/1987; Average, Texas-Oklahoma: 09/1987 to date.

United States Cattle on Feed, 1000+ Capacity Feedlots, on First of Month   In Thousands of Head

Year	Jan.	Feb.	Mar.	Apr.	May	June	July	Aug.	Sept.	Oct.	Nov.	Dec.
2005	11,299	11,342	11,154	10,873	10,641	10,771	10,394	10,093	10,000	10,482	11,473	11,726
2006	11,804	12,110	12,023	11,812	11,559	11,187	10,872	10,822	10,986	11,385	11,969	11,973
2007	11,974	11,726	11,599	11,644	11,297	11,272	10,737	10,299	10,302	10,967	11,769	12,099
2008	12,092	11,966	11,853	11,684	11,135	10,815	10,295	9,869	9,997	10,415	10,972	11,346
2009	11,234	11,288	11,228	11,162	10,822	10,407	9,752	9,637	9,900	10,474	11,134	11,277
2010	10,983	10,959	10,849	10,742	10,428	10,495	10,071	9,880	10,181	10,788	11,497	11,620
2011	11,513	11,571	11,386	11,257	11,175	10,902	10,433	10,579	10,700	11,282	11,889	12,055
2012	11,861	11,811	11,677	11,482	11,110	11,077	10,710	10,656	10,647	10,989	11,254	11,348
2013	11,172	11,070	10,845	10,924	10,760	10,767	10,375	10,025	9,876	10,110	10,585	10,724
2014[1]	10,523	10,678	10,790	10,873	10,648	10,594	10,127	9,837	9,799	10,058	10,633	10,873

[1] Preliminary.   *Source: Economic Research Service, U.S. Department of Agriculture (ERS-USDA)*

United States Cattle Placed on Feed, 1000+ Capacity Feedlots   In Thousands of Head

Year	Jan.	Feb.	Mar.	Apr.	May	June	July	Aug.	Sept.	Oct.	Nov.	Dec.	Total
2005	1,888	1,523	1,750	1,660	2,223	1,769	1,678	1,993	2,355	2,788	2,045	1,884	23,556
2006	2,199	1,588	1,837	1,619	1,903	1,946	1,958	2,290	2,227	2,430	1,884	1,714	23,595
2007	1,690	1,659	1,960	1,568	2,159	1,657	1,622	2,119	2,415	2,725	2,125	1,701	23,400
2008	1,787	1,723	1,736	1,536	1,900	1,518	1,656	2,061	2,281	2,438	2,016	1,647	22,299
2009	1,858	1,678	1,808	1,600	1,638	1,391	1,863	2,119	2,388	2,474	1,844	1,526	22,187
2010	1,822	1,674	1,856	1,634	2,030	1,628	1,758	2,271	2,463	2,505	1,959	1,789	23,389
2011	1,889	1,667	1,914	1,785	1,810	1,695	2,135	2,246	2,469	2,492	2,037	1,673	23,812
2012	1,847	1,714	1,792	1,521	2,084	1,664	1,922	2,007	2,004	2,180	1,943	1,576	22,254
2013	1,869	1,438	1,884	1,720	2,055	1,551	1,684	1,772	1,988	2,378	1,867	1,654	21,860
2014[1]	2,014	1,650	1,808	1,636	1,912	1,455	1,560	1,720	2,007	2,357	1,789	1,537	21,445

[1] Preliminary.   *Source: Economic Research Service, U.S. Department of Agriculture (ERS-USDA)*

CATTLE, LIVE - CME
Weekly Selected Futures as of 01/02/2015

WEEKLY SELECTED FUTURES
As of 01/02/2015

Chart High 171.975 on 10/31/2014
Chart Low 73.450 on 05/01/2006

Nearby Futures through Last Trading Day.

United States Cattle Marketings, 1000+ Capacity Feedlots[2]   In Thousands of Head

Year	Jan.	Feb.	Mar.	Apr.	May	June	July	Aug.	Sept.	Oct.	Nov.	Dec.	Total
2005	1,772	1,634	1,963	1,801	1,997	2,083	1,918	2,033	1,816	1,739	1,701	1,715	22,172
2006	1,810	1,602	1,958	1,785	2,160	2,198	1,950	2,067	1,760	1,765	1,797	1,625	22,477
2007	1,841	1,711	1,843	1,816	2,085	2,140	1,999	2,066	1,696	1,876	1,738	1,650	22,461
2008	1,853	1,776	1,842	2,010	2,140	1,978	2,037	1,884	1,812	1,814	1,575	1,683	22,404
2009	1,737	1,682	1,824	1,871	1,952	1,989	1,935	1,800	1,767	1,755	1,635	1,745	21,692
2010	1,776	1,716	1,903	1,857	1,865	1,997	1,901	1,923	1,802	1,734	1,774	1,830	22,078
2011	1,774	1,791	1,990	1,807	2,002	2,092	1,918	2,053	1,813	1,787	1,774	1,776	22,577
2012	1,816	1,755	1,918	1,815	2,017	1,965	1,913	1,955	1,598	1,837	1,761	1,678	22,028
2013	1,892	1,603	1,724	1,815	1,948	1,880	1,970	1,871	1,692	1,827	1,660	1,736	21,618
2014[1]	1,788	1,549	1,660	1,778	1,865	1,847	1,787	1,692	1,683	1,685	1,475	1,655	20,464

[1] Preliminary.   *Source: Economic Research Service, U.S. Department of Agriculture (ERS-USDA)*

Quarterly Trade of Live Cattle in the United States   In Head

	Imports					Exports				
Year	First Quarter	Second Quarter	Third Quarter	Fourth Quarter	Total	First Quarter	Second Quarter	Third Quarter	Fourth Quarter	Total
2005	336,216	348,368	342,661	788,293	1,815,538	5,580	6,446	5,977	3,604	21,607
2006	708,680	470,176	418,117	691,870	2,288,843	8,721	12,473	10,249	18,235	49,678
2007	629,157	518,173	462,359	885,276	2,494,965	13,723	15,112	10,441	27,107	66,383
2008	682,174	562,566	405,199	634,054	2,283,993	38,319	30,581	15,175	23,417	107,492
2009	612,188	423,742	342,988	622,956	2,001,874	6,903	18,153	16,354	16,613	58,023
2010	598,853	596,339	406,926	681,767	2,283,885	15,526	20,853	17,552	37,159	91,090
2011	580,696	488,356	376,602	661,649	2,107,303	35,446	41,142	45,749	71,771	194,108
2012	672,937	650,291	326,656	635,155	2,285,039	41,926	45,955	36,497	67,300	191,678
2013	590,946	475,884	311,315	653,841	2,031,986	32,040	51,163	39,512	42,093	164,808
2014[1]	600,761	563,169	415,309	780,517	2,359,756	27,590	25,995	25,818	28,338	107,741

[1] Preliminary.   *Source: Economic Research Service, U.S. Department of Agriculture (ERS-USDA)*

CATTLE AND CALVES

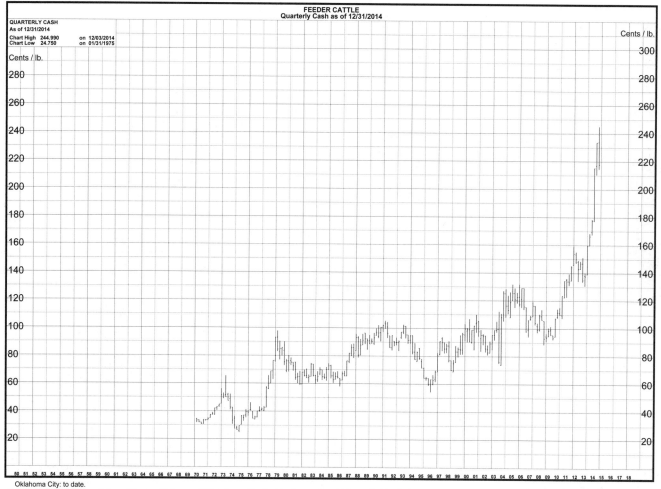

FEEDER CATTLE
Quarterly Cash as of 12/31/2014

QUARTERLY CASH
As of 12/31/2014

Chart High 244.990 on 12/03/2014
Chart Low 24.750 on 01/31/1975

Cents / lb.

Oklahoma City: to date.

Average Slaughter Steer Price, Choice 2-4, Nebraska Direct (1100-1300 Lb.) In Dollars Per 100 Pounds

Year	Jan.	Feb.	Mar.	Apr.	May	June	July	Aug.	Sept.	Oct.	Nov.	Dec.	Average
2008	88.63	90.85	89.28	89.04	93.86	95.55	98.83	99.14	97.37	90.61	90.40	83.66	92.27
2009	81.60	79.68	81.66	87.02	85.27	81.31	82.72	82.48	83.13	83.53	83.43	80.34	82.68
2010	83.46	87.41	92.93	99.58	97.93	92.25	93.12	96.42	97.22	97.85	99.89	102.30	95.03
2011	105.12	109.50	116.81	119.80	111.42	109.00	110.87	114.17	117.17	121.25	124.76	122.80	115.22
2012	123.73	125.74	127.16	122.26	122.07	119.27	114.95	119.50	125.14	125.61	125.75	125.65	123.07
2013	124.33	125.47	126.33	128.08	126.48	121.70	120.41	123.78	124.23	130.09	132.23	131.18	126.19
2014	143.33	146.45	151.93	149.01	146.19	149.55	158.57	158.35	159.86	164.91	170.04	163.09	155.11

Source: Economic Research Service, U.S. Department of Agriculture (ERS-USDA)

Average Price of Feeder Steers in Oklahoma City   In Dollars Per 100 Pounds

Year	Jan.	Feb.	Mar.	Apr.	May	June	July	Aug.	Sept.	Oct.	Nov.	Dec.	Average
2008	98.62	102.81	100.17	100.45	107.08	108.90	111.07	112.53	109.69	98.84	95.76	90.76	103.06
2009	95.57	93.19	92.47	98.05	99.58	97.74	100.65	100.39	97.75	93.56	93.33	93.29	96.30
2010	96.25	100.06	103.82	112.43	111.44	109.75	112.68	113.53	111.92	109.65	112.58	119.32	109.45
2011	125.33	127.22	130.02	133.94	128.32	126.90	136.72	134.25	132.02	137.54	142.47	144.22	133.25
2012	150.15	155.24	155.34	150.24	149.53	152.85	140.49	138.43	142.56	144.22	144.25	147.32	147.55
2013	147.99	142.75	136.98	136.75	133.75	135.73	144.26	152.68	156.92	161.92	165.05	166.20	148.41
2014	170.98	170.61	174.43	178.55	185.49	201.90	216.19	221.28	228.15	239.59	240.37	233.67	205.10

Source: Economic Research Service, U.S. Department of Agriculture (ERS-USDA)

Federally Inspected Slaughter of Cattle in the United States   In Thousands of Head

Year	Jan.	Feb.	Mar.	Apr.	May	June	July	Aug.	Sept.	Oct.	Nov.	Dec.	Total
2008	2,847	2,598	2,684	2,914	3,095	2,912	3,017	2,866	2,842	2,933	2,475	2,623	33,805
2009	2,668	2,479	2,681	2,724	2,806	2,936	2,878	2,738	2,766	2,829	2,556	2,704	32,765
2010	2,657	2,503	2,864	2,802	2,743	3,004	2,860	2,912	2,851	2,809	2,830	2,868	33,702
2011	2,687	2,580	2,913	2,678	2,778	3,058	2,728	3,053	2,830	2,804	2,739	2,706	33,555
2012	2,666	2,515	2,713	2,528	2,836	2,826	2,755	2,952	2,497	2,897	2,740	2,500	32,425
2013	2,785	2,315	2,545	2,689	2,823	2,693	2,856	2,778	2,568	2,851	2,527	2,518	31,947
2014[1]	2,634	2,204	2,413	2,556	2,597	2,568	2,562	2,463	2,490	2,591	2,210	2,398	29,684

[1] Preliminary.   *Source: National Agricultural Statistics Service, U.S. Department of Agriculture (NASS-USDA)*

CATTLE, FEEDER - CME
Weekly Nearest Futures as of 01/02/2015

WEEKLY NEAREST FUTURES
As of 01/02/2015

Chart High 245.200 on 10/09/2014
Chart Low 85.450 on 12/05/2008

Nearby Futures through Last Trading Day using Selected contract months: February, April, June, August, October and December.

Volume of Trading of Live Cattle Futures Chicago   In Thousands of Contracts

Year	Jan.	Feb.	Mar.	Apr.	May	June	July	Aug.	Sept.	Oct.	Nov.	Dec.	Total
2005	519.8	395.8	598.2	377.5	503.8	405.7	506.3	406.0	569.0	438.6	627.6	485.3	5,833.6
2006	783.0	498.8	849.5	570.0	817.5	709.7	718.8	670.4	698.3	631.9	757.8	504.0	8,209.7
2007	907.2	663.1	1,046.7	575.8	814.4	513.7	849.1	634.5	724.5	638.9	773.9	558.4	8,588.0
2008	982.6	596.4	954.2	724.4	936.2	731.3	1,006.4	738.2	998.2	801.1	773.9	558.4	9,801.4
2009	819.5	616.8	789.3	641.3	721.5	617.8	855.4	657.9	854.6	739.7	844.3	638.9	8,797.0
2010	901.0	782.9	1,167.2	863.2	1,204.5	785.8	923.8	868.3	1,158.8	827.1	1,066.3	783.9	11,332.7
2011	1,181.8	910.9	1,531.6	928.4	1,293.3	1,097.4	1,148.8	1,034.4	1,325.4	1,067.2	1,136.1	877.4	13,532.6
2012	1,179.7	1,078.3	1,516.9	1,180.1	1,399.6	1,022.4	1,293.1	1,097.1	1,185.9	977.2	1,090.4	964.8	13,985.4
2013	1,484.1	1,069.5	1,249.3	977.9	1,189.7	831.3	1,020.8	884.5	972.5	1,040.2	986.9	756.2	12,463.0
2014	1,381.4	970.0	1,270.2	847.7	1,139.3	1,126.6	1,503.5	1,023.5	1,303.4	1,061.5	962.5	1,009.4	13,599.1

Contract size = 40,000 lbs.   *Source: CME Group; Chicago Mercantile Exchange (CME)*

Average Open Interest of Live Cattle Futures in Chicago   In Contracts

Year	Jan.	Feb.	Mar.	Apr.	May	June	July	Aug.	Sept.	Oct.	Nov.	Dec.
2005	142,333	140,869	146,062	141,610	145,235	133,768	135,971	134,329	148,094	167,175	174,496	197,090
2006	225,313	220,947	220,042	240,567	261,496	235,783	231,914	213,918	214,583	205,776	211,814	224,501
2007	257,373	273,121	296,235	281,239	261,866	240,526	235,110	212,154	234,754	234,584	240,710	241,614
2008	252,555	273,397	276,043	285,956	298,370	298,937	300,862	278,808	265,436	227,860	215,054	211,836
2009	207,768	203,912	207,221	206,462	204,424	211,978	222,562	233,578	251,083	260,285	266,293	262,738
2010	276,265	294,225	343,951	362,939	362,895	327,910	323,477	339,349	344,298	317,349	321,039	332,858
2011	344,671	358,852	366,250	380,138	346,614	326,592	322,313	309,147	324,714	336,225	325,195	315,700
2012	333,921	350,623	358,333	351,179	337,579	318,041	305,336	290,534	294,356	289,303	327,964	331,211
2013	329,529	330,784	335,436	325,462	315,201	290,113	275,925	289,980	295,826	314,058	333,154	323,189
2014	354,327	371,310	369,611	352,639	345,372	352,223	343,096	313,046	315,722	313,134	317,289	286,556

Contract size = 40,000 lbs.   *Source: CME Group; Chicago Mercantile Exchange (CME)*

CATTLE AND CALVES

Beef Steer-Corn Price Ratio[1] in the United States

Year	Jan.	Feb.	Mar.	Apr.	May	June	July	Aug.	Sept.	Oct.	Nov.	Dec.	Average
2007	29.4	26.6	28.5	29.4	28.1	26.4	28.0	29.4	30.0	29.4	27.9	25.3	28.2
2008	23.5	20.8	19.8	17.9	18.2	17.6	19.0	19.0	19.8	21.3	21.3	20.9	19.9
2009	19.7	21.7	21.8	22.9	22.1	21.2	23.7	25.6	26.3	23.4	23.4	23.3	22.9
2010	23.9	25.5	27.0	29.6	28.6	27.8	27.5	26.9	24.4	22.9	22.2	21.6	25.7
2011	22.3	19.6	21.3	19.2	18.2	17.2	18.2	16.6	18.3	21.3	21.6	21.5	19.6
2012	21.4	20.9	20.8	20.2	19.7	19.5	16.4	15.7	18.1	18.7	18.3	18.6	19.0
2013	18.7	17.8	17.8	18.2	18.2	17.8	17.8	19.6	23.0	27.6	30.2	29.9	21.4
2014[1]	31.7	33.3	33.3	31.8	31.2	33.0	38.8	43.8	45.4	45.8	47.2	43.9	38.3

[1] Bushels of corn equal in value to 100 pounds of steers and heifers. [2] Preliminary. *Source: Economic Research Service, U.S. Department of Agriculture*

Farm Value, Income and Wholesale Prices of Cattle and Calves in the United States

	----- January 1 -----		Gross Income From C & C[2]	At Omaha				Feeder Heifers at Oklahoma	Cows, Boning Utility	Cows, Commercial	-- Wholesale Prices, Central U.S. --		Cow[6],
	Per Head Dollars	Total Million $	Million $	------- Steers -------		----- Heifers[4] -----					Choice	Select	Canner,
Year				Choice	Select	Select	Choice	City[5]	Sioux Falls[6]	Sioux Falls	700-850 lb.	700-850 lb.	Cutter
					Dollars per 100 Pounds								
2008	990	95,113	48,934	93.07	----	----	93.04	96.85	57.75	54.92	153.17	147.68	54.92
2009	872	82,436	44,261	82.70	----	----	82.71	90.49	50.87	47.94	140.77	135.70	46.00
2010	832	78,150	51,936	95.81	----	----	95.41	104.22	NA	NA	156.91	150.99	56.10
2011	947	87,786	63,467	111.52	----	----	111.55	125.56	NA	NA	181.29	173.31	68.30
2012	1,111	100,817	68,491	123.11	----	----	124.18	137.38	NA	NA	190.65	180.42	77.71
2013[1]	1,139	101,732		127.13	----	----	127.37	140.29	NA	NA	195.86	185.76	77.56
2014[1]					----	----		198.15	NA	NA	239.32	230.75	102.24

[1] Preliminary. [2] Excludes interfarm sales & Gov't. payments. Cash receipts from farm marketings + value of farm home consumption.
[3] 1,000 to 1,100 lb. [4] 1,000 to 1,200 lb. [5] 700 to 750 lb. [6] All weights.
Source: Economic Research Service, U.S. Department of Agriculture (NASS-USDA)

Average Price Received by Farmers for Beef Cattle in the United States   In Dollars Per 100 Pounds

Year	Jan.	Feb.	Mar.	Apr.	May	June	July	Aug.	Sept.	Oct.	Nov.	Dec.	Average
2007	84.30	86.10	91.60	93.70	92.80	88.80	89.00	91.40	93.10	90.90	89.90	89.20	90.07
2008	87.30	89.00	87.80	86.80	91.30	91.90	95.00	95.80	94.20	87.40	84.30	79.70	89.21
2009	80.10	78.90	79.10	83.80	83.20	80.10	80.90	80.40	80.50	79.20	79.60	78.50	80.36
2010	82.10	85.70	90.40	95.60	94.70	90.40	91.70	93.50	94.10	93.10	94.00	98.10	91.95
2011	107.00	108.00	115.00	119.00	112.00	107.00	111.00	111.00	112.00	117.00	120.00	120.00	113.25
2012	125.00	127.00	128.00	124.00	122.00	121.00	114.00	117.00	121.00	123.00	123.00	124.00	122.42
2013	126.00	123.00	125.00	125.00	126.00	122.00	120.00	121.00	122.00	127.00	130.00	130.00	124.75
2014[1]	138.00	144.00	148.00	148.00	146.00	147.00	156.00	158.00	157.00	161.00	167.00	164.00	152.83

[1] Preliminary. *Source: National Agricultural Statistics Service, U.S. Department of Agriculture (NASS-USDA)*

Average Price Received by Farmers for Calves in the United States   In Dollars Per 100 Pounds

Year	Jan.	Feb.	Mar.	Apr.	May	June	July	Aug.	Sept.	Oct.	Nov.	Dec.	Average
2007	115.00	114.00	122.00	125.00	124.00	124.00	126.00	127.00	126.00	123.00	122.00	120.00	122.33
2008	117.00	120.00	118.00	116.00	120.00	118.00	114.00	117.00	113.00	106.00	105.00	98.90	113.58
2009	106.00	104.00	106.00	109.00	111.00	109.00	108.00	108.00	105.00	103.00	104.00	105.00	106.50
2010	109.00	113.00	117.00	124.00	124.00	122.00	122.00	123.00	118.00	121.00	125.00	130.00	120.67
2011	136.00	139.00	148.00	147.00	137.00	133.00	138.00	134.00	132.00	145.00	153.00	157.00	141.58
2012	169.00	184.00	184.00	178.00	176.00	166.00	144.00	155.00	162.00	164.00	161.00	163.00	167.17
2013	168.00	170.00	163.00	159.00	157.00	152.00	162.00	178.00	200.00	190.00	192.00	197.00	174.00
2014[1]	208.00	209.00	216.00	222.00	229.00	249.00	257.00	271.00	279.00	307.00	305.00	303.00	254.58

[1] Preliminary. *Source: National Agricultural Statistics Board, U.S. Department of Agriculture (NASS-USDA)*

Federally Inspected Slaughter of Calves and Vealers in the United States   In Thousands of Head

Year	Jan.	Feb.	Mar.	Apr.	May	June	July	Aug.	Sept.	Oct.	Nov.	Dec.	Total
2007	73.3	65.6	69.6	55.8	58.0	60.3	61.7	64.5	54.8	63.7	57.5	59.9	744.7
2008	70.4	67.9	69.9	72.2	70.0	74.2	86.7	78.1	86.1	93.9	79.7	92.8	941.9
2009	83.6	73.0	78.8	67.1	64.2	76.0	78.9	75.6	79.9	82.2	80.0	91.1	930.4
2010	81.6	72.9	78.8	67.4	59.1	67.3	74.1	74.8	70.0	70.0	71.7	76.6	864.3
2011	70.8	67.9	71.8	57.9	60.0	71.5	72.4	78.9	72.5	71.5	71.9	71.8	838.9
2012	66.6	59.3	58.5	55.4	58.2	55.0	66.5	71.6	63.2	71.6	69.4	64.5	759.8
2013	69.9	58.7	61.6	57.7	57.6	56.7	69.1	63.5	62.0	68.5	59.7	65.8	750.8
2014[1]	62.0	51.5	52.9	48.0	45.9	44.6	47.8	43.0	41.8	42.6	35.2	42.2	557.5

[1] Preliminary. *Source: Crop Reporting Board, U.S. Department of Agriculture (CRB-USDA)*

Cement

Cement is made in a wide variety of compositions and is used in many different ways. The best-known cement is *Portland cement*, which is bound with sand and gravel to create concrete. Concrete is used to unite the surfaces of various materials and to coat surfaces to protect them from various chemicals. Portland cement is almost universally used for structural concrete. It is manufactured from lime-bearing materials, usually limestone, together with clays, blast-furnace slag containing alumina and silica or shale. The combination is usually approximately 60 percent lime, 19 percent silica, 8 percent alumina, 5 percent iron, 5 percent magnesia, and 3 percent sulfur trioxide. To slow the hardening process, gypsum is often added. In 1924, the name "Portland cement" was coined by Joseph Aspdin, a British cement maker, because of the resemblance between concrete made from his cement and Portland stone. The United States did not start producing Portland cement in any great quantity until the 20th century. Hydraulic cements are those that set and harden in water. Clinker cement is an intermediate product in cement manufacture. The production and consumption of cement is directly related to the level of activity in the construction industry.

Prices – The average value (F.O.B. mill) of Portland cement in 2014 rose by +3.7% yr/yr to $98.50 per ton, still well below the 2007 record high $104.00 per ton.

Supply – World production of hydraulic cement in 2014 rose +2.5% yr/yr to 4.180 billion tons, a new record high. The world's largest hydraulic cement producers were China with 59.8% of world production in 2014, India (6.7%), U.S. (2.0%), and Brazil (1.7%).

U.S. production of Portland cement in 2014 rose +7.7% yr/yr to 82.700, far below the 2005 record high of 93.904 million tons. U.S. shipments of finished Portland cement from mills in the U.S. in 2014 rose +9.3% to 82.505 million metric tons, but remained below the 2005 record high of 95.588 million metric tons.

Demand – U.S. consumption of cement in 2014 rose +9.1% to 89.100 million metric tons, but was still far below the 2005 record high of 128.260 million metric tons.

Trade – The U.S. relied on imports for 7% of its cement consumption in 2014. The two main suppliers of cement to the U.S. were Canada and Mexico. U.S. exports of cement in 2014 fell -22.2% yr/yr to 1.300 million metric tons.

World Production of Hydraulic Cement   In Thousands of Short Tons

Year	Brazil	China	France	Germany	India	Italy	Japan	Korea, South	Russia[3]	Spain	Turkey	United States	World Total
2007	46,551	1,361,170	22,300	33,382	170,000	47,542	67,685	52,182	59,939	54,720	49,553	96,850	2,810,000
2008	51,884	1,400,000	20,895	33,581	185,000	43,030	62,810	51,653	53,548	42,088	51,432	87,610	2,850,000
2009	51,748	1,644,000	17,974	32,461	205,000	36,317	54,800	50,126	44,266	29,505	53,973	64,843	3,040,000
2010	59,118	1,822,000	17,733	29,974	220,000	34,408	51,526	47,420	50,400	26,217	62,737	67,202	3,290,000
2011	64,093	2,099,000	19,270	29,203	250,000	33,120	51,291	48,249	56,200	22,178	63,405	68,639	3,650,000
2012	68,787	2,210,000	19,500	32,779	270,000	33,000	54,737	47,087	61,700	15,939	63,879	74,934	3,830,000
2013[1]	70,000	2,420,000		32,432	280,000	22,000	57,400	47,300	66,400		71,300	77,400	4,080,000
2014[2]	72,000	2,500,000		31,000	280,000	22,000	58,000	47,700	69,000		75,000	83,300	4,180,000

[1] Preliminary.   [2] Estimate.   *Source: U.S. Geological Survey (USGS)*

Salient Statistics of Cement in the United States

Year	Net Import Reliance as a % of Apparent Consump	Production Portland	Production Other[3]	Production Total	Capacity Used at Portland Mills %	Shipments --- From Mills Total (Mil. MT)	Shipments --- From Mills Value[4] (Mil. $)	Average Value (F.O.B. Mill) $ per MT	Stocks at Mills Dec. 31	Exports	Apparent Consumption	Imports for Consumption[5] by Country Canada	Imports for Consumption[5] by Country Japan	Imports for Consumption[5] by Country Mexico	Imports for Consumption[5] by Country Spain	Imports for Consumption[5] by Country Total
	--- 1,000 Metric tons ----								--------------------------- 1,000 Metric Tons -----------------------							
2007	19	91,144	4,320	95,464	78.2	114,000	11,900	104.00	8,890	886	116,550	5,326	5	1,684	29	22,468
2008	11	83,283	3,027	86,310	70.9	97,322	9,990	103.50	8,360	823	96,760	4,104	6	1,071	1	11,365
2009	8	61,939	1,990	63,929	49.9	71,489	7,020	99.00	6,080	884	71,510	3,426	1	366	----	6,767
2010	8	64,520	1,927	66,447	53.0	71,169	6,490	92.00	6,180	1,178	71,200	3,410	28	370	----	6,626
2011	7	66,136	1,759	67,895	54.1	73,402	6,440	89.50	6,270	1,414	72,200	3,416	1	354	6	6,418
2012[1]	7	72,222	1,929	74,151	59.9	79,951	7,020	89.50	6,920	1,749	77,900	3,709	1	300	38	6,893
2013[2]	7			76,804		83,291		95.00	6,580	1,670	81,700					7,095
2014[2]	7			82,700		89,100		98.50	6,100	1,300	89,100					7,920

[1] Preliminary.   [2] Estimate.   [3] Masonry, natural & pozzolan (slag-line).   [4] Value received F.O.B. mill, excluding cost of containers.   [5] Hydraulic & clinker cement for consumption.   [6] Less than 1/2 unit.   *Source: U.S. Geological Survey (USGS)*

Shipments of Finished Portland Cement from Mills in the United States   In Thousands of Metric Tons

Year	Jan.	Feb.	Mar.	Apr.	May	June	July	Aug.	Sept.	Oct.	Nov.	Dec.	Total
2008	5,503	5,323	6,347	7,768	8,064	8,182	8,640	7,974	7,822	8,291	6,021	4,555	84,490
2009	4,022	4,242	4,908	5,539	5,727	6,508	6,615	6,306	6,167	5,624	5,215	3,545	64,418
2010	3,167	3,133	5,012	6,051	5,776	6,459	6,144	6,673	6,226	6,461	5,411	3,853	64,366
2011	3,407	3,389	4,971	5,250	5,935	6,684	6,271	7,290	6,549	6,744	5,653	4,480	66,622
2012	4,257	4,376	5,566	6,173	6,859	6,985	6,709	7,455	6,341	7,372	6,095	4,341	72,528
2013	4,389	4,274	5,333	6,103	7,029	6,966	7,438	7,866	7,319	8,004	6,061	4,720	75,500
2014[1]	4,444	4,376	5,676	6,802	7,514	7,607	8,265	8,008	8,222	8,764	5,953		82,506

[1] Preliminary.   *Source: U.S. Geological Survey (USGS)*

Cheese

Since prehistoric times, humans have been making and eating cheese. Dating back as far as 6,000 BC, archaeologists have discovered that cheese had been made from cow and goat milk and stored in tall jars. The Romans turned cheese making into a culinary art, mixing sheep and goat milk and adding herbs and spices for flavoring. By 300 AD, cheese was being exported regularly to countries along the Mediterranean coast.

Cheese is made from the milk of cows and other mammals such as sheep, goats, buffalo, reindeer, camels, yaks, and mares. More than 400 varieties of cheese exist. There are three basic steps common to all cheese making. First, proteins in milk are transformed into curds, or solid lumps. Second, the curds are separated from the milky liquid (or whey) and shaped or pressed into molds. Finally, the shaped curds are ripened according to a variety of aging and curing techniques. Cheeses are usually grouped according to their moisture content into fresh, soft, semi-soft, hard, and very hard. Many classifications overlap due to texture changes with aging.

Cheese is a multi-billion-dollar a year industry in the U.S. Cheddar cheese is the most common natural cheese produced in the U.S., accounting for 35% of U.S. production. Cheeses originating in America include Colby, cream cheese, and Monterey Jack. Varieties other than American cheeses, mostly Italian, now have had a combined level of production that easily exceeds American cheeses.

Prices – Average monthly cheese prices at the CME Group in 2014 rose +19.6% yr/yr to 210.94 cents per pound, a new record high.

Supply – World production of cheese in 2015 is expected to rise +0.6% yr/yr to 18.022 million metric tons, well below the 2007 record high of 21.440 million metric tons. The European Union is the world's largest producer of cheese with 53.4% of the total world production in 2014. The U.S. production was the next largest with 28.7% of the total. U.S. production of cheese in 2013 (latest data available) rose +2.3% to 11.143 billion pounds, which was a new record high.

World Production of Cheese   In Thousands of Metric Tons

Year	Argentina	Australia	Brazil	Canada	Egypt	European Union	Japan	Mexico	New Zealand	Russia	Ukraine	United States	World Total
2006	480	362	528	359	408	8,676	40	145	292	405	210	4,320	16,328
2007	520	345	580	371	420	8,674	43	184	331	435	244	4,435	16,683
2008	525	344	607	370	----	8,717	47	188	288	430	249	4,496	16,301
2009	530	321	614	378	----	8,739	45	242	308	400	228	4,570	16,413
2010	540	319	648	383	----	8,959	48	264	268	438	212	4,737	16,858
2011	572	339	679	378	----	8,981	45	270	300	425	185	4,806	17,007
2012	564	330	700	386	----	9,287	47	264	328	446	145	4,938	17,460
2013	556	320	722	388	----	9,368	49	270	311	430	140	5,035	17,613
2014[1]	550	320	736	389	----	9,560	50	275	325	450	100	5,140	17,919
2015[2]	566	330	751	390	----	9,600	50	280	320	460	90	5,160	18,022

[1] Preliminary.   [2] Forecast.   NA = Not available.   *Source: Foreign Agricultural Service, U.S. Department of Agriculture (FAS-USDA)*

Production of Cheese in the United States   In Millions of Pounds

Year	American Whole Milk	American Part Skim	American Total	Swiss, Including Block	Munster	Brick	Limburger	Cream & Neufchatel Cheese	Italian Varieties	Blue Mond	All Other Varieties	Total of All Cheese[2]	Cottage Cheese Lowfat	Curd[3]	Creamed[4]
2004	3,739	----	3,739	281.3	72.8	8.1	.9	699.1	3,661.6	[5]	268.1	8,873	396.4	464.0	382.4
2005	3,808	----	3,808	300.1	77.9	8.9	.8	714.8	3,803.0	[5]	268.3	9,149	407.9	468.6	376.7
2006	3,913	----	3,913	314.5	95.5	8.6	.8	756.2	3,972.9	[5]	281.5	9,525	409.2	459.0	368.8
2007	3,877	----	3,877	313.7	103.6	7.4	.7	772.8	4,198.8	[5]	311.9	9,777	425.4	458.5	348.6
2008	4,109	----	4,109	294.0	117.2	6.9	.6	763.6	4,120.8	[5]	307.5	9,913	389.2	428.1	325.0
2009	4,203	----	4,203	322.3	115.5	9.4	[5]	766.9	4,180.6	[5]	270.0	10,074	389.0	432.3	342.4
2010	4,289	----	4,289	336.5	117.6	6.7	[5]	744.9	4,415.7	[5]	136.7	10,443	387.7	432.9	331.3
2011	4,227	----	4,227	329.1	146.6	11.4	[5]	714.6	4,585.3	[5]	147.5	10,595	381.5	423.7	322.1
2012[1]	4,358	----	4,358	320.6	152.6	12.5	[5]	807.7	4,633.6	[5]	146.6	10,890	386.1	424.1	323.2
2013[1]	4,419	----	4,419				[5]		4,794.7	[5]		11,143	374.5		310.7

[1] Preliminary.   [2] Excludes full-skim cheddar and cottage cheese.   [3] Includes cottage, pot, and baker's cheese with a butterfat content of less than 4%.
[4] Includes cheese with a butterfat content of 4 to 19 %.   [5] Included in All Other Varieties.   NA = Not available.
Source: Economic Research Service, U.S. Department of Agriculture ERS-USDA)

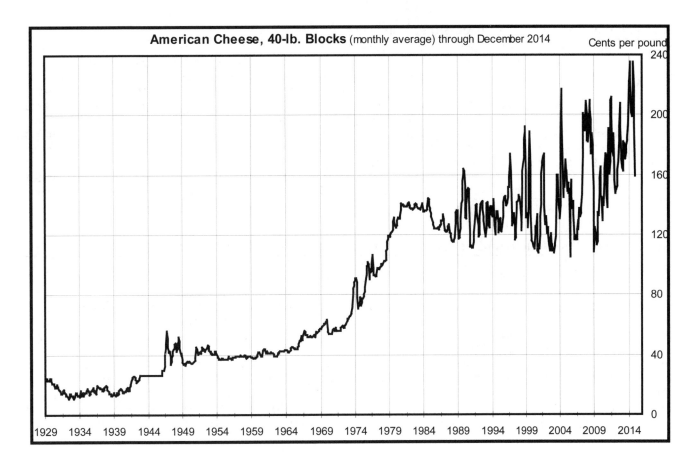

American Cheese, 40-lb. Blocks (monthly average) through December 2014 — Cents per pound

Average Price of Cheese, 40-lb. Blocks, Chicago Mercantile Exchange   In Cents Per Pound

Year	Jan.	Feb.	Mar.	Apr.	May	June	July	Aug.	Sept.	Oct.	Nov.	Dec.	Average
2005	162.7	149.3	153.2	154.1	147.7	150.7	105.4	142.5	156.4	144.7	137.6	142.2	145.5
2006	133.4	119.9	116.4	116.5	118.6	119.2	116.3	123.5	129.3	123.5	137.5	132.2	123.8
2007	131.8	134.1	138.2	146.3	172.1	201.0	191.4	195.5	199.3	189.6	209.3	200.8	175.8
2008	182.6	200.2	182.3	188.3	209.8	203.5	196.7	174.0	187.6	179.6	171.0	151.3	185.6
2009	108.3	121.7	124.6	120.5	113.9	113.5	115.2	134.7	132.9	147.1	157.9	165.0	129.6
2010	145.4	145.3	129.8	141.8	144.2	139.6	155.5	163.7	173.7	172.5	146.2	138.1	149.6
2011	151.4	190.6	181.3	160.4	168.6	210.0	211.5	197.3	175.6	172.3	187.2	161.7	180.6
2012	155.5	147.9	151.9	150.4	152.3	163.1	168.6	182.6	192.5	207.6	190.7	174.5	169.8
2013	169.7	164.2	162.4	182.3	180.5	171.4	170.7	174.9	179.6	182.4	184.8	194.3	176.4
2014[1]	222.3	219.5	235.5	224.4	201.6	202.4	198.7	218.2	235.0	219.3	195.1	159.4	210.9

[1] Preliminary.   Source: Economic Research Service, U.S. Department of Agriculture (ERS-USDA)

Average Price of American Cheese, Barrels, Chicago Mercantile Exchange   In Cents Per Pound

Year	Jan.	Feb.	Mar.	Apr.	May	June	July	Aug.	Sept.	Oct.	Nov.	Dec.	Average
2005	158.5	144.5	149.3	148.0	142.2	145.8	146.8	141.9	149.1	139.6	133.4	139.0	144.8
2006	130.1	117.4	112.4	113.0	116.7	118.2	112.7	122.2	129.0	124.3	138.1	128.6	121.9
2007	133.1	133.7	138.4	144.9	168.9	198.9	189.3	191.1	199.0	188.3	202.2	201.5	174.1
2008	187.7	195.6	179.8	180.1	207.1	205.6	188.9	169.8	185.2	180.3	169.8	153.0	183.6
2009	108.3	119.9	127.4	115.1	107.6	108.8	113.5	132.7	130.4	145.0	148.3	145.2	125.2
2010	146.8	141.8	127.8	138.5	142.0	136.5	151.6	160.1	171.1	171.2	145.2	137.5	147.5
2011	148.8	186.8	480.5	157.6	169.0	204.8	211.2	195.7	170.1	171.9	189.6	158.4	203.7
2012	153.6	148.2	151.5	145.2	147.0	158.7	168.3	178.9	187.8	202.4	183.9	166.3	166.0
2013	163.9	158.8	159.2	171.2	172.5	171.8	169.2	174.3	176.9	177.1	178.3	186.5	171.6
2014[1]	217.3	217.6	227.9	218.4	199.9	198.6	199.7	219.6	236.6	207.8	193.3	153.1	207.5

[1] Preliminary.   Source: Economic Research Service, U.S. Department of Agriculture (ERS-USDA)

CHEESE

Production of Cheese[2] in the United States   In Millions of Pounds

Year	Jan.	Feb.	Mar.	Apr.	May	June	July	Aug.	Sept.	Oct.	Nov.	Dec.	Total
2005	754.0	704.6	797.5	754.8	783.9	764.5	739.5	757.4	745.5	760.4	766.1	798.9	9,127
2006	782.7	720.5	820.8	793.6	820.0	796.1	775.4	795.1	788.6	812.3	798.1	831.1	9,534
2007	822.9	754.1	840.5	803.8	824.6	792.6	799.5	797.0	777.2	825.8	815.2	847.3	9,700
2008	812.7	784.6	834.7	810.2	831.8	809.4	813.2	820.7	796.5	843.5	824.0	859.0	9,840
2009	826.9	768.0	870.5	847.6	856.1	838.1	842.8	850.7	842.5	862.8	839.5	863.9	10,109
2010	842.5	779.0	895.3	864.6	881.0	883.3	878.0	871.2	873.2	882.2	884.5	908.5	10,443
2011	883.5	804.6	912.2	883.3	912.3	889.0	854.9	861.9	867.9	899.1	895.6	930.6	10,595
2012	911.9	861.5	956.2	899.4	918.1	901.1	883.0	891.4	871.5	930.5	914.2	951.3	10,890
2013	935.7	855.8	954.1	929.5	943.8	912.1	893.8	931.6	899.5	955.1	922.4	979.2	11,113
2014[1]	953.0	850.9	963.6	952.7	967.0	945.3	956.0	940.1	943.6	981.1	952.0	1,003.9	11,409

[1] Preliminary.   [2] Excludes cottage cheese.   *Source: National Agricultural Statistics Service, U.S. Department of Agriculture (NASS-USDA)*

Production of Other American Cheese[2] in the United States   In Millions of Pounds

Year	Jan.	Feb.	Mar.	Apr.	May	June	July	Aug.	Sept.	Oct.	Nov.	Dec.	Total
2005	322.3	292.2	331.5	327.6	332.5	321.4	316.0	312.0	301.8	312.3	313.2	330.1	3,813
2006	325.6	299.0	336.1	337.3	346.2	331.4	327.5	318.1	320.1	320.9	312.2	338.2	3,913
2007	339.6	306.2	339.4	325.9	332.5	315.5	324.7	311.9	299.6	321.3	324.7	336.4	3,878
2008	334.0	319.3	339.1	337.4	351.3	335.2	341.4	338.5	317.2	343.1	339.1	359.5	4,055
2009	357.2	323.4	364.4	354.8	368.0	356.9	354.7	347.1	342.9	349.4	331.6	352.2	4,202
2010	350.8	322.3	365.4	361.4	372.5	371.2	368.9	351.8	353.2	357.9	346.6	367.5	4,289
2011	357.0	327.3	363.5	355.8	369.1	362.1	349.0	337.5	337.5	351.7	348.3	367.9	4,227
2012	366.7	344.6	378.4	364.1	367.5	360.0	356.5	353.4	348.2	370.2	364.6	384.2	4,358
2013	376.3	346.7	384.7	376.7	387.5	362.9	345.7	381.1	347.4	371.5	356.1	381.4	4,418
2014[1]	380.4	340.7	379.3	376.8	391.3	375.1	378.5	374.0	362.6	383.3	372.9	387.1	4,502

[1] Preliminary.   [2] Includes Cheddar, Colby, Monterey, and Jack.   *Source: National Agricultural Statistics Service, U.S. Department of Agriculture*

Production of Cheddar Cheese in the United States   In Millions of Pounds

Year	Jan.	Feb.	Mar.	Apr.	May	June	July	Aug.	Sept.	Oct.	Nov.	Dec.	Total
2005	261.9	238.0	268.7	262.8	265.6	258.2	252.7	245.1	239.6	248.9	248.5	262.5	3,052
2006	265.8	241.5	267.8	271.7	274.2	263.4	266.0	250.4	254.2	249.4	247.2	273.1	3,125
2007	272.3	249.2	271.0	257.6	265.7	251.3	255.3	240.5	230.1	245.2	253.2	265.8	3,057
2008	262.4	251.3	265.3	268.0	273.7	259.3	264.9	256.0	235.4	255.3	258.0	283.9	3,133
2009	278.2	244.4	279.3	272.7	287.4	276.6	269.5	264.7	259.0	263.4	249.0	263.1	3,207
2010	268.8	245.1	283.7	272.4	287.7	286.2	275.6	261.4	257.2	265.5	256.6	274.8	3,235
2011	270.8	239.5	262.7	260.5	279.6	266.3	256.7	243.3	247.3	247.6	251.8	270.4	3,096
2012	272.0	253.0	274.8	264.6	268.4	259.9	258.8	250.9	243.6	262.7	259.1	278.9	3,147
2013	280.7	251.4	284.0	279.0	281.2	259.5	246.7	269.7	241.6	268.9	252.1	273.7	3,189
2014[1]	277.1	248.8	277.5	282.7	287.9	274.3	269.3	264.8	256.4	270.9	258.7	281.1	3,250

[1] Preliminary.   *Source: National Agricultural Statistics Service, U.S. Department of Agriculture (NASS-USDA)*

Production of Mozzarella Cheese in the United States   In Millions of Pounds

Year	Jan.	Feb.	Mar.	Apr.	May	June	July	Aug.	Sept.	Oct.	Nov.	Dec.	Total
2005	250.6	239.4	269.8	247.2	262.2	255.5	243.3	244.6	243.7	243.7	252.9	267.8	3,021
2006	259.9	240.5	273.4	262.3	265.8	260.9	255.3	261.2	258.7	266.3	259.1	281.0	3,145
2007	281.8	259.7	287.2	276.6	280.7	274.9	271.6	266.2	266.6	276.1	273.5	288.3	3,303
2008	281.2	265.3	285.7	273.8	270.9	260.0	259.5	258.0	258.3	263.9	260.1	278.0	3,215
2009	267.3	246.4	280.0	270.6	271.4	268.9	273.8	272.6	270.3	278.1	279.1	288.8	3,267
2010	283.0	258.4	299.4	287.4	293.1	289.7	290.2	290.5	290.3	291.2	298.6	307.9	3,479
2011	308.0	273.6	310.4	300.1	308.9	298.1	287.4	286.7	286.4	296.9	296.6	321.4	3,574
2012	311.7	291.3	318.5	302.2	305.9	299.4	291.7	286.0	286.4	296.9	297.5	324.6	3,612
2013	311.5	278.9	323.0	302.6	307.1	308.1	307.9	296.4	302.0	318.9	307.6	335.7	3,700
2014[1]	332.4	299.9	334.4	329.9	330.0	325.1	326.3	319.0	330.0	334.8	327.2	349.3	3,938

[1] Preliminary.   *Source: National Agricultural Statistics Service, U.S. Department of Agriculture (NASS-USDA)*

Cold Storage of All Varieties of Cheese in the United States, on First of Month   In Millions of Pounds

Year	Jan.	Feb.	Mar.	Apr.	May	June	July	Aug.	Sept.	Oct.	Nov.	Dec.
2005	705.8	713.8	723.7	749.2	780.8	815.6	823.4	837.2	812.9	769.0	755.9	720.8
2006	758.2	765.0	782.8	810.7	832.8	863.3	876.0	898.9	862.3	843.1	810.2	784.8
2007	817.4	850.0	875.7	892.9	894.3	898.9	891.2	886.0	846.2	820.4	810.6	805.9
2008	798.3	781.4	801.0	824.3	855.9	881.3	902.5	902.8	880.3	834.2	829.0	818.6
2009	852.0	882.4	892.5	915.2	938.9	970.3	987.4	1,000.2	997.6	983.9	969.2	961.7
2010	966.8	981.6	995.9	1,004.8	1,018.6	1,026.8	1,037.8	1,070.1	1,059.0	1,060.6	1,057.8	1,026.1
2011	1,047.9	1,052.4	1,035.3	1,029.5	1,040.1	1,049.2	1,051.4	1,084.9	1,065.4	1,046.0	1,017.6	977.8
2012	991.6	1,020.1	1,026.4	1,045.5	1,072.1	1,069.1	1,095.0	1,092.6	1,049.5	1,040.0	995.4	985.9
2013	1,023.1	1,032.2	1,068.8	1,105.7	1,121.3	1,150.0	1,149.4	1,146.1	1,100.4	1,070.7	1,019.7	996.6
2014[1]	1,009.4	1,015.1	1,010.1	1,018.3	1,037.6	1,065.5	1,055.4	1,054.9	1,041.4	1,013.8	995.7	1,017.2

Quantities are given in "net weight."   [1] Preliminary.   *Source: National Agricultural Statistics Service, U.S. Department of Agriculture (NASS-USDA)*

Cold Storage of Natural American Cheese in the United States, on First of Month   In Millions of Pounds

Year	Jan.	Feb.	Mar.	Apr.	May	June	July	Aug.	Sept.	Oct.	Nov.	Dec.
2005	481.1	484.2	505.0	527.3	553.8	582.7	590.1	603.5	582.0	554.8	541.6	516.7
2006	536.9	541.9	553.8	569.5	580.4	601.4	603.7	601.8	580.6	562.9	533.9	519.7
2007	534.2	546.7	565.1	571.9	586.2	576.7	565.9	563.9	548.8	540.4	524.1	518.0
2008	508.7	494.4	513.1	526.0	543.1	568.4	581.8	577.6	567.7	549.6	540.1	526.9
2009	538.1	533.4	541.7	548.6	577.4	586.1	602.0	605.0	598.7	596.2	579.8	583.1
2010	585.0	588.2	599.2	602.1	609.6	614.9	627.1	639.5	633.6	636.9	639.0	625.3
2011	630.8	637.9	621.0	611.2	622.1	622.7	619.1	648.8	647.3	639.2	619.4	584.0
2012	611.0	642.2	634.6	651.0	663.5	652.1	662.4	670.7	649.4	641.7	610.9	611.7
2013	635.6	643.2	661.0	684.7	698.7	714.6	710.6	702.0	668.4	661.0	626.2	614.0
2014[1]	618.3	630.8	628.7	639.1	648.9	656.4	655.2	660.4	648.8	631.3	623.3	635.8

Quantities are given in "net weight."   [1] Preliminary.   *Source: National Agricultural Statistics Service, U.S. Department of Agriculture (NASS-USDA)*

Cold Storage of Other Natural American Cheese in the United States, on First of Month   In Millions of Pounds

Year	Jan.	Feb.	Mar.	Apr.	May	June	July	Aug.	Sept.	Oct.	Nov.	Dec.
2005	198.8	203.6	191.2	199.4	205.3	209.4	210.6	211.2	209.1	190.0	188.5	180.4
2006	195.2	195.1	199.9	211.0	219.8	228.8	236.8	262.9	251.8	250.6	246.9	236.2
2007	254.1	272.9	278.6	286.8	277.0	292.0	291.9	289.5	269.3	253.3	257.9	260.5
2008	265.5	259.0	262.0	273.8	288.4	285.9	295.4	300.4	287.5	260.4	266.8	269.0
2009	291.3	325.8	327.5	343.4	338.7	362.2	362.3	371.9	375.5	364.6	365.8	354.4
2010	357.0	367.2	369.4	375.7	382.3	384.5	383.8	402.9	397.0	396.0	390.2	371.9
2011	385.6	378.1	379.7	385.7	386.6	392.8	397.9	401.9	384.5	375.5	366.0	354.9
2012	353.0	351.9	364.7	365.6	379.8	387.5	402.2	391.3	371.3	369.4	354.4	343.3
2013	355.8	358.6	377.6	390.5	394.1	406.4	407.4	411.5	400.0	379.7	365.6	356.5
2014[1]	366.4	358.8	354.5	351.8	360.4	378.6	372.2	369.9	365.5	356.8	346.7	357.0

Quantities are given in "net weight."   [1] Preliminary.   *Source: National Agricultural Statistics Service, U.S. Department of Agriculture (NASS-USDA)*

Cold Storage of Swiss Cheese in the United States, on First of Month   In Millions of Pounds

Year	Jan.	Feb.	Mar.	Apr.	May	June	July	Aug.	Sept.	Oct.	Nov.	Dec.
2005	26.0	26.0	27.5	22.5	21.7	23.5	22.7	22.5	21.8	24.3	25.9	23.7
2006	26.0	27.9	29.1	30.2	32.6	33.0	35.5	34.3	29.9	29.6	29.4	29.0
2007	29.1	30.4	32.0	34.2	31.2	30.5	33.3	32.6	28.1	26.7	28.6	27.4
2008	24.2	27.9	25.9	24.5	24.4	26.9	25.3	24.7	25.1	24.1	22.0	22.7
2009	22.6	23.1	23.3	23.2	22.9	22.1	23.1	23.3	23.4	23.1	23.5	24.3
2010	24.8	26.2	27.4	27.0	26.8	27.3	27.0	27.7	28.4	27.7	28.6	28.9
2011	31.5	36.3	34.6	32.6	31.4	33.7	34.4	34.2	33.6	31.3	32.2	30.1
2012	27.6	25.9	27.0	28.9	28.8	29.6	30.4	30.6	28.8	28.9	30.0	30.9
2013	31.7	30.4	30.1	30.6	28.5	29.1	31.3	32.7	32.0	30.0	27.9	26.1
2014[1]	24.7	25.4	26.9	27.4	28.3	30.5	28.0	24.6	27.1	25.7	25.6	24.4

Quantities are given in "net weight."   [1] Preliminary.   *Source: National Agricultural Statistics Service, U.S. Department of Agriculture (NASS-USDA)*

Chromium

Chromium (atomic symbol Cr) is a steel-gray, hard, and brittle, metallic element that can take on a high polish. Chromium and its compounds are toxic. Discovered in 1797 by Louis Vauquelin, chromium is named after the Greek word for color, *khroma*. Vauquelin also discovered that an emerald's green color is due to the presence of chromium. Many precious stones owe their color to the presence of chromium compounds.

Chromium is primarily found in chromite ore. The primary use of chromium is to form alloys with iron, nickel, or cobalt. Chromium improves hardness and resistance to corrosion and oxidation in iron, steel, and nonferrous alloys. It is a critical alloying ingredient in the production of stainless steel, making up 10% or more of the final composition. More than half of the chromium consumed is used in metallic products, and about one-third is used in refractories. Chromium is also used as a lustrous decorative plating agent, in pigments, leather processing, plating of metals, and catalysts.

Supply – World production of chromium in 2014 rose +0.7% yr/yr to 29.000 million metric tons, a new record high. The world's largest producers of chromium in 2014 were South Africa with 51.7% of world production, India with 10.3%, and Kazakhstan with 13.8%. India has emerged as a major producer of chromium in the past two decades. India's 2014 production level of 3.000 million metric tons was more than ten times the level of 360,000 metric tons seen 20 years earlier. South Africa's production in 2014 was up +9.5% yr/yr to a record high of 15.0 million metric tons and that is more than double the levels seen as recently as the early 1990s. Kazakhstan's production in 2014 was up 8.1% yr/yr to 4.000 million metric tons, a new record high.

Demand – Based on the most recently available data from 1994, the metallurgical and chemical industry accounts for about 94% of chromium usage in the U.S., with the remaining 6% used by the refractory industry.

Trade – The U.S. relied on imports for 72% of its chromium consumption in 2014. That is well below the record high of 91% posted back in the 1970s. U.S. chromium imports in 2012 (latest available data) rose +3.7% yr/yr to 413,980 metric tons. U.S. exports of chromium in 2012 (latest available data) rose +8.3% yr/yr to 27,700 metric tons.

World Mine Production of Chromite   In Thousands of Metric Tons (Gross Weight)

Year	Albania	Brazil	Cuba	Finland	India	Iran	Kazak-hstan	Mada-gascar	Philip-pines	South Africa	Turkey	Zim-babwe	World Total[1]
2005	183	617	34	571	3,255	224	3,581	141	38	7,552	688	820	19,200
2006	213	563	28	549	3,600	245	3,366	132	47	7,418	1,060	713	19,700
2007	200	628	----	556	3,320	186	3,687	78	32	9,647	1,679	664	22,500
2008	225	664	----	614	3,900	269	3,552	113	15	9,683	1,886	443	23,800
2009	284	365	----	247	3,760	269	3,544	133	14	7,561	1,574	194	19,500
2010	328	520	----	598	3,800	45	3,760	135	15	10,871	1,904	510	24,400
2011	331	543	----	693	3,850	100	3,800	67	23	10,721	2,901	599	25,800
2012	330	543	----	425	3,900	100	4,000	67	24	11,000	2,500	550	25,600
2013[1]			----		2,950		3,700			13,700	3,300		28,800
2014[2]			----		3,000		4,000			15,000	2,400		29,000

[1] Preliminary.   [2] Estimate.   *Source: U.S. Geological Survey (USGS)*

Salient Statistics of Chromite in the United States   In Thousands of Metric Tons (Gross Weight)

Year	Net Import Reliance as a % of Apparent Consumpn	Production of Ferro-chromium	Exports	Imports for Con-sumption	Reexports	Consumption by -- Primary Consumer Group -- Total	Metal-lurgical & Chemical	Refractory	Government[5] Stocks, Dec. 31 - Metal-lurgical & Chemical	Refractory	Total Stocks	$/Metric Ton - South Africa[3]	Turkish[4]
2005	68	W	57	353	----	W	W	W	4	70	73	NA	NA
2006	70	W	56	342	----	W	W	W	----	1	1	NA	NA
2007	67	W	60	328	----	W	W	W	----	----	----	NA	NA
2008	66	W	36	402	----	W	W	W	----	----	----	NA	NA
2009	12	W	17	181	----	W	W	W	----	----	----	NA	NA
2010	63	W	28	367	----	W	W	W	----	----	----	NA	NA
2011	67	W	26	399	----	W	W	W	----	----	----	NA	NA
2012[2]	69	W	28	414	----	W	W	W	----	----	----	NA	NA
2013[2]	63	W			----	W	W	W	----	----	----	NA	NA
2014[2]	72												

[1] Preliminary.   [2] Estimate.   [3] Cr_2O_3, 44% (Transvaal).   [4] 48% Cr_2O_3.   [5] Data through 1999 are for Consumer.   W = Withheld.
Source: U.S. Geological Survey (USGS)

Coal

Coal is a sedimentary rock composed primarily of carbon, hydrogen, and oxygen. Coal is a fossil fuel formed from ancient plants buried deep in the Earth's crust over 300 million years ago. Historians believe coal was first used commercially in China for smelting copper and for casting coins around 1,000 BC. Almost 92% of all coal consumed in the U.S. is burned by electric power plants, and coal accounts for about 55% of total electricity output. Coal is also used in the manufacture of steel. The steel industry first converts coal into coke, then combines the coke with iron ore and limestone, and finally heats the mixture to produce iron. Other industries use coal to make fertilizers, solvents, medicine, pesticides, and synthetic fuels.

There are four types of mined coal: anthracite (used in high-grade steel production), bituminous (used for electricity generation and for making coke), sub-bituminous, and lignite (both used primarily for electricity generation).

Coal futures trade at the CME Group. The contract trades in units of 1,550 tons and is priced in terms of dollars and cents per short ton.

Supply – U.S. production of bituminous coal in 2014 rose +1.2% yr/yr to 996.666 million tons, above last year's 20-year low of 984.842 million tons, but well below the 2008 record high of 1.172 billion tons.

Demand – U.S. consumption of coal in 2013 (latest data available) rose +4.0% to 925.106 million tons, below the 2007 record high of 1.128 billion tons.

Trade – U.S. exports of coal in 2013 (latest data available) fell -6.4% yr/yr to 1.176 billion short tons, below last year's record high of 1.257 billion short tons. U.S. imports fell -2.8% yr/yr to 8.906 million tons, well below the 2007 record high of 36.347 million tons. The major exporting destinations for the U.S. are Canada and Europe.

World Production of Primary Coal   In Thousands of Short Tons

Year	Australia	China	Colom-bia	Germany	India	Indonesia	Kazakh-stan	Poland	Russia	South Africa	Turkey	United States	World Total
2003	376,619	1,951,928	55,147	229,102	420,525	129,089	93,820	179,213	283,271	263,784	53,532	1,071,753	5,739,700
2004	388,231	2,132,343	59,186	232,673	446,683	158,418	95,912	178,260	285,437	267,666	51,122	1,112,099	6,043,692
2005	410,675	2,477,879	65,107	226,993	473,266	187,989	96,118	174,988	311,823	270,051	64,309	1,131,498	6,526,927
2006	425,313	2,647,755	72,307	220,554	500,193	257,187	106,555	171,135	313,680	269,817	70,829	1,162,750	6,865,647
2007	441,696	2,844,311	77,054	225,526	531,521	274,290	107,837	159,773	318,591	273,005	83,075	1,146,635	7,134,922
2008	432,383	3,099,061	81,022	214,268	570,010	274,218	122,436	157,993	336,163	278,017	87,526	1,171,809	7,470,959
2009	449,631	3,301,803	80,256	202,410	614,918	321,045	111,173	148,356	304,228	275,015	87,633	1,074,923	7,601,609
2010	467,823	3,560,635	81,957	200,955	619,843	358,251	122,278	146,257	354,615	280,562	80,909	1,084,368	7,999,455
2011[1]	443,390	3,878,012	94,582	207,853	633,774	397,202	128,364	152,680	354,869	278,617	83,904	1,095,628	8,443,803
2012[2]	463,783	4,025,377	98,603	217,144	649,644	488,112	138,918	158,197	390,152	285,832	76,622	1,016,458	8,694,754

[1] Preliminary.   [2] Estimate.   NA = Not available.   *Source: United Nations*

Production of Bituminous & Lignite Coal in the United States   In Thousands of Short Tons

Year	Alabama	Colorado	Illinois	Indiana	Kentucky	Montana	Ohio	Pennsyl-vania	Texas	West Virginia	Virginia	Wyoming	U.S. Total
2004	22,329	39,870	31,912	35,206	114,743	39,989	23,222	66,023	45,863	31,647	148,017	396,493	1,110,393
2005	21,453	38,510	32,014	34,457	120,029	40,354	24,718	65,852	45,939	27,964	153,655	404,319	1,129,794
2006	18,830	36,322	32,729	35,119	120,848	41,823	22,722	64,500	45,548	29,740	152,374	446,742	1,162,750
2007	19,522	36,384	32,857	35,003	115,530	43,390	22,575	63,621	41,948	25,462	153,522	453,568	1,145,067
2008	20,611	32,028	32,918	35,893	120,323	44,786	26,251	65,414	39,017	24,712	157,778	467,644	1,171,809
2009	18,796	28,267	33,748	35,655	107,338	39,486	27,501	57,979	35,093	21,019	137,127	431,107	1,074,923
2010	19,915	25,163	33,241	34,950	104,960	44,732	26,707	58,593	40,982	22,385	135,220	442,522	1,084,368
2011	19,071	26,890	37,770	37,426	108,766	42,008	28,166	57,051	45,904	22,523	134,662	438,673	1,095,628
2012[1]	19,321	28,566	48,486	36,720	90,862	36,694	26,328	52,384	44,178	18,965	120,425	401,442	1,016,458
2013[2]	18,411	23,789	52,124	38,945	79,949	42,231	25,762	52,187	42,559	16,710	112,910	388,345	983,964

[1] Preliminary.   [2] Estimate.   *Source: Energy Information Administration, U.S. Department of Energy (EIA-DOE)*

Production[2] of Bituminous Coal in the United States   In Thousands of Short Tons

Year	Jan.	Feb.	Mar.	Apr.	May	June	July	Aug.	Sept.	Oct.	Nov.	Dec.	Total
2005	93,728	89,926	102,147	93,271	90,151	95,371	91,841	97,824	95,628	93,688	95,021	92,901	1,131,497
2006	98,621	89,033	101,490	95,413	99,843	97,160	94,994	100,654	94,144	98,808	96,526	96,063	1,162,749
2007	99,784	88,580	97,677	93,084	97,038	95,566	93,003	100,627	92,404	98,825	96,910	93,138	1,146,636
2008	98,587	93,525	96,903	97,287	96,725	90,319	99,132	100,428	99,351	104,390	95,405	99,758	1,171,810
2009	97,022	89,688	96,062	89,072	85,236	88,708	90,847	90,308	88,185	88,002	85,564	86,229	1,074,923
2010	85,711	83,087	96,904	90,960	85,401	88,621	90,795	93,350	93,360	91,831	91,558	92,791	1,084,368
2011	91,355	85,575	96,548	88,563	86,850	88,878	85,498	95,495	94,013	94,643	94,109	94,101	1,095,628
2012	95,102	85,914	85,849	77,514	81,717	81,816	86,321	90,816	81,818	85,239	84,147	80,205	1,016,458
2013	82,713	77,586	84,568	78,909	83,271	81,031	84,518	90,199	82,878	80,603	80,576	77,990	984,842
2014[1]	82,964	75,294	86,929	82,976	83,788	79,063	84,429	87,327	83,563	84,145	80,774	85,414	996,666

[1] Preliminary.   [2] Includes small amount of lignite.   *Source: Energy Information Administration, U.S. Department of Energy (EIA-DOE)*

COAL

Production[2] of Pennsylvania Anthracite Coal   In Thousands of Short Tons

Year	Jan.	Feb.	Mar.	Apr.	May	June	July	Aug.	Sept.	Oct.	Nov.	Dec.	Total
2005	133	129	149	137	135	157	125	140	135	156	179	127	1,704
2006	138	121	147	117	128	125	124	140	115	134	126	123	1,538
2007	141	125	139	125	133	134	120	135	116	134	141	128	1,568
2008	131	126	127	160	162	103	147	146	148	168	140	154	1,712
2009	150	141	153	153	139	154	172	168	171	176	168	177	1,921
2010	129	128	156	158	140	151	161	169	168	131	140	143	1,776
2011	163	156	176	177	180	186	185	218	205	191	199	198	2,235
2012	198	185	193	205	213	206	210	224	195	186	179	174	2,368
2013	183	172	187	186	196	191	174	186	171	168	168	163	2,143
2014[1]	153	139	160	146	147	139	181	187	179				1,909

[1] Preliminary.   [2] Represents production in Pennsylvania only.   *Source: Energy Information Administration, U.S. Department of Energy (EIA-DOE)*

Salient Statistics of Coal in the United States   In Thousands of Short Tons

Year	Production	Imports	Consumption	Exports Brazil	Exports Canada	Exports Europe	Exports Asia	Exports Total	Total Ending Stocks[2]	Losses & Unaccounted For[3]
2004	1,112,099	27,280	1,107,255	4,361	17,760	15,211	7,475	47,998	154,006	6,887
2005	1,131,498	30,460	1,125,978	4,199	19,466	18,825	5,082	49,942	144,304	9,092
2006	1,162,750	36,246	1,112,292	4,534	19,889	20,805	2,008	49,647	186,946	8,824
2007	1,146,635	36,347	1,127,998	6,512	18,389	27,119	1,202	59,163	192,758	4,085
2008	1,171,809	34,208	1,120,548	6,380	22,979	40,306	5,269	81,519	205,112	5,740
2009	1,074,923	22,639	997,478	7,416	10,599	30,073	6,483	59,097	244,780	14,985
2010	1,084,368	19,353	1,048,514	7,925	11,400	38,208	17,896	81,716	231,740	182
2011	1,095,628	13,088	1,002,948	8,680	6,845	53,942	27,533	107,259	231,951	11,506
2012	1,016,458	9,159	889,185	7,954	7,211	66,399	32,512	125,746	238,853	14,980
2013[1]	983,964	8,906	925,106	8,610	7,110	60,755	27,245	117,659	197,467	1,684

[1] Preliminary.   [2] Producer & distributor and consumer stocks, excludes stocks held by retail dealers for consumption by the residential and commercial sector.   [3] Equals production plus imports minus the change in producer & distributor and consumer stocks minus consumption minus exports.
Source: Energy Information Administraion, U.S. Department of Energy (EIA-DOE)

Consumption and Stocks of Coal in the United States   In Thousands of Short Tons

Year	Consumption Electric Utilities Anthracite	Bituminous	Lignite	Total	Industrial Coke Plants	Other Industrial[2]	Residential and Commercial	Total	Stocks, Dec. 31 Consumer Electric Utilities	Coke Plants	Other Industrials	Producers and Distributors
2004	NA	NA	NA	1,016,268	23,670	62,195	5,122	1,107,255	106,669	1,344	4,842	41,151
2005	----	----	----	1,037,485	23,434	60,340	4,720	1,125,978	101,237	2,615	5,582	34,971
2006	----	----	----	1,026,636	22,957	59,472	3,226	1,112,292	140,964	2,928	6,506	36,548
2007	----	----	----	1,045,141	22,715	56,615	3,526	1,127,998	151,221	1,936	5,624	33,977
2008	----	----	----	1,040,580	22,070	54,393	3,506	1,120,548	161,589	2,331	6,007	34,688
2009	----	----	----	933,627	15,326	45,314	3,210	997,478	189,467	1,957	5,109	47,718
2010	----	----	----	975,052	21,092	49,289	3,081	1,048,514	174,917	1,925	4,525	49,820
2011	----	----	----	932,484	21,434	46,238	2,793	1,002,948	172,387	2,610	4,455	51,897
2012	----	----	----	823,551	20,751	42,838	2,045	889,185	185,116	2,522	4,475	46,157
2013[1]	----	----	----	858,351	21,474	43,331	1,951	925,106	147,973	2,200	4,108	42,692

[1] Preliminary.   [2] Including transportation.   [3] Excludes stocks held at retail dealers for consumption by the residential and commercial sector.
Source: Energy Information Administration, U.S. Department of Energy (EIA-DOE)

Average Prices of Coal in the United States   In Dollars Per Short Ton

Year	End-Use Sector Electric Utilities	Coke Plants	Other Industrial[2]	Imports[3]	Exports Steam	Metallurgical	Total Average[3]	Year	End-Use Sector Electric Utilities	Coke Plants	Other Industrial[2]	Imports[3]	Exports Steam	Metallurgical	Total Average[3]
2004	27.30	61.50	39.30	37.52	42.03	63.63	54.11	2009	----	143.01	64.87	63.91	73.63	117.73	101.44
2005	31.22	83.79	47.63	46.71	47.64	81.56	67.10	2010	----	153.59	64.38	71.77	65.54	145.44	120.41
2006	34.26	92.87	51.67	49.10	46.25	90.81	70.93	2011	----	184.44	70.62	103.32	80.42	185.99	148.86
2007	NA	94.97	54.42	47.64	47.90	88.99	70.25	2012	----	190.55	70.33	96.78	76.16	152.23	118.43
2008	NA	118.09	63.44	59.83	57.35	134.62	97.68	2013[1]	----	156.99	69.32	83.35	69.23	115.50	95.06

[1] Preliminary.   [2] Manufacturing plants only.   [3] Based on the free alongside ship (F.A.S.) value.
Source: Energy Information Administration, U.S. Department of Energy (EIA-DOE)

Trends in Bituminous Coal, Lignite and Pennsylvania Anthracite in the United States   In Thousands of Short Tons

	Bituminous Coal and Lignite				Labor Productivity			Pennsylvania Anthracite				Labor Productivity Short Tons	All Mines Labor Productivity Short Tons
	Production			Miners[1]	Under-Ground	Surface	Average	Under-Ground	Surface	Total	Miners[1]		
Year	Under-Ground	Surface	Total	Employd	Short Tons Per Miner Per Hour			Ground	Surface	Total	Employed	Miner/Hr.	Miner/Hr.
2004	367,557	743,552	1,112,099	73,912	3.96	10.57	6.80	271	1,408	1,679	890	.97	6.80
2005	368,612	762,190	1,131,498	79,283	3.62	10.04	6.36	264	1,296	1,560	891	.95	6.36
2006	359,022	802,976	1,161,998	82,959	3.37	10.19	6.26	239	1,132	1,371	869	.95	6.26
2007	351,790	793,690	1,145,480	81,278	3.34	10.25	6.27	224	1,199	1,423	910	.89	6.27
2008	357,079	813,322	1,170,401	86,859	3.15	9.82	5.96	227	2,455	2,682	929	.91	5.96
2009	332,062	740,174	1,072,236	87,592	2.99	9.22	5.61	176	1,555	1,731	941	.95	5.61
2010	337,155	745,357	1,082,512	86,057	2.89	9.47	5.55	139	1,566	1,705	928	.98	5.55
2011	345,606	748,372	1,093,978	91,482	2.72	8.97	5.19	166	1,965	2,131	952	1.11	5.19
2012	342,387	672,748	1,015,135	89,838	2.84	8.97	5.19	120	2,215	2,335	1,146	1.02	5.19
2013	341,685	641,191	982,876	80,396	3.07	9.69	5.53	95	1,965	2,060	1,095	1.01	5.53

[1] Excludes miners employed at mines producing less than 10,000 tons.
Source: Energy Information Administration, U.S. Department of Energy (EIA-DOE)

Average Mine Prices of Coal in the United States   In Dollars Per Short Ton

	Average Mine Prices by Method			Average Mine Prices by Rank				Bituminous & Lignite FOB Mines[2]	Anthracite FOB Mines[2]	All Coal CIF[3] Electric Utility Plants
Year	Under-ground	Surface	Total	Lignite	Sub-bituminous	Bituminous	Anthracite[1]			
2004	30.36	14.75	19.93	12.27	8.12	30.56	39.77	30.56	39.77	27.30
2005	36.42	17.37	23.59	13.49	8.68	36.80	41.00	36.80	41.00	31.22
2006	38.28	18.88	25.16	14.00	9.95	39.32	43.61	39.32	43.61	34.26
2007	40.29	19.41	26.20	14.89	10.69	40.80	52.24	40.80	52.24	36.06
2008	51.35	22.35	31.25	16.50	12.31	51.40	60.76	51.40	60.76	41.32
2009	55.77	23.24	33.24	17.26	13.35	55.44	57.10	55.44	57.10	44.47
2010	60.73	24.13	35.61	18.76	14.11	60.88	59.61	60.88	59.61	44.27
2011	70.47	27.00	41.01	18.77	14.07	68.50	75.70	68.50	75.70	46.29
2012	66.56	26.43	39.95	19.60	15.34	66.04	80.21	66.04	80.21	45.77
2013	60.98	24.50	37.24	19.96	14.86	60.61	87.82	60.61	87.82	45.21

[1] Produced in Pennsylvania.   [2] FOB = free on board.   [3] CIF = cost, insurance and freight.   W = Withheld data.
Source: Energy Information Adminstration, U.S. Department of Energy (EIA-DOE)

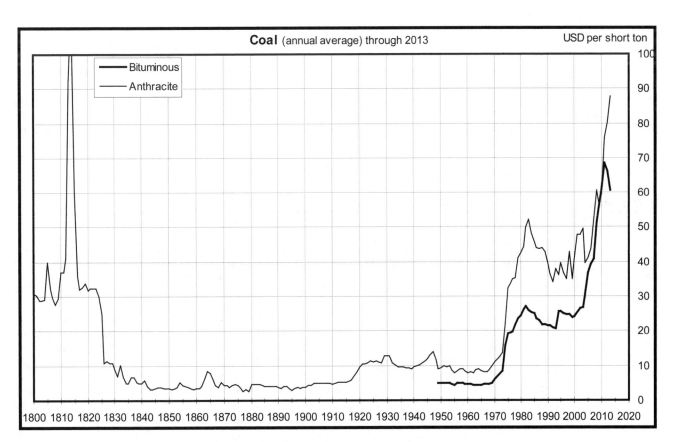

Coal (annual average) through 2013 — USD per short ton

Cobalt

Cobalt (atomic symbol Co) is a lustrous, silvery-white, magnetic, metallic element used chiefly for making alloys. Cobalt was known in ancient times and used by the Persians in 2250 BC to color glass. The name *cobalt* comes from the German word **kobalt** or **kobold**, meaning evil spirit. Miners gave cobalt its name because it was poisonous and troublesome since it polluted and degraded other mined elements, like nickel. In the 1730s, George Brandt first isolated metallic cobalt and was able to show that cobalt was the source of the blue color in glasses. In 1780, it was recognized as an element. Cobalt is generally not found in nature as a free metal and is instead found in ores. Cobalt is generally produced as a by-product of nickel and copper mining.

Cobalt is used in a variety of applications: high temperature steel alloys; fasteners in gas turbine engines; magnets and magnetic recording media; drying agents for paints and pigments; and steel-belted radial tires. Cobalt-60, an important radioactive tracer and cancer-treatment agent, is an artificially produced radioactive isotope of cobalt.

Prices – The price of cobalt in 2014 rose by +11.7% to $14.40 per pound, well below the 2008 record high of $39.01 per pound, but more than double the 20-year low of $6.91 per pound in 2002.

Supply – World production of cobalt in 2014 rose by +1.8% to a record high of 112,000 metric tons. The world's largest cobalt mine producers in 2014 were the Congo with 50.0% of world production, China (6.4%), Canada (6.3%), Australia (5.8%), and Russia (5.6%).

The U.S. does not specifically mine or refine cobalt although some cobalt is produced as a by-product of other mining operations. Imports, stock releases, and secondary materials comprise the U.S. cobalt supply. Secondary production includes extraction from super-alloy scrap, cemented carbide scrap, and spent catalysts. In the U.S. there are two domestic producers of extra-fine cobalt powder. One company produces the powder from imported primary metal and the other from recycled materials. There are only about seven companies that produce cobalt compounds. U.S. secondary production of cobalt in 2014 rose +1.9% yr/yr to 2,200 metric tons, well below the record high of 3,080 metric tons seen in 1998.

Demand – U.S. consumption of cobalt in 2013 (latest data) fell by -0.2% yr/yr to 8,400 metric tons, still below the 2005 record high of 11,800 metric tons. The largest use of cobalt by far was for super-alloys 48.0% of consumption in 2013 consumption. Other smaller-scaled applications for cobalt include cutting and wear-resistant materials (9.2%), welding materials (5.0%), and magnetic alloys (3.4%). Demand for some other uses is not available as proprietary information.

Trade – U.S. imports of cobalt in 2014 rose +11.4% to 11,700 metric tons, a new record high. In 2014 the U.S. relied on imports for 76% of its cobalt consumption, which is down from the 99% level seen in the early 1970s.

World Mine Production of Cobalt   In Metric Tons (Cobalt Content)

Year	Australia	Botswana	Brazil	Canada	China	Congo[3] (Kinshasa)	Cuba	Indonesia	Morocco	New Caledonia	Russia	Zambia	World Total
2005	4,590	326	1,400	5,767	2,100	24,500	4,798	1,600	1,600	1,769	6,300	9,300	65,200
2006	5,130	303	1,100	7,115	1,840	27,100	5,602	1,600	2,600	1,629	6,300	8,000	70,000
2007	4,730	242	2,725	8,692	6,100	25,400	4,540	1,600	1,800	2,250	6,300	7,500	73,700
2008	4,785	337	2,631	8,953	6,630	32,300	4,000	1,300	1,700	2,110	6,200	7,000	79,900
2009	4,345	342	2,075	3,919	6,000	40,000	4,600	1,200	2,200	2,000	6,100	4,900	79,900
2010	3,852	272	3,139	4,636	6,380	60,000	4,800	1,600	3,110	2,850	6,200	6,200	107,000
2011	3,848	149	3,623	6,836	6,800	60,000	5,100	1,600	2,159	3,100	6,100	5,400	110,000
2012	5,882	195	3,900	6,625	7,000	51,000	4,900	1,700	1,800	2,620	6,300	4,200	103,000
2013[1]	6,400		3,000	6,920	7,200	54,000	4,200		2,100	3,190	6,300	5,200	110,000
2014[2]	6,500		3,000	7,000	7,200	56,000	4,200			2,800	6,300	3,100	112,000

[1] Preliminary.   [2] Estimate.   [3] Formerly Zaire.   *Source: U.S. Geological Survey (USGS)*

Salient Statistics of Cobalt in the United States   In Metric Tons (Cobalt Content)

Year	Net Import Reliance As a % of Apparent Consump	Cobalt Secondary Production	Processor and Consumer Stocks Dec. 31	Imports for Consumption	Ground Coat Frit	Stainless & Heat Resisting	Catalysts	Super-alloys	Tool Steel	Magnetic Alloys	Pigments	Drier in Paints, etc	Cutting & Wear-Resistant Material	Welding Materials	Total Apparent Uses	Price $ Per Pound[4]
2004	77	2,300	719	8,720	W	W	W	3,650	W	396	W	W	765	627	9,950	23.93
2005	83	2,030	705	11,100	W	W	W	4,140	W	343	W	W	762	227	11,800	15.96
2006	82	2,010	1,180	11,600	W	W	W	4,170	W	386	W	W	808	224	11,000	17.22
2007	80	1,930	1,310	10,300	W	W	W	4,410	W	385	W	W	726	225	9,630	30.55
2008	81	1,930	1,160	10,700	W	W	W	4,320	W	368	W	W	827	226	10,100	39.01
2009	76	1,790	780	7,680	W	W	W	3,570	W	287	W	W	503	331	7,470	17.86
2010	81	2,000	880	11,100	W	W	W	3,740	W	357	W	W	696	364	8,030	20.85
2011	76	2,210	1,040	10,600	W	W	W	4,650	W	313	W	W	773	438	9,100	17.99
2012[2]	77	2,160	970	11,100	W	W	W	4,040	W	285	W	W	774	414	8,420	14.07
2013[2]	75	2,160	1,070	10,500											8,400	12.90

[1] Preliminary.   [2] Estimate.   [3] Or related usage.   [4] Annual spot for cathodes.   W = Withheld.   *Source: U.S. Geological Survey (USGS)*

Cocoa

Cocoa is the common name for a powder derived from the fruit seeds of the cacao tree. The Spanish called cocoa "the food of the gods" when they found it in South America 500 years ago. Today, it remains a valued commodity. Dating back to the time of the Aztecs, cocoa was mainly used as a beverage. The processing of the cacao seeds, also known as cocoa beans, begins when the harvested fruit is fermented or cured into a pulpy state for three to nine days. The cocoa beans are then dried in the sun and cleaned in special machines before they are roasted to bring out the chocolate flavor. After roasting, they are put into a crushing machine and ground into cocoa powder. Cocoa has a high food value because it contains as much as 20 percent protein, 40 percent carbohydrate, and 40 percent fat. It is also mildly stimulating because of the presence of theobromine, an alkaloid that is closely related to caffeine. Roughly two-thirds of cocoa bean production is used to make chocolate and one-third to make cocoa powder.

Four major West African cocoa producers, the Ivory Coast, Ghana, Nigeria and Cameroon, together account for about two-thirds of world cocoa production. Outside of West Africa, the major producers of cocoa are Indonesia, Brazil, Malaysia, Ecuador, and the Dominican Republic. Cocoa producers like Ghana and Indonesia have been making efforts to increase cocoa production while producers like Malaysia have been switching to other crops. Ghana has had an ongoing problem with black pod disease and with smuggling of the crop into neighboring Ivory Coast. Brazil was once one of the largest producers of cocoa but has had problems with witches' broom disease. In West Africa, the main crop harvest starts in the September-October period and can be extended into the January-March period. Cocoa trees reach maturity in 5-6 years but can live to be 50 years old or more. During the course of a growing season, the cocoa tree will produce thousands of flowers but only a few will develop into cocoa pods.

Cocoa futures and options are traded at ICE Futures U.S. and on the NYSE LIFFE European Derivatives Market. The futures contracts call for the delivery of 10 metric tons of cocoa and the contract is priced in US dollars per metric ton.

Prices – ICE cocoa futures prices (Barchart.com symbol CC) in January 2014 posted the low for the year of $2,629 on signs of ample supplies. Cocoa bean deliveries to ports in the Ivory Coast from Oct 1, 2013 through January 2014 were up +14% yr/yr to 1.086 MMT, the biggest deliveries in 9 years. Weakness was short-lived, though, as cocoa prices trended higher through Q3 and posted a 3-3/4 year high of $3,399 per metric ton in September 2014 on signs of strong global demand as U.S. Q2 2014 cocoa grindings rose +4.5% yr/yr and Asian Q2 cocoa grindings climbed +5.2% yr/yr. Also, cocoa found support on fears that the spread of the Ebola virus might curtail cocoa exports from West Africa. Cocoa prices then fell back through November 2014 after the International Cocoa Organization (ICCO) raised its 2013/14 global cocoa production estimate to a record high 4.37 MMT and said the global cocoa market will be in surplus by +53,000 MT, higher than a June 2014 estimate of a 75,000 MT deficit as the spread of Ebola failed to hurt West African cocoa supplies. Cocoa prices recovered in December 2014 after ICCO raised its 2013/14 global grindings estimate to a record 4.27 MMT from a May 2014 estimate of 4.195 MMT. Cocoa prices finished 2014 at $2,910 per metric ton, up +7.4% for the year.

Supply – The world production of cocoa beans in the 2013-14 crop year fell by -12.8% to 4.365 million metric tons. The world's largest cocoa producer by far is the Ivory Coast with 40.0% of total world production in 2013-14. The Ivory Coast's production in 2013-14, rose +5.5 yr/yr to 1.741 million metric tons. After the Ivory Coast the major producers are Ghana with 20.6% of total world production in 2013-14, Indonesia with 9.3%, Nigeria with 5.7%, and Brazil with 5.2%, Cameroon with 4.8%. Closing stocks of cocoa in the 2013-14 crop year rose +3.3% yr/yr to 1.659 metric tons.

Demand – World seasonal grindings of cocoa in 2013-14 rose +3.4% yr/yr to 4.268 million metric tons, a new record high. Europe is by far the largest global consumer of cocoa, consuming about 34% of the global crop.

Trade – U.S. imports of cocoa and cocoa products in 2014 (annualized through November) rose +1.3% yr/yr to 1.316 million metric tons, a new record high.

World Supply and Demand Cocoa   In Thousands of Metric Tons

Crop Year Beginning Oct. 1	Stocks Oct. 1	Net World Production[4]	Total Availability	Seasona Grindings	Closing Stocks	Stock Change	Stock/Consumption Ratio %
2005-06	1,644	3,808	5,452	3,522	1,892	248	53.7
2006-07	1,892	3,430	5,322	3,675	1,613	-279	43.9
2007-08	1,613	3,737	5,350	3,775	1,538	-75	40.7
2008-09	1,538	3,592	5,130	3,537	1,557	19	44.0
2009-10	1,557	3,634	5,191	3,737	1,418	-139	37.9
2010-11	1,418	4,309	5,727	3,938	1,746	328	44.3
2011-12	1,746	4,095	5,841	3,972	1,828	82	46.0
2012-13[1]	1,828	3,945	5,773	4,138	1,596	-232	38.6
2013-14[2]	1,596	4,355	5,951	4,281	1,626	30	38.0
2014-15[3]	1,626	4,232	5,858	4,207	1,609	-17	38.2

[1] Preliminary.   [2] Estimate.   [3] Forecast.   [4] Obtained by adjusting the gross world crop for a one percent loss in weight.
Source: International Cocoa Organization (ICO

COCOA

World Production of Cocoa Beans   In Thousands of Metric Tons

Crop Year Beginning Oct. 1	Brazil	Came-roon	Colom-bia	Côte d'Ivoire	Dominican Republic	Ecuador	Ghana	Indo-nesia	Malaysia	Mexico	Nigeria	Papau New Guinea	World Total
2005-06	209	140	37	1,286	31	94	740	749	28	36	441	48	4,044
2006-07	212	165	35	1,409	47	88	734	769	32	38	485	51	4,301
2007-08	202	213	40	1,230	43	86	615	740	35	40	361	49	3,898
2008-09	202	229	45	1,382	46	94	681	804	28	50	367	52	4,263
2009-10	218	236	45	1,223	55	121	711	810	18	60	364	59	4,207
2010-11	235	264	40	1,301	58	132	632	845	16	61	399	39	4,339
2011-12	249	239	44	1,559	54	224	700	712	5	83	391	48	4,679
2012-13[1]	253	256	50	1,650	72	133	879	936	4	83	383	39	5,003
2013-14[2]	228	211	49	1,746	70	220	897	375	5	30	248	40	4,355
2014-15[3]	215	205	51	1,720	72	230	810	380	5	30	235	42	4,233

[1] Preliminary.   [2] Estimate.   [3] Forecast.   *Source: Food and Agricultural Organization of the United Nations (FAO)*

World Consumption of Cocoa[4]   In Thousands of Metric Tons

Crop Year Beginning Oct. 1	Canada	Côte d'Ivoire	Brazil	European Union	Ghana	Indonesia	Japan	Malaysia	Singa-pore	Turkey	United States	Russia	World Total
2005-06	76	336	223	1,328	85	130	60	265	70	56	432	70	3,522
2006-07	66	360	226	1,390	121	140	50	301	87	64	418	65	3,675
2007-08	59	374	232	1,439	123	160	42	331	89	60	391	65	3,775
2008-09	55	419	216	1,357	133	120	41	278	80	57	361	54	3,537
2009-10	59	411	226	1,409	212	130	42	298	83	68	382	52	3,737
2010-11	62	361	239	1,492	230	190	40	305	83	70	401	61	3,938
2011-12	60	431	243	1,383	212	270	40	297	83	75	387	63	3,972
2012-13[1]	64	471	241	1,442	225	257	40	293	77	75	429	71	4,138
2013-14[2]	67	519	240	1,460	234	322	43	259	79	77	446	67	4,281
2014-15[3]	62	540	230	1,430	240	310	40	240	80	78	437	65	4,207

[1] Preliminary.   [2] Estimate.   [3] Forecast.   [4] Figures represent the "grindings" of cocoa beans in each country.
Source: International Cocoa Organization (ICO)

Imports of Cocoa Butter in Selected Countries   In Metric Tons

Year	Australia	Austria	Belgium	Canada	France	Germany	Italy	Japan	Nether-lands	Sweden	Switzer-land	United Kingdom	United States
2005	21,527	4,281	61,200	28,382	72,561	82,050	16,114	24,633	70,255	6,276	24,264	70,777	96,876
2006	19,172	4,729	68,173	23,803	75,572	82,726	16,285	25,603	82,864	5,774	25,725	48,447	96,455
2007	15,845	4,367	75,283	31,301	78,858	85,113	20,973	24,417	70,598	3,441	27,265	48,911	86,258
2008	14,970	4,847	64,782	23,516	69,153	85,605	21,706	23,368	72,786	3,993	27,193	42,879	102,868
2009	13,110	3,856	70,155	20,759	64,495	84,939	21,735	22,038	72,609	3,699	24,820	42,921	84,498
2010	15,024	4,929	65,336	20,885	57,639	88,713	22,439	19,365	70,529	6,416	26,462	50,639	102,878
2011	15,084	5,239	74,325	22,461	61,854	86,812	21,509	19,475	88,180	6,008	26,812	43,442	92,575
2012	15,970	5,155	75,410	24,091	70,648	90,832	25,999	26,563	71,541	6,219	26,429	51,542	72,086
2013	17,900	5,425	75,229	25,929	65,205	109,853	30,310	24,260	92,547	6,192	28,795	50,789	80,676
2014[1]	17,300	4,320	71,634	24,552	62,188	117,630	26,402	31,736	81,200	6,106	26,554	43,036	103,588

[1] Preliminary.   *Sources: Food and Agricultural Organization of the United Nations (FAO)*

Imports of Cocoa Liquor and Cocoa Powder in Selected Countries   In Metric Tons

	---------- Cocoa Liquor ----------						---------- Cocoa Powder ----------						
Year	France	Germany	Japan	Nether-lands	United Kingdom	United States	Denmark	France	Germany	Italy	Japan	Nether-lands	United States
2005	80,194	42,537	3,327	46,409	6,574	33,540	3,996	43,626	33,202	23,085	13,705	45,859	141,044
2006	86,767	43,918	14,684	43,885	6,541	24,359	3,053	39,833	41,050	22,485	15,831	34,770	145,820
2007	58,344	39,985	7,659	48,960	6,725	20,357	3,106	41,030	47,480	28,241	16,218	35,979	158,132
2008	58,469	60,364	8,438	44,435	6,603	20,135	3,046	45,652	47,232	28,576	18,050	24,364	156,028
2009	58,994	64,205	7,513	44,521	6,798	19,369	2,530	42,022	49,689	26,708	15,613	35,034	163,874
2010	60,808	77,908	5,950	57,146	10,030	36,686	2,549	53,861	54,056	26,161	18,765	45,047	172,904
2011	84,601	77,337	9,356	82,220	12,109	22,994	2,533	58,594	51,912	27,658	17,358	53,436	162,723
2012	83,829	81,121	9,349	71,604	14,908	20,457	2,195	53,286	52,448	25,370	17,199	44,698	161,085
2013	96,199	81,726	8,487	98,497	9,934	18,379	2,368	65,479	59,576	26,630	15,897	49,255	150,266
2014[1]	107,186	67,102	8,798	111,246	7,364	21,320	2,206	64,352	61,758	29,596	15,816	54,364	135,694

[1] Preliminary.   *Source: Food and Agricultural Organization of the United Nations (FAO)*

Imports of Cocoa and Products in the United States   In Thousands of Metric Tons

Year	Jan.	Feb.	Mar.	Apr.	May	June	July	Aug.	Sept.	Oct.	Nov.	Dec.	Total
2005	129	109	156	108	104	93	91	104	84	87	113	129	1,307
2006	114	104	109	94	92	86	108	140	103	91	90	124	1,255
2007	111	121	110	102	82	76	83	83	84	95	76	106	1,130
2008	108	115	109	87	80	65	88	82	79	90	84	128	1,114
2009	114	98	88	95	82	99	80	88	103	103	94	126	1,170
2010	154	100	134	85	94	78	80	84	110	89	100	115	1,222
2011	132	144	88	90	92	138	125	122	94	98	90	101	1,313
2012	147	152	115	99	83	91	92	96	83	92	88	100	1,238
2013	118	126	119	107	135	90	112	95	93	93	89	123	1,300
2014[1]	105	146	164	134	97	94	104	98	91	93	80	92	1,299

[1] Preliminary.   *Source: Foreign Agricultural Service, U.S. Department of Agriculture (FAS-USDA)*

Visible Stocks of Cocoa in Port of Hampton Road Warehouses[1], at End of Month   In Thousands of Bags

Year	Jan.	Feb.	Mar.	Apr.	May	June	July	Aug.	Sept.	Oct.	Nov.	Dec.
2005	31.1	30.9	28.6	28.0	28.0	27.4	27.4	27.4	27.4	27.4	27.4	27.4
2006	18.3	17.9	17.3	17.3	17.3	17.3	17.3	17.3	17.1	17.1	17.1	17.1
2007	16.8	16.8	16.8	16.8	16.8	16.8	16.8	15.6	15.6	15.6	15.6	15.6
2008	15.6	15.6	15.6	15.6	15.8	15.8	15.8	15.8	15.8	15.6	15.6	15.6
2009	14.9	14.9	14.9	14.9	14.9	14.9	13.7	13.7	13.7	13.7	13.7	13.7
2010	13.3	12.3	12.3	12.3	12.3	12.3	12.3	12.3	12.3	12.3	12.3	12.3
2011	10.4	12.3	12.3	12.3	12.3	12.3	12.3	12.3	11.6	11.6	11.6	11.6
2012	11.6	11.6	11.6	11.6	11.6	11.6	11.6	11.6	11.6	11.3	11.3	11.3
2013	11.3	11.3	11.3	9.6	9.6	9.6	10.5	10.5	5.1	9.6	9.5	9.6
2014	9.6	9.6	9.6	9.6	9.6	9.6	9.6	9.6	9.6	9.6	9.6	9.6

[1] Licensed warehouses approved by ICE.   *Source: ICE Futures U.S. (ICE)*

Visible Stocks of Cocoa in Philadelphia (Del. River) Warehouses[1], at End of Month   In Thousands of Bags

Year	Jan.	Feb.	Mar.	Apr.	May	June	July	Aug.	Sept.	Oct.	Nov.	Dec.
2005	1,588.9	1,809.8	2,066.3	2,264.5	2,434.3	2,258.3	2,465.0	2,481.0	2,470.5	2,385.2	2,382.8	2,566.4
2006	2,888.5	2,828.9	3,013.5	3,246.1	3,111.0	2,913.8	2,754.7	3,404.0	3,382.1	3,307.2	3,085.7	3,293.0
2007	3,488.8	4,113.3	4,326.8	4,324.0	4,226.5	3,860.3	3,437.9	3,106.8	2,883.0	2,660.0	2,327.4	2,334.5
2008	2,431.0	2,679.8	2,920.4	2,787.6	2,733.9	2,486.3	2,223.6	2,110.8	1,717.5	1,571.2	1,390.4	1,533.4
2009	2,062.7	2,339.1	2,292.6	2,530.2	2,456.1	2,405.8	2,137.2	2,059.1	1,938.5	1,931.4	2,105.8	2,196.4
2010	2,699.9	3,217.3	3,442.6	3,400.3	3,317.0	3,128.8	2,935.7	2,602.8	2,491.2	2,159.6	1,985.2	2,197.6
2011	2,551.7	2,900.4	2,856.1	2,633.1	2,546.0	2,971.6	3,388.2	3,089.4	3,055.1	2,758.3	2,559.1	2,856.1
2012	3,210.7	3,538.5	4,156.0	4,123.5	3,985.5	3,815.8	3,792.4	3,655.2	3,442.7	3,204.1	2,895.2	2,956.3
2013	3,070.3	3,690.7	3,924.4	3,884.4	4,110.6	4,035.9	3,945.1	3,897.9	3,583.0	3,170.0	2,921.9	3,050.1
2014	3,215.1	3,687.7	4,395.1	4,862.6	4,647.1	4,354.2	4,167.4	3,909.4	3,569.5	3,168.6	2,816.0	2,494.7

[1] Licensed warehouses approved by ICE.   *Source: ICE Futures U.S. (ICE)*

Visible Stocks of Cocoa in New York Warehouses[1], at End of Month   In Thousands of Bags

Year	Jan.	Feb.	Mar.	Apr.	May	June	July	Aug.	Sept.	Oct.	Nov.	Dec.
2005	201.2	446.3	495.9	677.7	813.6	916.5	805.2	625.2	457.2	430.3	388.3	599.2
2006	758.4	971.5	869.7	820.6	758.3	691.8	634.1	685.8	654.2	649.1	532.3	502.8
2007	532.2	460.2	632.6	667.1	611.9	605.4	577.7	530.5	496.8	442.2	394.8	343.2
2008	408.9	411.1	574.4	618.7	614.0	554.4	527.9	434.6	396.1	375.6	323.1	242.5
2009	291.7	413.2	423.9	472.0	501.5	557.3	672.2	664.2	653.9	726.0	714.6	722.3
2010	831.4	1,005.7	1,099.3	1,042.0	954.2	825.2	730.7	662.7	618.4	572.3	524.9	487.3
2011	499.4	604.9	701.2	711.1	639.3	661.5	719.8	734.1	807.6	884.8	875.5	857.6
2012	845.1	881.2	1,031.7	1,016.7	962.8	944.4	862.3	928.4	877.0	829.7	752.3	716.5
2013	679.9	619.6	621.1	708.3	779.6	779.6	717.2	660.4	589.3	529.2	451.3	475.6
2014	391.0	386.7	364.5	482.6	619.3	566.5	505.4	435.9	419.3	380.9	317.1	308.3

[1] Licensed warehouses approved by ICE.   *Source: ICE Futures U.S. (ICE)*

COCOA

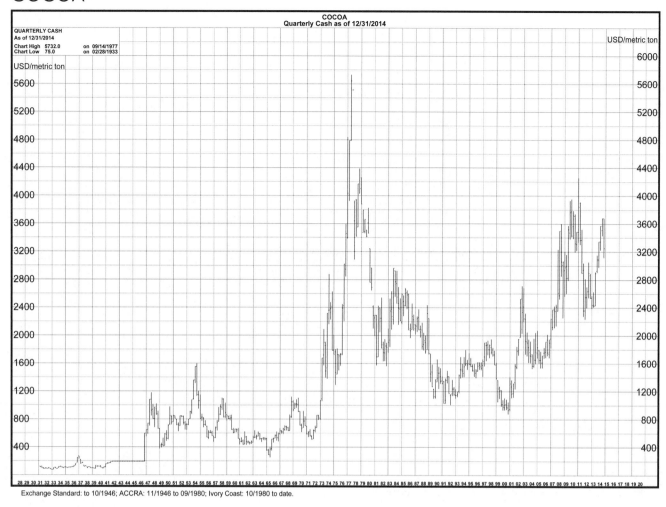

Exchange Standard: to 10/1946; ACCRA: 11/1946 to 09/1980; Ivory Coast: 10/1980 to date.

Average Cash Price of Cocoa, Ivory Coast in New York   In Dollars Per Metric Ton

Year	Jan.	Feb.	Mar.	Apr.	May	June	July	Aug.	Sept.	Oct.	Nov.	Dec.	Average
2005	1,740	1,827	1,950	1,744	1,656	1,687	1,625	1,626	1,640	1,598	1,585	1,670	1,696
2006	1,752	1,729	1,739	1,749	1,806	1,794	1,862	1,795	1,764	1,725	1,773	1,897	1,782
2007	1,883	1,996	2,120	2,169	2,214	2,225	2,361	2,185	2,242	2,198	2,251	2,396	2,187
2008	2,486	2,806	2,922	2,867	2,971	3,307	3,248	3,078	2,972	2,533	2,371	2,837	2,867
2009	2,985	2,977	2,781	2,830	2,699	2,892	3,047	3,186	3,427	3,634	3,596	3,782	3,153
2010	3,851	3,611	3,452	3,580	3,535	3,539	3,602	3,455	3,269	3,314	3,279	3,354	3,487
2011	3,507	3,937	3,992	3,697	3,565	3,360	3,422	3,312	3,199	2,949	2,831	2,396	3,347
2012	2,448	2,621	2,647	2,553	2,605	2,506	2,595	2,759	2,956	2,787	2,745	2,724	2,662
2013	2,519	2,455	2,428	2,492	2,566	2,494	2,521	2,672	2,819	2,988	2,996	3,099	2,671
2014	3,068	3,281	3,325	3,340	3,287	3,476	3,494	3,591	3,523	3,455	3,176	3,191	3,351

Source: Economic Research Service, U.S. Department of Agriculture (ERS-USDA)

Total Visible Stocks of Cocoa in Warehouses[1], at End of Month   In Thousands of Bags

Year	Jan.	Feb.	Mar.	Apr.	May	June	July	Aug.	Sept.	Oct.	Nov.	Dec.
2005	1,821.1	2,287.0	2,590.8	2,970.3	3,276.0	3,202.2	3,297.5	3,133.6	2,955.1	2,842.9	2,798.5	3,192.9
2006	3,665.1	3,818.4	3,900.5	4,249.5	4,021.8	3,737.7	3,512.1	4,375.5	4,271.5	4,166.7	3,811.4	4,194.0
2007	4,366.4	4,882.7	5,251.1	5,260.8	5,155.3	4,821.1	4,327.5	3,897.1	3,604.0	3,297.4	2,867.8	2,832.9
2008	3,140.9	3,453.9	3,917.9	3,757.7	3,648.4	3,322.8	3,003.3	2,771.8	2,322.7	2,114.2	1,875.9	1,950.5
2009	2,557.4	2,996.2	2,956.5	3,266.2	3,179.4	3,166.2	3,000.9	2,909.0	2,751.1	2,783.3	2,932.8	3,027.8
2010	3,639.8	4,330.1	4,727.3	4,636.9	4,477.2	4,170.8	3,901.1	3,492.1	3,318.1	2,884.6	2,645.7	2,801.8
2011	3,158.1	3,611.9	3,757.3	3,520.8	3,324.1	3,729.7	4,185.3	3,892.5	3,928.4	3,704.4	3,491.6	3,767.1
2012	4,108.5	4,627.0	5,393.6	5,343.0	5,149.2	4,947.6	4,834.9	4,758.7	4,483.8	4,161.4	3,753.2	3,763.1
2013	3,814.6	4,416.3	4,653.7	4,690.9	4,987.5	4,966.3	4,745.1	4,632.7	4,232.5	3,754.5	3,436.3	3,574.1
2014	3,648.9	4,117.1	4,800.1	5,384.4	5,305.6	4,960.0	4,711.8	4,384.1	4,027.5	3,588.3	3,171.9	2,824.9

[1] Licensed warehouses approved by ICE.   *Source: ICE Futures U.S. (ICE)*

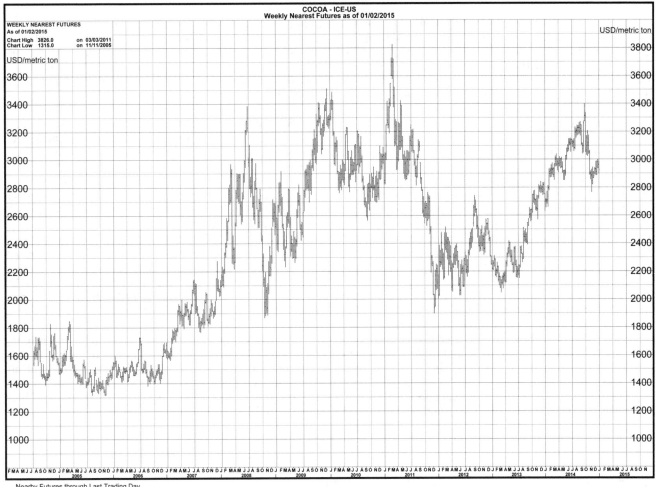

COCOA - ICE-US
Weekly Nearest Futures as of 01/02/2015

WEEKLY NEAREST FUTURES
As of 01/02/2015

Chart High 3826.0 on 03/03/2011
Chart Low 1315.0 on 11/11/2005

Nearby Futures through Last Trading Day.

Volume of Trading of Cocoa Futures in New York   In Contracts

Year	Jan.	Feb.	Mar.	Apr.	May	June	July	Aug.	Sept.	Oct.	Nov.	Dec.	Total
2005	185,624	239,511	231,917	249,209	134,330	288,809	151,339	252,868	222,122	182,337	283,663	161,198	2,582,927
2006	235,410	264,557	201,604	295,814	244,032	333,275	331,108	313,591	174,246	264,490	308,782	202,293	3,169,202
2007	239,568	338,998	273,605	333,551	212,318	328,646	242,710	378,897	213,143	265,018	273,419	235,410	3,335,283
2008	322,864	434,965	316,509	328,981	293,874	353,593	280,275	345,973	197,765	313,220	228,699	175,550	3,592,268
2009	265,308	282,200	242,110	279,621	214,640	303,030	216,046	292,552	188,138	289,133	338,296	175,892	3,086,966
2010	255,025	361,068	282,222	372,997	290,545	366,645	253,289	425,322	247,749	284,483	404,682	253,652	3,797,679
2011	395,349	401,740	390,590	423,879	357,282	454,217	328,156	571,410	335,481	388,486	554,320	347,142	4,948,052
2012	395,832	586,013	474,613	605,217	459,683	620,166	457,510	627,854	346,794	467,949	651,655	306,527	5,999,813
2013	505,589	598,270	425,547	752,332	541,022	792,100	504,933	646,114	379,515	484,417	621,749	332,158	6,583,746
2014	571,906	588,461	453,219	593,071	454,372	625,401	551,959	541,132	478,549	617,492	484,283	324,087	6,283,932

Source: ICE Futures U.S. (ICE)

Average Open Interest of Cocoa Futures in New York   In Contracts

Year	Jan.	Feb.	Mar.	Apr.	May	June	July	Aug.	Sept.	Oct.	Nov.	Dec.
2005	117,091	115,007	144,055	124,417	124,925	128,203	126,388	129,562	118,468	132,629	131,733	123,302
2006	131,527	127,471	129,426	129,814	131,035	138,004	154,163	134,942	139,544	153,485	136,329	140,099
2007	145,503	152,358	172,846	157,373	154,649	148,608	167,565	134,823	123,171	133,362	137,208	165,522
2008	188,039	182,389	166,939	136,591	146,759	160,366	151,896	134,715	127,674	122,381	113,422	113,240
2009	119,496	118,145	114,051	111,859	117,027	114,792	112,079	112,935	121,226	133,635	129,171	129,296
2010	137,675	127,994	129,562	128,298	130,258	119,074	124,335	119,070	127,315	138,385	136,708	137,345
2011	148,426	158,965	163,700	159,411	157,851	162,945	172,670	166,766	176,524	191,211	168,734	167,339
2012	171,138	165,555	170,143	178,362	183,549	174,848	186,439	190,328	202,142	202,142	189,765	193,643
2013	197,848	192,704	200,696	199,773	220,741	196,543	176,618	183,556	201,739	219,812	212,717	213,685
2014	210,130	216,867	215,297	206,091	204,253	216,264	214,879	213,149	208,448	199,236	177,425	186,443

Source: ICE Futures U.S. (ICE)

Coconut Oil and Copra

Coconut oil and copra come from the fruit of the coconut palm tree, which originated in Southeast Asia. Coconut oil has been used for thousands of years as cooking oil, and is still a staple in the diets of many people living in tropical areas. Until shortages of imported oil developed during WWII, Americans also used coconut oil for cooking.

Copra is the meaty inner lining of the coconut. It is an oil-rich pulp with a light, slightly sweet, nutty flavor. Copra is used mainly as a source of coconut oil and is also used shredded for baking. High-quality copra contains about 65% to 72% oil, and oil made from the copra is called crude coconut oil. Crude coconut oil is processed from copra by expeller press and solvent extraction. It is not considered fit for human consumption until it has been refined, which consists of neutralizing, bleaching and deodorizing it at high heat with a vacuum. The remaining oil cake obtained as a by-product is used for livestock feed.

Premium grade coconut oil, also called virgin coconut oil, is oil made from the first pressing without the addition of any chemicals. Premium grade coconut oil is more expensive than refined or crude oil because the producers use only selected raw materials and there is a lower production yield due to only one pressing.

Coconut oil accounts for approximately 20% of all vegetable oils used worldwide. Coconut oil is used in margarines, vegetable shortening, salad oils, confections, and in sports drinks to boost energy and enhance athletic performance. It is also used in the manufacture of soaps, detergents, shampoos, cosmetics, candles, glycerin and synthetic rubber. Coconut oil is very healthy, unless it is hydrogenated, and is easily digested.

Supply – World production of copra in 2014 fell -2.5% yr/yr to 5.246 million metric tons, remaining below the record high of 5.662 million metric tons posted in 2001. The world's largest producers of copra are the Philippines with 38.1% of world production, Indonesia with 29.2%, India with 13.3, and Mexico with 3.9%. World production of coconut oil in the 2013-14 marketing year fell -7.0% yr/yr to 3.209 million metric tons.

Demand – Virtually all of world production of copra goes for crushing into coconut meal and oil (over 99%). World consumption of coconut oil in 2013-14 fell by -4.1% yr/yr to 3.247 million metric tons, below the 2009-10 record high of 3.588 million metric tons.

Trade – Copra is generally crushed in the country of origin, meaning that less than 4% of copra itself is exported; the rest is exported in the form of coconut oil. World exports of coconut oil in 2013-14 fell by -8.7% yr/yr to 1.902 million metric tons, below the 2009-10 record high of 2.374 million metric tons.

World Production of Copra   In Thousands of Metric Tons

Year	India	Indonesia	Ivory Coast	Malaysia	Mexico	Mozam-bique	Papua New Guinea	Philip-pines	Sri Lanka	Thailand	Vanuatu	Vietnam	World Total
2005	690	1,460	45	48	209	50	112	2,100	67	72	30	50	5,252
2006	680	1,370	45	51	187	48	94	2,100	65	65	30	51	5,110
2007	670	1,570	45	49	217	46	97	1,880	69	68	30	54	5,121
2008	680	1,435	46	52	226	48	123	1,910	73	68	32	55	5,076
2009	680	1,520	46	54	228	48	100	2,040	89	69	31	55	5,284
2010	690	1,440	46	53	211	48	102	2,680	85	48	32	57	5,822
2011	680	1,400	46	51	209	48	115	1,700	87	44	32	57	4,798
2012[1]	670	1,550	46	58	216	49	85	2,030	90	48	32	57	5,252
2013[2]	640	1,460	46	79	207	50	80	2,270	90	49	32	57	5,381
2014[3]	700	1,530	46	70	205	52	95	2,000	90	49	32	57	5,246

[1] Preliminary.   [2] Estimate.   [3] Forecast.   *Source: The Oil World*

World Supply and Distribution of Coconut Oil   In Thousands of Metric Tons

	Production				World Exports	World Imports	Consumption						Ending Stocks		
Year	India	Indo-nesia	Malay-sia	Philip-pines	World Total			European Union	India	Indo-nesia	Philip-pines	United States	World Total	Philip-pines	United States	World Total
2004-05	416	881	42	1,263	3,164	2,116	2,067	814	434	175	253	361	3,083	73	110	402
2005-06	409	789	45	1,450	3,240	2,189	2,176	768	437	180	253	494	3,223	66	101	405
2006-07	402	960	47	1,220	3,178	1,924	1,909	704	417	187	351	435	3,173	105	58	396
2007-08	401	887	44	1,346	3,248	2,001	2,030	685	417	179	428	506	3,271	85	82	402
2008-09	396	851	44	1,239	3,099	1,766	1,795	632	411	181	441	419	3,087	145	83	442
2009-10	400	890	45	1,732	3,621	2,406	2,375	794	404	179	445	587	3,575	55	84	456
2010-11	398	847	50	1,240	3,090	1,948	1,974	730	409	153	336	474	3,238	70	62	334
2011-12[1]	393	914	47	1,208	3,123	1,922	1,907	594	402	138	375	487	3,057	110	77	385
2012-13[2]	380	850	51	1,624	3,451	2,084	2,082	716	381	200	523	520	3,387	100	82	447
2013-14[3]	400	937	52	1,265	3,210	1,903	1,899	700	400	164	465	515	3,247	90	77	406

[1] Preliminary.   [2] Estimate.   [3] Forecast.   *Source: The Oil World*

Supply and Distribution of Coconut Oil in the United States   In Millions of Pounds

| | --- Rotterdam --- | | Imports | | | | -------- Disapearance ------- | | | ------ Production of Coconut Oil (Refined) ------ | | | | |
| | Copra | Coconut Oil, CIF | For Con- | Stocks | Total | | Total | Edible | Inedible | | | Oct.- | Jan.- | April- | July- |
Year	Tonne ------ $ U.S. ------		sumption	Oct. 1	Supply	Exports	Domestic	Products	Products	Total	Dec.	Mar.	June	Sept.
2004-05	431	636	936	131	1,067	29	1,374	341	280	623.3	153.7	157.5	160.8	151.3
2005-06	387	583	1,127	242	1,369	58	1,323	366	270	599.9	141.9	156.2	160.5	141.4
2006-07	537	812	892	222	1,114	26	1,443	339	309	654.6	162.6	152.2	165.4	174.4
2007-08	867	1,306	1,196	128	1,325	28	1,383	373	447	627.4	139.9	165.9	161.1	160.5
2008-09	487	735	961	181	1,143	37	1,293	364	394	586.6	147.6	131.1	122.8	185.2
2009-10	613	921	1,338	183	1,521	41	1,836	441	W	833.0	190.1	214.9	211.2	216.8
2010-11	1,188	1,772	1,080	186	1,266	85	1,783	467	W	808.8	202.2	NA	NA	NA
2011-12	829	1,244	1,165	137	1,302	59	NA	NA	NA	NA	NA	NA	NA	NA
2012-13[1]	570	858	1,214	169	1,382	56	NA	NA	NA	NA	NA	NA	NA	NA
2013-14[2]	853	1,273	1,168	180	1,348	44	NA	NA	NA	NA	NA	NA	NA	NA

[1] Preliminary.   [2] Forecast.   Source: Bureau of Census, U.S. Department of Commerce

Consumption of Coconut Oil in End Products (Edible and Inedible) in the United States   In Millions of Pounds

Year	Jan.	Feb.	Mar.	Apr.	May	June	July	Aug.	Sept.	Oct.	Nov.	Dec.	Total
2002	55.4	41.3	50.8	59.3	53.9	46.4	50.7	51.8	45.9	54.3	56.1	49.4	615.4
2003	51.2	49.3	56.8	50.6	52.3	46.7	48.9	49.6	50.3	47.8	41.8	38.5	583.7
2004	50.0	51.7	58.5	54.6	48.5	55.6	52.9	55.1	48.9	48.2	64.3	51.7	640.0
2005	46.7	52.0	47.9	48.8	51.4	55.5	47.2	58.1	49.2	52.8	53.4	58.1	621.1
2006	70.4	62.7	50.4	47.5	50.7	51.6	43.1	51.6	43.8	49.6	44.4	40.8	606.4
2007	49.8	48.5	47.0	51.2	53.7	60.3	60.3	74.2	67.5	71.8	71.3	62.7	718.3
2008	63.6	72.1	64.8	74.4	69.7	70.4	65.8	67.6	65.8	63.0	63.6	53.6	794.5
2009	67.9	62.8	60.2	66.9	66.9	27.6	36.5	28.1	29.4	32.8	32.1	30.6	541.8
2010	41.0	36.6	45.3	34.9	39.8	38.6	37.2	40.4	32.1	41.4	39.9	70.8	498.0
2011[1]	34.6	37.0	40.6	38.0	39.0	37.0	26.7	NA	NA	NA	NA	NA	433.5

[1] Preliminary.   Source: Bureau of Census, U.S. Department of Commerce

Stocks of Coconut Oil (Crude and Refined) in the United States, on First of Month   In Millions of Pounds

Year	Jan.	Feb.	Mar.	Apr.	May	June	July	Aug.	Sept.	Oct.	Nov.	Dec.
2002	245.9	238.8	249.6	251.3	233.5	231.6	303.3	301.6	245.8	226.5	273.8	264.1
2003	195.2	194.0	214.3	224.9	223.7	187.8	162.2	202.9	195.6	218.9	184.6	186.1
2004	167.2	160.3	192.6	181.7	131.4	108.7	90.6	132.8	149.2	131.3	147.7	182.5
2005	225.9	163.7	188.4	191.0	170.6	187.7	263.5	250.4	253.7	242.1	252.3	273.3
2006	268.3	236.9	224.5	227.3	260.2	229.1	213.8	214.4	204.7	224.5	179.2	180.2
2007	214.4	228.5	261.5	223.1	191.8	157.9	171.2	154.4	127.7	128.4	142.5	212.6
2008	205.6	192.9	180.9	191.9	223.9	203.9	187.8	181.5	180.4	182.2	163.3	174.6
2009	164.1	183.7	215.6	167.2	143.9	138.0	134.8	133.2	102.3	182.3	159.0	154.7
2010	220.2	204.5	172.1	144.6	119.3	120.3	172.2	179.3	197.1	185.8	166.7	167.2
2011[1]	181.5	150.2	162.7	154.6	150.0	157.6	158.4	190.9	NA	NA	NA	NA

[1] Preliminary.   Source: Bureau of Census, U.S. Department of Commerce

Average Price of Coconut Oil (Crude) Tank Cars in New York   In Cents Per Pound

Year	Jan.	Feb.	Mar.	Apr.	May	June	July	Aug.	Sept.	Oct.	Nov.	Dec.	Average
2004	32.00	33.38	34.56	39.20	45.00	46.00	46.00	46.00	39.25	32.65	31.25	31.25	38.05
2005	31.05	31.00	32.67	35.00	34.67	34.00	33.00	33.00	33.00	35.00	29.13	27.75	32.44
2006	27.75	27.75	27.75	27.75	27.75	27.75	27.75	27.75	29.25	30.75	32.25	34.95	29.10
2007	35.75	36.00	36.00	37.50	40.13	45.75	48.00	NA	42.50	45.16	45.38	46.32	41.68
2008	58.02	62.33	70.98	67.38	67.38	71.73	70.33	59.62	55.82	47.73	37.46	35.51	58.69
2009	35.25	33.14	30.07	31.58	37.84	37.34	32.78	35.00	35.75	35.75	35.75	35.53	34.65
2010	36.20	35.75	37.88	41.99	43.60	44.00	46.49	54.31	55.94	63.65	69.00	79.50	50.69
2011	87.00	92.50	85.00	91.80	95.50	96.50	87.00	81.75	74.40	57.75	57.00	61.00	80.60
2012	68.25	68.00	64.90	63.63	59.25	54.00	52.75	50.30	47.75	43.75	41.40	38.88	54.40
2013[1]	39.38	41.25	39.30	38.00	38.20	40.75	41.50	41.50	46.00	45.00	59.30	61.00	44.26

[1] Preliminary.   Source: Economic Research Service, U.S. Department of Agriculture (ERS-USDA)

Coffee

Coffee is one of the world's most important cash commodities. Coffee is the common name for any type of tree in the genus madder family. It is actually a tropical evergreen shrub that has the potential to grow 100 feet tall. The coffee tree grows in tropical regions between the Tropics of Cancer and Capricorn in areas with abundant rainfall, year-round warm temperatures averaging about 70 degrees Fahrenheit, and no frost. In the U.S., the only areas that produce any significant amount of coffee are Puerto Rico and Hawaii. The coffee plant will produce its first full crop of beans at about 5 years old and then be productive for about 15 years. The average coffee tree produces enough beans to make about 1 to 1 ½ pounds of roasted coffee per year. It takes approximately 4,000 handpicked green coffee beans to make a pound of coffee. Wine was actually the first drink made from the coffee tree using the coffee cherries, honey, and water. In the 17th century, the first coffee house, also known as a "penny university" because of the price per cup, opened in London. The London Stock Exchange grew from one of these first coffee houses.

Coffee is generally classified into two types of beans: arabica and robusta. The most widely produced coffee is arabica, which makes up about 70 percent of total production. It grows mostly at high altitudes of 600 to 2,000 meters, with Brazil and Colombia being the largest producers. Arabic coffee is traded at the Intercontinental Exchange (ICE). The stronger of the two types is robusta. It is grown at lower altitudes with the largest producers being Indonesia, West Africa, Brazil, and Vietnam. Robusta coffee is traded on the LIFFE exchange.

Ninety percent of the world coffee trade is in green (unroasted) coffee beans. Seasonal factors have a significant influence on the price of coffee. There is no extreme peak in world production at any one time of the year, although coffee consumption declines by 12 percent or more below the year's average in the warm summer months. Therefore, coffee imports and roasts both tend to decline in spring and summer and pick up again in fall and winter.

The very low prices for coffee in 2000-03 created serious problems for coffee producers. When prices fall below the costs of production, there is little or no economic incentive to produce coffee. The result is that coffee trees are neglected or completely abandoned. When prices are low, producers cannot afford to hire the labor needed to maintain the trees and pick the crop at harvest. The result is that trees yield less due to reduced use of fertilizer and fewer employed coffee workers. One effect is a decline in the quality of the coffee that is produced. Higher quality Arabica coffee is often produced at higher altitudes, which entails higher costs. It is this coffee that is often abandoned. Although the pressure on producers can be severe, the market eventually comes back into balance as supply declines in response to low prices.

Coffee prices are subject to upward spikes in June, July and August due to possible freeze scares in Brazil during the winter months in the Southern Hemisphere. The Brazilian coffee crop is harvested starting in May and extending for several weeks into what are the winter months in Brazil. A major freeze in Brazil occurs roughly every five years on average.

Coffee futures and options are traded on ICE Futures U.S., the Bolsa de Mercadorias & Futuros (BM&F), and the NYSE-LIFFE European Derivatives Market. Coffee futures are traded on the CME Group, the Singapore Exchange, and the Tokyo Grain Exchange (TGE).

Prices – ICE Arabica coffee futures prices (Barchart.com symbol KC) rallied sharply through Q1 of 2014 on Brazil drought concerns and posted a 2-year high of 215.70 cents per pound in April 2014. Weather data showed that January 2014 was the driest January in Brazil since 1954. This prompted researcher Volcafe to cut its Brazil 2014/15 coffee crop estimate to 45.5 million bags from a December 2013 estimate of 51 million bags and to raise its 2014/15 global coffee ending stocks estimate to a deficit of -11 million bags from a December 2013 projection for a +5.3 million bag surplus. Coffee prices retreated to a 1-year low in July 2014 of 157.80 cents per pound as much-needed rains fell in Brazil and after data from the Green Coffee Association (GCA) showed ample supplies as U.S. green coffee inventories rose to a 6-year high in June of 5.655 million bags, up +8.7% yr/yr. Coffee prices then rallied into Q4 and posted a 3-year high of 225.50 cents per pound in October 2014 on concern that Brazil's 2014/15 output would fall for a third year, the first 3-year output decline since 1965. The International Coffee Organization (ICO) also raised its 2014/15 global coffee deficit forecast to -8 million to -10 million bags, a 9-year high. Coffee finished 2014 up 50% for the year at 166.60 cents per pound.

Supply – World coffee production in the 2014-15 marketing year (July-June) fell -1.8% yr/yr to 149.801 million bags (1 bag equals 60 kilograms or 132.3 pounds), below the 2012-13 record high of 154.816 million bags. Coffee ending stocks in the 2014-1 marketing year fell -9.0% to 36.495 million bags.

Brazil is the world's largest coffee producer by far with 51.200 million bags of production in 2014-15, which was 34.2% of total world production. Other key producers include Vietnam with 19.6% of the world's production Columbia with 8.3%, and Indonesia with 5.9%. Brazil's coffee production in 2014-15 fell -6.1% yr/yr to 51.200 million bags. Vietnam has become a major coffee producer in recent years, boosting its production to 29.350 million bags in 2014-15, up from less than a million bags in 1990.

Demand – U.S. coffee consumption in 2013 (latest data) rose +3.4% to 25.684 million bags, a new record high.

Trade – World coffee exports in 2014-15 rose +0.7% yr/yr to 119.919 million bags, a new record high. The world's largest exporters of coffee in 2014-15 were Brazil with 28.0% of world exports, Vietnam with 22.2%, and Columbia with 9.9%. U.S. coffee imports in 2014 rose +3.0% yr/yr from the previous year to 26.463 million bags, a new record high. The key countries from which the U.S. imported coffee in 2013 (latest data) were Brazil (which accounted for 23.7% of U.S. imports), Columbia (16.5%), Mexico (7.5%), and Guatemala (6.6%).

World Supply and Distribution of Coffee for Producing Countries   In Thousands of 60 Kilogram Bags

Year	Beginning Stocks	Production	Imports	Total Supply	Total Exports	Bean Exports	Rst/Grn Exports	Soluble Exports	Domestic Use	Ending Stocks
2005-06	41,374	117,518	91,336	250,228	93,661	85,061	179	8,421	123,635	32,932
2006-07	32,932	133,622	97,246	263,800	104,718	95,544	148	9,026	123,039	36,043
2007-08	36,043	123,955	98,023	258,021	98,100	88,021	234	9,845	128,188	31,733
2008-09	31,733	136,196	97,895	265,824	100,885	91,240	215	9,430	125,016	39,923
2009-10	39,923	128,601	101,334	269,858	102,857	91,745	228	10,884	137,739	29,262
2010-11	29,262	140,417	106,772	276,451	113,409	99,901	211	13,297	134,087	28,955
2011-12	28,955	143,897	109,102	281,954	114,377	100,642	285	13,450	141,604	25,973
2012-13[1]	25,973	154,816	113,346	294,135	116,527	102,123	366	14,038	141,973	35,635
2013-14[2]	35,635	152,512	113,422	301,569	119,043	104,798	371	13,874	142,416	40,110
2014-15[3]	40,110	149,801	114,131	304,042	119,919	105,219	380	14,320	147,628	36,495

[1] Preliminary.   [2] Estimate.   [3] Forecast.   132.276 Lbs. Per Bag   *Source: Foreign Agricultural Service, U.S. Department of Agriculture (FAS-USDA)*

World Production of Green Coffee   In Thousands of 60 Kilogram Bags

Crop Year	Brazil	Colombia	Costa Rica	Cote d'Ivoire	El Salvador	Ethiopia	Guatemala	India	Indonesia	Mexico	Uganda	Vietnam	World Total
2005-06	36,100	11,953	1,751	2,062	1,387	4,500	3,715	4,570	9,450	4,200	2,175	16,335	117,518
2006-07	46,700	12,164	1,782	2,447	1,400	5,000	4,050	4,800	7,500	4,500	2,905	19,500	133,622
2007-08	39,100	12,515	1,867	2,098	1,650	5,000	4,110	4,365	8,000	4,350	3,490	18,000	123,955
2008-09	53,300	8,664	1,580	1,853	1,550	5,500	3,980	4,375	10,000	4,550	3,260	16,980	136,196
2009-10	44,800	8,100	1,475	2,350	1,300	6,000	4,010	4,825	10,500	4,150	2,870	18,500	128,601
2010-11	54,500	8,525	1,575	1,600	1,860	6,125	3,960	5,035	9,325	4,000	3,212	19,415	140,417
2011-12	49,200	7,655	1,775	1,600	1,200	6,320	4,410	5,230	8,300	4,300	3,075	26,000	143,897
2012-13[1]	57,600	9,927	1,675	1,750	1,250	6,325	4,010	5,303	10,500	4,650	3,600	26,500	154,816
2013-14[2]	54,500	12,075	1,425	1,575	550	6,345	3,415	5,075	9,500	3,800	3,850	29,833	152,512
2014-15[3]	51,200	12,500	1,525	1,600	675	6,350	3,615	5,100	8,800	3,900	4,000	29,350	149,801

[1] Preliminary.   [2] Estimate.   [3] Forecast.   132.276 Lbs. Per Bag   *Source: Foreign Agricultural Service, U.S. Department of Agriculture (FAS-USDA)*

World Exportable[4] Production of Green Coffee   In Thousands of 60 Kilogram Bags

Crop Year	Brazil	Colombia	Cote d'Ivoire	Ethiopia	Guatemala	Honduras	India	Indonesia	Mexico	Peru	Uganda	Vietnam	World Total
2005-06	24,543	10,678	2,010	2,750	3,325	2,850	3,800	8,060	2,485	2,270	2,000	15,748	93,661
2006-07	29,260	11,155	2,095	3,000	3,980	3,370	3,660	6,490	2,865	4,200	2,700	18,840	104,718
2007-08	27,290	11,525	1,890	2,800	3,915	3,440	3,660	6,360	2,610	2,660	3,210	15,735	98,100
2008-09	31,475	8,935	1,555	3,000	3,815	3,050	2,950	7,700	2,735	3,830	3,050	15,565	100,885
2009-10	29,780	7,435	2,045	3,250	3,890	3,200	4,265	8,750	2,480	3,150	2,670	18,670	102,857
2010-11	35,010	8,385	985	3,235	3,725	3,900	5,515	9,720	2,460	3,880	3,150	18,640	113,409
2011-12	29,843	7,360	1,620	3,140	3,840	5,290	5,223	7,450	3,365	5,140	3,000	24,495	114,377
2012-13[1]	30,660	8,855	1,680	3,280	3,770	4,480	4,858	8,900	3,603	4,100	3,575	24,643	116,527
2013-14[2]	34,130	11,035	1,465	3,285	3,175	3,940	4,800	7,800	2,606	4,100	3,600	26,788	119,043
2014-15[3]	33,530	11,875	1,525	3,300	3,310	4,800	5,025	6,900	2,916	3,200	3,800	26,630	119,919

[1] Preliminary.   [2] Estimate.   [3] Forecast.   [4] Marketing year begins in October in some countries and April or July in others.   Exportable production represents total harvested production minus estimated domestic consumption.   132.276 Lbs. Per Bag
Source: Foreign Agricultural Service, U.S. Department of Agriculture (FAS-USDA)

Coffee[2] Imports in the United States   In Thousands of 60 Kilogram Bags

Year	Brazil	Colombia	Costa Rica	Republic	Ecuador	El Salvador	Ethiopia	Guatemala	Indonesia	Mexico	Peru	Venezuela	World Total
2005	4,464	4,090	920	2	74	406	177	1,752	1,599	1,285	587	0	21,791
2006	4,795	3,904	751	60	147	435	250	1,654	1,677	1,528	850	2	22,659
2007	4,968	4,064	823	35	123	565	234	1,815	1,122	1,495	919	25	23,216
2008	4,970	4,245	953	35	40	657	348	1,901	1,351	1,427	963	93	23,217
2009	5,642	3,425	750	56	65	463	202	1,739	1,318	1,642	854	7	22,465
2010	6,302	3,017	715	6	56	366	306	1,311	1,352	1,371	882	7	23,165
2011	6,971	3,552	707	26	73	657	283	1,576	990	1,639	1,051	0	24,912
2012	5,582	3,009	749	77	45	397	207	1,787	1,328	1,989	863	0	24,841
2013	6,090	4,241	762	34	54	427	268	1,696	1,344	1,923	869	4	25,683
2014[1]	7,326	4,607	671	23	71	205	293	1,390	1,117	1,392	873		26,209

[1] Preliminary.   132.276 Lbs. Per Bag   *Source: Bureau of Census, U.S. Department of Commerce*

COFFEE

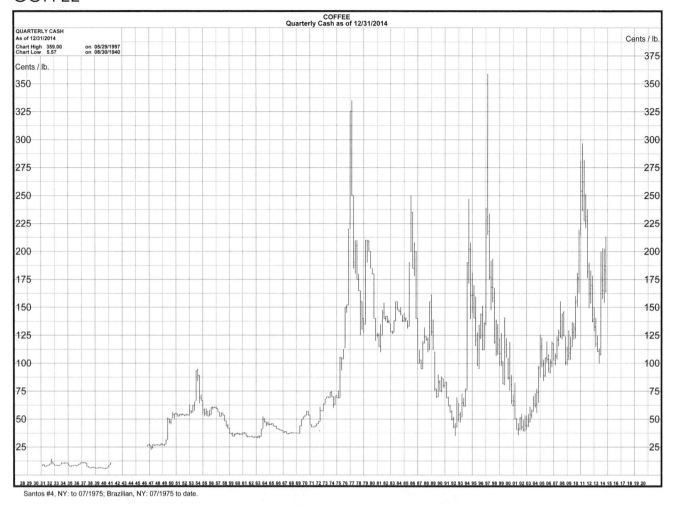

COFFEE
Quarterly Cash as of 12/31/2014

QUARTERLY CASH
As of 12/31/2014

Chart High 359.00 on 05/29/1997
Chart Low 5.57 on 08/30/1940

Cents / lb.

Santos #4, NY: to 07/1975; Brazilian, NY: 07/1975 to date.

Monthly Coffee Imports in the United States   In Thousands of 60 Kilogram Bags (132.276 Lbs. Per Bag)

Year	Jan.	Feb.	Mar.	Apr.	May	June	July	Aug.	Sept.	Oct.	Nov.	Dec.	Total
2005	1,939	1,942	2,072	1,965	1,893	1,891	1,781	1,606	1,481	1,718	1,699	1,803	21,791
2006	1,853	1,647	2,043	1,672	2,007	1,916	1,780	2,091	2,089	1,894	1,834	1,833	22,659
2007	2,167	1,760	1,992	2,016	1,888	1,743	2,005	2,249	2,037	2,038	1,712	1,608	23,216
2008	1,985	1,867	2,119	2,073	2,034	1,913	1,980	1,856	1,973	1,863	1,542	2,012	23,217
2009	1,872	1,680	1,998	1,978	2,042	2,197	2,357	1,895	1,661	1,605	1,389	1,793	22,465
2010	1,705	1,696	1,989	1,989	2,036	1,988	1,870	2,095	1,863	1,826	2,054	2,053	23,165
2011	2,058	1,913	2,389	2,187	2,105	2,092	2,050	1,830	1,871	2,013	2,138	2,267	24,912
2012	2,376	1,891	2,186	1,945	2,172	2,081	2,269	2,246	2,055	1,803	1,893	1,923	24,841
2013	2,198	1,935	2,084	2,161	2,628	2,281	2,461	2,184	1,873	1,936	1,827	2,116	25,684
2014[1]	1,916	1,897	2,405	2,491	2,544	2,467	2,356	2,356	2,169	2,025	1,631	1,950	26,209

[1] Preliminary.   *Source: Bureau of the Census, U.S. Department of Commerce*

Average Price of Brazilian[1] Coffee in New York   In Cents Per Pound

Year	Jan.	Feb.	Mar.	Apr.	May	June	July	Aug.	Sept.	Oct.	Nov.	Dec.	Average
2005	94.00	108.05	117.03	112.82	111.89	105.08	94.66	95.66	87.02	94.54	99.35	96.23	101.36
2006	115.89	109.51	103.52	105.89	99.00	91.26	91.01	98.90	97.36	97.39	109.34	115.60	102.89
2007	111.99	109.78	102.34	100.84	99.66	105.89	105.25	112.47	116.43	120.95	118.99	124.06	110.72
2008	126.26	142.25	130.45	123.15	125.18	130.52	131.10	131.85	126.82	104.57	102.74	95.22	122.51
2009	101.43	100.45	97.48	101.46	113.13	109.81	104.55	114.01	114.12	122.84	126.21	131.23	111.39
2010	128.11	121.61	125.28	124.94	121.66	136.18	146.74	152.91	162.02	163.86	179.16	186.05	145.71
2011	209.26	237.43	257.24	271.39	266.02	247.19	242.66	251.78	251.70	230.62	233.13	225.59	243.67
2012	222.41	211.95	188.15	177.20	170.39	151.55	171.69	158.75	162.59	155.77	146.35	138.80	171.30
2013	139.36	133.37	129.74	130.11	129.82	116.91	114.89	111.97	106.33	103.58	98.82	100.48	117.95
2014	107.49	142.75	174.89	182.89	170.89	154.02	154.00	171.99	168.11	181.58	169.10	157.87	161.30

[1] And other Arabicas.   *Source: Foreign Agricultural Service, U.S. Department of Agriculture (FAS-USDA)*

Average Monthly Retail[1] Price of Coffee in the United States   In Cents Per Pound

Year	Jan.	Feb.	Mar.	Apr.	May	June	July	Aug.	Sept.	Oct.	Nov.	Dec.	Average
2007	328.8	345.6	347.5	343.7	330.8	340.7	352.9	349.7	NA	NA	360.7	368.5	346.9
2008	NA	NA	NA	NA	NA	NA	NA	NA	NA	NA	NA	NA	NA
2009	NA	NA	NA	NA	NA	NA	NA	NA	NA	NA	NA	366.9	366.9
2010	381.1	373.6	356.5	364.1	366.4	369.7	385.7	393.5	417.4	417.5	446.7	414.6	390.6
2011	441.7	421.8	464.2	510.1	512.9	523.4	554.7	576.6	565.1	551.1	563.6	543.7	519.1
2012	549.7	538.2	555.8	551.3	559.6	558.2	572.3	569.3	569.3	588.8	606.6	592.1	567.6
2013	590.2	574.2	601.4	567.4	567.8	558.8	539.4	521.4	509.1	514.9	504.0	494.8	545.3
2014	502.5	500.2	500.5	520.4	515.3	467.0	509.9	516.7	521.5	503.2	471.3	459.0	499.0

[1] Roasted in 13.1 to 20 ounce cans.   *Source: Foreign Agricultural Service, U.S. Department of Agriculture (FAS-USDA)*

Average Price of Colombian Mild Arabicas[1] in the United States   In Cents Per Pound

Year	Jan.	Feb.	Mar.	Apr.	May	June	July	Aug.	Sept.	Oct.	Nov.	Dec.	Average
2007	127.54	125.54	119.92	117.51	116.14	122.35	122.32	126.68	131.51	137.71	133.81	139.87	126.74
2008	143.37	161.30	151.48	142.41	143.51	150.60	151.56	154.23	150.20	133.37	133.40	134.72	145.85
2009	148.88	149.58	162.00	190.94	225.58	195.27	192.11	181.61	169.90	175.16	180.08	199.38	180.87
2010	214.55	208.36	206.37	195.18	197.76	229.06	230.88	241.77	239.26	225.83	239.59	256.52	223.76
2011	280.05	289.49	300.93	314.26	301.48	290.19	286.46	288.43	283.51	256.86	259.74	254.41	283.82
2012	258.70	248.09	224.69	215.85	207.66	184.45	203.31	189.27	191.54	182.73	172.55	167.67	203.88
2013	170.64	164.74	163.46	164.52	161.14	148.56	147.70	142.47	135.93	130.14	123.92	125.82	148.25
2014	133.51	173.96	213.63	223.79	213.45	196.14	194.91	210.42	202.77	219.27	203.71	191.53	198.09

[1] ICO monthly and composite indicator prices on the New York Market, 1979 ICA Agreement basis.   *Source: Foreign Agricultural Service, U.S. Department of Agriculture (FAS-USDA)*

Average Price of Other Mild Arabicas[1] in the United States   In Cents Per Pound

Year	Jan.	Feb.	Mar.	Apr.	May	June	July	Aug.	Sept.	Oct.	Nov.	Dec.	Average
2007	124.40	122.34	116.44	114.59	112.35	118.76	116.80	123.53	128.04	134.43	130.28	136.47	123.20
2008	139.10	158.03	148.07	138.06	139.32	144.90	145.13	146.03	141.50	122.04	120.76	116.87	138.32
2009	128.03	128.63	127.76	134.44	147.34	145.17	137.87	146.87	145.67	151.95	150.23	155.86	141.65
2010	154.40	155.92	162.13	171.32	174.21	193.52	205.25	212.80	222.10	215.84	227.96	237.33	194.40
2011	262.94	288.08	294.48	303.59	293.06	277.78	269.18	273.54	274.38	248.49	249.50	243.40	273.20
2012	239.43	225.49	201.85	193.35	186.35	169.79	190.77	175.97	179.60	172.37	160.64	154.65	187.52
2013	158.27	153.00	152.96	152.96	151.43	138.86	138.44	135.63	132.78	128.83	122.75	127.05	141.08
2014	135.03	176.28	216.06	226.99	215.24	198.91	198.59	214.50	212.01	227.06	212.93	200.59	202.85

[1] ICO monthly and composite indicator prices on the New York Market, 1979 ICA Agreement basis.   *Source: Foreign Agricultural Service, U.S. Department of Agriculture (FAS-USDA)*

Average Price of Robustas 1976[1] in the United States   In Cents Per Pound

Year	Jan.	Feb.	Mar.	Apr.	May	June	July	Aug.	Sept.	Oct.	Nov.	Dec.	Average
2007	80.55	80.97	78.95	81.64	86.06	94.76	93.47	88.51	93.61	97.34	92.28	91.37	88.29
2008	100.68	117.10	122.44	112.06	109.58	112.16	115.09	113.48	106.67	89.69	92.81	83.99	106.31
2009	85.77	81.66	77.48	76.50	77.00	75.88	74.83	75.04	77.31	76.68	73.08	74.68	77.16
2010	75.09	73.49	72.53	76.26	76.21	82.51	89.95	89.06	87.11	90.57	97.94	98.32	84.09
2011	106.03	114.62	122.46	121.55	126.30	122.15	116.58	119.00	113.47	107.34	108.18	114.23	115.99
2012	109.40	111.25	113.60	111.71	116.01	113.34	113.37	113.01	110.87	109.89	102.94	102.26	110.64
2013	105.79	109.70	112.47	107.58	105.76	97.05	102.41	100.73	93.48	90.01	85.67	95.30	100.50
2014	92.93	101.14	111.90	110.68	108.35	104.63	107.23	105.07	105.57	109.39	106.81	103.51	105.60

[1] ICO monthly and composite indicator prices on the New York Market, 1979 ICA Agreement basis.   *Source: Foreign Agricultural Service, U.S. Department of Agriculture (FAS-USDA)*

Average Price of Composite 1979[1] in the United States   In Cents Per Pound

Year	Jan.	Feb.	Mar.	Apr.	May	June	July	Aug.	Sept.	Oct.	Nov.	Dec.	Average
2007	105.81	104.18	100.09	99.30	100.09	107.03	106.20	107.98	113.20	115.71	114.43	118.16	107.68
2008	122.33	138.82	136.17	126.55	126.76	130.51	132.78	131.14	126.69	108.31	107.88	103.07	124.25
2009	108.39	107.60	105.87	111.61	123.05	119.05	112.90	117.45	116.40	121.09	119.67	124.96	115.67
2010	126.85	123.37	125.30	126.89	128.10	142.20	153.41	157.46	163.61	161.56	173.90	184.26	147.24
2011	197.35	216.03	224.33	231.24	227.97	215.58	210.36	212.19	213.04	193.90	193.66	189.02	210.39
2012	188.90	182.29	167.77	160.46	157.68	145.31	159.07	148.50	151.28	147.12	136.35	131.31	156.34
2013	135.38	131.51	131.38	129.55	126.96	117.58	118.93	116.45	111.82	107.03	100.99	106.56	119.51
2014	110.75	137.81	165.03	170.58	163.94	151.92	152.50	163.08	161.79	172.88	162.17	150.66	155.26

[1] ICO monthly and composite indicator prices on the New York Market, 1979 ICA Agreement basis.   *Source: Foreign Agricultural Service, U.S. Department of Agriculture (FAS-USDA)*

COFFEE

Nearby Futures through Last Trading Day.

Volume of Trading of Coffee "C" Futures in New York   In Contracts

Year	Jan.	Feb.	Mar.	Apr.	May	June	July	Aug.	Sept.	Oct.	Nov.	Dec.	Total
2005	280,912	469,605	356,855	459,018	240,989	428,227	224,531	404,307	259,177	266,697	376,844	220,616	3,987,778
2006	357,994	416,964	326,256	429,249	322,932	476,542	289,027	481,870	238,953	313,459	492,904	261,362	4,407,512
2007	334,593	468,712	383,506	474,542	373,291	600,122	361,467	596,622	373,925	484,038	468,987	208,818	5,128,623
2008	419,096	729,397	515,528	556,002	354,887	642,074	317,917	512,002	381,241	384,451	383,346	250,575	5,446,516
2009	309,386	406,786	328,940	404,635	305,326	435,239	244,504	388,567	244,371	332,043	535,063	300,489	4,235,349
2010	336,188	544,197	388,468	586,602	372,641	791,873	384,464	601,583	336,930	370,233	519,808	255,209	5,488,196
2011	390,345	471,890	408,416	516,121	388,052	555,238	332,701	577,095	391,134	420,084	483,740	239,722	5,174,538
2012	401,399	578,415	541,098	628,814	494,615	642,772	466,738	581,141	406,023	503,577	603,866	277,026	6,125,484
2013	555,032	758,665	468,082	904,549	609,068	742,238	590,940	703,755	347,915	423,480	700,471	319,834	7,124,029
2014	567,574	1,140,881	596,963	736,494	458,676	596,745	404,407	619,641	394,952	583,259	562,039	349,933	7,011,564

Contract size = 37,500 lbs.   *Source: ICE Futures U.S. (ICE)*

Average Open Interest of Coffee "C" Futures in New York   In Contracts

Year	Jan.	Feb.	Mar.	Apr.	May	June	July	Aug.	Sept.	Oct.	Nov.	Dec.
2005	102,163	107,715	117,419	105,245	96,063	94,139	93,303	89,662	85,518	86,489	81,525	81,234
2006	102,195	102,614	99,982	102,882	104,230	120,907	120,007	107,928	105,175	111,392	117,469	123,259
2007	128,158	132,849	141,033	146,723	159,011	157,086	168,019	163,288	162,445	173,426	158,146	160,331
2008	176,128	193,555	179,957	160,544	150,017	146,166	147,056	133,178	126,573	132,112	116,643	118,223
2009	129,577	130,101	135,143	134,290	134,827	127,263	107,711	100,880	97,935	114,065	118,016	123,699
2010	129,749	126,850	124,238	133,961	136,711	151,959	169,669	156,086	143,454	139,801	138,738	134,477
2011	139,619	133,869	123,270	120,639	113,874	109,539	108,411	108,089	114,318	119,559	107,527	102,687
2012	113,404	131,880	149,533	151,527	148,352	147,775	137,737	137,322	141,421	147,434	141,940	141,395
2013	151,087	161,116	170,696	168,341	164,440	167,032	153,493	151,666	154,791	160,797	159,934	146,729
2014	146,800	162,005	169,201	160,266	162,103	163,163	161,218	156,931	154,752	168,847	156,410	155,382

Contract size = 37,500 lbs.   *Source: ICE Futures U.S. (ICE)*

Coke

Coke is the hard and porous residue left after certain types of bituminous coals are heated to high temperatures (up to 2,000 degrees Fahrenheit) for about 17 hours. It is blackish-gray and has a metallic luster. The residue is mostly carbon. Coke is used as a reducing agent in the smelting of pig iron and the production of steel. Petroleum coke is made from the heavy tar-like residue of the petroleum refining process. It is used primarily to generate electricity.

Supply – Production of petroleum coke in the U.S. in 2014 (annualized through April) rose +0.3% yr/yr to 318.799 million barrels, a three-decade high but well below the U.S. production record of 369.305 million barrels posted back in 1957. U.S. stocks of coke at coke plants (Dec 31) in 2013 (latest data available) rose +43.9% yr/yr to 872,000 short tons.

Trade – U.S. coke exports in 2013 (latest data available) fell -13.8% yr/yr to 840.042 tons, and over a third of those exports went to Canada. U.S. coke imports in 2013 fell -87.9% yr/yr to 137.533 thousand short tons. About 20% of the imports were from Japan.

Salient Statistics of Coke in the United States   In Thousands of Short Tons

| | Coke and Breeze Production at Coke Plants By Census Division | | | | | | | | Producer and Distributor | Exports | | Imports | |
Year	Middle Atlantic	East North Central	East South Central	Other	Total	Coke Total	Breeze Total	Con-sumption[2]	Stocks Dec. 31	Canada	Total	Japan	Total
2008	W	7,578	W	9,153	16,731	15,646	1,085	17,006	916	758	1,959	604	3,603
2009	W	5,972	W	5,796	11,768	11,143	625	10,323	776	419	1,307	46	347
2010	W	8,385	W	7,803	16,188	15,022	1,166	14,847	702	400	1,463	245	1,214
2011	W	8,907	W	7,624	16,531	15,420	1,110	15,825	745	407	970	141	1,418
2012	W	9,355	W	6,784	16,139	15,172	967	15,472	606	404	974	50	1,135
2013[1]	W	8,864	W	7,362	16,226	15,320	906	14,351	872	278	840	1	138

[1] Preliminary.   [2] Equal to production plus imports minus the change in producer and distributor stocks minus exports.
W = Withheld.   *Source: Energy Information Administration, U.S. Department of Energy (EIA-DOE)*

Production of Petroleum Coke in the United States   In Thousands of Barrels

Year	Jan.	Feb.	Mar.	Apr.	May	June	July	Aug.	Sept.	Oct.	Nov.	Dec.	Total
2008	25,862	22,994	24,616	24,100	25,432	25,801	26,691	25,993	21,350	24,796	25,196	25,875	298,706
2009	25,902	21,991	25,071	24,741	24,402	25,339	25,205	24,862	24,364	23,823	22,490	23,857	292,047
2010	23,127	20,913	24,490	23,911	25,878	25,618	26,761	26,089	23,986	24,674	24,394	26,437	296,278
2011	25,976	20,975	24,952	23,904	25,635	25,745	27,115	27,363	25,962	26,460	26,271	26,882	307,240
2012	25,427	23,451	24,656	24,774	26,408	25,602	26,785	26,670	25,385	26,477	26,303	28,543	310,481
2013	26,197	22,792	25,535	25,051	26,308	27,314	28,718	28,243	26,440	26,890	26,215	28,168	317,871
2014[1]	26,979	23,225	26,073	26,851	26,716	26,020	29,087	28,017	26,498	26,383	26,383		318,799

[1] Preliminary.   *Source: Energy Information Administration, U.S. Department of Energy (EIA-DOE)*

Coal Receipts and Average Prices at Coke Plants in the United States

| | Coal Receipts at Coke Plants By Census Division, in Thousands of Short Tons | | | | | Average Price of Coal Receipts at Coke Plants By Census Division, In Dollars per Short Ton | | | | |
Year	Middle Atlantic	East North Central	East South Central	Other	Total	Middle Atlantic	East North Central	East South Central	Other	Total
2008	W	10,362	W	12,067	22,429	W	122.18	W	W	118.09
2009	W	7,772	W	7,333	15,105	W	150.93	W	W	143.01
2010	W	11,081	W	10,000	21,081	W	164.08	W	W	153.59
2011	W	12,251	W	9,822	22,073	W	195.13	W	W	184.44
2012	W	12,157	W	8,705	20,862	W	198.78	W	W	190.55
2013[1]	W	11,815	W	9,295	21,110	W	157.52	W	W	156.99

[1] Preliminary.   W = Withheld.   *Source: Energy Information Administration, U.S. Department of Energy (EIA-DOE)*

Coal Carbonized and Coke and Breeze Stocks at Coke Plants in the United States   In Thousands of Short Tons

| | Coal Carbonized at Coke Plants By Census Division | | | | | Stocks at Coke Plants, Dec. 31 By Census Division | | | | | | |
Year	Middle Atlantic	East North Central	East South Central	Other	Total	Middle Atlantic	East North Central	East South Central	Other	Total	Coke Total	Breeze Total
2008	W	10,228	W	11,842	22,070	W	658	W	335	993	916	77
2009	W	7,849	W	7,477	15,326	W	538	W	320	858	776	82
2010	W	10,952	2,068	8,072	21,092	W	545	W	240	785	702	83
2011	W	11,673	W	9,761	21,434	W	571	W	236	807	745	62
2012	W	12,125	W	8,626	20,751	W	513	W	194	707	606	101
2013[1]	W	11,948	W	9,526	21,474	W	739	W	344	1,083	872	211

[1] Preliminary.   W = Withheld.   *Source: Energy Information Administration, U.S. Department of Energy (EIA-DOE)*

Copper

The word *copper* comes from name of the Mediterranean island Cyprus that was a primary source of the metal. Dating back more than 10,000 years, copper is the oldest metal used by humans. From the Pyramid of Cheops in Egypt, archeologists recovered a portion of a water plumbing system whose copper tubing was found in serviceable condition after more than 5,000 years.

Copper is one of the most widely used industrial metals because it is an excellent conductor of electricity, has strong corrosion-resistance properties, and is very ductile. It is also used to produce the alloys of brass (a copper-zinc alloy) and bronze (a copper-tin alloy), both of which are far harder and stronger than pure copper. Electrical uses of copper account for about 75% of total copper usage, and building construction is the single largest market (the average U.S. home contains 400 pounds of copper). Copper is biostatic, meaning that bacteria will not grow on its surface, and it is therefore used in air-conditioning systems, food processing surfaces, and doorknobs to prevent the spread of disease.

Copper futures and options are traded at the CME Group, and the London Metal Exchange (LME). Copper futures are traded on the Moscow Exchange, the Shanghai Futures Exchange (SHFE), the Singapore Exchange (SGX), and the Singapore Mercantile Exchange (SMX). The CME copper futures contract calls for the delivery of 25,000 pounds of Grade 1 electrolyte copper and is priced in terms of cents per pound.

Prices – CME copper futures prices (Barchart.com symbol HG) posted the high for the 2014 in January at $3.4660 per pound and subsequently fell to a then 3-1/2 year low of $2.9275 per pound in March due to a slump in Chinese demand as China 2013 copper imports fell -2.3% yr/yr to 4.54 MMT. Copper prices recovered into mid-year as supplies tightened when LME copper inventories fell to a 5-3/4 year low and Shanghai copper inventories slid to a 2-1/2 year low. Copper prices then trended lower into the end of the year as the dollar index surged to an 8-1/2 year high and on global economic concerns as the Asian and European economies slowed. U.S. economic strength was not enough to stop the slide in copper prices which finished 2014 down -17.5% at $2.8350 per pound.

Supply – World production of copper in 2014 rose by +2.2% yr/yr to 18.700 million metric tons, which was a new record high. The largest producer of copper was Chile with 31.0% of the world's production, followed by China with 8.7%, Peru with 7.5%, the U.S. with 7.3%, and Australia with 5.4%. U.S. production of refined copper in 2014 rose +7.8% yr/yr to 1.070 million short tons, which was far below the record U.S. production level of 2.490 million short tons seen in 1998.

Demand – U.S. consumption of copper in 2012 (latest data) rose +1.1% to 1.780 million metric tons. The primary users of copper in the U.S. by class of consumer are wire rod mills with about 72% of usage, brass mills with 24% of usage, and nominal use of 2% or less by each of foundries, ingot makers, and chemical plants.

Trade – U.S. exports of refined copper in 2014 fell -7.8% to 104,544 metric tons, below the 17-year high of 159,950 metric tons seen in 2012. U.S. imports of copper in 2014 fell -15.7% yr/yr to 618,720 metric tons, below the record high of 1.1 million metric tons in 2006.

World Mine Production of Copper (Content of Ore)   In Thousands of Metric Tons

Year	Australia	Canada[3]	Chile	China	Indonesia	Mexico	Peru	Poland	Russia	South Africa	United States[3]	Zambia	World Total[2]
2005	916.3	595.4	5,320.5	777	1,064.2	429.1	1,009.9	512.0	700	88.6	1,140	432.0	15,000
2006	858.8	603.3	5,360.8	889	818.0	327.5	1,048.5	497.0	725	89.5	1,200	474.0	15,100
2007	870.0	596.2	5,557.0	946	796.9	335.5	1,190.3	452.0	740	97.0	1,170	509.0	15,500
2008	886.0	607.0	5,327.6	1090	632.6	268.6	1,267.9	429.0	750	108.7	1,310	534.0	15,600
2009	854.0	494.5	5,394.4	1070	998.5	227.7	1,276.2	439.0	676	107.6	1,180	698.0	16,000
2010	870.0	525.0	5,418.6	1200	878.4	270.1	1,247.1	425.4	703	102.6	1,110	686.0	16,100
2011	958.0	566.2	5,262.8	1310	543.0	443.6	1,235.2	426.7	713	96.6	1,110	668.0	16,100
2012	958.0	579.0	5,430.0	1630	360.0	440.0	1,300.0	427.0	883		1,170	690.0	16,900
2013[1]	990.0	632.0	5,780.0	1600	504.0	480.0	1,380.0	429.0	833		1,250	760.0	18,300
2014[2]	1,000.0	680.0	5,800.0	1620	400.0	520.0	1,400.0	425.0	850		1,370	730.0	18,700

[1] Preliminary.   [2] Estimate.   [3] Recoverable.   *Source: U.S. Geological Survey (USGS)*

Commodity Exchange Inc. Warehouse Stocks of Copper, on First of Month   In Thousands of Short Tons

Year	Jan.	Feb.	Mar.	Apr.	May	June	July	Aug.	Sept.	Oct.	Nov.	Dec.
2005	48.2	45.8	46.8	43.3	30.1	22.0	15.3	11.0	9.3	7.2	3.7	3.7
2006	6.8	11.7	30.4	20.7	16.7	9.5	7.9	6.8	12.4	22.3	23.2	31.3
2007	34.0	36.2	37.0	36.4	33.7	27.2	22.1	21.8	20.7	20.1	19.0	18.0
2008	14.1	14.0	13.1	11.9	10.8	11.1	11.0	5.4	5.4	9.9	9.9	24.5
2009	NA	40.2	45.3	46.5	54.1	56.8	59.8	54.1	53.5	55.0	55.0	70.7
2010	94.5	94.5	94.5	102.0	101.2	101.9	101.9	100.4	95.3	84.9	74.3	70.8
2011	65.0	73.2	82.9	84.7	82.5	80.7	80.7	82.8	85.8	88.5	89.9	87.7
2012	90.1	89.7	91.2	86.5	75.1	59.1	53.3	48.1	49.8	50.3	56.6	63.6
2013	70.7	74.1	75.0	76.2	85.6	79.8	71.7	64.6	36.5	31.1	26.3	19.1
2014	13.0	19.2	13.6	20.0	18.3	16.4	19.7	23.9	28.0	34.2	29.8	28.1

Source: CME Group; New York Mercantile Exchange (NYMEX)

Salient Statistics of Copper in the United States   In Thousands of Metric Tons

	New Copper Produced						Imports[5]		Exports				Blister &	Apparent Consumption	
	From Domestic Ores -		From		Secon-				Ore,			Primary	Material	Refined	Primary
			Refin-	Foreign	Total	dary Re-	Unmanu-		Concen-			Producers	in	Copper	& Old
Year	Mines	Smelters	eries	Ores	New	covery	factured	Refined	trate[6]	Refined[7]	COMEX	(Refined)	Solution	(Reported)	Copper[8]
2005	1,140	523	524	130	1,210	183	1,230	1,000	137	40	6	64	44	2,270	2,420
2006	1,200	501	531	144	1,210	151	1,320	1,070	108	106	31	194	19	2,110	2,200
2007	1,170	617	702	62	1,270	158	1,100	829	134	51	14	130	26	2,140	2,270
2008	1,310	574	603	109	1,220	156	934	724	301	37	31	199	24	2,020	1,990
2009	1,180	597	588	48	1,110	138	788	664	151	81	90	434	16	1,650	1,580
2010	1,110	601	606	21	1,060	143	760	605	137	78	59	384	21	1,760	1,760
2011	1,110	538	545	W	992	153		670	252	40	80	409	13	1,760	1,730
2012	1,170				962	164		630	301	159				1,760	1,770
2013[1]	1,250				993	180		734	348	113				1,820	1,770
2014[2]	1,370				1,070	180		600	390	100				1,830	1,810

[1] Preliminary.   [2] Estimate.   [3] Also from matte, etc., refinery reports.   [4] From old scrap only.   [5] For consumption.   [6] Blister (copper content).
[7] Ingots, bars, etc.   [8] Old scrap only.   W = Withheld.   *Source: U.S. Geological Survey (USGS)*

Consumption of Refined Copper[3] in the United States   In Thousands of Metric Tons

	By-Products						By Class of Consumer						Total
		Wire	Ingots and	Cakes			Wire Rod	Brass	Chemical	Ingot		Miscel-	Con-
Year	Cathodes	Bars	Ingot Bars	& Slabs	Billets	Other[4]	Mills	Mills	Plants	Makers	Foundries	laneous[5]	sumption
2002	2,140.0	W	22.8	72.6	W	126.0	1,710.0	593.0	1.0	4.6	19.8	35.7	2,370.0
2003	2,070.0	W	22.3	41.8	W	153.0	1,640.0	587.0	1.0	4.6	21.9	36.7	2,290.0
2004	2,160.0	W	21.4	57.0	W	173.0	1,780.0	573.0	1.2	4.6	21.0	35.2	2,410.0
2005	2,040.0	W	28.8	35.3	W	167.0	1,680.0	528.0	1.2	4.5	20.2	39.3	2,270.0
2006	1,910.0	W	30.8	37.1	W	135.0	1,570.0	490.0	1.0	4.5	21.4	24.1	2,110.0
2007	1,930.0	W	28.8	42.7	W	135.0	1,610.0	476.0	1.0	4.5	19.4	25.7	2,140.0
2008	1,820.0	W	28.6	45.0	W	130.0	1,490.0	479.0	0.3	4.5	20.4	24.7	2,020.0
2009	1,450.0	W	27.4	43.6	W	125.0	1,140.0	454.0	0.4	4.5	19.1	30.1	1,650.0
2010[1]	1,570.0	W	22.5	44.1	W	127.0	1,250.0	459.0	0.4	4.5	18.2	34.6	1,760.0
2011[2]	1,580.0	W	2.5	43.8	W	136.0	1,270.0	430.0	1.5	5.0	17.7	37.5	1,760.0

[1] Preliminary.   [2] Estimate.   [3] Primary & secondary.   [4] Includes Wirebars and Billets.   [5] Includes iron and steel plants, primary smelters producing alloys other than copper, consumers of copper powder and copper shot, and other manufacturers.   W = Withheld.
Source: U.S. Geological Survey (USGS)

Salient Statistics of Recycling Copper in the United States

	New Scrap[1]	Old Scrap[2]	Recycled Metal[3]	Apparent Supply	Percent Recycled	New Scrap[1]	Old Scrap[2]	Recycled Metal[3]	Apparent Supply
Year	In Thousands of Metric Tons					Value in Millions of Dollars			
2003	738	206	944	3,170	29.8	1,390	387	1,770	5,950
2004	774	191	965	3,330	29.0	2,290	565	2,850	9,830
2005	769	183	953	3,190	30.0	2,940	701	3,640	12,200
2006	819	150	968	3,010	32.1	5,680	1,040	6,720	20,900
2007	772	162	933	3,050	30.6	5,580	1,170	6,750	22,000
2008	700	159	859	2,700	31.8	4,930	1,120	6,050	18,900
2009	639	138	777	2,220	35.0	3,400	734	4,130	11,800
2010	642	143	785	2,400	32.7	4,930	1,100	6,030	18,400
2011	649	153	802	2,380	33.7	5,810	1,370	7,180	21,300
2012	629	163	792	2,400	33.0	5,090	1,320	6,410	19,400

[1] Scrap that results from the manufacturing process.   [2] Scrap that results from consumer products.   [3] Metal recovered from new plus old scrap.
Source: U.S. Geological Survey (USGS)

Copper Refined from Scrap in the United States   In Thousands of Metric Tons

Year	Jan.	Feb.	Mar.	Apr.	May	June	July	Aug.	Sept.	Oct.	Nov.	Dec.	Total
2005	4.4	4.4	4.2	4.2	3.8	3.6	3.9	3.6	3.6	3.8	3.8	3.9	47.1
2006	3.8	3.7	3.8	3.7	3.7	3.7	3.7	3.7	3.8	3.7	3.7	3.8	44.8
2007	3.9	3.9	3.4	3.5	3.4	3.4	3.4	3.4	3.5	3.4	3.6	3.5	42.1
2008	4.1	4.2	4.1	4.3	4.6	5.0	4.3	4.5	4.3	4.6	4.6	4.6	53.2
2009	5.4	4.8	4.4	4.4	4.0	4.2	4.1	2.9	3.0	3.0	3.0	3.2	46.4
2010	2.9	3.2	2.8	3.3	3.0	3.3	3.2	3.5	3.3	3.2	3.2	2.9	37.7
2011	3.8	3.0	3.2	3.0	3.2	3.1	3.0	3.2	3.0	3.1	3.0	2.6	37.3
2012	3.1	3.4	3.0	3.0	2.9	3.0	2.8	2.8	3.1	4.5	4.0	3.9	39.3
2013	3.9	3.7	4.6	4.8	4.9	4.9	4.7	3.8	3.8	4.0	4.0	4.5	51.3
2014[1]	3.9	3.9	3.8	4.0	3.8	3.9	3.9	3.4	4.2	3.9			46.3

[1] Preliminary.   *Source: U.S. Geological Survey (USGS)*

COPPER

Imports of Refined Copper into the United States   In Thousands of Metric Tons

Year	Jan.	Feb.	Mar.	Apr.	May	June	July	Aug.	Sept.	Oct.	Nov.	Dec.	Total
2005	85.2	66.5	75.8	63.7	107.0	64.7	75.8	79.4	79.4	99.4	101.0	106.0	1,003.9
2006	138.0	108.0	80.1	69.1	100.0	94.1	91.4	101.0	106.0	96.4	58.3	56.5	1,098.9
2007	87.3	76.4	68.4	65.8	80.1	58.9	66.6	77.7	68.5	66.9	54.5	NA	841.2
2008	58.6	57.8	53.6	59.8	63.6	48.9	77.5	86.9	54.5	49.7	51.0	61.7	723.6
2009	76.4	67.7	80.0	53.9	52.6	35.7	54.2	36.4	56.0	39.9	55.2	55.5	663.5
2010	60.3	61.3	46.2	46.7	46.7	61.6	66.0	37.7	35.3	45.6	34.4	63.3	605.1
2011	57.4	50.5	66.2	73.1	65.5	45.5	69.5	32.3	64.3	46.7	50.3	48.9	670.2
2012	37.8	51.1	47.1	51.6	52.4	57.2	53.4	49.5	46.2	52.7	64.7	86.8	650.5
2013	86.8	64.6	88.2	55.6	83.6	69.2	70.0	50.2	42.8	40.3	33.9	48.5	733.7
2014[1]	42.9	36.2	45.1	56.2	54.1	53.0	62.9	46.7	59.9	58.6			618.7

[1] Preliminary.   Source: U.S. Geological Survey (USGS)

Exports of Refined Copper from the United States   In Thousands of Metric Tons

Year	Jan.	Feb.	Mar.	Apr.	May	June	July	Aug.	Sept.	Oct.	Nov.	Dec.	Total
2005	4.5	3.2	2.8	1.9	7.2	4.3	3.0	2.7	1.8	3.3	3.3	3.0	40.9
2006	5.6	7.3	6.8	9.6	6.3	13.1	6.0	9.6	9.3	13.7	6.2	12.6	106.1
2007	3.1	2.7	5.1	3.6	3.9	6.6	3.6	3.4	5.4	7.1	3.0	NA	51.8
2008	6.0	5.7	6.3	3.2	1.9	1.4	2.0	2.0	1.5	3.2	1.7	1.6	36.5
2009	.9	1.7	3.8	6.5	21.4	19.2	8.9	6.3	4.0	2.1	3.0	3.2	80.9
2010	6.2	13.9	13.6	10.4	4.7	4.5	4.2	5.3	7.0	1.5	1.2	5.7	78.2
2011	1.6	5.0	3.1	2.1	3.5	1.9	1.9	5.1	2.1	2.4	6.9	4.7	40.4
2012	9.6	18.3	26.0	37.9	33.0	10.2	4.9	5.7	4.3	3.2	3.3	3.5	160.0
2013	3.5	5.3	5.1	5.4	5.7	4.9	8.3	17.1	14.9	10.3	15.2	17.7	113.4
2014[1]	9.4	9.0	8.6	5.5	7.7	6.3	10.2	8.4	11.0	11.1			104.5

[1] Preliminary.   Source: U.S. Geological Survey (USGS)

Production of Refined Copper in the United States   In Thousands of Short Tons

Year	Jan.	Feb.	Mar.	Apr.	May	June	July	Aug.	Sept.	Oct.	Nov.	Dec.	Total
2005	102.0	102.0	104.0	105.0	109.0	101.0	100.0	102.0	103.0	104.0	108.0	115.0	1,255
2006	99.9	101.0	117.0	109.0	113.0	114.0	100.0	101.0	102.0	89.8	94.4	108.0	1,249
2007	101.0	97.1	116.0	113.0	116.0	112.0	116.0	117.0	108.0	120.0	91.5	103.0	1,311
2008	109.0	107.0	108.0	102.0	107.0	102.0	98.7	107.0	108.0	110.0	107.0	113.0	1,279
2009	105.0	96.7	95.9	93.7	91.8	90.3	94.4	97.6	94.3	101.0	98.0	101.0	1,160
2010	96.2	91.3	95.2	89.5	85.4	89.3	95.6	94.4	94.2	90.1	84.1	89.2	1,095
2011	86.8	76.3	84.9	79.7	82.9	86.4	79.2	79.7	93.6	89.6	95.1	96.5	1,031
2012	88.5	82.4	78.4	74.4	78.2	68.3	82.6	87.9	82.4	94.1	92.9	91.3	1,001
2013	89.3	76.2	85.7	88.5	83.0	80.3	83.8	85.3	81.1	94.8	92.8	99.2	1,040
2014[1]	96.0	86.7	87.8	94.8	98.9	97.8	103.0	99.9	90.7	79.3			1,122

Recoverable Copper Content.   [1] Preliminary.   Source: U.S. Geological Survey (USGS)

Mine Production of Recoverable Copper in the United States   In Thousands of Metric Tons

Year	---------- Recoverable Copper ----------			---------- Contained Copper ----------		
	Arizona	Others[2]	Total	Electrowon	Concentrates[3]	Total
2005	691.0	449.1	1,139.4	554.6	602.6	1,157.3
2006	712.2	485.1	1,197.5	530.3	690.1	1,219.0
2007	731.4	437.6	1,168.8	504.1	690.0	1,193.3
2008	836.2	472.0	1,307.7	507.8	826.4	1,335.1
2009	711.4	470.3	1,181.8	476.4	727.6	1,203.9
2010	703.2	406.0	1,109.2	428.3	700.9	1,128.9
2011	751.3	361.0	1,112.5	448.9	689.7	1,138.4
2012	763.3	404.1	1,167.9	471.0	724.0	1,196.4
2013	794.9	453.2	1,249.0	474.7	803.6	1,279.2
2014[1]	876.0	470.3	1,346.4	990.8	881.6	1,382.4

[1] Preliminary.   [2] Includes production from Alaska, Idaho, Missouri, Montana, Nevada, New Mexico, and Utah.   [3] Includes copper content of precipitates and other metal concentrates.   Source: U.S. Geological Survey (USGS)

Production of Recoverable Copper in Arizona   In Thousands of Short Tons

Year	Jan.	Feb.	Mar.	Apr.	May	June	July	Aug.	Sept.	Oct.	Nov.	Dec.	Total
2005	58.5	54.2	62.1	62.0	65.3	61.7	54.4	55.2	53.5	53.4	53.3	57.4	691.0
2006	55.9	52.7	60.8	58.9	62.0	60.5	60.4	59.9	59.3	59.7	60.8	61.3	712.2
2007	57.6	52.2	58.9	60.2	63.5	63.0	65.5	66.3	62.8	62.1	60.1	59.2	731.4
2008	63.0	57.9	64.7	68.0	68.7	67.9	71.2	74.7	72.9	78.4	73.1	75.7	836.2
2009	65.8	57.3	57.8	53.7	58.7	59.0	62.7	58.2	56.5	60.7	59.0	62.0	711.4
2010	62.6	53.1	56.6	56.6	61.5	58.6	59.1	56.2	57.7	60.0	57.6	63.6	703.2
2011	57.3	53.0	60.8	59.3	66.5	63.9	61.9	65.0	64.4	66.5	67.1	65.6	751.3
2012	62.8	64.5	65.7	64.6	65.2	56.7	60.7	66.2	60.9	64.0	67.5	64.5	763.3
2013	65.7	57.7	66.5	64.1	70.7	64.6	68.2	65.1	66.6	68.5	65.9	71.3	794.9
2014[1]	69.7	66.6	75.0	70.1	66.7	73.0	75.1	77.1	74.8	81.9			876.0

[1] Preliminary.   Source: U.S. Geological Survey (USGS)

Copper Stocks in the United States at Yearend   In Metric Tons

Year	Crude Copper[2]	Refined Copper						Total Refined
		Refineries[3]	Wire-rod Mills[3]	Brass Mills[3]	Other[4]	Comex	LME[5]	
2004	51.4	10.3	20.3	21.5	3.6	43.7	35.0	134.0
2005	44.3	8.2	21.3	24.6	5.8	6.2	0.8	66.8
2006	18.8	28.1	21.5	34.5	5.8	30.9	75.6	196.0
2007	26.3	21.8	20.6	10.4	5.8	13.5	60.6	133.0
2008	19.8	15.7	22.6	8.3	5.8	31.3	106.0	190.0
2009	15.5	23.7	25.3	7.6	3.2	90.0	283.0	433.0
2010	21.1	10.3	19.7	6.4	4.3	58.6	284.0	384.0
2011	13.0	8.4	24.0	6.9	4.4	79.8	286.0	409.0
2012	12.3	12.9	28.1	6.5	4.3	64.1	120.0	236.0
2013[1]	12.7	15.0	32.6	6.7	4.2	15.0	185.0	258.0

[1] Preliminary.   [2] Copper content of blister and anode.   [3] Stocks of refined copper as reported; no estimates are made for nonrespondents.   [4] Monthly estimates based on reported and 2011 annual data, comprising stocks at ingot makers, chemical plants, foundries, and miscellaneous manufacturers.
[5] London Metal Exchange Ltd., U.S. warehouses.   Source: U.S. Geological Survey (USGS)

Stocks of Crude Copper[2] in the United States, at End of Month   In Thousands of Metric Tons

Year	Jan.	Feb.	Mar.	Apr.	May	June	July	Aug.	Sept.	Oct.	Nov.	Dec.
2005	66.1	46.7	42.3	42.5	38.2	45.2	33.3	43.8	51.7	50.9	42.9	44.3
2006	17.3	21.7	15.2	18.8	40.6	18.6	23.9	20.5	27.3	24.3	19.0	18.8
2007	24.7	22.3	24.4	26.0	27.0	33.5	29.9	30.1	28.9	21.5	22.3	26.3
2008	29.0	21.1	15.7	15.1	14.3	30.5	16.0	10.8	11.8	14.1	16.3	19.8
2009	24.7	16.0	21.3	25.2	22.5	23.8	26.1	32.5	27.1	28.9	28.2	15.5
2010	25.8	25.2	25.5	24.4	23.8	18.1	23.7	22.4	19.9	17.6	23.4	21.1
2011	25.2	24.8	24.7	24.9	27.2	20.1	20.1	13.0	14.3	18.5	14.5	13.0
2012	10.9	14.2	16.5	19.2	15.0	12.6	12.3	12.5	16.7	19.7	18.6	12.3
2013	8.6	20.1	17.9	21.8	28.7	11.5	12.8	10.7	11.2	14.2	15.3	12.7
2014[1]	13.4	13.8	18.4	15.1	23.7	17.6	11.8	17.8	17.3	13.1		

[1] Preliminary.   [2] Copper content of blister and anode.   Source: U.S. Geological Survey (USGS)

Stocks of Refined Copper in the United States, at End of Month   In Thousands of Metric Tons

Year	Jan.	Feb.	Mar.	Apr.	May	June	July	Aug.	Sept.	Oct.	Nov.	Dec.
2005	143.0	136.0	129.0	125.0	113.0	101.0	91.9	80.5	70.2	65.7	60.9	66.8
2006	82.1	106.0	109.0	90.2	86.4	75.6	84.3	89.5	102.0	111.0	157.0	196.0
2007	198.0	193.0	174.0	148.0	116.0	105.0	104.0	103.0	102.0	106.0	113.0	133.0
2008	100.0	90.1	71.1	62.7	62.1	61.6	69.7	91.1	109.0	118.0	146.0	190.0
2009	258.0	289.0	337.0	337.0	312.0	284.0	293.0	298.0	323.0	339.0	379.0	433.0
2010	467.0	487.0	467.0	455.0	434.0	431.0	422.0	407.0	381.0	364.0	356.0	384.0
2011	282.0	383.0	372.0	366.0	365.0	359.0	368.0	370.0	377.0	383.0	387.0	409.0
2012	393.0	358.0	309.0	268.0	235.0	210.0	199.0	192.0	187.0	194.0	203.0	236.0
2013	261.0	275.0	308.0	325.0	318.0	314.0	306.0	292.0	273.0	260.0	250.0	258.0
2014[1]	246.0	239.0	258.0	246.0	222.0	201.0	198.0	202.0	214.0	207.0		

[1] Preliminary.   Source: U.S. Geological Survey (USGS)

COPPER

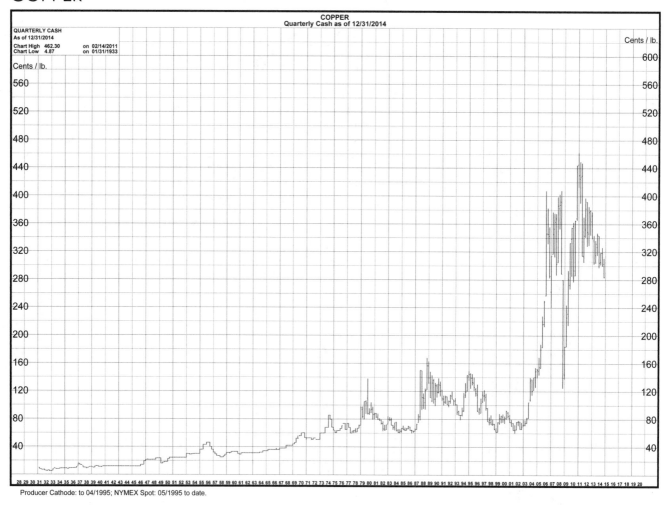

COPPER
Quarterly Cash as of 12/31/2014

QUARTERLY CASH
As of 12/31/2014
Chart High 462.30 on 02/14/2011
Chart Low 4.87 on 01/31/1933

Cents / lb.

Producer Cathode: to 04/1995; NYMEX Spot: 05/1995 to date.

Producers' Price of Electrolytic (Wirebar) Copper, Delivered to U.S. Destinations   In Cents Per Pound

Year	Jan.	Feb.	Mar.	Apr.	May	June	July	Aug.	Sept.	Oct.	Nov.	Dec.	Average
2005	151.25	152.89	154.68	155.42	154.19	168.31	169.62	178.39	182.00	197.61	208.60	224.25	174.77
2006	225.07	230.74	238.31	302.74	382.65	346.65	368.49	359.91	353.01	345.83	322.45	307.00	315.24
2007	263.89	265.67	298.65	356.76	355.24	346.59	370.42	343.65	351.87	364.48	318.93	306.74	328.57
2008	325.53	364.78	385.98	399.96	383.39	375.08	382.31	349.89	320.54	224.32	174.59	145.09	319.29
2009	153.55	155.38	176.45	209.36	215.36	233.23	243.36	285.81	285.91	292.24	307.45	320.57	239.89
2010	337.71	315.88	343.54	356.46	315.33	299.00	312.18	337.50	357.31	382.81	390.16	419.69	347.30
2011	439.85	454.13	436.70	435.63	410.49	415.91	445.11	412.86	378.78	339.15	349.89	348.73	405.60
2012	371.87	389.59	389.13	377.51	362.32	340.76	349.95	348.05	378.12	374.24	356.44	368.84	367.24
2013	372.47	371.83	351.31	332.72	337.45	325.95	321.50	335.18	334.13	334.93	328.07	339.43	340.41
2014	342.10	334.93	315.05	313.99	320.45	317.04	329.34	322.01	315.28	309.62	308.64	296.45	318.74

Source: American Metal Market (AMM)

Dealers' Buying Price of No. 2 Heavy Copper Scrap in Chicago   In Cents Per Pound

Year	Jan.	Feb.	Mar.	Apr.	May	June	July	Aug.	Sept.	Oct.	Nov.	Dec.	Average
2005	90.00	90.00	90.00	90.00	90.00	94.09	100.00	100.00	100.00	100.00	100.00	129.52	97.80
2006	137.50	137.50	139.46	145.00	145.00	171.36	175.25	185.89	184.10	192.09	192.85	183.30	165.78
2007	155.83	153.92	164.32	197.83	210.09	203.60	216.83	219.89	213.97	224.72	210.20	191.87	196.92
2008	198.21	210.00	238.21	246.82	247.02	237.50	240.00	233.93	226.07	141.85	97.50	87.02	200.34
2009	80.00	92.24	104.32	124.40	134.00	155.23	166.59	182.02	192.50	194.40	203.55	224.61	154.49
2010	245.13	220.92	258.37	275.68	244.50	214.32	214.64	255.68	260.36	273.93	277.50	268.29	250.78
2011	285.00	292.50	299.13	295.00	290.72	295.23	315.00	311.41	293.69	241.55	261.50	256.97	286.48
2012	262.50	287.75	292.50	283.93	280.00	259.64	262.50	262.50	275.39	282.50	270.25	281.39	275.07
2013	287.74	292.24	287.02	272.50	263.18	269.00	255.23	260.55	265.00	274.63	272.76	277.76	273.13
2014	287.02	277.50	266.55	262.73	270.36	269.07	270.64	268.26	262.64	257.24	255.50	240.31	265.65

Source: American Metal Market (AMM)

Nearby Futures through Last Trading Day using selected contract months: March, May, July, September and December.

Volume of Trading of Copper Futures in New York   In Thousands of Contracts

Year	Jan.	Feb.	Mar.	Apr.	May	June	July	Aug.	Sept.	Oct.	Nov.	Dec.	Total
2005	199.9	391.9	298.2	469.8	288.4	475.8	227.9	435.8	252.7	265.2	458.3	186.8	3,950.8
2006	234.3	401.4	284.5	407.0	260.4	321.6	182.2	310.0	189.4	216.4	320.8	153.4	3,281.3
2007	241.3	334.0	264.5	402.8	292.4	367.2	272.4	451.6	225.6	289.3	412.9	199.1	3,753.2
2008	345.5	459.5	298.5	466.5	344.5	462.0	382.1	463.2	349.5	403.8	414.4	228.4	4,618.1
2009	343.5	446.0	361.0	592.9	373.6	661.9	499.5	746.2	511.2	599.7	809.3	454.0	6,399.0
2010	645.5	996.3	772.6	1,049.0	894.7	1,051.1	724.9	980.5	604.4	822.3	1,132.3	631.8	10,305.7
2011	777.6	1,079.7	931.9	1,079.4	915.2	1,170.7	765.9	1,312.5	1,142.5	1,268.8	1,234.6	812.7	12,491.5
2012	1,131.5	1,572.7	1,222.8	1,768.1	1,491.4	1,790.3	1,163.1	1,478.0	1,084.8	1,137.7	1,469.8	848.6	16,158.8
2013	1,163.8	1,547.7	1,199.1	2,262.6	1,646.6	1,760.9	1,307.1	1,696.7	913.6	1,265.4	1,443.0	920.9	17,127.4
2014	1,049.9	1,236.2	1,401.8	1,422.9	933.0	1,434.3	1,081.3	1,276.8	1,089.7	1,269.0	1,458.9	927.6	14,581.5

Source: CME Group; New York Mercantile Exchange (NYMEX)

Average Open Interest of Copper Futures in New York   In Contracts

Year	Jan.	Feb.	Mar.	Apr.	May	June	July	Aug.	Sept.	Oct.	Nov.	Dec.
2005	85,363	96,537	116,004	120,138	98,240	106,218	109,156	109,481	102,652	106,829	110,972	104,062
2006	102,227	93,813	93,069	97,283	83,758	75,841	74,471	72,158	69,004	72,023	72,517	68,402
2007	69,972	70,373	69,324	78,919	80,834	79,257	88,691	78,113	72,469	86,909	78,385	71,626
2008	81,778	94,021	101,503	105,050	98,787	103,055	109,591	96,254	76,523	80,961	76,869	71,809
2009	82,402	85,831	90,636	103,517	106,511	111,555	111,849	118,935	117,782	127,204	146,612	149,621
2010	147,311	126,659	131,619	151,712	132,069	134,323	132,119	140,543	142,628	160,288	156,869	162,683
2011	162,325	157,918	138,261	134,959	122,036	128,861	148,876	130,312	120,015	126,973	124,770	115,634
2012	134,294	159,589	152,255	154,073	147,975	149,350	138,220	148,201	147,632	153,484	148,322	148,754
2013	160,188	174,428	166,007	179,530	162,279	180,744	165,350	160,513	149,129	150,400	162,528	160,424
2014	160,638	155,280	153,880	153,104	148,544	148,751	171,388	153,255	146,669	170,902	167,274	155,661

Source: CME Group; New York Mercantile Exchange (NYMEX)

Corn

Corn is a member of the grass family of plants and is a native grain of the American continents. Fossils of corn pollen that are over 80,000 years old have been found in lake sediment under Mexico City. Archaeological discoveries show that cultivated corn existed in the southwestern U.S. for at least 3,000 years, indicating that the indigenous people of the region cultivated corn as a food crop long before the Europeans reached the New World. Corn is a hardy plant that grows in many different areas of the world. It can grow at altitudes as low as sea level and as high as 12,000 feet in the South American Andes Mountains. Corn can also grow in tropical climates that receive up to 400 inches of rainfall per year, or in areas that receive only 12 inches of rainfall per year. Corn is used primarily as livestock feed in the United States and the rest of the world. Other uses for corn are alcohol additives for gasoline, adhesives, corn oil for cooking and margarine, sweeteners, and as food for humans. Corn is the largest crop in the U.S., both in terms of the value of the crop and of the acres planted.

The largest futures and options market for corn is at the CME Group. Corn futures and options also trade at ICE Futures U.S., the Bolsa de Mercadorias & Futuros (BM&F), the JSE Securities Exchange, the Mercado a Termino de Buenos Aires (MTBA), and the NYSE LIFFE European Derivatives Market. Corn futures are traded on the Budapest Stock Exchange (BSE), the Dalian Commodity Exchange (DCE), the Kansai Commodities Exchange, the Moscow Exchange, Rosario Futures Exchange, and the Tokyo Grain Exchange (TGE). The CME futures contract calls for the delivery of 5000 bushels of No. 2 yellow corn at par contract price, No. 1 yellow at 1-1/2 cents per bushel over the contract price, or No. 3 yellow at 1-1/2 cents per bushel below the contract price.

Prices – CME corn futures prices (Barchart.com electronic symbol code ZC) trended higher into May 2014 and posted a 1-1/2 year high of $5.1950 a bushel. Strong foreign demand for U.S. corn pushed prices higher into May. In April, 2013/14 cumulative U.S. 2013/14 corn exports were up by a whopping 100% yr/yr, which prompted the USDA to hike its U.S. 2013/14 corn export forecast to a 2-year high of 1.75 billion bushels. However, ideal spring weather in the U.S. led to early corn plantings and the USDA in May projected a record U.S. 2014/15 corn crop of 13.935 billion bushels and record global 2014/15 corn production of 979 MMT. Also, supplies were more than adequate after the USDA raised its U.S. quarterly corn stocks on March 1 to a 4-year high of 7.01 billion bushels and projected 2014/15 global corn ending stocks would climb to a record 181.79 MMT. Signs of record corn production and supplies sent corn prices cascading lower from May into October by more than -$2.00 a bushel when they posted a 5-1/4 year low of $3.1825 a bushel. In October, the USDA raised its U.S. 2014/15 corn production estimate to a record 14.475 billion bushels and raised its 2014/15 U.S. corn ending stocks estimate to 2.081 billion

bushels, a 21-year high. The USDA also raised its 2014/15 global corn production estimate to a record 990.69 MMT and raised its 2014/15 global corn ending stocks estimate to a record 190.58 MMT. Corn prices bottomed in October, though, due to the slow pace of the U.S. corn harvest. The USDA Crop Progress report showed 31% of the U.S. corn crop was harvested as of Oct 19, well below the 5-year average of 53%. This caused the USDA in November to unexpectedly cut its U.S. 2014/15 corn production estimate to 14.407 billion bushels and reduce its U.S. corn ending stocks estimate to 2.088 billion bushels. Stronger domestic demand helped push corn prices up to a 6-month high in December after U.S. ethanol production rose to a record 992,000 bpd in the week ended Dec 19. Prices finished 2014 down 5.9% at $3.97 a bushel.

Supply – World production of corn in the 2014-15 marketing year rose +0.1% to 988.077 million metric tons, a new record high. The world's largest corn producers are the U.S. with 36.5% of world production, China (21.8%), and Brazil (7.6%). Corn production in both China and Brazil has nearly tripled since 1980. Production in the U.S. over that same time frame has risen by about 50%. The world area harvested with corn in 2014-15 fell -1.6% yr/yr to 317.2 million hectares, below last year's 14-year high of 322.4 million hectares. World ending stocks of corn and coarse grains in 2014-15 rose +7.7% to 226.0 million metric tons.

U.S. corn production estimates for the 2014-15 marketing year (Sep-Aug) rose by +2.8% yr/yr to 14.215 billion bushels. U.S. farmers harvested 83.136 million acres of corn for grain usage in 2014-15, which was down -4.9% yr/yr. U.S. corn yield in 2014-15 rose +8.2% to 171.0 bushels per acre. U.S. 2014-15 ending stocks rose by +68.4% to 2.080 billion bushels. The largest corn producing states in the U.S. in 2014 were Iowa with 16.7% of U.S. production, Illinois (16.5%), Nebraska (11.3%), Minnesota (8.3%), and Indiana (7.6%). The value of the U.S. corn crop in 2013-14 (latest data) was $62.716 billion.

Demand – World consumption of corn and rough grains in 2014-15 rose +1.5% yr/yr to 1.256 billion metric tons, a new record high. The U.S. distribution tables for corn show that in 2014-15 the largest category of usage, aside from animal feed, is for ethanol production (alcohol fuel) with 5.125 billion bushels, which is 78.5% of total non-feed usage. That was down -0.1% yr/yr. Corn usage for ethanol is more than seven times the usage in 2000. After ethanol, the largest non-feed usage categories are for high fructose corn syrup (HFCS) with 7.5% of U.S. usage, glucose and dextrose sugars (4.5%), corn starch (3.8%), cereal and other corn products (3.1%), and alcoholic beverages (2.2%).

Trade – U.S. exports of corn in 2014-15 fell -4.2% to 1.983 billion bushels. The largest destination countries for U.S. corn exports are Japan, which accounted for 36% of U.S. corn exports, Mexico (27%), and Venezuela (6%).

World Production of Corn or Maize   In Thousands of Metric Tons

Crop Year Beginning Oct. 1	Argentina	Brazil	Canada	China	Egypt	European Union	India	Mexico	Romania	South Africa	Ukraine	United States	World Total
2005-06	15,800	41,700	9,332	139,365	5,932	63,168	14,710	19,500	10,300	6,935	7,167	282,263	700,696
2006-07	22,500	51,000	8,990	151,600	6,149	55,629	15,100	22,350	8,500	7,300	6,426	267,503	716,621
2007-08	22,017	58,600	11,649	152,300	6,174	49,355	18,960	23,600	----	13,164	7,421	331,177	795,539
2008-09	15,500	51,000	10,643	165,914	6,645	64,821	19,730	24,226	----	12,567	11,447	305,911	799,712
2009-10	25,000	56,100	9,796	163,974	6,280	59,151	16,720	20,374	----	13,420	10,486	331,921	824,942
2010-11	25,200	57,400	12,043	177,245	6,500	58,272	21,730	21,058	----	10,924	11,919	315,618	835,379
2011-12	21,000	73,000	11,359	192,780	5,500	68,123	21,760	18,726	----	12,759	22,838	312,789	888,163
2012-13[1]	27,000	81,500	13,060	205,614	5,800	58,896	22,260	21,591	----	12,365	20,922	273,192	867,996
2013-14[2]	25,000	79,300	14,194	218,490	5,800	64,259	24,190	22,960	----	14,750	30,900	351,272	987,686
2014-15[3]	22,000	75,000	11,500	215,500	5,750	73,960	22,000	23,000	----	13,500	27,000	361,091	988,077

[1] Preliminary.   [2] Estimate.   [3] Forecast.   *Source: Foreign Agricultural Service, U.S. Department of Agriculture (FAS-USDA)*

World Supply and Demand of Coarse Grains   In Millions of Metric Tons/Hectares

Crop Year Beginning Oct. 1	Area Harvested	Yield	Production	World Trade	Total Consumption	Ending Stocks	Stocks as % of Consumption[3]
2005-06	298.7	3.30	981.0	108.4	994.5	165.8	16.7
2006-07	305.1	3.20	988.5	114.5	1,013.1	141.2	13.9
2007-08	316.7	3.40	1,079.8	128.7	1,056.2	164.7	15.6
2008-09	314.7	3.50	1,109.5	110.4	1,080.0	194.2	18.0
2009-10	307.8	3.60	1,118.1	118.8	1,113.9	198.4	17.8
2010-11	306.0	3.60	1,099.4	116.0	1,130.1	167.8	14.8
2011-12	317.6	3.60	1,157.0	133.4	1,156.4	168.4	14.6
2012-13	315.8	3.60	1,136.9	132.2	1,136.5	168.8	14.9
2013-14[1]	322.4	4.00	1,278.3	162.4	1,237.3	209.8	17.0
2014-15[2]	317.2	4.00	1,272.4	148.4	1,256.3	226.0	18.0

[1] Preliminary.   [2] Estimate.   [3] Represents the ratio of marketing year ending stocks to total consumption.   *Source: Foreign Agricultural Service, U.S. Department of Agriculture (FAS-USDA)*

Acreage and Supply of Corn in the United States   In Millions of Bushels

Crop Year Beginning Sept. 1	Planted	Harvested For Grain	Harvested For Silage	Yield Per Harvested Acre Bushels	Carry-over, Sept. 1 On Farms	Carry-over, Sept. 1 Off Farms	Supply Beginning Stocks	Supply Production	Supply Imports	Total Supply
	In Thousands of Acres									
2005-06	81,759	75,107	5,920	147.9	820.5	1,293.5	2,114	11,112	9	13,235
2006-07	78,327	70,648	6,477	149.1	749.5	1,217.7	1,967	10,531	12	12,510
2007-08	93,527	86,520	6,060	150.7	460.1	843.5	1,304	13,038	20	14,362
2008-09	85,982	78,570	5,965	153.9	500.0	1,124.2	1,624	12,092	14	13,729
2009-10	86,382	79,490	5,605	164.7	607.5	1,065.8	1,673	13,110	8	14,774
2010-11	88,192	81,446	5,567	152.8	485.1	1,222.7	1,708	12,447	28	14,161
2011-12	91,936	83,989	5,935	147.2	315.0	812.7	1,128	12,360	29	13,471
2012-13	97,291	87,365	7,419	123.1	313.7	675.3	989	10,755	160	11,904
2013-14[1]	95,365	87,451	6,281	158.1	275.0	546.2	821	13,829	36	14,686
2014-15[2]	90,597	83,136	6,371	171.0	462.0	769.9	1,232	14,216	25	15,472

[1] Preliminary.   [2] Estimate.   *Source: Economic Research Service, U.S. Department of Agriculture (ERS-USDA)*

Production of Corn (For Grain) in the United States, by State   In Millions of Bushels

Year	Illinois	Indiana	Iowa	Kansas	Michigan	Minnesota	Missouri	Nebraska	Ohio	South Dakota	Texas	Wisconsin	Total
2005	1,708.9	888.6	2,162.5	465.8	288.9	1,191.9	329.7	1,270.5	464.8	470.1	210.9	429.2	11,112.1
2006	1,817.5	844.7	2,050.1	345.0	286.7	1,102.9	362.9	1,178.0	470.6	312.3	175.5	400.4	10,531.1
2007	2,283.8	981.0	2,376.9	507.8	287.8	1,146.1	457.8	1,472.0	541.5	542.1	291.6	442.8	13,037.9
2008	2,130.1	873.6	2,188.8	486.4	295.3	1,180.8	381.6	1,393.7	421.2	585.2	253.8	394.6	12,091.6
2009	2,053.2	933.7	2,420.6	598.3	309.3	1,244.1	446.8	1,575.3	546.4	706.7	254.8	448.3	13,110.1
2010	1,946.8	898.0	2,153.3	581.3	315.0	1,292.1	369.0	1,469.1	533.0	569.7	301.6	502.2	12,446.9
2011	1,946.8	839.5	2,356.4	449.4	335.1	1,201.2	350.0	1,536.0	508.8	653.4	136.7	517.9	12,359.6
2012	1,286.3	597.0	1,876.9	375.3	314.2	1,374.5	247.5	1,292.2	438.0	535.3	200.0	396.0	10,755.1
2013	2,100.4	1,031.9	2,140.2	504.0	345.7	1,294.3	435.2	1,614.0	649.0	802.8	265.2	439.4	13,829.0
2014[1]	2,350.0	1,084.8	2,367.4	566.2	355.8	1,177.8	628.7	1,602.1	610.7	787.4	294.5	485.2	14,215.5

[1] Preliminary.   *Source: National Agricultural Statistics Service, U.S. Department of Agriculture (NASS-USDA)*

CORN

Quarterly Supply and Disappearance of Corn in the United States In Millions of Bushels

Crop Year Beginning Sept. 1	Beginning Stocks	Pro-duction	Imports[3]	Total Supply	Food & Alcohol	Seed	Feed & Residual	Total	Exports[3]	Total Disap-pearance	Gov't Owned[4]	Privately Owned[5]	Total Stocks
						Domestic Use						**Ending Stocks**	
2010-11	1,708	12,447	27.7	14,182	6,403	23.0	4,798	11,224	1,831	13,055	----	----	1,128
Sept.-Nov.	1,708	12,447	5.3	14,160	1,582	0	2,069	3,651	452	4,103	----	----	10,057
Dec.-Feb.	10,057	----	8.5	10,065	1,577	0	1,562	3,139	403	3,542	----	----	6,523
Mar.-May	6,523	----	10.4	6,534	1,618	20.2	715	2,354	510	2,864	----	----	3,670
June-Aug.	3,670	----	3.5	3,673	1,625	2.8	452	2,080	466	2,546	----	----	1,128
2011-12	1,128	12,314	29.4	13,471	6,396	24.5	4,520	10,941	1,541	12,482	----	----	989
Sept.-Nov.	1,128	12,314	4.1	13,446	1,611	0	1,782	3,393	406	3,799	----	----	9,647
Dec.-Feb.	9,647	----	3.9	9,651	1,636	0	1,547	3,183	444	3,627	----	----	6,023
Mar.-May	6,023	----	10.7	6,034	1,601	23.6	861	2,486	400	2,886	----	----	3,148
June-Aug.	3,148	----	10.7	3,159	1,548	1.0	330	1,879	291	2,170	----	----	989
2012-13	989	10,755	159.9	11,904	6,013	24.6	4,315	10,353	730	11,083	----	----	821
Sept.-Nov.	989	10,755	34.8	11,779	1,466	0	2,060	3,525	221	3,746	----	----	8,033
Dec.-Feb.	8,033	----	45.4	8,078	1,430	0	1,087	2,517	161	2,678	----	----	5,400
Mar.-May	5,400	----	40.2	5,440	1,545	22.4	921	2,488	186	2,674	----	----	2,766
June-Aug.	2,766	----	39.6	2,806	1,573	2.2	247	1,822	162	1,985	----	----	821
2013-14[1]	821	13,829	35.8	14,686	6,478	23.0	5,036	11,537	1,917	13,454	----	----	1,232
Sept.-Nov.	821	13,829	14.5	14,665	1,550	0	2,312	3,862	350	4,212	----	----	10,453
Dec.-Feb.	10,453	----	6.6	10,459	1,605	0	1,453	3,058	393	3,451	----	----	7,008
Mar.-May	7,008	----	8.6	7,017	1,646	21.9	859	2,528	637	3,165	----	----	3,852
June-Aug.	3,852	----	6.1	3,858	1,677	1.1	411	2,089	537	2,626	----	----	1,232
2014-15[2]	1,232	14,216	25.0	15,472	6,622	23.2	5,250	11,895	1,750	13,645	----	----	1,827
Sept.-Nov.	1,232	14,216	5.0	15,452	1,632	0	2,209	3,842	408	4,250	----	----	11,203

[1] Preliminary.   [2] Estimate.   [3] Uncommitted inventory.   [4] Includes quantity under loan and farmer-owned reserve.   *Source: Economic Research Service, U.S. Department of Agriculture (ERS-USDA)*

Corn Production Estimates and Cash Price in the United States

Year	Aug. 1	Sept. 1	Oct. 1	Nov. 1	Final	St. Louis No. 2 Yellow	Omaha No. 2 Yellow	Gulf Ports No. 2 Yellow	Kansas City No. 2 White	Chicago No. 2 Yellow	Average Farm Price[2]	Value of Pro-duction (Mil. $)
	Corn for Grain Production Estimates In Thousands of Bushels					**Dollars Per Bushel**						
2005-06	10,349,841	10,638,661	10,857,440	11,032,105	11,112,072	2.19	1.88	2.69	2.11	2.10	2.01	22,198
2006-07	10,975,740	11,113,766	10,905,194	10,744,806	10,531,123	3.60	3.33	3.95	4.18	3.46	3.13	32,083
2007-08	13,053,617	13,307,999	13,318,102	13,167,741	13,037,875	5.05	4.84	5.54	5.19	4.98	4.45	54,667
2008-09	12,287,875	12,072,365	12,199,908	12,019,894	12,091,648	3.88	3.80	4.39	4.13	3.89	4.05	49,313
2009-10	12,760,986	12,954,500	13,018,058	12,920,928	13,110,062	3.69	3.49	4.14	3.71	3.64	3.53	46,734
2010-11	13,365,225	13,159,700	12,663,949	12,539,646	12,446,865	6.51	6.29	7.04	6.55	6.38	5.51	64,643
2011-12	12,914,085	12,497,070	12,432,910	12,309,936	12,359,612	6.95	6.65	7.22	7.37	6.73	6.36	76,940
2012-13	10,778,589	10,727,364	10,705,729	10,725,191	10,755,111	6.94	7.20	7.58	7.52	7.17	6.88	74,155
2013-14	13,763,025	13,843,320	NA	13,988,720	13,828,964	4.90	4.35	5.16	4.63	4.47	4.47	61,928
2014-15[1]	14,031,915	14,395,350	14,474,920	14,407,420	14,215,532	3.70	3.44	4.36	3.66	3.70	3.64	52,372

[1] Preliminary.   [2] Season-average price based on monthly prices weigthed by monthly marketings.
Source: Economic Research Service, U.S. Department of Agriculture (ERS-USDA)

Distribution of Corn in the United States In Millions of Bushels

Crop Year Beginning Sept. 1	HFCS	Glucose & Dextrose	Starch	Fuel	Bev-rage[3]	Seed	Cereal & Other Products	Total	Livestock Feed[4]	Exports (Including Grain Equiv. of Products)	Domestic Disap-pearance	Total Utilization
	Food, Seed and Industrial Use		**Alcohol**									
2005-06	529	229	275	1,603	135	19.9	190	2,961	6,152	2,133.8	9,134	11,268
2006-07	510	239	272	2,117	136	23.8	190	3,464	5,591	2,125.4	9,081	11,207
2007-08	490	236	262	3,049	135	21.8	192	4,387	5,858	2,437.4	10,300	12,737
2008-09	489	245	234	3,709	134	21.9	192	5,025	5,182	1,848.9	10,207	12,056
2009-10	512	257	250	4,591	134	22.3	194	5,961	5,125	1,980.0	11,086	13,066
2010-11	521	272	258	5,019	135	23.0	197	6,426	4,799	1,829.9	11,225	13,055
2011-12	513	297	254	5,000	137	24.5	203	6,428	4,557	1,542.5	10,985	12,528
2012-13	493	291	249	4,641	140	24.6	199	6,039	4,333	731.4	10,377	11,108
2013-14[1]	480	305	225	5,130	140	23.0	201	6,504	5,200	1,925.0	11,600	13,050
2014-15[2]	490	300	250	5,125	142	23.2	200	6,530		1,750.0		

[1] Preliminary.   [2] Estimate.   [3] Also includes nonfuel industrial alcohol.   [4] Feed and waste (residual, mostly feed).
Source: Economic Research Service, U.S. Department of Agriculture (ERS-USDA)

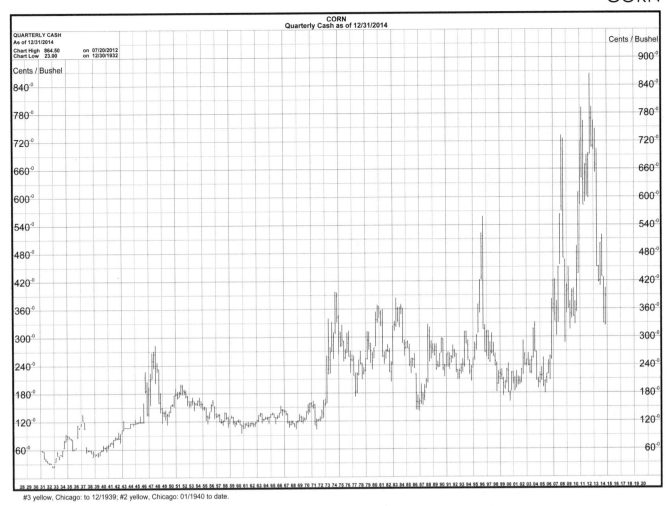

CORN
Quarterly Cash as of 12/31/2014

QUARTERLY CASH
As of 12/31/2014

Chart High 864.50 on 07/20/2012
Chart Low 23.00 on 12/30/1932

Cents / Bushel

#3 yellow, Chicago: to 12/1939; #2 yellow, Chicago: 01/1940 to date.

Average Cash Price of Corn, No. 2 Yellow in Central Illinois   In Dollars Per Bushel

Year	Sept.	Oct.	Nov.	Dec.	Jan.	Feb.	Mar.	Apr.	May	June	July	Aug.	Average
2005-06	1.75	1.67	1.75	1.89	1.98	2.07	2.04	2.18	2.22	2.15	2.22	2.07	2.00
2006-07	2.21	2.82	3.43	3.53	3.66	3.90	3.76	3.36	3.52	3.68	3.03	3.08	3.33
2007-08	3.15	3.28	3.66	4.03	4.55	4.91	5.15	5.59	5.58	6.55	5.97	5.04	4.79
2008-09	5.00	3.69	3.42	3.33	3.61	3.46	3.60	3.69	3.98	3.97	3.22	3.21	3.68
2009-10	3.10	3.52	3.62	3.59	3.52	3.39	3.40	3.36	3.43	3.24	3.49	3.77	3.45
2010-11	4.51	5.19	5.33	5.65	6.10	6.69	6.59	7.33	7.08	7.17	6.96	7.30	6.33
2011-12	6.77	6.23	6.26	5.96	6.25	6.41	6.46	6.34	6.27	6.30	7.85	8.15	6.60
2012-13	7.70	7.48	7.39	7.23	7.17	7.15	7.33	6.57	6.83	6.94	6.61	5.98	7.03
2013-14	4.78	4.20	4.10	4.13	4.13	4.33	4.64	4.98	4.72	4.37	3.74	3.59	4.31
2014-15[1]	3.16	3.09	3.45	3.75	3.67								3.42

[1] Preliminary.   *Source: Economic Research Service, U.S. Department of Agriculture (ERS-USDA)*

Average Cash Price of Corn, No. 2 Yellow at Gulf Ports[2]   In Dollars Per Bushel

Year	Sept.	Oct.	Nov.	Dec.	Jan.	Feb.	Mar.	Apr.	May	June	July	Aug.	Average
2005-06	2.47	2.58	2.44	2.61	2.61	2.72	2.67	2.74	2.81	2.78	2.90	2.92	2.69
2006-07	3.05	3.82	4.17	4.08	4.19	4.50	3.81	3.88	4.07	4.20	3.73	3.84	3.95
2007-08	4.05	4.17	4.35	4.58	5.25	5.59	5.99	6.26	6.18	7.29	6.74	5.97	5.54
2008-09	5.94	4.65	4.18	4.02	4.39	4.15	4.18	4.29	4.58	4.56	3.86	3.87	4.39
2009-10	3.82	4.25	4.36	4.18	4.25	4.11	4.04	3.99	4.15	3.88	4.15	4.46	4.14
2010-11	5.23	5.99	6.05	6.36	6.73	7.44	7.38	8.11	7.82	7.89	7.64	7.88	7.04
2011-12	7.50	6.98	6.97	6.57	6.94	7.10	7.13	6.96	6.84	6.79	8.46	8.44	7.22
2012-13	8.15	8.16	8.18	7.85	7.70	7.70	7.85	7.11	7.50	7.58	7.10	6.07	7.58
2013-14	5.27	5.13	5.06	5.06	5.03	5.32	5.65	5.65	5.51	5.14	4.64	4.48	5.16
2014-15[1]	4.14	4.15	4.54	4.55	4.44								4.36

[1] Preliminary.   [2] Barge delivered to Louisiana Gulf.   *Source: Economic Research Service, U.S. Department of Agriculture (ERS-USDA)*

CORN

Weekly Outstanding Export Sales and Cumulative Exports of U.S. Corn — In Thousands of Metric Tons

Marketing Year 2013/2014 Week Ending	Weekly Exports	Accumulated Exports	Net Sales	Outstanding Sales	Marketing Year 2014/2015 Week Ending	Weekly Exports	Accumulated Exports	Net Sales	Outstanding Sales
Sep 05, 2013	171,159	171,159	1,208,648	12,612,059	Sep 04, 2014	695,470	695,470	1,904,615	11,684,066
Sep 12, 2013	518,809	689,968	437,384	12,530,634	Sep 11, 2014	722,401	1,417,871	659,665	11,621,330
Sep 19, 2013	479,132	1,169,100	640,139	12,691,641	Sep 18, 2014	1,038,629	2,456,500	836,379	11,419,080
Sep 26, 2013	546,226	1,715,326	775,189	12,920,604	Sep 25, 2014	620,444	3,076,944	638,016	11,436,652
Oct 03, 2013	618,032	2,333,358	1,341,445	13,644,017	Oct 02, 2014	978,110	4,055,054	784,772	11,243,314
Oct 10, 2013		2,333,358		13,644,017	Oct 09, 2014	901,691	4,956,745	1,922,827	12,264,450
Oct 17, 2013		2,333,358		13,644,017	Oct 16, 2014	676,683	5,633,428	1,031,197	12,618,964
Oct 24, 2013	1,915,090	4,248,448	4,376,201	16,105,128	Oct 23, 2014	829,506	6,462,934	489,820	12,279,278
Oct 31, 2013	592,518	4,840,966	1,600,901	17,113,511	Oct 30, 2014	443,994	6,906,928	478,163	12,313,447
Nov 07, 2013	463,789	5,304,755	1,202,862	17,852,584	Nov 06, 2014	600,780	7,507,708	505,348	12,218,015
Nov 14, 2013	579,651	5,884,406	768,436	18,041,369	Nov 13, 2014	386,944	7,894,652	908,689	12,739,760
Nov 21, 2013	698,971	6,583,377	1,004,981	18,347,379	Nov 20, 2014	616,403	8,511,055	944,914	13,068,271
Nov 28, 2013	729,944	7,313,321	281,476	17,898,911	Nov 27, 2014	746,431	9,257,486	1,170,654	13,492,494
Dec 05, 2013	741,420	8,054,741	459,397	17,616,888	Dec 04, 2014	678,339	9,935,825	962,778	13,776,933
Dec 12, 2013	692,095	8,746,836	825,794	17,750,587	Dec 11, 2014	754,018	10,689,843	693,460	13,716,375
Dec 19, 2013	1,283,937	10,030,773	1,414,281	17,880,931	Dec 18, 2014	746,913	11,436,756	1,653,124	14,622,586
Dec 26, 2013	844,375	10,875,148	154,543	17,191,099	Dec 25, 2014	667,828	12,104,584	895,059	14,849,817
Jan 02, 2014	540,298	11,415,446	92,262	16,743,063	Jan 01, 2015	510,397	12,614,981	387,648	14,727,068
Jan 09, 2014	674,530	12,089,976	821,021	16,889,554	Jan 08, 2015	400,204	13,015,185	818,809	15,145,673
Jan 16, 2014	799,075	12,889,051	693,032	16,783,511	Jan 15, 2015	762,448	13,777,633	2,185,432	16,568,657
Jan 23, 2014	1,004,126	13,893,177	1,837,865	17,617,250	Jan 22, 2015	831,085	14,608,718	956,705	16,694,277
Jan 30, 2014	747,346	14,640,523	1,700,115	18,570,019	Jan 29, 2015	714,792	15,323,510	844,892	16,824,377
Feb 06, 2014	952,540	15,593,063	1,269,827	18,887,306	Feb 05, 2015	618,912	15,942,422	1,003,137	17,208,602
Feb 13, 2014	744,952	16,338,015	691,439	18,833,793	Feb 12, 2015	696,217	16,638,639	932,164	17,444,549
Feb 20, 2014	853,097	17,191,112	840,809	18,821,505	Feb 19, 2015				
Feb 27, 2014	1,138,147	18,329,259	1,518,009	19,201,367	Feb 26, 2015				
Mar 06, 2014	858,097	19,187,356	634,144	18,977,414	Mar 05, 2015				
Mar 13, 2014	927,117	20,114,473	745,804	18,796,101	Mar 12, 2015				
Mar 20, 2014	1,204,002	21,318,475	1,382,279	18,974,378	Mar 19, 2015				
Mar 27, 2014	1,425,650	22,744,125	960,635	18,509,363	Mar 26, 2015				
Apr 03, 2014	1,217,389	23,961,514	658,700	17,950,674	Apr 02, 2015				
Apr 10, 2014	1,047,984	25,009,498	538,881	17,441,571	Apr 09, 2015				
Apr 17, 2014	1,621,051	26,630,549	618,937	16,439,457	Apr 16, 2015				
Apr 24, 2014	1,215,972	27,846,521	937,920	16,161,405	Apr 23, 2015				
May 01, 2014	1,415,068	29,261,589	161,266	14,907,603	Apr 30, 2015				
May 08, 2014	1,023,306	30,284,895	343,002	14,227,299	May 07, 2015				
May 15, 2014	1,159,120	31,444,015	507,869	13,576,048	May 14, 2015				
May 22, 2014	1,166,201	32,610,216	577,311	12,987,158	May 21, 2015				
May 29, 2014	1,159,512	33,769,728	550,683	12,378,329	May 28, 2015				
Jun 05, 2014	1,070,502	34,840,230	409,696	11,717,523	Jun 04, 2015				
Jun 12, 2014	1,122,957	35,963,187	109,031	10,703,597	Jun 11, 2015				
Jun 19, 2014	1,088,533	37,051,720	255,431	9,870,495	Jun 18, 2015				
Jun 26, 2014	909,536	37,961,256	290,696	9,251,655	Jun 25, 2015				
Jul 03, 2014	1,207,083	39,168,339	362,998	8,407,570	Jul 02, 2015				
Jul 10, 2014	907,900	40,076,239	573,725	8,073,395	Jul 09, 2015				
Jul 17, 2014	992,508	41,068,747	291,540	7,372,427	Jul 16, 2015				
Jul 24, 2014	865,458	41,934,205	173,781	6,680,750	Jul 23, 2015				
Jul 31, 2014	1,071,719	43,005,924	120,877	5,729,908	Jul 30, 2015				
Aug 07, 2014	721,823	43,727,747	-117,130	4,890,955	Aug 06, 2015				
Aug 14, 2014	1,114,592	44,842,339	70,160	3,846,523	Aug 13, 2015				
Aug 21, 2014	1,002,720	45,845,059	-32,678	2,811,125	Aug 20, 2015				
Aug 28, 2014	1,022,551	46,867,610	-7,489	1,781,085	Aug 27, 2015				
Sep 04, 2014	507,483	47,375,093	67,812	1,341,414					

Source: Foreign Agricultural Service, U.S. Department of Agriculture (FAS-USDA)

Average Price Received by Farmers for Corn in the United States   In Dollars Per Bushel

Year	Sept.	Oct.	Nov.	Dec.	Jan.	Feb.	Mar.	Apr.	May	June	July	Aug.	Average
2005-06	1.90	1.82	1.77	1.92	2.00	2.02	2.06	2.11	2.17	2.14	2.14	2.09	2.01
2006-07	2.20	2.55	2.88	3.01	3.05	3.44	3.43	3.39	3.49	3.53	3.32	3.26	3.13
2007-08	3.28	3.29	3.44	3.77	3.98	4.54	4.70	5.14	5.27	5.47	5.25	5.26	4.45
2008-09	5.01	4.37	4.26	4.11	4.36	3.87	3.85	3.85	3.96	4.01	3.60	3.33	4.05
2009-10	3.25	3.61	3.65	3.60	3.66	3.55	3.55	3.41	3.48	3.41	3.49	3.65	3.53
2010-11	4.08	4.32	4.55	4.82	4.94	5.65	5.53	6.36	6.32	6.38	6.33	6.88	5.51
2011-12	6.38	5.73	5.83	5.86	6.07	6.28	6.35	6.34	6.34	6.37	7.14	7.63	6.36
2012-13	6.89	6.78	7.01	6.87	6.96	7.04	7.13	6.97	6.97	6.97	6.79	6.21	6.88
2013-14	5.40	4.63	4.37	4.41	4.42	4.35	4.51	4.71	4.71	4.49	4.05	3.63	4.47
2014-15[1]	3.48	3.56	3.58	3.78	3.81								3.64

[1] Preliminary.   *Source: Economic Research Service, U.S. Department of Agriculture (ERS-USDA)*

Corn Price Support Data in the United States

Crop Year Beginning Sept. 1	National Average Loan Rate[3] --- Dollars Per Bushel -----	Target Price	Placed Under Loan	% of Pro- duction	Acquired by CCC	Owned by CCC Aug. 31	CCC Owned	Under CCC Loan	Quantity Pledged (Thousands of Bushels)	Face Amount (Thousands of Dollars)
			-- Millions of Bushels -----------------------------				(As of Dec. 31)			
2004-05	1.95	2.63	1,366	11.6	25	0	12	----	40,814	87,053
2005-06	1.95	2.63	1,064	9.6	2	2	12	----	47,595	99,406
2006-07	1.95	2.63	1,108	10.5	0	0	1	----	31,873	65,968
2007-08	1.95	2.63	1,217	9.3	0	0	1	----	1,217,822	2,332,929
2008-09	1.95	2.63	1,074	8.9	0	0	30	----	1,078,175	2,025,300
2009-10	1.95	2.63	934	7.1	0	0	9	----	940,474	1,707,092
2010-11	1.95	2.63	801	6.4	0	0	0	----	38,062	76,121
2011-12[1]	1.95	2.63	572	4.6	----	----				
2012-13[2]	1.95	2.63			----	----				
2013-14[2]	1.95									

[1] Preliminary.   [2] Estimate.   [3] Findley or announced loan rate.   NA = Not available.
Source: National Agricultural Statistics Service, U.S. Department of Agriculture (NASS-USDA)

U.S. Exports[1] of Corn (Including Seed), By Country of Destination   In Thousands of Metric Tons

Crop Year Beginning Oct. 1	Algeria	Canada	Egypt	Israel	Japan	Mexico	Korea, South	Russia	Saudi Arabia	Spain	Taiwan	Vene- zuela	Total
2004-05	1,036	2,210	3,738	393	15,036	2,210	5,935	13	126	14	4,446	90	45,262
2005-06	1,255	1,901	4,156	725	16,361	6,755	5,866	15	619	8	4,519	133	56,038
2006-07	940	2,142	3,522	844	14,840	8,886	3,873	9	540	3	4,213	514	54,159
2007-08	898	3,051	2,971	1,207	15,043	9,526	8,380	7	985	10	3,792	1,085	60,593
2008-09	95	1,810	2,445	138	15,491	7,710	5,735		440	3	3,713	1,145	47,658
2009-10	64	1,935	2,961	330	14,616	8,243	6,795		706	3	3,012	1,121	49,642
2010-11		962	2,939	679	13,762	7,476	6,059		574	330	2,731	852	45,109
2011-12		718	298	29	11,703	9,878	3,189		361	1	1,500	1,398	38,329
2012-13		451		0	6,511	4,861	296		345	9	514	1,079	18,176
2013-14[2]	76	577	2,874	469	12,336	10,901	5,323		1,030	693	1,763	1,058	50,565

[1] Excludes exports of corn by-products.   [2] Preliminary.   *Source: Foreign Agricultural Service, U.S. Department of Agriculture (FAS-USDA)*

Stocks of Corn (Shelled and Ear) in the United States   In Millions of Bushels

Year	On Farms Mar. 1	June 1	Sept. 1	Dec. 1	Off Farms Mar. 1	June 1	Sept. 1	Dec. 1	Total Stocks Mar. 1	June 1	Sept. 1	Dec. 1
2005	4,137.0	2,462.3	820.5	6,325.0	2,619.3	1,858.5	1,293.5	3,490.0	6,756.3	4,320.8	2,114.0	9,815.0
2006	4,055.0	2,350.5	749.5	5,627.0	2,932.3	2,011.2	1,217.7	3,305.7	6,987.3	4,361.7	1,967.2	8,932.7
2007	3,330.0	1,826.6	460.1	6,530.0	2,738.3	1,706.8	843.5	3,748.1	6,068.3	3,533.4	1,303.6	10,278.1
2008	3,780.0	1,970.9	500.0	6,482.0	3,078.7	2,057.1	1,124.2	3,590.1	6,858.7	4,028.0	1,624.2	10,072.1
2009	4,085.0	2,205.4	607.5	7,405.0	2,869.1	2,056.0	1,065.8	3,497.5	6,954.1	4,261.4	1,673.3	10,902.5
2010	4,548.0	2,131.4	485.1	6,302.0	3,145.8	2,178.7	1,222.7	3,754.8	7,693.8	4,310.1	1,707.8	10,056.8
2011	3,384.0	1,681.5	315.0	6,175.0	3,139.2	1,988.3	812.7	3,472.5	6,523.2	3,669.8	1,127.6	9,647.5
2012	3,192.0	1,482.0	313.7	4,586.0	2,831.4	1,666.2	675.3	3,446.7	6,023.4	3,148.2	989.0	8,032.7
2013	2,669.2	1,260.1	275.0	6,380.0	2,730.7	1,506.1	546.2	4,072.5	5,399.9	2,766.2	821.2	10,452.5
2014[1]	3,860.5	1,863.2	462.0	7,087.0	3,147.6	1,988.5	769.9	4,115.7	7,008.1	3,851.7	1,231.9	11,202.7

[1] Preliminary.   *Source: National Agricultural Statistics Service, U.S. Department of Agriculture (NASS-USDA)*

CORN

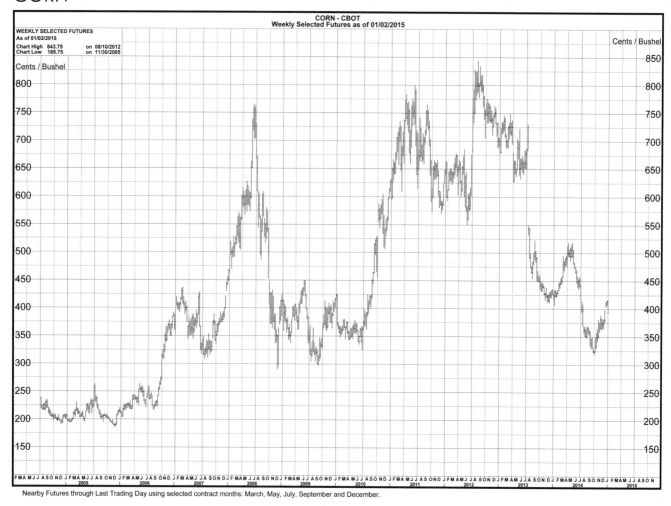

CORN - CBOT
Weekly Selected Futures as of 01/02/2015

WEEKLY SELECTED FUTURES
As of 01/02/2015

Chart High 843.75 on 08/10/2012
Chart Low 185.75 on 11/30/2005

Cents / Bushel

Nearby Futures through Last Trading Day using selected contract months: March, May, July, September and December.

Volume of Trading of Corn Futures in Chicago   In Thousands of Contracts

Year	Jan.	Feb.	Mar.	Apr.	May	June	July	Aug.	Sept.	Oct.	Nov.	Dec.	Total
2005	1,467.8	2,680.8	2,278.1	2,519.1	2,188.3	3,446.1	2,626.0	2,993.6	1,618.5	1,504.2	2,892.2	1,750.3	27,965.1
2006	2,494.6	3,599.1	3,041.0	3,507.5	3,773.1	4,693.4	3,743.6	4,226.9	3,760.5	5,300.2	6,279.4	2,820.6	47,239.9
2007	5,166.5	5,111.6	4,959.0	6,095.4	4,519.9	6,090.9	4,035.7	4,344.1	3,128.9	3,306.5	4,615.6	3,145.9	54,520.2
2008	4,213.2	5,808.2	4,350.8	6,501.1	4,876.9	7,593.8	5,402.2	4,989.1	3,934.7	4,572.5	4,448.6	3,266.2	59,957.1
2009	3,041.3	4,487.1	3,684.9	4,567.6	4,151.8	5,636.8	4,765.8	4,441.8	3,153.8	4,374.0	5,509.1	3,134.9	50,948.8
2010	4,025.9	5,217.5	3,935.4	6,466.0	4,240.6	6,207.8	4,863.8	6,899.6	7,033.7	7,501.1	9,169.7	4,280.4	69,841.4
2011	5,981.0	7,473.1	7,552.4	8,715.1	5,676.9	8,639.5	5,119.3	6,834.9	5,385.7	5,568.2	8,003.4	4,055.2	79,004.8
2012	6,194.8	7,388.6	6,538.5	7,418.0	6,162.5	8,027.0	6,825.3	6,003.0	4,164.7	4,701.6	6,406.8	3,353.5	73,184.3
2013	5,151.4	6,347.6	4,929.5	7,089.9	4,937.7	5,823.6	4,824.9	6,128.2	3,436.3	4,919.5	7,695.2	3,039.0	64,322.6
2014	5,790.8	7,614.4	5,772.2	6,996.2	4,613.5	6,677.8	4,938.4	5,781.3	3,784.4	5,875.4	7,406.4	4,151.6	69,402.4

Contract size = 5,000 bu.   *Source: CME Group; Chicago Board of Trade (CBT)*

Average Open Interest of Corn Futures in Chicago   In Thousands of Contracts

Year	Jan.	Feb.	Mar.	Apr.	May	June	July	Aug.	Sept.	Oct.	Nov.	Dec.
2005	629.3	654.1	659.7	673.8	677.3	702.4	713.1	733.6	714.2	794.4	852.5	774.2
2006	875.3	1,048.8	1,066.0	1,176.0	1,288.2	1,327.8	1,360.2	1,347.2	1,302.1	1,312.6	1,405.7	1,381.5
2007	1,448.2	1,498.8	1,427.3	1,345.9	1,257.6	1,244.1	1,213.4	1,132.8	1,108.5	1,161.7	1,202.6	1,211.5
2008	1,383.2	1,463.1	1,421.8	1,445.3	1,409.2	1,396.1	1,279.9	1,170.4	1,050.9	995.5	967.6	820.5
2009	806.7	801.1	767.8	823.3	860.6	971.7	894.1	862.6	850.1	923.9	1,002.9	969.2
2010	1,105.4	1,149.6	1,124.2	1,169.6	1,196.2	1,204.5	1,161.3	1,324.5	1,405.8	1,509.8	1,629.6	1,511.5
2011	1,595.6	1,697.7	1,598.8	1,617.6	1,439.8	1,406.3	1,196.7	1,244.3	1,214.8	1,220.0	1,268.5	1,156.4
2012	1,209.5	1,289.9	1,312.4	1,330.4	1,212.9	1,125.0	1,138.0	1,211.6	1,175.6	1,247.8	1,282.1	1,168.4
2013	1,187.9	1,275.3	1,264.8	1,270.8	1,160.8	1,196.6	1,135.7	1,166.2	1,114.6	1,252.2	1,335.0	1,193.8
2014	1,284.5	1,343.4	1,318.8	1,396.1	1,338.9	1,370.7	1,332.4	1,316.6	1,254.5	1,289.5	1,298.1	1,216.6

Contract size = 5,000 bu.   *Source: CME Group; Chicago Board of Trade (CBT)*

Corn Oil

Corn oil is a bland, odorless oil produced by refining the crude corn oil that is mechanically extracted from the germ of the plant seed. High-oil corn, the most common type of corn used to make corn oil, typically has an oil content of 7% or higher compared to about 4% for normal corn. Corn oil is widely used as cooking oil, for making margarine and mayonnaise, and for making inedible products such as soap, paints, inks, varnishes, and cosmetics. For humans, studies have shown that no vegetable oil is more effective than corn oil in lowering blood cholesterol levels.

Prices –The average monthly price of corn oil (wet mill price in Chicago) in the 2013-14 marketing year (Oct-Sep) fell into the range of 37.5-40.5 cents per pound from 46.66 cents per pound in the 2012-13 marketing year, still well below the 2007-08 record high of 69.37 cents per pound.

Seasonally, prices tend to be highest around March/April and lowest late in the calendar year.

Supply – U.S. corn oil production in the 2013-14 marketing year rose +4.3% yr/yr to 3.300 billion pounds, a new record high Seasonally, production tends to peak around December and March and reaches a low in July. U.S. stocks in the 2013-14 marketing year (beginning Oct 1) remained unchanged at 165.0 million pounds.

Demand – U.S. usage (domestic disappearance) in 2013-14 rose +6.6% to 2.345 billion pounds.

Exports – U.S. corn oil exports in 2013-14 fell -2.5% to 1.000 billion pounds. U.S. corn oil imports in 2013-14 fell by -25.0% to 45.000 million pounds.

Supply and Disappearance of Corn Oil in the United States   In Millions of Pounds

	Supply				Baking and Frying Fats	Salad and Cooking Oil	Margarine	Total Edible Products	Domestic Disappearance	Exports	Total Disappearance
Year	Stocks Oct. 1	Production	Imports	Total Supply							
2004-05	153	2,396	49.1	2,598	W	1,466	W	1,690	1,653	789	2,442
2005-06	156	2,483	45.0	2,683	W	1,407	W	1,607	1,685	799	2,483
2006-07	200	2,560	43.1	2,803	W	1,335	W	1,735	1,832	793	2,625
2007-08	179	2,507	45.2	2,731	W	1,722	W	1,606	1,756	769	2,525
2008-09	205	2,418	43.5	2,667	W	1,722	W	1,591	1,568	814	2,382
2009-10	286	2,485	37.0	2,808	W	1,930	W	1,589	1,895	774	2,669
2010-11	139	2,515	47.6	2,701	W	2,375	W	1,691	1,670	792	2,461
2011-12	240	3,010	45.8	3,296	NA	NA	NA	NA	2,127	1,003	3,131
2012-13[1]	165	3,165	60.0	3,390	NA	NA	NA	NA	2,200	1,025	3,225
2013-14[2]	165	3,300	45.0	3,510	NA	NA	NA	NA	2,345	1,000	3,345

[1] Preliminary.   [2] Estimate.   W = Withheld.   *Source: Economic Research Service, U.S. Department of Agriculture (ERS-USDA)*

Production[2] of Crude Corn Oil in the United States   In Millions of Pounds

Year	Oct.	Nov.	Dec.	Jan.	Feb.	Mar.	Apr.	May	June	July	Aug.	Sept.	Total
2004-05	208.8	187.1	191.0	205.2	182.5	206.6	217.2	188.2	211.5	206.7	198.5	189.0	2,392
2005-06	207.5	199.9	200.3	209.2	184.8	217.6	191.7	218.7	206.7	215.3	222.0	209.0	2,483
2006-07	228.7	216.0	226.1	224.7	187.9	216.4	194.1	214.4	212.7	219.8	209.5	209.4	2,560
2007-08	213.5	213.0	214.0	205.4	193.7	222.5	190.7	220.9	193.7	214.9	217.3	207.3	2,507
2008-09	206.3	210.6	198.7	200.3	199.8	218.8	189.4	202.5	189.0	186.0	201.4	215.8	2,419
2009-10	212.9	205.2	203.2	197.9	188.1	212.4	214.7	205.4	214.7	216.8	213.6	200.1	2,485
2010-11[1]	205.1	211.2	198.9	220.9	199.4	218.1	203.1	215.0	216.3	205.7			2,512

[1] Preliminary.   [2] Not seasonally adjusted.   *Source: Bureau of the Census, U.S. Department of Commerce*

Average Corn Oil Price, Wet Mill in Chicago   In Cents Per Pound

Year	Oct.	Nov.	Dec.	Jan.	Feb.	Mar.	Apr.	May	June	July	Aug.	Sept.	Average
2005-06	27.50	27.08	26.08	25.22	23.65	22.61	23.19	25.25	25.70	25.75	25.42	24.71	25.18
2006-07	24.70	26.47	28.05	28.05	28.66	29.08	29.93	31.56	34.71	37.25	39.61	43.61	31.81
2007-08	52.50	56.32	59.47	63.67	74.89	83.55	87.09	87.29	82.33	76.64	60.00	48.71	69.37
2008-09	34.76	31.06	26.88	25.19	29.05	29.64	31.31	37.23	39.57	36.30	35.23	36.83	32.75
2009-10	37.59	38.12	40.02	40.34	37.54	38.37	38.50	38.50	38.93	39.29	41.48	42.85	39.29
2010-11	47.50	51.96	54.71	57.91	63.39	67.72	68.89	68.33	66.70	62.00	62.00	57.95	60.76
2011-12	54.24	53.98	53.36	54.00	56.30	59.31	60.75	58.05	52.90	54.76	57.26	58.21	56.09
2012-13	54.75	51.93	50.63	52.06	51.71	47.76	47.06	45.23	42.50	38.91	38.93	38.46	46.66
2013-14	37.85	38.79	38.31	38.79	41.07	43.19	41.94	41.02	40.01	39.02	38.00	35.17	39.43
2014-15[1]	34.50	33.96	33.68	34.86									34.25

[1] Preliminary.   *Source: Economic Research Service, U.S. Department of Agriculture (ERS-USDA)*

Cotton

Cotton is a natural vegetable fiber that comes from small trees and shrubs of a genus belonging to the mallow family, one of which is the common American Upland cotton plant. Cotton has been used in India for at least the last 5,000 years and probably much longer, and was also used by the ancient Chinese, Egyptians, and North and South Americans. Cotton was one of the earliest crops grown by European settlers in the U.S.

Cotton requires a long growing season, plenty of sunshine and water during the growing season, and then dry weather for harvesting. In the United States, the Cotton Belt stretches from northern Florida to North Carolina and westward to California. In the U.S., planting time varies from the beginning of February in Southern Texas to the beginning of June in the northern sections of the Cotton Belt. The flower bud of the plant blossoms and develops into an oval boll that splits open at maturity. At maturity, cotton is most vulnerable to damage from wind and rain. Approximately 95% of the cotton in the U.S. is now harvested mechanically with spindle-type pickers or strippers and then sent off to cotton gins for processing. There it is dried, cleaned, separated, and packed into bales.

Cotton is used in a wide range of products from clothing to home furnishings to medical products. The value of cotton is determined according to the staple, grade, and character of each bale. Staple refers to short, medium, long, or extra-long fiber length, with medium staple accounting for about 70% of all U.S. cotton. Grade refers to the color, brightness, and amount of foreign matter and is established by the U.S. Department of Agriculture. Character refers to the fiber's diameter, strength, body, maturity (ratio of mature to immature fibers), uniformity, and smoothness. Cotton is the fifth leading cash crop in the U.S. and is one of the nation's principal agricultural exports. The weight of cotton is typically measured in terms of a "bale," which is deemed to equal 480 pounds.

Cotton futures and options are traded on ICE Futures U.S. Cotton futures are also traded on the CME Group, Moscow Exchange, Multi Commodity Exchange of India (MCX), National Commodity & Derivatives Exchange (NCDEX), Turkish Derivatives Exchange, and the Zhengzhou Commodity Exchange. The ICE futures contract calls for the delivery of 50,000 pounds net weight (approximately 100 bales) of No. 2 cotton with a quality rating of Strict Low Middling and a staple length of 1-and-2/32 inch. Delivery points include Texas (Galveston and Houston), New Orleans, Memphis, and Greenville/Spartanburg in South Carolina.

Prices – ICE cotton futures prices (Barchart.com symbol CT) pushed upward in Q1-2014 and posted the high for the year in March at 97.35 cents a pound, a 3-year high, after the USDA in its March WASDE report cut its U.S. 2013/14 cotton production estimate to a 4-year low of 12.87 million bales (-25.5% yr/yr). U.S. supplies were also tight after the USDA in April cut its U.S. 2013/14 ending stocks estimate to a 24-year low of 2.5 million bales. Cotton prices then fell sharply from May into September as global supplies remained plentiful and Chinese cotton

demand weakened. The USDA in July's WASDE report raised its 2014/15 world cotton ending stocks estimate to a record 105.68 million bales and China Jan-May 2014 cotton imports had plunged -45.1% to 1.175 MMT. Cotton prices fell further in Q3 after China said it would restrict cotton imports in 2015 to encourage textile producers to use domestic supplies after government purchases over the past three years had built China's domestic cotton stockpiles to a record 13.4 MMT. Cotton prices posted the low for the year in November at 57.84 cents per pound on burgeoning global supplies after the USDA raised its 2014/15 global cotton ending stocks estimate to a record 107.36 million bales. Cotton prices finished 2014 down -28.8% at 60.27 cents a pound.

Supply – World cotton production in 2014-15 fell -1.1% yr/yr to 118.978 million bales (480 pounds per bale), below 2011-12 record high of 127.280 million bales. The world's largest cotton producers were China with 25.2% of world production in 2014-15, India with 26.1%, the U.S. with 13.4%, and Pakistan with 8.2%. World beginning stocks in 2013-14 (latest data) rose +21.6% yr/yr to 89.157 million bales, a new record high.

The U.S. cotton crop in 2014-15 rose +24.6% yr/yr to 16.084 million bales, which was well below the 2005-06 record high of 23.890 million bales. U.S. farmers harvested 9.707 million acres of cotton in 2014-15, up +28.7% yr/yr. The U.S. cotton yield in 2014-15 fell -3.2% to 795 pounds per acre, not far behind the 2007-08 record high of 879 pounds per acre. The leading U.S. producing states of Upland cotton are Texas with 37.4% of U.S. production in 2014, Georgia (15.5%), Mississippi (6.4%), Arkansas (5.1%), California (4.7%), Alabama (4.1%), and Missouri (3.5%). U.S. production of cotton cloth has fallen sharply by almost half in the past decade due to the movement of the textile industry out of the U.S. to low-wage foreign countries.

Demand – World consumption of cotton in 2014-15 rose +3.7% yr/yr to 112.500 million bales, but still below the 2006-07 record high of 121.986. Consumption of cotton continues to move toward countries with low wages, where the raw cotton is utilized to produce textiles and other cotton products. The largest consumers of cotton in 2014-15 were China (32.9% of world total), India (21.3%), and Pakistan (9.4%). U.S. consumption of cotton by mills in 2014-15 rose +7.0% yr/yr to 3.800 million bales, and accounted for 27.5% of U.S. production. The remaining 72.5% of U.S. cotton production went for exports.

Trade – World exports of cotton in 2014-15 fell -15.9% yr/yr to 34.288 million bales, which was below the 2005-06 record high of 44.854 million bales. The U.S. is the world's largest cotton exporter by far and accounts for 29.2% of world cotton exports. Key world cotton importers include China with 20.4% of total world imports in 2014-15, Bangladesh with 13.0%, Turkey and Vietnam each with 10.5%, and Indonesia with 9.1%. U.S. cotton exports in 2013-14 (latest data) rose by +21.9% yr/yr to 10.412 million bales. The main destinations for U.S. exports in 2013-14 were China (25.4%), Mexico (9.7%), Indonesia (6.7%), South Korea and Thailand each with (4.4%).

Supply and Distribution of All Cotton in the United States In Thousands of 480-Pound Bales

Crop Year Beginning Aug. 1	Acre			Supply								Farm Price[5]	"A" Index Price[6]	Value of Production
	Planted	Harvested	Yield	Beginning Stocks[3]	Pro-duction[4]	Imports	Total	Mill Use	Exports	Total	Unac-counted	Ending Stocks			
	--- 1,000 Acres ---		Lbs./Acre												Million USD
2005-06	14,245	13,803	831	5,495	23,890	28	29,413	5,871	17,673	23,544	200	6,069	49.7	56.19	5,695.2
2006-07	15,274	12,732	814	6,069	21,588	19	27,676	4,935	12,959	17,894	-303	9,479	48.4	59.22	5,013.2
2007-08	10,827	10,489	879	9,479	19,207	12	28,698	4,584	13,634	18,218	-429	10,051	61.3	73.02	5,652.9
2008-09	9,471	7,569	813	10,051	12,815	0	22,866	3,541	13,261	16,802	263	6,337	49.1	61.10	3,021.5
2009-10	9,150	7,529	777	6,337	12,188	0	18,525	3,550	12,037	15,587	14	2,947	64.8	78.13	3,788.0
2010-11	10,974	10,699	812	2,947	18,104	9	21,060	3,900	14,376	18,276	-182	2,600	84.6	164.29	7,348.1
2011-12	14,735	9,461	790	2,600	15,573	19	18,192	3,300	11,714	15,014	172	3,350	93.5		6,986.0
2012-13	12,264	9,322	892	3,350	17,314	10	20,675	3,500	13,026	16,526	-348	3,800	75.7		6,291.8
2013-14[1]	10,407	7,544	821	3,900	12,909	13	16,822	3,550	10,530	14,080	-192	2,450	82.5		5,191.5
2014-15[2]	11,037	9,707	795	2,450	16,084	10	18,857	3,800	10,000	13,800	43	5,100	59-67		5,069.0

[1] Preliminary. [2] Estimate. [3] Excludes preseason ginnings (adjusted to 480-lb. bale net weight basis). [4] Includes preseason ginnings. [5] Marketing year average price. [6] Average of 5 cheapest types of SLM 1 3/32" staple length cotton offered on the European market.
Source: Economic Research Service, U.S. Department of Agriculture (ERS-USDA)

World Production of All Cotton In Thousands of 480-Pound Bales

Crop Year Beginning Aug. 1	Australia	Brazil	Burkina	China	Greece	India	Mexico	Pakistan	Turkey	Turkmen-istan	United States	Uzbek-istan	World Total
2005-06	2,750	4,700	1,367	28,400	1,975	19,050	635	9,850	3,550	975	23,890	5,550	116,358
2006-07	1,350	7,000	1,300	35,500	1,550	22,500	650	9,580	3,800	1,400	21,588	5,350	123,015
2007-08	625	7,360	675	37,000	1,550	24,700	620	8,550	3,100	1,350	19,207	5,350	120,570
2008-09	1,525	5,480	850	36,700	1,150	23,300	567	8,540	1,930	1,550	12,825	4,600	108,296
2009-10	1,775	5,450	700	32,000	940	24,500	475	9,240	1,750	1,470	12,183	3,900	103,369
2010-11	4,200	9,000	650	30,500	940	27,200	732	8,640	2,110	1,750	18,102	4,100	117,640
2011-12	5,500	8,700	800	34,000	1,330	29,000	1,180	10,600	3,440	1,400	15,573	4,200	127,280
2012-13	4,600	6,000	1,175	35,000	1,194	28,500	1,036	9,300	2,650	1,600	17,314	4,500	123,561
2013-14[1]	4,100	8,000	1,250	32,750	1,369	31,000	924	9,500	2,300	1,500	12,909	4,100	120,293
2014-15[2]	2,200	7,000	1,300	30,000	1,285	31,000	1,220	9,800	3,200	1,450	15,923	4,000	118,978

[1] Preliminary. [2] Estimate. *Source: Foreign Agricultural Service, U.S. Department of Agriculture (FAS-USDA)*

World Stocks and Trade of Cotton In Thousands of 480-Pound Bales

Crop Year Beginning Aug. 1	Beginning Stocks				Imports					Exports			
	United States	Uzbek-istan	China	World Total	Bang-ladesh	Indo-nesia	Mexico	Turkey	World Total	India	United States	Uzbek-istan	World Total
2005-06	5,495	1,298	18,388	60,726	2,450	2,200	1,744	3,501	44,673	3,675	17,673	4,800	44,712
2006-07	6,069	1,248	22,536	61,801	3,250	2,400	1,353	4,029	38,255	4,875	12,959	4,500	37,464
2007-08	9,479	1,198	20,536	63,103	3,600	2,700	1,530	3,267	39,436	7,500	13,634	4,200	38,951
2008-09	10,051	1,348	20,504	62,362	3,800	2,400	1,315	2,919	30,608	2,360	13,261	3,000	30,104
2009-10	6,337	1,948	21,366	62,226	4,000	2,700	1,393	4,394	37,077	6,550	12,037	3,800	35,522
2010-11	2,947	948	14,246	47,383	4,250	2,600	1,196	3,350	36,765	5,000	14,376	2,650	35,393
2011-12	2,600	1,148	10,603	50,608	3,300	2,500	1,000	2,382	45,319	11,080	11,714	2,500	45,857
2012-13	3,350	1,498	31,081	73,697	3,900	3,137	950	3,692	46,301	7,761	13,026	3,200	46,681
2013-14[1]	3,800	1,348	50,361	90,002	4,100	2,989	1,040	4,246	40,584	9,255	10,530	2,700	40,768
2014-15[2]	2,450	1,248	62,707	101,638	4,450	3,100	1,025	3,600	34,248	5,000	10,000	2,300	34,288

[1] Preliminary. [2] Estimate. *Source: Foreign Agricultural Service, U.S. Department of Agriculture (FAS-USDA)*

World Consumption of All Cottons in Specified Countries In Thousands of 480-Pound Bales

Crop Year Beginning Aug. 1	Bangla-desh	Brazil	China	India	Indonesia	Mexico	Pakistan	Thailand	Turkey	United States	Uzbek-istan	Vietnam	World Total
2005-06	2,505	4,302	43,500	16,700	2,225	2,125	11,525	2,075	7,000	5,671	800	750	115,244
2006-07	3,210	4,423	48,000	18,100	2,425	2,125	12,025	1,975	7,300	5,238	900	975	122,504
2007-08	3,510	4,450	48,500	18,600	2,650	2,025	12,025	1,975	6,100	5,013	1,000	1,200	121,796
2008-09	3,710	4,050	42,750	17,750	2,400	1,875	11,125	1,625	4,950	3,278	1,000	1,250	108,936
2009-10	4,010	4,250	50,000	19,750	2,650	1,925	10,425	1,800	5,900	3,536	1,100	1,600	119,767
2010-11	4,210	4,150	46,000	20,550	2,650	1,725	9,925	1,725	5,600	4,082	1,250	1,625	115,787
2011-12	3,510	3,850	38,000	19,450	2,450	1,725	10,025	1,325	5,600	3,128	1,350	1,675	103,653
2012-13	3,910	3,950	36,000	20,850	3,050	1,825	10,775	1,525	6,050	3,848	1,450	2,250	106,876
2013-14[1]	4,160	4,050	34,500	22,850	3,050	1,875	10,425	1,575	6,300	3,742	1,500	3,200	108,473
2014-15[2]	4,360	3,850	37,000	24,000	3,100	1,900	10,525	1,475	6,400	3,783	1,500	3,400	112,500

[1] Preliminary. [2] Estimate. *Source: Foreign Agricultural Service, U.S. Department of Agriculture (FAS-USDA)*

COTTON

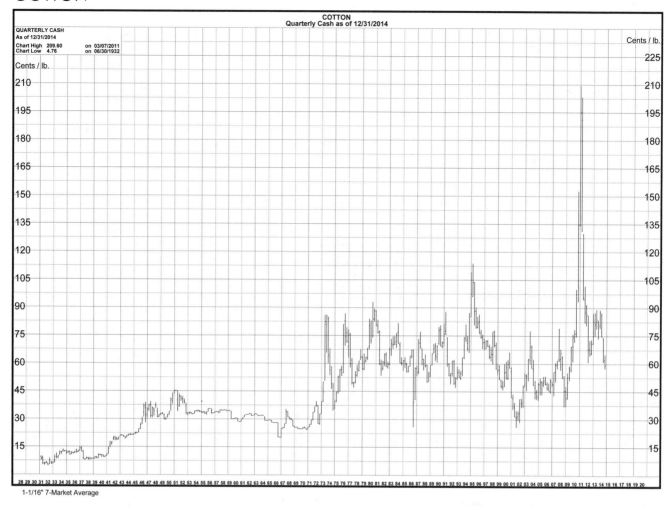

COTTON
Quarterly Cash as of 12/31/2014

QUARTERLY CASH
As of 12/31/2014

Chart High 209.60 on 03/07/2011
Chart Low 4.76 on 06/30/1932

Cents / lb.

1-1/16" 7-Market Average

Average Price of SLM 1-1/16", Cotton/5 at Designated U.S. Markets   In Cents Per Pound (Net Weight)

Year	Aug.	Sept.	Oct.	Nov.	Dec.	Jan.	Feb.	Mar.	Apr.	May	June	July	Average
2005-06	45.38	47.43	51.02	48.80	49.53	51.91	52.39	50.04	49.00	47.00	47.90	47.15	48.96
2006-07	48.65	46.80	45.15	46.32	49.85	49.90	48.77	49.21	46.97	44.62	50.35	57.50	48.67
2007-08	53.46	57.08	59.06	59.59	59.44	63.34	65.92	69.27	63.91	60.67	63.34	62.85	61.49
2008-09	60.93	56.72	46.90	39.83	42.07	44.87	41.81	38.53	45.11	52.92	50.80	53.98	47.87
2009-10	53.77	55.78	60.44	64.90	68.11	65.93	68.08	74.54	75.46	74.70	75.19	76.16	67.76
2010-11	81.16	91.53	108.26	126.62	135.46	144.79	177.65	195.79	181.98	151.93	144.77	113.03	137.75
2011-12	102.89	102.06	97.63	93.59	85.99	89.83	85.17	83.14	83.37	72.51	67.35	66.14	85.81
2012-13	69.97	69.38	68.03	67.34	70.61	73.33	76.87	82.80	80.94	79.84	82.18	81.62	75.24
2013-14	83.36	81.25	77.37	74.43	78.75	81.43	83.21	86.70	85.48	83.20	78.54	69.63	80.28
2014-15[1]	64.99	64.83	63.51	59.64	59.38	58.19							61.76

[1] Preliminary.   [2] Grade 41, leaf 4, staple 34, mike 35-36 and 43-49 , strength 23.5-26.4.   *Source: Agricultural Marketing Service,*
U.S. Department of Agriculture (AMS-USDA)

Average Spot Cotton, 1-3/32", Price (SLM) at Designated U.S. Markets[2]   In Cents Per Pound (Net Weight)

Year	Aug.	Sept.	Oct.	Nov.	Dec.	Jan.	Feb.	Mar.	Apr.	May	June	July	Average
2005-06	50.59	52.81	56.01	53.78	54.47	56.69	57.16	55.03	54.07	52.02	52.97	52.35	54.00
2006-07	53.80	51.95	50.20	51.13	54.71	54.75	53.66	54.05	51.59	49.12	54.71	61.59	53.44
2007-08	57.53	61.15	63.08	63.71	63.50	67.22	69.73	72.68	67.25	63.99	66.67	66.17	65.22
2008-09	64.25	60.01	50.52	43.76	45.95	48.76	45.67	42.40	49.02	56.81	54.70	57.94	51.65
2009-10	57.77	59.82	64.58	69.23	72.59	70.45	72.47	79.02	79.81	78.99	79.37	80.30	72.03
2010-11	87.38	95.48	112.06	130.62	139.68	148.24	181.61	199.76	185.94	155.89	148.73	117.00	141.87
2011-12	106.41	105.50	100.97	97.13	89.53	94.10	89.52	87.76	88.07	77.26	72.12	70.91	89.94
2012-13	74.76	74.19	72.87	72.06	75.42	77.99	81.37	87.28	85.39	84.29	86.63	86.07	79.86
2013-14	87.80	85.65	83.66	78.84	83.15	85.69	87.45	90.94	89.71	87.41	82.74	73.89	84.74
2014-15[1]	68.94	68.70	67.32	63.13	62.12								66.04

[1] Preliminary.   *Source: Agricultural Marketing Service, U.S. Department of Agriculture (AMS-USDA)*

Average Spot Cotton Prices[2], C.I.F. Northern Europe   In U.S. Cents Per Pound

Crop Year Beginning Aug. 1	Argentina "C"[3] 1 1/16" M 1 3/32"	Australia M 1 3/32"	Cotlook Index A	Cotlook Index B	Egypt Giza[4] 81 M 1 3/32"	Greece M 1 3/32"	Mexico[5] M 1 3/32"	Pakistan Sind/ Punjab[6]	Tanzania AR[7] Type 3	Turkey Izmir[8] 1 3/32"	U.S. Calif. ACALA SJV[9]	U.S. Memphis Terr.[10] M 1 3/32"	U.S. Orleans/ Texas[11] M 1 1/32"
1990-1	77.06	85.58	82.90	77.80	177.43	84.24	84.46	77.19	89.62	81.32	92.84	88.13	80.35
1991-2	55.08	65.97	63.05	58.50	128.10	65.90	68.19	58.14	68.90	74.66	74.47	66.35	63.41
1992-3	64.31	64.01	57.70	53.70	99.24	56.92	----	52.66	62.24	----	68.37	63.08	58.89
1993-4	80.20	72.81	70.60	67.30	88.35	58.81	----	54.42	69.83	59.80	77.55	72.80	69.78
1994-5	101.88	81.05	92.75	92.40	93.70	88.64	82.65	73.75	----	----	106.40	98.67	95.70
1995-6	82.98	93.75	85.61	81.06	----	84.95	94.94	81.86	96.20	90.38	103.49	94.71	90.37
1996-7	79.71	83.24	78.59	74.80	----	75.85	79.60	73.37	79.22	----	89.55	82.81	79.77
1997-8	69.96	77.49	72.19	70.69	----	72.03	81.70	72.93	84.04	----	85.11	78.12	74.74
1998-9	57.19	66.48	58.94	54.26	----	58.66	65.78	----	72.70	----	78.57	74.20	70.95
1999-00[1]	----	61.97	52.85	49.55	----	51.71	56.43	----	55.67	----	68.76	66.29	55.67

[1] Preliminary.   [2] Generally for prompt shipment.   [3] 1-1/32" prior to January 20, 1984; 1-1/16" since.   [4] Dendera until 1969/70; Giza 67 1969/70 until December 1983; Giza 69/75/81 until November 1990; Giza 81 since.   [5] S. Brazil Type 5, 1-1/32" prior to 1968-69; 1-1/16" until 1987/88; Brazilian Type 5/6, 1-1/16" since.   [6] Punjab until 1979/80; Sind SG until June 1984; Sind/Punjab SG until January 1985; Afzal 1" until January 1986; Afzal 1-1/32" since.   [7] No. 1 until 1978/79; No. 1/2 until February 1986; AR' Mwanza No. 3 until January 1992; AR' Type 3 since.   [8] Izmir ST 1 White 1-1/16" RG prior to 1981/82; 1-3/32" from 1981/82 until January 1987; Izmir/Antalya ST 1 White 1-3/32" RG since.   [9] SM 1-3/32" prior to 1975/76; SM 1-1/8" since.   [10] SM 1-1/16" prior to 1981/82; Middling 1-3/32" since.   [11] Middling 1" prior to 1988/89; Middling 1-1/32" since.
Source: International Cotton Advisory Committee (ICAC)

Average Producer Price Index of Gray Cotton Broadwovens   Index 1982 = 100

Year	Jan.	Feb.	Mar.	Apr.	May	June	July	Aug.	Sept.	Oct.	Nov.	Dec.	Average
2004	109.9	111.2	110.6	111.5	112.3	112.6	113.7	113.2	113.5	113.6	113.3	112.5	112.3
2005	112.6	112.0	111.9	111.8	111.2	111.2	111.1	111.2	111.2	111.3	110.9	111.1	111.5
2006	111.1	110.5	109.9	109.9	110.1	110.1	110.1	110.1	110.1	110.0	110.0	109.9	110.1
2007	110.0	109.9	109.9	110.1	109.8	109.9	109.9	109.9	109.9	110.0	109.9	109.9	109.9
2008	110.1	110.1	110.1	110.1	110.0	109.9	110.2	111.7	111.7	111.7	111.6	111.4	110.7
2009	111.0	111.0	111.0	107.2	107.2	107.2	107.2	107.5	107.5	107.5	108.9	108.9	108.5
2010	109.8	113.7	113.7	113.7	114.9	116.6	119.0	118.8	118.8	118.8	119.1	119.1	116.3
2011	144.8	145.4	147.0	153.5	154.3	154.3	162.1	162.0	161.3	148.5	148.5	141.1	151.9
2012	139.1	139.2	139.2	135.0	135.0	135.2	126.1	126.1	126.1	124.7	123.6	122.7	131.0
2013[1]	122.6	122.3	123.3	126.9	126.4	126.4	126.4	126.4	126.4	127.2	127.7		131.0

[1] Preliminary.   *Source: Bureau of Labor Statistics (0337-01), U.S. Department of Commerce*

Average Spot Prices of U.S. Cotton,[2] Base Quality (SLM) at Designated Markets   In Cents Per Pound

Crop Year Beginning Aug. 1	Dallas (EastTex.-Okl.)	Fresno (San Joaquin Valley)	Greenville (Southeast)	Greenwood (South Delta)	Lubbock (West Texas)	Memphis (North Delta)	Phoenix Desert (Southwest)	Average
2005-06	47.69	50.06	49.65	49.63	47.78	49.67	48.26	48.96
2006-07	48.17	48.58	49.90	49.46	48.06	49.46	47.08	48.67
2007-08	60.89	60.57	63.95	62.67	60.64	62.67	59.07	61.50
2008-09	47.08	49.10	48.97	47.99	46.93	47.99	47.03	47.87
2009-10	66.57	67.20	70.13	69.30	66.38	69.30	65.40	67.76
2010-11	135.51	138.91	139.70	139.10	135.11	139.02	137.91	137.88
2011-12	83.30	86.74	87.75	86.95	83.31	86.91	85.73	85.81
2012-13	77.50	76.56	76.56	73.79	73.68	73.89	74.74	75.24
2013-14	82.74	81.85	81.85	79.27	79.14	78.23	78.88	80.28
2014-15[1]	63.17	62.28	62.28	75.22	60.86	61.09	61.67	61.75

[1] Preliminary   [2] Prices are for mixed lots, net weight, uncompressed in warehouse.
Source: Agricultural Marketing Service, U.S. Department of Agriculture (AMS-USDA)

Average Price[1] Received by Farmers for Upland Cotton in the United States   In Cents Per Pound

Year	Aug.	Sept.	Oct.	Nov.	Dec.	Jan.	Feb.	Mar.	Apr.	May	June	July	Average
2005-06	42.1	44.3	48.5	48.5	48.0	48.6	48.9	50.0	48.5	46.4	47.4	46.8	47.3
2006-07	45.8	47.3	45.9	47.4	49.0	49.4	47.4	46.4	46.3	44.0	45.4	45.2	46.6
2007-08	44.9	52.0	55.5	57.4	59.6	61.5	63.0	63.0	65.5	64.6	64.0	66.2	59.8
2008-09	58.5	61.1	58.8	54.8	53.3	46.0	41.2	40.4	44.7	44.9	45.0	43.6	49.4
2009-10	47.7	55.0	58.5	59.5	63.4	60.8	65.0	65.0	66.7	66.6	68.5	68.5	62.1
2010-11	77.2	74.7	77.3	81.5	81.2	82.1	92.9	84.4	86.7	83.2	83.3	82.5	82.3
2011-12	94.0	93.5	92.2	92.6	88.9	90.1	92.3	90.0	90.4	84.4	77.1	76.6	88.5
2012-13	71.4	70.7	69.8	69.2	71.8	72.9	76.9	77.5	78.4	78.3	79.3	80.9	74.8
2013-14	76.9	74.6	77.8	75.9	77.2	77.5	79.0	79.4	80.5	79.4	81.5	82.1	78.5
2014-15[2]	70.5	69.5	64.0	62.2	60.4	58.6							64.2

[1] Weighted average by sales.   [2] Preliminary.   *Source: Agricultural Marketing Service, U.S. Department of Agriculture (AMS-USDA)*

COTTON

Purchases Reported by Exchanges in Designated U.S. Spot Markets[1]   In Running Bales

Crop Year Beginning Aug. 1	Aug.	Sept.	Oct.	Nov.	Dec.	Jan.	Feb.	Mar.	Apr.	May	June	July	Market Total
2004-05	135,568	46,749	91,390	263,999	369,597	402,504	445,448	424,472	210,285	93,471	95,154	20,398	2,599,035
2005-06	67,318	63,884	138,910	220,961	363,287	434,818	183,744	183,273	62,703	73,726	117,934	60,708	1,971,266
2006-07	87,527	58,849	111,619	112,634	214,384	174,852	140,273	125,562	207,478	310,748	168,730	137,204	1,849,860
2007-08	85,183	133,709	126,008	149,748	197,651	359,180	303,523	95,053	104,513	64,281	119,022	46,555	1,784,426
2008-09	79,487	75,191	89,246	92,960	113,117	149,362	106,701	175,099	265,718	92,969	66,390	77,746	1,383,986
2009-10	34,279	54,457	57,362	179,007	199,006	75,580	175,053	69,900	34,523	9,790	13,412	1,732	904,101
2010-11	1,431	5,498	69,122	126,009	153,780	130,932	59,520	27,102	10,609	27,288	33,804	7,581	652,676
2011-12	9,762	31,213	95,360	122,388	131,642	227,089	115,427	119,698	25,990	20,764	20,687	36,712	956,732
2012-13	38,533	55,227	81,437	408,050	417,927	382,992	112,442	62,556	65,991	27,923	25,573	12,135	1,690,786
2013-14	20,398	26,066	52,042	198,579	433,317	345,007	141,663						2,067,386

[1] Seven markets.   *Source: Agricultural Marketing Service, U.S. Department of Agriculture (AMS-USDA)*

Production of Cotton (Upland and American-Pima) in the United States   In Thousands of 480-Pound Bales

Year	Alabama	Arizona	Arkansas	California	Georgia	Louisiana	Mississippi	Missouri	North Carolina	South Carolina	Tennessee	Texas	Total American-Pima
2005	848	615	2,202	1,065	2,140	1,098	2,147	864	1,437	410	1,122	8,440	630.5
2006	675	556	2,525	779	2,334	1,241	2,107	985	1,285	433	1,368	5,800	765.4
2007	416	514	1,896	650	1,660	699	1,318	764	783	160	600	8,250	851.8
2008	469	405	1,296	367	1,600	281	683	698	755	246	530	4,450	430.8
2009	345	443	852	240	1,860	349	415	502	763	207	492	4,620	399.9
2010	480	610	1,176	380	2,250	437	848	685	951	376	681	7,840	504.1
2011	685	800	1,277	556	2,465	511	1,200	741	1,026	519	813	3,500	851.2
2012	745	605	1,297	508	2,910	478	993	731	1,225	593	743	5,000	779.8
2013[1]	590	480	720	333	2,320	326	719	496	766	360	414	4,170	634.2
2014[2]	660	465	820	235	2,500	410	1,035	570	1,005	520	492	5,980	588.0

[1] Preliminary.   [2] Forecast.   *Source: Agricultural Statistics Board, U.S. Department of Agriculture (ASB-USDA)*

Cotton Production and Yield Estimates in the United States

Year	Forecasts of Production (1,000 Bales of 480 Lbs.[1]) Aug.1	Sept.1	Oct. 1	Nov. 1	Dec. 1	Jan. 1	Actual Crop	Forecasts of Yield (Lbs. Per Harvested Acre) Aug.1	Sept.1	Oct. 1	Nov. 1	Dec. 1	Jan. 1	Actual Yield
2005	21,291	22,282	22,717	23,161	23,703	----	23,890	748	782	797	813	832	----	831
2006	20,431	20,345	20,659	21,299	21,297	----	21,588	765	762	774	798	798	----	814
2007	17,346	17,812	18,154	18,862	18,987	----	19,207	783	811	826	859	864	----	879
2008	13,767	13,846	13,711	13,528	13,613	----	12,815	842	849	849	837	843	----	813
2009	13,207	13,438	12,998	12,496	12,592	----	12,188	816	816	807	776	782	----	777
2010	18,534	18,841	18,873	18,418	18,268	----	18,104	837	839	841	821	814	----	812
2011	16,554	16,556	16,608	16,300	15,827	----	15,573	822	807	809	794	771	----	790
2012	17,651	17,109	17,287	17,447	17,257	----	17,314	784	786	795	802	793	----	892
2013	13,053	12,899	NA	13,105	13,069	----	12,909	813	796	NA	808	806	----	821
2014	17,502	16,538	16,255	16,397	15,923	----	16,084	820	803	790	797	773	----	795

[1] Net weight bales.   *Source: Agricultural Statistics Board, U.S. Department of Agriculture (ASB-USDA)*

Supply and Distribution of Upland Cotton in the United States   In Thousands of 480-Pound Bales

Crop Year Beginning Aug. 1	Area Planted 1,000 Acres	Area Harvested 1,000 Acres	Yield Lbs./Acre	Supply Beginning Stocks[3]	Supply Production	Supply Imports	Total Supply	Disappearance Mill Use	Disappearance Exports	Disappearance Total	Ending Stocks	Farm Price[5] Cents/ Lb.
2004-05	13,409	12,809	843	3,384	22,505	8	25,897	6,629	13,683	20,312	5,482	43.1
2005-06	13,975	13,534	825	5,482	23,260	9	28,751	5,820	17,115	22,935	5,991	47.3
2006-07	14,948	12,408	806	5,991	20,822	10	26,824	4,896	12,324	17,220	9,291	46.6
2007-08	10,535	10,201	864	9,291	18,355	6	27,652	4,548	12,801	17,349	9,895	59.8
2008-09	9,297	7,400	803	9,895	12,385	0	22,279	3,512	13,029	16,541	6,032	49.4
2009-10	9,008	7,391	766	6,032	11,788	0	17,820	3,529	11,343	14,872	2,929	62.1
2010-11	10,770	10,497	805	2,929	17,600	2	20,531	3,874	13,881	17,755	2,572	82.3
2011-12	14,428	9,156	772	2,572	14,722	19	17,307	3,278	11,120	14,398	3,081	88.5
2012-13[1]	12,076	9,135	869	3,081	16,535	5	19,621	3,430	12,785	16,215	3,386	74.8
2013-14[2]	10,206	7,465	807	3,386	12,551		16,311	3,475	10,350	13,825	2,481	

[1] Preliminary.   [2] Estimate.   [3] Excludes preseason ginnings (adjusted to 480-lb. bale net weight basis).   [4] Includes preseason ginnings.
[5] Marketing year average price.   *Source: Economic Research Service, U.S. Department of Agriculture (ERS-USDA)*

COTTON #2 - ICE-US
Weekly Selected Futures as of 01/02/2015

WEEKLY SELECTED FUTURES
As of 01/02/2015

Chart High 227.00 on 03/07/2011
Chart Low 36.70 on 11/12/2008

Nearby Futures through Last Trading Day using selected contract months: March, May, July, October and December.

Volume of Trading of Cotton #2 Futures in New York   In Contracts

Year	Jan.	Feb.	Mar.	Apr.	May	June	July	Aug.	Sept.	Oct.	Nov.	Dec.	Total
2005	356,817	407,277	317,486	465,210	306,971	456,584	171,139	189,584	271,268	290,650	408,580	207,424	3,848,990
2006	311,926	495,729	375,624	515,709	330,785	601,971	184,482	259,259	268,847	308,584	587,710	249,781	4,490,407
2007	366,579	713,894	375,964	765,244	439,838	745,901	428,059	445,099	435,529	520,221	759,829	338,822	6,334,979
2008	684,489	971,319	730,160	651,281	427,731	690,183	281,522	306,004	418,279	401,064	426,785	174,146	6,162,963
2009	276,977	326,853	272,091	373,379	274,983	372,124	187,347	177,989	228,815	347,989	509,375	227,073	3,574,995
2010	321,331	570,117	344,389	567,774	365,998	550,206	327,296	331,579	440,411	600,977	887,594	425,234	5,732,906
2011	457,454	719,075	590,294	602,903	325,606	536,555	293,608	290,265	307,617	350,452	598,711	215,914	5,288,454
2012	471,729	605,161	499,276	660,539	564,011	826,818	308,028	339,672	349,649	584,358	632,610	288,501	6,130,352
2013	599,171	738,954	474,475	725,015	494,848	729,167	282,565	464,074	273,354	487,233	588,624	297,544	6,155,024
2014	544,180	602,542	446,810	568,063	399,736	611,785	362,461	338,548	460,119	477,742	584,383	337,560	5,733,929

Contract size = 50,000 lbs.   *Source: ICE Futures U.S. (ICE)*

Average Open Interest of Cotton #2 Futures in New York   In Contracts

Year	Jan.	Feb.	Mar.	Apr.	May	June	July	Aug.	Sept.	Oct.	Nov.	Dec.
2005	92,651	94,047	118,183	120,416	103,446	93,818	92,284	99,959	105,874	117,889	103,466	100,660
2006	118,234	129,108	129,728	141,156	165,386	170,190	161,719	166,806	178,539	184,002	170,275	164,797
2007	177,495	199,342	214,628	225,473	223,839	212,296	214,893	206,042	215,820	239,217	229,629	219,185
2008	264,235	279,240	286,505	259,800	258,309	239,935	219,979	216,387	211,933	177,277	146,431	127,380
2009	130,049	120,331	128,054	128,973	134,079	120,861	122,153	127,019	136,585	165,683	180,594	182,489
2010	178,305	166,475	185,608	190,458	184,193	171,459	160,118	201,962	231,513	235,834	217,587	201,510
2011	204,871	198,798	176,675	180,626	150,430	148,695	138,168	144,300	150,834	155,592	149,292	146,219
2012	156,940	180,632	183,618	186,859	188,255	185,629	171,383	180,207	183,282	199,026	179,969	165,382
2013	185,106	201,378	205,753	188,311	181,012	173,729	162,260	191,013	178,447	203,972	172,006	164,247
2014	180,149	171,213	178,245	178,514	190,808	169,165	152,321	167,437	181,359	190,436	181,192	175,349

Contract size = 50,000 lbs.   *Source: ICE Futures U.S. (ICE)*

COTTON

Daily Rate of Upland Cotton Mill Consumption[2] on Cotton-System Spinning Spindles in the United States
In Thousands of Running Bales

Crop Year Beginning Aug. 1	Aug.	Sept.	Oct.	Nov.	Dec.	Jan.	Feb.	Mar.	Apr.	May	June	July	Average
2002-03	28.0	28.3	27.9	27.4	27.2	26.5	26.8	26.4	26.0	25.0	24.3	24.7	26.5
2003-04	23.0	22.7	22.6	23.0	22.7	22.4	23.1	23.1	22.8	23.1	23.2	24.2	23.0
2004-05	25.1	25.1	24.9	24.4	25.2	24.8	23.7	23.7	24.0	23.6	25.2	24.4	24.5
2005-06	23.2	22.0	22.6	21.2	20.5	22.9	23.1	22.4	20.7	20.2	19.9	19.5	21.5
2006-07	18.9	18.8	18.5	W	W	W	W	W	W	W	W	W	18.7
2007-08	W	W	W	W	W	16.7	17.0	16.0	17.2	16.6	16.9	16.4	16.7
2008-09	17.4	15.9	16.7	14.3	9.4	13.0	11.2	11.5	11.7	12.2	11.8	12.8	13.1
2009-10	12.8	10.6	13.0	12.9	10.3	13.2	12.8	12.4	12.9	13.6	13.2	13.1	12.6
2010-11[1]	13.8	13.7	14.6	13.4	11.7	14.4	14.0	13.5	13.3	13.5	13.4	12.2	13.5
2011-12[1]	NA	NA	NA	NA	NA	NA	NA	NA	NA	NA	NA	NA	NA

[1] Preliminary.　[2] Not seasonally adjusted.　W = Withheld.　*Source: Bureau of the Census: U.S. Department of Commerce*

Consumption of American and Foreign Cotton in the United States　In Thousands of Running Bales

Year	Aug.	Sept.	Oct.	Nov.	Dec.	Jan.	Feb.	Mar.	Apr.	May	June	July	Total
2002-03	574	733	585	545	598	671	556	708	541	523	616	456	7,106
2003-04	476	599	482	468	504	478	475	609	461	473	582	446	6,053
2004-05	484	604	483	460	500	470	472	601	469	463	581	449	6,035
2005-06	454	574	472	415	438	452	476	593	430	422	531	381	5,637
2006-07	385	492	389	357	370	361	363	461	371	371	476	348	4,744
2007-08	358	467	366	343	362	423	341	402	346	333	430	329	4,499
2008-09	349	399	333	285	234	261	230	302	230	251	311	254	3,439
2009-10	263	280	261	266	267	266	259	313	261	275	338	270	3,318
2010-11[1]	286	351	303	274	301	287	280	337	266	270	334	244	3,533
2011-12[1]	NA	NA	NA	NA	NA	NA	NA	NA	NA	NA	NA	NA	NA

[1] Preliminary.　*Source: Bureau of the Census, U.S. Department of Commerce*

Exports of All Cotton[2] from the United States　In Thousands of Running Bales

Year	Aug.	Sept.	Oct.	Nov.	Dec.	Jan.	Feb.	Mar.	Apr.	May	June	July	Total
2005-06	1,407	742	533	763	1,236	946	1,541	2,195	1,758	1,725	1,906	1,903	16,655
2006-07	688	412	487	599	812	683	824	1,266	1,269	1,385	2,174	1,745	12,342
2007-08	1,116	1,337	883	977	781	981	945	955	1,096	1,360	1,292	1,427	13,150
2008-09	994	983	1,159	923	747	733	813	1,128	1,442	1,475	1,266	1,106	13,179
2009-10	885	809	664	570	778	942	1,174	1,447	1,175	1,354	1,344	1,373	12,515
2010-11	1,023	467	449	1,141	1,688	2,057	1,839	2,085	1,561	1,163	706	533	14,714
2011-12	302	303	422	776	930	1,284	1,585	1,672	1,322	1,242	942	785	11,564
2012-13	743	743	494	732	1,099	1,549	1,798	1,721	1,449	1,387	914	692	13,322
2013-14	766	533	415	608	977	1,417	1,345	1,351	1,080	872	606	446	10,416
2014-15[1]	498	381	355	573	1,025								6,796

[1] Preliminary.　*Source: Foreign Agricultural Service, U.S. Department of Agriculture (FAS-USDA)*

U.S. Exports of American Cotton to Countries of Destination　In Thousands of 480-Pound Bales

Crop Year Beginning Aug. 1	Canada	China	Hong Kong	Indo-nesia	Italy	Japan	Korea, South	Mexico	Philip-pines	Taiwan	Thailand	United Kingdom	Total
2003-04	303	4,919	169	889	63	284	469	1,620	100	527	396	20	13,758
2004-05	305	4,085	274	1,138	75	301	643	1,589	110	846	711	60	14,436
2005-06	178	9,095	280	933	33	265	431	1,511	46	660	530	23	18,039
2006-07	101	3,641	238	928	36	265	307	1,200	39	429	456	0	12,219
2007-08	40	4,491	177	1,261	62	376	361	1,432	26	390	838	0	13,972
2008-09	19	3,770	184	1,057	23	158	302	1,320	52	436	615	----	13,179
2009-10	9	3,886	69	660	21	150	353	1,490	51	424	605	----	12,515
2010-11	10	4,863	47	889	53	186	513	1,245	37	357	712	1	14,714
2011-12[1]	3	6,281	45	329	15	97	329	957	16	271	275	0	11,564
2012-13[2]	2	5,611	104	533	8	120	352	980	31	419	355	0	13,322

[1] Preliminary.　[2] Estimate.　*Source: Foreign Agricultural Service, U.S. Department of Agriculture (FAS-USDA)*

Cotton[1] Government Loan Program in the United States

Crop Year Beginning Aug. 1	Support Price --- Cents Per Lb. ---	Target Price	Put Under Support Ths Bales	% of Production	Acquired ----- Ths. Bales -----	Owned July 31	Crop Year Beginning Aug. 1	Support Price --- Cents Per Lb. ---	Target Price	Put Under Support Ths Bales	% of Production	Acquired ----- Ths. Bales -----	Owned July 31
2003-04	52.00	72.4	10,466	57.3	16	0	2008-09	52.00	71.3	10,005	78.1	4	0
2004-05	52.00	72.4	17,092	73.5	8	0	2009-10	52.00	71.3	8,278	67.9	0	0
2005-06	52.00	72.4	17,783	74.4	181	11	2010-11	52.00	71.3	11,403	63.0	0	0
2006-07	52.00	72.4	17,839	82.6	79	0	2011-12[2]	52.00	71.3				
2007-08	52.00	72.4	14,636	76.2	169	0	2012-13[2]	52.00	71.3				

[1] Upland. [2] Preliminary. NA = Not applicable. *Source: Economic Research Service, U.S. Department of Agriculture (ERS-USDA)*

Production of Cotton Cloth[1] in the United States   In Millions of Square Yards

Year	First Quarter	Second Quarter	Third Quarter	Fourth Quarter	Total	Year	First Quarter	Second Quarter	Third Quarter	Fourth Quarter	Total
2002	893	912	894	825	3,524	2007	521	507	488	453	1,969
2003	836	780	662	620	2,898	2008	447	460	451	393	1,751
2004	648	644	640	614	2,547	2009	336	357	320	307	1,320
2005	672	640	653	664	2,629	2010	327	321	340	328	1,315
2006	583	609	551	487	2,230	2011[2]	347	331	X	X	1,356

[1] Cotton broadwoven goods over 12 inches in width. [2] Preliminary. *Source: Bureau of Census, U.S. Department of Commerce*

Cotton Ginnings[1] in the United States To: In Thousands of Running Bales

Crop Year	Aug. 1	Sept. 1	Sept. 15	Oct. 1	Oct. 15	Nov. 1	Nov. 15	Dec. 1	Dec. 15	Jan. 1	Jan. 15	Feb. 1	Total Crop
2005-06	69	592	976	2,314	4,556	8,691	12,569	15,991	18,401	20,108	21,282	22,255	23,253
2006-07	23	406	996	2,572	5,039	8,604	11,833	15,139	17,657	19,212	20,062	20,559	20,998
2007-08	W	182	375	1,566	3,793	7,072	10,099	12,593	14,341	15,700	16,690	17,585	18,713
2008-09	13	335	476	797	2,027	4,358	6,800	8,928	10,463	11,572	12,094	12,370	12,462
2009-10	5	110	175	234	552	2,189	4,957	7,873	9,728	10,812	11,383	11,706	11,832
2010-11	W	287	747	2,284	4,716	7,947	10,576	13,170	15,126	16,442	17,138	17,518	17,643
2011-12	203	822	1,095	1,734	3,467	6,440	9,214	11,668	13,064	13,949	14,458	14,805	15,153
2012-13	60	473	756	1,552	2,943	6,307	9,394	12,263	14,194	15,327	16,029	16,547	16,834
2013-14	W	132	274	486	1,101	3,038	5,723	8,260	10,459	11,402	12,053	12,391	12,521
2014-15[2]	1	367	696	1,154	2,108	4,807	7,530	10,248	12,602	14,249	15,057	15,548	

[1] Excluding linters. [2] Preliminary. W = Withheld. *Source: National Agricultural Statistics Service, U.S. Department of Agriculture (NASS-USDA)*

Fiber Prices in the United States   In Cents Per Pound

Year	Cotton[1] Actual	Cotton[1] Raw[5] Equivalent	Rayon[2] Actual	Rayon[2] Raw[5] Equivalent	Polyester[3] Actual	Polyester[3] Raw[5] Equivalent	Price Ratios[4] In Percent Cotton/ Rayon	Price Ratios[4] In Percent Cotton/ Polyester
2000	64.06	71.17	97.58	101.65	57.08	59.46	70.0	119.1
2001	47.08	52.32	98.50	102.61	60.42	62.93	52.0	83.0
2002	45.56	50.63	97.83	101.91	61.17	63.72	50.0	79.0
2003	62.54	69.49	90.25	94.01	60.67	63.20	74.1	111.0
2004	60.42	67.13	99.08	103.21	62.67	65.28	66.5	103.5
2005	54.75	60.00	114.58	119.36	67.75	70.57	51.0	86.2
2006	56.70	63.00	113.00	117.71	69.00	71.86	53.5	88.0
2007	61.97	68.86	113.00	117.71	74.00	77.08	58.5	89.3
2008[6]	73.79	82.01	113.00	117.71	74.00	77.08	69.7	121.1
Jan.	73.32	81.47	113.00	117.71	74.00	77.08	69.2	120.3
Feb.	74.25	82.54	113.00	117.71	74.00	77.08	70.1	121.8
Mar.	NA	NA	NA	NA	NA	NA	NA	NA
Apr.	NA	NA	NA	NA	NA	NA	NA	NA
May	NA	NA	NA	NA	NA	NA	NA	NA
June	NA	NA	NA	NA	NA	NA	NA	NA
July	NA	NA	NA	NA	NA	NA	NA	NA
Aug.	NA	NA	NA	NA	NA	NA	NA	NA
Sept.	NA	NA	NA	NA	NA	NA	NA	NA
Oct.	NA	NA	NA	NA	NA	NA	NA	NA
Nov.	NA	NA	NA	NA	NA	NA	NA	NA
Dec.								

[1] SLM-1 1/16" at group B Mill points, net weight. [2] 1.5 and 3.0 denier, regular rayon staples. [3] Reported average market price for 1.5 denier polyester staple for cotton blending. [4] Raw fiber equivalent. [5] Actual prices converted to estimated raw fiber equivalent as follows: cotton, divided by 0.90, rayon and polyester, divided by 0.96. [6] Preliminary.
Source: Economic Research Service, U.S. Department of Agriculture (ERS-USDA)

Cottonseed and Products

Cottonseed is crushed to produce both oil and meal. Cottonseed oil is typically used for cooking oil and cottonseed meal is fed to livestock. Before the cottonseed is crushed for oil and meal, it is de-linted of its linters. Linters are used for padding in furniture, absorbent cotton swabs, and for the manufacture of many cellulose products. The sediment left by cottonseed oil refining, called foots, provides fatty acids for industrial products. The value of cottonseeds represents a substantial 18% of a cotton producer's income.

Prices – The average monthly price of cottonseed oil in 2014 rose by +33.4% yr/yr to 62.15 cents per pound, still below the 2008 record high of 68.09 cents per pound. The average monthly price of cottonseed meal in 2013 (latest data available) rose by +10.0% yr/yr to $334.81 per short ton, a new record high.

Supply – World production of cottonseed in the 2013-

14 marketing year fell -3.8% yr/yr to 43.416 million metric tons, below the 2011-12 record high. The world's largest cottonseed producers are India with 27.4%, China with 25.3% of world production, Pakistan with 9.6%, and the U.S. with 8.9%. U.S. production of cottonseed in the 2014-15 marketing year rose by +25.1% yr/yr to 5.258 million tons. U.S. production of cottonseed oil in 2014-15 rose by +23.0% yr/yr to 775 million pounds, but still below the 12-year high of 957 million pounds posted in 2004-05.

Demand – U.S. cottonseed crushed (consumed) in the U.S. in the 2014-15 marketing year rose by +21.3% to 2.425 million tons, which was still far below the levels of over 4 million tons seen in the 1970s.

Trade – U.S. exports of cottonseed in 2014-15 rose +32.4% to 290,000 short tons, while imports were down -49.5% yr/yr to 100,000 short tons.

World Production of Cottonseed   In Thousands of Metric Ton

Crop Year Beginning Oct. 1	Argentina	Australia	Brazil	China	Egypt	Greece	India	Mexico	Pakistan	Turkey	United States	Former USSR	World Total
2005-06	230	770	1,816	10,171	399	677	8,200	221	4,428	1,291	7,414	3,165	42,953
2006-07	300	330	2,498	13,409	372	520	9,300	249	4,065	1,477	6,666	3,100	45,866
2007-08	271	180	2,422	13,571	389	500	10,400	209	3,695	1,321	5,977	3,158	45,248
2008-09	214	466	1,785	13,330	185	420	9,800	201	3,760	1,077	3,901	3,070	41,132
2009-10	374	547	1,786	11,351	174	449	9,800	151	4,138	1,021	3,764	2,918	39,101
2010-11	568	1,269	3,084	10,627	187	310	10,800	239	3,665	1,200	5,532	3,013	43,552
2011-12	390	1,694	3,028	11,718	219	490	11,800	410	4,347	1,300	4,872	3,070	47,177
2012-13[1]	285	1,408	2,076	11,800	155	425	11,300	355	4,164	1,220	5,140	3,049	45,111
2013-14[2]	450	1,330	2,323	11,000	140	475	11,900	280	4,150	1,150	3,813	2,943	43,416

[1] Preliminary. [2] Estimate. *Source: The Oil World*

Salient Statistics of Cottonseed in the United States   In Thousands of Short Tons

Crop Year Beginning Aug. 1	Stocks	Production	Total Supply	Crush	Exports	Other	Total	Farm Price USD/Ton	Value of Production Mil. USD	Products Produced	Total
2006-07	602	7,348	7,950	2,680	616	4,165	7,461	111	814.2	849	1,241
2007-08	489	6,589	7,080	2,706	599	3,132	6,437	162	1,069.8	856	1,262
2008-09	643	4,300	4,943	2,240	190	1,999	4,429	223	962.7	669	938
2009-10	514	4,149	4,687	1,901	296	2,149	4,345	158	670.0	617	883
2010-11	342	6,098	6,440	2,563	275	2,984	5,822	161	988.7	835	1,163
2011-12	618	5,370	6,059	2,400	133	3,096	5,629	260	1,413.3	755	1,090
2012-13	430	5,666	6,278	2,500	191	3,094	5,786	245-265	1,456.2	800	1,125
2013-14[1]	492	4,203	4,893	2,000	219	2,250	4,468		1,054.0	630	900
2014-15[2]	425	5,314	5,839	2,000	275	3,075	5,350		1,055.4		

[1] Preliminary.   [2] Estimate.   *Source: Economic Research Service, U.S. Department of Agriculture (ERS-USDA)*

Average Wholesale Price of Cottonseed Meal (41% Solvent)[2] in Memphis   In Dollars Per Short Ton

Year	Jan.	Feb.	Mar.	Apr.	May	June	July	Aug.	Sept.	Oct.	Nov.	Dec.	Average
2006	172.50	152.50	148.75	144.38	131.50	135.00	132.50	134.50	139.00	132.40	131.88	152.50	142.28
2007	161.00	174.75	185.50	148.25	137.00	131.25	137.50	144.75	167.50	183.40	176.25	196.67	161.99
2008	273.60	292.00	245.00	230.00	240.50	293.25	333.00	290.00	292.00	238.75	225.00	229.50	265.22
2009	237.50	236.25	213.00	212.50	236.25	306.00	305.00	315.00	308.00	250.00	260.00	283.75	263.60
2010	286.25	253.75	213.00	175.00	171.25	176.00	183.75	198.00	200.00	225.31	235.00	240.63	213.16
2011	245.63	258.75	256.50	240.00	275.50	307.50	313.13	342.50	345.63	255.63	240.50	220.63	275.16
2012	213.00	190.00	225.00	240.63	270.00	294.38	350.50	407.50	393.75	343.00	376.88	345.00	304.14
2013	327.50	279.38	301.88	314.50	311.88	329.38	344.50	330.00	374.38	355.00	345.00	401.88	334.61
2014[1]	375.63	388.75	401.25	405.50	416.88	412.50	359.50	310.00	360.63	346.88	313.13	332.50	368.60

[1] Preliminary.   *Source: Economic Research Service, U.S. Department of Agriculture (ERS-USDA)*

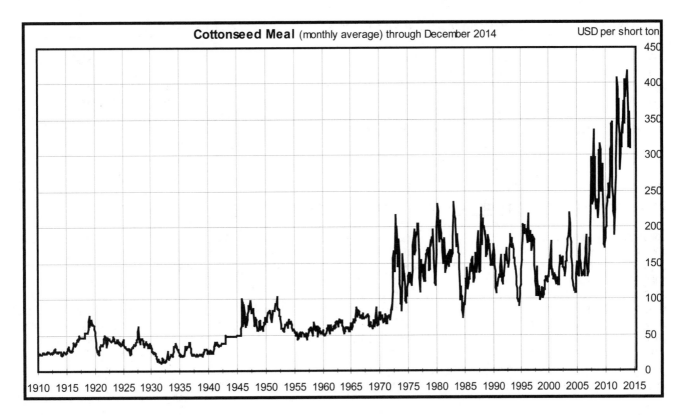

Cottonseed Meal (monthly average) through December 2014   USD per short ton

Supply and Distribution of Cottonseed Oil in the United States   In Millions of Pounds

Crop Year Beginning Oct. 1	Supply				Disappearance			Per Capita Consumption of Salad & Cooking Oils --- In Lbs. ---	Utilization Food Uses			Prices	
	Stocks	Pro-duction	Imports	Total Supply	Domestic	Exports	Total		Short-ening	Salad & Cooking Oils	Total	U.S.[3] (Crude) --- $/Metric Ton ---	Rott[4] (Cif)
2008-09	147	669	0	815	502	192	694	54	W	638	638	820	829
2009-10	121	617	0	738	551	94	646	51	W	509	509	888	895
2010-11	93	835	0	928	599	164	763	54	123	521	644	1,201	1,258
2011-12	165	755	10.0	930	572	259	830		NA	NA		1,173	1,188
2012-13	100	800	20.0	920	599	221	820		NA	NA		1,071	1,121
2013-14[1]	100	630	32.0	762	514	148	662					1,337	
2014-15[2]	100	640	20.0	760	510	150	660					923	

[1] Preliminary.   [2] Estimate.   [3] Valley Points FOB; Tank Cars.   [4] Rotterdam; US, PBSY, fob gulf.   W = Withheld.
Source: Economic Research Service, U.S. Department of Agriculture (ERS-USDA)

Consumption of Crude Cottonseed Oil, in Refining[2], in the United States   In Millions of Pound

Year	Oct.	Nov.	Dec.	Jan.	Feb.	Mar.	Apr.	May	June	July	Aug.	Sept.	Total
2005-06	72.7	79.0	75.1	70.9	64.0	71.1	58.2	71.6	61.2	52.6	61.4	52.4	790.2
2006-07	65.7	55.7	61.4	63.9	55.3	63.7	60.1	63.6	54.1	56.3	56.5	55.6	711.9
2007-08	59.6	60.9	61.7	74.0	70.2	68.0	70.9	62.2	52.3	55.3	57.1	52.8	744.8
2008-09	47.2	56.4	63.5	58.3	58.4	57.5	44.0	48.1	50.6	36.9	39.3	37.5	597.6
2009-10	32.6	46.2	51.6	45.0	41.4	43.9	38.5	42.7	39.5	W	45.6	47.4	517.6
2010-11[1]	38.7	60.1	59.0	56.6	51.6	60.2	56.4	56.8	56.0	45.6	NA	NA	649.4
2011-12[1]	NA	NA	NA	NA	NA	NA	NA	NA	NA	NA	NA	NA	NA

[1] Preliminary.   *Source: U.S. Bureau of Census, U.S. Department of Commerce*

Exports of Cottonseed Oil (Crude and Refined) from the United States   In Thousands of Pounds

Year	Jan.	Feb.	Mar.	Apr.	May	June	July	Aug.	Sept.	Oct.	Nov.	Dec.	Total
2008	11,089	21,546	25,577	11,565	12,436	17,019	17,441	11,300	17,263	22,083	20,819	18,611	206,747
2009	14,423	20,981	15,258	19,313	12,296	14,087	12,070	10,915	11,370	8,506	14,923	8,455	162,597
2010	6,880	9,414	7,075	6,728	6,450	4,234	3,539	5,523	12,740	20,331	16,878	7,038	106,827
2011	8,142	11,103	19,150	17,085	15,053	9,531	11,479	14,273	13,515	25,841	31,753	18,691	195,617
2012	18,674	12,596	31,375	19,626	20,622	24,030	17,908	21,029	16,715	21,956	17,805	15,878	238,213
2013	19,609	20,389	16,582	21,550	21,218	19,353	15,042	15,886	15,403	15,674	13,338	11,323	205,366
2014[1]	13,367	19,061	18,084	20,542	8,709	7,165	2,486	5,895	12,517	12,384	12,014	14,206	146,429

[1] Preliminary.   *Source: Economic Research Service, U.S. Department of Agriculture (ERS-USDA)*

COTTONSEED AND PRODUCTS

Cottonseed Crushed (Consumption) in the United States   In Thousands of Short Tons

Year	Aug.	Sept.	Oct.	Nov.	Dec.	Jan.	Feb.	Mar.	Apr.	May	June	July	Total
2003-04	138.7	98.9	251.6	254.8	252.0	265.2	242.3	278.0	217.1	240.2	217.7	182.4	2,639
2004-05	193.8	141.0	247.9	260.3	263.5	283.1	266.3	270.2	287.7	221.0	266.6	221.6	2,923
2005-06	240.7	170.3	272.2	289.4	296.9	291.3	245.0	276.7	235.0	280.3	227.2	203.4	3,028
2006-07	204.8	158.2	252.4	223.3	236.7	251.2	222.5	249.1	230.8	243.2	204.6	203.3	2,680
2007-08	173.4	163.8	242.5	241.2	252.1	267.5	264.1	236.3	245.2	233.4	190.3	193.1	2,703
2008-09	202.3	147.4	175.2	206.5	230.0	234.3	217.6	206.5	170.7	168.1	158.1	133.2	2,250
2009-10	107.1	92.8	131.2	169.2	189.7	202.4	184.6	187.0	180.0	191.3	141.2	124.0	1,900
2010-11[1]	151.0	143.9	172.8	245.7	251.3	249.0	229.4	258.8	235.6	235.6	211.1	178.3	2,563
2011-12[1]	NA	NA	NA	NA	NA	NA	NA	NA	NA	NA	NA	NA	NA

[1] Preliminary.   Source: Economic Research Service, U.S. Department of Agriculture (ERS-USDA)

Production of Cottonseed Cake and Meal in the United States   In Thousands of Short Tons

Year	Aug.	Sept.	Oct.	Nov.	Dec.	Jan.	Feb.	Mar.	Apr.	May	June	July	Total
2003-04	74.9	59.5	112.3	111.0	112.5	113.9	105.1	123.4	94.2	104.7	97.7	91.0	1,200
2004-05	95.3	82.5	105.4	110.4	118.7	125.7	119.3	120.4	124.4	103.6	121.0	106.2	1,333
2005-06	116.4	91.1	109.6	134.6	129.3	128.8	108.2	119.4	104.5	129.3	107.2	99.0	1,377
2006-07	102.0	83.0	118.8	101.8	102.4	115.3	101.8	114.6	105.9	112.6	97.4	102.3	1,258
2007-08	81.3	87.3	112.5	111.0	111.9	125.6	119.9	116.3	110.4	103.2	86.8	90.7	1,257
2008-09	96.5	76.9	74.8	89.7	103.5	102.7	99.2	90.8	76.6	73.0	75.6	60.7	1,020
2009-10	46.9	40.8	60.9	73.4	82.1	92.2	81.0	78.6	76.8	87.2	59.9	53.0	833
2010-11[1]	63.2	74.9	82.2	103.8	112.0	107.7	104.0	113.5	106.8	110.1	98.0	82.7	1,159
2011-12[1]	NA	NA	NA	NA	NA	NA	NA	NA	NA	NA	NA	NA	NA

[1] Preliminary.   Source: Bureau of Census, U.S. Department of Commerce

Production of Crude Cottonseed Oil[2] in the United States   In Millions of Pounds

Year	Aug.	Sept.	Oct.	Nov.	Dec.	Jan.	Feb.	Mar.	Apr.	May	June	July	Total
2003-04	45.0	40.7	77.5	78.2	79.0	82.4	75.7	87.2	67.0	73.8	66.7	59.7	833
2004-05	68.6	58.1	77.1	82.2	81.4	88.7	83.4	84.3	90.7	71.3	81.6	69.5	937
2005-06	84.3	62.0	86.9	95.7	90.9	92.8	77.2	87.8	70.9	90.4	70.4	68.1	977
2006-07	68.4	59.2	77.1	71.7	73.9	78.6	67.1	78.1	72.5	77.2	65.2	66.7	856
2007-08	58.2	62.5	77.5	73.8	76.8	83.5	82.1	77.1	77.1	70.3	58.5	60.3	858
2008-09	64.4	55.0	49.4	64.4	71.2	70.4	68.4	65.9	53.5	57.2	58.7	39.6	718
2009-10	34.5	35.5	38.3	54.1	59.1	59.8	55.9	60.0	51.5	59.8	41.1	36.6	586
2010-11[1]	48.0	52.9	54.3	79.1	79.8	79.3	71.4	84.6	77.3	80.0	70.6	59.4	837
2011-12[1]	NA	NA	NA	NA	NA	NA	NA	NA	NA	NA	NA	NA	NA

[1] Preliminary.   [2] Not seasonally adjusted.   Source: Bureau of Census, U.S. Department of Commerce

Production of Refined Cottonseed Oil in the United States   In Millions of Pounds

Year	Aug.	Sept.	Oct.	Nov.	Dec.	Jan.	Feb.	Mar.	Apr.	May	June	July	Total
2003-04	38.5	34.6	59.8	63.5	61.4	64.3	58.4	68.3	55.1	55.1	52.4	43.8	655
2004-05	53.4	52.0	59.7	66.1	66.9	73.4	68.8	66.6	72.3	52.7	64.6	56.6	753
2005-06	71.2	54.7	72.8	78.5	74.7	70.3	63.8	70.8	57.8	71.2	60.8	52.3	799
2006-07	61.0	52.0	65.2	55.3	61.1	63.5	55.3	62.9	58.9	63.5	54.0	56.1	709
2007-08	56.4	55.5	59.6	60.9	61.6	73.8	70.0	67.8	70.5	62.1	52.3	55.2	746
2008-09	56.9	52.6	46.9	56.3	63.2	57.9	58.1	57.2	43.7	47.9	50.3	36.7	628
2009-10	39.2	37.5	32.6	46.2	51.6	44.9	41.4	43.9	38.5	42.7	39.5	W	500
2010-11[1]	45.6	47.3	38.7	60.1	59.0	56.6	51.6	60.2	56.4	56.7	56.0	45.6	634
2011-12[1]	NA	NA	NA	NA	NA	NA	NA	NA	NA	NA	NA	NA	NA

[1] Preliminary.   Source: Bureau of the Census, U.S. Department of Commerce

Stocks of Cottonseed Oil (Crude and Refined) in the U.S., at End of Month   In Millions of Pounds

Year	Aug.	Sept.	Oct.	Nov.	Dec.	Jan.	Feb.	Mar.	Apr.	May	June	July
2003-04	50.5	36.0	51.9	56.1	68.7	85.9	100.6	117.6	116.8	125.7	121.0	123.0
2004-05	123.3	109.0	106.6	110.6	111.3	116.6	122.0	112.9	121.2	111.5	90.0	86.2
2005-06	90.6	76.4	69.0	76.1	74.0	84.0	99.0	108.5	103.3	110.8	105.8	95.6
2006-07	98.9	101.1	93.2	92.3	106.8	119.2	117.0	112.2	124.5	126.1	119.5	160.2
2007-08	132.9	105.8	92.8	91.6	94.9	114.3	138.4	143.5	156.1	161.4	158.7	143.1
2008-09	153.8	146.6	139.7	124.7	120.0	126.7	134.1	149.4	151.4	160.9	144.7	150.3
2009-10	141.0	120.6	98.1	85.4	114.2	112.2	122.7	130.4	126.6	128.8	121.2	97.5
2010-11[1]	78.6	84.9	72.1	78.0	109.7	139.6	152.1	163.5	163.2	180.1	189.1	180.7
2011-12[1]	NA	NA	NA	NA	NA	NA	NA	NA	NA	NA	NA	NA

[1] Preliminary.   Source: Bureau of the Census, U.S. Department of Commerce

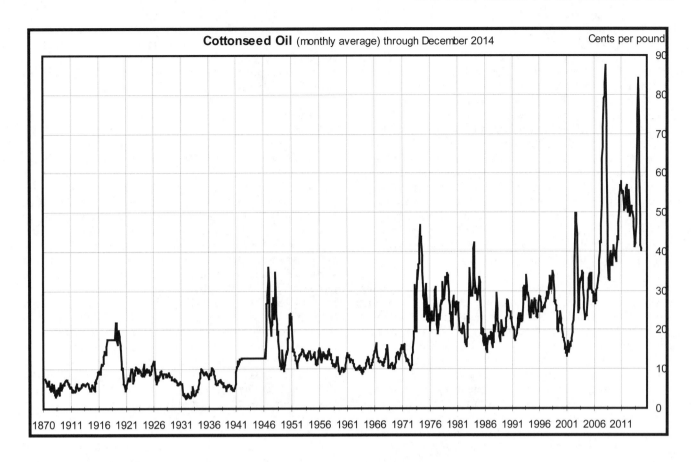

Cottonseed Oil (monthly average) through December 2014   Cents per pound

Average Price of Crude Cottonseed Oil, PBSY, Greenwood, MS.[1] in Tank Cars   In Cents Per Pound

Year	Jan.	Feb.	Mar.	Apr.	May	June	July	Aug.	Sept.	Oct.	Nov.	Dec.	Average
2005	23.70	24.38	28.19	29.80	30.63	33.13	34.15	30.44	31.25	34.44	34.09	30.50	30.39
2006	29.63	29.50	29.75	27.05	28.06	27.25	29.20	26.69	27.13	27.44	30.25	30.75	28.56
2007	31.00	32.69	33.00	34.38	37.75	40.00	42.44	42.15	46.56	52.20	63.60	66.63	43.53
2008	71.69	78.60	78.94	79.75	82.75	87.56	86.06	72.55	62.44	46.45	37.38	32.88	68.09
2009	35.70	33.19	32.63	37.38	39.90	38.75	36.55	39.13	36.44	37.90	40.69	41.40	37.47
2010	39.00	39.13	39.88	38.75	37.38	40.00	42.45	43.69	43.00	47.20	50.75	54.00	42.94
2011	55.92	56.75	55.50	57.70	56.06	55.25	54.75	54.75	55.35	51.56	50.50	51.10	54.60
2012	52.19	54.56	55.95	56.88	52.00	50.05	53.75	54.65	55.50	51.31	49.05	50.06	53.00
2013	50.94	51.56	50.20	49.94	49.75	48.25	46.19	43.10	42.81	41.19	42.05	43.19	46.60
2014[1]	47.10	57.81	69.94	75.00	84.25	83.31	73.15	61.25	49.63	41.45	40.75	40.31	60.33

[1] Preliminary.   *Source: Economic Research Service, U.S. Department of Agriculture (ERS-USDA)*

Exports of Cottonseed Oil to Important Countries from the United States   In Thousands of Metric Tons

Year	Canada	Dominican Republic	Egypt	Guate- mala	Japan	Mexico	Nether- lands	El Salvador	Korea, South	Turkey	Venez- uela	Total
2005	12.7	0	0	0	1.0	.1	6.5	0	0	0	0	21.5
2006	10.0	.0	0	.0	1.3	14.1	11.2	0	0	0	.1	40.2
2007	24.0	.1	0	0	7.1	17.3	11.6	0	0	0	.0	66.5
2008	40.8	.1	0	0	9.0	14.5	22.3	0	0	0	0	93.8
2009	37.0	0	0	0	2.6	8.7	18.1	.1	.2	0	0	73.8
2010	17.6	0	0	0	1.4	.9	26.0	0	0	0	0	48.5
2011	39.8	.0	0	0	0	.9	45.8	0	0	.0	0	88.7
2012	30.7	.0	0	0	.5	0	73.9	.2	0	.0	0	108.0
2013	22.4	0	0	0	.2	.0	63.5	1.2	0	.3	0	93.1
2014[1]	11.8	0	0	0	2.1	0	36.4	.9	0	.2	0	66.4

[1] Preliminary.   *Source: Foreign Agricultural Service, U.S. Department of Agriculture (FAS-USDA)*

Currencies

A "currency" rate involves the price of the base currency (e.g., the dollar) quoted in terms of another currency (e.g., the yen), or in terms of a basket of currencies (e.g., the dollar index). The world's major currencies have traded in a floating exchange rate regime ever since the Bretton-Woods international payments system broke down in 1971 when President Nixon broke the dollar's peg to gold. The two key factors affecting a currency's value are central bank monetary policy and the trade balance. An easy monetary policy (low interest rates) is bearish for a currency because the central bank is aggressively pumping new currency reserves into the marketplace and because foreign investors are not attracted to the low interest rate returns available in the country. By contrast, a tight monetary policy (high interest rates) is bullish for a currency because of the tight supply of new currency reserves and attractive interest rate returns for foreign investors.

The other key factor driving currency values is the nation's current account balance. A current account surplus is bullish for a currency due to the net inflow of the currency, while a current account deficit is bearish for a currency due to the net outflow of the currency. Currency values are also affected by economic growth and investment opportunities in the country. A country with a strong economy and lucrative investment opportunities will typically have a strong currency because global companies and investors want to buy into that country's investment opportunities. Futures on major currencies and on cross-currency rates are traded primarily at the CME Group.

Dollar – The dollar index traded sideways in the first half of 2014 but then rallied very sharply starting in August, closing the year up +13.2%. The dollar index rallied further in early 2015 and posted a new 11-1/2 year high. The dollar index rallied sharply in 2014 as the Fed progressively tapered its third quantitative easing program (QE3) and then ended the program altogether in October 2014. By contrast, the Bank of Japan (BOJ) expanded its QE program during 2014 and the European Central Bank (ECB) during 2014 saw increased pressure that finally resulted in a QE announcement in January 2015. The Fed's tighter monetary policy than the ECB or BOJ was a powerful bullish factor for the dollar. In addition, the markets are expecting the Fed to start raising interest rates way before either the ECB or BOJ. The dollar in 2014 also saw support from the better performance of the U.S. economy relative to the economies of its competitors. Although the U.S. GDP growth of +2.4% in 2014 was rather tepid, it was much better than the Eurozone's GDP growth rate of +0.8% in 2014 and Japan's zero growth rate.

Euro – EUR/USD edged to a 3-year high of $1.40/euro in May 2014 but then proceeded to plunge through the remainder of the year and into early 2015, posting an 11-1/2 year low in January 2015. EUR/USD closed 2014 down -12.0% at $1.21/euro. EUR/USD plunged in the latter half of 2014 when it became clear that the U.S. Federal Reserve would end its QE3 program in October 2014 while the ECB was coming under increasing pressure to implement a large-scale quantitative easing (QE) program. The ECB in January 2015 finally announced a large-scale QE program involving the purchase of 60 billion euros of sovereign bonds per month, totaling at least 1.1 trillion euros. The ECB implemented two interest rate cuts in 2014 that brought ECB's refinancing rate down to a negligible 0.05% by September 2014. The ECB was forced to cut rates and implement a QE program in response to the weak Eurozone economy and increased deflation risks. The Eurozone economy in 2014 recovered to only +0.8% after negative GDP growth rates in 2012-13 caused by the Eurozone sovereign debt crisis. Meanwhile, the Eurozone CPI in January 2015 fell into deflationary territory at -0.6% y/y and the core CPI fell to a record low of +0.6% y/y.

Yen – USD/JPY traded sideways in the first half of 2014 but then rallied sharply in the latter half of 2014 as the dollar index rallied against most other currencies in the world. USD/JPY closed up +13.7% in 2014 and posted a 7-1/2 year high of 121.84 yen/dollar in December 2014. The yen was weak against the dollar in 2014 as the Bank of Japan battled a mid-year recession and expanded its already-massive quantitative easing program. The Japanese economy experienced a recession in mid-2014 (Q2 GDP -7.3%, Q3 GDP -1.6%) due to the government's hike in the sales tax to 8% from 5% in April 2014. While Japan was experiencing a recession and while the Bank of Japan was expanding its QE program, the U.S. economy was gaining momentum and the Federal Reserve was ending its QE program. The outlook for Japan remains grim given weak economic growth combined with a massive government debt level.

BRITISH POUND - IMM
Weekly Nearest Futures as of 01/02/2015

WEEKLY NEAREST FUTURES
As of 01/02/2015
Chart High 2.1138   on 11/09/2007
Chart Low   1.3492   on 01/23/2009

Nearby Futures through Last Trading Day.

U.S. Dollars per British Pound

Year	Jan.	Feb.	Mar.	Apr.	May	June	July	Aug.	Sept.	Oct.	Nov.	Dec.	Average
2005	1.8783	1.8883	1.9034	1.8961	1.8538	1.8179	1.7518	1.7947	1.8078	1.7649	1.7355	1.7454	1.8198
2006	1.7665	1.7478	1.7446	1.7690	1.8693	1.8435	1.8451	1.8934	1.8858	1.8766	1.9124	1.9634	1.8431
2007	1.9585	1.9586	1.9479	1.9874	1.9834	1.9870	2.0344	2.0112	2.0202	2.0453	2.0709	2.0168	2.0018
2008	1.9692	1.9640	2.0012	1.9815	1.9662	1.9675	1.9897	1.8870	1.7997	1.6899	1.5290	1.4869	1.8526
2009	1.4484	1.4417	1.4197	1.4727	1.5460	1.6379	1.6387	1.6532	1.6312	1.6196	1.6610	1.6230	1.5661
2010	1.6160	1.5621	1.5059	1.5337	1.4658	1.4758	1.5302	1.5652	1.5575	1.5858	1.5953	1.5599	1.5461
2011	1.5789	1.6137	1.6158	1.6385	1.6338	1.6219	1.6150	1.6359	1.5776	1.5773	1.5799	1.5587	1.6039
2012	1.5522	1.5806	1.5829	1.6009	1.5909	1.5556	1.5598	1.5718	1.6113	1.6073	1.5964	1.6144	1.5854
2013	1.5961	1.5468	1.5083	1.5309	1.5287	1.5498	1.5184	1.5505	1.5875	1.6089	1.6112	1.6383	1.5646
2014	1.6468	1.6566	1.6617	1.6747	1.6841	1.6916	1.7075	1.6700	1.6303	1.6077	1.5773	1.5631	1.6476

Average.   Source: FOREX

Volume of Trading of British Pound Futures in Chicago   In Thousands of Contracts

Year	Jan.	Feb.	Mar.	Apr.	May	June	July	Aug.	Sept.	Oct.	Nov.	Dec.	Total
2005	376.7	410.5	628.7	453.3	555.5	763.5	640.2	735.3	1,034.5	887.8	1,080.6	1,203.1	8,769.8
2006	1,013.7	1,012.0	1,479.2	1,207.6	1,465.1	1,262.1	963.1	1,262.2	1,486.2	1,387.1	1,563.9	1,997.4	16,099.5
2007	1,639.3	1,485.2	2,151.4	1,330.1	1,705.8	2,066.0	1,946.6	1,964.1	1,668.3	1,729.8	1,793.9	1,319.3	20,799.8
2008	1,541.0	1,442.5	1,886.1	1,979.0	1,633.7	2,058.8	1,896.4	1,805.7	2,151.8	1,584.1	1,240.3	1,278.1	20,497.4
2009	1,446.3	1,457.1	1,721.8	1,509.2	1,736.4	2,609.0	2,127.0	2,126.5	2,644.3	2,864.8	2,389.1	2,222.4	24,853.8
2010	2,258.4	2,538.3	3,253.0	2,367.8	3,139.4	2,906.1	2,170.7	2,349.4	2,541.7	2,305.1	2,299.2	2,091.1	30,220.2
2011	2,520.0	2,519.3	2,933.2	2,170.3	2,578.2	2,683.0	2,159.4	2,348.8	2,732.7	2,313.8	2,015.5	2,054.4	29,028.8
2012	1,688.5	2,010.0	2,445.6	2,058.2	2,510.7	2,495.4	2,189.7	2,168.2	2,372.3	2,133.3	1,941.9	2,152.6	26,166.3
2013	2,460.2	2,647.5	2,948.2	2,172.0	2,678.5	3,067.9	2,504.8	2,298.1	2,348.2	2,002.0	1,936.9	2,173.5	29,237.8
2014	2,123.0	2,139.8	2,315.4	1,415.6	1,592.2	2,547.6	1,728.8	1,781.2	3,181.2	2,283.2	1,740.6	1,986.6	24,835.4

Contract size = 62,500 GBP.   Source: CME Group; Chicago Mercantile Exchange (CME)

Average Open Interest of British Pound Futures in Chicago   In Contracts

Year	Jan.	Feb.	Mar.	Apr.	May	June	July	Aug.	Sept.	Oct.	Nov.	Dec.
2005	67,140	70,872	81,799	80,850	88,397	79,278	75,387	73,199	81,479	79,854	84,884	91,497
2006	83,051	97,226	83,641	83,275	106,555	98,417	91,563	129,334	120,737	106,288	145,026	157,837
2007	147,183	152,892	135,618	130,611	130,861	145,405	157,336	124,948	110,905	118,737	128,761	96,974
2008	87,465	94,154	98,154	109,464	158,836	126,688	100,775	105,857	112,717	110,761	113,147	93,313
2009	81,141	84,191	88,354	82,933	91,683	92,365	90,994	98,358	88,658	104,344	96,882	83,847
2010	86,016	116,480	136,357	122,843	145,514	136,099	126,486	138,872	97,056	89,011	95,465	80,042
2011	92,434	118,770	118,434	114,166	111,901	103,047	106,501	100,953	142,668	174,087	162,814	206,391
2012	198,201	190,107	167,722	159,541	191,394	150,584	115,951	115,580	166,427	165,761	156,794	188,125
2013	165,256	184,350	248,526	201,357	202,681	172,212	145,625	145,596	167,475	181,110	186,634	226,964
2014	207,609	232,142	231,703	226,479	236,374	262,034	246,579	231,599	184,224	135,955	160,534	165,669

Contract size = 62,500 GBP.   Source: CME Group; Chicago Mercantile Exchange (CME)

CURRENCIES

CANADIAN DOLLAR - IMM
Weekly Nearest Futures as of 01/02/2015

WEEKLY NEAREST FUTURES
As of 01/02/2015

Chart High 1.1043 on 11/07/2007
Chart Low .7653 on 03/09/2009

Nearby Futures through Last Trading Day.

Canadian Dollars per U.S. Dollar

Year	Jan.	Feb.	Mar.	Apr.	May	June	July	Aug.	Sept.	Oct.	Nov.	Dec.	Average
2005	1.2248	1.2386	1.2157	1.2368	1.2553	1.2402	1.2239	1.2048	1.1781	1.1777	1.1813	1.1619	1.2116
2006	1.1573	1.1488	1.1571	1.1440	1.1094	1.1139	1.1287	1.1191	1.1161	1.1281	1.1365	1.1531	1.1343
2007	1.1757	1.1708	1.1687	1.1351	1.0948	1.0655	1.0512	1.0585	1.0260	0.9752	0.9680	1.0021	1.0743
2008	1.0114	1.0001	1.0031	1.0130	0.9999	1.0170	1.0133	1.0539	1.0582	1.1797	1.2204	1.2337	1.0670
2009	1.2244	1.2449	1.2638	1.2244	1.1502	1.1274	1.1225	1.0878	1.0812	1.0547	1.0587	1.0558	1.1413
2010	1.0435	1.0561	1.0233	1.0052	1.0415	1.0397	1.0433	1.0408	1.0335	1.0180	1.0128	1.0081	1.0305
2011	0.9939	0.9875	0.9767	0.9574	0.9682	0.9771	0.9558	0.9814	1.0023	1.0201	1.0253	1.0238	0.9891
2012	1.0132	0.9970	0.9934	0.9929	1.0106	1.0275	1.0137	0.9930	0.9788	0.9872	0.9969	0.9899	0.9995
2013	0.9919	1.0094	1.0240	1.0185	1.0206	1.0315	1.0404	1.0404	1.0354	1.0367	1.0488	1.0637	1.0301
2014	1.0947	1.1054	1.1106	1.0992	1.0890	1.0825	1.0734	1.0922	1.1007	1.1214	1.1332	1.1542	1.1047

Average.   *Source: FOREX*

Volume of Trading of Canadian Dollar Futures in Chicago   In Thousands of Contracts

Year	Jan.	Feb.	Mar.	Apr.	May	June	July	Aug.	Sept.	Oct.	Nov.	Dec.	Total
2005	548.6	483.0	678.0	592.9	555.2	761.5	562.2	566.3	914.2	671.3	736.0	861.0	7,930.2
2006	695.1	648.6	1,040.9	654.9	816.6	1,043.4	658.3	811.0	1,073.7	805.8	960.8	1,070.4	10,279.6
2007	795.9	724.5	1,089.4	749.9	949.9	1,348.4	1,101.2	1,015.5	1,226.6	1,054.0	1,238.3	931.2	12,224.8
2008	960.2	957.8	1,202.2	948.1	958.2	1,151.9	932.0	966.4	1,240.9	812.9	601.8	645.8	11,378.0
2009	625.5	685.7	1,040.2	964.4	1,222.0	1,691.7	1,318.6	1,319.2	1,644.8	1,626.3	1,569.5	1,773.2	15,481.2
2010	1,391.4	1,623.9	1,989.7	1,742.0	2,329.7	2,120.7	1,774.7	1,839.7	1,905.7	1,841.7	1,889.4	1,635.3	22,083.8
2011	1,477.5	1,505.0	2,143.4	1,403.3	1,943.9	2,213.2	1,557.3	2,545.8	2,479.4	2,000.8	1,624.9	1,522.3	22,416.7
2012	1,441.3	1,790.3	2,203.3	1,812.6	2,260.5	2,546.9	1,947.1	1,871.8	2,213.3	1,713.8	1,467.8	1,530.9	22,799.4
2013	1,472.2	1,439.5	1,815.4	1,502.0	1,770.9	1,891.0	1,434.3	1,327.6	1,256.7	1,077.0	986.0	1,455.2	17,427.8
2014	1,495.5	1,064.6	1,572.7	903.8	917.2	1,253.6	1,064.6	1,057.9	1,612.2	1,569.7	1,189.3	1,392.5	15,093.5

Contract size = 100,000 CAD.   *Source: CME Group; Chicago Mercantile Exchange (CME)*

Average Open Interest of Canadian Dollar Futures in Chicago   In Contracts

Year	Jan.	Feb.	Mar.	Apr.	May	June	July	Aug.	Sept.	Oct.	Nov.	Dec.
2005	74,703	84,753	93,986	77,680	95,229	79,464	86,451	101,128	120,542	108,095	106,773	122,584
2006	103,427	118,978	103,066	92,541	114,587	107,605	89,443	91,591	112,788	99,209	121,729	146,474
2007	151,511	144,025	140,775	119,430	163,570	180,961	147,966	132,910	136,952	145,923	120,912	99,261
2008	86,448	99,650	109,567	103,486	115,665	103,145	95,618	120,175	116,163	103,135	94,297	66,313
2009	59,962	70,940	70,863	63,119	83,214	88,873	87,203	98,521	91,989	97,587	89,022	94,758
2010	106,475	92,349	143,969	148,414	125,802	102,117	87,121	100,655	101,319	113,964	116,126	110,800
2011	123,984	139,328	141,949	141,548	124,951	108,081	118,209	111,898	102,180	118,239	127,296	143,821
2012	119,930	126,823	147,325	128,867	141,093	120,545	101,536	134,628	225,238	185,312	168,662	167,449
2013	142,358	161,037	216,418	167,325	145,528	128,346	126,955	115,698	127,754	114,266	121,783	158,005
2014	159,815	152,844	144,262	119,310	123,899	117,918	125,230	111,259	91,900	100,526	106,812	106,069

Contract size = 100,000 CAD.   *Source: CME Group; Chicago Mercantile Exchange (CME)*

EURO FX - IMM
Weekly Nearest Futures as of 01/02/2015

WEEKLY NEAREST FUTURES
As of 01/02/2015

Chart High 1.5988 on 07/15/2008
Chart Low 1.1661 on 11/17/2005

Nearby Futures through Last Trading Day.

Euro per U.S. Dollar

Year	Jan.	Feb.	Mar.	Apr.	May	June	July	Aug.	Sept.	Oct.	Nov.	Dec.	Average
2005	1.3110	1.3020	1.3178	1.2940	1.2685	1.2156	1.2049	1.2299	1.2246	1.2030	1.1796	1.1861	1.2448
2006	1.2121	1.1940	1.2033	1.2282	1.2773	1.2665	1.2693	1.2811	1.2734	1.2623	1.2893	1.3200	1.2564
2007	1.2989	1.3087	1.3249	1.3512	1.3511	1.3422	1.3720	1.3620	1.3918	1.4234	1.4681	1.4561	1.3709
2008	1.4722	1.4759	1.5527	1.5760	1.5560	1.5569	1.5765	1.4954	1.4367	1.3286	1.2723	1.3518	1.4709
2009	1.3253	1.2805	1.3074	1.3207	1.3675	1.4014	1.4087	1.4267	1.4565	1.4817	1.4926	1.4577	1.3939
2010	1.4270	1.3681	1.3574	1.3427	1.2536	1.2212	1.2803	1.2899	1.3092	1.3899	1.3640	1.3227	1.3272
2011	1.3374	1.3661	1.4018	1.4472	1.4324	1.4400	1.4289	1.4339	1.3754	1.3727	1.3551	1.3148	1.3921
2012	1.2910	1.3238	1.3213	1.3164	1.2788	1.2546	1.2293	1.2403	1.2873	1.2969	1.2837	1.3124	1.2863
2013	1.3306	1.3340	1.2956	1.3025	1.2978	1.3202	1.3090	1.3320	1.3362	1.3638	1.3496	1.3704	1.3285
2014	1.3616	1.3669	1.3827	1.3811	1.3733	1.3600	1.3538	1.3315	1.2895	1.2680	1.2474	1.2307	1.3289

Average.   *Source: FOREX*

Volume of Trading of Euro FX Futures in Chicago   In Thousands of Contracts

Year	Jan.	Feb.	Mar.	Apr.	May	June	July	Aug.	Sept.	Oct.	Nov.	Dec.	Total
2005	2,646.0	2,266.4	2,772.9	2,992.0	2,771.6	3,656.1	2,732.6	2,765.1	3,206.6	2,613.6	3,164.2	2,943.6	34,530.7
2006	2,956.0	2,563.9	3,411.2	2,984.4	4,496.3	3,765.7	2,789.0	3,229.5	3,364.0	3,123.5	3,790.4	4,316.6	40,790.4
2007	3,701.9	3,032.1	4,427.3	2,979.1	3,337.4	3,877.6	3,560.5	4,074.2	3,286.6	3,831.5	3,793.1	3,161.6	43,063.1
2008	3,669.9	3,327.5	4,709.2	4,596.3	4,537.8	5,312.0	4,661.3	5,009.7	6,216.8	4,556.3	3,607.9	3,447.8	53,652.6
2009	3,574.5	3,903.4	4,564.5	3,155.7	3,758.9	5,261.4	4,675.6	4,220.4	5,123.9	5,429.9	5,419.9	5,305.7	54,393.6
2010	5,407.6	6,439.6	7,562.4	7,157.1	9,578.8	7,913.1	6,006.4	6,418.2	7,294.2	7,476.0	8,241.8	6,737.2	86,232.4
2011	7,402.8	6,451.9	7,437.7	5,453.1	7,657.0	7,504.8	6,906.8	8,061.0	8,376.7	7,008.3	6,638.4	5,338.4	84,236.8
2012	5,611.6	5,984.0	6,055.0	4,864.4	6,510.0	7,165.7	5,311.9	5,059.1	5,927.6	5,197.0	5,281.1	4,440.5	67,407.7
2013	5,675.6	6,088.9	6,391.7	5,480.1	6,055.8	5,970.9	5,093.7	4,390.9	4,120.9	3,988.5	4,047.7	3,981.0	61,285.6
2014	4,422.1	3,733.1	4,781.4	3,046.6	3,338.3	4,261.9	3,048.4	3,507.4	6,106.3	5,900.3	4,564.9	5,486.6	52,197.2

Contract size = 125,000 EUR.   *Source: CME Group; Chicago Mercantile Exchange (CME)*

Average Open Interest of Euro FX Futures in Chicago   In Contracts

Year	Jan.	Feb.	Mar.	Apr.	May	June	July	Aug.	Sept.	Oct.	Nov.	Dec.
2005	135,748	152,110	140,879	130,131	154,751	163,584	142,826	148,309	149,184	142,879	171,035	160,065
2006	133,092	150,085	152,674	166,920	196,057	177,700	155,865	173,151	155,567	152,410	182,079	214,241
2007	173,989	196,963	205,366	217,899	222,019	204,945	218,401	221,095	221,268	207,644	221,736	204,536
2008	179,767	206,661	200,084	178,993	211,068	193,878	170,675	153,423	163,948	180,955	169,315	144,926
2009	127,134	156,321	141,863	110,261	124,438	130,793	129,062	133,469	156,493	168,629	169,331	155,488
2010	169,083	199,832	211,780	216,500	285,206	251,763	226,656	242,448	198,817	203,635	198,138	172,703
2011	190,755	202,950	225,190	244,014	257,695	222,331	184,688	178,500	231,100	228,018	251,778	297,070
2012	301,627	288,301	275,581	277,812	349,794	369,192	321,319	318,368	276,124	220,770	225,676	217,375
2013	214,230	236,476	211,778	220,576	242,334	232,139	217,712	237,132	250,358	270,275	239,030	258,190
2014	251,507	285,722	289,786	266,980	270,902	302,019	322,167	390,128	429,750	434,763	467,267	427,194

Contract size = 125,000 EUR.   *Source: CME Group; Chicago Mercantile Exchange (CME)*

CURRENCIES

JAPANESE YEN - IMM
Weekly Nearest Futures as of 01/02/2015

WEEKLY NEAREST FUTURES
As of 01/02/2015
Chart High 1.3264   on 10/31/2011
Chart Low   .8087   on 06/15/2007

Nearby Futures through Last Trading Day.

Japanese Yen per U.S. Dollar

Year	Jan.	Feb.	Mar.	Apr.	May	June	July	Aug.	Sept.	Oct.	Nov.	Dec.	Average
2005	103.29	104.98	105.35	107.19	106.71	108.75	111.92	110.62	111.19	114.84	118.42	118.39	110.14
2006	115.53	117.92	117.31	116.97	111.77	114.65	115.69	115.95	117.14	118.61	117.28	117.43	116.35
2007	120.45	120.40	117.33	118.96	120.82	122.65	121.47	116.78	115.08	115.92	110.92	112.37	117.76
2008	107.71	107.11	100.80	102.69	104.33	106.88	106.87	109.41	106.62	100.15	96.80	91.13	103.37
2009	90.33	92.86	97.74	98.94	96.49	96.67	94.46	94.90	91.40	90.32	89.12	89.99	93.60
2010	91.13	90.17	90.71	93.49	91.88	90.81	87.56	85.38	84.38	81.79	82.58	83.23	87.76
2011	82.61	82.57	81.65	83.18	81.14	80.47	79.29	77.05	76.88	76.68	77.54	77.83	79.74
2012	76.93	78.60	82.54	81.28	79.69	79.36	78.98	78.68	78.16	79.00	81.04	83.86	79.84
2013	89.19	93.11	94.88	97.75	100.97	97.30	99.64	97.80	99.18	97.85	100.12	103.55	97.61
2014	103.80	102.12	102.34	102.51	101.83	102.07	101.75	102.97	107.37	108.03	116.37	119.42	105.88

Average. *Source: FOREX*

Volume of Trading of Japanese Yen Futures in Chicago   In Thousands of Contracts

Year	Jan.	Feb.	Mar.	Apr.	May	June	July	Aug.	Sept.	Oct.	Nov.	Dec.	Total
2005	789.9	718.8	1,045.2	915.4	876.2	1,263.0	946.9	1,012.4	1,285.4	963.7	1,001.0	1,653.9	12,471.7
2006	1,221.1	1,128.7	1,950.5	1,385.9	1,890.9	1,905.3	1,317.9	1,395.9	1,965.8	1,525.1	1,852.8	2,137.5	19,677.4
2007	1,602.2	2,006.6	3,286.7	1,771.1	1,802.4	2,777.8	3,083.8	3,954.2	2,860.7	2,493.1	3,125.2	2,056.6	30,820.4
2008	3,013.2	2,558.7	3,384.5	2,632.6	2,502.9	3,193.9	2,898.0	2,428.9	3,446.2	3,117.8	1,937.5	1,730.2	32,844.4
2009	1,644.2	1,802.9	1,796.0	1,469.3	1,600.9	1,932.6	2,061.8	1,924.0	2,260.9	2,157.6	1,916.7	2,182.7	22,749.6
2010	2,321.3	2,382.1	2,664.8	2,397.2	3,481.7	3,094.9	2,712.4	2,591.6	3,065.3	2,171.1	2,484.6	2,495.8	31,862.8
2011	2,542.6	2,572.2	3,764.0	2,438.4	2,297.9	2,563.3	2,023.5	2,701.8	2,393.6	2,135.9	1,425.0	1,510.9	28,369.1
2012	1,445.7	1,772.5	2,609.4	1,752.1	1,820.9	2,037.7	1,397.4	1,721.5	2,223.2	1,912.0	2,189.4	2,638.8	23,520.6
2013	3,831.3	4,175.7	3,820.2	4,510.5	4,431.7	5,387.8	2,849.1	2,885.5	3,045.1	2,564.9	2,379.8	2,880.5	42,762.3
2014	3,335.1	2,865.2	3,324.4	2,335.1	2,285.1	2,615.9	2,143.3	2,335.6	3,904.6	4,728.3	3,791.3	4,650.1	38,314.0

Contract size = 12,500,000 JPY.   *Source: CME Group; Chicago Mercantile Exchange (CME)*

Average Open Interest of Japanese Yen Futures in Chicago   In Contracts

Year	Jan.	Feb.	Mar.	Apr.	May	June	July	Aug.	Sept.	Oct.	Nov.	Dec.
2005	164,708	155,593	132,268	134,802	172,574	164,580	161,763	170,290	159,227	186,631	202,939	191,591
2006	168,309	198,855	203,450	201,459	210,578	197,160	191,480	218,893	239,426	258,509	242,216	265,490
2007	312,252	338,933	246,715	234,352	303,537	347,031	302,278	272,937	227,242	225,047	202,361	195,324
2008	197,886	233,558	224,932	176,577	171,298	171,516	185,657	207,309	168,119	142,938	128,891	130,118
2009	112,194	108,893	90,828	79,142	86,624	81,378	95,456	80,087	119,014	118,478	123,821	110,809
2010	116,578	121,216	117,096	131,315	143,384	111,812	129,460	135,623	130,539	142,646	133,612	111,840
2011	112,265	119,793	118,104	123,251	102,290	101,702	121,491	128,615	135,195	151,744	147,224	168,945
2012	162,827	160,215	161,521	145,491	143,219	151,494	127,493	147,320	152,104	136,446	176,769	226,165
2013	203,930	217,961	246,456	211,493	222,136	199,960	182,942	168,128	184,355	160,423	204,490	251,937
2014	217,565	201,386	190,296	174,544	163,960	170,679	163,460	202,088	234,084	205,740	233,431	252,694

Contract size = 12,500,000 JPY.   *Source: CME Group; Chicago Mercantile Exchange (CME)*

SWISS FRANC - IMM
Weekly Nearest Futures as of 01/02/2015

WEEKLY NEAREST FUTURES
As of 01/02/2015

Chart High 1.4167 on 08/09/2011
Chart Low   .7548   on 11/17/2005

Nearby Futures through Last Trading Day.

Swiss Francs per U.S. Dollar

Year	Jan.	Feb.	Mar.	Apr.	May	June	July	Aug.	Sept.	Oct.	Nov.	Dec.	Average
2005	1.1802	1.1906	1.1763	1.1955	1.2183	1.2663	1.2935	1.2626	1.2657	1.2872	1.3100	1.3056	1.2460
2006	1.2781	1.3056	1.3044	1.2822	1.2185	1.2319	1.2362	1.2319	1.2440	1.2597	1.2351	1.2102	1.2532
2007	1.2438	1.2385	1.2179	1.2128	1.2217	1.2329	1.2076	1.2034	1.1847	1.1743	1.1229	1.1397	1.2000
2008	1.1001	1.0894	1.0116	1.0141	1.0443	1.0363	1.0278	1.0843	1.1091	1.1429	1.1923	1.1393	1.0826
2009	1.1280	1.1635	1.1540	1.1472	1.1057	1.0810	1.0784	1.0677	1.0399	1.0218	1.0117	1.0304	1.0858
2010	1.0341	1.0719	1.0660	1.0682	1.1325	1.1263	1.0531	1.0392	1.0012	0.9688	0.9852	0.9671	1.0428
2011	0.9567	0.9495	0.9187	0.8964	0.8733	0.8404	0.8221	0.7810	0.8734	0.8963	0.9086	0.9335	0.8875
2012	0.9377	0.9119	0.9129	0.9131	0.9397	0.9574	0.9771	0.9685	0.9394	0.9327	0.9388	0.9212	0.9375
2013	0.9243	0.9215	0.9465	0.9368	0.9564	0.9330	0.9446	0.9255	0.9232	0.9032	0.9126	0.8937	0.9268
2014	0.9039	0.8934	0.8805	0.8830	0.8888	0.8955	0.8977	0.9100	0.9367	0.9526	0.9641	0.9769	0.9152

Average.   *Source: FOREX*

Volume of Trading of Swiss Franc Futures in Chicago   In Thousands of Contracts

Year	Jan.	Feb.	Mar.	Apr.	May	June	July	Aug.	Sept.	Oct.	Nov.	Dec.	Total
2005	444.3	389.1	575.5	605.0	521.4	753.4	546.4	596.4	888.8	765.9	797.1	901.2	7,784.5
2006	803.5	745.9	1,129.0	837.5	1,011.3	993.3	771.2	1,014.8	1,046.8	919.6	1,078.1	1,118.9	11,470.0
2007	994.4	998.5	1,418.5	959.4	1,100.0	1,507.0	1,660.0	1,588.2	1,113.7	1,129.8	1,067.3	941.8	14,478.7
2008	1,090.5	1,082.4	1,311.8	1,350.7	1,362.8	1,789.1	1,650.0	1,330.3	1,578.9	1,042.4	574.0	651.3	14,814.2
2009	677.7	624.5	813.9	641.5	731.2	1,094.1	844.8	727.0	1,015.2	1,098.5	1,206.6	1,143.5	10,618.6
2010	1,046.8	954.5	1,218.2	1,105.8	1,299.4	1,066.8	813.5	806.1	997.7	847.7	940.4	914.3	12,011.2
2011	848.8	1,025.6	1,266.4	827.0	928.5	1,074.6	936.2	1,098.0	643.1	539.6	489.5	561.4	10,238.7
2012	552.9	773.9	1,034.3	865.2	1,140.5	1,163.6	870.0	855.3	827.8	623.8	599.5	604.6	9,911.3
2013	767.5	643.9	850.4	696.4	1,085.0	938.7	665.1	677.3	688.4	711.0	632.6	705.7	9,061.8
2014	714.1	552.0	819.7	535.8	607.3	792.8	721.4	758.5	1,121.3	1,026.6	834.4	1,154.5	9,638.5

Contract size = 125,000 CHF.   *Source: CME Group; Chicago Mercantile Exchange (CME)*

Average Open Interest of Swiss Franc Futures in Chicago   In Contracts

Year	Jan.	Feb.	Mar.	Apr.	May	June	July	Aug.	Sept.	Oct.	Nov.	Dec.
2005	51,858	56,240	50,827	41,322	55,995	78,794	72,596	67,489	66,009	75,088	91,072	98,443
2006	80,904	107,509	101,445	82,280	98,416	89,254	67,127	69,406	83,545	97,034	89,039	74,522
2007	83,176	103,073	70,627	66,246	89,737	121,557	108,394	118,597	100,948	73,433	81,366	73,025
2008	67,993	67,786	71,972	60,528	65,029	58,511	56,337	61,521	53,448	39,448	42,315	31,420
2009	26,083	32,701	33,518	28,613	34,585	40,027	35,918	39,324	49,537	51,736	52,912	41,890
2010	36,523	41,531	36,834	38,093	49,842	48,989	52,203	55,870	58,484	53,703	45,087	44,460
2011	42,658	46,656	62,300	65,373	70,315	61,349	50,716	20,516	33,972	25,587	29,848	44,100
2012	40,696	48,122	50,263	40,932	59,311	68,970	60,351	56,214	47,686	36,825	43,328	47,914
2013	42,982	44,119	58,519	49,385	59,413	47,741	36,890	38,631	39,298	51,347	45,586	53,657
2014	42,329	48,122	56,682	47,081	49,564	42,368	38,273	52,798	61,701	58,348	60,929	63,108

Contract size = 125,000 CHF.   *Source: CME Group; Chicago Mercantile Exchange (CME)*

CURRENCIES

United States Merchandise Trade Balance[2]   In Millions of Dollars

Year	Jan.	Feb.	Mar.	Apr.	May	June	July	Aug.	Sept.	Oct.	Nov.	Dec.	Total
2005	-61,181	-63,446	-58,949	-62,621	-61,685	-63,601	-63,343	-63,929	-70,530	-73,179	-69,822	-70,516	-782,802
2006	-72,871	-67,493	-68,017	-68,707	-71,283	-69,728	-72,687	-74,214	-71,279	-65,954	-65,796	-69,259	-837,288
2007	-65,776	-66,380	-70,644	-68,670	-67,895	-68,735	-69,198	-67,060	-67,714	-68,299	-71,741	-69,084	-821,196
2008	-71,650	-74,110	-70,917	-74,315	-73,868	-72,286	-77,628	-71,541	-70,455	-70,138	-53,601	-51,983	-832,492
2009	-47,164	-37,359	-38,976	-39,544	-35,595	-36,844	-42,838	-41,816	-45,296	-45,350	-49,072	-49,840	-509,694
2010	-48,966	-51,997	-51,498	-52,540	-53,634	-59,026	-53,171	-58,069	-57,546	-54,054	-52,393	-55,783	-648,677
2011	-62,494	-59,400	-59,642	-57,913	-63,202	-65,602	-61,880	-61,972	-59,455	-60,906	-62,890	-65,289	-740,645
2012	-66,927	-59,838	-66,673	-64,375	-63,928	-59,936	-59,939	-61,411	-57,593	-60,163	-64,888	-56,424	-742,095
2013	-61,192	-60,688	-55,680	-58,758	-63,352	-54,973	-58,021	-58,527	-61,387	-57,742	-54,765	-56,583	-701,668
2014[1]	-59,112	-59,955	-62,202	-65,243	-62,751	-60,249	-59,261	-59,485	-62,346	-61,166	-59,000	-65,017	-735,787

[1] Preliminary.   [2] Not seasonally adjusted.   *Source: Bureau of Economic Analysis, U.S. Department of Commerce (BEA)*

Index of Real Trade-Weighted Dollar Exchange Rates for Total Agriculture[3]   (2000 = 100)

Year		Jan.	Feb.	Mar.	Apr.	May	June	July	Aug.	Sept.	Oct.	Nov.	Dec.
2007	U.S. Markets	110.2	110.2	110.3	109.7	109.0	108.7	107.4	107.3	105.8	103.7	102.7	103.0
	U.S. Competitors	107.1	106.6	106.3	104.6	104.3	104.4	102.4	103.4	101.7	98.8	97.1	97.2
2008	U.S. Markets	102.4	101.2	100.0	99.9	100.3	100.8	100.2	101.1	102.7	107.9	108.2	106.5
	U.S. Competitors	96.7	95.7	93.1	92.3	92.9	93.2	92.3	95.1	98.9	106.2	109.1	105.4
2009	U.S. Markets	107.8	110.8	112.3	109.1	106.3	106.3	105.6	104.4	103.7	102.2	101.6	101.3
	U.S. Competitors	107.5	110.9	110.4	107.7	104.2	102.4	101.7	100.1	98.7	96.7	95.9	96.8
2010	U.S. Markets	101.2	101.8	100.8	100.1	102.2	102.5	101.2	100.2	99.3	96.8	96.6	97.1
	U.S. Competitors	97.7	100.1	99.7	99.5	103.9	105.6	102.3	101.2	99.7	95.7	96.4	97.7
2011	U.S. Markets	96.6	96.3	96.1	95.2	95.2	95.1	94.2	94.9	96.9	97.5	97.4	97.6
	U.S. Competitors	97.1	95.9	94.8	92.6	93.2	92.8	92.8	93.1	96.6	97.1	97.6	99.0
2012	U.S. Markets	97.3	94.7	96.8	96.9	98.1	99.1	98.0	97.4	96.6	96.1	96.3	95.6
	U.S. Competitors	99.7	96.9	98.0	98.4	101.0	102.8	102.8	102.1	100.3	99.4	99.8	98.2
2013	U.S. Markets	96.0	97.5	98.3	97.9	98.2	99.1	99.8	99.8	100.0	98.8	99.0	99.3
	U.S. Competitors	97.5	97.7	99.3	98.7	99.3	100.2	100.9	100.8	100.8	98.6	99.5	99.3
2014[1]	U.S. Markets	99.8	100.0	100.1	99.3	99.0	99.1	98.9	99.1	100.1	101.2	102.8	104.6
	U.S. Competitors	102.0	102.2	101.3	100.7	101.0	101.7	101.5	102.6	104.8	106.7	108.2	109.4

[1] Preliminary.   [2] Forecast.   [3] Real indexes adjust nominal exchange rates for differences in rates of inflation, to avoid the distortion caused by high-inflation countries. A higher value means the dollar has appreciated. Federal Reserve Board Index of trade-weighted value of the U.S. dollar against 10 major currencies. Weights are based on relative importance in world financial markets.
Source: Bureau of Economic Analysis, U.S. Department of Commerce (BEA)

United States Balance on Current Account[2]   In Millions of Dollars

Year	First Quarter	Second Quarter	Third Quarter	Fourth Quarter	Annual
2005	-153,426	-181,357	-201,511	-209,141	-745,435
2006	-180,164	-205,586	-231,744	-189,232	-806,726
2007	-180,513	-189,443	-184,747	-163,940	-718,643
2008	-157,640	-179,309	-198,042	-151,650	-686,641
2009	-78,808	-89,655	-111,626	-100,703	-380,792
2010	-90,728	-117,666	-133,393	-102,143	-443,930
2011	-96,914	-125,168	-127,016	-110,245	-459,343
2012	-101,806	-126,482	-129,483	-102,978	-460,749
2013	-81,022	-113,093	-118,705	-87,434	-400,254
2014[1]	-86,131	NA	NA	NA	-344,524

[1] Estimate.   [2] Not seasonally adjusted.   *Source: Bureau of Economic Analysis, U.S. Department of Commerce (BEA)*

Merchandise Trade and Current Account Balances[3]   In Billions of Dollars

	Merchanise Trade Balance					Current Account Balance				
Year	Canada	Germany	Japan	Switzerland	United Kingdom	Canada	Germany	Japan	Switzerland	United Kingdom
2006	35.2	164.6	54.7	32.6	-65.0	17.9	180.9	171.4	58.4	-71.0
2007	30.5	235.9	73.6	44.8	-73.6	11.2	249.9	211.1	38.8	-62.2
2008	28.3	228.9	8.2	58.3	-61.4	3.6	226.7	160.0	8.5	-24.6
2009	-20.2	163.2	18.8	56.7	-36.3	-40.3	199.1	145.6	54.6	-30.9
2010	-30.6	182.8	65.5	59.3	-50.9	-56.6	202.8	203.8	82.5	-62.0
2011	-22.3	185.8	-54.3	68.5	-37.4	-49.1	224.2	118.4	58.9	-36.0
2012	-36.2	204.7	-118.0	65.9	-54.9	-62.3	243.4	65.5	70.2	-94.9
2013	-34.3	217.6	-126.3	70.3	-34.6	-55.6	253.8	42.5	83.3	-85.6
2014[1]	-32.9	203.5	-105.4	75.1	-29.9	-54.3	238.6	60.2	86.4	-67.9
2015[2]	-25.7	190.9	-91.4	78.7	-25.1	-47.8	224.8	78.0	91.0	-65.9

[1] Estimate.   [2] Projection.   [3] Not seasonally adjusted.   *Source: Organization for Economic Cooperation and Development (OECD)*

EURO / SWISS FRANC
Weekly Cash as of 01/02/2015

WEEKLY CASH
As of 01/02/2015
Chart High 1.6828 on 10/11/2007
Chart Low 1.0074 on 08/09/2011

EURO / BRITISH POUND
Weekly Cash as of 01/02/2015

WEEKLY CASH
As of 01/02/2015
Chart High .98020 on 12/29/2008
Chart Low .65360 on 01/23/2007

BRITISH POUND / JAPANESE YEN
Weekly Cash as of 01/02/2015

WEEKLY CASH
As of 01/02/2015
Chart High 251.092 on 07/20/2007
Chart Low 116.868 on 09/22/2011

EURO / JAPANESE YEN
Weekly Cash as of 01/02/2015

WEEKLY CASH
As of 01/02/2015
Chart High 169.96 on 07/23/2008
Chart Low 94.12 on 07/24/2012

Forex.

Diamonds

The diamond, which is the mineral form of carbon, is the hardest, strongest natural material known on earth. The name *diamond* is derived from *adamas*, the ancient Greek term meaning "invincible." Diamonds form deep within the Earth's crust and are typically billions of years old. Diamonds have also have been found in and near meteorites and their craters. Diamonds are considered precious gemstones but lower grade diamonds are used for industrial applications such as drilling, cutting, grinding and polishing.

Supply – World production of natural gem diamonds in 2013 (latest data available) fell by -0.2% yr/yr to 91.800 million carats, but still down from the 2006 record high of 93.900 million carats (one carat equals 1/5 gram or 200 milligrams). The world's largest producers of natural gem diamonds are Russia with 22.6% of world production in 2013, Botswana with 15.3%, Angola with 8.6%, Namibia with 1.6%, and Sierra Leone with 0.3%. World production of natural industrial diamonds in 2012 (latest data available) was up +2.6% yr/yr to 36.000 million carats. World production of synthetic diamonds in 2012 remained the same yr/yr at 4.380 million carats. The main producer of synthetic diamonds was China with 91.3% of world production.

Trade – The U.S. in 2014 relied on net imports for 86% of its consumption of natural diamonds.

World Production of Natural Gem Diamonds   In Thousands of Carats

Year	Angola	Australia	Botswana	Brazil	Central African Republic	China	Congo (Kinshasa)	Ghana	Namibia	Russia	Suerra Leone	South Africa	World Total
2008	8,020	149	22,600	80	302	69	33,402	643	2,435	21,900	223	5,160	114,000
2009	8,310	156	12,400	21	249	46	21,298	376	1,192	20,600	241	2,460	80,200
2010	7,530	100	15,400	25	241	17	20,166	334	1,693	20,700	306	3,550	90,100
2011	7,500	78	16,000	46	259	[3]	19,249	302	1,256	20,900	280	2,820	87,800
2012[1]	7,500	92	14,400	46	293	2	21,524	233	1,629	20,700	325	2,830	92,000
2013[2]	7,900	70	14,000	30	200				1,500	20,700	300	2,800	91,800

[1] Preliminary.   [2] Estimate.   [3] Less than 1/2 unit.   *Source: U.S. Geological Survey (USGS)*

World Production of Natural Industrial Diamonds[4]   In Thousands of Carats

Year	Angola	Australia	Botswana	Brazil	Central African Republic	China	Congo[3] (Kinshasa)	Ghana	Russia	Sierra Leone	South Africa	Venezuela	World Total
2007	970	18,960	8,000	600	93	970	22,600	168	15,000	241	9,100	70	77,700
2008	891	14,800	9,680	600	75	1,000	88	120	15,000	149	7,740	6	49,100
2009	924	15,400	5,320	600	62	1,000	54	75	14,100	160	3,680	5	40,000
2010	836	9,880	6,610	600	60	1,000	305	67	14,200	175	5,320	1	38,200
2011[1]	833	7,750	6,870	600	65	1,000	61	67	14,300	143	4,230	----	35,100
2012[2]	833	9,090	6,170	----	73	----	41	----	14,200	135	4,246	----	36,000

[1] Preliminary.   [2] Estimate.   [3] Formerly Zaire.   *Source: U.S. Geological Survey (USGS)*

World Production of Synthetic Diamonds   In Thousands of Carats

Year	Belarus	China	France	Ireland	Japan	Russia	South Africa	Sweden	Ukraine	United States	World Total
2006	25,000	3,900,000	3,000	60,000	34,000	80,000	60,000	20,000	8,000	128,000	4,320,000
2007	25,000	4,000,000	3,000	60,000	34,000	80,000	60,000	20,000	8,000	130,000	4,420,000
2008	25,000	4,000,000	3,000	60,000	34,000	80,000	60,000	20,000	4,000	131,000	4,420,000
2009	25,000	4,000,000	3,000	60,000	34,000	80,000	60,000	20,000	NA	91,000	4,370,000
2010[1]	25,000	4,000,000	3,000	60,000	34,000	80,000	60,000	20,000	NA	93,000	4,380,000
2011[2]	25,000	4,000,000	3,000	60,000	34,000	80,000	60,000	20,000	NA	98,200	4,380,000

[1] Preliminary.   [2] Estimate.   *Source: U.S. Geological Survey (USGS)*

Salient Statistics of Industrial Diamonds in the United States   In Millions of Carats

	Bort, Grit & Powder & Dust Natural and Synthetic							Stones (Natural)					Net Import Reliance
	Production						Price					Price	% of
	Manu-factured	Secon-dary	Imports for Con-sumption	Exports & Reexports	In Manu-factured Products	Gov't Sales	Apparent Con-sumption	Value of Imports $/Carat	Secon-dary Pro-duction	Imports for Con-sumption	Exports & Reexports	Gov't Sales	Apparent Con-sumption	Value of Imports $/Carat	Con-sumption
Year	Diamond													
2009	260.0	33.5	246.0	67.0	----	----	251.0	.17	----	1.4	----	----	3.0	13.31	71
2010		33.4	596.0	113.0	----	----	556.0	.14	----	1.7	----	----	3.0	18.78	87
2011		34.7	726.0	148.0	----	----	654.0	.13	----	2.5	----	----	4.0	19.67	88
2012		36.5	595.0	155.0	----	----	520.0	.13	----	2.3	----	----	4.0	15.30	85
2013[2]		38.1	728.0	134.0	----	----	678.0	.11	----	1.9	----	----		15.50	88
2014[2]		44.1	716.0	152.0			656.0	.11		2.5				12.30	86

[1] Preliminary.   [2] Estimate.   [3] Less than 1/2 unit.   *Source: U.S. Geological Survey (USGS)*

Eggs

Eggs are a low-priced protein source and are consumed worldwide. Each commercial chicken lays between 265-280 eggs per year. In the United States, the grade and size of eggs are regulated under the federal Egg Products Inspection Act (1970). The grades of eggs are AA, A, and B, and must have sound, whole shells and must be clean. The difference among the grades of eggs is internal and mostly reflects the freshness of the egg. Table eggs vary in color and can be determined by the color of the chicken's earlobe. For example, chickens with white earlobes lay white eggs and chickens with reddish-brown earlobes lay brown eggs. In the U.S., egg size is determined by the weight of a dozen eggs, not individual eggs, and range from Peewee to Jumbo. Store-bought eggs in the shell stay fresh for 3 to 5 weeks in a home refrigerator, according to the USDA.

Eggs are primarily used as a source of food, although eggs are also widely used for medical purposes. Fertile eggs, as a source of purified proteins, are used to produce many vaccines. Flu vaccines are produced by growing single strains of the flu virus in eggs, which are then extracted to make the vaccine. Eggs are also used in biotechnology to create new drugs. The hen's genetic make-up can be altered so the whites of the eggs are rich in tailored proteins that form the basis of medicines to fight cancer and other diseases. The U.S. biotech company Viragen and the Roslin Institute in Edinburgh have produced eggs with 100 mg or more of the easily-extracted proteins used in new drugs to treat various illnesses including ovarian and breast cancers.

Prices – The average monthly price of all eggs received by farmers in the U.S. in 2014 rose by +15.7% yr/yr to 125.9 cents per dozen, a new record high.

Supply – World egg production in 2012 (latest data available) was 1.249 billion eggs, up +1.7% yr/yr. The world's largest egg producers at that time were China with 39.2% of world production, the U.S. with 7.4%, Mexico with 3.7%, Japan with 3.4%, Russia and Brazil each with 3.3%. U.S. egg production in 2014 rose +2.4% to 98.854 billion eggs, a new record high. The average number of hens and pullets on U.S. farms in 2013 (latest data available) rose by +2.9% yr/yr to 356.923 million, a new record high.

Demand – U.S. consumption of eggs in 2013 (latest data available) rose +1.1% yr/yr to 6.729 billion dozen eggs, a new record high. U.S. consumption of eggs is up sharply by about 20% from ten years earlier, reflecting the increased popularity of eggs in American diets. U.S. per capita egg consumption in 2015 is forecasted to rise +1.9% yr/yr to 265.2 eggs per year per person. Per capita egg consumption was at a high of 277.2 eggs in 1970, then fell sharply in the 1990s to a low of 174.9 in 1995, and then began rebounding in 1997 to current levels of about 250 eggs per year.

Trade – U.S. imports of eggs in 2013 (latest data available) fell -8.6% yr/yr to 16.9 million dozen eggs. U.S. exports of eggs in 2013 rose +23.3% yr/yr to 371.9 million dozen eggs, a new record high.

World Production of Eggs   In Millions of Eggs

Year	Brazil	China	France	Germany	Italy	Japan	Mexico	Russia	Spain	Ukraine	United Kingdom	United States	World Total
2004	32,319	403,000	15,757	12,353	13,054	41,346	40,033	35,562	15,213	11,883	10,704	89,091	1,045,088
2005	33,499	414,480	15,502	12,028	12,896	41,377	40,494	36,691	13,122	12,955	10,608	90,027	1,066,202
2006	35,207	412,080	15,138	12,137	12,123	41,611	45,801	37,651	13,122	14,122	10,224	91,800	1,087,906
2007	35,584	429,980	14,640	11,974	12,929	43,050	45,817	37,889	13,095	13,978	9,972	91,044	1,120,299
2008	36,893	459,000	13,355	12,103	13,393	42,567	46,744	37,804	12,896	14,809	10,404	90,012	1,162,306
2009	38,438	466,225	14,601	10,754	14,509	41,750	47,206	39,188	13,166	15,303	10,319	90,408	1,182,668
2010	38,961	473,100	15,094	10,191	13,157	41,900	47,623	40,392	12,896	16,865	11,274	91,482	1,209,074
2011[1]	40,731	477,940	14,088	11,955	13,482	41,377	49,170	40,778	12,997	18,428	11,201	91,855	1,228,433
2012[2]	41,676	490,000	14,227	12,430	13,661	41,780	46,361	41,548	11,000	18,843	10,806	92,275	1,249,111

[1] Preliminary.   [2] Forecast.   [3] Selected countries.   *Source: Food and Agricultural Organization of the United Nations (FAO)*

Salient Statistics of Eggs in the United States

	--- Hens & Pullets ---		Rate of Lay	----- Eggs -----			Total					----- Consumption -----	
	On Farm Dec. 1[3]	Average Number During Year	Per Layer During Year[4]	Total Produced	Price in cents Per Dozen	Value of Production[5]	Egg Production	Imports[6]	Exports[6]	Used for Hatching	Total	Per Capita Eggs[6]
Year	----- Thousands -----		(Number)	----- Millions -----		Million USD	-------------------- Million Dozen --------------------					Number
2006	348,719	347,880	263	91,328	58.2	4,432	7,650	7.9	202.1	992.2	6,467	259.7
2007	344,492	346,498	263	91,101	88.5	6,719	7,587	14.3	250.3	1,016.3	6,336	251.7
2008	339,643	339,131	266	90,239	109.0	8,239	7,501	14.3	206.3	996.3	6,307	248.3
2009	339,526	337,848	268	90,737	82.1	6,191	7,547	10.5	242.2	955.3	6,359	248.2
2010	341,551	340,335	269	91,811	86.5	6,553	7,656	21.8	258.4	982.2	6,436	247.9
2011	338,472	338,475	271	92,450	97.7	7,356	7,715	20.9	276.5	950.1	6,501	250.0
2012	346,965	341,052	274	94,364	100.1	7,929	7,877	18.5	301.7	940.8	6,659	254.3
2013[1]	356,923	354,844	275	97,555	108.8	8,499	8,046	16.9	371.9	959.9	6,729	255.2
2014[2]	362,809	360,873	277	99,768	125.9							

[1] Preliminary.   [2] Forecast.   [3] All layers of laying age.   [4] Number of eggs produced during the year divided by the average number of all layers of laying age on hand during the year.   [5] Value of sales plus value of eggs consumed in households of producers. 6/ Shell-egg equivalent of eggs and egg products.
Source: National Agricultural Statistics Service, U.S. Department of Agriculture (NASS-USDA)

EGGS

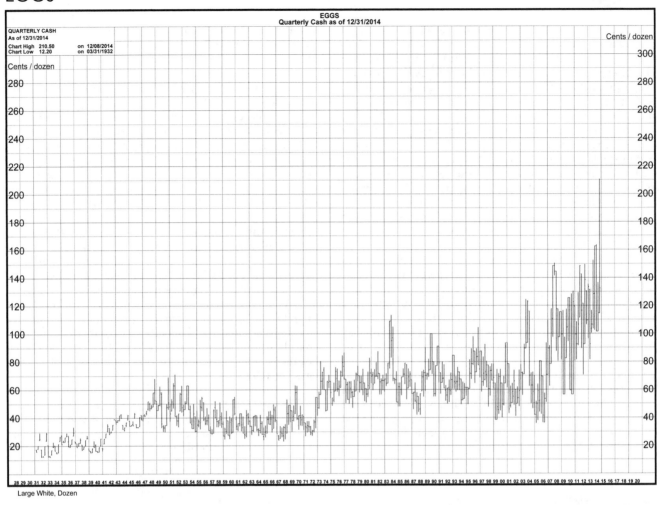

QUARTERLY CASH
As of 12/31/2014
Chart High 210.50 on 12/08/2014
Chart Low   12.20   on 03/31/1932

Cents / dozen

Cents / dozen

Large White, Dozen

Average Price Received by Farmers for All Eggs in the United States   In Cents Per Dozen

Year	Jan.	Feb.	Mar.	Apr.	May	June	July	Aug.	Sept.	Oct.	Nov.	Dec.	Average
2005	55.8	55.1	52.6	47.4	45.6	45.2	52.7	47.1	63.6	51.1	65.0	71.9	54.4
2006	61.0	49.5	67.0	51.2	42.7	54.7	43.5	55.0	53.4	54.1	81.2	80.7	57.8
2007	91.5	78.1	82.8	72.9	78.0	73.4	94.5	86.6	107.0	93.5	126.0	136.0	93.4
2008	129.0	131.0	138.0	103.0	86.8	106.0	84.1	96.3	99.6	102.0	102.0	99.9	106.5
2009	103.0	80.9	81.6	92.0	61.7	59.4	70.8	75.8	74.4	80.0	101.0	105.0	82.1
2010	103.0	91.7	116.0	79.4	63.3	61.9	70.9	78.9	68.4	83.6	113.0	108.0	86.5
2011	85.0	95.4	84.9	105.0	82.2	88.6	88.0	115.0	102.0	102.0	102.0	122.0	97.7
2012	87.9	88.5	99.5	86.5	82.8	90.7	96.9	113.0	122.0	102.0	118.0	113.0	100.1
2013	106.0	99.3	115.0	88.5	117.0	93.0	104.0	108.0	103.0	104.0	132.0	136.0	108.8
2014[1]	112.0	140.0	124.0	128.0	117.0	109.0	125.0	108.0	105.0	114.0	152.0	177.0	125.9

[1] Preliminary.   Source: Economic Research Service, U.S. Department of Agriculture (ERS-USDA)

Average Wholesale Price of Shell Eggs (Large) Delivered, Chicago   In Cents Per Dozen

Year	Jan.	Feb.	Mar.	Apr.	May	June	July	Aug.	Sept.	Oct.	Nov.	Dec.	Average
2005	54.78	60.26	48.32	42.00	41.57	40.72	51.38	42.78	61.19	48.38	62.41	70.21	52.00
2006	65.40	46.08	65.11	57.11	41.32	56.14	40.30	57.46	54.97	55.64	84.38	87.65	59.30
2007	91.75	92.71	89.23	80.00	83.55	69.60	99.95	97.37	117.50	101.89	128.93	147.70	100.02
2008	144.55	142.70	150.15	115.23	90.64	107.33	95.43	100.07	108.98	103.85	110.50	109.50	114.91
2009	113.40	92.29	85.64	99.26	64.55	72.41	73.55	85.69	80.17	86.14	110.75	114.41	89.86
2010	111.50	107.55	116.80	84.81	64.15	69.68	73.74	88.73	83.17	76.88	124.79	124.73	93.88
2011	100.20	99.08	86.37	106.05	87.31	86.95	92.70	114.07	105.93	111.79	112.50	130.07	102.75
2012	106.25	91.47	98.59	96.10	76.55	92.50	105.45	131.33	119.50	114.28	123.93	123.90	106.65
2013	112.93	112.92	114.30	97.86	105.45	89.75	104.77	106.82	106.50	106.41	133.60	150.21	111.79
2014[1]	113.10	135.97	133.93	145.98	116.21	115.83	122.16	116.02	111.93	117.11	143.18	194.45	130.49

[1] Preliminary.   Source: National Agricultural Statistics Service, U.S. Department of Agriculture (NASS-USDA)

Total Egg Production in the United States   In Millions of Eggs

Year	Jan.	Feb.	Mar.	Apr.	May	June	July	Aug.	Sept.	Oct.	Nov.	Dec.	Total
2005	7,626	6,928	7,738	7,407	7,572	7,346	7,563	7,528	7,348	7,665	7,514	7,793	90,028
2006	7,727	6,980	7,843	7,543	7,637	7,401	7,645	7,647	7,430	7,678	7,549	7,815	90,895
2007	7,675	6,951	7,806	7,472	7,622	7,380	7,599	7,594	7,393	7,726	7,542	7,808	90,568
2008	7,646	7,114	7,675	7,373	7,564	7,367	7,599	7,551	7,339	7,625	7,490	7,778	90,121
2009	7,678	6,903	7,737	7,472	7,607	7,360	7,590	7,593	7,376	7,696	7,569	7,853	90,434
2010	7,724	6,935	7,839	7,578	7,716	7,484	7,719	7,765	7,514	7,698	7,573	7,927	91,472
2011	7,833	7,013	7,840	7,617	7,773	7,503	7,732	7,719	7,503	7,783	7,612	7,987	91,915
2012	7,892	7,283	7,916	7,653	7,850	7,582	7,798	7,869	7,625	7,965	7,874	8,226	93,533
2013	8,125	7,321	8,195	7,929	8,139	7,857	8,082	8,178	7,969	8,267	8,098	8,489	96,649
2014[1]	8,397	7,452	8,324	8,117	8,335	8,054	8,395	8,394	8,094	8,435	8,325	8,731	99,053

[1] Preliminary.   *Source: National Agricultural Statistics Service, U.S. Department of Agriculture (NASS-USDA)*

Per Capita Disappearance of Eggs[4] in the United States   In Number of Eggs

Year	First Quarter	Second Quarter	Third Quarter	Fourth Quarter	Total	Total Consumption (Million Dozen)	Year	First Quarter	Second Quarter	Third Quarter	Fourth Quarter	Total	Total Consumption (Million Dozen)
2004	63.7	63.9	64.1	65.5	258.0	6,306	2010	61.5	61.4	62.2	62.8	247.9	6,436
2005	63.4	63.0	63.5	65.0	257.2	6,344	2011	61.3	61.5	62.8	64.3	250.0	6,501
2006	64.1	63.7	63.9	64.7	259.7	6,467	2012	63.3	62.3	63.3	65.4	254.3	6,659
2007	62.2	61.7	62.4	63.8	251.7	6,336	2013[1]	63.5	62.6	63.9	65.1	255.2	6,729
2008	61.8	61.3	62.0	63.8	248.3	6,307	2014[2]	63.8	64.6	65.4	66.4	260.2	
2009	62.0	61.5	61.4	62.9	248.2	6,359	2015[3]	65.4	65.8	66.1	67.8	265.2	

[1] Preliminary.   [2] Estimate.   [3] Forecast.   *Source: Economic Research Service, U.S. Department of Agriculture (ERS-USDA)*

Egg-Feed Ratio[1] in the United States

Year	Jan.	Feb.	Mar.	Apr.	May	June	July	Aug.	Sept.	Oct.	Nov.	Dec.	Average
2005	7.2	7.4	6.3	5.2	4.6	4.4	5.9	5.1	9.3	6.6	10.3	11.3	7.0
2006	8.5	5.9	9.8	6.3	4.2	7.1	4.6	7.5	6.9	6.4	10.6	10.1	7.3
2007	11.7	8.4	9.1	7.6	8.1	6.4	10.7	9.5	12.3	10.2	13.9	13.9	10.2
2008	12.7	11.1	11.8	7.4	5.8	7.3	5.4	6.6	7.7	8.9	9.4	9.2	8.6
2009	9.0	7.0	7.2	8.4	4.3	3.8	5.6	6.5	6.8	7.3	10.0	10.3	7.2
2010	10.1	8.9	12.2	7.0	5.1	5.0	6.0	6.9	4.6	6.5	9.5	8.1	7.5
2011	5.8	6.0	5.1	6.4	4.5	4.9	4.9	6.7	6.3	6.8	6.8	8.7	6.1
2012	5.1	5.0	5.7	4.5	5.0	4.8	4.8	5.6	7.0	5.6	6.6	6.3	5.5
2013	5.6	5.0	6.1	4.2	6.3	4.4	5.3	6.1	6.4	7.3	10.4	10.7	6.5
2014[1]	8.0	10.9	8.9	8.9	7.9	7.3	9.6	8.6	9.0	10.5	15.1	17.7	10.2

[1] Pounds of laying feed equivalent in value to one dozen eggs.   [2] Preliminary.   *Source: Economic Research Service, U.S. Department of Agriculture (ERS-USDA)*

Hens and Pullets of Laying Age (Layers) in the United States, on First of Month   In Thousands

Year	Jan.	Feb.	Mar.	Apr.	May	June	July	Aug.	Sept.	Oct.	Nov.	Dec.
2005	347,273	348,412	349,117	344,759	342,346	341,247	338,424	338,674	339,984	341,803	343,789	347,917
2006	349,763	349,930	350,452	350,453	346,809	343,596	341,733	340,728	342,309	343,946	345,090	348,719
2007	349,192	348,563	349,081	347,280	343,835	341,057	339,373	340,648	340,604	341,322	343,909	344,492
2008	345,535	343,891	342,666	341,320	340,318	339,867	337,416	335,094	335,396	333,534	336,301	339,643
2009	341,373	341,388	340,716	341,067	339,239	334,953	333,064	332,371	332,808	334,917	336,671	339,526
2010	341,411	339,747	341,191	342,969	339,635	339,018	340,442	339,384	340,749	336,691	337,300	341,551
2011	344,255	340,247	339,296	342,237	339,520	336,232	336,559	334,997	335,794	334,826	336,909	338,472
2012	340,522	339,826	340,926	343,073	341,885	341,486	338,416	337,525	339,302	341,076	345,269	346,965
2013	344,920	344,916	347,025	348,468	344,363	345,740	343,944	349,862	351,870	349,950	352,971	356,923
2014[1]	360,079	358,861	349,930	352,293	352,673	351,542	351,348	357,659	357,607	358,299	358,201	362,809

[1] Preliminary.   *Source: National Agricultural Statistics Service, U.S. Department of Agriculture (NASS-USDA)*

EGGS

Eggs Laid Per Hundred Layers in the United States   In Number of Eggs

Year	Jan.	Feb.	Mar.	Apr.	May	June	July	Aug.	Sept.	Oct.	Nov.	Dec.	Average
2005	2,192	1,986	2,230	2,156	2,215	2,162	2,234	2,218	2,155	2,236	2,172	2,234	2,183
2006	2,210	1,994	2,238	2,164	2,212	2,160	2,240	2,239	2,165	2,228	2,176	2,234	2,188
2007	2,200	1,993	2,242	2,162	2,226	2,169	2,235	2,229	2,168	2,255	2,191	2,255	2,194
2008	2,218	2,072	2,244	2,163	2,224	2,175	2,260	2,252	2,194	2,277	2,216	2,283	2,215
2009	2,249	2,024	2,269	2,197	2,256	2,203	2,281	2,283	2,209	2,292	2,239	2,303	2,234
2010	2,267	2,036	2,291	2,220	2,273	2,203	2,271	2,283	2,218	2,284	2,231	2,311	2,241
2011	2,289	2,064	2,301	2,234	2,300	2,230	2,303	2,301	2,238	2,317	2,254	2,351	2,265
2012	2,320	2,140	2,315	2,234	2,297	2,229	2,307	2,325	2,241	2,321	2,275	2,347	2,279
2013	2,327	2,090	2,326	2,259	2,329	2,249	2,315	2,331	2,271	2,352	2,281	2,354	2,290
2014[1]	2,335	2,103	2,341	2,274	2,337	2,264	2,354	2,347	2,261	2,354	2,309	2,388	2,306

[1] Preliminary.   *Source: National Agricultural Statistics Service, U.S. Department of Agriculture (NASS-USDA)*

Egg-Type Chicks Hatched by Commercial Hatcheries in the United States   In Thousands

Year	Jan.	Feb.	Mar.	Apr.	May	June	July	Aug.	Sept.	Oct.	Nov.	Dec.	Total
2005	38,339	34,365	41,883	37,646	38,999	35,078	34,721	38,548	33,812	35,450	32,300	35,925	437,066
2006	35,230	33,473	38,910	35,549	39,827	37,475	32,860	35,779	37,048	36,345	31,623	33,254	427,373
2007	36,176	37,071	38,672	39,634	37,744	40,421	35,927	36,969	35,386	36,310	36,219	36,033	446,562
2008	40,156	38,429	42,189	42,329	41,829	40,704	37,234	35,594	37,179	40,288	34,247	37,585	467,763
2009	37,826	36,809	41,752	42,808	40,772	41,980	36,227	38,078	40,310	37,392	34,525	39,502	467,981
2010	39,815	38,854	44,189	47,132	44,039	41,474	38,831	37,172	39,761	41,965	38,794	38,367	490,393
2011	40,587	37,412	43,600	42,956	42,946	38,918	36,948	41,428	39,803	37,616	37,503	38,889	478,606
2012	41,290	40,523	43,101	43,202	44,564	38,829	35,968	42,269	38,319	37,901	36,492	40,985	483,443
2013	43,454	41,840	43,600	45,423	49,468	41,584	39,225	38,231	41,668	42,406	41,750	41,144	509,793
2014[1]	44,134	40,323	43,818	45,115	49,003	43,470	42,123	39,458	43,309	44,416	36,539	42,980	514,688

[1] Preliminary.   *Source: National Agricultural Statistics Service, U.S. Department of Agriculture (NASS-USDA)*

Cold Storage Holdings of Frozen Eggs in the United States, on First of Month   In Millions of Pounds[2]

Year	Jan.	Feb.	Mar.	Apr.	May	June	July	Aug.	Sept.	Oct.	Nov.	Dec.
2005	19.1	18.6	17.9	18.5	18.9	17.7	19.7	19.6	19.9	18.8	17.6	17.6
2006	21.0	22.5	24.5	20.8	23.3	21.0	22.1	23.6	21.6	19.0	16.3	17.1
2007	16.5	17.2	15.7	14.6	14.3	15.2	17.4	17.5	18.5	17.7	17.6	15.2
2008	14.7	12.0	16.7	16.3	16.0	12.4	16.1	21.1	20.8	21.9	22.4	21.3
2009	22.6	22.6	22.1	20.3	18.2	21.7	21.7	22.6	22.6	21.6	22.9	21.2
2010	23.6	24.3	24.1	21.6	22.4	22.4	25.0	24.7	24.7	26.1	25.6	22.9
2011	25.4	26.8	28.1	27.3	27.7	29.0	33.8	33.9	31.0	31.9	33.9	33.0
2012	36.5	37.4	36.3	33.7	32.5	34.5	40.2	38.7	35.9	31.4	29.0	27.3
2013	27.4	29.7	28.6	27.1	29.3	28.9	30.6	26.1	30.1	33.6	33.8	29.8
2014[1]	30.4	34.7	34.6	29.0	27.4	28.3	30.1	31.5	29.8	31.1	32.0	30.3

[1] Preliminary.   [2] Converted on basis 39.5 pounds frozen eggs equals 1 case.   *Source: National Agricultural Statistics Service, U.S. Department of Agriculture (NASS-USDA)*

Electric Power Production by Electric Utilities in the United States   In Millions of Kilowatt Hours

Year	Jan.	Feb.	Mar.	Apr.	May	June	July	Aug.	Sept.	Oct.	Nov.	Dec.	Total
2005	212,654	185,283	196,136	178,408	197,082	221,116	239,381	238,790	211,139	193,687	188,255	212,914	2,474,845
2006	204,976	192,304	197,249	184,803	204,107	223,950	243,526	242,624	200,655	193,321	189,435	206,705	2,483,655
2007	218,288	197,329	197,229	184,017	202,783	218,554	234,728	246,147	209,641	197,285	189,498	208,631	2,504,130
2008	220,229	197,368	194,959	185,415	201,811	225,775	239,383	230,563	201,631	186,930	184,192	207,111	2,475,367
2009	216,218	179,859	184,963	174,130	189,695	213,482	221,545	222,452	193,720	184,019	179,276	213,417	2,372,776
2010	222,362	195,895	188,491	172,441	199,835	228,551	243,756	240,185	203,521	178,917	179,858	217,820	2,471,632
2011	220,900	188,700	195,148	183,567	196,994	225,535	253,142	242,540	199,144	181,359	176,515	197,306	2,460,850
2012	196,498	176,554	175,331	169,095	194,593	210,514	242,595	229,579	191,871	178,825	178,834	194,884	2,339,173
2013	204,308	178,510	187,573	172,366	188,659	210,788	230,218	226,603	196,318	180,417	179,433	205,119	2,360,312
2014[1]	222,427	190,724	193,861	170,037	192,471	212,588	227,208	225,079	193,157	176,012	180,173		2,382,259

[1] Preliminary.   *Source: Energy Information Administration, U.S. Department of Energy (EIA-DOE)*

Electric Power

The modern electric utility industry began in the 1800s. In 1807, Humphry Davy constructed a practical battery and demonstrated both incandescent and arc light. In 1831, Michael Faraday built the first electric generator proving that rotary mechanical power could be converted into electric power. In 1879, Thomas Edison perfected a practical incandescent light bulb. The electric utility industry evolved from gas and electric carbon-arc commercial and street lighting systems. In 1882, in New York City, Thomas Edison's Pearl Street electricity generating station established the industry by displaying the four key elements of a modern electric utility system: reliable central generation, efficient distribution, successful end use, and a competitive price.

Electricity is measured in units called watts and watt-hours. Electricity must be used when it is generated and cannot be stored to any significant degree. That means the power utilities must match the level of electricity generation to the level of demand in order to avoid wasteful over-production. The power industry has been deregulated to some degree in the past decade and now major utility companies sell power back and forth across major national grids in order to meet supply and demand needs. The rapid changes in the supply-demand situation mean that the cost of electricity can be very volatile.

Electricity futures trade at the CME Group. The futures contract is a financially settled contract, which is priced based on electricity prices in the PJM western hub at 111 delivery points, mainly on the utility transmission systems of Pennsylvania Electric Co. and the Potomac Electric Co. The contract is priced in dollars and cents per megawatt hours.

Supply – U.S. electricity production in 2014 (annualized through September) rose +0.9% yr/yr to 2.382 trillion kilowatt-hours. That was well below the record high of 3.212 trillion kilowatt-hours in 1998 and indicated that recent electricity production has been reduced by more efficient production and distribution systems, and to some extent by conservation of electricity by both business and residential consumers.

U.S. electricity generation in 2014 required the use of 8.590 billion cubic feet of natural gas (+0.9% yr/yr), 867 million tons of coal (+0.8% yr/yr), and 55 million barrels of fuel oil (+17.8% yr/yr).

In terms of kilowatt-hours, coal is the most widely used source of electricity production in the U.S. accounting for 40.3% of electricity production in 2013 (latest data available), followed by natural gas (26.2%), nuclear (20.2%), hydro (6.8%), and fuel oil (0.6%). Alternative sources of fuel for electricity generation that are gaining favor include geothermal, biomass, solar, wind, etc. but so far account for only 5.7% of total electricity production in the U.S.

Demand – Residential use of electricity accounts for the largest single category of electricity demand with usage of 1.374 trillion kilowatt hours in 2012 (latest data available) accounting for 37.2% of overall usage. Business users in total use more electricity than residential users, but business users are broken into the categories of commercial with 35.9% of usage and industrial with 26.7% of usage.

World Net Generation of Electricity   In Billions of Kilowatt Hours

Year	Brazil	Canada	China	France	Germany	India	Japan	Korea, South	Russia	Spain	United Kingdom	United States	World Total
2003	358.9	572.3	1,810.3	533.7	567.5	599.7	982.1	323.9	866.5	244.2	372.6	3,883.2	15,904.2
2004	381.2	582.3	2,103.5	540.6	579.2	644.8	1,010.2	345.7	883.7	259.4	368.7	3,970.6	16,691.9
2005	395.7	606.3	2,370.1	544.9	576.9	675.7	1,020.2	363.9	899.3	268.9	370.6	4,055.4	17,330.0
2006	411.9	592.6	2,714.8	542.8	593.5	727.4	1,038.5	379.1	939.9	280.0	368.4	4,064.7	18,032.9
2007	437.2	612.9	3,087.3	538.5	597.9	775.9	1,077.8	402.4	958.4	286.5	367.6	4,156.7	18,866.7
2008	454.5	614.6	3,280.7	544.0	595.2	796.1	1,012.9	419.1	982.5	295.6	360.4	4,119.4	19,157.2
2009	458.6	595.0	3,507.5	507.3	556.7	856.1	985.6	426.0	937.8	278.3	348.9	3,950.3	19,093.3
2010	506.8	585.8	4,051.9	540.3	591.2	912.3	1,044.2	468.3	980.9	285.4	354.8	4,125.1	20,437.0
2011[1]	530.4	626.6	4,547.1	531.6	572.3	1,006.3	1,032.2	489.7	996.8	278.1	341.5	4,100.1	21,182.4
2012[2]	537.6	616.2	4,768.3	533.3	585.2	1,052.5	966.4	499.7	1,012.5	280.0	335.7	4,047.8	21,531.7

[1] Preliminary.   [2] Estimate.   NA = Not avaliable.   *Source: Energy Information Administration, U.S. Department of Energy (EIA-DOE)*

World Consumption of Electricity   In Billions of Kilowatt Hours

Year	Brazil	Canada	China	France	Germany	India	Italy	Japan	Korea, South	Russia	United Kingdom	United States	World Total
2003	336.9	528.2	1,676.8	435.5	537.2	427.4	295.0	932.4	312.9	742.6	342.7	3,662.0	14,452.3
2004	353.3	534.1	1,955.4	447.0	548.4	471.0	302.1	961.3	332.9	763.5	343.0	3,715.9	15,135.9
2005	367.9	547.8	2,193.3	452.3	543.0	497.1	306.7	969.8	350.2	774.3	351.0	3,811.0	15,719.7
2006	382.5	534.0	2,522.0	447.6	548.1	547.1	313.8	988.3	364.5	816.5	348.4	3,816.8	16,400.8
2007	404.2	561.5	2,870.8	450.1	552.0	593.3	314.7	1,026.9	387.0	840.7	345.0	3,890.2	17,181.2
2008	419.6	561.6	3,054.1	462.5	545.0	621.3	314.6	961.6	403.0	855.6	343.3	3,865.2	17,453.4
2009	418.4	523.8	3,270.3	446.5	519.4	669.2	297.4	935.1	409.2	816.1	323.6	3,723.8	17,388.1
2010	455.7	526.3	3,781.5	474.2	547.2	725.5	306.8	994.8	450.2	858.5	330.9	3,886.4	18,679.9
2011[1]	478.8	543.7	4,264.3	442.7	543.7	803.0	311.3	983.2	472.3	869.3	320.2	3,882.6	19,396.6
2012[2]	483.5	524.8	4,467.9	451.1	540.1	864.7	303.1	921.0	482.4	889.3	319.1	3,832.3	19,710.4

[1] Preliminary.   [2] Estimate.   NA = Not avaliable.   *Source: Energy Information Administration, U.S. Department of Energy (EIA-DOE)*

ELECTRIC POWER

World Installed Capacity of Electricity   In Billions of Kilowatt Hours

Year	Brazil	Canada	China	France	Germany	India	Italy	Japan	Russia	Spain	United Kingdom	United States	World Total
2003	86.4	119.0	397.6	116.7	124.3	131.5	78.1	268.7	215.3	71.8	77.8	948.4	3,843.9
2004	90.7	119.7	448.8	116.9	126.7	139.0	81.3	273.4	216.9	69.7	79.8	962.9	3,983.6
2005	93.3	122.5	524.2	115.8	128.1	147.2	85.5	275.3	218.1	76.6	82.4	978.0	4,123.0
2006	96.8	124.2	631.0	115.7	132.2	155.4	89.5	276.8	220.6	81.3	83.6	986.2	4,303.4
2007	100.2	125.3	725.4	116.6	136.2	168.9	93.6	277.2	223.2	88.8	83.5	994.9	4,478.5
2008	103.5	126.4	806.4	117.7	142.7	176.8	98.6	279.9	222.8	93.7	84.8	1,010.2	4,650.1
2009	105.4	131.6	890.4	119.2	150.9	189.2	101.4	282.5	224.1	96.7	86.7	1,025.4	4,853.0
2010	113.6	132.2	987.3	124.4	162.5	207.7	106.5	284.9	228.1	91.8	92.9	1,039.1	5,081.4
2011[1]	119.1	132.8	1,084.7	127.4	167.6	237.9	118.5	287.3	231.6	101.4	92.0	1,051.3	5,314.5
2012[2]	121.7	135.0	1,174.3	129.3	177.1	254.7	124.2	293.3	234.4	105.3	93.8	1,063.0	5,549.6

[1] Preliminary.   [2] Estimate.   NA = Not avaliable.   *Source: Energy Information Administration, U.S. Department of Energy (EIA-DOE)*

Electricity in the United States   In Billions of Kilowatt Hours

	Net Generation				Trade			T&D Losses[6] and Unaccounted for[7]	End Use		
Year	Electric Power Sector[2]	Commercial Sector[3]	Industrial Sector[4]	Total	Imports[5]	Exports[5]	Net Imports[5]		Retail Sales[8]	Direct Use[9]	Total
2005	3,902.2	8.5	144.7	4,055.4	43.9	19.2	24.8	269.2	3,661.0	150.0	3,811.0
2006	3,908.1	8.4	148.3	4,064.7	42.7	24.3	18.4	266.3	3,669.9	146.9	3,816.8
2007	4,005.3	8.3	143.1	4,156.7	51.4	20.1	31.3	297.8	3,764.6	125.7	3,890.2
2008	3,974.3	7.9	137.1	4,119.4	57.0	24.2	32.8	287.1	3,733.0	132.2	3,865.2
2009	3,809.8	8.2	132.3	3,950.3	52.2	18.1	34.1	260.6	3,596.9	126.9	3,723.8
2010	3,972.4	8.6	144.1	4,125.1	45.1	19.1	26.0	264.6	3,754.5	131.9	3,886.4
2011	3,948.2	10.1	141.9	4,100.1	52.3	15.0	37.3	254.8	3,749.8	132.8	3,882.6
2012	3,890.4	11.3	146.1	4,047.8	59.3	12.0	47.3	262.7	3,694.7	137.7	3,832.3
2013	3,898.8	11.5	147.9	4,058.2	63.6	11.3	52.3	279.3	3,691.8	139.4	3,831.2
2014[1]	3,964.7	12.0	141.0	4,117.8	60.7	13.8	46.9	263.6	3,767.2	133.8	3,901.1

[1] Preliminary.   [2] Electricity-only and combined-heat-and-power (CHP) plants within the NAICS 22 category whose primary business is to sell electricity, or electricity and heat, to the public.   [3] Commercial combined-heat-and-power (CHP) and commercial electricity-only plants.   [4] Industrial combined-heat-and-power (CHP) and industrial electricity-only plants.   [5] Electricity transmitted across U.S. borders. Net imports equal imports minus exports.   [6] Transmission and distribution losses.   [7] Data collection frame differences and nonsampling error.   [8] Electricity retail sales to ultimate customers by electric utilities and other energy service providers.   [9] Use of electricity that is 1) self-generated, 2) produced by either the same entity that consumes the power or an affiliate, and 3) used in direct support of a service or industrial process located within the same facility or group of facilities that house the generating equipment. Direct use is exclusive of station use.   *Source: U.S. Geological Survey (USGS)*

Electricity Net Generation in the United States by Sector   In Millions of Kilowatt Hours

	Fossil Fuels				Nuclear electric power	Hydro-electric Pumped Storage[6]	Renewable Energy						Total
	Coal[2]	Petro-leum[3]	Natural Gas[4]	Other Gases[5]			Conventional Hydro-electric Power	Biomass: Wood[7]	Biomass: Waste[8]	Geo-thermal	Solar/ PV[9]	Wind	
2005	2,012,873	122,225	760,960	13,464	781,986	-6,558	270,321	38,856	15,420	14,692	550	17,811	4,055,423
2006	1,990,511	64,166	816,441	14,177	787,219	-6,558	289,246	38,762	16,099	14,568	508	26,589	4,064,702
2007	2,016,456	65,739	896,590	13,453	806,425	-6,896	247,510	39,014	16,525	14,637	612	34,450	4,156,745
2008	1,985,801	46,243	882,981	11,707	806,208	-6,288	254,831	37,300	17,734	14,840	864	55,363	4,119,388
2009	1,755,904	38,937	920,979	10,632	798,855	-4,627	273,445	36,050	18,443	15,009	891	73,886	3,950,331
2010	1,847,290	37,061	987,697	11,313	806,968	-5,501	260,203	37,172	18,917	15,219	1,212	94,652	4,125,060
2011	1,733,430	30,182	1,013,689	11,566	790,204	-6,421	319,355	37,449	19,222	15,316	1,818	120,177	4,100,141
2012	1,514,043	23,190	1,225,894	11,898	769,331	-4,950	276,240	37,799	19,823	15,562	4,327	140,822	4,047,765
2013	1,585,998	26,863	1,113,665	12,271	789,017	-4,424	269,136	39,937	19,957	16,517	9,252	167,665	4,058,209
2014[1]	1,612,515	31,736	1,129,725	11,404	790,278	-5,780	261,198	42,134	19,403	16,252	19,167	177,656	4,117,768

[1] Preliminary.   [2] Anthracite, bituminous coal, subbituminous coal, lignite, waste coal, and coal synfuel.   [3] Distillate fuel oil, residual fuel oil, petroleum coke, jet fuel, kerosene, other petroleum, waste oil, and propane.   [4] Natural gas, plus a small amount of supplemental gaseous fuels.   [5] Blast furnace gas, and other manufactured and waste gases derived from fossil fuels.   [6] Pumped storage facility production minus energy used for pumping.   [7] Wood and wood-derived fuels.   [8] Municipal solid waste from biogenic sources, landfill gas, sludge waste, agricultural byproducts, and other biomass.   [9] Solar thermal and photovoltaic (PV) energy.   *Source: U.S. Geological Survey (USGS)*

Total Electricity Net Generation in the United States   In Billions of Kilowatt Hours

Year	Jan.	Feb.	Mar.	Apr.	May	June	July	Aug.	Sept.	Oct.	Nov.	Dec.	Total
2004	346.5	314.3	308.8	290.6	327.4	345.1	377.3	368.4	335.6	312.5	302.1	341.9	3,970.6
2005	343.1	298.5	317.5	289.6	315.1	363.7	402.3	404.9	350.2	316.4	306.1	348.1	4,055.4
2006	328.7	307.3	318.7	297.9	330.6	364.3	410.4	407.8	332.1	321.6	309.2	336.3	4,064.7
2007	353.5	323.2	320.5	303.1	330.2	362.8	393.2	421.8	355.4	332.6	314.1	346.3	4,156.7
2008	363.0	325.1	324.6	305.9	325.2	373.1	402.9	389.0	338.1	318.5	310.0	343.9	4,119.4
2009	355.0	300.9	310.6	289.5	311.3	347.7	372.5	381.2	327.4	307.0	296.6	350.5	3,950.3
2010	361.0	319.7	312.2	287.8	327.9	375.8	409.7	408.9	346.0	307.9	306.0	362.1	4,125.1
2011	362.9	313.1	318.7	302.4	323.6	367.7	418.7	406.5	337.9	308.7	304.1	335.7	4,100.1
2012	339.5	309.4	309.1	295.2	336.5	360.8	414.6	395.7	334.6	311.7	306.0	334.6	4,047.8
2013[1]	348.5	309.4	325.3	298.1	321.8	356.2	393.8	384.0	340.3	314.7	313.8		3,705.9

[1] Preliminary.   *Source: Energy Information Administration, U.S. Department of Energy (EIA-DOE)*

Imports[2] of Electricity in the United States   In Billions of Kilowatt Hours

Year	Jan.	Feb.	Mar.	Apr.	May	June	July	Aug.	Sept.	Oct.	Nov.	Dec.	Total
2005	3.2	3.0	3.4	3.0	3.3	3.6	4.4	5.0	3.7	3.7	3.8	3.9	43.9
2006	3.9	3.4	3.7	3.4	3.7	3.8	4.7	4.7	2.2	2.7	2.9	3.7	42.7
2007	3.5	4.2	3.9	4.0	4.6	4.5	5.5	5.4	3.8	3.6	4.3	4.1	51.4
2008	5.0	4.6	4.8	4.1	5.3	6.1	6.0	5.8	4.9	3.6	3.3	3.5	57.0
2009	4.3	3.9	2.9	3.3	4.1	4.7	5.5	5.8	4.5	4.7	3.8	4.6	52.2
2010	5.3	4.4	4.4	3.9	3.1	4.1	4.3	3.6	2.9	2.5	2.7	4.0	45.1
2011	4.3	3.7	4.0	3.8	4.9	4.5	6.0	5.6	4.0	3.7	3.5	4.3	52.3
2012	4.1	3.6	4.2	5.0	5.5	5.4	6.7	6.3	4.9	4.4	4.7	4.4	59.3
2013	5.0	4.6	5.2	4.6	5.5	5.7	6.4	6.5	5.2	4.9	5.1	4.9	63.6
2014[1]	5.0	4.0	5.1	4.3	4.9	4.9	5.8	6.2	5.5	4.9			60.7

[1] Preliminary.   [2] Electricity transmitted across U.S. borders. Net imports equal imports minus exports.   *Source: Energy Information Administration, U.S. Department of Energy (EIA-DOE)*

Exports[2] of Electricity in the United States   In Billions of Kilowatt Hours

Year	Jan.	Feb.	Mar.	Apr.	May	June	July	Aug.	Sept.	Oct.	Nov.	Dec.	Total
2005	1.7	1.2	1.1	1.2	1.8	2.0	1.6	1.5	1.9	1.8	1.7	1.9	19.2
2006	2.4	1.8	2.0	2.0	2.3	2.4	1.6	1.6	2.2	2.3	2.2	1.4	24.3
2007	1.6	1.4	2.1	1.2	1.2	1.3	1.7	1.9	2.5	1.6	1.8	2.0	20.1
2008	1.8	1.5	2.7	1.3	3.0	3.4	1.7	1.5	1.8	2.0	2.1	1.4	24.2
2009	2.3	1.5	1.7	1.5	1.4	1.6	1.4	1.4	1.4	1.4	1.3	1.4	18.1
2010	1.2	1.0	1.3	1.3	1.7	1.6	1.5	1.8	2.4	2.1	1.9	1.4	19.1
2011	1.6	1.5	1.5	1.6	1.3	1.3	1.3	1.0	1.0	0.9	1.1	0.9	15.0
2012	0.9	0.9	1.2	1.3	1.2	1.2	1.0	0.9	0.9	0.7	0.8	1.1	12.0
2013	1.0	0.8	0.9	1.2	0.9	0.8	1.0	0.9	0.7	1.0	0.9	1.1	11.3
2014[1]	1.3	1.3	1.9	1.3	0.8	1.1	1.1	0.9	0.8	1.0			13.8

[1] Preliminary.   [2] Electricity transmitted across U.S. borders. Net imports equal imports minus exports.   *Source: Energy Information Administration, U.S. Department of Energy (EIA-DOE)*

Total End Use of Electricity in the United States   In Billions of Kilowatt Hours

Year	Jan.	Feb.	Mar.	Apr.	May	June	July	Aug.	Sept.	Oct.	Nov.	Dec.	Total
2005	322.0	291.2	299.4	276.1	285.8	332.5	369.9	376.9	343.2	308.6	285.8	319.7	3,811.0
2006	317.4	292.3	301.9	279.5	299.5	333.9	375.7	381.9	329.4	303.7	289.0	312.6	3,816.8
2007	326.4	310.8	301.7	285.2	303.1	333.3	363.7	384.9	348.1	318.4	296.4	318.2	3,890.2
2008	338.3	315.8	305.8	288.7	299.1	339.6	372.6	364.1	332.5	302.5	287.9	318.3	3,865.2
2009	331.7	296.5	294.0	275.3	285.0	315.5	349.5	356.9	322.1	298.1	278.4	320.8	3,723.8
2010	342.9	308.6	303.4	277.1	294.3	341.9	380.7	384.0	338.9	298.4	285.4	330.7	3,886.4
2011	345.3	306.9	302.4	285.6	298.7	339.9	382.8	385.0	337.5	298.6	286.1	313.6	3,882.6
2012	322.6	298.0	294.7	281.3	308.3	336.6	383.5	377.2	329.5	301.9	289.5	309.2	3,832.3
2013	329.6	299.7	306.2	285.5	298.0	329.0	367.9	362.6	332.4	303.1	290.9	326.4	3,831.2
2014[1]	351.1	319.6	311.1	283.3	298.6	330.3	359.0	359.8	334.3	303.7			3,901.1

[1] Preliminary.   *Source: Energy Information Administration, U.S. Department of Energy (EIA-DOE)*

Ethanol

World Production of Fuel Ethanol   In Thousands of Barrels per Day

Year	Australia	Brazil	Canada	China	Colombia	France	Germany	India	Jamaica	Spain	Thailand	United States	World Total
2003	----	249.4	4.0	13.8	----	1.7	----	3.3	2.6	3.0	----	182.9	465.3
2004	----	251.7	4.0	17.2	----	1.7	0.4	3.5	2.0	4.0	0.1	221.5	510.9
2005	0.4	276.4	4.4	20.7	0.5	2.5	2.8	3.7	2.2	5.0	1.2	254.7	585.0
2006	1.3	306.1	4.4	28.0	4.6	5.0	7.4	4.1	5.2	7.0	2.2	318.6	715.9
2007	1.4	388.7	13.8	28.7	4.7	9.3	6.8	4.5	4.9	7.0	3.0	425.4	924.5
2008	2.5	466.3	15.0	34.4	4.4	16.0	10.0	5.0	6.4	6.0	5.7	605.6	1,215.2
2009	3.5	449.8	20.0	37.5	5.6	17.0	13.0	1.7	6.9	8.0	7.2	713.5	1,323.2
2010	4.7	486.0	24.0	36.7	4.8	18.0	13.0	0.9	2.0	8.0	7.8	867.4	1,521.0
2011[1]	5.5	392.0	30.0	38.9	6.0	17.4	13.3	6.3	3.0	8.0	8.4	908.6	1,490.5
2012[2]	5.3	402.5	32.7	43.2	8.5	17.0	13.4	5.3	----	7.9	8.1	875.6	1,470.1

[1] Preliminary.   [2] Estimate.   *Source: Renewable Fuels Association*

Salient Statistics of Ethanol in the United States

Year	Ethanol Plants	Ethanol Production Capacity (mgy)	Plants Under Con-struction	Capacity Under Construction (mgy)	Farmer Owned Plants	Farmer Owned Capacity (mgy)	Percent of Total Capacity Farmer	Farmer Owned UC Plants	Farmers Owned UC Capacity	Percent of Total UC Capacity	States with Ethanol Plants
2005	81	3,643.7	16	754.0	40	1,388.6	38	10	450	60	18
2006	95	4,336.4	31	1,778.0	46	1,677.1	39	4	187	11	20
2007	110	5,493.4	76	5,635.5	46	1,677.1	39	4	187	11	21
2008	139	7,888.4	61	5,536.0	49	1,948.6	28	13	771	12	21
2009	170	12,475.4	24	2,066.0	NA	NA	NA	NA	NA	NA	26
2010	189	13,028.4	15	1,432.0	----	----	----	----	----	----	26
2011	204	14,071.4	10	560.0	----	----	----	----	----	----	29
2012	209	14,906.9	2	140.0	----	----	----	----	----	----	29
2013[1]	211	14,837.4	2	50.0	----	----	----	----	----	----	28
2014[2]	210	14,879.5	7	167.0	----	----	----	----	----	----	28

[1] Preliminary.   [2] Estimate.   *Source: Renewable Fuels Association*

Production of Fuel Ethanol in the United States   In Thousands of Barrels

Year	Jan.	Feb.	Mar.	Apr.	May	June	July	Aug.	Sept.	Oct.	Nov.	Dec.	Total
2005	7,461	6,847	7,530	7,135	7,357	7,463	8,007	8,050	7,841	8,335	8,259	8,676	92,961
2006	8,935	8,463	9,333	8,663	9,086	9,531	9,791	10,235	10,088	10,512	10,442	11,215	116,294
2007	11,621	10,795	11,892	11,716	12,573	12,553	13,083	13,581	13,402	14,221	14,568	15,258	155,263
2008	16,058	15,527	17,527	17,152	18,756	17,651	19,040	20,059	19,338	20,048	20,139	20,342	221,637
2009	19,561	18,255	20,121	19,374	21,024	21,125	22,887	23,136	22,218	23,467	24,122	25,134	260,424
2010	25,625	23,802	26,486	25,384	26,244	25,632	26,584	26,964	26,221	27,471	27,747	28,457	316,617
2011	28,467	25,300	28,178	26,538	27,720	27,224	27,541	27,976	26,588	28,013	28,383	29,718	331,646
2012	29,038	26,647	27,548	26,346	27,616	26,513	25,236	26,092	24,376	24,976	24,744	25,582	314,714
2013	24,778	22,494	25,620	25,601	27,197	26,722	26,923	26,279	25,564	27,995	27,915	29,405	316,493
2014[1]	28,344	25,401	28,116	27,837	29,039	28,759	29,413	28,665	27,577	28,641			338,150

[1] Preliminary.   *Source: Energy Information Administration, U.S. Department of Energy (EIA-DOE)*

Stocks of Fuel Ethanol in the United States   In Thousands of Barrels

Year	Jan.	Feb.	Mar.	Apr.	May	June	July	Aug.	Sept.	Oct.	Nov.	Dec.
2005	6,142	6,261	6,605	6,861	6,810	6,064	5,926	5,398	5,317	5,591	5,723	5,563
2006	6,099	7,268	8,626	8,990	7,767	6,675	7,706	9,133	9,725	9,723	9,232	8,760
2007	8,656	8,765	8,539	8,807	8,966	9,171	9,866	11,011	11,555	11,449	11,218	10,535
2008	11,383	11,173	12,288	12,572	13,297	13,323	13,448	14,771	16,110	15,214	15,286	14,226
2009	14,514	15,834	16,411	15,322	14,173	13,974	14,223	14,671	15,283	14,933	15,578	16,594
2010	18,251	19,297	20,222	20,042	19,851	18,565	17,809	17,380	17,437	17,278	18,150	17,941
2011	20,826	21,016	21,593	21,065	20,609	19,217	18,788	18,123	18,465	18,038	18,308	18,238
2012	21,475	22,393	22,583	22,050	21,635	21,239	20,224	19,180	19,921	18,626	19,992	20,350
2013	19,894	19,009	18,410	17,370	16,804	16,428	17,072	16,945	15,986	15,750	15,569	16,424
2014[1]	17,086	16,834	17,349	17,356	18,117	18,664	18,665	18,471	18,660	17,265		

[1] Preliminary.   *Source: Energy Information Administration, U.S. Department of Energy (EIA-DOE)*

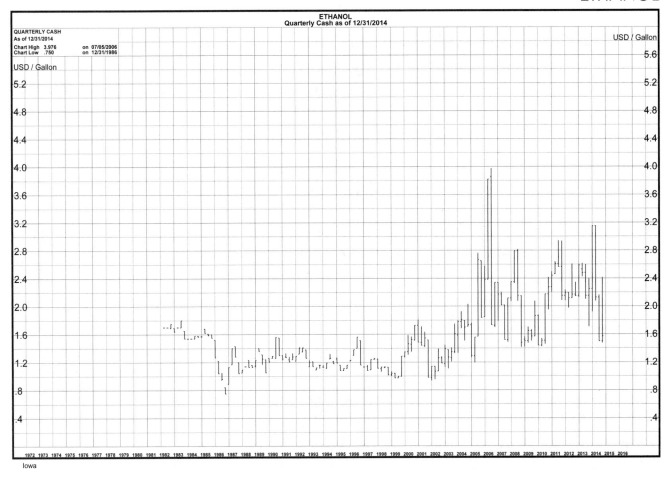

ETHANOL
Quarterly Cash as of 12/31/2014

QUARTERLY CASH
As of 12/31/2014
Chart High 3.976 on 07/05/2006
Chart Low .750 on 12/31/1986

USD / Gallon

Iowa

Average Price of Ethanol in the United States[1]   In Dollars Per Gallon

Year	Jan.	Feb.	Mar.	Apr.	May	June	July	Aug.	Sept.	Oct.	Nov.	Dec.	Average
2007	2.144	1.899	2.185	2.159	2.169	2.089	1.970	1.849	1.581	1.523	1.739	1.950	1.938
2008	2.188	2.129	2.316	2.455	2.485	2.535	2.642	2.224	2.150	1.846	1.648	1.493	2.176
2009	1.518	1.488	1.461	1.497	1.553	1.673	1.585	1.535	1.540	1.798	1.984	1.962	1.633
2010	1.817	1.689	1.515	1.439	1.508	1.523	1.507	1.692	2.012	2.120	2.331	2.108	1.772
2011	2.268	2.292	2.435	2.564	2.546	2.600	2.718	2.830	2.745	2.596	2.825	2.324	2.562
2012	2.128	2.089	2.177	2.152	2.107	2.002	2.399	2.532	2.397	2.296	2.301	2.265	2.237
2013	2.197	2.331	2.473	2.478	2.553	2.571	2.430	2.287	2.346	2.096	1.942	2.314	2.335
2014	2.073	1.946	2.478	2.800	2.237	2.225	2.100	2.096	1.827	1.561	2.019	1.995	2.113

[1] Northeast and Northwest Iowa.   *Source: Agricultural Marketing Service, U.S. Department of Agriculture (AMS-USDA)*

Volume of Trading of Ethanol Futures in Chicago   In Contracts

Year	Jan.	Feb.	Mar.	Apr.	May	June	July	Aug.	Sept.	Oct.	Nov.	Dec.	Total
2009	2,969	2,116	7,158	4,673	4,031	5,535	4,707	4,843	7,439	6,530	6,521	10,646	67,168
2010	9,629	9,887	19,404	12,659	12,794	17,809	15,406	15,073	13,694	13,176	11,952	11,242	162,725
2011	12,857	15,589	18,387	16,665	21,406	25,489	22,550	22,026	22,766	21,370	19,710	20,131	238,946
2012	19,054	17,458	25,690	26,004	38,420	41,795	35,450	23,875	23,434	26,077	26,094	27,562	330,913
2013	29,052	31,990	37,290	40,033	30,116	30,695	27,053	22,140	16,027	13,413	13,413	11,025	302,247
2014	18,334	20,874	20,547	24,319	20,168	24,842	18,015	17,399	20,134	22,580	18,380	16,753	242,345

Contract size = 29,000 US gallons.   *Source: CME Group; Chicago Board of Trade (CBT)*

Month-End Open Interest of Ethanol Futures in Chicago   In Contracts

Year	Jan.	Feb.	Mar.	Apr.	May	June	July	Aug.	Sept.	Oct.	Nov.	Dec.
2009	3,146	3,228	4,644	4,145	4,381	4,174	3,877	4,631	4,940	5,575	5,932	6,904
2010	7,186	8,478	7,827	8,603	10,531	11,833	11,720	10,118	10,013	8,267	7,437	7,209
2011	8,259	8,200	7,507	7,748	8,275	9,240	9,619	10,325	9,462	10,658	10,355	9,985
2012	10,608	11,343	12,268	12,209	12,570	11,157	12,113	11,273	10,809	11,013	10,573	8,587
2013	9,154	11,207	11,408	10,271	10,071	9,266	8,301	6,655	5,429	4,015	3,409	3,143
2014	5,047	5,498	5,726	7,472	6,981	6,483	6,599	6,287	6,363	6,646		

Contract size = 29,000 US gallons.   *Source: CME Group; Chicago Board of Trade (CBT)*

ETHANOL

World Production of Biodiesel — In Thousands of Barrels per Day

Year	Argentina	Austria	Belgium	Brazil	China	France	Germany	Indonesia	Italy	Spain	Thailand	United States	World Total
2003	0.2	0.6	----	----	0.1	7.3	14.0	----	5.3	2.0	----	0.9	34.1
2004	0.2	1.1	----	----	0.1	7.7	20.0	----	6.2	2.2	----	1.8	43.8
2005	0.2	1.6	----	----	0.8	8.4	33.0	0.2	7.7	3.2	0.4	5.9	71.2
2006	0.6	2.4	0.5	1.2	4.0	11.6	52.0	0.4	11.6	1.2	0.4	16.3	124.6
2007	3.6	5.2	3.2	7.0	2.0	18.7	57.0	1.0	9.2	3.5	1.2	32.0	178.8
2008	13.9	4.2	5.4	20.1	5.0	34.4	55.0	2.0	13.1	4.3	7.7	44.1	262.1
2009	23.1	6.1	8.1	27.7	10.2	41.0	45.0	5.7	15.6	13.0	10.5	34.0	311.7
2010	36.0	5.7	8.5	41.1	9.8	37.0	49.0	12.8	14.5	16.0	11.4	22.0	345.4
2011[1]	47.3	6.2	8.7	46.1	14.7	34.0	57.2	31.0	11.2	11.0	10.9	63.0	425.3
2012[2]	47.9	7.0	8.7	46.7	15.7	32.7	54.7	37.9	9.8	8.7	15.5	64.0	431.3

[1] Preliminary.   [2] Estimate.   *Source: Renewable Fuels Association*

Production of Biodiesel in the United States — In Thousands of Barrels (mbbl)

Year	Jan.	Feb.	Mar.	Apr.	May	June	July	Aug.	Sept.	Oct.	Nov.	Dec.	Average
2006	312	269	368	385	531	612	540	689	598	549	520	590	5,963
2007	692	564	775	765	958	943	1,237	1,298	1,224	1,188	993	1,026	11,663
2008	1,197	1,074	1,188	1,268	1,292	1,445	1,604	1,623	1,501	1,465	1,438	1,052	16,147
2009	1,011	780	599	624	689	761	1,030	1,070	1,158	1,364	1,511	1,455	12,052
2010	633	696	804	814	760	644	657	653	723	676	528	588	8,177
2011	842	961	1,419	1,692	1,838	1,938	2,183	2,273	2,284	2,508	2,494	2,604	23,035
2012	1,751	1,887	2,251	2,237	2,428	2,223	2,127	2,176	1,949	1,792	1,363	1,406	23,588
2013	1,640	1,672	2,412	2,548	2,645	2,699	3,072	3,086	3,025	3,272	3,080	3,217	32,368
2014[1]	1,612	2,183	2,325	2,219	2,409	2,454	3,119	2,510	2,631	2,715			29,012

[1] Preliminary.   *Source: Energy Information Administration, U.S. Department of Energy (EIA-DOE)*

Stocks of Biodiesel in the United States — In Thousands of Barrels (Mbbl)

Year	Jan.	Feb.	Mar.	Apr.	May	June	July	Aug.	Sept.	Oct.	Nov.	Dec.
2009	664	424	665	632	600	581	511	511	527	553	531	711
2010	1,049	1,039	1,057	1,009	1,016	968	830	771	682	650	676	672
2011	1,016	1,217	1,381	1,408	1,576	1,524	1,748	1,834	1,617	1,965	1,877	2,012
2012	2,510	2,895	2,893	2,783	2,710	2,348	2,262	2,011	2,059	2,183	1,865	2,083
2013	2,090	2,093	2,491	2,588	2,598	2,565	2,793	3,099	3,051	2,970	4,029	4,506
2014[1]	4,171	3,928	4,074	3,764	3,334	2,995	3,358	2,998	2,743	2,867		

[1] Preliminary.   *Source: Energy Information Administration, U.S. Department of Energy (EIA-DOE)*

Imports of Biodiesel in the United States — In Thousands of Barrels (mbbl)

Year	Jan.	Feb.	Mar.	Apr.	May	June	July	Aug.	Sept.	Oct.	Nov.	Dec.	Average
2007	237	148	114	179	110	364	269	409	299	428	245	539	3,341
2008	598	838	274	688	513	512	526	907	908	721	612	404	7,501
2009	261	158	383	52	117	138	58	126	123	159	105	165	1,845
2010	42	32	62	46	83	56	33	54	71	19	31	35	564
2011	50	39	55	54	49	50	64	67	67	85	69	241	890
2012	48	72	25	32	75	132	166	55	108	60	9	71	853
2013	38	88	439	372	410	698	358	385	781	1,177	1,641	1,765	8,152
2014[1]	233	175	257	146	563	233	493	571	352	507			4,236

[1] Preliminary.   *Source: Energy Information Administration, U.S. Department of Energy (EIA-DOE)*

Exports of Biodiesel in the United States — In Thousands of Barrels (mbbl)

Year	Jan.	Feb.	Mar.	Apr.	May	June	July	Aug.	Sept.	Oct.	Nov.	Dec.	Average
2007	103	173	293	605	543	418	895	644	515	583	965	741	6,478
2008	1,100	1,384	1,172	1,592	1,364	1,758	1,421	1,606	1,452	1,333	1,181	766	16,129
2009	1,150	1,166	203	154	417	366	581	397	224	424	819	431	6,332
2010	306	144	448	234	260	314	206	233	135	137	59	113	2,588
2011	224	91	204	229	198	120	147	74	199	136	135	40	1,799
2012	258	125	189	230	320	392	426	403	295	209	65	143	3,056
2013	16	37	176	371	563	587	429	687	511	415	408	476	4,675
2014[1]	135	141	91	261	208	263	320	264	136	40			2,231

[1] Preliminary.   *Source: Energy Information Administration, U.S. Department of Energy (EIA-DOE)*

Fertilizer

Fertilizer is a natural or synthetic chemical substance, or mixture, that enriches soil to promote plant growth. The three primary nutrients that fertilizers provide are nitrogen, potassium, and phosphorus. In ancient times, and still today, many commonly used fertilizers contain one or more of the three primary ingredients: manure (containing nitrogen), bones (containing small amounts of nitrogen and large quantities of phosphorus), and potash (containing potassium).

At least fourteen different nutrients have been found essential for crops. These include three organic nutrients (carbon, hydrogen, and oxygen, which are taken directly from air and water), three primary chemical nutrients (nitrogen, phosphorus, and potassium), and three secondary chemical nutrients (magnesium, calcium, and sulfur). The others are micronutrients or trace elements and include iron, manganese, copper, zinc, boron, and molybdenum.

Prices – The average price of ammonia, a key source of ingredients for fertilizers, fell by -6.7% yr/yr in 2013 to $540 per metric ton, below the 2008 record high of $590 per metric ton. The average price of potash in the U.S. in 2012 (latest data) fell by -2.7% yr/yr to $710.00 per metric ton, below the 2009 record high of $800.00 per metric ton.

Supply – World production of nitrogen (as contained in ammonia) in 2014 rose +0.7% 144.000 million metric tons, a new record high. The world's largest producers of nitrogen in 2014 were China with 33.3% of world production, India (8.3%), Russia (7.2%), and the U.S. (6.4%). U.S. nitrogen production in 2014 rose +0.3% to 9.200 million metric tons.

World production of phosphate rock, basic slag and guano in 2014 fell -2.2% yr/yr to 220.000 million metric tons. The world's largest producers of phosphate rock in 2014 were China (with 45.5% of world production), Morocco (13.6%), U.S. (12.3%), and Russia (4.6%). U.S. production in 2014 fell -13.4% y/y to 27.100 million metric tons.

World production of marketable potash in 2014 rose +1.5% yr/yr to 35.000 million metric tons. The world's largest producers of potash in 2014 were Canada with 28.0% of world production, Russia (17.7%), China (12.6%), and Belarus (12.3%). U.S. production of potash in 2014 fell -11.5% yr/yr to 850,000 metric tons.

Demand – U.S. consumption of nitrogen in 2012 (latest data available) rose +6.0% yr/yr to 12.300 million metric tons, a new decade record high. U.S. consumption of phosphate rock in 2014 fell -2.2% yr/yr to 30.600 million metric tons. U.S. consumption of potash in 2014 rose +5.8% yr/yr to 5.500 million metric tons, below 2008's decade high of 6.700 million metric tons.

Trade – U.S. imports of nitrogen in 2014 rose +4.0% yr/yr to 5.160 million metric tons and the U.S. relied on imports for 36% of consumption. U.S. imports of phosphate rock in 2014 rose +0.4% yr/yr to 2.570 million metric tons. U.S. imports of potash in 2014 fell -1.1% to 4.600 million metric tons, but was still higher than the 4-decade low of 2.400 million metric tons posted in 2009. Imports accounted for 84% of U.S. consumption.

World Production of Ammonia   In Thousands of Metric Tons of Contained Nitrogen

Year	Canada	China	France	Germany	India	Indonesia	Japan	Mexico	Nether-lands	Poland	Russia	United States	Total
2006	4,100	40,660	616	2,718	10,900	4,300	1,091	487	1,800	2,007	10,500	8,190	125,000
2007	3,688	42,480	800	2,746	11,000	4,400	1,114	714	1,800	1,995	10,500	8,540	130,000
2008	3,920	41,140	800	2,819	11,100	4,500	1,244	737	----	2,000	10,425	7,870	123,000
2009	3,611	42,290	2,970	2,363	11,200	4,600	1,021	861	----	1,600	10,441	7,700	121,000
2010	3,620	40,870	3,517	2,677	11,500	4,800	1,178	824	----	1,700	10,400	8,290	127,000
2011	3,946	43,250	3,500	2,821	11,800	5,000	1,211	766	----	1,900	10,400	9,350	133,000
2012	3,942	45,520	2,644	2,823	12,000	5,100	1,055	880	1,800	2,100	10,300	8,730	136,000
2013[1]	3,840	47,300	2,640	2,820	12,000	5,200	1,150		1,800	2,100	10,300	9,170	143,000
2014[2]	3,900	48,000	2,600	2,800	12,000	5,200	1,200		1,800	2,100	10,300	9,200	144,000

[1] Preliminary.   [2] Estimate.   Source: U.S. Geological Survey (USGS)

Salient Statistics of Nitrogen[3] (Ammonia) in the United States   In Thousands of Metric Tons

Year	Net Import Reliance As a % of Apparent Consumption	Production[3] (Fixed) Fertilizer	Production[3] (Fixed) Non-fertilizer	Total	Imprts[4] (Fixed)	Exports	Nitrogen[5] Compounds Produced	Nitrogen[5] Compounds Consumption	Stocks, Dec. 31 - Ammonia	Stocks, Dec. 31 - Fixed Nitrogen Compounds	Ammonia Consumption (Apparent)	Average Price ($/Metric Ton) Urea FOB Gulf[6] Coast	Average Price Urea FOB Corn Belt	Average Price Ammonium Nitrate: FOB Corn Belt	Ammonia FOB Gulf Coast
2006	41	7,270	921	8,190	5,920	194	9,083	11,000	201	485	14,000	265-280	295-305	250-260	302
2007	43	7,610	930	8,540	6,530	145	9,485	12,000	157	407	15,000	435-445	465-490	590-620	307
2008	42	6,730	1,140	7,870	6,020	192	8,605	11,500	302	794	13,500	190-210	270-330	450-650	590
2009	38	6,470	1,240	7,700	4,530	16	8,071	10,500	167	364	12,300	307-315	350-360	340-390	251
2010	40	7,130	1,160	8,290	5,540	36	8,597	11,200	165	328	13,800	370-380	415-440	640-685	396
2011	37	8,170	1,180	9,350	5,600	26	8,759	11,600	178	NA	14,900	360-375	410-450	670-710	531
2012	37	7,600	1,140	8,730	5,170	31	8,579	12,300	180	NA	13,900	393-410	440-480	760-820	579
2013[1]	34			9,170	4,960	196			240		13,900				540
2014[2]	36			9,200	5,160	95			190		14,300				

[1] Preliminary.   [2] Estimate.   [3] Anhydrous ammonia, synthetic.   [4] For consumption.   [5] Major downstream nitrogen compounds.   [6] Granular.
Source: U.S. Geological Survey (USGS)

World Production of Phosphate Rock, Basic Slag & Guano   In Thousands of Metric Tons (Gross Weight)

Year	Brazil	China	Egypt	Israel	Jordan	Morocco	Russia	Senegal	Syria	Togo	Tunisia	United States	World Total
2005	5,450	30,400	2,144	3,236	6,375	28,788	11,000	1,455	3,500	1,350	8,220	36,100	150,000
2006	5,932	38,600	2,177	2,949	5,805	27,400	11,000	584	3,664	1,650	7,801	30,100	151,000
2007	6,185	45,400	3,890	3,069	5,552	27,800	11,400	691	3,678	750	8,005	29,700	160,000
2008	6,727	50,700	5,523	3,088	6,266	24,861	10,400	645	2,629	842	7,692	30,200	166,000
2009	6,084	60,200	6,627	2,697	5,282	18,307	9,500	949	2,128	726	7,398	26,400	162,000
2010	6,192	68,000	3,435	3,135	6,529	26,603	11,000	1,079	3,167	695	7,281	25,800	184,000
2011	6,738	81,000	4,746	3,105	7,623	28,052	11,000	1,411	3,541	866	3,350	28,100	201,000
2012	6,740	95,300	6,236	3,513	6,383	27,100	10,000	1,381	1,534	1,110	2,230	30,100	215,000
2013[1]	6,000	108,000	6,500	3,500	5,400	26,400	10,000	800	500	1,110	3,500	31,200	225,000
2014[2]	6,750	100,000	6,000	3,610	6,000	30,000	10,000	700	1,000	1,200	5,000	27,100	220,000

[1] Preliminary.   [2] Estimate.   *Source: U.S. Geological Survey (USGS)*

Salient Statistics of Phosphate Rock in the United States   In Thousands of Metric Tons

Year	Mine Production	Marketable Production	Value Million Dollars	Imports for Consumption	Exports	Apparent Consumption	Producer Stocks, Dec. 31	Avg. Price FOB Mine $/Metric Ton	Avg. Price of Florida & N. Carolina $/Met. Ton - FOB Mine (-60% to +74%) - Domestic	Export	Average
2005	151,000	36,100	1,070	2,630	----	37,800	6,970	29.61	29.67	NA	29.60
2006	111,000	30,100	919	2,420	----	32,600	7,070	30.49	W	NA	30.52
2007	126,000	29,700	1,520	2,670	----	33,800	4,970	51.10	W	NA	51.36
2008	124,000	30,200	2,320	2,750	----	31,600	6,340	76.76	W	NA	76.64
2009	107,000	26,400	3,360	2,000	----	27,500	8,120	127.19	W	NA	NA
2010	106,000	25,800	1,980	2,400	----	30,500	5,620	76.69	W	NA	NA
2011	129,000	28,100	2,720	3,350	----	32,000	4,580	96.64	W	NA	NA
2012	150,000	30,100	3,080	3,080	----	30,400	6,700	102.54	W	NA	NA
2013[1]		31,200		2,560	----	31,300	9,000	91.11	W	NA	NA
2014[2]		27,100		2,570	----	30,600	6,800	90.00	W	NA	NA

[1] Preliminary.   [2] Estimate.   *Source: U.S. Geological Survey (USGS)*

World Production of Marketable Potash   In Thousands of Metric Tons (K_2O Equivalent)

Year	Belarus	Brazil	Canada	Chile	China	Germany	Israel	Jordan	Russia	Spain	United Kingdom	United States	World Total
2005	4,844	405	10,140	547	1,500	3,664	2,224	1,115	7,131	575	439	1,200	33,800
2006	4,605	403	8,518	496	1,800	3,625	2,187	1,036	5,740	435	420	1,100	30,400
2007	4,972	424	11,085	515	2,600	3,637	2,182	1,096	6,430	435	427	1,100	34,900
2008	4,968	383	10,455	559	2,750	3,280	2,170	1,223	5,992	435	411	1,100	33,700
2009	2,485	453	4,318	691	3,200	1,825	1,656	683	3,727	481	411	720	20,600
2010	5,223	448	9,788	964	3,600	3,024	1,790	1,185	6,283	419	427	930	34,100
2011	7,304	424	11,055	861	3,800	3,215	1,736	1,355	6,498	436	470	1,000	38,200
2012	4,906	425	8,984	1,053	4,100	3,120	2,154	1,094	5,472	436	470	900	33,100
2013[1]	4,240	430	10,100	1,050	4,300	3,200	2,100	1,080	6,100	420	470	960	34,500
2014[2]	4,300	350	9,800	1,100	4,400	3,000	2,500	1,100	6,200	420	470	850	35,000

[1] Preliminary.   [2] Estimate.   *Source: U.S. Geological Survey (USGS)*

Salient Statistics of Potash in the United States   In Thousands of Metric Tons (K_2O Equivalent)

Year	Net Import Reliance As a % of Apparent Consump	Production	Sales by Producers	Value Million Dollars	Imports for Consumption	Exports	Apparent Consumption	Producer Stocks Dec. 31	Avg Value of Product	Avg Value of K_2O Equiv	Avg. Price[3] (Metric Ton)
2005	80	1,200	1,200	410.0	4,920	200	5,900	----	165.00	350.00	280.00
2006	79	1,100	1,100	410.0	4,470	332	5,200	----	170.00	375.00	290.00
2007	81	1,100	1,200	480.0	4,970	199	5,900	----	185.00	400.00	400.00
2008	84	1,100	1,100	740.0	5,800	222	6,700	----	305.00	675.00	700.00
2009	73	720	630	500.0	2,220	303	2,500	----	330.00	800.00	800.00
2010	83	930	1,000	660.0	4,760	297	5,500	----	275.00	630.00	605.00
2011	83	1,000	990	740.0	4,980	202	5,800	----	320.00	745.00	730.00
2012	82	900	980	750.0	4,240	234	5,000	----	340.00	765.00	710.00
2013[1]	82	960	880		4,650	289	5,200	----		720.00	
2014[2]	84	850	950		4,600	100	5,500	----		730.00	

[1] Preliminary.   [2] Estimate.   [3] Unit of K_2O, standard 60% muriate F.O.B. mine.   *Source: U.S. Geological Survey (USGS)*

Fish

Fish are the primary source of protein for a large portion of the world's population. The worldwide yearly harvest of all sea fish (including aquaculture) is between 85 and 130 million metric tons. There are approximately 20,000 species of fish, of which 9,000 are regularly caught. Only 22 fish species are harvested in large amounts. Ground-fish, which are fish that live near or on the ocean floor, account for about 10% of the world's fishery harvest, and include cod, haddock, pollock, flounder, halibut and sole. Large pelagic fish such as tuna, swordfish, marlin, and mahi-mahi, account for about 5% of world harvest. The fish eaten most often in the United States is canned tuna.

Rising global demand for fish has increased the pressure to harvest more fish to the point where all 17 of the world's major fishing areas have either reached or exceeded their limits. Atlantic stocks of cod, haddock and blue-fin tuna are all seriously depleted, while in the Pacific, anchovies, salmon and halibut are all over-fished. Aquaculture, or fish farming, reduces pressure on wild stocks and now accounts for nearly 20% of world harvest.

Supply – The U.S. grand total of fishery products in 2012 fell -1.7% to 20.757 billion pounds, below last year's record high. The U.S. total domestic catch in 2012 fell -2.3% to 9.634 billion pounds, and that comprised 46.4% of total U.S. supply. Of the U.S. total domestic catch in 2012, 64.0% of the catch was finfish for human consumption, 22.4% of the catch was a variety of fish for industrial use, and 13.6% was shellfish for human consumption. The principal species of U.S. fishery landings in 2012 were Pollock (with 2.826 billion pounds landed), Menhaden (1.770 billion pounds), Pacific Salmon (635 million pounds), Flounder (707 million pounds), and Sea Herring (276 million pounds).

About 30% of the fish harvested in the world are processed directly into fishmeal and fish oil. Fishmeal is used primarily in animal feed. Fish oil is used in both animal feed and human food products. World fishmeal production in the 2013-14 marketing year rose by +9.5% to 4.727 million metric tons. World production of fish oil in 2013-14 rose +5.2% to 912.000 thousand metric tons. Peru and Chile are by far the world's largest producers of fishmeal and fish oil.

Trade – U.S. imports of fishery products in 2012 fell -1.1% yr/yr to 11.122 billion pounds, below the 2010 record high of 11.517 billion pounds a new record high, comprising 53.6% of total U.S. supply.

					----------------- Domestic Catch -----------------					---------------------- Imports ----------------------			
			For		Percent				For		Percent			For
	Grand	- For Human Food -		Industrial		of Grand	- For Human Food -		Industrial		of Grand	- For Human Food -		Industrial
Year	Total	Finfish	Shellfish[3]	Use[4]	Total	Total	Finfish	Shellfish[3]	Use[4]	Total	Total	Finfish	Shellfish[3]	Use[4]
2007	20,561	13,339	4,914	2,308	9,309	45.3	6,415	1,075	1,819	11,252	54.7	6,925	3,838	489
2008	19,200	12,295	4,742	2,163	8,326	43.4	5,590	1,043	1,692	10,874	56.6	6,705	3,699	471
2009	18,899	11,700	4,936	2,262	8,031	42.5	4,930	1,268	1,833	10,868	57.5	6,771	3,668	430
2010	19,748	12,505	5,055	2,188	8,231	41.7	5,216	1,310	1,705	11,517	58.3	7,288	3,746	483
2011	21,106	13,644	5,088	2,374	9,858	46.7	6,540	1,369	1,949	11,248	53.3	7,104	3,719	425
2012	20,757	13,159	4,907	2,692	9,634	46.4	6,163	1,314	2,157	11,123	53.6	6,996	3,592	535
2013[1]	20,998	13,787	4,795	2,416	9,880	47.1	6,777	1,275	1,827	11,118	52.9	7,009	3,520	589

[1] Preliminary. [2] Live weight, except percent. [3] For univalue and bivalues mollusks (conchs, clams, oysters, scallops, etc.) the weight of meats, excluding the shell is reported. [4] Fish meal and sea herring. *Source: Fisheries Statistics Division, U.S. Department of Commerce*

Fisheries -- Landings of Principal Species in the United States   In Millions of Pounds

	--- Fish ---									-------------------------- Shellfish --------------------------					
	Cod,			Herring,	Man-		Salmon,			Clams		Lobsters	Oysters	Scallops	
Year	Atlantic	Flounder	Halibut	Sea	haden	Pollock	Pacific	Tuna	Whiting	(Meats)	Crabs	American	----- (Meats) -----		Shrimp
2007	17	483	70	233	1,484	3,085	885	51	14	116	294	81	38	59	281
2008	19	663	67	259	1,341	2,298	658	48	14	108	325	82	30	54	257
2009	20	575	60	313	1,568	1,883	705	49	17	101	326	97	36	58	301
2010	18	624	56	253	1,472	1,959	788	48	18	89	350	115	28	58	259
2011	18	707	43	276	1,875	2,827	780	50	17	86	369	126	29	59	313
2012	11	703	34	270	1,771	2,887	636	60	16	91	367	150	33	57	303
2013[1]	5	717	30	298	1,467	3,014	1,069	56	14	91	332	149	45	41	283

[1] Preliminary. *Source: National Marine Fisheries Service, U.S. Department of Commerce*

U.S. Fisheries: Quantity & Value of Domestic Catch & Consumption & World Fish Oil Production

	-------------------------- Disposition --------------------------					For	For			Fish	World[2]
	Fresh &			For Meal,		Human	Industrial	Ex-vessel	Average	Per Capita	Fish Oil
	Frozen	Canned	Cured	Oil, etc.	Total	Food	Products	Value[3]	Price	Consumption	Production
Year	------------------------------- Millions of Pounds -------------------------------							- Million $ -	- Cents /Lb. -	- - Pounds - -	- 1,000 Tons -
2007	7,450	514	121	1,224	9,309	7,490	1,819	4,192	45.0	16.3	1,055
2008	6,538	336	138	1,313	8,325	6,633	1,692	4,383	52.6	16.0	1,075
2009	6,204	392	103	1,332	8,031	6,198	1,833	3,891		16.0	1,040
2010	6,515	373	102	1,241	8,231	6,526	1,705	4,520		15.8	887
2011	7,817	371	52	1,618	9,858	7,909	1,949	5,289			1,068
2012	7,541	299	82	1,712	9,634	7,477	2,157	5,103			921
2013[1]	8,019	365	45	1,451	9,880	8,053	1,827	5,490			902

[1] Preliminary. [2] Crop years on a marketing year basis. [3] At the Dock Prices. Source: Fisheries Statistics Division, U.S. Department of Commerce

FISH

Imports of Seafood Products into the United States In Thousands of Pounds

Year	Trout, fresh and frozen	Atlantic salmon, fresh	Pacific salmon, fresh[2]	Atlantic salmon, frozen	Pacific salmon, frozen[2]	Atlantic salmon, fillets	Salmon, canned and prepared[3]	Tilapia[4]	Shrimp, frozen	Shrimp, fresh and prepared[5]	Oysters[6]	Mussels[6]	Clams[6]	Scallops[6]
2006	10,215	171,848	20,905	5,137	52,161	257,970	27,456	348,707	920,922	385,701	24,599	50,796	34,454	60,792
2007	11,717	178,778	17,577	6,619	52,643	265,078	30,470	383,153	912,953	317,735	24,041	53,091	30,618	56,627
2008	9,137	182,929	12,843	6,219	52,407	250,282	28,468	395,559	943,989	304,907	20,544	54,261	33,143	57,800
2009	12,021	198,260	12,278	7,844	61,750	220,550	32,444	404,132	896,045	321,372	20,503	57,062	37,657	56,262
2010	16,326	203,913	18,956	6,058	80,859	178,871	27,222	474,967	914,925	321,800	23,802	56,921	40,145	51,865
2011	11,082	192,231	19,704	5,694	85,406	201,601	25,167	433,162	948,460	323,579	26,779	63,813	44,832	56,804
2012	19,616	222,313	9,770	4,828	65,491	276,703	27,539	503,644	923,109	253,456	18,566	75,384	45,518	34,021
2013[1]	18,713	190,427	12,153	5,604	71,480	317,975	37,070	504,698	871,693	249,318	19,830	70,916	48,705	60,429

[1] Preliminary.   [2] Includes salmon with no specific species noted.   [3] Includes smoked and cured salmon.   [4] Frozen whole fish plus fresh and frozen fillets.   [5] Canned, breaded or otherwise prepared.   [6] Fresh or prepared.   *Source: Bureau of the Census, U.S. Department of Commerce*

Exports of Seafood Products From the United States In Thousands of Pounds

Year	Trout, fresh and frozen	Atlantic salmon, fresh	Pacific salmon, fresh[2]	Atlantic salmon, frozen	Pacific salmon, frozen[2]	Salmon, canned and prepared[3]	Shrimp, frozen	Shrimp, fresh and prepared[4]	Oysters[5]	Mussels[5]	Clams[5]	Scallops[5]
2006	875	8,759	19,869	106	219,019	137,538	7,544	12,944	6,241	2,525	12,257	29,110
2007	817	7,303	15,778	257	300,386	139,103	8,723	14,153	6,231	1,896	12,470	23,908
2008	1,107	17,705	16,198	247	277,331	138,048	7,902	17,684	7,241	1,855	14,366	24,694
2009	978	14,039	11,661	173	263,564	115,974	7,841	12,842	6,396	1,498	12,907	26,183
2010	667	20,958	18,128	205	316,240	112,952	6,155	11,269	7,658	1,069	12,789	24,615
2011	503	7,537	20,881	667	337,058	137,878	9,980	16,439	10,376	1,141	13,526	32,136
2012	1,779	17,234	20,934	380	222,889	92,838	14,951	9,260	7,781	931	14,056	28,756
2013[1]	2,148	15,574	24,129	223	359,561	101,469	14,764	7,904	7,624	1,043	18,114	21,206

[1] Preliminary.   [2] Includes salmon with no specific species noted.   [3] Includes smoked and cured salmon.   [4] Canned, breaded, or prepared.   [5] Fresh or prepared.   *Source: Bureau of the Census, U.S. Department of Commerce*

World Production of Fish Meal In Thousands of Metric Tons

Year	Chile	Denmark	European Union	Iceland	Japan	Norway	Peru	Russia	South Africa	Spain	Thailand	United States	World Total
2006-07	798.5	164.8	386.3	149.6	204.0	173.1	1,400.1	67.3	88.6	40.9	429.0	258.1	5,185.3
2007-08	740.8	161.9	375.6	140.0	202.0	141.3	1,426.9	70.3	80.7	35.0	421.0	223.9	5,028.8
2008-09	685.9	177.5	389.5	106.3	209.2	119.9	1,442.6	74.9	69.8	33.0	436.0	222.6	4,953.0
2009-10	470.1	182.5	394.6	89.3	200.9	160.6	1,189.6	84.8	84.8	31.2	488.0	201.7	4,737.3
2010-11	564.1	176.2	394.0	96.6	185.7	113.0	1,286.0	82.8	90.0	30.4	503.0	277.4	5,045.9
2011-12[1]	464.5	90.0	307.2	130.3	189.8	86.0	1,413.8	82.2	96.2	30.0	489.0	278.6	5,056.6
2012-13[2]	336.6	140.4	368.2	123.0	206.0	101.0	775.0	84.2	28.4	30.5	462.5	229.1	4,315.7
2013-14[3]	330.0	112.5	338.8	85.0	208.0	97.5	1,250.0	85.0	76.8	30.1	450.0	215.0	4,727.4

[1] Preliminary.   [2] Estimate.   [3] Forecast.   *Source: The Oil World*

World Production of Fish Oil In Thousands of Metric Tons

Year	Canada	Chile	China	Denmark	Iceland	Japan	Norway	Peru	Africa	Russia	United States	World Total	Fish Oil CIF[4] $ Per Tonne
2006-07	5.2	179.7	13.0	52.6	49.6	66.9	41.5	307.9	4.5	3.9	71.4	1,008.2	885
2007-08	5.4	181.5	12.5	63.5	72.1	64.3	42.9	298.6	4.0	4.0	81.7	1,077.0	1,612
2008-09	5.5	178.4	14.0	67.5	71.5	63.6	38.8	302.1	4.2	4.0	80.7	1,061.3	855
2009-10	5.6	107.4	15.4	67.1	44.0	62.0	49.8	238.4	6.4	4.1	54.1	950.0	994
2010-11	5.7	131.6	16.7	61.9	53.1	55.7	49.3	237.9	5.0	4.2	69.1	952.5	1,502
2011-12[1]	6.0	117.5	17.8	35.2	59.9	56.2	36.0	307.4	5.8	4.3	56.5	1,033.5	1,718
2012-13[2]	6.2	91.1	18.7	46.8	57.0	57.2	33.0	137.6	2.2	4.4	75.1	867.0	2,190
2013-14[3]	6.3	98.2	20.0	39.0	46.0	59.0	31.8	200.0	5.0	4.5	65.0	912.0	1,733

[1] Preliminary.   [2] Estimate.   [3] Forecast.   [4] Any origin, N.W. Europe.   *Source: The Oil World*

Monthly Production of Catfish--Round Weight Processed--in the United States In Thousands of Pounds (Live Weight)

Year	Jan.	Feb.	Mar.	Apr.	May	June	July	Aug.	Sept.	Oct.	Nov.	Dec.	Total
2007	46,079	44,083	45,477	37,954	38,867	37,275	39,168	42,626	39,519	45,890	40,307	39,001	496,246
2008	45,992	47,634	47,908	45,018	44,326	43,265	42,583	40,985	39,057	43,344	36,869	32,616	509,597
2009	36,406	37,702	44,912	40,768	39,925	39,370	40,966	39,490	36,408	40,191	36,211	33,751	466,100
2010	40,042	40,977	46,650	37,111	38,244	38,656	39,302	39,231	39,494	40,455	36,683	34,838	471,683
2011	35,076	27,782	30,372	23,605	24,749	24,337	26,595	30,680	30,271	32,446	25,814	22,598	334,325
2012	25,843	26,950	28,098	22,463	25,009	23,938	25,056	24,886	24,535	28,596	22,124	22,653	300,151
2013	29,458	29,959	NA	NA	NA	NA	NA	NA	NA	NA	NA	NA	356,502
2014[1]	NA	NA	NA	NA	NA	NA	NA	NA	NA	NA	NA	NA	NA

[1] Preliminary.   NA = Not available.   *Source: Economic Research Service, U.S. Department of Agriculture ERS-USDA)*

Average Price Paid to Producers for Farm-Raised Catfish in the United States   In Cents Per Pound (Live Weight)

Year	Jan.	Feb.	Mar.	Apr.	May	June	July	Aug.	Sept.	Oct.	Nov.	Dec.	Average
2007	83.7	83.8	83.8	84.1	84.0	81.7	76.2	73.1	69.7	68.2	66.6	65.0	76.7
2008	65.8	68.8	74.3	75.7	77.6	79.4	81.8	82.7	82.7	82.5	82.3	82.1	78.0
2009	81.0	77.0	77.3	76.3	76.2	76.3	77.1	76.9	77.2	76.8	76.5	76.3	77.1
2010	76.4	76.5	78.5	80.4	79.6	78.6	78.8	79.0	81.6	83.2	84.1	86.1	80.2
2011	93.1	100.3	107.5	114.1	116.9	123.1	125.2	127.7	127.5	126.2	125.7	125.1	117.7
2012	124.8	122.9	120.1	116.7	103.8	93.4	84.3	79.8	79.3	80.3	82.2	83.0	97.6
2013	81.9	82.2	NA	NA	NA	NA	NA	NA	NA	NA	NA	NA	82.1
2014[1]	NA	NA	NA	NA	NA	NA	NA	NA	NA	NA	NA	NA	NA

[1] Preliminary.   NA = Not available.   *Source: Economic Research Service, U.S. Department of Agriculture (ERS-USDA)*

Sales of Fresh Catfish in the United States   In Thousands of Pounds

Year	Jan.	Feb.	Mar.	Apr.	May	June	July	Aug.	Sept.	Oct.	Nov.	Dec.	Total
Whole													
2008	3,338	3,585	3,194	2,908	2,868	2,612	2,552	2,605	2,227	2,830	2,302	2,517	33,538
2009	2,537	2,752	3,137	2,733	2,551	2,546	2,582	2,332	2,321	2,830	2,352	2,461	31,134
2010	2,811	3,156	3,743	3,046	2,844	2,730	2,277	2,582	2,518	2,863	2,297	2,434	33,301
2011	2,488	2,046	2,614	2,259	2,061	2,025	1,484	1,701	1,635	2,024	2,021	1,878	24,236
2012	2,219	2,323	2,353	2,004	2,107	2,097	2,206	2,076	2,086	2,546	2,204	2,295	26,516
2013[1]	2,859	2,480	NA	NA	NA	NA	NA	NA	NA	NA	NA	NA	32,034
Fillets[2]													
2008	4,489	4,922	4,823	4,145	4,000	4,761	3,943	3,803	3,503	3,723	3,083	3,075	48,270
2009	3,795	3,732	4,196	3,894	3,864	3,621	3,649	3,554	3,444	3,495	2,989	3,038	43,271
2010	3,607	4,221	3,905	3,495	3,720	3,475	3,411	3,606	3,456	3,343	2,791	3,045	42,075
2011	3,220	2,650	2,880	2,351	2,199	2,105	2,227	2,199	2,047	2,173	1,892	1,877	27,820
2012	2,231	2,349	2,399	2,150	2,234	2,148	2,218	2,474	2,433	2,400	1,913	1,934	26,883
2013[1]	2,372	2,543	NA	NA	NA	NA	NA	NA	NA	NA	NA	NA	29,490
Other[3]													
2008	913	819	755	786	736	704	653	665	642	713	717	568	8,671
2009	709	810	797	684	751	783	646	709	644	685	616	611	8,445
2010	695	735	807	668	713	641	631	650	647	621	516	564	7,888
2011	615	535	556	551	485	461	456	462	444	476	423	420	5,884
2012	473	515	529	475	497	445	459	476	449	479	422	425	5,644
2013[1]	530	566	NA	NA	NA	NA	NA	NA	NA	NA	NA	NA	6,576

[1] Preliminary.   [2] Includes regular, shank and strip fillets; excludes breaded products.   [3] Includes steaks, nuggets and all other products not reported.
NA = Not available.   *Source: Economic Research Service, U.S. Department of Agriculture (ERS-USDA)*

Prices of Fresh Catfish in the United States   In Dollars Per Pound

Year	Jan.	Feb.	Mar.	Apr.	May	June	July	Aug.	Sept.	Oct.	Nov.	Dec.	Average
Whole													
2008	1.49	1.50	1.56	1.59	1.60	1.68	1.68	1.76	1.73	1.71	1.72	1.66	1.64
2009	1.72	1.67	1.65	1.68	1.70	1.64	1.66	1.69	1.66	1.59	1.57	1.57	1.65
2010	1.55	1.49	1.50	1.55	1.55	1.58	1.67	1.58	1.63	1.57	1.61	1.71	1.58
2011	1.90	2.06	2.17	2.28	2.40	2.49	2.64	2.61	2.65	2.54	2.42	2.45	2.38
2012	2.44	2.44	2.42	2.35	2.25	2.12	2.04	1.95	1.89	1.84	1.81	1.78	2.11
2013[1]	1.81	1.83	NA	NA	NA	NA	NA	NA	NA	NA	NA	NA	1.82
Fillets[2]													
2008	2.90	2.88	2.96	3.03	3.10	3.08	3.25	3.33	3.33	3.31	3.30	3.31	3.15
2009	3.30	3.24	3.24	3.23	3.23	3.22	3.21	3.21	3.20	3.19	3.18	3.19	3.22
2010	3.16	3.10	3.18	3.22	3.25	3.26	3.25	3.22	3.24	3.29	3.32	3.32	3.23
2011	3.47	3.75	4.18	4.43	4.55	4.60	4.84	4.77	4.88	4.86	4.84	4.78	4.50
2012	4.73	4.68	4.68	4.57	4.35	4.09	3.87	3.76	3.72	3.74	3.73	3.73	4.14
2013[1]	3.70	3.68	NA	NA	NA	NA	NA	NA	NA	NA	NA	NA	3.69
Other[3]													
2008	1.46	1.51	1.57	1.61	1.65	1.80	1.81	1.77	1.76	1.73	1.68	1.62	1.66
2009	1.64	1.52	1.61	1.75	1.60	1.68	1.64	1.64	1.67	1.64	1.66	1.67	1.64
2010	1.66	1.60	1.65	1.81	1.76	1.71	1.72	1.72	1.69	1.68	1.74	1.75	1.71
2011	1.77	1.95	2.07	2.14	2.24	2.29	2.17	2.26	2.29	2.25	2.23	2.20	2.16
2012	2.15	2.11	2.10	2.14	1.91	1.97	1.87	1.84	1.85	1.85	1.80	1.80	1.95
2013[1]	1.82	1.78	NA	NA	NA	NA	NA	NA	NA	NA	NA	NA	1.80

[1] Preliminary.   [2] Includes regular, shank and strip fillets; excludes breaded products.   [3] Includes steaks, nuggets and all other products not reported.
NA = Not available.   *Source: Economic Research Service, U.S. Department of Agriculture (ERS-USDA)*

Flaxseed and Linseed Oil

Flaxseed, also called linseed, is an ancient crop that was cultivated by the Babylonians around 3,000 BC. Flaxseed is used for fiber in textiles and to produce oil. Flaxseeds contain approximately 35% oil, of which 60% is omega-3 fatty acid. Flaxseed or linseed oil is obtained through either the expeller extraction or solvent extraction method. Manufacturers filter the processed oil to remove some impurities and then sell it as unrefined. Unrefined oil retains its full flavor, aroma, color, and naturally occurring nutrients. Flaxseed oil is used for cooking and as a dietary supplement as well as for animal feed. Industrial linseed oil is not for internal consumption due to possible poisonous additives and is used for making putty, sealants, linoleum, wood preservation, varnishes, and oil paints.

Prices – The average monthly price received by U.S. farmers for flaxseed in the 2014-15 marketing year (through December 2014) fell by -12.1% yr/yr to $12.25 per bushel, below the record high of $14.08 per bushel posted in the 2012-13 marketing year.

Supply – World production of flaxseed in the 2013-14 (latest data available) marketing year rose by +11.3% yr/yr to 2.242 million metric tons, still well below the 9-year high of 2.864 million metric tons in 2005-06. The world's largest producer of flaxseed is the former USSR with 29.1% of world production in 2013-14, followed by Canada (31.8%), China (14.7%), India (6.2%), and the U.S. (3.8%). U.S. production of flaxseed in 2014-15 rose +89.8% to 6.368 million bushels, up from the 2011-12 record low of 2.791 million bushels. North Dakota is by far the largest producing state for flaxseed and accounted for 91.2% of flaxseed production in 2014, followed by South Dakota and Montana both with 1.4% of production.

World production of linseed oil in 2013-14 (latest data available) rose by +2.1% yr/yr to 619.000 million metric tons. The world's largest producers of linseed oil are China (with 26.0% of world production in 2013-14), Belgium (17.3%), the U.S. (14.5%), and Germany (7.8%). U.S. production of linseed oil in 2013-14 fell by -4.7% yr/yr to 205.000 million pounds.

Demand – U.S. distribution of flaxseed in 2013-14 fell by -7.8% yr/yr to 11.841 million bushels. The breakdown was 88.7% for crushing into meal and oil, 3.8% for residual, 5.5% for exports and 2.0% for seed.

Trade – U.S. exports of flaxseed in 2013-14 fell by -36.3% yr/yr to 650,000 thousand bushels. U.S. imports of flaxseed in 2013-14 rose by +22.6% yr/yr to 8.500 million bushels.

World Production of Flaxseed   In Thousands of Metric Tons

Crop Year	Argentina	Australia	Bangladesh	Canada	China	Egypt	France	Hungary	India	Romania	United States	Former USSR	World Total
2004-05	36	10	3	592	460	31	13	2	200	3	263	98	2,008
2005-06	54	10	3	1,150	475	28	25	3	210	----	480	105	2,870
2006-07	38	7	9	1,040	480	27	43	2	200	----	280	157	2,551
2007-08	13	8	8	660	480	12	34	2	190	----	150	135	1,942
2008-09	19	8	8	861	475	12	15	1	150	----	145	145	2,098
2009-10	52	8	7	930	318	8	21	1	169	1	189	206	2,181
2010-11	32	7	7	419	340	12	36	1	146	1	230	336	1,819
2011-12[1]	21	7	7	399	359	5	31	1	152	3	71	802	2,136
2012-13[2]	17	7	6	489	350	5	26	----	149	4	146	571	2,014
2013-14[3]	20	7	7	712	330	7	17	1	140	6	85	653	2,242

[1] Preliminary.   [2] Estimate.   [3] Forecast.   *Source: The Oil World*

Supply and Distribution of Flaxseed in the United States   In Thousands of Bushels

Crop Year Beginning June 1	Planted	Harvested	Yield Per Acre (Bushels)	Beginning Stocks	Production	Imports	Total Supply	Seed	Crush	Exports	Residual	Total
	---- 1,000 Acres ----			-------- Supply --------				-------- Distribution --------				
2005-06	983	955	20.6	863	19,695	4,256	24,814	659	16,400	3,780	440	21,279
2006-07	813	767	14.4	3,535	11,019	5,464	20,018	287	14,900	1,788	599	17,574
2007-08	354	349	16.9	2,444	5,896	8,019	16,359	287	11,700	2,221	640	14,847
2008-09	354	340	16.8	1,512	5,716	4,794	12,022	257	8,150	432	631	9,470
2009-10	317	314	23.6	2,552	7,423	6,283	16,258	341	12,000	1,752	608	14,701
2010-11	421	418	21.7	1,557	9,056	6,040	16,653	144	11,635	2,130	573	14,483
2011-12	178	173	16.1	2,170	2,791	8,286	13,247	279	10,500	654	694	12,127
2012-13[1]	349	336	17.3	1,120	5,798	6,932	13,761	181	11,000	1,020	637	12,837
2013-14[2]	181	172	19.5	924	3,356	8,500	12,780	243	10,500	650	448	11,841
2014-15[3]	311	302	21.1		6,368							

[1] Preliminary.   [2] Estimate.   [3] Forecast.   NA = not avaliable.   *Source: Economic Research Service, U.S. Department of Agriculture (ERS-USDA)*

Supply and Distribution of Linseed Meal in the United States   In Millions of Pounds

Crop Year Beginning June 1	Stocks June 1	Production	Imports	Total Supply	Domestic Disappear-ance	Exports	Total Disappearance	Ending Stocks	Average Price at Minneapolis (34% Protein) Cents/Lb.
2004-05	5	245	23	273	206	62	268	5	114.24
2005-06	5	295	18	318	269	44	313	5	124.69
2006-07	5	268	17	290	275	10	285	5	124.61
2007-08	5	211	9	225	210	10	220	5	191.54
2008-09	5	147	10	162	130	28	157	5	227.66
2009-10	5	216	3	224	210	10	219	5	217.24
2010-11	5	209	7	221	208	7	216	5	223.23
2011-12	5	189	8	202	194	3	197	5	238.35
2012-13[1]	5	198	6	209	199	5	204	5	320.13
2013-14[2]	5	189	2	196	186	5	191	5	335-375

[1] Preliminary.   [2] Forecast.   *Source: Economic Research Service, U.S. Department of Agriculture (ERS-USDA)*

Supply and Distribution of Linseed Oil in the United States   In Millions of Pounds

Crop Year Beginning June 1	Stocks June 1	Production	Total Supply	Exports	Domestic Disappearance	Total Disappearance	Average Price at Minneapolis Cents/Lb.
2004-05	20	265	301	107	149	256	59.5
2005-06	45	320	375	98	248	346	54.0
2006-07	29	291	328	76	202	278	44.4
2007-08	51	228	291	74	191	265	70.3
2008-09	26	159	191	66	52	118	86.5
2009-10	73	234	312	103	172	275	67.5
2010-11	37	227	270	102	130	232	68.0
2011-12	38	205	248	89	124	213	68.0
2012-13[1]	35	215	255	94	126	220	66.5-69.5
2013-14[2]	35	205	245	75	135	210	

[1] Preliminary.   [2] Forecast.   *Source: Economic Research Service, U.S. Department of Agriculture (ERS-USDA)*

World Production and Price of Linseed Oil   In Thousands of Metric Tons

Year	Argen-tina	Bang-ladesh	Belgium	China	Egypt	Germany	India	Japan	United Kingdom	United States	Former USSR	World Total	Rotterdam Ex-TankUSD $/Tonne
2004-05	6.9	0.6	97.9	127.0	12.0	37.9	62.7	6.8	3.5	135.5	16.3	625.7	1,191
2005-06	13.1	2.6	97.9	137.6	14.8	65.2	63.7	5.7	3.5	147.7	16.2	695.0	686
2006-07	5.0	4.3	118.9	146.6	11.2	59.3	52.0	6.2	5.3	140.3	15.8	693.9	809
2007-08	2.8	2.8	114.6	87.3	8.5	53.6	48.2	4.6	2.8	98.1	18.1	574.5	1,635
2008-09	2.1	2.3	77.4	121.3	6.4	37.7	47.9	2.6	3.2	84.8	14.2	524.3	975
2009-10	1.7	2.1	96.9	157.7	5.2	34.5	45.2	2.0	2.6	115.7	22.0	598.8	1,114
2010-11	1.9	2.0	107.2	120.4	4.3	40.9	41.4	1.6	5.9	108.0	27.0	560.9	1,451
2011-12	1.1	2.3	108.8	135.5	4.3	49.5	41.1	1.6	5.6	105.5	30.8	631.8	1,267
2012-13[1]	1.6	2.0	107.2	143.0	2.9	44.8	38.6	1.7	4.9	99.2	28.0	606.3	1,217
2013-14[2]	----	----	107.2	161.0	3.6	48.0	37.2	2.3	5.6	89.7	28.0	619.0	1,183

[1] Preliminary.   [2] Forecast.   *Source: The Oil World*

Production of Flaxseed in the United States, by States   In Thousands of Bushels

Year	Minnesota	North Dakota	South Dakota	Montana	Total
2005	132	18,165	480	918	19,695
2006	126	10,368	228	297	11,019
2007	72	5,548	96	180	5,896
2008	69	5,491	84	72	5,716
2009	63	7,032	168	160	7,423
2010	56	8,536	209	255	9,056
2011	45	2,426	112	208	2,791
2012	45	5,478	119	119	5,798
2013	76	2,920	120	120	3,356
2014[1]	48	5,805	90	90	6,368

[1] Preliminary.   *Source: National Agricultural Statistics Service, U.S. Department of Agriculture (NASS-USDA)*

FLAXSEED AND LINSEED OIL

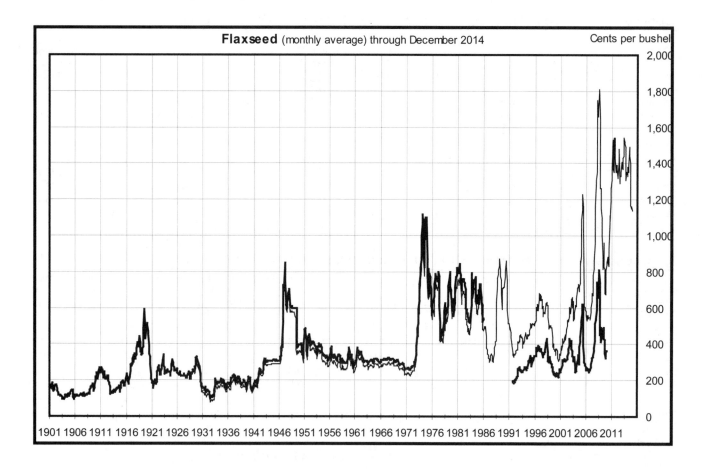

Flaxseed (monthly average) through December 2014 — Cents per bushel

Average Price Received by Farmers for Flaxseed in the United States   In Dollars Per Bushel

Year	July	Aug.	Sept.	Oct.	Nov.	Dec.	Jan.	Feb.	Mar.	Apr.	May	June	Average
2005-06	10.40	6.28	6.10	6.05	5.94	5.81	5.64	5.59	5.31	5.56	5.59	5.40	6.14
2006-07	5.47	5.50	5.46	5.41	5.38	5.73	6.03	6.39	6.79	6.72	7.08	7.81	6.15
2007-08	8.14	8.64	9.55	11.60	12.90	13.10	13.50	16.00	17.50	16.60	16.90	18.00	13.54
2008-09	18.10	16.50	15.60	12.60	12.60	11.50	11.00	9.98	8.84	8.13	8.96	9.59	11.95
2009-10	8.28	8.14	6.79	6.78	8.12	8.40	8.53	8.57	8.82	8.53	8.34	9.26	8.21
2010-11	10.70	11.10	10.80	11.90	12.60	13.10	13.80	15.30	13.70	13.50	14.20	15.40	13.01
2011-12	15.40	14.30	13.50	13.90	13.90	13.50	13.70	13.20	13.30	14.10	14.80	12.90	13.88
2012-13	13.30	13.30	13.30	13.50	14.10	13.80	13.70	14.30	14.40	14.90	15.40	15.20	14.10
2013-14	15.10	14.90	13.10	13.50	13.40	13.40	13.30	13.80	13.50	13.90	14.90	14.40	13.93
2014-15[1]	14.00	13.30	11.70	11.50	11.60	11.40	11.70						12.17

[1] Preliminary.   *Source: National Agricultural Statistics Service, U.S. Department of Agriculture (NASS-USDA)*

Average Price of Linseed Meal (34% protein) at Minneapolis   In Dollars Per Ton

Year	July	Aug.	Sept.	Oct.	Nov.	Dec.	Jan.	Feb.	Mar.	Apr.	May	June	Average
2005-06	159.40	157.80	99.00	100.40	113.60	118.00	127.30	130.20	129.00	126.60	119.10	116.90	124.78
2006-07	111.50	101.10	92.80	100.80	118.10	123.30	134.20	156.40	156.30	149.00	135.10	132.00	125.88
2007-08	135.80	123.90	131.40	170.20	184.60	186.80	242.70	250.00	247.10	253.70	240.30	265.40	202.66
2008-09	273.70	231.30	200.00	160.80	164.00	189.60	248.80	270.00	231.90	233.50	263.10	250.00	226.39
2009-10	226.90	217.00	195.20	185.00	220.00	256.50	228.75	222.50	201.50	200.83	202.75	189.50	212.20
2010-11	199.38	204.00	200.00	208.75	237.50	234.38	255.00	256.25	236.50	225.63	231.88	254.38	228.64
2011-12	260.63	247.50	239.38	243.75	239.00	221.25	209.00	193.75	216.25	256.25	279.00	287.50	241.11
2012-13	343.00	358.75	340.63	334.00	297.50	335.83	296.00	303.75	303.75	309.00	331.88	340.00	324.51
2013-14	382.50	317.50	400.00	363.75	316.25	328.75	330.00	377.50	413.75	388.00	355.00	323.75	358.06
2014-15[1]	295.00	252.50	302.50	214.38	283.75	287.50	250.00						269.38

[1] Preliminary.   *Source: Economic Research Service, U.S. Department of Agriculture (ERS-USDA)*

Fruits

A fruit is any seed-bearing structure produced from a flowering plant. A widely used classification system divides fruit into fleshy or dry types. Fleshy fruits are juicy and include peaches, mangos, apples, and blueberries. Dry fruits include tree nuts such as almonds, walnuts, and pecans. Some foods that are commonly called vegetables, such as tomatoes, squash, peppers and eggplant, are technically fruits because they develop from the ovary of a flower.

Worldwide, over 430 million tons of fruit are produced each year and are grown everywhere except the Arctic and the Antarctic. The tropics, because of their abundant moisture and warm temperatures, produce the most diverse and abundant fruits. Mexico and Chile produce more than half of all the fresh and frozen fruit imported into the U.S. In the U.S., the top three fruits produced are oranges, grapes, and apples. Virtually all U.S. production of almonds, pistachios, and walnuts occurs in California, which leads the U.S. in tree nut production.

Prices – Overall fruit prices were fairly strong in 2013 (latest data available) with the fresh fruit Consumer Price Index (CPI) rising +2.0% to 343.2 and the processed fruit CPI index rising +1.2% to 153.8. Individual fruit prices, however, were mixed in 2012: Red Delicious Apples (+0.7% to $1.386 per pound), bananas (-0.4% to 60.0 cents per pound), Anjou pears (-11.1% to $1.253 per pound),

Thompson seedless grapes (+2.2% to $2.490 per pound), lemons (+1.1% to $1.582 per pound), grapefruit (-2.8% to $1.048 per pound), navel oranges (+9.3% to $1.151 cents per pound), and Valencia oranges (+2.3% to $1.032 per pound).

Supply – U.S. commercial production of selected fruits in 2013 rose +4.3% to 30.038 million short tons. By weight, grapes accounted for 28.7% of that U.S. fruit production figure, followed by oranges at 27.5%, and apples at 17.4%. The value of U.S. fruit production in 2013 rose +3.3% yr/yr to $28.496 billion.

Demand – U.S. per capita fresh fruit consumption in 2013 rose +2.1% to 110.47 pounds per year, a new record high. The highest per capita consumption categories for non-citrus fruits in 2013 were bananas (28.09 pounds) and apples (17.31 pounds).

Per capital consumption of citrus fruits were oranges (10.46 pounds), tangerines & tangelos (3.96 pounds), lemons (3.48 pounds), and grapefruit (2.80 pounds). The utilization breakdown for 2013 shows that total U.S. non-citrus fruit was used for fresh fruit (39.9%), wine (26.1%), dried fruit (11.9%), canned fruit (6.9%), juice (6.9%), and frozen fruit (4.1%). The value of utilized non-citrus fruit production in 2013 rose +3.7%yr/yr to $16.111 billion.

Commercial Production for Selected Fruits in the United States   In Thousands of Short Tons

Year	Apples	Cherries[2]	Cran-berries	Grapes	Grape-fruit	Lemons	Nect-arines	Oranges	Peach-es	Pears	Pine-apple[3]	Prunes & Plums	Straw-berries	Tang-elos	Tang-erines	Total All Fruits
2007	4,545	437	328	7,057	1,627	798	283	7,625	1,127	873	W	405	1,223	56	361	27,145
2008	4,817	355	393	7,319	1,548	619	303	10,076	1,135	870	W	544	1,266	68	527	30,150
2009	4,853	623	346	7,307	1,304	912	220	9,128	1,104	957	W	627	1,401	52	443	29,761
2010	4,646	408	340	7,471	1,238	882	233	8,243	1,150	814	----	543	1,426	41	596	28,400
2011	4,713	450	386	7,448	1,264	920	225	8,905	1,072	966	----	617	1,451	52	657	29,587
2012	4,491	467	402	7,527	1,153	850	189	8,982	977	851	----	564	1,506	52	644	28,815
2013[1]	5,221	479	448	8,606	1,204	912	162	8,269	902	877	----	373	1,500	45	984	30,039

[1] Preliminary.   [2] Sweet and tart.   [3] Utilized production.   *Source: Economic Research Service, U.S. Department of Agriculture (ERS-USDA)*

Utilized Production for Selected Fruits in the United States   In Thousands of Short Tons

Year	Citrus[2]	Utilized Production — Noncitrus	Tree nuts[3]	Total	Citrus[2]	Value of Production — Noncitrus	Tree nuts[3]	Total
	In Thousands of Short Tons				In Thousands of Dollars			
2007	10,467	17,048	2,000	29,515	3,147,755	11,436,449	4,273,279	18,857,483
2008	12,838	17,603	2,144	32,585	3,240,263	11,270,860	3,828,207	18,339,330
2009	11,839	18,069	2,014	31,923	2,741,963	11,811,298	4,172,838	18,726,099
2010	11,000	17,879	2,374	31,253	2,965,231	12,367,607	5,862,688	21,195,526
2011	11,798	18,147	2,584	32,529	3,240,896	13,910,375	7,007,694	24,158,965
2012	11,681	17,622	2,636	31,939	3,712,817	15,529,828	8,337,826	27,580,471
2013[1]	11,114	19,383	2,659	33,156	3,170,508	16,111,277	9,214,560	28,496,345

[1] Preliminary.   [2] Year harvest was completed.   [3] Tree nuts on an in-shell equivalent.
Source: Economic Research Service, U.S. Department of Agriculture (ERS-USDA)

Annual Average Retail Prices for Selected Fruits in the United States   In Dollars Per Pound

Year	Red Delicious Apples	Bananas	Anjou Pears	Thompson Seedless Grapes	Lemons	Grapefruit	Oranges — Navel	Valencias
2007	1.115	.510	1.273	2.172	1.857	.964	1.284	1.074
2008	1.319	.609	1.331	2.154	2.006	.966	1.116	1.016
2009	1.182	.611	1.305	2.161	1.520	.903	1.050	.956
2010	1.220	.580	1.287	2.145	1.634	.927	1.062	1.017
2011	1.350	.610	1.409	2.283	1.581	.976	1.096	1.009
2012	1.377	.602	1.253	2.437	1.565	1.078	1.053	----
2013[1]	1.386	.600	----	2.490	1.582	1.048	1.151	1.032

[1] Estimate.   *Source: Economic Research Service, U.S. Department of Agriculture (ERS-USDA)*

FRUITS

Utilization of Noncitrus Fruit Production, and Value in the United States   1,000 Short Tons (Fresh Equivalent)

Year	Utilized Production	Fresh	Canned	Dried	Juice	Frozen	Wine	Other Processed	Value of Utilized Production $1,000
2004	16,823	7,168	1,710	1,425	1,418	685	3,819	290	8,553,060
2005	18,272	7,188	1,575	2,101	1,555	712	4,551	277	9,805,757
2006	16,816	6,930	1,400	2,219	1,256	710	3,726	235	10,510,417
2007	17,048	7,013	1,453	2,030	1,277	748	3,921	278	11,436,449
2008	17,603	7,248	1,406	2,413	1,228	682	3,944	290	11,270,860
2009	18,069	7,562	1,394	2,148	1,235	742	4,373	269	11,811,298
2010	17,879	7,458	1,386	2,318	1,103	706	4,270	298	12,367,607
2011	18,147	7,702	1,301	2,399	1,153	737	4,154	316	13,910,375
2012	17,622	7,303	1,101	2,094	978	641	4,704	285	15,529,828
2013[1]	19,383	7,732	1,345	2,297	1,338	789	5,066	372	16,111,277

[1] Preliminary.   *Source: Economic Research Service, U.S. Department of Agriculture (ERS-USDA)*

Average Price Indexes for Fruits in the United States

Year	Index of all Fruit & Nut Prices Received by Growers (1990-92=100)	Fresh Fruit	Dried Fruit	Canned Fruits and Juices	Frozen Fruits and Juices	Fresh Fruit	Processed Fruit
		Producer Price Index — 1982 = 100				*Consumer Price Index — 1982-84 = 100*	
2004	124	104.9	NA	143.1	113.3	286.8	114.0
2005	128	102.8	NA	148.1	112.4	297.4	118.4
2006	154	111.0	----	153.0	119.7	315.2	121.5
2007	158	123.4	----	168.3	138.5	329.5	128.0
2008	149	122.9	----	179.0	146.7	345.4	141.1
2009	140	110.4	----	186.9	150.5	324.4	141.9
2010	148	123.8	----	187.3	148.7	322.3	138.2
2011	169	117.7	----	195.4	160.0	333.1	149.6
2012	189	119.0	----	203.8	168.9	336.6	152.0
2013[1]	----	121.2	----	206.4	170.3	343.2	153.8

[1] Estimate.   NA = Not availavle.   *Source: Economic Research Service, U.S. Department of Agriculture (ERS-USDA)*

Fresh Fruit: Per Capita Consumption[1] in the United States   In Pounds

Year	Oranges	Tangerines & Tangelos	Lemons	Grapefruit	Total	Apples	Apricots	Avocados	Bananas	Cherries	Cran-berries
	Cutrus Fruit					*Noncitrus Fruit*					
2004	10.80	2.77	3.12	4.14	22.68	18.79	.12	3.17	25.78	.99	.11
2005	11.42	2.50	2.95	2.65	21.60	16.66	.13	3.46	25.18	.87	.09
2006	10.25	2.69	4.15	2.31	21.64	17.73	.08	3.50	25.11	1.06	.09
2007	7.46	2.56	2.81	2.84	17.93	16.39	.16	3.50	25.95	1.22	.10
2008	9.93	3.08	1.97	3.16	20.61	15.90	.13	3.83	25.04	1.00	.10
2009	9.06	3.16	3.12	2.80	20.68	16.25	.14	4.25	22.01	1.56	.09
2010	9.68	3.77	2.79	2.76	21.58	15.32	.12	4.00	25.61	1.31	.06
2011	9.97	3.97	3.46	2.71	22.62	15.42	.12	5.10	25.54	1.30	.06
2012	10.54	3.99	3.94	2.37	23.42	16.00	.10	5.61	26.99	1.50	.07
2013[2]	10.46	3.96	3.48	2.80	23.66	17.31	.11	5.54	28.09	.98	.08

[1] All data on calendar-year basis except for citrus fruits; apples, August; grapes and pears, July; grapefruit, September; lemons, August of prior year; all other citrus, November.   [2] Preliminary.   *Source: Economic Research Service, U.S. Department of Agriculture (ERS-USDA)*

Fresh Fruit: Per Capita Consumption[1] in the United States   In Pounds

Year	Grapes	Kiwifruit	Mangos	& Peaches	Pears	Pineapples	Papaya	Prunes	Straw-berries	Total Noncitrus	Total Fruit
	Noncitrus Fruit Continued										
2004	7.80	.41	2.02	5.15	2.96	4.43	1.03	1.12	5.47	79.88	102.56
2005	8.60	.45	1.88	4.83	2.91	4.90	.94	1.11	5.83	78.27	99.88
2006	7.59	.47	2.10	4.58	3.19	5.20	1.04	1.02	6.14	79.46	101.11
2007	8.01	.44	2.10	4.46	3.09	5.02	1.08	1.01	6.26	79.37	97.31
2008	8.52	.46	2.10	5.08	3.11	5.07	.98	.92	6.45	79.52	100.13
2009	7.92	.50	2.02	4.41	3.19	5.09	1.20	.73	7.17	77.48	98.16
2010	8.18	.50	2.24	4.73	2.91	5.70	1.17	.78	7.23	80.96	102.54
2011	7.61	.58	2.53	4.47	3.21	5.72	1.05	.87	7.36	82.24	104.86
2012	7.58	.55	2.49	3.91	2.76	6.42	.97	.63	7.84	84.76	108.18
2013[2]	7.77	.48	2.87	3.08	2.84	6.74	1.12	.57	7.86	86.80	110.47

[1] All data on calendar-year basis except for citrus fruits; apples, August; grapes and pears, July; grapefruit, September; lemons, August of prior year; all other citrus, November.   [2] Preliminary.   *Source: Economic Research Service, U.S. Department of Agriculture (ERS-USDA)*

Average Price Received by Growers for Grapefruit in the United States   In Dollars Per Box

Year	Jan.	Feb.	Mar.	Apr.	May	June	July	Aug.	Sept.	Oct.	Nov.	Dec.	Average
2005	14.40	12.52	10.58	10.69	12.28	18.06	16.62	13.50	16.77	10.69	8.83	10.02	12.91
2006	11.06	9.92	8.18	8.12	11.41	10.98	11.16	9.42	11.38	11.17	8.34	7.98	9.93
2007	5.66	4.02	2.91	2.10	4.49	9.89	8.95	7.53	8.55	10.06	9.93	5.97	6.67
2008	4.67	3.30	2.70	2.89	4.94	6.61	5.59	4.58	5.50	10.64	5.49	4.52	5.12
2009	4.19	3.74	3.61	2.99	6.21	8.23	7.15	6.15	6.55	16.41	10.78	8.82	7.07
2010	8.86	7.10	5.93	4.19	4.05	5.40	1.30	0.50	4.70	7.62	12.06	8.06	5.81
2011	6.94	6.31	5.69	5.27	7.55	9.50	8.20	7.10	9.50	8.67	7.90	7.18	7.48
2012	6.83	6.79	6.91	10.20	9.62	15.43	13.23	10.33	10.13	12.49	7.68	6.87	9.71
2013	7.19	5.71	4.29	4.33	8.26	8.76	6.66	6.36	8.76	7.96	8.54	7.51	7.03
2014[1]	7.30	5.60	5.16	4.79	7.89	7.69	7.19	5.99	8.59	14.27	9.13	6.96	7.55

On-tree equivalent.   [1]Preliminary.   *Source: National Agricultural Statistics Service, U.S. Department of Agriculture (NASS-USDA)*

Average Price Received by Growers for Lemons in the United States   In Dollars Per Box

Year	Jan.	Feb.	Mar.	Apr.	May	June	July	Aug.	Sept.	Oct.	Nov.	Dec.	Average
2005	7.63	7.77	9.19	12.18	5.46	20.08	12.32	11.75	10.88	9.32	8.14	5.58	10.03
2006	3.78	9.42	9.44	13.50	15.09	16.98	18.88	21.19	27.80	28.83	20.71	12.98	16.55
2007	11.50	27.69	8.68	9.18	8.14	13.04	13.64	31.67	33.08	37.98	29.80	23.89	20.69
2008	23.90	29.41	23.67	22.13	20.54	27.04	24.17	24.64	21.33	11.08	10.40	7.86	20.51
2009	5.90	2.62	1.80	4.26	5.68	11.34	12.21	20.79	17.60	15.59	14.60	11.81	10.35
2010	9.88	8.48	8.68	10.06	9.13	11.24	12.59	16.60	19.72	19.92	18.51	9.51	12.86
2011	8.84	3.91	5.70	8.54	10.26	12.32	16.16	21.99	17.98	12.87	14.10	14.29	12.25
2012	12.97	11.38	12.51	15.55	17.19	16.10	17.29	11.89	14.94	16.38	13.96	11.60	14.31
2013	10.65	7.28	7.08	9.18	14.77	16.35	18.98	28.45	27.85	32.77	26.65	23.52	18.63
2014[1]	21.17	20.96	24.22	25.87	26.36	30.80	37.58	39.16	36.72	41.41	33.57	21.68	29.96

On-tree equivalent.   [1]Preliminary.   *Source: National Agricultural Statistics Service, U.S. Department of Agriculture (NASS-USDA)*

Average Price Received by Growers for Tangelos in the United States   In Dollars Per Box

Year	Jan.	Feb.	Mar.	Apr.	May	June	July	Aug.	Sept.	Oct.	Nov.	Dec.	Average
2005	1.99	1.51	NQ	NQ	NQ	NQ	NQ	NQ	NQ	NQ	3.93	7.66	3.77
2006	4.81	2.70	1.00	NQ	NQ	NQ	NQ	NQ	NQ	NQ	6.69	8.19	4.68
2007	8.52	9.01	NQ	NQ	NQ	NQ	NQ	NQ	NQ	NQ	5.08	2.78	6.35
2008	2.18	1.87	NQ	NQ	NQ	NQ	NQ	NQ	NQ	NQ	4.71	2.92	2.92
2009	1.28	-0.40	NQ	NQ	NQ	NQ	NQ	NQ	NQ	NQ	6.68	4.49	3.01
2010	3.83	4.00	NQ	NQ	NQ	NQ	NQ	NQ	NQ	NQ	NQ	5.56	4.46
2011	5.70	5.75	NQ	NQ	NQ	NQ	NQ	NQ	NQ	NQ	6.53	6.63	6.15
2012	13.79	10.67	NQ	NQ	NQ	NQ	NQ	NQ	NQ	NQ	7.44	12.89	11.20
2013	9.02	NQ	NQ	NQ	NQ	NQ	NQ	NQ	NQ	NQ	10.34	8.74	9.37
2014[1]	7.85	NQ	NQ	NQ	NQ	NQ	NQ	NQ	NQ	NQ	NQ	9.33	8.59

On-tree equivalent.   [1]Preliminary.   NQ = No quote.   *Source: National Agricultural Statistics Service, U.S. Department of Agriculture (NASS-USDA)*

Average Price Received by Growers for Tangerines in the United States   In Dollars Per Box

Year	Jan.	Feb.	Mar.	Apr.	May	June	July	Aug.	Sept.	Oct.	Nov.	Dec.	Average
2005	14.21	13.50	13.57	16.86	16.21	NQ	NQ	NQ	NQ	14.55	13.66	12.69	14.41
2006	10.39	10.21	7.96	6.52	5.88	NQ	NQ	NQ	12.62	10.39	16.25	14.81	10.56
2007	14.05	14.19	12.98	14.68	17.01	NQ	NQ	NQ	NQ	12.75	20.06	18.63	15.54
2008	12.19	13.72	11.70	7.95	4.13	NQ	NQ	NQ	NQ	14.16	17.47	12.31	11.70
2009	13.71	18.37	14.38	14.91	NQ	NQ	NQ	NQ	NQ	9.87	18.61	19.56	15.63
2010	15.25	8.12	12.07	15.91	NQ	NQ	NQ	NQ	NQ	10.38	27.06	21.53	15.76
2011	16.93	14.68	13.23	13.53	NQ	NQ	NQ	NQ	NQ	8.35	15.74	20.11	14.65
2012	14.73	18.68	24.11	NQ	NQ	NQ	NQ	NQ	NQ	12.70	18.60	21.86	18.45
2013	19.94	20.57	25.04	NQ	NQ	NQ	NQ	NQ	NQ	NQ	NQ	24.41	22.49
2014[1]	22.15	26.32	25.75	NQ	NQ	NQ	NQ	NQ	NQ	28.45	28.52	24.61	25.97

On-tree equivalent.   [1]Preliminary.   NQ = No quote.   *Source: National Agricultural Statistics Service, U.S. Department of Agriculture (NASS-USDA)*

FRUITS

Average Price Received by Growers for Grapes in the United States In Dollars Per Box

Year	Jan.	Feb.	Mar.	Apr.	May	June	July	Aug.	Sept.	Oct.	Nov.	Dec.	Average
2005	NQ	NQ	NQ	NQ	1,270	980	530	530	620	610	490	390	678
2006	NQ	NQ	NQ	NQ	NQ	2,400	1,030	880	910	830	930	1,320	1,186
2007	NQ	NQ	NQ	NQ	NQ	770	660	680	790	940	1,200	1,710	964
2008	NQ	NQ	NQ	NQ	420	590	660	530	480	370	360	300	464
2009	NQ	NQ	NQ	NQ	1,380	1,120	610	310	470	630	630	1,220	796
2010	NQ	NQ	NQ	NQ	NQ	650	460	430	420	430	500	750	520
2011	NQ	NQ	NQ	NQ	NQ	1,080	1,480	960	820	790	980	1,040	1,021
2012	NQ	NQ	NQ	NQ	NQ	1,410	1,030	980	1,130	1,540	1,770	1,780	1,377
2013	NQ	NQ	NQ	NQ	NQ	NQ	NQ	NQ	NQ	NQ	NQ	NQ	NQ
2014[1]	NQ	NQ	NQ	NQ	NQ	1,910	1,860	1,530	1,400	1,610	1,630	1,650	1,656

Fresh. [1]Preliminary. NQ = No quote. *Source: National Agricultural Statistics Service, U.S. Department of Agriculture (NASS-USDA)*

Average Price Received by Growers for Peaches in the United States In Dollars Per Box

Year	Jan.	Feb.	Mar.	Apr.	May	June	July	Aug.	Sept.	Oct.	Nov.	Dec.	Average
2005	NQ	NQ	NQ	NQ	756	596	576	743	622	NQ	NQ	NQ	659
2006	NQ	NQ	NQ	NQ	NQ	809	721	746	589	NQ	NQ	NQ	716
2007	NQ	NQ	NQ	NQ	937	562	579	593	563	NQ	NQ	NQ	647
2008	NQ	NQ	NQ	NQ	960	537	485	510	468	NQ	NQ	NQ	592
2009	NQ	NQ	NQ	NQ	846	794	644	676	655	NQ	NQ	NQ	723
2010	NQ	NQ	NQ	NQ	1,080	587	573	568	506	NQ	NQ	NQ	663
2011	NQ	NQ	NQ	NQ	1,290	705	666	704	564	NQ	NQ	NQ	786
2012	NQ	NQ	NQ	NQ	1,100	836	780	737	689	NQ	NQ	NQ	828
2013	NQ	NQ	NQ	NQ	NQ	NQ	NQ	NQ	NQ	NQ	NQ	NQ	NQ
2014[1]	NQ	NQ	NQ	NQ	NQ	1,220	1,130	1,020	858	NQ	NQ	NQ	1,057

Fresh. [1]Preliminary. NQ = No quote. *Source: National Agricultural Statistics Service, U.S. Department of Agriculture (NASS-USDA)*

Average Price Received by Growers for Pears in the United States In Dollars Per Box

Year	Jan.	Feb.	Mar.	Apr.	May	June	July	Aug.	Sept.	Oct.	Nov.	Dec.	Average
2005	455	475	474	479	498	NQ	667	583	540	440	458	443	501
2006	404	392	339	356	419	596	759	286	283	568	570	563	461
2007	541	517	544	597	651	714	584	374	380	526	514	557	542
2008	560	552	537	527	525	654	638	546	543	628	582	574	572
2009	539	473	452	462	518	642	537	424	383	481	449	398	480
2010	381	368	350	426	533	640	598	496	485	622	548	587	503
2011	639	636	625	599	571	565	561	576	490	533	512	474	565
2012	428	386	301	286	353	594	673	583	601	692	686	713	525
2013	774	778	753	NQ	NQ	NQ	NQ	NQ	NQ	NQ	NQ	NQ	768
2014[1]	NQ	NQ	NQ	592	686	893	800	704	706	698	684	705	719

Fresh. [1]Preliminary. *Source: National Agricultural Statistics Service, U.S. Department of Agriculture (NASS-USDA)*

Average Price Received by Growers for Strawberries in the United States In Dollars Per Box

Year	Jan.	Feb.	Mar.	Apr.	May	June	July	Aug.	Sept.	Oct.	Nov.	Dec.	Average
2005	139.00	112.00	60.90	44.70	54.90	56.40	50.60	65.40	84.30	85.00	102.00	85.00	78.35
2006	142.00	99.90	68.80	61.10	61.80	51.40	64.00	63.70	77.60	72.90	96.10	189.00	87.36
2007	131.00	147.00	88.90	64.90	68.60	66.10	53.00	79.30	57.40	80.00	116.00	171.00	93.60
2008	194.00	131.00	95.30	65.50	83.30	61.90	65.90	91.00	70.10	72.00	87.60	208.00	102.13
2009	116.00	128.00	91.10	78.90	76.10	62.80	74.80	73.50	75.00	108.00	87.60	210.00	98.48
2010	218.00	179.00	116.00	75.70	78.90	67.70	62.00	81.70	73.30	87.60	139.00	285.00	121.99
2011	217.00	126.00	99.20	93.50	80.80	72.70	89.20	78.80	87.60	66.90	84.40	153.00	104.09
2012	137.00	113.00	103.00	94.40	82.70	74.40	74.00	85.00	87.60	90.10	139.00	222.00	108.52
2013	109.00	123.00	117.00	NA	NA	NA	NA	NA	NA	NA	NA	NA	116.33
2014[1]	NA	NA	NA	87.60	96.10	91.80	89.30	92.70	133.00	112.00	152.00	209.00	118.17

Fresh. [1]Preliminary. *Source: National Agricultural Statistics Service, U.S. Department of Agriculture (NASS-USDA)*

Cold Storage Stocks of Frozen Blackberries[2] in the United States, on First of Month   In Thousands of Pounds

Year	Jan.	Feb.	Mar.	Apr.	May	June	July	Aug.	Sept.	Oct.	Nov.	Dec.
2005	29,634	25,465	21,450	18,580	13,950	10,824	10,041	33,883	33,669	32,441	31,371	27,874
2006	25,677	25,365	25,417	19,575	18,023	15,825	14,397	31,908	32,164	31,326	30,528	28,310
2007	26,743	25,604	24,726	22,748	20,937	18,456	18,641	43,124	46,102	44,603	42,769	36,000
2008	32,000	27,355	25,578	22,673	19,206	16,257	15,989	36,058	40,136	39,871	35,328	31,335
2009	26,148	22,370	20,797	17,505	15,256	13,742	11,081	39,708	40,099	37,329	34,855	32,393
2010	27,630	25,010	23,056	21,793	19,425	16,174	12,879	26,312	31,930	32,384	28,823	26,794
2011	23,857	18,649	14,941	14,603	13,864	13,113	11,946	20,833	36,913	38,718	37,111	33,876
2012	31,909	26,925	24,149	21,359	19,248	18,076	15,138	40,692	40,867	39,689	37,508	36,152
2013	35,272	33,021	25,975	24,247	21,792	17,887	18,727	40,606	39,237	37,880	33,468	32,048
2014[1]	30,066	28,823	27,183	22,994	21,110	21,107	22,053	42,581	35,020	37,494	34,756	32,368

[1] Preliminary.   [2] Includes IQF, Pails and Tubs, Barrels (400lbs net), and Concentrate.   *Source: Economic Research Service, U.S. Department of Agriculture (ERS-USDA)*

Cold Storage Stocks of Frozen Blueberries in the United States, on First of Month   In Thousands of Pounds

Year	Jan.	Feb.	Mar.	Apr.	May	June	July	Aug.	Sept.	Oct.	Nov.	Dec.
2005	85,109	77,105	68,419	53,737	41,516	34,673	28,198	62,282	111,198	109,229	97,204	88,008
2006	77,360	68,466	58,454	47,039	36,613	28,909	26,785	62,220	123,072	114,351	110,139	99,826
2007	98,719	83,196	75,709	65,398	56,362	45,921	37,700	84,342	154,880	147,570	134,715	125,577
2008	114,114	100,696	94,652	78,106	66,604	58,282	51,960	69,783	172,145	182,478	174,334	164,703
2009	153,445	141,089	130,964	115,615	100,820	87,790	81,404	106,327	189,893	189,628	173,849	154,647
2010	141,883	123,579	109,095	93,342	75,482	61,331	57,332	100,100	163,387	155,105	140,707	129,877
2011	116,485	104,091	93,103	80,016	65,583	50,865	57,467	76,551	167,015	174,805	160,156	147,757
2012	136,966	124,003	114,066	96,723	85,700	73,717	82,218	148,315	238,510	234,207	215,588	196,702
2013	171,296	165,932	152,187	137,358	119,814	100,876	103,559	166,382	260,094	251,279	235,007	217,393
2014[1]	201,834	172,718	150,626	130,825	117,065	98,716	102,012	171,661	269,537	265,303	240,830	229,225

[1] Preliminary.   *Source: Economic Research Service, U.S. Department of Agriculture (ERS-USDA)*

Cold Storage Stocks of Frozen Cherries[2] in the United States, on First of Month   In Thousands of Pounds

Year	Jan.	Feb.	Mar.	Apr.	May	June	July	Aug.	Sept.	Oct.	Nov.	Dec.
2005	76,570	74,505	69,829	56,106	47,832	39,172	27,701	136,042	150,216	139,969	131,846	117,828
2006	110,359	102,319	92,935	78,660	71,560	61,316	47,806	137,736	143,082	133,717	123,486	112,606
2007	110,361	97,425	88,896	76,170	66,958	58,337	48,989	168,436	158,643	153,812	142,039	132,845
2008	126,646	117,609	109,423	100,479	87,495	75,690	63,055	118,790	137,994	120,386	113,867	108,046
2009	101,892	96,533	90,052	79,608	69,139	59,714	53,206	128,571	193,312	185,263	179,608	167,716
2010	156,136	145,923	136,313	124,138	113,941	103,008	96,431	161,826	150,298	136,233	128,236	118,223
2011	110,166	97,223	87,153	71,167	62,380	50,776	40,803	96,444	124,645	108,842	98,395	90,339
2012	83,622	73,371	65,185	54,211	44,684	32,532	26,924	59,120	51,815	50,514	49,966	56,135
2013	51,161	44,651	38,315	33,746	26,644	19,127	14,227	114,938	150,224	139,064	128,171	114,676
2014[1]	112,101	99,639	91,631	82,926	71,746	58,869	50,181	103,362	178,542	164,429	153,521	144,280

[1] Preliminary.   [2] Tart (ripe tart pitted).   *Source: Economic Research Service, U.S. Department of Agriculture (ERS-USDA)*

Cold Storage Stocks of Frozen Peaches in the United States, on First of Month   In Thousands of Pounds

Year	Jan.	Feb.	Mar.	Apr.	May	June	July	Aug.	Sept.	Oct.	Nov.	Dec.
2005	69,665	58,340	51,616	41,581	33,336	24,672	17,559	17,771	45,220	72,567	73,327	61,957
2006	61,937	41,079	36,253	34,552	32,246	29,955	21,848	21,197	38,302	61,098	74,673	70,200
2007	73,133	68,955	62,954	60,635	52,576	35,415	29,501	35,881	63,129	89,711	84,584	77,439
2008	75,780	68,716	62,681	52,331	41,348	34,291	27,422	37,217	54,995	87,006	87,140	82,656
2009	76,356	69,001	59,525	45,757	40,755	34,667	29,049	32,155	48,217	59,280	56,959	57,070
2010	52,278	48,051	48,298	44,625	41,204	40,744	31,570	30,403	52,904	64,624	63,093	60,595
2011	56,317	52,137	46,376	39,799	35,267	31,398	27,005	28,034	56,462	77,798	73,554	73,053
2012	66,344	60,950	60,096	48,374	44,074	39,734	35,430	36,517	59,775	70,173	67,100	55,085
2013	50,717	45,535	40,062	33,489	28,880	22,290	19,137	36,193	59,642	72,610	73,147	65,548
2014[1]	61,092	53,367	47,862	39,621	32,936	25,714	19,497	34,001	54,810	63,033	57,543	52,384

[1] Preliminary.   *Source: Economic Research Service, U.S. Department of Agriculture (ERS-USDA)*

FRUITS

Cold Storage Stocks of Frozen Raspberries[2] in the United States, on First of Month   In Thousands of Pounds

Year	Jan.	Feb.	Mar.	Apr.	May	June	July	Aug.	Sept.	Oct.	Nov.	Dec.
2005	42,252	31,933	29,359	27,061	23,413	21,716	28,213	83,470	76,319	70,147	65,406	59,127
2006	55,801	50,804	46,381	39,472	34,752	30,989	36,572	85,911	78,993	64,459	60,612	56,486
2007	52,208	45,239	39,593	34,686	33,569	30,317	27,572	72,044	60,685	52,212	44,626	39,369
2008	33,681	27,326	25,349	19,566	15,043	12,548	10,744	49,092	55,382	49,094	45,873	41,861
2009	34,083	29,155	25,817	24,155	20,797	18,742	15,963	75,263	65,422	59,133	52,459	48,339
2010	41,572	38,012	30,972	28,317	25,137	20,192	19,296	67,816	63,950	59,331	53,098	46,875
2011	42,151	37,949	33,062	28,151	27,424	23,199	21,531	66,893	73,113	71,489	65,330	62,067
2012	56,868	51,127	45,651	38,328	34,302	31,284	26,663	77,169	73,056	68,773	61,981	56,825
2013	53,505	44,526	39,815	32,916	31,666	26,920	25,369	72,447	82,984	79,479	72,788	65,095
2014[1]	62,102	52,730	45,071	38,418	33,673	31,353	30,226	87,492	81,541	74,858	67,095	62,337

[1] Preliminary .   [2] Red: Includes IQF, Pails and Tubs, Barrels (400 lbs net), and Concentrate.   *Source: Economic Research Service, U.S. Department of Agriculture (ERS-USDA)*

Cold Storage Stocks of Frozen Strawberries[2] in the United States, on First of Month   In Thousands of Pounds

Year	Jan.	Feb.	Mar.	Apr.	May	June	July	Aug.	Sept.	Oct.	Nov.	Dec.
2005	293,560	251,980	213,406	173,610	198,041	237,150	359,214	418,138	384,593	324,809	279,229	245,559
2006	218,762	193,324	159,547	127,657	148,933	227,983	382,403	400,725	357,189	294,710	260,489	232,352
2007	202,475	185,241	166,281	150,460	250,998	306,734	443,993	476,180	436,899	401,274	349,491	308,867
2008	280,186	256,852	236,353	182,162	205,462	258,745	331,009	379,197	347,910	329,502	296,064	271,843
2009	235,241	198,713	182,112	151,904	212,641	281,133	390,580	423,878	412,766	389,377	364,611	342,063
2010	322,452	289,623	269,111	236,089	273,591	274,438	358,348	421,410	385,612	355,255	322,577	297,494
2011	263,147	233,644	203,393	177,108	180,773	244,433	333,190	384,184	367,425	350,563	348,285	323,160
2012	291,697	259,308	224,105	199,485	206,876	305,961	399,764	424,417	414,358	399,632	381,561	343,201
2013	302,987	265,250	240,083	218,149	334,359	397,352	421,128	463,698	428,160	392,032	345,152	320,036
2014[1]	279,977	240,382	215,168	211,064	233,147	257,783	357,526	362,127	330,666	294,969	270,553	236,828

[1] Preliminary.   [2] Includes IQF and Poly, Pails and Tubs, Barrels and Drums, and Juice Stock.   *Source: Economic Research Service, U.S. Department of Agriculture (ERS-USDA)*

Cold Storage Stocks of Other Frozen Fruit in the United States, on First of Month   In Thousands of Pounds

Year	Jan.	Feb.	Mar.	Apr.	May	June	July	Aug.	Sept.	Oct.	Nov.	Dec.
2005	405,492	365,236	308,868	270,956	240,512	211,448	188,746	181,378	164,671	158,923	439,479	435,833
2006	421,491	399,423	353,776	301,890	274,713	249,472	224,001	212,044	160,851	172,959	424,987	495,447
2007	458,222	396,189	371,397	319,167	276,074	254,816	232,344	215,691	196,806	209,121	451,052	498,790
2008	464,609	425,313	402,895	350,167	312,823	269,330	251,309	234,242	206,201	219,247	537,319	527,876
2009	509,807	467,363	414,907	360,587	343,101	311,835	286,675	246,058	215,985	198,200	551,910	530,591
2010	486,760	449,112	399,408	355,773	318,497	289,097	246,690	209,745	174,476	225,587	502,560	473,224
2011	439,996	404,540	367,245	345,131	294,806	254,167	217,588	189,747	150,499	160,415	452,421	452,416
2012	423,367	388,229	360,867	331,923	294,833	256,890	220,723	194,871	170,723	224,022	525,515	510,323
2013	493,200	444,506	417,678	382,611	355,428	316,247	284,810	277,685	238,619	224,171	470,098	589,226
2014[1]	575,025	528,790	475,527	440,532	389,071	341,283	305,249	286,727	264,490	293,231	542,534	576,843

[1] Preliminary.   *Source: Economic Research Service, U.S. Department of Agriculture (ERS-USDA)*

Cold Storage Stocks of Total Frozen Fruit in the United States, on First of Month   In Millions of Pounds

Year	Jan.	Feb.	Mar.	Apr.	May	June	July	Aug.	Sept.	Oct.	Nov.	Dec.
2005	1,093.9	984.9	874.3	748.8	708.1	684.5	765.8	1,045.6	1,060.2	988.1	1,204.5	1,124.4
2006	1,067.1	972.0	863.5	747.0	710.9	740.3	849.1	1,057.4	1,027.2	963.3	1,179.7	1,192.4
2007	1,136.5	1,019.9	950.7	853.6	882.8	866.8	949.6	1,218.4	1,226.8	1,200.0	1,352.4	1,319.9
2008	1,239.5	1,140.3	1,068.7	920.5	866.2	839.8	864.1	1,043.1	1,125.7	1,130.7	1,393.6	1,337.5
2009	1,245.6	1,134.2	1,038.1	911.0	916.8	910.6	973.2	1,154.3	1,257.8	1,200.7	1,501.1	1,428.2
2010	1,328.6	1,226.0	1,125.9	1,014.5	971.8	902.7	921.1	1,124.3	1,118.5	1,113.1	1,335.7	1,259.8
2011	1,165.1	1,060.7	950.9	847.7	770.1	750.6	785.5	953.4	1,058.5	1,063.6	1,317.2	1,269.3
2012	1,189.3	1,082.2	989.1	881.4	813.3	835.1	889.5	1,077.5	1,145.4	1,178.0	1,425.6	1,342.3
2013	1,246.6	1,123.5	1,030.1	934.9	985.0	962.6	954.1	1,251.3	1,335.0	1,270.0	1,431.1	1,489.0
2014[1]	1,405.6	1,261.1	1,140.4	1,052.0	981.1	912.1	972.2	1,176.0	1,317.9	1,286.1	1,461.4	1,426.8

[1] Preliminary.   *Source: Economic Research Service, U.S. Department of Agriculture (ERS-USDA)*

Gas

Natural gas is a fossil fuel that is colorless, shapeless, and odorless in its pure form. It is a mixture of hydrocarbon gases formed primarily of methane, but it can also include ethane, propane, butane, and pentane. Natural gas is combustible, clean burning, and gives off a great deal of energy. Around 500 BC, the Chinese discovered that the energy in natural gas could be harnessed. They passed it through crude bamboo-shoot pipes and then burned it to boil sea water to create potable fresh water. Around 1785, Britain became the first country to commercially use natural gas produced from coal for streetlights and indoor lights. In 1821, William Hart dug the first well specifically intended to obtain natural gas and he is generally regarded as the "father of natural gas" in America. There is a vast amount of natural gas estimated to still be in the ground in the U.S. Natural gas as a source of energy is significantly less expensive than electricity per Btu.

Natural gas futures and options are traded at the CME Group. The CME natural gas futures contract calls for the delivery of natural gas representing 10,000 million British thermal units (mmBtu) at the Henry Hub in Louisiana, which is the nexus of 16 intra-state and inter-state pipelines. The contract is priced in terms of dollars per mmBtu. CME also has basic swap futures contracts available for 30 different natural gas pricing locations versus the benchmark Henry Hub location. Natural gas futures are also listed on the ICE Futures Europe exchange.

Prices – CME natural gas futures (Barchart.com symbol code NG) on the nearest-futures chart in 2014 rallied to a 6-year high in February 2014 but then traded lower the rest of the year to close the year down -31.7% at $2.889 per mmBtu, which was only moderately above the record low of 1.902 posted in April 2012.

Supply – U.S. recovery of natural gas in 2013 (latest data available) rose +2.1% to a record high of 30.167 billion cubic feet. The top U.S. producing states for natural gas were Texas with 29.4% of U.S. production in 2013, Louisiana with 9.2%, Wyoming with 7.2%, Oklahoma with 8.4%, and New Mexico with 4.8%. In 2014 the world's largest natural gas producers were the U.S. with 2,276,915 terajoules and Russia with 1,732,577 terajoules of production.

Demand – U.S.- delivered consumption of natural gas in 2013 rose +2.0% yr/yr to 23.879 billion cubic feet, of which about 34.1% was delivered to electrical utility plants, 31.3% to industrial establishments, 20.7% to residences, and 13.8% to commercial establishments.

Trade – U.S. imports of natural gas (consumed) in 2013 fell -8.1% yr/yr to 2.883 billion cubic feet, down from the 2007 record high of 4,607 billion cubic feet. U.S. exports of natural gas in 2013 fell -2.9% yr/yr to 1,572 billion cubic feet, below last year's record high of 1,618 billion cubic feet.

World Dry Natural Gas Production   In Billion Cubic Feet

Year	Algeria	Canada	China	Indonesia	Iran	Nether-lands	Norway	Qatar	Russia	Saudi Arabia	United States	Uzbek-istan	World Total
2004	2,830	6,483	1,439	2,028	2,963	3,035	2,948	1,383	20,991	2,319	18,591	2,114	95,642
2005	3,151	6,561	1,763	2,001	3,655	2,773	3,072	1,617	21,224	2,516	18,051	2,108	98,395
2006	3,079	6,548	2,067	2,199	3,836	2,730	3,094	1,790	21,736	2,594	18,504	2,216	101,588
2007	2,996	6,416	2,446	2,422	3,952	2,687	3,168	2,232	21,595	2,628	19,266	2,302	104,143
2008	3,055	6,046	2,685	2,472	4,107	2,957	3,503	2,719	21,515	2,841	20,159	2,387	107,761
2009	2,876	5,634	2,975	2,557	4,986	2,786	3,664	3,154	19,303	2,770	20,624	2,169	105,179
2010	2,988	5,390	3,334	2,841	5,161	3,131	3,756	4,166	21,536	3,096	21,316	2,123	112,574
2011	2,923	5,218	3,629	2,693	5,361	2,851	3,580	5,198	22,213	3,258	22,902	2,226	116,255
2012[1]	3,053	5,070	3,666	2,559	5,649	2,843	4,156	5,523	21,764	3,508	24,058	2,222	118,910
2013[2]		5,129	4,135			3,052	3,840		21,359	3,637	24,282		

[1] Preliminary.   [2] Estimate.   *Source: Energy Information Administration, U.S. Department of Energy (EIA-DOE)*

Marketed Production of Natural Gas in the United States, by States   In Million Cubic Feet

Year	Alaska	Arkansas	California	Colorado	Kansas	Louisiana	New Mexico	Oklahoma	Pennsyl-vania	Texas	Wyoming	Total
2005	487,282	190,533	317,637	1,133,086	377,229	1,296,048	1,645,166	1,639,310	168,501	5,276,401	1,639,317	18,927,095
2006	444,724	270,293	315,209	1,202,821	371,044	1,361,119	1,609,223	1,688,985	175,950	5,548,022	1,816,201	19,409,674
2007	433,485	269,886	307,160	1,242,571	365,877	1,365,333	1,517,922	1,783,682	182,277	6,123,180	2,047,882	20,196,346
2008	398,442	446,457	296,469	1,389,399	374,310	1,377,969	1,446,204	1,886,710	198,295	6,960,693	2,274,850	21,112,053
2009	397,077	679,952	276,575	1,499,070	354,440	1,548,607	1,383,004	1,901,556	273,869	6,818,973	2,335,328	21,647,936
2010	374,226	926,639	286,841	1,578,379	324,720	2,210,099	1,292,185	1,827,328	572,902	6,715,294	2,305,525	22,381,873
2011	356,225	1,072,212	250,177	1,637,576	309,124	3,029,206	1,237,303	1,888,870	1,310,592	7,112,863	2,159,422	24,036,352
2012	351,259	1,146,168	246,822	1,709,376	296,299	2,955,437	1,215,773	2,023,461	2,256,696	7,475,495	2,022,275	25,283,278
2013	338,182	1,139,654	252,310	1,604,860	292,467	2,371,489	1,241,465	2,143,988	3,259,042	7,545,401	1,858,207	25,690,878
2014[1]	341,998					1,982,470	1,227,969	2,310,114		7,750,187	1,807,618	27,259,815

[1] Preliminary.   *Source: Energy Information Administration, U.S. Department of Energy (EIA-DOE)*

GAS

World Production of Natural Gas Plant Liquids   Thousand Barrels per Day

Year	Algeria	Canada	Mexico	Saudi Arabia	Russia	United States	Persian Gulf[2]	OAPEC[3]	OPEC-12[4]	OPEC-11[4]	World
2005	265	645	337	1,860	457	1,717	2,282	2,524	2,844	2,834	7,926
2006	270	685	338	1,860	472	1,739	2,289	2,554	2,859	2,837	8,178
2007	260	726	328	1,940	486	1,783	2,313	2,582	2,907	2,883	8,394
2008	250	677	318	2,080	500	1,784	2,339	2,592	2,928	2,894	8,538
2009	325	640	326	1,980	539	1,910	2,427	2,744	3,099	3,057	8,673
2010	340	597	332	1,920	574	2,074	2,669	2,972	3,366	3,316	8,930
2011	322	591	334	1,920	611	2,216	2,825	2,958	3,405	3,350	9,139
2012	342	611	318	1,920	647	2,408	2,943	3,164	3,622	3,567	9,527
2013[1]	300	639	320	1,920	684	2,606					9,668

Average.   [1] Preliminary.   [2] Bahrain, Iran, Iraq, Kuwait, Qatar, Saudi Arabia, and the United Arab Emirates.   [3] Organization of Arab Petroleum Exporting Countries: Algeria, Iraq, Kuwait, Libya, Qatar, Saudi Arabia, and the United Arab Emirates.   [4] OPEC-12: Organization of the Petroleum Exporting Countries: Algeria, Angola, Indonesia, Iran, Iraq, Kuwait, Libya, Nigeria, Qatar, Saudi Arabia, the United Arab Emirates, and Venezuela. OPEC-11 does not include Angola.   *Source: Energy Information Administration, U.S. Department of Energy (EIA-DOE)*

Recoverable Reserves and Deliveries of Natural Gas in the United States   In Billions of Cubic Feet

Year	Gross Withdrawals	Recoverable Reserves of Natural Gas Dec. 31[2]	Residential	Commercial	Electric Utility Plants[3]	Industrial	Total	Lease & Plant Fuel	Used as Pipline Fuel	Heating Value BTU per Cubic Foot
2005	23,457	204,385	4,827	2,999	5,869	6,597	22,011	1,112	584	1,028
2006	23,535	211,085	4,368	2,832	6,222	6,512	21,685	1,142	584	1,028
2007	24,664	237,726	4,722	3,013	6,655	6,655	21,256	1,226	621	1,027
2008	25,636	244,656	4,892	3,153	6,686	6,670	21,409	1,220	648	1,027
2009	26,057	272,509	4,779	3,119	6,873	6,167	20,965	1,275	670	1,025
2010	26,816	304,625	4,782	3,103	7,387	6,826	22,127	1,286	674	1,023
2011	28,479	334,067	4,714	3,155	7,574	6,994	22,467	1,323	688	1,022
2012[1]	29,542		4,149	2,895	9,111	7,224	23,409	1,396	728	1,024
2013[1]	30,167		4,940	3,289	8,153	7,463	23,879	1,413	742	

[1] Preliminary.   [2] Estimated proved recoverable reserves of dry natural gas.   [3] Figures include gas other than natural (impossible to segregate); therefore, shown separately from other consumption.   *Source: Energy Information Administration, U.S. Department of Energy (EIA-DOE)*

Gas Utility Sales in the United States by Types and Class of Service   In Trillions of BTUs

Year	Total Utility Sales	Number of Customers (Millions)	Residential	Commercial	Industrial	Electric Generation	Other	Total	Residential	Commercial	Industrial	Electric Generation	Other
			Class of Service					Revenue - Million $ From Sales to Customers					
2000	9,232	61.3	4,741	2,077	1,698	709	6	59,243	35,828	13,338	7,432	2,612	33
2001	8,667	61.4	4,525	2,053	1,461	620	8	69,150	42,454	16,848	7,513	2,286	49
2002	8,864	62.0	4,589	2,055	1,748	459	13	57,112	35,062	13,512	6,840	1,639	59
2003	8,927	62.6	4,722	2,125	1,672	397	11	72,606	43,664	17,349	9,478	2,048	68
2004	8,766	63.3	4,566	2,075	1,763	351	12	79,929	47,275	18,689	11,230	2,653	83
2005	8,848	64.4	4,516	2,056	1,654	610	12	96,909	55,680	22,653	13,751	4,718	107
2006	8,222	65.0	4,117	1,861	1,576	606	62	91,928	53,961	21,557	12,006	3,921	484
2007[1]	8,565	65.4	4,418	1,943	1,522	626	57	92,131	55,027	21,248	11,323	4,076	457
2008[2]	8,594	65.5	4,541	2,009	1,410	614	21	102,641	60,195	23,592	13,205	5,406	243

[1] Preliminary.   [2] Estimate.   *Source: American Gas Association (AGA)*

Salient Statistics of Natural Gas in the United States

Year	Marketed Production	Extraction Loss	Dry Production	Storage Withdrawals	Imports (Consumed) Supply	Total Supply	Consumption	Exports	Added to Storage	Total Disposition	Wellhead Price	Imports	Exports	Residential	Commercial	Industrial	Electric Utilities
	Supply — In Billions of Cubic Feet						Disposition				Average Price Delivered to Customers — Dollars Per Thousand Cubic Feet						
2006	19,410	906	18,504	2,493	4,186	26,089	21,685	724	2,924	25,333	6.39	6.88	6.83	13.73	12.00	7.87	7.11
2007	20,196	930	19,266	3,325	4,608	28,129	23,104	822	3,133	27,059	6.25	6.87	6.92	13.08	11.34	7.68	7.31
2008	21,112	953	20,159	3,374	3,984	28,470	23,277	963	3,340	27,581	7.97	8.70	8.58	13.89	12.23	9.65	9.26
2009	21,648	1,024	20,624	2,966	3,751	28,366	22,910	1,072	3,315	27,297	3.67	4.19	4.47	12.14	10.06	5.33	4.93
2010	22,382	1,066	21,316	3,274	3,741	29,397	24,087	1,137	3,291	28,515	4.48	4.52	5.02	11.39	9.47	5.49	5.27
2011	24,036	1,134	22,902	3,074	3,469	30,579	24,477	1,506	3,422	29,405	3.95	4.24	4.64	11.03	8.91	5.13	4.89
2012	25,283	1,250	24,033	2,818	3,138	31,239	25,538	1,619	2,854	30,011	2.75	2.88	3.25	10.65	8.10	3.88	3.54
2013[1]	25,691	1,357	24,334		2,883	28,574	26,131	1,572	3,156	30,859	3.73	3.83	4.08	10.32	8.08	4.64	4.49
2014[2]	27,260	1,553	25,707		2,442	29,702	24,096	1,370	3,695	29,161	4.37	5.49	5.53	10.97	8.90	5.53	5.19

[1] Preliminary.   [2] Estimate.   *Source: Energy Information Administration, U.S. Department of Energy (EIA-DOE)*

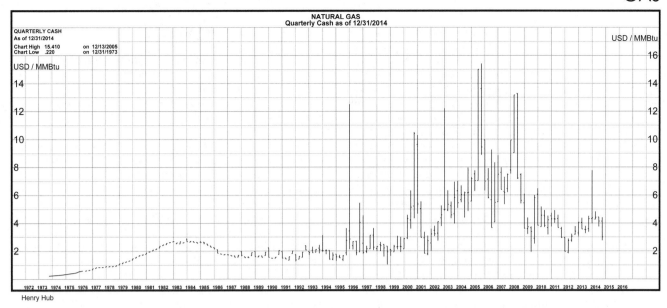

Henry Hub

Average Price of Natural Gas at Henry Hub   In Dollars Per MMBtu

Year	Jan.	Feb.	Mar.	Apr.	May	June	July	Aug.	Sept.	Oct.	Nov.	Dec.	Average
2005	6.13	6.13	6.91	7.22	6.48	7.15	7.63	9.46	11.87	13.42	10.28	13.05	8.81
2006	8.65	7.54	6.90	7.16	6.23	6.19	6.22	7.14	4.90	5.84	7.36	6.73	6.74
2007	6.60	7.92	7.10	7.59	7.63	7.35	6.21	6.23	6.08	6.78	7.15	7.13	6.98
2008	7.98	8.54	9.44	10.13	11.28	12.68	11.06	8.25	7.67	6.73	6.67	5.81	8.85
2009	5.23	4.52	3.95	3.50	3.83	3.81	3.39	3.15	3.01	4.02	3.70	5.33	3.95
2010	5.77	5.33	4.29	4.03	4.15	4.81	4.62	4.31	3.91	3.43	3.73	4.24	4.38
2011	4.49	4.09	3.97	4.24	4.30	4.55	4.42	4.05	3.89	3.57	3.25	3.17	4.00
2012	2.67	2.51	2.16	1.95	2.43	2.46	2.96	2.84	2.85	3.31	3.55	3.34	2.75
2013	3.33	3.34	3.82	4.17	4.04	3.82	3.63	3.43	3.62	3.67	3.62	4.24	3.73
2014	4.69	6.01	4.86	4.61	4.55	4.57	4.01	3.88	3.92	3.78	4.09	3.40	4.36

Source: Energy Information Administration, U.S. Department of Energy (EIA-DOE)

Volume of Trading of Natural Gas Futures in New York   In Thousands of Contracts

Year	Jan.	Feb.	Mar.	Apr.	May	June	July	Aug.	Sept.	Oct.	Nov.	Dec.	Total
2005	1,442.2	1,490.4	1,653.3	1,586.0	1,504.1	1,931.9	1,528.4	2,044.4	1,587.6	1,433.1	1,449.5	1,491.7	19,142.5
2006	1,609.9	1,833.9	1,682.2	1,911.6	2,272.5	1,920.6	1,786.2	2,428.7	2,017.7	1,935.1	1,799.6	1,832.0	23,030.0
2007	2,597.6	2,417.5	1,922.6	2,163.2	2,266.2	2,683.7	2,346.7	3,049.9	2,468.5	3,044.3	2,452.0	2,374.2	29,786.3
2008	2,921.9	3,330.7	2,983.6	3,382.9	3,168.0	3,379.1	4,274.0	3,756.1	3,458.5	3,151.7	2,539.9	2,384.3	38,730.5
2009	2,343.7	2,780.6	2,989.9	2,493.1	3,479.0	4,486.6	3,979.4	4,445.9	5,597.7	5,594.7	4,413.7	5,347.2	47,951.4
2010	4,501.7	4,557.7	4,690.9	5,740.4	4,729.9	5,911.9	5,267.7	5,791.0	5,428.1	5,920.0	5,780.8	6,002.9	64,323.1
2011	6,468.6	6,123.2	7,284.0	6,432.0	6,015.2	6,759.5	5,317.9	6,904.9	6,363.8	7,199.9	6,117.1	5,878.3	76,864.3
2012	9,328.0	8,723.2	6,798.8	7,488.9	8,660.3	8,639.0	7,412.7	8,579.0	7,272.7	9,259.2	6,262.3	6,375.6	94,799.5
2013	7,329.4	6,910.3	8,343.9	9,484.9	6,796.2	6,271.5	5,626.2	6,944.2	5,741.2	6,991.3	5,618.2	8,225.0	84,282.5
2014	8,872.0	8,301.5	4,804.4	5,114.8	5,031.3	5,425.1	5,022.7	5,374.9	5,623.7	6,087.8	7,965.4	6,554.8	74,178.4

Contract size = 10,000 MMBtu.   *Source: CME Group; New York Mercantile Exchange (NYMEX)*

Average Open Interest of Natural Gas Futures in New York   In Thousands of Contracts

Year	Jan.	Feb.	Mar.	Apr.	May	June	July	Aug.	Sept.	Oct.	Nov.	Dec.
2005	401.8	405.7	458.0	479.9	480.3	472.6	498.4	524.2	544.2	551.1	545.3	551.4
2006	545.2	582.2	634.1	700.6	795.4	851.7	883.5	938.0	940.3	931.9	903.4	889.8
2007	905.4	839.1	761.7	747.7	752.6	787.1	823.1	776.7	778.5	749.5	789.4	843.4
2008	881.8	942.1	906.5	875.5	885.2	946.7	964.0	922.5	915.6	859.3	744.8	702.9
2009	693.3	709.0	652.4	649.9	678.4	709.2	737.5	731.6	713.8	710.0	713.6	719.6
2010	762.0	786.4	839.2	855.4	860.8	817.7	783.9	819.2	812.4	800.8	783.7	774.4
2011	820.8	917.0	922.1	948.1	956.5	980.4	977.0	990.3	952.1	969.6	977.2	981.2
2012	1,122.7	1,241.6	1,226.2	1,271.3	1,221.7	1,177.7	1,120.4	1,089.0	1,106.9	1,184.3	1,166.7	1,157.0
2013	1,172.0	1,196.1	1,315.3	1,539.1	1,511.7	1,434.8	1,389.5	1,356.6	1,306.4	1,263.8	1,271.2	1,302.4
2014	1,278.0	1,246.6	1,160.8	1,104.7	1,021.9	1,032.9	1,017.1	962.3	970.3	914.8	952.5	939.1

Contract size = 10,000 MMBtu.   *Source: CME Group; New York Mercantile Exchange (NYMEX)*

Gasoline

Gasoline is a complex mixture of hundreds of lighter liquid hydrocarbons and is used chiefly as a fuel for internal-combustion engines. Petroleum crude, or crude oil, is still the most economical source of gasoline with refineries turning more than half of every barrel of crude oil into gasoline. The three basic steps to all refining operations are the separation process (separating crude oil into various chemical components), conversion process (breaking the chemicals down into molecules called hydrocarbons), and treatment process (transforming and combining hydrocarbon molecules and other additives). Another process, called *hydro treating*, removes a significant amount of sulfur from finished gasoline as is currently required by the state of California.

Octane is a measure of a gasoline's ability to resist pinging or knocking noise from an engine. Most gasoline stations offer three octane grades of unleaded fuel—regular at 87 (R+M)/2, mid-grade at 89 (R+M)/2, and premium at 93 (R+M)/2. Additional refining steps are needed to increase the octane, which increases the retail price. This does not make the gasoline any cleaner or better, but yields a different blend of hydrocarbons that burn more slowly.

In an attempt to improve air quality and reduce harmful emissions from internal combustion engines, Congress in 1990 amended the Clean Air Act to mandate the addition of ethanol to gasoline. Some 2 billion gallons of ethanol are now added to gasoline each year in the U.S. The most common blend is E10, which contains 10% ethanol and 90% gasoline. Auto manufacturers have approved that mixture for use in all U.S. vehicles. Ethanol is an alcohol-based fuel produced by fermenting and distilling crops such as corn, barley, wheat and sugar.

Gasoline futures and options trade at the CME Group. The CME gasoline futures contract calls for the delivery of 1,000 barrels (42,000 gallons) of unleaded gasoline in the New York harbor and is priced in terms of dollars and cents per gallon.

Prices – CME gasoline futures prices (Barchart.com symbol code RB) traded mildly higher in the first half of 2014 but then plunged through year-end to close 2014 down -47.2% at $1.4721 per gallon.

The average monthly retail price of regular unleaded gasoline in 2014 (through November) fell -4.5% yr/yr to $3.36 per gallon. The average monthly retail price of unleaded premium motor gasoline in the U.S. in 2014 (through November) fell -3.4% to $3.71 per gallon. The average monthly refiner price of finished aviation gasoline to end users in 2014 (through September) rose +4.6% yr/yr to $4.14 per gallon.

Supply – U.S. production of gasoline in 2014 (through November, annualized) rose +4.0% yr/yr to 9.599 million barrels per day. Gasoline stocks in November of 2014 were 29.532 million barrels, down from 37.548 million barrels in November of 2013.

Demand – U.S. consumption of finished motor gasoline in 2014 (through November, annualized) rose +1.3% yr/yr to 8.958 million barrels per day, below 2007's record high of 9.284 million barrels per day.

World Production of Motor Gasoline   In Thousands of Barrels Per Day

Year	Brazil	Canada	China	France	Germany	India	Italy	Japan	Mexico	Russia	United Kingdom	United States	World Total
2003	322.0	787.1	1,119.6	392.5	612.3	257.0	486.4	1,006.0	415.0	685.1	523.8	8,501.3	20,809.9
2004	337.8	769.7	1,219.4	391.3	612.1	256.8	478.8	999.6	442.2	710.9	567.7	8,723.3	21,487.4
2005	348.5	754.0	1,269.7	379.5	636.7	245.4	488.0	1,009.1	436.1	748.1	523.7	8,317.5	21,373.2
2006	369.9	721.8	1,304.0	401.9	626.9	293.0	455.3	998.0	435.0	803.2	496.4	8,363.7	21,277.8
2007	393.9	760.7	1,378.7	389.2	609.9	331.1	480.6	1,004.6	436.7	820.2	493.4	8,357.8	21,291.9
2008	364.1	701.3	1,483.3	386.8	587.3	374.4	460.4	975.3	430.0	832.0	471.0	8,548.3	21,406.5
2009	373.6	717.8	1,710.8	365.8	559.9	527.1	434.0	981.6	454.5	837.3	473.0	8,785.6	22,251.4
2010	398.9	719.2	1,720.1	316.7	499.2	610.8	438.0	1,014.2	407.7	840.1	466.0	9,058.6	22,298.8
2011[1]		670.4		303.5	499.3		450.3	943.4	387.2		461.0	9,057.6	
2012[2]		687.4		276.0	478.7		395.7	919.9	404.4		406.9	8,926.3	

[1] Preliminary.   [2] Estimate.   *Source: Energy Information Administration, U.S. Department of Energy (EIA-DOE)*

World Imports of Motor Gasoline   In Thousands of Barrels Per Day

Year	Australia	Canada	Indo-nesia	Iran	Malaysia	Mexico	Nether-lands	Nigeria	Saudi Arabia	Singa-pore	United Kingdom	United States	World Total
2003	39.8	45.3	65.4	95.0	56.1	119.9	181.1	126.3	10.0	108.0	46.9	517.9	2,643.8
2004	59.6	65.0	99.7	142.6	54.7	161.7	182.5	136.9	----	161.6	50.2	496.4	2,891.6
2005	57.5	83.1	125.2	156.0	66.3	214.2	212.4	128.1	41.1	166.6	55.1	602.7	3,235.6
2006	56.1	99.9	128.9	172.9	76.3	245.7	243.5	126.4	79.2	172.4	87.8	475.2	3,216.2
2007	46.8	75.6	145.3	119.8	73.3	284.7	172.4	135.4	75.2	200.0	75.6	412.6	3,038.2
2008	70.7	94.2	94.8	130.0	78.1	309.5	225.2	107.4	108.0	230.3	53.7	301.6	3,035.1
2009	77.1	89.1	199.3	132.5	74.0	307.6	234.1	140.0	102.9	20.2	77.8	223.4	2,947.2
2010	47.3	79.9	219.0	117.2	75.0	354.4	217.2	117.6	86.2	53.9	85.3	134.3	2,969.1
2011[1]	57.2	90.4				386.2	240.5				88.0	104.8	
2012[2]	57.3	62.2				366.2	276.2				111.5	44.1	

[1] Preliminary.   [2] Estimate.   *Source: Energy Information Administration, U.S. Department of Energy (EIA-DOE)*

World Exports of Motor Gasoline   In Thousands of Barrels Per Day

Year	Canada	France	Germany	India	Italy	Nether-lands	Russia	Singa-pore	United Kingdom	United States	Vene-zuela	Virgin Islands	World Total
2003	160.7	89.0	96.2	69.6	122.5	319.5	91.7	182.1	129.8	125.4	65.3	156.2	2,936.2
2004	156.2	163.8	121.5	67.5	131.9	340.4	98.3	240.4	169.3	124.3	178.0	158.9	3,368.4
2005	161.4	179.1	132.1	53.1	173.1	376.4	138.4	332.0	152.5	135.5	172.0	159.3	3,677.5
2006	138.8	161.7	129.7	86.4	167.5	400.5	147.4	330.2	162.1	141.8	132.0	131.6	3,691.5
2007	147.4	147.1	125.5	105.3	218.7	297.8	140.4	376.5	169.7	127.0	115.1	140.1	3,585.4
2008	129.3	182.6	132.2	126.8	196.6	357.1	104.3	428.7	162.6	171.7	117.0	131.9	3,660.8
2009	136.5	148.4	125.5	228.1	166.8	376.0	105.2	216.8	177.2	195.4	127.5	115.8	3,593.9
2010	149.7	133.2	112.1	317.3	192.7	382.9	69.2	254.4	208.4	295.8	9.5	107.9	3,597.6
2011[1]	130.7	118.5	109.6		187.2	348.7			214.3	478.8			
2012[2]	138.4	107.9	114.9		201.8	448.9			196.5	408.9			

[1] Preliminary.   [2] Estimate.   *Source: Energy Information Administration, U.S. Department of Energy (EIA-DOE)*

Production of Finished Motor Gasoline in the United States   In Thousand Barrels per Day

Year	Jan.	Feb.	Mar.	Apr.	May	June	July	Aug.	Sept.	Oct.	Nov.	Dec.	Average
2005	8,157	8,194	8,119	8,549	8,475	8,589	8,352	8,326	8,129	7,953	8,468	8,503	8,318
2006	8,189	7,969	7,765	8,032	8,613	8,957	8,624	8,610	8,465	8,210	8,335	8,567	8,361
2007	8,348	8,012	8,101	8,122	8,491	8,686	8,504	8,547	8,320	8,276	8,353	8,501	8,355
2008	8,516	8,495	8,373	8,560	8,700	8,564	8,523	8,513	7,855	8,889	8,722	8,850	8,547
2009	8,445	8,408	8,646	8,724	8,793	9,068	8,952	8,856	8,829	8,770	8,905	9,006	8,784
2010	8,348	8,510	8,913	9,062	9,113	9,211	9,500	9,426	9,143	9,049	9,134	9,252	9,055
2011	8,714	8,866	8,908	8,978	9,157	9,289	9,166	9,264	9,140	8,932	9,141	9,128	9,057
2012	8,385	8,606	8,705	8,720	8,950	9,157	9,073	9,237	8,888	9,176	9,156	9,051	8,925
2013	8,718	8,926	8,971	9,042	9,299	9,472	9,374	9,340	9,190	9,484	9,476	9,495	9,232
2014[1]	8,999	9,259	9,533	9,733	9,823	9,890	10,052	9,734	9,418	9,541	9,541	9,670	9,599

[1] Preliminary.   *Source: Energy Information Administration, U.S. Department of Energy (EIA-DOE)*

Disposition of Finished Motor Gasoline, Total Product Supplied in the United States   In Thousand Barrels per Day

Year	Jan.	Feb.	Mar.	Apr.	May	June	July	Aug.	Sept.	Oct.	Nov.	Dec.	Average
2005	8,813	8,861	8,994	9,128	9,278	9,373	9,534	9,537	8,915	9,036	9,115	9,296	9,157
2006	8,839	8,911	9,054	9,154	9,308	9,478	9,607	9,564	9,236	9,267	9,244	9,338	9,250
2007	8,886	9,006	9,178	9,215	9,434	9,491	9,640	9,582	9,254	9,236	9,229	9,251	9,284
2008	8,810	8,866	9,066	9,112	9,251	9,110	9,150	9,134	8,497	9,024	8,904	8,927	8,988
2009	8,623	8,836	8,903	9,029	9,084	9,180	9,260	9,295	8,911	8,986	8,906	8,931	8,995
2010	8,520	8,579	8,793	9,108	9,162	9,311	9,301	9,255	9,112	9,016	8,816	8,911	8,990
2011	8,370	8,604	8,799	8,796	8,817	9,067	9,031	8,925	8,744	8,649	8,537	8,683	8,752
2012	8,190	8,598	8,582	8,741	8,979	8,996	8,810	9,154	8,561	8,701	8,483	8,389	8,682
2013	8,331	8,395	8,641	8,855	9,033	9,078	9,146	9,124	8,946	8,944	8,923	8,670	8,841
2014[1]	8,206	8,699	8,684	8,979	9,016	9,034	9,220	9,287	8,775	9,196	8,930	9,245	8,939

[1] Preliminary.   *Source: Energy Information Administration, U.S. Department of Energy (EIA-DOE)*

Stocks of Finished Gasoline[2] on Hand in the United States, at End of Month   In Millions of Barrels

Year	Jan.	Feb.	Mar.	Apr.	May	June	July	Aug.	Sept.	Oct.	Nov.	Dec.
2005	145.6	146.4	136.4	141.1	140.7	140.9	133.6	122.5	127.3	131.3	135.4	135.8
2006	142.2	137.9	124.2	115.4	121.5	119.1	117.9	116.6	120.5	112.8	113.8	116.1
2007	124.3	116.0	109.2	108.5	114.5	116.6	114.2	110.6	113.2	108.8	110.5	111.4
2008	117.4	119.9	110.6	106.2	106.0	107.3	102.3	97.8	92.6	95.9	96.9	98.3
2009	95.3	86.9	85.9	86.0	83.5	88.6	86.1	86.7	84.7	79.4	83.0	84.9
2010	87.2	83.6	81.9	78.1	75.2	71.8	71.9	72.4	70.2	65.1	65.5	63.3
2011	69.6	67.8	61.2	54.6	56.4	55.5	53.3	54.5	56.3	55.1	57.6	60.6
2012	61.6	58.7	54.1	50.5	50.0	51.9	52.0	48.3	47.8	49.7	52.6	55.2
2013	55.2	53.1	47.3	45.1	46.4	48.6	49.7	47.7	39.8	37.6	37.5	39.0
2014[1]	39.8	37.7	34.3	30.7	31.1	28.9	28.3	27.5	28.8	27.4	29.5	30.6

[1] Preliminary.   [2] Includes oxygenated and other finished.   *Source: Energy Information Administration, U.S. Department of Energy (EIA-DOE)*

GASOLINE

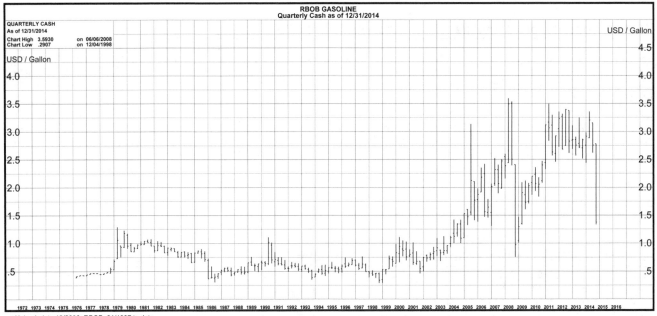

RBOB GASOLINE
Quarterly Cash as of 12/31/2014

QUARTERLY CASH
As of 12/31/2014
Chart High 3.5930 on 06/06/2008
Chart Low .2907 on 12/04/1998

USD / Gallon

Unleaded: to 12/2006; RBOB: 01/1997 to date.

Average Spot Price of Unleaded Gasoline in New York   In Cents Per Gallon

Year	Jan.	Feb.	Mar.	Apr.	May	June	July	Aug.	Sept.	Oct.	Nov.	Dec.	Average
2005	123.85	122.42	143.90	147.06	137.06	151.02	158.89	191.13	214.78	170.87	147.73	159.88	155.72
2006	173.39	149.98	175.87	214.62	204.68	206.50	223.99	203.23	158.42	152.00	158.71	166.70	182.34
2007	141.63	164.55	193.58	210.05	224.09	218.30	213.51	199.83	209.72	216.93	242.33	232.69	205.60
2008	233.09	238.37	249.09	277.45	309.23	329.79	315.86	290.20	280.69	190.84	129.29	97.18	245.09
2009	115.11	121.66	128.84	137.77	169.79	190.79	174.74	193.01	178.43	192.30	198.63	192.00	166.09
2010	204.28	199.38	214.86	222.10	201.35	201.13	200.38	195.01	197.47	216.07	224.31	238.74	209.59
2011	244.61	252.95	283.48	316.55	302.77	283.41	302.40	282.05	281.44	276.53	263.11	263.19	279.37
2012	281.87	302.35	315.95	320.96	287.24	262.17	275.67	302.71	326.56	296.81	284.34	272.56	294.10
2013	286.04	305.47	291.21	272.68	274.46	274.54	291.78	293.30	260.38	248.87	245.11	252.01	274.65
2014	254.77	267.72	271.44	280.08	278.26	289.58	272.45	263.14	260.50	217.93	193.75	142.35	249.33

Source: Energy Information Administration, U.S. Department of Energy (EIA-DOE)

Average Refiner Price of Finished Motor Gasoline to End Users[2] in the United States   In Cents Per Gallon

Year	Jan.	Feb.	Mar.	Apr.	May	June	July	Aug.	Sept.	Oct.	Nov.	Dec.	Average
2005	139.5	146.8	163.7	180.3	171.4	172.1	185.0	208.0	241.7	226.2	182.4	173.9	182.6
2006	187.2	183.3	198.3	233.1	245.8	243.6	252.8	248.6	207.6	178.9	178.8	186.8	212.1
2007	179.1	184.2	213.8	240.5	266.9	256.9	248.8	232.0	233.7	235.0	261.4	255.2	234.0
2008	257.1	256.6	278.3	298.4	331.6	358.0	356.8	327.9	320.7	253.7	161.7	121.9	276.9
2009	135.8	146.8	150.3	160.1	185.6	218.7	206.7	215.7	208.6	210.4	217.3	214.4	189.2
2010	224.0	217.3	230.1	237.0	235.3	225.1	224.7	225.0	221.9	231.9	237.8	251.4	230.1
2011	261.5	271.2	307.2	334.0	341.9	318.4	317.2	313.4	309.0	298.0	292.2	280.8	303.7
2012	291.4	308.7	338.9	340.5	328.9	306.1	298.1	324.8	335.7	326.1	299.4	282.8	315.1
2013	285.0	322.1	323.3	310.2	318.8	318.4	314.6	309.7	305.9	289.3	275.9	275.9	304.1
2014[1]	281.6	291.3	310.4	321.4	324.5	326.5	312.8	301.6	293.6	267.0	240.4		297.4

[1] Preliminary.   [2] Excludes aviation and taxes.   *Source: Energy Information Administration, U.S. Department of Energy (EIA-DOE)*

Average Retail Price of All-Types[2] Motor Gasoline[3] in the United States   In Cents Per Gallon

Year	Jan.	Feb.	Mar.	Apr.	May	June	July	Aug.	Sept.	Oct.	Nov.	Dec.	Average
2005	186.6	196.0	210.7	232.5	225.7	221.8	235.7	254.8	296.9	283.0	238.7	223.0	233.8
2006	235.9	235.4	244.4	280.1	299.3	296.3	304.6	303.3	263.7	231.9	228.7	238.0	263.5
2007	232.1	233.3	263.9	290.9	317.6	310.0	301.3	283.3	283.9	284.3	311.8	306.9	284.9
2008	309.6	308.3	330.7	349.1	381.3	411.5	414.2	383.8	374.9	322.5	220.8	174.2	331.7
2009	183.8	197.9	200.0	210.7	231.4	268.1	259.4	267.7	262.6	261.3	270.9	267.1	240.1
2010	277.9	270.9	282.9	290.6	291.5	278.3	278.3	279.5	275.4	284.3	289.9	303.1	283.6
2011	313.9	321.5	359.4	386.3	398.2	375.3	370.3	368.0	366.4	352.1	347.5	332.9	357.7
2012	344.7	362.2	391.8	397.6	383.9	360.2	350.2	375.9	390.8	383.9	354.2	338.6	369.5
2013	340.7	374.8	379.2	364.7	368.2	369.3	368.7	365.8	361.6	343.4	331.0	333.3	358.4
2014[1]	337.8	342.2	359.0	371.7	374.5	375.0	369.0	354.0	346.3	324.1	294.5	261.8	342.5

[1] Preliminary.   [2] Also includes types of motor oil not shown separately.   [3] Including taxes   *Source: Energy Information Administration, U.S. Department of Energy (EIA-DOE)*

114

BLENDSTOCK GASOLINE (RBOB) - NYMEX
Weekly Nearest Futures as of 01/02/2015

WEEKLY NEAREST FUTURES
As of 01/02/2015

Chart High 3.6310 on 07/11/2008
Chart Low .7850 on 12/24/2008

USD / Gallon

Nearby Futures through Last Trading Day.

Volume of Trading of Gasoline, RBOB[1] Futures in New York — In Thousands of Contracts

Year	Jan.	Feb.	Mar.	Apr.	May	June	July	Aug.	Sept.	Oct.	Nov.	Dec.	Total
2005	974.6	1,000.9	1,193.5	1,252.5	1,060.2	1,104.7	1,103.2	1,341.3	1,221.3	999.2	928.1	989.0	13,168.4
2006	1,149.6	1,233.0	1,259.1	1,079.6	1,122.7	1,039.8	939.8	1,145.5	891.4	839.6	838.1	966.0	12,504.2
2007	1,172.9	1,272.2	1,722.5	1,826.7	2,134.5	1,811.8	1,770.2	1,872.8	1,627.3	1,706.1	1,531.3	1,343.2	19,791.4
2008	1,660.6	1,887.5	2,111.9	1,986.3	1,917.6	1,854.4	1,621.6	1,667.7	1,862.1	1,452.9	1,193.4	1,306.4	20,522.6
2009	1,597.7	1,592.3	1,594.4	1,612.9	1,841.8	2,060.8	1,748.6	1,773.9	1,600.3	2,082.5	1,908.8	1,746.5	21,160.5
2010	1,979.2	1,978.8	2,318.0	2,829.9	2,537.8	2,186.6	1,946.1	2,402.3	2,325.4	2,614.0	2,529.1	2,251.3	27,898.7
2011	2,315.2	2,274.1	2,342.8	2,592.4	3,390.6	2,720.4	2,078.4	2,874.5	2,745.1	2,791.8	2,780.3	2,223.6	31,129.3
2012	2,899.2	2,844.2	3,480.0	3,789.4	3,257.2	3,107.9	2,844.9	3,043.1	3,015.4	3,298.3	2,674.1	2,350.2	36,603.8
2013	2,981.2	3,000.0	3,079.8	3,578.7	3,090.8	2,566.9	3,105.3	2,810.5	2,516.6	2,664.8	2,777.1	2,298.6	34,470.3
2014	2,470.9	2,417.0	2,562.7	3,316.9	3,240.6	2,679.3	3,001.7	2,894.1	3,173.3	3,170.5	2,713.6	2,775.9	34,416.5

[1] Data thru September 2005 are Unleaded, October 2005 thru December 2006 are Unleaded and RBOB.
Contract size = 42,000 US gallons. *Source: CME Group; New York Mercantile Exchange (NYMEX)*

Average Open Interest of Gasoline, RBOB[1] Futures in New York — In Contracts

Year	Jan.	Feb.	Mar.	Apr.	May	June	July	Aug.	Sept.	Oct.	Nov.	Dec.
2005	162,432	161,603	172,012	166,620	145,587	148,482	156,730	156,282	140,270	134,833	138,659	144,396
2006	157,562	173,978	168,067	165,233	150,913	138,578	146,173	135,367	131,771	124,963	128,906	135,085
2007	161,557	161,335	166,936	170,675	172,870	183,443	189,084	184,342	188,954	196,730	206,392	208,238
2008	230,032	253,303	241,781	250,852	264,988	256,220	238,170	219,229	198,263	162,480	172,267	194,234
2009	192,691	187,748	199,423	204,956	220,450	215,256	200,537	217,625	205,517	219,883	256,151	238,789
2010	262,247	258,312	304,437	320,529	275,659	245,923	239,242	246,901	241,014	270,830	282,949	273,638
2011	280,084	274,277	275,857	293,452	280,369	251,349	245,309	250,244	268,974	273,495	280,706	275,994
2012	312,848	345,884	374,449	348,606	306,453	293,802	258,931	273,299	290,070	279,312	276,945	282,942
2013	312,415	328,903	318,974	301,346	283,215	277,107	270,359	271,797	264,119	232,420	240,735	246,590
2014	252,519	274,087	283,756	310,549	332,460	314,754	307,808	274,978	283,206	310,119	334,015	349,589

[1] Data thru September 2005 are Unleaded, October 2005 thru December 2006 are Unleaded and RBOB.
Contract size = 42,000 US gallons. *Source: CME Group; New York Mercantile Exchange (NYMEX)*

GASOLINE

Average Retail Price of Unleaded Premium Motor Gasoline[2] in the United States   In Cents per Gallon

Year	Jan.	Feb.	Mar.	Apr.	May	June	July	Aug.	Sept.	Oct.	Nov.	Dec.	Average
2005	201.7	210.5	225.1	246.8	240.3	236.5	250.2	270.1	313.0	300.1	256.0	239.3	249.1
2006	252.1	251.9	260.3	296.7	316.9	313.9	321.9	320.7	281.9	249.3	245.9	255.0	280.5
2007	250.1	250.9	281.8	309.3	334.8	328.1	320.0	301.8	302.1	303.7	330.7	326.4	303.3
2008	329.1	327.2	350.2	369.0	400.3	431.9	435.0	404.5	394.0	343.2	243.3	195.1	351.9
2009	203.6	218.2	219.7	230.9	251.1	288.3	280.6	288.7	284.5	282.6	291.7	288.2	260.7
2010	298.7	292.2	303.5	311.3	312.4	300.0	299.7	301.5	296.8	305.5	310.9	323.4	304.7
2011	334.5	342.4	380.7	407.4	419.2	397.2	391.5	389.3	388.7	374.5	370.0	355.3	379.2
2012	366.3	384.0	413.8	419.4	406.2	382.5	372.6	399.1	414.0	407.9	378.2	362.6	392.2
2013	364.6	399.0	403.8	390.1	393.6	395.7	395.1	391.9	388.1	370.2	358.5	360.4	384.3
2014[1]	365.1	369.4	385.8	398.6	402.0	402.7	397.6	383.5	375.8	354.7	326.2	294.0	371.3

[1] Preliminary.   [2] Including taxes.   *Source: Energy Information Administration, U.S. Department of Energy (EIA-DOE)*

Average Retail Price of Unleaded Regular Motor Gasoline[2] in the United States   In Cents per Gallon

Year	Jan.	Feb.	Mar.	Apr.	May	June	July	Aug.	Sept.	Oct.	Nov.	Dec.	Average
2005	182.3	191.8	206.5	228.3	221.6	217.6	231.6	250.3	292.7	278.5	234.3	218.6	229.5
2006	231.5	231.0	240.1	275.7	294.7	291.7	299.9	298.5	258.9	227.2	224.1	233.4	258.9
2007	227.4	228.5	259.2	286.0	313.0	305.2	296.1	278.2	278.9	279.3	306.9	302.0	280.1
2008	304.7	303.3	325.8	344.1	376.4	406.5	409.0	378.6	369.8	317.3	215.1	168.9	326.6
2009	178.7	192.8	194.9	205.6	226.5	263.1	254.3	262.7	257.4	256.1	266.0	262.1	235.0
2010	273.1	265.9	278.0	285.8	286.9	273.6	273.6	274.5	270.4	279.5	285.2	298.5	278.8
2011	309.1	316.7	354.6	381.6	393.3	370.2	365.4	363.0	361.2	346.8	342.3	327.8	352.7
2012	339.9	357.2	386.8	392.7	379.2	355.2	345.1	370.7	385.6	378.6	348.8	333.1	364.4
2013	335.1	369.3	373.5	359.0	362.3	363.3	362.8	360.0	355.6	337.5	325.1	327.7	352.6
2014[1]	332.0	336.4	353.2	365.9	369.1	369.5	363.3	348.1	340.3	318.2	288.7	256.0	336.7

[1] Preliminary.   [2] Including taxes.   *Source: Energy Information Administration, U.S. Department of Energy (EIA-DOE)*

Average Retail Price of All-Types[2] Motor Gasoline[3] in the United States   In Cents per Gallon

Year	Jan.	Feb.	Mar.	Apr.	May	June	July	Aug.	Sept.	Oct.	Nov.	Dec.	Average
2005	186.6	196.0	210.7	232.5	225.7	221.8	235.7	254.8	296.9	283.0	238.7	223.0	233.8
2006	235.9	235.4	244.4	280.1	299.3	296.3	304.6	303.3	263.7	231.9	228.7	238.0	263.5
2007	232.1	233.3	263.9	290.9	317.6	310.0	301.3	283.3	283.9	284.3	311.8	306.9	284.9
2008	309.6	308.3	330.7	349.1	381.3	411.5	414.2	383.8	374.9	322.5	220.8	174.2	331.7
2009	183.8	197.9	200.0	210.7	231.4	268.1	259.4	267.7	262.6	261.3	270.9	267.1	240.1
2010	277.9	270.9	282.9	290.6	291.5	278.3	278.3	279.5	275.4	284.3	289.9	303.1	283.6
2011	313.9	321.5	359.4	386.3	398.2	375.3	370.3	368.0	366.4	352.1	347.5	332.9	357.7
2012	344.7	362.2	391.8	397.6	383.9	360.2	350.2	375.9	390.8	383.9	354.2	338.6	369.5
2013	340.7	374.8	379.2	364.7	368.2	369.3	368.7	365.8	361.6	343.4	331.0	333.3	358.4
2014[1]	337.8	342.2	359.0	371.7	374.5	375.0	369.0	354.0	346.3	324.1	294.5	261.8	342.5

[1] Preliminary.   [2] Also includes types of motor oil not shown separately.   [3] Including taxes.   *Source: Energy Information Administration, U.S. Department of Energy (EIA-DOE)*

Average Refiner Price of Finished Aviation Gasoline to End Users[2] in the United States   In Cents per Gallon

Year	Jan.	Feb.	Mar.	Apr.	May	June	July	Aug.	Sept.	Oct.	Nov.	Dec.	Average
2005	173.8	186.7	201.5	221.7	212.1	211.6	223.0	238.6	280.8	270.8	218.6	219.3	221.5
2006	239.1	232.4	247.3	286.9	301.3	305.7	310.3	305.8	253.2	238.5	235.3	234.9	265.9
2007	217.9	228.5	262.7	296.9	309.6	297.8	305.3	282.3	290.0	285.5	306.7	297.5	281.7
2008	298.7	295.4	329.6	335.8	361.5	396.5	392.9	379.2	383.7	297.5	223.0	181.4	322.9
2009	185.7	197.4	197.7	215.0	242.3	270.7	260.7	276.4	268.4	269.3	284.5	279.9	245.7
2010	291.4	285.5	310.3	320.1	312.9	298.1	302.8	296.7	289.3	300.0	309.5	321.8	303.2
2011	332.3	337.4	376.7	413.2	409.1	391.3	402.7	392.0	391.5	369.7	362.0	W	379.8
2012	373.2	W	413.3	431.3	W	W	W	409.1	426.2	406.4	356.1	359.9	396.9
2013	W	406.0	402.2	386.0	390.0	419.1	422.4	429.8	398.2	365.3	367.3	367.8	395.8
2014[1]	W	414.2	W	W	W	W	W	W	W	W	W	W	414.2

[1] Preliminary.   [2] Excluding taxes.   NA = Not available.   W = Withheld proprietary data.   *Source: Energy Information Administration, U.S. Department Energy (EIA-DOE)*

Gold

Gold is a dense, bright yellow metallic element with a high luster. Gold is an inactive substance and is unaffected by air, heat, moisture, and most solvents. Gold has been coveted for centuries for its unique blend of rarity, beauty, and near indestructibility. The Egyptians mined gold before 2,000 BC. The first known, pure gold coin was made on the orders of King Croesus of Lydia in the sixth century BC.

Gold is found in nature in quartz veins and secondary alluvial deposits as a free metal. Gold is produced from mines on every continent with the exception of Antarctica, where mining is forbidden. Because it is virtually indestructible, much of the gold that has ever been mined still exists above ground in one form or another. The largest producer of gold in the U.S. by far is the state of Nevada, with Alaska and California running a distant second and third.

Gold is a vital industrial commodity. Pure gold is one of the most malleable and ductile of all the metals. It is a good conductor of heat and electricity. The prime industrial use of gold is in electronics. Another important sector is dental gold where it has been used for almost 3,000 years. Other applications for gold include decorative gold leaf, reflective glass, and jewelry.

In 1792, the United States first assigned a formal monetary role for gold when Congress put the nation's currency on a bimetallic standard, backing it with gold and silver. Under the gold standard, the U.S. government was willing to exchange its paper currency for a set amount of gold, meaning the paper currency was backed by a physical asset with real value. However, President Nixon in 1971 severed the convertibility between the U.S. dollar and gold, which led to the breakdown of the Bretton Woods international payments system. Since then, the prices of gold and of paper currencies have floated freely. U.S. and other central banks now hold physical gold reserves primarily as a store of wealth.

Gold futures and options are traded at the CME Group, NYSE-LIFFE U.S., the Bolsa de Mercado & Futuros (BM&F), EUREX, JSE Securities Exchange, and the Moscow Exchange. Gold futures are traded on the Hong Kong Exchanges & Clearing, the Indonesia Commodity & Derivatives Exchange (ICDX), the Multi Commodity Exchange of India (MCX), the Korea Exchange, Shanghai Futures Exchange (SHFE), and the Singapore Exchange (SGX). The CME gold futures contract calls for the delivery of 100 troy ounces of gold (0.995 fineness), and the contract trades in terms of dollars and cents per troy ounce.

Prices – CME gold futures prices (Barchart.com symbol GC) started 2014 on firm footing and rose to the high for the year in February of $1,392 an ounce, a 15-month high. The Bank of Japan's expansion of its emergency lending programs for another year boosted demand for gold as an alternative asset. Gold prices then traded sideways to lower through Q2 as the dollar strengthened on indications that the Fed would continue to taper QE3. Gold prices sold off in Q4 and slid to the low for the year in November at $1,130 an ounce, a 4-3/4 year low. The main bearish factors for gold were the rally in the dollar index to an 8-1/2 year high by year-end and strength in stocks as the S&P 500 continued to post record highs, which curbed safe-haven demand for gold. Also, the plunge in crude oil to a 5-1/2 year low reduced inflation expectations and undercut demand for gold as an inflation hedge. Fund support for gold slid throughout 2014 as long gold positions in ETFs by December fell to a 5-year low. Gold finished 2014 down -1.5% at $1,184 an ounce.

Supply – World mine production of gold rose +2.1% yr/yr to 2.860 million kilograms in 2014, a new record high (1 kilogram = 32.1507 troy ounces). The world's largest producers of gold in 2014 were China with 15.7% of world production, followed by Australia (9.4%), Russia (8.6%), the U.S (7.4%), and Peru and South Africa each with (5.2%).

Gold mine production has been moving lower in most major gold-producing countries such as South Africa, Australia, and the U.S. For example, South Africa's production of 150,000 kilograms in 2014 was down -6.3% yr/yr and that was about one-third the production levels of more than 600,000 kilograms seen in the 1980s and early 1990s. On the other hand, China's gold production in 2014 rose +4.7% to a record 450,000 kilograms. U.S. gold mine production in 2014 fell -8.3% yr/yr to 211,000 kilograms, just above 2009 production level which was the lowest production since 1988. U.S. refinery production of gold from domestic and foreign ore sources in 2014 fell -10.3% yr/yr to 200,000 kilograms. U.S. refinery production of gold from secondary scrap sources in 2014 fell -4.8% yr/yr to 200,000 kilograms.

Demand – U.S. consumption of gold in 2014 rose +3.1% yr/yr to 165,000 kilograms. The most recent data available from the early 1990s showed that 71% of that gold demand came from jewelry and the arts, 22% from industrial uses, and 7% from dental uses.

Trade – U.S. exports of gold (excluding coinage) in 2014 fell -37.8% yr/yr to 430,000 kilograms, below the 2012 record high of 695,000 kilograms. U.S. imports of gold for consumption in 2014 remained unchanged yr/yr at 315,000 kilograms, below the 2012 record high of 326,000 kilograms.

World Mine Production of Gold   In Kilograms (1 Kilogram = 32.1507 Troy Ounces)

Year	Australia	Brazil	Canada	China	Ghana	Indonesia	Papua New Guinea	Peru	Russia	South Africa	United States	Uzbek-istan	World Total
2006	247,000	43,082	103,513	245,000	69,817	93,176	58,349	202,826	159,340	272,128	252,000	85,000	2,370,000
2007	247,000	49,613	102,211	275,000	83,558	117,851	57,549	170,236	156,975	252,598	238,000	85,000	2,350,000
2008	215,000	54,666	94,909	285,000	73,819	64,390	67,463	179,870	172,031	212,571	233,000	85,000	2,300,000
2009	224,000	60,330	96,573	320,000	67,818	140,488	63,600	183,995	192,832	197,628	223,000	90,000	2,480,000
2010	261,000	62,047	102,147	345,000	72,441	106,316	62,900	164,084	189,000	188,702	231,000	90,000	2,580,000
2011	260,000	65,209	101,975	362,000	82,919	96,100	61,760	166,187	199,642	180,184	234,000	91,000	2,670,000
2012	250,000	65,000	103,713	403,000	86,540	58,800	53,100	161,325	217,800	160,000	235,000	93,000	2,690,000
2013[1]	265,000	71,000	124,000	430,000	90,000	61,000	57,000	151,000	230,000	160,000	230,000	98,000	2,800,000
2014[2]	270,000	70,000	160,000	450,000	90,000	65,000	60,000	150,000	245,000	150,000	211,000	102,000	2,860,000

[1] Preliminary.   [2] Estimate.   *Source: U.S. Geological Survey (USGS)*

GOLD

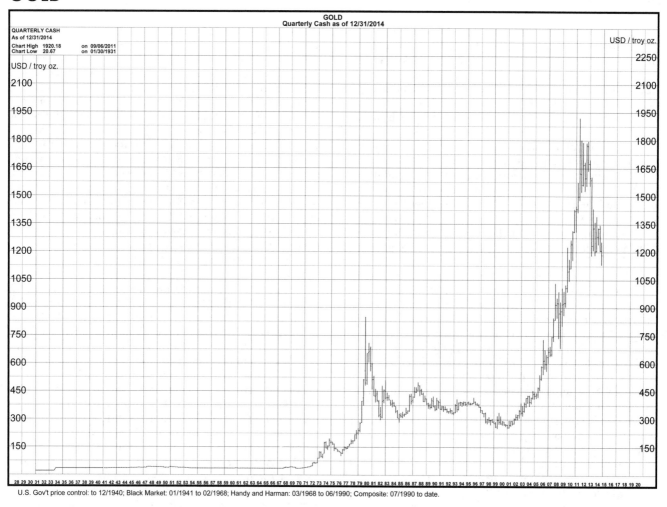

QUARTERLY CASH
As of 12/31/2014
Chart High 1920.18 on 09/06/2011
Chart Low 20.67 on 01/30/1931

USD / troy oz.

U.S. Gov't price control: to 12/1940; Black Market: 01/1941 to 02/1968; Handy and Harman: 03/1968 to 06/1990; Composite: 07/1990 to date.

Salient Statistics of Gold in the United States   In Kilograms (1 Kilogram = 32.1507 Troy Ounces)

Year	Mine Pro- duction	Value Million $	Domestic & Foreign Ores	Secondary (Old Scrap)	Exports, Excluding Coinage	Imports for Con- sumption	Treasury Depart- ment[3]	Futures Exchange	Industry	Official World Reserves[4]	Dental	Indus- trial[5]	Jewelry & Arts	Total
2005	256,000	3,670.0	195,000	81,300	324,000	341,000	8,140,000	211,000	2,040	30,800	----	----	----	183,000
2006	252,000	4,910.0	181,000	89,100	389,000	263,000	8,140,000	234,000	2,000	30,400	----	----	----	185,000
2007	238,000	5,350.0	176,000	135,000	519,000	170,000	8,140,000	229,000	1,140	29,900	----	----	----	180,000
2008	233,000	6,550.0	168,000	181,000	567,000	231,000	8,140,000	265,000	W	28,700	----	----	----	176,000
2009	223,000	7,000.0	170,000	189,000	381,000	320,000	8,140,000	305,000	9,200	30,400	----	----	----	173,000
2010	231,000	9,130.0	175,000	198,000	383,000	616,000	8,140,000	361,000	6,810	30,700	----	----	----	180,000
2011	234,000	11,800.0	220,000	263,000	644,000	550,000	8,140,000	353,000	6,470	31,100	----	----	----	168,000
2012	235,000	12,600.0	222,000	215,000	695,000	326,000	8,140,000	344,000	4,070	31,700	----	----	----	147,000
2013[1]	230,000		223,000	210,000	691,000	315,000	8,140,000				----	----	----	160,000
2014[2]	211,000		200,000	200,000	430,000	315,000	8,140,000							165,000

[1] Preliminary.   [2] Estimate.   [3] Includes gold in Exchange Stabilization Fund.   [4] Held by market economy country central banks and governments and international monetary orgainzations.   [5] Including space and defense.   NA = Not available.   *Source: U.S. Geological Survey (USGS)*

Monthly Average Gold Price (Handy & Harman) in New York   Dollars Per Troy Ounce

Year	Jan.	Feb.	Mar.	Apr.	May	June	July	Aug.	Sept.	Oct.	Nov.	Dec. Average
2005	424.39	423.15	433.91	429.23	422.53	430.66	424.33	438.03	456.52	469.90	474.87	510.01	444.79
2006	549.27	555.02	557.09	610.41	673.97	596.15	634.89	632.10	596.76	585.78	627.12	629.38	604.00
2007	630.97	664.43	655.30	679.20	667.86	655.40	665.83	665.21	714.79	749.73	806.68	803.20	696.55
2008	890.47	923.25	966.30	909.70	886.29	889.49	940.16	838.30	830.30	806.62	754.95	816.09	870.99
2009	859.98	943.20	924.27	890.50	927.34	945.67	934.31	949.34	996.76	1,043.16	1,122.03	1,212.50	979.09
2010	1,116.74	1,095.26	1,114.36	1,147.70	1,204.50	1,232.92	1,192.25	1,217.11	1,272.02	1,342.02	1,370.46	1,389.70	1,224.59
2011	1,359.39	1,371.13	1,424.01	1,478.55	1,511.63	1,528.66	1,576.70	1,757.21	1,765.99	1,665.36	1,743.83	1,645.50	1,569.00
2012	1,656.88	1,743.10	1,673.77	1,649.72	1,588.34	1,598.98	1,592.98	1,627.97	1,747.24	1,748.69	1,719.98	1,684.18	1,669.32
2013	1,670.17	1,628.47	1,592.85	1,490.22	1,415.91	1,342.36	1,288.31	1,349.30	1,346.63	1,316.19	1,276.94	1,220.65	1,411.50
2014	1,244.53	1,300.60	1,336.08	1,298.45	1,288.74	1,279.10	1,310.59	1,295.13	1,236.14	1,222.49	1,175.33	1,200.62	1,265.65

Source: U.S. Geological Survey (USGS)

Nearby Futures through Last Trading Day using selected contract months: February, April, June, August, October and December.

Volume of Trading of Gold Futures in New York (COMEX)   In Thousands of Contracts

Year	Jan.	Feb.	Mar.	Apr.	May	June	July	Aug.	Sept.	Oct.	Nov.	Dec.	Total
2005	1,502.3	944.4	1,599.0	858.1	1,451.7	1,240.0	1,432.4	1,234.4	1,380.2	1,174.0	1,852.7	1,221.5	15,890.6
2006	2,018.8	1,162.7	2,052.7	1,302.9	2,071.0	1,148.6	1,487.2	804.5	884.7	857.1	1,284.7	842.7	15,917.6
2007	1,929.8	1,455.9	2,195.9	1,405.2	2,336.6	1,610.8	2,292.2	1,710.7	2,024.6	2,584.4	3,837.1	1,677.2	25,060.4
2008	4,041.7	2,617.6	3,901.8	2,765.5	3,328.0	2,624.0	4,269.9	3,066.1	4,109.4	3,045.1	2,687.1	1,921.1	38,377.4
2009	3,073.0	2,444.2	3,385.0	1,808.4	2,766.7	2,305.0	2,846.2	1,815.6	2,831.4	3,216.7	4,564.3	4,083.1	35,139.5
2010	4,574.3	3,616.1	4,385.6	2,932.3	4,824.1	3,024.7	4,097.3	2,184.9	2,732.1	3,858.8	5,530.4	2,969.7	44,730.3
2011	4,724.6	2,740.4	4,512.3	3,145.2	4,955.3	3,078.9	4,278.2	6,406.6	5,300.5	3,026.4	4,105.3	2,901.9	49,175.6
2012	4,146.5	3,506.7	4,860.6	2,834.8	4,913.7	3,479.4	3,732.7	2,793.5	3,460.8	3,147.0	4,380.3	2,637.3	43,893.3
2013	4,221.1	3,632.3	3,906.6	5,218.8	5,312.3	3,744.7	4,647.2	3,466.7	3,331.9	3,458.2	3,577.1	2,777.7	47,294.6
2014	3,754.8	2,607.5	4,200.3	2,692.9	3,631.1	2,508.1	3,848.3	2,381.8	3,205.8	3,703.7	4,676.8	3,307.6	40,518.8

Contract size = 100 oz.   *Source: CME Group; New York Mercantile Exchange (NYMEX)*

Average Open Interest of Gold in New York (COMEX)   In Contracts

Year	Jan.	Feb.	Mar.	Apr.	May	June	July	Aug.	Sept.	Oct.	Nov.	Dec.
2005	277,112	263,191	301,758	283,546	277,469	275,508	268,068	304,000	339,269	356,526	334,562	331,527
2006	348,949	338,851	331,223	350,380	336,735	288,309	316,969	309,186	320,850	330,152	346,141	335,204
2007	350,958	387,321	372,781	377,094	405,645	401,337	379,066	339,923	394,400	479,735	530,775	500,409
2008	556,302	487,373	471,320	418,693	435,847	401,914	460,178	382,302	378,216	321,545	290,706	280,402
2009	331,891	359,420	376,201	341,491	366,468	382,960	380,301	383,826	454,286	493,909	522,556	504,102
2010	512,723	469,214	489,600	521,976	574,107	579,416	561,781	541,408	595,118	619,536	626,630	589,823
2011	556,448	479,014	507,118	522,520	513,744	504,841	522,091	517,064	494,932	438,488	453,477	424,014
2012	426,896	445,515	434,210	402,740	423,294	417,783	424,790	400,896	471,946	469,628	461,382	430,717
2013	442,707	435,425	437,300	416,489	431,460	383,314	424,302	388,278	380,768	382,216	395,583	383,980
2014	397,700	381,045	404,828	369,755	395,313	385,660	400,977	365,066	381,961	400,455	433,102	372,432

Contract size = 100 oz.   *Source: CME Group; New York Mercantile Exchange (NYMEX)*

GOLD

Commodity Exchange, Inc. (COMEX) Depository Warehouse Stocks of Gold   In Thousands of Troy Ounces

Year	Jan. 1	Feb. 1	Mar. 1	Apr. 1	May 1	June 1	July 1	Aug. 1	Sept. 1	Oct. 1	Nov. 1	Dec. 1
2005	5,795.6	5,962.6	5,913.9	5,960.7	6,156.7	6,036.6	5,751.0	5,713.8	6,008.5	6,737.1	6,351.5	6,614.3
2006	6,657.7	7,320.9	7,518.9	7,426.6	7,334.4	7,796.0	8,031.2	8,199.0	7,980.8	7,695.2	7,565.8	7,491.1
2007	7,534.5	7,459.2	7,487.2	7,302.5	7,624.8	7,633.1	7,276.1	7,130.5	7,077.1	7,211.9	7,346.7	7,366.1
2008	7,492.5	7,588.0	7,371.3	7,623.1	7,760.4	7,588.9	7,611.6	8,266.0	8,442.8	8,594.9	8,171.8	8,540.3
2009	8,548.5	8,556.8	8,635.9	8,508.6	8,322.6	8,725.8	8,893.4	9,144.6	9,173.0	9,316.2	9,316.2	9,508.9
2010	9,679.4	9,679.4	9,679.4	10,022.9	10,184.3	10,736.8	10,923.5	11,112.1	10,816.9	10,896.7	11,311.9	11,488.4
2011	11,694.3	11,401.9	11,075.3	11,033.0	11,140.8	11,310.3	11,439.7	11,431.5	11,559.8	11,246.8	11,236.9	11,301.8
2012	11,469.4	11,434.6	11,405.2	11,350.5	10,895.2	10,978.4	10,831.7	10,806.6	10,844.5	11,009.3	11,243.3	11,151.0
2013	11,058.7	11,009.3	10,289.3	9,279.4	8,129.2	8,054.9	7,534.5	6,991.4	7,013.2	6,862.8	7,153.7	7,247.9
2014	7,828.1	7,081.3	7,177.1	7,740.8	7,935.6	8,262.7	8,298.5	8,684.3	9,927.3	9,127.3	8,056.0	7,928.7

Source: CME Group; New York Mercantile Exchange (NYMEX)

Central Gold Bank Reserves   In Millions of Troy Ounces

Year	Belgium	Canada	France	Germany	Italy	Japan	Netherlands	Switzerland	United Kingdom	United States	Industrial Total	Developing Oil	Developing Non-Oil	IMF[2]	Bank for Int'l Settlements	World Total
2005	7.3	0.1	90.9	110.2	78.8	24.6	22.3	41.5	10.0	261.6	----	----	----	----	----	991.5
2006	7.3	0.1	87.4	110.0	78.8	24.6	20.6	41.5	10.0	261.5	----	----	----	----	----	979.7
2007	7.3	0.1	83.7	109.9	78.8	24.6	20.0	36.8	10.0	261.5	----	----	----	----	----	963.5
2008	7.3	0.1	80.1	109.7	78.8	24.6	19.7	33.4	10.0	261.5	----	----	----	----	----	964.1
2009	7.3	0.1	78.3	109.5	78.8	24.6	19.7	33.4	10.0	261.5	----	----	----	----	----	980.9
2010	7.3	0.1	78.3	109.3	78.8	24.6	19.7	33.4	10.0	261.5	----	----	----	----	----	991.6
2011	7.3	0.1	78.3	109.2	78.8	24.6	19.7	33.4	10.0	261.5	----	----	----	----	----	1,003.7
2012	7.3	0.1	78.3	109.0	78.8	24.6	19.7	33.4	10.0	261.5	----	----	----	----	----	1,019.4
2013	7.3	0.1	78.3	108.9	78.8	24.6	19.7	33.4	10.0	261.5	----	----	----	----	----	1,025.3
2014[1]	7.3	0.1	78.3	108.8	78.8	24.6	19.7	33.4	10.0	261.5	----	----	----	----	----	

[1] Preliminary.   [2] International Monetary Fund.   *Source: American Metal Market (AMM)*

Mine Production of Recoverable Gold in the United States   In Kilograms

Year	Arizona	California	Idaho	Montana	Nevada	Alaska	Colorado	South Dakota	New Mexico	Utah	Other States	Total
2004	W	3,260	W	W	216,000	W	W	W	W	W	38,740	258,000
2005	W	W	W	W	212,000	W	W	W	W	W	44,200	256,000
2006	W	W	W	W	206,000	W	W	W	W	W	45,800	252,000
2007	W	W	W	W	186,000	W	W	W	W	W	52,400	238,000
2008	W	W	W	W	178,000	W	W	W	W	W	55,400	233,000
2009	W	W	W	W	161,000	W	W	W	W	W	62,500	223,000
2010	W	W	W	W	166,000	28,100	W	W	W	W	36,900	231,000
2011	W	W	W	W	172,000	25,800	W	W	W	W	36,100	234,000
2012	W	W	W	W	175,000	27,700	W	W	W	W	31,400	235,000
2013[1]	W	W	W	W	170,000	32,200	W	W	W	W	27,800	230,000

[1] Preliminary.   W = Withheld proprietary data, included in "Other States."   *Source: U.S. Geological Survey (USGS)*

U.S. Exports of Gold   In Kilograms

Year	Australia	Canada	China	Germany	Hong Kong	India	Mexico	South Africa	Switzerland	Thailand	United Arab Emirates	United Kingdom	Total
2003	----	2,160	32	624	98	11	11,600	8	237,000	1[1]	1,050	94,500	352,000
2004	5,250	18,100	45	77	30	10	12,500	14	174,000	23	7,910	29,300	257,000
2005	1,980	738	49	1,940	6,270	2,500	5,980	----	197,000	5,980	22,200	64,900	324,000
2006	6,010	1,530	3	124	2,320	67	7,430	----	213,000	505	10,200	145,000	389,000
2007	2,470	9,210	10	664	1,170	17,000	5,890	----	266,000	1,330	20,000	191,000	519,000
2008	12,300	11,800	219	305	4,280	18,800	4,660	5,270	296,000	8,510	20,700	181,000	568,000
2009	26,700	3,110	51	832	844	21,000	3,120	----	103,000	----	147	220,000	381,000
2010	14,200	8,750	558	1,390	18,400	30,900	2,270	9,510	113,000	5,000	3,080	170,000	383,000
2011	18,200	1,460	5,150	1,440	111,000	15,500	5,160	11,900	105,000	21,200	10,300	161,000	474,000
2012	5,140	18,400	1,200	2,230	133,000	66,900	7,040	8,260	280,000	9,280	64,200	137,000	692,000

[1] Less than 1/2 unit.   *Source: U.S. Geological Survey (USGS)*

Gold in British Pound
Ratio Spread (a / b)

Gold in Euro
Ratio Spread (a / b)

Gold in Japanese Yen
Ratio Spread (a / b)

Gold in Swiss Franc
Ratio Spread (a / b)

Grain Sorghum

Grain sorghums include milo, kafir, durra, feterita, and kaoliang. Grain sorghums are tolerant of drought by going into dormancy during dry and hot conditions and then resuming growth as conditions improve. Grain sorghums are a staple food in China, India, and Africa but in the U.S. they are mainly used as livestock feed. The two key U.S. producing states are Texas and Kansas, each with about one-third of total U.S. production. U.S. sorghum production has become more popular with the breeding of dwarf grain sorghum hybrids which are only about 3 feet tall (versus up to 10 feet tall for wild sorghum) and are easier to harvest with a combine. The U.S. sorghum crop year begins September 1.

Prices – The monthly average price for sorghum grain received by U.S. farmers in the 2014-15 marketing year (Sep-Aug) fell by -13.9% yr/yr to $6.68 per hundred pounds (annualized through December 2014). The value of U.S. grain sorghum production in the 2013-14 (latest data) marketing year rose +5.9% to $1.695 billion.

Supply – World production of sorghum in the 2014-15 marketing year rose +3.1% to 62.125 million metric tons, below the 13-year high of 65.909 million metric tons posted in 2007-08. U.S. grain sorghum production in 2014-15 rose

+10.3% yr/yr to 432.575 million bushels. Sorghum acreage harvested in 2014-15 is forecasted to fall -2.8% to 6.401 million acres, above the 2006-07 figure of 4.937 acres which was the smallest sorghum acreage since the late 1930s. Yield in 2014-15 was 67.6 bushels per acre, but that was still below the record high of 73.2 bushels per acre in 2007-08.

Demand – World utilization (consumption) of grain sorghum in the 2014-15 marketing year rose +5.6% to 62.021 million metric tons. The biggest consumers are Mexico utilizing 12.6% of the world supply and the U.S. utilizing 6.8% of the world supply.

Trade – World exports of sorghum in the 2014-15 marketing year rose +24.0% to 9.368 million metric tons, below the 21-year high of 9.773 million metric tons seen in 2007-08. U.S. exports in 2014-15 rose +27.5% yr/yr to 6.858 million metric tons, accounting for 73.2% of total world exports. Argentina is the world's other major exporter with 1.200 million metric tons of exports in 2014-15, accounting for 12.8% of total world exports. World imports of sorghum in 2014-15 rose +33.8% yr/yr to 8.865 million metric tons. Major world importers are Mexico and Japan.

World Supply and Demand of Grain Sorghum   In Thousands of Metric Tons

Crop Year	Exports Argen-tina	Exports Non-U.S.	Exports U.S.	Exports Total	Imports Japan	Imports Mexico	Imports Unac-counted	Imports Total	Total Pro-duction	Utilization China	Utilization Mexico	Utilization U.S.	Utilization Total	Ending Stocks Non-U.S.	Ending Stocks U.S.	Ending Stocks Total
2009-10	1,771	6,591	41	6,632	39	1,649	----	6,292	57,200	1,900	950	5,866	58,553	3,624	1,048	4,672
2010-11	1,702	6,726	34	6,760	111	1,418	----	6,722	61,163	2,200	1,250	5,277	59,904	5,182	697	5,879
2011-12	3,083	6,412	113	6,525	22	1,481	----	5,032	57,183	2,200	950	3,916	56,933	4,053	583	4,636
2012-13[1]	1,783	5,412	124	5,536	62	1,897	----	6,764	57,771	3,200	1,200	4,796	58,880	4,380	385	4,765
2013-14[2]	1,200	7,329	229	7,558	84	1,003	----	6,625	60,261	6,800	1,300	4,109	58,754	4,445	864	5,309
2014-15[3]	1,200	9,218	150	9,368	50	1,000	----	8,865	62,125	8,800	1,300	4,191	62,021	5,055	808	5,863

[1] Preliminary.   [2] Estimate.   [3] Forecast.   *Source: Foreign Agricultural Service, U.S. Department of Agriculture (FAS-USDA)*

Salient Statistics of Grain Sorghum in the United States

Crop Year Beginning Sept. 1	Acreage Planted[4] for All Purposes	For Grain Acreage Harvested	For Grain Pro-duction (1,000 Bushels)	For Grain Yield Per Harvested Acre (Bushels)	For Grain Price in Cents Per Bushel	For Grain Value of Pro-duction (Million $)	For Silage Acreage Harvested (1,000 Acres)	For Silage Pro-duction (1,000 Tons)	For Silage Yield Per Harvested Acre (Tons)	Sorghum Grain Stocks Dec. 1 On Farms	Sorghum Grain Stocks Dec. 1 Off Farms	Sorghum Grain Stocks June 1 On Farms	Sorghum Grain Stocks June 1 Off Farms
2009-10	6,633	5,520	382,983	69.4	322	1,207.1	254	3,680	14.5	48,000	202,759	10,700	77,162
2010-11	5,404	4,813	345,625	71.8	502	1,617.9	268	3,370	12.6	30,500	207,168	3,140	76,894
2011-12	5,481	3,929	214,443	54.6	599	1,268.5	224	2,298	10.3	27,850	123,101	4,120	54,405
2012-13[1]	6,259	4,995	247,742	49.6	633	1,606.2	353	4,196	11.9	17,600	122,247	2,710	38,398
2013-14[2]	8,076	6,585	392,331	59.6	375-445	1,716.9	380	5,420	14.3	32,950	198,441	4,500	87,924
2014-15[3]	7,138	6,401	432,575	67.6		1,670.4	315	4,123	13.1	30,500	198,586		

[1] Preliminary.   [2] Estimate.   [3] Forecast.   *Source: Foreign Agricultural Service, U.S. Department of Agriculture (FAS-USDA)*

Production of All Sorghum for Grain in the United States, by States   In Thousands of Bushels

Year	Arkansas	Colo-rado	Illinois	Kansas	Louis-iana	Miss-issippi	Missouri	Nebraska	New Mexico	Okla-homa	South Dakota	Texas	Total
2009	2,923	6,750	2,952	224,400	5,330	770	3,698	13,020	2,300	12,320	7,320	98,400	382,983
2010	2,695	7,520	3,168	171,000	7,410	650	2,574	6,750	4,488	13,000	5,270	119,000	345,625
2011	6,480	4,900	1,820	110,000	10,788	3,700	2,376	6,580	1,344	1,680	6,600	56,350	214,443
2012	11,340	3,000	1,620	81,900	12,300	3,864	3,190	3,540	798	4,940	5,880	112,100	247,742
2013	12,750	5,760	1,880	168,150	12,091	5,828	4,920	9,715	2,312	14,850	22,000	128,800	392,331
2014[1]	16,005	8,400	2,226	199,800	8,928	8,400	7,373	13,120	2,520	17,360	9,450	137,250	432,575

[1] Preliminary.   *Source: National Agricultural Statistics Service, U.S. Department of Agriculture (NASS-USDA)*

Quarterly Supply and Disappearance of Grain Sorghum in the United States   In Millions of Bushels

Crop Year Beginning Sept. 1	Supply				Disappearance						Ending Stocks		
					Domestic Use								
	Beginning Stocks	Pro-duction	Imports[3]	Total Supply	Food & Alcohol	Seed	Feed & Residual	Total	Exports[3]	Total Disap-pearance	Gov't Owned[4]	Privately Owned[5]	Total Stocks
2011-12	27.5	213.0	.1	240.5	84.2	.8	69.2	154.2	63.4	217.6	----	----	23.0
Sept.-Nov.	27.5	213.0	.0	240.4	24.5	0	42.9	67.4	22.1	89.5	----	----	151.0
Dec.-Feb.	151.0	----	.0	151.0	25.5	0	5.7	31.2	11.8	42.9	----	----	108.1
Mar.-May	108.1	----	.1	108.1	25.9	.6	15.4	41.9	7.7	49.6	----	----	58.5
June-Aug.	58.5	----	.0	58.5	8.3	.2	5.3	13.8	21.8	35.6	----	----	23.0
2012-13	23.0	247.7	9.6	280.3	94.3	.9	93.6	188.8	76.3	265.1	----	----	15.2
Sept.-Nov.	23.0	247.7	1.1	271.8	24.9	0	79.7	104.6	27.3	131.9	----	----	139.8
Dec.-Feb.	139.8	----	.1	139.9	24.9	0	4.3	29.2	19.1	48.4	----	----	91.5
Mar.-May	91.5	----	5.5	97.1	25.4	.5	16.5	42.4	13.6	55.9	----	----	41.1
June-Aug.	41.1	----	2.9	44.0	19.1	.4	-6.9	12.6	16.2	28.9	----	----	15.2
2013-14[1]	15.2	392.3	.1	407.6	69.0	1.0	91.8	161.8	211.8	373.5	----	----	34.0
Sept.-Nov.	15.2	392.3	.0	407.5	45.0	0	97.7	142.7	33.4	176.1	----	----	231.4
Dec.-Feb.	231.4	----	.0	231.4	10.0	0	1.9	11.9	43.7	55.7	----	----	175.7
Mar.-May	175.7	----	.0	175.7	11.5	.5	4.9	16.9	66.4	83.3	----	----	92.4
June-Aug.	92.4	----	.1	92.5	2.5	.5	-12.8	-9.8	68.2	58.5	----	----	34.0
2014-15[2]	34.0	432.6	.2	466.8	44.1	.9	120.0	165.0	270.0	435.0	----	----	31.8
Sept.-Nov.	34.0	432.6	.2	466.8	28.0	0	126.3	154.3	83.5	237.7	----	----	229.1

[1] Preliminary.   [2] Estimate.   [3] Uncommitted inventory.   [4] Includes quantity under loan and farmer-owned reserve.   *Source: Economic Research Service, U.S. Department of Agriculture (ERS-USDA)*

Average Price of Sorghum Grain, No. 2, Yellow in Kansas City   In Dollars Per Hundred Pounds (Cwt.)

Year	Sept.	Oct.	Nov.	Dec.	Jan.	Feb.	Mar.	Apr.	May	June	July	Aug.	Average
2007-08	5.68	5.60	6.13	7.34	8.36	8.86	9.13	9.70	9.65	11.63	10.10	8.37	8.38
2008-09	8.43	5.92	5.49	5.19	5.67	5.48	5.51	5.76	6.37	6.29	4.66	4.75	5.79
2009-10	4.81	5.49	5.72	6.44	5.81	5.58	5.69	5.64	5.77	5.50	6.03	6.59	5.75
2010-11	8.23	9.10	9.40	9.91	10.62	11.62	11.37	12.64	12.08	12.21	12.27	12.97	11.04
2011-12	11.79	10.90	11.30	10.91	11.27	11.36	11.14	10.61	10.04	9.90	12.96	13.46	11.30
2012-13	12.74	12.65	12.88	12.74	12.74	12.59	12.63	11.38	11.82	11.97	11.00	8.61	11.98
2013-14	8.15	7.57	7.40	7.52	7.62	8.08	8.64	8.89	8.74	7.98	6.79	6.05	7.79
2014-15[1]	5.31	5.67	6.71	7.25	6.93								6.37

[1] Preliminary.   *Source: Economic Research Service, U.S. Department of Agriculture (ERS-USDA)*

Exports of Grain Sorghum, by Country of Destination from the United States   In Metric Tons

Year	Canada	Ecuador	Eritrea (Ethiopia)	Israel	Japan	Jordan	Mexico	South Africa	Spain	Sudan	Turkey	World Total
2007-08	5,775	----	27,600	137,284	505,919	125	1,150,231	45,498	1,929,955	303,818	----	6,653,444
2008-09	4,987	----	28,170	----	313,179	----	2,476,004	41,000	----	268,160	----	3,585,632
2009-10	3,928	----	----	20,681	818,807	----	2,475,084	21,000	----	344,283	----	4,015,978
2010-11	3,704	----	----	134,990	327,689	----	2,364,880	23,039	482,697	191,658	----	3,803,830
2011-12	2,379	----	----	----	127,396	----	1,153,494	20,000	295	108,480	----	1,529,460
2012-13[1]	3,251	----	----	----	220,070	----	1,336,805	38,720	35,500	178,240	813	2,099,325
2013-14[2]	5,299	----	----	----	254,692	----	135,236	47,363	18,910	94,063	----	5,793,416

[1] Preliminary.   [2] Estimate.   *Source: Economic Research Service, U.S. Department of Agriculture (ERS-USDA)*

Grain Sorghum Price Support Program and Market Prices in the United States

	Price Support Operations						Effective Base[3] (Million Acres)	Partici-pation Rate[4] % of Base	No. 2 Yellow ($ Per Cwt.)			
	Price Support		Aquired by CCC	Owned by CCC at Year End	Basic Loan Rate	Target Price	Findley Loan Rate			Kansas City	Texas High Plains	Los Angeles	Gulf Ports
Year	Quantity	% of Pro-duction											
	Million Cwt.				Dollars Per Bushel								
2006-07	1.9	1.2	0	0	3.48	4.59	1.95	11.8	----	5.75	6.09	----	7.39
2007-08	1.8	.7	0	0	3.48	4.59	1.95	11.7	----	8.38	8.49	----	9.81
2008-09	4.5	1.7	0	0	3.48	4.59	1.95	11.5	----	5.79	5.44	----	7.18
2009-10	1.8	.8	0	0	3.48	4.59	1.95	----	----	5.75	5.73	----	7.74
2010-11	.5	.3	0	0	3.48	4.70	1.95	----	----	11.04	10.61	----	11.92
2011-12[1]	.3	.2	----	----	3.48	4.70	1.95	----	----	11.30	10.92	----	12.33
2012-13[2]	----	----	----	----	3.48	4.70	1.95	----	----	11.98	----	----	12.66

[1] Preliminary.   [2] Estimate.   [3] National effective crop acreage base as determined by ASCS.   [4] Percentage of effective base acres enrolled in acreage reduction programs.   5/ Beginning with the 1996-7 marketing year, target prices are no longer applicable.   *Source: Economic Research Service, U.S. Department of Agriculture (ERS-USDA)*

Hay

Hay is a catchall term for forage plants, typically grasses such as timothy and Sudan-grass, and legumes such as alfalfa and clover. Alfalfa and alfalfa mixtures account for nearly half of all hay production. Hay is generally used to make cured feed for livestock. Curing, which is the proper drying of hay, is necessary to prevent spoilage. Hay, when properly cured, contains about 20% moisture. If hay is dried excessively, however, there is a loss of protein, which makes it less effective as livestock feed. Hay is harvested in virtually all of the lower 48 states.

Prices – The average monthly price of hay received by U.S. farmers in the first eight months of the 2014-15 marketing year (May/April) through December 2014 rose by +1.3% yr/yr to $181.00 per ton, down from the record high of $189.67 per ton seen in 2012-13. The farm production value of hay produced in 2013-14 (latest data) was $20.211 million.

Supply – U.S. hay production in 2014-15 rose +3.6% yr/yr to 139.789 million tons. U.S. farmers harvested 57.092 million acres of hay in 2014-15, down -1.4% yr/yr. The yield in 2014-15 was 2.45 tons per acre, below the 2004-05 record high of 2.55. U.S. carryover (May 1) in 2013-14 (latest data) fell -33.8% to 14.156 million tons.

The largest hay producing states in the U.S. for 2014 were Texas, (with 8.4% of U.S. hay production), California (5.3%), Missouri (5.1%), South Dakota (4.8%), Oklahoma (4.4%), Nebraska (4.3%), and North Dakota (3.9%).

Salient Statistics of All Hay in the United States

Crop Year Beginning May 1	Acres Harvested (1,000 Acres)	Yield Per Acre (Tons)	Pro-duction	Carry-over May 1	Disap-pearance	Supply Per Animal Unit	Disap-pearance	Animal Units Fed[3] (Millions)	Farm Price ($ Per Ton)	Farm Pro-duction Value Million $	Alfalfa (Certified)	Timothy	Red Clover	Sudan-grass
			------ Millions of Tons ------			----- In Tons -----					---------- Dollars Per Cwt. ----------			
2009-10	59,775	2.47	147.7	22.1	148.5	2.41	2.11	70.4	109.8	14,716	379.00	149.00	289.00	72.50
2010-11	59,872	2.43	145.6	20.9	143.9	2.40	2.08	69.3	116.1	14,656	379.00	135.00	213.00	73.60
2011-12	55,633	2.36	131.1	22.2		2.26	1.95	67.9	176.7	18,251				
2012-13	54,653	2.14	117.1	21.4		2.10	1.89	67.2	189.7	18,613				
2013-14[1]	57,897	2.33	135.0	14.2		2.24		67.1	178.5	19,815				
2014-15[2]	57,092	2.45	139.8							19,185				

[1] Preliminary. [2] Estimate. [3] Roughage-consuming animal units fed annually. NA = Not available.
Source: Economic Research Service, U.S. Department of Agriculture (ERS-USDA)

Production of All Hay in the United States, by States   In Thousands of Tons

Year	California	Idaho	Iowa	Minne-sota	Missouri	New York	North Dakota	Ohio	Okla-homa	South Dakota	Texas	Wisconsin	Total
2009	8,890	5,528	4,002	5,250	8,040	6,235	5,240	2,876	5,278	7,830	8,250	4,430	147,700
2010	8,304	5,460	3,760	5,400	7,512	6,349	5,321	2,871	5,953	7,335	10,800	4,526	145,624
2011	7,980	5,070	3,460	5,530	6,250	5,624	5,224	2,772	2,330	8,625	4,440	4,075	131,144
2012	8,130	4,730	2,780	3,995	5,580	4,457	3,156	2,214	3,880	3,740	9,460	3,350	117,072
2013	7,646	4,976	3,377	3,895	7,921	4,935	5,090	2,495	4,981	5,905	8,880	3,760	135,002
2014[1]	7,388	4,881	3,675	4,486	7,100	6,028	5,460	2,710	6,121	6,665	11,746	4,866	139,798

[1] Preliminary.   *Source: Agricultural Statistics Board, U.S. Department of Agriculture (ASB-USDA)*

Hay Production and Farm Stocks in the United States   In Thousands of Short Tons

Year	Alfalfa & Mixtures	All Others	All Hay	Corn for Silage[1]	Sorghum Silage[1]	Farm Stocks May 1	Farm Stocks Dec. 1
2009	71,072	76,628	147,700	108,209	3,680	22,065	107,222
2010	67,971	77,653	145,624	107,314	3,370	20,931	102,134
2011	65,332	65,812	131,144	108,926	2,298	22,217	90,726
2012	50,600	66,472	117,072	116,148	4,196	21,381	76,547
2013	57,217	77,785	135,002	118,296	5,420	14,156	89,304
2014[2]	61,446	78,352	139,798	128,048	4,123	19,176	92,052

[1] Not included in all tame hay. [2] Preliminary. *Source: Agricultural Statistics Board, U.S. Department of Agriculture (ASB-USDA)*

Mid-Month Price Received by Farmers for All Hay (Baled) in the United States   In Dollars Per Ton

Year	May	June	July	Aug.	Sept.	Oct.	Nov.	Dec.	Jan.	Feb.	Mar.	Apr.	Average
2009-10	130.0	123.0	116.0	104.0	105.0	105.0	105.0	105.0	106.0	104.0	107.0	108.0	109.8
2010-11	116.0	114.0	112.0	110.0	112.0	111.0	110.0	111.0	112.0	116.0	126.0	143.0	116.1
2011-12	171.0	163.0	170.0	179.0	180.0	185.0	174.0	174.0	172.0	177.0	183.0	192.0	176.7
2012-13	201.0	183.0	184.0	183.0	185.0	191.0	190.0	189.0	188.0	192.0	195.0	195.0	189.7
2013-14	203.0	199.0	190.0	177.0	174.0	174.0	168.0	163.0	162.0	168.0	173.0	191.0	178.5
2014-15[1]	202.0	197.0	192.0	185.0	176.0	173.0	164.0	159.0	152.0				177.8

[1] Preliminary. [2] Marketing year average. *Source: Economic Research Service, U.S. Department of Agriculture (ERS-USDA)*

Heating Oil

Heating oil is a heavy fuel oil that is derived from crude oil. Heating oil is also known as No. 2 fuel oil and accounts for about 25% of the yield from a barrel of crude oil. That is the second largest "cut" after gasoline. The price to consumers of home heating oil is generally comprised of 42% for crude oil, 12% for refining costs, and 46% for marketing and distribution costs (Source: EIA's Petroleum Marketing Monthly, 2001). Generally, a $1 increase in the price of crude oil translates into a 2.5-cent per gallon rise in heating oil. Because of this, heating oil prices are highly correlated with crude oil prices, although heating oil prices are also subject to swift supply and demand shifts due to weather changes or refinery shutdowns.

The primary use for heating oil is for residential heating. In the U.S., approximately 8.1 million households use heating oil as their main heating fuel. Most of the demand for heating oil occurs from October through March. The Northeast region, which includes the New England and the Central Atlantic States, is most reliant on heating oil. This region consumes approximately 70% of U.S. heating oil. However, demand for heating oil has been dropping as households switch to a more convenient heating source like natural gas. In fact, demand for heating oil is down by about 10 billion gallons/year from its peak use in 1976 (Source: American Petroleum Institute).

Refineries produce approximately 85% of U.S. heating oil as part of the "distillate fuel oil" product family, which includes heating oil and diesel fuel. The remainder of U.S. heating oil is imported from Canada, the Virgin Islands, and Venezuela.

Recently, a team of Purdue University researchers developed a way to make home heating oil from a mixture of soybean oil and conventional fuel oil. The oil blend is made by replacing 20% of the fuel oil with soybean oil, potentially saving 1.3 billion gallons of fuel oil per year. This soybean heating oil can be used in conventional furnaces without altering existing equipment. The soybean heating oil is relatively easy to produce and creates no sulfur emissions.

The "crack-spread" is the processing margin earned when refiners buy crude oil and refine it into heating oil and gasoline. The crack-spread ratio commonly used in the industry is the 3-2-1, which involves buying 1 heating oil contract and 2 gasoline futures contracts, and then selling 3 crude oil contracts. As long as the crack spread is positive, it is profitable for refiners to buy crude oil and refine it into products.

Heating oil futures and options trade at the CME Group. The heating oil futures contract calls for the delivery of 1,000 barrels of fungible No. 2 heating oil in the New York harbor. In London, heating oil and gas/oil futures and options are traded on ICE Futures Europe. Futures are also traded on the Multi Commodity Exchange of India (MCX).

Prices – CME heating oil futures prices (Barchart. com symbol code HO) on the nearest-futures chart traded sideways in the first half of 2014 but then plunged in the latter half of the year to post a new 5-year low and close 2014 down -40.2% at $1.8336 per gallon.

Supply – U.S. production of distillate fuel oil in 2014 (through November, annualized) rose by +3.3% yr/yr to 4.888 million barrels per day, a new record high. Stocks of distillate fuel oil in November 2014 were 126.093 million barrels. U.S. production of residual fuel in 2014 (through November, annualized) fell by -7.2% yr/yr to an average of 432,000 barrels per day, which was less than half the production level of over 1 million barrels per day produced in the 1970s. U.S. stocks of residual fuel oil as of January 1, 2014 rose +3.5% to 36.788 million barrels, down from the 2007 record of 42.329 million barrels.

Demand – U.S. usage of distillate fuel oil in 2014 (through November, annualized) rose +4.1% yr/yr to 3.985 million barrels per day, but remained well below 2007's record high of 4.198 million barrels per day.

Trade – U.S. imports of distillate fuel oil in 2014 (through November, annualized) rose +22.8% to an average of 190,000 barrels per day, down from the 2006 record high of 365,000 barrels per day. U.S. exports of distillate fuel oil in 2007 (latest data available) rose by +2.7% yr/yr to a 13-year high average of 221 barrels per day. U.S. imports of residual fuel oil in 2013 (latest data) fell -11.3% yr/yr to 227,000 barrels per day, which was less than a third of the levels of over 1 million barrels per day seen back in the 1970s.

World Production of Distillate Fuel Oil   In Thousands of Barrels Per Day

Year	Brazil	Canada	China	France	Germany	India	Italy	Japan	Korea, South	Russia	Saudi Arabia	United States	World Total
2003	608.3	635.4	1,744.9	716.0	994.2	919.7	791.4	1,175.8	568.2	1,103.0	590.6	3,707.2	22,101.7
2004	674.6	643.9	2,070.5	708.5	1,015.8	967.2	795.2	1,172.1	591.9	1,129.8	641.8	3,814.3	23,061.4
2005	684.8	631.0	2,267.9	695.8	1,079.9	991.7	818.6	1,182.6	643.7	1,227.1	647.6	3,954.4	23,949.4
2006	663.0	627.5	2,398.9	701.5	1,060.0	1,081.6	804.1	1,130.2	664.9	1,312.3	694.6	4,040.4	24,241.4
2007	673.6	636.4	2,520.2	711.1	1,035.4	1,206.5	838.4	1,119.4	707.6	1,260.1	653.4	4,133.0	24,382.2
2008	705.2	629.3	2,740.6	753.8	1,019.1	1,297.7	817.9	1,135.3	730.9	1,407.8	677.9	4,293.8	25,448.4
2009	731.7	602.3	2,921.9	676.6	969.3	1,507.5	773.6	1,035.9	726.0	1,375.1	623.8	4,048.0	24,931.0
2010	711.7	618.3	3,052.0	616.3	918.1	1,607.9	809.3	1,020.2	744.0	1,431.2	633.4	4,223.3	25,445.9
2011[1]		604.3		626.9	911.4		776.6	961.5	810.6			4,488.8	
2012[2]		627.2		533.7	937.9		737.6	924.7	854.3			4,549.3	

[1] Preliminary.   [2] Estimate.   *Source: Energy Information Administration, U.S. Department of Energy (EIA-DOE)*

HEATING OIL

World Imports of Distillate Fuel Oil   In Thousands of Barrels Per Day

Year	Australia	Belgium	France	Germany	Indonesia	Nether-lands	Singa-pore	Spain	Turkey	United Kingdom	United States	Vietnam	World Total
2003	42.6	136.1	275.6	299.0	145.6	191.0	124.3	220.6	55.6	71.6	333.3	95.1	4,058.8
2004	63.0	164.7	329.0	267.4	130.1	204.1	112.5	240.9	77.8	85.9	325.5	111.6	4,297.2
2005	81.7	198.1	383.1	278.1	170.2	197.1	78.9	270.0	84.7	100.5	328.8	120.4	4,496.9
2006	105.7	166.8	321.9	332.9	176.1	278.9	125.2	278.1	131.5	164.8	364.7	110.8	4,937.4
2007	105.2	149.4	272.5	190.3	229.7	191.1	127.0	294.5	162.3	168.7	304.1	132.5	5,064.1
2008	147.8	156.4	292.1	317.2	211.6	250.9	178.6	246.3	169.8	152.6	212.9	132.6	5,477.7
2009	144.0	124.6	380.2	297.0	146.7	333.5	155.0	234.1	186.2	127.5	225.1	132.9	5,491.3
2010	141.7	111.8	414.0	318.9	183.4	385.2	181.1	220.7	197.9	193.0	228.4	100.5	5,925.3
2011[1]	176.6	161.7	408.0	278.9		375.1		174.1	207.5	191.4	178.8		
2012[2]	202.0	128.3	469.9	276.1		384.2		136.4	226.1	218.6	126.3		

[1] Preliminary.   [2] Estimate.   *Source: Energy Information Administration, U.S. Department of Energy (EIA-DOE)*

World Exports of Distillate Fuel Oil   In Thousands of Barrels Per Day

Year	Belgium	Germany	India	Italy	Japan	Korea, South	Kuwait	Nether-lands	Russia	Singa-pore	Taiwan	United States	World Total
2003	151.6	129.4	126.3	195.8	16.2	166.4	227.1	420.0	613.7	294.4	92.7	106.8	4,536.1
2004	167.0	166.1	148.5	193.8	29.4	185.8	225.3	411.2	614.3	294.0	119.9	109.6	4,703.4
2005	182.3	204.4	173.0	195.2	64.1	234.3	221.2	430.4	649.2	300.0	149.2	138.4	5,063.6
2006	162.1	223.0	238.0	173.3	70.5	250.6	185.5	496.6	752.6	341.3	150.0	215.1	5,436.1
2007	177.9	250.9	292.4	208.1	137.2	281.9	194.0	421.0	751.9	359.3	176.5	267.7	5,313.9
2008	171.7	203.2	300.2	170.2	220.5	357.6	190.2	464.7	767.8	406.8	181.1	528.3	5,891.5
2009	140.2	181.8	377.3	168.2	215.7	343.6	152.8	562.3	812.9	346.3	206.6	587.4	6,196.6
2010	142.4	138.8	415.6	189.1	197.4	358.0	151.8	636.1	851.0	376.8	176.1	656.0	6,209.2
2011[1]	156.2	132.2		153.6	160.0	436.8		631.1				854.1	
2012[2]	160.7	128.9		178.8	120.4	481.8		608.5				1,007.2	

[1] Preliminary.   [2] Estimate.   *Source: Energy Information Administration, U.S. Department of Energy (EIA-DOE)*

Production of Distillate Fuel Oil in the United States   In Thousand Barrels per Day

Year	Jan.	Feb.	Mar.	Apr.	May	June	July	Aug.	Sept.	Oct.	Nov.	Dec.	Average
2005	3,777	3,797	3,874	4,028	4,179	4,274	4,236	4,108	3,570	3,585	3,966	4,044	3,953
2006	3,840	3,941	3,736	3,833	4,105	4,107	4,065	4,234	4,300	4,090	4,070	4,159	4,040
2007	4,256	4,582	4,334	4,214	4,068	4,114	4,026	4,146	4,161	4,213	4,074	4,193	4,198
2008	4,130	3,980	3,953	4,287	4,459	4,587	4,523	4,466	3,681	4,435	4,489	4,511	4,292
2009	4,284	4,231	3,939	4,132	4,093	4,047	3,929	3,965	4,099	3,984	4,018	3,877	4,050
2010	3,551	3,658	3,835	4,156	4,375	4,408	4,425	4,404	4,341	4,315	4,503	4,670	4,220
2011	4,303	4,033	4,326	4,189	4,283	4,471	4,656	4,668	4,576	4,539	4,902	4,919	4,489
2012	4,500	4,408	4,263	4,352	4,547	4,632	4,660	4,600	4,566	4,510	4,669	4,884	4,549
2013	4,480	4,281	4,284	4,416	4,767	4,792	4,934	4,930	4,888	4,815	5,050	5,122	4,730
2014[1]	4,656	4,572	4,754	4,980	5,020	4,889	5,014	5,030	4,923	4,656	5,012	5,236	4,895

[1] Preliminary.   *Source: Energy Information Administration; U.S. Department of Energy (EIA-DOE)*

Stocks of Distillate Fuel in the United States, on First of Month   In Millions of Barrels

Year	Jan.	Feb.	Mar.	Apr.	May	June	July	Aug.	Sept.	Oct.	Nov.	Dec.
2005	121.9	117.3	105.4	105.4	112.4	119.7	133.3	139.1	127.7	124.7	133.7	136.0
2006	139.4	135.6	120.5	116.5	124.0	129.9	137.5	145.1	149.3	142.8	140.6	143.7
2007	139.6	123.7	120.0	121.3	125.1	123.8	130.3	134.6	134.2	134.4	134.8	133.9
2008	131.0	117.6	107.8	107.1	113.9	121.7	130.9	133.0	127.7	127.6	135.9	146.0
2009	143.7	148.1	145.3	150.1	156.7	162.7	165.9	168.6	172.7	171.2	171.1	166.0
2010	163.5	155.3	146.8	144.8	150.0	157.9	166.6	170.3	166.7	161.5	162.0	164.3
2011	163.1	154.1	149.2	142.9	144.8	143.9	154.5	155.1	153.4	142.3	143.9	149.2
2012	147.2	139.3	133.7	124.7	121.4	119.9	126.5	127.3	127.4	118.7	118.0	134.8
2013	131.3	122.0	118.7	118.8	122.1	122.5	126.0	129.1	129.3	118.0	121.1	127.5
2014[1]	114.5	112.9	115.3	116.8	121.8	121.7	125.6	128.1	131.3	120.1	126.1	136.1

[1] Preliminary.   *Source: Energy Information Administration; U.S. Department of Energy (EIA-DOE)*

Imports of Distillate Fuel Oil in the United States   In Thousand of Barrels per Day

Year	Jan.	Feb.	Mar.	Apr.	May	June	July	Aug.	Sept.	Oct.	Nov.	Dec.	Average
2005	353	344	257	264	281	236	243	263	275	507	486	435	329
2006	552	388	292	297	437	297	361	363	438	307	288	355	365
2007	352	334	360	322	272	273	318	346	261	288	245	241	301
2008	309	249	249	266	188	180	181	109	195	166	203	262	213
2009	368	327	269	166	206	245	191	166	205	177	164	224	226
2010	462	293	179	220	189	237	170	246	189	163	178	219	229
2011	337	206	190	191	170	127	157	148	179	128	138	175	179
2012	157	142	137	98	113	87	117	112	86	88	188	190	126
2013	213	174	146	238	168	121	107	123	132	128	145	164	155
2014[1]	283	336	324	180	186	121	129	143	126	120	136	230	193

[1] Preliminary.   Source: Energy Information Administration, U.S. Department of Energy (EIA-DOE)

Disposition of Distillate Fuel Oil, Total Product Supplied in the United States   In Thousand of Barrels per Day

Year	Jan.	Feb.	Mar.	Apr.	May	June	July	Aug.	Sept.	Oct.	Nov.	Dec.	Average
2005	4,223	4,202	4,349	4,101	4,037	4,038	3,854	4,020	4,116	4,079	4,061	4,339	4,118
2006	4,159	4,308	4,395	4,065	4,072	4,019	3,950	4,162	4,141	4,315	4,180	4,268	4,170
2007	4,256	4,582	4,334	4,214	4,068	4,114	4,026	4,146	4,161	4,213	4,074	4,193	4,198
2008	4,192	4,281	4,161	4,106	3,931	3,763	3,688	3,659	3,740	4,182	3,872	3,783	3,947
2009	4,079	3,864	3,744	3,455	3,436	3,513	3,395	3,426	3,560	3,654	3,596	3,861	3,632
2010	3,701	3,854	3,835	3,759	3,639	3,743	3,544	3,830	3,886	3,773	3,873	4,176	3,801
2011	3,958	3,913	4,045	3,755	3,699	3,947	3,564	4,009	3,936	4,003	4,109	3,853	3,899
2012	3,861	3,923	3,715	3,719	3,756	3,732	3,557	3,743	3,674	3,852	3,848	3,529	3,742
2013	4,062	3,984	3,769	3,854	3,749	3,663	3,621	3,693	3,725	4,039	3,893	3,887	3,828
2014[1]	4,272	4,182	4,046	3,972	3,937	3,880	3,860	3,817	3,909	4,238	3,879	3,887	3,990

[1] Preliminary.   Source: Energy Information Administration, U.S. Department of Energy (EIA-DOE)

World Production of Residual Fuel Oil   In Thousands of Barrels Per Day

Year	Brazil	China	India	Iran	Italy	Japan	Korea, South	Mexico	Russia	Saudi Arabia	United States	Vene-zuela	World Total
2003	318.9	430.8	376.0	476.7	304.9	649.8	548.9	392.0	1,079.4	464.0	659.9	218.3	11,261.6
2004	323.4	461.7	407.8	470.2	308.9	576.1	544.4	369.7	1,114.1	472.1	655.5	278.0	11,285.3
2005	335.5	403.1	407.4	480.2	330.5	576.6	571.2	352.2	1,193.3	487.6	627.6	265.7	11,499.7
2006	332.0	408.1	408.7	480.8	306.5	552.9	560.8	325.9	1,238.1	495.9	635.3	279.1	11,344.1
2007	265.2	358.9	459.9	459.2	307.0	526.0	496.5	302.1	1,235.1	477.8	672.7	267.3	10,763.4
2008	298.7	317.0	322.7	486.4	259.0	512.8	405.4	289.3	1,260.9	477.8	619.9	280.2	10,332.9
2009	289.3	351.1	375.0	478.6	233.0	423.2	336.6	316.8	1,332.1	497.6	598.2	312.5	10,109.0
2010	297.8	389.1	427.9	480.5	197.4	388.1	341.2	322.9	1,238.1	445.4	584.9	272.1	9,804.5
2011[1]					159.8	398.4	336.6	308.0			537.4		
2012[2]					172.7	461.2	281.3	273.9			500.6		

[1] Preliminary.   [2] Estimate.   Source: Energy Information Administration, U.S. Department of Energy (EIA-DOE)

Supply and Disposition of Residual Fuel Oil in the United States

Year	Supply Total Production	Supply Imports	Disposition Stock Change	Disposition Exports	Disposition Product Supplied	Ending Stocks (Million Barrels)	Average Sales to End Users[3] (Cents per Gallon)
2004	655	426	12	205	865	42	73.9
2005	628	530	-14	251	920	37	104.8
2006	635	350	14	283	689	42	121.8
2007	673	372	-13	309	723	39	137.4
2008	620	349	NA	NA	622	36	196.4
2009	598	331	NA	NA	511	37	134.1
2010	585	366	----	----	535	41	171.3
2011	537	328	----	----	461	34	240.1
2012	501	256	----	----	369	34	259.2
2013[1]	466	227	----	----	314	37	

(In Tousands of Barrels Per Day)

[1] Preliminary.   [2] Less than +500 barrels per day and greater than -500 barrels per day.   [3] Refiner price excluding taxes.
Source: Energy Information Administration, U.S. Department of Energy (EIA-DOE)

HEATING OIL

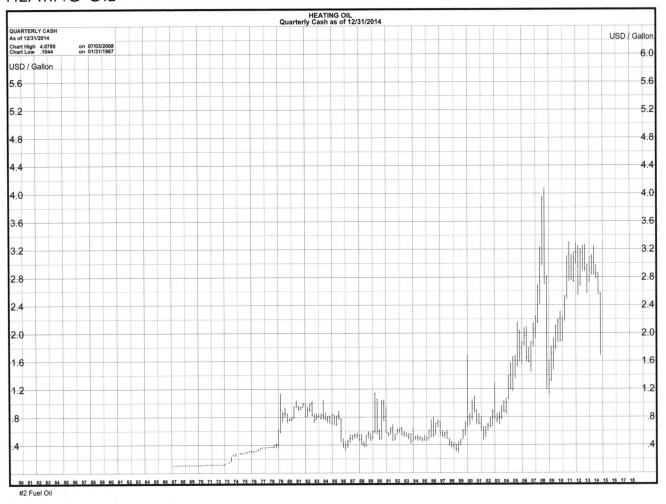

QUARTERLY CASH
As of 12/31/2014

Chart High 4.0785   on 07/03/2008
Chart Low   .1044   on 01/31/1967

HEATING OIL
Quarterly Cash as of 12/31/2014

USD / Gallon

#2 Fuel Oil

Production of Residual Fuel Oil in the United States   In Thousands of Barrels per Day

Year	Jan.	Feb.	Mar.	Apr.	May	June	July	Aug.	Sept.	Oct.	Nov.	Dec.	Average
2005	701	691	619	598	645	673	614	594	555	530	642	674	628
2006	670	635	644	643	580	645	658	652	619	597	624	656	635
2007	667	650	656	658	647	628	708	698	698	689	694	676	672
2008	588	643	662	710	734	695	584	579	485	575	588	597	620
2009	585	571	583	475	605	613	586	631	604	672	624	624	598
2010	633	632	581	598	615	559	576	554	588	528	564	595	585
2011	552	529	526	534	538	553	563	604	516	530	516	486	537
2012	500	548	577	525	509	538	486	495	508	481	458	388	501
2013	395	504	569	508	488	469	481	417	434	420	446	455	466
2014[1]	480	428	463	422	455	456	402	439	410	416	461	385	435

[1] Preliminary.   *Source: Energy Information Administration, U.S. Department of Energy (EIA-DOE)*

Average Price of Heating Oil #2   In Cents Per Gallon

Year	Jan.	Feb.	Mar.	Apr.	May	June	July	Aug.	Sept.	Oct.	Nov.	Dec.	Average
2005	132.01	134.26	155.44	152.35	140.89	161.20	163.71	180.75	196.50	188.75	168.67	170.32	162.07
2006	174.99	163.68	177.70	198.27	197.17	191.76	192.30	198.25	169.17	154.53	165.00	167.85	179.22
2007	151.99	169.48	174.05	186.30	188.47	200.31	206.99	198.36	218.06	228.32	258.79	257.54	203.22
2008	255.64	264.17	306.80	322.96	361.64	379.99	375.67	317.16	290.76	222.44	185.15	138.93	285.11
2009	146.43	127.78	128.30	135.95	147.87	174.72	163.18	186.59	173.05	193.34	198.48	197.22	164.41
2010	205.23	197.52	208.47	221.26	203.78	203.44	197.75	202.24	209.48	224.23	231.74	246.43	212.63
2011	260.35	276.38	303.39	319.56	295.14	296.51	306.92	294.27	291.99	295.00	305.24	288.75	294.46
2012	304.52	319.41	321.46	314.72	291.23	262.01	282.00	304.59	312.95	313.83	301.07	295.91	301.98
2013	307.20	316.69	294.68	272.78	268.82	274.24	288.63	295.81	296.13	294.22	292.28	303.25	292.06
2014	306.33	306.56	291.24	288.78	286.03	288.22	277.58	275.35	263.32	242.37	224.93	185.55	269.69

Source: Energy Information Administration, U.S. Department of Energy (EIA-DOE)

ULSD NY HARBOR - NYMEX
Weekly Nearest Futures as of 01/02/2015

WEEKLY NEAREST FUTURES
As of 01/02/2015

Chart High 4.1586   on 07/11/2008
Chart Low   1.1252   on 03/11/2009

USD / Gallon

Nearby Futures through Last Trading Day.

Volume of Trading of Heating Oil #2 Futures in New York   In Thousands of Contracts

Year	Jan.	Feb.	Mar.	Apr.	May	June	July	Aug.	Sept.	Oct.	Nov.	Dec.	Total
2005	1,090.6	1,046.1	1,204.2	1,062.5	999.7	1,193.5	1,058.5	1,150.4	1,165.1	1,019.5	1,009.5	1,136.0	13,135.6
2006	1,157.5	1,131.2	1,121.7	974.8	1,185.1	1,114.0	1,027.1	1,166.1	1,235.9	1,291.1	1,228.6	1,357.5	13,990.6
2007	1,655.6	1,507.5	1,370.3	1,326.0	1,462.2	1,605.8	1,478.9	1,579.8	1,394.7	1,687.2	1,544.1	1,467.0	18,079.0
2008	1,611.7	1,726.3	1,763.3	1,639.2	1,825.3	1,651.9	1,571.3	1,641.9	1,578.0	1,646.4	1,297.3	1,630.4	19,583.1
2009	1,789.0	1,512.9	1,670.1	1,633.3	1,644.5	1,809.7	2,004.2	1,652.6	1,777.3	1,975.9	1,921.9	2,035.1	21,426.5
2010	2,096.3	1,872.5	2,230.6	2,459.2	2,493.3	2,305.2	1,963.7	2,409.5	2,548.9	2,230.9	2,165.8	2,194.1	26,970.1
2011	2,545.9	2,600.7	2,805.0	2,206.5	2,645.6	2,624.9	2,022.6	2,843.7	2,889.1	2,964.2	3,071.0	2,619.4	31,838.6
2012	3,149.6	3,203.3	2,953.3	2,693.2	2,913.9	3,172.8	2,875.1	3,071.6	2,812.8	3,887.9	2,913.4	2,440.8	36,087.7
2013	3,122.0	2,801.6	2,900.0	3,057.7	2,852.8	2,540.0	2,700.0	2,490.4	2,384.5	2,932.3	2,608.5	2,359.7	32,749.6
2014	3,400.6	2,893.3	2,533.8	2,209.6	2,253.3	2,483.3	2,857.3	2,719.9	2,875.9	3,409.5	3,123.5	3,177.4	33,937.5

Contract size = 42,000 US gallons.   *Source: CME Group; New York Mercantile Exchange (NYMEX)*

Average Open Interest of Heating Oil #2 Futures in New York   In Contracts

Year	Jan.	Feb.	Mar.	Apr.	May	June	July	Aug.	Sept.	Oct.	Nov.	Dec.
2005	155,528	152,479	174,437	179,923	176,770	185,831	182,710	185,185	174,229	172,772	178,199	178,008
2006	170,094	165,627	168,415	170,955	171,732	169,123	179,773	185,648	208,848	221,942	228,152	216,033
2007	219,690	219,715	209,805	208,829	210,128	224,289	239,109	218,913	235,403	232,165	224,475	209,578
2008	202,976	220,716	230,646	227,140	224,480	218,004	223,645	221,733	212,561	212,981	224,465	224,359
2009	237,894	252,753	261,552	259,008	260,646	283,068	294,270	308,022	311,296	312,653	322,505	309,113
2010	317,506	306,607	319,389	310,085	311,994	313,624	304,866	305,549	325,342	327,588	319,732	308,661
2011	306,262	312,145	305,872	310,288	310,053	316,026	306,360	307,607	323,485	303,460	291,931	274,679
2012	273,761	299,758	286,319	296,190	314,645	323,256	313,376	320,011	332,853	316,594	303,742	280,933
2013	297,517	316,763	297,280	304,306	307,574	291,583	287,422	290,885	284,372	280,863	298,480	292,422
2014	281,102	294,144	280,719	263,461	269,766	285,931	313,266	353,133	373,004	390,505	391,923	355,367

Contract size = 42,000 US gallons.   *Source: CME Group; New York Mercantile Exchange (NYMEX)*

Hides and Leather

Hides and leather have been used since ancient times for boots, clothing, shields, armor, tents, bottles, buckets, and cups. Leather is produced through the tanning of hides, pelts, and skins of animals. The remains of leather have been found in the Middle East dating back at least 7,000 years.

Today, most leather is made of cowhide but it is also made from the hides of lamb, deer, ostrich, snakes, crocodiles, and even stingray. Cattle hides are the most valuable byproduct of the meat packing industry. U.S. exports of cowhides bring more than $1 billion in foreign trade, and U.S. finished leather production is worth about $4 billion.

Prices – The average monthly price of wholesale cattle hides (packer heavy native steers FOB Chicago) in 2014 rose +12.2% yr/yr to 110.19 cents per pound, a new record high.

Supply – World production of cattle and buffalo hides in 2012 (latest data) rose by +0.2% yr/yr to 8.905, down from 2009's record high of 9.135 million metric tons. The world's largest producers of cattle and buffalo hides in 2012 were the U.S. with 12.6% of world production, Brazil with 9.5%, and Argentina with 3.8%. U.S. new supply of cattle hides from domestic slaughter in 2009 (latest data available) fell 3.0% yr/yr to 33.338 million hides, which is far below the record high of 43.582 million hides posted in 1976.

U.S. production of leather footwear has been dropping off sharply in recent years due to the movement of production offshore to lower cost producers. U.S. production of leather footwear in 2003 (latest data available) fell -46% yr/yr to 22.3 million pairs and was a mere 4% of the 562.3 million pairs produced in 1970.

Demand – World consumption of cowhides and skins in 2000, the last reporting year for the series, rose +1.4% to 4,774 metric tons, which was a record high for the data series, which goes back to 1984. The world's largest consumers of cowhides and skins in 2000 were the U.S. with 13.0% of world consumption, Italy (10.6%), Brazil (8.9%), Mexico, (6.0%), Argentina (6.0%), and South Korea (5.9%).

Trade – U.S. net exports of cattle hides in 2013 (latest data) rose +34.9% yr/yr to 25.899 million hides, a new record high. The total value of U.S. leather exports in 2004 (latest data) rose +16.8% yr/yr to $1.344 billion. The largest destinations for U.S. exports in 2013 were South Korea (which took 16.0% of U.S. exports), Taiwan (6.7%), Mexico (5.4%), Italy (1.5%), and Thailand (1.1%). World imports of cowhides and skins in 2000 (latest data) rose +2.8% yr/yr to a record high of 2,058 metric tons. The world's largest importers of cowhides and skins in 2000 were South Korea (with 13% of world imports in 2000), Italy (11%) and Taiwan (7%).

World Production of Cattle and Buffalo Hides   In Thousands of Metric Tons

Year	Argentina	Australia	Brazil	Canada	Colombia	France	Germany	Italy	Mexico	Russia	United Kingdom	United States	World Total
2003	375	256	770	88	72	160	141	130	180	229	63	1,093	8,193
2004	429	243	792	111	80	150	145	128	191	223	66	1,009	8,310
2005	428	245	850	112	86	148	132	126	192	203	68	1,016	8,409
2006	403	233	886	104	85	143	135	124	197	183	74	1,076	8,592
2007	449	252	914	96	88	142	132	122	199	180	75	1,086	8,771
2008	440	239	874	96	94	143	132	115	202	182	75	1,104	8,822
2009	482	236	856	93	84	144	132	115	207	179	75	1,103	8,939
2010	356	230	855	94	80	145	132	115	213	177	75	1,130	8,945
2011[1]	326	230	849	85	86	145	132	116	220	163	75	1,123	8,889
2012[2]	336	230	849	78	86	138	132	118	220	163	75	1,123	8,905

[1] Preliminary.   [2] Forecast.   *Source: Food and Agricultural Organization of the United Nations (FAO-UN)*

Salient Statistics of Hides and Leather in the United States   In Thousands of Equivalent Hides

Year	New Supply of Cattle hides — Domestic Slaughter — Federally Inspected	Unin- spected[4]	Total Production	Net Exports	Wholesale Prices - Cents Per Pound - Heavy Native Cows[2]	Heavy Native[3] Steers	Production All U.S. Tanning	Cattle- hide	Value of Leather Exports ($1,000)	Wholesale Leather Indicies (1982 = 100) Men	Women	Footwear Pro- duction[5]	Exports
	----- Thousands of Equivalent Hides -----						In 1,000 Equiv. Hides			---- (1982 = 100) ----		----- Million Pairs -----	
2001	34,771	599	35,370	21,750	85.52	85.8	14,212	13,779	1,221,131	158.4	133.8	55,600	19,472
2002	35,120	614	35,735	19,484	85.73	82.3		16,403	1,161,944	158.8	133.5	41,100	21,582
2003	34,907	587	35,493	18,177	88.34	83.8		17,470	1,150,212	161.4	132.1	22,300	21,319
2004	32,156	573	32,728	17,388	57.07	67.1		15,492	1,344,017	161.7	129.2		21,464
2005	31,832	556	32,388		57.89	65.6				163.5	132.1		
2006	33,145	553	33,698		60.30	68.9				164.6	134.2		
2007	33,721	543	34,264	24,394	65.70	72.0				167.0	137.0		
2008	33,805	560	34,365	22,213	58.35	63.9				173.7	139.7		
2009[1]	32,765	573	33,338	22,126	29.00	45.3				177.6	139.9		
2010[1]				23,378	63.44	71.9				180.9	141.0		

[1] Preliminary.   [2] Central U.S., heifers.   [3] F.O.B. Chicago.   [4] Includes farm slaughter; diseased & condemned animals & hides taken off fallen animals.
[5] Other than rubber.   *Sources: Leather Industries of America (LIA); Bureau of Labor Statistics, U.S. Department of Commerce (BLS)*

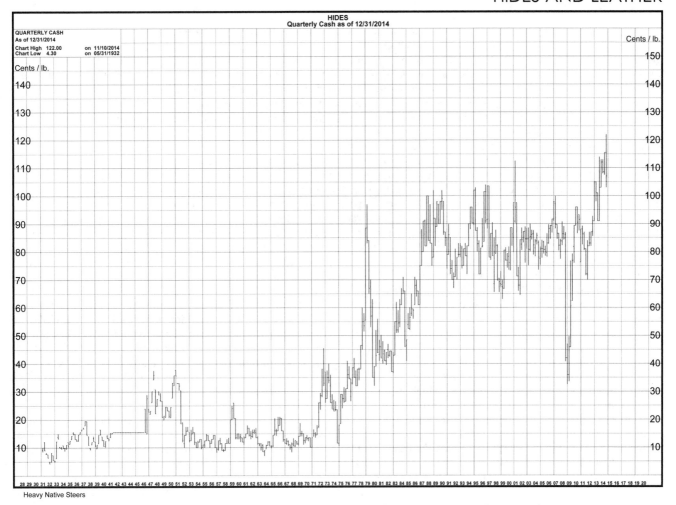

HIDES
Quarterly Cash as of 12/31/2014

QUARTERLY CASH
As of 12/31/2014

Chart High 122.00 on 11/10/2014
Chart Low 4.30 on 05/31/1932

Heavy Native Steers

Imports and Exports of All Cattle Hides in the United States   In Thousands of Hides

	----- Imports -----		-- U.S. Exports - by Country of Destination --										
Year	Canada	Total	Canada	Italy	Japan	Korea, South	Mexico	Portugal	Romania	Spain	Taiwan	Thailand	Total
2004	6,171	9,000	346	417	468	4,218	1,419	4	0	16	1,842	684	18,795
2005	2,897	4,517	141	568	334	4,048	1,288	2	0	8	1,730	652	19,231
2006	1,786	2,491	57	523	277	3,455	1,225	5	0	41	1,902	441	20,059
2007	1,243	1,986	91	191	234	2,867	1,243	3	0	44	1,260	724	17,687
2008	1,182	1,863	113	265	175	2,346	1,135		0	99	795	453	16,015
2009	975	1,475	345	407	189	2,379	1,510	11	0	62	1,249	574	16,661
2010	1,064	1,388	193	1,010	148	2,042	1,423	1	0	90	1,446	460	15,440
2011	932	1,306	179	1,703	347	3,000	1,062	5	0	51	1,194	382	18,799
2012	1,209	1,610	97	547	211	3,473	1,264	2	0	3	983	400	19,204
2013[1]	1,008	1,622	62	378	237	4,148	1,408	17	0	18	1,753	272	25,899

[1] Preliminary.   *Source: Leather Industries of America*

Wholesale Price of Hides (Packer Heavy Native Steers) F.O.B. Chicago   In Cents Per Pound

Year	Jan.	Feb.	Mar.	Apr.	May	June	July	Aug.	Sept.	Oct.	Nov.	Dec.	Average
2005	78.14	80.90	79.04	80.45	79.49	83.07	82.70	81.78	80.58	80.44	80.07	79.03	80.47
2006	79.28	81.01	83.86	84.95	87.76	88.07	87.93	87.15	88.29	88.08	88.81	90.50	86.31
2007	93.75	95.85	95.66	98.13	97.68	93.19	87.36	86.95	86.14	83.08	84.72	83.83	90.53
2008	79.55	79.43	82.79	85.58	85.82	87.01	87.55	87.49	85.10	85.31	78.38	44.98	80.75
2009	43.75	43.09	34.55	36.22	38.33	46.84	53.76	73.02	68.86	65.35	74.23	77.51	54.63
2010	79.31	78.31	83.78	91.83	93.38	93.69	92.86	91.36	88.90	90.68	90.44	90.90	88.79
2011	78.24	81.78	85.20	88.18	84.12	86.26	85.60	85.66	82.40	79.54	76.76	72.10	82.15
2012	72.19	78.90	83.55	84.32	85.95	83.71	84.10	85.89	83.66	86.48	88.52	91.10	84.03
2013	91.45	97.00	96.81	103.14	99.66	98.93	99.32	95.39	91.50	94.39	106.00	105.38	98.25
2014	104.76	107.00	110.62	112.00	108.90	108.14	108.59	112.00	114.43	114.37	114.29	107.16	110.19

Source: National Agricultural Statistics Service, U.S. Department of Agriculture (NASS-USDA)

Hogs

Hogs are generally bred twice a year in a continuous cycle designed to provide a steady flow of production. The gestation period for hogs is 3-1/2 months and the average litter size is 9 pigs. The pigs are weaned at 3-4 weeks of age. The pigs are then fed so as to maximize weight gain. The feed consists primarily of grains such as corn, barley, milo, oats, and wheat. Protein is added from oilseed meals. Hogs typically gain 3.1 pounds per pound of feed. The time from birth to slaughter is typically 6 months. Hogs are ready for slaughter at about 254 pounds, producing a dressed carcass weight of around 190 pounds and an average 88.6 pounds of lean meat. The lean meat consists of 21% ham, 20% loin, 14% belly, 3% spareribs, 7% Boston butt roast and blade steaks, and 10% picnic, with the remaining 25% going into jowl, lean trim, fat, miscellaneous cuts, and trimmings. Futures on lean hogs are traded at the CME Group. The futures contract is settled in cash based on the CME Lean Hog Index price, meaning that no physical delivery of hogs occurs. The CME Lean Hog Index is based on the 2-day average net price of slaughtered hogs at the average lean percentage level.

Prices – CME lean hog futures prices (Barchart.com electronic symbol HE) had a parabolic rally the first half of 2014 on concern about future pork production due to Porcine Epidemic Diarrhea (PED) virus, which has a near 100% mortality rate for piglets. Going into Q2, the PED virus had spread throughout 30 U.S. states and killed more than 8 million pigs since April 2013, and spread to hog farms in Canada, Japan, South Korea and Taiwan. USDA data confirmed the seriousness of the virus when the Q1 Quarterly Hogs & Pigs report showed that the U.S. hog inventory on March 1, 2013 had fallen -3.3% yr/yr to 62.9 million hogs, a 7-year low. The rally stalled briefly in May after USDA slaughter data showed hog weights had risen to 222.04 lbs, the highest since the USDA began tracking the data in 2002. Hog futures prices then surged to a record 133.900 cents a pound in July, the highest since hog futures began trading in 1964. Hog prices then plunged the rest of the year as record-high pork prices decimated consumer demand. Also, containment of the PED virus hammered hog prices after USDA data showed only 239 cases of the virus reported on U.S. pig farms in September, the fewest in 11 months. Hog futures prices ended 2014 down -4.9% at 81.200 cents per pound.

Supply – World pork production in 2014 rose +1.6% to 110.606 million metric tons. The USDA is forecasting a rise of +1.1% to 111.845 million metric tons in 2015. The world's largest pork producers are China with 51% of world production in 2014, the European Union with 20%, and the U.S. with 9%.

U.S. pork production in 2014 fell -1.9% to 10.329 million metric tons. The USDA is forecasting that U.S. pork production in 2015 will rise by +5.1% to 10.858 million metric tons. The number of hogs and pigs on U.S. farms in 2014 (Dec 1) rose by +2.1% to 67.775 million, well below more than 6-decade high of 68.117 in 2007. The federally-inspected hog slaughter in the U.S. in 2014 fell -4.6% to 106.122 million head, well below the 2008 record high of 115.421 million head.

Demand – World consumption of pork in 2014 rose by +1.3% to 109.882 million metric tons. The USDA is forecasting an increase of +1.2% in 2015 to 111.174 million metric tons. U.S. consumption of pork in 2014 fell by -2.4% to 8.455 million metric tons. The USDA is forecasting a +5.0% increase in U.S. pork consumption in 2015 to 8.874 million metric tons.

Trade – World pork exports in 2014 fell -1.4% to 6.936 million metric tons. The USDA is forecasting that world pork exports in 2015 will increase by +3.7% to 7.196 million metric tons. The world's largest pork exporters are the U.S. with 33% of world exports in 2014, the European Union with 31%, Canada with 17%, and Brazil with 8%. U.S. pork exports in 2014 rose by +2.4% to 2.321 million metric tons and the USDA is forecasting a rise of +2.6% in 2015 to 2.381 million metric tons.

World pork imports in 2014 fell -6.3% to 6.245 million metric tons. The USDA is forecasting that world pork imports will rise by +1.2% to 6.323 million metric tons in 2015. The world's largest pork importers are Japan, which accounted for 21% of world imports in 2014, Mexico (13%), and China (13%).

Salient Statistics of Pigs and Hogs in the United States

	Pig Crop						Value of Hogs on Farms, Dec. 1		Hog Marketings (1,000 Head)	Quantity Produced (Live Wt.) (Mil. Lbs.)	Value of Production (Million$)	Hogs Slaughtered, Thousand Head — Commercial				
	Spring[3]			Fall[4]												
Year	Sows Farrowed --- 1,000 Head ---	Pig Crop	Pigs Per Litter	Sows Farrowed --- 1,000 Head ---	Pig Crop	Pigs Per Litter	$ Per Head	Total Million $				Federally Inspected	Other	Total	Farm	Total
2005	5,716	51,330	8.98	5,818	52,635	9.05	95.0	5,834	129,056	27,416	13,607	102,519	1,063	103,582	109	103,690
2006	5,768	52,242	9.06	5,862	53,376	9.11	90.0	5,599	132,262	28,149	12,702	103,689	1,048	104,737	105	104,842
2007	5,935	54,266	9.14	6,312	58,608	9.28	73.0	4,986	137,519	29,606	13,468	108,138	1,034	109,172	106	109,278
2008	6,123	57,019	9.31	6,103	58,011	9.51	89.0	5,958	148,986	31,411	14,457	115,421	1,026	116,446	106	116,553
2009	6,029	57,564	9.55	5,874	56,978	9.70	83.0	5,417	150,107	31,359	12,590	112,612	1,001	113,614	114	113,727
2010	5,801	56,326	9.71	5,824	57,359	9.85	106.0	6,899	144,486	30,437	16,095	109,315	948	110,263	107	110,370
2011	5,760	57,118	9.92	5,857	58,720	10.03	----	----	145,665	31,066	20,176	109,956	904	110,860	96	110,957
2012	5,759	57,749	10.03	5,810	58,906	10.14	----	----	151,353	31,961	20,224	112,265	896	113,162	83	113,245
2013[1]	5,595	57,020	10.19	5,670	58,115	10.25	----	----	152,726	32,222	21,409	111,248	833	112,081	71	112,152
2014[2]	5,573	53,821	9.66	5,777	58,907	10.20	----	----				106,122	756	106,878		106,878

[1] Preliminary.   [2] Estimate.   [3] December-May.   [4] June-November.   *Source: Economic Research Service, U.S. Department of Agriculture (ERS-USDA)*

World Hog Numbers in Specified Countries as of January 1   In Thousands of Head

Year	Brazil	Canada	China	European Union	Japan	Korea, South	Mexico	Philip- pines	Russia	Taiwan	Ukraine	United States	World Total
2006	32,938	15,110	433,191	159,924	9,620	8,098	8,911	13,041	13,812	7,172	7,052	61,463	806,215
2007	33,147	14,980	418,504	163,039	9,759	8,518	9,021	13,693	16,185	7,092	8,055	62,516	801,621
2008	32,947	14,080	439,895	160,918	9,745	8,742	9,401	----	16,340	----	7,020	68,177	775,866
2009	33,892	12,700	462,913	153,707	9,899	8,223	9,310	----	16,165	----	6,526	67,048	786,499
2010	35,122	12,465	469,960	152,780	10,000	8,721	8,979	----	17,236	----	7,577	64,887	793,811
2011	36,652	12,615	464,600	152,361	9,768	8,449	9,007	----	17,231	----	7,960	64,725	789,544
2012	38,336	12,625	468,627	149,809	9,735	8,171	9,276	----	17,258	----	7,373	66,259	793,743
2013	38,577	12,610	475,922	146,982	9,685	9,916	9,510	----	18,816	----	7,577	66,224	802,200
2014[1]	38,844	12,955	474,113	146,129	9,537	9,912	9,876	----	19,081	----	7,922	64,775	798,509
2015[2]	39,042	13,280	475,000	145,500	9,400	9,175	9,625	----	19,000	----	7,650	65,400	798,058

[1] Preliminary.   [2] Forecast.   *Source: Foreign Agricultural Service, U.S. Department of Agriculture (FAS-USDA)*

Hogs and Pigs on Farms in the United States on December 1   In Thousands of Head

Year	Georgia	Illinois	Indiana	Iowa	Kansas	Minne- sota	Missouri	Nebraska	North Carolina	Ohio	South Dakota	Wisconsin	Total
2005	270	4,000	3,250	16,600	1,790	6,600	2,700	2,850	9,800	1,560	1,490	430	61,449
2006	245	4,200	3,350	17,300	1,840	6,900	2,800	3,050	9,500	1,690	1,270	450	62,490
2007	265	4,350	3,700	19,400	1,880	7,700	3,150	3,350	10,200	1,830	1,460	440	68,177
2008	235	4,350	3,550	19,900	1,740	7,500	3,150	3,350	9,700	1,940	1,280	360	67,148
2009	195	4,250	3,600	19,000	1,810	7,200	3,100	3,100	9,600	2,010	1,190	350	64,887
2010	160	4,400	3,650	19,100	1,820	7,700	2,900	3,150	9,000	2,040	1,290	340	64,925
2011	155	4,650	3,800	20,000	1,890	7,800	2,750	3,150	8,900	2,200	1,400	340	66,361
2012	155	4,600	3,800	20,600	1,900	7,650	2,750	3,000	9,000	2,050	1,200	320	66,374
2013	141	4,550	3,650	20,200	1,750	7,800	2,750	3,050	8,500	2,200	1,200	295	64,775
2014[1]	153	4,600	3,600	20,900	1,800	7,850	2,750	3,100	8,600	2,150	1,250	300	66,050

[1] Preliminary.   *Source: National Agricultural Statistics Service, U.S. Department of Agriculture (NASS-USDA)*

Hog-Corn Price Ratio[2] in the United States

Year	Jan.	Feb.	Mar.	Apr.	May	June	July	Aug.	Sept.	Oct.	Nov.	Dec.	Average
2005	25.1	26.0	25.3	25.6	27.7	24.4	23.6	26.2	26.0	25.8	24.6	23.1	25.3
2006	20.4	21.1	20.8	19.6	22.2	25.1	23.5	24.7	22.2	18.2	15.6	14.5	20.7
2007	14.0	13.8	13.1	14.0	15.2	15.4	15.7	15.7	14.3	12.9	11.0	10.5	13.8
2008	9.3	9.3	8.6	8.6	10.5	9.8	10.3	11.5	10.5	11.1	9.6	10.2	9.9
2009	9.8	11.3	11.4	11.4	11.3	10.8	12.0	11.2	11.6	10.5	11.0	12.5	11.2
2010	13.2	13.8	14.7	16.6	17.9	17.1	16.8	16.8	15.0	12.3	10.5	10.9	14.6
2011	11.3	10.9	11.4	10.7	10.9	10.9	11.3	11.0	10.5	12.0	11.0	10.8	11.1
2012	10.5	10.4	10.3	9.9	9.9	11.0	10.1	8.8	8.1	9.1	8.7	9.1	9.7
2013	9.2	9.2	8.3	8.9	9.8	10.7	11.2	11.9	13.1	14.8	14.6	13.9	11.3
2014[1]	13.8	15.1	18.2	18.9	17.6	18.9	23.0	22.9	21.8	21.6	18.6	17.0	19.0

[1] Preliminary.   [2] Bushels of corn equal in value to 100 pounds of hog, live weight.   *Source: Economic Research Service, U.S. Department of Agriculture (ERS-USDA)*

Cold Storage Holdings of Frozen Pork[2] in the United States, on First of Month   In Millions of Pounds

Year	Jan.	Feb.	Mar.	Apr.	May	June	July	Aug.	Sept.	Oct.	Nov.	Dec.
2005	482.9	496.8	538.2	540.2	562.8	511.2	488.6	442.9	408.5	425.6	440.7	431.3
2006	421.3	527.7	528.0	505.0	520.0	477.0	412.6	417.8	415.6	458.4	488.4	468.5
2007	442.5	484.3	483.2	494.8	528.5	492.0	467.9	455.9	458.3	484.9	494.8	474.6
2008	458.7	574.9	611.8	657.3	663.4	579.4	530.1	505.3	502.7	526.2	528.0	526.7
2009	555.6	606.9	624.5	594.1	612.3	584.5	577.9	539.7	530.1	528.7	516.3	482.8
2010	471.1	492.3	515.9	513.1	483.7	446.0	413.0	391.2	388.5	424.3	481.7	468.0
2011	475.8	538.8	574.2	574.4	549.3	548.3	495.1	454.3	442.9	491.9	488.7	495.1
2012	484.5	585.3	622.7	610.3	659.7	636.0	592.9	549.6	585.8	630.4	603.5	558.7
2013	551.5	606.4	633.4	647.8	701.0	658.9	565.1	543.7	549.0	567.8	565.0	546.2
2014[1]	554.3	618.7	654.7	575.5	583.9	575.8	537.4	533.3	543.7	550.6	533.1	492.8

[1] Preliminary.   [2] Excludes lard.   *Source: Economic Research Service, U.S. Department of Agriculture (ERS-USDA)*

HOGS

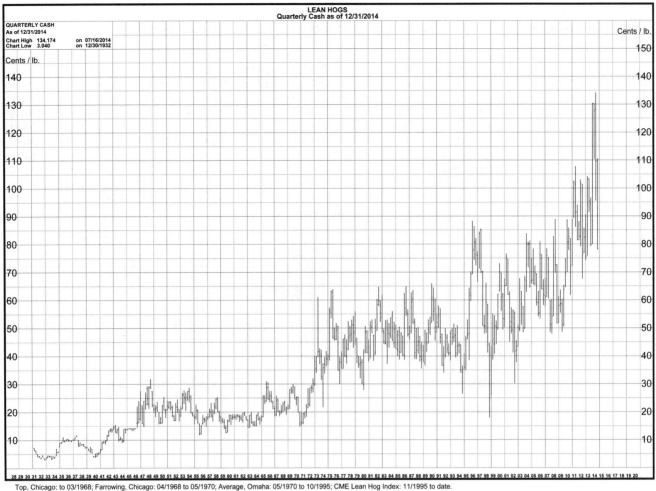

LEAN HOGS
Quarterly Cash as of 12/31/2014

QUARTERLY CASH
As of 12/31/2014
Chart High 134.174 on 07/16/2014
Chart Low 3.040 on 12/30/1932

Cents / lb.

Top, Chicago: to 03/1968; Farrowing, Chicago: 04/1968 to 05/1970; Average, Omaha: 05/1970 to 10/1995; CME Lean Hog Index: 11/1995 to date.

Average Price of Hogs, National Base 51-52% lean   In Dollars Per Hundred Pounds (Cwt.)

Year	Jan.	Feb.	Mar.	Apr.	May	June	July	Aug.	Sept.	Oct.	Nov.	Dec.	Average
2005	53.36	51.11	51.30	51.00	55.40	49.86	49.96	51.60	49.98	47.49	37.70	44.81	49.46
2006	41.37	43.17	43.34	41.45	49.00	54.90	51.89	53.32	50.28	47.57	45.97	44.84	47.26
2007	44.04	48.60	45.47	48.43	54.40	54.82	52.39	52.01	46.61	41.96	36.95	39.40	47.09
2008	36.77	42.74	39.40	45.06	57.75	54.71	56.48	62.56	52.76	47.06	38.90	39.80	47.83
2009	41.43	42.43	42.47	42.83	43.18	42.21	42.74	36.56	37.41	37.65	40.12	45.82	41.24
2010	49.81	48.98	52.43	57.43	63.13	58.23	58.25	61.49	60.64	52.41	47.00	50.92	55.06
2011	55.56	61.62	62.63	68.10	68.41	69.88	71.65	76.09	65.45	68.44	63.40	62.14	66.11
2012	62.18	63.94	61.86	58.99	58.51	67.87	69.93	65.00	50.85	59.06	57.67	59.16	61.25
2013	61.22	61.59	54.28	57.71	66.03	72.65	72.88	71.03	67.84	64.95	60.21	58.16	64.05
2014[1]	58.36	63.88	83.82	89.09	81.76	85.35	57.00	80.39	74.36	75.24	63.76	61.24	72.85

[1] Preliminary.   Source: Economic Research Service, U.S. Department of Agriculture (ERS-USDA)

Average Price Received by Farmers for Hogs in the United States   In Cents Per Pound

Year	Jan.	Feb.	Mar.	Apr.	May	June	July	Aug.	Sept.	Oct.	Nov.	Dec.	Average
2005	53.2	50.7	51.2	51.1	54.9	49.5	49.8	51.0	49.4	47.0	43.5	44.3	49.6
2006	40.7	42.6	42.8	41.3	48.2	53.8	50.2	51.6	48.9	46.5	44.9	43.5	46.3
2007	42.7	47.5	44.9	47.3	53.1	54.3	52.2	51.3	46.8	42.4	37.9	39.6	46.7
2008	37.2	42.2	40.3	44.4	55.3	53.4	54.3	60.7	52.6	48.5	40.7	41.9	47.6
2009	42.8	43.8	43.9	44.0	44.6	43.3	43.3	37.3	37.7	37.8	40.3	45.0	42.0
2010	48.4	48.9	52.1	56.5	62.2	58.2	58.5	58.2	61.0	53.3	47.8	52.3	54.8
2011	55.8	61.4	62.9	67.8	68.6	69.7	71.7	75.8	67.1	68.7	64.4	63.5	66.5
2012	63.5	65.5	65.2	62.8	62.8	70.2	72.1	66.9	55.7	62.0	61.1	62.4	64.2
2013	63.8	64.5	59.2	61.8	68.6	74.4	75.8	74.2	70.7	68.5	63.6	61.5	67.2
2014[1]	61.2	65.5	81.9	88.8	82.8	84.8	93.3	83.2	75.7	77.0	66.7	64.3	77.1

[1] Preliminary.   Source: Economic Research Service, U.S. Department of Agriculture (ERS-USDA)

Quarterly Hogs and Pigs Report in the United States, 10 States   In Thousands of Head

Year[2]	Inventory[3]	Breeding[3]	Market[3]	Farrowings	Pig Crop	Year[2]	Inventory[3]	Breeding[3]	Market[3]	Farrowings	Pig Crop
2005	60,975	5,969	55,005	11,535	103,965	2010	64,887	5,850	59,037	11,626	113,685
I	60,975	5,969	55,005	2,835	25,343	I	64,887	5,850	59,037	2,872	27,596
II	59,699	5,941	53,757	2,882	25,986	II	63,568	5,760	57,808	2,929	28,730
III	60,732	5,977	54,754	2,918	26,449	III	64,650	5,788	58,862	2,944	28,871
IV	61,846	5,972	55,873	2,900	26,187	IV	65,971	5,770	60,201	2,881	28,488
2006	61,449	6,011	55,438	11,629	105,618	2011	64,625	5,778	59,147	11,616	115,838
I	61,449	6,011	55,438	2,841	25,662	I	64,625	5,778	59,147	2,843	27,866
II	60,326	6,025	54,301	2,927	26,580	II	63,684	5,788	57,896	2,917	29,252
III	61,687	6,060	55,627	2,912	26,519	III	65,320	5,803	59,517	2,927	29,355
IV	62,914	6,079	56,835	2,949	26,857	IV	67,234	5,806	61,428	2,929	29,365
2007	62,490	6,087	56,402	12,248	112,873	2012	66,361	5,803	60,558	11,567	116,655
I	62,490	6,087	56,402	2,905	26,395	I	66,361	5,803	60,558	2,813	28,037
II	61,896	6,149	55,746	3,030	27,870	II	64,787	5,820	58,967	2,945	29,712
III	63,947	6,169	57,777	3,133	29,095	III	66,609	5,862	60,747	2,921	29,587
IV	67,275	6,208	66,708	3,180	29,513	IV	68,172	5,788	62,384	2,888	29,319
2008	68,177	6,233	61,944	12,226	115,030	2013	66,374	5,819	60,555	11,264	115,135
I	68,177	6,233	61,944	3,071	28,388	I	66,374	5,819	60,555	2,788	28,099
II	67,218	6,200	61,018	3,052	28,631	II	65,071	5,834	59,237	2,806	28,921
III	67,400	6,131	61,269	3,075	29,240	III	65,188	5,884	59,304	2,890	29,862
IV	68,196	6,061	62,135	3,028	28,771	IV	66,906	5,816	61,090	2,780	28,253
2009	67,148	6,062	61,087	11,903	114,542	2014[1]	64,775	5,757	59,018	11,350	112,728
I	67,148	6,062	61,087	3,011	28,552	I	64,775	5,757	59,018	2,763	26,326
II	65,819	5,992	59,828	3,018	29,012	II	61,494	5,851	55,643	2,810	27,495
III	66,809	5,968	60,842	2,959	28,718	III	61,568	5,855	55,713	2,906	29,534
IV	66,716	5,875	60,842	2,915	28,260	IV	65,131	5,920	59,211	2,871	29,373

[1] Preliminary.   [2] Quarters are Dec. preceding year-Feb.(I), Mar.-May(II), June-Aug.(III) and Sept.-Nov.(IV).
[3] Beginning of period.   Source: National Agricultural Statistics Service, U.S. Department of Agriculture (NASS-USDA)

Federally Inspected Hog Slaughter in the United States   In Thousands of Head

Year	Jan.	Feb.	Mar.	Apr.	May	June	July	Aug.	Sept.	Oct.	Nov.	Dec.	Total
2005	8,402	8,031	8,858	8,369	7,939	8,470	7,582	8,888	8,778	9,027	9,038	9,138	102,519
2006	8,834	7,978	9,148	7,884	8,450	8,256	7,805	8,991	8,738	9,541	9,276	8,788	103,689
2007	9,281	8,040	9,119	8,389	8,680	8,218	8,312	9,296	8,683	10,555	9,964	9,601	108,138
2008	10,474	9,297	9,579	9,911	8,981	8,801	9,373	9,170	9,878	10,654	9,250	10,053	115,421
2009	9,846	8,840	9,574	9,353	8,379	9,101	9,062	9,250	9,848	10,230	9,385	9,742	112,612
2010	8,838	8,619	9,947	8,980	7,897	8,968	8,396	9,030	9,257	9,651	9,895	9,838	109,315
2011	9,036	8,440	9,795	8,559	8,470	8,866	8,089	9,440	9,603	9,822	9,968	9,868	109,956
2012	9,467	8,975	9,454	8,757	9,212	8,481	8,493	9,858	9,376	10,770	10,030	9,393	112,265
2013	9,885	8,526	9,252	9,292	9,147	8,132	9,003	9,474	8,952	10,341	9,579	9,665	111,248
2014[1]	9,726	8,609	8,614	8,794	8,561	8,040	8,394	8,199	8,762	9,880	8,754	9,788	106,122

[1] Preliminary. Source: National Agricultural Statistics Service, U.S. Department of Agriculture (NASS-USDA)

Average Live Weight of all Hogs Slaughtered Under Federal Inspection   In Pounds Per Head

Year	Jan.	Feb.	Mar.	Apr.	May	June	July	Aug.	Sept.	Oct.	Nov.	Dec.	Average
2005	270	270	271	271	270	269	265	263	265	269	272	272	269
2006	273	272	272	272	271	267	264	262	267	269	272	271	269
2007	271	270	271	270	269	267	265	264	267	270	273	272	269
2008	273	271	271	270	268	266	263	261	266	270	271	271	268
2009	272	272	272	272	272	270	268	268	270	272	272	270	271
2010	272	271	272	273	273	271	269	267	271	276	278	278	273
2011	278	278	278	277	276	273	268	266	271	276	279	278	275
2012	279	278	279	279	277	274	269	269	271	274	276	276	275
2013	277	277	277	277	276	274	271	271	273	279	283	283	277
2014[1]	284	283	285	287	287	285	284	283	283	286	287	287	285

[1] Preliminary. Source: National Agricultural Statistics Service, U.S. Department of Agriculture (NASS-USDA)

HOGS

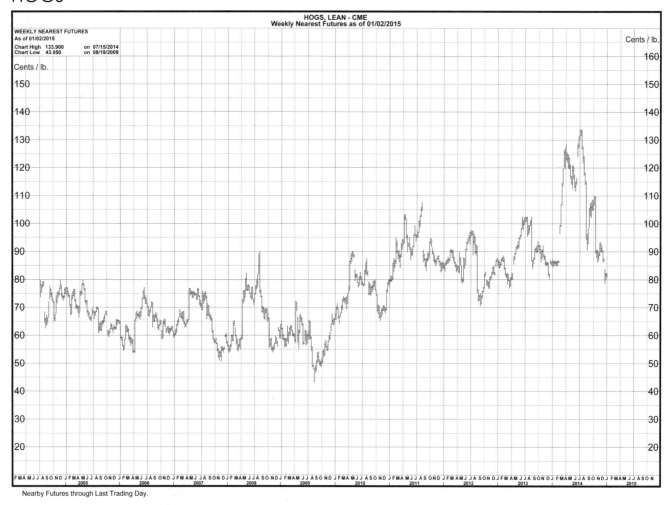

HOGS, LEAN - CME
Weekly Nearest Futures as of 01/02/2015

WEEKLY NEAREST FUTURES
As of 01/02/2015

Chart High 133.900 on 07/15/2014
Chart Low 43.050 on 08/18/2009

Nearby Futures through Last Trading Day.

Volume of Trading of Lean Hog Futures in Chicago   In Thousands of Contracts

Year	Jan.	Feb.	Mar.	Apr.	May	June	July	Aug.	Sept.	Oct.	Nov.	Dec.	Total
2005	347.5	237.1	380.7	287.8	412.7	398.2	354.8	315.9	391.1	295.8	421.7	310.2	4,153.5
2006	561.2	319.8	597.9	357.0	659.0	826.3	578.7	478.8	577.4	533.5	649.3	342.2	6,481.0
2007	687.6	449.6	721.0	423.2	621.0	744.8	865.4	559.1	591.6	485.1	730.0	386.4	7,264.8
2008	800.6	527.1	809.7	736.4	796.7	938.7	968.4	617.9	781.6	506.8	576.3	445.1	8,505.1
2009	614.9	390.1	593.6	503.2	620.3	727.6	644.1	510.7	657.8	540.6	590.1	426.2	6,819.1
2010	672.2	464.9	706.3	567.4	740.5	803.0	763.6	627.9	808.6	683.5	753.5	485.3	8,076.5
2011	879.9	660.3	925.1	661.0	881.2	991.4	901.0	770.6	1,047.8	785.7	857.7	608.4	9,970.0
2012	908.4	715.1	1,093.7	882.7	1,312.9	1,189.3	1,082.5	819.3	979.4	869.2	949.2	660.3	11,461.9
2013	999.0	808.0	1,017.5	832.9	1,100.6	1,151.0	1,076.2	778.1	1,155.6	861.5	833.8	662.8	11,277.0
2014	940.1	880.1	1,402.3	760.6	893.0	937.5	1,046.6	818.8	1,000.4	674.1	708.0	593.8	10,655.3

Contract size = 40,000 lbs.   *Source: Chicago Mercantile Exchange (CME)*

Average Open Interest of Lean Hog Futures in Chicago   In Contracts

Year	Jan.	Feb.	Mar.	Apr.	May	June	July	Aug.	Sept.	Oct.	Nov.	Dec.
2005	102,580	97,550	95,841	94,008	96,662	91,871	97,160	95,841	107,617	113,754	116,005	124,492
2006	133,258	144,506	145,020	144,250	157,259	158,276	157,899	165,781	176,336	174,971	188,965	179,057
2007	174,424	182,146	178,296	174,233	176,897	177,274	174,144	176,425	175,093	179,402	204,475	206,458
2008	212,644	227,377	219,938	232,309	252,497	242,588	238,162	231,283	206,602	171,506	168,129	159,600
2009	137,693	122,594	126,377	134,363	143,493	135,606	131,683	130,844	143,952	152,820	164,819	174,739
2010	194,351	179,300	197,407	217,304	217,779	190,933	197,940	214,535	230,240	209,159	198,160	200,932
2011	218,818	243,878	226,344	233,168	222,193	221,633	242,921	253,224	247,476	273,568	257,632	246,758
2012	243,120	256,724	262,970	259,367	268,655	258,585	231,982	224,131	237,138	219,733	230,592	242,093
2013	244,228	226,691	235,834	229,097	247,125	279,932	297,930	306,652	326,192	302,314	282,782	263,509
2014	266,366	282,321	288,484	265,981	256,474	248,869	248,878	234,967	237,877	236,417	230,578	216,735

Contract size = 40,000 lbs.   *Source: Chicago Mercantile Exchange (CME)*

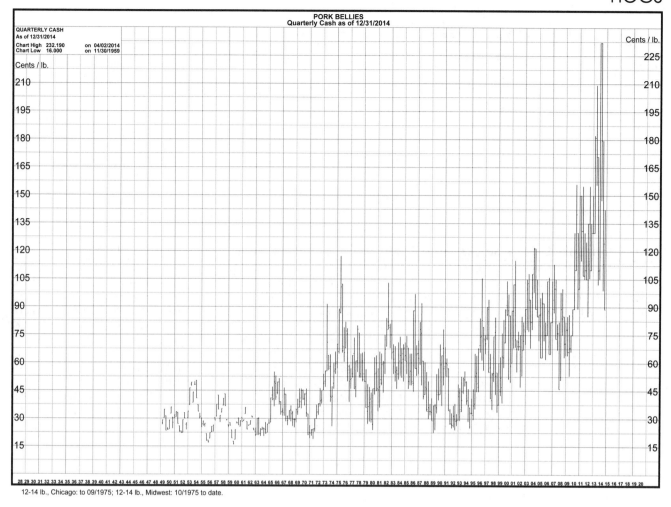

PORK BELLIES
Quarterly Cash as of 12/31/2014

12-14 lb., Chicago: to 09/1975; 12-14 lb., Midwest: 10/1975 to date.

Average Price of Pork Bellies (12-14 lbs.), Central, U.S.   In Cents Per Pound

Year	Jan.	Feb.	Mar.	Apr.	May	June	July	Aug.	Sept.	Oct.	Nov.	Dec.	Average
2005	78.00	82.13	84.20	78.13	87.31	68.73	77.48	94.00	89.67	84.07	78.82	75.00	81.46
2006	75.00	71.83	78.67	78.83	87.00	101.25	94.29	90.67	82.56	75.44	78.64	79.50	82.81
2007	86.25	96.08	93.25	93.47	106.30	101.06	99.83	86.58	80.42	71.58	75.69	77.08	88.97
2008	75.56	78.94	67.26	61.08	79.00	64.54	78.75	74.17	63.50	77.00	57.25	61.25	69.86
2009	69.88	71.00	65.25	77.50	57.00	50.00	80.36	42.25	45.83	47.33	60.50	64.00	60.91
2010	82.00	73.50	89.00	NA	NA	NA	73.50	122.50	88.00	76.67	143.00	94.50	93.63
2011	110.00	NA	143.00	147.00	143.00	119.00	121.00	135.09	133.00	111.00	91.33	NA	125.34
2012	96.50	NA	90.00	80.00	NA	NA	NA	146.00	NA	NA	NA	123.50	107.20
2013	NA	NA	NA	151.44	161.60	175.55	163.12	177.24	149.62	134.99	128.41	127.35	152.15
2014[1]	124.07	137.58	176.77	191.73	156.63	173.03	174.29	139.46	120.57	127.81	111.33	107.00	145.02

[1] Preliminary.   *Source: Economic Research Service, U.S. Department of Agriculture (ERS-USDA)*

Average Price of Pork Loins (12-14 lbs.)[2], Central, U.S.   In Cents Per Pound

Year	Jan.	Feb.	Mar.	Apr.	May	June	July	Aug.	Sept.	Oct.	Nov.	Dec.	Average
2005	116.08	114.83	115.88	115.03	133.45	115.62	115.03	119.82	111.31	103.78	96.72	101.12	113.22
2006	95.00	96.21	101.31	107.25	112.77	124.61	114.95	109.35	99.58	99.27	92.02	101.15	104.46
2007	100.96	112.08	101.04	108.99	121.61	113.58	111.78	111.66	100.18	93.41	88.25	86.46	104.17
2008	87.70	90.22	90.33	108.10	130.43	115.19	117.11	128.86	114.54	111.10	92.88	93.10	106.63
2009	94.96	94.83	90.46	92.10	97.73	91.58	101.03	90.33	89.08	85.98	82.63	103.03	92.81
2010	110.94	104.08	108.14	122.64	137.62	114.17	118.47	132.73	120.09	110.36	104.06	108.22	115.96
2011	119.02	119.98	123.08	131.20	138.84	136.21	139.57	149.33	131.78	131.07	116.40	117.61	129.51
2012	116.21	118.22	123.09	119.81	128.27	149.14	127.43	119.00	108.86	117.45	105.20	105.56	119.85
2013	107.12	111.73	108.86	106.77	120.28	138.64	129.84	128.96	116.92	115.78	107.25	106.24	116.53
2014[1]	115.27	128.19	165.28	147.55	135.39	153.75	167.79	150.01	153.69	152.92	117.50	115.00	141.86

[1] Preliminary.   *Source: Economic Research Service, U.S. Department of Agriculture (ERS-USDA)*

HOGS

Average Retail Price of Bacon, Sliced   In Dollars Per Pound

Year	Jan.	Feb.	Mar.	Apr.	May	June	July	Aug.	Sept.	Oct.	Nov.	Dec.	Average
2005	3.37	3.40	3.36	3.33	3.56	3.46	3.48	3.44	3.40	3.33	3.26	3.33	3.39
2006	3.36	3.39	3.40	3.34	3.31	3.40	3.51	3.56	3.55	3.61	3.44	3.46	3.44
2007	3.51	3.57	3.46	3.50	3.65	3.66	3.72	3.80	3.78	3.88	3.66	3.69	3.66
2008	3.65	3.62	3.62	3.55	3.64	3.66	3.61	3.84	3.73	3.75	3.60	3.67	3.66
2009	3.73	3.62	3.59	3.58	3.66	3.62	3.64	3.59	3.59	3.60	3.50	3.57	3.61
2010	3.63	3.64	3.67	3.64	3.86	4.05	4.21	4.35	4.57	4.77	4.70	4.16	4.11
2011	4.25	4.37	4.54	4.66	4.77	4.84	4.76	4.77	4.82	4.59	4.64	4.55	4.63
2012	4.57	4.66	4.60	4.53	4.39	4.33	4.37	4.61	4.69	4.66	4.64	4.64	4.56
2013	4.72	4.83	4.91	4.89	5.09	5.33	5.49	5.62	5.68	5.71	5.62	5.54	5.29
2014[1]	5.56	5.46	5.55	5.69	6.05	6.11	6.01	6.07	5.95	5.76	5.57	5.53	5.78

[1] Preliminary.   Source: Economic Research Service, U.S. Department of Agriculture (ERS-USDA)

Frozen Pork Belly Storage Stocks in the United States, on First of Month   In Thousands of Pounds

Year	Jan.	Feb.	Mar.	Apr.	May	June	July	Aug.	Sept.	Oct.	Nov.	Dec.
2005	56,026	61,528	72,324	77,718	88,367	80,033	66,775	45,254	16,175	8,094	9,421	22,490
2006	40,707	54,902	58,861	61,628	62,665	58,803	46,056	30,506	11,962	10,199	15,597	30,553
2007	41,917	46,227	46,643	55,160	61,796	57,294	47,214	31,619	21,410	17,050	20,356	34,328
2008	54,746	70,647	79,282	98,896	100,189	87,428	74,372	57,964	31,878	21,270	21,696	33,490
2009	51,593	69,166	75,668	72,940	79,543	78,801	76,333	60,238	48,958	38,481	37,127	44,638
2010	56,764	53,584	55,552	58,762	49,656	44,201	35,369	21,380	7,202	4,817	23,248	37,696
2011	50,677	51,326	50,900	52,487	53,185	57,123	48,645	29,503	15,162	9,297	8,734	26,599
2012	41,469	53,685	61,577	66,031	74,927	65,648	49,034	27,962	14,210	15,668	18,720	23,837
2013	36,037	36,425	42,976	51,473	56,352	54,829	42,033	28,177	19,335	23,491	26,674	48,298
2014[1]	80,367	87,171	87,675	79,721	83,579	85,888	83,936	64,644	45,562	34,311	29,006	35,894

[1] Preliminary.   Source: National Agricultural Statistics Service, U.S. Department of Agriculture (NASS-USDA)

United States Imports of Honey   In Metric Tons

Year	Argentina	Canada	Chile	Brazil	India	Malaysia	Mexico	Taiwan	Turkey	Ukraine	Uruguay	Vietnam	World Total
2007	20,379	12,103	13,961	453	7,671	1,891	3,192	753	167	502	1,893	15,707	105,676
2008	10,043	13,598	17,305	5	13,648	4,150	1,411	3,983	54	84	227	19,378	104,984
2009	10,899	17,709	8,302	15	13,137	9,068	1,625	5,576	73	635	19	17,430	95,475
2010	17,414	10,036	11,053	79	18,462	15,396	3,325	1,755	37	440	852	20,738	113,930
2011	33,502	14,981	7,148	21	26,912	2,326	2,846	903	183	453	7,083	27,826	130,764
2012	42,482	11,303	15,971	1,706	21,454	2,067	6,179	1,324	1,073	1,302	10,877	20,700	141,027
2013[1]	44,239	11,677	9,400	853	25,867	36	5,648	1,827	1,897	3,308	8,710	33,586	152,883

[1] Preliminary.   Source: Foreign Agricultural Service, U.S. Department of Agriculture (FAS-USDA)

Average Price of Honey, by Color Class in the United States   In Cents Per Pound

	Co-op and Private					Retail					All				
Year	Water White, Extra White, White	Extra Light Amber	Light Amber, Amber, Dark Amber	All Other Honey, Area Special-ties	All Honey	Water White, Extra White, White	Extra Light Amber	Light Amber, Amber, Dark Amber	All Other Honey, Area Special-ties	All Honey	Water White, Extra White, White	Extra Light Amber	Light Amber, Amber, Dark Amber	All Other Honey, Area Special-ties	All Honey
2007	103.0	97.5	93.8	132.7	99.9	172.8	188.0	218.3	291.1	204.6	104.6	106.4	112.5	175.6	107.7
2008	138.9	135.2	127.4	143.3	135.4	195.0	209.7	240.5	326.8	224.7	141.2	140.7	142.0	205.9	142.1
2009	142.6	144.5	135.1	179.8	141.5	252.6	252.5	291.4	414.3	283.7	144.0	150.4	148.2	247.9	147.3
2010	157.5	151.1	148.9	172.1	154.1	297.1	266.3	330.5	471.4	311.6	159.8	157.6	167.0	208.1	161.9
2011	170.1	164.4	165.7	182.6	167.7	274.1	307.1	315.4	461.0	314.7	172.9	171.1	183.4	225.2	176.5
2012	192.3	195.4	183.0	213.4	191.3	323.9	303.5	352.4	519.5	348.0	194.2	200.2	205.8	281.6	199.2
2013[1]	211.2	203.4	194.1	219.0	204.7	313.6	333.4	393.9	471.2	373.5	212.6	207.6	214.0	241.1	212.1

[1] Preliminary.   Source: National Agricultural Statistics Service, U.S. Department of Agriculture (NASS-USDA)

138

Honey

Honey is the thick, supersaturated sugar solution produced by bees to feed their larvae. It is composed of fructose, glucose and water in varying proportions and also contains several enzymes and oils. The color of honey varies due to the source of nectar and age of the honey. Light colored honeys are usually of higher quality than darker honeys. The average honeybee colony can produce more than 700 pounds of honey per year but only 10 percent is usually harvested by the beekeeper. The rest of the honey is consumed by the colony during the year. American per capita honey consumption is 1 pound per person per year. Honey is said to be humanity's oldest sweet, and beeswax the first plastic.

Honey is used in many ways, including direct human consumption, baking, and medicine. Honey has several healing properties. Its high sugar content nourishes injured tissues, thus enhancing faster healing time. Honey's phytochemicals create a form of hydrogen peroxide that cleans out the wound, and the thick consistency protects the wound from contact with air. Honey has also proven superior to antibiotic ointments for reducing rates of infection in people with burns.

Prices – U.S. average domestic honey prices in 2013 (latest data) rose by +6.5% to a record high of 212.1 cents per pound. The value of U.S. honey production in 2013 rose +11.9% to $317.087 million, a new record high.

Supply – World production of honey in 2013 rose +2.9% to 1.663 million metric tons, a new record high. The major producer of honey by far is China with 466.300 metric tons in 2013 which is 28.0% of total world production. Other major producers in 2013 were the U.S. with 67,812 metric tons, Russia with 68,446, Argentina with 80,000 metric tons, and Mexico with 56,907 metric tons.

U.S. production of honey in 2013 rose +5.1% to 149.499 million pounds, remaining well below the 14-year high of 220.339 million pounds posted in 2000. Stocks rose by +19.9% to 38.160 million pounds in 2013 (Jan 1), which is a down from 2000's decade high of 220.339 million pounds. Yield per colony in 2013 rose +1.1% to 56.6 pounds per colony. The number of colonies in 2013 rose +4.0% to 2.640, just below the 2010 decade record high of 2.692.

Trade – U.S. imports of honey in 2013 rose by +8.5% to 323.6 million pounds, a new record high. U.S. exports of honey are generally small and in 2013 they totaled only 11.9 million pounds, which was only 2.3% of U.S. production.

World Production of Honey   In Metric Tons

Year	Argentina	Australia	Brazil	Canada	China	Germany	Japan	Mexico	Russia	United States	World Total
2007	81,000	18,000	34,747	31,489	354,000	18,266	3,373	55,459	53,655	67,286	1,461,918
2008	72,000	17,600	37,792	29,440	400,000	15,727	3,384	55,271	57,440	74,293	1,520,956
2009	62,000	16,595	38,974	31,920	402,000	16,460	2,656	56,071	53,598	66,413	1,510,323
2010	59,000	16,150	38,073	33,710	409,149	23,178	2,639	55,684	51,535	80,042	1,546,710
2011	76,000	10,000	41,793	35,520	446,089	25,831	2,684	57,783	60,010	67,294	1,614,020
2012	80,000	10,500	33,932	41,113	462,203	15,699	2,763	58,602	64,898	64,544	1,616,820
2013[1]	80,000	10,500	35,365	34,640	466,300	15,700	2,800	56,907	68,446	67,812	1,663,800

[1] Preliminary.   Source: Food and Agricultural Organization of the United Nations (FAO)

Salient Statistics of Honey in the United States   In Millions of Pounds

Year	Number of Colonies (1,000)	Yield Per Colony (Pounds)	Stocks Jan. 1	Total U.S. Production	Imports for Consumption	Domestic Disappearance	Exports	Total Supply	Placed Under Loan	CCC Take Over	Net Gov't. Expenditure[3] (Million $)	Domestic Avg. Price All Honey - Cents Per Pound -	National Avg. Price Support	Per Capita Consumption (Pounds)
2008	2,342	69.9	51.2	163.8	231.4	----	10.1	446.4	----	----	----	142.1	----	----
2009	2,498	58.6	37.5	146.4	210.5	----	9.7	394.4	----	----	----	147.3	----	----
2010	2,692	65.6	45.0	176.5	251.2	----	9.6	472.6	----	----	----	161.9	----	----
2011	2,491	59.6	36.8	148.4	288.3	----	11.9	473.4	----	----	----	176.5	----	----
2012[1]	2,539	56.0	31.8	142.3	298.1	----	12.3	472.3	----	----	----	199.2	----	----
2013[2]	2,640	56.6	38.2	149.5	323.6	----	11.9	511.2	----	----	----	212.1	----	----

[1] Preliminary.   [2] Forecast.   [3] Fiscal year.   Source: Economic Research Service, U.S. Department of Agriculture (ERS-USDA)

Production and Yield of Honey in the United States

Year	California	Florida	Minnesota	North Dakota	South Dakota	Total	Value of Production ($1,000)	California	Florida	Minnesota	North Dakota	South Dakota	Average
	--------------- Production in Thousands of Pounds ---------------							------------------ Yield Per Colony in Pounds ------------------					
2008	18,360	11,850	9,516	36,000	21,375	163,789	232,744	51	79	78	90	95	69.9
2009	11,715	11,560	7,930	34,650	17,820	146,416	215,671	33	68	65	77	66	58.6
2010	27,470	13,800	8,448	46,410	15,370	176,462	285,692	67	69	66	91	58	65.6
2011	17,760	10,980	6,360	32,660	16,500	148,357	261,850	48	61	53	71	66	59.6
2012	11,550	12,352	8,375	33,120	16,380	142,296	283,454	35	64	67	69	63	56.0
2013[1]	10,890	13,420	7,540	33,120	14,840	149,499	317,087	33	61	58	69	56	56.6

[1] Preliminary.   Source: National Agricultural Statistics Service, U.S. Department of Agriculture (NASS-USDA)

Interest Rates - U.S.

U.S. interest rates can be characterized in two main ways, by credit quality and by maturity. Credit quality refers to the level of risk associated with a particular borrower. U.S. Treasury securities, for example, carry the lowest risk. Maturity refers to the time at which the security matures and must be repaid. Treasury securities carry the full spectrum of maturities, from short-term cash management bills, to T-bills (4-weeks, 3-months, 6-months), T-notes (2-year, 3-year, 5-year, 7-year, and 10-year), and 30-year T-bonds. The most active futures markets are the 10-year T-note futures, 30-year T-bond futures, and Eurodollar futures, all of which are traded at the CME Group.

Prices – CME 10-year T-note futures prices posted a 3-1/2 year low in December 2013, but then rallied moderately during 2014 to post a new 1-1/2 year high. T-note prices traded sideways in the first half of 2014 as Fed policy remained steady and the U.S. economy picked up some steam. However, T-note prices then rallied and broke out to a new 1-1/2 year high in the latter part of the year due to the plunge in inflation expectations caused by the free-fall in crude oil prices.

T-note prices during 2014 were supported by the Fed's continued extraordinarily easy monetary policy as the Fed kept its federal funds rate target near zero all year. The Fed during 2014 progressively cut the size of its third quantitative easing program (QE3) by $10 billion per month at each FOMC meeting, finally making the final $15 billion cut at its October 2014 meeting. The end of QE3 did not have much impact on the T-note market since the Fed had been progressively cutting QE3 for over a year and had clearly telegraphed its intention to end QE3 in

October 2014. The Fed is now keeping its balance sheet asset level unchanged near $4.5 trillion by rolling-over maturing securities.

Meanwhile, the plunge in crude oil prices in the latter part of 2014 had a bullish impact on the T-note market since inflation expectations fell sharply. The 10-year breakeven inflation expectations rate, which measures the difference between nominal and inflation-adjusted TIPS T-notes, posted a 7-year high of 3.00% at the beginning of 2014 but then fell as low as 1.60% in January 2015 after crude oil prices plunged. The plunge in crude oil prices pushed the headline U.S. inflation indexes lower and also put downward pressure on the core inflation indexes because fuel prices are such a key cost for a wide variety of products and services. The disinflation pressures caused by the plunge in crude oil prices also gave the Fed more flexibility to extend its extraordinarily easy monetary policy, which was a further supportive factor for T-note prices.

U.S. interest rates continue to trade at extraordinarily low levels due to the Fed's zero interest rate policy, low inflation, and weak global economic growth. However, the question is whether long-term interest rates will see significant upward pressure over the next few years as the global economy gains traction and as the Fed starts to drain excess reserves and raise interest rates. The federal funds market is currently expecting the Fed's first 25 basis point (bp) rate hike to 0.50% by November 2015. The market is then expecting three 25 bp rate hikes in 2016 and three more 25 bp rate hikes in 2017, thus bringing the federal funds rate up to 2.00% by the end of 2017. Those rate hikes would put significant downward pressure on T-note prices.

U.S. Producer Price Index[2] for All Commodities   1982 = 100

Year	Jan.	Feb.	Mar.	Apr.	May	June	July	Aug.	Sept.	Oct.	Nov.	Dec.	Average
2005	150.9	151.6	153.7	155.0	154.3	154.3	156.3	157.6	162.2	166.2	163.7	163.0	157.4
2006	164.3	161.8	162.2	164.3	165.8	166.1	166.8	167.9	165.4	162.2	164.6	165.6	164.8
2007	164.0	166.8	169.3	171.4	173.3	173.8	175.1	172.4	173.5	174.7	179.0	178.6	172.7
2008	181.0	182.7	187.9	190.9	196.6	200.5	205.5	199.0	196.9	186.4	176.8	170.9	189.6
2009	171.2	169.3	168.1	169.1	170.8	174.1	172.5	175.0	174.1	175.2	177.4	178.1	172.9
2010	181.9	181.0	183.3	184.4	184.8	183.5	184.1	184.9	184.9	186.6	187.7	189.7	184.7
2011	192.7	195.8	199.2	203.1	204.1	203.9	204.6	203.2	203.7	201.1	201.4	199.8	201.1
2012	200.7	201.6	204.2	203.7	201.9	199.8	200.1	202.7	204.4	203.5	201.8	201.5	202.2
2013	202.5	204.3	204.0	203.5	204.1	204.3	204.4	204.2	203.9	202.5	201.2	202.0	203.4
2014[1]	203.8	205.7	207.0	208.3	208.0	208.3	208.0	207.0	206.5	203.6	201.2	197.6	205.4

[1] Preliminary.   [2] Not seasonally adjusted.   *Source: Bureau of Labor Statistics, U.S. Department of Commerce (BLS)*

U.S. Consumer Price Index[2] for All Urban Consumers   1982-84 = 100

Year	Jan.	Feb.	Mar.	Apr.	May	June	July	Aug.	Sept.	Oct.	Nov.	Dec.	Average
2005	190.7	191.8	193.3	194.6	194.4	194.5	195.4	196.4	198.8	199.2	197.6	196.8	195.3
2006	198.3	198.7	199.8	201.5	202.5	202.9	203.5	203.9	202.9	201.8	201.5	201.8	201.6
2007	202.4	203.5	205.4	206.7	207.9	208.4	208.3	207.9	208.5	208.9	210.2	210.0	207.3
2008	211.1	211.7	213.5	214.8	216.6	218.8	220.0	219.1	218.8	216.6	212.4	210.2	215.3
2009	211.1	212.2	212.7	213.2	213.9	215.7	215.4	215.8	216.0	216.2	216.3	215.9	214.5
2010	216.7	216.7	217.6	218.0	218.2	218.0	218.0	218.3	218.4	218.7	218.8	219.2	218.1
2011	220.2	221.3	223.5	224.9	226.0	225.7	225.9	226.5	226.9	226.4	226.2	225.7	224.9
2012	226.7	227.7	229.4	230.1	229.8	229.5	229.1	230.4	231.4	231.3	230.2	229.6	229.6
2013	230.3	232.2	232.8	232.5	232.9	233.5	233.6	233.9	234.1	233.5	233.1	233.0	233.0
2014[1]	233.9	234.8	236.3	237.1	237.9	238.3	238.3	237.9	238.0	237.4	236.2	234.8	236.7

[1] Preliminary.   [2] Not seasonally adjusted.   *Source: Bureau of Labor Statistics, U.S. Department of Commerce (BLS)*

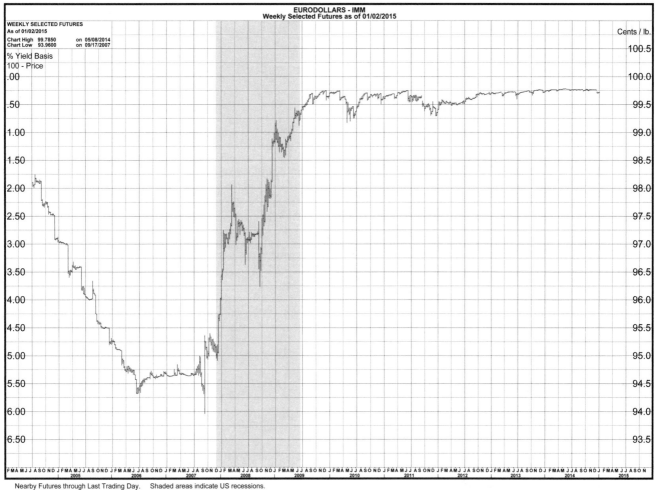

EURODOLLARS - IMM
Weekly Selected Futures as of 01/02/2015

Nearby Futures through Last Trading Day.   Shaded areas indicate US recessions.

Volume of Trading of 3-month Eurodollar Futures in Chicago   In Thousands of Contracts

Year	Jan.	Feb.	Mar.	Apr.	May	June	July	Aug.	Sept.	Oct.	Nov.	Dec.	Total
2005	27,793.8	28,549.2	34,472.4	42,437.2	36,599.9	37,997.0	26,794.7	32,920.8	45,483.5	35,148.8	34,775.7	27,382.0	410,355
2006	35,602.4	34,218.0	47,463.8	37,752.2	44,154.6	45,443.4	36,794.1	45,126.7	45,180.3	46,453.5	42,700.7	41,187.7	502,077
2007	43,204.2	46,365.8	63,154.7	39,567.7	50,305.2	58,372.0	53,290.3	77,539.0	49,528.8	45,862.8	53,795.1	40,484.5	621,470
2008	70,787.1	59,378.2	60,956.1	56,371.5	48,683.4	60,086.5	54,178.8	36,521.6	58,497.7	40,508.5	24,515.5	26,489.2	596,974
2009	31,370.9	29,422.6	35,280.3	29,706.3	34,665.5	51,021.4	40,062.0	36,483.1	39,604.4	40,397.6	32,914.4	36,656.6	437,585
2010	36,569.3	37,746.7	47,459.2	52,132.3	57,806.8	36,986.7	32,120.3	34,582.2	38,196.5	34,205.0	55,512.9	47,637.1	510,955
2011	42,213.1	51,117.3	62,877.0	49,748.5	46,199.0	62,516.2	46,462.8	61,739.9	38,864.4	34,186.8	39,340.0	28,821.7	564,087
2012	41,620.4	38,145.0	46,496.1	32,895.5	40,756.4	38,105.8	28,199.5	34,119.2	37,238.4	35,652.7	26,998.6	26,210.8	426,438
2013	40,800.6	32,152.3	37,526.2	30,235.7	51,371.9	69,283.3	41,177.9	38,851.4	51,413.1	43,321.9	39,422.5	41,693.4	517,250
2014	54,761.3	38,750.1	57,945.4	46,118.3	54,063.9	55,196.8	57,448.5	47,862.5	67,835.8	86,823.2	34,561.6	62,937.8	664,305

Contract size = $1,000,000.   *Source: CME Group; International Monetary Market (IOM), division of the Chicago Mercantile Exchange (CME)*

Average Open Interest of 3-month Eurodollar Futures in Chicago   In Thousands of Contracts

Year	Jan.	Feb.	Mar.	Apr.	May	June	July	Aug.	Sept.	Oct.	Nov.	Dec.
2005	7,163.3	7,858.5	8,124.1	8,244.1	8,604.5	8,045.7	7,416.0	8,044.7	8,054.2	8,471.9	9,264.8	9,145.1
2006	8,833.5	9,574.0	9,586.0	9,679.6	10,126.2	9,995.4	9,572.4	10,153.9	9,949.4	9,809.8	10,345.5	10,201.1
2007	9,682.3	10,400.5	10,847.9	10,827.1	11,895.5	11,285.2	11,166.9	11,416.3	10,782.6	10,019.4	10,631.2	10,515.5
2008	11,033.0	11,206.7	10,356.6	9,225.3	9,282.5	9,266.0	9,589.0	9,882.1	8,953.0	8,141.7	8,286.9	7,389.1
2009	6,772.8	6,857.6	6,371.3	6,055.5	6,480.5	6,383.2	6,540.1	6,748.5	6,659.5	6,937.8	7,382.3	6,876.4
2010	6,957.6	7,607.2	7,643.6	7,850.9	7,728.4	7,297.3	7,652.9	7,876.1	7,528.6	7,953.2	8,245.8	7,433.0
2011	7,675.5	8,820.5	9,086.9	9,494.8	10,101.6	10,117.4	10,018.2	9,997.3	9,011.2	8,239.0	8,624.3	8,123.4
2012	7,787.5	8,387.6	8,508.1	8,593.1	8,776.6	8,213.4	7,889.8	7,858.5	8,210.5	8,269.0	8,508.1	8,292.0
2013	8,320.7	8,898.0	9,261.8	9,350.3	9,681.0	9,020.2	8,685.1	9,291.6	9,141.1	9,420.5	10,163.4	10,422.3
2014	10,142.7	10,022.8	10,453.9	10,875.2	11,635.9	11,593.8	12,101.1	12,734.0	13,139.9	11,819.9	11,685.4	10,902.1

Contract size = $1,000,000.   *Source: CME Group; International Monetary Market (IOM), division of the Chicago Mercantile Exchange (CME)*

INTEREST RATES - U.S.

T-NOTE, 2-YEAR - CBOT
Weekly Nearest Futures as of 01/02/2015

Nearby Futures through Last Trading Day.   Shaded areas indicate US recessions.

Volume of Trading of 2-Year U.S. Treasury Note Futures in Chicago   In Thousands of Contracts

Year	Jan.	Feb.	Mar.	Apr.	May	June	July	Aug.	Sept.	Oct.	Nov.	Dec.	Total
2005	953.7	1,997.5	1,706.1	1,548.3	2,306.3	1,811.4	1,153.0	2,144.2	2,118.0	1,344.1	2,451.5	1,671.3	21,205
2006	2,053.3	3,223.3	3,206.5	2,090.0	4,690.9	2,837.1	2,525.1	4,461.0	2,768.3	2,422.9	4,826.4	2,862.0	37,967
2007	2,892.6	5,666.6	5,321.4	3,128.3	7,197.4	5,495.7	4,793.7	10,567.2	4,788.1	4,771.2	8,849.7	5,138.5	68,610
2008	7,526.1	10,092.8	7,515.4	5,102.6	8,195.6	7,207.2	6,366.1	7,529.6	8,126.5	5,355.3	4,067.9	2,225.8	79,311
2009	2,117.4	3,797.2	2,486.1	2,219.7	4,409.0	3,818.7	3,094.7	5,931.9	3,915.7	5,012.4	7,205.5	4,150.6	48,159
2010	4,487.2	8,143.4	6,164.3	6,164.1	9,494.2	4,398.8	4,083.6	6,491.7	3,719.2	3,189.8	6,849.9	3,791.0	66,977
2011	4,172.3	9,276.8	7,161.9	5,363.7	8,520.4	6,814.1	5,166.5	9,198.7	3,990.7	3,743.3	6,105.9	2,664.6	72,179
2012	3,162.6	6,083.1	4,858.3	3,568.9	6,748.6	3,626.2	3,831.4	6,593.6	3,575.3	3,318.0	6,615.1	3,127.6	55,109
2013	4,249.9	7,408.8	3,786.5	3,169.7	8,812.1	4,703.0	3,008.5	6,380.5	4,134.8	3,133.0	5,982.2	3,046.9	57,816
2014	4,004.9	4,637.1	4,670.2	4,402.3	8,206.8	4,404.6	3,913.5	9,120.7	6,155.0	6,801.9	8,643.1	5,054.0	70,014

Contract size = $200,000.   *Source: CME Group; Chicago Board of Trade (CBT)*

Average Open Interest of 2-Year U.S. Treasury Note Futures in Chicago   In Thousands of Contracts

Year	Jan.	Feb.	Mar.	Apr.	May	June	July	Aug.	Sept.	Oct.	Nov.	Dec.
2005	287.3	345.7	329.6	307.0	341.5	372.9	362.3	371.1	364.4	351.3	357.3	363.2
2006	437.8	489.3	469.0	489.5	607.6	541.1	595.1	701.4	683.6	680.7	698.4	716.0
2007	764.5	826.7	896.3	1,003.3	1,125.5	965.1	1,016.8	985.4	902.3	993.1	1,043.6	997.3
2008	1,101.2	1,313.0	1,187.3	1,110.0	1,166.8	972.5	895.4	922.6	783.7	735.0	648.0	503.4
2009	505.7	495.1	473.4	487.5	514.2	535.3	627.8	741.6	772.4	935.2	1,052.2	911.8
2010	885.7	982.1	891.3	1,001.7	1,022.3	900.3	847.1	805.6	708.2	734.8	710.8	664.9
2011	711.7	900.2	892.0	1,031.0	1,066.2	1,030.5	1,012.9	976.2	772.3	714.5	748.0	698.8
2012	781.4	904.4	842.3	835.7	975.7	928.1	953.8	1,012.6	963.5	942.0	1,030.2	1,015.8
2013	998.1	1,046.5	989.2	916.5	945.3	816.8	791.7	864.5	863.5	925.2	978.2	866.6
2014	858.0	934.8	942.0	1,077.5	1,153.4	1,051.2	1,164.8	1,400.5	1,546.2	1,425.6	1,432.8	1,292.8

Contract size = $200,000.   *Source: CME Group; Chicago Board of Trade (CBT)*

T-NOTE, 5-YEAR - CBOT
Weekly Nearest Futures as of 01/02/2015

WEEKLY NEAREST FUTURES
As of 01/02/2015

Chart High 125 2/64   on 09/04/2012
Chart Low   102 63/64 on 07/05/2006

% Yield Basis
6% 5-Yr

Cents / lb.

Nearby Futures through Last Trading Day.   Shaded areas indicate US recessions.

Volume of Trading of 5-Year U.S. Treasury Note Futures in Chicago   In Thousands of Contracts

Year	Jan.	Feb.	Mar.	Apr.	May	June	July	Aug.	Sept.	Oct.	Nov.	Dec.	Total
2005	7,797.7	11,168.4	11,848.9	10,720.3	12,320.4	9,164.3	7,698.0	12,662.9	10,999.9	8,510.5	11,996.4	7,021.1	121,909
2006	9,388.4	12,141.7	11,865.2	7,869.8	12,971.9	9,368.7	8,102.0	13,347.5	9,369.3	8,730.9	13,423.5	8,291.5	124,870
2007	9,208.6	14,410.2	14,156.0	8,372.3	15,673.4	13,243.1	13,001.7	22,354.8	11,376.0	12,495.6	21,271.6	10,644.1	166,207
2008	15,479.7	20,790.4	17,424.0	12,474.7	17,616.2	14,904.3	14,514.1	15,085.6	16,979.1	10,079.8	8,057.9	4,721.7	168,127
2009	4,821.3	8,349.9	7,388.4	5,837.7	9,658.3	8,314.8	8,034.1	10,588.0	8,259.3	9,242.9	10,231.8	7,664.7	98,391
2010	7,434.9	11,815.6	10,096.3	9,631.3	16,093.0	10,212.4	9,662.0	13,062.2	9,627.7	9,404.1	14,828.5	10,282.0	132,150
2011	10,654.1	16,398.4	16,604.1	11,371.9	17,958.8	16,524.9	13,314.4	21,004.3	12,074.6	11,607.0	15,320.7	7,729.7	170,563
2012	9,260.0	14,543.1	12,251.9	8,980.8	14,647.3	10,565.4	7,291.7	13,493.4	10,510.3	9,281.0	13,968.6	8,549.0	133,342
2013	12,206.3	18,750.5	11,971.1	11,023.9	23,914.4	17,072.7	11,763.4	18,021.9	13,464.8	10,198.2	16,397.4	10,543.6	175,328
2014	13,081.6	18,022.0	16,060.6	14,088.2	20,473.5	13,605.3	14,182.4	20,546.3	16,596.0	20,858.3	15,933.0	12,981.8	196,429

Contract size = $100,000.   *Source: CME Group; Chicago Board of Trade (CBT)*

Average Open Interest of 5-Year U.S. Treasury Note Futures in Chicago   In Thousands of Contracts

Year	Jan.	Feb.	Mar.	Apr.	May	June	July	Aug.	Sept.	Oct.	Nov.	Dec.
2005	1,160.2	1,237.0	1,325.0	1,383.0	1,320.9	1,127.9	1,247.7	1,450.3	1,190.2	1,342.0	1,397.6	1,126.8
2006	1,105.1	1,404.8	1,238.0	1,257.2	1,326.0	1,264.7	1,258.3	1,409.8	1,341.3	1,413.8	1,484.4	1,423.8
2007	1,468.1	1,499.6	1,481.0	1,614.9	1,763.5	1,601.5	1,586.9	1,648.0	1,564.9	1,666.1	1,932.4	1,841.2
2008	1,940.6	2,101.2	1,923.8	1,850.9	1,851.0	1,669.6	1,574.5	1,600.7	1,483.4	1,378.1	1,267.1	1,057.8
2009	965.5	964.7	897.8	812.7	860.8	774.2	761.1	831.9	800.3	770.9	854.0	831.6
2010	805.1	939.1	942.4	937.2	1,045.8	932.2	940.4	1,095.6	925.0	1,012.8	1,136.6	1,010.9
2011	1,075.8	1,293.9	1,223.4	1,364.8	1,524.6	1,576.9	1,513.4	1,435.6	1,326.7	1,200.4	1,277.5	1,261.2
2012	1,398.3	1,444.8	1,390.1	1,306.6	1,384.1	1,144.6	1,145.8	1,236.3	1,330.2	1,399.5	1,461.6	1,506.2
2013	1,532.5	1,653.7	1,733.6	1,847.6	1,842.2	1,535.0	1,584.4	1,641.0	1,668.5	1,745.1	1,968.7	1,865.1
2014	1,939.7	2,002.5	1,959.1	2,036.7	2,126.3	2,070.6	2,130.6	2,190.1	2,130.5	1,992.7	1,993.5	1,844.4

Contract size = $100,000.   *Source: CME Group; Chicago Board of Trade (CBT)*

INTEREST RATES - U.S.

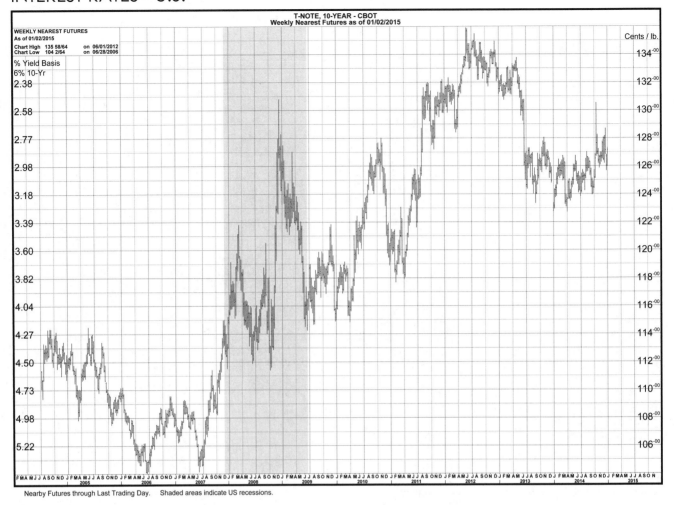

T-NOTE, 10-YEAR - CBOT
Weekly Nearest Futures as of 01/02/2015

WEEKLY NEAREST FUTURES
As of 01/02/2015

Chart High 135 58/64 on 06/01/2012
Chart Low 104 2/64 on 06/28/2006

% Yield Basis
6% 10-Yr

Cents / lb.

Nearby Futures through Last Trading Day.   Shaded areas indicate US recessions.

Volume of Trading of 10-year U.S. Treasury Note Futures in Chicago   In Thousands of Contracts

Year	Jan.	Feb.	Mar.	Apr.	May	June	July	Aug.	Sept.	Oct.	Nov.	Dec.	Total
2005	13,901.3	19,565.4	21,132.8	19,487.3	22,688.8	16,778.7	13,894.5	20,120.1	18,348.2	15,357.3	20,705.4	13,144.2	215,124
2006	17,188.6	21,262.7	22,739.9	17,241.5	26,174.6	20,311.2	16,645.2	24,796.6	22,125.2	20,602.6	28,413.8	18,070.1	255,572
2007	21,492.5	30,367.2	30,210.2	18,529.8	34,343.9	37,171.0	32,361.3	38,785.6	24,375.6	25,280.4	36,890.7	19,421.3	349,229
2008	28,924.8	33,426.2	23,331.5	19,043.9	27,414.0	22,591.8	22,903.0	21,069.7	23,265.1	15,101.1	11,826.6	7,873.1	256,771
2009	9,778.0	14,548.1	15,116.1	11,893.7	17,309.8	16,994.6	16,420.7	19,292.8	16,099.0	19,268.8	19,037.2	14,093.3	189,852
2010	16,865.3	23,588.6	19,582.2	22,070.6	35,156.5	24,198.2	22,294.5	30,744.0	26,070.6	22,947.9	29,360.3	20,840.2	293,719
2011	22,260.8	27,531.8	29,500.1	20,162.8	31,149.4	31,897.7	25,851.1	39,911.1	24,612.4	23,559.8	26,614.2	14,351.4	317,403
2012	19,336.4	26,546.0	24,188.9	20,706.8	32,255.6	24,036.4	16,688.1	25,178.8	18,527.4	18,740.5	23,319.0	15,473.1	264,997
2013	24,720.9	33,572.4	24,606.7	23,859.0	43,005.7	32,912.7	21,673.6	31,715.3	23,332.3	21,265.7	27,463.8	17,800.2	325,928
2014	23,218.1	29,772.2	27,675.3	25,202.1	34,569.3	24,098.5	23,402.1	34,087.3	28,122.5	39,126.2	28,205.8	23,001.4	340,481

Contract size = $100,000.   *Source: CME Group; Chicago Board of Trade (CBT)*

Average Open Interest of 10-year U.S. Treasury Note Futures in Chicago   In Thousands of Contracts

Year	Jan.	Feb.	Mar.	Apr.	May	June	July	Aug.	Sept.	Oct.	Nov.	Dec.
2005	1,671.3	1,888.6	1,980.2	2,003.5	2,140.8	1,869.0	1,859.3	1,992.8	1,749.4	1,677.7	1,778.6	1,635.6
2006	1,700.0	1,990.4	2,048.7	2,259.7	2,321.0	2,054.2	2,087.1	2,265.3	2,271.5	2,408.2	2,398.2	2,236.0
2007	2,343.6	2,367.3	2,294.0	2,586.9	2,878.3	2,853.9	2,871.5	2,820.5	2,269.5	2,497.2	2,661.6	2,313.2
2008	2,431.2	2,517.6	2,179.8	2,073.7	2,144.6	1,978.8	1,802.6	1,835.2	1,658.2	1,385.2	1,226.4	1,074.2
2009	1,034.9	1,027.6	1,007.0	1,010.0	1,132.3	1,070.9	1,056.2	1,139.7	1,120.2	1,239.1	1,327.5	1,203.9
2010	1,292.9	1,420.4	1,423.8	1,632.0	1,838.8	1,756.8	1,802.2	1,973.0	1,686.3	1,617.2	1,527.4	1,335.3
2011	1,360.1	1,521.3	1,563.5	1,643.4	1,854.0	1,834.0	1,843.5	1,937.7	1,627.4	1,504.3	1,505.7	1,460.6
2012	1,647.6	1,847.4	1,796.4	1,804.4	1,949.8	1,806.5	1,787.3	1,640.5	1,593.8	1,685.3	1,783.4	1,674.9
2013	1,815.9	2,089.8	2,125.6	2,230.3	2,331.8	2,132.2	2,199.4	2,308.6	2,031.6	2,079.2	2,341.3	2,261.2
2014	2,260.5	2,426.0	2,433.4	2,526.5	2,720.3	2,591.6	2,679.0	2,853.2	2,705.4	2,776.0	2,855.5	2,652.6

Contract size = $100,000.   *Source: CME Group; Chicago Board of Trade (CBT)*

Nearby Futures through Last Trading Day.   Shaded areas indicate US recessions.

Volume of Trading of 30-year U.S. Treasury Bond Futures in Chicago   In Thousands of Contracts

Year	Jan.	Feb.	Mar.	Apr.	May	June	July	Aug.	Sept.	Oct.	Nov.	Dec.	Total
2005	6,134.8	8,973.5	8,573.7	7,293.5	8,558.9	7,407.2	5,367.0	7,771.3	7,193.6	6,450.4	7,928.8	5,274.0	86,927
2006	7,044.8	8,511.6	8,980.6	6,969.2	10,354.4	7,564.5	5,854.2	8,736.7	7,553.9	6,375.1	9,461.6	6,348.2	93,755
2007	7,108.8	10,060.2	10,338.3	6,108.4	10,578.5	11,338.4	9,452.1	11,439.3	6,864.4	7,232.1	11,146.2	5,963.6	107,630
2008	9,667.3	11,646.2	8,739.1	5,835.3	9,173.4	7,176.8	7,429.4	7,521.6	7,830.0	5,559.1	5,267.6	3,618.7	89,465
2009	3,805.9	6,062.7	4,525.5	3,224.8	6,465.1	5,192.0	4,995.2	7,238.3	4,297.6	5,133.4	6,978.4	4,313.9	62,233
2010	4,617.8	7,345.1	5,748.7	6,033.7	10,457.5	5,899.4	5,711.8	9,165.6	6,774.8	6,806.7	9,379.5	5,569.2	83,510
2011	6,272.2	8,551.9	7,823.2	5,528.4	9,231.3	8,358.3	6,471.5	11,892.5	7,487.1	6,694.3	9,057.7	4,969.9	92,339
2012	6,143.3	8,623.0	7,335.2	5,890.8	11,326.7	9,060.1	6,493.7	8,685.7	6,680.1	6,866.2	8,530.8	6,109.6	91,745
2013	7,892.2	10,758.6	7,691.9	8,269.7	13,337.5	9,601.6	5,788.0	8,792.7	6,759.6	6,193.9	7,712.2	5,165.3	97,963
2014	5,871.1	8,211.2	6,867.7	6,259.9	9,648.8	7,044.9	6,719.0	9,948.4	7,678.1	10,370.2	7,827.0	6,741.8	93,188

Contract size = $100,000.   *Source: CME Group; Chicago Board of Trade (CBT)*

Average Open Interest of 30-year U.S. Treasury Bond Futures in Chicago   In Contracts

Year	Jan.	Feb.	Mar.	Apr.	May	June	July	Aug.	Sept.	Oct.	Nov.	Dec.
2005	674,170	792,247	749,403	710,061	735,910	665,235	579,724	600,565	595,736	586,653	618,647	574,121
2006	601,094	662,314	622,927	739,601	858,812	760,240	760,749	813,905	763,092	737,070	810,426	803,020
2007	816,747	903,121	852,305	875,810	949,173	980,004	988,995	991,513	915,693	948,940	1,022,623	947,588
2008	1,033,106	1,041,505	979,695	893,308	941,317	879,149	891,111	880,157	877,623	756,790	731,186	754,687
2009	726,062	733,323	712,813	708,243	724,577	706,818	696,641	727,674	749,290	739,723	777,241	704,259
2010	656,438	676,778	648,845	663,991	740,180	663,330	682,310	738,206	669,950	683,476	654,901	563,632
2011	552,937	613,356	609,003	573,206	702,197	668,848	628,174	661,826	647,168	618,884	634,941	597,183
2012	612,937	615,616	583,579	576,419	661,058	664,479	636,745	610,065	570,346	564,706	623,227	586,502
2013	551,333	632,060	630,148	681,045	667,210	568,046	574,724	626,392	630,549	644,843	696,333	656,867
2014	666,663	716,926	712,174	722,390	780,781	738,607	758,214	870,115	860,417	870,759	850,561	889,272

Contract size = $100,000.   *Source: CME Group; Chicago Board of Trade (CBT)*

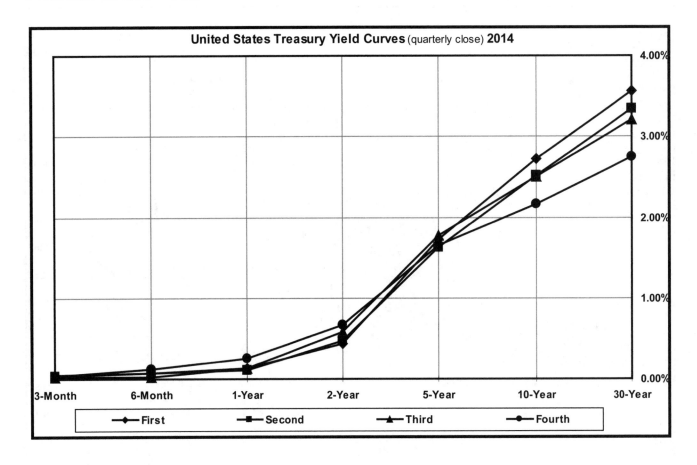

United States Treasury Yield Curves (quarterly close) **2014**

Legend: ◆ First ■ Second ▲ Third ● Fourth

X-axis: 3-Month, 6-Month, 1-Year, 2-Year, 5-Year, 10-Year, 30-Year
Y-axis: 0.00%, 1.00%, 2.00%, 3.00%, 4.00%

U.S. Federal Funds Rate   In Percent

Year	Jan.	Feb.	Mar.	Apr.	May	June	July	Aug.	Sept.	Oct.	Nov.	Dec.	Average
2005	2.28	2.50	2.63	2.79	3.00	3.04	3.26	3.50	3.62	3.78	4.00	4.16	3.21
2006	4.29	4.49	4.59	4.79	4.94	4.99	5.24	5.25	5.25	5.25	5.25	5.24	4.96
2007	5.25	5.26	5.26	5.25	5.25	5.25	5.26	5.02	4.94	4.76	4.49	4.24	5.02
2008	3.94	2.98	2.61	2.28	1.98	2.00	2.01	2.00	1.81	0.97	0.39	0.16	1.93
2009	0.15	0.22	0.18	0.15	0.18	0.21	0.16	0.16	0.15	0.12	0.12	0.12	0.16
2010	0.11	0.13	0.16	0.20	0.20	0.18	0.18	0.19	0.19	0.19	0.19	0.18	0.18
2011	0.17	0.16	0.14	0.10	0.09	0.09	0.07	0.10	0.08	0.07	0.08	0.07	0.10
2012	0.08	0.10	0.13	0.14	0.16	0.16	0.16	0.13	0.14	0.16	0.16	0.16	0.14
2013	0.14	0.15	0.14	0.15	0.11	0.09	0.09	0.08	0.08	0.09	0.08	0.09	0.11
2014	0.07	0.07	0.08	0.09	0.09	0.10	0.09	0.09	0.09	0.09	0.09	0.12	0.09

Source: Bureau of Economic Analysis, U.S. Department of Commerce (BEA)

U.S. Municipal Bond Yield[1]   In Percent

Year	Jan.	Feb.	Mar.	Apr.	May	June	July	Aug.	Sept.	Oct.	Nov.	Dec.	Average
2005	4.41	4.35	4.57	4.46	4.31	4.23	4.31	4.32	4.29	4.48	4.57	4.46	4.40
2006	4.37	4.41	4.44	4.58	4.59	4.60	4.61	4.39	4.27	4.30	4.14	4.11	4.40
2007	4.23	4.22	4.15	4.26	4.31	4.60	4.56	4.64	4.51	4.39	4.46	4.42	4.40
2008	4.27	4.64	4.93	4.70	4.58	4.69	4.68	4.69	4.86	5.50	5.23	5.56	4.86
2009	5.07	4.90	4.99	4.78	4.56	4.81	4.72	4.60	4.24	4.20	4.37	4.21	4.62
2010	4.33	4.36	4.36	4.41	4.29	4.36	4.32	4.03	3.87	3.87	4.40	4.92	4.29
2011	5.28	5.15	4.92	4.99	4.59	4.51	4.52	4.02	4.01	4.13	4.05	3.95	4.51
2012	3.68	3.66	3.91	3.95	3.77	3.94	3.78	3.74	3.73	3.65	3.46	3.48	3.73
2013	3.60	3.72	3.96	3.92	3.72	4.27	4.56	4.82	4.79	4.56	4.60	4.73	4.27
2014	4.59	4.44	4.46	4.35	4.29	4.35	4.33	4.23	4.13	3.96	3.96	3.70	4.23

[1] 20-bond average.   *Source: Bureau of Economic Analysis, U.S. Department of Commerce (BEA)*

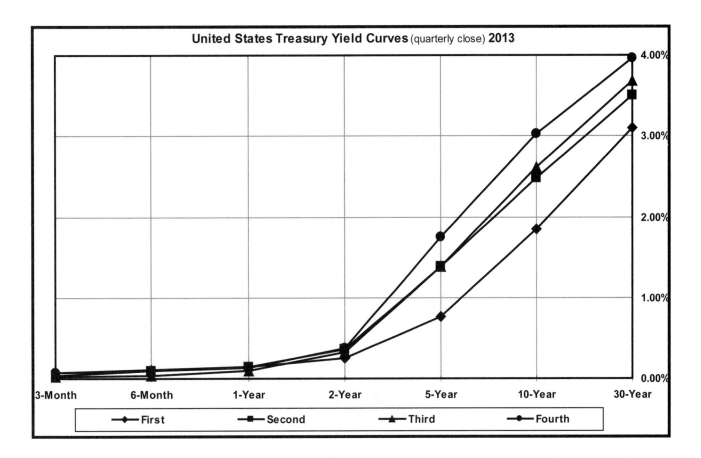

United States Treasury Yield Curves (quarterly close) **2013**

◆ First   ■ Second   ▲ Third   ● Fourth

U.S. Industrial Production Index[1]   1997 = 100

Year	Jan.	Feb.	Mar.	Apr.	May	June	July	Aug.	Sept.	Oct.	Nov.	Dec.	Average
2005	94.7	95.3	95.2	95.3	95.5	95.9	95.8	95.9	94.0	95.2	96.1	96.7	95.5
2006	96.8	96.8	97.1	97.4	97.3	97.7	97.8	98.0	97.8	97.7	97.6	98.6	97.6
2007	98.2	99.3	99.3	100.1	100.1	100.1	100.1	100.3	100.7	100.2	100.8	100.8	100.0
2008	100.5	100.3	100.0	99.2	98.8	98.6	98.1	96.5	92.5	93.2	92.2	89.6	96.6
2009	87.5	87.0	85.7	84.9	84.1	83.8	84.5	85.4	86.0	86.2	86.6	87.0	85.7
2010	88.0	88.2	88.9	89.2	90.6	90.8	91.4	91.7	91.9	91.6	91.8	92.6	90.6
2011	92.6	92.1	93.0	92.6	92.9	93.1	93.7	94.1	94.2	94.7	94.8	95.2	93.6
2012	96.0	96.4	96.0	96.8	97.1	97.2	97.7	97.1	97.4	97.3	98.3	98.4	97.1
2013	98.4	99.0	99.5	99.3	99.4	99.6	99.4	100.0	100.7	100.8	101.4	101.6	99.9
2014[1]	101.3	102.3	103.1	103.2	103.7	104.1	104.5	104.5	105.2	105.1	106.3	106.0	104.1

[1] Total Index of the Federal Reserve Index of Quantity Output, seasonally adjusted.   [2] Preliminary.   *Source: Bureau of Economic Analysis, U.S. Department of Commerce (BEA)*

U.S. Gross National Product, National Income, and Personal Income   In Billions of Constant Dollars[1]

	Gross Domestic Product					National Income					Personal Income				
Year	First Quarter	Second Quarter	Third Quarter	Fourth Quarter	Total	First Quarter	Second Quarter	Third Quarter	Fourth Quarter	Total	First Quarter	Second Quarter	Third Quarter	Fourth Quarter	Total
2005	12,816	12,976	13,207	13,383	13,095	10,983	11,120	11,325	11,536	11,241	10,355	10,515	10,694	10,877	10,610
2006	13,650	13,803	13,911	14,068	13,858	11,865	11,956	12,062	12,139	12,006	11,206	11,326	11,436	11,591	11,390
2007	14,235	14,425	14,572	14,690	14,480	12,227	12,324	12,329	12,410	12,322	11,816	11,944	12,043	12,180	11,996
2008	14,673	14,817	14,844	14,547	14,720	12,476	12,516	12,545	12,187	12,431	12,362	12,513	12,474	12,374	12,431
2009	14,381	14,342	14,384	14,564	14,418	12,007	11,996	12,122	12,374	12,125	12,039	12,099	12,057	12,134	12,082
2010	14,681	14,889	15,058	15,230	14,964	12,457	12,621	12,869	13,012	12,740	12,187	12,366	12,496	12,669	12,429
2011	15,238	15,461	15,587	15,785	15,518	13,091	13,256	13,455	13,607	13,352	13,025	13,142	13,295	13,346	13,202
2012	15,957	16,095	16,269	16,333	16,163	13,914	13,985	14,078	14,301	14,070	13,651	13,776	13,829	14,295	13,888
2013	16,502	16,619	16,872	17,078	16,768	14,376	14,512	14,651	14,770	14,577	13,977	14,131	14,247	14,312	14,167
2014[2]	17,044	17,328	17,600	17,701	17,418	14,734	14,973	15,245		14,984	14,485	14,661	14,811	14,960	14,729

[1] Seasonally adjusted at annual rates.   [2] Preliminary.   *Source: Bureau of Economic Analysis, U.S. Department of Commerce (BEA)*

U.S. Money Supply M1[2]   In Billions of Dollars

Year	Jan.	Feb.	Mar.	Apr.	May	June	July	Aug.	Sept.	Oct.	Nov.	Dec.	Average
2005	1,367.3	1,371.2	1,370.7	1,357.8	1,365.1	1,378.5	1,367.7	1,377.9	1,378.2	1,376.8	1,376.0	1,374.8	1,371.8
2006	1,380.0	1,378.7	1,383.1	1,380.8	1,386.3	1,372.7	1,370.5	1,372.8	1,364.0	1,370.9	1,370.7	1,367.5	1,374.8
2007	1,372.6	1,363.1	1,366.2	1,377.4	1,379.6	1,364.6	1,368.8	1,377.2	1,375.2	1,380.4	1,371.2	1,374.9	1,372.6
2008	1,378.4	1,380.2	1,388.5	1,390.6	1,392.1	1,400.2	1,418.4	1,408.5	1,462.1	1,475.2	1,514.0	1,603.7	1,434.3
2009	1,583.8	1,566.9	1,578.5	1,610.9	1,615.7	1,653.2	1,660.5	1,662.4	1,664.8	1,678.9	1,681.9	1,693.9	1,637.6
2010	1,674.8	1,699.2	1,711.8	1,698.5	1,708.8	1,726.0	1,724.4	1,751.1	1,765.9	1,780.8	1,826.1	1,835.8	1,741.9
2011	1,853.1	1,872.4	1,890.8	1,900.8	1,936.6	1,951.7	2,005.5	2,117.1	2,127.1	2,139.6	2,160.5	2,159.6	2,009.6
2012	2,202.3	2,212.2	2,228.7	2,245.3	2,251.0	2,262.3	2,314.6	2,346.5	2,383.6	2,415.5	2,423.2	2,457.7	2,311.9
2013	2,467.6	2,470.4	2,474.8	2,511.0	2,522.0	2,518.0	2,545.7	2,557.4	2,579.0	2,620.3	2,622.0	2,654.0	2,545.2
2014[1]	2,682.7	2,718.5	2,745.9	2,772.4	2,785.3	2,814.3	2,840.7	2,814.4	2,857.5	2,861.2	2,874.8	2,907.3	2,806.3

[1] Preliminary.   [2] *M1* -- The sum of currency held outside the vaults of depository institutions, Federal Reserve Banks, and the U.S. Treasury; travelers checks; and demand and other checkable deposits issued by financial institutions (except demand deposits due to the Treasury and depository institutions), minus cash items in process of collection and Federal Reserve float. Seasonally adjusted.   *Source: Board of Governors of the Federal Reserve System*

U.S. Money Supply M2[2]   In Billions of Dollars

Year	Jan.	Feb.	Mar.	Apr.	May	June	July	Aug.	Sept.	Oct.	Nov.	Dec.	Average
2005	6,395.1	6,403.3	6,413.0	6,426.1	6,443.5	6,476.2	6,508.0	6,540.8	6,574.7	6,608.8	6,625.7	6,652.4	6,505.6
2006	6,695.0	6,719.6	6,734.7	6,771.2	6,778.3	6,815.8	6,857.2	6,887.5	6,914.1	6,962.9	6,998.4	7,041.8	6,848.0
2007	7,079.9	7,096.2	7,131.0	7,203.0	7,218.1	7,250.7	7,280.6	7,357.2	7,375.3	7,387.8	7,414.0	7,445.5	7,269.9
2008	7,480.0	7,565.8	7,633.5	7,676.8	7,688.9	7,705.4	7,750.2	7,764.0	7,832.3	7,938.6	7,990.2	8,168.5	7,766.2
2009	8,250.9	8,281.9	8,349.7	8,353.5	8,411.1	8,418.5	8,421.0	8,419.3	8,414.5	8,440.7	8,474.5	8,472.5	8,392.3
2010	8,437.1	8,488.3	8,487.3	8,519.5	8,572.0	8,586.4	8,592.9	8,640.5	8,664.3	8,712.8	8,738.9	8,774.1	8,601.2
2011	8,815.8	8,867.0	8,911.9	8,976.0	9,025.6	9,103.9	9,289.0	9,496.4	9,511.1	9,541.0	9,586.6	9,628.0	9,229.4
2012	9,714.8	9,758.1	9,801.4	9,849.0	9,883.1	9,951.0	10,029.9	10,098.3	10,180.6	10,239.1	10,299.1	10,423.6	10,019.0
2013	10,451.9	10,448.6	10,518.9	10,552.5	10,586.4	10,639.1	10,700.7	10,754.6	10,809.5	10,920.5	10,929.8	10,984.9	10,691.5
2014[1]	11,037.5	11,118.9	11,162.6	11,218.8	11,283.8	11,331.8	11,405.0	11,440.5	11,481.0	11,520.7	11,562.3	11,625.2	11,349.0

[1] Preliminary.   [2] *M2* -- M1 plus savings deposits (including money market deposit accounts) and small-denomination (less than $100,000) time deposits issued by financial institutions; and shares in retail money market mutual funds (funds with initial investments of less than $50,000), net of retirement accounts. Seasonally adjusted.   *Source: Board of Governors of the Federal Reserve System*

U.S. Money Supply MZM[2]   In Billions of Dollars

Year	Jan.	Feb.	Mar.	Apr.	May	June	July	Aug.	Sept.	Oct.	Nov.	Dec.	Average
2005	6,655.7	6,644.0	6,635.5	6,641.5	6,638.6	6,668.9	6,702.1	6,727.0	6,764.3	6,798.4	6,805.2	6,835.7	6,709.7
2006	6,874.5	6,883.1	6,888.8	6,919.6	6,923.4	6,963.0	7,000.0	7,026.2	7,053.6	7,108.9	7,152.0	7,227.3	7,001.7
2007	7,245.9	7,265.6	7,323.5	7,416.9	7,465.0	7,528.5	7,599.8	7,750.7	7,868.7	7,968.1	8,060.0	8,130.9	7,635.3
2008	8,179.6	8,395.3	8,556.7	8,643.0	8,684.4	8,734.0	8,782.1	8,790.0	8,793.2	8,829.6	8,946.9	9,170.1	8,708.7
2009	9,325.3	9,399.0	9,500.4	9,532.3	9,621.4	9,635.0	9,643.4	9,614.8	9,590.7	9,575.9	9,576.6	9,539.5	9,546.2
2010	9,490.9	9,502.6	9,448.9	9,415.6	9,439.7	9,447.9	9,476.3	9,551.4	9,599.9	9,661.5	9,707.5	9,736.3	9,539.9
2011	9,745.8	9,790.1	9,873.0	9,978.1	10,062.0	10,132.3	10,296.2	10,428.1	10,474.1	10,515.0	10,564.2	10,620.4	10,206.6
2012	10,705.7	10,750.6	10,816.3	10,864.3	10,910.6	10,981.0	11,071.8	11,164.5	11,257.6	11,318.5	11,382.9	11,527.5	11,062.6
2013	11,584.5	11,590.6	11,655.4	11,699.3	11,740.9	11,812.2	11,891.1	11,954.6	12,037.9	12,144.6	12,160.3	12,201.9	11,872.8
2014[1]	12,254.8	12,336.5	12,385.3	12,417.2	12,492.0	12,539.7	12,622.5	12,658.8	12,708.8	12,774.4	12,831.4	12,914.2	12,578.0

[1] Preliminary.   [2] *MZM* (money, zero maturity): M2 minus small-denomination time deposits, plus institutional money market mutual funds (that is, those included in M3 but excluded from M2). The label MZM was coined by William Poole (1991); the aggregate itself was proposed earlier by Motley (1988). Seasonally adjusted.   *Source: Board of Governors of the Federal Reserve System*

U.S. Money Supply M3[2]   In Billions of Dollars

Year	Jan.	Feb.	Mar.	Apr.	May	June	July	Aug.	Sept.	Oct.	Nov.	Dec.	Average
1997	5,013.2	5,041.7	5,080.2	5,119.8	5,147.1	5,177.4	5,235.8	5,291.4	5,332.3	5,376.3	5,417.1	5,460.5	5,224.4
1998	5,508.8	5,541.3	5,611.5	5,647.3	5,686.9	5,728.4	5,750.0	5,815.0	5,882.0	5,953.7	6,010.1	6,051.9	5,765.6
1999	6,080.7	6,129.5	6,133.6	6,172.3	6,201.0	6,237.7	6,269.0	6,299.1	6,323.0	6,378.4	6,464.1	6,551.8	6,270.0
2000	6,605.5	6,642.2	6,704.0	6,767.3	6,776.9	6,823.6	6,875.2	6,945.0	7,003.5	7,027.0	7,038.3	7,117.6	6,860.5
2001	7,237.2	7,308.5	7,372.0	7,507.8	7,564.1	7,644.7	7,691.9	7,696.3	7,853.2	7,897.8	7,973.0	8,035.4	7,648.5
2002	8,063.9	8,109.3	8,117.3	8,142.6	8,175.1	8,190.8	8,244.2	8,298.1	8,331.5	8,368.9	8,498.8	8,568.0	8,259.0
2003	8,588.1	8,628.7	8,648.8	8,686.0	8,741.9	8,791.6	8,888.7	8,918.2	8,906.5	8,896.8	8,880.3	8,872.3	8,787.3
2004	8,930.2	9,000.3	9,080.7	9,149.6	9,243.8	9,275.7	9,282.7	9,314.4	9,351.8	9,359.4	9,395.1	9,433.0	9,234.7
2005	9,487.2	9,531.6	9,565.3	9,620.9	9,665.0	9,725.3	9,762.4	9,864.6	9,950.8	10,032.0	10,078.5	10,154.0	9,786.5
2006[1]	10,242.8	10,298.7	Discontinued										10,270.8

[1] Preliminary.   [2] *M3* -- M2 plus large-denomination ($100,000 or more) time deposits; repurchase agreements issued by depository institutions; Eurodollar deposits, specifically, dollar-denominated deposits due to nonbank U.S. addresses held at foreign offices of U.S. banks worldwide and all banking offices in Canada and the United Kingdom; and institutional money market mutual funds (funds with initial investments of $50,000 or more). Seasonally adjusted.   *Source: Board of Governors of the Federal Reserve System*

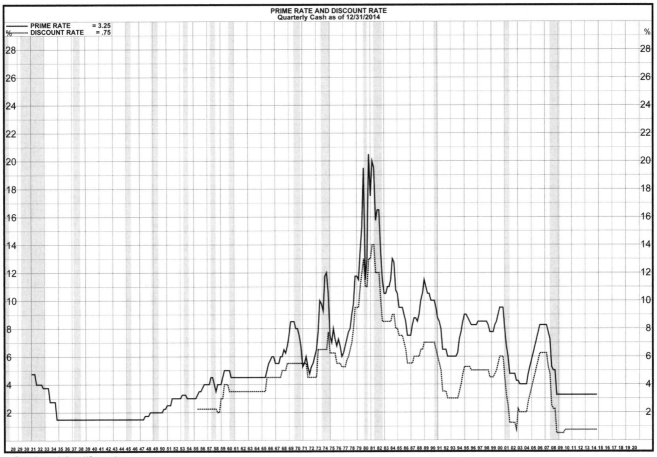

PRIME RATE AND DISCOUNT RATE
Quarterly Cash as of 12/31/2014

PRIME RATE = 3.25
DISCOUNT RATE = .75

Shaded areas indicate US recessions.

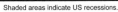

MUNICIPAL BONDS AND CORPORATE AAA BOND YIELDS
Quarterly Cash as of 12/25/2014

MUNICIPAL BOND YIELD = 3.65
CORPORATE AAA BOND YIELD = 3.72

Shaded areas indicate US recessions.

149

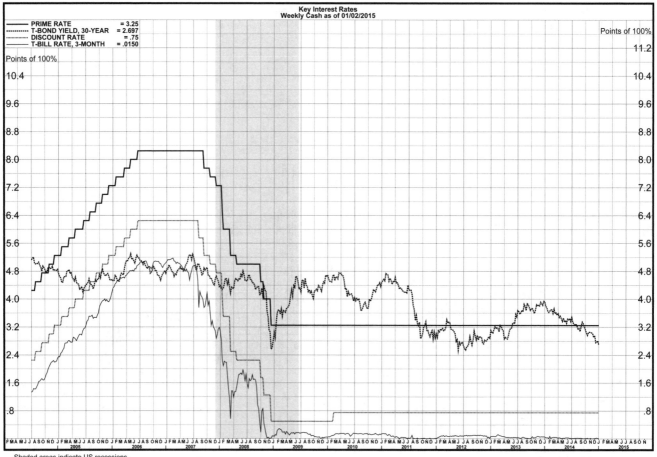

Points of 100%

Shaded areas indicate US recessions.

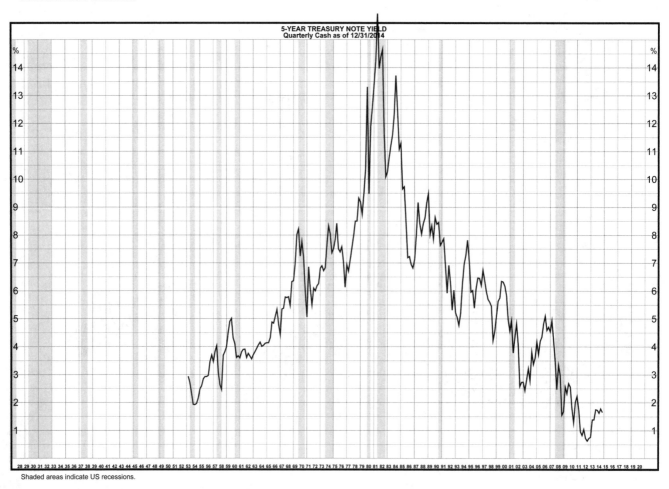

Shaded areas indicate US recessions.

Interest Rates - Worldwide

Interest rate futures contracts are widely traded throughout the world. The most popular futures contracts are generally the 10-year government bond and the 3-month interest rate contracts. In Europe, futures on German interest rates are traded at the Eurex Exchange. Futures on UK interest rates are traded at the Liffe Exchange in London. Futures on Canadian interest rates are traded at the Montreal Exchange. Futures on Japanese interest rates are traded at the Singapore Exchange (SGX) and at the Tokyo Stock Exchange. A variety of other interest rate futures contracts are traded throughout the rest of the world (please see the front of this Yearbook for a complete list).

Euro-Zone – Interest rates in the Eurozone dropped very sharply in 2014 as the Eurozone sovereign debt crisis receded, allowing not only German and French yields to drop but also the yields of fiscally-troubled Eurozone countries such as Spain, Italy, and Portugal. The German 10-year bund yield fell from 1.93% at the beginning of 2014 to a record low of 0.30% by early 2015. The French 10-year bond yield fell to 0.54% by early 2015.

By early 2015, the 10-year bond yields fell to 1.50% for Spain and 1.57% for Italy. By early 2015, 10-year bond yields also fell to 2.21% for Portugal and 1.09% for Ireland, which were near or below the U.S. 10-year T-note yield of 2.11% at the time. That illustrated that investors were much less worried about the Eurozone debt crisis since they were willing to take a lower yield on an Irish bond then they would for a U.S. bond.

Greek voters in early 2015 voted the anti-austerity Syriza party into power. Even though the Syriza party initially demanded a write-down of its debt load and the end of its bailout conditions, the markets did not panic and virtually no contagion risk spread to other Eurozone countries. Eurozone officials and Greece in February 2015 agreed on a 4-month extension of its bailout program to the end of June 2015 to give time to negotiate a new long-term bailout package.

The ECB in 2014 cut its refinancing rate twice, once in June 2014 by 10 bp to 0.15% and again in September by another 10 bp to 0.05%. The ECB also took the rather drastic step of cutting its deposit rate to the negative level of -0.20% in September. The ECB in January 2015 also announced a large quantitative easing (QE) program involving the purchase of 60 billion euros per month of sovereign bonds. The ECB said it intends for the program to last from March 2015 through September 2016 and for the program to total at least 1.1 trillion euros. The ECB's rate cuts and QE program were instrumental in driving down Eurozone bond yields.

Eurex Euro Bunds rallied fairly steadily in 2014, posting a new record high and closing the year up +16.70 points at 155.87. Bullish factors for bund prices in 2014 included (1) the threat of deflation with the CPI dropping into negative territory by early 2015, (2) the weak Eurozone GDP growth rate during 2014 of +0.8%, and (3) the ECB's QE program and its cut in the refinancing rate to 0.05%. The German 10-year bund yield during 2014 fell sharply to

close the year at 0.54%, down 139 basis points from 1.93% at the end of 2013. The 10-year bund yield in early 2015 then continued to fall and hit a new record low of 0.30% on January 30, 2015.

UK – The Liffe 10-year Gilt futures contract during 2014 rallied from a 6-1/2 year low of 106.00 in January 2014 to close the year up +12.97 points at 119.53. The 10-year gilt yield fell sharply by 126 basis points during 2014 from 3.02% at the beginning of the year to 1.76% at the end of 2014. The sharp drop in the UK gilt yield was driven by the same forces that drove U.S. and Eurozone bond yields sharply lower, i.e., weak global economic growth, expansionary monetary policy, and a sharp drop in inflation expectations tied in part to the plunge in crude oil prices. The Bank of England left its monetary policy unchanged during 2014. The BOE left the base rate at 0.50% where it has been since early 2009. The BOE did not engage in bond purchases during 2014 and left its asset purchase target at 375 billion pounds all year. UK GDP growth in 2014 improved to +2.7% from +1.7% in 2013 as the UK economy gained traction, posting the best growth rate since 2006. The UK core CPI fell during 2014 and the relatively low level of +1.3% seen in December 2014 meant that the BOE was not under pressure to raise interest rates in response to stronger UK GDP growth.

Canada – The Montreal Exchange's Canadian 10-year government note futures contract started out 2014 at a 3-1/2 year low but then rallied sharply during the year to close +11.78 points higher at 138.52. The Canadian 10-year government bond yield moved sharply lower to close the year down -97 basis points at 1.79%. The Canadian 10-year government bond yield fell during 2014 along with other G-7 bond in response to weak global economic growth and falling inflation. The Bank of Canada (BOC) during 2014 left its policy interest rate unchanged at 1.00%, the same level that prevailed since September 2010. However, the Bank of Canada finally cut its policy rate by 25 bp to 0.75% in January 2015 in response to lower inflation and the hit that Canada's economy took from the late 2014 plunge in oil prices. Canada's GDP weakened to 2.2% in Q4-2014 from the strong average growth rate of +3.3% seen in Q2-Q3 2014, thus drawing the easing move from the Bank of Canada.

Japan – SGX 10-year JGB futures rallied steadily during 2014, closing the year up +4.57 points at 147.84. JGB futures rallied further in early 2015 to post a new record high of 148.67. Japan's 10-year government bond (JGB) yield fell steadily during 2014 by 42 basis points from 0.75% at the beginning of the year to close the year at 0.33%. The 10-year JGB yield then fell further in early 2015 to a new record low of 0.20%. Factors leading to the sharp decline in yields included (1) the shaky Japanese economy which experienced a recession in the middle of 2014 in response to the April 2014 hike in the sales tax to 8% from 5%, (2) the Bank of Japan's aggressive bond buying program that soaked up JGBs, and (3) the sharp decline in inflation expectations tied to the plunge in crude oil prices. Japan's GDP fell to unchanged in 2014 from +1.6% in 2013 and is expected to recover to only +1.0% in 2015.

GILT, LONG - ICE-LIFF
Weekly Nearest Futures as of 01/02/2015

WEEKLY NEAREST FUTURES
As of 01/02/2015

Chart High 133.63 on 12/28/2011
Chart Low 102.90 on 07/06/2007

% Yield Basis
6% 10-Yr

Points of 100%

Nearby Futures through Last Trading Day.

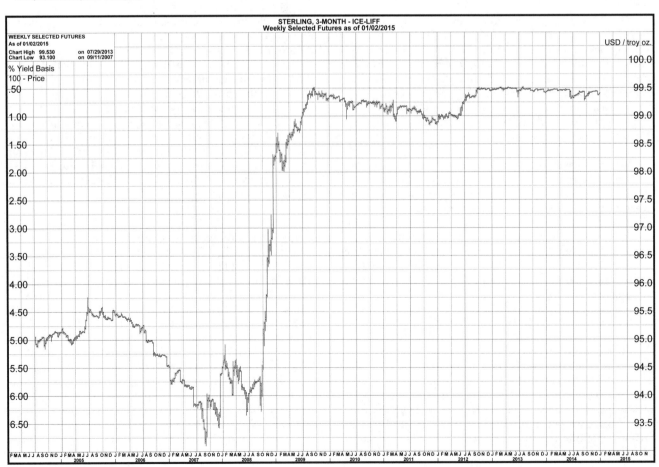

STERLING, 3-MONTH - ICE-LIFF
Weekly Selected Futures as of 01/02/2015

WEEKLY SELECTED FUTURES
As of 01/02/2015

Chart High 99.530 on 07/29/2013
Chart Low 93.100 on 09/11/2007

% Yield Basis
100 - Price

USD / troy oz.

Nearby Futures through Last Trading Day.

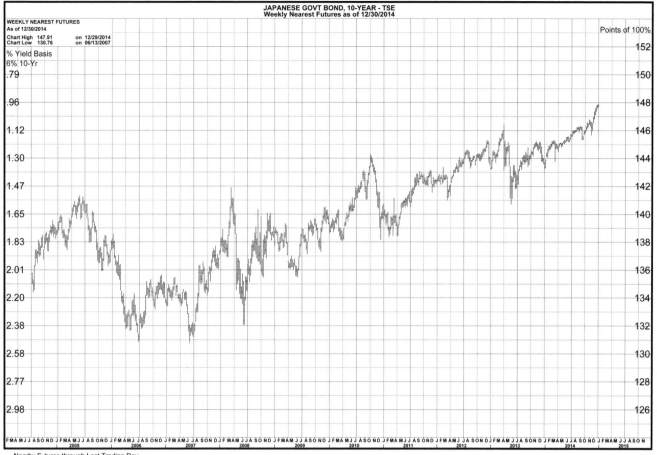

JAPANESE GOVT BOND, 10-YEAR - TSE
Weekly Nearest Futures as of 12/30/2014

WEEKLY NEAREST FUTURES
As of 12/30/2014

| Chart High | 147.91 | on 12/29/2014 |
| Chart Low | 130.76 | on 06/13/2007 |

Points of 100%

% Yield Basis
6% 10-Yr

Nearby Futures through Last Trading Day.

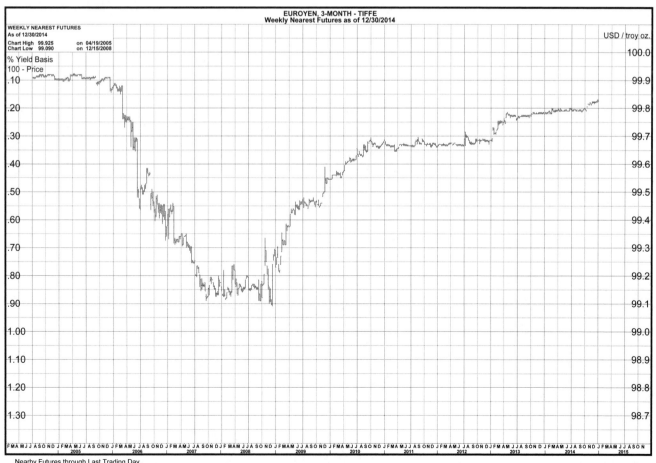

EUROYEN, 3-MONTH - TIFFE
Weekly Nearest Futures as of 12/30/2014

WEEKLY NEAREST FUTURES
As of 12/30/2014

| Chart High | 99.925 | on 04/19/2005 |
| Chart Low | 99.090 | on 12/15/2008 |

USD / troy oz.

% Yield Basis
100 - Price

Nearby Futures through Last Trading Day.

153

INTEREST RATES - WORLDWIDE

CANADIAN GOVT BOND, 10-YR - ME
Weekly Nearest Futures as of 01/02/2015

WEEKLY NEAREST FUTURES
As of 01/02/2015

Chart High 140.440 on 07/23/2012
Chart Low 108.830 on 06/12/2007

% Yield Basis
6% 10-Yr

Points of 100%

Nearby Futures through Last Trading Day.

CAN. BANKERS' ACCEPTANCE, 3-MO - ME
Weekly Selected Futures as of 01/02/2015

WEEKLY SELECTED FUTURES
As of 01/02/2015

Chart High 99.640 on 05/21/2009
Chart Low 94.895 on 09/12/2007

% Yield Basis
100 - Price

USD / troy oz.

Nearby Futures through Last Trading Day.

Australia -- Economic Statistics   Percentage Change from Previous Period

Year	Real GDP	Nominal GDP	Real Private Consump-tion	Real Public Consump-tion	Grossed Fixed Invest-ment	Real Total Domestic Demand	Real Exports of Goods & Services	Real Imports of Goods & Services	Consumer Prices[3]	Unem-ployment Rate
2007	4.7	9.0	5.5	3.2	9.5	7.0	3.3	13.0	2.4	4.4
2008	2.5	9.2	2.0	4.7	8.0	3.7	3.6	11.2	4.4	4.2
2009	1.6	1.5	.7	1.6	-2.1	-.6	2.3	-8.9	1.8	5.6
2010	2.3	8.4	3.0	3.6	4.2	4.0	5.3	14.4	2.9	5.2
2011	2.6	6.5	3.3	2.5	7.1	4.6	-.8	10.6	3.4	5.1
2012	3.6	3.0	3.2	3.2	8.9	4.7	6.3	6.3	1.7	5.2
2013	2.4	3.4	2.2	1.0	-1.1	.6	6.5	-1.2	2.1	5.7
2014[1]	3.1	4.1	3.2	.6	.6	2.1	6.7	4.3	2.1	6.1
2015[2]	2.5	5.5	3.7	.7	1.1	2.5	7.5	4.5	1.9	6.3

[1] Estimate.   [2] Projection.   [3] National accounts implicit private consumption deflator.   *Source: Organization for Economic Co-operation and Development (OECD)*

Canada -- Economic Statistics   Percentage Change from Previous Period

Year	Real GDP	Nominal GDP	Real Private Consump-tion	Real Public Consump-tion	Grossed Fixed Invest-ment	Real Total Domestic Demand	Real Exports of Goods & Services	Real Imports of Goods & Services	Consumer Prices[3]	Unem-ployment Rate
2007	2.0	5.3	4.3	2.8	3.2	3.6	1.1	5.8	2.1	6.0
2008	1.2	5.1	2.9	4.6	1.6	2.9	-4.5	.8	2.4	6.1
2009	-2.7	-4.8	.4	3.3	-11.5	-2.8	-13.1	-12.4	.3	8.3
2010	3.4	6.1	3.4	2.7	11.5	5.4	6.9	13.6	1.8	8.0
2011	3.0	5.8	2.3	.8	4.2	2.3	4.7	5.7	2.9	7.5
2012	1.9	3.4	1.9	1.1	4.3	2.2	1.5	3.1	1.5	7.3
2013	2.0	2.8	2.3	1.3	.7	1.6	1.9	1.6	1.0	7.1
2014[1]	2.4	3.7	2.3	1.1	3.0	2.2	4.6	4.1	1.6	7.0
2015[2]	2.6	4.4	2.7	1.0	2.2	2.2	5.7	4.4	2.0	6.9

[1] Estimate.   [2] Projection.   [3] National accounts implicit private consumption deflator.   *Source: Organization for Economic Co-operation and Development (OECD)*

France -- Economic Statistics   Percentage Change from Previous Period

Year	Real GDP	Nominal GDP	Real Private Consump-tion	Real Public Consump-tion	Grossed Fixed Invest-ment	Real Total Domestic Demand	Real Exports of Goods & Services	Real Imports of Goods & Services	Consumer Prices[3]	Unem-ployment Rate
2007	2.3	4.9	2.3	1.5	6.4	3.1	2.3	5.5	1.6	8.0
2008	.1	2.3	.2	1.2	.1	.1	-.6	.6	3.2	7.4
2009	-2.9	-2.4	.4	2.6	-10.4	-2.6	-11.9	-9.5	.1	9.2
2010	1.9	2.6	1.5	1.8	1.2	1.7	9.0	8.6	1.7	9.3
2011	2.1	3.3	.5	.5	3.0	2.0	5.6	5.3	2.3	9.2
2012	.4	1.6	-.3	1.4	-1.2	-.9	2.5	-.9	2.2	9.8
2013	.4	1.6	.5	1.6	-2.4	.4	.3	1.1	1.0	10.6
2014[1]	.4	1.8	.9	.9	.6	1.1	3.1	3.3	1.2	10.8
2015[2]	.8	2.6	1.4	.5	2.8	1.4	5.3	4.4	1.2	10.7

[1] Estimate.   [2] Projection.   [3] National accounts implicit private consumption deflator.   *Source: Organization for Economic Co-operation and Development (OECD)*

Germany -- Economic Statistics   Percentage Change from Previous Period

Year	Real GDP	Nominal GDP	Real Private Consump-tion	Real Public Consump-tion	Grossed Fixed Invest-ment	Real Total Domestic Demand	Real Exports of Goods & Services	Real Imports of Goods & Services	Consumer Prices[3]	Unem-ployment Rate
2007	3.4	5.1	-.2	1.4	5.0	1.9	8.3	5.6	2.3	8.7
2008	.8	1.6	.7	3.2	.6	1.0	2.3	3.0	2.8	7.5
2009	-5.6	-4.0	.3	3.0	-11.6	-2.2	-13.0	-7.8	.2	7.8
2010	3.9	4.9	1.0	1.3	5.2	2.3	14.8	12.3	1.2	7.1
2011	3.7	4.7	2.3	1.0	7.1	2.8	8.1	7.5	2.5	6.0
2012	.6	2.4	.7	1.0	-1.3	-.2	3.8	1.8	2.1	5.5
2013	.2	2.7	1.1	1.0	-1.0	.8	.6	1.3	1.7	5.4
2014[1]	1.5	3.0	1.8	1.7	4.3	2.2	3.6	5.0	1.8	5.4
2015[2]	1.1	3.6	1.9	1.8	4.7	2.4	4.6	5.8	2.0	5.2

[1] Estimate.   [2] Projection.   [3] National accounts implicit private consumption deflator.   *Source: Organization for Economic Co-operation and Development (OECD)*

Italy -- Economic Statistics   Percentage Change from Previous Period

Year	Real GDP	Nominal GDP	Real Private Consumption	Real Public Consumption	Grossed Fixed Investment	Real Total Domestic Demand	Real Exports of Goods & Services	Real Imports of Goods & Services	Consumer Prices[3]	Unemployment Rate
2007	1.5	4.0	1.1	1.0	1.3	1.3	5.6	4.6	2.0	6.1
2008	-1.0	1.3	-.8	.6	-3.8	-1.2	-2.8	-2.9	3.5	6.8
2009	-5.5	-3.6	-1.6	.8	-11.8	-4.5	-17.7	-13.6	.8	7.8
2010	1.7	2.1	1.5	-.4	.5	2.0	11.2	12.3	1.6	8.4
2011	.6	2.0	-.3	-1.2	-1.6	-.8	6.9	1.4	2.9	8.4
2012	-2.3	-.9	-4.1	-2.7	-8.4	-5.3	1.9	-7.5	3.3	10.7
2013	-1.9	-.5	-2.4	-.2	-5.9	-3.0	.0	-3.9	1.4	12.1
2014[1]	-.4	1.7	.0	.1	.1	.0	3.6	1.8	1.3	12.4
2015[2]	.2	2.2	.8	-.1	3.7	1.1	4.9	4.2	1.0	12.1

[1] Estimate.   [2] Projection.   [3] National accounts implicit private consumption deflator.   *Source: Organization for Economic Co-operation and Development (OECD)*

Japan -- Economic Statistics   Percentage Change from Previous Period

Year	Real GDP	Nominal GDP	Real Private Consumption	Real Public Consumption	Grossed Fixed Investment	Real Total Domestic Demand	Real Exports of Goods & Services	Real Imports of Goods & Services	Consumer Prices[3]	Unemployment Rate
2007	2.2	1.2	.9	1.1	.3	1.1	8.7	2.3	.1	3.8
2008	-1.0	-2.3	-.9	-.1	-4.1	-1.3	1.4	.3	1.4	4.0
2009	-5.5	-6.0	-.7	2.3	-10.6	-4.0	-24.2	-15.7	-1.3	5.0
2010	4.7	2.4	2.8	1.9	-.2	2.9	24.4	11.1	-.7	5.0
2011	-.5	-2.5	.4	1.4	1.1	.3	-.4	5.9	-.3	4.6
2012	1.5	1.1	2.3	2.4	4.4	2.8	-.1	5.5	.0	4.3
2013	1.5	1.3	1.8	1.4	3.5	1.9	1.9	2.4	.2	4.0
2014[1]	.4	2.7	1.0	.2	1.4	.9	7.8	4.1	2.3	3.9
2015[2]	.8	2.3	1.3	-.9	.2	.7	7.2	4.9	1.8	3.8

[1] Estimate.   [2] Projection.   [3] National accounts implicit private consumption deflator.   *Source: Organization for Economic Co-operation and Development (OECD)*

Switzerland -- Economic Statistics   Percentage Change from Previous Period

Year	Real GDP	Nominal GDP	Real Private Consumption	Real Public Consumption	Grossed Fixed Investment	Real Total Domestic Demand	Real Exports of Goods & Services	Real Imports of Goods & Services	Consumer Prices[3]	Unemployment Rate
2007	4.1	6.4	2.2	.9	5.4	1.6	9.9	6.2	.7	3.6
2008	2.3	5.0	1.2	-2.5	.7	.5	2.9	-.3	2.4	3.3
2009	-2.1	-2.4	1.8	3.3	-8.0	.0	-7.7	-5.2	-.5	4.3
2010	3.0	3.3	1.7	.2	4.8	2.7	7.7	8.4	.7	4.4
2011	1.8	2.2	1.1	1.2	4.5	1.7	3.8	4.2	.2	3.9
2012	1.1	1.2	2.4	3.2	-.4	1.2	2.5	3.1	-.7	4.1
2013	1.9	1.9	2.6	1.7	.9	1.3	2.3	1.1	-.4	4.4
2014[1]	1.5	2.8	2.4	1.0	2.6	2.3	3.5	4.1	.2	4.4
2015[2]	1.5	3.5	2.7	1.1	2.8	2.5	5.0	5.1	.6	4.1

[1] Estimate.   [2] Projection.   [3] National accounts implicit private consumption deflator.   *Source: Organization for Economic Co-operation and Development (OECD)*

United Kingdom -- Economic Statistics   Percentage Change from Previous Period

Year	Real GDP	Nominal GDP	Real Private Consumption	Real Public Consumption	Grossed Fixed Investment	Real Total Domestic Demand	Real Exports of Goods & Services	Real Imports of Goods & Services	Consumer Prices[3]	Unemployment Rate
2007	2.6	5.8	2.7	.7	7.5	3.4	-2.1	-1.5	2.3	5.4
2008	-.3	2.4	-1.0	2.1	-6.9	-1.5	1.1	-1.7	3.6	5.7
2009	-4.3	-3.1	-3.6	.7	-16.7	-5.9	-8.7	-10.7	2.2	7.6
2010	1.9	4.8	1.0	.5	2.8	2.1	6.7	7.9	3.3	7.9
2011	1.6	3.5	-.4	.0	-2.4	-.2	4.5	.3	4.5	8.1
2012	.7	1.8	1.2	1.7	.9	.9	1.0	3.1	2.8	7.9
2013	1.7	3.5	1.7	.4	-2.5	1.1	2.6	1.9	2.6	7.8
2014[1]	3.0	4.0	1.8	-.7	6.4	2.1	4.4	3.5	2.4	7.5
2015[2]	2.7	4.4	2.0	-.3	7.0	2.2	4.3	3.5	2.3	7.2

[1] Estimate.   [2] Projection.   [3] National accounts implicit private consumption deflator.   *Source: Organization for Economic Co-operation and Development (OECD)*

Iron and Steel

Iron (atomic symbol Fe) is a soft, malleable, and ductile metallic element. Next to aluminum, iron is the most abundant of all metals. Pure iron melts at about 1535 degrees Celsius and boils at 2750 degrees Celsius. Archaeologists in Egypt discovered the earliest iron implements dating back to about 3000 BC, and iron ornaments were used even earlier.

Steel is an alloy of iron and carbon, often with an admixture of other elements. The physical properties of various types of steel and steel alloys depend primarily on the amount of carbon present and how it is distributed in the iron. Steel is marketed in a variety of sizes and shapes, such as rods, pipes, railroad rails, tees, channels, and I-beams. Steel mills roll and form heated ingots into the required shapes. The working of steel improves the quality of the steel by refining its crystalline structure and making the metal tougher. There are five classifications of steel: carbon steels, alloy steels, high-strength low-alloy steels, stainless steel, and tool steels.

Iron Ore futures are traded at the CME Group and the Multi Commodity Exchange of India (MCX).

Prices –In 2014 the average wholesale price for No. 1 heavy-melting steel scrap in Chicago rose +2.5% to $365.71 per metric ton. In January 2014, the price hit $414.29 per metric ton but then moved lower the rest of the year.

Supply – World production of iron ore in 2014 rose by +3.5% to 3.220 billion metric tons, which was a new record high. The world's largest producers of iron ore are China with 46.6% of world production, Australia with 20.5%, and Brazil with 9.9%. The U.S. accounted for only 1.8% of world iron ore production in 2014. World production of raw steel (ingots and castings) in 2014 rose +1.9 % yr/yr to 1,650 million metric tons, with the largest producers being China with 49.7% of world production, Japan with 6.7%, and Russia with 4.3%.

U.S. production of steel ingots in 2014 rose by +1.4% to 77.800 million short tons, up from the 2009 record low of 59.400 million short tons. U.S. production of pig iron (excluding ferro-alloys) in 2014 (annualized through October) fell -5.3% to 32.436 million short tons.

Demand – U.S. consumption of ferrous scrap and pig iron rose +2.4% yr/yr in 2012 (latest data) to 104.080 million metric tons, above the record low of 84.660 million metric tons seen in 2009. The largest consumers of ferrous scrap and pig iron were the manufacturers of pig iron and steel ingots and castings with 91.1% of consumption at 94.780 million metric tons in 2012. Iron foundries and miscellaneous users accounted for 8.4% of consumption and manufacturers of steel castings (scrap) accounted for 0.6% of consumption.

Trade – The U.S. imported 5.140 million metric tons of iron ore in 2012, down -2.5% yr/yr from 5.270 million metric tons in 2011. The bulk of U.S. iron ore imports came from Canada (74.1% with 3.810 million metric tons), Brazil (14.4% with 739,000 metric tons), and Venezuela (1.5% with 75,000 metric tons).

World Production of Raw Steel (Ingots and Castings)   In Thousands of Metric Tons

Year	Brazil	Canada	China	France	Germany	Italy	Japan	Rep. of Korea	Russia	Ukraine	United Kindom	United States	World Total
2005	31,631	15,327	353,240	19,481	44,524	29,061	112,471	47,820	66,186	38,636	13,210	94,900	1,140,000
2006	30,901	15,493	419,150	19,857	47,224	31,550	116,266	48,455	70,816	40,899	13,931	98,200	1,250,000
2007	33,782	15,572	489,290	19,252	48,550	31,990	120,203	51,517	72,389	42,830	14,300	98,100	1,350,000
2008	33,726	14,845	500,490	17,874	45,833	30,477	118,739	53,322	68,700	37,279	13,538	91,900	1,330,000
2009	26,506	9,245	572,180	12,836	32,671	19,737	87,534	48,752	59,800	29,855	10,079	59,400	1,230,000
2010	33,033	13,003	637,230	15,416	43,830	25,751	109,599	58,914	66,800	33,559	9,709	80,500	1,430,000
2011	35,200	12,891	685,280	15,800	44,284	28,700	107,601	68,519	68,100	35,332	9,478	86,400	1,520,000
2012	35,000	13,507	716,540	15,607	42,661	27,227	107,232	70,000	68,500	32,912	9,819	88,700	1,550,000
2013[1]	35,000		779,000	16,000	43,000		111,000	81,000	69,000	33,000	12,000		1,620,000
2014[2]	34,000		820,000	17,000	44,000		111,000	65,000	71,000	26,000	12,000		1,650,000

[1] Preliminary.   [2] Estimate.   *Source: U.S. Geological Survey (USGS)*

Average Wholesale Prices of Iron and Steel in the United States

	No. 1 Heavy Melting Steel Scrap		Sheet Bars			Pittsburg Prices					
	Pittsburg	Chicago	Hot Rolled	Hot Rolled	Cold Finished	Hot Rolled Strip	Carbon Steel Plates	Cold Rolled Strip	Galvan-ized Sheets	Rail Road Steel Scrap[2]	Used Steel Cans[3]
Year	----- $ Per Gross Ton -----		--- Cents Per Pound ---							---- $ Per Gross Ton ----	
2002	101.06	89.92	16.46	----	23.26	----	----	----	22.00	NA	66.71
2003	128.32	113.82	14.80	----	25.15	----	----	----	20.08	----	116.21
2004	221.05	220.13	30.84	----	38.67	----	----	----	36.69	----	192.80
2005	199.10	196.75	27.83	----	44.96	----	----	----	33.77	----	172.00
2006	222.39	225.21	29.78	----	44.02	----	----	----	38.09	----	212.63
2007	250.98	262.80	26.89	----	45.26	----	----	----	38.25	----	244.65
2008	365.62	357.88	44.56	----	61.67	----	----	----	54.91	----	314.63
2009	204.21	206.14	24.60	----	42.10	----	----	----	34.23	----	121.84
2010	339.54	334.48	31.65	----	50.82	----	----	----	41.72	----	296.91
2011[1]	408.64	417.00	38.02	----	63.63	----	----	----	48.45	----	391.50

[1] Preliminary.   [2] Specialties scrap.   [3] Consumer buying prices.   NA = Not available.   *Source: American Metal Market (AMM)*

IRON AND STEEL

Salient Statistics of Steel in the United States   In Thousands of Short Tons

Year	Pig Iron Production	Producer Price Index for Steel Mill Products (1982=100)	Raw Steel Production By Type of Furnace Basic Oxygen	Open Hearth	Electric[2]	Stainless	Carbon	Alloy	Total	Net Shipments Steel Mill Products	Total Steel Products Exports	Imports
2005	40,036	159.7	45,231	----	57,599	1,903	96,636	4,935	102,830	103,474	9,393	32,108
2006	37,900	174.1	39,298	----	50,346	2,712	98,656	6,823	108,246	99,300	8,830	41,100
2007	36,300	182.9	36,147	----	53,161	2,392	98,987	6,768	108,136	96,500	10,100	30,200
2008	33,700	220.6	41,336	----	58,532	2,127	92,703	6,404	101,301	89,400	12,200	29,000
2009	19,000	165.2	21,274	----	39,793	1,786	60,847	2,888	65,477	56,400	8,420	14,700
2010	26,800	191.7	30,975	----	54,343	2,425	81,129	5,159	88,735	75,700	11,000	21,700
2011	30,200	216.2	34,943	----	57,430	2,282	87,192	5,754	95,239	83,300	12,200	25,900
2012	30,100	208.0	36,817	----	57,761	2,183	90,278	5,258	97,774	87,000	12,500	30,400
2013	30,300	195.0								86,600	11,500	29,200
2014[1]	29,000	200.1								89,000	11,000	39,000

[1] Preliminary.   [2] Includes crucible steels.   *Sources: American Iron & Steel Institute (AISI); U.S. Geological Survey (USGS)*

Production of Steel Ingots, Rate of Capability Utilization[1] in the United States   In Percent

Year	Jan.	Feb.	Mar.	Apr.	May	June	July	Aug.	Sept.	Oct.	Nov.	Dec.	Average
2005	90.9	92.9	88.4	89.2	84.2	79.8	77.1	81.3	86.4	89.3	88.1	85.0	86.1
2006	85.6	89.5	92.8	91.4	92.5	92.1	88.7	88.7	91.2	86.2	81.5	75.0	87.9
2007	78.2	87.8	86.3	85.0	88.4	88.6	87.0	87.7	86.5	88.5	88.5	88.1	86.7
2008	90.3	91.6	89.7	90.3	91.1	90.3	88.8	90.4	84.5	70.5	50.7	40.9	80.8
2009	42.6	45.5	42.9	40.8	42.8	46.9	52.4	57.7	62.1	62.3	61.4	60.9	51.5
2010	64.2	71.1	73.2	74.0	74.8	75.4	69.6	68.1	70.2	67.3	68.3	68.4	70.4
2011	73.2	75.4	75.0	74.2	72.7	76.2	75.0	75.7	76.1	71.9	73.0	75.2	74.5
2012	77.6	80.7	79.6	80.9	79.2	74.8	73.3	76.3	70.4	68.0	70.1	71.7	75.2
2013	76.5	78.3	76.2	76.7	76.5	76.1	77.3	77.6	78.3	76.5	76.2	74.0	76.7
2014[2]	75.8	77.9	77.7	76.6	77.3	78.5	79.6	80.2	78.1	76.5	77.2		77.8

[1] Based on tonnage capability to produce raw steel for a full order book.   [2] Preliminary.   *Sources: American Iron and Steel Institute (AISI); U.S. Geological Survey (USGS)*

Production of Steel Ingots in the United States   In Thousands of Short Tons

Year	Jan.	Feb.	Mar.	Apr.	May	June	July	Aug.	Sept.	Oct.	Nov.	Dec.	Total
1997	8,735	8,266	9,175	8,882	9,048	8,662	8,692	8,818	9,006	9,128	9,116	9,071	107,488
1998	9,510	9,087	9,839	9,524	9,483	8,863	8,832	9,194	8,548	8,681	7,710	8,013	107,643
1999	8,422	7,837	8,854	8,643	8,914	8,413	8,619	8,993	8,650	9,574	9,357	9,604	105,882
2000	9,838	9,170	10,009	9,843	10,097	9,592	9,411	9,213	8,830	8,978	8,054	7,982	111,015
2001	8,475	8,122	8,932	8,685	8,832	8,550	8,459	8,525	8,263	8,125	7,226	6,695	98,889
2002	8,050	7,609	8,261	8,214	8,401	8,414	8,510	8,918	8,916	9,015	8,340	8,329	100,976
2003	8,617	8,175	8,817	8,692	8,047	8,534	8,163	8,096	8,026	8,514	8,347	8,414	100,442
2004	8,656	8,400	9,268	8,901	9,163	9,006	9,164	9,314	9,234	9,551	8,989	8,660	108,305
2005	9,123	8,419	9,028	8,757	8,543	7,837	7,896	8,330	8,562	9,032	8,629	8,599	102,754
2006[1]	8,918	8,506	9,770	9,382	9,811	9,458	9,324	9,320	9,282	8,922	8,169	7,760	108,621

[1] Preliminary.   *Source: American Iron and Steel Institute (AISI)*

Shipments of Steel Products[1] by Market Classifications in the United States   In Thousands of Short Tons

Year	Appliances Utensils & Cutlery	Automotive	Containers, Packaging & Shipping Materials	Construction Including Maint.	Contactors Products	Electrical Equipment	Export	Machinery, Industrial Equip. & Tools	Oil and Gas	Rail Transportation	Steel for Converting & Processing[2]	Steel Service Center & Distributors	All Other[3]	Total Shipments
1997	1,635	15,251	4,163	15,885	[5]	2,434	2,610	2,355	3,811	1,410	11,263	27,800	17,241	105,858
1998	1,729	15,842	3,829	15,289	[5]	2,255	2,556	2,147	2,649	1,657	9,975	27,751	16,741	102,420
1999	1,712	15,639	3,768	14,685	[5]	2,260	2,292	1,547	1,544	876	7,599	21,439	32,840	106,201
2000	1,530	14,697	3,684	14,763	[5]	2,039	2,752	1,513	2,268	994	7,753	22,537	35,093	109,624
2001	1,675	12,767	3,193	16,339	[5]	1,694	2,281	1,210	2,134	720	7,462	23,887	26,086	99,448
2002	1,734	12,562	3,251	15,729	[5]	1,336	1,844	1,137	1,658	751	7,201	22,828	29,160	99,191
2003	1,891	11,937	2,949	14,403	[5]	1,200	2,572	1,108	1,800	799	6,798	24,266	35,905	105,628
2004	1,919	12,527	2,978	15,114	[5]	1,139	2,426	1,332	2,043	957	7,295	25,385	38,969	112,085
2005	1,895	13,031	2,504	15,858	[5]	1,088	2,592	1,300	2,056	1,019	7,559	23,213	31,359	103,474
2006[4]	1,781	14,003	2,535	17,544	[5]	1,228	3,068	1,360	2,459	1,242	8,531	23,706	31,153	108,609

[1] All grades including carbon, alloy and stainless steel.   [2] Net total after deducting shipments to reporting companines for conversion or resale.
[3] Includes agricultural; bolts, nuts rivets & screws; forgings (other than automotive); shipbuilding & marine equipment; aircraft; mining, quarrying & lumbering; other domestic & commercial equipment machinery; ordnance & other direct military; and shipments of non-reporting companies.
[4] Preliminary.   [5] Included in Construction.   *Source: American Iron and Steel Institute (AISI)*

Net Shipments of Steel Products[2] in the United States   In Thousands of Short Tons

Year	Cold Finished Bars	Rails & Accessories	Wire Drawn	Tin Mill Products	Plates Cut & Coils	Sheet & Strip[3] Galv, Hot Dipped	Hot Rolled Bars	Pipe & Tubing	Structural Shapes & Steel Piling	Rein-forcing Bars	Hot Rolled Sheets	Cold Rolled Sheets	Carbon	Alloy	Stainless
1997	1,809	875	619	4,057	8,855	12,439	8,153	6,548	6,029	6,188	18,221	13,322	97,509	6,282	2,067
1998	1,780	938	725	3,714	8,864	13,481	8,189	5,409	5,595	5,909	15,715	13,185	94,536	5,847	2,037
1999	1,775	646	611	3,771	8,200	14,870	8,078	4,772	5,995	6,183	17,740	13,874	98,694	5,421	2,086
2000	1,756	783	579	3,742	8,898	14,917	7,901	5,385	7,402	6,893	19,236	14,802	102,141	5,379	2,104
2001	1,369	630	481	3,202	8,349	14,310	7,032	5,377	6,789	6,976	18,866	12,352	92,314	4,789	1,837
2002	1,404	789	733	3,419	8,769	14,944	6,581	4,809	6,729	6,359	19,243	12,673	92,518	4,779	1,894
2003	1,426	739	684	3,513	9,230	15,221	6,486	4,597	7,437	7,970	22,218	13,485	98,772	4,901	1,952
2004	1,520	843	428	3,247	10,740	16,306	7,181	5,328	7,812	8,274	23,106	14,762	105,161	4,851	2,073
2005	1,495	920	560	2,874	10,274	15,249	6,674	5,096	8,070	7,464	20,569	12,793	97,884	5,183	1,903
2006[1]	1,487	1,016	603	2,880	10,827	16,358	7,595	5,426	8,652	7,419	20,862	13,281	101,572	4,956	2,081

[1] Preliminary.   [2] All grades, including carbon, alloy and stainless steel.   *Source: American Iron and Steel Institute (AISI)*

World Production of Pig Iron (Excludes Ferro-Alloys)   In Thousands of Metric Tons

Year	Belgium	Brazil	China	France	Germany	India	Italy	Japan	Russia	Ukraine	United Kingdom	United States	World Total
2005	7,254	33,884	343,750	12,705	28,854	27,125	11,423	83,058	49,175	30,747	10,236	37,200	858,000
2006	7,516	32,452	412,450	13,013	30,360	28,300	11,497	84,270	51,683	32,926	10,736	37,900	939,000
2007	6,576	35,571	476,520	12,426	31,149	28,800	11,100	86,771	51,523	35,647	10,960	36,300	1,020,000
2008	7,125	34,871	470,670	11,372	29,111	29,000	10,373	86,171	48,300	30,982	10,137	33,700	998,000
2009	3,087	25,135	552,830	8,105	20,104	34,000	5,719	66,943	43,930	25,682	7,674	19,000	986,000
2010	4,688	25,000	597,330	10,137	28,560	38,685	8,549	82,283	48,200	27,361	7,235	26,800	1,100,000
2011	4,725	31,000	640,510	9,700	27,943	43,600	9,800	81,028	48,000	28,881	6,600	30,200	1,180,000
2012	4,072	27,000	657,900	9,531	27,048	48,000	9,418	81,405	49,000	28,514	7,252	32,100	1,180,000
2013[1]		26,000	709,000	10,000	27,000	50,000		84,000	51,000	29,000	10,000	30,000	1,180,000
2014[2]		26,000	710,000	11,000	28,000	54,000		84,000	51,000	25,000	10,000	29,000	1,190,000

[1] Preliminary.   [2] Estimate.   *Source: U.S. Geological Survey (USGS)*

Production of Pig Iron (Excludes Ferro-Alloys) in the United States   In Thousands of Short Tons

Year	Jan.	Feb.	Mar.	Apr.	May	June	July	Aug.	Sept.	Oct.	Nov.	Dec.	Total
2005	3,773	3,592	4,030	3,397	3,395	2,962	2,895	3,183	3,127	3,237	3,310	3,135	40,036
2006	3,519	3,421	3,765	3,612	3,816	3,667	3,540	3,525	3,544	3,403	3,059	2,909	41,780
2007	2,850	2,610	3,040	3,010	3,130	3,120	3,080	3,010	3,010	3,200	2,940	3,160	36,160
2008	2,900	3,110	3,280	3,240	3,210	3,020	3,090	3,290	2,900	2,770	2,040	1,690	34,540
2009	1,450	1,510	1,630	1,410	1,370	1,380	1,840	2,090	1,930	2,510	2,240	2,410	21,770
2010	2,350	2,530	2,870	2,030	2,830	2,800	2,450	2,490	2,600	2,150	2,470	2,340	29,910
2011	2,400	2,490	2,790	2,550	2,870	2,820	2,520	2,610	2,540	3,010	2,990	3,190	32,780
2012	3,080	3,050	3,430	2,920	3,320	2,970	2,930	2,860	2,440	2,260	2,820	2,900	34,980
2013	3,060	2,760	3,040	2,800	2,880	2,760	2,760	2,890	2,880	2,870	2,760	2,780	34,240
2014[1]	2,430	2,450	2,820	2,580	2,710	2,760	2,930	2,920	2,740	2,690			32,436

[1] Preliminary.   *Source: American Iron and Steel Institute*

Salient Statistics of Ferrous Scrap and Pig Iron in the United States   In Thousands of Metric Tons

| | Consumption: Ferrous Scrap & Pig Iron Charged To | | | | | | | | | | | Stocks, Dec. 31 Ferrous Scrap & Pig Iron at Consumers | |
| | Mfg. of Pig Iron & Steel Ingots & Castings | | | Iron Foundries & Misc. Users | | | Mfg. of Steel | All Uses | | | Imports of | Exports of | | |
Year	Scrap	Pig Iron	Total	Scrap	Pig Iron	Total	Castings (Scrap)	Ferrous Scrap	Pig Iron	Grand Total	Scrap[2]	Scrap[3]		Total
2003	55,200	39,700	96,670	4,460	655	5,119	2,680	61,900	41,000	104,670	3,480	10,800	4,410	381	4,791
2004	57,100	38,000	96,590	8,490	1,020	9,514	1,330	66,500	39,100	107,100	4,660	11,800	5,400	721	6,121
2005	54,600	36,900	93,240	9,010	1,090	10,103	1,810	65,400	38,000	105,150	3,840	13,000	4,970	664	5,897
2006	54,500	36,700	92,730	9,370	857	10,232	1,640	65,600	37,600	104,740	4,820	14,900	4,210	787	5,309
2007	54,600	36,500	93,140	9,080	1,290	10,374	1,380	65,000	37,800	104,850	3,700	16,500	4,140	771	5,275
2008	56,600	33,500	92,050	7,760	844	8,608	2,070	66,400	34,400	102,760	3,600	21,500	4,340	885	5,660
2009	47,600	28,300	77,240	838	17	859	838	53,100	30,200	84,660	2,990	22,400	3,070	506	3,810
2010	53,100	34,100	88,690	5,180	1,910	7,093	1,810	60,100	36,000	97,590	3,780	20,500	3,330	418	3,909
2011	56,400	34,900	92,920	5,960	1,970	7,933	756	63,100	36,900	101,620	4,010	24,300	3,980	423	4,529
2012[1]	55,800	35,400	94,780	6,710	1,980	8,693	639	63,100	37,400	104,080	3,720	21,400	4,160	405	4,712

[1] Preliminary.   [2] Includes tinplate and terneplate.   [3] Excludes used rails for rerolling and other uses and ships, boats, and other vessels for scrapping.
Source: U.S. Geological Survey (USGS)

IRON AND STEEL

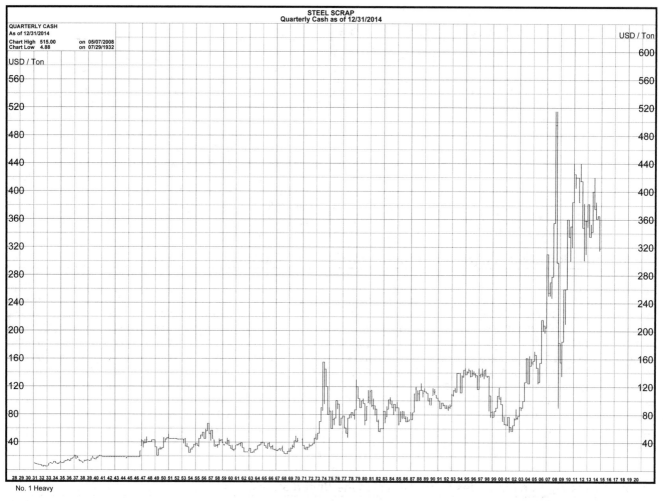

STEEL SCRAP
Quarterly Cash as of 12/31/2014

QUARTERLY CASH
As of 12/31/2014

Chart High 515.00 on 05/07/2008
Chart Low 4.88 on 07/29/1932

USD / Ton

No. 1 Heavy

Consumption of Pig Iron in the United States, by Type of Furance or Equipment   In Thousands of Metric Tons

Year	Open Hearth	Electric	Cupola	Basic Oxygen Process	Air & Other Furnace	Direct Casting	Total
2003	----	2,310	792	37,900	W	36	41,000
2004	----	3,030	354	35,700	W	36	39,100
2005	----	3,040	528	34,400	W	36	38,000
2006	----	3,380	435	33,800	W	36	37,600
2007	----	3,980	401	33,400	8	36	37,800
2008	----	3,350	401	30,600	5	36	33,600
2009	----	4,140	148	25,900	----	36	30,200
2010	----	4,740	55	31,200	----	16	36,000
2011	----	5,410	76	31,300	12	36	36,900
2012[1]	----	5,790	57	31,500	10	36	37,400

[1] Preliminary.   W = Withheld.   *Source: U.S. Geological Survey (USGS)*

Wholesale Price of No. 1 Heavy Melting Steel Scrap in Chicago   In Dollars Per Metric Ton

Year	Jan.	Feb.	Mar.	Apr.	May	June	July	Aug.	Sept.	Oct.	Nov.	Dec.	Average
2005	203.00	190.00	190.00	217.14	180.95	124.32	135.50	189.78	241.19	204.29	246.25	242.43	197.07
2006	222.70	237.76	237.07	245.00	249.23	249.23	245.25	204.41	207.25	202.55	197.90	203.55	225.16
2007	225.24	252.37	305.00	291.90	255.36	254.71	250.71	257.04	268.74	265.65	252.10	273.42	262.69
2008	334.00	338.70	352.57	482.73	513.10	498.10	510.45	466.43	313.62	188.00	91.67	169.29	354.89
2009	183.00	176.68	157.73	150.00	179.25	185.00	230.00	244.29	257.86	244.76	216.32	251.05	206.33
2010	297.63	305.00	352.83	360.00	338.75	335.00	305.00	325.91	347.14	324.29	338.00	380.00	334.13
2011	429.00	427.37	425.00	425.00	407.86	419.32	420.00	420.00	420.00	411.43	388.75	408.68	416.87
2012	436.25	417.50	415.00	406.43	405.00	358.86	310.05	372.30	361.95	320.43	349.20	358.17	375.93
2013	358.00	350.89	375.71	363.86	342.82	336.20	351.36	351.18	343.35	344.61	370.26	395.16	356.95
2014	414.29	396.00	378.10	383.64	373.67	362.90	362.55	363.00	364.71	350.13	322.11	317.43	365.71

Source: American Metal Market (AMM)

World Production of Iron Ore[3]   In Thousands of Metric Tons (Gross Weight)

Year	Australia	Brazil	Canada	China	India	Maur-itania	Russia	South Africa	Sweden	Ukraine	United States	Venezuela	World Total
2005	262,000	281,462	30,387	420,000	152,000	11,133	96,764	39,542	23,300	68,570	54,329	21,200	1,550,000
2006	275,000	317,800	33,543	601,000	177,000	10,658	102,000	41,326	23,300	74,000	52,700	22,100	1,830,000
2007	299,000	354,674	32,744	707,000	207,000	11,817	105,000	42,083	24,700	77,900	52,500	20,700	2,040,000
2008	342,000	350,707	32,102	824,000	213,033	11,296	99,900	48,983	27,713	72,688	53,600	20,650	2,210,000
2009	394,000	298,528	31,704	880,000	217,155	10,524	92,000	55,313	20,389	66,476	26,700	24,100	2,230,000
2010	433,000	372,120	37,001	1,070,000	210,006	11,534	95,900	58,709	27,917	78,171	49,900	22,200	2,590,000
2011	488,000	398,131	35,705	1,330,000	177,256	11,160	104,000	58,057	22,968	80,581	54,700	27,000	2,930,000
2012	521,000	398,150	39,427	1,310,000	143,710	12,000	105,000	63,000	23,000	81,966	54,000	27,000	2,930,000
2013[1]	609,000	317,000	43,000	1,450,000	150,000		105,000	72,000	26,000	82,000	53,000		3,110,000
2014[2]	660,000	320,000	41,000	1,500,000	150,000		105,000	78,000	26,000	82,000	58,000		3,220,000

[1] Preliminary.   [2] Estimate.   [3] Iron ore, iron ore concentrates and iron ore agglomerates.   *Source: U.S. Geological Survey (USGS)*

Salient Statistics of Iron Ore[3] in the United States   In Thousands of Metric Tons

Year	Net Import Reliance As a % of Apparent Consump	Production Total	Lake Superior	Other Regions	Ship-ments	Value Million $ (at Mine)	Average Value $ at Mine Per Ton	Stock, Dec. 31 Mines	Con-suming Plants	Lake Erie Docks	Imports	Exports	Con-sumption	Total
2005	4	54,300	NA	NA	53,200	2,370.0	44.50	2,040	----	----	13,000	11,800	60,100	532.0
2006	8	52,700	NA	NA	52,700	2,840.0	53.88	1,650	----	----	11,500	8,270	58,200	611.0
2007	E	52,500	NA	NA	50,900	3,040.0	59.64	2,090	----	----	9,400	9,310	54,700	543.0
2008	E	53,600	NA	NA	53,600	3,770.0	70.43	4,070	----	----	9,250	11,100	51,900	918.0
2009	E	26,700	NA	NA	27,600	2,560.0	92.76	5,060	----	----	3,870	3,920	31,000	376.0
2010	E	49,900	----	----	50,600	5,000.0	98.79	3,470	----	----	6,420	10,000	42,300	703.0
2011	E	54,700	----	----	55,600	5,530.0	99.45	3,260	----	----	5,300	11,100	46,300	841.0
2012	E	54,000	----	----	52,900	5,190.0	98.16	3,110	----	----	5,200	11,200	46,900	758.0
2013[1]	E	53,000	----	----	52,700		104.90	2,290	----	----	3,200	11,000	48,800	
2014[2]	E	57,500	----	----	54,200		101.00	4,500	----	----	5,500	13,000	49,500	

[1] Preliminary.   [2] Estimate.   [3] Usable iron ore exclusive of ore containing 5% or more manganese and includes byproduct ore.
NA = Not available.   *Source: U.S. Geological Survey (USGS)*

U.S. Imports (for Consumption) of Iron Ore[2]   In Thousands of Metric Tons

Year	Australia	Brazil	Canada	Chile	Mauritania	Peru	Sweden	Venezuela	Total
2003	128	4,980	6,970	296	----	77	88	21	12,600
2004	[3]	5,020	5,830	244	----	56	111	262	11,800
2005	1	4,180	7,510	270	----	33	133	148	13,000
2006	8	4,530	6,240	283	----	52	[3]	23	11,500
2007	----	3,210	5,520	279	----	140	141	58	9,400
2008	----	2,620	5,900	215	----	59	88	68	9,250
2009	----	188	3,140	203	----	34	31	21	3,870
2010	----	506	4,490	131	----	14	54	251	6,420
2011	----	562	3,910	165	----	----	----	279	5,270
2012[1]	----	739	3,810	104	----	44	72	75	5,140

[1] Preliminary.   [2] Including agglomerates.   [3] Less than 1/2 unit.   *Source: U.S. Geological Survey (USGS)*

Iron Ore Stocks in the United States, at End of Month   In Thousands of Metric Tons

Year	Jan.	Feb.	Mar.	Apr.	May	June	July	Aug.	Sept.	Oct.	Nov.	Dec.
2005	4,060	6,770	8,410	7,690	7,730	7,370	7,420	7,240	6,550	5,840	6,250	5,750
2006	6,750	9,620	11,900	11,100	10,800	10,100	9,353	8,760	8,090	8,120	7,590	5,880
2007	7,330	10,100	11,800	11,000	10,300	9,870	9,340	8,700	7,950	7,660	7,110	6,490
2008	6,930	9,820	12,400	11,300	9,950	9,370	8,170	6,910	6,110	5,800	5,830	6,630
2009	8,680	10,900	12,500	12,300	10,600	9,010	7,410	5,990	5,430	5,130	3,900	3,120
2010	3,760	6,080	7,040	6,070	5,400	4,160	3,730	3,240	3,150	3,410	3,320	2,860
2011	4,250	7,470	9,750	9,250	8,970	8,200	7,060	6,380	5,140	4,660	4,250	3,390
2012	3,200	6,750	8,910	7,730	6,410	5,340	3,850	2,980	2,660	2,970	3,020	2,200
2013	3,290	6,580	8,960	7,830	6,350	5,390	4,130	3,320	2,770	2,110	2,470	3,690
2014[1]	5,200	8,820	11,900	13,200	12,000	10,900	9,350	7,770	6,890	6,180		

[1] Preliminary.   *Source: U.S. Geological Survey (USGS)*

Lard

Lard is the layer of fat found along the back and underneath the skin of a hog. The hog's fat is purified by washing it with water, melting it under constant heat, and straining it several times. Lard is an important byproduct of the meatpacking industry. It is valued highly as cooking oil because there is very little smoke when it is heated. However, demand for lard in cooking is declining because of the trend toward healthier eating. Lard is also used for medicinal purposes such as ointments, plasters, liniments, and occasionally as a laxative for children. Lard production is directly proportional to commercial hog production, meaning the largest producers of hogs are the largest producers of lard.

Prices – The average monthly wholesale price of lard in 2014 fell by -12.0% to 43.36 per pound, well below the 2011 record high of 54.55 per pound.

Supply – World production of lard in the 2013-14 marketing year rose by +1.6% yr/yr to 8.424 million metric tons, which was a new record high. The world's largest lard producers were China (with 44.0% of world production), the U.S (7.0%), Germany (6.6%), the former USSR (6.2%), Brazil (5.3%), Spain (3.5%), and Poland (2.6%). U.S. production of lard in 2012-13 fell -0.2% yr/yr to 1.319 billion pounds.

Demand – U.S. consumption of lard in 2011 fell -4.9% to 348.654 million pounds, down from 2008 record high of 490.602 million pounds. The current level of consumption is less than 20% of the consumption of 1.574 billion pounds in 1971.

Exports – U.S. exports of lard in 2012-13 rose by +18.4% to 64.8 million pounds, and accounted for only 7% of U.S. production.

World Production of Lard   In Thousands of Metric Tons

Year	Brazil	Canada	China	France	Germany	Italy	Japan	Poland	Romania	Spain	United States	Ex-USSR	World Total
2005-06	368.9	126.5	3,371.0	151.3	471.3	200.9	55.9	266.4	66.7	282.1	541.3	330.5	7,653.5
2006-07	382.5	126.1	3,181.3	152.2	501.2	207.7	54.2	270.9	76.2	300.5	552.7	369.5	7,636.8
2007-08	386.0	123.7	3,192.7	153.0	520.1	208.7	54.7	249.9	75.0	308.5	605.3	385.1	7,733.1
2008-09	404.9	120.4	3,280.9	140.6	532.9	207.9	52.9	208.9	72.1	297.8	597.3	383.6	7,694.2
2009-10	413.1	122.7	3,402.7	136.5	554.9	210.4	52.6	220.4	71.9	287.2	576.7	423.4	7,895.3
2010-11	421.2	125.0	3,468.0	136.6	566.7	208.4	51.0	234.3	76.2	302.2	586.9	448.2	8,052.2
2011-12[1]	427.5	126.4	3,560.8	133.2	561.5	208.4	51.4	222.7	76.5	309.3	599.7	466.2	8,178.2
2012-13[2]	434.6	125.4	3,627.5	132.1	560.3	213.0	51.3	213.9	74.1	301.9	598.7	495.6	8,295.8
2013-14[3]	443.1	126.0	3,708.2	134.3	559.2	208.4	51.7	218.0	73.8	297.7	589.4	524.2	8,424.7

[1] Preliminary.   [2] Estimate.   [3] Forecast.   *Source: The Oil World*

Supply and Distribution of Lard in the United States   In Millions of Pounds

Year	Production	Stocks Oct. 1	Total Supply	Domestic	Baking or Frying Fats	Margarine[3]	Exports	Total Disappearance	Direct Use	Per Capita (Lbs.)
2004-05	1,117.0	13.3	1,136.0	487.8	W	6.0	289.2	777.0	220.2	0.7
2005-06	1,193.3	13.8	1,207.1	694.8	W	3.0	93.8	788.6	459.7	1.5
2006-07	1,218.5	9.4	1,227.9	718.5	W	W	71.9	790.4	498.6	1.7
2007-08	1,334.4	14.2	1,348.6	756.8	W	W	72.9	829.7	486.7	1.6
2008-09	1,316.8	13.9	1,330.7	800.9	W	W	81.4	882.3	310.3	1.0
2009-10	1,271.4	17.5	1,288.9	775.8	W	W	71.6	847.4	479.8	1.5
2010-11	1,293.9	25.6	1,319.5	794.2	W	W	76.6	870.8	NA	NA
2011-12[1]	1,322.1	20.0	1,342.1	830.1	W	W	54.8	884.9	NA	NA
2012-13[2]	1,319.9	20.0	1,339.9	816.8	W	W	64.8	881.6	NA	NA

[1] Preliminary.   [2] Forecast.   [3] Includes edible tallow.   W = Withheld.
Source: Economic Research Service, U.S. Department of Agriculture (ERS-USDA)

Consumption of Lard (Edible and Inedible) in the United States   In Millions of Pounds

Year	Jan.	Feb.	Mar.	Apr.	May	June	July	Aug.	Sept.	Oct.	Nov.	Dec.	Total
2002	26.4	26.1	21.8	26.7	24.8	21.2	22.9	26.4	23.6	26.4	28.1	28.7	303.2
2003	22.6	22.3	23.4	21.4	23.3	24.0	23.0	21.4	22.5	24.3	20.2	21.0	269.5
2004	22.9	25.8	25.9	23.9	23.5	22.0	19.1	19.7	21.3	22.4	21.9	19.9	268.1
2005	19.0	15.4	21.4	18.7	19.9	20.4	18.9	19.5	20.1	19.7	22.2	17.9	233.1
2006	15.7	16.4	20.6	21.4	20.2	16.7	14.9	17.7	17.8	18.9	22.3	20.9	223.4
2007	21.6	16.2	22.2	19.7	20.5	20.8	22.8	23.9	22.8	31.1	29.7	31.4	282.8
2008	34.8	32.2	44.6	50.7	50.8	44.4	47.8	39.7	44.0	37.5	31.7	32.2	490.6
2009	23.4	17.3	26.8	26.0	26.3	25.8	21.3	20.5	25.4	32.4	29.9	27.0	302.3
2010	22.2	W	38.8	W	30.4	30.8	30.4	32.4	30.1	31.1	30.4	28.8	366.6
2011[1]	22.2	26.3	36.0	W	28.8	29.6	31.4	W	W	W	W	W	348.7

[1] Preliminary.   *Source: Bureau of the Census, U.S. Department of Commerce*

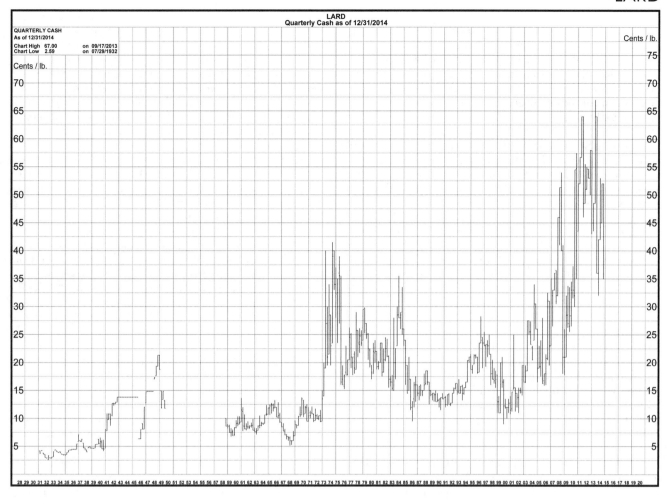

LARD
Quarterly Cash as of 12/31/2014

QUARTERLY CASH
As of 12/31/2014

Chart High 67.00   on 09/17/2013
Chart Low   2.59   on 07/29/1932

Average Wholesale Price of Lard--Loose, Tank Cars, in Chicago   In Cents Per Pound

Year	Jan.	Feb.	Mar.	Apr.	May	June	July	Aug.	Sept.	Oct.	Nov.	Dec.	Average
2005	22.10	18.30	17.71	20.72	22.95	21.30	18.08	17.75	20.97	27.38	27.76	18.60	21.14
2006	17.16	16.44	16.82	18.00	17.13	17.63	22.21	29.91	31.86	23.55	20.78	22.58	21.17
2007	23.00	23.82	30.75	27.71	28.60	32.64	36.00	35.77	36.00	35.09	33.78	32.66	31.32
2008	33.01	38.33	46.00	43.04	42.27	44.93	52.82	46.50	41.73	37.07	26.40	20.00	39.34
2009	25.36	20.31	19.49	23.36	29.00	30.06	27.63	32.20	29.73	25.75	30.07	28.75	26.81
2010	28.60	28.25	32.95	33.95	34.24	32.98	31.42	33.33	43.59	46.64	37.32	38.30	35.13
2011	48.50	49.60	52.00	51.50	54.31	56.75	63.00	58.96	61.33	61.10	48.86	48.71	54.55
2012	NA	52.55	54.60	52.59	54.82	54.83	53.00	NA	NA	51.60	57.00	NA	53.87
2013	52.45	45.56	NA	43.50	44.50	48.50	53.25	56.89	64.78	43.00	48.00	41.50	49.27
2014	33.00	38.00	40.67	53.00	NA	45.00	NA	46.50	50.67	48.00	42.81	35.91	43.36

Source: Economic Research Service, U.S. Department of Agriculture (ERS-USDA)

Cold Storage Holdings of all Lard[1] in the United States, on First of Month   In Millions of Pounds

Year	Jan.	Feb.	Mar.	Apr.	May	June	July	Aug.	Sept.	Oct.	Nov.	Dec.
2002	13.2	18.0	16.4	16.5	20.3	22.4	18.9	18.3	12.0	10.5	14.6	11.3
2003	10.5	14.0	19.6	18.7	16.5	13.5	11.9	9.7	8.4	9.3	10.1	12.4
2004	13.3	19.8	18.6	20.3	20.5	15.0	12.9	10.8	10.3	11.8	11.4	13.2
2005	13.7	14.6	20.6	19.0	17.8	12.3	12.0	12.3	12.5	13.0	12.2	14.7
2006	9.6	11.5	13.7	13.6	9.3	9.9	13.0	12.4	13.0	11.5	16.1	16.0
2007	16.4	14.9	13.3	18.5	10.9	14.6	11.3	12.8	11.0	9.2	14.6	18.8
2008	14.0	22.4	20.4	22.9	23.0	19.5	22.7	13.6	18.0	17.8	16.1	20.4
2009	12.1	13.6	15.4	16.2	14.5	18.8	17.3	21.6	20.5	26.7	18.5	15.4
2010	13.9	14.5	21.0	22.9	26.1	15.7	19.4	17.9	14.1	13.8	15.6	15.5
2011[2]	17.5	20.5	25.3	20.9	26.2	19.9	23.4	23.9	NA	NA	NA	NA

[1] Stocks in factories and warehouses (except that in hands of retailers).   [2] Preliminary.   *Source: Bureau of the Census, U.S. Department of Commerce*

Lead

Lead (atomic symbol Pb) is a dense, toxic, bluish-gray metallic element, and is the heaviest stable element. Lead was one of the first known metals. The ancients used lead in face powders, rouges, mascaras, paints, condiments, wine preservatives, and water supply plumbing. The Romans were slowly poisoned from lead because of its diverse daily usage.

Lead is usually found in ore with zinc, silver, and most often copper. The most common lead ore is galena, containing 86.6% lead. Cerussite and angleside are other common varieties of lead. More than half of the lead currently used comes from recycling.

Lead is used in building construction, bullets and shot, tank and pipe lining, storage batteries, and electric cable sheathing. Lead is used extensively as a protective shielding for radioactive material (e.g., X-ray apparatus) because of its high density and nuclear properties. Lead is also part of solder, pewter, and fusible alloys.

Lead futures and options are traded on the London Metal Exchange (LME). Lead futures are traded on the Multi Commodity Exchange of India (MCX), and the Shanghai Futures Exchange (SHFE). The LME lead futures contract calls for the delivery of 25 metric tons of at least 99.970% purity lead ingots (pigs). The contract is priced in U.S. dollars per metric ton. Lead first started trading on the LME in 1903.

Prices – The average price of pig lead among U.S. producers reached a record high of $1.2474 per pound in 2007 but has since remained below that level. Pig lead prices in 2014 closed the year down -2.5% at $1.0789 per pound.

Supply – World smelter production of lead (both primary and secondary) in 2012 (latest data) rose +1.0% yr/yr to 10.200 million metric tons to post a new record high production level. The world's largest smelter producers of lead (both primary and secondary) are China with 46.1% of world production in 2012, followed by the U.S. with 12.0%, Germany with 4.2%, and with the UK, Canada, and Japan, each with about 3%.

U.S. mine production of recoverable lead rose +0.6% yr/yr to 336,000 metric tons in 2012 (latest data available). Missouri was responsible for 94% of U.S. production, with the remainder produced mainly by Idaho and Montana. Lead recovered from scrap in the U.S. (secondary production fell -5.0% yr/yr in 2014 (annualized through November) to 1.134 million metric tons, down from the 2008 record high of 1.220 metric tons. The amount of lead recovered from scrap is almost three times the amount of lead produced in the U.S. from mines (primary production). The value of U.S. secondary lead production in 2012 fell -8.2% yr/yr to $2.790 billion, still below the 2007 record high of $3.040 billion.

Demand – U.S. lead consumption in 2014 (annualized through November) rose +21.1% to 1.764 million metric tons, a new record high.

Trade – The U.S. relied on imports for 30% of its lead consumption in 2014. U.S. imports of lead pigs and bars in 2013 (latest data) rose +43.3% yr/yr to 500,000 metric tons. U.S. lead exports in 2012 were comprised of ore concentrate (214,000 metric tons), unwrought lead (47,000 metric tons), scrap (25,900 metric tons), and wrought lead (6,300 metric tons).

World Smelter (Primary and Secondary) Production of Lead — In Thousands of Metric Tons

Year	Australia[3]	Belgium[4]	Canada[3]	China[2]	France	Germany	Italy	Japan	Mexico[3]	Spain	United Kingdom[3]	United States	World Total
2004	268.0	63.0	241.2	1,940.0	105.6	359.2	202.0	282.9	217.4	105.6	245.9	1,280	7,040
2005	263.0	83.4	230.2	2,390.0	105.0	417.7	211.5	274.6	226.5	110.0	304.4	1,300	7,660
2006	233.0	101.4	250.5	2,720.0	100.2	379.0	190.5	280.0	212.5	129.0	318.7	1,310	8,100
2007	229.0	117.2	236.7	2,790.0	100.2	405.1	210.0	276.3	212.0	128.0	263.0	1,303	8,320
2008	248.0	109.0	259.1	3,200.0	88.0	415.1	211.8	279.5	243.8	125.0	283.0	1,275	8,730
2009	229.0	109.0	258.9	3,710.0	88.0	390.6	149.0	247.8	254.4	125.0	279.0	1,213	8,860
2010	204.0	121.0	272.9	4,200.0	88.0	404.0	149.0	267.2	286.0	165.0	294.0	1,255	9,530
2011[1]	213.0	121.0	282.3	4,600.0	88.0	429.0	149.0	248.6	317.7	172.0	294.0	1,248	10,100
2012[2]	184.0	121.0	278.1	4,700.0	88.0	430.0	149.0	252.0	405.0	125.0	294.0	1,221	10,200

[1] Preliminary.   [2] Estimate.   [3] Refinded & bullion.   [4] Includes scrap.   *Source: U.S. Geological Survey (USGS)*

Consumption of Lead in the United States, by Products — In Metric Tons

Year	Ammun-ition	Bearing Metals	Pipes, Traps & Bends[2]	Cable Covering	Calking Lead	Casting Metals	Other Metal Products[3]	Total Other Oxides[4]	Sheet Lead	Solder	Storage Battery Grids, Post, etc.	Oxides	Brass and Bronze	Total Con-sumption
2004	61,500	1,300	W	W	W	17,900	W	25,700	31,600	7,440	657,000	630,000	2,390	1,480,000
2005	61,300	1,180	1,220	W	W	30,400	22,200	14,100	29,100	8,370	579,000	705,000	2,100	1,490,000
2006	65,700	1,240	1,440	W	W	29,900	23,400	16,000	28,400	7,280	586,000	710,000	3,130	1,490,000
2007	69,400	1,410	1,230	W	W	31,500	23,600	15,800	28,600	7,220	640,000	738,000	2,870	1,570,000
2008	67,400	1,250	1,190	W	W	20,100	7,670	10,700	26,400	6,610	575,000	715,000	2,460	1,440,000
2009	67,900	1,100	1,130	W	W	15,900	5,790	10,100	25,400	6,450	389,000	750,000	1,370	1,290,000
2010	65,700	1,230	990	W	W	16,400	8,800	9,760	23,400	6,420	478,000	806,000	1,410	1,430,000
2011	75,100	1,150	6,110	W	W	16,000	23,100	9,760	7,170	6,170	417,000	837,000	1,620	1,410,000
2012[1]	73,900	1,090	6,240	W	W	16,700	18,500	9,740	7,390	6,280	449,000	745,000	1,300	1,360,000

[1] Preliminary.   [2] Including building.   [3] Including terne metal, type metal, and lead consumed in foil, collapsible tubes, annealing, plating, galvanizing and fishing weights.   [4] Includes paints, glass and ceramic products, and other pigments and chemicals.   W = Withheld.
Source: U.S. Geological Survey (USGS)

Salient Statistics of Lead in the United States   In Thousands of Metric Tons

Year	Net Import Reliance as a % of Apparent Consump	Production --- of Refined Lead From --- Domestic Ores[3]		Foreighn Ores[3]		Total Primary	Total Value of Refined Million $	--- Secondary Lead Recovered --- As Soft Lead	In Anti- monial Lead	In Other Alloys	Total	Total Value of Secondary Million USD	- Stocks, Dec. 31 - Primary		Con- sumer[4]	Average Price - Cents Per Pound - New York	London
2005	E	143	W			143	----	869	271	4.5	1,150	1,550	W		46.8	61.03	44.23
2006	E	153	W			153	----	948	200	12.4	1,160	1,980	W		54.8	77.40	58.00
2007	E	123	W			123	----	1,020	160	2.4	1,180	3,220	W		51.6	123.84	117.00
2008	E	135	W			135	----	1,000	140	2.4	1,140	3,040	W		72.5	120.33	94.79
2009	13	103	W			103	----	960	151	----	1,110	2,130	W		63.3	86.87	77.95
2010	13	115	W			115	----	968	174	----	1,140	2,740	W		64.8	108.91	97.42
2011	19	118	W			118	----	966	167	----	1,130	3,040	W		46.6	121.70	108.92
2012	18	111	W			111	----	873	236	----	1,110	2,790	W		72.0	114.00	93.50
2013[1]	26	114	W			114	----			----	1,150		W		70.0	114.00	97.20
2014[2]	30	1	W			1	----			----	1,150		W		60.0	----	86.00

[1] Preliminary.   [2] Estimate.   [3] And base bullion.   [4] Also at secondary smelters.   W = Withheld.   E = Net exporter.
Source: U.S. Geological Survey (USGS)

U.S. Foreign Trade of Lead   In Thousands of Metric Tons

Year	---- Exports ---- Ore Con- centrate	Un- wrought Lead[3]	Wrought Lead[4]	Scrap	Ash & Re- sidues[5]	--- Imports for Consumption --- Ores, Flue Dust or Fume & Mattes	Base Bullion	Pigs & Bars	Re- claimed Scrap, Etc.	Value Million $	--- General Import From: --- Ore, Flue, Dust & Matte Aus- tralia	Can- ada	Peru	Pigs & Bars Can- ada	Mexico	Peru
2004	292.0	58.6	23.8	56.3	----	----	----	197.0	4.8	235.3	----	----	----	166.0	8.8	7.3
2005	390.2	45.5	19.0	67.3	----	----	----	298.0	3.3	334.8	----	----	----	190.0	15.2	23.9
2006	297.6	52.7	15.8	120.9	----	----	0.5	331.0	1.6	450.8	----	----	----	222.0	15.8	34.6
2007	300.0	51.8	4.6	129.0	----	----	2.0	263.0	2.4	591.4	----	----	----	208.0	35.6	16.5
2008	277.0	68.1	6.2	175.0	----	----	2.7	309.0	1.3	681.6	----	----	----	219.0	58.1	10.6
2009	287.0	77.6	4.3	140.0	----	----	0.8	251.0	1.3	418.8	----	----	----	205.0	41.1	1.0
2010	299.0	77.7	5.6	43.5	----	----	0.6	271.0	3.7	575.9	----	----	----	237.0	29.4	----
2011	223.0	40.1	7.0	31.1	----	----	0.4	313.0	2.4	718.4	----	----	----	250.0	56.0	0.1
2012[1]	214.0	47.0	6.3	25.9	----	1.5	1.0	349.0	2.9	715.9	----	----	----	240.0	56.1	0.0
2013[2]	210.0	48.0		34.9	----	0.0	1.9	500.0								

[1] Preliminary.   [2] Estimate.   [3] And lead alloys.   [4] Blocks, pigs, etc.   [5] Less than 1/2 unit.   *Source: U.S. Geological Survey (USGS)*

Annual Mine Production of Recoverable Lead in the United States   In Metric Tons

Year	Total	Idaho	Missouri	Montana	Other States	Missouri's % of Total
2003	449,000	W	432,000	W	17,200	96%
2004	430,000	W	407,000	W	23,400	95%
2005	426,000	W	397,000	W	29,500	93%
2006	419,000	W	393,000	W	26,100	94%
2007	434,000	W	400,000	W	34,200	92%
2008	399,000	W	360,000	W	38,600	90%
2009	395,000	W	370,000	W	24,900	94%
2010	356,000	W	W	W	W	W
2011[1]	334,000	W	W	W	W	W
2012[2]	336,000	W	W	W	W	W

[1] Preliminary.   [2] Estimate.   W = Withheld, included in Other States.   *Source: U.S. Geological Survey (USGS)*

Mine Production of Recoverable Lead in the United States   In Thousands of Metric Tons

Year	Jan.	Feb.	Mar.	Apr.	May	June	July	Aug.	Sept.	Oct.	Nov.	Dec.	Total
2005	31.1	31.1	34.6	35.2	33.4	41.4	39.5	37.4	38.2	37.9	34.6	37.9	432.3
2006	36.7	33.3	38.1	33.6	33.4	33.9	36.6	36.3	37.0	38.0	35.0	29.6	421.5
2007	38.1	33.9	36.7	31.6	36.9	34.5	38.7	41.3	34.6	39.4	31.5	37.1	434.3
2008	38.0	36.9	36.1	33.0	31.0	34.4	37.8	34.2	33.8	29.1	27.8	33.7	405.8
2009	33.8	30.5	32.8	34.7	33.6	33.7	29.9	35.7	35.6	36.9	28.5	32.8	398.5
2010	31.8	28.6	32.7	31.5	29.7	26.5	29.5	26.9	30.1	31.3	27.8	30.0	356.4
2011	30.4	25.1	29.5	32.5	27.4	27.2	29.3	24.4	29.2	25.2	28.1	30.7	339.0
2012	28.7	27.9	27.6	27.3	27.6	28.1	27.5	29.7	27.0	27.5	27.7	29.1	335.7
2013	27.0	25.7	26.0	28.6	28.9	28.0	28.5	28.7	29.6	27.2	25.7	28.6	332.5
2014[1]	30.3	26.6	28.8	31.3	32.8	29.6	30.5	30.4					360.5

[1] Preliminary.   *Source: U.S. Geological Survey (USGS)*

LEAD

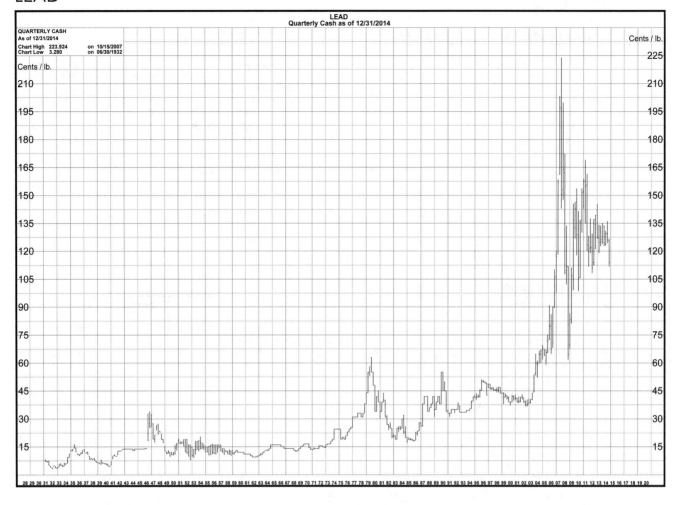

Average Price of Pig Lead, U.S. Primary Producers (Common Corroding)[1]   In Cents Per Pound

Year	Jan.	Feb.	Mar.	Apr.	May	June	July	Aug.	Sept.	Oct.	Nov.	Dec.	Average
2005	50.46	52.20	54.00	53.25	53.41	53.26	47.22	47.53	49.76	54.01	54.68	59.63	52.45
2006	66.16	67.16	63.28	61.58	61.16	51.92	56.07	61.48	69.24	77.64	82.09	86.22	67.00
2007	83.62	88.42	94.72	98.73	103.14	117.95	148.17	148.47	153.50	175.59	159.80	124.81	124.74
2008	125.37	146.72	141.77	134.92	106.42	88.93	93.68	92.49	90.49	73.02	65.52	49.58	100.74
2009	57.27	55.74	61.81	67.86	70.02	80.87	81.05	91.57	104.06	105.75	109.61	110.96	83.05
2010	113.15	102.18	104.73	108.78	92.43	83.23	89.48	99.29	104.31	113.11	113.59	114.22	103.21
2011	123.37	122.83	124.67	130.68	117.43	121.38	129.14	116.63	111.36	95.84	97.61	100.19	115.93
2012	103.68	105.11	101.81	100.71	98.42	91.70	92.52	93.54	106.29	112.62	113.81	117.08	103.11
2013	120.19	121.68	112.79	106.17	105.82	109.38	106.18	111.56	107.53	108.72	107.97	109.40	110.62
2014	110.40	108.69	106.23	107.71	107.99	108.35	112.31	114.44	108.97	105.16	104.11	100.29	107.89

[1] New York Delivery.   *Source: American Metal Market*

Refiners Production[1] of Lead in the United States   In Metric Tons

Year	Jan.	Feb.	Mar.	Apr.	May	June	July	Aug.	Sept.	Oct.	Nov.	Dec.	Total
2001	NA	NA	NA	NA	NA	NA	NA	NA	NA	NA	NA	NA	290,000
2002	NA	NA	NA	NA	NA	NA	NA	NA	NA	NA	NA	NA	262,000
2003	NA	NA	NA	NA	NA	NA	NA	NA	NA	NA	NA	NA	245,000
2004	NA	NA	NA	NA	NA	NA	NA	NA	NA	NA	NA	NA	NA
2005	NA	NA	NA	NA	NA	NA	NA	NA	NA	NA	NA	NA	143,000
2006	NA	NA	NA	NA	NA	NA	NA	NA	NA	NA	NA	NA	143,000
2007	NA	NA	NA	NA	NA	NA	NA	NA	NA	NA	NA	NA	NA
2008	NA	NA	NA	NA	NA	NA	NA	NA	NA	NA	NA	NA	NA
2009	NA	NA	NA	NA	NA	NA	NA	NA	NA	NA	NA	NA	NA
2010[2]	NA	NA	NA	NA	NA	NA	NA	NA	NA	NA	NA	NA	NA

[1] Represents refined lead produced from domestic ores by primary smelters plus small amounts of secondary material passing through these smelters. Includes GSA metal purchased for remelt.   [2] Preliminary.   NA = Not available.   *Source: U.S. Geological Survey (USGS)*

Total Stocks of Lead[1] in the United States at Refiners, at End of Month   In Metric Tons

Year	Jan.	Feb.	Mar.	Apr.	May	June	July	Aug.	Sept.	Oct.	Nov.	Dec.
2005	66,500	65,200	63,200	63,000	61,400	60,700	61,500	56,200	58,300	60,900	61,900	61,400
2006	59,300	59,700	59,800	60,100	61,500	60,100	49,000	48,000	47,900	48,900	49,900	50,900
2007	50,000	49,000	49,000	49,300	37,900	46,800	54,300	54,100	58,700	56,400	59,100	63,100
2008	53,100	50,800	53,600	50,900	51,600	49,900	46,100	52,500	52,300	55,500	69,100	69,900
2009	70,600	70,100	77,900	68,100	70,200	65,600	56,300	53,800	54,500	55,200	59,100	61,700
2010	60,200	60,200	55,700	50,700	55,500	57,200	57,600	59,100	59,800	58,700	67,700	67,400
2011	67,100	53,000	53,200	61,100	62,600	61,500	62,800	60,500	58,800	56,300	53,500	54,800
2012	58,700	63,300	54,800	54,000	51,800	56,600	62,600	65,700	63,400	63,800	56,000	57,500
2013	69,900	76,200	83,100	94,300	98,000	93,400	83,600	81,400	77,400	69,300	65,100	69,400
2014[1]	68,100	63,600	65,400	65,700	64,000	66,600	62,500	74,000				

[1] Preliminary.   [2] Secondary smelters and consumers.   *Source: U.S. Geological Survey (USGS)*

Total[2] Lead Consumption in the United States   In Thousands of Metric Tons

Year	Jan.	Feb.	Mar.	Apr.	May	June	July	Aug.	Sept.	Oct.	Nov.	Dec.	Total
2005	125.0	117.0	109.0	108.0	134.0	130.0	124.0	129.0	126.0	126.0	126.0	126.0	1,480
2006	124.0	130.0	129.0	128.0	128.0	128.0	125.0	126.0	127.0	128.0	126.0	126.0	1,525
2007	130.0	128.0	129.0	128.0	131.0	139.0	131.0	134.0	132.0	137.0	132.0	127.0	1,578
2008	140.0	136.0	130.0	135.0	135.0	141.0	134.0	129.0	134.0	136.0	127.0	126.0	1,603
2009	123.0	119.0	116.0	124.0	116.0	117.0	116.0	115.0	118.0	122.0	121.0	117.0	1,424
2010	120.0	118.0	114.0	115.0	117.0	118.0	116.0	117.0	118.0	117.0	118.0	117.0	1,405
2011	131.0	118.0	118.0	133.0	132.0	133.0	132.0	133.0	132.0	132.0	132.0	131.0	1,557
2012	122.0	130.0	135.0	123.0	121.0	122.0	120.0	122.0	121.0	122.0	122.0	123.0	1,483
2013	146.0	123.0	118.0	117.0	117.0	117.0	116.0	118.0	117.0	119.0	115.0	134.0	1,457
2014[1]	159.0	159.0	148.0	153.0	148.0	146.0	131.0	132.0					1,764

[1] Preliminary.   [1] Represents total consumption of primary & secondary lead as metal, in chemicals, or in alloys.   *Source: U.S. Geological Survey (USGS)*

Lead Recovered from Scrap in the United States   In Thousands of Metric Tons (Lead Content)

Year	Jan.	Feb.	Mar.	Apr.	May	June	July	Aug.	Sept.	Oct.	Nov.	Dec.	Total
2005	94.4	95.1	86.8	86.8	87.1	94.6	94.7	94.8	93.0	95.9	96.4	92.4	1,112.0
2006	90.2	96.7	97.4	98.2	99.5	95.7	94.9	97.0	95.6	98.4	98.4	95.9	1,157.9
2007	99.0	96.5	98.6	93.5	94.5	100.0	103.0	103.0	101.0	104.0	104.0	94.6	1,191.7
2008	104.0	98.2	102.0	100.0	105.0	102.0	92.0	102.0	91.7	100.0	122.0	101.0	1,219.9
2009	97.3	99.0	101.0	90.2	91.6	93.8	97.0	97.2	90.9	96.3	98.0	98.0	1,150.3
2010	96.2	95.2	92.1	86.3	89.8	92.9	94.2	98.0	95.6	101.0	100.0	96.3	1,137.6
2011	104.0	96.2	95.5	104.0	101.0	100.0	102.0	103.0	95.4	95.9	98.8	99.6	1,195.4
2012	102.0	101.0	97.8	98.0	99.4	102.0	100.0	98.0	97.3	100.0	100.0	99.2	1,194.7
2013	104.0	96.7	100.0	97.3	100.0	98.1	97.2	100.0	99.5	104.0	102.0	95.0	1,193.8
2014[1]	92.1	91.1	97.3	96.3	94.5	94.5	96.9	93.8					1,134.8

[1] Preliminary.   *Source: U.S. Geological Survey (USGS)*

Domestic Shipments[1] of Lead in the United States, by Refiners   In Thousands of Short Tons

Year	Jan.	Feb.	Mar.	Apr.	May	June	July	Aug.	Sept.	Oct.	Nov.	Dec.	Total
1989	29.3	28.5	32.2	35.7	45.1	36.4	32.8	41.5	40.0	44.2	40.2	31.1	437.1
1990	39.3	33.9	39.1	33.5	38.4	32.9	32.6	38.9	36.6	38.9	37.9	31.7	433.7
1991	35.4	33.8	34.3	39.8	33.9	26.0	31.8	37.9	35.1	35.7	28.7	26.7	399.2
1992	31.3	23.9	30.4	26.3	25.6	27.2	27.3	28.7	26.3	28.5	26.3	21.7	323.5
1993	24.6	23.6	32.5	30.0	31.3	35.1	28.9	34.0	35.5	35.5	31.7	33.5	376.2
1994	35.9	32.8	35.2	32.7	34.7	36.7	31.6	33.4	34.8	34.3	34.0	33.3	409.3
1995	36.5	30.3	35.1	31.1	33.7	31.9	28.6	40.3	34.9	40.9	33.2	29.8	406.4
1996	37.2	32.4	29.5	30.2	29.4	26.7	27.7	33.5	30.1	33.5	28.1	27.6	366.0
1997[2]	31.5	27.8	24.7	35.2	39.2	36.1	33.4	29.4	26.4	31.5	30.4	28.1	377.8
1998[2]	Data no longer available.												

[1] Includes GSA metal.   [2] Preliminary.   *Source: American Metal Market (AMM)*

Lumber and Plywood

Humans have utilized lumber for construction for thousands of years, but due to the heaviness of timber and the manual methods of harvesting, large-scale lumbering didn't occur until the mechanical advances of the Industrial Revolution. Lumber is produced from both hardwood and softwood. Hardwood lumber comes from deciduous trees that have broad leaves. Most hardwood lumber is used for miscellaneous industrial applications, primarily wood pallets, and includes oak, gum, maple, and ash. Hardwood species with beautiful colors and patterns are used for such high-grade products as furniture, flooring, paneling, and cabinets and include black walnut, black cherry, and red oak. Wood from cone-bearing trees is called softwood, regardless of its actual hardness. Most lumber from the U.S. is softwood. Softwoods, such as southern yellow pine, Douglas fir, ponderosa pine, and true firs, are primarily used as structural lumber such as 2x4s and 2x6s, poles, paper and cardboard.

Plywood consists of several thin layers of veneer bonded together with adhesives. The veneer sheets are layered so that the grain of one sheet is perpendicular to that of the next, which makes plywood exceptionally strong for its weight. Most plywood has from three to nine layers of wood. Plywood manufacturers use both hard and soft woods, although hardwoods serve primarily for appearance and are not as strong as those made from softwoods. Plywood is primarily used in construction, particularly for floors, roofs, walls, and doors. Homebuilding and remodeling account for two-thirds of U.S. lumber consumption. The price of lumber and plywood is highly correlated with the strength of the U.S. home-building market.

The forest and wood products industry is dominated by Weyerhaeuser Company (ticker symbol WY), which has about $20 billion in annual sales. Weyerhaeuser is a forest products conglomerate that engages not only in growing and harvesting timber, but also in the production and distribution of forest products, real estate development, and construction of single-family homes. Forest products include wood products, pulp and paper, and containerboard. The timberland segment of the business manages 7.2 million acres of company-owned land and 800,000 acres of leased commercial forestlands in North America. The company's Canadian division has renewable, long-term licenses on about 35 million acres of forestland in five Canadian provinces. In order to maximize its long-term yield from its acreage, Weyerhaeuser engages in a number of forest management activities such as extensive planting, suppression of non-merchantable species, thinning, fertilization, and operational pruning.

Lumber futures and options are traded at the CME Group. The CME's lumber futures contract calls for the delivery of 111,000 board feet (one 73 foot rail car) of random length 8 to 12 foot 2 x 4s, the type used in construction. The contract is priced in terms of dollars per thousand board feet.

Prices – CME lumber futures prices (Barchart.com electronic symbol code LS) on the nearest-futures chart in 2014 faded further from the 9-year high of $409.00 per thousand board feet posted in early 2013. Lumber futures fell in the first half of 2014 to a 1-1/2 year low but then recovered somewhat in the second half of 2014 to close the year -8.1% at $331.10 per thousand board feet.

Supply – The U.S. led the world in the production of industrial round wood and in 2013 production rose +0.4% yr/yr to 293.583 million cubic meters, followed by Russia with 180.379 million cubic meters (+1.7% yr/yr) and Canada with 146.741 million cubic meters (unchanged yr/yr). The U.S. also led the world in the production of plywood with 9.680 million cubic meters of production in 2013 (+2.0% yr/yr), followed by Russia with 3.304 million cubic meters (+4.9% yr/yr), and then Japan with 2.761 million cubic meters (+12.3% yr/yr). U.S. softwood lumber production in latest data from the series of 2006 (latest data annualized through November) fell -4.4% yr/yr to 38.503 billion board feet.

Trade – World exports of plywood in 2013 rose by +2.7% yr/yr to 26.060 million cubic meters. The world's largest exporter of plywood is Russia with a 6.7% share of world plywood exports in 2013, followed by Finland (3.5%) and Belgium (1.4%). Russian production of plywood in 2012 (latest data) fell by -1.6% to 1.574 million cubic meters. U.S. exports of plywood accounted for 3.6% of world exports in 2013 and rose by +3.6% yr/yr to 929,000 cubic meters.

World exports of industrial roundwood in 2013 rose by +14.3% yr/yr to 128.444 million cubic meters. Russia was the world's largest exporter of roundwood in 2013 with a 14.8% share of world exports, followed by the U.S. with an 12.8% share, and Canada with a 5.5% share. Russian exports of industrial roundwood in 2013 rose by +7.9% yr/yr to 19.045 million cubic meters. U.S. exports of industrial roundwood in 2013 rose by +16.3% yr/yr to 16.476 million cubic meters.

World Production of Industrial Roundwood by Selected Countries In Thousands of Cubic Meters

Year	Austria	Canada	Czech Republic	Finland	France	Germany	Poland	Romania	Russia	Spain	Sweden	Turkey	United States
2004	12,943	205,273	14,411	49,281	28,187	48,657	29,337	12,794	164,266	14,235	61,400	11,225	418,131
2005	12,786	200,247	14,285	47,116	27,944	50,905	28,531	11,542	167,580	13,351	92,300	11,202	423,456
2006	14,430	181,010	16,333	45,521	28,592	54,000	28,767	9,454	175,500	14,109	58,700	12,253	412,134
2007	16,521	161,390	16,738	51,406	29,817	68,029	32,461	11,572	189,770	12,546	72,300	13,674	378,771
2008	16,772	136,096	14,307	45,965	27,724	46,806	30,470	9,517	149,256	14,427	64,900	14,462	336,895
2009	12,144	113,306	13,769	36,701	29,081	38,987	30,475	8,587	146,310	11,900	59,200	14,252	292,091
2010	13,281	138,802	14,771	45,977	29,634	45,388	31,343	10,548	161,595	10,969	66,300	15,695	283,549
2011	13,631	146,735	13,467	45,526	28,387	45,358	32,200	10,345	175,625	11,528	66,000	16,423	297,653
2012[1]	12,831	146,741	13,041	44,614	24,945	42,863	32,972	11,050	177,455	11,627	63,599	17,701	292,473
2013[2]	12,433	146,741	13,149	49,331	24,451	42,052	33,795	10,092	180,379	12,323	63,000	16,762	293,583

[1] Preliminary.   [2] Estimate.   *Source: Food and Agriculture Organization of the United Nations (FAO)*

Imports of Industrial Roundwood by Selected Countries In Thousands of Cubic Meters

Year	Austria	Belgium	Canada	Finland	France	Germany	Italy	Norway	Poland	Portugal	Spain	Sweden	United States
2004	8,812	2,879	5,961	12,961	2,175	2,227	4,614	2,866	943	364	2,973	9,398	2,437
2005	8,629	3,188	6,274	16,031	2,344	3,005	4,755	3,145	2,009	362	3,640	8,686	3,569
2006	9,102	3,284	5,787	14,655	2,601	3,669	4,486	2,333	1,814	335	3,841	6,664	2,922
2007	8,722	4,094	5,100	12,942	3,181	4,692	4,299	2,539	2,088	746	3,965	7,364	2,242
2008	7,550	3,669	4,608	13,371	2,358	5,758	3,478	1,808	1,868	521	2,860	6,781	1,430
2009	8,036	3,031	4,636	3,761	1,503	4,534	2,703	933	1,874	473	1,868	4,676	696
2010	8,041	4,193	4,745	6,256	1,690	7,656	3,198	1,288	2,289	855	1,839	6,276	816
2011	7,427	4,326	4,275	5,736	1,454	7,005	3,328	1,355	3,419	1,717	2,135	6,724	959
2012[1]	7,319	4,338	4,495	5,457	1,368	6,567	2,802	940	2,469	1,644	1,727	6,855	1,167
2013[2]	8,214	4,507	4,799	6,694	1,241	7,979	2,691	661	2,270	2,428	2,047	7,542	1,021

[1] Preliminary.   [2] Estimate.   *Source: Food and Agricultural Organization of the United Nations (FAO)*

Exports of Industrial Roundwood by Selected Countries In Thousands of Cubic Meters

Year	Canada	Czech Republic	Estonia	France	Germany	Hungary	Latvia	Lithuania	Russia	Slovakia	Sweden	Switzerland	United States
2004	3,899	2,858	2,297	3,851	5,589	1,137	4,136	1,178	41,553	1,142	1,522	1,741	10,402
2005	5,592	2,942	1,806	3,862	6,819	871	3,919	1,131	48,020	1,691	3,095	1,416	9,815
2006	4,640	2,679	1,606	3,695	7,557	1,095	3,419	1,061	50,900	1,218	3,004	1,667	9,638
2007	3,560	2,384	1,502	3,966	7,674	1,054	3,690	1,671	49,100	1,457	3,808	2,005	9,949
2008	2,839	1,906	1,469	3,547	7,037	661	3,193	1,171	36,784	2,192	2,349	1,155	10,200
2009	2,723	2,596	1,080	5,047	3,857	684	2,503	673	21,700	2,538	1,177	575	9,619
2010	4,019	1,743	2,250	6,665	3,726	873	4,158	1,329	20,983	2,434	1,217	796	9,641
2011	5,706	3,487	2,610	6,380	3,658	881	4,401	1,844	20,429	2,533	846	926	9,405
2012[1]	6,094	3,912	2,392	4,571	3,398	858	4,107	1,464	17,652	2,085	794	801	14,169
2013[2]	7,005	4,292	2,747	4,713	3,239	1,072	3,737	1,809	19,045	2,662	915	740	16,476

[1] Preliminary.   [2] Estimate.   *Source: Food and Agricultural Organization of the United Nations (FAO)*

U.S. Housing Starts: Seasonally Adjusted Annual Rate In Thousands

Year	Jan.	Feb.	Mar.	Apr.	May	June	July	Aug.	Sept.	Oct.	Nov.	Dec.	Average
2005	2,144	2,207	1,864	2,061	2,025	2,068	2,054	2,095	2,151	2,065	2,147	1,994	2,073
2006	2,273	2,119	1,969	1,821	1,942	1,802	1,737	1,650	1,720	1,491	1,570	1,649	1,812
2007	1,409	1,480	1,495	1,490	1,415	1,448	1,354	1,330	1,183	1,264	1,197	1,037	1,342
2008	1,084	1,103	1,005	1,013	973	1,046	923	844	820	777	652	560	900
2009	490	582	505	478	540	585	594	586	585	534	588	581	554
2010	614	604	636	687	583	536	546	599	594	543	545	539	586
2011	630	517	600	554	561	608	623	585	650	610	711	694	612
2012	723	704	695	753	708	757	740	754	847	915	833	976	784
2013	896	951	994	848	915	831	898	885	863	936	1,105	1,034	930
2014[1]	897	928	950	1,063	984	909	1,098	963	1,028	1,092	1,015	1,081	1,001

[1] Preliminary.   Total Privately owned.   *Source: Bureau of the Census, U.S. Department of Commerce*

LUMBER AND PLYWOOD

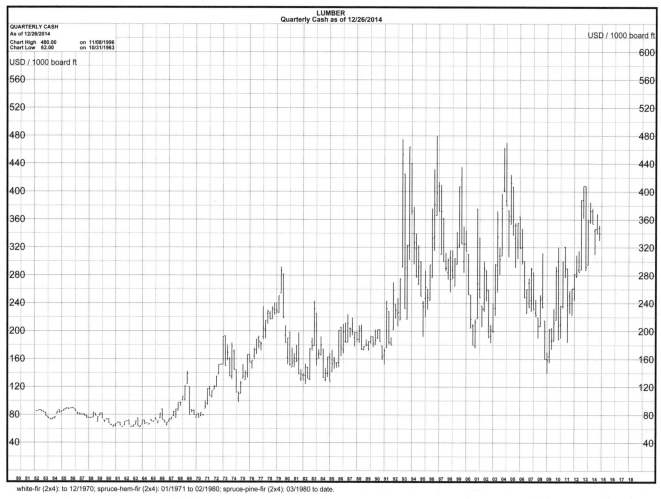

LUMBER
Quarterly Cash as of 12/26/2014

QUARTERLY CASH
As of 12/26/2014

Chart High 480.00   on 11/08/1996
Chart Low   62.00   on 10/31/1963

USD / 1000 board ft

white-fir (2x4): to 12/1970; spruce-hem-fir (2x4): 01/1971 to 02/1980; spruce-pine-fir (2x4): 03/1980 to date.

Average Price of Lumber in the United States   In Dollars per Thousand Board Feet

Year	Jan.	Feb.	Mar.	Apr.	May	June	July	Aug.	Sept.	Oct.	Nov.	Dec.	Average
2005	366.25	412.25	415.25	379.80	351.50	358.50	337.40	303.00	341.80	311.00	328.25	341.40	353.87
2006	357.00	344.50	329.40	332.50	320.75	298.60	291.75	271.25	271.60	238.00	242.75	251.60	295.81
2007	259.25	255.00	243.20	242.00	246.25	282.00	273.50	265.60	239.00	223.75	240.20	226.50	249.69
2008	206.50	203.00	200.50	214.25	238.20	244.00	259.50	283.40	247.25	194.40	180.75	164.50	219.69
2009	150.60	158.00	154.75	166.00	161.80	193.00	185.00	200.25	186.25	191.00	210.00	223.67	181.69
2010	238.50	287.00	281.50	312.00	272.50	207.50	203.40	219.75	231.75	245.80	275.33	283.80	254.90
2011	307.25	286.25	294.25	269.50	227.25	222.75	254.50	231.75	250.80	236.50	230.25	248.00	254.92
2012	253.50	262.67	280.75	281.25	305.50	300.00	294.25	310.20	292.33	298.00	339.50	370.00	299.00
2013	382.25	377.33	401.50	386.60	325.50	298.40	312.25	326.00	346.75	360.25	381.80	364.25	355.24
2014	373.20	364.00	362.75	339.00	342.00	323.75	351.50	361.00	355.25	347.00	333.75	337.75	349.25

Source: National Agricultural Statistics Service, U.S. Department of Agriculture (NASS-USDA)

Average Price of Plywood in the United States   In Dollars per Thousand Board Feet

Year	Jan.	Feb.	Mar.	Apr.	May	June	July	Aug.	Sept.	Oct.	Nov.	Dec.	Average
2005	317.50	387.00	387.50	321.00	291.00	301.25	255.80	252.50	380.20	388.25	274.75	295.00	320.98
2006	304.25	277.50	275.20	258.00	236.75	221.80	185.75	179.75	138.39	169.00	171.50	158.80	214.72
2007	145.50	148.00	141.40	149.75	148.25	169.00	191.00	176.20	164.25	165.50	177.60	149.00	160.45
2008	139.25	132.20	141.50	143.25	185.60	204.75	189.50	212.80	197.50	177.60	173.25	158.75	171.33
2009	151.00	163.00	150.75	148.00	140.80	153.75	174.00	186.00	176.50	158.00	171.25	186.33	163.28
2010	191.50	220.00	233.00	353.75	330.00	206.25	217.20	171.25	164.50	183.00	189.33	196.40	221.35
2011	210.75	196.75	189.25	178.25	167.25	180.25	171.25	192.25	188.60	190.75	185.00	192.00	186.86
2012	201.00	194.67	213.25	212.50	233.75	252.00	257.50	331.00	343.33	300.00	343.75	354.50	269.77
2013	401.50	412.67	430.00	410.00	354.33	279.25	256.25	254.40	244.75	263.00	244.00	227.75	314.83
2014	226.60	215.00	214.50	210.33	233.00	210.25	212.25	215.40	222.00	222.00	219.00	204.00	217.03

Source: National Agricultural Statistics Service, U.S. Department of Agriculture (NASS-USDA)

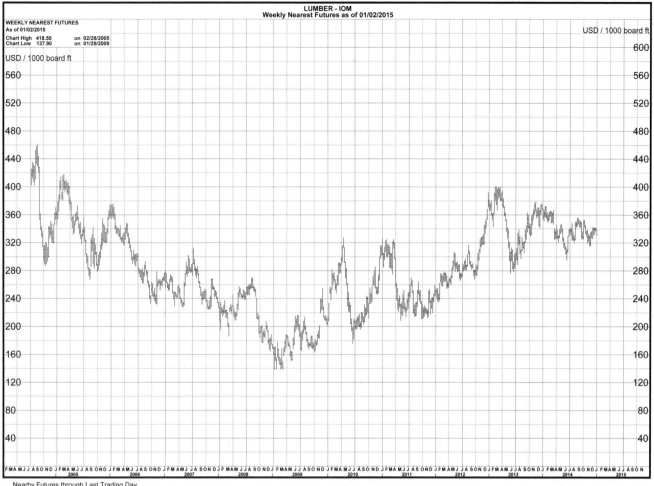

LUMBER - IOM
Weekly Nearest Futures as of 01/02/2015

WEEKLY NEAREST FUTURES
As of 01/02/2015

Chart High 418.50 on 02/28/2005
Chart Low 137.90 on 01/29/2009

USD / 1000 board ft

USD / 1000 board ft

Nearby Futures through Last Trading Day.

Volume of Trading of Random Lumber Futures in Chicago   In Contracts

Year	Jan.	Feb.	Mar.	Apr.	May	June	July	Aug.	Sept.	Oct.	Nov.	Dec.	Total
2005	20,838	20,257	24,595	20,360	17,338	17,115	16,244	19,590	22,895	15,896	23,404	17,709	236,241
2006	26,803	19,152	18,504	21,358	21,619	23,959	21,568	23,800	22,618	24,804	22,385	24,454	271,024
2007	26,214	28,328	24,741	26,433	31,540	28,545	23,462	28,610	24,841	33,876	29,738	28,361	334,689
2008	31,401	43,338	37,899	50,586	37,909	38,362	41,612	40,693	32,155	36,226	20,277	27,155	437,613
2009	18,478	29,930	22,193	25,349	24,351	34,027	24,340	29,548	22,271	33,768	21,817	31,155	317,227
2010	25,483	26,365	20,928	32,393	24,763	29,446	18,360	24,660	26,107	31,689	23,662	28,046	311,902
2011	22,691	25,642	25,141	32,161	20,134	30,740	18,440	32,615	28,562	26,650	22,589	33,968	319,333
2012	20,678	33,593	25,208	30,526	24,563	26,638	23,663	32,211	19,595	31,797	24,513	31,538	324,523
2013	26,219	29,842	18,671	26,472	23,349	19,914	18,572	18,118	19,271	17,021	11,100	15,073	243,622
2014	13,001	14,025	12,632	14,563	13,365	17,276	10,119	14,977	11,766	16,481	8,933	13,333	160,471

Contract size = 110,000 board feet.   *Source: CME Group; Chicago Mercantile Exchange (CME)*

Average Open Interest of Random Lumber Futures in Chicago   In Contracts

Year	Jan.	Feb.	Mar.	Apr.	May	June	July	Aug.	Sept.	Oct.	Nov.	Dec.
2005	3,759	5,169	5,040	4,705	3,463	3,576	3,401	4,227	3,913	3,883	4,713	5,202
2006	5,893	5,144	4,084	4,959	4,586	5,449	5,317	6,429	5,912	6,351	6,121	7,018
2007	6,466	7,807	7,684	8,680	7,726	8,206	7,130	7,666	6,493	9,356	8,960	9,731
2008	9,827	13,134	13,385	14,637	14,801	14,275	14,417	14,016	12,110	9,466	7,744	8,084
2009	7,912	7,937	6,852	7,732	7,815	9,039	7,910	8,873	9,248	9,593	10,174	9,557
2010	9,674	10,231	9,538	10,571	8,358	9,402	8,675	9,498	8,812	9,707	9,620	10,018
2011	11,235	10,223	9,471	9,813	10,090	10,408	9,233	10,170	9,465	10,314	9,663	10,768
2012	9,261	10,228	10,192	9,962	9,226	7,885	7,666	9,259	8,153	8,275	10,713	10,624
2013	9,354	8,222	8,609	7,345	5,872	6,726	5,816	5,539	5,699	4,816	4,672	4,086
2014	3,945	4,602	4,618	5,020	4,422	5,013	4,080	4,419	3,751	3,698	4,610	4,289

Contract size = 110,000 board feet.   *Source: CME Group; Chicago Mercantile Exchange (CME)*

LUMBER AND PLYWOOD

Production of Plywood by Selected Countries   In Thousands of Cubic Meters

Year	Austria	Canada	Finland	France	Germany	Italy	Japan	Poland	Romania	Russia	Spain	Sweden	United States
2004	186	2,344	1,350	435	283	485	3,149	342	117	2,246	375	71	14,833
2005	195	2,322	1,305	415	236	390	3,212	361	126	2,556	557	92	14,449
2006	178	2,252	1,415	431	235	334	3,314	385	188	2,614	468	92	13,651
2007	258	2,639	1,410	378	229	420	3,073	440	107	2,777	450	72	12,402
2008	268	2,225	1,273	360	174	421	2,586	391	152	2,592	250	56	10,376
2009	163	1,810	800	265	193	337	2,287	312	212	2,107	233	65	8,934
2010	273	2,005	980	271	232	310	2,645	402	266	2,689	267	60	9,397
2011	216	1,794	1,010	258	218	310	2,486	411	331	3,040	299	84	9,365
2012[1]	216	1,824	1,020	324	178	280	2,459	388	472	3,150	255	53	9,493
2013[2]	216	1,792	1,090	271	161	225	2,761	430	665	3,304	275	53	9,680

[1] Preliminary.   [2] Estimate.   *Source: Food and Agricultural Organization of the United Nations (FAO)*

Imports of Plywood by Selected Countries   In Thousands of Cubic Meters

Year	Austria	Belgium	Canada	Denmark	France	Germany	Italy	Japan	Nether- lands	Sweden	Switzer- land	United Kingdom	United States
2004	144	624	350	413	383	1,214	581	5,122	542	164	140	1,474	5,900
2005	140	521	690	371	411	1,142	532	4,732	526	189	145	1,456	6,181
2006	140	610	685	280	445	1,314	575	5,046	603	197	128	1,497	6,393
2007	172	672	1,827	358	459	1,516	588	4,064	608	240	126	1,624	4,397
2008	133	633	2,149	402	581	1,459	530	3,583	635	192	131	1,486	3,059
2009	116	527	861	229	397	1,066	417	2,948	457	144	53	1,164	2,647
2010	155	544	1,909	219	544	1,288	485	3,255	495	152	68	1,264	2,551
2011	196	593	1,554	262	492	1,423	463	3,809	620	185	74	1,330	2,632
2012[1]	209	533	1,621	270	374	1,336	420	3,645	476	173	86	1,285	3,113
2013[2]	145	537	1,458	266	367	1,338	428	3,765	399	155	99	1,374	3,184

[1] Preliminary.   [2] Estimate.   *Source: Food and Agricultural Organization of the United Nations (FAO)*

Exports of Plywood by Selected Countries   In Thousands of Cubic Meters

Year	Austria	Baltic States	Belgium	Canada	Finland	France	Germany	Italy	Nether- lands	Poland	Russia	Spain	United States
2004	265	255	474	1,027	1,234	192	265	201	46	171	1,438	114	525
2005	287	253	423	1,118	1,173	196	287	146	40	177	1,527	117	503
2006	311	282	470	950	1,250	225	321	239	60	137	1,577	124	492
2007	285	318	386	964	1,229	227	368	295	55	148	1,503	162	443
2008	278	197	470	583	1,083	275	342	184	51	133	1,326	213	506
2009	278	211	374	306	683	162	277	148	49	117	1,334	122	529
2010	304	289	440	301	833	163	337	218	50	133	1,512	141	871
2011	353	302	437	359	863	127	355	228	63	141	1,600	165	837
2012[1]	334	310	368	287	855	143	298	201	89	169	1,575	152	914
2013[2]	339	312	369	426	920	141	293	192	71	181	1,758	169	929

[1] Preliminary.   [2] Estimate.   *Source: Food and Agricultural Organization of the United Nations (FAO)*

Magnesium

Magnesium (atomic symbol Mg) is a silvery-white, light, and fairly tough, metallic element and is relatively stable. Magnesium is one of the alkaline earth metals. Magnesium is the eighth most abundant element in the earth's crust and the third most plentiful element found in seawater. Magnesium is ductile and malleable when heated, and with the exception of beryllium, is the lightest metal that remains stable under ordinary conditions. First isolated by the British chemist Sir Humphrey Davy in 1808, magnesium today is obtained mainly by electrolysis of fused magnesium chloride.

Magnesium compounds, primarily magnesium oxide, are used in the refractory material that line the furnaces used to produce iron and steel, nonferrous metals, glass, and cement. Magnesium oxide and other compounds are also used in the chemical, agricultural, and construction industries. Magnesium's principal use is as an alloying addition for aluminum. These aluminum-magnesium alloys are used primarily in beverage cans. Due to their lightness and considerable tensile strength, the alloys are also used in structural components in airplanes and automobiles.

Prices – The average price of magnesium in 2014 fell -2.1% to $2.04 per pound, well below the 2008 record high of $3.38 per pound.

Supply – World primary production of magnesium in 2014 rose +3.4% yr/yr to 907,000 metric tons, a new record high. The current level of magnesium production has more than tripled since the mid-1970s when 1976's production was 249,367 metric tons.

The world's largest primary producers of magnesium in 2012 were China with 800,000 metric tons, Russia with 28,000 metric tons, and Israel with 30,000 metric tons. The U.S. production amount is not available because it is considered proprietary data but is probably less than about 50,000 metric tons. China's production has increased over the past 10 years from 70,500 metric tons in 1998 to a new record high of 800,000 metric tons in 2014. By 2006 Canada's production had grown by more than seven-fold from the mid-1980s, but that fell sharply in 2007 to 16,300 metric tons and down to 2,000 in 2008.

Demand – Total U.S. consumption of primary magnesium in 2012 (latest data available) rose +10.2% to 59,200 from 53,700 metric tons. U.S. consumption of magnesium for structural products in 2012 fell -52.9% yr/yr to 12,681 metric tons. Of the structural product consumption category, 84.9% was for castings and the remaining 15.1% was for wrought products. U.S. consumption of magnesium for aluminum alloys fell -7.5% yr/yr in 2012 to 23,500 metric tons. The consumption of magnesium for other uses rose +26.2% yr/yr in 2012 to 35,700 metric tons.

Trade – U.S. exports of magnesium in 2014 rose +11.8% yr/yr to 18,000 metric tons, well above the 2005 record low of 9,650 metric tons. U.S. imports of magnesium in 2014 rose +19.8% yr/yr to 55,000 metric tons.

World Production of Magnesium (Primary)   In Metric Tons

Year	Brazil	Canada	China	Israel	Kazakhstan	Russia	Serbia	Ukraine	United States	Total
2009	16,000	----	501,000	19,405	21,000	29,000	----	2,000	W	588,000
2010	16,000	----	654,000	23,309	21,000	29,000	----	2,000	W	745,000
2011	16,000	----	661,000	26,284	21,000	29,000	----	2,000	W	755,000
2012	16,000	----	698,000	27,292	21,000	20,000	----	2,000	W	787,000
2013[1]	16,000	----	770,000	28,000	23,000	32,000	----	----	W	877,000
2014[2]	16,000	----	800,000	30,000	21,000	28,000	----	----	W	907,000

[1] Preliminary.   [2] Estimate.   W = Withheld.   *Source: U.S. Geological Survey (USGS)*

Salient Statistics of Magnesium in the United States   In Metric Tons

Year	Production Primary (Ingot)	Production Secondary New Scrap	Production Secondary Old Scrap	Total	Total Exports[3]	Imports for Consumption	Stocks Dec. 31[4]	Price $ Per Pound[5]	Domestic Consumption of Primary Magnesium Structural Products Castings	Domestic Consumption of Primary Magnesium Structural Products Wrought	Total	Aluminum Alloys	Other Uses	Total
2009	W	48,100	20,500	68,600	19,600	47,300	W	2.30	19,617	1,090	20,707	23,000	7,200	30,200
2010	W	51,300	20,500	72,000	14,800	52,700	W	2.43	20,187	2,120	22,307	23,800	9,600	33,400
2011	W	43,100	24,100	67,200	12,300	48,400	W	2.13	23,191	3,720	26,911	25,400	28,300	53,700
2012	W	52,000	25,200	77,100	18,300	50,800	W	2.20	10,761	1,920	12,681	23,500	35,700	59,200
2013[1]	W	54,000	25,100	79,100	16,100	45,900	W	2.13						
2014[2]	W			82,000	18,000	55,000	W	2.15						

[1] Preliminary.   [2] Estimate.   [3] Metal & alloys in crude form & scrap.   [4] Estimate of Industry Stocks, metal.   [5] Magnesium ingots (99.8%), f.o.b. Valasco, Texas.   [6] Distributive or sacrificial purposes.   W = Withheld proprietary data.   *Source: U.S. Geological Survey (USGS)*

Average Price of Magnesium   In Dollars Per Pound

Year	Jan.	Feb.	Mar.	Apr.	May	June	July	Aug.	Sept.	Oct.	Nov.	Dec.	Average
2010	2.43	2.65	2.65	2.68	2.65	2.65	2.67	2.66	2.63	2.60	2.55	2.55	2.61
2011	2.55	2.53	2.53	2.53	2.53	2.58	2.42	2.40	2.40	2.22	2.19	2.20	2.42
2012	2.14	2.13	2.13	2.13	2.15	2.15	2.15	2.15	2.15	2.15	2.15	2.15	2.14
2013	2.13	2.13	2.13	2.07	2.05	2.07	2.07	2.03	2.05	2.08	2.08	2.08	2.08
2014	2.08	2.06	2.05	2.05	2.05	2.03	2.02	2.02	2.02	2.02	2.02	2.02	2.04

Source: American Metal Market (AMM)

Manganese

Manganese (atomic symbol Mn) is a silvery-white, very brittle, metallic element used primarily in making alloys. Manganese was first distinguished as an element and isolated in 1774 by Johan Gottlieb Gahn. Manganese dissolves in acid and corrodes in moist air.

Manganese is found in the earth's crust in the form of ores such as rhodochrosite, franklinite, psilomelane, and manganite. Pyrolusite is the principal ore of manganese. Pure manganese is produced by igniting pyrolusite with aluminum powder or by electrolyzing manganese sulfate.

Manganese is used primarily in the steel industry for creating alloys, the most important ones being ferromanganese and spiegeleisen. In steel, manganese improves forging and rolling qualities, strength, toughness, stiffness, wear resistance, and hardness. Manganese is also used in plant fertilizers, animal feed, pigments, and dry cell batteries.

Prices – The average monthly price of ferromanganese (high carbon, FOB plant) in 2014 fell by -0.4% yr/yr to $1.059.90 per gross ton, well below the 2008 record high of $2,953.84 per gross ton. The 2014 price, however, is still about two times the 25-year low price of $447.44 per gross ton posted as recently as 2001.

Supply – World production of manganese ore in 2012 (latest data available) rose by +0.4% to a record high of 47.100 million metric tons. The world's largest producers of manganese ore are China with 30.8% of world production in 2012, South Africa with 19.0%, Australia with 16.0%, Gabon with 7.7%, and the India with 4.7%. China's production in 2012 rose by +3.6% yr/yr to 14.500 million metric tons.

Demand – U.S. consumption of manganese ore in 2014 fell -4.4% to 500,000 metric tons. U.S. consumption of ferromanganese in 2014 rose +0.5% yr/yr to 370,000 metric tons, a new record high. The 2014 figure is about 25% of the U.S. consumption in the early 1970s.

Trade – The U.S. still relies on imports for 100% of its manganese consumption, as it has since 1985. U.S. imports of manganese ore for consumption in 2014 fell -21.7% yr/yr to 430,000 metric tons, up from 2009's 18-year low of 269,000 metric tons. U.S. imports of ferromanganese for consumption in 2014 rose +8.8% yr/yr to 360,000 metric tons. U.S. imports of silico-manganese in 2014 rose +36.8% yr/yr to 450,000 metric tons, up from 2009's 27-year low of 130,000 metric tons. The primary sources of U.S. imports of manganese ore in 2012 (latest data) were Gabon with 67.3% imports and South Africa with 20.5%.

World Production of Manganese Ore — In Thousands of Metric Tons (Gross Weight)

Year	Australia[2] 37-53[4]	Brazil 37[4]	China 20-30[4]	Gabon 45-53[4]	Georgia[5] 29-30[4]	Ghana 32-34[4]	India 10-54[4]	Kazakhstan[5] 29-30[4]	Mexico 27-50[4]	South Africa 30-48+[4]	Ukraine[5] 30-35[4]	Other	World Total
2003	2,564	2,544	4,600	2,000	----	1,509	1,650	2,361	320	3,501	2,591	547	24,200
2004	3,431	3,143	5,500	2,460	----	1,597	1,776	2,318	377	4,282	2,362	656	27,900
2005	3,136	3,200	7,500	2,859	----	1,715	2,386	2,208	369	4,612	2,260	745	31,000
2006	4,556	3,390	8,000	3,000	----	1,659	2,084	2,531	346	5,213	1,606	752	33,100
2007	5,289	1,570	10,000	3,300	----	1,854	2,016	1,003	423	5,996	1,720	1,270	34,500
2008	4,812	3,200	11,000	3,248	----	914	2,293	1,117	472	6,807	1,447	1,700	37,900
2009	4,451	2,575	12,000	1,992	----	882	2,347	982	330	4,579	932	1,660	33,800
2010	6,474	3,215	13,000	3,201	----	1,529	2,858	1,094	485	7,172	1,589	1,850	44,100
2011	6,963	3,480	14,000	4,070	----	1,729	2,542	1,096	468	8,652	972	1,720	46,900
2012[1]	7,531	3,330	14,500	3,637	----	1,244	2,225	1,056	515	8,943	1,039	1,650	47,100

[1] Preliminary. [2] Metallurgical Ore. [3] Concentrate. [4] Ranges of percentage of manganese. *Source: U.S. Geological Survey (USGS)*

Salient Statistics of Manganese in the United States — In Thousands of Metric Tons (Gross Weight)

Year	Net Import Reliance As a % of Apparent Consump	Manganese Ore (35% or More Manganese) Imports for Consumption	Exports	Consumption	Stocks Dec. 31[3]	Ferromanganese Imports for Consumption	Exports	Consumption	Avg Price Mn. Metallurgical Ore $/Lg. Ton Unit[4]	Silicomanganese Exports	Imports
2005	100	656	13	368	337	255	14	286	4.39	0.9	327.0
2006	100	572	2	365	153	358	22	297	3.22	0.9	400.0
2007	100	602	29	351	190	315	29	272	3.10	3.3	414.0
2008	100	571	48	464	255	448	23	304	12.15	7.1	365.0
2009	100	269	15	422	115	153	24	242	7.95	18.8	130.0
2010	100	489	14	450	168	326	19	292	9.64	9.4	297.0
2011	100	552	1	532	250	348	5	303	7.88	8.5	348.0
2012	100	506	2	538	203	401	5	382	6.04	5.9	348.0
2013[1]	100	549	1	523	217	331	2	368	6.00	6.0	329.0
2014[2]	100	430	1	500	200	360	7	370		2.0	450.0

[1] Preliminary. [2] Estimate. [3] Including bonded warehouses; excludes Gov't stocks; also excludes small tonnages of dealers' stocks.
[4] 46-48% Mn, C.I.F. U.S. Ports. *Source: U.S. Geological Survey (USGS)*

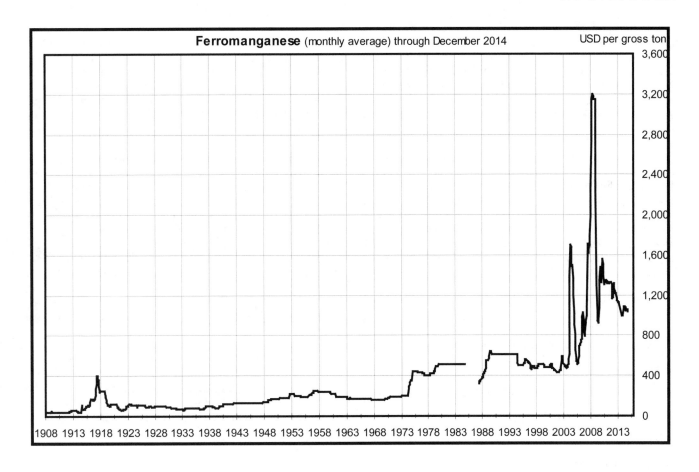

Ferromanganese (monthly average) through December 2014   USD per gross ton

Imports[3] of Manganese Ore (20% or More Mn) in the United States   In Metric Tons (Mn Content)

Year	Australia	Brazil	Gabon	Mexico	Morocco	South Africa	Total	Customs Value ($1,000)
2003	12,900	7	123,000	1,520	----	36,900	175,000	27,000
2004	27,700	----	188,000	1,640	----	13,200	234,000	37,700
2005	21,300	7,020	252,000	4,320	----	33,100	334,000	58,200
2006	12,800	5,800	120,000	1,320	----	91,200	270,000	53,900
2007	34,900	20,000	170,000	3,670	----	53,600	298,000	57,600
2008	51,900	34,400	181,000	----	----	14,600	289,000	154,000
2009	15,400	1,540	96,500	671	9	----	154,000	82,600
2010	65,200	3,440	125,000	1,050	791	40,100	255,000	133,000
2011[1]	70,500	4,750	183,000	1,640	454	5,530	266,000	145,000
2012[2]	15,000	3,970	152,000	2,200	2,670	46,400	226,000	101,000

[1] Preliminary.   [2] Estimate.   [3] Imports for consumption.   *Source: U.S. Geological Survey (USGS)*

Average Price of Ferromanganese[1]   In Dollars Per Gross Ton -- Carloads

Year	Jan.	Feb.	Mar.	Apr.	May	June	July	Aug.	Sept.	Oct.	Nov.	Dec.	Average
2005	904.50	818.68	739.46	651.67	586.19	547.39	528.13	512.07	522.14	550.24	597.75	694.05	637.69
2006	707.25	712.50	737.50	759.00	764.55	870.23	987.50	1,025.00	1,021.25	946.25	836.25	790.00	846.44
2007	834.29	930.00	949.55	1,000.00	1,074.43	1,633.33	1,705.00	1,620.00	1,620.00	1,656.96	1,700.00	1,785.53	1,375.76
2008	1,978.57	2,262.75	2,734.29	3,145.45	3,200.00	3,200.00	3,175.00	3,150.00	3,150.00	3,150.00	3,150.00	3,150.00	2,953.84
2009	2,225.00	1,300.00	1,300.00	1,038.10	950.00	928.18	955.45	1,071.43	1,344.52	1,481.67	1,431.84	1,365.26	1,282.62
2010	1,326.58	1,387.50	1,530.43	1,559.09	1,507.00	1,389.09	1,310.00	1,320.45	1,327.38	1,345.00	1,345.00	1,345.00	1,391.04
2011	1,336.25	1,320.00	1,320.00	1,327.62	1,321.43	1,315.00	1,315.00	1,327.39	1,330.00	1,330.00	1,330.00	1,303.95	1,323.05
2012	1,171.50	1,179.38	1,285.23	1,317.86	1,280.68	1,263.34	1,238.45	1,220.33	1,214.48	1,202.39	1,171.25	1,144.58	1,224.12
2013	1,140.00	1,128.16	1,128.81	1,121.14	1,076.94	1,071.25	1,037.50	1,037.50	1,031.88	1,000.00	1,000.00	1,000.00	1,064.43
2014	1,006.19	1,066.50	1,088.58	1,090.00	1,080.00	1,078.22	1,041.25	1,060.00	1,053.34	1,055.22	1,060.00	1,039.53	1,059.90

[1] Domestic standard, high carbon, FOB plant, carloads.   *Source: American Metal Market (AMM)*

Meats

U.S. commercial red meat includes beef, veal, lamb, and pork. Red meat is a good source of iron, vitamin B12, and protein, and eliminating it from the diet can lead to iron and zinc deficiencies. Today, red meat is far leaner than it was 30 years ago due to newer breeds of livestock that carry less fat. The leanest cuts of beef include tenderloin, sirloin, and flank. The leanest cuts of pork include pork tenderloin, loin chops, and rib chops.

The USDA (United States Department of Agriculture) grades various cuts of meat. "Prime" is the highest USDA grade for beef, veal, and lamb. "Choice" is the grade designation below Prime for beef, veal, and lamb. "Commercial" and "Cutter" grades are two of the lower designations for beef, usually sold as ground meat, sausage, and canned meat. "Canner" is the lowest USDA grade designation for beef and is used primarily in canned meats not sold at retail.

Supply – World meat production in 2015 is expected to rise +0.2% to a new record high of 170.584 million metric tons. China is projected to be the world's largest meat producer in 2015 with 63.750 million metric tons of production (up +1.2% yr/yr), accounting for 37.2% of world production.

U.S. production of meat in 2014 is expected to fall -2.3% yr/yr to 48.135 billion pounds, below the 2008 record high of 50.362 billion pounds. U.S. production of beef in 2015 is expected to fall -1.7% yr/yr to 23.830 billion pounds, which will be just moderately below the record high of 27.192 billion pounds in 2002. Beef accounted for 50.4% of all U.S. meat production. U.S. production of pork in 2015 is expected to rise +4.6% yr/yr to 23.895, a new record high. Pork accounts for 47.5% of U.S. meat production. Veal accounts for only 0.3% of U.S. meat production, and lamb and mutton account for only 0.4% of U.S. meat production.

Demand – U.S. per capita meat consumption in 2014 is expected to fall by -2.8% yr/yr to 101.5 pounds per person per year, below the 2006-07 record low of 117.5 pounds per person reflecting the trend towards eating more chicken and fish and the availability of meat substitutes. Per capita beef consumption in 2015 is expected to fall -3.0% yr/yr to 52.7 pounds per person per year, which was about half the record high of 127.5 pounds seen in 1976. Per capita pork consumption in 2015 is expected to rise +1.3% yr/yr to 47.1 pounds per person per year, and remain above the 2011 record low of 45.7 pounds. Per capita consumption of veal is negligible at 0.4 pounds per person and lamb/mutton consumption is also negligible at 0.8 pound per person.

Trade – World red meat exports in 2015 are expected to rise +2.6% to 17.139 million metric tons, a new record high. The world's largest red meat exporters will be the U.S. with 20.6% of world exports expected in 2015, Brazil with 17.1%, European Union with 14.3%, India with 11.4%, Australia with 9.5%, and Canada with 9.0%.

World Total Meat Production[4]   In Thousands of Metric Tons

Year	Argentina	Australia	Brazil	Canada	China[4]	European Union	India	Mexico	New Zealand	Russia	South Africa	United States	World Total
2006	3,362	2,571	11,855	3,077	52,272	30,276	2,450	2,659	699	2,894	898	21,539	153,472
2007	3,576	2,554	12,293	3,024	49,012	31,233	2,490	2,752	658	3,070	869	22,059	152,760
2008	3,424	2,483	12,039	3,090	52,337	30,852	2,700	2,828	695	3,226	861	22,762	156,595
2009	3,669	2,430	12,065	3,033	55,263	29,933	2,950	2,867	671	3,304	866	22,333	158,484
2010	2,899	2,468	12,310	3,055	57,243	30,728	3,125	2,920	690	3,416	1,031	22,232	161,520
2011	2,831	2,473	12,257	2,953	57,079	31,067	3,308	3,006	651	3,424	1,029	22,314	161,782
2012	2,951	2,504	12,637	2,900	60,050	30,234	3,491	3,060	674	3,555	1,031	22,402	165,538
2013	3,266	2,719	12,955	2,868	61,630	29,726	3,800	3,089	670	3,780	1,033	22,276	168,298
2014[1]	3,270	2,875	13,264	2,880	63,025	29,875	4,100	3,040	695	4,040	1,033	21,455	170,204
2015[2]	3,335	2,705	13,709	2,870	63,750	29,840	4,250	3,055	700	4,220	1,033	21,726	170,584

[1] Preliminary. [2] Forecast. [3] Data through 2000, includes beef, veal, pork, sheep and goat meat. Beginning 2001, excludes sheep and goat.
[4] Predominately pork production. *Source: Foreign Agricultural Service, U.S. Department of Agriculture (FAS-USDA)*

Production and Consumption of Red Meats in The United States

	Beef Commercial Production - Million Pounds -	Beef Consumption Total	Beef Consumption Per Capita Lbs.	Veal Commercial Production - Million Pounds -	Veal Consumption Total	Veal Consumption Per Capita Lbs.	Lamb & Mutton Commercial Production - Million Pounds -	Lamb & Mutton Consumption Total	Lamb & Mutton Consumption Per Capita Lbs.	Pork (Excluding Lard) Commercial Production - Million Pounds -	Pork Consumption Total	Pork Consumption Per Capita Lbs.	All Meats Commercial Production - Million Pounds -	All Meats Consumption Total	All Meats Consumption Per Capita Lbs.
Year															
2005	24,787	27,754	66.0	165	164	0.6	191	355	1.0	20,705	19,112	50.0	45,848	47,385	117.0
2006	26,256	28,137	65.9	156	155	0.4	190	356	1.1	21,074	19,055	49.4	47,675	47,703	116.8
2007	26,523	28,141	65.2	146	145	0.4	189	385	1.1	21,962	19,763	50.8	48,820	48,434	117.5
2008	26,664	27,194	62.5	152	150	0.4	180	343	1.0	23,367	19,431	49.5	50,362	47,118	113.3
2009	26,068	26,836	61.1	147	147	0.4	177	338	1.0	23,020	19,870	50.1	49,412	47,191	112.6
2010	26,304	26,390	59.6	145	150	0.4	168	317	0.9	22,437	19,077	47.8	49,183	45,935	108.6
2011	26,195	25,538	57.3	136	137	0.4	153	295	0.8	22,758	18,382	45.7	49,358	44,370	104.3
2012	25,913	25,755	57.4	125	123	0.3	161	299	0.8	23,253	18,607	45.9	49,553	44,787	104.5
2013[1]	25,720	25,475	56.3	118	119	0.3	161	324	0.9	23,187	19,095	46.8	49,296	45,044	104.4
2014[2]	24,249	24,440	54.3							22,852	19,177	46.5	48,135	44,042	101.5

[1] Preliminary. [2] Estimate. [3] Forecast. *Source: Economic Research Service, U.S. Department of Agriculture (ERS-USDA)*

Total Red Meat Imports[3] (Carcass Weight Equivalent) of Principal Countries   In Thousands of Metric Tons

Year	Brazil	Canada	European Union	Egypt	Hong Kong	Japan	Korea, South	Mexico	Philip-pines	Russia	Taiwan	United States	World Total
2006	28	326	292	845	366	1,832	708	829	162	1,922	128	1,848	11,754
2007	30	412	293	683	391	1,896	755	854	196	2,032	120	1,823	12,242
2008	29	424	166	528	464	1,926	725	943	238	2,334	141	1,528	13,069
2009	35	427	180	547	523	1,835	705	1,000	233	1,929	182	1,569	12,130
2010	36	426	260	467	501	1,919	748	983	292	1,974	188	1,432	12,547
2011	41	486	217	384	584	1,999	1,071	859	284	1,965	188	1,297	13,035
2012	63	542	250	369	655	1,996	872	921	273	2,077	148	1,371	13,568
2013	60	516	195	391	872	1,983	763	1,015	317	1,886	170	1,419	14,103
2014[1]	66	490	240	372	1,000	2,070	850	1,050	345	1,285	195	1,648	14,121
2015[2]	76	495	260	365	1,110	2,015	890	1,070	360	1,200	210	1,633	14,372

[1] Preliminary.   [2] Forecast.   [3] Data through 2000, includes beef, veal, pork, sheep and goat meat. Beginning 2001, excludes sheep and goat.
Source: Foreign Agricultural Service, U.S. Department of Agriculture (FAS-USDA)

Total Red Meat Exports[3] (Carcass Weight Equivalent) of Principal Countries   In Thousands of Metric Tons

Year	Argentina	Australia	Brazil	Canada	China	Denmark	France	India	Ireland	Nether-lands	New Zealand	United States	World Total
2006	553	1,490	2,723	1,558	629	1,461	681	530	8	24	1,878	461	12,815
2007	506	1,454	2,919	1,490	431	1,381	678	496	8	52	2,075	386	12,780
2008	398	1,455	2,426	1,623	281	1,878	672	533	11	24	3,015	361	13,764
2009	623	1,404	2,303	1,603	270	1,506	609	514	9	27	2,735	376	13,066
2010	278	1,409	2,177	1,682	329	2,042	917	530	6	20	2,958	347	13,826
2011	214	1,451	1,924	1,623	299	2,595	1,268	503	8	35	3,619	320	15,029
2012	165	1,443	2,185	1,578	277	2,461	1,411	517	18	52	3,552	360	15,406
2013	187	1,629	2,434	1,578	274	2,476	1,765	529	13	41	3,439	338	16,163
2014[1]	191	1,812	2,615	1,545	306	2,405	1,850	570	11	30	3,500	385	16,711
2015[2]	201	1,627	2,935	1,535	332	2,445	1,950	575	11	31	3,526	435	17,139

[1] Preliminary.   [2] Forecast.   [3] Data through 2000, includes beef, veal, pork, sheep and goat meat. Beginning 2001, excludes sheep and goat.
Source: Foreign Agricultural Service, U.S. Department of Agriculture (FAS-USDA)

Exports and Imports of Meats in the United States (Carcass Weight Equivalent)[3]

	Exports				Imports			
Year	Beef and Veal	Lamb and Mutton	Pork[3]	All Meat	Beef and Veal	Lamb and Mutton	Pork[3]	All Meat
2006	1,145	18	2,995	4,158	3,085	190	990	4,265
2007	1,434	9	3,141	4,585	3,052	203	968	4,223
2008	1,996	12	4,667	6,660	2,538	183	832	3,553
2009	1,935	16	4,126	6,045	2,626	171	834	3,631
2010	2,299	16	4,223	6,539	2,297	166	859	3,322
2011	2,785	----	5,196	7,981	2,057	162	803	3,022
2012	2,452	----	5,380	7,832	2,220	154	802	3,176
2013	2,590	----	4,992	7,582	2,250	173	880	3,303
2014[1]	2,584	----	4,841	7,425	2,848	180	1,008	4,036
2015[2]	2,525	----	5,250	7,775	2,700	166	910	3,776

[1] Preliminary.   [2] Estimate.   [3] Includes meat content of minor meats and of mixed products.
Source: Economic Research Service, U.S. Department of Agriculture (FAS-USDA)

Average Wholesale Prices of Meats in the United States   In Cent Per Pound

Year	Composite Retail Price of Beef, Choice, Grade 3	of Pork[3]	Wholesale Value[4] Beef	Wholesale Value[4] Pork	Net Farm Value[5] of Pork	Cow Beef Canner & Cutter, Central US	Boxed Beef Cut-out, Choice1-3, Central US 550-700 Lb.	Pork Carcass Cut-out, U.S., No. 2	Lamb Carcass, Choice-Prime, E. Coast, 55-65 lbs.	Pork[6] Loins, Central US 14-18 lbs.	Skinned Ham, Central US 17-20 lbs.	Pork Bellies, Central US 12-14 lbs.
2005	409.22	282.69	226.10	124.90	88.00	NA	145.78	69.84	209.88	113.22	64.07	81.46
2006	397.02	280.72	228.17	121.38	83.27	NA	146.82	67.62	199.10	104.46	64.04	82.81
2007	415.85	287.03	231.08	121.44	81.98	NA	149.80	67.54	215.96	104.17	57.96	88.97
2008	432.58	293.65	235.04	124.73	82.48	NA	153.17	69.24	226.63	106.63	63.52	69.86
2009	425.81	291.97	217.18	111.19	71.56	NA	140.77	58.13	225.45	92.81	51.34	60.91
2010	438.40	311.36	241.08	141.16	95.68	NA	156.91	81.25	263.02	115.96	76.41	93.63
2011	480.73	343.35	275.82	158.89	113.93	NA	181.29	93.69	364.95	129.51	82.19	123.60
2012	498.59	346.67	290.59	147.10	104.88	NA	190.36	84.65	329.48	119.85	73.04	107.20
2013[1]	528.93	364.39	298.48	157.58	110.07	NA	195.64	91.69	281.52	116.53	79.12	152.15
2014[2]	597.03	401.88	364.71	187.66	131.80	NA	239.00	110.19	338.54	141.86	106.65	145.02

[1] Preliminary.   [2] Estimate.   [3] Sold as retail cuts (ham, bacon, loin, etc.).   [4] Quantity equivalent to 1 pound of retail cuts.
[5] Portion of gross farm value minus farm by-product allowance.   *Source: Economic Research Service, U.S. Department of Agriculture (ERS-USDA)*

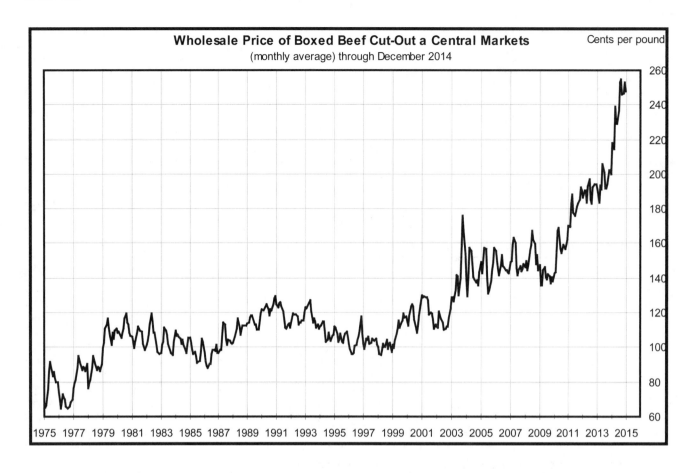

Wholesale Price of Boxed Beef Cut-Out a Central Markets   Cents per pound

(monthly average) through December 2014

Average Wholesale Price of Boxed Beef Cut-Out[2], Choice 1-3, at Central US   In Cents Per Pound

Year	Jan.	Feb.	Mar.	Apr.	May	June	July	Aug.	Sept.	Oct.	Nov.	Dec.	Average
2005	148.93	143.02	150.66	157.34	156.82	140.02	131.19	132.85	137.97	144.30	148.81	157.49	145.78
2006	155.60	149.71	144.94	141.83	147.45	153.09	147.01	146.22	144.69	144.79	143.64	142.92	146.82
2007	149.15	149.54	159.23	163.23	160.20	145.59	141.47	144.51	146.99	144.09	145.39	148.25	149.80
2008	146.41	149.63	144.42	147.47	156.07	159.10	167.33	162.31	159.56	148.03	153.29	144.42	153.17
2009	147.68	136.03	135.91	144.42	146.22	140.22	139.59	142.13	140.94	137.15	140.60	138.35	140.77
2010	142.87	143.22	155.73	167.37	168.80	156.54	154.53	156.67	159.20	156.58	159.25	162.20	156.91
2011	169.96	169.82	182.52	188.05	177.96	176.02	178.44	181.12	183.05	185.34	192.51	190.72	181.29
2012	186.77	190.46	190.54	183.43	192.84	197.24	185.25	183.00	192.09	194.19	194.22	194.25	190.36
2013	191.12	183.60	193.79	191.01	205.64	200.83	191.87	191.66	194.01	202.33	202.01	199.77	195.64
2014[1]	218.00	214.43	239.03	229.14	228.96	236.60	252.87	254.83	246.14	246.80	253.18	248.00	239.00

[1] Preliminary.   [2] Data through 2004: 550-750 pounds; beginning 2005: 600-900 pounds.   *Source: Economic Research Service, U.S. Department of Agriculture (ERS-USDA)*

Production (Commercial) of All Red Meats in the United States   In Millions of Pounds (Carcass Weight)

Year	Jan.	Feb.	Mar.	Apr.	May	June	July	Aug.	Sept.	Oct.	Nov.	Dec.	Total
2005	3,648.2	3,423.7	3,878.2	3,619.7	3,713.4	3,962.0	3,613.6	4,100.4	3,929.8	3,925.3	3,942.7	3,953.6	45,711
2006	3,899.6	3,489.9	4,112.2	3,614.8	4,063.8	4,136.2	3,790.6	4,257.6	3,950.0	4,197.3	4,151.3	3,874.5	47,538
2007	4,093.8	3,615.3	4,012.3	3,753.4	4,075.5	4,027.5	3,940.4	4,325.7	3,863.7	4,615.6	4,300.2	4,059.9	48,683
2008	4,417.7	3,967.3	4,089.8	4,298.2	4,222.1	4,050.0	4,250.1	4,095.2	4,273.0	4,529.3	3,869.5	4,162.8	50,225
2009	4,170.2	3,827.0	4,141.8	4,085.1	3,919.5	4,162.0	4,124.5	4,077.0	4,262.7	4,391.2	3,963.8	4,148.7	49,274
2010	3,915.9	3,735.8	4,281.2	4,012.3	3,731.2	4,176.5	3,955.5	4,125.9	4,160.1	4,262.1	4,329.2	4,352.9	49,039
2011	4,041.1	3,809.9	4,346.8	3,867.8	3,914.8	4,218.8	3,792.2	4,303.5	4,192.1	4,270.6	4,258.9	4,215.2	49,232
2012	4,122.9	3,914.0	4,171.4	3,855.3	4,182.7	4,022.5	3,945.3	4,391.0	3,948.0	4,580.1	4,309.3	3,996.9	49,439
2013	4,348.4	3,673.2	3,994.3	4,091.6	4,151.4	3,859.7	4,158.0	4,203.2	3,937.9	4,509.5	4,119.5	4,136.0	49,183
2014[1]	4,248.9	3,653.1	3,814.8	3,976.9	3,952.8	3,824.0	3,906.9	3,795.3	3,958.8	4,319.3	3,759.3	4,136.2	47,346

[1] Preliminary.   *Source: Economic Research Service, U.S. Department of Agriculture (ERS-USDA)*

Production (Commercial) of Beef in the United States   In Millions of Pounds (Carcass Weight)

Year	Jan.	Feb.	Mar.	Apr.	May	June	July	Aug.	Sept.	Oct.	Nov.	Dec.	Total
2005	1,915.6	1,767.4	2,041.7	1,887.8	2,074.0	2,227.0	2,082.8	2,319.0	2,158.0	2,080.7	2,071.3	2,057.3	24,683
2006	2,051.0	1,826.9	2,203.7	1,969.2	2,309.0	2,446.1	2,213.6	2,450.0	2,169.9	2,236.4	2,226.6	2,049.6	26,152
2007	2,166.0	1,952.5	2,118.2	2,015.0	2,285.1	2,348.5	2,256.7	2,450.6	2,094.7	2,443.0	2,228.8	2,061.4	26,421
2008	2,232.7	2,038.6	2,100.5	2,255.4	2,380.1	2,263.4	2,371.6	2,266.8	2,269.9	2,340.9	1,959.3	2,082.0	26,561
2009	2,117.9	1,986.0	2,144.0	2,133.4	2,179.4	2,289.0	2,271.2	2,184.2	2,234.1	2,275.7	2,016.1	2,134.4	25,965
2010	2,081.8	1,955.2	2,211.2	2,139.2	2,087.2	2,320.0	2,229.6	2,286.6	2,252.2	2,234.9	2,235.5	2,270.9	26,304
2011	2,122.9	2,020.4	2,266.2	2,052.5	2,131.9	2,375.0	2,134.1	2,386.9	2,215.2	2,215.1	2,148.8	2,126.3	26,195
2012	2,113.1	2,008.9	2,159.5	1,990.6	2,231.9	2,250.7	2,201.4	2,368.6	2,015.5	2,344.8	2,207.5	2,020.1	25,913
2013	2,260.0	1,873.7	2,038.6	2,127.3	2,228.0	2,161.4	2,293.5	2,241.6	2,073.6	2,316.5	2,057.3	2,046.5	25,718
2014[1]	2,141.1	1,788.9	1,938.4	2,042.8	2,071.6	2,068.7	2,085.9	2,024.4	2,067.4	2,171.5	1,850.6	2,000.7	24,252

[1] Preliminary.   *Source: Economic Research Service, U.S. Department of Agriculture (ERS-USDA)*

Production (Commercial) of Pork in the United States   In Millions of Pounds (Carcass Weight)

Year	Jan.	Feb.	Mar.	Apr.	May	June	July	Aug.	Sept.	Oct.	Nov.	Dec.	Total
2005	1,704.8	1,629.2	1,803.7	1,703.4	1,611.4	1,706.5	1,505.0	1,752.3	1,743.0	1,816.2	1,843.2	1,866.3	20,685
2006	1,820.5	1,637.0	1,877.5	1,618.3	1,726.0	1,663.3	1,552.6	1,780.2	1,753.7	1,932.0	1,896.4	1,796.4	21,054
2007	1,898.5	1,636.3	1,861.0	1,711.5	1,762.6	1,654.1	1,659.5	1,850.0	1,746.0	2,145.1	2,045.2	1,972.7	21,943
2008	2,159.0	1,902.7	1,962.0	2,015.6	1,815.5	1,761.8	1,852.5	1,803.9	1,975.8	2,159.9	1,886.1	2,052.1	23,347
2009	2,027.0	1,817.3	1,969.7	1,925.0	1,716.8	1,847.7	1,828.5	1,868.9	2,002.1	2,089.0	1,921.7	1,985.3	22,999
2010	1,809.7	1,757.5	2,040.1	1,849.1	1,621.3	1,831.7	1,702.2	1,815.3	1,883.5	2,002.7	2,068.0	2,055.4	22,437
2011	1,896.2	1,768.1	2,054.4	1,790.7	1,759.7	1,820.0	1,637.1	1,892.1	1,954.4	2,033.2	2,086.7	2,065.6	22,758
2012	1,987.3	1,883.0	1,987.7	1,841.9	1,926.8	1,750.5	1,721.9	1,998.1	1,911.2	2,210.7	2,079.2	1,954.2	23,253
2013	2,065.5	1,779.0	1,932.7	1,941.8	1,900.0	1,677.1	1,840.8	1,938.7	1,844.1	2,169.9	2,041.3	2,066.5	23,197
2014[1]	2,086.1	1,844.4	1,854.5	1,910.5	1,859.5	1,734.3	1,799.3	1,752.1	1,871.9	2,126.7	1,890.7	2,114.5	22,845

[1] Preliminary.   *Source: Economic Research Service, U.S. Department of Agriculture (ERS-USDA)*

Cold Storage Holdings of All[2] Meats in the United States, on First of Month   In Millions of Pounds

Year	Jan.	Feb.	Mar.	Apr.	May	June	July	Aug.	Sept.	Oct.	Nov.	Dec.
2005	979.0	965.0	953.2	928.0	908.5	847.0	847.8	850.8	842.9	884.9	900.1	882.1
2006	877.2	1,012.4	987.3	959.8	979.1	940.8	880.9	915.5	918.2	969.4	994.0	1,009.9
2007	946.6	977.3	963.4	943.5	970.3	925.7	919.7	943.5	958.7	991.8	1,003.2	968.4
2008	961.6	1,047.5	1,072.6	1,106.9	1,103.9	1,024.5	983.8	960.5	970.9	1,009.4	1,027.8	1,037.8
2009	1,078.5	1,096.2	1,084.9	1,045.3	1,050.6	1,030.1	1,043.1	1,014.7	980.2	984.0	968.4	936.8
2010	924.9	938.4	941.9	921.8	876.3	837.8	816.1	808.6	803.4	844.7	918.6	925.3
2011	939.9	1,017.4	1,050.6	1,036.6	1,009.5	1,014.9	949.4	894.2	896.7	944.9	929.3	961.1
2012	961.5	1,092.6	1,118.7	1,139.8	1,201.0	1,157.7	1,087.6	1,039.1	1,047.7	1,082.8	1,060.9	1,023.4
2013	1,043.8	1,114.8	1,148.1	1,182.4	1,238.0	1,166.3	1,071.3	1,035.5	1,005.0	1,041.0	1,033.0	1,021.9
2014[1]	1,022.2	1,077.0	1,093.6	1,012.3	1,015.9	981.4	930.1	939.1	934.0	970.8	956.5	930.3

[1] Preliminary.   [2] Includes beef and veal, mutton and lamb, pork and products, rendered pork fat, and miscellaneous meats. Excludes lard.
Source: Economic Research Service, U.S. Department of Agriculture (ERS-USDA)

Cold Storage Holdings of Frozen Beef in the United States, on First of Month   In Millions of Pounds

Year	Jan.	Feb.	Mar.	Apr.	May	June	July	Aug.	Sept.	Oct.	Nov.	Dec.
2005	484.3	453.3	400.2	372.3	329.4	318.2	342.1	385.2	410.6	438.8	439.2	429.9
2006	434.4	465.9	440.6	436.2	441.3	446.3	449.1	479.2	484.5	491.9	485.7	520.3
2007	482.1	470.6	458.9	427.2	417.3	411.5	430.3	467.7	480.9	486.7	488.0	475.3
2008	482.5	450.8	436.5	426.7	416.4	420.4	428.1	430.8	441.2	454.5	471.0	481.6
2009	492.6	462.5	435.5	425.9	410.7	417.9	434.8	444.8	420.1	428.9	427.7	430.9
2010	430.3	426.3	404.5	384.6	369.5	362.8	374.2	388.8	387.4	396.8	414.6	435.2
2011	445.0	461.7	459.8	445.5	443.2	447.6	432.8	415.2	428.6	427.6	417.0	443.8
2012	457.2	485.1	470.8	503.2	517.9	497.9	468.7	461.1	432.8	424.9	430.3	441.8
2013	465.7	484.6	490.0	511.2	510.1	482.6	481.2	462.6	430.2	445.2	440.1	450.8
2014[1]	439.4	429.3	409.5	405.8	402.3	377.6	358.2	367.9	346.6	378.2	380.9	400.8

[1] Preliminary.   *Source: Economic Research Service, U.S. Department of Agriculture (ERS-USDA)*

Mercury

Mercury (atomic symbol Hg) was known to the ancient Hindus and Chinese, and was also found in Egyptian tombs dating back to 1500 BC. The ancient Greeks used mercury in ointments, and the Romans used it in cosmetics. Alchemists thought mercury turned into gold when it hardened.

Mercury, also called quicksilver, is a heavy, silvery, toxic, transitional metal. Mercury is the only common metal that is liquid at room temperatures. When subjected to a pressure of 7,640 atmospheres (7.7 million millibars), mercury becomes a solid. Mercury dissolves in nitric or concentrated sulfuric acid, but is resistant to alkalis. It is a poor conductor of heat. Mercury has superconductivity when cooled to sufficiently low temperatures. It has a freezing point of about −39 degrees Celsius and a boiling point of about 357 degrees Celsius.

Mercury is found in its pure form or combined in small amounts with silvers, but is found most often in the ore cinnabar, a mineral consisting of mercuric sulfide. By heating the cinnabar ore in air until the mercuric sulfide breaks down, pure mercury metal is produced. Mercury forms alloys called amalgams with all common metals except iron and platinum. Most mercury is used for the manufacture of industrial chemicals and for electrical and electronic applications. Other uses for mercury include its use in gold recovery from ores, barometers, diffusion pumps, laboratory instruments, mercury-vapor lamps, pesticides, batteries, and catalysts. A decline in mercury production and usage since the 1970s reflects a trend for using mercury substitutes due to its toxicity.

Prices – The average monthly price of mercury in 2014 fell by -20.8% yr/yr to $2.724.99 per flask (34.5 kilograms) from the record yearly high of $3.438.59 posted in 2013.

Supply – World mine production of mercury in 2014 fell by -0.5% yr/yr to 1,870 metric tons, down from the 15-year high of 2,250 metric tons in 2010. The record low of 1,150 metric tons was posted in 2006. The world's largest miners of mercury are China with 85.6% of world production and Kyrgyzstan with 5.4%. China's production in 2010 was a record high of 1,600 metric tons. China's record low of 190 metric tons was posted in 2001.

Demand – The breakdown of domestic consumption of mercury by particular categories is no longer available. However, as of 1997 records showed that chlorine and caustic soda accounted for 46% of U.S. mercury consumption, followed by wiring devices and switches (17%), dental equipment (12%), electrical lighting (8%), and measuring control instruments (7%). Substitutes for mercury include lithium and composite ceramic materials.

Trade – U.S. foreign trade in mercury has been relatively small but U.S. imports of mercury in 2014 rose +31.6% yr/yr to 50 metric tons, well below the 2010 14-year high of 294 metric tons. By contrast the U.S.'s record high imports were in 1974 at 1,799 metric tons. U.S. imports were mostly from Chile and Peru. U.S. exports of mercury in 2012 (latest data) fell by -22.6% to 103 metric tons, but still above 2007's 13-year low of 84 metric tons.

World Mine Production of Mercury   In Metric Tons (1 tonne = 29.008216 flasks)

Year	Chile (byproduct)	China	Finland	Kyrgyzstan	Mexico	Morocco	Peru (exports)	Russia	Tajikistan	United States	World Total
2005	----	1,100	20	200	6	10	102	50	30	NA	1,520
2006	----	760	20	250	8	10	22	50	30	NA	1,150
2007	----	800	20	250	8	10	34	50	30	NA	1,200
2008	----	1,300	20	250	21	10	136	50	30	NA	1,820
2009	88	1,430	6	140	15	10	107	50	30	NA	1,960
2010	176	1,600	9	99	15	10	159	50	30	NA	2,250
2011	90	1,500	----	113	----	9	53	50	30	NA	2,000
2012	52	1,350	----	75	----	8	17	50	32	NA	1,810
2013[1]	50	1,600	----	100	----	5	45	50	32	NA	1,880
2014[2]	50	1,600		100			40	50	30	NA	1,870

[1] Preliminary. [2] Estimate. NA = Not available. W = Withheld. *Source: U.S. Geological Survey (USGS)*

Salient Statistics of Mercury in the United States   In Metric Tons

Year	Producing Mines	Secondary Production — Industrial	Secondary Production — Government[3]	NDS[4] Shipments	Consumer & Dealer Stocks, Dec. 31	Industrial Demand	Exports	Imports
2006	NA	NA	----	----	19	38	390	94
2007	NA	NA	----	----	18	31	84	67
2008	NA	NA	----	----	24	NA	732	155
2009	NA	NA	----	----	30	NA	753	206
2010	NA	NA	----	----	NA	NA	459	294
2011	NA	NA	----	----	NA	NA	133	110
2012	NA	NA	----	----	NA	NA	103	249
2013[1]	NA	NA	----	----	NA	NA	[5]	38
2014[2]	NA	NA	----	----	NA	NA	----	50

[1] Preliminary. [2] Estimate. [3] Secondary mercury shipped from the Department of Energy. [4] National Defense Stockpile. [5] Less than 1/2 unit. NA = Not available. *Source: U.S. Geological Survey (USGS)*

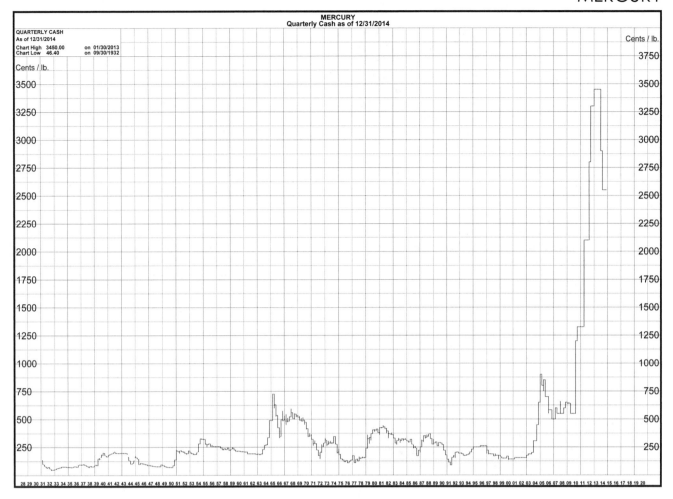

Average Price of Mercury in New York   In Dollars Per Flask of 76 Pounds (34.5 Kilograms)

Year	Jan.	Feb.	Mar.	Apr.	May	June	July	Aug.	Sept.	Oct.	Nov.	Dec.	Average
2005	678.57	747.50	867.39	873.81	850.00	817.05	759.52	750.00	813.64	730.95	700.00	700.00	774.04
2006	700.00	700.00	691.30	552.50	574.02	582.50	582.50	582.50	582.50	576.59	513.64	500.00	594.84
2007	500.00	500.00	500.00	500.00	500.00	573.81	600.00	600.00	572.50	550.00	550.00	550.00	541.36
2008	550.00	550.00	550.00	550.00	550.00	550.00	550.00	550.00	590.91	600.00	645.00	650.00	573.83
2009	650.00	647.00	640.00	640.00	642.86	640.00	640.00	640.00	603.18	550.00	550.00	550.00	616.09
2010	550.00	550.00	550.00	550.00	828.57	1,129.55	1,213.64	1,293.18	1,325.00	1,325.00	1,325.00	1,325.00	997.08
2011	1,325.00	1,325.00	1,325.00	1,325.00	1,325.00	1,325.00	1,370.24	2,073.91	2,100.00	2,100.00	2,100.00	2,100.00	1,649.51
2012	2,100.00	2,100.00	2,100.00	2,100.00	2,547.83	2,800.00	2,800.00	2,800.00	3,100.00	3,300.00	3,300.00	3,300.00	2,695.65
2013	3,313.05	3,450.00	3,450.00	3,450.00	3,450.00	3,450.00	3,450.00	3,450.00	3,450.00	3,450.00	3,450.00	3,450.00	3,438.59
2014	3,269.57	3,175.00	2,991.67	2,850.00	2,563.64	2,550.00	2,550.00	2,550.00	2,550.00	2,550.00	2,550.00	2,550.00	2,724.99

Source: American Metal Market (AMM)

Mercury Consumed in the United States   In Metric Tons

Year	Batteries[3]	Chlorine & Caustic Soda	Catalysts, Misc.	Dental Equip.	Electrical Lighting[3]	General Lab Use	Measuring Control Instrument	Paints	Wiring Devices & Switches[3]	Other Uses	Grand Total
1989	250	379	40	39	31	18	87	192	141	32	1,212
1990	106	247	29	44	33	32	108	14	70	38	720
1991	18	184	26	41	39	30	90	6	71	49	554
1992	13	209	20	42	55	28	80	----	82	92	621
1993	10	180	18	35	38	26	65	----	83	103	558
1994	6	135	25	24	27	24	53	----	79	110	483
1995	----	154	----	32	30	----	43	----	84	93	436
1996[1]	----	136	----	31	29	----	41	----	49	86	372
1997[2]	----	160	----	40	29	----	24	----	57	36	346
	Data No Longer Available

[1] Preliminary.   [2] Estimate.   W = Withheld proprietary data.   *Source: U.S. Geological Survey (USGS)*

Milk

Evidence of man's use of animal milk as food was discovered in a temple in the Euphrates Valley near Babylon, dating back to 3,000 BC. Humans drink the milk produced from a variety of domesticated mammals, including cows, goats, sheep, camels, reindeer, buffaloes, and llama. In India, half of all milk consumed is from water buffalo. Camels' milk spoils slower than other types of milk in the hot desert, but the vast majority of milk used for commercial production and consumption comes from cows.

Milk directly from a cow in its natural form is called raw milk. Raw milk is processed by spinning it in a centrifuge, homogenizing it to create a consistent texture (i.e., by forcing hot milk under high pressure through small nozzles), and then sterilizing it through pasteurization (i.e., heating to a high temperature for a specified length of time to destroy pathogenic bacteria). Condensed, powdered, and evaporated milk are produced by evaporating some or all of the water content. Whole milk contains 3.5% milk fat. Lower-fat milks include 2% low-fat milk, 1% low- fat milk, and skim milk, which has only 1/2 gram of milk fat per serving.

The CME Group has three different milk futures contracts: Milk Class III which is milk used in the manufacturing of cheese, Milk Class IV which is milk used in the production of butter and all dried milk products, and Nonfat Dry Milk which is used in commercial or consumer cooking or to reconstitute nonfat milk by the consumer. The Milk Class III contract has the largest volume and open interest.

Prices – The average monthly price received by farmers for all milk sold to plants in 2014 rose by +19.6% yr/yr to $23.98 per hundred pounds, a new record high.

Supply – World milk production in 2015 is expected to rise +2.1% to 582.521 million metric tons. The biggest producers will be the European Union with 26.1% of world production, India with 25.2%, and the U.S. with 16.5%. U.S. 2014 milk production in pounds is expected to rise +2.4% yr/yr to 205.994 billion pounds, setting a new record high. The number of dairy cows on U.S. farms has fallen sharply in the past 3 decades from the 12 million seen in 1970. In 2014, there were 9.255 million dairy cows on U.S. farms, down -0.4% yr/yr. Dairy farmers have been able to increase milk production even with fewer cows because of a dramatic increase in milk yield per cow. In 2014, the average cow produced 22,259 pounds of milk per year, more than double the 9,751 pounds seen in 1970.

Demand – Per capita consumption of milk in the U.S. fell to a new record low of 204 pounds per year in 2008 (latest data), down sharply by -26% from 277 pounds in 1977. The utilization breakdown for 2002 (latest data) shows the largest manufacturing usage categories are cheese (64.504 billion pounds of milk) and creamery butter (30.250 billion pounds).

Trade – U.S. imports of milk in 2014 rose +13.5% yr/yr to 4.200 billion pounds, still well below the record high of 7.500 billion pounds posted in 2005-06.

World Fluid Milk Production (Cow's Milk)   In Thousands of Metric Tons

Year	Argentina	Australia	Brazil	China	European Union	India	Japan	Mexico	New Zealand	Russia	Ukraine	United States	World Total
2007	9,550	9,500	26,750	36,334	136,874	105,000	8,007	10,829	15,918	32,200	12,262	84,211	507,541
2008	10,010	9,500	27,820	35,450	137,848	109,000	7,982	11,077	15,580	32,500	11,762	86,173	505,471
2009	10,350	9,326	28,795	29,625	137,720	112,000	7,910	11,036	16,983	32,600	11,610	85,821	504,523
2010	10,600	9,327	29,948	30,528	139,492	117,000	7,721	11,201	17,173	31,847	11,249	87,488	514,379
2011	11,470	9,568	30,715	31,980	142,920	123,000	7,474	11,213	18,965	31,646	11,085	89,020	529,717
2012	11,679	9,811	31,490	33,960	143,750	129,000	7,631	11,434	20,567	31,831	11,378	91,010	544,651
2013	11,519	9,400	32,380	35,750	144,850	134,500	7,508	11,411	20,200	30,529	11,488	91,271	551,738
2014[1]	11,404	9,700	33,350	37,500	151,450	140,500	7,315	11,599	21,742	29,900	11,510	93,531	570,369
2015[2]	11,746	9,800	34,500	38,984	151,750	146,500	7,350	11,760	22,120	29,300	11,470	96,252	582,521

[1] Preliminary.   [2] Forecast.   *Source: Foreign Agricultural Service, U.S. Department of Agriculture (FAS-USDA)*

Salient Statistics of Milk in the United States   In Millions of Pounds

Year	Number of Milk Cows on Farms[3] (Thousands)	Production Per Cow[4] (Pounds)	Production Total[4]	Beginning Stocks[5]	Imports	Total Supply	Exports[5]	Fed to Calves	Humans	Total Use	All Milk, Wholesale	Milk, Eligible for Fluid Market	Milk, Manufacturing Grade	Per Capita Consumption[6] (Fluid Milk in Lbs)
2007	9,158	20,266	185,602	9,500	7,200	202,302	5,700	952	184,565	191,217	19.13	19.13	18.18	206
2008	9,315	20,396	189,992	10,356	5,300	205,648	8,700	944	188,917	198,561	18.30	18.28	17.98	204
2009	9,200	20,576	189,320	10,045	5,600	204,965	4,500	901	188,322	193,723	12.84	12.84	12.18	
2010	9,117	21,149	192,819	11,334	4,100	208,253	8,100	873	191,863	200,836	16.27	16.29	14.79	
2011	9,194	21,346	196,245	10,800	3,500	210,545	9,400	867	195,192	205,459	20.14	----	----	
2012	9,232	21,696	200,324	10,900	4,100	215,324	8,800	858	199,362	209,020	18.48	----	----	
2013[1]	9,215	21,413	201,218	12,200	3,700	217,118	12,400	880			20.04	----	----	
2014[2]	9,255	22,259	205,994	11,200	4,200	221,394	12,300				23.98	----	----	

[1] Preliminary.   [2] Estimate.   [3] Average number on farms during year including dry cows, excluding heifers not yet fresh.   [4] Excludes milk sucked by calves.   [5] Government and commercial.   [6] Product pounds of commercial sales and on farm consumption.
Source: Economic Research Service, U.S. Department of Agriculture (ERS-USDA)

Milk-Feed Price Ratio[1] in the United States   In Pounds

Year	Jan.	Feb.	Mar.	Apr.	May	June	July	Aug.	Sept.	Oct.	Nov.	Dec.	Average
2005	3.45	3.50	3.35	3.18	2.93	2.87	2.93	3.08	3.27	3.42	3.45	3.28	3.23
2006	3.17	2.93	2.70	2.48	2.32	2.35	2.33	2.48	2.61	2.53	2.44	2.43	2.56
2007	2.45	2.33	2.39	2.51	2.54	2.88	3.16	3.19	3.19	3.10	3.05	2.85	2.80
2008	2.65	2.24	2.07	1.88	1.81	1.88	1.90	1.81	1.90	2.02	2.01	1.92	2.01
2009	1.60	1.51	1.56	1.59	1.48	1.45	1.57	1.80	2.00	2.11	2.26	2.42	1.78
2010	2.33	2.36	2.18	2.19	2.17	2.26	2.31	2.36	2.36	2.40	2.23	1.98	2.26
2011	1.96	2.01	2.12	1.81	1.73	1.87	1.91	1.83	1.84	1.82	1.89	1.81	1.88
2012	1.72	1.56	1.48	1.41	1.34	1.38	1.34	1.37	1.59	1.74	1.74	1.65	1.53
2013	1.57	1.52	1.48	1.54	1.53	1.52	1.53	1.68	1.88	2.10	2.27	2.30	1.74
2014[1]	2.46	2.60	2.56	2.43	2.24	2.20	2.36	2.61	2.97	2.91	2.74	2.38	2.54

[1] Pounds of 16% protein mixed dairy feed equal in value to one pound of whole milk.   [2] Preliminary.   *Source: Economic Research Service, U.S. Department of Agriculture (ERS-USDA)*

Milk Production[2] in the United States   In Millions of Pounds

Year	Jan.	Feb.	Mar.	Apr.	May	June	July	Aug.	Sept.	Oct.	Nov.	Dec.	Total
2005	14,614	13,530	15,206	15,047	15,697	15,087	14,978	14,896	14,260	14,611	14,209	14,854	176,989
2006	15,343	14,238	15,966	15,538	16,068	15,324	15,168	15,061	14,481	14,857	14,523	15,231	181,798
2007	15,605	14,321	16,132	15,763	16,180	15,476	15,714	15,525	14,871	15,370	15,013	15,632	185,602
2008	15,976	15,176	16,458	16,125	16,707	15,942	15,995	15,757	15,129	15,615	15,212	15,900	189,992
2009	16,135	14,754	16,485	16,148	16,805	15,935	16,018	15,737	15,038	15,420	15,070	15,775	189,320
2010	16,020	14,758	16,614	16,416	17,040	16,353	16,436	16,094	15,540	15,900	15,498	16,150	192,819
2011	16,393	15,077	16,989	16,652	17,278	16,518	16,479	16,422	15,783	16,278	15,820	16,556	196,245
2012	17,016	16,310	17,718	17,232	17,601	16,676	16,585	16,403	15,687	16,267	16,008	16,821	200,324
2013	17,109	15,759	17,677	17,249	17,813	16,935	16,788	16,789	15,831	16,475	16,003	16,790	201,218
2014[1]	17,293	15,920	17,833	17,468	18,080	17,313	17,442	17,211	16,495	17,066	16,555	17,318	205,994

[1] Preliminary.   [2] Excludes milk sucked by calves.   *Source: Economic Research Service, U.S. Department of Agriculture (ERS-USDA)*

Milk Cows[2] in the United States   In Thousands of Head

Year	Jan.	Feb.	Mar.	Apr.	May	June	July	Aug.	Sept.	Oct.	Nov.	Dec.	Total
2005	9,000	8,996	9,009	9,030	9,042	9,050	9,053	9,060	9,066	9,060	9,056	9,063	9,040
2006	9,081	9,088	9,106	9,116	9,129	9,139	9,119	9,114	9,107	9,107	9,111	9,126	9,112
2007	9,135	9,136	9,142	9,132	9,138	9,144	9,153	9,159	9,166	9,181	9,196	9,217	9,158
2008	9,276	9,287	9,295	9,307	9,318	9,321	9,335	9,331	9,323	9,324	9,333	9,334	9,315
2009	9,312	9,289	9,283	9,282	9,270	9,228	9,191	9,162	9,123	9,094	9,085	9,082	9,200
2010	9,089	9,092	9,099	9,108	9,119	9,129	9,135	9,123	9,121	9,123	9,125	9,141	9,117
2011	9,160	9,163	9,180	9,182	9,194	9,196	9,198	9,200	9,201	9,212	9,213	9,223	9,194
2012	9,242	9,257	9,271	9,273	9,263	9,241	9,222	9,217	9,195	9,189	9,201	9,218	9,232
2013	9,222	9,223	NA	NA	NA	NA	9,235	9,229	9,208	9,203	9,198	9,202	9,215
2014[1]	9,210	9,212	9,221	9,238	9,254	9,267	9,271	9,265	9,269	9,269	9,280	9,302	9,255

[1] Preliminary.   [2] Includes dry cows, excludes heifers not yet fresh.   *Source: Economic Research Service, U.S. Department of Agriculture (ERS-USDA)*

Milk Per Cow[2] in the United States   In Pounds

Year	Jan.	Feb.	Mar.	Apr.	May	June	July	Aug.	Sept.	Oct.	Nov.	Dec.	Total
2005	1,624	1,504	1,688	1,666	1,735	1,668	1,656	1,643	1,572	1,613	1,569	1,639	19,577
2006	1,690	1,567	1,753	1,705	1,760	1,676	1,663	1,653	1,590	1,631	1,594	1,669	19,951
2007	1,708	1,567	1,765	1,726	1,771	1,692	1,717	1,695	1,622	1,674	1,633	1,696	20,266
2008	1,722	1,634	1,771	1,733	1,793	1,710	1,713	1,689	1,623	1,675	1,630	1,703	20,396
2009	1,733	1,588	1,776	1,740	1,812	1,726	1,744	1,718	1,649	1,695	1,658	1,737	20,576
2010	1,763	1,623	1,826	1,802	1,869	1,791	1,799	1,764	1,704	1,743	1,698	1,767	21,149
2011	1,790	1,645	1,851	1,814	1,879	1,796	1,792	1,785	1,715	1,767	1,717	1,795	21,346
2012	1,841	1,762	1,911	1,858	1,900	1,805	1,798	1,780	1,706	1,770	1,740	1,825	21,696
2013	1,855	1,709	NA	NA	NA	NA	1,818	1,819	1,719	1,790	1,740	1,825	21,413
2014[1]	1,878	1,728	1,934	1,891	1,954	1,868	1,881	1,858	1,780	1,841	1,784	1,862	22,259

[1] Preliminary.   [2] Excludes milk sucked by calves.   *Source: Economic Research Service, U.S. Department of Agriculture (ERS-USDA)*

MILK

Average Price Received by Farmers for All Milk (Sold to Plants)   In Dollars Per Hundred Pounds (Cwt.)

Year	Jan.	Feb.	Mar.	Apr.	May	June	July	Aug.	Sept.	Oct.	Nov.	Dec.	Average
2005	15.90	15.50	15.60	15.20	14.70	14.40	14.80	14.80	15.30	15.60	15.10	14.80	15.14
2006	14.50	13.50	12.60	12.10	11.90	11.90	11.70	12.00	13.00	13.60	13.90	14.20	12.91
2007	14.50	14.90	15.60	16.60	18.00	20.20	21.60	21.60	21.80	21.40	21.90	21.50	19.13
2008	20.50	19.10	18.10	18.00	18.30	19.30	19.30	18.40	18.20	17.80	17.10	15.50	18.30
2009	13.30	11.60	11.80	11.90	11.60	11.30	11.30	12.10	13.00	14.30	15.40	16.50	12.84
2010	16.10	15.90	14.80	14.60	15.00	15.40	15.90	16.70	17.70	18.50	17.90	16.70	16.27
2011	16.70	19.10	20.40	19.60	19.60	21.10	21.80	22.10	21.10	20.00	20.50	19.70	20.14
2012	19.00	17.70	17.20	16.80	16.20	16.30	16.90	18.20	18.90	21.60	22.10	20.80	18.48
2013	19.90	19.50	19.10	19.50	19.70	19.50	19.10	19.60	20.10	20.90	21.60	22.00	20.04
2014[1]	23.50	24.90	25.20	25.30	24.20	23.20	23.30	24.10	25.70	24.90	23.00	20.40	23.98

[1] Preliminary.   *Source: Economic Research Service, U.S. Department of Agriculture (ERS-USDA)*

Production of Nonfat Dry Milk in the United States   In Thousands of Pounds

Year	Jan.	Feb.	Mar.	Apr.	May	June	July	Aug.	Sept.	Oct.	Nov.	Dec.	Total
2005	93,261	97,275	109,299	104,876	124,329	124,206	108,865	86,679	70,954	73,554	89,095	103,711	1,186,104
2006	111,278	117,998	128,867	130,613	132,935	116,846	88,594	73,193	63,278	69,989	76,914	113,567	1,224,072
2007	108,023	96,818	112,867	123,022	115,381	118,173	122,193	102,993	89,844	100,242	99,994	108,930	1,298,480
2008	119,102	118,268	135,244	132,998	128,921	134,386	135,614	115,180	85,516	120,961	134,780	155,237	1,516,207
2009	158,286	125,902	137,301	141,397	150,452	146,065	133,175	107,049	87,808	92,800	102,156	126,720	1,509,111
2010	129,679	118,999	138,305	152,945	154,757	136,990	131,704	119,562	109,286	114,595	116,653	139,043	1,562,518
2011	114,896	106,785	124,065	145,323	147,290	145,125	131,502	113,299	103,115	99,751	119,686	148,640	1,499,477
2012	152,085	171,394	189,227	190,728	193,362	168,394	140,169	106,014	84,498	95,064	115,854	157,660	1,764,449
2013	142,799	137,674	146,576	160,117	150,531	124,635	116,616	106,039	107,002	85,830	101,185	125,570	1,504,574
2014[1]	138,858	140,559	162,649	158,614	162,780	148,424	166,416	118,668	114,930	135,114	151,378	163,112	1,761,502

[1] Preliminary.   *Source: Economic Research Service, U.S. Department of Agriculture (ERS-USDA)*

Production of Dry Whey in the United States   In Thousands of Pounds

Year	Jan.	Feb.	Mar.	Apr.	May	June	July	Aug.	Sept.	Oct.	Nov.	Dec.	Total
2005	85,936	79,665	91,775	91,260	94,083	89,357	89,143	87,438	83,948	82,186	84,844	86,187	1,045,822
2006	88,391	89,695	100,953	95,662	97,295	89,701	95,226	91,547	86,271	87,434	84,079	91,128	1,097,382
2007	96,757	89,662	98,340	96,812	99,346	94,656	95,549	94,454	88,164	88,895	93,605	97,621	1,133,861
2008	91,772	88,023	97,923	96,747	97,046	92,331	89,821	87,372	82,614	85,248	86,463	91,272	1,086,632
2009	79,395	74,668	82,785	83,218	87,125	92,639	93,640	82,555	79,006	81,709	79,361	85,059	1,001,160
2010	85,766	78,206	92,496	87,728	89,255	86,045	87,529	81,519	77,718	77,888	79,506	89,327	1,012,983
2011	90,192	82,035	94,304	92,037	91,293	83,740	81,752	79,759	76,800	77,517	77,614	83,074	1,010,117
2012	95,588	89,274	88,348	84,014	86,760	83,819	79,807	77,543	74,810	77,195	72,559	89,181	998,898
2013	90,663	80,471	87,631	85,400	79,654	79,564	79,515	75,832	72,334	71,460	74,176	84,320	961,020
2014[1]	70,010	62,092	71,504	75,754	82,480	79,310	73,475	69,555	70,735	70,194	69,982	75,987	871,078

[1] Preliminary.   Excludes all modified dry whey products.   *Source: Economic Research Service, U.S. Department of Agriculture (ERS-USDA)*

Production of Whey Protein Concentrate in the United States   In Thousands of Pounds

Year	Jan.	Feb.	Mar.	Apr.	May	June	July	Aug.	Sept.	Oct.	Nov.	Dec.	Total
2005	29,624	27,638	31,382	32,926	31,296	33,023	32,109	31,021	32,829	33,293	33,226	35,559	383,926
2006	37,162	34,436	37,766	37,525	37,373	36,190	35,704	35,024	34,581	34,581	33,116	34,266	427,724
2007	33,280	30,166	35,075	33,104	33,460	33,046	33,252	30,970	31,372	32,283	32,252	35,327	393,587
2008	32,825	33,358	35,830	35,170	36,469	34,274	35,813	34,369	33,314	36,624	34,086	35,709	417,841
2009	35,177	32,340	35,259	32,971	34,705	34,572	35,221	35,284	34,810	35,830	34,061	34,785	415,015
2010	34,765	31,417	37,775	36,265	36,811	35,307	36,441	35,142	36,005	35,583	34,952	37,447	427,910
2011	34,871	32,701	36,809	34,668	36,669	36,292	34,683	35,248	35,571	37,323	36,818	39,285	430,938
2012	38,845	35,064	41,433	39,077	38,417	39,942	35,590	36,804	37,469	38,627	37,735	40,471	459,474
2013	39,262	36,941	41,742	40,396	43,391	41,501	40,265	39,461	39,386	45,542	43,194	46,567	497,648
2014[1]	47,041	42,174	44,796	45,725	45,986	43,795	44,486	44,797	41,843	46,498	45,768	47,314	540,223

[1] Preliminary.   *Source: Economic Research Service, U.S. Department of Agriculture (ERS-USDA)*

MILK (CLASS III) - CME
Weekly Nearest Futures as of 01/02/2015

WEEKLY NEAREST FUTURES
As of 01/02/2015

Chart High 24.60   on 10/01/2014
Chart Low   9.24   on 02/03/2009

Nearby Futures through Last Trading Day.

Volume of Trading of Class III Milk Futures in Chicago   In Contracts

Year	Jan.	Feb.	Mar.	Apr.	May	June	July	Aug.	Sept.	Oct.	Nov.	Dec.	Total
2005	28,126	23,757	18,519	18,261	14,083	13,244	13,235	11,452	8,434	11,069	10,921	11,408	182,509
2006	23,025	26,229	21,112	9,975	19,374	18,328	15,205	18,627	15,148	23,892	20,264	13,958	225,137
2007	26,017	22,343	26,109	33,860	34,154	35,602	19,918	22,058	28,078	20,241	23,638	19,441	311,459
2008	29,875	19,221	19,877	23,359	27,767	28,652	22,218	29,485	24,902	31,238	19,601	28,559	304,754
2009	29,313	21,085	22,708	19,126	21,625	26,902	26,248	21,781	20,214	25,391	17,874	28,369	280,636
2010	28,947	22,118	25,828	22,661	21,808	16,183	19,302	17,900	19,066	25,489	33,175	25,383	277,860
2011	48,169	40,246	37,892	16,713	24,145	30,885	27,495	37,989	29,503	25,880	25,522	24,175	368,614
2012	27,318	27,399	31,079	21,345	22,468	19,617	27,152	28,798	23,819	25,021	22,239	18,242	294,497
2013	22,182	20,654	25,964	29,668	24,403	22,482	23,762	28,680	19,519	24,806	21,210	30,611	293,941
2014	37,317	27,468	31,390	23,084	22,764	21,118	26,702	28,532	38,651	33,233	25,464	42,936	358,659

Contract size = 200,000 lbs.   *Source: CME Group; Chicago Mercantile Exchange (CME)*

Average Open Interest of Class III Milk Futures in Chicago   In Contracts

Year	Jan.	Feb.	Mar.	Apr.	May	June	July	Aug.	Sept.	Oct.	Nov.	Dec.
2005	23,986	25,755	24,490	22,744	22,465	22,190	21,407	20,965	19,390	19,244	19,583	20,268
2006	24,077	28,425	30,871	31,894	30,767	30,737	30,795	29,771	27,567	27,523	27,893	27,064
2007	26,542	30,517	32,057	33,766	37,342	39,254	37,426	34,841	34,108	31,402	31,279	30,368
2008	30,376	30,478	29,534	29,651	29,781	33,265	33,597	36,122	37,165	36,678	36,744	36,815
2009	37,081	36,447	33,843	30,337	28,648	28,695	27,551	25,535	24,131	23,388	23,538	24,950
2010	27,126	29,049	30,462	29,520	29,035	28,974	27,487	26,200	26,869	25,722	28,261	30,694
2011	33,741	38,813	38,723	34,509	33,021	35,150	35,730	36,553	33,284	31,322	33,127	33,472
2012	32,511	33,482	31,516	28,476	26,706	24,376	24,511	26,462	26,559	25,497	22,784	20,226
2013	19,320	20,206	21,408	23,180	22,062	21,456	21,802	23,267	23,463	22,153	22,480	24,287
2014	26,264	28,094	29,393	28,695	27,114	26,298	26,128	29,218	32,844	36,731	39,197	43,959

Contract size = 200,000 lbs.   *Source: CME Group; Chicago Mercantile Exchange (CME)*

Molybdenum

Molybdenum (atomic symbol Mo) is a silvery-white, hard, malleable, metallic element. Molybdenum melts at about 2610 degrees Celsius and boils at about 4640 degrees Celsius. Swedish chemist Carl Wilhelm Scheele discovered molybdenum in 1778.

Molybdenum occurs in nature in the form of molybdenite and wulfenite. Contributing to the growth of plants, it is an important trace element in soils. Approximately 70% of the world supply of molybdenum is obtained as a by-product of copper mining. -Molybdenum is chiefly used as an alloy to strengthen steel and resist corrosion. It is used for structural work, aircraft parts, and forged automobile parts because it withstands high temperatures and pressures and adds strength. Other uses include lubricants, a refractory metal in chemical applications, electron tubing, and as a catalyst.

Prices – The average monthly U.S. merchant price of molybdic oxide in 2014 rose +12.4% yr/yr to $11.70 per pound. That was far below the 2005 record high of $32.70 per pound.

Supply – World production of molybdenum in 2014 rose +3.1% yr/yr to 266,000 metric tons. The 18-year low of 122,000 metric tons was seen in 2002. The world's largest producers of molybdenum are China with 37.6% of world production in 2014, the U.S. with 24.6%, and Chile with 14.7%

U.S. production of molybdenum concentrate in 2014 rose +7.9% yr/yr to 65,500 metric tons, well above the 29-year low of 32,300 metric tons posted in 2002. U.S. net production of molybdic oxide in 2009 (latest data available) rose +1.9% to 32,100 metric tons. U.S. net production of molybdenum metal powder is now being withheld as proprietary data but in 2008 the figure was 1,640 metric tons.

Demand – U.S. consumption of molybdenum concentrate in 2010 (latest data available) rose by +57.4% yr/yr to 48,000 metric tons, remaining well above the 14-year low of 21,200 metric tons posted in 2002. U.S. consumption of molybdenum concentrate has more than doubled over the last 13 years. U.S. consumption of molybdenum primary products in 2013 (latest data available) rose by +2.0% yr/yr to 20,100 metric tons.

Trade – U.S. imports of molybdenum concentrate for consumption in 2012 (latest available data) fell by -17.8% yr/yr to 12,000 metric tons, still well above the 16-year low of 4,710 metric tons posted in 2002.

World Mine Production of Molybdenum   In Metric Tons (Contained Molybdenum)

Year	Armenia	Canada[3]	Chile	China	Iran	Kazakhstan	Mexico	Mongolia	Peru	Russia	United States	Uzbekisten	World Total
2008	4,472	8,602	33,687	81,000	6,597	----	7,811	1,780	16,721	3,600	55,900	500	221,000
2009	4,365	8,721	34,925	93,500	4,447	----	10,166	2,140	12,297	3,800	47,800	500	223,000
2010	4,335	8,648	37,186	93,600	7,000	----	10,849	2,198	16,963	3,800	59,400	500	247,000
2011	4,817	8,326	40,889	103,000	7,000	----	10,787	1,960	19,141	3,900	63,700	550	264,000
2012	4,900	9,005	35,090	104,000	6,300	----	11,000	1,903	16,790	3,900	60,400	550	259,000
2013[1]	6,700	7,620	38,700	101,000	4,000	----	12,100	1,900	18,100	4,800	60,700	530	258,000
2014[2]	6,700	9,500	39,000	100,000	6,300	----	11,000	2,000	18,100	4,800	65,500	550	266,000

[1] Preliminary. [2] Estimate. [3] Shipments. *Source: U.S. Geological Survey (USGS)*

Salient Statistics of Molybdenum in the United States   In Metric Tons (Contained Molybdenum)

| | | Concentrate | | | | | | | Primary Products[4] | | | | | | |
| | | Shipments | | | | | | | Net Production | | | Shipments | | | |
Year	Production	Total (Including Exports)	Value Million $	For Exports	Consumption	Imports For Consumption	Stocks Dec. 31[3]	Grand Total	Molybolic Oxide[5]	Molybdenum Metal Powder	Avg Price Value $ / Kg.[6]	Domestic Destinations	To Oxide for Exports, Gross Weight	Consumption	Producer Stocks, Dec. 31
2007	57,000	57,100	----	----	43,900	12,400	2,630	31,100	29,500	1,620	66.79	48,700	14,900	21,000	3,140
2008	55,900	57,800	----	----	44,500	10,200	1,690	33,200	31,500	1,640	62.99	51,300	16,700	21,100	3,680
2009	47,800	63,700	----	----	W	7,520	2,550	33,700	32,100	W	25.84	43,300	10,600	17,700	3,660
2010	59,400	59,400	----	----	W	12,900	2,200	42,100	W	W	34.83	51,100	6,040	19,200	W
2011	63,700	62,800	----	----	W	14,600	3,520	45,500	W	W	34.34	W	4,840	19,100	W
2012[1]	61,500	60,200	----	----	W	12,000	W		W	W	28.09	W	1,590	19,700	W
2013[2]	60,700										22.85			20,100	W

[1] Preliminary. [2] Estimate. [3] At mines & at plants making molybdenum products. [4] Comprises ferromolybdenum, molybdic oxide, & molybdenum salts & metal. [5] Includes molybdic oxide briquets, molybdic acid, molybdenum trioxide, all other. [6] U.S. producer price per kilogram of molybdenum oxide contained in technical-grade molybdic oxide. W = Withheld proprietary data. E = Net exporter. *Source: U.S. Geological Survey (USGS)*

US Merchant Price of Molybdic Oxide   In Dollars Per Pound

Year	Jan.	Feb.	Mar.	Apr.	May	June	July	Aug.	Sept.	Oct.	Nov.	Dec.	Average
2008	32.74	32.88	32.88	32.88	32.88	32.88	32.88	33.17	33.75	33.75	15.58	10.62	29.74
2009	9.78	9.61	9.03	8.55	9.08	10.34	11.56	17.35	15.24	13.22	10.86	11.15	11.31
2010	14.04	15.91	17.68	17.89	17.34	14.60	14.13	15.57	16.20	15.20	15.65	16.03	15.85
2011	16.73	17.63	17.70	17.36	17.25	16.87	14.95	14.83	14.70	13.80	13.24	13.47	15.71
2012	13.87	14.56	14.38	14.21	14.09	13.53	12.79	11.69	11.68	10.87	10.76	11.06	12.79
2013	11.71	11.44	11.11	11.05	11.10	11.06	9.87	9.29	9.50	9.36	9.67	9.75	10.41
2014	9.92	10.26	10.29	11.60	14.05	14.72	13.55	13.25	12.84	10.59	9.78	9.59	11.70

Source: American Metal Market (AMM)

Nickel

Nickel (atomic symbol Ni) is a hard, malleable, ductile metal that has a silvery tinge that can take on a high polish. Nickel is somewhat ferromagnetic and is a fair conductor of heat and electricity. Nickel is primarily used in the production of stainless steel and other corrosion-resistant alloys. Nickel is used in coins to replace silver, in rechargeable batteries, and in electronic circuitry. Nickel plating techniques, like electro-less coating or single-slurry coating, are employed in such applications as turbine blades, helicopter rotors, extrusion dies, and rolled steel strip.

Nickel futures and options trade at the London Metal Exchange (LME). The nickel futures contract calls for the delivery of 6 metric tons of primary nickel with at least 99.80% purity in the form of full plate, cut cathodes, pellets or briquettes. The contract is priced in terms of U.S. dollars per metric ton.

Prices – Nickel prices posted a record high of $17.75 per pound in 2007 but have since remained well below that level. Nickel prices in 2014 closed up +12.5% at $8.28 per pound.

Supply – World mine production of nickel in 2014 fell -8.8% yr/yr to 2.400 million metric tons, below last year's record high of 2.630 million metric tons. The current levels are almost triple the production seen in 1970. The world's largest mine producers of nickel in 2014 were Philippines (with 18.3% of world production), Russia (10.8%), Indonesia (10.0%), and Canada (10%). In 2011 (latest data available) U.S. secondary nickel production rose +9.0% to 89,300 metric tons, below the 2006 decade high of 103,630 metric tons.

Demand – U.S. consumption of nickel in 2014 rose +25.6% to 250,000 metric tons. The primary U.S. nickel consumption use is for stainless and heat-resisting steels, which accounted for 61.7% of U.S. consumption in 2011 (latest data). Other consumption uses in 2011 were super alloys (11.1%), nickel alloys (9.7%), alloy steels (4.1%) electro-plating anodes (3.6%), copper base alloys (1.1%), and chemicals (0.5%).

Trade – The U.S. relied on imports for 54% of its nickel consumption in 2014, up from 46% in 2013. U.S. imports of primary and secondary nickel in 2014 rose +29.7% to 197,500 metric tons, well above the 2009 record low of 117,600 metric tons. U.S. exports of primary and secondary nickel in 2014 fell -5.6% to 67,800 metric tons.

World Mine Production of Nickel   In Metric Tons (Contained Nickel)

Year	Australia[3]	Botswana	Brazil	Canada	China	Dominican Republic	Greece	Indonesia	New Caledonia	Philippines	Russia	South Africa	Total
2008	199,200	28,940	67,116	259,651	79,500	31,300	18,646	219,300	102,583	84,000	266,569	31,675	1,610,000
2009	165,000	28,595	41,059	136,594	84,800	----	10,203	202,800	92,570	161,300	261,791	34,605	1,450,000
2010	168,500	28,000	108,983	158,376	79,600	----	16,345	235,800	129,894	233,000	269,277	39,960	1,710,000
2011	215,000	26,000	109,000	219,612	89,800	21,693	21,710	290,000	131,071	270,000	267,393	39,810	1,960,000
2012	246,000	26,000	139,000	205,000	93,300	15,200		228,000	132,000	424,000	255,000	45,900	2,200,000
2013[1]	234,000		138,000	223,000	95,000	15,800		440,000	164,000	446,000	275,000	51,200	2,630,000
2014[2]	220,000		126,000	233,000	100,000			240,000	165,000	440,000	260,000	54,700	2,400,000

[1] Preliminary.   [2] Estimate.   [3] Content of nickel sulfate and concentrates.   *Source: U.S. Geological Survey (USGS)*

Salient Statistics of Nickel in the United States   In Metric Tons (Contained Nickel)

Year	Net Import Reliance As a % of Apparent Consumption	Production - Plant[4]	Secondary[5]	Alloy Sheets	Cast Iron	Copper Base Alloys	Electro-plating Anodes	Nickel Alloys	Stainless & Heat Resisting Steels	Super Alloys	Chemicals	Apparent Consumption	Stocks, Dec. 31 At Consumer Plants	Stocks, Dec. 31 At Producer Plants	Primary & Secondary Exports	Primary & Secondary Imports	Avg. Price LME $/Lb.
2007	17	----	93,940	7,130	212	5,720	10,300	17,900	127,000	22,000	2,880	119,000	14,050	5,690	116,100	141,200	16.88
2008	32	----	86,750	8,680	232	4,930	9,560	22,200	110,400	22,900	844	128,000	15,700	5,860	106,200	149,100	9.57
2009	22	----	79,830	6,330	204	2,870	11,500	20,100	104,000	13,000	1,740	164,000	14,030	5,490	97,030	117,600	6.65
2010	41	----	81,950	1,370	292	3,550	7,200	16,000	117,000	20,700	919	196,000	17,350	6,240	92,900	152,800	9.89
2011	48	----	89,300	7,850	64	2,110	6,910	18,800	119,000	21,500	956	213,000	18,710	6,610	77,200	159,300	10.38
2012[1]	49	----	----	----	----	----	----	----	----	----	----	218,000	16,600	6,380	68,900	155,300	7.95
2013[2]	46	----	----	----	----	----	----	----	----	----	----	199,000	18,500	9,730	71,800	152,300	6.81

[1] Exclusive of scrap.   [2] Preliminary.   [3] Estimate.   [4] Smelter & refinery.   [5] From purchased scrap (ferrous & nonferrous).
W = Withheld proprietary data.   NA = Not available.   *Source: U.S. Geological Survey (USGS)*

Average Price of Nickel[1] in the United States   In Cents Per Pound

Year	Jan.	Feb.	Mar.	Apr.	May	June	July	Aug.	Sept.	Oct.	Nov.	Dec.	Average
2010	929.69	958.30	1,124.71	1,290.79	1,130.91	1,006.54	1,041.32	1,109.42	1,153.47	1,186.36	1,133.19	1,174.23	1,103.24
2011	1,242.88	1,361.67	1,298.06	1,275.63	1,180.33	1,090.85	1,154.75	1,077.02	1,000.59	933.70	891.56	899.85	1,117.24
2012	977.36	1,000.39	913.14	869.82	828.25	800.53	783.19	763.76	835.67	834.31	787.80	841.55	852.98
2013	846.82	858.29	812.99	765.63	732.69	701.86	676.33	702.50	679.63	692.78	679.12	694.11	736.90
2014	703.14	708.28	774.92	855.13	943.44	906.85	927.94	907.24	883.35	778.75	773.39	784.30	828.89

[1] Plating material, briquettes.   *Source: American Metal Market (AMM)*

Oats

Oats are seeds or grains of a genus of plants that thrive in cool, moist climates. There are about 25 species of oats that grow worldwide in the cooler temperate regions. The oldest known cultivated oats were found inside caves in Switzerland and are believed to be from the Bronze Age. Oats are usually sown in early spring and harvested in mid to late summer, but in southern regions of the northern hemisphere, they may be sown in the fall. Oats are used in many processed foods such as flour, livestock feed, and furfural, a chemical used as a solvent in various refining industries. The oat crop year begins in June and ends in May. Oat futures and options are traded at the CME Group.

Prices – CME oat futures prices (Barchart.com electronic symbol ZO) on the nearest-futures chart rallied to a record high of $5.6375 per bushel in March 2014, but then fell sharply during the remainder of the year to post a 2-1/2 year low and close the year of 2014 down -14.3% at $3.0375 per bushel. Regarding cash prices, the average monthly price received by farmers for oats in the U.S. in the first eight months of the 2014-15 marketing year (June/May) fell -13.0% yr/yr to $3.28 per bushel.

Supply – World oat production in 2014-15 fell -5.4% yr/yr to 22.333 million metric tons, moderately above the record low of 19.625 million metric tons posted in 2010-11. World annual oat production in the past three decades has dropped very sharply from levels above 50 million metric tons in the early 1970s. The world's largest oat producers

are the European Union with 35.3% of world production in 2014-15, Russia 22.4%, Canada with 13.0%, and Australia with 5.2%.

U.S. oat production in the 2014-15 marketing year rose +7.8% yr/yr to 69.684 million bushels, above the 2011-12 record low of 53.649 million bushels. U.S. oat production has fallen sharply from levels mostly above 1 billion bushels seen from the early 1900s into the early 1960s. U.S. farmers harvested 1.029 million acres of oats in 2014-15, which was down -2.0% from the previous year's record low. That is down from the almost 40 million acres harvested back in the 1950s. The oat yield in 2014-15 rose +5.6% to 67.7 bushels per acre. Oat stocks in the U.S. as of September 2014 were up +17.1% yr/yr to a 74.310 million bushels. The largest U.S. oat-producing states in 2013 were the states of Wisconsin (12.5% of U.S. production), Minnesota (11.3%), North Dakota (11.0%), Iowa (5.1%), Pennsylvania (5.0%), and Michigan (4.0%).

Demand – U.S. usage of oats in 2014-15 fell -5.5% yr/yr to 164.000 million bushels, above the 2011-12 record low of 106.360 million bushels. Regarding U.S. usage of oats in 2014-15, 51.8% was for feed and residual, 42.1% for food, alcohol and industrial, 4.9% for seed, and 1.2% for exports.

Trade – U.S. exports of oats rose +27.6% yr/yr to 2.000 million bushels in 2014-15. U.S. imports of oats in 2014-15 rose +2.9% yr/yr to 100.000 million bushels, below the 2007 record high of 123.29 million bushels.

World Production of Oats   In Thousands of Metric Tons

Crop Year	Argentina	Australia	Belarus	Brazil	Canada	China	European Union	Norway	Russia	Turkey	Ukraine	United States	World Total
2005-06	350	1,690	609	522	3,283	700	8,017	279	4,545	270	791	1,667	23,827
2006-07	400	748	555	406	3,852	400	7,835	248	4,860	209	690	1,357	22,674
2007-08	472	1,502	580	238	4,618	643	8,690	276	5,384	189	544	1,313	25,536
2008-09	291	1,160	605	239	4,273	530	9,000	328	5,835	196	944	1,307	25,637
2009-10	182	1,162	552	253	2,912	580	8,641	276	5,401	218	731	1,321	23,334
2010-11	660	1,128	442	379	2,451	525	7,500	299	3,218	204	458	1,188	19,645
2011-12	345	1,262	448	354	3,158	600	7,927	231	5,332	218	506	728	22,308
2012-13[1]	496	1,121	422	361	2,812	600	7,909	236	4,027	210	630	892	21,105
2013-14[2]	445	1,326	352	380	3,906	580	8,388	236	4,932	210	467	938	23,602
2014-15[3]	460	1,150	450	380	2,910	600	7,869	236	5,000	210	580	1,011	22,333

[1] Preliminary.   [2] Estimate.   [3] Forecast.   *Source: Foreign Agricultural Service, U.S. Department of Agriculture (FAS-USDA)*

Official Oats Crop Production Reports in the United States   In Thousands of Bushels

Year	July 1	Aug. 1	Sept. 1	Oct. 1	Dec. 1	Final	Year	July 1	Aug. 1	Sept. 1	Oct. 1	Dec. 1	Final
2003	147,895	151,345	----	----	----	144,383	2009	91,277	91,960	----	----	----	93,081
2004	121,860	127,950	----	----	----	115,695	2010	87,726	87,239	----	----	----	81,190
2005	131,314	127,819	----	----	----	114,878	2011	56,551	57,489	----	----	----	53,649
2006	110,322	107,423	----	----	----	93,522	2012	65,276	66,519	----	----	----	61,486
2007	100,921	98,341	----	----	----	90,430	2013	74,459	75,210	----	----	----	64,642
2008	92,872	89,897	----	----	----	89,135	2014[1]	75,507	77,267	----	----	----	69,684

[1] Preliminary.   *Source: National Agricultural Statistics Service, U.S. Department of Agriculture (NASS-USDA)*

Oat Stocks in the United States   In Thousands of Bushels

	On Farms				Off Farms				Total Stocks			
Year	Mar. 1	June 1	Sept. 1	Dec. 1	Mar. 1	June 1	Sept. 1	Dec. 1	Mar. 1	June 1	Sept. 1	Dec. 1
2005	43,500	25,350	71,700	60,100	38,946	32,592	41,803	35,617	82,446	57,942	113,503	95,717
2006	42,200	25,190	60,800	53,000	32,673	27,376	39,284	45,889	74,873	52,566	100,084	98,889
2007	33,900	18,400	53,650	43,100	37,158	32,198	34,710	51,331	71,058	50,598	88,360	94,431
2008	31,000	16,100	52,800	42,600	47,988	50,674	66,296	72,322	78,988	66,774	119,096	114,922
2009	30,200	17,480	54,500	43,000	65,250	66,619	73,875	67,629	95,450	84,099	128,375	110,629
2010	30,900	17,600	46,250	34,100	67,091	62,716	70,722	66,911	97,991	80,316	116,972	101,011
2011	26,950	14,580	31,000	24,900	59,361	53,049	47,391	54,235	86,311	67,629	78,391	79,135
2012	19,750	11,120	34,100	26,100	55,044	43,869	50,872	47,051	74,794	54,989	84,972	73,151
2013	18,900	11,380	37,150	25,650	33,726	24,957	26,339	22,394	52,626	36,337	63,489	48,044
2014[1]	19,800	9,710	41,400	31,300	15,323	15,029	32,910	30,907	35,123	24,739	74,310	62,207

[1] Preliminary.   *Source: National Agricultural Statistics Service, U.S. Department of Agriculture (NASS-USDA)*

Supply and Utilization of Oats in the United States   In Millions of Bushels

	Acreage					Total	Feed &	Food, Alcohol &			Total	Ending	Farm	Findley Loan	Target
Crop Year Beginning June 1	Planted	Harvested	Yield Per Acre	Production	Imports	Supply	Residual	Industrial	Seed	Exports	Use	Stocks	Price	Rate	Price
	1,000 Acres		(Bushels)			In Millions of Bushels							Dollars Per Bushel		
2005-06	4,246	1,823	63.0	114.9	91.2	264.0	135.7	62.9	10.8	2.1	211.4	52.6	1.63	1.33	1.44
2006-07	4,168	1,566	59.8	93.5	106.2	252.3	124.9	64.5	9.7	2.6	201.7	50.6	1.87	1.33	1.44
2007-08	3,763	1,504	60.1	90.4	123.3	264.3	120.2	66.0	8.5	2.9	197.5	66.8	2.63	1.33	1.44
2008-09	3,247	1,400	63.7	89.1	114.6	270.5	108.1	66.1	8.9	3.3	186.4	84.1	3.15	1.33	1.44
2009-10	3,404	1,379	67.5	93.1	94.9	272.1	115.2	66.2	8.2	2.2	191.8	80.3	2.02	1.33	1.44
2010-11	3,138	1,263	64.3	81.2	85.1	247.3	102.9	67.2	6.8	2.9	179.7	67.6	2.52	1.39	1.79
2011-12	2,496	939	57.1	53.6	94.1	211.8	78.5	68.8	7.2	2.4	156.9	54.9	3.49	1.39	1.79
2012-13	2,700	1,005	61.2	61.5	92.9	209.3	95.6	68.1	7.9	1.4	172.9	36.3	3.89	1.39	1.79
2013-14[1]	2,980	1,009	64.1	64.6	97.2	198.2	96.9	66.2	8.8	1.6	173.5	24.7	3.45-3.75	1.39	1.79
2014-15[2]	2,723	1,029	67.7	69.7	100.0	194.4	85.0	69.0	8.0	2.0	164.0	30.4			

[1] Preliminary.   [2] Forecast.   [3] Less than 500,000 bushels.   NA = Not available.
Source: Economic Research Service, U.S. Department of Agiculture (ERS-USDA)

Production of Oats in the United States, by States   In Thousands of Bushels

Year	Illinois	Iowa	Michigan	Minnesota	Nebraska	New York	North Dakota	Ohio	Pennsylvania	South Dakota	Texas	Wisconsin	Total
2005	3,160	9,875	4,575	12,710	4,380	4,050	14,160	3,600	6,050	12,960	4,730	13,760	114,878
2006	3,080	8,360	4,030	11,200	2,025	4,958	4,920	4,125	7,040	5,415	3,700	14,490	93,522
2007	1,488	4,757	3,080	10,800	2,135	3,480	15,340	3,100	4,480	9,360	4,000	10,720	90,430
2008	2,100	4,875	3,960	11,900	2,450	4,224	6,630	3,500	4,640	8,760	5,000	11,780	89,135
2009	1,625	6,175	3,465	12,070	2,070	4,620	11,220	3,375	4,880	6,570	2,820	13,260	93,081
2010	1,950	4,340	4,080	11,385	1,700	3,886	6,405	3,500	4,720	7,560	4,160	9,860	81,190
2011	1,360	3,250	1,920	5,940	1,300	1,700	4,420	2,052	2,760	4,130	2,100	7,130	53,649
2012	1,140	3,770	2,100	8,370	1,026	3,250	6,510	2,576	3,965	3,060	3,185	7,800	61,486
2013	1,725	3,960	1,860	5,985	1,625	3,082	8,370	1,575	3,100	9,240	1,840	6,825	64,642
2014[1]	2,000	3,520	2,760	7,875	1,600	2,520	7,665	2,457	3,480	9,300	1,710	8,680	69,684

[1] Preliminary.   *Source: National Agricultural Statistics Service, U.S. Department of Agriculture (NASS-USDA)*

Average Cash Price of No. 2 Heavy White Oats in Toledo   In Dollars Per Bushel

Year	Jan.	Feb.	Mar.	Apr.	May	June	July	Aug.	Sept.	Oct.	Nov.	Dec.	Average
1996-97	NQ	2.45	2.34	2.19	2.02	1.96	1.96	1.99	2.16	2.26	2.12	2.08	2.14
1997-98	2.12	1.79	1.84	1.80	1.77	NQ	NQ	NQ	NQ	NQ	NQ	NQ	1.86
1998-99	NQ	NQ	NQ	NQ	NQ	NQ	NQ	NQ	NQ	NQ	NQ	NQ	NQ
1999-00	NQ	NQ	NQ	NQ	NQ	NQ	NQ	NQ	NQ	NQ	NQ	NQ	NQ
2000-01	NQ	NQ	NQ	NQ	NQ	NQ	NQ	NQ	NQ	NQ	NQ	NQ	NQ
2001-02	NQ	NQ	NQ	NQ	NQ	NQ	NQ	NQ	NQ	NQ	NQ	NQ	NQ
2002-03	NQ	NQ	NQ	NQ	NQ	NQ	NQ	NQ	NQ	NQ	NQ	NQ	NQ
2003-04	NQ	NQ	NQ	NQ	NQ	NQ	NQ	NQ	NQ	NQ	NQ	NQ	NQ
2004-05	NQ	NQ	NQ	NQ	NQ	NQ	NQ	NQ	NQ	NQ	NQ	NQ	NQ
2005-06[1]	NQ	NQ	NQ										

[1] Preliminary.   NQ = No quotes.   *Source: Economic Research Service, U.S. Department of Agriculture (ERS-USDA)*

OATS

Volume of Trading in Oats Futures in Chicago   In Contracts

Year	Jan.	Feb.	Mar.	Apr.	May	June	July	Aug.	Sept.	Oct.	Nov.	Dec.	Total
2005	26,439	35,921	36,808	35,199	24,696	33,748	28,353	26,134	17,708	27,080	32,687	26,766	351,539
2006	25,667	40,534	30,437	35,799	39,362	42,812	35,751	30,790	25,700	43,724	51,304	25,435	427,315
2007	42,231	41,327	41,259	46,054	31,288	43,157	32,977	30,240	24,565	29,484	48,488	21,671	432,741
2008	44,184	61,469	44,478	47,918	37,813	52,116	27,923	32,074	19,009	31,829	23,978	18,797	441,588
2009	17,494	34,259	19,035	34,277	25,365	41,961	19,370	24,801	20,076	29,720	29,328	18,619	314,305
2010	31,060	32,283	23,890	37,409	21,363	54,174	26,097	23,735	22,430	25,743	30,649	15,754	344,587
2011	28,513	41,210	32,798	35,451	25,962	42,810	17,687	26,037	24,613	23,352	41,624	9,259	349,316
2012	19,267	27,361	29,511	22,787	28,013	31,967	16,898	20,154	15,311	22,011	28,859	17,431	279,570
2013	21,246	34,411	16,949	31,035	16,891	28,267	18,156	16,459	17,388	21,863	22,977	9,316	254,958
2014	18,860	30,902	18,786	18,113	11,938	19,491	11,446	13,556	11,300	16,754	21,918	7,480	200,544

Contract size = 5,000 bu.   *Source: CME Group; Chicago Board of Trade (CBT)*

Average Open Interest of Oats in Chicago   In Contracts

Year	Jan.	Feb.	Mar.	Apr.	May	June	July	Aug.	Sept.	Oct.	Nov.	Dec.
2005	7,691	8,482	7,346	8,110	7,746	7,686	7,779	6,721	5,847	6,914	7,565	9,385
2006	10,200	11,697	10,960	10,961	13,529	14,128	13,965	11,620	11,178	13,483	14,714	13,818
2007	16,176	18,406	19,178	19,255	18,061	17,909	14,824	13,387	14,158	14,251	13,223	10,914
2008	13,696	14,812	14,764	15,097	15,957	16,802	16,667	15,027	14,740	15,495	15,108	16,848
2009	16,519	16,927	14,367	15,142	13,304	14,380	13,805	13,649	13,684	13,526	13,593	11,976
2010	12,601	13,869	15,662	17,612	17,244	16,838	10,329	10,956	11,664	13,477	13,452	11,707
2011	13,104	14,297	13,191	13,677	12,577	12,457	12,287	13,127	14,082	15,902	16,557	12,802
2012	13,363	11,924	10,849	10,879	11,516	11,021	9,959	10,708	11,328	11,802	11,567	10,439
2013	10,568	11,022	10,619	9,356	8,634	10,207	8,659	9,000	9,941	10,805	9,767	8,937
2014	10,414	11,168	9,529	8,350	7,356	7,793	7,292	8,382	8,987	9,787	9,813	8,151

Contract size = 5,000 bu.   *Source: CME Group; Chicago Board of Trade (CBT)*

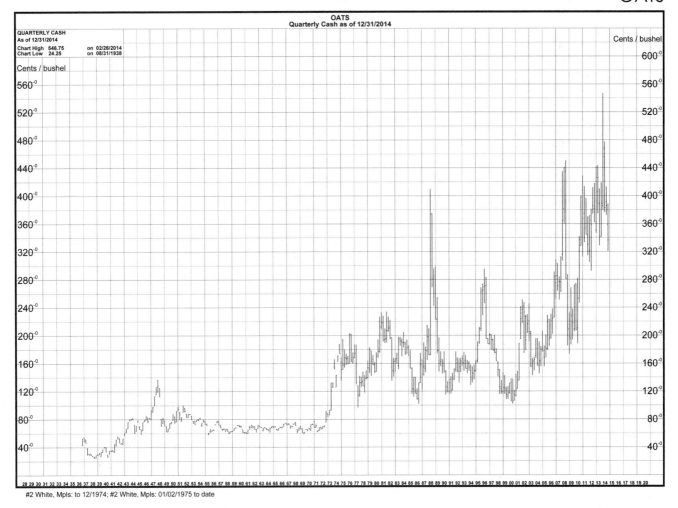

OATS
Quarterly Cash as of 12/31/2014

QUARTERLY CASH
As of 12/31/2014

Chart High 546.75 on 02/26/2014
Chart Low   24.25   on 08/31/1938

Cents / bushel

Cents / bushel

#2 White, Mpls: to 12/1974; #2 White, Mpls: 01/02/1975 to date

Average Cash Price of No. 2 Heavy White Oats in Minneapolis   In Dollars Per Bushel

Year	June	July	Aug.	Sept.	Oct.	Nov.	Dec.	Jan.	Feb.	Mar.	Apr.	May	Average
2005-06	1.88	1.88	1.88	1.88	1.88	1.88	2.19	2.12	2.06	1.97	2.00	2.13	1.98
2006-07	2.21	2.25	2.06	2.17	2.43	2.70	2.81	2.78	2.65	2.84	2.82	2.76	2.54
2007-08	2.90	2.69	2.61	2.68	2.70	2.79	2.95	3.24	3.66	3.82	3.75	3.96	3.15
2008-09	4.07	4.07	NQ	NQ	NQ	2.14	2.13	2.18	1.89	1.97	2.01	2.33	2.53
2009-10	2.33	2.15	2.12	2.03	2.34	2.56	2.44	2.56	2.30	2.19	2.10	1.98	2.26
2010-11	2.39	2.58	2.69	3.14	3.56	3.54	3.93	3.88	4.08	3.55	3.83	3.55	3.39
2011-12	3.68	3.68	3.69	3.72	3.51	3.36	3.16	3.30	3.46	3.48	3.55	3.48	3.50
2012-13	3.37	3.95	3.99	3.89	3.98	3.85	3.79	3.94	4.07	4.26	4.13	3.99	3.93
2013-14	4.21	3.84	3.78	3.40	3.57	3.79	4.30	3.80	4.64	4.66	4.58	4.03	4.05
2014-15[1]	3.88	3.85	3.83	3.86	3.68	3.53	3.26	3.49					3.67

[1] Preliminary.   NQ = No qoute.   *Source: Economic Research Service, U.S. Department of Agriculture (ERS-USDA)*

Average Price Received by Farmers for Oats in the United States   In Dollars Per Bushel

Year	June	July	Aug.	Sept.	Oct.	Nov.	Dec.	Jan.	Feb.	Mar.	Apr.	May	Average
2005-06	1.75	1.59	1.49	1.54	1.59	1.64	1.73	1.73	1.82	1.82	1.75	1.85	1.69
2006-07	1.90	1.78	1.67	1.70	1.77	2.05	2.01	2.20	2.35	2.40	2.46	2.49	2.07
2007-08	2.54	2.32	2.24	2.47	2.45	2.63	2.69	2.88	3.19	3.43	3.47	3.63	2.83
2008-09	3.56	3.44	3.16	3.29	3.26	3.00	3.12	2.77	2.69	2.77	2.37	2.64	3.01
2009-10	2.37	2.03	1.86	1.82	2.03	2.02	2.22	2.19	2.10	2.29	2.25	2.19	2.11
2010-11	2.11	2.11	2.09	2.30	2.55	3.07	2.94	3.13	3.27	3.28	3.54	3.55	2.83
2011-12	3.42	3.35	3.20	3.67	3.69	3.38	3.57	3.56	3.47	3.77	3.84	4.12	3.59
2012-13	3.80	3.70	3.82	3.76	3.93	3.88	3.90	4.06	4.14	4.20	4.43	4.45	4.01
2013-14	3.93	3.88	3.67	3.57	3.49	3.63	3.59	3.70	3.77	4.11	3.94	3.98	3.77
2014-15[1]	3.72	3.50	3.25	3.20	3.13	2.96	3.20	3.02					3.25

[1] Preliminary.   *Source: National Agricultural Statistics Service, U.S. Department of Agriculture (NASS-USDA)*

Olive Oil

Olive oil is derived from the fruit of the olive tree and originated in the Mediterranean area. Olives designated for oil are picked before ripening in the fall. Olive picking is usually done by hand. The olives are then weighed and washed in cold water. The olives, along with their oil-rich pits, are then crushed and kneaded until a homogeneous paste is formed. The paste is spread by hand onto metal plates, which are then stacked and pressed hydraulically to yield a liquid. The liquid is then centrifuged to separate the oil. It takes 1,300 to 2,000 olives to produce 1 quart of olive oil. The best olive oil is still produced from the first pressing, which is usually performed within 24 to 72 hours after harvest and is called extra virgin olive oil.

Supply – World production of olive oil (pressed oil) in the marketing year 2013-14 rose +33.0% to 3.440 million metric tons, slightly below the 2011-12 record high of 3.630 million metric tons. The world's largest producers of olive oil in 2013-14 were Spain (with 54.9% of world production), Italy (13.9%), Greece (5.1%), Syria (4.3%), Turkey (4.2%),

and Morocco (3.7%). Production levels in the various countries vary considerably from year-to-year depending on weather and crop conditions.

Demand – World consumption of olive oil in the 2013-14 marketing year rose +1.3% yr/yr to 3.165 million metric tons, below the 2011-12 record high of 3.351 million metric tons. The U.S. is the world's largest consumer of olive oil with 9.7% of world consumption in 2013-14. The U.S. consumption of olive oil set a new record high of 308,000 metric tons.

Trade – World olive oil imports in 2013-14 fell -3.7% to 910,000 metric tons. The U.S. was the world's largest importer in 2013-14 with 305,000 metric tons, representing 33.5% of world imports. World olive oil exports in 2013-14 fell -3.7% to 905,000 metric tons. The world's largest exporters were Spain (with 33.2% of world exports), Italy (25.4%), Tunisia (9.4%), and Turkey (5.5%).

World Production of Olive Oil (Pressed Oil)   In Thousands of Metric Tons

Crop Year	Algeria	Argen-tina	Greece	Italy	Jordan	Libya	Morocco	Portugal	Spain	Syria	Tunisia	Turkey	World Total
2005-06	32.0	23.0	455.5	635.0	23.0	9.0	81.0	35.5	887.0	110.0	236.5	119.0	2,711.6
2006-07	21.5	15.0	398.0	532.0	39.0	11.0	81.0	51.3	1,139.0	171.5	172.5	174.5	2,916.7
2007-08	24.0	27.0	353.2	553.0	22.5	13.0	92.0	39.3	1,280.0	111.0	183.0	79.0	2,886.5
2008-09	61.5	23.0	329.0	586.0	20.0	15.0	92.0	57.0	1,125.3	142.0	179.0	140.0	2,888.0
2009-10	26.5	17.0	346.0	557.7	29.5	15.0	151.5	57.5	1,494.5	163.0	170.0	157.0	3,298.2
2010-11	67.0	20.0	334.0	551.8	28.0	15.0	137.0	67.9	1,512.9	196.0	140.0	174.0	3,384.4
2011-12[1]	39.5	32.0	322.6	576.0	20.5	15.0	126.5	82.3	1,701.9	165.0	202.0	205.0	3,630.1
2012-13[2]	66.0	17.0	393.9	440.5	22.5	15.0	107.0	64.6	709.6	155.0	240.0	209.0	2,586.0
2013-14[3]	62.0	30.0	174.0	477.0	26.0	15.0	128.5	91.0	1,890.0	147.0	94.0	145.0	3,440.0

[1] Preliminary.   [2] Estimate.   [3] Forecast.   *Source: The Oil World*

World Imports and Exports of Olive Oil (Pressed Oil)   In Thousands of Metric Tons

Crop Year	Australia	Brazil	Italy	Japan	Spain	United States	World Total	Greece	Italy	Spain	Tunisia	Turkey	World Total
				Imports						Exports			
2005-06	32.7	26.0	136.6	30.2	51.1	242.0	700.9	9.8	203.6	114.6	123.3	56.0	686.1
2006-07	42.1	36.6	154.1	32.0	71.3	262.5	801.6	17.8	208.6	148.5	220.7	47.2	804.2
2007-08	27.8	42.9	119.4	30.4	41.8	264.5	737.6	12.0	197.9	158.8	187.4	18.3	740.8
2008-09	29.0	41.4	82.6	33.3	12.1	276.5	713.1	13.4	195.9	179.0	152.2	27.9	717.5
2009-10	35.6	51.3	56.8	42.6	17.9	272.0	739.9	13.7	213.8	208.0	115.3	27.2	731.5
2010-11	32.0	65.0	57.5	37.7	16.5	292.0	800.3	14.4	243.3	229.2	109.0	12.9	808.1
2011-12[1]	31.9	71.0	73.9	45.6	21.4	317.4	893.4	18.1	254.9	285.8	149.5	19.4	904.8
2012-13[2]	28.8	74.9	79.8	54.0	61.5	298.8	945.0	20.1	235.3	223.5	178.3	80.7	940.0
2013-14[3]	28.0	76.0	75.0	55.0	25.0	305.0	910.0	15.0	230.0	300.0	85.0	50.0	905.0

[1] Preliminary.   [2] Estimate.   [3] Forecast.   *Source: The Oil World*

World Consumption and Ending Stocks of Olive Oil (Pressed Oil)   In Thousands of Metric Tons

Crop Year	Brazil	Morocco	Syria	Tunisia	Turkey	United States	World Total	European Union	Morocco	Syria	Tunisia	Turkey	World Total
		Consumption							Ending Stocks				
2005-06	26.0	60.4	117.8	46.2	68.1	232.7	2,865.6	863.4	3.0	55.0	110.0	8.0	1,079.9
2006-07	36.6	71.8	128.3	26.8	90.3	244.2	3,003.8	782.3	14.0	43.0	38.0	45.0	990.2
2007-08	42.9	77.9	105.2	28.1	97.8	258.7	3,038.1	741.0	25.0	5.0	8.0	8.0	842.9
2008-09	41.4	92.8	112.0	29.8	105.2	266.3	3,072.6	541.0	34.0	8.0	9.0	15.0	697.9
2009-10	51.3	89.4	133.4	32.0	116.8	272.1	3,184.9	577.0	85.0	20.0	33.0	28.0	819.6
2010-11	65.0	96.7	135.7	34.5	129.2	284.7	3,292.3	575.0	90.0	47.0	30.0	60.0	903.9
2011-12[1]	71.0	103.3	138.6	38.8	145.7	298.2	3,351.8	750.6	105.0	50.0	44.0	100.0	1,170.8
2012-13[2]	74.9	111.3	140.5	40.9	148.3	305.4	3,125.7	249.6	90.0	38.0	65.0	80.0	636.0
2013-14[3]	76.0	115.0	141.0	36.2	125.1	308.0	3,165.0	601.6	85.0	21.0	38.0	50.0	916.0

[1] Preliminary.   [2] Estimate.   [3] Forecast.   *Source: The Oil World*

Onions

Onions are the bulbs of plants in the lily family. Onions can be eaten raw, cooked, pickled, used as a flavoring or seasoning, or dehydrated. Onions rank in the top 10 vegetables produced in the U.S. in terms of dollar value. Since 1629, onions have been cultivated in the U.S., but are believed to be indigenous to Asia.

The two main types of onions produced in the U.S. are yellow and white onions. Yellow varieties comprise approximately 75% of all onions grown for bulb production in the U.S. Onions that are planted as a winter crop in warm areas are milder in taste and odor than onions planted during the summer in cooler regions.

Prices – Onion prices in 2014 averaged $15.20 per hundred pounds, up +1.3% yr/yr.

Supply – U.S. production in 2014 rose +8.3% to 7.541 billion pounds, still below the 2004 record high of 8.307 billion pounds. The farm value of the U.S. production crop in 2013 rose +2.9% to 969,183, well below the 2006 record high of $1.084 billion. U.S. farmers harvested 142.650 acres, down -0.5% yr/yr, a new decade low. The yield in 2014 was 529 pounds per acre.

Demand – U.S. per capita consumption of onions in 2012 (latest data) rose +3.4% yr/yr to 21.3 pounds.

Trade – U.S. exports of fresh onions in 2012 (latest data) totaled 648 million pounds, and imports totaled 849 million pounds.

Salient Statistics of Onions in the United States

Crop Year	Harvested Acres	Yield Per Acre	Pro-duction 1,000 Cwt.	Price Per Cwt.	Farm Value $1,000	Jan. 1 Pack Frozen	Anual Pack Frozen	Imports Canned	Exports (Fresh)	Imports (Fresh)	Per Capita[3] Utilization -- Lbs., Farm Weight -- All	Fresh
						----------------------------- In Millions of Pounds -----------------------------						
2007	160,080	497	79,638	11.10	816,061	44.9	----	14.0	550.8	902.5	22.6	21.6
2008	153,490	489	75,120	11.90	834,386	39.4	----	19.7	612.2	714.2	21.7	20.2
2009	151,060	500	75,599	15.00	1,054,227	36.2	----	18.9	561.2	681.6	21.5	19.6
2010	149,270	493	73,599	15.60	1,049,704	39.0	----	17.7	713.5	869.1	21.1	19.6
2011	147,630	502	74,097	10.90	742,236	37.5	----	18.8	700.9	868.9	20.6	19.1
2012[1]	148,250	487	71,495	14.20	942,340	73.7	----	21.1	648.0	849.4	21.3	19.8
2013[2]	143,340	486	69,654	15.00	969,183	58.0	----					

[1] Preliminary. [2] Forecast. [3] Includes fresh and processing. *Source: Economic Research Service, U.S. Department of Agiculture (ERS-USDA)*

Production of Onions in the United States   In Thousands of Hundredweight (Cwt.)

Crop Year	Arizona	California	Texas	Total (All)	California	Colo-rado	Idaho	Mich-igan	Minne-sota	Mexico	New York	Oregon, Malheur	Texas	Total (All)	Grand Total
	---------------- Spring ----------------				-- Summer --										
2008	660	2,860	2,403	9,498	13,303	2,850	6,192	1,008	----	----	4,141	8,662	----	65,622	75,120
2009	576	2,460	3,003	8,523	14,287	2,739	6,512	1,330	----	----	4,275	7,840	----	67,076	75,599
2010	----	2,542	2,666	7,484	13,050	2,880	6,840	880	----	----	3,087	8,588	----	66,115	73,599
2011	----	2,520	3,360	8,845	12,980	2,864	7,176	816	----	----	1,891	8,249	----	65,252	74,097
2012	----	2,480	3,090	8,008	12,354	2,604	6,205	644	----	----	2,480	7,950	----	63,487	71,495
2013	----	2,720	3,492	9,209	11,700	1,700	7,380	810	----	----	2,015	7,848	----	60,445	69,654
2014[1]	----	2,992	2,340	7,917	16,120	1,638	6,400	975	----	----	2,788	7,600	----	67,501	75,418

[1] Preliminary. *Source: Agricultural Statistics Board, U.S. Department of Agriculture (ASB-USDA)*

Cold Storage Stocks of Frozen[2] Onions in the United States, on First of Month   In Thousands of Pounds

Year	Jan.	Feb.	Mar.	Apr.	May	June	July	Aug.	Sept.	Oct.	Nov.	Dec.
2009	36,192	35,247	34,714	32,696	32,860	33,258	31,005	31,252	34,647	36,935	40,862	42,488
2010	38,967	38,348	35,231	29,333	26,484	25,109	25,119	23,805	30,594	32,146	29,197	30,444
2011	37,504	33,942	34,401	43,066	49,076	58,596	53,773	56,913	68,638	74,735	58,288	68,902
2012	73,678	68,208	67,465	71,295	72,894	75,430	75,960	74,299	82,451	62,101	65,917	59,641
2013	58,030	53,882	55,947	52,566	52,835	51,059	50,557	53,048	50,048	50,252	49,506	52,770
2014[1]	49,806	50,425	47,054	46,423	46,175	50,046	55,773	64,252	60,862	52,736	50,282	45,791

[1] Preliminary. *Source: National Agricultural Statistics Service, U.S. Department of Agiculture (NASS-USDA)*

Average Price Received by Growers for Onions in the United States   In Dollars Per Hundred Pounds (Cwt.)

Year	Jan.	Feb.	Mar.	Apr.	May	June	July	Aug.	Sept.	Oct.	Nov.	Dec.	Season Average
2009	9.47	8.44	6.99	18.40	13.40	18.00	10.80	8.56	9.27	8.19	7.93	7.83	15.00
2010	11.20	15.00	34.20	29.90	19.30	16.10	16.30	13.10	11.70	9.61	12.10	11.60	15.60
2011	12.40	9.97	8.04	10.80	15.10	22.40	19.00	9.46	8.59	7.82	9.35	9.48	10.90
2012	6.59	4.90	7.07	18.80	26.30	21.30	27.50	30.50	11.10	10.10	12.40	17.50	14.20
2013	32.30	28.80	21.10	NQ	NQ	NQ	NQ	NQ	NQ	NQ	NQ	NQ	15.00
2014[1]	NQ	NQ	NQ	25.10	19.70	15.10	22.10	14.00	11.90	10.20	9.12	9.56	

[1] Preliminary.   NQ = Not quoted. *Source: Economic Research Service, U.S. Department of Agiculture (ERS-USDA)*

Oranges and Orange Juice

The orange tree is a semi-tropical, non-deciduous tree, and the fruit is technically a hesperidium, a kind of berry. The three major varieties of oranges include the sweet orange, the sour orange, and the mandarin orange (or tangerine). In the U.S., only sweet oranges are grown commercially. Those include Hamlin, Jaffa, navel, Pineapple, blood orange, and Valencia. Sour oranges are mainly used in marmalade and in liqueurs such as triple sec and curacao.

Frozen Concentrated Orange Juice (FCOJ) was developed in 1945, which led to oranges becoming the main fruit crop in the U.S. The world's largest producer of orange juice is Brazil, followed by Florida. Two to four medium-sized oranges will produce about 1 cup of juice, and modern mechanical extractors can remove the juice from 400 to 700 oranges per minute. Before juice extraction, orange oil is recovered from the peel. Approximately 50% of the orange weight is juice, the remainder is peel, pulp, and seeds, which are dried to produce nutritious cattle feed.

The U.S. marketing year for oranges begins December 1 of the first year shown (e.g., the 2005-06 marketing year extends from December 1, 2005 to November 30, 2006). Orange juice futures prices are subject to upward spikes during the U.S. hurricane season (officially June 1 to November 30), and the Florida freeze season (late-November through March).

Frozen concentrated orange juice future and options are traded on ICE Futures U.S. The ICE orange juice futures contract calls for the delivery of 15,000 pounds of orange solids and is priced in terms of cents per pound.

Prices – ICE orange juice futures prices (Barchart.com symbol OJ) in 2014 trended higher into April and posted the high for 2014 at 168.30 cents, a 2-3/4 year high. FCOJ prices gained on shrinking U.S. output as the USDA in April cut its U.S. 2013/14 orange production estimate to 110 million boxes, the lowest in 29 years, as greening disease decimated the orange crop. FCOJ prices then ratcheted lower into November and posted their low for 2014 at 124.10 cents as high prices crushed demand. U.S. orange-juice retail sales in the four weeks ended September 27 dropped to 36.65 million gallons, down -9% yr/yr and the lowest for the period since 2002. FCOJ prices recovered into year-end as dry weather in Brazil, the world's largest orange producer, damaged orange groves, and after the USDA cut its U.S. 2013/14 orange crop estimate to 104.6 million boxes, a 29-year low. FCOJ prices finished 2014 up +2.6% at 140.05 cents.

Supply – World production of oranges in the 2014-15 marketing year fell -4.3% yr/yr to 48.797 million metric tons. The world's largest producers of oranges in 2014-15 were Brazil with 33.4% of world production, followed by the U.S. (12.5%), and Mexico (8.8%).

U.S. production of oranges in 2013-14 (latest data) fell -17.7% yr/yr to 156.376 million boxes (1 box equals 90 lbs.) Florida's production in 2013-14 fell -21.7% yr/yr to 104.600 million boxes and California's production fell -8.3% to 50.000 million boxes.

World Production of Oranges   In Thousands of Metric Tons

Year	Argen-tina	Australia	Brazil	Egypt	Greece	Italy	Mexico	Morocco	South Africa	Spain	Turkey	United States	World Total
2005-06	840	470	17,993	2,120	1,017	2,261	4,157	784	1,167	2,376	1,445	8,212	50,253
2006-07	990	419	18,482	2,054	----	----	4,248	721	1,412	----	1,536	6,917	49,520
2007-08	940	403	16,850	2,138	----	----	4,297	732	1,526	----	1,427	9,141	50,720
2008-09	900	430	17,014	2,372	----	----	4,193	790	1,445	----	1,430	8,281	50,818
2009-10	770	380	15,830	2,401	----	----	4,051	823	1,459	----	1,690	7,478	49,151
2010-11	850	300	22,603	2,430	----	----	4,080	904	1,428	----	1,710	8,078	55,942
2011-12	565	390	20,482	2,350	----	----	3,666	850	1,466	----	1,650	8,166	53,830
2012-13[1]	550	435	16,361	2,450	----	----	4,400	784	1,560	----	1,600	7,502	49,917
2013-14[2]	600	430	16,850	2,570	----	----	4,400	1,001	1,620	----	1,700	6,153	51,008
2014-15[3]	900	430	16,320	2,630	----	----	4,300	750	1,600	----	1,550	6,097	48,797

[1] Preliminary. [2] Estimate. [3] Forecast.   NA = Not available.   *Source: Foreign Agricultural Service, U.S. Department of Agriculture (FAS-USDA)*

Salient Statistics of Oranges & Orange Juice in the United States

	---------- Production[4] ----------			Farm Price $ Per Box	Farm Value Million $	-------- Florida Crop Processed ----------				Frozen Concentrated Orange Juice - Florida ----------			
Year	California	Florida	Total U.S.			Frozen Concen-trates	Chilled Products	Total Pro-cessed	Yield Per Box Gallons[5]	Carry-in	Pack	Total Supply	Total Season Movement
	-------- Million Boxes ---------					-------------- Million Boxes ---------------				---- In Millions of Gallons (42 Deg. Brix) ----			
2004-05	64.5	149.8	216.5	6.68	1,475.4	54.3	88.5	143.9	1.6	151.8	86.3	238.1	175.2
2005-06	61.0	147.7	210.8	8.60	1,829.9	51.9	88.7	141.7	1.6	107.8	85.2	193.0	160.8
2006-07	46.0	129.0	177.3	12.56	2,216.5	48.0	74.5	123.4	1.6	67.2	79.6	146.8	149.2
2007-08	62.0	170.2	234.4	9.36	2,198.8	80.8	84.7	165.5	1.7	52.1	135.6	187.7	137.7
2008-09	46.5	162.5	210.7	9.22	1,970.1	72.5	82.6	156.2	1.7	108.0	153.9	261.9	143.9
2009-10	57.5	133.7	192.8	10.24	1,997.2	52.7	74.9	128.2	1.6	118.0	82.3	200.3	130.2
2010-11	62.5	140.5	204.9	10.90	2,230.4	51.8	82.6	135.2	1.6	95.0	82.1	177.1	148.5
2011-12[1]	58.0	146.7	206.1	12.70	2,621.6	65.4	75.5	141.3	1.6	51.6	175.4	227.0	124.3
2012-13[2]	54.5	133.6	189.9	10.85	2,073.4	48.0	79.2	128.2	1.6	61.1	127.9	189.0	108.4
2013-14[3]	50.0	104.6	156.4	12.35	1,960.1	22.7	76.0	99.5	1.6				

[1] Preliminary. [2] Estimate. [3] Forecast. 4/ Fruit ripened on trees, but destroyed prior to picking not included. [5] 42 deg. Brix equivalent.
Source: Economic Research Service, U.S. Department of Agriculture (ERS-USDA); Florida Department of Citrus

ORANGE JUICE FCOJ-1 - ICE-US
Weekly Nearest Futures as of 01/02/2015

WEEKLY NEAREST FUTURES
As of 01/02/2015

Chart High 226.95 on 01/23/2012
Chart Low 64.60 on 02/17/2009

Nearby Futures through Last Trading Day.

Volume of Trading of Frozen Concentrated Orange Juice Futures in New York   In Contracts

Year	Jan.	Feb.	Mar.	Apr.	May	June	July	Aug.	Sept.	Oct.	Nov.	Dec.	Total
2005	54,140	85,349	57,557	87,595	40,785	94,913	61,610	92,195	46,868	117,355	50,098	113,574	902,039
2006	65,978	98,034	82,293	92,312	73,517	87,429	63,429	84,160	50,871	95,955	54,975	74,743	923,696
2007	70,773	84,076	63,417	87,759	59,937	84,150	50,721	78,502	48,392	103,218	45,539	69,308	845,792
2008	57,421	78,860	52,166	80,331	43,942	70,780	51,859	67,402	41,353	78,327	29,013	59,058	710,512
2009	28,514	63,757	31,766	67,156	30,396	81,964	56,197	65,286	40,276	86,071	28,426	77,186	656,995
2010	55,002	62,671	42,726	73,654	36,599	63,734	37,098	64,224	50,953	72,996	34,959	96,967	691,583
2011	39,184	63,134	43,077	63,680	41,142	89,150	28,260	80,733	32,920	59,502	24,493	62,335	627,610
2012	59,578	68,746	29,672	58,405	42,001	56,218	28,654	57,465	31,796	51,993	36,729	65,518	586,775
2013	46,432	54,711	37,532	67,361	31,399	63,622	26,724	43,047	29,937	40,275	24,295	39,684	505,019
2014	27,695	39,560	29,605	51,337	24,033	51,811	21,141	36,438	18,068	35,974	26,840	34,565	397,067

Contract size = 15,000 lbs.   *Source: ICE Futures U.S. (ICE)*

Average Open Interest of Frozen Concentrated Orange Juice Futures in New York   In Contracts

Year	Jan.	Feb.	Mar.	Apr.	May	June	July	Aug.	Sept.	Oct.	Nov.	Dec.
2005	33,821	33,619	30,008	32,523	26,171	28,730	32,221	29,034	23,603	28,602	34,966	35,795
2006	30,485	35,479	36,603	36,617	34,418	29,180	27,169	29,872	29,515	30,852	29,873	28,342
2007	29,484	28,370	32,312	29,430	28,830	31,917	30,457	29,540	28,335	29,599	26,608	27,412
2008	24,919	26,603	29,806	32,831	32,102	33,136	28,353	31,133	29,112	31,060	28,254	28,802
2009	27,889	28,234	26,905	27,982	29,370	31,608	30,602	31,281	28,806	30,805	29,677	34,210
2010	35,442	34,435	35,991	31,854	29,524	29,143	26,424	27,037	27,400	29,340	28,707	29,996
2011	31,885	31,086	27,618	27,153	31,594	36,039	35,046	28,253	23,967	25,308	27,118	27,105
2012	26,892	23,743	21,892	20,278	22,652	25,461	21,779	23,214	23,078	23,687	22,412	24,458
2013	20,672	20,900	18,819	20,972	20,719	22,432	19,760	19,241	16,646	15,809	14,609	14,636
2014	15,542	15,905	16,793	18,372	18,487	17,605	13,552	13,068	12,175	13,385	13,798	12,089

Contract size = 15,000 lbs.   *Source: ICE Futures U.S. (ICE)*

ORANGES AND ORANGE JUICE

Cold Storage Stocks of Orange Juice Concentrate[2] in the U.S., on First of Month   In Millions of Pounds

Year	Jan.	Feb.	Mar.	Apr.	May	June	July	Aug.	Sept.	Oct.	Nov.	Dec.
2005	1,468.8	1,553.8	1,578.9	1,578.2	1,652.4	1,668.1	1,548.8	1,501.6	1,397.3	1,243.3	1,139.9	1,027.5
2006	1,044.7	1,065.9	1,076.8	1,005.7	1,087.5	1,157.7	1,104.1	1,002.6	888.8	776.0	714.3	650.3
2007	678.2	726.0	751.1	825.1	901.5	960.7	909.7	849.1	761.2	620.4	582.2	563.7
2008	682.5	837.8	942.4	1,031.9	1,210.6	1,442.7	1,514.9	1,424.9	1,319.4	1,199.7	1,086.0	1,034.6
2009	1,088.0	1,193.2	1,261.2	1,291.4	1,415.4	1,497.2	1,519.7	1,404.3	1,316.7	1,252.2	1,150.3	1,127.2
2010	1,185.2	1,289.7	1,300.4	1,305.1	1,377.6	1,434.2	1,353.1	1,235.7	1,133.9	1,036.8	903.6	795.3
2011	809.7	834.7	869.2	842.0	835.2	864.5	797.3	732.0	641.5	588.9	522.3	479.6
2012	632.1	710.1	788.8	889.0	1,006.7	1,057.6	956.6	857.9	773.6	675.6	606.4	598.0
2013	695.4	781.6	875.4	946.8	1,021.3	1,042.3	996.2	915.0	864.6	795.8	785.9	732.6
2014[1]	739.5	750.5	799.3	813.0	877.8	872.9	853.7	815.9	773.0	712.0	721.9	676.8

[1] Preliminary.   [2] Adjusted to 42.0 degrees Brix equivalent (9.896 pounds per gallon).   Source: Agricultural Statistics Board, U.S. Department of Agriculture (ASB-USDA)

Producer Price Index of Frozen Orange Juice Concentrate   1982 = 100

Year	Jan.	Feb.	Mar.	Apr.	May	June	July	Aug.	Sept.	Oct.	Nov.	Dec.	Average
2005	103.3	103.3	105.0	109.0	109.0	109.0	109.3	109.3	108.1	107.9	108.4	126.4	109.0
2006	138.3	142.1	150.1	160.9	161.0	164.1	172.3	174.8	185.4	197.6	208.9	208.7	172.0
2007	198.1	191.7	198.5	179.6	187.7	184.1	173.6	171.5	152.9	159.3	162.6	168.2	177.3
2008	168.0	166.6	160.0	159.2	159.3	159.6	126.0	121.8	121.4	116.8	115.2	124.3	141.5
2009	124.6	124.4	124.4	117.6	125.0	118.0	118.0	119.8	119.1	119.0	119.0	128.8	121.5
2010	141.3	141.1	141.5	144.5	144.5	144.5	144.7	145.0	150.0	150.4	150.4	150.6	145.7
2011	164.1	163.9	163.9	169.6	169.8	170.4	170.8	188.8	187.6	181.7	190.5	175.7	174.7
2012	177.5	188.7	184.9	173.4	170.7	133.5	131.6	130.0	127.0	125.5	123.1	132.0	149.8
2013	130.8	122.6	123.0	124.1	145.6	148.6	145.5	149.2	149.2	136.7	140.1	140.9	138.0
2014[1]	138.3	139.0	135.1	184.0	184.4	184.6	184.5	184.0	190.2	183.4	178.3	178.1	172.0

[1] Preliminary.   Source: Bureau of Labor Statistics, U.S. Department of Labor (BLS)

Average Price Received by Farmers for Oranges (Equivalent On-Tree) in the U.S.   In Dollars Per Box

Year	Jan.	Feb.	Mar.	Apr.	May	June	July	Aug.	Sept.	Oct.	Nov.	Dec.	Average
2005	3.39	3.69	4.84	4.80	5.11	5.43	6.55	4.90	4.29	4.04	5.90	4.46	4.78
2006	5.16	5.27	5.78	6.44	7.13	7.05	6.56	12.03	17.96	13.89	6.95	7.28	8.46
2007	8.25	8.11	10.58	10.62	11.12	11.07	8.95	8.81	7.84	9.60	8.14	5.80	9.07
2008	5.77	5.83	6.20	6.40	7.01	6.75	5.79	4.78	5.92	5.57	7.53	5.39	6.08
2009	5.74	6.04	7.08	6.54	6.61	7.04	7.38	8.58	W	W	11.61	6.13	7.28
2010	6.41	6.78	7.97	7.49	8.00	8.85	7.10	7.49	6.88	6.96	11.47	6.66	7.67
2011	6.58	6.50	6.77	7.00	7.53	8.46	7.74	7.53	7.60	8.47	8.86	7.29	7.53
2012	7.65	8.25	8.52	9.53	10.35	12.49	9.60	7.81	9.08	9.57	8.92	6.64	9.03
2013	6.85	7.05	7.84	8.46	9.27	12.85	10.64	10.00	12.24	12.94	13.07	6.93	9.85
2014[1]	8.24	11.80	12.73	10.32	11.20	13.87	14.79	15.62	13.74	9.97	14.88	9.12	12.19

[1] Preliminary.   Source: Economic Research Service, U.S. Department of Agriculture (ERS-USDA)

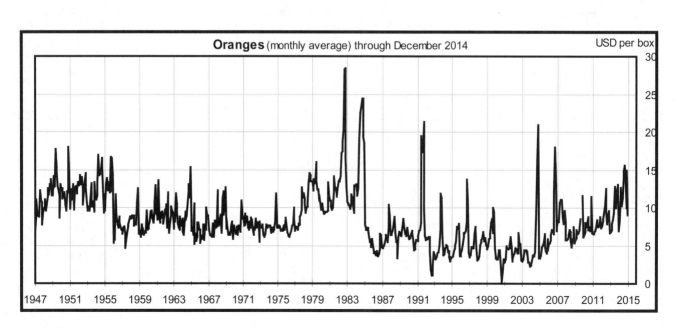

Palm Oil

Palm oil is an edible vegetable oil produced from the flesh of the fruit of the oil palm tree. The oil palm tree is a tropical palm tree that is a native of the west coast of Africa and is different from the coconut palm tree. The fruit of the oil palm tree is reddish, about the size of a large plum, and grows in large bunches. A single seed, the palm kernel, is contained in each fruit. Oil is extracted from both the pulp of the fruit (becoming palm oil) and the kernel (palm kernel oil). About 1 metric ton of palm kernel oil is obtained for every 10 metric tons of palm oil.

Palm oil is commercially used in soap, ointments, cosmetics, detergents, and machinery lubricants. It is also used worldwide as cooking oil, shortening, and margarine. Palm kernel oil is a lighter oil and is used exclusively for food use. Crude palm oil and crude palm kernel oil are traded on the Bursa Malaysia Derivatives Berhad (BMD). Futures are also traded on the Dalian Commodity Exchange (DCE), Indonesia Commodity & Derivatives Exchange (ICDX), and the National Commodity & Derivatives Exchange (NCDEX).

Prices – The monthly average wholesale price of palm oil (CIF, bulk, U.S. ports) in 2013 fell by -14.5% yr/yr to 41.13 cents per pound, below the 2011 record high of 55.98 cents per pound.

Supply – World production of palm oil in the 2014-15 marketing year rose by +6.3% to 62.793 million metric tons. World palm oil production has grown by over twenty times the production level of 1.922 million metric tons seen back in 1970. Indonesia and Malaysia are the world's two major global producers of palm oil. Indonesian production rose +8.2% to a record high of 33.000 million metric tons in 2014-15 and Indonesian production accounted for 52.6% of world production. Malaysian production in 2014-15 rose +5.4% to a record high of 21.250 million metric tons and Malaysian production accounted for 33.8% of world production. Other smaller global producers include Thailand with 3.6% of world production, Columbia with 1.7% and Nigeria with 1.5%.

Demand – U.S. total disappearance of palm oil in 2013-14 rose +11.8% yr/yr to 1.300 million metric tons which was a new record high.

Trade – World palm oil exports in 2014-15 rose by +5.4% to 44.567 million metric tons, which was a new record high. The world's largest exporters are Indonesia with a 50.0% share of world exports and Malaysia with a share of 40.4%. World palm oil imports in 2014-15 rose +6.9% to 42.521 million metric tons. The world's largest importers are India with a 20.9% share of world imports and European Union with a 16.5% share.

World Production of Palm Oil   In Thousands of Metric Tons

Crop Year	Brazil	Colom-bia	Costa Rica	Cote d'Ivoire	Ecuador	Guate-mala	Honduras	Indonesia	Malaysia	Nigeria	Papua New Guinea	Thailand	World Total
2005-06	170	660	181	236	340	92	180	15,560	15,485	800	310	784	35,767
2006-07	190	714	189	281	352	125	195	16,600	15,290	810	422	1,170	37,359
2007-08	205	733	199	289	396	153	278	18,000	17,567	820	447	1,050	41,186
2008-09	230	778	207	345	418	194	280	20,500	17,259	850	501	1,540	44,190
2009-10	250	805	227	330	429	177	275	22,000	17,763	850	527	1,287	46,107
2010-11	270	753	242	300	380	231	320	23,600	18,211	850	582	1,832	48,836
2011-12	310	945	260	400	473	291	395	26,200	18,202	850	582	1,892	52,111
2012-13[1]	340	1,140	265	390	540	323	410	28,500	19,321	910	610	2,135	56,144
2013-14[2]	340	1,042	270	400	565	350	430	30,500	20,161	930	630	2,150	59,059
2014-15[3]	340	1,070	270	400	575	355	440	33,000	21,250	930	630	2,250	62,793

[1] Preliminary.   [2] Estimate.   [3] Forecast.   *Source: The Oil World*

World Trade of Palm Oil   In Thousands of Metric Tons

Crop Year	China	Germany	India	Nether-lands	Pakistan	United Kingdom	Total	Hong Kong	Indonesia	Malaysia	Guinea	Sing-apore	Total
2004-05	4,319	766	3,342	1,438	1,683	869	26,328	59	9,862	13,585	322	223	26,152
2005-06	5,182	662	2,820	1,589	1,728	885	27,885	14	11,590	13,718	317	206	28,088
2006-07	5,543	711	3,664	1,710	1,743	734	29,157	27	12,465	13,768	406	185	29,598
2007-08	5,559	654	5,019	2,011	1,860	595	32,609	11	14,100	15,041	385	199	32,757
2008-09	6,297	1,000	6,875	2,097	1,870	426	35,890	19	16,209	15,990	494	198	35,565
2009-10	5,853	1,038	6,606	1,950	1,970	436	36,522	2	16,596	16,610	470	201	36,571
2010-11	5,975	1,083	6,684	1,871	1,975	400	38,100	3	17,167	17,151	530	166	38,130
2011-12[1]	5,950	931	7,473	2,240	2,109	420	40,367	2	18,631	17,587	559	110	40,354
2012-13[2]	6,680	1,177	8,312	2,788	2,172	472	43,962	4	21,029	18,524	507	83	44,030
2013-14[3]	6,400	1,200	7,900	2,350	2,220	450	42,261	3	20,900	17,150	530	83	42,355

[1] Preliminary.   [2] Estimate.   [3] Forecast.   *Source: The Oil World*

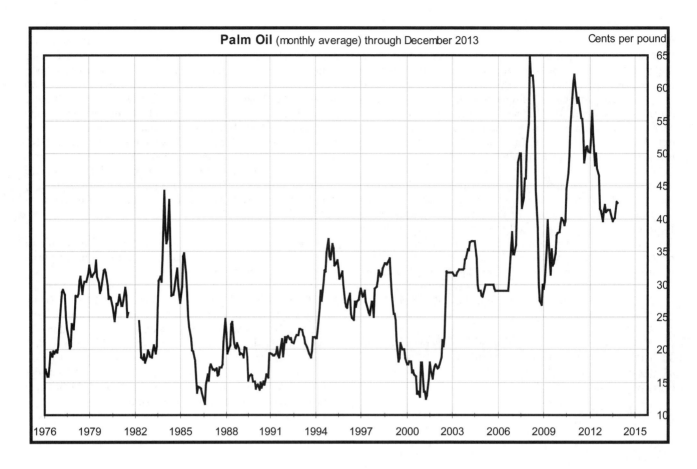

Palm Oil (monthly average) through December 2013 — Cents per pound

Supply and Distribution of Palm Oil in the United States   In Thousands of Metric Tons

Crop Year Beginning Oct. 1	Stocks Oct. 1	Imports	Total Supply	Consumption Edible Products	Consumption Inedible Products	Consumption Total End Products	Total Disappearance	Exports	U.S. Import Value[4]	Malaysia, F.O.B., RBD	Palm Kernel Oil, Malaysia, C.I.F Rotterdam
				-------- In Millions of Pounds --------					--------- U.S. $ Per Metric Ton -----------		
2005-06	76.4	603.8	680.2	436.4	W	436.4	555.6	30.6	----	452	583
2006-07	94.0	692.0	786.0	568.5	W	568.5	635.8	58.7	----	685	768
2007-08	91.5	954.7	1,046.2	789.3	W	789.3	934.7	38.3	----	1053	1248
2008-09	73.2	1,035.5	1,108.7	973.6	W	973.6	917.0	62.1	----	628	662
2009-10	129.6	996.6	1,126.2	1,140.8	W	1,140.8	894.6	80.9	----	807	972
2010-11	150.7	979.7	1,130.4	1,049.7	W	1,049.7	887.6	97.8	----	1146	1741
2011-12	145.0	1,030.1	1,175.1	NA	NA	NA	965.0	83.8	----	1053	1220
2012-13[1]	126.3	1,285.1	1,411.4	NA	NA	NA	1,163.1	103.3	----	835	836
2013-14[2]	145.0	1,390.0	1,535.0	NA	NA	NA	1,300.0	80.0	----	905	1186
2014-15[3]	155.0								----		

[1] Preliminary. [2] Estimate. [3] Forecast. [4] Market value in the foreign country, excluding import duties, ocean freight and marine insurance.
W = Withheld. *Sources: The Oil World; Economic Research Service, U.S. Department of Agriculture (ERS-USDA)*

Average Wholesale Palm Oil Prices, CIF, Bulk, U.S. Ports   In Cents Per Pound

Year	Jan.	Feb.	Mar.	Apr.	May	June	July	Aug.	Sept.	Oct.	Nov.	Dec.	Average
2004	34.00	35.38	35.25	36.40	36.50	36.50	36.50	36.50	34.00	30.00	29.00	29.00	34.09
2005	28.20	28.00	28.67	30.00	30.00	30.00	30.00	30.00	30.00	30.00	29.25	29.00	29.43
2006	29.00	29.00	29.00	29.00	29.00	29.00	29.00	29.00	29.00	29.00	31.00	35.75	29.73
2007	38.00	34.50	34.50	36.00	42.38	48.63	50.00	NA	41.67	43.19	46.20	46.20	41.93
2008	51.48	54.66	64.63	61.96	61.90	59.70	55.41	44.43	38.52	30.11	27.41	26.91	48.09
2009	29.98	29.32	30.32	35.46	39.86	36.45	31.40	35.39	32.90	33.24	34.66	37.53	33.88
2010	37.83	37.91	39.35	40.11	39.60	38.97	39.64	44.57	47.00	49.55	54.00	58.60	43.93
2011	60.88	62.06	60.44	57.80	58.44	57.56	55.40	55.25	53.25	48.63	51.00	51.05	55.98
2012	50.25	50.19	52.60	56.56	52.94	48.20	50.06	47.75	46.63	41.44	41.25	39.69	48.13
2013	41.38	42.06	41.00	41.38	41.35	41.31	40.19	39.70	40.00	40.19	42.65	42.38	41.13

Source: Economic Research Service, U.S. Department of Agriculture (ERS-USDA)

Paper

The earliest known paper that is still in existence was made from cotton rags around 150 AD. Around 800 AD, paper made its appearance in Egypt but was not manufactured there until 900 AD. The Moors introduced the use of paper to Europe, and around 1150, the first papermaking mill was established in Spain, followed by England in 1495, and the U.S. in 1690.

During the 17th and 18th centuries, the increased usage of paper created a shortage of cotton rags, which were the only source for papermaking. The solution to this problem lead to the introduction of the ground-wood process of pulp-making in 1840 and the first chemical pulp process 10 years later.

Today, the paper and paperboard industries, including newsprint, are sensitive to the economic cycle. As the economy strengthens, paper use increases, and vice versa.

Prices – The average monthly index price (1982 = 100) for paperboard in 2014 rose +2.0% yr/yr to 248.6, a new record high. The average monthly producer price index of standard newsprint paper in 2014 fell by -1.2% to 129.0, well below the 12-year high of 151.8 posted in 2006.

Supply – U.S. production of paper and paperboard in 2013 fell -0.4% yr/yr to 74.228 million metric tons. The U.S. is the world's largest producer of paper and paperboard by far, followed by Germany with 22.393 million metric tons and Canada with 11.133 million metric tons.

U.S. production of newsprint fell by –2.4% yr/yr to a record low of 414.6 metric tons per month in 2005 which is the latest data available. U.S. production of newsprint is second in the world, after Canada, which had production of 657.167 metric tons per month in 2005.

Production of Paper and Paperboard by Selected Countries   In Thousands of Metric Tons

Year	Austria	Canada	Finland	France	Germany	Italy	Nether-lands	Norway	Russia/3	Spain	Sweden	United Kingdom	United States
2008	5,153	15,789	13,126	9,404	22,828	9,467	2,977	1,900	7,700	6,414	11,663	4,983	80,178
2009	4,606	12,823	10,602	8,332	20,870	8,404	2,609	1,577	7,373	5,700	10,932	4,293	71,356
2010	5,009	12,755	11,758	8,830	23,072	9,087	2,859	1,695	5,606	6,193	11,410	4,300	77,689
2011	4,901	12,057	11,329	8,527	22,706	9,130	2,748	1,496	7,549	6,203	11,298	4,342	76,431
2012	5,004	10,756	10,694	8,354	22,603	8,588	2,761	1,209	7,661	6,177	11,417	4,292	74,492
2013[1]	4,837	11,133	10,592	8,308	22,393	8,536	2,814	1,079	7,490	6,118	10,782	4,600	74,228

[1] Preliminary.   Source: Food and Agriculture Organization of the United Nations (FAO)

Production of Newsprint by Selected Countires (Monthly Average)   In Thousands of Metric Tons

Year	Australia	Brazil	Canada	China	Finland	France	Germany	India	Japan	Rep. of Korea	Russia/3	Sweden	United States
2009	NA	NA	NA	403.6	NA	NA	207.3	80.7	287.9	124.8	167.3	200.6	NA
2010	NA	NA	NA	358.9	NA	NA	213.4	80.9	280.1	132.6	162.8	201.2	NA
2011	NA	NA	NA	296.3	NA	NA	213.4	74.4	267.1	130.6	160.8	188.2	NA
2012	NA	NA	NA	326.1	NA	NA	184.3	NA	271.1	126.1	151.7	167.7	NA
2013[1]	NA	NA	NA	305.4	NA	NA	176.4	NA	268.2	124.1	132.1	127.4	NA
2014[2]	NA	NA	NA	274.6	NA	NA	NA	NA	262.9	118.8	138.6	104.8	NA

[1] Preliminary.   [2] Estimate.   NA = Not available.   Source: Food and Agriculture Organization of the United Nations (FAO)

Index Price of Paperboard   (1982 = 100)

Year	Jan.	Feb.	Mar.	Apr.	May	June	July	Aug.	Sept.	Oct.	Nov.	Dec.	Average
2008	209.7	209.8	209.7	209.7	209.7	210.3	211.5	226.0	229.5	230.0	229.6	229.1	217.9
2009	224.6	221.3	216.7	211.8	205.3	203.0	202.8	202.0	202.4	199.1	198.8	197.9	207.1
2010	198.0	210.3	212.6	214.5	229.2	231.4	232.2	232.3	236.3	234.2	233.7	233.8	224.9
2011	233.6	230.6	230.7	230.6	230.0	232.0	232.6	231.6	231.6	230.0	226.3	226.4	230.5
2012	226.4	226.3	225.9	226.1	226.0	225.9	224.9	226.1	226.6	230.3	235.5	235.7	228.0
2013	235.7	235.8	236.8	236.8	241.1	246.4	247.7	249.3	249.0	249.0	248.8	248.3	243.7
2014[1]	249.0	249.6	249.7	249.2	249.3	249.3	249.2	248.8	247.6	247.3	246.9	246.9	248.6

[1] Preliminary.   Source: Bureau of Labor Statistics, U.S. Department of Commerce (BLS) (0914)

Producer Price Index of Standard Newsprint   (1982 = 100)

Year	Jan.	Feb.	Mar.	Apr.	May	June	July	Aug.	Sept.	Oct.	Nov.	Dec.	Average
2008	125.8	129.6	133.4	136.2	142.7	146.5	151.0	156.1	158.6	162.4	167.6	166.1	148.0
2009	162.3	158.9	153.0	141.1	129.6	120.3	107.5	105.3	105.5	107.7	111.0	114.6	126.4
2010	116.5	116.9	118.3	114.8	122.3	124.8	128.6	129.5	132.5	133.5	135.3	134.7	125.6
2011	137.3	137.8	136.2	136.1	136.0	137.5	135.2	137.1	138.2	138.1	138.8	138.4	137.2
2012	138.9	138.6	143.9	144.1	144.1	138.7	138.4	138.2	138.3	138.1	137.9	138.1	139.8
2013	136.3	132.6	130.1	129.7	129.1	127.8	130.8	129.6	129.4	129.9	131.3	130.3	130.6
2014[1]	130.7	130.5	130.2	129.2	128.3	129.2	129.1	129.0	128.7	128.4	127.9	127.1	129.0

[1] Preliminary.   Source: Bureau of Labor Statistics, U.S. Department of Commerce (BLS) (0913-02)

Peanuts and Peanut Oil

Peanuts are the edible seeds of a plant from the pea family. Although called a nut, the peanut is actually a legume. Ancient South American Inca Indians were the first to grind peanuts to make peanut butter. Peanuts originated in Brazil and were later brought to the U.S. via Africa. The first major use of peanuts was as feed for pigs. It wasn't until the Civil War that peanuts were used as human food when both Northern and Southern troops used the peanut as a food source during hard times. In 1903, Dr. George Washington Carver, a talented botanist who is considered the "father of commercial peanuts," introduced peanuts as a rotation crop in cotton-growing areas. Carver discovered over 300 uses for the peanut including shaving cream, leather dye, coffee, ink, cheese, and shampoo.

Peanuts come in many varieties, but there are four basic types grown in the U.S.: Runner, Spanish, Valencia, and Virginia. Over half of Runner peanuts are used to make peanut butter. Spanish peanuts are primarily used to make candies and peanut oil. Valencia peanuts are the sweetest of the four types. Virginia peanuts are mainly roasted and sold in and out of the shell.

Peanut oil is extracted from shelled and crushed peanuts through hydraulic pressing, expelled pressing, or solvent extraction. Crude peanut oil is used as a flavoring agent, salad oil, and cooking oil. Refined, bleached and deodorized peanut oil is used for cooking and in margarines and shortenings. The by-product called press cake is used for cattle feed along with the tops of the plants after the pods are removed. The dry shells can be burned as fuel.

Prices – The average monthly price received by farmers for peanuts (in the shell) in the first six months of the 2013-14 marketing year (Aug/July) fell -17.7% to 24.7 cents per pound. The record high is 34.7 cents posted in 1990-91. The average monthly price of peanut oil in the 2013-14 marketing year (through January 2014) fell -26.1% yr/yr to 64.86 cents per pound, below the 2007-08 record high of 100.91 cents per pound.

Supply – World peanut production in 2014-15 fell -1.8% to 39.129 million metric tons, slightly below last year's record high of 39.835 million metric tons. The world's largest peanut producers are China with 42.2% of world production, India with 12.8%, Nigeria with 7.7% and U.S. with 6.0%. U.S. peanut production in the 2014-15 marketing year rose by +24.9% to 5.210 billion pounds, below the 2012-13 record high of 6.763 billion pounds.

U.S. farmers harvested 1.325 million acres of peanuts in 2014-15, up +27.0% yr/yr. That was below the 16-year high harvest of 1.629 million acres in 2005-06. U.S. peanut yield in 2014-15 fell -1.7% yr/yr to 3,932 pounds per acre, slightly below the 2012-13 record high of 4,217 pounds per acre. The largest peanut producing states in the U.S.in 2014 are Georgia (with 46.5% of U.S. production), Florida (12.8%), Alabama (10.6%), Texas (9.4%), and North Carolina (7.7%). U.S. crude peanut oil production in 2012 (latest data) rose +36.6% to 209.820 million pounds, which was only about 40% of the record high level of 358,195 million pounds posted in 1996.

Demand – U.S. disposition of peanuts in 2014-15 fell by -1.9% yr/yr to 5.077 billion pounds. Of that disposition, 57.9% of the peanuts went for food, 19.7% for exports, 12.5% for crushing into peanut oil, and 9.9% for seed, loss and residual. The most popular type of peanut grown in the U.S. is the Runner peanut with 89.0% of U.S. production in 2013-14. This was followed by the Virginia peanut with 9.8% of production and the Spanish peanut far behind with only 1.2% of production. Peanut butter is a primary use for Runner and Virginia peanuts. It accounts for 61.2% of Runner peanut usage and 42.8% of Virginia peanut usage. In lagging third place, only about 5% of Spanish peanuts are used for peanut butter. Snack peanuts is also a key usage category and accounts for 42.1% of Virginia peanut usage, 25.9% of Spanish peanut usage, and 18.3% of Runner peanut usage. Candy accounts for 63.0% of Spanish peanut usage, 19.2% of Runner peanut usage, and 8.5% of Virginia peanut usage.

Trade – U.S. exports of peanuts in 2014-15 fell -8.8% yr/yr to 1.000 billion pounds. U.S. imports of peanuts fell by -26.1% yr/yr in 2014-15 to 65 million pounds.

World Production of Peanuts (in the Shell)   In Thousands of Metric Tons

Crop Year	Argen-tina	Burma	Came-roon	China	India	Indo-nesia	Nigeria	Senegal	Sudan	Tanzania	United States	Vietnam	World Total
2005-06	510	1,039	346	14,342	6,300	1,170	3,478	703	520	294	2,209	489	35,852
2006-07	775	1,024	414	12,887	5,385	1,200	3,062	460	555	350	1,571	463	32,688
2007-08	800	1,088	449	13,027	6,800	1,150	2,847	331	564	408	1,666	510	34,051
2008-09	860	1,202	484	14,286	6,250	1,250	2,873	731	716	341	2,342	534	37,132
2009-10	836	1,305	503	14,708	4,900	1,250	2,978	1,033	942	348	1,675	525	36,121
2010-11	1,033	1,362	536	15,644	5,850	1,250	3,799	1,286	763	465	1,886	441	39,816
2011-12	1,023	1,399	564	16,046	5,500	1,165	2,963	528	1,185	651	1,660	471	38,328
2012-13	1,016	1,372	570	16,692	5,000	1,145	3,070	693	1,032	810	3,064	493	40,119
2013-14[1]	997	1,400	550	16,972	5,650	1,160	3,000	710	850	800	1,893	530	39,835
2014-15[2]	1,000	1,400	550	16,500	5,000	1,150	3,000	725	850	800	2,363	550	39,129

[1] Preliminary.   [2] Estimate.   *Source: Foreign Agricultural Service, U.S. Department of Agriculture (FAS-USDA)*

Salient Statistics of Peanuts in the United States

Crop Year Beginning Aug. 1	Acreage Planted	Acreage Harvested for Nuts	Average Yield Per Acre In Lbs.	Production (1,000 Lbs)	Season Farm Price (Cents Lb.)	Farm Value (Million Dollars)	In Thousands of Pounds			
							Exports		Imports	
	------- 1,000 Acres -------						Unshelled	Shelled	Unshelled	Shelled
2005-06	1,657.0	1,629.0	2,989	4,869,860	17.3	843.4	491,000	----	32,100	----
2006-07	1,243.0	1,210.0	2,863	3,464,250	17.7	612.8	603,000	----	61,000	----
2007-08	1,230.0	1,195.0	3,130	3,740,650	20.5	758.6	750,000	----	73,000	----
2008-09	1,534.0	1,507.0	3,426	5,162,400	23.0	1,193.6	727,000	----	86,000	----
2009-10	1,116.0	1,079.0	3,421	3,691,650	21.7	793.1	592,000	----	72,000	----
2010-11	1,288.0	1,255.0	3,312	4,156,840	22.5	938.6	606,000	----	65,000	----
2011-12	1,140.6	1,080.6	3,386	3,658,590	31.8	1,168.6	546,000	----	254,000	----
2012-13	1,638.0	1,604.0	4,211	6,753,880	29.2-30.8	2,026.3	1,175,000	----	115,000	----
2013-14[1]	1,067.0	1,043.0	4,001	4,173,170		1,055.1	650,000	----	65,000	----
2014-15[2]	1,354.0	1,325.0	3,932	5,210,100		1,122.3				

[1] Preliminary. [2] Estimate. Source: Economic Research Service, U.S. Department of Agriculture (ERS-USDA)

Supply and Disposition of Peanuts (Farmer's Stock Basis) & Support Program in the United States

Crop Year Beginning Aug. 1	Supply				Disposition				Government Support Program			
	Pro- duction	Imports	Stocks Aug. 1	Total	Exports	Crushed for Oil	Seed, Loss & Residual	Food	Total Disap- pearance	Support Price	Addi- tional	Amount Put ---- Under Support ---
												Quantity (Mil. Lbs.)	% of Pro- duction
	------------------------------- In Millions of Pounds -------------------------------								--- Cents Per Lb. ---			
2006-07	3,464	61	2,167	5,692	603	513	471	2,585	4,172	NA	NA	1,694	97.9
2007-08	3,741	73	1,520	5,265	750	496	471	2,517	4,234	NA	NA	1,363	74.2
2008-09	5,162	86	1,031	6,280	727	445	407	2,571	4,150	----	----	2,073	80.5
2009-10	3,692	72	2,130	5,894	592	435	569	2,675	4,271	----	----	1,674	90.7
2010-11	4,157	65	1,829	6,050	606	587	350	2,840	4,382	----	----	1,811	87.1
2011-12	3,659	254	1,516	5,428	546	604	470	2,805	4,425	----	----		
2012-13	6,754	119	1,003	7,876	1,190	656	524	2,735	5,105	----	----		
2013-14[1]	4,173	88	2,771	7,032	1,096	663	530	2,886	5,174	----	----		
2014-15[2]	5,210	65	1,858	7,133	1,050	656	514	2,954	5,174	----	----		

[1] Preliminary. [2] Estimate. Source: Economic Research Service, U.S. Department of Agriculture (ERS-USDA)

Production of Peanuts (Harvested for Nuts) in the United States, by States   In Thousands of Pounds

Crop Year	Alabama	Florida	Georgia	Mississippi	New Mexico	North Carolina	Oklahoma	South Carolina	Texas	Virginia	Total
2005	613,250	410,400	2,130,000	44,800	66,500	288,000	107,910	168,000	975,000	66,000	4,869,860
2006	407,500	300,000	1,598,500	46,400	43,200	268,800	62,700	168,000	514,750	54,400	3,464,250
2007	400,350	321,300	1,622,400	59,400	32,000	261,000	57,800	173,600	691,900	52,500	3,740,650
2008	675,500	448,000	2,329,000	81,900	25,600	358,900	63,000	265,200	834,900	80,400	5,162,400
2009	495,000	336,000	1,797,800	54,000	21,700	244,200	42,900	148,800	506,850	44,400	3,691,650
2010	481,000	472,500	1,959,150	63,000	34,000	232,200	70,350	224,000	586,800	33,840	4,156,840
2011	489,700	549,500	1,645,750	56,000	19,800	291,600	54,600	240,900	249,240	61,500	3,658,590
2012	876,000	760,500	3,343,400	215,600	26,000	427,180	80,300	417,300	525,600	82,000	6,753,880
2013	489,900	517,450	1,887,180	122,100	21,700	315,900	59,200	273,000	423,540	63,200	4,173,170
2014[1]	553,600	668,000	2,423,100	124,000	15,500	399,900	44,000	410,400	488,950	82,650	5,210,100

[1] Preliminary. Source: Agricultural Statistics Board, U.S. Department of Agriculture (ASB-USDA)

Supply and Reported Uses of Shelled Peanuts and Products in the United States   In Thousands of Pounds

Crop Year Beginning Aug. 1	Shelled Peanuts -- Stocks, Aug. 1 --		Shelled Peanuts ----- Production -----		Reported Used (Shelled Peanuts - Raw Basis)					Shelled Peanuts Crushed[6]	Crude Oil Pro- duction	Cake & Meal Production
					Edible Grades Used In							
	Edible	Oil Stock[2]	Edible	Oil Stock[2]	Candy[3]	Snack[4]	Butter[5]	Other Products	Total			
2005-06	501,868	15,305	2,411,471	357,600	376,777	454,324	974,223	12,092	1,817,416	407,817	181,085	232,868
2006-07	510,097	21,499	2,415,495	347,243	373,684	415,131	993,445	9,397	1,791,657	385,375	166,450	223,537
2007-08	528,918	33,401	2,291,603	319,186	320,467	425,166	1,012,263	10,676	1,768,572	372,980	158,144	211,733
2008-09	431,593	39,508	2,442,345	253,778	316,275	367,478	1,102,698	9,840	1,796,291	334,296	142,666	190,748
2009-10	554,295	35,498	2,457,434	280,888	315,595	352,963	1,191,821	15,840	1,876,219	326,779	139,903	185,452
2010-11	473,878	43,380	2,450,639	357,130	395,452	395,177	1,213,229	16,890	2,020,748	441,017	190,110	250,043
2011-12	466,310	52,883	2,399,094	345,565	394,678	390,068	1,197,748	19,661	2,002,155	453,835	188,479	250,037
2012-13	547,965	33,883	3,125,786	351,284	381,914	400,429	1,227,859	20,664	2,030,866	493,205	210,702	270,328
2013-14[1]	519,824	25,364	3,098,392	373,008	395,726	429,796	1,218,170	29,103	2,072,795	497,272	209,808	268,554

[1] Preliminary. [2] Includes straight run oil stock peanuts. [3] Includes peanut butter made by manufacturers for own use in candy. [4] Formerly titled "Salted Peanuts." [5] Includes peanut butter made by manufacturers for own use in cookies and sandwiches, but excludes peanut butter used in candy.
[6] All crushings regardless of grade. Source: National Agricultural Statistics Service, U.S. Department of Agriculture (NASS-USDA)

PEANUTS AND PEANUT OIL

Shelled Peanuts (Raw Basis) Used in Primary Products, by Type   In Thousands of Pounds

| Crop Year Beginning Aug. 1 | Virginia | | | | Runner | | | | Spanish | | | |
	Candy[2]	Peanuts	Butter[3]	Total	Candy[2]	Peanuts	Butter[3]	Total	Candy[2]	Peanuts	Butter[3]	Total
2004-05	25,466	70,216	112,027	209,411	349,437	367,671	824,876	1,562,692	14,793	12,894	1,611	29,435
2005-06	25,738	81,617	123,402	231,893	335,748	361,176	849,176	1,557,025	15,291	11,531	W	28,498
2006-07	29,542	75,858	113,689	220,196	329,806	328,167	869,014	1,535,250	14,335	11,104	W	36,211
2007-08	27,909	71,059	125,497	225,445	279,564	344,551	878,026	1,511,807	12,994	9,556	W	31,321
2008-09	26,342	52,925	110,737	191,770	276,212	303,730	981,546	1,569,531	13,721	10,823	W	34,990
2009-10	17,361	50,812	W	198,497	286,277	290,358	1,056,699	1,646,454	11,957	11,793	W	31,269
2010-11	16,070	62,708	W	211,194	365,260	319,529	1,076,521	1,774,346	14,122	12,940	W	35,207
2011-12	17,856	78,333	W	203,958	360,797	303,631	1,091,541	1,770,809	16,025	8,104	W	27,390
2012-13	17,731	83,722	82,981	192,888	347,428	309,860	1,143,108	1,812,591	16,755	6,847	W	25,389
2013-14[1]	17,109	85,298	86,759	202,536	W	337,934	1,128,206	1,844,490	15,996	6,564	W	W

[1] Preliminary.   [2] Includes peanut butter made by manufacturers for own use in candy.   [3] Includes peanut butter made by manufacturers for own use in cookies and sandwiches, but excludes peanut butter used in candy.
Source: National Agricultural Statistics Service, U.S. Department of Agriculture (NASS-USDA)

Production, Consumption, Stocks and Foreign Trade of Peanut Oil in the United States   In Millions of Pounds

| Crop Year Beginning Aug. 1 | Production | | Consumption | | Stocks, Dec. 31 | | Imports for Con-sumption | Exports |
	Crude	Refined	In Refining	In End Products	Crude	Refined		
2002-03	267.7	166.3	W	277.6	52.9	3.5	----	----
2003-04	180.7	115.8	W	203.8	23.0	1.8	----	----
2004-05	135.7	91.0	W	181.9	40.3	2.4	----	----
2005-06	188.0	119.9	W	152.1	15.4	3.7	----	----
2006-07	173.8	115.1	W	W	35.5	5.6	----	----
2007-08	168.7	111.2	W	W	14.1	1.8	----	----
2008-09	150.8	99.9	W	W	17.6	3.0	----	----
2009-10[1]	146.3	96.6	W	W	18.1	2.1	----	----
2010-11[2]	196.9	132.0	W	W	----	----	----	----
2011-12[2]	NA	NA	NA	NA	NA	NA	----	----

[1] Preliminary.   [2] Forecast.   W = Withheld.   *Source: Bureau of the Census, U.S. Department of Commerce*

Farmer Stock Equivalent Total[2/3] Stocks of Peanuts in the United States at End of Month   In Million Pounds

Crop Year	Aug.	Sept.	Oct.	Nov.	Dec.	Jan.	Feb.	Mar.	Apr.	May.	June	July
2005-06	1,089.0	1,359.6	3,471.8	4,482.8	4,416.2	4,112.6	3,847.5	3,494.8	3,179.6	2,815.9	2,459.6	2,166.6
2006-07	1,854.5	1,791.2	3,202.6	4,119.5	3,942.2	3,648.0	3,318.9	2,929.0	2,587.4	2,223.1	1,897.7	1,520.1
2007-08	1,173.6	1,073.9	2,752.7	3,401.0	3,199.8	2,898.1	2,622.8	2,322.2	1,967.5	1,625.4	1,331.0	1,031.3
2008-09	718.7	1,042.8	3,212.5	4,301.6	4,367.0	4,074.4	3,818.6	3,448.3	3,085.4	2,763.7	2,447.5	2,130.1
2009-10	1,837.6	1,657.4	2,922.1	3,973.0	3,862.4	3,602.9	3,541.8	3,153.2	2,785.9	2,451.9	2,158.8	1,828.7
2010-11	1,502.4	1,778.9	3,651.7	4,150.9	3,887.3	3,565.5	3,258.3	2,867.1	2,443.1	2,148.3	1,820.9	1,515.9
2011-12	1,171.5	1,252.4	2,888.2	3,389.3	3,237.9	2,938.7	2,652.9	2,333.0	1,966.5	1,553.1	1,261.8	1,003.3
2012-13	669.6	1,623.1	5,050.1	5,758.2	5,570.7	5,184.7	4,792.2	4,382.6	3,953.0	3,559.0	3,202.7	2,770.7
2013-14	2,427.0	2,172.4	3,776.3	4,641.5	4,710.1	4,299.6	3,919.4	3,505.5	3,092.3	2,741.2	2,304.4	1,857.8
2014-15[1]	1,426.7	1,330.5	4,248.1	4,717.9	4,573.9	4,284.1						

[1] Preliminary.   [2] Excludes stocks on farms. Includes stocks owned by or held for account of peanut producers and CCC in commercial storage facilities. Farmer stock on net weight basis.   [3] Actual farmer stock, plus roasting stock, plus shelled peanuts.   W = Withheld.   *Source: Agricultural Marketing Service, U.S. Department of Agriculture (AMS-USDA)*

Farmer Stock Peanuts[2], Total All Types, in the United States at End of Month   In Millions of Pounds

Crop Year	Aug.	Sept.	Oct.	Nov.	Dec.	Jan.	Feb.	Mar.	Apr.	May.	June	July
2005-06	444.0	787.0	2,878.9	3,885.8	3,739.0	3,361.2	2,999.9	2,608.2	2,281.2	1,964.1	1,653.8	1,402.6
2006-07	1,085.2	994.4	2,383.5	3,269.5	3,109.8	2,770.3	2,436.4	2,064.0	1,728.1	1,378.9	1,080.9	730.1
2007-08	446.6	431.5	2,186.1	2,821.3	2,614.7	2,236.8	1,872.4	1,514.5	1,168.1	855.5	585.4	346.9
2008-09	123.8	606.4	2,693.9	3,692.9	3,698.4	3,345.2	3,019.4	2,643.5	2,316.6	2,013.7	1,652.7	1,360.0
2009-10	1,037.5	859.2	2,113.7	3,143.5	3,035.0	2,783.8	2,656.9	2,258.7	1,903.9	1,595.4	1,286.0	991.4
2010-11	711.4	1,064.9	2,900.3	3,394.2	3,178.3	2,852.9	2,501.4	2,066.1	1,657.1	1,343.8	1,027.3	769.0
2011-12	472.0	613.8	2,300.1	2,780.8	2,581.2	2,239.4	1,888.5	1,514.2	1,145.2	772.3	507.9	272.8
2012-13	98.2	1,164.8	4,442.1	5,098.6	4,865.5	4,447.0	4,032.1	3,548.0	3,073.4	2,629.0	2,266.4	1,925.0
2013-14	1,527.6	1,296.5	2,909.0	3,790.8	3,876.1	3,472.0	3,045.7	2,615.1	2,195.8	1,819.1	1,423.3	1,059.5
2014-15[1]	661.8	573.0	3,517.7	4,046.4	3,949.9	3,633.5						

[1] Preliminary.   [2] Excludes stocks on farms. Includes stocks owned by or held for account of peanut producers and CCC in commercial storage facilities. Farmer stock on net weight basis.   *Source: Agricultural Marketing Service, U.S. Department of Agriculture (AMS-USDA)*

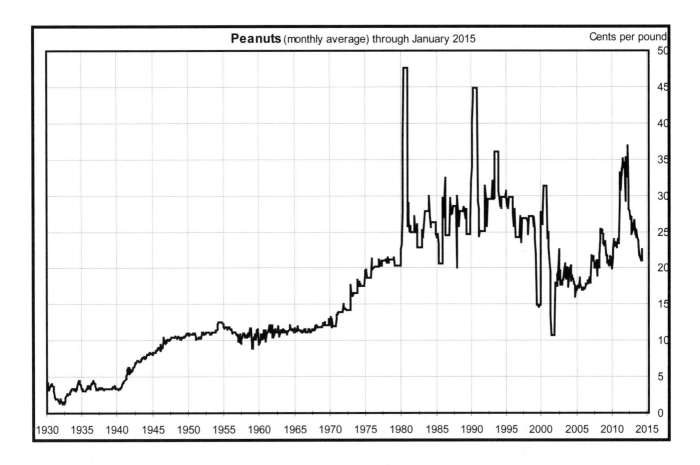

Peanuts (monthly average) through January 2015 — Cents per pound

Average Price[2] Received by Farmers for Peanuts (in the Shell) in the United States   In Cents Per Pound

Year	Jan.	Feb.	Mar.	Apr.	May	June	July	Aug.	Sept.	Oct.	Nov.	Dec.	Average[1]
2005-06	17.0	17.0	17.4	17.5	17.4	17.3	18.6	16.9	17.4	17.3	17.0	17.0	17.3
2006-07	17.0	17.3	17.2	17.2	17.6	17.8	17.8	17.8	18.3	17.9	18.1	18.7	17.7
2007-08	18.0	18.6	21.4	21.7	21.3	21.6	21.0	20.7	20.0	20.4	20.1	21.1	20.5
2008-09	18.9	21.0	20.6	20.1	21.7	23.9	25.3	25.4	25.2	24.8	24.7	23.4	22.9
2009-10	23.1	23.3	23.7	21.7	21.7	20.7	21.0	20.6	20.4	20.5	21.6	21.5	21.7
2010-11	20.7	19.9	21.4	22.3	24.0	23.0	23.5	23.4	23.1	22.8	23.3	23.9	22.6
2011-12	23.4	23.5	28.9	33.2	30.8	33.7	32.9	34.8	35.1	33.8	34.4	34.5	31.6
2012-13	29.3	35.2	33.7	32.6	36.9	31.2	28.2	27.8	26.8	27.1	27.0	24.7	30.0
2013-14	25.1	25.3	26.0	26.6	24.6	25.4	24.2	25.2	24.2	23.8	W	21.7	24.7
2014-15[1]	22.1	21.5	21.0	21.4	21.0	22.5							

[1] Preliminarly.   [2] Weighted average by sales.   *Source: National Agricultural Statistics Service, U.S. Department of Agriculture (NASS-USDA)*

Average Price of Domestic Crude Peanut Oil (in Tanks) F.O.B. Southeast Mills   In Cents Per Pound

Year	Jan.	Feb.	Mar.	Apr.	May	June	July	Aug.	Sept.	Oct.	Nov.	Dec.	Average
2005-06	45.50	45.50	45.00	42.50	42.50	42.50	42.50	42.50	43.75	45.00	47.30	49.25	44.48
2006-07	52.67	52.50	50.00	49.25	46.25	48.20	52.63	55.63	62.56	69.63	70.00	73.00	56.86
2007-08	76.75	93.20	98.50	97.33	99.00	100.00	104.38	104.80	107.00	110.00	110.00	110.00	100.91
2008-09	97.00	90.00	85.25	79.10	75.00	62.50	58.75	56.60	57.00	60.70	62.00	54.00	69.83
2009-10	51.20	52.00	52.20	59.00	59.50	58.75	63.60	67.63	67.75	67.80	68.38	68.81	61.39
2010-11	71.40	75.13	77.90	80.06	79.63	77.50	78.70	82.81	78.50	88.05	95.56	97.50	81.90
2011-12	97.00	98.75	96.10	95.81	95.00	96.60	102.38	106.13	111.00	110.00	110.00	104.50	101.94
2012-13	103.00	99.90	98.56	96.75	86.00	79.05	77.50	80.00	82.75	84.00	83.00	82.00	87.71
2013-14	81.00	78.70	75.38	65.70	62.06	59.06	57.75	57.20	58.25	58.63	62.80	61.75	64.86
2014-15[1]	59.95	60.63	60.13	56.15									59.22

[1] Preliminary.   *Source: Agricultural Marketing Service, U.S. Department of Agriculture (AMS-USDA)*

Pepper

The pepper plant is a perennial climbing shrub that originated in India and Sri Lanka. Pepper is considered the world's most important spice and has been used to flavor foods for over 3,000 years. Pepper was once considered so valuable that it was used to ransom Rome from Attila the Hun. Black pepper alone accounts for nearly 35% of the world's spice trade. Unlike many other popular herbs and spices, pepper can only be cultivated in tropical climates. The pepper plant produces a berry called a peppercorn. Both black and white pepper are obtained from the same plant. The colors of pepper are determined by the maturity of the berry at harvest and by different processing methods.

Black pepper is picked when the berries are still green and immature. The peppercorns are then dried in the sun until they turn black. White pepper is picked when the berries are fully ripe and bright red. The red peppercorns are then soaked, washed to remove the skin of the berry, and dried to produce a white to yellowish-white peppercorn. Black pepper has a slightly hotter flavor and stronger aroma than white pepper. Piperine, an alkaloid of pyridine, is the active ingredient in pepper that makes it hot.

Black pepper oil is obtained from crushed berries using solvent extraction. Black pepper oil is used in the treatment of pain, chills, flu, muscular aches, and in some perfumes. It is also helpful in promoting digestion in the colon.

The world's key pepper varieties are known by their place of origin. Popular types of pepper include Lampong

Black and Muntok White from Indonesia, Brazilian Black, and Malabar Black and Tellicherry from India.

Pepper futures are traded on the National Commodity & Derivatives Exchange (NCDEX) and the Singapore Mercantile Exchange (SMX).

Production – World production of pepper in 2013 rose by +4.6% yr/yr to 472,526 metric tons. The world's largest pepper producer is Vietnam with a 34.5% share of world production, followed by Indonesia with a 18.8% share and India with a 11.2% share. Pepper production in 2013 in Vietnam rose by +4.5% yr/yr to 163,000 metric tons. Pepper production in 2013 rose by +1.0% yr/yr in Indonesia to 88,700 metric tons.

Trade – The world's largest exporters of pepper in 2011 (latest data available) were Vietnam (with 123,800 metric tons of exports), India (37,419), Indonesia (36,487), Brazil (32,696), and Malaysia (14,237). U.S. imports of black pepper in 2008 (latest data) fell -2.6% yr/yr to 49,625 metric tons. The primary source of U.S. imports of black pepper in 2008 was Indonesia which accounted for 41% of U.S. imports, followed by India with 20%, and Brazil with 17%. Imports from Malaysia have dropped by over 95% since 2003. U.S. imports of white pepper in 2008 rose by +25.1% yr/yr to 6,960 metric tons. The primary source of U.S. imports of white pepper was Indonesia, which accounted for 69% of U.S. imports, followed by Malaysia with 5%, Brazil with 1%, and China with 1%.

World Production of Pepper   In Metric Tons

Year	Brazil	Cambodia	China	India	Indonesia	Madagascar	Malaysia	Mexico	Philippines	Sri Lanka	Thailand	Vietnam	World Total
2006	80,316	2,278	24,000	92,900	77,534	5,443	19,092	4,915	3,678	18,600	12,156	102,570	466,456
2007	77,770	2,373	26,000	69,000	80,420	5,200	20,145	6,854	3,270	19,390	10,419	116,090	461,825
2008	69,600	2,557	27,000	47,010	80,420	4,264	22,218	6,653	3,426	22,870	5,852	128,000	444,207
2009	65,398	2,375	28,262	47,400	82,834	5,010	23,210	6,269	3,432	25,300	6,730	140,000	457,972
2010	52,137	2,356	30,210	51,020	83,700	5,018	24,227	3,640	3,348	26,620	6,391	137,000	448,638
2011	44,610	2,304	29,192	52,000	87,100	4,092	25,600	3,453	3,369	25,770	4,395	146,000	450,429
2012[1]	43,345	2,400	31,200	41,000	87,841	5,000	26,000	3,025	3,248	24,950	3,504	156,000	451,632
2013[2]	42,312	2,498	31,410	53,000	88,700	5,000	26,500	3,199	2,716	26,730	2,791	163,000	472,526

[1] Preliminary.   [2] Estimate.   Source: Food and Agricultural Organization of the United Nations (FAO-UN)

World Imports of Pepper   In Metric Tons

Year	European Union	France	Germany	India	Japan	Netherlands	Pakistan	Russia	Singapore	United Arab Em.	United Kingdom	United States	World Total
2004	62,638	8,693	27,459	15,695	8,146	14,226	6,814	7,698	10,316	1,514	5,464	65,990	278,781
2005	60,380	9,210	22,731	18,858	8,993	13,183	5,165	9,356	12,936	510	6,840	66,895	284,509
2006	66,394	9,439	26,031	16,897	9,208	15,409	6,424	10,099	15,847	3,422	9,105	70,539	304,571
2007	65,870	8,656	31,460	13,301	9,108	14,745	5,332	7,473	13,154	10,071	7,201	63,941	292,133
2008	60,948	8,812	28,084	11,567	7,781	13,090	7,562	9,589	13,144	10,782	8,066	64,789	295,355
2009	60,786	8,357	26,219	17,444	8,785	15,765	6,564	9,358	12,437	10,782	7,761	65,855	308,996
2010[1]	64,950	9,719	28,948	11,913	8,908	19,856	7,267	10,244	10,130	10,782	10,269	70,470	315,287
2011[2]	61,905	8,827	25,480	13,548	8,855	18,331	8,893	8,603	11,923	2,572	10,799	68,489	314,240

[1] Preliminary.   [2] Estimate.   Source: Food and Agricultural Organization of the United Nations (FAO-UN)

World Exports of Pepper   In Metric Tons

Year	Brazil	European Union	Germany	India	Indonesia	Malaysia	Mexico	Netherlands	Singapore	Sri Lanka	United States	Vietnam	World Total
2004	43,003	5,714	8,736	15,429	32,364	19,788	5,785	10,357	17,659	4,852	4,370	111,000	302,262
2005	38,424	5,116	8,092	21,470	34,531	18,097	4,485	10,417	12,190	8,131	4,601	109,900	300,987
2006	42,200	5,684	9,802	35,499	36,953	16,610	6,593	11,655	15,231	7,596	3,876	115,000	333,689
2007	38,679	5,644	9,387	47,464	38,447	15,165	4,081	11,342	16,007	6,940	5,310	83,000	309,983
2008	36,728	9,157	14,350	39,645	52,407	13,592	5,376	9,705	12,363	6,237	5,364	90,300	322,688
2009	35,770	5,900	10,850	26,281	50,642	13,153	6,175	9,974	9,570	6,576	5,472	134,300	342,403
2010[1]	30,761	6,524	11,128	25,847	62,599	14,107	6,590	9,153	9,777	12,236	5,605	116,859	343,075
2011[2]	32,696	7,134	11,031	37,419	36,487	14,237	5,998	10,848	9,119	5,057	7,110	123,800	330,857

[1] Preliminary.   [2] Estimate.   Source: Food and Agricultural Organization of the United Nations (FAO-UN)

Petroleum

Crude oil is petroleum that is acquired directly from the ground. Crude oil was formed millions of years ago from the remains of tiny aquatic plants and animals that lived in ancient seas. Ancient societies such as the Persians, 10th century Sumatrans, and pre-Columbian Indians believed that crude oil had medicinal benefits. Around 4,000 BC in Mesopotamia, bitumen, a tarry crude, was used as caulking for ships, as a setting for jewels and mosaics, and as an adhesive to secure weapon handles. The walls of Babylon and the famed pyramids were held together with bitumen, and Egyptians used it for embalming. During the 19th century in America, an oil find was often met with dismay. Pioneers who dug wells to find water or brine, were disappointed when they struck oil. It wasn't until 1854, with the invention of the kerosene lamp, that the first large-scale demand for petroleum emerged. Crude oil is a relatively abundant commodity. The world has produced approximately 650 billion barrels of oil, but another trillion barrels of proved reserves have yet to be extracted. Crude oil was the world's first trillion-dollar industry and accounts for the single largest product in world trade.

Crude Oil futures and options are traded at the CME Group, the ICE Futures Europe, and the JSE Securities Exchange. Futures are also traded at the Dubai Mercantile Exchange (DME), the Multi Commodity Exchange of India (MCX), the Thailand Futures Exchange, and the Tokyo Commodity Exchange (TOCOM). The CME trades two main types of crude oil: light sweet crude oil and Brent crude oil. The light sweet futures contract calls for the delivery of 1,000 barrels of crude oil in Cushing, Oklahoma. Light sweet crude is preferred by refiners because of its low sulfur content and relatively high yield of high-value products such as gasoline, diesel fuel, heating oil, and jet fuel. The Brent blend crude is based on a light, sweet North Sea crude oil. Brent blend crude production is approximately 500,000 barrels per day, and is shipped from Sullom Voe in the Shetland Islands.

Prices – CME West-Texas Intermediate crude oil prices (Barchart.com symbol CL) started 2014 on a weak note as they fell to a 6-month low of $91.24 a barrel in January as U.S. crude output ramped up to a 25-year high of 8.111 million bpd. Crude prices then gained traction and rallied into Q2 when they posted the high for the year at $107.73 a barrel, a 15-month high. Crude found support as crude inventories shrank at Cushing, OK, the delivery point of WTI futures, to a 5-1/3 year low. Chinese demand was robust as well with China Jan-Apr 2014 crude imports up +11.5% yr/yr at 102.61 MMT as China stockpiled crude oil for its strategic petroleum reserve. In addition, supply concerns arose after Islamic militants extended control over northern areas of Iraq, the second-largest producer in OPEC. Crude prices then began a steep decline the second-half of the year on a confluence of bearish factors. Economic concerns arose after the World Bank in June cut its global 2014 GDP forecast to 2.8% from a January estimate of 3.2%. The dollar index soared throughout 2014 to an 8-year high, and militants failed to extend their insurgency to southern Iraq, where 75% of the country's oil output is located. The slide in crude prices picked up steam in November after OPEC failed to cut crude production at its November meeting. U.S. crude production continued to increase to a 40-year high of 9.137 million bpd in December as new oil extraction technologies such as fracking and horizontal drilling boosted output. Crude prices finished 2014 down -46% at $53.27 a barrel.

Supply – World crude oil production in 2013 (latest data) rose +0.1% yr/yr to 76.047 million barrels per day, which was a new record high. The world's largest oil producers in 2013 were Russia (with 13.2%), Saudi Arabia (12.8%), the United States (9.8%), China (5.5%), and Canada (4.1%). U.S. crude oil production in 2013 rose +15.4% yr/yr to 7.478 million barrels per day. Alaskan production in 2013 fell −2.1% yr/yr to 515,000 barrels per day, the lowest level since 1977 and far below the peak level of 2.017 million barrels per day seen in 1988.

Demand – U.S. demand for crude oil in 2013 rose +2.2% yr/yr to 15.321 million barrels per day, which was well below the 2004 record high of 15.475. Most of that demand went for U.S. refinery production of products such as gasoline fuel, diesel fuel, aviation fuel, heating oil, kerosene, asphalt, and lubricants.

Trade – The U.S. is still highly dependent on imports of crude oil to meet its energy needs even though U.S. imports in 2013 fell -9.4% yr/yr to 7.729 million barrels per day, down from the 2005 record high of 10.126.

World Production of Crude Petroleum   In Thousands of Barrels Per Day

Year	Canada	China	Iran	Iraq	Kuwait	Mexico	Nigeria	Russia	Saudi Arabia	United Arab Em	United States	Vene-zuela	World Total
2004	2,398	3,485	4,001	2,011	2,376	3,476	2,329	8,805	9,101	2,478	5,441	2,557	72,468
2005	2,369	3,609	4,139	1,878	2,529	3,423	2,627	9,043	9,550	2,535	5,181	2,565	73,628
2006	2,525	3,673	4,028	1,996	2,535	3,345	2,440	9,247	9,152	2,636	5,088	2,511	73,253
2007	2,628	3,729	3,912	2,086	2,464	3,143	2,350	9,437	8,722	2,603	5,077	2,490	72,852
2008	2,579	3,790	4,050	2,375	2,586	2,839	2,165	9,357	9,261	2,681	5,000	2,464	73,661
2009	2,579	3,796	4,037	2,391	2,350	2,646	2,208	9,495	8,250	2,413	5,350	2,319	72,670
2010	2,741	4,078	4,080	2,399	2,300	2,621	2,455	9,694	8,900	2,415	5,482	2,216	74,459
2011	2,901	4,059	4,054	2,626	2,530	2,600	2,550	9,774	9,458	2,679	5,645	2,300	74,534
2012[1]	3,138	4,085	3,387	2,983	2,635	2,593	2,520	9,922	9,832	2,804	6,497	2,300	75,960
2013[2]	3,325	4,164	3,113	3,054	2,650	2,562	2,367	10,054	9,693	2,820	7,442	2,300	76,048

Includes lease condensate.   [1] Preliminary.   [2] Estimate.   Source: Energy Information Administration, U.S. Department of Energy (EIA-DOE)

PETROLEUM

World Imports of Crude Petroleum   In Thousands of Barrels Per Day

Year	China	France	Germany	India	Italy	Japan	Korea, South	Nether-lands	Singa-pore	Spain	United Kingdom	United States	World Total
2003	1,806	1,707	2,129	1,789	1,687	4,089	2,141	971	750	1,146	972	9,665	41,200
2004	2,449	1,707	2,209	1,912	1,742	4,019	2,268	1,044	881	1,187	1,120	10,088	43,444
2005	2,599	1,683	2,246	1,938	1,786	4,146	2,265	1,046	1,046	1,191	1,044	10,126	44,072
2006	2,905	1,634	2,193	2,156	1,740	3,949	2,389	954	1,012	1,209	1,029	10,118	43,976
2007	3,264	1,620	2,136	2,412	1,763	3,997	2,367	978	963	1,150	998	10,031	44,314
2008	3,578	1,667	2,122	2,557	1,666	3,972	2,333	988	1,006	1,179	1,041	9,783	44,124
2009	4,082	1,442	1,975	3,185	1,540	3,444	2,320	967	1,078	1,055	957	9,013	43,042
2010	4,754	1,298	1,876	3,272	1,592	3,473	2,372	1,027	1,137	1,061	965	9,213	43,677
2011[1]		1,296	1,820		1,448	3,366	2,515	982		1,047	1,012	8,935	
2012[2]		1,147	1,881		1,387	3,457	2,549	1,000		1,178	1,086	8,527	

Includes lease condensate.   [1] Preliminary.   [2] Estimate.   *Source: Energy Information Administration, U.S. Department of Energy (EIA-DOE)*

World Exports of Crude Petroleum   In Thousands of Barrels Per Day

Year	Angola	Canada	Iran	Iraq	Kuwait	Mexico	Nigeria	Norway	Russia	Saudi Arabia	United Arab Em	Vene-zuela	World Total
2003	860	1,230	2,296	912	1,249	2,114	2,164	2,731	4,520	6,873	1,848	1,535	39,964
2004	1,011	1,336	2,556	1,600	1,479	2,118	2,176	2,682	5,211	7,143	2,172	1,587	43,274
2005	1,220	1,360	2,497	1,381	1,690	2,022	2,260	2,339	5,222	7,216	2,107	2,418	43,361
2006	1,393	1,440	2,540	1,480	1,760	2,002	2,190	2,176	5,106	7,036	2,324	2,349	43,322
2007	1,659	1,506	2,618	1,618	1,645	1,808	2,120	1,981	5,172	6,969	2,289	2,225	42,533
2008	1,849	1,551	2,475	1,767	1,785	1,505	1,932	1,674	5,120	7,299	2,339	1,861	42,137
2009	1,909	1,493	2,297	1,903	1,495	1,312	2,115	1,772	4,891	6,250	2,181	1,594	42,002
2010	1,928	1,449	2,377	1,914	1,395	1,460	2,341	1,602	4,888	6,844	2,142	1,645	42,769
2011[1]		1,684				1,421		1,423					
2012[2]		1,756				1,333		1,303					

Includes lease condensate.   [1] Preliminary.   [2] Estimate.   *Source: Energy Information Administration, U.S. Department of Energy (EIA-DOE)*

World Production of Petroleum Products   In Thousands of Barrels Per Day

Year	Brazil	Canada	China	Germany	India	Italy	Japan	Korea, South	Russia	Saudi Arabia	United Kingdom	United States	World Total
2003	2,095	2,154	5,124	2,466	2,461	2,054	4,338	2,282	3,995	1,859	1,799	17,794	78,079
2004	2,137	2,181	6,178	2,540	2,700	2,048	4,241	2,395	4,153	1,985	1,897	18,271	81,229
2005	2,180	2,119	6,354	2,617	2,746	2,116	4,360	2,502	4,361	2,087	1,823	17,800	82,575
2006	2,167	2,086	6,495	2,580	2,895	2,050	4,262	2,559	4,549	2,289	1,757	17,975	82,642
2007	2,185	2,134	7,019	2,543	3,121	2,112	4,215	2,552	4,568	2,145	1,719	17,994	81,623
2008	2,008	2,029	7,069	2,484	3,226	1,971	4,136	2,535	4,802	2,103	1,678	18,146	81,774
2009	2,236	1,962	8,209	2,333	3,837	1,823	3,863	2,476	4,934	1,934	1,584	17,882	72,444
2010	2,108	2,016	8,983	2,198	4,216	1,887	3,857	2,537	4,812	1,935	1,549	18,452	83,799
2011[1]		1,906		2,184		1,791	3,658	2,685			1,594	18,673	
2012[2]		1,927		2,206		1,692	3,645	2,790			1,453	18,564	

Includes lease condensate.   [1] Preliminary.   [2] Estimate.   *Source: Energy Information Administration, U.S. Department of Energy (EIA-DOE)*

Supply and Disposition of Crude Oil in the United States   In Thousands of Barrels Per Day

	Supply						Stock		Disposition		Ending Stocks		
	-- Field Production --		------------ Imports ------------			Unaccounted for Crude	Withdrawal[3]		Refinery				Other
	Total Domestic	Alaskan	Total	SPR[2]	Other	Oil	SPR[2]	Other	Inputs	Exports	Total	SPR[2]	Primary
Year	--- In Thousands of Barrels Per Day ---										--- In Millions of Barrels ---		
2006	5,088	741	10,118	8	10,089	8	11	-37	15,242	25	1,001	689	312
2007	5,077	722	10,031	7	----	----	----	----	15,156	27	983	697	286
2008	5,000	683	9,783	19	----	----	----	----	14,648	29	1,028	702	326
2009	5,353	645	9,013	56	----	----	----	----	14,336	44	1,052	727	325
2010	5,471	600	9,213	----	----	----	----	----	14,724	42	1,060	727	333
2011	5,652	561	8,935	----	----	----	----	----	14,806	47	1,027	696	331
2012	6,486	526	8,527	----	----	----	----	----	14,999	67	1,061	695	365
2013[1]	7,443	515	7,719	----	----	----	----	----	15,315	120	1,054	696	358

[1] Preliminary.   [2] Strategic Petroleum Reserve.   [3] A negative number indicates a decrease in stocks and a positive number indicates an increase.
Source: Energy Information Administration, U.S. Department of Energy (EIA-DOE)

Crude Petroleum Refinery Operations Ratio[2] in the United States   In Percent of Capacity

Year	Jan.	Feb.	Mar.	Apr.	May	June	July	Aug.	Sept.	Oct.	Nov.	Dec.	Average
2005	91.3	90.6	90.8	92.8	94.2	97.1	94.2	92.7	83.6	81.3	89.3	89.4	90.6
2006	87.0	86.5	85.8	88.0	91.2	93.0	92.5	93.2	93.0	87.9	88.0	90.6	89.7
2007	88.2	84.7	87.1	88.1	89.7	88.5	91.2	90.8	88.9	87.4	88.9	88.7	88.5
2008	85.8	85.0	83.2	86.2	88.8	89.5	88.8	87.1	74.6	85.3	85.8	83.9	85.3
2009	82.3	81.5	81.5	82.7	84.0	86.0	84.2	84.1	84.9	81.5	81.1	81.3	82.9
2010	79.9	81.1	83.2	88.7	88.2	90.7	91.2	89.1	86.5	82.5	86.5	88.4	86.3
2011	84.8	80.0	84.4	82.9	85.3	89.0	90.2	90.3	88.7	84.9	87.0	86.5	86.2
2012	85.6	86.5	85.6	86.6	90.6	92.5	92.5	91.1	87.6	87.1	88.6	90.4	88.7
2013	83.8	81.7	84.0	85.8	88.2	91.7	92.6	91.5	90.7	86.9	90.6	92.0	88.3
2014[1]	87.2	86.6	85.8	90.7	90.2	90.3	94.6	93.7	91.8	87.7	92.0	94.2	90.4

[1] Preliminary.   [2] Based on the ration of the daily average crude runs to stills to the rated capacity of refineries per day.   *Source: Energy Information Administration, U.S. Department of Energy (EIA-DOE)*

Crude Oil Refinery Inputs in the United States   In Thousands of Barrels Per Day

Year	Jan.	Feb.	Mar.	Apr.	May	June	July	Aug.	Sept.	Oct.	Nov.	Dec.	Average
2005	15,254	15,142	15,214	15,494	15,905	16,401	15,850	15,664	13,986	13,646	15,032	15,046	15,220
2006	14,805	14,581	14,582	14,928	15,516	15,843	15,702	15,792	15,739	15,008	15,009	15,354	15,238
2007	14,992	14,435	14,840	15,045	15,380	15,248	15,671	15,685	15,226	14,933	15,151	15,202	15,151
2008	14,804	14,625	14,364	14,799	15,263	15,417	15,255	14,947	12,759	14,552	14,606	14,352	14,645
2009	14,146	14,134	14,118	14,382	14,483	14,850	14,636	14,593	14,710	14,095	13,898	13,983	14,336
2010	13,666	13,950	14,314	15,131	15,215	15,382	15,519	15,110	14,740	14,000	14,637	14,976	14,720
2011	14,423	13,676	14,451	14,231	14,718	15,294	15,589	15,556	15,275	14,570	14,960	14,842	14,799
2012	14,374	14,615	14,476	14,609	15,097	15,637	15,665	15,325	14,910	14,843	15,085	15,330	14,997
2013	14,567	14,230	14,703	14,864	15,305	15,833	16,042	15,793	15,636	14,991	15,633	16,069	15,306
2014[1]	15,300	15,122	15,126	15,867	15,945	15,818	16,532	16,455	16,060	15,338	16,043	16,392	15,833

[1] Preliminary.   *Source: Energy Information Administration, U.S. Department of Energy (EIA-DOE)*

Production of Major Refined Petroleum Products in Continental United States   In Millions of Barrels

| Year | Asphalt | -------- Fuel Oil -------- | | | Gasoline | Jet Fuel | Kero-sene | Natural Gas Plant Liquids | Lubri-cants | --------- Liquified Gasses --------- | | |
		Aviation Gasoline	Distillate	Residual						Total	at L.P.G.[2]	AT L.P.G.[3]
2004	185.6	6.2	1,397.6	238.0	3,013	566.3	23.2	662.7	62.0	797.2	561.3	235.9
2005	186.0	6.1	1,441.4	227.9	3,014	561.5	23.6	623.9	60.8	736.9	527.2	209.8
2006	184.8	6.6	1,478.1	231.5	3,036	540.4	17.3	633.4	66.8	757.6	537.8	219.9
2007	166.1	6.0	1,507.7	244.4	3,045	528.6	12.7	648.3	65.1	789.0	552.8	236.2
2008	150.9	5.5	1,569.5	227.1	3,072	539.5	12.0	651.9	63.2	786.1	556.2	229.9
2009	131.0	5.0	1,476.7	218.6	3,199	510.2	6.9	688.5	55.4	821.1	591.3	229.8
2010	132.1	5.4	1,384.7	200.8	3,298	519.7	7.2	730.4	47.6	869.3	631.7	237.6
2011	129.6	5.4	1,405.1	175.3	3,189	520.2	4.4	825.0	45.3	915.5	689.1	226.4
2012	124.5	5.0	1,369.8	126.2	3,185	512.2	1.4	830.7	41.4	992.0	762.6	229.4
2013[1]	117.0	4.2	1,727.0	170.4	3,347	547.8	4.0	809.0	59.8	1,162.2	933.1	229.1

[1] Preliminary.   [2] Gas processing plants.   [3] Refineries.   *Source: Energy Information Administration, U.S. Department of Energy (EIA-DOE)*

Stocks of Petroleum and Products in the United States on January 1   In Millions of Barrels

| Year | Crude Petroleum | Strategic Reserve | -- Refined Products -- | | | | | | | | | | - Motor Gasoline - | |
			Total	Asphalt	Aviation Gasoline	Fuel Oil Distillate	Residual	Finished Gasoline	Jet Fuel	Kero-sene	Gases[2]	Lubri-cants	Total	Finished[3]
2005	961.9	675.6	405.6	22.1	1.3	126.0	42.4	143.1	40.2	4.9	111.0	10.4	----	143
2006	1,007.8	684.5	403.6	21.0	1.2	136.0	37.3	134.8	41.8	5.1	117.6	9.7	----	135
2007	998.4	688.6	405.9	28.8	1.4	143.7	42.4	118.3	39.1	3.4	125.2	12.4	----	118
2008	982.8	696.9	374.3	22.2	1.2	133.5	38.6	110.0	39.5	2.8	105.5	10.6	----	110
2009	1,026.1	701.8	367.8	20.3	1.2	145.9	36.2	98.2	38.2	2.2	126.9	10.7	----	98
2010	1,051.8	726.6	375.1	17.9	1.0	164.7	37.8	85.9	43.4	2.5	113.2	8.9	----	86
2011	1,058.5	726.5	357.4	19.9	1.1	164.5	41.3	63.4	43.2	2.4	121.3	8.2	----	63
2012	1,026.8	696.0	332.7	19.6	1.1	149.7	34.1	61.4	41.7	2.4	111.1	9.9	----	61
2013	1,060.3	695.3	313.6	22.1	1.0	134.7	33.9	56.8	39.5	1.7	140.9	9.6	----	57
2014[1]	1,053.6	696.0	291.3	21.4	0.9	127.3	37.7	39.7	37.2	1.9	112.7	10.1	----	40

[1] Preliminary.   [2] Includes ethane & ethylene at plants and refineries.   [3] Includes oxygenated.
Source: Energy Information Administration, U.S. Department of Energy (EIA-DOE)

PETROLEUM

Stocks of Crude Petroleum in the United States, on First of Month   In Millions of Barrels

Year	Jan.	Feb.	Mar.	Apr.	May	June	July	Aug.	Sept.	Oct.	Nov.	Dec.
2005	965.7	984.2	1,008.0	1,029.5	1,030.1	1,024.3	1,017.2	1,010.3	1,000.0	1,007.4	1,008.1	1,008.2
2006	1,006.8	1,027.4	1,028.8	1,035.5	1,029.2	1,024.6	1,019.4	1,020.7	1,020.6	1,027.9	1,023.1	1,000.9
2007	1,013.2	1,006.2	1,019.5	1,031.4	1,043.6	1,044.3	1,027.0	1,011.0	1,003.9	1,001.4	995.0	983.0
2008	994.6	1,001.1	1,015.0	1,021.2	1,007.9	1,001.7	1,002.4	1,009.7	1,006.4	1,014.5	1,023.4	1,027.7
2009	1,055.1	1,063.1	1,079.7	1,089.7	1,081.2	1,071.2	1,069.5	1,059.7	1,060.1	1,057.6	1,063.0	1,051.8
2010	1,063.4	1,069.8	1,085.8	1,089.9	1,088.5	1,092.1	1,084.2	1,085.9	1,089.3	1,094.1	1,079.0	1,060.0
2011	1,071.6	1,075.0	1,086.8	1,093.1	1,094.9	1,082.3	1,064.6	1,043.2	1,026.1	1,032.9	1,032.8	1,026.6
2012	1,039.4	1,044.4	1,069.1	1,078.8	1,083.9	1,083.9	1,068.6	1,058.4	1,064.9	1,071.3	1,074.4	1,060.8
2013	1,073.5	1,080.9	1,088.1	1,091.8	1,088.2	1,071.7	1,062.5	1,059.5	1,067.1	1,079.8	1,072.5	1,053.6
2014[1]	1,059.7	1,069.3	1,079.7	1,086.5	1,085.0	1,074.9	1,059.7	1,051.6	1,051.9	1,073.0	1,078.5	1,084.7

[1] Preliminary.   Source: Energy Information Administration; U.S. Department of Energy

Production of Crude Petroleum in the United States   In Thousands of Barrels Per Day

Year	Jan.	Feb.	Mar.	Apr.	May	June	July	Aug.	Sept.	Oct.	Nov.	Dec.	Average
2005	5,441	5,494	5,601	5,556	5,581	5,460	5,240	5,218	4,204	4,534	4,837	4,984	5,179
2006	5,106	5,045	5,045	5,128	5,161	5,160	5,102	5,059	5,037	5,106	5,105	5,166	5,102
2007	5,123	5,125	5,106	5,189	5,197	5,096	5,024	4,914	4,884	5,043	5,017	5,056	5,065
2008	5,100	5,122	5,151	5,117	5,102	5,098	5,133	4,894	3,930	4,669	5,024	5,056	4,950
2009	5,154	5,260	5,227	5,273	5,379	5,281	5,402	5,418	5,547	5,501	5,427	5,451	5,360
2010	5,399	5,546	5,513	5,377	5,398	5,384	5,313	5,445	5,608	5,596	5,558	5,614	5,479
2011	5,482	5,386	5,603	5,554	5,619	5,587	5,420	5,648	5,595	5,877	6,010	6,028	5,651
2012	6,153	6,262	6,297	6,296	6,342	6,252	6,391	6,318	6,574	6,941	7,044	7,081	6,496
2013	7,086	7,101	7,173	7,365	7,285	7,243	7,472	7,469	7,745	7,684	7,877	7,858	7,447
2014[1]	7,955	8,083	8,224	8,516	8,577	8,637	8,686	8,743	8,902	9,051	9,020	9,128	8,627

[1] Preliminary.   Source: Energy Information Administration, U.S. Department of Energy (EIA-DOE)

U.S. Foreign Trade of Petroleum and Products   In Thousands of Barrels Per Day

	---------------- Exports ----------------		--- Imports ---				
Year	Total[2]	Petroleum Products	Crude	Petroleum Products	Distillate Fuel Oil	Residual Fuel Oil	Net Imports[3]
2004	1,048	1,021	10,088	3,057	325	426	12,097
2005	1,165	1,133	10,126	3,588	329	530	12,549
2006	1,317	1,292	10,118	3,517	365	350	12,390
2007	1,433	1,405	10,031	2,761	304	372	12,035
2008	1,802	1,773	9,783	2,570	213	349	11,113
2009	2,024	1,980	9,013	2,122	225	331	9,667
2010	2,353	2,311	9,213	1,986	228	366	9,440
2011	2,986	2,939	8,935	2,062	179	328	8,518
2012	3,205	3,137	8,527	1,740	126	256	7,444
2013[1]	3,473	3,377	7,729	-8,110	154	227	-3,473

[1] Preliminary.   [2] Includes crude oil.   [3] Equals imports minus exports.
Source: Energy Information Administration, U.S. Department of Energy (EIA-DOE)

Domestic First Purchase Price of Crude Petroleum at Wells[2]   In Dollars Per Barrel

Year	Jan.	Feb.	Mar.	Apr.	May	June	July	Aug.	Sept.	Oct.	Nov.	Dec.	Average
2005	40.18	42.19	47.56	47.26	44.03	49.83	53.35	58.90	59.64	56.99	53.20	53.24	50.53
2006	57.85	55.69	55.59	62.51	64.31	64.36	67.72	67.21	59.36	53.26	52.42	55.03	59.61
2007	49.32	52.94	54.95	58.20	58.90	62.35	69.23	67.78	73.16	79.32	87.16	85.29	66.55
2008	87.06	89.41	98.44	106.64	118.55	127.47	128.08	112.83	98.50	73.22	53.67	36.80	94.22
2009	35.00	34.14	42.46	45.22	52.69	63.08	60.43	65.28	65.27	69.82	71.99	70.42	56.32
2010	72.89	72.74	75.77	78.80	70.90	70.77	71.37	72.07	71.23	76.02	79.20	83.98	74.65
2011	85.66	86.69	99.19	108.80	102.46	97.30	97.82	89.00	90.22	92.28	100.18	98.71	95.69
2012	98.99	102.04	105.42	103.62	95.57	83.59	86.10	92.53	95.98	92.24	89.64	89.81	94.63
2013	94.89	95.04	95.85	94.72	95.00	94.05	101.61	103.14	102.45	96.18	88.70	91.85	96.12
2014[2]	89.59	96.89	96.18	96.47	95.69	98.70	96.67	90.72	87.34	78.83	71.07		90.74

[1] Preliminary.   [2] Buyers posted prices.   Source: Energy Information Administration, U.S. Department of Energy (EIA-DOE)

Refiner Sales Prices of Residual Fuel Oil   In Cents Per Gallon

Year	Jan.	Feb.	Mar.	Apr.	May	June	July	Aug.	Sept.	Oct.	Nov.	Dec.	Average
2007	117.2	121.4	122.1	125.8	135.9	142.1	153.9	158.4	161.0	166.1	183.2	194.8	148.5
2008	203.9	200.4	204.8	222.1	234.9	265.8	294.5	300.5	266.6	216.6	165.4	121.1	224.7
2009	116.4	120.0	118.3	117.4	121.3	144.0	148.8	164.1	168.9	171.7	173.9	181.3	145.5
2010	185.2	186.2	186.2	188.7	189.8	187.4	185.8	189.5	188.3	191.3	202.5	221.5	191.9
2011	230.2	245.1	265.4	274.1	278.6	290.5	287.7	289.6	288.2	289.1	285.3	289.1	276.1
2012	296.5	307.0	315.9	320.1	317.0	308.3	292.6	304.1	297.0	296.9	289.5	281.4	302.2
2013	287.4	301.7	294.9	287.5	283.9	278.5	276.8	275.9	283.9	NA	NA	NA	285.6
2014[1]	NA	NA	NA	NA	290.2	288.8	297.7	W	275.6	257.3	229.4		273.2

Sulfur 1% or less, excluding taxes.   [1] Preliminary.   *Source: Energy Information Administration, U.S. Department of Energy (EIA-DOE)*

Refiner Sales Prices of No. 2 Fuel Oil   In Cents Per Gallon

Year	Jan.	Feb.	Mar.	Apr.	May	June	July	Aug.	Sept.	Oct.	Nov.	Dec.	Average
2007	161.2	172.9	178.1	191.0	194.9	201.4	207.1	202.1	213.3	226.0	256.9	257.0	205.2
2008	256.4	260.7	297.7	319.5	353.6	376.2	380.2	328.7	300.3	240.0	194.7	157.9	288.8
2009	154.8	142.7	135.8	139.7	146.8	174.4	165.8	180.4	177.4	191.8	200.4	198.9	167.4
2010	207.5	198.6	210.0	221.4	212.9	203.7	200.1	204.1	209.3	222.1	230.8	243.5	213.7
2011	258.5	273.7	299.6	316.7	303.9	295.6	302.4	292.7	292.7	291.5	305.0	292.8	293.8
2012	302.7	316.6	321.1	315.3	297.6	263.5	277.4	298.8	312.8	315.5	304.9	300.3	302.2
2013	306.9	316.8	297.7	279.3	270.8	274.1	289.4	295.4	297.3	295.5	291.0	301.1	292.9
2014[1]	305.9	305.1	297.9	291.1	288.3	287.8	282.5	278.4	270.1	247.6	237.1		281.1

Excluding taxes.   [1] Preliminary.   *Source: Energy Information Administration, U.S. Department of Energy (EIA-DOE)*

Refiner Sales Prices of No. 2 Diesel Fuel   In Cents Per Gallon

Year	Jan.	Feb.	Mar.	Apr.	May	June	July	Aug.	Sept.	Oct.	Nov.	Dec.	Average
2007	169.5	182.4	197.9	211.6	210.1	214.7	222.0	219.3	232.2	242.6	269.8	259.9	219.3
2008	258.0	273.8	315.8	335.6	371.2	385.9	387.6	333.8	316.0	251.4	195.5	146.9	297.6
2009	148.0	132.6	131.5	145.6	153.1	182.8	174.5	193.7	184.8	197.8	203.7	199.7	170.7
2010	207.8	202.5	216.3	231.2	217.7	212.0	209.8	216.1	219.0	232.5	239.2	248.6	221.1
2011	262.1	282.0	313.4	329.6	311.6	307.9	313.5	303.2	303.5	303.5	315.7	292.7	303.2
2012	301.8	316.3	330.8	325.2	303.9	274.1	290.7	320.6	327.8	326.5	311.7	302.2	311.0
2013	304.6	325.9	308.2	296.9	295.8	292.3	301.5	308.4	309.5	300.6	294.9	299.8	303.2
2014[1]	298.1	309.1	303.1	302.7	298.7	297.3	292.1	290.0	280.6	263.9	255.8		290.1

Excluding taxes.   [1] Preliminary.   *Source: Energy Information Administration, U.S. Department of Energy (EIA-DOE)*

Refiner Sales Prices of Kerosine-Type Jet Fuel   In Cents Per Gallon

Year	Jan.	Feb.	Mar.	Apr.	May	June	July	Aug.	Sept.	Oct.	Nov.	Dec.	Average
2007	172.7	176.6	184.6	202.1	207.9	211.4	216.7	215.1	225.6	235.3	265.6	265.5	214.9
2008	266.5	267.4	310.6	331.5	364.2	391.2	397.8	339.3	327.8	256.9	197.4	147.0	299.8
2009	147.2	135.2	126.6	142.5	146.0	178.0	175.9	189.4	182.2	191.7	206.0	201.2	168.5
2010	212.1	199.9	212.9	224.7	218.6	209.4	210.0	213.8	213.1	226.3	234.2	245.9	218.4
2011	258.5	278.3	309.5	325.9	318.8	310.1	309.0	304.0	302.5	296.2	308.9	295.1	301.4
2012	305.9	318.6	329.6	325.5	307.6	274.7	285.0	312.9	324.5	318.2	301.5	298.2	308.5
2013	309.3	325.0	303.6	288.4	276.3	278.4	289.9	299.5	301.7	292.8	286.8	297.8	295.8
2014[1]	296.4	298.1	293.9	291.1	293.2	291.7	288.2	288.2	282.3	254.7	240.9		283.5

Excluding taxes.   [1] Preliminary.   *Source: Energy Information Administration, U.S. Department of Energy (EIA-DOE)*

Refiner Sales Prices of Propane[2]   In Cents Per Gallon

Year	Jan.	Feb.	Mar.	Apr.	May	June	July	Aug.	Sept.	Oct.	Nov.	Dec.	Average
2007	99.5	103.3	104.9	106.7	111.2	109.4	115.9	116.7	124.8	135.1	147.1	146.1	118.4
2008	151.9	146.9	149.5	157.1	167.5	176.1	183.3	166.7	156.5	124.2	100.5	91.6	147.7
2009	97.4	89.0	80.5	71.9	72.8	83.8	76.0	83.7	92.3	100.4	108.8	117.8	89.5
2010	133.2	132.4	117.9	114.4	109.8	104.9	101.2	108.4	115.1	125.3	127.7	132.2	118.5
2011	138.0	140.1	140.3	143.3	151.5	150.3	151.3	152.2	155.7	151.1	149.8	144.4	147.3
2012	134.1	128.2	129.3	116.3	95.0	76.2	80.9	87.5	91.0	97.9	95.5	89.4	101.8
2013	92.8	95.3	95.2	94.9	93.2	86.1	90.3	105.9	111.4	115.4	121.9	134.2	103.1
2014[1]	164.1	165.4	119.8	112.1	105.7	105.4	107.5	105.5	109.7	104.4	96.6		117.8

[1] Preliminary.   [2] Consumer Grade, Excluding taxes.   *Source: Energy Information Administration, U.S. Department of Energy (EIA-DOE)*

PETROLEUM

CRUDE OIL, LIGHT - NYMEX
Weekly Nearest Futures as of 01/02/2015

WEEKLY NEAREST FUTURES
As of 01/02/2015

Chart High 147.27 on 07/11/2008
Chart Low 32.40 on 12/19/2008

USD / barrel

Nearby Futures through Last Trading Day.

Volume of Trading of Crude Oil Futures in New York   In Thousands of Contracts

Year	Jan.	Feb.	Mar.	Apr.	May	June	July	Aug.	Sept.	Oct.	Nov.	Dec.	Total
2005	4,352	4,032	5,721	5,404	5,045	5,326	4,629	6,091	5,252	5,022	4,488	4,288	59,650
2006	5,482	5,594	5,937	5,285	5,861	5,134	4,500	5,409	6,067	7,492	7,555	6,739	71,053
2007	10,367	9,092	10,069	9,287	9,487	9,862	9,656	10,647	10,670	12,390	11,307	8,692	121,526
2008	10,815	10,100	12,577	11,066	13,497	12,453	11,321	10,589	11,554	11,638	8,662	9,910	134,183
2009	11,369	11,411	11,340	10,106	9,939	11,367	11,924	11,823	11,462	13,179	11,600	11,906	137,428
2010	10,894	12,772	13,298	17,433	17,591	14,458	11,427	14,494	16,018	14,423	13,429	12,416	168,652
2011	17,948	17,757	15,675	12,089	15,126	15,815	11,571	17,178	13,488	14,785	13,609	9,994	175,036
2012	12,557	14,693	13,290	10,627	12,402	12,593	10,870	11,687	10,572	11,660	11,055	8,524	140,532
2013	12,028	11,540	10,515	13,354	13,825	13,111	15,384	12,849	11,139	13,792	10,569	9,586	147,691
2014	11,162	9,862	11,700	11,467	10,283	11,398	13,174	11,016	12,824	15,939	12,176	14,091	145,091

Contract size = 1,000 bbl.   *Source: CME Group; New York Mercantile Exchange (NYMEX)*

Average Open Interest of Crude Oil Futures in New York   In Thousands of Contracts

Year	Jan.	Feb.	Mar.	Apr.	May	June	July	Aug.	Sept.	Oct.	Nov.	Dec.
2005	707.9	745.2	829.2	833.8	799.0	785.4	820.1	901.6	870.6	848.7	832.3	841.3
2006	903.5	927.5	954.2	1,000.4	1,055.7	1,016.2	1,068.7	1,164.0	1,181.8	1,168.7	1,176.6	1,200.0
2007	1,284.9	1,281.7	1,314.3	1,328.0	1,390.4	1,431.6	1,523.6	1,477.4	1,483.3	1,447.1	1,451.8	1,362.3
2008	1,393.5	1,384.6	1,428.5	1,393.8	1,396.5	1,351.8	1,277.9	1,224.1	1,171.2	1,076.8	1,139.7	1,160.9
2009	1,232.4	1,223.3	1,190.2	1,163.0	1,159.6	1,180.5	1,170.7	1,176.0	1,174.2	1,231.2	1,207.8	1,200.4
2010	1,303.5	1,304.8	1,324.1	1,375.8	1,416.3	1,307.3	1,252.7	1,262.3	1,338.2	1,419.1	1,414.1	1,380.0
2011	1,494.0	1,540.7	1,551.4	1,565.5	1,591.3	1,531.0	1,517.1	1,521.8	1,433.7	1,406.6	1,332.6	1,321.5
2012	1,374.6	1,475.5	1,565.8	1,561.7	1,520.9	1,446.8	1,408.6	1,473.6	1,575.5	1,574.3	1,548.8	1,514.8
2013	1,504.5	1,636.4	1,690.3	1,751.8	1,753.7	1,813.5	1,835.7	1,872.0	1,896.1	1,821.8	1,682.1	1,631.0
2014	1,607.4	1,628.5	1,653.4	1,654.8	1,633.4	1,703.8	1,687.6	1,572.7	1,518.4	1,495.4	1,464.1	1,450.3

Contract size = 1,000 bbl.   *Source: CME Group; New York Mercantile Exchange (NYMEX)*

Plastics

Plastics are moldable, chemically fabricated materials produced mostly from fossil fuels, such as oil, coal, or natural gas. The word plastic is derived from the Greek *plastikos*, meaning "to mold," and the Latin *plasticus*, meaning "capable of molding." Leo Baekeland created the first commercially successful thermosetting synthetic resin in 1909. More than 50 families of plastics have since been produced.

All plastics can be divided into either thermoplastics or thermosetting plastics. The difference is the way in which they respond to heat. Thermoplastics can be repeatedly softened by heat and hardened by cooling. Thermosetting plastics harden permanently after being heated once.

Prices – The average monthly producer price index (1982=100) of plastic resins and materials in the U.S. in 2014 rose +5.1% yr/yr to 257.8, a new record high. The average monthly producer price index of thermoplastic resins in the U.S. in 2014 rose +5.8% yr/yr to 263.0, a new record high. The average monthly producer price index of thermosetting resins in the U.S. in 2014 rose +1.3% to 244.4, a new record high.

Supply – Total U.S. plastics production in 2013 (latest data) rose +1.5% yr/yr to 107.522 billion pounds, which was well below the 2007 record high of 115.793 billion pounds.

U.S. plastics production has more than doubled in the past two decades. By sector, the thermoplastics sector is by far the largest, with 2013 production rising +1.2% yr/yr to 92.547 billion pounds and accounting for 1.5% of total U.S. plastic production. Production in the thermosetting plastic sector (polyester unsaturated, phenolic, and epoxy) rose +3.1% yr/yr in 2013 to 14.975 billion pounds and accounted for 13.9% of total U.S. plastics production. The category of "other plastics" fell -14.7% to 11.952 billion pounds and accounted for 12% of total U.S. plastics production in 2008 (latest data available).

Demand – Total usage of plastic resins by important markets in 2013 (latest data) in the U.S. rose by +1.0% to 75.714 billion pounds. The breakdown by market shows that the largest single consumption category is "Packaging" with 2.573 billion pounds of usage in 2013, accounting for 34.0% of total U.S. consumption. After packaging, the largest categories are "Consumer and Industrial" (19.9% of U.S. consumption), and "Building and Construction" (16.2% of U.S. consumption).

Trade – U.S. exports of plastics in 2013 fell -1.1% yr/yr to 14.224 billion pounds, below the 2011 record high of 14.858 billion pounds. U.S. exports accounted for 18.8% of U.S. supply disappearance in 2013.

Plastics Production by Resin in the United States   In Millions of Pounds

	----------- Thermosets -------------				------------------------------- Thermoplastics ----------------------------------								Total		
Year	Polyester Unsaturated	Phenolic	Epoxy	Total Thermosets	Thermoplastic Polyester	Polyvinyl Chloride	Polystyrene	Polypropylene	Nylon	Low Density Polyethylene[1]	High Density Polyethylene	Total Thermoplastics	Selected Plastics	Other Plastics	Total Plastics
2004	3,294	4,200	658	8,152	8,632	15,883	6,765	18,523	1,357	20,390	17,519	92,317	100,469	13,471	113,940
2005	3,359	4,689	609	8,657	7,749	15,259	6,293	17,965	1,252	19,736	16,155	87,524	96,181	13,595	109,776
2006	3,430	4,809	624	8,863	8,290	14,919	6,269	18,775	1,270	20,926	17,645	91,204	100,067	13,970	114,037
2007	3,471	4,838	642	8,951	8,745	14,606	6,015	19,445	1,295	21,511	18,222	92,835	101,786	14,007	115,793
2008	2,798	4,233	583	15,091	8,159	12,789	5,220	16,768	1,148	19,061	16,247	86,455	89,594	11,952	101,546
2009	NA	NA	535	12,713	NA	12,754	4,865	16,623	943	19,793	16,956	85,983	98,696	NA	98,696
2010	NA	NA	610	13,214	NA	14,017	5,055	17,254	1,027	20,530	16,887	89,592	102,806	NA	102,806
2011	NA	NA	613	13,800	NA	14,434	5,472	16,418	1,106	20,130	17,116	89,408	103,208	NA	103,208
2012	NA	NA	545	14,519	NA	15,310	5,452	16,326	1,193	20,328	17,738	91,426	105,945	NA	105,945
2013	NA	NA	499	14,975	NA	15,373	5,405	16,427	1,238	20,772	17,899	92,547	107,522	NA	107,522

[1] Includes LDPE and LLDPE.   *Source: American Plastics Council (APC)*

Total Resin Sales and Captive Use by Important Markets   In Millions of Pounds (Dry Weight Basis)

Year	Adhesive, Inks & Coatings	Building & Construction	Consumer & Industrial	Electrical & Electronics	Exports	Furniture & Furnishings	Industrial & Machinary	Packaging	Transportation	Other	Total
2004	1,196	15,676	18,714	3,096	9,900	3,458	1,042	25,952	4,899	2,168	86,101
2005	1,160	15,483	17,400	2,917	9,790	3,406	1,087	25,144	4,711	2,133	83,231
2006	1,078	15,486	17,823	2,641	10,244	3,332	1,004	26,280	4,559	2,031	84,478
2007	1,069	14,289	17,193	1,980	12,346	3,091	943	26,527	3,312	1,604	82,354
2008	937	12,313	15,461	1,755	11,962	2,671	834	24,097	2,751	1,375	74,156
2009	798	11,102	14,717	1,519	14,691	1,877	678	23,702	1,971	972	72,025
2010	846	10,914	14,782	1,561	14,488	1,894	774	25,041	2,558	1,200	74,057
2011	801	11,036	14,743	1,618	14,858	1,818	781	25,302	2,649	1,206	74,811
2012	350	11,712	14,937	1,701	14,380	1,469	838	25,577	2,720	1,255	74,939
2013	353	12,233	15,026	1,728	14,224	1,470	851	25,734	2,772	1,323	75,714

[1] Included in other.   *Source: American Plastics Council (APC)*

PLASTICS

Average Producer Price Index of Plastic Resins and Materials (066) in the United States (1982 = 100)

Year	Jan.	Feb.	Mar.	Apr.	May	June	July	Aug.	Sept.	Oct.	Nov.	Dec.	Average
2005	190.3	190.8	192.1	192.3	190.3	186.3	185.0	183.4	188.2	203.9	208.6	205.2	193.0
2006	203.9	200.0	198.9	194.3	195.9	198.5	199.2	202.3	202.4	200.0	196.2	189.1	198.4
2007	187.6	185.5	187.0	192.1	193.8	196.9	198.6	198.7	198.0	199.3	205.9	207.5	195.9
2008	209.7	209.6	210.8	212.1	216.4	219.1	229.2	233.3	227.1	222.3	200.3	190.3	215.0
2009	184.6	190.1	188.6	183.5	185.9	185.9	194.4	194.5	196.4	194.5	194.5	196.8	190.8
2010	195.0	206.4	208.2	222.4	213.1	208.1	212.7	211.1	210.7	215.0	210.3	208.4	210.1
2011	213.2	218.8	223.2	229.1	239.5	238.4	236.7	233.8	235.3	229.2	231.5	227.2	229.7
2012	232.0	234.9	238.0	239.6	238.7	236.3	233.8	234.8	231.8	234.4	234.2	233.9	235.2
2013	239.7	244.1	247.1	245.9	244.6	245.4	244.4	245.1	245.5	245.8	247.9	247.7	245.3
2014[1]	250.6	253.8	256.6	257.5	257.3	255.2	257.1	259.4	262.4	263.1	261.7	259.0	257.8

[1] Preliminary.   *Source: Bureau of Labor Statistics, U.S. Department of Commerce (BLS)*

Average Producer Price Index of Thermoplastic Resins (0662) in the United States (1982 = 100)

Year	Jan.	Feb.	Mar.	Apr.	May	June	July	Aug.	Sept.	Oct.	Nov.	Dec.	Average
2005	193.2	193.8	195.3	194.9	192.0	187.0	185.4	183.7	189.3	208.4	213.7	209.4	195.5
2006	207.9	202.8	201.5	195.6	197.6	201.1	201.6	205.1	205.0	201.6	196.8	188.1	200.4
2007	186.0	183.4	185.3	190.7	193.0	196.2	198.2	198.4	197.6	199.3	206.6	208.2	195.2
2008	209.9	209.9	211.5	213.2	218.4	221.2	232.4	236.5	229.0	223.5	197.6	187.1	215.9
2009	179.3	187.1	185.9	180.3	183.1	183.2	193.2	192.9	194.5	192.2	192.8	194.9	188.3
2010	193.2	206.8	208.8	225.7	214.9	208.8	214.3	212.6	212.1	217.2	211.7	209.3	211.3
2011	214.7	221.1	226.0	232.6	244.6	242.1	239.9	236.3	238.1	230.9	233.6	228.6	232.4
2012	234.3	237.6	241.1	242.9	241.7	238.8	235.6	236.8	233.2	236.2	236.1	235.4	237.5
2013	242.8	247.4	250.7	249.4	247.7	248.7	246.7	247.7	249.2	249.6	251.8	251.7	248.6
2014[1]	254.9	258.5	261.7	262.8	262.1	260.0	262.3	265.0	268.3	269.1	267.6	263.9	263.0

[1] Preliminary.   *Source: Bureau of Labor Statistics, U.S. Department of Commerce (BLS)*

Average Producer Price Index of Thermosetting Resins (0663) in the United States (1982 = 100)

Year	Jan.	Feb.	Mar.	Apr.	May	June	July	Aug.	Sept.	Oct.	Nov.	Dec.	Average
2005	189.9	190.3	190.5	193.5	195.8	195.8	195.5	194.6	196.1	197.5	199.9	200.2	195.0
2006	200.0	200.8	200.8	201.7	201.6	200.5	202.1	203.6	204.2	206.3	206.6	206.3	202.9
2007	207.8	208.3	207.8	211.7	210.0	212.6	212.3	212.4	211.9	211.6	214.7	216.8	211.5
2008	221.4	220.7	220.0	219.0	218.5	220.3	224.8	229.3	229.8	229.6	228.3	220.7	223.5
2009	226.7	219.3	216.2	213.5	213.9	213.7	213.5	215.5	219.7	220.0	216.2	220.0	217.4
2010	218.0	216.8	217.1	216.7	216.1	217.2	216.3	215.2	215.3	215.4	215.3	216.1	216.3
2011	218.0	219.4	220.6	223.0	224.8	231.9	233.0	233.7	234.0	233.9	233.8	233.4	228.3
2012	233.2	234.0	235.1	235.9	236.4	236.6	238.1	237.6	238.6	238.6	238.1	239.3	236.8
2013	236.4	240.1	241.8	241.4	241.8	241.8	246.2	245.6	239.7	239.9	240.7	240.2	241.3
2014[1]	241.5	242.6	243.4	243.7	245.9	244.3	243.5	244.2	245.6	245.6	244.6	247.3	244.4

[1] Preliminary.   *Source: Bureau of Labor Statistics, U.S. Department of Commerce (BLS)*

Average Producer Price Index of Styrene Plastics Materials (0662-06) in the United States (1982 = 100)

Year	Jan.	Feb.	Mar.	Apr.	May	June	July	Aug.	Sept.	Oct.	Nov.	Dec.	Average
1995	129.0	127.0	132.5	134.7	135.9	137.5	135.1	133.2	132.1	130.1	127.9	126.1	131.8
1996	125.7	123.5	125.0	118.3	120.1	122.7	123.4	123.3	123.6	122.8	122.0	120.9	122.6
1997	120.6	123.1	123.0	121.6	121.6	121.6	122.7	117.7	118.0	116.5	113.5	113.7	119.5
1998	113.3	113.9	115.5	114.9	114.1	112.8	111.3	111.2	107.6	107.9	107.1	106.3	111.3
1999	103.5	102.4	103.5	104.7	103.0	102.3	103.1	101.5	101.4	99.8	99.4	100.5	102.1
2000	103.0	104.3	110.5	113.0	116.2	116.9	118.5	116.5	115.0	114.1	112.1	110.4	112.5
2001	110.5	109.2	107.9	108.0	101.8	99.9	97.6	95.7	87.3	89.4	90.0	85.4	98.6
2002	85.7	85.8	87.9	88.5	90.4	91.7	93.7	100.6	100.5	108.9	108.1	103.9	95.5
2003[1]	102.9	110.2	119.5	127.2	126.7	119.1	118.0	113.3	112.8	113.6	113.7	111.6	115.7
2004[1]	Data no longer available												

[1] Preliminary.   *Source: Bureau of Labor Statistics, U.S. Department of Commerce (BLS)*

Platinum-Group Metals

Platinum (atomic symbol Pt) is a relatively rare, chemically inert metallic element that is more valuable than gold. Platinum is a grayish-white metal that has a high fusing point, is malleable and ductile, and has a high electrical resistance. Chemically, platinum is relatively inert and resists attack by air, water, single acids, and ordinary reagents. Platinum is the most important of the six-metal group, which also includes ruthenium, rhodium, palladium, osmium, and iridium. The word "platinum" is derived from the Spanish word *platina* meaning silver.

Platinum is one of the world's rarest metals with new mine production totaling only about 5 million troy ounces a year. All the platinum mined to date would fit in the average-size living room. Platinum is mined all over the world with supplies concentrated in South Africa. South Africa accounts for nearly 80% of world supply, followed by Russia, and North America.

Because platinum will never tarnish, lose its rich white luster, or even wear down after many years, it is prized by the jewelry industry. The international jewelry industry is the largest consumer sector for platinum, accounting for 51% of total platinum demand. In Europe and the U.S., the normal purity of platinum is 95%. Ten tons of ore must be mined and a five-month process is needed to produce one ounce of pure platinum.

The second major consumer sector for platinum is for auto catalysts, with 21% of total platinum demand. Catalysts in autos are used to convert most of vehicle emissions into less harmful carbon dioxide, nitrogen, and water vapor. Platinum is also used in the production of hard disk drive coatings, fiber optic cables, infra-red detectors, fertilizers, explosives, petrol additives, platinum-tipped spark plugs, glassmaking equipment, biodegradable elements for household detergents, dental restorations, and in anti-cancer drugs.

Palladium (atomic symbol Pd) is very similar to platinum and is part of the same general metals group. Palladium is mined with platinum, but it is somewhat more common because it is also a by-product of nickel mining. The primary use for palladium is in the use of automotive catalysts, with that sector accounting for about 63% of total palladium demand. Other uses for palladium include electronic equipment (21%), dental alloys (12%), and jewelry (4%).

Rhodium (atomic symbol Rh), another member of the platinum group, is also used in the automotive industry in pollution control devices. To some extent palladium has replaced rhodium. Iridium (atomic symbol Ir) is used to process catalysts and it has also found use in some auto catalysts. Iridium and ruthenium (atomic symbol Ru) are used in the production of polyvinyl chloride. As the prices of these metals change, there is some substitution. Therefore, strength of platinum prices relative to palladium should lead to the substitution of palladium for platinum in catalytic converters.

Platinum futures and options are traded at the CME Group, the JSE Securities Exchange, and the Moscow Exchange. Platinum futures are also traded on the Multi Commodity Exchange of India (MCX), the National Commodity & Derivatives Exchange (NCDEX), and the Tokyo Commodity Exchange (TOCOM). Palladium futures and options are traded at the CME Group. Palladium futures are also traded on the Moscow Exchange and the Tokyo Commodity Exchange (TOCOM). The CME platinum futures contract calls for the delivery of 50 troy ounces of platinum (0.9995 fineness) and the contract trades in terms of dollars and cents per troy ounce. The CME palladium futures contract calls for the delivery of 50 troy ounces of palladium (0.9995 fineness) and the contract is priced in terms of dollars and cents per troy ounce.

Prices – CME platinum futures prices (Barchart.com symbol PL) on the nearest futures chart reached a record high of $2308.80 per troy ounce in early 2008, but then plunged below $800 by late-2008 due to the global financial crisis. Platinum prices rebounded higher during 2009-2011 and posted a 5-year high of $1918.50 in Aug 2011, but then trended lower during 2012-14. Platinum futures prices in late 2014 fell to a 5-year low and closed the year down -11.8% at $1208.9 per troy ounce.

CME palladium futures prices (Barchart.com symbol PA) rallied to a record high of $912.0 in September 2014 but then fell back to close the year of 2014 up +11.1% at $789.40 per troy ounce.

Supply – World mine production of platinum in 2014 fell -12.0% yr/yr to 161,000 kilograms, and remained below the record high of 217,000 kilograms in 2006. South Africa is the world's largest producer of platinum by far with 68.3% of world production in 2014, followed by Russia (15.5%), Zimbabwe (6.8%), Canada (4.5%) and the U.S. (2.3%). World mine production of palladium in 2014 fell -6.4% to 190,000 kilograms, which was still below the record high production level of 222,000 in 2006. The world's largest palladium producers are Russia with 42.6% of world production in 2014, South Africa with 31.6%, Canada with 9.0%, and the U.S. with 6.4%. World production of platinum group metals other than platinum and palladium in 2012 (latest data available) fell by -7.2% yr/yr to 67,900 kilograms, but still below the 2007 record high of 79,600 kilograms.

U.S. mine production of platinum in 2014 fell -1.9% yr/yr to 3,650 kilograms, but still below the record high of 4,390 kilograms posted in 2002. U.S. mine production of palladium in 2014 fell -3.2% yr/yr to 12,200 kilograms, well below the record high of 14,800 kilograms posted in 2002. U.S. refinery production of scrap platinum and palladium in 2012 (latest data available) rose +13.9% to 37,600 kilograms, a new 13-year high.

Demand – The total of platinum-group metals sold to consuming industries in the U.S. in 2004 (latest data available) rose +7.1% to 91,434 kilograms. The two main U.S. industries that use platinum are the auto industry, which accounted for about 74% of U.S. platinum usage in 2004, and the jewelry industry, which accounted for about 26% of U.S. platinum usage.

Trade – U.S. imports of refined platinum and palladium in 2014 for consumption fell -22.5% yr/yr to 253,735 kilograms. U.S. exports of refined platinum and palladium in 2014 rose +5.2% yr/yr to 41,700 kilograms, well below the record high of 103,590 kilograms in 2006. The U.S. relied on imports for 85% of its platinum and palladium consumption in 2014.

PLATINUM-GROUP METALS

World Mine Production of Platinum   In Kilograms

Year	Australia	Canada	Colombia[3]	Finland	Japan	Russia	Serbia/Montenegro	Africa	United States	Zimbabwe	World Total
2005	111	6,075	1,082	800	760	29,000	3	163,711	3,920	4,834	211,000
2006	209	8,510	1,438	800	760	29,000	2	168,125	4,290	4,998	218,000
2007	142	8,000	1,526	461	1,000	27,000	2	160,940	3,860	5,306	209,000
2008	120	8,500	1,370	214	1,442	25,000	----	146,140	3,580	5,642	193,000
2009	230	4,000	929	265	1,417	24,500	12	140,819	3,830	6,849	184,000
2010	130	3,500	997	500	1,331	25,000	----	147,790	3,450	8,800	192,000
2011	130	8,000	1,231	400	1,765	25,900	----	148,008	3,700	10,826	200,000
2012	90	7,000	1,025	400	1,500	24,600	6	133,000	3,670	11,000	183,000
2013[1]		7,000				25,500		131,000	37,520	12,400	183,000
2014[2]		7,200				25,000		110,000	3,650	11,000	161,000

[1] Preliminary.   [2] Estimate.   [3] Placer platinum.   W = Withheld.   *Source: U.S. Geological Survey (USGS)*

World Mine Production of Palladium and Other Group Metals   In Kilograms

Year	Australia	Canada	Finland	Japan	Russia	Serbia/Montenegro	South Africa	United States	Zimbabwe	Total	Russia	South Africa	World Total
2005	550	10,415	----	5,400	97,400	19	82,961	13,300	3,879	216,000	15,500	56,309	77,700
2006	750	10,493	----	5,400	98,400	15	86,265	14,400	4,022	222,000	15,600	53,138	74,600
2007	600	14,100	----	6,505	96,800	15	83,643	12,800	4,180	224,000	14,500	59,449	76,500
2008	580	14,700	342	7,526	87,700	70	75,537	11,900	4,386	206,000	12,500	53,999	69,100
2009	800	7,000	560	6,675	83,200	38	75,117	12,700	5,680	195,000	11,900	55,456	69,500
2010	650	6,200	1,493	6,107	84,700	22	82,222	11,600	7,000	203,000	12,000	57,292	71,500
2011	600	14,300	1,058	7,534	84,300	20	82,731	12,400	8,241	213,000	12,500	58,111	73,200
2012	300	12,200	1,100	7,000	82,000	4	74,000	12,300	9,000	201,000	12,000	53,000	67,900
2013[1]		16,500			80,000		75,000	12,600	9,600	203,000			
2014[2]		17,000			81,000		60,000	12,200	10,000	190,000			

[1] Preliminary.   [2] Estimate.   *Source: U.S. Geological Survey (USGS)*

Salient Statistics of Platinum and Allied Metals[3] in the United States   In Kilograms

Year	Net Import Reliance as a % of Apparent Consump	Mine Production Platinum	Mine Production Palladium	Refinery Production (Secondary)	Total Refined	Refiner, Importer & Dealer Stocks as of Dec. 31 — Platinum	Palladium	Other[4]	Total	Imports Refined	Total	Exports Refined	Total	Apparent Consumptio
2005	93	3,920	13,300	11,580	11,580	261	----	189	450	284,849	----	49,395	----	----
2006	90	4,290	14,400	12,530	12,530	261	----	111	372	287,756	----	103,590	----	----
2007	91	3,860	12,800	16,340	16,340	261	----	18	279	362,733	----	81,100	----	----
2008	89	3,580	11,900	15,050	15,050	261	----	18	279	334,961	----	50,430	----	----
2009	95	3,830	12,700	15,030	15,030	261	----	18	279	286,688	----	51,140	----	----
2010	91	3,450	11,600	12,230	12,230	261	----	18	279	253,206	----	61,040	----	----
2011	89	3,700	12,400	33,000	33,000	261	----	18	279	257,138	----	45,820	----	----
2012	90	3,670	12,300	37,600	37,600	261	----	18	279	276,460	----	43,510	----	----
2013[1]	84	3,720	12,600							327,297	----	39,640	----	----
2014[2]	85	3,650	12,200							253,735		41,700		

[1] Preliminary.   [2] Estimate.   [3] Includes platinum, palladium, iridium, osmium, rhodium, and ruthenium.   [4] Includes iridium, osmium, rhodium, and ruthenium.   W = Withheld.   *Source: U.S. Geological Survey (USGS)*

Average Producer Price of Rhodium in the United States   In Dollars Per Troy Ounce

Year	Jan.	Feb.	Mar.	Apr.	May	June	July	Aug.	Sept.	Oct.	Nov.	Dec.	Average
2005	1,420.48	1,595.00	1,557.73	1,509.05	1,558.10	1,837.50	1,974.75	2,061.96	2,463.57	2,751.90	2,933.75	3,015.71	2,056.63
2006	3,134.29	3,493.68	3,876.74	4,465.53	5,543.41	4,898.86	4,602.11	4,647.83	4,824.75	4,930.00	4,883.75	5,390.00	4,557.58
2007	5,738.64	5,947.50	6,065.91	6,293.75	6,144.55	6,107.62	6,050.48	6,104.78	6,201.32	6,258.70	6,648.75	6,815.00	6,198.08
2008	7,042.27	8,531.25	9,248.75	9,065.91	9,553.57	9,775.00	9,385.23	6,247.62	4,501.19	2,460.87	1,393.06	1,214.29	6,534.92
2009	1,147.62	1,178.95	1,169.32	1,346.90	1,417.50	1,463.64	1,490.91	1,671.43	1,650.00	1,782.95	2,332.89	2,410.71	1,588.57
2010	2,668.75	2,483.75	2,514.57	2,846.43	2,768.75	2,484.09	2,341.67	2,148.86	2,203.57	2,279.76	2,341.25	2,361.98	2,453.62
2011	2,436.90	2,475.00	2,396.74	2,340.00	2,120.24	2,067.05	1,982.50	1,876.09	1,817.86	1,625.00	1,660.00	1,475.00	2,022.70
2012	1,390.00	1,513.75	1,484.09	1,383.25	1,345.91	1,250.00	1,224.52	1,123.26	1,175.00	1,184.78	1,137.50	1,091.50	1,275.30
2013	1,123.64	1,226.00	1,254.00	1,184.32	1,127.95	1,037.00	988.64	1,000.23	1,000.00	987.83	958.50	916.43	1,067.05
2014	1,047.73	1,068.00	1,092.14	1,134.52	1,071.67	1,118.81	1,187.27	1,375.24	1,310.48	1,228.70	1,224.44	1,206.36	1,172.11

Source: American Metal Market (AMM)

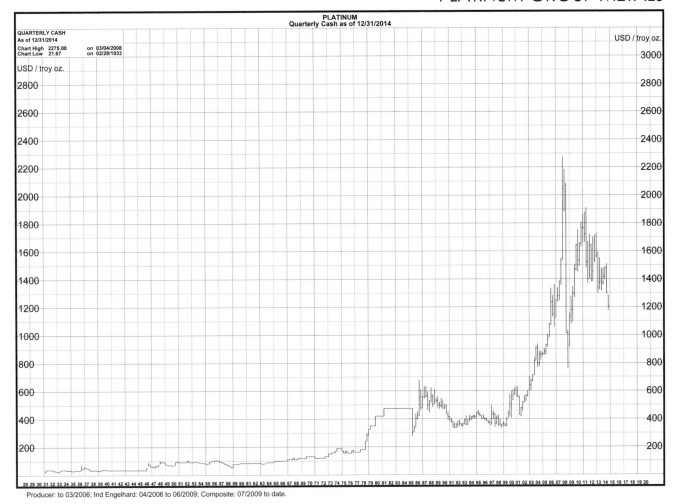

PLATINUM
Quarterly Cash as of 12/31/2014

QUARTERLY CASH
As of 12/31/2014

Chart High 2275.00   on 03/04/2008
Chart Low   21.67   on 02/28/1933

USD / troy oz.

Producer: to 03/2006; Ind Engelhard: 04/2006 to 06/2009; Composite: 07/2009 to date.

Average Merchant's Price of Platinum in the United States   In Dollars Per Troy Ounce

Year	Jan.	Feb.	Mar.	Apr.	May	June	July	Aug.	Sept.	Oct.	Nov.	Dec.	Average
2005	861.80	867.40	870.23	867.71	869.00	883.23	876.60	901.04	918.10	933.76	964.00	9,890.48	1,641.95
2006	1,032.48	1,045.16	1,044.39	1,105.00	1,264.05	1,192.73	1,233.03	1,236.74	1,183.30	1,085.32	1,183.73	1,124.79	1,144.23
2007	1,151.90	1,206.47	1,222.77	1,280.90	1,306.50	1,289.14	1,307.38	1,267.30	1,313.00	1,413.87	1,449.45	1,492.47	1,308.43
2008	1,585.09	2,002.55	2,043.65	1,991.32	2,053.57	2,042.24	1,904.68	1,492.52	1,221.71	917.13	841.22	842.40	1,578.17
2009	949.76	1,037.26	1,084.59	1,169.57	1,134.45	1,220.41	1,163.82	1,248.24	1,294.71	1,335.86	1,401.26	1,447.20	1,207.26
2010	1,567.15	1,525.63	1,602.65	1,718.33	1,633.45	1,556.77	1,530.57	1,543.82	1,598.57	1,692.29	1,702.35	1,715.05	1,615.55
2011	1,790.62	1,828.68	1,773.26	1,804.00	1,792.24	1,771.45	1,766.65	1,810.52	1,745.43	1,539.81	1,607.65	1,461.81	1,724.34
2012	1,510.85	1,664.50	1,660.05	1,590.85	1,474.45	1,450.05	1,425.86	1,455.70	1,629.89	1,639.26	1,578.85	1,583.00	1,555.28
2013	1,646.43	1,676.95	1,586.30	1,497.23	1,478.95	1,431.20	1,405.14	1,496.50	1,454.05	1,415.52	1,423.85	1,355.25	1,488.95
2014	1,423.73	1,411.30	1,457.52	1,435.38	1,461.07	1,457.81	1,497.05	1,449.90	1,362.10	1,263.61	1,213.00	1,222.48	1,387.91

Source: American Metal Market (AMM)

Average Dealer Price[1] of Palladium in the United States   In Dollars Per Troy Ounce

Year	Jan.	Feb.	Mar.	Apr.	May	June	July	Aug.	Sept.	Oct.	Nov.	Dec.	Average
2005	188.45	184.15	200.09	200.76	191.38	188.50	186.95	188.13	191.19	209.71	246.35	266.24	203.49
2006	275.95	291.58	312.70	355.74	372.82	319.36	320.21	332.57	324.40	315.18	326.91	328.00	322.95
2007	339.81	344.26	352.27	370.35	369.50	370.76	368.67	344.61	337.63	368.70	366.75	355.42	357.39
2008	376.95	473.65	490.35	449.05	438.29	453.57	428.27	318.29	250.19	193.30	212.61	178.00	355.21
2009	189.81	207.63	203.73	228.29	230.45	247.18	250.64	278.38	295.86	324.45	354.84	376.60	265.66
2010	437.15	429.16	464.48	535.33	495.05	465.18	459.86	493.45	543.24	596.33	687.75	760.05	530.59
2011	797.48	823.47	766.48	777.30	743.38	774.55	794.80	766.57	710.14	620.45	637.70	650.57	738.57
2012	664.28	708.05	689.86	660.65	624.68	617.95	582.95	607.04	664.00	637.78	639.20	694.95	649.28
2013	716.62	755.68	761.20	710.27	723.91	716.70	725.18	746.23	711.75	727.61	737.20	721.45	729.48
2014	738.59	733.90	783.19	804.62	829.67	841.19	880.95	884.10	844.57	784.30	783.78	810.71	809.96

[1] Based on wholesale quantities, prompt delivery.   Source: American Metal Market (AMM)

PLATINUM-GROUP METALS

PLATINUM - NYMEX
Weekly Selected Futures as of 01/02/2015

WEEKLY SELECTED FUTURES
As of 01/02/2015

Chart High 2308.80   on 03/04/2008
Chart Low   761.80   on 10/27/2008

USD / troy oz.

Nearby Futures through Last Trading Day.

Volume of Trading of Platinum Futures in New York   In Contracts

Year	Jan.	Feb.	Mar.	Apr.	May	June	July	Aug.	Sept.	Oct.	Nov.	Dec.	Total
2005	15,410	20,253	41,297	16,267	20,135	55,588	25,132	26,604	52,535	21,827	30,447	50,684	376,179
2006	20,604	27,572	42,804	17,215	34,684	45,985	16,220	21,428	44,000	21,182	46,754	34,671	373,119
2007	20,534	26,975	59,099	26,457	35,525	66,968	35,371	35,975	58,091	34,100	36,126	66,324	501,545
2008	54,479	71,978	84,901	41,283	54,476	66,398	43,127	47,539	74,165	38,107	30,011	69,079	675,543
2009	31,090	35,199	82,949	30,849	34,962	104,413	46,045	48,650	134,462	55,865	63,896	134,504	802,884
2010	85,446	83,630	176,594	91,365	133,781	144,344	71,314	74,099	188,874	99,204	151,998	185,858	1,486,507
2011	123,012	97,150	235,375	105,524	113,655	216,647	95,589	188,066	293,142	156,172	136,109	232,822	1,993,263
2012	150,111	172,872	252,464	136,954	181,216	283,780	138,326	217,759	371,411	211,656	183,154	322,051	2,621,754
2013	280,979	275,013	335,276	277,634	243,442	388,436	188,942	216,194	341,340	222,190	185,380	307,949	3,262,775
2014	217,465	194,296	389,315	182,628	239,397	379,860	210,163	179,938	399,265	271,921	211,153	360,542	3,235,943

Contract size = 50 oz.   *Source: CME Group; New York Mercantile Exchange (NYMEX)*

Average Open Interest of Platinum Futures in New York   In Contracts

Year	Jan.	Feb.	Mar.	Apr.	May	June	July	Aug.	Sept.	Oct.	Nov.	Dec.
2005	6,800	7,486	8,047	8,132	8,496	10,109	8,497	11,729	12,478	13,024	12,377	11,327
2006	10,625	9,995	8,407	9,486	9,681	8,265	8,575	9,889	9,076	7,276	8,332	8,186
2007	8,810	10,752	11,154	13,413	15,173	15,033	16,641	12,347	12,341	15,199	14,427	15,404
2008	17,912	15,770	12,966	12,977	15,869	15,821	14,198	12,325	13,904	15,111	16,530	17,267
2009	18,300	20,041	20,388	20,506	21,045	23,755	21,952	25,303	28,571	31,236	33,730	33,542
2010	34,160	34,637	36,720	37,368	33,840	30,242	28,369	31,026	35,528	38,402	36,959	37,115
2011	40,572	41,823	35,986	35,925	36,214	35,150	32,278	37,063	39,229	37,910	38,779	42,652
2012	43,893	44,519	43,028	40,337	45,372	50,530	50,160	53,902	57,555	63,289	60,641	62,626
2013	64,184	70,544	64,608	63,193	63,406	62,590	61,937	65,515	61,739	59,391	59,092	63,028
2014	59,980	63,324	69,278	65,308	68,150	68,004	71,271	64,416	64,103	59,701	61,768	65,647

Contract size = 50 oz.   *Source: CME Group; New York Mercantile Exchange (NYMEX)*

PALLADIUM - NYMEX
Weekly Selected Futures as of 01/02/2015

WEEKLY SELECTED FUTURES
As of 01/02/2015

Chart High 912.00 on 09/02/2014
Chart Low 160.00 on 12/05/2008

Nearby Futures through Last Trading Day.

Volume of Trading of Palladium Futures in New York In Contracts

Year	Jan.	Feb.	Mar.	Apr.	May	June	July	Aug.	Sept.	Oct.	Nov.	Dec.	Total
2005	7,728	43,268	16,979	13,316	46,112	13,594	17,185	49,268	17,747	21,680	50,643	24,403	321,923
2006	28,447	59,279	32,573	23,135	64,863	25,857	13,464	41,123	16,222	14,351	47,797	11,005	378,116
2007	23,636	62,815	14,987	25,166	69,089	16,322	15,072	65,106	16,975	26,385	52,411	13,029	400,993
2008	26,954	105,845	49,411	24,750	66,939	18,934	26,245	53,692	25,253	28,627	43,879	13,299	483,828
2009	14,284	41,726	14,509	17,332	51,635	23,403	25,689	57,502	25,393	29,401	71,228	28,719	400,821
2010	48,438	90,368	48,314	58,104	134,435	45,840	45,847	87,366	55,399	69,623	156,495	61,355	901,584
2011	72,121	121,271	94,402	85,897	132,608	80,665	66,290	139,208	80,932	72,895	119,732	73,508	1,139,529
2012	74,977	125,721	75,910	61,833	136,033	67,710	59,308	123,731	85,209	84,730	145,835	77,483	1,118,480
2013	126,987	198,821	87,681	122,520	181,016	93,497	77,175	163,892	82,470	99,944	182,133	69,880	1,486,016
2014	87,502	158,760	136,126	111,648	195,880	101,610	97,809	208,474	126,132	115,708	161,947	72,356	1,573,952

Contract size = 100 oz.   *Source: CME Group; New York Mercantile Exchange (NYMEX)*

Average Open Interest of Palladium Futures in New York In Contracts

Year	Jan.	Feb.	Mar.	Apr.	May	June	July	Aug.	Sept.	Oct.	Nov.	Dec.
2005	12,824	13,821	12,946	13,116	13,345	13,527	13,794	14,465	13,340	13,488	14,676	14,477
2006	14,353	16,632	15,426	17,783	18,002	14,251	14,087	13,166	11,247	11,836	12,511	11,210
2007	13,794	16,132	15,587	18,126	19,682	18,288	18,152	18,035	16,062	16,286	17,194	14,820
2008	18,184	20,999	20,227	19,571	19,197	17,106	15,223	13,821	14,294	14,656	13,435	12,688
2009	12,442	12,596	12,230	14,237	15,594	16,288	17,150	20,669	21,877	21,881	22,650	22,692
2010	23,356	22,566	22,944	23,905	23,152	21,271	19,732	19,808	23,036	24,706	24,747	23,089
2011	22,340	22,939	21,584	21,325	20,376	20,615	21,809	21,576	19,590	19,074	19,368	18,558
2012	18,051	21,035	20,978	21,174	22,931	21,951	22,676	23,304	19,987	20,172	22,005	25,798
2013	31,036	37,519	37,181	37,118	36,554	36,219	35,682	38,564	34,971	37,152	39,264	36,781
2014	39,059	40,226	41,494	42,071	43,466	39,964	43,791	44,286	38,776	33,587	34,170	32,060

Contract size = 100 oz.   *Source: CME Group; New York Mercantile Exchange (NYMEX)*

Potatoes

The potato is a member of the nightshade family. The leaves of the potato plant are poisonous and a potato will begin to turn green if left too long in the light. This green skin contains solanine, a substance that can cause the potato to taste bitter and even cause illness in humans.

In Peru, the Inca Indians were the first to cultivate potatoes around 200 BC. The Indians developed potato crops because their staple diet of corn would not grow above an altitude of 3,350 meters. In 1536, after conquering the Incas, the Spanish Conquistadors brought potatoes back to Europe. At first, Europeans did not accept the potato because it was not mentioned in the Bible and was therefore considered an "evil" food. But after Marie Antoinette wore a crown of potato flowers, it finally became a popular food. In 1897, during the Alaskan Klondike gold rush, potatoes were so valued for their vitamin C content that miners traded gold for potatoes. The potato became the first vegetable to be grown in outer space in October 1995.

The potato is a highly nutritious, fat-free, cholesterol-free and sodium-free food, and is an important dietary staple in over 130 countries. A medium-sized potato contains only 100 calories. Potatoes are an excellent source of vitamin C and provide B vitamins as well as potassium, copper, magnesium, and iron. According to the U.S. Department of Agriculture, "a diet of whole milk and potatoes would supply almost all of the food elements necessary for the maintenance of the human body."

Potatoes are one of the largest vegetable crops grown in the U.S., and are grown in all fifty states. The U.S. ranks about 4th in world potato production. The top three types of potatoes grown extensively in the U.S. are white, red, and Russets (Russets account for about two-thirds the U.S. crop). Potatoes in the U.S. are harvested in all four seasons, but the vast majority of the crop is harvested in fall. Potatoes harvested in the winter, spring and summer are used mainly to supplement fresh supplies of fall-harvested potatoes and are also important to the processing industries. The four principal categories for U.S. potato exports are frozen, potato chips, fresh, and dehydrated. Fries account for approximately 95% of U.S. frozen potato exports.

Prices – The average monthly price received for potatoes by U.S. farmers in 2014 fell -5.4% to $9.19 per hundred pounds, below last year's record high of $9.71.

Supply –The total potato crop in 2014 rose+0.7% to 44.276 billion pounds, well below the record high of 50.936 billion pounds posted in 2000. The fall crop in 2014 rose by +1.2% to 40.619 billion pounds and it accounted for 91.7% of the total crop. Stocks of the fall crop (as of Dec 1, 2014) were 26.340 billion pounds. In 2014, the spring crop rose +2.1% to 2.260 billion pounds, the summer crop fell -8.6% to 1.575 billion pounds, and the winter crop (annualized through 2014) rose +3.3% to 408.329 million pounds.

The largest producing states for the fall 2014 crop were Idaho (with 33.3% of the crop), Washington (24.9%), Wisconsin (6.6%), North Dakota (5.9%), and Colorado (5.8%). For the spring crop, the largest producing states were California with 51.6% of the crop and Florida with 31.1% of the crop. Farmers harvested 1.049 million acres in 2014, down -0.1% yr/yr and slightly above the 2010 record low of 1.008 million acres. The yield per harvested acre in 2014 rose +2.9% to 42,600 pounds per acre.

Demand – Total utilization of potatoes in 2013 (latest data) fell -6.1% yr/yr to 43.465 billion pounds, up from the 2010 record low of 40.427 billion pounds. The breakdown shows that the largest consumption category for potatoes is frozen French fries with 34.4% of total consumption, followed closely by table stock (25.8%), chips and shoestrings (14.9%), and dehydration (11.8%). U.S. per capita consumption of potatoes in 2013 rose +1.7% to 116.7 pounds, below the record high of 145.0 pounds per capita seen in 1996.

Trade – U.S. exports of potatoes in 2011 (latest data) rose +16.2% to 944,494 thousand pounds, a new record high. U.S. imports in 2011 rose +19.2% to 909,645 thousand pounds, down from the 2008 record high of 1.071 million pounds.

Salient Statistics of Potatoes in the United States

	---- Acreage ----		Yield Per	Total	---- Used Where Grown ---- (Farm Disposition)				---- Value of ----			Stocks	- Foreign Trade[4] -		Consumption[4] Per Capita	
Crop Year	Planted	Harvest-ed	Harvested Acre	Pro-duction	Seed & Feed	Shrinkage & Loss	Sold[2]	Farm Price	Pro-duction[3]	Sales	Jan. 1 (1,000	Exports (Fresh)	Imports	Fresh	Total
	--- 1,000 Acres ---		Cwt.	--------- In Thousands of Cwt. ---------				($ Cwt.)	---- Million $ ----		Cwt)	-- Millions of Lbs. --		-- In Pounds --	
2005	1,109	1,087	390	423,926	4,791	28,519	390,616	7.04	2,982	2,750	220,500	586,226	631,252	41.3	125.4
2006	1,139	1,120	393	440,698	4,750	29,639	406,309	7.31	3,209	2,970	225,800	600,715	611,229	38.6	123.7
2007	1,142	1,122	396	444,873	4,105	29,561	411,209	7.51	3,340	3,089	232,300	615,784	923,574	38.7	124.4
2008	1,060	1,047	396	415,055	4,138	26,438	384,478	9.09	3,770	3,494	213,200	616,290	1,071,973	37.8	118.3
2009	1,071	1,044	414	432,601	4,535	29,135	398,931	8.25	3,558	3,292	234,300	682,190	794,611	36.7	113.5
2010	1,026	1,008	401	404,273	4,220	24,990	375,063	9.20	3,722	3,449	209,400	812,748	762,876	36.8	113.9
2011	1,099	1,077	399	429,647	4,142	27,755	397,750	9.37	4,041	3,743	NA	944,494	909,645	34.1	110.3
2012	1,155	1,139	408	464,970	4,869	28,356	429,541	8.63	4,017	3,728	NA				
2013[1]	1,064	1,051	414	434,652	4,323	26,211	404,118	9.71	4,223	3,930					
2014[1]	1,061	1,050	426	446,693					3,848						

[1] Preliminary. [2] For all purposes, including food, seed processing & livestock feed. [3] Farm weight basis, excluding canned and frozen potatoes.
[4] Calendar year. *Source: Economic Research Service, U.S. Department of Agriculture (ERS-USDA)*

218

Cold Storage Stocks of All Frozen Potatoes in the United States, on First of Month — In Millions of Pounds

Year	Jan.	Feb.	Mar.	Apr.	May	June	July	Aug.	Sept.	Oct.	Nov.	Dec.
2005	1,074.8	1,168.8	1,152.8	1,093.7	1,174.3	1,178.1	1,190.5	1,154.9	1,121.3	1,180.4	1,200.0	1,122.5
2006	1,051.1	1,076.2	1,147.0	1,158.9	1,176.6	1,104.9	1,108.1	996.4	964.1	1,009.6	1,066.6	1,052.1
2007	954.8	1,041.3	1,063.6	1,116.2	1,102.2	1,070.7	1,078.2	991.8	1,000.4	1,080.0	1,133.8	1,078.4
2008	1,012.4	1,089.1	1,117.5	1,087.7	1,134.4	1,074.9	1,190.0	1,107.5	1,126.7	1,180.8	1,200.5	1,212.1
2009	1,098.6	1,171.0	1,192.1	1,226.8	1,221.4	1,203.2	1,245.1	1,187.5	1,094.8	1,130.2	1,162.9	1,108.1
2010	1,043.8	1,091.3	1,113.6	1,100.5	1,093.7	1,077.3	1,141.9	1,063.9	1,036.3	1,070.1	1,122.9	1,127.5
2011	1,018.9	1,095.0	1,102.9	1,086.1	1,070.3	1,073.8	1,073.8	1,073.8	1,073.8	1,073.8	1,073.8	1,073.8
2012	999.9	1,072.0	1,111.7	1,129.0	1,138.7	1,091.6	1,161.5	1,065.7	1,019.8	1,123.4	1,184.7	1,144.2
2013	1,110.4	1,175.1	1,232.7	1,226.8	1,222.4	1,181.3	1,270.3	1,138.4	1,091.3	1,137.6	1,175.3	1,150.8
2014[1]	1,095.3	1,104.8	1,124.1	1,044.3	1,009.2	983.4	1,012.8	924.2	936.6	1,039.7	1,099.5	1,105.6

[1] Preliminary.   Source: Agricultural Statistics Board, U.S. Department of Agriculture (ASB-USDA)

Potato Crop Production Estimates, Stocks and Disappearance in the United States — In Millions of Cwt.

	Crop Production Estimates			Total Storage Stocks[2]								Fall Crop — 1,000 Cwt.				
	Total Crop			Fall Crop			Following Year						Disappearance	Stocks	Average Price	Value of Sales
Year	Oct. 1	Nov. 1	Dec. 1	Oct. 1	Nov. 1	Dec. 1	Jan. 1	Feb. 1	Mar. 1	Apr. 1	May 1	Production	(Sold)	Dec. 1	($/Cwt.)	($1,000)
2005	----	421.3	----	----	382.2	253.8	220.5	189.1	155.5	115.7	75.9	378,732	351,083	253,800	6.53	2,290,850
2006	----	434.8	----	----	390.9	258.9	225.8	192.2	159.5	120.9	79.1	389,527	365,863	258,900	6.67	2,442,474
2007	----	448.0	----	----	408.3	265.5	232.3	199.3	163.4	125.5	84.0	397,753	374,617	265,500	7.04	2,636,885
2008	----	415.1	----	----	373.5	243.7	213.2	183.9	152.7	115.8	78.1	369,866	349,580	243,700	8.49	2,967,871
2009	----	429.7	----	----	391.5	265.8	234.3	203.5	169.7	128.7	89.6	383,962	361,316	265,800	7.62	2,751,550
2010	----	399.2	----	----	361.4	240.2	209.4	180.3	148.5	111.0	72.0	357,191	339,051	240,200	8.79	2,981,528
2011	----	429.6	----	----	391.2	253.0	NA	187.5	NA	115.7	NA	391,180	360,620	253,000	8.87	3,197,096
2012	----	467.2	----	----	422.0	271.5	NA	204.6	NA	NA	NA	420,030	385,767	271,500	8.05	3,111,362
2013	----	439.7	----	----	401.5	NA	NA	NA	NA	119.1	NA	395,275		NA		
2014[1]	----	442.8	----	----	406.2	267.4	NA	203.7				408,329		267,400		

[1] Preliminary.   [2] Held by growers and local dealers in the fall producing areas.
Source: Agricultural Statistics Board, U.S. Department of Agriculture (ASB-USDA)

Production of Potatoes by Seasonal Groups in the United States — In Thousands of Cwt.

	Winter	Spring			Summer			Fall								
Year	Total	California	Florida	Total	Mexico	Virgina	Total	Colorado	Idaho	Maine	Minnesota	North Dakota	Oregan	Washington	Wisconsin	Total
2005	4,892	6,116	6,527	18,724	----	1,029	17,567	22,910	118,288	15,455	17,630	20,500	22,023	95,480	27,880	378,732
2006	4,495	6,044	6,441	19,766	----	1,512	18,166	22,686	128,915	17,980	20,400	25,480	18,533	89,900	29,370	389,527
2007	2,258	6,123	7,807	19,817	----	1,134	15,997	20,981	130,010	16,668	21,560	23,660	20,294	100,800	28,160	397,753
2008	2,530	6,930	7,952	20,132	----	1,254	13,805	21,907	116,475	14,769	20,400	22,680	18,674	93,000	25,730	369,866
2009	2,132	7,175	7,700	21,321	----	1,416	14,321	22,080	132,500	15,263	20,700	19,125	21,460	87,230	28,980	383,962
2010	NA	10,935	7,950	24,797	----	952	12,971	21,528	112,970	15,892	17,010	22,000	20,058	88,440	24,293	357,191
2011	NA	10,920	9,112	25,573	----	1,180	12,894	21,291	128,760	14,310	16,685	18,865	23,342	97,600	25,938	391,180
2012	----	11,600	8,917	26,736	----	1,350	18,204	19,980	141,820	16,088	18,800	25,200	22,935	95,940	30,360	420,030
2013	----	10,865	7,080	22,137	----	819	17,240	20,304	131,131	15,660	17,325	22,620	21,582	96,000	26,040	395,275
2014[1]	----	11,656	7,032	22,608	----	1,125	15,756	23,735	135,920	15,150	16,800	24,255	22,562	101,475	27,090	408,329

[1] Preliminary.   Source: Agricultural Statistics Board, U.S. Department of Agriculture (ASB-USDA)

Utilization of Potatoes in the United States — In Thousands of Cwt.

	Sales								Other Sales			Non-Sales			
		For Processing										Used on			
Crop Year	Table Stock	Chips, Shoe-strings	Dehyd-ration	Frozen French Fries	Other Frozen Products	Canned Potatoes	Other Canned Products[2]	Starch & Flour	Live-stock Feed	Seed	Total Sales	Farms Where Grown	Shrink-age & Loss	Total Non-Sales	Total
2004	130,418	50,068	48,541	131,592	23,003	2,843	984	1,531	1,942	22,915	413,837	3,601	37,408	42,204	456,041
2005	114,123	52,294	43,387	126,429	25,376	2,174	958	1,622	1,999	22,254	390,616	3,595	28,519	33,310	423,926
2006	113,335	64,377	48,809	126,083	24,229	1,957	930	1,369	1,610	23,610	406,309	3,520	29,639	34,389	440,698
2007	110,860	54,343	49,021	139,624	26,571	2,504	800	4,029	1,160	22,297	411,209	2,986	29,561	33,666	444,875
2008	109,351	50,988	40,646	134,123	19,519	2,070	790	5,288	803	20,900	384,478	3,315	26,438	30,576	415,055
2009	116,326	42,548	44,477	138,589	21,004	1,983	748	6,504	6,533	20,219	398,931	3,346	29,135	33,670	432,601
2010	107,407	54,508	34,164	135,703	13,374	1,659	700	6,334	593	20,621	375,063	3,002	24,990	29,210	404,273
2011	102,655	58,703	45,511	144,626	15,188	1,650	716	6,013	825	21,863	397,750	3,012	27,755	31,897	429,647
2012	118,535	59,304	49,894	142,993	20,635	1,741	734	7,919	4,080	23,706	429,541	3,286	28,356	33,225	462,766
2013[1]	104,326	60,210	47,827	139,007	19,176	651	660	8,579	1,251	22,431	404,118	3,215	26,211	30,534	434,652

[1] Preliminary.   [2] Hash, stews and soups.   Source: Agricultural Statistics Board, U.S. Department of Agriculture (ASB-USDA)

POTATOES

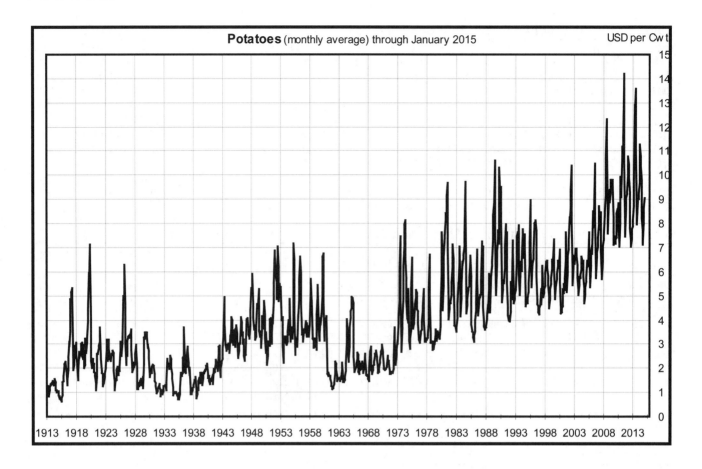

Potatoes (monthly average) through January 2015 — USD per Cwt

Average Price Received by Farmers for Potatoes in the U.S. — In Dollars Per Hundred Pounds (Cwt.)

Year	Jan.	Feb.	Mar.	Apr.	May	June	July	Aug.	Sept.	Oct.	Nov.	Dec.	Season Average
2005	5.59	5.79	6.44	6.20	6.23	6.29	7.63	7.02	5.69	5.37	6.26	6.83	7.04
2006	7.07	6.76	8.50	8.35	7.83	8.41	10.46	8.23	6.12	5.76	6.59	6.79	7.31
2007	7.06	7.42	7.93	8.71	7.95	7.75	8.48	6.85	5.81	5.68	6.47	7.02	7.51
2008	7.33	7.51	8.37	8.45	9.16	10.78	12.33	11.33	8.65	7.60	8.77	9.30	9.09
2009	9.40	8.87	9.27	9.81	9.62	9.48	9.81	9.61	8.27	7.11	7.22	7.47	8.25
2010	7.17	7.34	7.42	8.42	8.57	8.25	8.83	7.78	7.22	7.03	8.01	9.94	9.20
2011	9.08	9.26	10.74	11.17	11.17	11.59	14.19	10.47	8.05	7.46	8.58	9.06	9.37
2012	9.23	9.31	9.98	10.75	10.44	9.93	9.29	7.80	7.31	7.02	7.39	7.74	8.63
2013	7.87	8.12	8.72	9.63	12.89	12.57	13.56	11.15	8.48	7.96	8.87	9.02	9.71
2014[1]	9.02	9.28	9.66	11.29	10.77	10.38	9.81	8.22	7.70	7.13	7.99	8.64	

[1] Preliminary.   *Source: Agricultural Statistics Board, U.S. Department of Agriculture (ASB-USDA)*

Per Capita Utilization of Potatoes in the United States — In Pounds (Farm Weight)

Year	Total	Fresh	Freezing	Chips & Shoe-string	Dehy-drating	Canning	Total Processing
			--- Processing ---				
2004	134.5	45.8	57.3	16.4	13.8	1.2	88.7
2005	125.4	41.3	54.3	16.1	12.8	0.9	84.1
2006	123.6	38.6	53.2	18.6	12.4	0.8	85.0
2007	124.4	38.7	53.2	18.6	13.0	0.9	85.6
2008	118.3	37.8	51.5	15.7	12.4	0.9	80.5
2009	113.5	36.7	50.4	13.7	11.8	0.8	76.8
2010	114.0	36.8	50.2	15.0	11.2	0.7	77.2
2011	110.3	34.1	48.2	16.8	10.6	0.7	76.3
2012[1]	114.8	34.4	48.8	17.0	13.9	0.8	80.4
2013[2]	116.7	36.1	50.3	16.7	12.9	0.8	80.6

[1] Preliminary.   [2] Forecast.   *Source: Agricultural Statistics Board, U.S. Department of Agriculture (ASB-USDA)*

Potatoes Processed[1] in the United States, Eight States   In Thousands of Cwt.

States	Storage Season	to Dec. 1	to Jan. 1	to Feb. 1	to Mar. 1	to Apr. 1	to May 1	to June 1	Entire Season
Idaho and Oregon-Malheur Co.	2005-06	22,840	29,300	35,970	43,300	50,820	57,830	65,030	77,360
	2006-07	27,090	34,070	41,350	49,840	56,650	63,680	71,220	85,630
	2007-08	26,230	33,250	40,310	48,660	55,460	63,000	70,700	88,030
	2008-09	22,380	28,980	35,430	42,150	49,030	55,570	62,940	77,340
	2009-10	23,110	29,180	35,170	42,050	49,200	56,100	62,930	79,400
	2010-11	21,040	26,840	32,700	39,240	46,180	52,830	59,440	70,050
	2011-12	28,060	34,800	41,800	49,460	56,680	63,800	71,510	84,780
	2012-13	27,900	34,740	41,890	49,980	57,750	65,430	73,430	89,780
	2013-14	25,770	32,060	39,090	46,320	53,755	61,780	70,425	85,280
Maine[2]	2005-06	1,365	1,880	2,485	3,090	3,800	4,450	5,130	6,825
	2006-07	1,755	2,360	2,910	3,465	4,185	4,810	5,470	7,560
	2007-08	1,700	2,170	2,815	3,440	3,990	4,670	5,240	7,550
	2008-09	1,635	2,240	2,895	3,515	4,005	4,795	5,540	7,545
	2009-10	1,575	2,060	2,680	3,265	3,915	4,550	5,260	7,160
	2010-11	1,860	2,390	3,000	3,620	4,320	4,980	5,645	7,490
	2011-12	1,860	2,380	3,095	3,695	4,360	4,940	5,345	6,790
	2012-13	1,890	2,380	3,005	3,600	4,290	5,075	5,740	7,720
	2013-14	1,570	1,990	2,510	3,060	3,680	4,240	4,800	6,315
Washington & Oregon-Other	2005-06	30,310	35,895	40,545	48,290	55,320	61,855	69,360	78,550
	2006-07	30,980	37,060	41,290	49,930	56,690	63,170	70,410	77,355
	2007-08	30,595	36,940	42,350	50,165	57,160	67,690	72,380	82,770
	2008-09	32,560	38,050	42,795	49,865	56,350	62,635	70,625	81,260
	2009-10	25,395	31,245	36,530	43,780	50,130	56,700	64,805	75,690
	2010-11	27,670	33,570	38,815	46,700	53,660	60,145	67,655	77,940
	2011-12	31,750	38,165	44,475	51,630	58,515	65,320	73,040	84,105
	2012-13	31,295	37,730	43,820	51,765	57,915	64,500	70,470	80,400
	2013-14	31,575	37,990	45,420	52,690	59,025	64,905	72,325	80,655
Other States[3]	2005-06	11,055	14,070	17,005	19,895	22,520	25,270	27,740	35,535
	2006-07	14,355	17,800	21,415	24,690	28,205	31,560	35,040	43,565
	2007-08	15,040	17,535	20,755	23,900	26,650	29,710	32,600	39,430
	2008-09	12,480	15,120	18,165	21,030	24,025	26,515	29,590	37,285
	2009-10	10,865	13,565	16,305	18,995	21,600	24,355	27,375	34,240
	2010-11	11,820	14,785	17,435	20,370	23,215	25,775	28,690	35,430
	2011-12	14,205	16,770	19,525	21,930	24,910	27,230	29,960	36,200
	2012-13	14,270	16,765	19,785	22,520	25,170	28,320	31,100	40,395
	2013-14	11,365	14,280	17,470	20,475	23,695	26,990	30,195	37,425
Total	2005-06	65,570	81,145	96,005	114,575	132,460	149,405	167,260	198,270
	2006-07	74,210	91,320	107,895	127,050	145,760	163,250	182,170	214,225
	2007-08	73,565	89,895	106,230	126,165	143,260	165,070	180,920	217,780
	2008-09	68,975	84,280	99,155	116,400	133,220	149,285	168,420	203,005
	2009-10	60,945	76,050	90,685	108,090	124,845	141,705	160,370	196,490
	2010-11	62,390	77,585	91,950	109,930	127,375	143,730	161,430	190,910
	2011-12	75,875	92,115	108,895	126,715	144,465	161,290	179,855	211,875
	2012-13	75,355	91,615	108,500	127,865	145,125	163,325	180,740	218,295
	2013-14	70,280	86,320	104,490	122,545	140,155	157,915	177,745	209,675
Dehy-drated[4]	2005-06	11,920	15,655	19,225	22,765	26,605	30,065	34,130	41,625
	2006-07	14,590	19,250	23,635	27,885	32,210	36,480	40,915	49,375
	2007-08	12,815	16,785	21,040	25,350	29,500	33,650	37,975	46,660
	2008-09	10,675	14,490	18,335	21,465	24,875	28,195	31,870	39,345
	2009-10	10,985	14,035	17,150	19,895	23,155	26,630	30,045	38,915
	2010-11	7,960	10,795	13,645	16,485	19,415	22,740	25,855	32,700
	2011-12	13,375	16,845	20,875	24,410	28,070	31,533	35,310	42,585
	2012-13	13,965	17,640	22,000	26,105	30,135	34,610	38,945	47,305
	2013-14	12,065	15,875	19,835	23,380	27,140	31,095	34,895	44,385

[1] Total quantity received and used for processing regardless of the State in which the potatoes were produced. Amount excludes quantities used for potato chips in Maine, Michigan and Wisconsin.   [2] Includes Maine grown potatoes only.   [3] Colorado, Minnesota, , Nevada, North Dakota and Wisconsin.
[4] Dehydrated products except starch and flour. Included in above totals. Includes CO, ID, NV, ND, OR, WA, and WI.
Source: National Agricultural Statistics Service, U.S. Department of Agriculture (NASS-USDA)

Rice

Rice is a grain that is cultivated on every continent except Antarctica and is the primary food for half the people in the world. Rice cultivation probably originated as early as 10,000 BC in Asia. Rice is grown at varying altitudes (sea level to about 3,000 meters), in varying climates (tropical to temperate), and on dry to flooded land. The growth duration of rice plants is 3-6 months, depending on variety and growing conditions. Rice is harvested by hand in developing countries or by combines in industrialized countries. Asian countries produce about 90% of rice grown worldwide.

Rough rice futures and options are traded at the CME Group. Rice futures are also traded on the Kansai Commodities Exchange, the Moscow Exchange, the Tokyo Grain Exchange (TGE), and the Zhengzhou Commodity Exchange.

Prices – CME rough rice prices (Barchart.com electronic symbol ZR) on the nearest-futures chart traded sideways in early 2014 but then fell sharply to a 4-year low by October and closed the year of 2014 down -25.9% at $11.490 per hundred pounds. Regarding cash prices, the average monthly price of rice received by farmers in the U.S. in the first six months of the 2014-15 marketing year (i.e., August 2014 through January 2015) fell by -10.6% yr/yr to $14.38 per hundred pounds (cwt.).

Supply – World rice production in the 2014-15 marketing year fell -0.3% to 708.879 million metric tons, below last year's record high of 711.183 million metric tons. The world's largest rice producers were China with 29.1% of world production in 2014-15, India with 21.6%, Indonesia with 8.1%, Bangladesh with 7.3%, Vietnam with 6.4%, and Thailand with 4.4%. U.S. production of rice in 2014-15 rose +16.4 % yr/yr to 221.035 million cwt (hundred pounds), below the 2010-11 record high of 243.104 million cwt (hundred pounds).

Demand – World utilization of rice in 2014-15 rose +0.6% to a record high of 480.328 million metric tons. U.S. rice consumption in 2014-15 rose +4.8% yr/yr to 131.0 million cwt (hundred pounds), below the 2010-11 record high of 136.5 million cwt (hundred pounds).

Trade – World exports of rice in 2014-15 rose +0.9% yr/yr to 42.569 million metric tons, a new record high. The world's largest rice exporters are Thailand with 26.6% of world exports, India with 20.4%, Vietnam 15.7%, Pakistan with 9.2%, the U.S. with 6.7%, and Burma with 3.6%. U.S. rice imports in 2014-15 fell -4.7% yr/yr to 22.0 million cwt (hundred pounds), but still below the 2007-08 record high of 23.9 million cwt. U.S. rice exports in 2014-15 rose +11.1% yr/yr to 103.0 million cwt.

World Rice Supply and Distribution   In Thousands of Metric Tons

	------ Imports ------						---- Utilization ----			--- Ending Stocks ---		
Crop Year	Brazil	European Union	Indo-nesia	Iran	Nigeria	Saudi Arabia	Total	China	India	Total	China	India	Total
2008-09	675	1,345	250	1,670	1,750	1,072	27,395	133,000	91,090	436,014	38,546	19,000	92,400
2009-10	688	1,336	1,150	1,300	1,750	1,069	28,180	134,320	85,508	435,550	40,534	20,500	94,618
2010-11	632	1,408	3,098	1,950	2,400	1,059	33,003	135,000	90,206	442,787	42,574	23,500	99,611
2011-12	730	1,301	1,960	1,575	3,200	1,193	35,755	139,600	93,334	455,630	45,023	25,100	106,830
2012-13[1]	641	1,395	650	2,100	2,800	1,326	36,406	144,000	94,031	465,787	46,826	25,440	110,079
2013-14[2]	700	1,530	1,225	1,650	2,800	1,450	39,309	146,300	99,180	477,283	46,814	22,500	106,863
2014-15[3]	700	1,500	1,300	1,700	3,500	1,325	39,567	148,000	99,000	480,328	46,914	16,800	99,000

[1] Preliminary.   [2] Estimate.   [3] Forecast.   Source: Foreign Agricultural Service, U.S. Department of Agriculture (FAS-USDA)

World Production of Rough Rice   In Thousands of Metric Tons

Year	Bang-ladesh	Brazil	Burma	China	India	Indo-nesia	Japan	Korea	Pakistan	Philip-pines	Thailand	Vietnam	World Total
2008-09	46,805	12,603	17,500	191,900	148,785	59,395	11,029	6,468	10,351	17,071	30,076	38,904	668,340
2009-10	46,505	11,660	18,191	195,100	133,648	57,276	10,592	6,502	10,201	15,511	30,697	39,989	656,603
2010-11	47,555	13,676	17,281	195,714	143,984	56,349	10,604	5,810	7,501	16,729	30,700	42,194	671,413
2011-12	50,555	11,600	17,927	201,000	157,981	57,480	10,503	5,616	9,301	17,000	31,000	43,443	696,263
2012-13[1]	50,735	11,819	18,305	204,286	157,876	57,559	10,654	5,405	8,701	18,140	30,606	44,059	703,606
2013-14[2]	51,590	12,206	18,683	203,614	159,826	57,165	10,758	5,632	10,051	18,822	31,000	45,058	711,183
2014-15[3]	51,905	12,206	18,984	206,429	153,015	57,480	10,577	5,637	9,751	19,365	31,061	45,200	708,879

[1] Preliminary.   [2] Estimate.   [3] Forecast.   Source: Foreign Agricultural Service, U.S. Department of Agriculture (FAS-USDA)

World Exports of Rice (Milled Basis)   In Thousands of Metric Tons

Year	Argen-tina	Australia	Burma	China	European Union	Guyana	India	Pakistan	Thailand	United States	Uruguay	Vietnam	World Total
2008-09	554	15	1,052	747	135	182	2,090	2,910	8,570	3,032	987	5,950	28,955
2009-10	488	59	700	650	240	241	2,082	4,000	9,047	3,516	711	6,734	31,359
2010-11	700	389	1,075	500	255	298	2,774	3,385	10,647	3,516	966	7,000	35,183
2011-12	593	457	1,357	441	209	260	10,376	3,456	6,945	3,200	971	7,717	39,909
2012-13[1]	533	440	1,163	341	203	265	10,869	3,578	6,722	3,385	1,012	6,700	39,252
2013-14[2]	600	460	1,550	257	245	346	10,300	3,900	10,300	2,985	890	6,500	42,202
2014-15[3]	600	400	1,550	400	220	500	8,700	3,900	11,300	3,294	950	6,700	42,569

[1] Preliminary.   [2] Estimate.   [3] Forecast.   Source: Foreign Agricultural Service, U.S. Department of Agriculture (FAS-USDA)

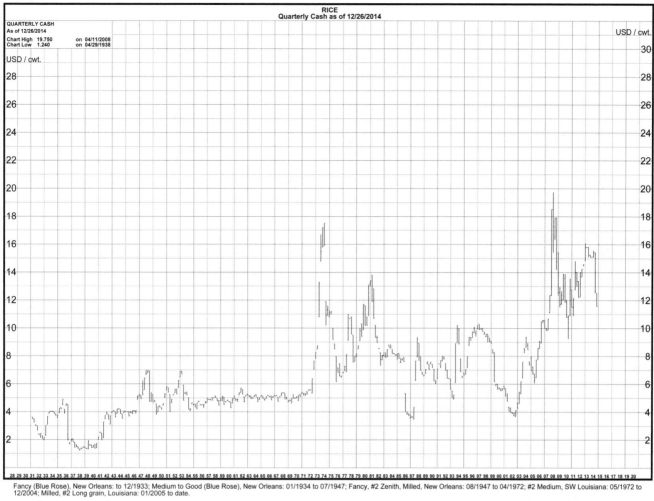

RICE
Quarterly Cash as of 12/26/2014

QUARTERLY CASH
As of 12/26/2014

Chart High 19.750   on 04/11/2008
Chart Low   1.240   on 04/29/1938

USD / cwt.

Fancy (Blue Rose), New Orleans: to 12/1933; Medium to Good (Blue Rose), New Orleans: 01/1934 to 07/1947; Fancy, #2 Zenith, Milled, New Orleans: 08/1947 to 04/1972; #2 Medium, SW Louisiana: 05/1972 to 12/2004; Milled, #2 Long grain, Louisiana: 01/2005 to date.

Average Wholesale Price of Rice No. 2 (Medium)[1] Southwest Louisiana   In Dollars Per Cwt. Bagged

Year	Jan.	Feb.	Mar.	Apr.	May	June	July	Aug.	Sept.	Oct.	Nov.	Dec.	Average
2004-05	18.60	15.69	15.23	15.13	15.13	16.31	14.88	14.88	14.88	14.88	14.88	14.94	15.45
2005-06	17.00	17.50	18.45	20.13	21.38	22.50	22.50	22.50	22.50	22.50	22.50	22.35	20.98
2006-07	21.94	22.00	22.00	23.50	23.50	23.50	23.50	23.50	23.50	23.50	23.50	23.50	23.12
2007-08	23.50	23.50	23.30	23.25	23.25	23.25	24.31	27.45	34.00	39.00	40.00	40.00	28.73
2008-09	40.63	43.10	43.25	43.06	42.88	43.25	43.25	42.15	42.25	42.25	42.25	42.25	42.55
2009-10	41.05	35.75	33.25	33.05	32.75	32.75	32.63	32.15	31.56	30.35	29.25	28.88	32.79
2010-11	28.35	28.16	29.69	32.70	33.75	34.15	34.75	34.75	34.00	33.75	33.75	33.75	32.63
2011-12	33.75	33.75	32.55	32.06	31.50	30.70	30.31	29.75	29.75	29.75	29.75	29.75	31.11
2012-13	29.75	29.75	29.75	29.75	29.75	29.75	30.19	30.38	30.38	30.38	30.38	30.38	30.05
2013-14[2]	30.44	30.50	32.00	32.00	32.00	32.00	32.00						31.56

[1] U.S. No. 2 -- broken not to exceed 4%.   [2] Preliminary.   *Source: Economic Research Service, U.S. Department of Agriculture (ERS-USDA)*

Average Price Received by Farmers for Rice (Rough) in the United States   In Dollars Per Hundred Pounds (Cwt.)

Year	Jan.	Feb.	Mar.	Apr.	May	June	July	Aug.	Sept.	Oct.	Nov.	Dec.	Average[2]
2005-06	6.58	6.76	6.99	7.46	7.49	7.80	8.02	8.05	8.16	8.03	8.41	8.18	7.66
2006-07	8.81	9.03	9.65	10.10	9.91	10.40	10.10	10.00	10.20	10.00	10.00	10.10	9.86
2007-08	10.10	10.30	10.70	11.40	11.50	12.40	12.60	13.60	14.60	15.90	16.50	16.80	13.03
2008-09	18.10	16.90	18.10	19.40	18.60	18.20	16.00	15.60	15.00	14.60	14.70	14.20	16.62
2009-10	14.70	14.60	14.30	14.00	14.40	15.00	14.80	14.30	14.30	13.80	13.20	12.60	14.17
2010-11	11.60	11.10	11.50	12.50	13.80	14.00	13.40	13.00	13.10	12.70	12.10	12.90	12.64
2011-12	13.60	14.40	14.70	15.00	14.70	15.20	14.10	14.10	14.40	14.10	14.20	14.40	14.41
2012-13	14.60	14.30	14.40	14.60	14.80	15.30	15.00	15.20	15.40	15.50	15.50	15.60	15.02
2013-14	15.80	15.60	15.80	16.20	16.50	17.10	16.50	16.10	16.10	16.20	16.20	16.10	16.18
2014-15[1]	15.40	14.80	13.90	14.40	13.40	14.60							14.42

[1] Preliminary.   [2] Weighted average by sales.   *Source: Economic Research Service, U.S. Department of Agriculture (ERS-USDA)*

RICE

Salient Statistics of Rice, Rough & Milled (Rough Equivalent) in the United States   In Millions of Cwt.

Crop Year Beginning Aug. 1	Supply				Disappearance							Government Support Program					
					Domestic						Total	CCC	Put Under	Loan Rate ($ Per Cwt.)			
	Stocks Aug. 1	Pro-duction	Imports	Total Supply	Food	Brewers	Seed	Total	Resi-dual	Exports	Disap-pearance	Stocks July 31	Price Support	Rough[3]			Milled Long
														Long	Med-ium	All Classes	
2009-10	30.4	219.9	19.0	269.3	119.9	[4]	4.5	124.4	[4]	108.4	232.8	0	----	6.50	6.50	6.50	9.94
2010-11	36.5	243.1	18.3	297.9	133.6	[4]	3.3	136.9	[4]	112.5	249.5	0	----	6.50	6.50	6.50	9.91
2011-12	48.5	184.9	19.4	252.8	107.5	[4]	3.3	110.8	[4]	100.9	211.7	----	----	6.50	6.50	6.50	9.93
2012-13	41.1	199.9	21.1	262.1	116.0	[4]	3.1	119.0	[4]	106.6	225.7	----	----	6.50	6.50	6.50	10.13
2013-14[1]	36.4	190.0	23.1	249.5	121.3	[4]	3.6	125.0	[4]	92.7	217.6	----	----	6.50	6.50	6.50	10.34
2014-15[2]	31.8	221.0	22.0	274.9	NA	[4]	NA	131.0	[4]	103.0	234.0			6.50	6.50	6.50	

[1] Preliminary.   [2] Forecast.   [3] Loan rate for each class of rice is the sum of the whole kernels' loan rate weighted by its milling yield (average 56%) and the broken kernels' loan rate weighted by its milling yield (average 12%).   [4] Included in Food.

Source: Economic Research Service, U.S. Department of Agriculture (ERS-USDA)

Acreage, Yield, Production and Prices of Rice in the United States

Crop Year Beginning Aug. 1	Acreage Harvested 1,000 Acres			Yield Per Harvested Acre (In Lbs.)		Production 1,000 Cwt.			Value of Pro-duction ($1,000)	Wholesale Prices $ Per Cwt.		Milled Rice, Average C.I.F. Rotterdam		
	Southern States	Cali-fornia	United States	Cali-fornia	United States	Southern States	Cali-fornia	United States		Arkan-sas[2]	Hous-ton[3]	U.S. No. 2[4]	Thai "A"[5]	Thai "B"[5]
												$ Per Metric Ton		
2009-10	2,547	556	3,103	8,600	7,085	172,046	47,804	219,850	3,209,236	31.47	26.52	----	----	----
2010-11	3,062	553	3,615	8,020	6,725	198,778	44,326	243,104	3,183,213	33.21	27.52	----	----	----
2011-12	2,037	580	2,617	8,350	7,067	136,539	48,402	184,941	2,737,423	30.64	28.47	----	----	----
2012-13	2,122	557	2,679	8,150	7,463	154,526	45,413	199,939	3,067,365	28.27	28.46	----	----	----
2013-14	1,907	562	2,469	8,480	7,694	142,312	47,641	189,953	3,181,993	28.98	30.29	----	----	----
2014-15[1]	2,488	431	2,919	8,580	7,572	184,042	36,993	221,035	3,104,623			----	----	----

[1] Preliminary.   [2] F.O.B. mills, Arkansas, medium.   [3] Houston, Texas (long grain).   [4] Milled, 4%, container, FAS.
[5] SWR, 100%, bulk.   NA = Not available.   *Source: Economic Research Service, U.S. Department of Agriculture (ERS-USDA)*

U.S. Exports of Milled Rice, by Country of Destination   In Thousands of Metric Tons

Trade Year Beginning October	Canada	Haiti	Iran	Ivory Coast	Jamaica	Mexico	Nether-lands	Peru	Saudi Arabia	South Africa	Switzer-land	United Kingdom	Total
2008-09	207.8	239.7	31.7	15.3	26.4	790.9	6.9	.3	129.8	.7	1.3	57.1	3,388
2009-10	220.0	327.5	.0	.4	28.3	827.0	4.4	3.2	116.1	1.2	.3	65.5	4,260
2010-11	229.1	324.1		1.9	23.3	942.0	5.1	1.5	120.3	1.7	.6	47.4	3,920
2011-12	219.9	287.3	3.1	.3	9.1	804.2	5.6	.7	133.4	2.1	.3	36.2	3,578
2012-13	231.6	365.0	125.7	14.9	2.7	885.8	4.6	.3	126.2	2.6	.6	21.4	3,848
2013-14[1]	244.6	346.0	.2	13.5	2.3	741.5	5.4	6.8	105.9	2.3	.6	23.5	3,341

[1] Preliminary.   *Source: Economic Research Service, U.S. Department of Agriculture (ERS-USDA)*

U.S. Rice Exports by Export Program   In Thousands of Metric Tons

Year	PL 480	Section 416	CCC Credit Pro-grams[2]	CCC African Relief Exports	EEP[3]	Export Pro-grams[4]	Exports Outside Specified Export Programs	Total U.S. Rice Exports	% Export Programs as a Share of Total Exports
2005	128	0	----	0	0	159	4,099	4,258	4
2006	59	0	----	0	0	107	3,917	4,024	3
2007	103	0	----	0	0	142	3,174	3,316	4
2008	65	0	----	0	0	91	3,818	3,909	2
2009[1]	44	0	----	0	0	54	3,358	3,411	2
2010[1]	----	----	----	----	----	----	----	----	----

[1] Preliminary.   [2] May not completely reflect exports made under these programs.   [3] Sales not shipments.   [4] Adjusted for estimated overlap between CCC export credit and EEP shipments.   *Source: Economice Research Service, U.S. Department of Agriculture (ERS-USDA)*

Production of Rice (Rough) in the United States, by Type and Variety   In Thousands of Cwt.

Year	Long Grain	Medium Grain	Short Grain	Total	Year	Long Grain	Medium Grain	Short Grain	Total
2005	177,527	42,408	3,300	223,235	2010	183,296	57,144	2,664	243,104
2006	146,214	43,802	3,720	193,736	2011	116,352	65,562	3,027	184,941
2007	143,235	51,063	4,090	198,388	2012	144,280	51,819	3,840	199,939
2008	153,257	47,166	3,310	203,733	2013	131,896	54,915	3,142	189,953
2009	152,725	63,291	3,834	219,850	2014[1]	162,379	56,391	2,265	221,035

[1] Preliminary.   *Source: National Agricultural Statistics Service, U.S. Department of Agriculture (NASS-USDA)*

Rubber

Rubber is a natural or synthetic substance characterized by elasticity, water repellence, and electrical resistance. Pre-Columbian Native South Americans discovered many uses for rubber such as containers, balls, shoes, and waterproofing for fabrics such as coats and capes. The Spaniards tried to duplicate these products for many years but were unsuccessful. The first commercial application of rubber began in 1791 when Samuel Peal patented a method of waterproofing cloth by treating it with a solution of rubber and turpentine. In 1839, Charles Goodyear revolutionized the rubber industry with his discovery of a process called vulcanization, which involves combining rubber and sulfur and heating the mixture.

Natural rubber is obtained from latex, a milky white fluid, from the Hevea Brasiliensis tree. The latex is gathered by cutting a chevron shape through the bark of the rubber tree. The latex is collected in a small cup, with approximately 1 fluid ounce per cutting. The cuttings are usually done every other day until the cuttings reach the ground. The tree is then allowed to renew itself before a new tapping is started. The collected latex is strained, diluted with water, and treated with acid to bind the rubber particles together. The rubber is then pressed between rollers to consolidate the rubber into slabs or thin sheets and is air-dried or smoke-dried for shipment.

During World War II, natural rubber supplies from the Far East were cut off, and the rubber shortage accelerated the development of synthetic rubber in the U.S. Synthetic rubber is produced by chemical reactions, condensation or polymerization, of certain unsaturated hydrocarbons. Synthetic rubber is made of raw material derived from petroleum, coal, oil, natural gas, and acetylene and is almost identical to natural rubber in chemical and physical properties.

Rubber futures are traded on the National Commodity & Derivatives Exchange (NCDEX), the Shanghai Futures Exchange (SHFE) and the Tokyo Commodity Exchange (TOCOM).

Prices – The average monthly price for spot crude rubber (No.1 smoked sheets, ribbed, plantation rubber), basis in New York, in 2010 (for two months annualized) was up by +80.7% to a record high of 175.93 cents per pound. A 3-decade low of 33.88 cents per pound was seen as recently as 2001 during that recessionary year.

Supply – World production of natural rubber in 2013 (latest data) rose +3.4% to 11.965 million metric tons. The world's largest producers of natural rubber in 2013 were Thailand with 32.3% of world production, Indonesia (26.0%), Vietnam (7.9%), India (7.5%), China (7.2%), and Malaysia (6.9%).

World production of synthetic rubber in 2010 (latest data) rose by +14.2% to 14.002 million metric tons. The world's largest producers of synthetic rubber in 2010 were the U.S. with 16.6% of world production, Japan (11.3%), Russia (8.2%), and Germany (6.7%). U.S. production of synthetic rubber in 2010 rose +18.3% to 2.322 million metric tons up from the 14-year low of 2.064 million metric tons posted in 2001.

Demand – World consumption of natural rubber in 2010 (latest data) rose by +14.4% to 10.671 million metric tons. The largest consumers of natural rubber in 2010 were the U.S. with 8.5% of consumption, Japan with 6.9%, and France, Germany, and the UK with a combined 6.0%. The world's consumption of natural rubber has tripled since 1970. World consumption of synthetic rubber in 2010 rose by +15.2% to 13.751 million metric tons. The largest consumers of synthetic rubber in 2010 were the U.S. with 12.6% of consumption, Japan with 7.1%, and France, Germany, and the UK with a combined 7.2%. The world's consumption of synthetic rubber has more than doubled since 1970.

U.S. consumption of natural rubber in 2010 (latest data) rose by +32.2% to 908,200 thousand metric tons. U.S. consumption of natural rubber has more than doubled since 1970. U.S. consumption of synthetic rubber in 2010 rose +19.6% to 1.731 million metric tons. The U.S. consumption of synthetic rubber has remained about the same as it was in 1970.

Trade – World exports of natural rubber in 2011 (latest data) rose +9.9% to a record 7.499 million metric tons. The world's largest exporters of natural rubber in 2011 were Indonesia with 34.0% of world exports and Thailand with 28.3% of world exports. U.S. imports of natural rubber in 2014 rose +2.0% to 946,034 thousand metric tons. U.S. exports of synthetic rubber in 2010 (latest data) rose +19.2% to 1.163 million metric tons, below the 2007 record high of 1.317 million metric tons.

World Production of Natural Rubber   In Thousands of Metric Tons

Year	Brazil	China	Côte d'Ivoire	India	Indonesia	Liberia	Malaysia	Nigeria	Philippines	Sri Lanka	Thailand	Vietnam	Total
2004	98.8	574.7	136.8	749.7	2,065.8	114.5	1,168.7	142.0	102.7	94.7	3,006.7	419.0	8,942.1
2005	103.7	513.6	170.1	802.6	2,270.9	111.0	1,126.0	158.6	104.2	104.4	2,979.7	481.6	9,219.7
2006	105.4	538.0	178.3	852.9	2,637.2	93.5	1,283.6	142.5	116.0	109.1	3,070.5	555.4	9,989.2
2007	111.4	588.4	188.5	825.3	2,755.2	120.8	1,199.6	143.0	133.3	117.6	3,024.2	605.8	10,141.6
2008	120.9	547.9	203.0	864.5	2,751.3	84.8	1,072.4	110.4	135.6	129.2	3,166.9	660.0	10,228.7
2009	127.0	618.9	209.5	831.4	2,440.4	59.5	857.0	145.0	129.0	136.0	3,090.3	711.3	9,758.0
2010	134.0	690.8	235.0	862.0	2,734.9	62.1	939.2	143.5	130.4	153.0	3,051.8	751.7	10,326.2
2011	164.5	750.9	238.7	800.0	2,990.2	63.0	996.2	143.5	140.5	158.2	3,348.9	789.6	11,098.9
2012[1]	177.1	802.3	256.6	900.0	3,012.3	63.0	922.8	143.5	110.8	150.6	3,625.0	877.1	11,570.1
2013[2]	185.7	864.8	289.6	900.0	3,107.5	63.0	826.4	143.5	111.2	130.4	3,863.0	949.1	11,965.8

[1] Preliminary.   [2] Estimate.   *Source: Food and Agricultural Organization of the United Nations (FAO-UN)*

RUBBER

World Imports of Natural Rubber   In Metric Tons

Year	Brazil	Canada	China	European Union	Germany	Italy	Malaysia	Mexico	Pakistan	Rep of Korea	United Kingdom	United States	Total
2002	13,088	3,739	121,675	131,419	34,468	35,623	261,628	27,380	22,291	24,833	19,067	205,635	934,629
2003	11,735	8,489	155,256	135,080	33,683	38,137	293,924	25,457	23,152	25,467	16,904	113,882	917,637
2004	12,345	18,959	211,127	163,733	60,530	34,402	303,345	23,483	26,860	24,189	20,042	112,514	1,056,492
2005	12,358	17,657	201,498	160,790	56,039	34,518	303,852	22,469	24,235	23,636	24,348	97,156	1,002,099
2006	12,100	19,771	280,618	156,403	81,842	35,949	330,408	22,937	29,645	22,964	22,818	68,215	1,124,669
2007	13,024	20,366	256,643	188,138	114,432	38,012	361,713	22,527	22,497	23,399	22,635	89,160	1,204,584
2008	13,649	20,552	257,702	183,293	75,878	34,597	341,173	22,928	22,293	21,342	22,772	93,714	1,145,247
2009	14,003	14,233	312,771	127,146	67,388	24,955	357,254	18,918	16,634	21,036	15,620	69,930	1,104,422
2010[1]	17,180	22,241	262,089	134,922	40,107	24,604	348,487	20,323	17,218	21,316	19,031	53,222	1,027,843
2011[2]	17,752	23,058	280,663	119,973	31,817	24,123	306,561	19,433	14,819	19,252	20,376	49,264	974,899

[1] Preliminary.   [2] Estimate.   *Source: Food and Agricultural Organization of the United Nations (FAO-UN)*

World Exports of Natural Rubber   In Metric Tons

Year	Belgium	Cameroon	Hong Kong	Germany	Guatemala	India	Indonesia	Malaysia	Myanmar	Netherlands	Thailand	United States	Total
2002	5,002	7,816	9,536	8,553	13,861	3,299	8,637	77,974	22,600	1,106	438,889	8,136	621,553
2003	6,386	8,502	8,403	10,253	12,136	8,627	12,526	76,866	30,000	927	491,926	21,795	703,055
2004	8,193	9,115	10,230	13,560	12,870	5,403	11,755	73,331	31,500	600	853,403	8,624	1,051,981
2005	11,138	9,482	9,627	9,255	20,096	11,125	4,014	55,602	34,000	1,449	814,613	4,094	1,001,822
2006	22,047	9,553	10,262	7,178	17,234	6,763	8,334	58,211	407	16,952	947,755	1,987	1,130,351
2007	42,653	9,173	8,487	10,563	22,800	13,069	7,610	56,704	947	16,650	887,544	5,365	1,118,072
2008	31,402	6,396	5,723	6,732	20,355	13,141	8,547	44,599	1,388	22,650	836,404	5,888	1,031,926
2009	13,266	6,614	3,813	5,076	19,821	7,690	9,147	38,752	1,170	5,857	1,007,957	3,386	1,149,039
2010[1]	14,255	8,160	3,224	6,039	20,603	7,407	12,929	47,773	1,886	694	898,454	5,369	1,056,340
2011[2]	26,934	6,627	2,031	6,273	22,742	9,943	9,502	41,586	1,378	3,127	876,382	7,279	1,037,161

[1] Preliminary.   [2] Estimate.   *Source: Food and Agricultural Organization of the United Nations (FAO-UN)*

World Imports of Natural Dry Rubber   In Metric Tons

Year	Brazil	Canada	China	European Union	France	Germany	Italy	Japan	Malaysia	Rep of Korea	Spain	United States	Total
2002	131,646	156,089	985,965	1,117,621	248,610	244,889	124,583	770,473	195,172	298,965	178,377	1,007,538	5,235,204
2003	150,077	140,140	1,222,944	1,248,305	314,400	262,320	126,255	793,889	142,204	315,808	183,802	1,005,904	5,674,079
2004	171,015	133,676	1,224,415	1,172,116	239,751	210,307	137,872	795,542	148,800	328,117	187,364	1,045,540	5,751,954
2005	183,329	142,460	1,347,662	1,185,635	240,984	248,544	137,884	842,766	173,950	346,866	185,521	1,071,864	6,107,819
2006	166,448	129,971	1,465,027	1,194,464	230,784	246,444	139,991	879,987	190,200	341,772	175,035	943,348	6,210,335
2007	208,453	123,287	1,490,358	1,233,869	233,711	261,495	136,895	842,246	245,317	354,553	199,911	939,367	6,359,097
2008	220,959	121,907	1,506,462	1,103,069	208,921	234,608	123,850	839,170	219,637	337,790	181,472	958,558	6,180,191
2009	138,010	91,646	1,500,896	744,649	131,546	189,322	80,071	584,577	381,483	311,067	126,787	634,888	5,314,528
2010[1]	232,161	128,087	1,724,502	1,032,820	171,252	367,791	103,302	731,498	329,683	366,255	177,182	891,688	6,512,283
2011[2]	205,351	124,911	1,935,738	1,151,216	192,644	392,475	117,765	770,804	360,872	382,908	171,838	999,373	7,179,256

[1] Preliminary.   [2] Estimate.   *Source: Food and Agricultural Organization of the United Nations (FAO-UN)*

World Exports of Natural Dry Rubber   In Metric Tons

Year	Côte d'Ivoire	Germany	Guatemala	India	Indonesia	Liberia	Malaysia	Nigeria	Philippines	Sri Lanka	Thailand	Vietnam	Total
2002	123,527	17,814	22,481	36,781	1,487,352	109,000	808,900	24,000	44,559	34,676	2,053,817	351,000	5,316,644
2003	129,080	16,049	24,258	42,045	1,648,394	107,000	868,018	22,000	55,241	34,648	2,307,742	345,000	5,829,936
2004	137,539	18,995	32,106	31,999	1,862,506	114,500	1,360,977	29,000	43,305	38,460	2,167,961	513,300	6,545,316
2005	155,981	13,634	36,304	48,197	2,019,768	111,000	1,091,505	25,000	41,088	30,595	2,137,538	249,423	6,125,611
2006	172,437	22,006	33,059	41,014	2,277,663	93,500	1,073,193	24,000	33,833	46,022	2,109,080	246,081	6,342,028
2007	182,397	40,572	45,474	39,294	2,399,146	120,800	960,241	33,792	30,417	46,083	2,077,771	247,331	6,425,892
2008	199,721	28,113	53,008	26,031	2,286,910	84,800	870,997	25,900	36,323	42,476	1,995,524	212,850	6,077,168
2009	218,555	56,089	57,770	12,787	1,982,116	59,500	664,306	31,700	24,899	50,246	1,731,787	239,580	5,378,189
2010[1]	238,701	96,979	55,695	8,601	2,338,986	70,620	853,108	42,435	36,355	46,924	1,834,828	782,213	6,824,472
2011[2]	259,459	130,568	65,351	28,154	2,546,237	70,339	904,494	58,088	42,209	41,052	2,120,597	816,600	7,499,130

[1] Preliminary.   [2] Estimate.   *Source: Food and Agricultural Organization of the United Nations (FAO-UN)*

Rye

Rye is a cereal grain and a member of the grass family. Hardy varieties of rye have been developed for winter planting. Rye is most widely grown in northern Europe and Asia. In the U.S., rye is used as an animal feed and as an ingredient in bread and some whiskeys. Bread using rye was developed in northern Europe in the Middle Ages where bakers developed dark, hearty bread consisting of rye, oat and barley flours. Those were crops that grew more readily in the wet and damp climate of northern Europe, as opposed to wheat which fares better in the warmer and drier climates in central Europe. Modern rye bread is made with a mixture of white and rye flours. Coarsely ground rye flour is also used in pumpernickel bread and helps provide the dark color and course texture, along with molasses. The major producing states are North and South Dakota, Oklahoma, and Georgia. The crop year runs from June to May.

Supply – World rye production in 2014-15 marketing year fell by -5.2% yr/yr to 15.001 million metric tons, above from the 2006-07 record low of 12.402 million metric tons. The world's largest producers of rye are the European Union with 58.6% of world production in 2014-15, followed by Russia with 26.7%, Belarus with 5.3%, and the Ukraine with 3.0%. U.S. production of rye accounted for only 1.2% of world production.

U.S. production of rye in 2014 fell -5.7% to 7.189 million bushels, far below the production levels of over 20 million bushels seen from the late 1800s through the 1960s. U.S. production of rye fell off in the 1970s, and fell to a record low of 6.311 million bushels in 2007.

U.S. acreage harvested with rye in 2014-15 fell -7.2% yr/yr to 258,000 acres. U.S. farmers in the late 1800s through the 1960s typically harvested more than 1 million acres of rye, showing how domestic planting of rye has dropped off sharply in the past several decades. Rye yield in 2014-15 fell -1.8% to 27.9 bushels per acre, well below the record high of 33.1 bushels per acre posted in 1984-85. Modern rye production yields are, however, more than double the levels seen prior to the 1960s.

Demand – Total U.S. domestic usage of rye in 2014-15 rose +1.4% yr/yr to 16.975 million bushels. The breakdown of domestic usage shows that 44.0% of rye in 2014-15 was used for feed and residual, 20.4% for food, 17.9% for seed, and 17.7% for industry.

Trade – World exports of rye in the 2014-15 marketing year fell -6.8% yr/yr to 412,000 metric tons, still above the record low of 270,000 metric tons in 2008-09. The largest exporters were the European Union with 175,000 metric tons and Canada with 100,000 metric tons of exports. World imports of rye fell -2.8% to 424,000 metric tons. U.S. imports of rye in 2014-15 fell -2.1% yr/yr to 229,000 metric tons.

World Production of Rye   In Thousands of Metric Tons

Crop Year	Argen-tina	Australia	Belarus	Canada	European Union	Kazak-hstan	Romania	Russia	Switzer-land	Turkey	Ukraine	United States	World Total
2005-06	55	20	1,155	330	7,693	24	----	3,622	9	270	1,054	191	14,499
2006-07	55	20	1,072	383	6,546	30	----	2,959	9	271	584	183	12,183
2007-08	77	20	1,305	252	7,683	68	----	3,909	10	241	562	160	14,367
2008-09	55	35	1,492	297	9,266	40	----	4,505	12	247	1,051	211	17,308
2009-10	55	34	1,227	281	9,955	75	----	4,333	16	343	954	172	17,518
2010-11	40	33	735	237	7,576	42	----	1,642	14	365	464	190	11,408
2011-12	45	40	801	241	6,900	28	----	2,967	13	366	579	154	12,248
2012-13[1]	40	40	1,082	337	8,763	50	----	2,132	11	370	676	166	13,771
2013-14[2]	52	20	648	223	10,188	43	----	3,360	11	350	638	194	15,829
2014-15[3]	40	20	800	195	8,790	50	----	4,000	11	350	450	183	15,001

[1] Preliminary.   [2] Estimate.   [3] Forecast.   Source: Foreign Agricultural Service, U.S. Department of Agriculture (FAS-USDA)

World Imports and Exports of Rye   In Thousands of Metric Tons

| | --------------------- Imports --------------------- | | | | | | --------------------- Exports --------------------- | | | | | |
Year	European Union	Japan	Korea, South	Turkey	Russia	United States	World Total	Belarus	Canada	European Union	Russia	United States	World Total
2005-06	8	279	7	2	49	139	617	50	132	357	----	----	608
2006-07	25	258	8	18	32	150	582	50	208	418	26	2	706
2007-08	98	83	6	13	----	179	413	75	191	74	119	6	468
2008-09	9	57	7	8	----	100	209	50	76	111	16	8	267
2009-10	----	103	7	----	----	108	246	25	124	97	12	2	316
2010-11	21	101	11	----	150	141	458	150	189	108	----	4	492
2011-12	290	46	11	3	----	152	531	25	166	58	238	4	505
2012-13[1]	98	27	12	----	25	228	455	25	192	113	133	8	489
2013-14[2]	77	37	8	----	25	234	436	25	117	169	75	7	442
2014-15[3]	75	40	10	----	25	229	424	25	100	175	100	7	412

[1] Preliminary.   [2] Estimate.   [3] Forecast.   Source: Foreign Agricultural Service, U.S. Department of Agriculture (FAS-USDA)

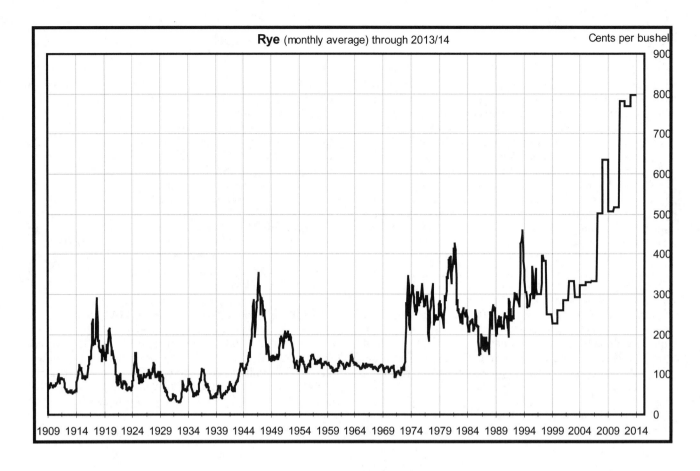

Production of Rye in the United States   In Thousands of Bushels

Year	Georgia	Kansas	Mich-igan	Minne-sota	Neb-raska	Dakota	Okla-homa	Penn-ylvania	Carolina	Dakota	Texas	Wis-consin	Total
2005	810	2	2	2	2	2	1,400	2	2	2	2	2	7,537
2006	650	2	2	2	2	2	1,040	2	2	2	2	2	7,193
2007	800	2	2	2	2	2	1,080	2	2	2	2	2	6,311
2008	1,200	2	2	2	2	2	1,045	2	2	2	2	2	7,979
2009	525	2	2	2	2	2	560	2	2	2	2	2	6,993
2010	960	2	2	2	2	2	1,500	2	2	2	2	2	7,431
2011	945	2	2	2	2	2	825	2	2	2	2	2	6,326
2012	575	2	2	2	2	2	1,680	2	2	2	2	2	6,542
2013	1,080	2	2	2	2	2	1,600	2	2	2	2	2	7,626
2014[1]	540	2	2	2	2	2	495	2	2	2	2	2	7,189

[1] Preliminary.   [2] Estimates not published beginning in 2000.   *Source: Agricultural Statistics Board, U.S. Department of Agriculture (ASB-USDA)*

Salient Statistics of Rye in the United States   In Thousands of Bushels

Crop Year Beginning June 1	Supply				Disappearance							Acreage		Yield Per Harvested Acre (Bushels)
	Stocks June 1	Pro-duction	Imports	Total Supply	Domestic Use					Total Disap-pearance		Planted	Harvested for Grain	
					Food	Industry	Seed	Feed & Residual	Total	Exports		---- **1,000 Acres** ----		
2005-06	793	7,537	5,481	13,811	3,300	3,000	3,000	3,791	13,091	14	13,105	1,433	279	27.0
2006-07	706	7,193	5,899	13,798	3,300	3,000	3,000	3,947	13,247	70	13,317	1,396	274	26.3
2007-08	481	6,311	7,064	13,856	3,300	3,000	3,000	3,909	13,209	251	13,460	1,334	252	25.0
2008-09	396	7,979	3,953	12,328	3,300	3,000	3,000	2,203	11,503	316	11,819	1,260	269	29.7
2009-10	509	6,993	4,251	11,753	3,300	3,000	3,000	1,448	10,748	73	10,821	1,241	252	27.8
2010-11	932	7,431	5,552	13,915	3,300	3,000	3,000	3,665	12,965	149	13,114	1,211	265	28.0
2011-12	801	6,326	5,994	13,121	3,310	3,000	3,010	3,192	12,512	157	12,669	1,266	242	26.1
2012-13[1]	452	6,542	8,966	15,960	3,400	3,000	3,020	6,231	15,651	310	15,961	1,300	248	28.0
2013-14[2]	401	7,626	9,227	17,254	3,430	3,000	3,030	7,284	16,744	268	17,012	1,451	278	27.4
2014-15[3]	285	7,189	9,000	16,474	3,460	3,000	3,040	7,475	16,975	250	17,225	1,434	258	27.9

[1] Preliminary.   [2] Estimate.   [3] Forecast   *Source: Economic Research Service, U.S. Department of Agriculture (ERS-USDA)*

Salt

Salt, also known as sodium chloride, is a chemical compound that is an essential element in the diet of humans, animals, and even many plants. Since prehistoric times, salt has been used to preserve foods and was commonly used in the religious rites of the Greeks, Romans, Hebrews, and Christians. Salt, in the form of salt cakes, served as money in ancient Ethiopia and Tibet. As long ago as 1450 BC, Egyptian art shows records of salt production.

The simplest method of obtaining salt is through the evaporation of salt water from areas near oceans or seas. In most regions, rock salt is obtained from underground mining or by wells sunk into deposits. Salt is soluble in water, is slightly soluble in alcohol, but is insoluble in concentrated hydrochloric acid. In its crystalline form, salt is transparent and colorless, shining with an ice-like luster.

Prices – Salt prices in 2014 (FOB mine, vacuum and open pan) rose +0.8% yr/yr to $180.00 per ton, just below the record high of $180.08 posted in 2010.

Supply – World production of salt in 2014 rose +2.7% yr/yr to 269.000 million metric tons. The world's largest salt producers were China with 26.4% and the U.S. with 16.4% of world production in 2014. U.S. salt production in 2014 rose +9.4% yr/yr to 44.100 million metric tons.

Demand – U.S. consumption of salt in 2014 rose +12.4% to 61.600 million metric tons, a new record high.

Trade – The U.S. relied on imports for 28% of its salt consumption in 2014, a new record high. U.S. imports of salt for consumption in 2014 rose +51.3% yr/yr to 18.000 million metric tons, a new record high. U.S. exports of salt in 2014 rose by +61.9% to 850,000 metric tons, with the bulk of those exports going to Canada.

World Production of All Salt   In Thousands of Metric Tons

Year	Australia	Canada	China	France	Germany	India	Italy	Mexico	Poland	Spain	United Kingdom	United States	World Total
2007	10,855	11,862	59,760	6,140	18,806	16,000	2,214	8,400	3,522	4,350	5,800	44,600	266,000
2008	11,160	14,386	66,640	6,240	15,833	16,000	2,200	8,809	4,023	4,303	5,565	48,000	276,000
2009	10,316	14,615	66,630	6,200	18,939	16,500	3,471	7,445	3,831	4,201	6,166	46,000	279,000
2010	11,968	10,537	70,380	5,867	19,676	17,000	4,006	8,431	4,097	4,450	6,666	43,300	280,000
2011	11,744	12,756	67,420	5,430	17,432	16,000	2,912	8,812	4,282	4,504	6,700	45,000	286,000
2012	10,821	10,845	70,000	6,100	14,800	17,000	2,200	10,800	3,810	4,500	6,700	37,200	259,000
2013[1]	11,000	12,200	70,000	6,100	11,900	16,000		10,800	4,430	4,440	6,700	40,300	262,000
2014[2]	11,000	13,300	71,000	6,000	12,000	17,000		9,500	4,400	4,500	6,800	44,100	269,000

[1] Preliminary.   [2] Estimate.   *Source: U.S. Geological Survey (USGS)*

Salient Statistics of the Salt Industry in the United States   In Thousands of Metric Tons

Year	Net Import Reliance As a % of Apparent Consumption	Average Value FOB Mine Vacuum & Open Pan ($ Per Ton)	Production Total	Open & Vacuum Pan	Solar	Rock	Brine	Sold or Used, Producers Open & Vacuum Pan	Rock	Brine	Total Salt	Imports for Consumption Value[3] Million $	Imports for Consumption	Exports Total	Exports To Canada	Apparent Consumption
2007	15	154.95	44,500	4,420	3,650	16,800	19,700	4,310	18,400	19,600	45,500	1,520.0	8,640	833	588	53,300
2008	21	158.59	48,000	4,200	4,070	20,900	18,900	4,120	21,100	18,800	47,400	1,690.0	13,900	1,030	896	60,200
2009	24	178.67	46,000	4,030	3,880	20,300	17,800	3,960	18,200	17,800	43,100	1,750.0	14,700	1,450	1,360	56,400
2010	24	180.08	43,300	4,100	3,120	17,600	18,500	4,020	17,900	18,500	43,500	1,690.0	12,900	595	451	55,800
2011	22	174.00	45,000	4,080	3,230	18,500	19,200	4,000	18,500	19,200	45,500	1,770.0	13,800	846	754	58,500
2012	22	169.93	37,200	4,240	2,760	13,300	16,900	4,200	11,300	16,900	34,900	1,460.0	9,880	809	728	44,000
2013[1]	21	178.65	40,300								43,400		11,900	525		54,800
2014[2]	28	180.00	44,100								44,500		18,000	850		61,600

[1] Preliminary.   [2] Estimate.   [3] Values are f.o.b. mine or refinery & do not include cost of cooperage or containers.   *Source: U.S. Geological Survey (USGS)*

Salt Sold or Used by Producers in the U.S. by Classes & Consumers or Uses   In Thousands of Metric Tons

Year	Chemical[2]	Tanning Leather	Textile & Dyeing	Meat Packers[3]	Canning	Baking	Agricultural Distribution	Feed Dealers	Feed Manufacturers	Rubber	Oil & Pulp	Paper	Metal Processing	Water Treatment	Grocery Stores	Water Conditioning Distrib.	Ice Control and/or Stabilization
2005	19,700	55	149	398	211	204	227	1,140	477	65	2,210	81	107	1,140	803	511	21,000
2006	18,400	50	121	380	208	203	211	1,090	502	66	2,150	72	49	952	770	489	12,400
2007	21,500	41	98	305	198	149	385	1,160	457	6	211	61	36	1,030	943	522	20,800
2008	18,600	37	78	283	190	144	436	1,260	405	6	286	77	42	1,330	992	464	22,600
2009	17,900	32	48	271	215	324	357	1,310	377	5	314	58	24	1,010	812	469	16,900
2010	20,200	39	59	275	258	364	359	1,330	425	5	325	59	26	913	761	461	18,700
2011	18,500	42	49	260	195	162	375	1,170	438	5	322	67	44	311	706	493	19,600
2012[1]	16,800	36	41	248	182	160	253	1,010	392	7	441	61	53	446	591	472	11,100

[1] Preliminary.   [2] Chloralkali producers and other chemical.   *Source: U.S. Geological Survey (USGS)*

Sheep and Lambs

Sheep and lambs are raised for both their wool and meat. In countries that have high wool production, there is also demand for sheep and lamb meat due to the easy availability. Production levels have declined in New Zealand and Australia, but that has been counteracted by a substantial increase in China.

Prices – The average monthly price received by farmers for lambs in the U.S. in 2011 (latest data) rose by +42.7% to 177.33 cents per pound, a new record high. The average monthly price received by U.S. farmers for sheep in 2011 (latest data) rose by +27.7% to 64.33 cents per pound, a new record high. The average monthly wholesale price of slaughter lambs (choice) at San Angelo, Texas in 2014 rose

by +40.8% to 157.62 cents per pound, which was below the record high of 160.75 cents per pound posted in 2010.

Supply – World sheep and goat numbers in 2013 (latest data) rose by +0.1% to 2.138 billion head, a new record high. The world's largest producers of sheep and goats are China with 16.7% of world production in 2013, India (9.3%), Turkey with (1.7%), and United Kingdom (1.5%). The number of sheep and lambs on U.S. farms in 2015 (Jan 1) is projected to rise +0.7% to 5.280 million head. The U.S. states with the most sheep and lambs are Texas (with 13.6% of the U.S. total), California (11.4%), Colorado (8.0%), Wyoming (6.5%), and Utah (5.5%).

World Sheep and Goat Numbers in Specified Countries on January 1   In Thousands of Head

Year	Argentina	Australia	China	India	Kazakhstan	New Zealand	Romania	Russia	South Africa	Spain	Turkey	United Kingdom	World Total
2004	19,358	104,127	340,511	192,061	12,247	39,424	8,125	17,030	31,732	25,743	32,203	35,937	1,930,474
2005	19,697	104,525	366,400	198,507	13,409	40,024	8,086	17,771	31,690	25,654	31,811	35,345	1,999,970
2006	20,038	94,328	372,927	205,171	14,335	40,227	8,298	18,213	31,383	25,408	31,822	34,820	2,016,796
2007	20,430	88,211	369,216	212,098	15,350	38,572	8,405	19,675	31,347	25,086	32,260	34,041	2,065,465
2008	20,238	82,638	368,126	209,732	16,080	34,184	9,334	21,503	31,623	22,912	31,749	33,223	2,070,301
2009	19,528	76,140	369,744	207,387	16,770	32,466	9,780	21,770	31,347	22,652	29,568	31,533	2,070,524
2010	19,062	71,586	372,756	205,065	17,370	32,658	10,059	21,986	30,776	21,455	26,923	31,177	2,073,520
2011	19,011	76,599	362,996	202,766	18,092	31,218	9,658	21,820	30,468	19,696	29,383	31,728	2,108,319
2012[1]	18,650	78,272	366,464	200,242	17,633	31,353	9,770	22,858	30,533	18,977	32,310	32,313	2,137,079
2013[2]	18,950	79,098	357,871	197,800	17,561	30,867	10,100	24,180	31,200	18,729	35,782	32,954	2,138,683

[1] Preliminary.   [2] Forecast.   *Source: Food and Agricultural Organization of the United Nations (FAO-UN)*

Salient Statistics of Sheep & Lambs in the United States (Average Live Weight)   In Thousands of Head

Year	Inventory, Jan. 1 - Without New Crop Lambs	Inventory, Jan. 1 - With New Crop Lambs	Lamb Crop	Total Supply	Marketings[3] Sheep	Marketings[3] Lambs	Slaughter Farm	Slaughter Commercial	Slaughter Total[4]	Net Exports	Total Disappearance	Production (Live Weight) (Mil. Lbs.)	Farm Value Jan. 1 Total
2005	6,135	6,135	4,117	10,252	669	4,200	64	2,698	2,762	----	----	473.3	798.2	130.0
2006	6,230	6,230	3,950	10,180	692	4,196	69	2,699	2,768	----	----	463.1	872.4	141.0
2007	6,165	6,273	3,895	10,168	780	3,927	85	2,694	2,778	----	----	473.1	818.5	134.0
2008	5,950	6,055	3,710	9,765	737	3,652	92	2,556	2,647	----	----	417.0	823.4	138.0
2009	5,747	5,855	3,690	9,545	625	3,532	95	2,516	2,611	----	----	421.6	765.2	133.0
2010	5,620	5,727	3,600	9,327	645	3,429	95	2,458	2,553	----	----	405.3	761.1	135.0
2011	5,480	5,589	3,510	9,099	----	----	93	2,164	2,258	----	----	----	938.4	170.0
2012	5,365	5,474	3,455	8,929	----	----	93	2,183	2,275	----	----	----	----	----
2013[1]	5,335	5,442	3,370	8,812	----	----	94	2,319	2,412	----	----	----	----	----
2014[2]	5,245	5,356	3,440	8,796			95	2,104	2,199					

[1] Preliminary.   [2] Estimate.   [3] Excludes interfarm sales.   [4] Includes all commercial and farm.
Source: Economic Research Service, U.S. Department of Agriculture (ERS-USDA)

Sheep and Lambs[3] on Farms in the United States on January 1   In Thousands of Head

Year	California	Colorado	Idaho	Iowa	Minnesota	Montana	Mexico	Ohio	Dakota	Texas	Utah	Wyoming	Total
2007	610	400	260	235	150	290	130	141	380	1,050	295	460	6,165
2008	620	420	235	225	145	270	130	125	340	960	280	425	5,950
2009	660	410	210	200	140	255	120	130	305	870	290	420	5,747
2010	610	370	220	210	130	245	120	128	325	830	290	375	5,620
2011	600	370	235	200	130	230	110	129	265	850	280	365	5,480
2012	570	460	240	195	150	225	100	126	285	650	305	370	5,365
2013	570	435	235	175	135	235	100	121	275	700	295	375	5,335
2014	590	365	250	155	135	220	81	117	270	730	280	355	5,245
2015[1]	600	420	260	175	130	215	90	121	255	720	290	345	5,280

[1] Preliminary.   [2] Includes sheep & lambs on feed for market and stock sheep & lambs.   *Source: Economic Research Service, U.S. Department of Agriculture (ERS-USDA)*

Average Wholesale Price of Slaughter Lambs (Choice[2]) at San Angelo Texas In Dollars Per Hundred Pounds (Cwt.)

Year	Jan.	Feb.	Mar.	Apr.	May	June	July	Aug.	Sept.	Oct.	Nov.	Dec.	Average
2006	86.75	76.87	67.47	60.60	68.16	70.94	74.00	84.00	85.30	85.18	85.40	83.00	77.31
2007	81.00	82.27	84.50	85.25	84.20	77.40	86.38	86.19	89.44	84.90	84.83	92.92	84.94
2008	86.63	88.82	83.25	74.70	77.75	86.75	88.81	88.13	89.54	85.55	85.46	95.83	85.94
2009	88.74	89.25	92.75	89.38	95.23	93.91	88.00	88.88	88.17	89.50	89.66	92.25	90.48
2010	95.04	106.63	109.95	112.00	104.47	102.05	109.17	112.15	125.38	129.69	138.50	156.67	116.81
2011	164.19	182.63	177.15	152.88	160.20	160.88	169.47	162.13	152.80	154.00	156.80	135.83	160.75
2012	147.40	148.13	141.94	136.75	128.50	116.00	116.00	75.00	80.88	96.20	84.67	88.67	113.35
2013	114.25	109.57	109.57	88.90	92.50	93.76	90.85	86.50	104.38	146.50	143.09	163.33	111.93
2014[1]	165.00	168.38	154.88	150.97	135.17	160.83	150.23	152.94	164.90	159.25	162.00	166.83	157.62

[1] Preliminary.   Source: Economic Research Service, U.S. Department of Agriculture (ERS-USDA)

Federally Inspected Slaughter of Sheep & Lambs in the United States   In Thousands of Head

Year	Jan.	Feb.	Mar.	Apr.	May	June	July	Aug.	Sept.	Oct.	Nov.	Dec.	Total
2006	210	193	240	234	215	200	191	213	205	223	212	212	2,547
2007	204	194	267	203	205	188	191	212	197	232	223	212	2,529
2008	202	202	219	207	195	181	193	186	207	209	180	213	2,393
2009	179	169	210	213	167	185	189	187	207	201	200	217	2,323
2010	173	167	249	175	167	194	178	185	186	185	201	200	2,261
2011	151	146	184	192	166	168	150	183	163	161	172	167	2,000
2012	154	155	180	166	164	155	165	186	161	190	166	173	2,012
2013	165	150	184	175	188	168	193	190	167	187	170	185	2,120
2014[1]	167	155	177	204	177	175	189	161	173	187	157	183	2,104

[1] Preliminary.   Source: Economic Research Service, U.S. Department of Agriculture (ERS-USDA)

Cold Storage Holdings of Lamb and Mutton in the United States, on First of Month   In Thousands of Pounds

Year	Jan.	Feb.	Mar.	Apr.	May	June	July	Aug.	Sept.	Oct.	Nov.	Dec.
2006	9,967	15,730	15,777	15,454	15,247	15,215	15,126	15,254	15,353	15,228	15,452	15,862
2007	15,769	15,640	15,570	15,996	18,206	16,644	15,410	13,811	15,692	14,734	13,944	13,096
2008	12,918	15,177	18,157	17,118	17,783	18,411	19,598	19,723	21,147	20,796	21,331	21,659
2009	21,001	19,469	18,279	19,274	19,801	19,694	21,568	20,062	19,045	17,426	15,301	15,052
2010	14,519	11,759	12,922	16,313	16,453	20,448	22,972	22,059	19,859	18,046	16,189	16,500
2011	15,206	13,278	12,582	12,874	13,279	15,062	18,097	21,034	21,209	22,218	20,021	19,014
2012	16,857	19,275	20,851	21,846	19,711	19,680	22,460	24,291	24,233	23,453	23,210	18,978
2013	21,379	18,768	19,833	17,624	21,463	19,793	19,307	23,324	21,988	23,444	23,967	21,697
2014[1]	24,508	25,658	26,191	28,076	26,536	25,208	31,119	33,968	40,157	39,693	38,686	31,366

[1] Preliminary.   Source: Economic Research Service, U.S. Department of Agriculture (ERS-USDA)

Average Price Received by Farmers for Sheep in the United States   In Dollars Per Hundred Pounds (Cwt.)

Year	Jan.	Feb.	Mar.	Apr.	May	June	July	Aug.	Sept.	Oct.	Nov.	Dec.	Average
2004	43.80	40.80	36.70	36.70	36.00	31.30	37.10	37.30	41.20	40.40	41.40	44.60	38.94
2005	53.50	52.40	49.00	45.10	43.70	41.20	41.00	43.00	43.70	43.60	46.20	49.30	45.98
2006	47.70	45.90	40.10	35.20	32.50	28.20	27.60	27.90	32.20	31.40	30.30	34.80	34.48
2007	37.10	37.30	36.60	34.20	30.80	28.20	29.20	28.30	26.70	25.50	27.10	30.20	30.93
2008	31.90	29.90	28.70	28.40	25.40	24.50	26.10	26.60	24.50	21.70	27.30	32.90	27.33
2009	31.40	31.90	32.10	34.70	31.70	28.90	29.60	31.30	29.70	29.80	36.30	44.40	32.65
2010	52.40	54.80	51.30	49.40	46.20	42.10	43.80	47.60	48.70	48.40	54.20	65.70	50.38
2011	81.90	76.00	NA	68.80	55.40	50.80	56.50	66.80	58.40	NA	NA	NA	64.33
2012[1]	NA	NA	NA	NA	NA	NA	NA	NA	NA	NA	NA	NA	NA

[1] Preliminary.   Source: Economic Research Service, U.S. Department of Agriculture (ERS-USDA)

Average Price Received by Farmers for Lambs in the United States   In Dollars Per Hundred Pounds (Cwt.)

Year	Jan.	Feb.	Mar.	Apr.	May	June	July	Aug.	Sept.	Oct.	Nov.	Dec.	Average
2004	104.00	106.00	103.00	100.00	103.00	105.00	101.00	97.90	100.00	97.70	99.90	101.00	101.54
2005	114.00	114.00	114.00	114.00	114.00	114.00	110.00	109.00	110.00	108.00	107.00	100.00	110.67
2006	96.10	97.80	92.10	87.20	88.90	92.10	93.40	95.40	98.30	98.50	95.60	94.00	94.12
2007	96.50	94.80	95.50	97.10	97.10	96.80	98.70	97.90	99.00	97.00	97.10	98.40	97.16
2008	97.50	96.50	97.40	99.40	101.00	102.00	103.00	99.90	99.40	97.40	100.00	101.00	99.54
2009	100.00	100.00	100.00	101.00	102.00	104.00	102.00	97.10	98.10	96.80	97.70	98.70	99.78
2010	102.00	106.00	115.00	118.00	122.00	119.00	122.00	127.00	135.00	137.00	142.00	146.00	124.25
2011	149.00	155.00	169.00	181.00	181.00	189.00	194.00	189.00	189.00	NA	NA	NA	177.33
2012[1]	NA	NA	NA	NA	NA	NA	NA	NA	NA	NA	NA	NA	NA

[1] Preliminary.   Source: Economic Research Service, U.S. Department of Agriculture (ERS-USDA)

Silk

Silk is a fine, tough, elastic fiber produced by caterpillars, commonly called silkworms. Silk is one of the oldest known textile fibers. Chinese tradition credits Lady Hsi-Ling-Shih, wife of the Emperor Huang Ti, with the discovery of the silkworm and the invention of the first silk reel. Dating to around 3000 BC, a group of ribbons, threads, and woven fragments was found in China. Also found, along the lower Yangzi River, were 7,000 year-old spinning tools, silk thread, and fabric fragments.

Silk filament was first woven into cloth in Ancient China. The Chinese successfully guarded this secret until 300AD, when Japan, and later India, learned the secret. In 550 AD, two Nestorian monks were sent to China to steal mulberry seeds and silkworm eggs, which they hid in their walking staffs, and then brought them back to Rome. By the 17th century, France was the silk center of the West. Unfortunately, the silkworm did not flourish in the English climate, nor has it ever flourished in the U.S.

Sericulture is the term for the raising of silkworms. The blind, flightless moth, Bombyx mori, lays more than 500 tiny eggs. After hatching, the tiny worms eat chopped mulberry leaves continuously until they are ready to spin their cocoons. After gathering the complete cocoons, the first step in silk manufacturing is to kill the insects inside the cocoons with heat. The cocoons are then placed in boiling water to loosen the gummy substance, sericin,

holding the filament together. The filament is unwound, and then rewound in a process called reeling. Each cocoon's silk filament is between 600 and 900 meters long. Four different types of silk thread may be produced: organzine, crepe, tram, and thrown singles. During the last 30 years, in spite of the use of man-made fibers, world silk production has doubled.

Raw silk is traded on the Kansai Agricultural Commodities Exchange (KANEX) in Japan. Dried cocoons are traded on the Chuba Commodity Exchange (CCE). Raw silk and dried cocoons are traded on the Yokohama Commodity Exchange.

Supply – World production of silk in 2013 (latest data), fell -0.4% yr/yr to 167,913 metric tons, below last year's record high of 168,511 metric tons. China is the world's largest producer of silk by far with a 75.0% share of world production in 2013. Other key producers include India with 14.1% of world production, Vietnam (3.8%), and Thailand (1.0%).

Trade – In 2011 (latest data), the world's largest exporters of silk were China with 82.7 % of world exports, North Korea with 0.7%, and Japan with 0.4%. In 2011, the world's largest importers of silk were India (with 48.8% of world imports), Japan (5.0%), Italy (6.2%), and Japan (4.9%).

World Production of Raw Silk   In Metric Tons

Year	Brazil	China	India	Iran	Japan	North Korea	Rep. of Korea	Kyrgy-zstan	Thailand	Turkmen-istan	Uzbek-istan	Viet Nam	World Total
2004	1,750	104,800	15,742	900	263	350	3	17	1,600	4,500	1,200	12,323	145,943
2005	1,200	111,950	16,500	900	150	350	3	50	1,600	4,500	1,200	11,475	152,448
2006	1,250	123,491	17,305	900	117	350	3	50	1,600	4,500	1,200	10,413	163,774
2007	1,300	125,001	18,475	900	105	350	3	50	1,600	4,500	1,200	10,110	166,189
2008	1,000	126,001	18,320	900	120	350	3	50	1,600	4,500	1,200	7,746	164,385
2009	800	126,001	18,370	900	150	400	3	50	1,600	4,500	1,200	7,367	163,941
2010	600	126,001	19,690	900	130	400	3	50	1,600	4,500	1,200	7,107	164,779
2011	500	126,001	20,410	900	280	400	3	50	1,600	4,500	1,200	7,057	165,500
2012[1]	400	126,001	23,060	900	280	400	3	50	1,600	4,500	1,200	7,517	168,511
2013[2]	400	126,001	23,679	900	280	400		50	1,600	4,500	1,200	6,300	167,913

[1] Preliminary.   [2] Estimate.   NA = Not avaliable.   *Source: Food and Agricultural Organization of the United Nations (FAO-UN)*

World Trade of Silk by Selected Countries   In Metric Tons

	---------------------------------- Imports ----------------------------------						---------------------------------- Exports ----------------------------------					
Year	France	Hong Kong	India	Italy	Japan	Korea, South	World Total	Brazil	China	Hong Kong	Japan	Korea, South	World Total
2002	262	38	9,054	2,363	2,025	1,845	18,548	4	14,701	102	2	170	16,117
2003	147	67	9,258	2,219	1,949	1,648	18,439	2	13,931	31	96	296	15,866
2004	181	3	7,948	1,983	1,581	1,338	16,607	7	11,288	20	688	227	14,321
2005	262	14	8,383	1,974	1,406	1,359	18,114	36	10,972	11	202	219	13,699
2006	212	3	5,565	2,146	1,295	1,095	15,215	4	6,712	4	11	223	10,008
2007	150	2	7,922	1,463	791	989	15,931	18	13,756	2	10	277	15,696
2008	191		8,392	1,040	932	724	16,371	13	13,431	----	16	137	14,903
2009	111	17	7,338	501	733	656	12,552	8	9,227	16	8	100	10,860
2010	109	34	4,525	698	737	645	10,012	6	8,509	34	36	57	10,406
2011[1]	110	9	5,597	711	563	533	11,481		7,122	----	35	59	8,608

[1] Preliminary.   *Source: Food and Agricultural Organization of the United Nations (FAO-UN)*

Silver

Silver is a white, lustrous metallic element that conducts heat and electricity better than any other metal. In ancient times, many silver deposits were on or near the earth's surface. Before 2,500 BC, silver mines were worked in Asia Minor. Around 700 BC, ancient Greeks stamped a turtle on their first silver coins. Silver assumed a key role in the U.S. monetary system in 1792 when Congress based the currency on the silver dollar. However, the U.S. discontinued the use of silver in coinage in 1965. Today Mexico is the only country that uses silver in its circulating coinage.

Silver is the most malleable and ductile of all metals, with the exception of gold. Silver melts at about 962 degrees Celsius and boils at about 2212 degrees Celsius. Silver is not very chemically active, although tarnishing occurs when sulfur and sulfides attack silver, forming silver sulfide on the surface of the metal. Because silver is too soft in its pure form, a hardening agent, usually copper, is mixed into the silver. Copper is usually used as the hardening agent because it does not discolor the silver. The term "sterling silver" refers to silver that contains at least 925 parts of silver per thousand (92.5%) to 75 parts of copper (7.5%).

Silver is usually found combined with other elements in minerals and ores. In the U.S., silver is mined in conjunction with lead, copper, and zinc. In the U.S., Nevada, Idaho, Alaska, and Arizona are the leading silver-producing states. For industrial purposes, silver is used for photography, electrical appliances, glass, and as an antibacterial agent for the health industry.

Silver futures and options are traded at the CME Group, the NYSE-LIFFE U.S., the EUREX, and the Moscow Exchange. Silver futures are also traded on the Hong Kong Mercantile Exchange (HKMEx), the JSE Securities Exchange, the Multi Commodity Exchange of India (MCX), the National Commodity & Derivatives Exchange (NCDEX), the Shanghai Futures Exchange, and the Tokyo Commodity Exchange (TOCOM). The CME silver futures contract calls for the delivery of 5,000 troy ounces of silver (0.999 fineness) and is priced in terms of dollars and cents per troy ounce.

Prices – CME silver futures prices (Barchart.com symbol SI) moved higher in Q1-2014 and posted the high for the year at $22.18 an ounce in February 2014. Silver prices found support on increased demand for precious metals as an alternative asset after the BOJ expanded its emergency lending programs and extended them for another year. Silver then moved sideways into Q3 as a rally in the dollar limited the upside and pressured silver prices. Silver slumped in Q4 and plummeted to a 5-1/2 year low of $14.10 an ounce in December. Besides dollar strength, silver prices in Q4 were undercut by (1) a rally in stocks as the S&P 500 continued to post record highs, and (2) reduced inflation expectations after crude oil plunged to a 5-1/2 year low. Fund liquidation was another negative factor as long silver holdings in ETFs fell to the low for the year low in December. Silver prices finished 2014 down -19.5% at $15.57 an ounce.

Supply – World mine production of silver in 2014 rose +0.4% yr/yr to a new record high of 26,100 metric tons, continuing to show some improvement after flat production figures in 2000-03. The world's largest silver producers in 2014 were Mexico with 18.0% of world production, China (16.1%), Peru (14.2%), Australia (7.3%), Russia (6.5%), and Bolivia (5.0%). U.S. production of refined silver in 2014 (through August, annualized) rose by +2.6% to 5,008 metric tons, down from the 2011 record high of 6,375 metric tons.

Demand – U.S. consumption of silver in 2009 (latest data) fell –11.8% yr/yr to 164.4 million troy ounces. The largest consumption of silver is for electrical contacts and conductors with 31.9% of total usage, followed by coinage (20.6%), photographic materials (13.4%), jewelry (7.1%), and brazing alloys and solders (3.2%). The world's largest consuming nation of silver for industrial purposes is the U.S. with 20% of world consumption in 2004 (latest data), followed by Japan (16%), India (10%), and Italy (7%).

Trade – U.S. exports of refined silver in 2011 (latest data) rose +27.5% yr/yr to 29.064 million troy ounces, which is about half of the record high of 99.022 million troy ounces seen in 1997. The major destinations for U.S. silver exports are Japan (17.3%), South Korea (14.3%), and Canada (11.0%). U.S. imports of silver ore and concentrates in 2011 rose from 104,000 troy ounces to 2.707 million troy ounces. U.S. imports of refined silver bullion in 2011 rose +2.2% yr/yr to 168.788 million troy ounces. The bulk of those imports came from Mexico (67.515 million troy ounces), Canada (40.509 million troy ounces), and Chile (3.122 million troy ounces).

World Mine Production of Silver   In Thousands of Kilograms (Metric Ton)

Year	Australia	Bolivia	Canada[3]	Chile	China	Kazak-hstan	Mexico	Peru	Poland	Russia	Sweden	United States	World Total[2]
2005	2,417	420	1,124	1,400	2,500	832	2,894	3,206	1,263	1,350	310	1,230	20,800
2006	1,727	472	995	1,607	2,600	806	2,970	3,471	1,266	974	268	1,160	20,100
2007	1,879	525	860	1,936	2,700	723	3,135	3,494	1,199	911	270	1,280	20,800
2008	1,926	1,114	728	1,405	2,800	646	3,236	3,686	1,161	1,132	265	1,250	21,400
2009	1,635	1,326	631	1,301	2,900	618	3,554	3,854	1,207	1,313	265	1,250	22,200
2010	1,864	1,259	596	1,287	3,500	551	4,411	3,640	1,181	1,356	270	1,280	23,800
2011	1,725	1,214	572	1,291	3,700	645	4,500	3,414	1,167	1,350	270	1,120	23,300
2012	1,730	1,210	663	1,190	3,900		5,360	3,480	1,150	1,500		1,060	25,500
2013[1]	1,840	1,290	627	1,170	4,100		4,860	3,670	1,200	1,720		1,040	26,000
2014[2]	1,900	1,300	646	1,200	4,200		4,700	3,700	1,200	1,700		1,170	26,100

[1] Preliminary.   [2] Estimate.   [3] Shipments.   *Source: U.S. Geological Survey (USGS)*

SILVER

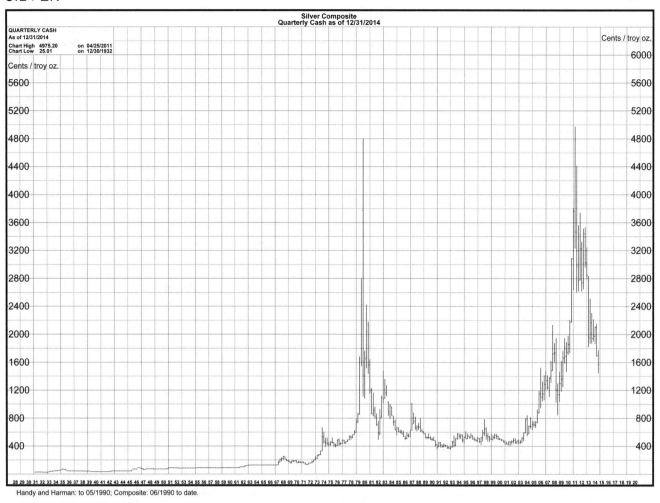

QUARTERLY CASH
As of 12/31/2014
Chart High 4975.20 on 04/25/2011
Chart Low 25.01 on 12/30/1932

Silver Composite
Quarterly Cash as of 12/31/2014

Cents / troy oz.

Handy and Harman: to 05/1990; Composite: 06/1990 to date.

Average Price of Silver in New York (Handy & Harman)　In Cents Per Troy Ounce (.999 Fine)

Year	Jan.	Feb.	Mar.	Apr.	May	June	July	Aug.	Sept.	Oct.	Nov.	Dec.	Average
2005	665.45	709.18	728.50	715.74	705.29	733.64	704.40	702.72	719.33	769.90	786.35	865.88	733.87
2006	918.48	952.13	1,037.52	1,263.71	1,337.84	1,077.41	1,121.24	1,225.39	1,159.93	1,161.55	1,298.45	1,329.83	1,156.96
2007	1,286.63	1,394.58	1,316.27	1,373.23	1,319.27	1,315.48	1,295.21	1,233.22	1,292.92	1,372.17	1,467.15	1,431.24	1,341.45
2008	1,605.90	1,766.63	1,921.60	1,751.57	1,704.90	1,703.95	1,806.41	1,457.81	1,219.33	1,042.72	986.78	1,031.66	1,499.94
2009	1,139.90	1,343.68	1,311.50	1,252.02	1,411.30	1,465.93	1,338.64	1,443.05	1,648.74	1,726.34	1,787.68	1,765.68	1,469.54
2010	1,775.05	1,587.21	1,717.11	1,816.83	1,841.90	1,853.43	1,793.98	1,849.25	2,061.12	2,346.86	2,657.20	2,933.00	2,019.41
2011	2,855.15	3,085.61	3,594.61	4,264.45	3,702.67	3,584.09	3,832.95	4,035.17	3,802.10	3,206.33	3,336.08	3,028.07	3,527.27
2012	3,095.25	3,421.95	3,296.32	3,154.65	2,882.00	2,810.29	2,739.74	2,891.35	3,379.18	3,328.57	3,271.00	3,177.13	3,120.62
2013	3,112.05	3,027.53	2,878.90	2,525.25	2,301.95	2,111.53	1,968.66	2,208.02	2,249.40	2,201.43	2,072.35	1,962.29	2,384.95
2014	1,987.52	2,086.53	2,071.60	1,973.64	1,934.19	1,989.24	2,092.25	1,973.56	1,837.10	1,716.33	1,596.61	1,629.48	1,907.34

Source: American Metal Market (AMM)

Average Price of Silver in London (Spot Fix)　In Pence Per Troy Ounce (.999 Fine)

Year	Jan.	Feb.	Mar.	Apr.	May	June	July	Aug.	Sept.	Oct.	Nov.	Dec.	Average
2005	354.28	375.57	382.74	377.48	380.46	403.56	402.10	391.55	397.90	436.23	453.10	496.09	404.26
2006	519.94	544.76	594.70	714.36	715.69	584.44	607.69	647.19	615.09	618.97	678.96	677.31	626.59
2007	656.95	712.03	675.74	690.95	665.15	662.06	636.65	613.19	639.99	670.90	708.45	709.65	670.14
2008	815.50	899.50	960.24	883.98	867.12	866.05	907.89	772.57	677.51	617.03	645.37	693.86	800.55
2009	787.02	931.98	923.81	850.16	912.88	894.99	816.90	872.89	1,010.76	1,065.91	1,076.27	1,087.91	935.96
2010	1,098.45	1,016.07	1,140.22	1,184.58	1,256.63	1,255.90	1,172.41	1,181.47	1,323.37	1,479.95	1,665.70	1,880.21	1,304.58
2011	1,808.34	1,912.09	2,224.65	2,602.69	2,266.24	2,209.81	2,373.37	2,466.59	2,410.10	2,032.85	2,111.63	1,942.66	2,196.75
2012	1,994.05	2,164.96	2,082.42	1,970.51	1,811.54	1,806.56	1,756.42	1,839.55	2,097.22	2,070.91	2,049.00	1,967.97	1,967.59
2013	1,949.80	1,957.31	1,908.68	1,649.50	1,505.82	1,362.47	1,296.54	1,424.04	1,416.94	1,368.26	1,286.22	1,197.73	1,526.94
2014	1,206.90	1,259.53	1,246.67	1,178.50	1,148.47	1,175.94	1,225.31	1,181.77	1,126.82	1,067.60			1,181.75

Source: American Metal Market (AMM)

SILVER 5,000 TROY OZ - COMEX
Weekly Selected Futures as of 01/02/2015

WEEKLY SELECTED FUTURES
As of 01/02/2015

Chart High 4982.00 on 04/25/2011
Chart Low 642.00 on 01/10/2005

Nearby Futures through Last Trading Day.

Volume of Trading of Silver Futures in New York (COMEX)   In Thousands of Contracts

Year	Jan.	Feb.	Mar.	Apr.	May	June	July	Aug.	Sept.	Oct.	Nov.	Dec.	Total
2005	285.4	513.6	370.3	485.8	392.2	621.6	334.9	601.0	455.0	425.0	652.9	398.5	5,536.4
2006	495.6	624.5	562.3	807.3	513.8	508.7	255.8	452.6	268.4	244.2	424.8	275.1	5,433.1
2007	364.6	589.3	479.9	635.0	417.3	680.6	404.1	784.0	469.5	581.1	1,018.5	393.2	6,817.1
2008	719.3	989.6	881.8	913.0	581.0	860.0	722.7	953.1	792.1	594.3	578.0	332.4	8,917.2
2009	415.6	652.2	433.8	575.7	418.4	869.1	476.6	842.9	657.0	809.6	1,159.3	680.3	7,990.5
2010	755.9	1,065.2	750.2	994.8	936.9	1,079.3	642.8	978.6	757.1	1,314.2	2,282.2	1,269.6	12,826.7
2011	1,429.7	1,674.7	1,685.7	3,014.6	2,461.1	1,768.9	1,325.0	1,982.8	1,220.4	952.6	1,327.4	765.6	19,608.6
2012	826.9	1,478.7	1,120.1	1,224.1	1,028.2	1,416.8	804.5	1,231.9	1,068.8	874.2	1,437.3	804.2	13,315.7
2013	1,021.7	1,346.4	780.3	1,980.5	1,172.0	1,555.4	932.3	1,652.5	958.1	948.4	1,270.3	857.7	14,475.6
2014	915.0	1,498.8	973.7	1,388.9	883.1	1,459.4	957.2	1,216.7	990.8	1,013.7	1,435.4	964.7	13,697.5

Contract size = 5,000 oz.   *Source: CME Group; New York Mercantile Exchange (NYMEX), COMEX Division*

Average Open Interest of Silver Futures in New York (COMEX)   In Contracts

Year	Jan.	Feb.	Mar.	Apr.	May	June	July	Aug.	Sept.	Oct.	Nov.	Dec.
2005	97,744	98,644	101,200	103,562	104,680	124,317	124,521	121,133	117,121	135,335	146,409	136,502
2006	131,767	129,928	132,140	137,121	110,400	110,631	98,733	110,635	102,159	105,167	114,132	105,741
2007	105,692	122,515	113,749	118,275	109,070	120,179	117,817	118,292	110,958	123,781	144,897	146,891
2008	174,969	182,076	157,971	143,333	123,649	128,645	136,866	131,931	110,333	97,927	91,983	84,986
2009	87,525	96,902	92,756	93,855	95,420	106,283	99,018	103,076	122,052	133,409	137,261	124,797
2010	126,921	118,619	112,234	123,849	122,547	129,561	118,619	126,117	145,022	153,013	148,547	133,596
2011	133,030	138,901	135,793	143,245	124,278	118,740	115,246	117,217	109,908	103,939	107,600	100,220
2012	103,766	108,478	110,777	117,254	113,514	122,240	122,555	124,907	125,957	140,254	145,146	141,906
2013	143,032	141,751	149,900	156,813	145,964	147,042	133,417	130,278	113,116	116,266	130,050	133,668
2014	137,682	145,743	141,847	157,064	152,154	161,079	161,447	161,613	168,883	172,012	169,706	148,854

Contract size = 5,000 oz.   *Source: CME Group; New York Mercantile Exchange (NYMEX), COMEX Division*

SILVER

Mine Production of Recoverable Silver in the United States   In Metric Tons

Year	Arizona	Cali-fornia	Colo-rado	Idaho	Missouri	Montana	Nevada	New Mexico	South Dakota	Wash-ington	Other States	Total
2005	W	W	W	W	W	W	276	W	W	W	949	1,230
2006	W	W	W	W	W	W	260	W	W	W	895	1,160
2007	W	W	W	W	W	W	243	W	W	W	1,040	1,280
2008	W	W	W	W	W	W	235	W	W	W	1,020	1,250
2009	W	W	W	W	W	W	203	W	W	W	1,040	1,250
2010	W	W	W	W	W	W	224	W	W	W	1,050	1,280
2011	W	W	W	W	W	W	209	W	W	W	913	1,120
2012	W	W	W	W	W	W	250	W	W	W	805	1,060
2013	W	W	W	W	W	W	255	W	W	W	791	1,050
2014[1]	W	W	W	W	W	W	272	W	W	W	694	966

[1] Preliminary.   W = Withheld proprietary data; included in "Other States".   *Source: U.S. Geological Survey (USGS)*

Commodity Exchange, Inc. (COMEX) Warehouse of Stocks of Silver   In Thousands of Troy Ounces

Year	Jan.	Feb.	Mar.	Apr.	May	June	July	Aug.	Sept.	Oct.	Nov.	Dec.
2005	103,590	102,390	101,494	103,627	103,995	104,257	104,719	109,467	115,588	116,687	116,257	117,608
2006	119,974	124,793	127,898	125,763	123,627	108,443	102,268	102,086	103,634	105,451	105,313	107,770
2007	111,071	113,970	117,637	126,433	131,343	130,497	139,935	132,106	133,057	133,474	133,891	134,533
2008	130,072	135,414	135,037	135,881	133,512	134,896	135,959	138,061	137,821	135,719	130,204	127,170
2009	125,536	123,902	124,121	123,615	119,910	120,879	118,519	117,818	117,796	116,159	116,159	112,494
2010	110,588	110,588	110,588	115,786	116,178	119,452	114,015	110,244	110,765	111,075	107,785	107,393
2011	104,548	103,594	102,549	105,495	102,014	100,968	101,720	104,176	104,085	106,012	107,096	110,415
2012	126,218	129,403	130,318	137,073	142,125	143,150	145,933	139,218	140,678	142,047	142,362	145,284
2013	148,205	154,577	162,830	164,163	166,050	165,749	166,746	164,711	163,771	165,329	169,012	169,985
2014	173,927	179,297	182,831	179,791	174,483	175,267	175,517	175,317	179,292	182,194	181,185	177,008

Source: CME Group; New York Mercantile Exchange (NYMEX), COMEX Division

Production[2] of Refined Silver in the United States, from All Sources   In Metric Tons

Year	Jan.	Feb.	Mar.	Apr.	May	June	July	Aug.	Sept.	Oct.	Nov.	Dec.	Total
2005	402	505	515	568	450	558	556	440	356	376	485	439	5,650
2006	506	434	500	445	381	554	489	431	349	387	209	305	4,990
2007	401	405	445	436	476	452	335	438	290	388	267	339	4,671
2008	325	360	394	460	401	417	420	428	460	445	422	393	4,925
2009	456	182	270	326	337	394	363	495	535	676	530	778	5,342
2010	553	504	794	503	510	356	383	534	439	460	547	441	6,024
2011	626	512	748	477	485	462	493	491	499	522	426	634	6,375
2012	559	443	443	419	457	426	423	375	344	385	407	393	5,073
2013	505	438	421	486	376	337	415	365	364	450	292	431	4,880
2014[1]	431	334	347	399	450	418	456	386	506	447			5,009

[1] Preliminary.   [2] Includes U.S. mine production of recoverable silver plus imports of refined silver.   *Source: U.S. Geological Survey (USGS)*

U.S. Exports of Refined Silver to Selected Countries   In Thousands of Troy Ounces

Year	Canada	France	Germany	Hong Kong	Japan	Korea, South	Singa-pore	Switzer-land	United Arab Emirates	United Kingdom	Uruguay	Other Countries	Total
2002	466	----	1	4	466	----	10	727	----	14,532	----	11,990	28,196
2003	524	3	----	3	17	16	2	630	----	3,086	----	2,534	6,816
2004	7,009	1	3	24	585	1	166	2,321	----	3	108	2,125	12,346
2005	3,729	----	25	3	1	18	95	2,829	----	1,145	563	1,302	9,709
2006	5,433	----	874	----	547	----	120	1,218	2	37,937	----	----	50,797
2007	3,762	3	1,537	1,804	801	25	103	990	----	1,061	498	----	23,373
2008	4,051	----	1,283	5	2,115	1,424	131	527	----	1,929	437	10	20,512
2009	395	1	1,399	159	2	1,816	113	823	----	1,765	----	3	12,989
2010	3,376	----	2,247	139	1,241	1,974	1,010	733	----	1,331	----	28	22,794
2011[1]	3,189	----	389	284	5,015	4,147	566	1,270	----	1,813	----	55	29,064

[1] Preliminary.   [2] Included in "Other Countries", if any.   NA = Not available.   *Source: American Bureau of Metal Statistics, Inc. (ABMS)*

U.S. Imports of Silver From Selected Countries   In Thousands of Troy Ounces

Year	Canada	Mexico	Other Countries	Total	Canada	Chile	Mexico	Peru	Uruguay	Other Countries	Total
2002	149	1,813	----	1,961	48,868	2,331	67,837	6,430	----	6,350	131,815
2003	82	----	----	82	41,795	1,987	62,050	18,261	----	12,223	136,316
2004	71	----	----	71	37,616	2,042	59,156	17,297	----	4,774	120,884
2005	14	----	----	14	41,474	2,514	65,908	20,319	----	4,173	134,387
2006	----	----	----	----	47,261	1,106	73,945	13,214	----	2,077	137,602
2007	----	----	12	12	34,722	1,206	78,125	18,358	----	2,942	135,352
2008	----	----	1	1	25,109	2,234	76,196	16,075	----	4,485	124,099
2009	----	----	----	3	24,016	4,019	52,405	6,559	----	3,022	90,020
2010	104	----	----	104	51,119	2,578	82,947	9,999	----	26,003	172,646
2011[1]	2,707	----	----	2,707	40,509	3,122	67,515	952	----	56,690	168,788

[1] Preliminary.   [2] Included in "Other Countries", if any.   NA = Not available.   Source: American Bureau of Metal Statistics, Inc. (ABMS)

World Silver Consumption   In Millions of Troy Ounces

	--- Industrial Uses ---										--- Coinage ---							
Year	Canada	France	Germany	India	Italy	Japan	Mexico	United Kingdom	United States	World Total	Austria	Canada	France	Germany	Mexico	United States	Total Coinage	World Total
1995	2.0	30.0	43.6	101.3	49.5	112.7	16.9	31.6	148.7	752.7	.5	.7	1.2	2.4	.6	9.0	24.7	777.4
1996	2.0	26.9	41.0	122.2	51.7	112.1	20.3	33.8	155.0	785.8	.5	.7	.3	4.6	.5	7.1	23.3	809.1
1997	2.2	28.3	42.3	122.9	56.1	119.9	23.3	34.9	166.3	828.2	.4	.6	.3	3.7	.4	6.5	28.5	856.7
1998	2.3	28.4	38.4	114.7	55.9	112.8	21.7	38.6	162.6	801.2	.3	1.1	.3	10.0	.2	7.0	27.8	829.0
1999	2.1	26.6	35.1	121.5	61.8	122.5	21.3	39.3	175.2	838.7	.3	1.4	.3	7.0	.4	10.7	29.2	867.8
2000	2.0	28.8	31.8	131.0	65.1	135.0	16.6	42.7	179.1	871.8	.3	1.0	.4	8.8	.6	13.4	32.1	904.0
2001	2.0	28.7	32.4	154.0	58.2	119.3	15.9	45.9	157.3	836.5	.3	.9	.4	8.1	1.1	12.3	30.5	867.0
2002	2.1	27.1	29.4	122.5	56.0	118.7	17.0	43.1	161.6	807.0	.4	1.0	.5	6.0	1.1	15.3	31.6	838.6
2003	2.2	25.6	29.4	122.5	55.0	115.9	18.7	44.1	160.8	817.5	.4	.3	.5	10.3	1.1	14.5	35.8	853.4
2004[2]	2.1	12.0	30.7	79.2	54.8	125.1	18.6	52.2	164.8	807.0	.5	1.3	.5	10.3	.9	15.5	41.1	836.6

[2] Preliminary.   NA = Not available.   *Source: The Silver Institute*

Consumption of Silver in the United States, by End Use   In Millions of Troy Ounces

Year	Brazing Alloys & Solders	Catalysts	Batteries	Mirrors	Electrical Contacts & Conductors	Photographic Materials	Silverplate	Jewelry	Sterling Ware	Total Net Industrial Consumption	Coinage	Total Consumption
2000	8.7	6.3	5.2	2.6	51.5	70.2	4.5	6.1	5.6	178.8	13.4	192.2
2001	8.3	6.1	5.3	2.5	34.1	65.5	4.0	4.9	4.6	157.3	12.3	169.6
2002	8.4	NA	NA	NA	37.6	64.8	[3]	13.7	[3]	161.7	15.3	177.0
2003	7.9	NA	NA	NA	39.5	58.9	[3]	15.1	[3]	160.8	14.5	175.3
2004	7.3	NA	NA	NA	47.4	55.2	[3]	15.4	[3]	164.8	15.5	180.3
2005	7.7	NA	NA	NA	52.1	56.4	[3]	15.7	[3]	172.8	16.6	189.4
2006	7.2	NA	NA	NA	55.0	46.4	[3]	15.0	[3]	168.2	17.6	185.8
2007	7.7	NA	NA	NA	57.7	35.9	[3]	14.2	[3]	164.2	16.0	180.2
2008	7.2	NA	NA	NA	61.4	29.3	[3]	13.0	[3]	161.0	25.4	186.4
2009[1]	5.2	NA	NA	NA	52.4	22.0	[3]	11.6	[3]	130.5	33.9	164.4

[1] Preliminary.   [3] Included in Jewelry beginning 2002.   NA = Not available.   *Source: American Metal Market*

Soybean Meal

Soybean meal is produced through processing and separating soybeans into oil and meal components. If the soybeans are of particularly good quality, then the processor can get more meal weight by including more hulls in the meal while still meeting a 48% protein minimum. Soybean meal can be further processed into soy flour and isolated soy protein, but the bulk of soybean meal is used as animal feed for poultry, hogs and cattle. Soybean meal accounts for about two-thirds of the world's high-protein animal feed, followed by cottonseed and rapeseed meal, which together account for less than 20%. Soybean meal consumption has been moving to record highs in recent years. The soybean meal marketing year begins in October and ends in September.

Soybean meal futures and options are traded at the CME Group. The CME soybean meal futures contract calls for the delivery of 100 tons of soybean meal produced by conditioning ground soybeans and reducing the oil content of the conditioned product and having a minimum of 48.0% protein, minimum of 0.5% fat, maximum of 3.5% fiber, and maximum of 12.0% moisture.

Soybean crush – The term soybean "crush" refers to both the physical processing of soybeans and also to the dollar-value premium received for processing soybeans into their component products of meal and oil. The conventional model says that processing 60 pounds (one bushel) of soybeans produces 11 pounds of soybean oil, 44 pounds of 48% protein soybean meal, 3 pounds of hulls, and 1 pound of waste. The Gross Processing Margin (GPM) or crush equals (0.22 times Soybean Meal Prices in dollars per ton) + (11 times Soybean Oil prices in cents/pound) – Soybean prices in $/bushel. A higher crush value will occur when the price of the meal and oil products are strong relative to soybeans, e.g., because of supply disruptions or because of an increase in demand for the products. When the crush value is high, companies will have a strong incentive to buy raw soybeans and boost the output of the products. That supply increase should eventually bring the crush value back into line with the long-term equilibrium.

Prices – CME soybean meal futures prices (Barchart.com electronic symbol ZM) showed some strength in early 2014 but then fell sharply and posted a 3-year low in October 2014, finally closing the year down -16.7% at $364.6 per short ton.

Supply – World soybean meal production in 2014-15 rose +5.7% yr/yr to a new record high of 199.494 million metric tons. The world's largest soybean meal producers are China with 29.6% of world production in 2014-15, the U.S. with 19.5%, Argentina with 14.8%, and Brazil with 14.5%. U.S. production of soybean meal in 2014-15 rose +5.2% yr/yr to 42.785 million short tons, below the 2006-07 record high of 43.054. U.S. soybean meal stocks in 2014-15 (Oct 1) fell -9.1% yr/yr to 250,000 short tons, below the decade high of 383,000 short tons in 2001-02.

Demand – World consumption of soybean meal in 2014-15 rose +5.1% yr/yr to 194.341 million metric tons, a new record high. The European Union accounted for 15.0% of that consumption and the U.S. accounted for 14.1%. U.S. consumption of soybean meal in 2014-15 rose +2.4% yr/yr to 27.398 million metric tons.

Trade – World exports of soybean meal in 2014-15 rose +6.5% to 63.507 million metric tons. Argentina accounted for 43.8% of world exports and the U.S. accounted for 18.3%. World imports of soybean meal in 2014-15 rose +5.2% yr/yr to 60.288 million metric tons. U.S. exports of soybean meal in 2014-15 rose +10.8% yr/yr to 12.800 million short tons. U.S. imports of soybean meal in 2014-15 fell -50.9% yr/yr to 165,000 short tons, remaining well below the record high of 285,000 short tons seen in 2003-04.

Supply and Distribution of Soybean Meal in the United States   In Thousands of Short Tons

Crop Year Beginning Oct. 1	For Stocks Oct. 1	Pro-duction	Total Supply	Domestic	Exports	Total	Decatur 48% Protein Solvent	Decatur 44% Protein Solvent	Brazil FOB 45-46% Protein	Rotter-dam CIF
2005-06	172	41,244	41,557	33,195	8,048	41,243	174.17	192	176	215
2006-07	314	43,054	43,524	34,374	8,804	43,178	205.44	226	199	276
2007-08	343	42,284	42,768	33,232	9,242	42,474	335.94	370	337	469
2008-09	294	39,102	39,484	30,752	8,497	39,249	331.17	365	333	401
2009-10	235	41,707	42,101	30,640	11,159	41,800	311.27	343	327	391
2010-11	302	39,251	39,731	30,278	9,104	39,381	345.52	381	383	418
2011-12	350	41,025	41,591	31,548	9,743	41,291	393.53	434	442	461
2012-13[1]	300	39,875	40,420	29,031	11,114	40,145	468.11	516	489	538
2013-14[2]	275	40,685	41,296	29,496	11,550	41,046	415-455	517	524	546
2014-15[3]	250	43,100	43,600	30,500	12,800	43,300				

[1] Preliminary.   [2] Estimate.   [3] Forecast.   *Source: Economic Research Service, U.S. Department of Agriculture (ERS-USDA)*

World Production of Soybean Meal   In Thousands of Metric Tons

Crop Year	Argen-tina	Bolivia	Brazil	China	European Union	India	Japan	Mexico	Para-guay	Russia	Taiwan	United States	World Total
2005-06	25,012	1,468	21,920	27,296	10,904	5,381	2,280	2,945	927	530	1,607	37,416	146,431
2006-07	26,061	1,332	24,110	28,465	11,693	5,255	2,299	3,010	1,025	632	1,605	39,037	153,821
2007-08	27,071	925	24,890	31,280	11,808	6,705	2,218	2,930	1,092	825	1,525	38,359	158,751
2008-09	24,363	1,145	24,700	32,475	10,223	5,960	1,895	2,850	1,140	1,176	1,510	35,473	152,169
2009-10	26,624	1,200	26,120	38,644	9,950	6,240	1,908	2,850	1,225	1,535	1,581	37,836	165,277
2010-11	29,312	1,420	28,160	43,560	9,633	7,440	1,647	2,870	1,235	1,708	1,620	35,608	174,427
2011-12	27,945	1,580	29,510	48,288	9,668	7,720	1,483	2,910	705	1,891	1,588	37,217	180,452
2012-13	26,089	1,720	27,310	51,440	10,432	7,920	1,447	2,890	2,310	1,923	1,510	36,174	181,287
2013-14[1]	27,950	1,580	27,980	54,531	10,737	6,640	1,465	3,088	2,750	2,333	1,512	36,909	188,780
2014-15[2]	29,575	1,740	29,000	59,004	10,750	6,800	1,491	3,325	2,820	2,364	1,550	38,828	199,494

Crop year beginning October 1.   [1] Preliminary.   [2] Forecast.   Source: Foreign Agricultural Service, U.S. Department of Agriculture (FAS-USDA)

World Exports of Soybean Meal   In Thousands of Metric Tons

Crop Year	Argen-tina	Bolivia	Brazil	Canada	China	European Union	India	Korea, South	Norway	Para-guay	Russia	United States	World Total
2005-06	24,222	1,186	12,895	129	357	714	4,268	----	160	785	1	7,301	52,245
2006-07	25,625	1,178	12,715	137	867	544	4,143	----	144	1,096	2	7,987	54,699
2007-08	26,816	763	12,138	120	634	422	5,285	9	148	1,072	50	8,384	56,063
2008-09	24,025	1,103	13,109	82	1,017	464	3,808	116	153	1,076	14	7,708	52,844
2009-10	24,914	1,114	12,985	126	1,181	471	3,117	75	165	1,124	3	10,125	55,606
2010-11	27,615	1,097	13,987	210	472	609	4,800	72	152	1,043	28	8,238	58,545
2011-12	26,043	1,208	14,678	173	966	884	4,391	38	165	523	10	8,845	58,275
2012-13	23,667	1,480	13,242	246	1,365	536	4,354	115	148	2,149	80	10,139	57,837
2013-14[1]	24,960	1,260	13,948	241	2,017	310	2,742	179	142	2,500	350	10,478	59,630
2014-15[2]	27,830	1,350	14,100	250	1,700	390	2,550	150	145	2,570	350	11,612	63,507

Crop year beginning October 1.   [1] Preliminary.   [2] Forecast.   Source: Foreign Agricultural Service, U.S. Department of Agriculture (FAS-USDA)

World Imports of Soybean Meal   In Thousands of Metric Tons

Crop Year	Algeria	European Union	Iran	Indo-nesia	Japan	Korea, South	Malaysia	Mexico	Peru	Philippines	Thailand	Vietnam	World Total
2005-06	631	22,947	509	2,071	1,601	1,773	862	1,728	853	1,646	2,042	1,722	51,426
2006-07	622	22,362	817	2,237	1,737	1,870	907	1,780	853	1,743	2,275	2,291	52,812
2007-08	724	24,619	900	2,429	1,747	1,761	917	1,401	787	1,627	1,935	2,296	54,860
2008-09	727	21,153	1,311	2,339	1,812	1,813	933	1,518	902	1,575	2,160	2,526	51,686
2009-10	850	20,879	1,524	2,507	2,106	1,737	1,076	1,209	1,072	1,719	2,513	2,879	53,480
2010-11	1,074	21,877	1,742	3,069	2,208	1,658	1,028	1,500	1,059	1,972	2,318	2,719	56,908
2011-12	892	20,872	2,192	3,278	2,282	1,571	1,078	1,548	1,113	1,833	2,928	2,276	57,046
2012-13	1,333	16,941	2,099	3,367	1,765	1,654	1,276	1,295	1,099	1,970	2,874	2,980	53,853
2013-14[1]	1,300	18,175	2,683	3,700	1,976	1,826	1,400	1,425	1,150	2,250	2,665	3,100	57,297
2014-15[2]	1,370	19,300	2,800	3,900	2,100	1,880	1,425	1,420	1,240	2,350	2,900	3,200	60,288

Crop year beginning October 1.   [1] Preliminary.   [2] Forecast.   Source: Foreign Agricultural Service, U.S. Department of Agriculture (FAS-USDA)

U.S. Exports of Soybean Cake & Meal by Country of Destination   In Thousands of Metric Tons

Year	Algeria	Australia	Canada	Dominican Republic	Italy	Japan	Mexico	Nether-lands	Philip-pines	Russia	Spain	Vene-zuela	Total
2005	63.0	74.9	1,155.9	264.2	0.2	523.4	1,356.3	10.1	442.0	16.8	5.0	112.5	6,352
2006	18.4	54.3	1,390.4	423.6	1.3	481.1	1,705.7	6.5	519.4	31.1	----	27.9	7,479
2007	39.5	1.2	1,467.4	448.7	0.1	451.3	1,638.4	8.2	626.9	31.8	0.6	49.3	7,922
2008	50.1	45.3	1,365.0	368.5	58.5	385.8	1,447.3	36.8	551.2	27.3	0.0	545.0	7,996
2009	----	121.9	1,154.3	362.4	48.5	366.3	1,323.0	0.2	803.4	20.0	90.0	487.1	8,791
2010	----	208.0	1,069.3	384.4	28.1	389.2	1,382.3	0.8	860.3	22.0	50.6	571.0	9,318
2011	17.4	0.5	1,048.5	358.4	33.7	338.6	1,423.7	0.4	869.5	22.6	0.2	636.1	7,821
2012	16.5	41.8	1,073.0	393.9	63.2	211.6	1,343.0	0.2	1,305.9	25.1	50.5	705.8	9,691
2013	17.3	69.0	895.1	331.6	229.6	180.2	1,269.5	0.9	1,120.6	0.1	198.4	755.1	10,161
2014[1]	3.0	0.1	971.0	352.2	277.0	212.0	1,592.9	1.6	1,107.1	15.0	267.2	842.6	10,245

[1] Preliminary.   Source: Foreign Agricultural Service, U.S. Department of Agriculture (FAS-USDA)

SOYBEAN MEAL

Nearby Futures through Last Trading Day.

Volume of Trading of Soybean Meal Futures in Chicago   In Thousands of Contracts

Year	Jan.	Feb.	Mar.	Apr.	May	June	July	Aug.	Sept.	Oct.	Nov.	Dec.	Total
2005	658.7	857.6	713.4	661.8	571.3	1,025.0	632.8	693.4	602.9	497.9	694.0	715.8	8,324.6
2006	506.9	605.0	575.3	785.6	716.8	976.1	801.5	819.1	807.7	906.1	1,064.2	785.7	9,350.0
2007	768.9	1,018.8	822.1	985.7	798.9	1,217.3	1,107.9	1,025.1	1,028.6	1,016.4	1,218.8	1,204.7	12,213.3
2008	1,260.6	1,235.1	1,240.4	1,257.7	922.5	1,359.0	1,258.6	1,074.5	1,069.3	1,020.3	837.1	818.9	13,354.2
2009	909.2	988.7	841.7	1,195.1	1,071.4	1,390.1	1,146.6	1,071.8	974.6	1,012.1	1,222.7	1,056.6	12,880.8
2010	994.1	1,134.5	1,330.1	1,264.3	850.7	1,349.0	1,134.2	1,057.8	1,136.4	1,054.7	1,590.7	1,156.3	14,052.8
2011	1,115.7	1,437.9	1,475.1	1,546.9	1,141.0	1,642.3	1,211.5	1,485.3	1,726.2	1,329.8	1,511.7	1,296.8	16,920.2
2012	1,182.2	1,484.7	1,545.3	1,914.5	1,481.2	1,812.1	1,848.1	1,594.8	1,389.8	1,263.9	1,436.3	1,234.5	18,187.4
2013	1,520.3	1,758.3	1,277.9	1,985.6	1,558.3	1,839.5	1,919.1	1,797.3	1,433.2	1,632.4	1,881.6	1,633.7	20,237.2
2014	1,519.1	1,918.1	1,409.7	1,711.2	1,138.3	1,811.9	1,703.3	1,664.5	1,613.9	2,456.8	2,070.8	1,619.8	20,637.3

Contract size = 100 tons.   *Source: CME Group; Chicago Board of Trade (CBT)*

Average Open Interest of Soybean Meal Futures in Chicago   In Contracts

Year	Jan.	Feb.	Mar.	Apr.	May	June	July	Aug.	Sept.	Oct.	Nov.	Dec.
2005	154,984	165,403	146,326	133,578	129,372	149,882	122,088	109,976	121,833	135,970	140,102	140,959
2006	127,922	132,833	147,837	172,905	181,823	182,940	196,236	230,082	236,351	206,002	216,854	206,762
2007	201,214	227,905	213,708	216,258	212,398	217,576	210,612	201,339	219,046	225,683	248,277	251,133
2008	234,286	234,695	225,607	218,126	199,422	216,039	208,444	178,191	163,511	152,968	138,111	124,898
2009	118,930	121,722	110,580	123,445	160,515	190,481	174,733	167,301	155,388	150,639	159,393	165,141
2010	170,924	198,651	200,438	196,464	177,726	187,838	197,981	200,131	208,773	195,256	201,589	194,033
2011	203,340	215,886	213,717	226,365	228,210	223,375	180,790	176,598	187,326	186,973	204,468	206,053
2012	193,344	187,100	226,979	261,896	251,386	253,037	263,064	255,541	235,650	211,525	217,752	222,206
2013	248,644	287,037	281,914	262,103	264,520	305,549	285,970	266,192	267,963	272,131	279,717	274,139
2014	272,424	307,186	312,283	321,497	310,358	320,237	309,536	319,263	340,910	362,209	382,227	353,605

Contract size = 100 tons.   *Source: CME Group; Chicago Board of Trade (CBT)*

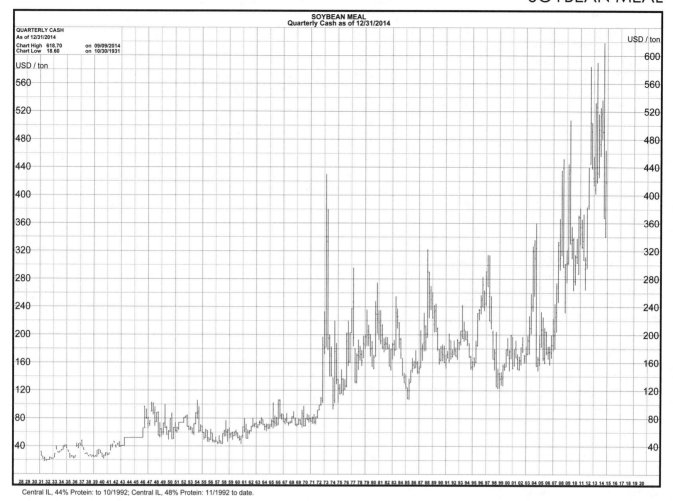

SOYBEAN MEAL
Quarterly Cash as of 12/31/2014

QUARTERLY CASH
As of 12/31/2014

Chart High 618.70   on 09/09/2014
Chart Low   18.60   on 10/30/1931

Central IL, 44% Protein: to 10/1992; Central IL, 48% Protein: 11/1992 to date.

Average Price of Soybean Meal (48% Solvent) in Decatur Illinois   In Dollars Per Short Ton -- Bulk

Year	Jan.	Feb.	Mar.	Apr.	May	June	July	Aug.	Sept.	Oct.	Nov.	Dec.	Average
2005-06	166.22	170.32	193.17	183.64	176.73	175.07	174.64	175.77	176.83	168.97	159.76	168.87	174.17
2006-07	177.71	190.67	180.63	190.36	208.81	205.26	189.37	198.66	229.70	222.05	217.63	254.41	205.44
2007-08	260.55	280.76	314.78	331.28	345.87	331.57	329.94	325.48	390.72	412.25	355.35	352.70	335.94
2008-09	260.66	267.37	268.24	306.85	297.42	292.22	324.27	380.37	418.47	373.18	405.27	379.68	331.17
2009-10	325.69	328.18	333.93	314.23	295.79	277.61	291.21	287.85	305.78	325.56	331.76	317.65	311.27
2010-11	321.92	341.78	351.93	368.54	358.59	345.43	335.87	342.30	347.45	346.52	349.60	336.32	345.52
2011-12	301.45	290.37	281.65	310.65	330.37	365.95	394.29	415.17	422.59	515.82	564.69	529.37	393.53
2012-13	488.46	465.64	459.40	431.39	440.66	437.33	422.07	465.72	496.78	544.59	464.90	500.39	468.11
2013-14	443.63	451.13	498.10	479.54	509.25	495.71	514.01	519.38	501.72	450.79	490.32	525.72	489.94
2014-15	381.50	441.39	431.73	380.03									408.66

Source: Economic Research Service, U.S. Department of Agriculture (ERS-USDA)

Average Price of Soybean Meal (44% Solvent) in Decatur Illinois   In Dollars Per Short Ton -- Bulk

Year	Jan.	Feb.	Mar.	Apr.	May	June	July	Aug.	Sept.	Oct.	Nov.	Dec.	Average
1992-93	168.6	170.9	176.4	175.6	167.5	172.4	175.6	181.7	181.3	217.6	206.9	186.5	181.8
1993-94	180.6	195.7	192.5	185.9	184.4	182.0	176.4	191.1	183.0	168.1	165.6	162.5	180.7
1994-95	156.4	150.9	145.4	145.1	149.4	145.7	151.0	148.1	149.1	160.1	157.5	171.8	152.5
1995-96	183.4	194.1	213.6	220.5	216.7	215.7	237.9	232.3	227.9	242.3	251.1	265.5	225.1
1996-97	238.0	242.7	240.9	240.7	253.6	270.4	277.7	296.0	275.9	261.5	261.6	265.7	260.4
1997-98	216.0	231.6	214.9	193.1	182.1	165.3	152.8	150.3	157.8	173.3	135.7	126.9	175.0
1998-99	129.4	139.3	139.6	131.0	124.4	127.2	128.6	127.0	131.7	125.7	135.9	144.1	132.0
1999-00	147.2	148.1	145.4	155.0	163.6	166.6	168.1	180.1	170.2	156.8	151.4	166.9	160.0
2000-01	166.0	173.7	187.9	175.6	158.3	149.1	149.7	155.6	163.1	183.9	170.6	163.5	166.4
2001-02	157.7	157.2	146.6	Disc.	Disc.	Disc.	Disc.	Disc.	Disc.	Disc.	Disc.	Disc.	153.8

Source: Economic Research Service, U.S. Department of Agriculture (ERS-USDA)

Soybean Oil

Soybean oil is the natural oil extracted from whole soybeans. Typically, about 19% of a soybean's weight can be extracted as crude soybean oil. The oil content of U.S. soybeans correlates directly with the temperatures and amount of sunshine during the soybean pod-filling stages. Edible products produced with soybean oil include cooking and salad oils, shortening, and margarine. Soybean oil is the most widely used cooking oil in the U.S. It accounts for 80% of margarine production and for more than 75% of total U.S. consumer vegetable fat and oil consumption. Soy oil is cholesterol-free and high in polyunsaturated fat. Soy oil is also used to produce inedible products such as paints, varnish, resins, and plastics. Of the edible vegetable oils, soy oil is the world's largest at about 32%, followed by palm oil and rapeseed oil.

Soybean oil futures and options are traded at the CME Group. Soybean Oil futures are also traded at ICE Futures U.S., the Dalian Commodity Exchange (DCE), the JSE Securities Exchange, the Mercado a Termino de Buenos Aires (MTBA), the Multi Commodity Exchange of India (MCX), and the National Commodity & Derivatives Exchange (NCDEX).

Prices – CME soybean oil futures prices (Barchart.com electronic symbol ZL) on the nearest-futures chart showed some strength in early 2014 but then fell during the remainder of the year to post a new 5-year low and close the year of 2014 down -17.6% yr/yr at 31.97 cents per pound. Regarding cash prices for the year 2014-15 (through January 2015), the average monthly price of crude domestic soybean oil (in tank cars) in Decatur (F.O.B.) fell by -12.7% yr/yr to 33.37 cents per pound.

Supply – World production of soybean oil in 2014-15 rose +5.1% yr/yr to a new record high of 47.151 million metric tons. China accounts for 28.3% of world soybean oil production, while the U.S. accounts for 19.8%, and Argentina accounts for 15.4%. U.S. production of soybean oil in 2014-15 rose +2.7 % yr/yr to 20.680 billion pounds.

Demand – World consumption of soybean oil in 2014-15 rose +2.9% yr/yr to a new record high of 46.258 million metric tons. China accounted for 30.8% of world consumption, while the U.S. accounted for 18.0%, Brazil for 13.1%, and India for 7.5%. U.S. consumption of soybean oil in 2014-15 fell -2.7% yr/yr to 18.450 billion pounds.

Trade – World exports of soybean oil in 2014-15 rose +2.3% yr/yr to 9.445 million metric tons. U.S. exports of soybean oil in 2014-15 rose +11.9% yr/yr to 2.100 billion pounds, well below 2009-10 record high of 3.359 billion pounds.

World Production of Soybean Oil   In Thousands of Metric Tons

Crop Year	Argentina	Bolivia	Brazil	China	European Union	India	Japan	Mexico	Paraguay	Russia	Taiwan	United States	World Total
2005-06	5,998	335	5,430	6,149	2,512	1,205	579	665	224	120	373	9,248	34,860
2006-07	6,424	303	5,970	6,410	2,694	1,175	576	680	248	143	375	9,294	36,431
2007-08	6,627	211	6,160	7,045	2,720	1,499	563	661	264	187	363	9,335	37,744
2008-09	5,914	261	6,120	7,325	2,350	1,319	479	643	275	266	359	8,503	35,940
2009-10	6,476	277	6,470	8,726	2,290	1,381	480	643	296	349	376	8,897	38,851
2010-11	7,181	320	6,970	9,840	2,392	1,646	416	648	300	389	385	8,568	41,402
2011-12	6,839	355	7,310	10,914	2,359	1,708	380	657	172	430	376	8,954	42,732
2012-13	6,364	390	6,760	11,626	2,514	1,752	371	653	565	437	355	8,990	43,101
2013-14[1]	6,800	355	6,960	12,335	2,582	1,478	375	698	670	530	355	9,131	44,860
2014-15[2]	7,260	395	7,215	13,343	2,584	1,496	381	750	708	537	362	9,324	47,151

Crop year beginning October 1.   [1] Preliminary.   [2] Forecast.   *Source: Foreign Agricultural Service, U.S. Department of Agriculture (FAS-USDA)*

World Consumption of Soybean Oil   In Thousands of Metric Tons

Crop Year	Algeria	Argentina	Bangladesh	Brazil	China	Egypt	European Union	India	Iran	Korea, South	Mexico	United States	World Total
2005-06	25,012	1,468	21,920	27,296	10,904	5,381	2,280	2,945	927	530	1,607	37,416	146,431
2006-07	26,061	1,332	24,110	28,465	11,693	5,255	2,299	3,010	1,025	632	1,605	39,037	153,821
2007-08	27,071	925	24,890	31,280	11,808	6,705	2,218	2,930	1,092	825	1,525	38,359	158,751
2008-09	24,363	1,145	24,700	32,475	10,223	5,960	1,895	2,850	1,140	1,176	1,510	35,473	152,169
2009-10	26,624	1,200	26,120	38,644	9,950	6,240	1,908	2,850	1,225	1,535	1,581	37,836	165,277
2010-11	29,312	1,420	28,160	43,560	9,633	7,440	1,647	2,870	1,235	1,708	1,620	35,608	174,427
2011-12	27,945	1,580	29,510	48,288	9,668	7,720	1,483	2,910	705	1,891	1,588	37,217	180,452
2012-13	26,089	1,720	27,310	51,440	10,432	7,920	1,447	2,890	2,310	1,923	1,510	36,174	181,287
2013-14[1]	27,950	1,580	27,980	54,531	10,737	6,640	1,465	3,088	2,750	2,333	1,512	36,909	188,780
2014-15[2]	29,575	1,740	29,000	59,004	10,750	6,800	1,491	3,325	2,820	2,364	1,550	38,828	199,494

Crop year beginning October 1.   [1] Preliminary.   [2] Forecast.   *Source: Foreign Agricultural Service, U.S. Department of Agriculture (FAS-USDA)*

World Exports of Soybean Oil   In Thousands of Metric Tons

Crop Year	Argentina	Bolivia	Brazil	Canada	European Union	Malaysia	Paraguay	Russia	South Africa	Ukraine	United States	Vietnam	World Total
2005-06	5,597	220	2,466	23	273	135	187	1	7	8	523	----	9,788
2006-07	5,970	210	2,462	24	244	143	260	5	1	9	851	8	10,531
2007-08	5,789	143	2,388	50	335	123	260	10	3	8	1,320	----	10,841
2008-09	4,704	218	1,909	38	398	109	229	127	12	28	995	----	9,183
2009-10	4,453	230	1,449	47	386	126	243	170	30	44	1,524	----	9,160
2010-11	4,561	232	1,668	66	463	134	255	136	62	43	1,466	28	9,643
2011-12	3,794	224	1,885	73	742	157	127	142	69	53	664	73	8,469
2012-13	4,244	260	1,251	102	1,011	130	558	129	75	68	982	44	9,332
2013-14[1]	4,090	260	1,378	92	771	148	630	270	85	118	851	80	9,233
2014-15[2]	4,350	280	1,170	110	800	134	650	220	85	135	953	90	9,445

Crop year beginning October 1.   [1] Preliminary.   [2] Forecast.   *Source: Foreign Agricultural Service, U.S. Department of Agriculture (FAS-USDA)*

World Imports of Soybean Oil   In Thousands of Metric Tons

Crop Year	Algeria	Bangla-desh	China	Colom-bia	Egypt	European Union	India	Iran	Korea, South	Peru	Morocco	Vene-zuela	World Total
2005-06	310	262	1,516	163	240	719	1,727	600	265	302	372	285	9,077
2006-07	295	327	2,404	170	124	978	1,447	606	302	300	360	375	9,973
2007-08	383	401	2,727	184	482	1,038	733	545	296	292	421	400	10,397
2008-09	365	254	2,494	164	320	795	1,060	376	266	272	350	388	9,166
2009-10	402	349	1,514	184	243	547	1,598	275	318	352	379	302	8,717
2010-11	516	376	1,319	238	644	906	945	704	300	315	397	366	9,507
2011-12	438	420	1,502	257	----	386	1,174	411	343	344	367	415	7,954
2012-13	575	397	1,409	216	324	300	1,086	543	300	363	364	374	8,455
2013-14[1]	565	441	1,353	288	213	320	1,830	551	278	380	400	385	9,198
2014-15[2]	580	450	1,000	295	280	310	1,925	600	350	400	380	400	9,199

Crop year beginning October 1.   [1] Preliminary.   [2] Forecast.   *Source: Foreign Agricultural Service, U.S. Department of Agriculture (FAS-USDA)*

Supply and Distribution of Soybean Oil in the United States   In Millions of Pounds

| | | | | | Domestic Disappearance | | | | | | | | | |
| | | | | | Food | | | | | | Non-Food | | | |
Crop Year	Pro-duction	Imports	Stocks Oct. 1	Exports	Total Domestic	Short-ening	Mar-garine	Cooking & Salad Oils	Other Edible	Total Food	Paint & Varnish	Resins & Plastics	Total Non-Food	Total Disap-pearance
2005-06	20,387	35	1,699	1,153	17,959	7,799	848	8,657	NA	17,304	117	85	1,866	19,112
2006-07	20,489	37	3,010	1,877	18,574	6,225	961	8,708	NA	15,894	63	98	3,445	20,451
2007-08	20,580	65	3,085	2,911	18,335	5,271	902	9,612	NA	15,785	33	108	3,466	21,246
2008-09	18,745	90	2,485	2,193	16,265	4,445	W	10,321	NA	14,766	W	106	2,182	18,459
2009-10	19,615	103	2,861	3,359	15,814	3,895	W	9,595	NA	13,490	W	W	3,166	19,173
2010-11	18,888	159	3,406	3,233	16,794	3,670	W	9,541	NA	13,211	NA	NA	NA	20,027
2011-12	19,740	149	2,425	1,464	18,311	NA	NA	NA	NA	NA	NA	NA	NA	19,775
2012-13	19,820	196	2,540	2,164	18,686	NA	NA	NA	NA	NA	NA	NA	NA	20,851
2013-14[1]	20,130	165	1,705	1,877	18,958	NA	NA	NA	NA	NA	NA	NA	NA	20,835
2014-15[2]	20,580	160	1,165	2,050	18,350	NA	NA	NA	NA	NA	NA	NA	NA	20,550

Crop year beginning October 1.   [1] Preliminary .   [2] Forecast.   *Source: Economic Research Service, U.S. Department of Agriculture (ERS-USDA)*

U.S. Exports of Soybean Oil[1], by Country of Destination   In Metric Tons

Crop Year	Canada	Ecuador	Ethiopia	Haiti	India	Mexico	Morocco	Pakistan	Panama	Peru	Turkey	Vene-zuela	Total
2004-05	68,162	----	1,529	4,375	29,385	162,913	6,579	15,506	7,247	15,459	21	6,063	600,399
2005-06	76,342	2	3,270	3,972	23,031	108,515	21,951	12,000	1,546	19,588	4,032	38	523,153
2006-07	80,068	3	550	1,962	14,301	151,641	60,347	2	3,409	5,940	16	26,806	851,221
2007-08	90,361	3,009	2,141	14,138	11	269,249	107,323	----	6,817	183	73	82,035	1,320,430
2008-09	41,500	----	840	19,127	146,086	173,041	110,249	----	1,715	37,061	2,598	54,438	994,927
2009-10	41,390	----	720	24,616	162,342	211,456	231,996	6,795	5,151	92,004	54	52,702	1,523,384
2010-11	35,001	8,722	700	13,314	49	167,760	291,890	20,900	6,123	44,999	1,120	57,707	1,466,468
2011-12	25,417	15	890	3,156	12	151,224	159,917	----	2,307	7	1,092	22,942	664,111
2012-13	30,867	28	----	2,230	113,104	187,117	23,248	0	6,374	193	76	51,377	981,358
2013-14[2]	31,731	13	390	1,576	22	190,419	29,702	0	4,139	42,121	----	18,988	851,198

Crop year beginning October 1.   [1] Crude & Refined oil combined as such.   [2] Preliminary.   *Source: Foreign Agricultural Service, U.S. Department of Agriculture (FAS-USDA)*

SOYBEAN OIL

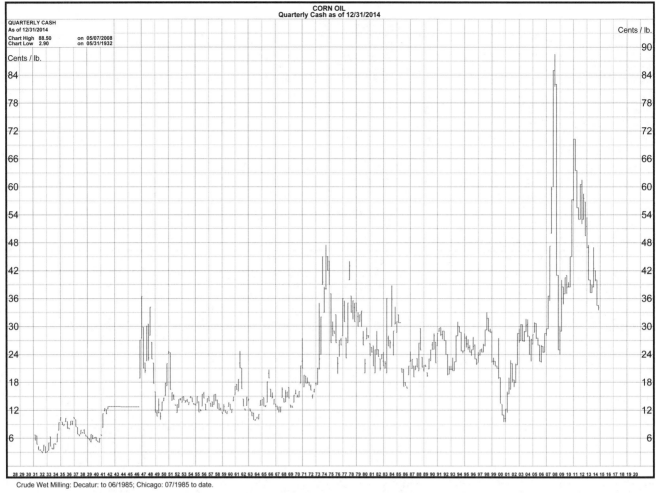

CORN OIL
Quarterly Cash as of 12/31/2014

QUARTERLY CASH
As of 12/31/2014

Chart High 88.50 on 05/07/2008
Chart Low 2.90 on 05/31/1932

Cents / lb.

Crude Wet Milling: Decatur: to 06/1985; Chicago: 07/1985 to date.

Consumption of Soybean Oil in End Products in the United States   In Millions of Pounds

Year	Jan.	Feb.	Mar.	Apr.	May	June	July	Aug.	Sept.	Oct.	Nov.	Dec.	Total
2002	1,461.5	1,395.3	1,568.0	1,505.1	1,549.7	1,492.4	1,490.5	1,545.5	1,543.7	1,710.2	1,587.2	1,458.8	18,308
2003	1,418.1	1,347.4	1,490.0	1,494.9	1,552.6	1,493.1	1,509.5	1,483.5	1,577.7	1,660.7	1,544.2	1,451.4	18,023
2004	1,388.1	1,417.6	1,555.2	1,468.0	1,506.7	1,421.1	1,429.2	1,473.6	1,483.2	1,558.3	1,533.7	1,368.9	17,604
2005	1,365.4	1,609.2	1,609.2	1,587.2	1,589.5	1,496.2	1,523.3	1,570.4	1,527.2	1,589.6	1,546.9	1,416.2	18,430
2006	1,505.2	1,368.8	1,661.4	1,561.1	1,634.9	1,653.2	1,575.5	1,746.2	1,727.9	1,775.6	1,638.6	1,571.5	19,420
2007	1,547.3	1,357.8	1,624.8	1,586.7	1,728.6	1,640.3	1,812.9	1,793.1	1,699.5	1,757.8	1,618.9	1,548.4	19,716
2008	1,623.6	1,476.9	1,625.3	1,580.9	1,510.8	1,528.4	1,589.8	1,624.2	1,559.2	1,662.7	1,500.3	1,348.5	18,630
2009	1,251.8	1,245.9	1,346.9	1,282.5	1,275.3	1,283.6	1,357.4	1,374.8	1,397.9	1,606.5	1,468.2	1,377.4	16,268
2010	1,231.8	1,227.6	1,350.0	1,215.6	1,183.4	1,232.8	1,229.6	1,274.4	1,262.6	1,342.1	1,293.8	1,192.1	15,036
2011[1]	1,222.6	1,190.1	1,458.3	1,413.2	1,421.6	1,500.8	1,508.7	NA	NA	NA	NA	NA	16,655

[1] Preliminary.   *Source: Bureau of the Census, U.S. Department of Commerce*

U.S. Exports of Soybean Oil (Crude and Refined)   In Millions of Pounds

Year	Jan.	Feb.	Mar.	Apr.	May	June	July	Aug.	Sept.	Oct.	Nov.	Dec.	Total
2005	77.0	217.2	74.6	74.8	71.9	68.5	52.4	137.3	65.9	76.3	154.1	107.8	1,178
2006	71.3	67.0	178.2	96.8	53.8	82.0	89.4	64.7	111.8	167.1	120.3	276.7	1,379
2007	176.4	118.2	75.2	102.7	121.3	123.5	202.0	202.3	190.8	132.9	198.0	391.3	2,035
2008	157.7	509.9	385.5	427.1	163.4	171.7	125.5	183.8	64.2	138.1	102.3	119.9	2,549
2009	96.4	145.9	161.3	350.3	277.9	86.5	247.6	302.9	164.2	332.1	241.1	390.3	2,797
2010	513.9	399.5	408.0	148.0	77.2	129.1	179.1	365.7	174.5	440.3	432.5	394.5	3,662
2011	466.3	301.2	330.1	188.6	91.7	129.7	120.0	114.6	223.6	78.0	107.8	59.6	2,211
2012	91.4	142.5	69.8	121.2	193.6	123.8	198.1	206.7	71.6	253.1	274.6	358.7	2,105
2013	258.9	339.9	136.7	136.0	79.4	75.5	70.7	92.8	88.0	71.4	129.1	320.7	1,799
2014[1]	267.1	276.2	195.5	93.0	45.9	78.7	198.0	119.0	75.6	159.3	231.4	233.8	1,973

[1] Preliminary.   *Source: Bureau of the Census, U.S. Department of Commerce*

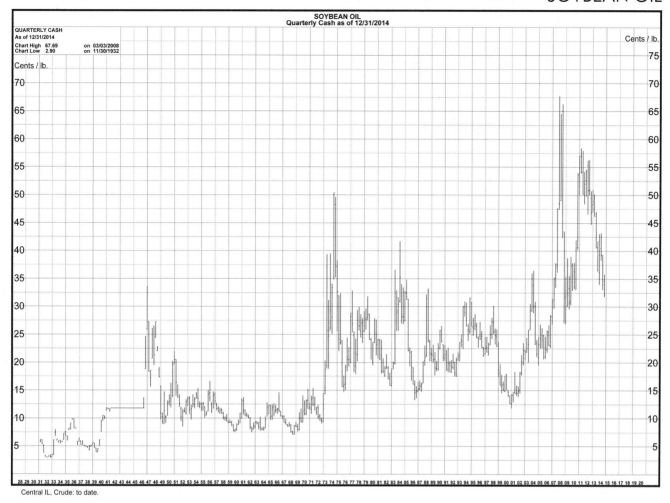

Central IL, Crude: to date.

Stocks of Soybean Oil (Crude and Refined) at Factories and Warehouses in the U.S. In Millions of Pounds

Year	Oct.	Nov.	Dec.	Jan.	Feb.	Mar.	Apr.	May	June	July	Aug.	Sept.
2001-02	2,877.2	2,724.9	2,787.4	2,868.1	3,038.5	2,896.4	2,952.7	2,856.8	2,943.2	2,735.9	2,529.7	2,521.7
2002-03	2,358.6	2,280.1	2,326.1	2,398.0	2,395.7	2,271.9	2,244.6	2,120.2	2,053.9	1,928.5	1,794.2	1,654.4
2003-04	1,490.6	1,411.8	1,530.4	1,579.9	1,945.6	1,988.0	1,855.9	1,644.1	1,651.6	1,514.0	1,412.0	1,180.6
2004-05	1,075.6	1,269.4	1,191.2	1,311.1	1,560.1	1,646.8	1,812.7	1,797.1	1,888.7	1,838.0	1,988.8	1,727.0
2005-06	1,699.0	1,883.5	1,851.8	2,190.5	2,498.7	2,673.4	2,718.1	2,755.4	2,885.0	2,919.2	3,106.1	3,061.2
2006-07	3,009.8	3,012.3	3,081.9	3,090.6	3,356.7	3,477.7	3,558.4	3,500.0	3,468.7	3,549.8	3,399.6	3,200.4
2007-08	3,085.2	3,224.9	3,235.2	3,277.0	3,408.0	3,278.3	3,083.5	2,925.8	2,989.0	2,906.0	2,793.2	2,567.4
2008-09	2,484.6	2,388.5	2,519.0	2,629.6	2,992.3	3,124.1	3,191.6	3,279.4	3,338.8	3,530.3	3,448.9	3,134.0
2009-10	2,860.5	2,809.4	2,990.5	3,150.5	3,221.7	3,295.7	3,317.6	3,152.1	3,521.9	3,597.5	3,594.1	3,337.8
2010-11[1]	3,405.8	3,285.0	3,349.5	3,531.9	3,415.4	3,375.5	3,409.8	3,342.1	3,177.3	3,153.1	3,128.9	2,868.1

On First of Month. [1] Preliminary. *Source: Economic Research Service, U.S. Department of Agriculture (ERS-USDA)*

Average Price of Crude Domestic Soybean Oil (in Tank Cars) F.O.B. Decatur In Cents Per Pound

Year	Oct.	Nov.	Dec.	Jan.	Feb.	Mar.	Apr.	May	June	July	Aug.	Sept.	Average
2005-06	24.26	22.52	21.00	21.63	22.21	23.21	22.98	24.76	24.20	25.86	24.80	23.54	23.41
2006-07	24.80	27.64	27.63	28.00	28.94	29.74	31.06	32.90	34.01	35.74	34.87	36.89	31.02
2007-08	38.10	42.68	45.16	49.77	56.68	57.27	56.58	58.27	62.43	60.54	50.78	46.09	52.03
2008-09	35.50	31.55	29.30	32.16	28.93	28.23	32.76	36.06	35.66	31.08	33.69	30.96	32.16
2009-10	33.15	36.59	36.81	34.88	34.69	36.39	37.11	35.41	34.47	35.07	37.57	39.21	35.95
2010-11	44.02	47.62	51.51	53.84	54.21	54.07	56.65	56.09	55.68	55.16	54.39	55.13	53.20
2011-12	51.73	51.44	50.17	50.99	52.36	53.43	54.96	50.69	48.65	51.96	52.65	53.81	51.90
2012-13	49.31	46.27	47.16	48.85	49.33	48.62	49.28	49.31	47.84	45.19	42.33	42.12	47.13
2013-14	39.66	39.58	37.63	34.95	37.11	40.82	41.87	40.68	39.84	37.60	35.04	33.99	38.23
2014-15[1]	34.10	33.45	32.56	32.33									33.11

[1] Preliminary. *Source: Economic Research Service, U.S. Department of Agriculture (ERS-USDA)*

SOYBEAN OIL

SOYBEAN OIL - CBOT
Weekly Nearest Futures as of 01/02/2015

WEEKLY NEAREST FUTURES
As of 01/02/2015
Chart High 71.26 on 03/04/2008
Chart Low 18.82 on 02/03/2005

Nearby Futures through Last Trading Day.

Volume of Trading of Soybean Oil Futures in Chicago   In Thousands of Contracts

Year	Jan.	Feb.	Mar.	Apr.	May	June	July	Aug.	Sept.	Oct.	Nov.	Dec.	Total
2005	475.1	799.9	579.6	636.3	565.5	852.3	548.3	637.1	594.8	607.1	672.8	707.4	7,676
2006	531.9	611.2	597.6	866.4	688.6	1,024.5	801.2	816.7	729.0	939.3	1,003.3	878.8	9,489
2007	784.1	1,091.9	765.0	1,218.3	805.3	1,476.9	1,113.7	1,092.0	947.7	1,213.6	1,324.4	1,337.9	13,171
2008	1,294.7	1,541.4	1,291.0	1,551.1	1,107.0	1,467.6	1,624.2	1,386.9	1,441.7	1,414.4	1,252.4	1,455.9	16,828
2009	1,211.9	1,518.5	1,189.8	1,429.7	1,202.9	1,993.4	1,543.9	1,400.4	1,217.9	1,342.1	1,527.1	1,554.4	17,132
2010	1,184.3	1,787.0	1,414.2	1,924.2	1,224.4	2,198.2	1,721.4	1,646.8	1,561.7	1,588.9	2,297.3	2,242.9	20,791
2011	1,660.1	2,427.9	2,153.7	2,276.7	1,613.1	2,427.4	1,616.1	1,924.0	2,027.5	1,866.4	2,296.1	1,867.6	24,157
2012	1,649.0	2,155.3	2,107.2	2,732.0	2,333.5	2,846.1	2,394.5	2,206.0	1,958.3	2,392.5	2,683.3	2,169.7	27,628
2013	2,043.6	2,403.6	1,465.9	2,453.7	1,831.6	2,213.7	1,918.7	1,850.1	1,560.5	1,908.5	2,263.2	1,892.7	23,806
2014	1,752.1	2,531.9	1,657.5	2,058.5	1,450.2	2,199.9	1,869.4	1,775.4	1,768.9	2,199.9	2,370.5	2,119.1	23,753

Contract size = 60,000 lbs.   *Source: CME Group; Chicago Board of Trade (CBT)*

Average Open Interest of Soybean Oil Futures in Chicago   In Contracts

Year	Jan.	Feb.	Mar.	Apr.	May	June	July	Aug.	Sept.	Oct.	Nov.	Dec.
2005	159,229	174,091	161,971	145,808	135,515	155,962	147,542	132,351	139,489	165,634	175,229	186,760
2006	171,317	183,717	192,643	204,132	244,580	241,962	276,251	269,208	259,464	256,153	279,091	273,375
2007	256,800	283,761	285,436	312,454	301,566	309,109	294,005	285,255	277,219	276,874	306,390	298,906
2008	289,892	292,918	287,995	275,016	253,974	259,416	258,412	254,496	256,621	257,226	252,077	220,725
2009	204,502	211,632	206,299	208,101	217,198	246,451	245,978	239,386	217,068	229,387	248,176	229,970
2010	219,042	283,115	282,973	290,577	299,379	319,098	284,484	292,426	290,685	325,697	358,850	347,185
2011	375,563	391,930	358,625	357,657	313,673	322,642	287,408	278,784	287,250	297,663	305,955	305,279
2012	296,889	314,752	340,827	380,916	386,924	377,817	329,673	332,182	314,359	322,262	347,898	310,982
2013	313,467	327,562	329,956	353,044	351,425	357,052	340,600	308,032	291,005	314,235	333,607	344,607
2014	364,056	339,211	302,398	326,545	313,757	333,690	325,337	347,395	373,086	391,486	395,330	365,382

Contract size = 60,000 lbs.   *Source: CME Group; Chicago Board of Trade (CBT)*

Soybeans

Soybean is the common name for the annual leguminous plant and its seed. The soybean is a member of the oilseed family and is not considered a grain. The soybean seeds are contained in pods and are nearly spherical in shape. The seeds are usually light yellow in color. The seeds contain 20% oil and 40% protein. Soybeans were an ancient food crop in China, Japan, and Korea and were only introduced to the U.S. in the early 1800s. Today, soybeans are the second largest crop produced in the U.S. behind corn. Soybean production in the U.S. is concentrated in the Midwest and the lower Mississippi Valley. Soybean crops in the U.S. are planted in May or June and are harvested in autumn. Soybean plants usually reach maturity 100-150 days after planting depending on growing conditions.

Soybeans are used to produce a wide variety of food products. The key value of soybeans lies in the relatively high protein content, which makes it an excellent source of protein without many of the negative factors of animal meat. Popular soy-based food products include whole soybeans (roasted for snacks or used in sauces, stews and soups), soy oil for cooking and baking, soy flour, protein concentrates, isolated soy protein (which contains up to 92% protein), soy milk and baby formula (as an alternative to dairy products), soy yogurt, soy cheese, soy nut butter, soy sprouts, tofu and tofu products (soybean curd), soy sauce (which is produced by a fermentation process), and meat alternatives (hamburgers, breakfast sausage, etc).

The primary market for soybean futures is at the CME Group. The CME's soybean contract calls for the delivery of 5,000 bushels of No. 2 yellow soybeans (at contract par), No. 1 yellow soybeans (at 6 cents per bushel above the contract price), or No. 3 yellow soybeans (at a 6 cents under the contract price). Soybean futures are also traded at exchanges in Brazil, Argentina, China, and Tokyo.

Prices – CME soybean futures prices (Barchart.com electronic symbol ZS) moved higher the first half of 2014 and posted the high for the year at $15.37 a bushel in May 2014, a 1-1/2 year high. Soybeans were supported by strong demand, tight U.S. supplies, and drought concerns in South America. U.S. soybean quarterly stocks on March 1, 2014 dropped to a 10-year low of 992.3 million bushels. In addition, the USDA in the May 2014 WASDE report raised its U.S. 2013/14 soybean export estimate to a record 1.6 billion bushels (+21% yr/yr), and forecast that 2014/15 U.S. soybean exports would climb to a new record of 1.625 billion bushels. The USDA also cut its global 2013/14 soybean production estimate to 283.79 MMT from 287.69 MMT due to drought in South America. Robust Chinese demand was supportive for soybean prices as China imported 28 MMT of U.S. soybeans from Sep 1, 2013 to Apr 24, 2014, up +33% yr/yr. China soybean imports in 2013 had previously climbed +8.6% yr/yr to a record 63.4 MMT. Soybeans plummeted into Q4 and posted the low for the year in October at $9.04 a bushel, a 5-year low. Exceptional weather led to ideal growing conditions as the USDA's Weekly Crop Progress showed that 72% of the U.S. soybean crop was in good-to-excellent condition as of Sep 7, up +20 points yr/yr and the best condition in 30 years. This led the USDA in the October WASDE report to raise its 2014/15 U.S. soybean production estimate to a record 3.927 billion bushels and raise its 21014/15 global soybean production estimate to a record 311.2 MMT. Supplies were also abundant after the USDA forecast U.S. 2014/15 soybean ending stocks at 450 million bushels, an 8-year high, and projected 2014/15 global soybean ending stocks at a record 90.67 MMT. The plunge in prices enticed foreign demand for U.S. supplies as U.S. October 2014 soybean exports rose to a record 9.2 MMT. This helped soybean prices recover into year-end, but they still finished 2014 down -22.4% at $10.19 a bushel.

Supply – World soybean production during the 2014-15 marketing year (Sep-Aug) rose by +10.8% yr/yr to 314.369 million metric tons. World soybean production has risen sharply from the 62 million metric ton level seen in 1980. The world's largest soybean producers were the U.S. with 34.5% of world production in 2014-15, Brazil (30.4%), Argentina (17.5%), China (3.8%), and India (3.3%). China's soybean production has roughly doubled since 1980. Brazil's production has risen just over four times since 1980.

U.S. soybean production in 2014-15 rose by +18.2% yr/yr to 3.968 billion bushels, a new record high. U.S. farmers harvested 83.061 million acres of soybeans in 2014-15, which rose +8.9% yr/yr, a new record high. The average yield in 2014-15 was up +8.6% yr/yr to 47.8 bushels per acre, a new record high. U.S. ending stocks for the 2014-15 marketing year fell by -34.6% to 92.0 million bushels.

Demand – Total U.S. distribution in 2014-15 rose +5.1% to 3.655 billion bushels. The distribution tables for U.S. soybeans for the 2014-15 marketing year show that 48.7% of U.S. soybean usage went for crushing into soybean oil and meal, 48.2% for exports, and 3.2% for seed and residual. The quantity of U.S. soybeans that went for crushing rose +2.7% yr/yr in 2014-15 to 1.780 billion bushels. The world soybean crush rose +5.1% yr/yr in 2014-15 to a new record high of 252.528 million metric tons, which was about double the level seen in 1993-94.

Trade – World exports of soybeans in 2014-15 rose +3.2% yr/yr to a new record high of 116.487 million metric tons. The world's largest soybean exporters in 2014-15 were the U.S. with 41.4% of world exports, Brazil with 39.5% of world exports, and Argentina with 6.9% of world exports. U.S. soybean exports in 2014-15 rose +7.5% yr/yr to a 48.172 million metric tons, a new record high. Brazil's soybean exports have more than doubled in the past decade and Canada's exports have almost tripled.

World imports in 2014-15 rose +2.2% yr/yr to a new record high of 112.988 million metric tons. The world's largest importers of soybeans in 2014-15 were China with 65.5% of world imports, the European Union with 11.3%, Mexico with 3.5%, and Japan with 2.6%. China's imports in 2014-15 rose +5.2% yr/yr to a record level of 74.000 million metric tons, which is far from negligible levels prior to 1994.

SOYBEANS

World Production of Soybeans   In Thousands of Metric Tons

Crop Year[4]	Argen-tina	Bolivia	Brazil	Canada	China	European Union	India	Para-guay	Ukraine	Uruguay	Russia	United States	World Total
2005-06	40,500	2,060	57,000	3,156	16,350	1,294	7,000	3,641	613	681	689	83,507	220,870
2006-07	48,800	1,650	59,000	3,466	15,080	1,402	7,690	5,581	890	865	807	87,001	236,309
2007-08	46,200	1,050	61,000	2,686	12,725	814	9,470	5,969	723	843	652	72,859	219,017
2008-09	32,000	1,600	57,800	3,336	15,540	747	9,300	3,647	813	1,170	744	80,749	212,084
2009-10	54,500	1,665	69,000	3,581	14,980	951	9,700	6,462	1,044	1,987	942	91,470	260,556
2010-11	49,000	2,300	75,300	4,445	15,080	1,198	10,100	7,128	1,680	1,855	1,222	90,663	264,246
2011-12	40,100	2,320	66,500	4,467	14,485	1,220	11,700	4,043	2,264	2,726	1,749	84,291	240,493
2012-13[1]	49,300	2,634	82,000	5,086	13,050	948	12,200	8,202	2,410	3,650	1,880	82,791	268,765
2013-14[2]	54,000	2,400	86,700	5,359	12,200	1,229	9,500	8,200	2,774	3,500	1,636	91,389	283,736
2014-15[3]	55,000	2,700	95,500	6,050	11,800	1,715	10,500	8,500	3,800	3,400	2,500	108,014	314,369

[1] Preliminary.   [2] Estimate.   [3] Forecast.   [4] Spilt year includes Northern Hemisphere crops harvested in the late months of the first year shown combined with Southern Hemisphere crops harvested in the early months of the following year.   *Sources: Foreign Agricultural Service, U.S. Department of Agriculture (FAS-USDA)*

World Crushings of Soybeans   In Thousands of Metric Tons

Crop Year	Argen-tina	Bolivia	Brazil	Canada	China	India	Indo-nesia	Mexico	Para-guay	Russia	Thailand	United States	World Total
2005-06	31,888	1,843	28,286	34,500	13,802	6,740	3,004	3,723	1,181	675	2,040	47,324	185,982
2006-07	33,586	1,670	31,109	35,970	14,801	6,585	3,033	3,800	1,305	805	2,040	49,198	195,578
2007-08	34,607	1,160	32,117	39,518	14,947	8,400	2,919	3,700	1,390	1,051	1,940	49,081	202,287
2008-09	31,243	1,435	31,869	41,035	12,940	7,450	2,497	3,600	1,450	1,497	1,920	45,230	193,618
2009-10	34,127	1,520	33,700	48,830	12,595	7,800	2,535	3,600	1,558	1,950	2,010	47,673	209,584
2010-11	37,614	1,800	36,330	55,000	12,430	9,300	2,149	3,625	1,570	2,170	2,060	44,851	221,312
2011-12	35,886	2,000	38,083	60,970	12,414	9,650	1,960	3,675	900	2,400	2,020	46,348	228,331
2012-13[1]	33,611	2,175	35,235	64,950	13,231	9,900	1,915	3,650	2,950	2,440	1,920	45,967	230,185
2013-14[2]	36,175	2,000	36,276	68,850	13,591	8,300	1,940	3,900	3,500	2,960	1,925	47,192	240,316
2014-15[3]	38,050	2,200	37,600	74,500	13,600	8,500	1,970	4,200	3,600	3,000	1,970	48,444	252,528

[1] Preliminary.   [2] Estimate.   [3] Forecast.   *Sources: Foreign Agricultural Service, U.S. Department of Agriculture (FAS-USDA)*

World Exports of Soybeans   In Thousands of Metric Tons

Crop Year	Argen-tina	Bolivia	Brazil	Canada	China	India	Para-guay	Russia	Serbia	Ukraine	United States	Uruguay	World Total
2005-06	7,249	58	25,911	1,326	354	6	2,380	3	3	224	25,579	653	63,852
2006-07	9,560	80	23,485	1,683	446	1	4,136	16	4	420	30,386	813	71,137
2007-08	13,839	79	25,364	1,753	453	12	4,100	5	1	190	31,538	818	78,321
2008-09	5,590	123	29,987	2,017	400	55	2,620	2	2	277	34,817	1,097	77,212
2009-10	13,088	50	28,578	2,247	184	15	4,070		5	263	40,798	1,940	91,440
2010-11	9,205	24	29,951	2,943	190	18	5,226	1	82	989	40,959	1,820	91,702
2011-12	7,368	322	36,257	2,933	275	39	3,574	90	17	1,338	37,156	2,607	92,157
2012-13[1]	7,738	544	41,904	3,470	266	115	5,518	97	6	1,323	35,846	3,532	100,534
2013-14[2]	7,841	300	46,829	3,471	215	183	4,400	30	35	1,260	44,815	3,340	112,829
2014-15[3]	8,000	275	46,000	3,700	300	150	4,520	100	70	1,900	48,172	3,180	116,487

[1] Preliminary.   [2] Estimate.   [3] Forecast.   *Sources: Foreign Agricultural Service, U.S. Department of Agriculture (FAS-USDA)*

World Imports of Soybeans   In Thousands of Metric Tons

Crop Year	China	Egypt	European Union	Indo-nesia	Japan	Korea, South	Mexico	Russia	Taiwan	Thailand	Turkey	Vietnam	World Total
2005-06	28,317	776	14,014	1,187	3,962	1,190	3,667	2	2,498	1,473	889	46	64,099
2006-07	28,726	1,328	15,181	1,309	4,094	1,231	3,844	34	2,436	1,532	1,217	74	68,906
2007-08	37,816	1,061	15,139	1,147	4,014	1,232	3,614	442	2,148	1,753	1,339	120	78,373
2008-09	41,098	1,575	13,213	1,393	3,396	1,167	3,327	837	2,216	1,510	1,076	184	77,426
2009-10	50,338	1,638	12,683	1,620	3,401	1,197	3,523	1,037	2,469	1,660	1,648	231	86,817
2010-11	52,339	1,644	12,472	1,898	2,917	1,239	3,498	1,000	2,454	2,139	1,351	932	88,760
2011-12	59,231	1,649	12,070	1,922	2,759	1,139	3,606	741	2,285	1,907	1,057	1,290	93,453
2012-13[1]	59,865	1,730	12,538	1,795	2,830	1,115	3,409	691	2,286	1,867	1,249	1,291	95,888
2013-14[2]	70,364	1,674	12,985	2,200	2,894	1,271	3,700	1,500	2,335	1,798	1,608	1,350	110,512
2014-15[3]	74,000	1,870	12,750	2,350	2,900	1,300	3,950	700	2,350	2,000	1,600	1,600	112,988

[1] Preliminary.   [2] Estimate.   [3] Forecast.   *Sources: Foreign Agricultural Service, U.S. Department of Agriculture (FAS-USDA)*

World Ending Stocks of Soybeans   In Thousands of Metric Tons

Crop Year	Argen- tina	Bolivia	Brazil	Canada	China	European Union	India	Japan	Para- guay	Turkey	Ukraine	United States	World Total
2005-06	15,892	313	17,668	636	4,573	733	155	172	93	270	28	12,229	53,950
2006-07	21,897	276	19,377	655	1,807	1,007	218	185	148	261	20	15,617	62,972
2007-08	20,945	51	20,246	174	2,472	707	146	262	491	382	30	5,580	52,485
2008-09	15,633	1	13,434	220	7,455	454	561	263	----	407	28	3,761	43,022
2009-10	21,039	1	17,480	305	13,209	541	1,076	239	674	701	146	4,106	60,450
2010-11	21,403	385	23,636	297	14,538	820	438	160	898	644	113	5,852	70,521
2011-12	16,300	293	13,024	232	15,909	800	800	128	357	398	240	4,610	54,223
2012-13[1]	21,813	118	15,330	178	12,378	233	1,135	184	38	460	299	3,825	57,145
2013-14[2]	29,000	127	16,530	282	14,427	219	606	231	230	406	286	2,503	66,160
2014-15[3]	34,851	262	25,830	657	14,027	344	656	266	450	426	387	11,159	90,780

[1] Preliminary.   [2] Estimate.   [3] Forecast.   *Sources: Foreign Agricultural Service, U.S. Department of Agriculture (FAS-USDA)*

Supply and Distribution of Soybeans in the United States   In Millions of Bushels

Crop Year Beginning Sept. 1	Stocks, Sept. 1 Farms	Stocks, Sept. 1 Mills, Elevators[3]	Total	Production	Total Supply	Crushings	Exports	Seed, Feed & Residual Use	Total Distri- bution
2005-06	99.7	156.0	255.7	3,063	3,322	1,739	940	194	2,873
2006-07	176.3	273.0	449.3	3,188	3,655	1,808	1,116	157	3,081
2007-08	143.0	430.8	573.8	2,676	3,261	1,803	1,159	94	3,056
2008-09	47.0	158.0	205.0	2,967	3,185	1,662	1,279	106	3,047
2009-10	35.1	103.1	138.2	3,359	3,512	1,752	1,499	110	3,361
2010-11	35.4	115.5	150.9	3,329	3,495	1,648	1,501	130	3,280
2011-12	48.5	166.5	215.0	3,094	3,325	1,703	1,365	87	3,155
2012-13	38.3	131.1	169.4	3,042	3,252	1,689	1,317	105	3,111
2013-14[1]	39.6	101.0	140.6	3,358	3,570	1,734	1,647	98	3,478
2014-15[2]	21.3	70.7	92.0	3,969	4,086	1,795	1,790	116	3,701

[1] Preliminary.   [2] Estimate.   [3] Also warehouses.   *Source: Economic Research Service, U.S. Department of Agriculture (ERS-USDA)*

Salient Statistics & Official Crop Production Reports of Soybeans in the United States   In Millions of Bushels

Year	Planted 1,000 Acres	Acreage Har- vested 1,000 Acres	Yield Per Acre (Bu.)	Farm Price ($/Bu.)	Farm Value (Million Dollars)	Yield of Oil (Lbs. Per Bushel Crushed)	Yield of Meal (Lbs. Per Bushel Crushed)	Crop Production Reports In Thousands of Bushels Aug. 1	Sept. 1	Oct. 1	Nov. 1	Dec. 1	Final
2005-06	72,032	71,251	43.0	5.63	17,269	11.64	43.83	2,791,133	2,856,449	2,967,075	3,043,116	----	3,063,237
2006-07	75,522	74,602	42.9	6.67	20,468	11.34	44.03	2,927,634	3,092,970	3,188,576	3,203,908	----	3,188,247
2007-08	64,741	64,146	41.7	11.02	26,974	11.54	43.95	2,625,274	2,618,796	2,598,046	2,594,275	----	2,675,822
2008-09	75,718	74,681	39.7	10.13	29,458	11.36	43.93	2,972,577	2,933,888	2,983,023	2,920,589	----	2,967,007
2009-10	77,451	76,372	44.0	9.61	32,145	11.10	43.82	3,199,172	3,245,292	3,250,113	3,319,270	----	3,359,011
2010-11	77,404	76,610	43.5	12.17	37,547	11.54	44.39	3,433,370	3,482,899	3,408,211	3,375,067	----	3,329,181
2011-12	75,046	73,776	41.9	13.13	38,498	----	----	3,055,882	3,085,340	3,059,987	3,045,558	----	3,093,524
2012-13	77,198	76,144	40.0	14.53	43,723	----	----	2,692,014	2,634,310	2,860,290	2,971,022	----	3,042,044
2013-14[1]	76,840	76,253	44.0	13.33	43,583	----	----	3,255,444	3,149,166	NA	3,257,746	----	3,357,984
2014-15[2]	83,701	83,061	47.8	10.33	40,289	----	----	3,815,679	3,913,079	3,926,812	3,958,272	----	3,968,823

[1] Preliminary.   [2] Forecast.   NA = Not available.   *Source: National Agricultural Statistics Service, U.S. Department of Agriculture (NASS-USDA)*

Stocks of Soybeans in the United States   In Thousands of Bushels

Year	On Farms Mar. 1	June 1	Sept. 1	Dec. 1	Off Farms Mar. 1	June 1	Sept. 1	Dec. 1	Total Stocks Mar. 1	June 1	Sept. 1	Dec. 1
2005	795,000	356,100	99,700	1,345,000	586,364	343,174	156,038	1,157,098	1,381,364	699,274	255,738	2,502,098
2006	872,000	495,500	176,300	1,461,000	797,206	495,199	273,026	1,240,366	1,669,206	990,699	449,326	2,701,366
2007	910,000	500,000	143,000	1,100,000	876,887	592,185	430,810	1,231,860	1,786,887	1,092,185	573,810	2,331,860
2008	593,000	226,600	47,000	1,189,000	840,982	449,543	158,034	1,086,432	1,433,982	676,143	205,034	2,275,432
2009	656,500	226,300	35,100	1,229,500	645,289	369,859	103,098	1,109,050	1,301,789	596,159	138,198	2,338,550
2010	609,200	232,600	35,400	1,091,000	660,868	338,523	115,485	1,187,084	1,270,068	571,123	150,885	2,278,084
2011	505,000	217,700	48,500	1,139,000	743,800	401,583	166,513	1,230,885	1,248,800	619,283	215,013	2,369,885
2012	555,000	179,000	38,250	910,000	819,488	488,465	131,120	1,056,161	1,374,488	667,465	169,370	1,966,161
2013	456,700	171,100	39,550	955,000	541,320	263,564	101,007	1,198,621	998,020	434,664	140,557	2,153,621
2014[1]	381,900	109,100	21,325	1,218,000	611,928	295,945	70,666	1,305,651	993,828	405,045	91,991	2,523,651

[1] Preliminary.   *Source: National Agricultural Statistics Service, U.S. Department of Agriculture (NASS-USDA)*

SOYBEANS

Commercial Stocks of Soybeans in the United States, on First of Month   In Millions of Bushels

Year	Jan.	Feb.	Mar.	Apr.	May	June	July	Aug.	Sept.	Oct.	Nov.	Dec.
2005	26.5	21.5	19.5	16.0	14.8	12.1	11.5	8.8	5.4	17.0	36.7	36.1
2006	36.8	30.2	26.1	25.7	17.6	20.5	14.6	14.5	14.5	19.0	40.1	43.7
2007	42.0	36.5	37.3	34.3	29.7	27.4	26.6	24.6	25.5	32.0	54.0	61.3
2008	51.1	45.5	41.8	36.3	28.2	25.6	19.2	14.8	11.4	19.6	40.5	46.1
2009	44.6	36.8	27.0	15.6	13.9	11.8	10.0	5.8	5.9	24.7	40.5	44.3
2010	30.0	28.5	20.1	22.3	10.8	8.0	8.2	4.5	3.3	19.2	45.0	32.0
2011	32.6	23.2	16.0	11.3	10.2	5.9	6.2	5.7	4.6	9.8	49.4	50.7
2012	42.7	34.8	29.9	28.5	27.1	23.8	16.6	10.4	5.2	18.8	41.6	33.8
2013	25.2	20.3	16.1	10.0	6.4	6.6	4.1	2.9	2.1	27.2	36.9	35.5
2014	30.7	20.4	15.5	12.2	7.0	5.1	5.2	2.3	----	----	----	----

This report was discontinued as of August 26, 2014.   *Source: Livestock Division, U.S. Department of Agriculture (LD-USDA)*

Production of Soybeans for Beans in the United States, by State   In Millions of Bushels

Year	Arkansas	Illinois	Indiana	Iowa	Ken-tucky	Mich-igan	Minn-esota	Miss-issippi	Missouri	Neb-raska	Ohio	Tenn-essee	Total
2005-06	102.0	439.4	263.6	525.0	53.3	76.6	306.0	58.0	181.7	235.3	201.6	41.8	3,063.2
2006-07	107.5	482.4	284.0	510.1	60.3	89.6	319.0	42.9	191.2	250.5	217.1	44.1	3,188.2
2007-08	101.5	360.2	220.3	448.8	30.3	70.7	267.3	58.3	175.1	196.4	199.3	19.2	2,675.8
2008-09	123.5	428.6	244.4	449.7	47.6	69.9	264.9	78.4	191.1	226.0	161.3	49.6	2,967.0
2009-10	122.6	430.1	266.6	486.0	68.2	79.6	284.8	77.1	230.6	259.4	222.0	68.9	3,359.0
2010-11	110.3	466.1	258.5	496.2	47.3	88.7	329.0	76.2	210.4	267.8	220.3	43.7	3,329.2
2011-12	126.3	423.2	240.7	475.3	57.7	85.4	274.6	70.2	190.2	261.4	217.9	40.3	3,093.5
2012-13	137.0	384.0	225.3	419.0	58.8	85.6	304.5	87.8	158.1	207.1	206.6	46.7	3,042.0
2013-14	140.9	474.0	267.3	420.9	83.0	85.4	278.0	91.5	202.0	255.2	222.3	72.1	3,358.0
2014-15[1]	160.5	547.7	307.4	505.7	84.0	92.0	305.3	114.4	260.4	288.9	254.1	74.1	3,968.8

[1] Preliminary.   *Source: Agricultural Statistics Board, U.S. Department of Agriculture (ASB-USDA)*

U. S. Exports of Soybeans   In Millions of Bushels

Year	Sept.	Oct.	Nov.	Dec.	Jan.	Feb.	Mar.	Apr.	May	June	July	Aug.	Total
2005-06	32.3	143.1	140.1	83.1	111.8	111.3	95.6	43.4	46.5	39.0	47.6	51.0	944.8
2006-07	64.9	182.7	126.4	122.7	147.3	126.5	97.0	71.2	42.0	48.9	37.9	49.6	1,117.1
2007-08	62.1	138.7	127.5	146.1	146.2	139.3	114.9	72.7	56.3	58.8	51.2	45.9	1,159.5
2008-09	34.3	179.4	173.4	171.0	153.0	159.2	101.7	82.0	60.1	60.6	49.9	55.4	1,280.0
2009-10	39.1	198.1	299.0	226.1	226.5	170.0	131.6	55.5	32.0	28.2	37.4	56.3	1,499.9
2010-11	68.2	296.4	257.8	195.9	185.5	169.5	125.9	66.4	34.7	31.5	30.4	43.6	1,505.8
2011-12	47.6	193.3	184.2	151.2	175.0	153.5	115.7	74.1	67.1	53.9	73.8	76.5	1,365.8
2012-13	96.8	268.7	253.4	184.7	194.9	146.3	67.9	35.1	22.1	19.5	13.7	17.4	1,320.3
2013-14	64.0	275.6	322.0	259.5	265.4	200.2	116.7	43.7	32.2	22.1	18.9	16.4	1,636.6
2014-15[1]	77.6	335.2	412.1	301.7									3,379.7

[1] Preliminary.   *Source: Economic Research Service, U.S. Department of Agriculture (ERS-USDA)*

Soybean Crushed (Factory Consumption) in the United States   In Millions of Bushels

Year	Jan.	Feb.	Mar.	Apr.	May	June	July	Aug.	Sept.	Oct.	Nov.	Dec.	Total
2005-06	133.2	157.7	151.5	148.4	152.4	136.3	149.5	135.5	146.2	137.4	148.5	142.1	1,738.7
2006-07	142.4	161.7	155.1	157.4	155.5	136.9	156.1	145.0	152.1	148.9	150.4	146.2	1,807.7
2007-08	147.3	163.7	156.3	164.1	160.5	146.5	156.0	147.5	152.6	141.0	139.3	128.6	1,803.4
2008-09	125.7	150.0	144.7	141.3	145.2	135.4	144.4	140.3	146.2	140.1	128.8	119.8	1,661.9
2009-10	113.3	163.5	168.7	173.1	167.2	153.9	156.1	136.5	133.0	129.2	129.4	128.1	1,752.0
2010-11	130.4	157.2	155.1	153.0	149.2	129.4	140.3	128.0	128.0	123.6	129.6	125.0	1,648.8
2011-12	----	516.6	----	----	524.0	----	----	453.9	----	----	299.0	----	1,793.5
2012-13	----	631.2	----	----	453.5	----	----	442.3	----	----	267.3	----	1,794.3
2013-14[1]	----	675.8	----	----	448.0	----	----	414.8	----	----	292.9	----	1,831.5
2014-15[1]	----	720.3	----	----	----	----	----	----	----	----	----	----	2,881.2

[1] Preliminary.   *Source: Economic Research Service, U.S. Department of Agriculture (ERS-USDA)*

SOYBEANS - CBOT
Weekly Nearest Futures as of 01/02/2015

WEEKLY NEAREST FUTURES
As of 01/02/2015

Chart High   1794.75   on 09/04/2012
Chart Low   498.50   on 02/04/2005

Nearby Futures through Last Trading Day.

Volume of Trading of Soybean Futures in Chicago   In Thousands of Contracts

Year	Jan.	Feb.	Mar.	Apr.	May	June	July	Aug.	Sept.	Oct.	Nov.	Dec.	Total
2005	1,398.6	2,085.8	1,959.9	1,656.5	1,454.6	2,577.3	1,675.4	1,487.2	1,069.1	1,765.0	1,241.5	1,845.1	20,216
2006	1,503.4	1,889.1	1,501.2	1,916.6	1,682.6	2,443.2	1,798.2	1,638.5	1,420.2	2,884.7	2,017.4	1,952.6	22,648
2007	1,976.3	2,620.6	2,251.0	2,641.2	2,107.2	3,461.3	2,734.6	2,323.7	2,315.2	3,680.4	2,521.3	3,093.5	31,726
2008	3,528.7	3,746.2	2,895.0	3,786.1	2,272.2	3,731.2	3,134.9	2,454.4	2,615.1	3,719.0	1,910.5	2,579.7	36,373
2009	2,773.7	2,892.5	2,576.2	3,638.9	2,635.5	3,439.7	2,845.7	2,417.6	2,348.2	3,996.4	2,820.8	3,373.7	35,759
2010	2,659.0	3,392.5	2,932.8	3,414.4	2,078.2	2,946.5	2,546.1	2,266.1	2,553.0	4,660.2	3,455.9	4,029.3	36,934
2011	3,572.5	4,577.6	3,906.0	4,143.1	2,790.6	3,822.9	2,708.7	3,332.7	4,053.1	5,309.5	3,004.7	3,922.4	45,144
2012	3,342.4	4,370.8	4,388.0	5,314.9	4,556.2	4,887.6	5,195.8	3,879.3	3,925.5	5,272.1	3,027.3	3,881.7	52,042
2013	3,628.0	4,568.4	3,193.0	4,516.5	3,522.9	3,644.1	3,328.3	4,132.9	3,442.2	5,288.6	3,401.3	4,054.9	46,721
2014	3,692.7	5,090.5	3,613.9	4,191.9	2,914.6	3,929.4	3,765.7	2,967.5	3,672.1	7,261.6	3,660.2	4,408.2	49,168

Contract size = 5,000 bu.   Source: CME Group; Chicago Board of Trade (CBT)

Average Open Interest of Soybean Futures in Chicago   In Contracts

Year	Jan.	Feb.	Mar.	Apr.	May	June	July	Aug.	Sept.	Oct.	Nov.	Dec.
2005	244,197	266,745	295,324	268,081	252,582	313,724	278,738	256,853	249,030	285,070	275,308	290,370
2006	315,640	359,379	354,211	374,507	375,124	371,155	336,000	348,321	361,643	384,069	394,259	414,374
2007	416,459	478,579	474,466	470,517	465,303	549,655	536,595	495,302	526,913	580,446	586,635	582,502
2008	563,927	598,278	543,451	506,423	458,047	489,069	446,006	388,939	364,679	348,438	312,905	304,252
2009	297,316	313,704	292,160	358,857	415,599	454,846	410,718	401,752	428,320	461,463	438,531	464,281
2010	446,212	465,666	434,272	477,138	459,342	462,796	470,087	514,703	553,196	633,086	624,213	643,091
2011	643,422	673,796	618,157	624,350	559,493	582,529	529,949	524,547	590,297	567,081	521,277	525,510
2012	474,050	532,738	623,973	793,781	787,884	769,806	805,353	748,382	732,388	704,191	609,007	588,185
2013	549,767	615,897	589,572	565,212	565,761	596,479	517,022	535,645	615,389	626,484	582,859	625,222
2014	589,906	675,981	649,898	645,604	601,103	616,406	622,020	642,043	724,924	766,218	664,485	668,492

Contract size = 5,000 bu.   Source: CME Group; Chicago Board of Trade (CBT)

SOYBEANS

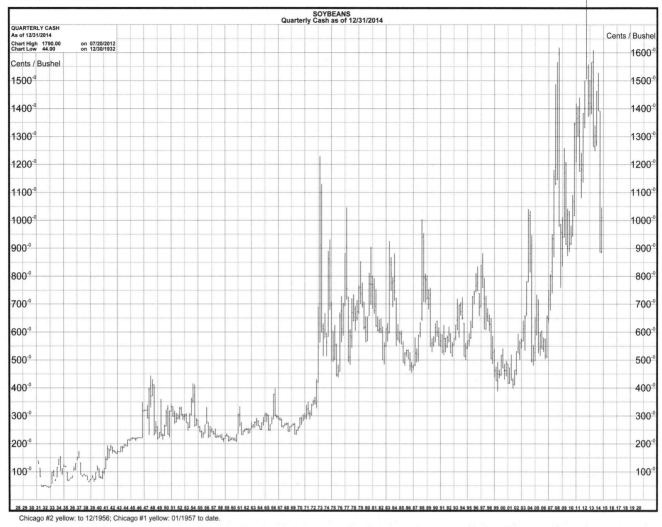

SOYBEANS
Quarterly Cash as of 12/31/2014

QUARTERLY CASH
As of 12/31/2014

Chart High 1790.00 on 07/20/2012
Chart Low 44.00 on 12/30/1932

Chicago #2 yellow: to 12/1956; Chicago #1 yellow: 01/1957 to date.

Average Cash Price of No. 1 Yellow Soybeans at Illinois Processor   In Cents Per Bushel

Year	Jan.	Feb.	Mar.	Apr.	May	June	July	Aug.	Sept.	Oct.	Nov.	Dec.	Average
2001-02	469	430	441	438	437	440	464	471	492	519	575	567	479
2002-03	579	541	575	566	570	590	580	611	640	635	601	589	590
2003-04	639	729	763	772	823	872	975	992	958	890	809	641	822
2004-05	562	519	534	545	539	544	628	622	644	701	703	639	598
2005-06	565	553	574	592	576	575	569	562	581	576	577	542	570
2006-07	535	580	661	657	683	735	730	718	749	792	801	804	704
2007-08	907	944	1,032	1,123	1,216	1,335	1,312	1,292	1,324	1,499	1,516	1,288	1,232
2008-09	1,140	903	893	868	991	938	917	1,025	1,166	1,237	1,096	1,136	1,026
2009-10	1,012	978	1,009	1,033	984	944	949	975	955	955	1,030	1,066	991
2010-11[1]	1,065	1,148	1,252	1,311	1,378	1,386	1,350	1,364	1,368	1,382	1,384	1,381	1,314

[1] Preliminary.   *Source: Economic Research Service, U.S. Department of Agriculture (ERS-USDA)*

Average Price Received by Farmers for Soybeans in the United States   In Dollars Per Bushel

Year	Jan.	Feb.	Mar.	Apr.	May	June	July	Aug.	Sept.	Oct.	Nov.	Dec.	Average
2005-06	5.77	5.67	5.62	5.78	5.87	5.67	5.57	5.52	5.68	5.62	5.61	5.23	5.63
2006-07	5.23	5.52	6.08	6.18	6.37	6.87	6.95	6.88	7.12	7.51	7.56	7.72	6.67
2007-08	8.15	8.36	9.42	10.00	9.95	11.70	11.40	12.00	12.10	13.10	13.30	12.80	11.02
2008-09	10.80	9.95	9.39	9.24	9.97	9.54	9.12	9.79	10.70	11.40	10.80	10.80	10.13
2009-10	9.75	9.43	9.53	9.80	9.79	9.41	9.39	9.47	9.41	9.45	9.79	10.10	9.61
2010-11	9.98	10.20	11.10	11.60	11.60	12.70	12.70	13.10	13.20	13.20	13.20	13.40	12.17
2011-12	12.20	11.80	11.70	11.50	11.90	12.20	13.00	13.80	14.00	13.90	15.40	16.20	13.13
2012-13	14.30	14.20	14.30	14.30	14.30	14.60	14.60	14.40	14.90	15.10	15.30	14.10	14.53
2013-14	13.30	12.50	12.70	13.00	12.90	13.20	13.70	14.30	14.40	14.40	13.10	12.40	13.33
2014-15[1]	10.90	9.97	10.20	10.30	10.30								10.33

[1] Preliminary.   *Source: Economic Research Service, U.S. Department of Agriculture (ERS-USDA)*

Stock Index Futures - U.S.

A stock index simply represents a basket of underlying stocks. Indexes can be either price-weighted or capitalization-weighted. In a price-weighted index, such as the Dow Jones Industrial Average, the individual stock prices are simply added up and then divided by a divisor, meaning that stocks with higher prices have a higher weighting in the index value. In a capitalization-weighted index, such as the Standard and Poor's 500 index, the weighting of each stock corresponds to the size of the company as determined by its capitalization (i.e., the total dollar value of its stock). Stock indexes cover a variety of different sectors. For example, the Dow Jones Industrial Average contains 30 blue-chip stocks that represent the industrial sector. The S&P 500 index includes 500 of the largest blue-chip U.S. companies. The NYSE index includes all the stocks that are traded at the New York Stock Exchange. The Nasdaq 100 includes the largest 100 companies that are traded on the Nasdaq Exchange. The most popular U.S. stock index futures contract is the E-mini S&P 500 futures contract, which is traded at the CME Group.

Prices – The S&P 500 index rallied steadily during 2014 and progressively posted new record highs. The S&P 500 index rallied by +11.4% in 2014, adding to the +30% rally seen in 2013. Through the end of 2014, the S&P 500 index rallied by a total of 162% from the early-2009 low seen during the global financial crisis.

The U.S. stock market in 2014 saw support from (1) the Fed's extraordinarily easy monetary policy, (2) the improvement in the U.S. economy, (3) the sharp drop in long-term Treasury yields, and (4) decent earnings growth. Those bullish factors overcame negative factors such as (1) end of the Fed's third quantitative easing program (QE3) in October 2014, (2) weak global economic growth, (3) weak U.S. wage growth, (4) the sharp rally in the dollar index in the latter half of 2014 that hurt U.S. export earnings, and (5) stretched stock market valuations.

The Federal Reserve's extraordinarily easy monetary policy in 2014 continued to provide strong support for the U.S. stock market. The Fed tapered its QE3 program during 2014 and ended the program altogether in October 2014. That ended the extra liquidity injections that helped to support asset prices in general. However, the Fed kept its federal funds rate target near zero all during 2014, thus helping to keep Treasury yields low. In fact, the 10-year T-note yield during 2014 fell sharply by 75 basis points from 3.00% at the beginning of the year to 2.25% by the end of 2014.

The plunge in crude oil prices that started in September 2014 initially had a negative impact on the overall U.S. stock indexes because of the plunge in oil company stocks, which are an important component in the S&P 500 index. However, the sharp drop in oil prices will eventually turn out to be very beneficial for most U.S. corporations due to lower fuel costs and higher profits. Lower oil prices are also putting more cash into the pockets of consumers, thus giving them more money to spend on various goods and services.

The U.S. stock market in 2014 saw continued support from decent earnings growth of +8% for the S&P 500 companies, which was unchanged from the +8% earnings growth seen in 2013. However, the forward price/earnings ratio for the S&P 500 index rose to 17.5 in late 2014, which was well above the 10-year average of 14.4 and close to the 30-year average.

Looking ahead, the U.S. stock market in 2015 faces some headwinds. First, valuations are a bit stretched and the market is expecting earnings growth of only +2% in 2015, providing little room on the upside for stock prices to rally. Second, the stock market later in 2015 will likely have to contend with the beginning of a series of interest rate hikes by the Federal Reserve. Third, the stock market has rallied sharply for more than three years without a downside correction of more than 15%.

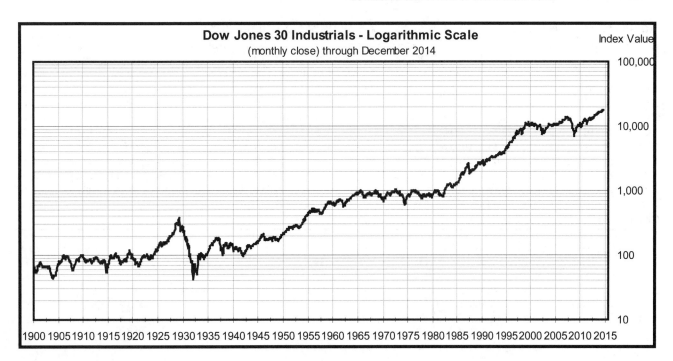

Dow Jones 30 Industrials - Logarithmic Scale
(monthly close) through December 2014

STOCK INDEX FUTURES - U.S.

Composite Index of Leading Indicators (1992 = 100)

Year	Jan.	Feb.	Mar.	Apr.	May	June	July	Aug.	Sept.	Oct.	Nov.	Dec.	Average
2005	101.8	102.2	101.7	101.8	102.1	103.1	102.9	103.1	102.4	103.3	104.2	104.2	102.7
2006	104.7	104.4	104.6	104.4	103.7	103.9	103.7	103.3	103.7	103.9	103.8	104.4	104.0
2007	104.0	103.7	104.1	103.9	104.0	103.9	104.6	103.6	103.7	103.2	102.8	102.6	103.7
2008	102.1	101.9	101.9	102.0	101.9	101.9	101.2	100.3	100.3	99.4	99.0	98.8	100.9
2009	98.8	98.3	98.1	99.2	100.6	101.3	102.5	103.1	104.2	104.7	105.8	106.2	101.9
2010	106.7	107.2	108.6	108.6	109.0	108.8	109.0	109.1	109.9	110.1	111.4	112.3	109.2
2011	91.8	92.7	93.7	93.7	94.2	94.2	94.4	93.7	93.2	93.8	94.1	92.2	93.5
2012	92.2	92.9	93.1	92.9	93.3	92.7	93.1	92.7	93.2	93.4	93.4	94.3	93.1
2013	94.8	95.3	95.1	95.8	96.0	96.1	96.5	97.2	98.2	98.5	99.4	113.8	98.1
2014[1]	113.7	114.3	115.4	115.8	116.5	117.2	118.4	118.5	119.2	119.9	120.3	120.8	117.5

[1] Preliminary.   *Source: The Conference Board*

Consumer Confidence, The Conference Board (2004 = 100)

Year	Jan.	Feb.	Mar.	Apr.	May	June	July	Aug.	Sept.	Oct.	Nov.	Dec.	Average
2005	105.1	104.4	103.0	97.5	103.1	106.2	103.6	105.5	87.5	85.2	98.3	103.8	100.3
2006	106.8	102.7	107.5	109.8	104.7	105.4	107.0	100.2	105.9	105.1	105.3	110.0	105.9
2007	110.2	111.2	108.2	106.3	108.5	105.3	111.9	105.6	99.5	95.2	87.8	90.6	103.4
2008	87.3	76.4	65.9	62.8	58.1	51.0	51.9	58.5	61.4	38.8	44.7	38.6	58.0
2009	37.4	25.3	26.9	40.8	54.8	49.3	47.4	54.5	53.4	48.7	50.6	53.6	45.2
2010	56.5	46.4	52.3	57.7	62.7	54.3	51.0	53.2	48.6	49.9	57.8	63.4	54.5
2011	64.8	72.0	63.8	66.0	61.7	57.6	59.2	45.2	46.4	40.9	55.2	64.8	58.1
2012	61.5	71.6	69.5	68.7	64.4	62.7	65.4	61.3	68.4	73.1	71.5	66.7	67.1
2013	58.4	68.0	61.9	69.0	74.3	82.1	81.0	81.8	80.2	72.4	72.0	77.5	73.2
2014[1]	79.4	78.3	83.9	81.7	82.2	86.4	90.3	93.4	89.0	94.1	91.0	93.1	86.9

[1] Preliminary.   *Source: The Conference Board (TCB) Copyrighted.*

Capacity Utilization Rates (Total Industry)   In Percent

Year	Jan.	Feb.	Mar.	Apr.	May	June	July	Aug.	Sept.	Oct.	Nov.	Dec.	Average
2005	79.7	80.1	80.0	80.0	80.0	80.2	80.0	80.0	78.3	79.2	79.8	80.2	79.8
2006	80.2	80.1	80.2	80.4	80.2	80.4	80.3	80.3	80.1	79.9	79.6	80.2	80.2
2007	79.7	80.4	80.3	80.7	80.6	80.5	80.4	80.4	80.7	80.3	80.7	80.8	80.5
2008	80.5	80.4	80.2	79.6	79.3	79.2	78.8	77.5	74.2	74.8	73.9	71.7	77.5
2009	70.0	69.6	68.5	67.9	67.2	66.9	67.6	68.3	68.9	69.2	69.7	70.1	68.7
2010	71.0	71.4	72.1	72.5	73.8	74.1	74.7	75.0	75.3	75.1	75.3	76.0	73.9
2011	76.0	75.6	76.3	75.8	76.0	76.1	76.4	76.6	76.6	76.8	76.7	76.8	76.3
2012	77.3	77.4	76.9	77.4	77.4	77.3	77.6	77.0	77.0	76.9	77.5	77.5	77.3
2013	77.4	77.8	78.0	77.8	77.8	77.8	77.5	77.8	78.3	78.2	78.5	78.5	78.0
2014[1]	78.1	78.6	79.1	79.0	79.1	79.2	79.3	79.1	79.4	79.1	79.8	79.4	79.1

[1] Preliminary.   *Source: Bureau of Economic Analysis, U.S. Department of Commerce (BEA)*

Manufacturers New Orders, Durable Goods   In Billions of Constant Dollars

Year	Jan.	Feb.	Mar.	Apr.	May	June	July	Aug.	Sept.	Oct.	Nov.	Dec.	Average
2005	193.00	194.90	187.38	194.71	206.10	209.60	196.78	205.61	204.19	210.22	222.33	220.10	203.74
2006	207.20	217.67	227.24	214.36	215.54	221.07	212.70	211.63	235.79	216.93	226.24	228.70	219.59
2007	218.18	221.09	228.25	233.45	228.00	229.41	239.56	234.48	226.24	229.45	232.57	242.96	230.30
2008	236.58	233.05	229.93	229.83	229.79	229.32	225.87	216.25	211.90	192.49	184.29	172.89	216.02
2009	151.75	145.10	144.46	144.41	149.92	146.12	157.12	157.53	157.97	162.39	161.27	158.51	153.05
2010	181.01	175.85	179.45	186.90	185.59	186.09	190.11	192.40	200.47	194.37	196.50	194.14	188.57
2011	204.66	194.49	212.48	201.68	206.56	201.52	210.26	217.27	209.45	209.97	217.77	226.37	209.37
2012	222.04	220.24	217.02	216.93	214.12	217.11	225.09	201.38	214.34	219.15	217.18	230.36	217.91
2013	220.18	230.27	213.82	224.07	231.72	243.78	224.33	225.29	233.99	231.08	241.44	229.81	229.15
2014[1]	224.01	229.86	238.42	240.48	238.34	244.84	299.86	245.00	243.20	243.82	238.58	229.83	243.02

[1] Preliminary.   *Source: Bureau of Economic Analysis, U.S. Department of Commerce (BEA)*

Corporate Profits After Tax -- Quarterly   In Billions of Dollars

Year	First Quarter	Second Quarter	Third Quarter	Fourth Quarter	Total	Year	First Quarter	Second Quarter	Third Quarter	Fourth Quarter	Total
2003	756.6	801.9	829.1	862.8	812.6	2009	1,044.0	1,060.6	1,178.3	1,227.3	1,127.6
2004	961.1	968.6	1,005.3	974.1	977.3	2010	1,313.7	1,314.8	1,426.6	1,448.4	1,375.9
2005	1,022.7	1,050.4	1,071.2	1,117.2	1,065.4	2011	1,279.9	1,406.6	1,475.6	1,588.0	1,437.5
2006	1,166.7	1,174.0	1,196.8	1,155.0	1,173.1	2012	1,526.6	1,551.2	1,600.4	1,593.8	1,568.0
2007	1,056.8	1,128.8	1,087.1	1,061.2	1,083.5	2013	1,564.5	1,644.4	1,673.1	1,648.4	1,632.6
2008	1,028.1	1,023.5	1,058.7	793.5	976.0	2014[1]	1,379.8	1,498.2	1,568.3		1,482.1

[1] Preliminary.   *Source: Bureau of Economic Analysis, U.S. Department of Commerce (BEA)*

Change in Manufacturing and Trade Inventories   In Billions of Dollars

Year	Jan.	Feb.	Mar.	Apr.	May	June	July	Aug.	Sept.	Oct.	Nov.	Dec.	Average
2005	130.5	84.6	60.3	40.0	218.4	-5.7	-66.0	57.9	272.9	81.3	78.8	305.6	54.5
2006	85.9	-49.7	129.5	82.7	169.3	169.3	92.2	93.2	65.9	22.9	28.3	4.2	85.2
2007	37.8	43.6	-17.0	59.5	68.1	55.0	75.6	62.7	87.7	23.8	53.3	96.3	53.4
2008	169.4	78.5	35.6	81.4	66.2	133.3	202.6	34.8	-64.9	-99.6		-250.0	35.2
2009	-170.2	-188.5	-232.1	-197.4	-196.7	-218.1	-159.1	-232.5	-46.8	59.8	75.6	-14.9	-126.7
2010	27.9	104.4	95.5	95.3	54.9	136.3	173.2	139.3	179.6	190.5	63.3	173.4	119.5
2011	167.1	129.1	226.8	154.7	184.1	50.0	75.1	114.0	-26.5	158.7	69.4	79.7	115.2
2012	139.9	118.4	47.8	46.5	56.8	27.0	128.1	85.0	118.2	60.8	37.4	33.6	75.0
2013	205.4	30.2	-18.8	66.4	-1.8	17.5	62.3	71.5	117.8	137.2	95.7	82.0	72.1
2014[1]	65.6	93.0	82.9	129.5	97.9	73.4	78.6	27.2	59.7	44.5	33.3	16.1	66.8

[1] Preliminary.   *Source: Bureau of Economic Analysis, U.S. Department of Commerce (BEA)*

Productivity: Index of Output per Hour, All Persons, Nonfarm Business -- Quarterly   (1992 = 100)

Year	First Quarter	Second Quarter	Third Quarter	Fourth Quarter	Total	Year	First Quarter	Second Quarter	Third Quarter	Fourth Quarter	Total
2003	87.1	88.3	90.2	91.0	89.1	2009	97.6	99.5	100.9	102.1	100.0
2004	91.0	91.9	92.2	92.5	91.9	2010	102.7	103.0	103.6	104.0	103.3
2005	93.5	93.4	94.1	94.2	93.8	2011	103.1	103.5	103.3	104.0	103.5
2006	94.8	94.7	94.2	95.0	94.7	2012	104.0	104.6	105.0	104.4	104.5
2007	95.1	95.7	96.8	97.2	96.2	2013	104.6	104.8	105.7	106.5	105.4
2008	96.2	97.2	97.4	96.8	96.9	2014[1]	105.2	106.0	107.0	106.4	106.1

[1] Preliminary.   *Source: Bureau of Economic Analysis, U.S. Department of Commerce (BEA)*

Civilian Unemployment Rate - U3

Year	Jan.	Feb.	Mar.	Apr.	May	June	July	Aug.	Sept.	Oct.	Nov.	Dec.	Average
2005	5.2	5.4	5.1	5.1	5.1	5.0	5.0	4.9	5.1	4.9	5.0	4.9	5.1
2006	4.7	4.8	4.7	4.7	4.6	4.6	4.8	4.7	4.6	4.4	4.5	4.5	4.6
2007	4.6	4.5	4.4	4.5	4.5	4.6	4.7	4.7	4.7	4.8	4.7	5.0	4.6
2008	5.0	4.8	5.1	5.0	5.4	5.5	5.8	6.1	6.2	6.6	6.9	7.4	5.8
2009	7.7	8.2	8.6	8.9	9.4	9.5	9.4	9.7	9.8	10.1	10.0	10.0	9.3
2010	9.7	9.8	9.9	9.9	9.6	9.4	9.5	9.5	9.5	9.5	9.8	9.4	9.6
2011	9.1	9.0	9.0	9.1	9.0	9.1	9.0	9.0	9.0	8.8	8.6	8.5	8.9
2012	8.2	8.3	8.2	8.2	8.2	8.2	8.2	8.1	7.8	7.8	7.8	7.9	8.1
2013	7.9	7.7	7.5	7.5	7.5	7.5	7.3	7.2	7.2	7.2	7.0	6.7	7.4
2014[1]	6.6	6.7	6.6	6.2	6.3	6.1	6.2	6.1	5.9	5.7	5.8	5.6	6.2

[1] Preliminary.   *Source: Bureau of Economic Analysis, U.S. Department of Commerce (BEA)*

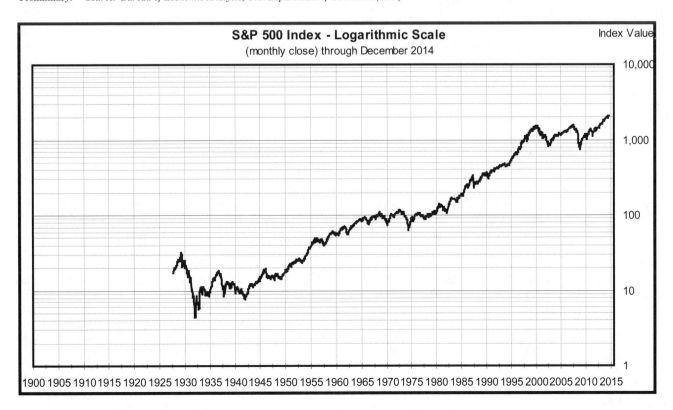

S&P 500 Index - Logarithmic Scale
(monthly close) through December 2014

Index Value

STOCK INDEX FUTURES - U.S.

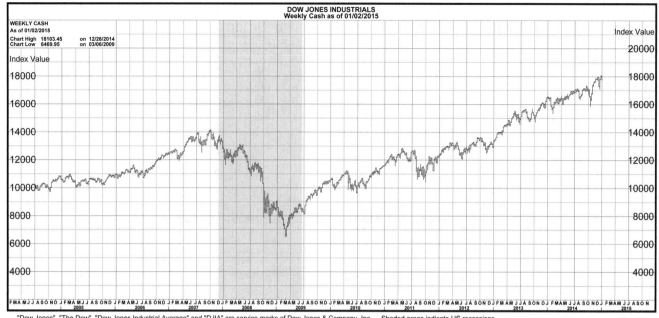

"Dow Jones", "The Dow", "Dow Jones Industrial Average" and "DJIA" are service marks of Dow Jones & Company, Inc.   Shaded areas indicate US recessions.

Average Value of Dow Jones Industrials Index (30 Stocks)

Year	Jan.	Feb.	Mar.	Apr.	May	June	July	Aug.	Sept.	Oct.	Nov.	Dec.	Average
2005	10,539.5	10,723.8	10,682.1	10,283.2	10,377.2	10,486.6	10,545.4	10,554.3	10,532.5	10,324.3	10,695.3	10,827.8	10,547.7
2006	10,872.5	10,971.2	11,144.5	11,234.7	11,333.9	10,998.0	11,032.5	11,257.4	11,533.6	11,963.1	12,185.2	12,377.6	11,408.7
2007	12,512.9	12,631.5	12,268.5	12,754.8	13,407.8	13,480.2	13,677.9	13,239.7	13,557.7	13,901.3	13,200.5	13,406.9	13,170.0
2008	12,537.4	12,419.6	12,193.9	12,656.6	12,812.5	12,056.7	11,322.4	11,530.8	11,114.1	9,176.7	8,614.6	8,595.6	11,252.6
2009	8,396.2	7,690.5	7,235.5	7,992.1	8,398.4	8,593.0	8,679.8	9,375.1	9,635.0	9,857.3	10,227.6	10,433.4	8,876.1
2010	10,471.2	1,021.5	10,677.5	11,052.2	10,500.2	10,159.3	10,222.2	10,350.4	10,598.1	11,044.5	11,198.6	11,465.3	9,896.7
2011	11,802.4	12,190.0	12,081.5	12,434.9	12,580.0	12,097.3	12,512.3	11,326.6	11,175.5	11,515.9	11,804.2	12,075.7	11,966.4
2012	12,550.9	12,889.1	13,079.5	13,030.8	12,721.1	12,544.9	12,814.1	13,134.9	13,418.5	13,380.7	12,896.4	13,144.2	12,967.1
2013	13,615.3	13,967.3	14,418.3	14,675.9	15,172.2	15,035.8	15,390.2	15,195.3	15,269.8	15,289.8	15,870.8	16,095.8	14,999.7
2014	16,243.6	15,958.4	16,308.6	16,399.5	16,567.3	16,843.8	16,988.3	16,775.2	17,098.1	16,701.9	17,649.0	17,754.2	16,774.0

Source: New York Stock Exchange (NYSE)

Volume of Trading of Dow Jones Industrials Index Futures in Chicago   In Contracts

Year	Jan.	Feb.	Mar.	Apr.	May	June	July	Aug.	Sept.	Oct.	Nov.	Dec.	Total
2005	149,353	107,824	226,113	157,010	124,999	192,165	96,885	121,793	188,541	133,636	108,737	180,349	1,787,405
2006	119,593	111,738	220,880	106,325	152,340	272,494	108,053	97,964	237,988	121,736	111,993	258,743	1,919,847
2007	97,032	97,537	231,466	76,661	127,981	197,380	101,710	119,985	135,432	95,101	91,014	112,518	1,483,817
2008	105,901	82,432	135,860	71,571	51,097	121,220	122,305	76,031	170,465	99,607	53,397	57,771	1,147,657
2009	32,235	36,568	54,497	35,502	32,590	50,874	27,114	17,541	47,003	18,659	13,769	29,232	395,584
2010	13,279	11,251	23,512	14,352	14,189	28,257	9,843	10,761	18,012	9,749	10,888	24,016	188,109
2011	14,006	12,520	30,645	22,807	16,017	38,755	19,825	27,233	40,956	11,931	14,659	37,343	286,697
2012	7,615	5,635	33,083	5,980	12,265	31,245	6,815	11,230	32,719	14,054	11,811	30,319	202,771
2013	10,802	10,989	21,803	9,017	4,578	16,342	10,751	8,949	30,100	15,738	4,009	23,827	166,905
2014	8,423	11,102	13,968	5,417	3,905	13,687	1,834	10,656	20,225	9,191	4,687	23,915	127,010

Contract value = $10.   *Source: Chicago Board of Trade (CBT)*

Average Open Interest of Dow Jones Industrials Index Futures in Chicago   In Contracts

Year	Jan.	Feb.	Mar.	Apr.	May	June	July	Aug.	Sept.	Oct.	Nov.	Dec.
2005	47,754	48,665	48,423	40,068	41,367	36,909	29,042	30,921	37,232	36,378	37,588	43,819
2006	39,641	39,943	43,595	43,351	45,756	53,833	56,451	58,799	60,497	61,996	63,061	69,927
2007	67,567	72,788	54,933	41,615	48,211	42,631	33,406	37,757	35,894	30,936	35,735	34,375
2008	27,564	32,212	33,736	29,240	31,425	32,987	31,175	34,663	36,423	26,685	27,638	23,708
2009	14,401	22,146	19,045	10,306	15,681	18,781	10,880	11,614	12,693	13,764	16,046	12,915
2010	12,142	13,855	10,785	7,616	11,884	10,945	7,250	8,945	7,325	5,155	7,631	7,591
2011	8,937	11,647	11,005	15,685	23,810	16,465	14,001	15,038	13,834	13,114	17,338	17,038
2012	11,338	12,478	13,704	11,329	14,604	16,009	12,248	11,646	14,912	13,543	14,519	13,868
2013	9,380	13,515	12,699	7,484	12,051	11,053	9,360	14,640	12,090	11,143	13,944	12,557
2014	9,861	13,110	9,992	4,946	4,878	6,345	3,370	5,383	7,712	9,132	10,879	10,044

Contract value = $10.   *Source: Chicago Board of Trade (CBT)*

The S&P 500® Index is a trademark of The McGraw-Hill Companies, Inc.   Shaded areas indicate US recessions.

Average Value of Standard & Poor's 500 Index

Year	Jan.	Feb.	Mar.	Apr.	May	June	July	Aug.	Sept.	Oct.	Nov.	Dec.	Average
2005	1,181.4	1,199.6	1,194.9	1,164.4	1,178.3	1,202.3	1,222.2	1,224.3	1,225.9	1,192.0	1,237.3	1,262.1	1,207.1
2006	1,278.7	1,276.7	1,293.7	1,302.2	1,290.0	1,253.1	1,260.2	1,287.2	1,317.8	1,363.3	1,388.6	1,416.4	1,310.7
2007	1,424.2	1,444.8	1,407.0	1,463.7	1,511.1	1,514.5	1,520.7	1,454.6	1,497.1	1,539.7	1,463.4	1,479.2	1,476.7
2008	1,378.8	1,354.9	1,316.9	1,370.5	1,403.2	1,341.3	1,257.3	1,281.5	1,217.0	968.8	883.0	877.4	1,220.9
2009	865.6	805.2	757.1	848.2	902.4	926.1	935.8	1,009.7	1,044.6	1,067.7	1,088.1	1,110.4	946.7
2010	1,123.6	1,089.2	1,152.1	1,197.3	1,125.1	1,083.4	1,079.8	1,087.3	1,122.1	1,171.6	1,198.9	1,241.5	1,139.3
2011	1,282.6	1,321.1	1,304.5	1,331.5	1,338.3	1,287.3	1,325.2	1,185.3	1,173.9	1,207.2	1,226.4	1,243.3	1,268.9
2012	1,300.6	1,352.5	1,389.2	1,386.4	1,341.3	1,323.5	1,359.8	1,403.5	1,443.4	1,437.8	1,394.5	1,422.3	1,379.6
2013	1,480.4	1,512.3	1,550.8	1,570.7	1,639.8	1,618.8	1,668.7	1,670.1	1,687.2	1,720.1	1,783.5	1,807.8	1,642.5
2014	1,822.4	1,817.0	1,863.5	1,864.3	1,889.8	1,947.1	1,973.1	1,961.5	1,993.2	1,937.3	2,044.6	2,054.3	1,930.7

Source: Index and Option Market (IOM), division of the Chicago Mercantile Exchange (CME)

Volume of Trading of S&P 500 Stock Index Futures in Chicago   In Thousands of Contracts

Year	Jan.	Feb.	Mar.	Apr.	May	June	July	Aug.	Sept.	Oct.	Nov.	Dec.	Total
2005	764.5	873.6	2,330.2	916.2	891.6	2,090.1	618.4	979.1	2,090.2	902.1	880.2	2,041.4	15,377
2006	711.3	772.9	2,198.8	607.5	1,122.0	2,321.6	726.3	890.8	1,883.1	686.3	935.6	1,988.6	14,845
2007	696.3	765.0	2,341.9	614.6	937.9	2,237.8	803.4	1,546.1	1,941.4	854.5	1,130.8	1,967.9	15,838
2008	1,187.3	907.8	2,374.7	761.0	768.2	1,978.9	921.9	729.7	2,491.2	1,588.1	942.0	2,112.2	16,763
2009	674.4	744.3	2,026.3	555.3	534.7	1,637.5	453.5	427.3	1,338.3	473.3	384.6	1,186.4	10,436
2010	403.6	432.0	1,084.5	363.5	650.7	1,195.3	412.7	433.1	1,027.9	296.8	415.8	974.1	7,690
2011	321.2	330.8	1,162.0	306.6	309.8	1,027.3	283.4	713.6	1,124.3	389.1	394.8	857.8	7,221
2012	228.2	222.9	812.5	233.0	301.8	818.9	243.5	247.9	729.7	192.4	257.1	744.9	5,033
2013	263.4	248.8	699.6	203.8	232.6	693.8	151.4	190.4	584.4	186.8	136.4	565.0	4,156
2014	200.5	193.0	525.4	137.2	145.7	500.1	136.0	118.4	518.8	229.3	152.7	510.1	3,367

Contract value = $250.   *Source: Index and Option Market (IOM), division of the Chicago Mercantile Exchange (CME)*

Average Open Interest of S&P 500 Stock Index Futures in Chicago   In Contracts

Year	Jan.	Feb.	Mar.	Apr.	May	June	July	Aug.	Sept.	Oct.	Nov.	Dec.
2005	678,739	686,413	719,141	681,149	697,818	700,618	656,266	653,430	669,849	642,704	657,097	681,868
2006	655,483	668,113	682,218	653,044	664,790	670,449	625,142	634,579	634,817	609,410	640,481	679,221
2007	634,075	639,584	654,891	634,576	662,438	652,951	602,222	643,716	663,165	595,908	623,469	623,631
2008	566,839	602,738	607,396	560,088	559,320	558,810	551,609	565,810	578,027	627,531	633,531	603,664
2009	518,589	583,132	566,284	439,705	467,060	456,209	391,596	393,499	400,489	386,593	398,242	379,761
2010	334,063	379,277	384,532	320,130	323,367	354,304	308,220	320,409	327,551	314,245	352,215	341,358
2011	295,221	328,406	351,308	312,007	326,135	314,542	277,586	351,944	367,322	292,018	295,609	285,435
2012	247,547	249,536	248,980	234,595	260,383	266,290	236,315	235,725	225,849	199,981	217,709	215,589
2013	193,514	217,014	202,882	169,581	189,144	203,898	162,175	170,134	196,824	159,233	167,647	168,253
2014	150,125	197,844	198,079	126,277	142,806	163,129	144,257	161,528	165,415	142,572	149,630	146,618

Contract value = $250.   *Source: Index and Option Market (IOM), division of the Chicago Mercantile Exchange (CME)*

STOCK INDEX FUTURES - U.S.

The NASDAQ 100® Index is a trademark of The Nasdaq Stock Market, Inc.   Shaded areas indicate US recessions.

Average Value of NASDAQ 100 Index

Year	Jan.	Feb.	Mar.	Apr.	May	June	July	Aug.	Sept.	Oct.	Nov.	Dec.	Average
2005	1,539.8	1,521.4	1,499.5	1,447.3	1,489.9	1,528.2	1,566.9	1,587.1	1,586.6	1,560.8	1,653.8	1,684.8	1,555.5
2006	1,714.0	1,671.3	1,678.7	1,714.7	1,637.7	1,560.1	1,501.5	1,534.3	1,621.2	1,704.2	1,770.3	1,780.7	1,657.4
2007	1,796.4	1,806.0	1,759.3	1,732.8	1,895.7	1,922.0	1,999.1	1,931.3	2,024.3	2,164.6	2,081.0	2,089.8	1,933.5
2008	1,886.4	1,784.9	1,748.2	1,868.3	1,991.0	1,950.3	1,831.0	1,905.0	1,710.0	1,328.6	1,199.1	1,188.2	1,699.2
2009	1,206.5	1,199.4	1,167.3	1,332.2	1,393.5	1,472.2	1,515.8	1,618.0	1,688.0	1,722.1	1,761.8	1,816.5	1,491.1
2010	1,850.2	1,784.7	1,920.6	2,011.0	1,892.7	1,847.2	1,827.2	1,839.1	1,939.9	2,066.0	2,148.4	2,211.4	1,944.9
2011	2,291.2	2,353.4	2,298.7	2,344.1	2,364.6	2,255.1	2,379.5	2,173.8	2,224.5	2,298.7	2,291.8	2,279.2	2,296.2
2012	2,404.3	2,567.0	2,699.0	2,716.1	2,589.0	2,549.9	2,605.7	2,739.1	2,820.9	2,735.9	2,616.6	2,658.8	2,641.9
2013	2,736.9	2,748.2	2,795.3	2,818.6	2,981.2	2,937.3	3,033.0	3,105.5	3,187.5	3,292.0	3,399.5	3,513.8	3,045.7
2014	3,557.9	3,615.0	3,661.1	3,554.5	3,621.1	3,792.1	3,926.7	3,979.4	4,070.3	3,964.6	4,221.1	4,260.8	3,852.0

Source: Index and Option Market (IOM), division of the Chicago Mercantile Exchange (CME)

Volume of Trading of NASDAQ 100 Index Futures in Chicago   In Contracts

Year	Jan.	Feb.	Mar.	Apr.	May	June	July	Aug.	Sept.	Oct.	Nov.	Dec.	Total
2005	254,437	198,956	375,435	217,304	170,882	281,483	125,500	159,789	289,113	200,952	155,141	253,066	2,682,058
2006	186,649	162,841	295,163	113,885	169,399	305,557	132,661	149,906	256,605	136,433	140,407	220,364	2,269,870
2007	122,055	111,962	255,491	73,881	97,857	226,877	94,964	124,717	178,645	112,930	121,891	162,108	1,683,378
2008	137,810	90,886	188,815	72,775	80,472	192,723	103,965	83,158	171,532	125,975	58,023	101,279	1,407,413
2009	61,110	61,943	119,432	47,289	53,465	76,479	46,606	55,012	84,170	45,122	48,519	57,772	756,919
2010	50,060	37,696	55,326	34,026	44,200	47,702	28,137	32,035	46,609	24,746	57,965	49,322	507,824
2011	36,142	21,771	58,401	35,746	27,603	43,952	38,356	50,565	57,793	39,421	31,144	31,693	472,587
2012	19,898	19,091	38,038	18,999	30,068	25,902	22,187	25,137	30,075	31,438	41,749	29,706	332,288
2013	18,447	25,571	21,117	28,743	13,116	25,790	16,558	12,803	19,171	21,573	10,037	21,106	234,032
2014	26,643	14,461	29,456	22,271	19,780	22,242	11,262	12,484	21,924	20,996	14,323	36,283	252,125

Contract value = $100.   *Source: Index and Option Market (IOM), division of the Chicago Mercantile Exchange (CME)*

Average Open Interest of NASDAQ 100 Index Futures in Chicago   In Contracts

Year	Jan.	Feb.	Mar.	Apr.	May	June	July	Aug.	Sept.	Oct.	Nov.	Dec.
2005	72,299	81,327	78,387	56,668	57,116	56,836	49,357	53,270	61,369	60,918	59,754	63,712
2006	61,254	62,994	69,322	60,603	65,224	65,908	54,289	57,585	54,235	53,832	68,347	61,397
2007	47,832	51,655	55,782	50,905	59,586	63,132	63,492	67,870	64,324	50,761	53,292	50,372
2008	42,272	52,260	51,385	31,738	37,017	34,864	28,456	30,588	27,761	27,770	31,473	29,459
2009	23,558	29,607	29,090	21,525	24,228	21,913	17,299	21,266	22,113	19,389	21,267	18,502
2010	15,446	28,890	20,717	17,115	23,509	19,880	12,821	18,414	18,068	22,008	29,505	19,916
2011	14,571	18,006	17,336	17,887	21,448	14,400	16,130	21,731	20,622	20,112	30,793	19,188
2012	12,254	17,696	15,464	13,363	21,065	13,429	7,749	13,354	18,588	10,769	22,194	19,077
2013	10,103	15,181	10,375	6,155	8,762	8,970	6,978	9,860	9,166	7,796	9,156	9,598
2014	11,113	16,080	14,989	14,562	20,045	10,907	4,271	6,602	6,715	8,232	11,112	11,967

Contract value = $100.   *Source: Index and Option Market (IOM), division of the Chicago Mercantile Exchange (CME)*

Average Value of Dow Jones Transportation Index (20 Stocks)

Year	Jan.	Feb.	Mar.	Apr.	May	June	July	Aug.	Sept.	Oct.	Nov.	Dec.	Average
2005	3,587.0	3,614.5	3,779.4	3,527.8	3,548.8	3,542.1	3,663.1	3,726.1	3,637.0	3,673.1	4,051.7	4,152.1	3,708.6
2006	4,224.5	4,362.5	4,519.5	4,679.6	4,761.4	4,663.1	4,636.1	4,291.1	4,363.3	4,654.7	4,761.6	4,660.0	4,548.1
2007	4,752.2	5,024.6	4,817.3	5,059.2	5,174.8	5,137.2	5,258.8	4,889.0	4,812.7	4,891.2	4,605.9	4,686.4	4,925.8
2008	4,348.7	4,720.0	4,641.9	4,996.9	5,304.5	5,166.7	4,899.2	5,057.0	4,889.3	3,815.4	3,518.5	3,369.2	4,560.6
2009	3,238.3	2,857.3	2,499.9	2,986.8	3,163.7	3,266.6	3,321.5	3,697.2	3,863.1	3,844.4	3,915.2	4,117.2	3,397.6
2010	4,119.6	3,971.7	4,308.5	4,597.7	4,427.6	4,259.5	4,217.9	4,280.6	4,439.9	4,670.6	4,846.8	5,067.4	4,434.0
2011	5,135.4	5,130.2	5,110.7	5,319.1	5,431.5	5,212.9	5,395.0	4,569.8	4,420.8	4,628.8	4,820.8	4,943.3	5,009.8
2012	5,206.5	5,245.1	5,225.4	5,239.7	5,121.6	5,050.9	5,117.2	5,088.7	5,038.1	5,041.0	5,056.3	5,218.7	5,137.4
2013	5,665.7	5,908.1	6,167.2	6,073.4	6,370.3	6,225.1	6,420.2	6,438.7	6,555.1	6,767.9	7,131.0	7,220.9	6,412.0
2014	7,361.9	7,235.3	7,512.0	7,587.8	7,854.6	8,135.4	8,308.7	8,272.8	8,534.2	8,308.9	9,033.8	9,025.7	8,097.6

Source: New York Stock Exchange (NYSE)

Average Value of Dow Jones Utilities Index (15 Stocks)

Year	Jan.	Feb.	Mar.	Apr.	May	June	July	Aug.	Sept.	Oct.	Nov.	Dec.	Average
2005	331.9	351.5	356.3	364.5	364.4	376.3	392.5	397.4	422.7	401.3	395.3	409.0	380.2
2006	416.7	408.2	401.7	392.1	401.0	409.2	424.1	436.9	430.1	439.8	449.1	458.5	422.3
2007	449.9	474.1	486.1	516.9	526.2	498.2	502.3	489.0	499.5	514.0	523.5	540.9	501.7
2008	518.8	499.0	480.3	506.2	516.7	519.1	500.8	472.4	446.3	370.1	368.1	362.7	463.4
2009	371.3	356.3	315.8	331.6	339.3	350.6	361.4	373.3	376.0	375.6	373.4	398.9	360.3
2010	393.8	371.9	378.1	384.3	372.7	366.9	379.8	389.8	396.6	404.8	400.5	400.8	386.7
2011	410.1	411.9	409.9	416.5	434.8	427.0	435.3	419.9	431.7	439.9	443.0	451.5	427.6
2012	451.0	451.3	454.8	459.4	467.9	475.6	485.0	479.3	471.5	479.2	449.7	453.9	464.9
2013	463.6	474.7	493.1	522.2	511.0	481.1	496.7	490.3	480.7	492.3	499.5	485.4	490.9
2014	491.9	513.0	519.8	540.7	540.0	556.0	557.5	547.2	555.3	569.2	596.5	609.7	549.7

Source: New York Stock Exchange (NYSE)

Volume of Trading of S&P 400 Midcap Stock Index Futures in Chicago   In Contracts

Year	Jan.	Feb.	Mar.	Apr.	May	June	July	Aug.	Sept.	Oct.	Nov.	Dec.	Total
2005	6,486	5,736	36,685	5,130	7,235	39,025	4,603	7,699	42,503	5,736	4,988	39,232	205,058
2006	5,668	3,739	34,668	3,671	4,619	31,924	2,656	3,311	23,289	3,718	6,409	29,596	153,268
2007	2,854	3,205	26,948	3,716	3,937	22,210	3,906	4,271	17,518	3,610	10,570	15,395	118,140
2008	5,581	3,286	14,864	2,796	3,124	15,896	4,670	3,369	19,246	6,432	4,397	13,563	97,224
2009	2,330	4,802	11,017	4,668	1,707	10,037	1,642	1,822	8,854	3,229	2,285	6,967	59,360
2010	1,852	3,043	5,412	1,019	3,956	6,944	1,580	2,582	4,072	2,330	1,117	4,560	38,467
2011	2,827	879	4,887	2,098	824	2,839	2,792	6,161	4,604	6,310	5,453	3,050	42,724
2012	1,421	1,630	3,042	1,996	1,789	1,710	1,932	2,079	2,978	502	3,289	1,814	24,182
2013	1,440	71	2,840	2,934	1,003	1,564	2,343	1,271	3,319	1,416	406	2,137	20,744
2014	1,281	2,655	1,034	1,672	1,128	606	441	1,111	1,726	6,111	2,001	1,537	21,303

Contract value = $500.   *Source: Index and Option Market (IOM), division of the Chicago Mercantile Exchange (CME)*

Average Open Interest of S&P 400 Midcap Stock Index Futures in Chicago   In Contracts

Year	Jan.	Feb.	Mar.	Apr.	May	June	July	Aug.	Sept.	Oct.	Nov.	Dec.
2005	13,078	13,313	14,861	11,812	11,832	13,811	12,380	12,420	14,477	12,890	12,955	13,822
2006	12,168	11,940	12,409	10,999	10,892	10,447	9,307	9,687	9,194	8,442	9,884	9,794
2007	7,793	8,143	8,267	7,972	9,187	8,425	6,729	6,671	6,951	6,166	8,580	8,839
2008	6,501	7,622	7,512	4,254	5,358	5,700	4,578	5,756	6,847	6,601	6,766	5,761
2009	3,785	4,755	5,227	4,433	4,580	3,781	2,481	2,887	2,847	2,586	2,273	2,437
2010	1,552	2,791	2,274	1,549	2,580	3,250	2,268	2,799	2,334	2,418	3,389	2,539
2011	2,112	2,802	2,290	1,682	1,727	1,558	2,090	4,372	3,291	4,399	5,756	3,581
2012	1,210	2,126	1,748	1,712	2,315	1,647	1,208	2,299	2,951	600	2,314	2,122
2013	857	1,477	1,034	1,211	1,580	1,436	1,239	1,590	1,160	517	438	758
2014	752	1,606	992	956	1,483	1,239	259	869	830	4,459	3,660	1,910

Contract value = $500.   *Source: Index and Option Market (IOM), division of the Chicago Mercantile Exchange (CME)*

STOCK INDEX FUTURES - U.S.

Volume of Trading of E-mini S&P 500 Index Futures in Chicago   In Thousands of Contracts

Year	Jan.	Feb.	Mar.	Apr.	May	June	July	Aug.	Sept.	Oct.	Nov.	Dec.	Total
2005	15,447	12,561	18,478	20,182	16,591	17,371	14,400	17,759	18,786	22,929	16,088	16,503	207,096
2006	18,716	16,095	21,357	18,174	24,750	30,359	21,629	19,107	21,986	22,377	23,616	19,760	257,927
2007	21,632	22,507	37,944	20,399	26,266	39,351	35,295	55,547	37,578	38,649	46,727	33,454	415,348
2008	55,257	40,368	56,108	38,472	36,217	49,724	53,375	36,400	76,696	84,259	56,426	50,587	633,889
2009	45,814	49,498	69,321	49,293	46,060	48,779	42,273	38,448	46,864	46,352	36,951	36,662	556,314
2010	40,765	42,986	46,644	43,563	64,388	61,258	44,454	42,196	46,366	41,921	45,468	35,320	555,329
2011	38,684	36,326	60,446	32,705	43,114	59,186	43,083	82,693	71,646	55,044	51,593	45,850	620,369
2012	34,720	32,505	44,161	35,956	47,447	54,942	38,614	33,377	38,685	36,912	39,528	37,433	474,279
2013	30,743	35,953	43,787	41,242	41,901	52,896	29,323	34,906	39,752	39,069	28,689	34,028	452,291
2014	33,770	33,265	43,038	34,460	27,653	33,330	33,263	28,020	40,843	54,465	22,223	40,608	424,938

Contract value = $50.   *Source: Index and Option Market (IOM), division of the Chicago Mercantile Exchange (CME)*

Average Open Interest of E-mini S&P 500 Index Futures in Chicago   In Thousands of Contracts

Year	Jan.	Feb.	Mar.	Apr.	May	June	July	Aug.	Sept.	Oct.	Nov.	Dec.
2005	827.3	901.7	1,013.6	943.3	1,014.9	986.8	932.6	1,060.8	1,110.1	1,042.2	1,166.4	1,211.3
2006	1,149.2	1,194.6	1,334.1	1,211.3	1,402.5	1,525.3	1,371.2	1,512.3	1,582.4	1,549.5	1,754.4	1,810.9
2007	1,625.6	1,825.1	2,037.4	1,943.7	2,088.7	2,060.5	1,735.6	2,105.4	2,151.5	1,972.4	2,095.4	2,172.5
2008	2,208.2	2,418.8	2,442.6	2,076.5	2,180.8	2,311.5	2,405.0	2,467.2	2,566.1	2,987.6	3,114.1	2,942.0
2009	2,512.9	2,896.4	3,123.3	2,489.2	2,680.4	2,690.2	2,429.6	2,622.9	2,582.3	2,397.1	2,593.6	2,688.5
2010	2,510.1	2,808.4	2,866.0	2,468.7	2,680.5	2,937.2	2,797.2	2,839.5	2,872.0	2,668.2	2,810.5	2,826.7
2011	2,581.7	2,829.5	2,960.3	2,704.1	2,762.3	2,887.0	2,578.6	3,318.6	3,424.6	3,008.7	2,955.1	2,903.6
2012	2,651.8	2,769.8	2,904.4	2,797.2	2,949.5	2,964.8	2,799.8	2,945.7	3,182.3	2,951.7	3,088.0	3,116.6
2013	2,872.7	3,117.0	3,199.6	3,038.9	3,279.6	3,245.5	2,778.0	2,910.8	2,954.2	2,717.7	2,848.0	2,973.0
2014	2,865.8	3,123.2	3,283.5	2,800.4	2,949.6	3,160.0	2,946.3	2,985.7	3,153.2	2,821.8	2,990.2	3,025.6

Contract value = $50.   *Source: Index and Option Market (IOM), division of the Chicago Mercantile Exchange (CME)*

Volume of Trading of E-mini NASDAQ 100 Index Futures in Chicago   In Thousands of Contracts

Year	Jan.	Feb.	Mar.	Apr.	May	June	July	Aug.	Sept.	Oct.	Nov.	Dec.	Total
2005	7,174	6,149	7,336	7,256	5,735	6,233	4,895	5,171	5,624	6,583	5,288	5,008	72,453
2006	6,628	5,803	7,479	5,459	7,386	8,258	6,741	6,315	7,074	6,769	6,333	5,696	79,940
2007	7,122	6,685	8,700	4,976	7,069	8,426	8,122	10,558	6,856	8,916	11,147	6,733	95,309
2008	11,604	8,072	9,677	6,988	7,042	9,912	10,151	7,607	11,523	12,287	7,300	6,571	108,734
2009	5,713	6,789	8,800	6,383	6,241	6,722	6,243	5,959	6,808	7,048	5,686	5,579	77,972
2010	6,712	6,180	6,448	5,938	8,666	8,055	6,905	6,619	7,366	6,249	5,997	4,505	79,638
2011	4,986	4,764	8,138	4,913	5,944	6,778	5,276	8,884	8,035	6,814	5,807	4,826	75,165
2012	3,623	4,274	6,069	5,655	6,429	6,101	4,853	4,449	5,149	5,579	5,845	5,506	63,531
2013	4,420	4,366	4,912	5,226	4,549	6,411	4,223	4,687	5,211	6,077	4,281	5,030	59,393
2014	5,641	5,236	7,514	7,766	5,541	5,253	5,306	4,774	7,104	10,105	4,014	7,221	75,476

Contract value = $20.   *Source: Index and Option Market (IOM), division of the Chicago Mercantile Exchange (CME)*

Average Open Interest of E-mini NASDAQ 100 Index Futures in Chicago   In Contracts

Year	Jan.	Feb.	Mar.	Apr.	May	June	July	Aug.	Sept.	Oct.	Nov.	Dec.
2005	339,077	419,715	382,805	310,664	331,447	290,759	270,134	325,508	307,007	365,277	382,667	371,388
2006	351,240	361,807	345,533	309,746	381,178	427,387	386,930	421,179	437,975	457,275	498,584	433,456
2007	360,663	354,765	423,270	396,080	463,422	454,010	418,512	429,654	451,180	415,073	439,054	408,021
2008	347,374	410,404	424,513	320,046	377,029	358,774	316,037	333,976	336,525	379,643	359,028	302,534
2009	245,830	281,273	302,750	256,064	286,754	284,962	272,424	332,576	341,802	321,653	329,991	338,692
2010	338,217	402,622	362,520	329,709	353,999	353,720	316,651	349,380	397,910	441,782	442,146	401,214
2011	367,204	361,772	350,534	351,601	370,994	321,623	346,518	350,282	369,902	321,427	325,938	308,063
2012	335,164	435,422	484,224	435,734	402,222	376,770	354,698	422,296	480,174	390,199	382,542	380,507
2013	313,000	337,571	376,894	365,878	419,450	381,375	361,111	391,874	393,462	380,763	406,143	439,961
2014	427,403	428,404	452,936	352,802	355,239	383,300	365,320	359,978	399,636	349,013	357,410	376,694

Contract value = $20.   *Source: Index and Option Market (IOM), division of the Chicago Mercantile Exchange (CME)*

Stock Index Futures - WorldWide

World stocks – World stock markets in 2014 closed mixed. The MSCI World Index, a benchmark for large companies based in 23 developed countries, closed up +2.9% in 2014, below the gains of +24.1% seen in 2013 and +13.2% in 2012. Supportive factors for world stocks in 2014 included (1) highly stimulative monetary policies in the U.S., Europe, and Japan, (2) decent global economic growth led by the U.S., and (3) respectable earnings growth. The Federal Reserve in October 2014 ended its third quantitative easing program but kept its key federal funds rate near zero all year. The European Central Bank cut its policy rate twice during 2014 to nearly zero and in January 2015 announced a large quantitative easing program. The Bank of Japan during 2014 expanded its quantitative easing program and kept its policy rate near zero.

China's economy in 2014 eased to a 24-year low of 7.4% as the Chinese economy downshifts into a lower gear due to bad loans, overcapacity in many industries, a weak real estate sector, and an attempt by the government to rein in the shadow banking system. Still, China's growth rate remained strong relative to other countries and helped support the overall world economy.

Small-Capitalization Stocks – The MSCI World Small-Cap Index, which tracks companies with market caps between $200 million and $1.5 billion, rose by just +0.4% in 2014, holding steady after the sharp gains of +30.4% in 2013 and +15.6% in 2012. The +0.4% gain in the MSCI World Small-Cap Index in 2014 was 2.5 percentage points less than the +2.9% gain in the large-cap MSCI World Index. The under-performance by small-caps was not surprising given that the stock indexes in 2014 barely chalked up positive gains. Small-caps, however, have outperformed large caps in four of the last six years (2009-2014).

World Industry Groups – The MSCI industry sectors in 2014 produced the following ranked annual returns: Health Care +16.3%, Information Technology +14.7%, Utilities +12.0%, Consumer Staples +6.0%, Consumer Discretionary +2.4%, Financials +0.9%, Industrials -1.3%, Telecom -5.0%, Materials -7.1%, and Energy -13.7%.

Only 5 of the 9 industry groups showed gains in 2014 as the post-recession rally lost some breadth. Defensive sectors fared well in 2014 with Health Care up +16.3%, Utilities up +12.0%, and Consumer Staples up +6.0%. Information Technology did well at +14.7% as innovation in the sector continued to drive returns. Consumer Discretionary (+2.4%) and Financials (+0.9%) eked out small gains. Industrials (-1.3%) and Materials (-7.1%) showed declines due to weak global economic growth. Energy plunged by -13.7% due to the free-fall in crude oil prices in late 2014.

Emerging markets – The MSCI Emerging Markets Free Index, which tracks companies based in 26 emerging countries, fell by -4.6% in 2014, adding to the -5.0% decline in 2013. The emerging markets saw weakness for the second straight year as they battled high inflation and were negatively impacted by (1) weak commodity and energy prices, and (2) reduced global liquidity as the U.S. Federal Reserve ended its third quantitative easing program.

G7 – The G7 stock markets in 2014 saw mixed results with five of the seven countries showing gains. The U.S. S&P 500 index showed the best results with a gain of +11.4%, which was not surprising given that the U.S. economy showed the strongest performance during the year. The Canadian Toronto Composite index came in second with a +7.4% as it piggy-backed on U.S. strength and was able to fend off the plunge in crude oil prices late in the year. Japan's Nikkei index came in third with an increase of +7.1% as the economy recovered in the fourth quarter from the mid-year recession on the sales tax hike. The Eurozone stock markets showed middling results as the Eurozone economy struggled to keep its head above water and as Greece caused trouble with its bailout program late in the year: Germany's Dax Index +2.7%, Italy's MIB Index +0.2%, France's CAC40 Index -0.5%. The UK FTSE 100 index in 2014 showed a -2.7% decline.

North America – In North America, the U.S. S&P 500 index (+11.4%) in 2014 outperformed Canada's Toronto Composite (+7.4%) and Mexico's Bolsa Index (+1.0%). The Toronto Composite index has now underperformed the S&P 500 index for four consecutive years after the 7-year streak (2004-2010) of outperforming the S&P 500.

Latin America – Five of the large Latin America stock markets showed increases in 2014 while four showed declines. The ranked returns are as follows: Argentina's Merval Index +59.1%, Venezuela's Stock Market Index +41.0%, Ecuador's Guayaqui Bolsa Index +13.2%, Costa Rica's Stock Market Index +10.7%, Chile's Stock Market Select Index +4.1%, Brazil's Bovespa Index -2.9%, Jamaica's Stock Exchange Index -5.2%, Peru's Lima General Index -6.1%, and Columbia's General Index -11.0%.

Europe – European stocks in 2014 closed on a weak note as the Eurozone economy struggled to recover as the Eurozone sovereign debt crisis receded. The Euro Stoxx 50 index eked out a gain of +2.9% in 2014, adding to the gains of +13.3% in 20313 and +8.8% in 2012. The ranked returns in 2014 were as follows: Spanish IBEX 35 index +3.7%, German DAX index +2.7%, Italian MIB index +0.2%, French CAC 40 index -0.5%, UK FTSE 100 index -2.7%.

Asia – The Asian stock markets in 2014 closed mixed. The MSCI Far East Index in 2014 fell by -2.3% after the gains of +23.4% seen in 2013 and +12.0% in 2012. Asian stocks in 2014 were led higher by sharp rallies in China (+52.9%) and India (+29.9%). The ranked closes for the Asian stock markets in 2014 were as follows: China's Shanghai Composite Index +52.9%, India's Mumbai Sensex 30 index +29.9%, Pakistan's 100 Index +27.2%, Philippines' Composite index +22.7%, Indonesia's Jakarta Composite Index +22.3%, New Zealand's Exchange 50 Index +17.5%, Thailand's Stock Exchange index +15.3%, Vietnam's Stock Index +8.1%, Taiwan's TAIEX Index +8.1%, Japan's Nikkei 225 Index +7.1%, Singapore's Straights Times Index +6.2%, Hong Kong's Hang Seng +1.3%, Australia's All-Ordinaries Index +0.7%, South Korea's Composite Index -4.8%, and Malaysia's Kuala Lumpur Composite index -5.7%.

STOCK INDEX FUTURES - WORLDWIDE

Comparison of International Indices   (2010=100)

Year	Jan.	Feb.	Mar.	Apr.	May	June	July	Aug.	Sept.	Oct.	Nov.	Dec. Average
United States
2008	126.7	125.5	123.2	127.9	129.5	121.8	114.4	116.5	112.3	92.7	87.0	86.9	113.7
2009	84.8	77.7	73.1	80.8	84.9	86.8	87.7	94.7	97.4	99.6	103.3	105.4	89.7
2010	105.8	10.3	107.9	111.7	106.1	102.7	103.3	104.6	107.1	111.6	113.2	115.8	100.0
2011	119.3	123.2	122.1	125.6	127.1	122.2	126.4	114.4	112.9	116.4	119.3	122.0	120.9
2012	126.8	130.2	132.2	131.7	128.5	126.8	129.5	132.7	135.6	135.2	130.3	132.8	131.0
2013	137.6	141.1	145.7	148.3	153.3	151.9	155.5	153.5	154.3	154.5	160.4	162.6	151.6
2014	164.1	161.2	164.8	165.7	167.4	170.2	171.7	169.5	172.8	168.8	178.3	179.4	169.5
Canada
2008	109.5	110.6	109.7	115.1	121.0	121.9	112.8	110.7	103.1	81.0	74.7	70.2	103.4
2009	73.6	69.9	68.9	76.4	83.1	85.9	85.3	89.6	93.2	93.5	94.5	95.9	84.2
2010	96.5	94.9	99.1	100.7	97.9	96.8	95.7	97.2	100.8	104.1	106.4	110.0	100.0
2011	110.9	115.2	115.4	115.7	112.8	108.7	110.1	102.6	100.5	98.8	99.7	98.2	107.4
2012	102.2	104.0	103.2	100.5	96.5	95.2	96.3	98.7	101.8	102.2	100.8	101.8	100.3
2013	104.9	105.5	105.8	101.9	104.3	101.2	103.4	104.6	106.2	108.2	111.0	110.5	105.6
2014	113.7	115.7	118.3	119.6	121.2	123.9	126.5	127.5	127.2	119.8	122.8	118.7	121.2
France
2008	137.5	129.3	123.8	130.7	133.9	124.5	114.4	117.7	112.6	92.7	87.7	85.2	115.8
2009	82.7	77.7	72.7	80.2	86.6	86.5	85.7	94.5	99.6	100.9	100.1	102.8	89.2
2010	104.7	98.4	104.7	106.0	95.0	94.9	94.4	96.5	99.4	101.4	101.9	102.7	100.0
2011	105.7	109.0	105.2	107.3	106.7	102.8	101.9	85.4	79.6	84.0	80.9	82.5	95.9
2012	86.7	91.3	93.1	86.7	82.3	81.5	85.4	91.5	93.1	91.7	92.4	96.9	89.4
2013	99.6	98.2	101.0	99.7	105.9	101.2	103.4	108.0	109.9	112.8	114.2	111.0	105.4
2014	113.4	114.8	115.8	118.4	119.7	120.7	116.4	113.4	118.1	110.2	113.7	113.7	115.7
Germany
2008	118.4	111.3	105.0	109.3	114.0	108.6	102.5	103.8	99.2	80.0	75.8	75.3	100.3
2009	73.3	68.9	64.2	73.0	79.0	79.7	80.0	87.2	90.2	91.8	91.2	94.3	81.1
2010	94.8	90.3	96.4	100.5	96.4	98.3	98.0	99.0	100.4	104.0	109.0	113.0	100.0
2011	113.8	117.9	112.4	116.8	118.5	115.7	117.9	95.7	87.3	94.9	94.2	94.8	106.7
2012	101.5	109.7	112.6	108.8	103.8	99.9	105.9	112.3	117.6	117.8	117.0	122.4	110.8
2013	125.2	123.9	127.9	124.8	134.4	130.7	131.9	134.7	137.3	142.2	148.2	149.3	134.2
2014	153.8	153.7	151.0	153.4	156.9	160.5	157.6	149.9	155.8	145.0	153.4	158.6	154.1
Italy
2008	170.5	160.7	151.2	158.6	159.6	146.3	134.3	135.4	130.5	104.4	97.8	91.2	136.7
2009	89.5	80.6	69.2	84.3	94.8	93.1	91.6	102.7	108.7	111.4	107.9	107.9	95.1
2010	109.7	101.4	106.8	108.2	94.4	93.8	96.3	97.2	97.8	99.8	98.0	96.6	100.0
2011	101.2	107.1	103.6	104.3	101.8	95.3	90.3	73.9	68.2	75.3	71.2	71.4	88.6
2012	73.0	78.1	78.9	69.8	63.9	63.0	64.6	69.8	75.3	74.3	73.2	75.8	71.6
2013	82.6	77.9	75.1	75.3	81.8	76.1	75.5	80.8	83.1	89.4	89.9	86.9	81.2
2014	92.8	95.1	98.9	102.8	100.4	103.9	99.4	94.4	99.1	91.7	92.1	91.2	96.8
Japan
2008	137.2	135.3	125.9	133.4	139.8	140.7	131.6	129.8	121.1	91.1	85.2	84.6	121.3
2009	83.2	76.9	77.6	87.6	93.0	98.0	96.8	104.2	102.9	100.6	96.3	101.6	93.2
2010	106.5	101.7	106.6	111.3	100.9	97.8	94.5	92.6	93.4	94.5	97.9	102.4	100.0
2011	104.4	106.1	98.4	96.4	96.4	95.3	99.9	90.6	86.9	87.3	85.0	85.0	94.3
2012	86.1	92.3	99.5	96.2	88.3	86.3	87.5	89.4	89.4	88.2	90.5	98.0	91.0
2013	107.4	113.2	122.4	132.1	144.8	130.9	143.0	137.1	143.6	143.2	149.2	156.4	135.3
2014	155.6	146.0	146.8	144.6	143.3	151.2	153.6	153.4	159.3	153.8	171.6	175.2	154.6
United Kingdom
2008	110.3	108.1	103.8	109.6	113.2	105.7	98.3	100.0	95.7	78.4	77.3	78.1	98.2
2009	78.3	74.5	68.8	74.0	80.4	79.5	80.0	87.0	92.1	94.4	95.9	97.1	83.5
2010	99.0	95.7	102.8	104.6	95.8	94.0	94.3	96.5	100.9	104.0	104.9	107.5	100.0
2011	109.2	110.1	107.1	109.9	108.6	105.9	108.1	96.4	95.6	98.9	98.8	100.2	104.1
2012	104.2	107.8	107.5	104.7	99.9	100.2	103.1	106.0	106.2	106.7	105.9	108.3	105.0
2013	112.7	115.5	117.7	116.3	121.6	115.2	119.2	119.3	119.8	120.2	122.4	120.2	118.4
2014	122.8	122.4	121.3	121.7	125.0	124.4	123.9	122.8	124.0	117.2	121.5	119.7	122.2

Not Seasonally Adjusted.   Source: Economic and Statistics Administration, U.S. Department of Commerce (ESA)

DAX® is Deutsche Börse's blue chip index for the German stock market. It comprises the 30 largest and most actively traded German companies.   Shaded areas indicate German recessions.

Average Value of Deutscher Aktienindex (DAX)

Year	Jan.	Feb.	Mar.	Apr.	May	June	July	Aug.	Sept.	Oct.	Nov.	Dec.	Average
2005	4,246.4	4,344.7	4,357.4	4,293.8	4,329.6	4,569.2	4,726.6	4,886.3	4,946.1	4,951.8	5,092.5	5,343.1	4,674.0
2006	5,494.0	5,762.5	5,861.7	6,010.0	5,845.8	5,495.3	5,594.2	5,750.3	5,901.0	6,161.3	6,368.7	6,492.6	5,894.8
2007	6,692.5	6,913.1	6,706.0	7,237.3	7,582.0	7,874.5	7,888.9	7,463.6	7,638.5	7,950.7	7,715.2	7,945.3	7,467.3
2008	7,323.7	6,886.7	6,499.6	6,762.7	7,056.1	6,716.8	6,341.5	6,421.5	6,137.0	4,946.8	4,692.0	4,657.9	6,203.5
2009	4,534.2	4,265.0	3,969.2	4,519.1	4,886.4	4,930.8	4,949.6	5,395.2	5,584.0	5,680.0	5,642.2	5,836.6	5,016.0
2010	5,863.2	5,584.7	5,965.1	6,215.3	5,966.6	6,080.8	6,061.3	6,122.4	6,214.9	6,436.3	6,744.4	6,991.9	6,187.2
2011	7,039.7	7,294.2	6,952.0	7,227.1	7,330.6	7,158.7	7,292.8	5,923.8	5,402.3	5,871.8	5,826.5	5,867.8	6,598.9
2012	6,278.3	6,789.6	6,966.5	6,731.9	6,424.8	6,184.0	6,549.6	6,949.8	7,274.4	7,288.2	7,238.6	7,576.2	6,854.3
2013	7,747.6	7,666.7	7,913.9	7,723.1	8,317.4	8,089.2	8,161.8	8,332.5	8,497.8	8,800.5	9,170.6	9,235.0	8,304.7
2014	9,516.8	9,509.5	9,339.9	9,490.0	9,709.5	9,927.4	9,751.8	9,273.1	9,638.7	8,971.9	9,490.3	9,812.3	9,535.9

Source: EUREX

The FTSE 100 Index covers 100 of the largest companies traded on the LSE.   Shaded areas indicate United Kingdom recessions.

Average Value of FTSE 100 Stock Index

Year	Jan.	Feb.	Mar.	Apr.	May	June	July	Aug.	Sept.	Oct.	Nov.	Dec.	Average
2005	4,826.5	4,998.8	4,961.5	4,887.8	4,928.9	5,050.3	5,228.4	5,311.0	5,392.6	5,292.9	5,458.2	5,547.2	5,157.0
2006	5,711.2	5,806.7	5,938.8	6,054.4	5,846.0	5,668.1	5,833.7	5,877.7	5,896.1	6,100.5	6,167.8	6,171.6	5,922.7
2007	6,237.8	6,362.5	6,204.9	6,433.9	6,569.8	6,598.0	6,561.9	6,177.2	6,345.1	6,599.3	6,326.7	6,433.5	6,404.2
2008	6,033.2	5,910.1	5,676.3	5,993.3	6,187.2	5,778.3	5,375.2	5,465.7	5,233.9	4,288.8	4,224.9	4,270.7	5,369.8
2009	4,281.9	4,074.4	3,760.2	4,046.3	4,393.8	4,349.3	4,374.5	4,755.6	5,033.1	5,161.2	5,242.3	5,309.5	4,565.2
2010	5,411.7	5,231.9	5,621.0	5,720.7	5,238.8	5,139.3	5,158.4	5,276.0	5,514.7	5,687.2	5,735.8	5,874.9	5,467.5
2011	5,971.3	6,021.1	5,858.2	6,007.9	5,938.0	5,792.2	5,909.8	5,271.3	5,228.5	5,408.6	5,402.5	5,480.1	5,690.8
2012	5,694.5	5,893.4	5,875.4	5,725.6	5,461.5	5,480.4	5,636.5	5,797.0	5,805.5	5,831.8	5,787.5	5,922.7	5,742.6
2013	6,161.9	6,316.4	6,435.6	6,361.0	6,647.4	6,299.4	6,517.9	6,521.5	6,552.4	6,572.0	6,694.3	6,573.0	6,471.0
2014	6,714.5	6,690.8	6,631.7	6,652.0	6,834.8	6,804.3	6,772.0	6,712.2	6,777.8	6,408.6	6,644.1	6,542.6	6,682.1

Source: Euronext LIFFE

STOCK INDEX FUTURES - WORLDWIDE

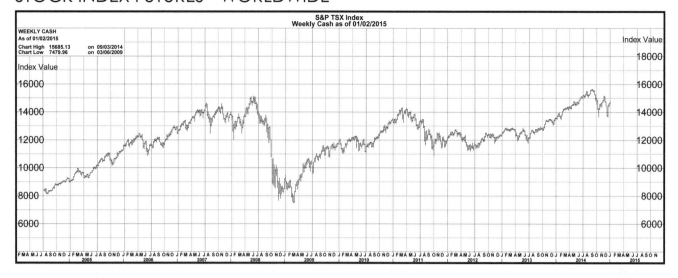

Average Value of S&P TSX Index

Year	Jan.	Feb.	Mar.	Apr.	May	June	July	Aug.	Sept.	Oct.	Nov.	Dec.	Average
2005	9,088	9,530	9,697	9,475	9,472	9,860	10,247	10,571	10,918	10,488	10,747	11,151	10,104
2006	11,662	11,770	11,972	12,291	11,923	11,341	11,659	12,035	11,770	11,970	12,422	12,854	11,972
2007	12,747	13,207	13,026	13,535	13,929	13,935	14,197	13,411	13,864	14,215	13,745	13,671	13,623
2008	13,216	13,353	13,245	13,891	14,613	14,719	13,623	13,364	12,450	9,774	9,024	8,473	12,479
2009	8,886	8,438	8,314	9,225	10,031	10,372	10,293	10,816	11,255	11,291	11,414	11,580	10,160
2010	11,654	11,454	11,967	12,154	11,816	11,680	11,559	11,729	12,164	12,569	12,843	13,275	12,072
2011	13,393	13,908	13,933	13,962	13,621	13,126	13,295	12,381	12,131	11,923	12,038	11,861	12,964
2012	12,332	12,553	12,464	12,135	11,644	11,496	11,627	11,921	12,286	12,338	12,163	12,290	12,104
2013	12,669	12,737	12,777	12,299	12,585	12,221	12,480	12,623	12,819	13,058	13,396	13,339	12,750
2014	13,728	13,964	14,281	14,441	14,636	14,961	15,268	15,389	15,353	14,461	14,825	14,330	14,636

Source: Toronto Stock Exchange

The CAC 40® is a free float market capitalization weighted index that reflects the performance of the 40 largest and most actively traded shares listed on Euronext Paris, and is the most widely used indicator of the Paris stock market.   Shaded areas indicate French recessions.

Average Value of CAC 40 Index

Year	Jan.	Feb.	Mar.	Apr.	May	June	July	Aug.	Sept.	Oct.	Nov.	Dec.	Average
2005	3,863.0	3,991.3	4,059.6	4,027.7	4,049.4	4,193.2	4,359.5	4,445.0	4,495.6	4,471.4	4,533.9	4,700.6	4,265.8
2006	4,839.7	4,976.6	5,111.9	5,188.6	5,073.2	4,789.2	4,910.6	5,073.3	5,157.9	5,338.8	5,414.5	5,448.1	5,110.2
2007	5,587.0	5,684.2	5,495.4	5,831.8	6,053.9	6,014.9	5,973.5	5,534.8	5,597.2	5,793.7	5,565.3	5,619.1	5,729.2
2008	5,153.6	4,845.2	4,641.1	4,900.2	5,020.2	4,664.6	4,287.2	4,409.9	4,220.5	3,474.7	3,287.2	3,192.2	4,341.4
2009	3,099.7	2,911.5	2,725.3	3,007.2	3,244.0	3,242.9	3,212.0	3,539.9	3,732.7	3,780.0	3,752.7	3,851.9	3,341.6
2010	3,925.2	3,687.1	3,922.2	3,973.7	3,561.5	3,558.0	3,539.3	3,616.9	3,723.6	3,799.4	3,818.4	3,848.5	3,747.8
2011	3,960.7	4,086.4	3,941.7	4,020.3	3,998.6	3,853.3	3,818.0	3,201.9	2,983.1	3,148.4	3,033.0	3,091.9	3,594.8
2012	3,250.6	3,420.4	3,490.0	3,248.8	3,084.4	3,055.9	3,199.6	3,427.4	3,490.9	3,435.7	3,461.5	3,631.8	3,349.7
2013	3,734.0	3,679.4	3,786.4	3,735.1	3,968.7	3,792.5	3,876.6	4,046.3	4,117.7	4,228.0	4,279.9	4,161.4	3,950.5
2014	4,248.4	4,301.1	4,338.1	4,437.3	4,484.8	4,522.0	4,362.0	4,249.6	4,425.3	4,129.8	4,261.0	4,262.2	4,335.1

Source: Euronext Paris

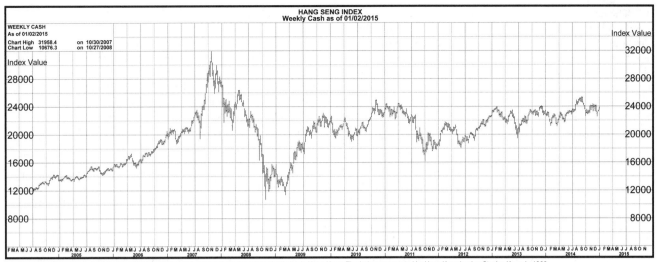

The Hang Seng Index is a freefloat-adjusted market capitalization-weighted stock market index in Hong Kong. The Index was created by Hong Kong banker Stanley Kwan in 1969.

Average Value of Hang Seng Index

Year	Jan.	Feb.	Mar.	Apr.	May	June	July	Aug.	Sept.	Oct.	Nov.	Dec.	Average
2005	13,644	13,914	13,774	13,661	13,825	13,996	14,463	15,128	15,192	14,644	14,761	15,065	14,339
2006	15,526	15,581	15,729	16,557	16,473	15,725	16,457	17,139	17,355	17,991	18,952	19,114	16,883
2007	20,197	20,484	19,339	20,439	20,727	21,214	22,878	22,321	24,997	29,153	28,287	28,053	23,174
2008	25,401	23,848	22,561	24,597	25,237	23,184	22,079	21,435	19,370	14,925	13,573	14,593	20,900
2009	13,794	13,167	12,795	15,029	17,124	18,342	18,904	20,475	20,920	21,654	22,219	21,748	18,014
2010	21,409	20,244	21,089	21,624	19,945	20,104	20,446	21,109	21,658	23,301	23,805	23,057	21,483
2011	23,865	23,197	23,110	24,009	23,133	22,342	22,280	20,334	19,007	18,352	18,865	18,586	21,423
2012	19,456	21,128	21,013	20,666	19,615	18,940	19,372	19,946	20,227	21,293	21,650	22,406	20,476
2013	23,471	23,148	22,518	22,054	22,933	21,064	21,299	22,009	22,933	23,102	23,305	23,371	22,601
2014	22,725	22,188	21,981	22,598	22,585	23,145	23,760	24,812	24,342	23,301	23,779	23,386	23,217

Source: Hong Kong Futures Exchange

The Nikkei Stock Average is owned by and proprietary to Nihon Keisai Shimbun.   Shaded areas indicate Japan recessions.

Average Value of Nikkei 225 Index

Year	Jan.	Feb.	Mar.	Apr.	May	June	July	Aug.	Sept.	Oct.	Nov.	Dec.	Average
2005	11,395	11,545	11,809	11,396	11,082	11,403	11,717	12,205	12,979	13,393	14,368	15,651	12,412
2006	16,086	16,188	16,312	17,233	16,322	14,990	15,148	15,787	15,934	16,519	16,101	16,791	16,117
2007	17,286	17,741	17,128	17,470	17,595	18,001	17,975	16,461	16,235	16,903	15,544	15,545	16,990
2008	13,731	13,548	12,603	13,358	13,995	14,085	13,169	12,989	12,124	9,117	8,531	8,464	12,143
2009	8,331	7,695	7,765	8,768	9,304	9,810	9,691	10,430	10,303	10,066	9,641	10,169	9,331
2010	10,662	10,175	10,671	11,140	10,104	9,786	9,457	9,268	9,347	9,455	9,797	10,254	10,010
2011	10,450	10,622	9,852	9,645	9,651	9,542	9,997	9,073	8,695	8,734	8,506	8,506	9,439
2012	8,617	9,242	9,962	9,627	8,843	8,638	8,761	8,950	8,949	8,827	9,060	9,814	9,108
2013	10,751	11,327	12,255	13,224	14,494	13,107	14,318	13,727	14,372	14,329	14,932	15,655	13,541
2014	15,578	14,618	14,695	14,475	14,343	15,132	15,379	15,359	15,948	15,394	17,179	17,542	15,470

Source: Singapore Exchange

Sugar

The white crystalline substance called "sugar" is the organic chemical compound sucrose, one of several related compounds all known as sugars. These include glucose, dextrose, fructose, and lactose. All sugars are members of the larger group of compounds called carbohydrates and are characterized by a sweet taste. Sucrose is considered a double sugar because it is composed of one molecule of glucose and one molecule of fructose. While sucrose is common in many plants, it occurs in the highest concentration in sugarcane (Saccharum officinarum) and sugar beets (Beta vulgaris). Sugarcane is about 7 to 18 percent sugar by weight while sugar beets are 8 to 22 percent.

Sugarcane is a member of the grass family and is a perennial. Sugarcane is cultivated in tropical and subtropical regions around the world roughly between the Tropics of Cancer and Capricorn. It grows best in hot, wet climates where there is heavy rainfall followed by a dry season. The largest cane producers are Florida, Louisiana, Texas, and Hawaii. On a commercial basis, sugarcane is not grown from seeds but from cuttings or pieces of the stalk.

Sugar beets, which are produced in temperate or colder climates, are annuals grown from seeds. Sugar beets do best with moderate temperatures and evenly distributed rainfall. The beets are planted in the spring and harvested in the fall. The sugar is contained in the root of the beet, but the sugars from beets and cane are identical. Sugar beet production takes place mostly in Europe, the U.S., China, and Japan. The largest sugar beet producing states are Minnesota, Idaho, North Dakota, and Michigan. Sugar beets are refined to yield white sugar and very little raw sugar is produced.

Sugar beets and sugarcane are produced in over 100 countries around the world. Of all the sugar produced, about 25% is processed from sugar beets and the remaining 75% is from sugar cane. The trend has been that production of sugar from cane is increasing relative to that produced from beets. The significance of this in that sugarcane is a perennial plant while the sugar beet is an annual, and due to the longer production cycle, sugarcane production and the sugar processed from that cane, may not be quite as responsive to changes in price.

Sugar futures are traded at the ICE Futures U.S., the Bolsa de Mercadorias & Futuros (BM&F), Kansai Commodities Exchange (KANEX), the Tokyo Grain Exchange (TGE), and the London International Financial Futures and Options Exchange (LIFFE).

Raw sugar is traded on the ICE exchange while white sugar is traded on the London International Financial Futures Exchange (LIFFE). The most actively traded contract is the No. 11 (World) sugar contract at the ICE exchange. The No. 11 contract calls for the delivery of 112,000 pounds (50 long tons) of raw cane centrifugal sugar from any of 28 foreign countries of origin and the United States. The ICE exchange also trades the No. 14 sugar contract (Domestic), which calls for the delivery of raw centrifugal cane sugar in the United States. Futures on white sugar are traded on the London International Financial Futures Exchange and call for the delivery of 50 metric tons of white beet sugar, cane crystal sugar, or refined sugar of any origin from the crop current at the time of delivery.

Prices – ICE World No. 11 Sugar prices on the nearest-futures chart (Barchart.com symbol SB) slid to a 4-1/2 year low in January 2014 of 14.70 cents per pound after the International Sugar Organization (ISO) raised its 2012/13 global sugar production estimate to a record 183.7 MMT and estimated a record 2012/13 global sugar surplus of 10.6 MMT. Also, the ISO predicted that sugar imports from China, the world's second-largest sugar consumer, would fall 36% yr/yr in 2014 to 2.35 MMT as the government phased out stockpiling after China sugar inventories soared to a record 6 MMT in 2013. In addition, India, the world's second-biggest sugar producer, said it would allow an additional 4 MMT of sugar exports in 2014 order to trim its sugar reserves that rose to a 5-year high of 8.85 MMT. Sugar prices recovered and moved to the high for 2014 in March at 18.40 cents per pound on Brazil drought concerns. Prices moved sideways through Q2 and then plunged in Q3, posting a 4-1/2 year low in September at 13.32 cents per pound. Thailand, the world's second-biggest sugar exporter, reported a record 2013/14 sugar harvest of 11.29 MMT and said it would export a record 9 MMT of sugar in 2014. The USDA estimated that despite a loss of Brazil sugar output from drought, 2014/15 global sugar ending stocks would be 42.2 MMT, the fifth straight year of surplus. Sugar prices recovered slightly into year-end and finished 2014 down -11.5% at 14.52 cents per pound.

Supply – World production of centrifugal (raw) sugar in the 2014-15 marketing year (Oct 1 to Sep 30) fell -1.5% to 172.458 million metric tons, below the 2012-13 record high of 177.557 million metric tons. The world's largest sugar producers in 2014-15 were Brazil with 20.8% of world production, India with 15.8%, and the European Union with 9.5%. U.S. centrifugal sugar production in 2014-15 rose +0.1% to 7.677 million metric tons. World ending stocks in 2014-15 fell -3.2% to 42.215 million metric tons. The stocks/consumption ratio fell -5.3% in 2014-15 to 24,700 metric tons. U.S. production of cane sugar in 2014-15 rose +2.1% to 3.740 million short tons and beet sugar production rose +1.6% yr/yr to 4.870 million short tons.

Demand – World domestic consumption of centrifugal (raw) sugar in 2014-15 rose by +2.2% yr/yr to a new record high of 170.996 million metric tons. U.S. domestic disappearance (consumption) of sugar in 2014-15 rose by +2.5% yr/yr to 12.244 million short tons. U.S. per capita sugar consumption in 2013-14 (latest data) rose +2.0% to 67.90 pounds per year, which was only about two-thirds of the levels seen in the early 1970s.

Trade – World exports of centrifugal sugar in 2014-15 fell -6.5% yr/yr to 53.697 million metric tons, below last year's record high of 57.437. The world's largest sugar exporter was Brazil, where exports in 2014-15 fell -8.4% yr/yr to 24.000 million metric tons, which accounted for 44.7% of total world exports. The next largest exporters are Thailand with 15.8% of world exports and Australia with 6.5%. U.S. sugar exports in 2014-15 fell -18.4% yr/yr to 250,000 short tons, which is down from the 15-year high of 422,000 seen in 2006-07. U.S. sugar imports in 2014-15 fell -6.3% yr/yr to 3.149 million short tons, down from the decade high of 3.355 in 2010-11.

World Production, Supply & Stocks/Consumption Ratio of Sugar   In 1000's of Metric Tons (Raw Value)

Marketing Year	Beginning Stocks	Production	Imports	Total Supply	Exports	Domestic Consumption	Ending Stocks	Stocks As a % of Consumption
2005-06	34,739	144,303	44,720	223,762	49,534	143,039	30,474	21.3
2006-07	30,474	164,278	44,142	238,979	50,759	149,452	36,736	24.6
2007-08	36,736	163,257	44,959	245,037	50,625	150,599	43,080	28.6
2008-09	43,080	143,833	42,333	229,767	44,962	153,461	30,303	19.7
2009-10	29,839	153,179	48,367	231,385	48,332	154,232	28,042	18.2
2010-11	28,042	162,189	49,339	239,570	53,857	155,763	29,281	18.8
2011-12	29,281	172,297	48,400	249,978	55,019	159,208	35,129	22.1
2012-13[1]	35,129	177,557	50,991	263,677	55,293	164,725	42,505	25.8
2013-14[2]	42,505	175,010	51,837	269,352	57,437	167,277	43,620	26.1
2014-15[3]	43,620	172,458	51,763	267,841	53,697	170,996	42,215	24.7

[1] Preliminary.   [2] Estimate.   [3] Forecast.   *Source: Foreign Agricultural Service, U.S. Department of Agriculture (FAS-USDA)*

World Production of Sugar (Centrifugal Sugar-Raw Value)   In Thousands of Metric Tons

Year	Australia	Brazil	China	Cuba	European Union	India	Indonesia	Mexico	Pakistan	Thailand	United States	Ukraine	World Total
2005-06	5,297	26,850	9,446	1,240	21,373	21,140	2,100	5,604	2,597	4,835	2,054	6,713	144,303
2006-07	5,212	31,450	12,855	1,200	17,987	30,780	1,900	5,633	3,615	6,720	2,850	7,662	164,278
2007-08	4,939	31,600	15,898	1,420	15,834	28,630	2,000	5,852	4,163	7,820	2,020	7,396	163,257
2008-09	4,814	31,850	13,317	1,340	14,290	15,950	2,053	5,260	3,512	7,200	1,710	6,833	143,833
2009-10	4,700	36,400	11,429	1,250	16,897	20,637	1,910	5,115	3,420	6,930	1,382	7,224	153,179
2010-11	3,700	38,350	11,199	1,150	15,939	26,574	1,770	5,495	3,920	9,663	1,540	7,104	162,189
2011-12	3,683	36,150	12,341	1,400	18,320	28,620	1,830	5,351	4,520	10,235	2,300	7,700	172,297
2012-13[1]	4,250	38,600	14,001	1,525	16,655	27,337	2,300	7,393	5,000	10,024	2,400	8,148	177,557
2013-14[2]	4,400	37,800	14,263	1,600	16,010	26,605	2,300	6,383	5,215	11,333	1,300	7,672	175,010
2014-15[3]	4,600	35,800	13,300	1,650	16,300	27,250	2,500	6,508	4,700	10,200	1,600	7,677	172,458

[1] Preliminary.   [2] Estimate.   [3] Forecast.   *Source: Foreign Agricultural Service, U.S. Department of Agriculture (FAS-USDA)*

World Stocks of Centrifugal Sugar at Beginning of Marketing Year   In Thousands of Metric Tons (Raw Value)

Year	Australia	Brazil	China	Cuba	European Union	India	Indonesia	Iran	Mexico	Philippines	Russia	United States	World Total
2005-06	343	585	1,757	215	5,339	5,160	1,120	542	2,045	239	580	1,208	34,739
2006-07	291	-285	703	225	5,088	4,000	1,170	932	1,294	253	470	1,540	30,474
2007-08	402	-485	1,401	155	2,720	11,701	570	1,292	1,718	262	440	1,632	36,736
2008-09	400	215	3,965	135	3,130	12,296	590	1,362	1,975	547	550	1,510	43,080
2009-10	487	-1,135	3,784	102	2,232	5,880	340	475	623	581	481	1,392	29,839
2010-11	413	-835	2,355	114	1,433	6,223	750	475	973	730	399	1,359	28,042
2011-12	193	-285	1,621	59	1,974	6,299	602	650	806	934	350	1,250	29,281
2012-13[1]	64	-285	4,140	109	3,303	7,163	409	640	1,024	932	390	1,795	35,129
2013-14[2]	83	-535	6,793	150	3,836	9,373	879	700	1,548	942	395	1,958	42,505
2014-15[3]	65	-195	8,832	160	3,396	8,018	1,564	750	881	932	400	1,629	43,620

[1] Preliminary.   [2] Estimate.   [3] Forecast.   *Source: Foreign Agricultural Service, U.S. Department of Agriculture (FAS-USDA)*

Centrifugal Sugar (Raw Value) Imported into Selected Countries   In Thousands of Metric Tons

Year	Algeria	Canada	China	European Union	Indonesia	Iran	Japan	Korea, South	Malaysia	Nigeria	Russia	United States	World Total
2005-06	1,130	1,445	1,234	2,630	1,800	1,450	1,385	1,669	1,414	1,200	2,900	3,124	44,720
2006-07	1,110	1,161	1,465	3,530	1,800	1,600	1,432	1,475	1,670	1,240	2,950	1,887	44,142
2007-08	1,105	1,445	972	2,948	2,420	1,200	1,477	1,805	1,425	1,485	3,100	2,377	44,959
2008-09	1,159	1,255	1,077	3,180	2,197	973	1,279	1,687	1,504	1,175	2,150	2,796	42,333
2009-10	1,260	1,114	1,535	2,561	3,200	1,643	1,199	1,617	1,527	1,431	2,223	3,010	48,367
2010-11	1,193	1,135	2,143	3,755	3,082	1,292	1,331	1,688	1,813	1,495	2,510	3,391	49,339
2011-12	1,594	1,103	4,430	3,552	3,027	1,079	1,230	1,668	1,720	1,399	510	3,294	48,400
2012-13[1]	2,014	1,156	3,802	3,790	3,570	1,553	1,330	1,806	1,966	1,450	735	2,925	50,991
2013-14[2]	1,854	1,053	4,330	3,300	4,085	1,629	1,415	1,909	1,897	1,470	1,250	3,362	51,837
2014-15[3]	1,850	1,300	3,800	3,500	3,800	1,600	1,415	1,945	1,925	1,470	1,500	3,149	51,763

[1] Preliminary.   [2] Estimate.   [3] Forecast.   *Source: Foreign Agricultural Service, U.S. Department of Agriculture (FAS-USDA)*

SUGAR

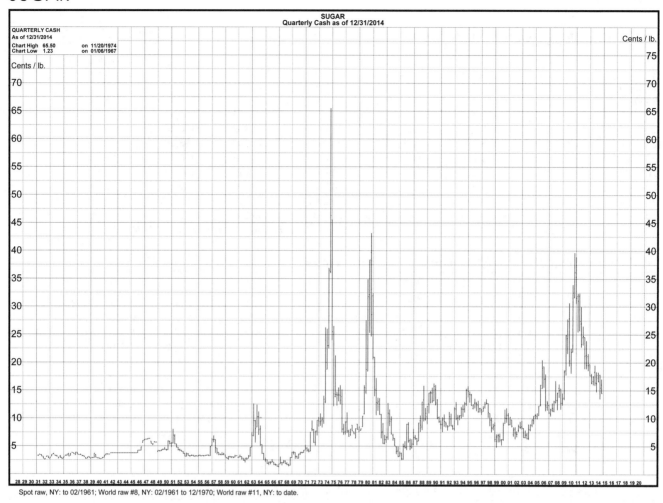

QUARTERLY CASH
As of 12/31/2014
Chart High 65.50 on 11/20/1974
Chart Low 1.23 on 01/06/1967

Cents / lb.

Spot raw, NY: to 02/1961; World raw #8, NY: 02/1961 to 12/1970; World raw #11, NY: to date.

Centrifugal Sugar (Raw Value) Exported From Selected Countries   In Thousands of Metric Tons

Year	Australia	Brazil	Colom-bia	Cuba	Dominican Republic	European Union	Guate-mala	India	Mauritius	South Africa	Swazi-land	Thailand	World Total
2005-06	4,208	17,090	988	730	251	8,345	1,391	1,510	548	1,230	320	2,242	49,534
2006-07	3,860	20,850	942	795	225	2,439	1,500	2,680	510	1,267	358	4,705	50,759
2007-08	3,700	19,500	661	960	217	1,656	1,333	6,014	443	1,154	350	4,914	50,625
2008-09	3,522	21,550	585	727	239	1,332	1,654	224	455	1,230	350	5,295	44,962
2009-10	3,600	24,300	870	538	261	2,647	1,815	225	271	754	350	4,930	48,332
2010-11	2,750	25,800	830	577	204	1,113	1,544	3,903	338	400	320	6,642	53,857
2011-12	2,800	24,650	876	830	211	2,343	1,619	3,764	389	271	315	7,898	55,019
2012-13[1]	3,100	27,650	542	794	165	1,662	1,911	964	406	356	363	6,693	55,293
2013-14[2]	3,290	26,200	800	850	222	1,450	1,950	2,810	445	868	373	7,500	57,437
2014-15[3]	3,500	24,000	800	850	233	1,500	1,950	1,500	430	800	385	8,500	53,697

[1] Preliminary.   [2] Estimate.   [3] Forecast.   *Source: Foreign Agricultural Service, U.S. Department of Agriculture (FAS-USDA)*

Average Wholesale Price of Refined Beet Sugar[2]--Midwest Market   In Cents Per Pound

Year	Jan.	Feb.	Mar.	Apr.	May	June	July	Aug.	Sept.	Oct.	Nov.	Dec.	Average
2005	23.50	23.50	23.25	23.80	24.75	25.88	26.00	26.75	40.10	40.00	40.00	36.90	29.54
2006	34.50	36.50	37.10	36.38	35.00	35.00	35.00	34.50	31.20	28.75	27.19	26.10	33.10
2007	25.50	25.00	24.90	25.00	25.00	25.00	25.38	25.60	25.38	25.00	24.50	24.50	25.06
2008	24.13	26.40	28.00	28.00	29.60	33.25	38.00	38.40	38.50	36.20	35.00	35.00	32.54
2009	35.00	35.00	35.00	34.25	34.40	35.50	35.40	38.00	42.00	42.60	45.00	45.00	38.10
2010	50.50	53.00	52.25	48.20	45.00	50.00	53.40	59.50	59.00	54.40	56.50	57.00	53.23
2011	54.50	54.00	56.50	56.80	54.00	55.00	55.40	57.00	58.60	59.00	58.75	55.10	56.22
2012	51.75	51.00	51.00	50.25	47.81	45.00	42.00	41.20	38.25	36.00	34.60	31.75	43.38
2013	30.50	28.50	27.60	26.63	26.30	26.50	26.00	25.50	26.25	27.38	28.00	27.50	27.22
2014[1]	26.50	26.25	26.50	29.75	31.60	35.00	36.00	36.60	37.50	36.60	36.00	36.00	32.86

[1] Preliminary.   [2] These are f.o.b. basis prices in bulk, not delivered prices.   *Source: Economic Research Service, U.S. Department of Agriculture (ERS-)*

Average Price of World Raw Sugar[1]   In Cents Per Pound

Year	Jan.	Feb.	Mar.	Apr.	May	June	July	Aug.	Sept.	Oct.	Nov.	Dec.	Average
2005	10.33	10.51	10.57	10.19	10.23	10.45	10.89	11.09	11.59	12.40	12.86	15.09	11.35
2006	17.27	18.93	18.01	18.21	17.83	16.19	16.61	13.58	12.42	12.09	12.38	12.47	15.50
2007	11.85	11.63	11.44	10.85	10.78	11.05	12.18	11.66	11.61	11.86	11.83	12.47	11.60
2008	13.75	15.16	14.60	13.68	12.23	13.29	14.90	15.58	14.74	12.99	12.87	12.31	13.84
2009	13.09	13.90	13.83	14.43	16.89	16.94	18.57	22.37	23.11	23.22	22.96	25.28	18.72
2010	28.94	27.29	21.36	19.87	19.59	21.24	23.42	25.09	31.19	34.80	35.44	36.10	27.03
2011	36.11	35.01	33.22	29.35	26.64	29.75	30.51	28.87	27.71	26.30	24.52	23.42	29.28
2012	24.05	25.81	24.73	22.98	20.25	20.44	22.76	20.53	19.47	20.39	19.31	19.50	21.69
2013	18.37	18.28	18.33	17.71	17.08	16.79	16.38	16.44	17.33	18.81	17.58	16.41	17.46
2014[1]	15.42	16.28	17.58	17.01	17.50	17.22	17.18	15.89	14.60	16.48	15.89	14.99	16.34

[1] Contract No. 11, f.o.b. stowed Caribbean port, including Brazil, bulk spot price.   [2] Preliminary.   *Source: Economic Research Service, U.S. Department of Agriculture (ERS-USDA)*

Average Price of Raw Sugar in New York (C.I.F., Duty/Free Paid, Contract #12 & #14)   In Cents Per Pound

Year	Jan.	Feb.	Mar.	Apr.	May	June	July	Aug.	Sept.	Oct.	Nov.	Dec.	Average
2005	20.57	20.36	20.54	21.21	21.96	21.89	21.94	20.49	21.10	21.71	21.83	21.74	21.28
2006	23.61	24.05	23.10	23.56	23.48	23.32	22.44	21.38	21.27	20.22	19.66	19.59	22.14
2007	20.03	20.59	20.85	20.91	21.27	21.33	22.72	21.80	21.42	20.56	20.25	20.12	20.99
2008	20.24	20.21	20.65	20.54	20.83	21.80	23.76	23.15	23.10	21.46	19.83	20.00	21.30
2009	20.15	19.83	19.75	21.58	21.64	22.47	23.02	26.18	28.91	30.48	31.86	33.30	24.93
2010	39.36	40.13	35.11	30.86	30.89	32.73	33.66	34.24	38.17	39.30	38.84	38.35	35.97
2011	38.46	39.69	39.65	38.32	35.04	35.65	37.93	40.16	40.15	38.19	37.92	36.32	38.12
2012	34.69	33.57	34.94	31.87	30.20	28.89	28.68	28.84	26.27	23.89	22.52	22.41	28.90
2013	21.20	20.72	20.82	20.38	19.51	19.31	19.22	20.97	21.05	21.82	20.61	19.95	20.46
2014[1]	20.27	21.65	22.03	24.33	24.66	25.65	24.78	25.64	25.36	26.41	24.26	24.81	24.15

[1] Preliminary.   *Source: Economic Research Service, U.S. Department of Agriculture (ERS-USDA)*

Supply and Utilization of Sugar (Cane and Beet) in the United States   In Thousands of Short Tons (Raw Value)

	Supply								Utilization						
	Production			Offshore Receipts							Net		Domestic Disappearance		
											Changes	Refining	In Poly-		Per
					Terri-		Beginning	Total	Total		in Invisible	Loss Ad-	hydric		Capita
Year	Cane	Beet	Total	Foreign	tories	Total	Stocks	Supply	Use	Exports	Stocks	justment	Alcohol[4]	Total	Pounds
2005-06	2,955	4,444	7,399	3,443	0	3,443	1,332	12,174	10,476	203	-67	0	51	10,340	63.1
2006-07	3,438	5,008	8,445	2,080	0	2,080	1,698	12,223	10,424	422	-132	0	53	10,135	62.2
2007-08	3,431	4,721	8,152	2,620	0	2,620	1,799	12,571	10,907	203	0	0	61	10,704	61.2
2008-09	3,317	4,214	7,531	3,082	0	3,082	1,664	12,277	10,743	136	0	0	46	10,607	65.1
2009-10	3,387	4,575	7,963	3,320	0	3,320	1,534	12,817	11,319	211	-45	0	35	11,152	63.4
2010-11	3,172	4,659	7,831	3,738	0	3,738	1,498	13,067	11,689	248	19	0	33	11,422	65.9
2011-12	3,588	4,900	8,488	3,632	0	3,632	1,378	13,498	11,519	269	-64	0	33	11,313	65.9
2012-13[1]	3,905	5,076	8,981	3,224	0	3,224	1,979	14,185	12,027	274	-23	0	185	11,776	66.6
2013-14[2]	3,663	4,794	8,457	3,742	0	3,742	2,158	14,357	12,561	306	0	0	346	12,255	67.9
2014-15[3]	3,740	4,870	8,610	3,504	0	3,504	1,796	13,910	12,244	250	0	0	35	11,994	

[1] Preliminary.   [2] Estimate.   [3] Forecast.   [4] Includes feed use.   *Source: Economic Research Service, U.S. Department of Agriculture (ERS-USDA)*

Sugar Cane for Sugar & Seed and Production of Cane Sugar and Molasses in the United States

	Acreage Harvested (1,000 Acres)	Yield of Cane Per Havested Acre Net Tons	Production			Sugar Yield Per Acre (Short Tons)	Farm Price ($ Per Ton)	Farm Value		Sugar Production			Molasses Made	
								of Cane Used for Sugar	of Cane Used for Sugar & Seed	Raw Value		Refined Basis		
			for Sugar	for Seed	Total					Total (1,000 Tons)	Per Ton of Cane (In Lbs.)	(1,000 Tons)	Edible	Total[3]
Year			---- 1,000 Tons ----					----- 1,000 Dollars -----					-- 1,000 Gallons --	
2005	921.9	28.9	24,728	1,878	26,606	3.49	28.4	701,920	754,529	2,991	----	----	----	----
2006	897.7	32.9	27,962	1,602	29,564	4.05	30.4	849,157	897,601	3,429	----	----	----	----
2007	879.6	34.1	28,273	1,696	29,969	4.17	29.4	831,218	880,616	3,454	----	----	----	----
2008	868.0	31.8	26,131	1,472	27,603	4.03	29.5	771,134	814,479	3,311	----	----	----	----
2009	873.9	34.8	28,484	1,938	30,432	4.16	34.8	NA	1,056,613	3,395	----	----	----	----
2010	877.5	31.2	25,663	1,697	27,360	3.83	41.7	NA	1,140,636	3,161	----	----	----	----
2011	872.6	33.5	27,738	1,486	29,224	4.35	47.2	NA	1,379,498	3,599	----	----	----	----
2012	902.4	35.7	30,500	1,727	32,227	4.56	41.9	1,280,799	1,348,361	3,898	----	----	----	----
2013[1]	910.8	33.8	29,023	1,738	30,761	4.50	31.4		962,807	3,853	----	----	----	----
2014[2]	874.1	35.3	29,328	1,541	30,869						----	----	----	----

[1] Preliminary.   [2] Estimate.   [3] Excludes edible molasses.   *Source: Economic Research Service, U.S. Department of Agriculture (ERS-USDA)*

SUGAR

U.S. Sugar Beets, Beet Sugar, Pulp & Molasses Produced from Sugar Beets and Raw Sugar Spot Prices

Year of Harvest	Planted	Harvested	Yield Per Harvested Acre (Sh. Tons)	Pro-duction (1,000 Tons)	Sugar Yield Per Acre (Sh. Tons)	Price[3] (Dollars)	Farm Value (1,000 $)	Equiv-alent Raw Value[4]	Refined Basis	World[5] Refined #5	#11 World	N.Y. Duty Paid	Wholesale List Price HFCS (42%) Midwest
	---- 1,000 Acres ----							- 1,000 Short Tons -		------ In Cents Per Pound -----			
2005	1,300	1,243	22.1	27,433	3.58	43.50	1,193,151	4,444	----	13.19	11.35	21.28	18.62
2006	1,366	1,304	26.1	34,064	3.84	44.20	1,506,985	5,008	----	19.01	15.50	22.14	19.35
2007	1,269	1,247	25.5	31,834	3.79	42.00	1,337,173	4,721	----	14.00	11.60	20.99	23.41
2008	1,091	1,005	26.8	26,881	4.15	48.00	1,294,144	4,166	----	15.96	13.84	21.30	27.57
2009	1,186	1,149	25.9	29,783	3.98	51.50	1,532,634	4,575	----	22.13	18.72	24.93	31.51
2010	1,172	1,156	27.7	32,034	4.03	66.90	2,142,162	4,800	----	27.78	27.03	35.97	26.56
2011	1,233	1,213	23.8	28,896	4.04	69.50	2,004,116		----	31.68	29.28	38.12	30.11
2012	1,230	1,204	29.3	35,224	4.22	66.40	2,338,789		----	26.50	21.69	28.90	32.92
2013[1]	1,198	1,154	28.4	32,789	4.25	46.90	1,536,422		----	22.17	17.46	20.46	35.86
2014[2]	1,162	1,147	27.4	31,386					----	20.05	16.34	24.15	29.96

[1] Preliminary. [2] Estimate. [3] Includes support payments, but excludes Gov't. sugar beet payments. [4] Refined sugar multiplied by factor of 1.07.
[5] F.O.B. Europe. *Source: Economic Research Service, U.S. Department of Agriculture (ERS-USDA)*

Sugar Deliveries and Stocks in the United States   In Thousands of Short Tons (Raw Value)

Year	Quota Allocation	Actual Imports	Cane Sugar Refineries Deliveries	Beet Sugar Factories Deliveries	Importers of Direct Con-sumption Sugar	Mainland Cane Sugar Mills[3]	Total Deliveries	Total Domestic Con-sumption	Cane Sugar Re-fineries	Beet Sugar Factories	CCC	Refiners' Raw	Mainland Cane Mills	Total
2005	----	----	5,136	4,710	197	----	10,043	10,212	368	1,753	28	245	1,635	4,029
2006	----	----	5,230	4,195	577	----	10,002	10,162	328	1,429	0	217	1,382	3,357
2007	----	----	5,123	4,707	116	----	9,946	10,173	452	1,792	0	358	1,437	4,039
2008	----	----	5,075	4,867	773	----	10,715	10,900	400	1,806	0	304	1,500	4,009
2009	----	----	5,493	4,324	667	----	10,485	10,657	440	1,464	0	468	1,612	3,984
2010	----	----	5,635	4,514	843	----	10,992	11,231	484	1,456	0	346	1,274	3,559
2011	----	----	5,572	4,552	995	----	11,118	11,370	466	1,691	0	257	1,455	3,869
2012	----	----	5,648	4,633	977	----	11,257	11,405	315	1,597	0	498	1,370	3,780
2013[1]	----	----	5,849	4,777	949	----	11,575	11,916	388	2,013	0	574	1,646	4,621
2014[2]	----	----	6,069	4,875	760	----	11,704	11,720	459	1,603	0	579	1,707	4,348

[1] Preliminary. [2] Estimate. [3] Sugar for direct consumption only. [4] Refined. *Source: Economic Research Service, U.S. Department of Agriculture (ERS-USDA)*

Sugar, Refined--Deliveries to End User in the United States   In Thousands of Short Tons

Year	Bakery & Cereal Products	Bev-erages	Confec-tionery[2]	Hotels, Restar. & Insti-tutions	Ice Cream & Dairy Products	Canned, Bottled & Frozen Foods	All Other Food Uses	Retail Grocers[3]	Wholesale Grocers[4]	Non-food Uses	Non-Industrial Uses	Industrial Uses	Total Deliveries
2005	2,297	237	1,131	115	587	336	606	1,262	2,401	92	4,026	5,286	9,312
2006	2,231	228	1,069	88	553	335	535	1,204	2,389	107	3,856	5,056	8,912
2007	2,399	312	1,110	74	609	360	569	1,211	2,411	102	3,888	5,460	9,348
2008	2,312	341	1,108	115	612	427	676	1,212	2,317	97	3,835	5,572	9,407
2009	2,286	351	1,085	127	587	427	573	1,241	2,360	84	3,907	5,393	9,300
2010	2,400	422	1,070	124	583	391	609	1,270	2,471	111	4,077	5,601	9,679
2011	2,324	404	1,048	120	622	411	625	1,239	2,511	128	4,104	5,562	9,665
2012	2,330	486	1,044	130	674	412	687	1,172	2,374	123	3,959	5,755	9,715
2013	2,296	547	1,149	112	678	399	760	1,109	2,427	117	4,040	5,947	9,987
2014[1]	2,435	598	1,142	118	756	434	853	1,193	2,151	118	3,965	6,336	10,300

[1] Preliminary. [2] And related products. [3] Chain stores, supermarkets. [4] Jobbers, sugar dealers.
Source: Economic Research Service, U.S. Department of Agriculture (ERS-USDA)

Deliveries[1] of All Sugar by Primary Distributors in the United States, by Quarters   In Thousands of Short Tons

Year	First Quarter	Second Quarter	Third Quarter	Fourth Quarter	Total	Year	First Quarter	Second Quarter	Third Quarter	Fourth Quarter	Total
2003	2,233	2,415	2,519	2,546	9,713	2009	2,431	2,649	2,823	2,754	10,657
2004	2,324	2,419	2,572	2,586	9,901	2010	2,565	2,759	3,074	2,833	11,231
2005	2,370	2,521	2,711	2,609	10,212	2011	2,649	2,809	3,131	2,781	11,370
2006	2,474	2,522	2,734	2,432	10,162	2012	2,663	2,915	2,954	2,873	11,405
2007	2,364	2,604	2,735	2,471	10,173	2013	2,720	2,954	3,014	3,229	11,916
2008	2,532	2,728	2,865	2,775	10,900	2014[2]	2,742	3,053	3,078	2,847	11,720

[1] Includes for domestic consumption and for export. [2] Preliminary. *Source: Economic Research Service, U.S. Department of Agriculture (ERS-USDA)*

SUGAR #11 - ICE-US
Weekly Selected Futures as of 01/02/2015

WEEKLY SELECTED FUTURES
As of 01/02/2015

Chart High 36.08 on 02/02/2011
Chart Low 7.50 on 02/28/2005

Cents / lb.

Nearby Futures through Last Trading Day using selected contract months: March, May, July and October.

Volume of Trading of World Sugar #11 Futures in New York   In Contracts

Year	Jan.	Feb.	Mar.	Apr.	May	June	July	Aug.	Sept.	Oct.	Nov.	Dec.	Total
2005	981.5	1,279.3	957.1	1,258.6	657.6	1,366.8	779.2	1,198.3	1,803.5	915.8	816.6	992.8	13,007
2006	1,444.2	1,601.2	1,092.2	1,467.4	1,147.7	1,459.1	825.0	1,278.6	1,746.7	1,095.7	918.7	1,024.0	15,101
2007	1,322.9	2,189.7	1,659.6	2,023.2	1,819.5	2,679.8	1,559.7	1,326.6	2,175.7	1,565.3	1,452.1	1,489.7	21,264
2008	3,566.7	3,280.8	2,237.7	2,889.5	1,941.8	3,067.4	1,820.2	1,721.4	2,540.9	1,629.9	1,085.5	1,238.1	27,020
2009	1,624.6	2,040.3	1,867.0	2,995.5	2,229.3	3,359.1	1,741.5	2,833.2	3,219.5	1,824.3	1,576.4	1,989.5	27,300
2010	2,348.9	2,986.5	2,772.9	2,754.5	1,730.0	2,936.0	1,840.3	2,184.6	3,366.7	1,978.1	2,629.3	1,524.7	29,053
2011	2,180.8	3,341.9	1,774.8	2,338.8	1,832.4	3,266.1	1,702.0	1,986.6	2,555.9	1,258.7	1,286.7	1,104.7	24,629
2012	1,999.3	2,765.1	2,316.0	2,765.4	1,941.5	3,460.7	2,251.7	2,049.8	2,736.2	1,781.4	1,633.1	1,426.4	27,127
2013	2,368.0	3,038.0	2,039.9	3,086.2	1,908.9	3,974.1	2,037.0	2,117.1	3,791.9	2,279.9	1,559.9	1,612.7	29,814
2014	2,461.6	4,157.3	2,477.4	2,857.3	1,906.5	3,370.3	1,981.4	1,853.3	3,657.9	1,651.3	1,518.6	1,383.7	29,277

Contract size = 112,000 lbs.   Source: ICE Futures U.S. (ICE)

Average Open Interest of World Sugar #11 Futures in New York   In Contracts

Year	Jan.	Feb.	Mar.	Apr.	May	June	July	Aug.	Sept.	Oct.	Nov.	Dec.
2005	375,713	391,006	357,056	352,521	355,922	366,568	404,141	473,757	468,737	464,829	478,097	523,820
2006	526,575	501,074	462,871	474,241	490,201	453,021	457,301	479,420	493,931	447,817	503,364	563,844
2007	632,783	695,426	652,346	686,648	738,708	695,249	674,318	667,523	656,128	681,403	763,910	835,526
2008	1,035,301	1,013,324	973,541	939,615	915,325	885,082	809,433	804,956	774,839	664,164	636,078	644,852
2009	664,303	656,033	644,829	681,177	703,355	764,799	735,556	838,638	821,646	770,085	772,808	813,238
2010	842,463	830,888	745,170	667,291	656,182	635,744	587,509	627,022	651,093	585,353	584,909	592,044
2011	619,904	648,027	597,384	613,301	583,047	627,566	630,027	598,737	544,893	489,135	495,699	533,588
2012	612,932	699,780	729,307	728,645	728,515	744,254	669,730	688,099	705,221	697,064	726,541	756,324
2013	796,708	824,203	804,682	852,113	846,873	901,021	848,276	878,813	870,124	818,823	803,346	810,753
2014	834,655	838,471	787,473	792,420	809,219	870,191	842,551	885,193	851,724	766,320	811,959	828,791

Contract size = 112,000 lbs.   Source: ICE Futures U.S. (ICE)

Sulfur

Sulfur (atomic symbol S) is an odorless, tasteless, light yellow, nonmetallic element. As early as 2000 BC, Egyptians used sulfur compounds to bleach fabric. The Chinese used sulfur as an essential component when they developed gunpowder in the 13th century.

Sulfur is widely found in both its free and combined states. Free sulfur is found mixed with gypsum and pumice stone in volcanic regions. Sulfur dioxide is an air pollutant released from the combustion of fossil fuels. The most important use of sulfur is the production of sulfur compounds. Sulfur is used in skin ointments, matches, dyes, gunpowder, and phosphoric acid.

Supply – World production of all forms of sulfur in 2014 rose +2.8% yr/yr to 72.400 million metric tons, just below the record high of 70.500 million metric tons posted in 2011. The world's largest producers of sulfur are China with 16.6% of world production, the U.S. with

13.5%, Russia with 10.1%, and Canada with 8.3%. U.S. production of sulfur in 2014 rose by +6.1% yr/yr to 9.770 million metric tons, still above the 2011 record low of 8.950 million metric tons.

Demand – U.S. consumption of all forms of sulfur fell -3.5% in 2014 to 11.000 million metric tons, well above the 4-decade low of 9.460 million metric tons seen in 2009. U.S. consumption of elemental sulfur in 2011 (latest data) rose +3.3% to 10.200 million metric tons. U.S. consumption of sulfuric acid in 2011 (latest data) rose by +9.6% yr/yr to 7.650 million metric tons.

Trade – U.S. exports of recovered sulfur in 2011 (latest data) fell -9.7% yr/yr to 1.310 million metric tons, but still above the 16-year low of 635,000 metric tons in 2006. U.S. imports of recovered sulfur in 2011 rose by +10.9% yr/yr to 3.270 million metric tons, a new record high.

World Production of Sulfur (All Forms)   In Thousands of Metric Tons

Year	Canada	China	France	Germany	Kazakh-stan	Japan	Mexico	Poland	Russia	Saudi Arabia	Spain	United States	World Total
2007	8,789	8,460	650	4,091	1,960	3,216	1,576	1,350	7,050	3,089	637	9,100	67,500
2008	8,156	8,610	650	4,167	2,030	3,334	1,740	1,280	6,450	3,163	637	9,300	68,800
2009	7,467	9,370	650	3,760	2,500	3,214	1,810	740	6,350	3,214	673	8,940	67,900
2010	7,260	9,600	650	3,713	2,700	3,292	1,790	1,020	6,350	3,200	676	9,110	68,100
2011	6,523	9,700	650	3,908	2,700	3,205	1,760	1,130	6,450	4,579	676	8,950	70,500
2012	6,183	9,900	650	3,818	2,700	3,247	1,810	1,150	6,550	4,092	681	9,000	68,100
2013[1]	6,370	10,500	650	3,880	2,850	3,300	1,810	1,080	7,250	3,900	270	9,210	70,400
2014[2]	6,000	12,000	650	3,900	2,850	3,300	1,810	1,100	7,300	4,000	270	9,770	72,400

[1] Preliminary.   [2] Estimate.   *Source: U.S. Geological Survey (USGS)*

Salient Statistics of Sulfur in the United States   In Thousands of Metric Tons (Sulfur Content)

	Production of												
	Native - Sulfur[3] - Frasch	Recovered		Total	By-product	Other Sulf. Acid	Imports	Exports	Producer	Apparent Consumption	Sales Value of Shipments		
		Petroleum & Cole	Natural Gas		Elemental Sulfur	Sulfuric Acid[4]	Com-pounds	Sulfuric Acid[4]	Sulfuric Acid[4]	Stocks, Dec. 31[5]	(All Forms)	F.O.B. Mine/Plant		
Year	Frasch			Total								Frasch	Recovered	Average Total
2007	----	7,000	1,280	8,280	817	----	9,100	2,600	336	187	11,900	----	----	36.49
2008	----	7,240	1,300	8,550	753	----	9,300	3,440	261	208	12,900	----	----	264.04
2009	----	6,970	1,220	8,190	749	----	8,940	1,270	254	231	9,520	----	----	1.73
2010	----	7,140	1,170	8,320	791	----	9,110	2,110	215	166	11,300	----	----	70.16
2011	----	7,080	1,130	8,230	720	----	8,950	2,670	332	175	11,700	----	----	159.88
2012	----	7,370	1,040	8,410	586	----	9,000	2,850	161	132	11,000	----	----	123.54
2013[1]	----	7,580	1,020	8,600	616	----	9,210	2,980	165	161	11,400	----	----	68.83
2014[2]	----	8,030	1,000	9,030	730	----	9,770	3,240	145	142	11,000	----	----	95.00

[1] Preliminary.   [2] Estimate.   [3] Or sulfur ore; Withheld included in natural gas.   [4] Basis 100% H2SO4, sulfur equivalent.   [5] Frasch & recovered.
W = Withheld proprietary data.   Source: U.S. Geological Survey (USGS)

Sulfur Consumption & Foreign Trade of the United States   In Thousands of Metric Tons (Sulfur Content)

	Consumption			Sulfuric Acid Sold or Used, by End Use[2]						Foreign Trade					
	Native Sulfur (Frasch)	Rec-overed Sulfur	Total Elemental Form	Pulpmills & Paper Products	Inorganic Chem-icals[3]	Synthetic Rubber & Plastic	Phosph-atic Fertilizers	Petro-leum Refining[4]	Frasch	Exports			Imports		
Year										Frasch	Re-covered	Value $1,000	Frasch	Re-covered	Value $1,000
2005	W	10,900	10,900	9,680	267	312	64	7,000	188	----	684	55,200	----	2,820	70,500
2006	W	10,600	10,600	8,750	246	426	250	6,220	262	----	635	43,800	----	2,950	70,400
2007	W	10,300	10,300	8,330	245	245	117	6,280	264	----	922	84,800	----	2,930	79,400
2008	----	----	10,600	7,680	187	293	69	5,690	244	----	952	272,000	----	3,000	753,000
2009	----	----	8,380	7,740	188	286	64	5,430	283	----	1,430	82,200	----	1,700	54,100
2010	----	----	9,870	6,980	79	31	6	5,700	368	----	1,450	171,000	----	2,950	214,000
2011	----	----	10,200	7,650	168	118	70	5,740	422	----	1,310	266,000	----	3,270	301,000
2012[1]	----	----	9,520	7,410	168	107	70	5,420	423	----	1,850	366,000	----	2,930	238,000

[1] Preliminary.   [2] Sulfur equivalent.   [3] Including inorganic pigments, paints & allied products, and other inorganic chemicals & products.
[4] Including other petroleum and coal products.   W = Withheld proprietary data.   NA = Not available.   *Source: U.S. Geological Survey (USGS)*

Sunflowerseed, Meal and Oil

Sunflowers are native to South and North America, but are now grown almost worldwide. Sunflower-seed oil accounts for approximately 14% of the world production of seed oils. Sunflower varieties that are commercially grown contain from 39% to 49% oil in the seed. Sunflower crops produce about 50 bushels of seed per acre on average, which yields approximately 50 gallons of oil.

Sunflower-seed oil accounts for around 80% of the value of the sunflower crop. Refined sunflower-seed oil is edible and used primarily as a salad and cooking oil and in margarine. Crude sunflower-seed oil is used industrially for making soaps, candles, varnishes, and detergents. Sunflower-seed oil contains 93% of the energy of U.S. No. 2 diesel fuel and is being explored as a potential alternate fuel source in diesel engines. Sunflower meal is used in livestock feed and when fed to poultry, increases the yield of eggs. Sunflower seeds are also used for birdfeed and as a snack for humans.

Prices – The average monthly price received by U.S. farmers for sunflower seeds in the first five months of the 2014-15 marketing year (Sep/Aug) fell -6.2% to $20.60 per hundred pounds, well below the 2011-12 record high of $28.96 per hundred pounds.

Supply – World sunflower-seed production in the 2014-15 fell -6.9% yr/yr to 39.951 million metric tons. The world's largest sunflower-seed producers are Ukraine

with 22.5% of world production, the European Union with 22.6%, Russia with 22.5%, Argentina and China each with 6.3%, Turkey with 3.0%, and the U.S. with 2.5%.

U.S. production of sunflower seeds in 2014-15 rose by +26.3% yr/yr to 1.164 million metric tons, far below the record production level of 3.309 million metric tons posted in 1979-80. U.S. farmers harvested 1.507 million acres of sunflowers in 2014-15, up +2.9% yr/yr, well below the 9-year high of 2.610 million acres posted in 2005-06. U.S sunflower yield in 2014-15 was 14.69 hundred pounds per acre, below 2009-10 record high of 15.54 hundred pounds per acre.

Demand – Total U.S. disappearance of sunflower seeds in 2014-15 rose +14.3% yr/yr to 1.221 million metric tons, of which 47.3% went to non-oil and seed use, 40.7% went to crushing for oil and meal, and 12.0% went to exports.

Trade – World sunflower-seed exports in 2014-15 rose +5.5% yr/yr to 2.106 million metric tons. The world's largest exporters are the European Union which accounted for 33.2% of world exports in 2014-15 and Moldova which accounted for 15.4% of world exports. World sunflower-seed imports in 2014-15 rose +15.7% yr/yr to 1.898 million metric tons. The world's largest importers are Turkey which accounted for 44.8% of world exports and Pakistan with 16.3% of world imports.

World Production of Sunflowerseed   In Thousands of Metric Tons

Crop Year	Argen-tina	China	European Union	India	Kazakh-stan	Pakistan	Russia	Serbia	South Africa	Turkey	Ukraine	United States	World Total
2007-08	4,650	1,187	4,847	1,120	206	604	5,650	260	872	700	4,200	1,301	27,365
2008-09	2,483	1,792	7,241	1,000	186	420	7,350	490	801	830	7,000	1,553	33,279
2009-10	2,232	1,956	6,985	820	368	325	6,425	400	490	800	7,600	1,377	31,770
2010-11	3,672	2,298	6,959	655	329	404	5,350	400	860	1,000	8,100	1,241	33,074
2011-12	3,341	2,313	8,456	620	409	750	9,627	415	522	925	9,800	925	39,680
2012-13	3,100	2,323	7,088	700	400	700	7,959	350	557	1,125	9,000	1,241	35,973
2013-14[1]	2,100	2,450	8,881	670	573	600	10,554	425	853	1,400	11,600	917	42,906
2014-15[2]	2,500	2,500	9,041	650	500	540	9,000	525	800	1,200	10,000	1,005	39,951

[1] Preliminary. [2] Forecast. *Source: Economic Research Service, U.S. Department of Agriculture (ERS-USDA)*

World Exports of Sunflowerseed   In Thousands of Metric Tons

Crop Year	Argen-tina	Canada	China	European Union	Israel	Kazakh-stan	Moldova	Russia	Serbia	Turkey	Ukraine	United States	World Total
2007-08	50	112	143	510	6	1	10	37	4	8	75	200	1,456
2008-09	74	88	109	494	6	1	131	160	10	13	767	184	2,146
2009-10	70	49	132	567	5	21	99	20	2	20	353	179	1,550
2010-11	75	46	175	597	6	1	218	8	10	26	444	160	1,777
2011-12	80	33	186	596	4	30	194	332	15	38	282	106	1,918
2012-13	84	44	158	521	4	31	196	31	50	38	127	136	1,438
2013-14[1]	80	49	173	680	4	140	375	130	128	33	70	120	1,996
2014-15[2]	80	45	230	700	4	100	325	50	155	40	200	163	2,106

[1] Preliminary. [2] Forecast. *Source: Economic Research Service, U.S. Department of Agriculture (ERS-USDA)*

World Imports of Sunflowerseed   In Thousands of Metric Tons

Crop Year	Belarus	Canada	Egypt	European Union	Iran	Mexico	Moldova	Morocco	Pakistan	Russia	Turkey	United States	World Total
2007-08	----	18	1	300	25	8	9	1	1	11	533	87	1,229
2008-09	10	20	11	635	42	14	1	80	190	12	446	70	1,863
2009-10	14	26	30	269	31	14	5	72	92	23	736	46	1,483
2010-11	35	33	49	379	26	15	1	89	37	42	705	41	1,565
2011-12	35	33	75	280	27	15	1	18	159	28	834	44	1,637
2012-13	12	27	59	209	30	14	1	37	2	28	628	54	1,306
2013-14[1]	15	25	53	340	45	15	153	10	187	35	583	65	1,641
2014-15[2]	40	25	60	250	45	15	146	15	310	30	850	59	1,898

[1] Preliminary. [2] Forecast. *Source: Economic Research Service, U.S. Department of Agriculture (ERS-USDA)*

SUNFLOWERSEED, MEAL AND OIL

World Production of Sunflowerseed Oil In Thousands of Metric Tons

Crop Year	Argen-tina	Burma	China	European Union	India	Pakistan	Russia	Serbia	South Africa	Turkey	Ukraine	United States	World Total
2007-08	1,758	130	130	1,902	360	224	2,130	115	310	544	1,795	287	10,181
2008-09	1,345	195	315	2,488	319	234	2,565	180	318	515	2,631	296	12,007
2009-10	1,146	205	324	2,613	255	170	2,505	170	241	626	2,975	331	12,139
2010-11	1,551	202	340	2,493	195	168	2,082	170	284	671	3,327	224	12,208
2011-12	1,565	140	348	2,800	205	340	3,552	170	272	718	3,933	149	14,734
2012-13	984	110	476	2,544	220	285	3,117	132	289	769	3,615	196	13,266
2013-14[1]	950	160	490	3,185	210	313	3,851	115	335	845	4,451	197	15,752
2014-15[2]	1,060	160	455	3,120	200	330	3,570	145	335	854	4,259	175	15,257

[1] Preliminary. [2] Forecast. *Source: Economic Research Service, U.S. Department of Agriculture (ERS-USDA)*

World Production of Sunflowerseed Meal In Thousands of Metric Tons

Crop Year	Argen-tina	Burma	China	European Union	India	Kazakh-stan	Pakistan	Russia	South Africa	Turkey	Ukraine	United States	World Total
2007-08	1,795	128	200	2,467	482	80	245	1,917	334	483	1,769	328	10,746
2008-09	1,390	188	484	3,238	426	86	325	2,306	342	460	2,600	335	12,859
2009-10	1,218	200	495	3,395	341	113	313	2,253	243	559	2,947	374	13,078
2010-11	1,632	198	519	3,348	260	100	317	1,874	287	597	3,304	253	13,239
2011-12	1,621	140	532	3,798	275	127	356	3,199	275	640	4,115	170	15,820
2012-13	1,021	110	726	3,570	294	125	293	2,808	293	685	3,607	224	14,270
2013-14[1]	980	160	745	3,930	280	140	322	3,466	340	753	4,433	226	16,347
2014-15[2]	1,090	160	698	4,020	265	132	340	3,215	340	762	4,259	240	16,279

[1] Preliminary. [2] Forecast. *Source: Economic Research Service, U.S. Department of Agriculture (ERS-USDA)*

Sunflowerseed Statistics in the United States In Thousands of Metric Tons

Crop Year Beginning Sept. 1	Acres Harvested (1,000)	Harvested Yield Per CWT	Farm Price ($/Metric Ton)	Value of Pro-duction (Million $)	Stocks, Sept. 1	Pro-duction	Imports	Total Supply	Crush	Exports	Non-Oil Use & Seed	Total Disap-pearance
2007-08	2,012	14.26	478	614.7	137	1,301	87	1,525	683	200	522	1,405
2008-09	2,396	14.29	481	704.1	120	1,553	70	1,743	661	184	675	1,520
2009-10	1,954	15.54	333	459.0	223	1,377	46	1,646	776	179	514	1,469
2010-11	1,874	14.60	514	633.8	177	1,241	41	1,459	588	160	594	1,342
2011-12	1,458	13.98	642	589.3	117	925	44	1,086	349	106	544	999
2012-13	1,840	14.87	560	700.0	87	1,264	54	1,405	451	136	664	1,251
2013-14[1]	1,465	13.80	472	443.3	154	922	65	1,141	463	117	488	1,068
2014-15[2]	1,508	14.69	474	504.6	73	1,164	71	1,308	497	147	577	1,221

[1] Preliminary. [2] Forecast. *Source: Economic Research Service, U.S. Department of Agriculture (ERS-USDA)*

Sunflower Oil Statistics in the United States In Thousands of Metric Tons

Crop Year Beginning Sept. 1	Stocks, Oct. 1	Production	Imports	Total Supply	Exports	Domestic Use	Total Disap-pearance	Price $ Per Metric Ton (Crude Mpls.)
2007-08	27	287	47	361	77	272	349	1,978
2008-09	12	296	30	338	91	197	288	1,170
2009-10	50	331	22	403	98	268	366	1,163
2010-11	37	224	47	308	38	243	281	1,824
2011-12	27	149	74	250	19	208	227	1,871
2012-13	23	196	32	251	28	200	228	1,473
2013-14[1]	23	197	35	255	37	195	232	1,305
2014-15[2]	23	175	45	243	27	193	220	

[1] Preliminary. [2] Forecast. *Source: Economic Research Service, U.S. Department of Agriculture (ERS-USDA)*

Sunflower Meal Statistics in the United States In Thousands of Metric Tons

Crop Year Beginning Sept. 1	Stocks, Oct. 1	Production	Imports	Total Supply	Exports	Domestic Use	Total Disap-pearance	Price USD Per Metric Ton 28% Protein
2007-08	5	328	----	333	17	311	333	183
2008-09	5	335	----	340	7	328	340	172
2009-10	5	374	----	379	6	368	379	164
2010-11	5	253	----	258	3	250	258	233
2011-12	5	170	----	175	3	167	175	264
2012-13	5	224	----	229	19	205	229	279
2013-14[1]	5	226	11	242	8	229	242	270
2014-15[2]	5	200	----	205	5	195	205	

[1] Preliminary. [2] Forecast. *Source: Economic Research Service, U.S. Department of Agriculture (ERS-USDA)*

Average Price Received by Farmers for Sunflower[2] in the United States   In Dollars Per Hundred Pounds (Cwt.)

Year	Sept.	Oct.	Nov.	Dec.	Jan.	Feb.	Mar.	Apr.	May	June	July	Aug.	Average
2007-08	17.70	17.80	18.30	19.20	19.10	24.20	25.90	24.50	27.40	28.10	28.40	26.40	23.08
2008-09	28.20	25.30	23.10	22.80	22.10	22.60	22.10	20.20	21.50	18.40	17.70	20.60	22.05
2009-10	13.90	16.20	14.20	14.80	15.50	16.70	15.80	15.80	14.90	15.10	15.40	14.50	15.23
2010-11	17.30	20.80	18.70	20.60	21.90	27.40	28.30	28.80	30.00	29.00	30.40	32.20	25.45
2011-12	32.90	29.60	29.00	29.60	28.90	29.50	28.80	28.40	27.80	27.20	27.00	28.80	28.96
2012-13	28.80	25.90	26.70	24.80	26.00	26.10	24.60	24.80	24.00	24.40	23.70	23.70	25.29
2013-14	22.60	23.00	20.70	18.80	19.60	22.90	21.50	22.30	24.10	22.70	22.10	22.40	21.89
2014-15[1]	20.20	22.80	19.80	19.60	19.30								20.34

[1] Preliminary.   [2] KS, MN, ND and SD average.   *Source: Economic Research Service, U.S. Department of Agriculture (ERS-USDA)*

Average Price of Crude Sunflower Oil at Minneapolis   In Cents Per Pound

Year	Sept.	Oct.	Nov.	Dec.	Jan.	Feb.	Mar.	Apr.	May	June	July	Aug.	Average
2007-08	70.50	73.50	84.80	86.50	90.00	96.00	96.75	93.00	97.40	99.50	97.50	91.40	89.74
2008-09	87.50	74.40	53.75	42.50	41.60	40.00	42.50	45.00	49.20	53.75	53.40	53.50	53.09
2009-10	53.25	52.20	53.00	52.00	52.00	52.00	51.25	51.60	52.50	55.75	53.60	53.75	52.74
2010-11	54.00	56.00	63.00	62.90	74.13	85.63	96.75	101.20	103.75	103.25	97.00	95.00	82.72
2011-12	94.80	92.50	91.00	91.00	88.75	86.00	82.00	79.00	80.00	80.20	78.00	75.00	84.85
2012-13	75.00	74.00	70.30	67.50	65.25	65.00	64.60	64.00	64.00	64.00	64.00	64.00	66.80
2013-14	63.75	60.50	57.40	57.00	57.00	57.00	58.00	59.00	59.00	57.50	61.00	63.00	59.18
2014-15[1]	63.00	63.00	61.75	58.00	63.00	65.63							62.40

[1] Preliminary.   *Source: Economic Research Service, U.S. Department of Agriculture (ERS-USDA)*

Average Price of Sunflower Meal (26% protein) in the United States   In Cents Per Pound

Year	Sept.	Oct.	Nov.	Dec.	Jan.	Feb.	Mar.	Apr.	May	June	July	Aug.	Average
2007-08	103.00	138.40	133.80	158.70	212.00	225.50	201.30	163.20	154.40	160.40	190.50	156.30	166.46
2008-09	179.40	161.10	146.90	150.00	164.40	161.90	134.40	130.00	141.30	187.50	170.60	147.50	156.25
2009-10	134.00	151.90	189.40	197.50	181.88	165.63	137.50	132.50	120.50	109.50	120.00	141.20	148.46
2010-11	165.00	190.63	211.50	217.50	205.63	209.38	210.00	196.25	203.13	240.63	241.25	247.00	211.49
2011-12	263.75	232.50	224.00	225.63	223.50	191.88	191.88	211.25	230.50	226.88	300.50	348.13	239.20
2012-13	354.38	287.00	269.38	266.67	252.00	237.50	231.25	222.00	215.00	233.13	245.50	221.25	252.92
2013-14	218.13	236.25	246.88	277.50	283.75	285.00	271.25	267.50	265.00	250.00	192.50	151.25	245.42
2014-15[1]	139.50	162.50	208.13	245.00	247.50	225.63							204.71

[1] Preliminary.   *Source: Economic Research Service, U.S. Department of Agriculture (ERS-USDA)*

Production of Sunflower in the United States   In Thousands of Pounds

Crop Year	California	Colorado	Kansas	Minnesota	Nebraska	North Dakota	Oklahoma	South Dakota	Texas	Total
2007	----	129,500	232,330	191,500	58,470	1,500,950	----	631,060	50,340	2,868,870
2008	----	153,400	278,900	163,850	82,900	1,511,400	----	1,049,300	92,400	3,422,840
2009	51,000	122,060	245,200	86,600	62,700	1,317,200	17,500	1,004,400	129,800	3,036,460
2010	40,500	167,950	186,060	116,800	83,400	1,254,980	17,180	772,750	95,950	2,735,570
2011	44,300	124,200	149,400	46,100	75,900	766,250	5,275	776,950	49,900	2,038,275
2012	68,575	52,720	97,950	93,925	26,460	1,430,460	4,720	859,250	102,000	2,736,060
2013	75,150	45,600	82,000	69,250	32,975	600,560	5,180	996,800	114,250	2,021,765
2014[1]	61,250	63,300	91,540	87,870	45,055	848,600	3,200	876,620	137,400	2,214,835

[1] Preliminary.   [2] Forecast.   *Source: Economic Research Service, U.S. Department of Agriculture (ERS-USDA)*

Production of Sunflower Oil in the United States   In Thousands of Pounds

Crop Year	California	Colorado	Kansas	Minnesota	Nebraska	North Dakota	Oklahoma	South Dakota	Texas	Total
2007	----	110,000	210,250	140,800	40,920	1,297,750	----	599,060	19,140	2,483,585
2008	----	128,700	254,200	113,150	55,900	1,329,900	----	970,100	59,400	2,993,510
2009	40,200	89,760	221,200	61,600	31,200	1,155,200	13,750	918,000	53,100	2,584,010
2010	31,050	124,200	144,900	76,500	23,400	1,000,100	15,750	616,000	33,600	2,074,500
2011	39,500	97,000	123,900	35,100	45,500	690,000	4,875	664,950	21,850	1,722,675
2012	65,075	40,120	74,750	70,300	20,650	1,283,500	4,180	761,600	39,600	2,359,775
2013	72,150	29,600	58,000	51,200	19,975	504,000	3,480	820,800	78,000	1,637,205
2014[1]	57,200	46,200	57,540	65,250	26,680	683,400	2,100	668,000	56,800	1,663,170

[1] Preliminary.   [2] Forecast.   *Source: Economic Research Service, U.S. Department of Agriculture (ERS-USDA)*

Tallow and Greases

Tallow and grease are derived from processing (rendering) the fat of cattle. Tallow is used to produce both edible and inedible products. Edible tallow products include margarine, cooking oil, and baking products. Inedible tallow products include soap, candles, and lubricants. Production of tallow and greases is directly related to the number of cattle produced. Those countries that are the leading cattle producers are also the largest producers of tallow. The American Fats and Oils Association provides specifications for a variety of different types of tallow and grease, including edible tallow, lard (edible), top white tallow, all beef packer tallow, extra fancy tallow, fancy tallow, bleachable fancy tallow, prime tallow, choice white grease, and yellow grease. The specifications include such characteristics as the melting point, color, density, moisture content, insoluble impurities, and others.

Prices– The monthly average price of tallow (inedible, No. 1 Packers-Prime, delivered Chicago) in 2013 (latest data) fell -11.0% yr/yr to 42.58 cents per pound. The wholesale price of inedible tallow in 2014 fell -9.2% yr/yr to 36.67 cents per pound.

Supply – World production of tallow and greases (edible and inedible) in 2013 (latest data), rose by +1.6% yr/yr to 8.491 million metric tons, which was below the 2007 record high of 8.530 million metric tons. The world's largest producer of tallow and greases by far is the U.S. with 42.1% of world production, followed by Brazil with 7.1%, Australia with 6.5%, and Canada with 3.1%.

U.S. production of edible tallow in 2013 (latest data) fell -0.6% yr/yr to 2.043 billion pounds, below last year's record high of 2.136 billion pounds. U.S. production of inedible tallow and greases in 2011 (latest data) fell -37.9% yr/yr to 3.653 billion pounds, well below the record high of 7.156 billion pounds posted in 2002.

Demand – U.S. consumption of inedible tallow and greases in 2011 (latest data) fell 0.9% yr/yr to 1.559 billion pounds, of which virtually all went for animal feed. U.S. consumption of edible tallow in 2013 (latest data) fell -0.3% yr/yr to 1.935 billion pounds, down from 2011 record high of 1.954 billion pounds. U.S. per capita consumption of edible tallow in 2010 (latest data) rose from 0.7 pounds per person to 3.3 pounds per person yr/yr, down from the 2000 and 2004 record high of 4.0 pounds.

Trade – U.S. exports of inedible tallow and grease in 2011 (latest data) fell -3.2% yr/yr to 341.551 million pounds, and accounted for 8.7% of total U.S. supply. U.S. exports of edible tallow in 2013 fell -5.2% yr/yr to 157 million pounds, and accounted for 7.5% of U.S. supply.

World Production of Tallow and Greases (Edible and Inedible)   In Thousands of Metric Tons

Year	Argentina	Australia	Brazil	Canada	France	Germany	Korea	Nether- lands	New Zealand	Russia	United Kingdom	United States	World Total
2004	178	486	528	343	166	124	15	113	192	181	124	3,714	8,247
2005	184	493	554	339	171	121	15	106	168	175	128	3,797	8,389
2006	181	503	574	285	195	124	16	107	187	179	135	3,808	8,474
2007	195	501	589	276	192	128	16	116	184	184	140	3,818	8,522
2008	189	499	564	261	196	131	16	122	189	189	138	3,695	8,389
2009	204	483	547	252	188	131	16	123	168	195	134	3,655	8,304
2010	160	488	566	262	200	134	16	131	169	199	141	3,575	8,328
2011	153	493	548	266	209	134	15	121	167	198	144	3,678	8,455
2012[1]	160	494	570	267	198	131	18	106	166	199	139	3,553	8,359
2013[2]	175	548	600	266	191	129	21	103	171	203	138	3,575	8,491

[1] Preliminary.   [2] Forecast.   *Source: Foreign Agricultural Service, U.S. Department of Agriculture (FAS-USDA)*

Salient Statistics of Tallow and Greases (Inedible) in the United States   In Millions of Pounds

	-------------------- Supply --------------------				---------------- Consumption ----------------			Wholesale Prices, Cents Per Lb.	
Year	Production	Stocks, Jan. 1	Total	Exports	Soap	Feed	Total	Edible, (Loose) Chicago	Inedible, Chicago No. 1
2004	6,173	282	6,455	336	W	2,536	2,536	19.8	18.0
2005	6,204	281	6,485	276	W	2,456	2,456	19.0	17.5
2006	6,460	309	6,769	331	W	2,585	2,585	18.6	16.9
2007	6,369	291	6,661	361	W	2,385	2,385	30.7	27.8
2008	6,224	350	6,573	319	W	2,095	2,095	38.0	34.2
2009	5,878	315	6,193	330	W	1,770	1,770	27.5	25.2
2010	5,887	286	6,174	353	W	1,574	1,574	35.1	33.3
2011	3,654	281	3,934	342	W	1,560	1,560	53.2	49.6
2012[1]	NA	NA	NA	NA	NA	NA	NA	47.8	43.8
2013[2]	NA	NA	NA	NA	NA	NA	NA	42.6	40.4

[1] Preliminary.   [2] Forecast.   *Source: Foreign Agricultural Service, U.S. Department of Agriculture (FAS-USDA)*

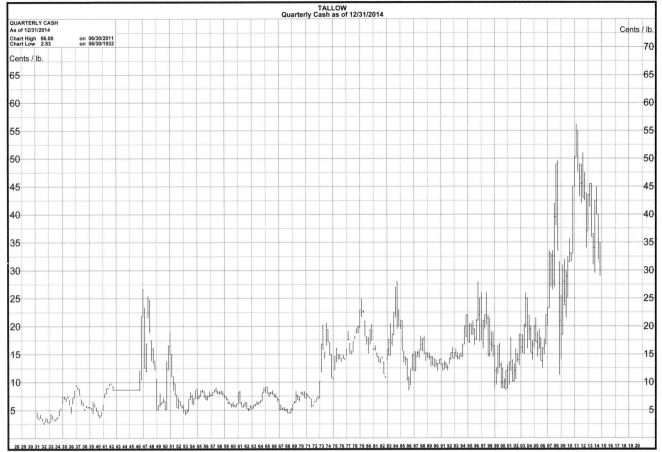

TALLOW
Quarterly Cash as of 12/31/2014

QUARTERLY CASH
As of 12/31/2014

Chart High 56.00 on 06/30/2011
Chart Low 2.53 on 06/30/1932

Cents / lb.

Spot raw, NY: to 02/1961; World raw #8, NY: 02/1961 to 12/1970; World raw #11, NY: to date.

Supply and Disappearance of Edible Tallow in the United States   In Millions of Pounds, Rendered Basis

	-------------------- Supply --------------------			------------------------------------- Disappearance -------------------------------------					
Year	Stocks, Jan. 1	Production	Total Supply	Domestic Disap- pearance	Exports	Total Disap- pearance	Direct Use	Baking or Frying Fats	Per Capita (Lbs.)
2004	24	1,818	1,842	1,565	255	1,820	1,163	W	4.0
2005	22	1,813	1,836	1,518	293	1,811	1,116	W	3.8
2006	25	1,861	1,893	1,583	275	1,858	1,160	W	3.9
2007	35	1,789	1,831	1,404	388	1,792	889	W	2.9
2008	39	1,794	1,863	1,648	185	1,833	896	W	2.9
2009	30	1,837	1,903	1,710	162	1,872	212	W	0.7
2010	31	1,859	1,913	1,693	183	1,876	1,050	W	3.4
2011	38	2,050	2,116	1,954	132	2,086	NA	NA	NA
2012[1]	30	2,055	2,136	1,940	166	2,106	NA	NA	NA
2013[2]	30	2,043	2,123	1,935	157	2,093	NA	NA	NA

[1] Preliminary.   [2] Forecast.   W = Withheld.   *Sources: Economic Research Service, U.S. Department of Agriculture (ERS-USDA); Bureau of the Census, U.S. Department of Commerce*

Average Wholesale Price of Tallow, Inedible, No. 1 Packers (Prime), Delivered, Chicago   In Cents Per Pound

Year	Jan.	Feb.	Mar.	Apr.	May	June	July	Aug.	Sept.	Oct.	Nov.	Dec.	Average
2005	16.20	16.03	18.73	20.95	19.38	18.23	15.11	15.31	17.54	17.40	17.96	16.67	17.46
2006	17.52	17.05	14.98	13.47	14.77	15.27	17.05	17.35	15.59	17.71	20.42	21.46	16.89
2007	22.02	20.78	21.74	25.04	29.16	33.08	32.58	27.67	30.14	31.29	32.87	27.64	27.83
2008	32.19	36.08	40.03	39.66	40.02	45.36	47.55	40.14	36.17	24.39	14.29	14.23	34.18
2009	22.86	19.57	16.72	21.83	25.80	29.53	26.17	31.75	30.44	22.27	25.89	29.09	25.16
2010	28.37	27.42	31.57	32.74	33.08	32.73	32.15	32.28	32.93	33.88	40.52	42.50	33.35
2011	47.83	47.61	49.49	51.59	52.33	54.52	53.69	49.36	50.02	47.36	44.35	47.21	49.61
2012	44.17	45.67	48.16	47.33	48.98	45.39	45.38	44.59	45.72	40.07	34.05	36.20	43.81
2013	40.00	40.00	42.42	43.06	41.67	45.00	45.39	42.74	40.53	33.37	35.14	35.14	40.37
2014[1]	31.95	31.61	38.52	42.60	44.57	42.04	39.96	39.85	34.90	29.51	32.47	32.09	36.67

[1] Preliminary.   *Sources: Economic Research Service, U.S. Department of Agriculture (ERS-USDA)*

Tea

Tea is the common name for a family of mostly woody flowering plants. The tea family contains about 600 species placed in 28 genera and they are distributed throughout the tropical and subtropical areas, with most species occurring in eastern Asia and South America. The tea plant is native to Southeast Asia. There are more than 3,000 varieties of tea, each with its own distinct character, and each is generally named for the area in which it is grown. Tea may have been consumed in China as long ago as 2700 BC and certainly since 1000 BC. In 2737 BC, the Chinese Emperor Shen Nung, according to Chinese mythology, was a scholar and herbalist. While his servant boiled drinking water, a leaf from the wild tea tree he was sitting under dropped into the water and Shen Nung decided to try the brew. Today, half the world's population drinks tea. Tea is the world's most popular beverage next to water.

Tea is a healthful drink and contains antioxidants, fluoride, niacin, folic acid, and as much vitamin C as a lemon. The average 5 oz. cup of brewed tea contains approximately 40 to 60 milligrams of caffeine (compared to 80 to 115 mg in brewed coffee). Decaffeinated tea has been available since the 1980s. Herbal tea contains no true tea leaves but is actually brewed from a collection of herbs and spices.

Tea grows mainly between the tropic of Cancer and the tropic of Capricorn, requiring 40 to 50 inches of rain per year and a temperature ideally between 50 to 86 degrees Fahrenheit. In order to rejuvenate the bush and keep it at a convenient height for the pickers to access, the bushes must be pruned every four to five years. A tea bush can produce tea for 50 to 70 years, but after 50 years, the yield is reduced.

The two key factors in determining different varieties of tea are the production process (sorting, withering, rolling, fermentation, and drying methods) and the growing conditions (geographical region, growing altitude, and soil type). Black tea, often referred to as fully fermented tea, is produced by allowing picked tea leaves to wither and ferment for up to 24 hours. After fermenting, the leaves are fired, which stops oxidation. Green tea, or unfermented tea, is produced by immediately and completely drying the leaves and omitting the oxidization process, thus allowing the tea to remain green in color.

Supply – World production of tea in 2013 (latest data) rose +6.2% to 5.345 million metric tons, a new record high. The world's largest producers of tea in 2013 were China (with 36.3% of world production), India (22.6%), Kenya (8.1%), Sri Lanka (6.4%), Turkey (4.0%), and Iran (3.0%).

Trade – U.S. tea imports in 2014 (annualized through May) fell -1.4% to 231,919 metric tons, below last year's record high of 216,844 metric tons. World tea imports in 2011 (latest data) rose +10.5% to 1.902 million metric tons. The world's largest tea importers were Russia (with 9.9% of total world imports), the United Kingdom (8.1%), the U.S. (6.7%), and Pakistan (6.3%). World exports of tea in 2011 fell -2.0% to 1.983 million metric tons. The world's largest exporters were China (with 16.5% of world exports), India (16.3%), Sri Lanka (16.2%), Kenya (15.5%), Vietnam (6.8%), Argentina (4.4%), and Indonesia (3.8%).

World Tea Production, in Major Producing Countries In Metric Tons

Year	Argentina	Bang-ladesh	China	India	Indo-nesia	Iran	Japan	Kenya	Malawi	Sri Lanka	Turkey	Ex-USSR[2]	World Total
2007	76,000	58,500	1,165,500	973,000	150,623	49,680	94,100	369,600	48,140	305,220	206,160	16,028	3,978,842
2008	80,142	59,000	1,274,980	987,000	153,971	165,717	96,500	345,800	41,637	318,700	198,046	13,354	4,232,490
2009	71,715	59,500	1,375,780	972,700	156,901	165,717	86,000	314,198	52,555	290,000	198,601	17,157	4,286,820
2010	92,417	60,000	1,467,470	991,182	150,342	165,717	85,000	399,006	51,589	331,400	235,000	14,766	4,606,070
2011	92,892	60,500	1,640,310	1,095,460	150,200	103,890	82,100	377,912	52,000	327,500	221,600	3,704	4,771,210
2012	82,813	60,000	1,804,660	1,135,070	143,400	158,000	85,900	369,400	53,500	330,000	225,000	3,258	5,034,970
2013[1]	105,000	64,000	1,939,460	1,208,780	148,100	160,000	84,800	432,400	54,000	340,230	212,400	3,958	5,345,520

[1] Preliminary. [2] Mostly Georgia and Azerbaijan. *Sources: Foreign Agricultural Service, U.S. Department of Agriculture (FAS-USDA); Food and Agriculture Organization of the United Nations (FAO-UN)*

World Exports of Tea from Producing Countries In Metric Tons

Year	Argentina	Bang-ladesh	Brazil	China	India	Indonesia	Kenya	Malawi	Papua New Guinea	Sri Lanka	Vietnam	Zim-babwe	Total
2005	68,270	12,560	3,407	288,814	159,121	102,294	347,971	44,600	6,900	307,793	88,000	4,825	1,719,251
2006	72,056	7,842	3,238	290,743	181,326	95,339	325,066	27,503	6,600	204,240	105,000	11,532	1,629,291
2007	75,767	5,269	3,298	294,329	193,459	83,659	374,329	54,397	6,400	190,203	114,000	6,840	1,787,039
2008	77,498	8,259	3,034	302,020	203,207	96,210	396,641	30,435	5,937	318,329	104,700	5,979	1,908,811
2009	69,816	5,339	2,326	307,434	203,863	92,304	331,594	47,356	6,250	288,528	133,000	7,874	1,822,236
2010[1]	85,695	1,981	2,542	307,777	234,560	87,101	417,661	49,999	4,581	312,908	136,515	10,023	2,022,821
2011[2]	86,650	945	1,965	327,650	322,548	75,450	306,678	46,007	4,224	321,074	133,900	11,221	1,983,182

[1] Preliminary. [2] Estimate. *Source: Food and Agriculture Organization of the United Nations (FAO-UN)*

Imports of Tea in the United States In Metric Tons

Year	Jan.	Feb.	Mar.	Apr.	May	June	July	Aug.	Sept.	Oct.	Nov.	Dec.	Total
2009	15,525	14,737	19,304	18,124	19,177	18,666	17,092	18,666	17,551	13,217	13,429	12,201	197,689
2010	14,752	15,682	18,907	20,421	20,967	19,845	19,856	19,150	18,747	15,722	14,465	13,815	212,329
2011	13,923	15,355	18,580	18,052	21,794	19,831	19,085	19,257	21,617	13,852	15,173	15,055	211,575
2012	15,091	15,277	16,211	16,716	21,047	20,510	21,292	19,525	22,502	15,871	13,926	13,306	211,272
2013	14,558	13,532	15,848	22,563	22,281	20,306	21,342	21,595	22,288	14,234	15,381	12,918	216,844
2014[1]	13,570	13,945	16,047	20,629	19,669	18,546	17,249	18,987	21,626	18,281	17,544	15,138	211,230

[1] Preliminary. *Source: Foreign Agricultural Service, U.S. Department of Agriculture (FAS-USDA)*

Tin

Tin (atomic symbol Sn) is a silvery-white, lustrous gray metallic element. Tin is soft, pliable and has a highly crystalline structure. When a tin bar is bent or broken, a crackling sound called a "tin cry" is produced due to the breaking of the tin crystals. People have been using tin for at least 5,500 years. Tin has been found in the tombs of ancient Egyptians. In ancient times, tin and lead were considered different forms of the same metal. Tin was exported to Europe in large quantities from Cornwall, England, during the Roman period, from approximately 2100 BC to 1500 BC. Cornwall was one of the world's leading sources of tin for much of its known history and into the late 1800s.

The principal ore of tin is the mineral cassiterite, which is found in Malaya, Bolivia, Indonesia, Thailand, and Nigeria. About 80% of the world's tin deposits occur in unconsolidated placer deposits in riverbeds and valleys, or on the sea floor, with only about 20% occurring as primary hard-rock lodes. Tin deposits are generally small and are almost always found closely allied to the granite from which it originates. Tin is also recovered as a by-product of mining tungsten, tantalum, and lead. After extraction, tin ore is ground and washed to remove impurities, roasted to oxidize the sulfides of iron and copper, washed a second time, and then reduced by carbon in a reverberatory furnace. Electrolysis may also be used to purify tin.

Pure tin, rarely used by itself, was used as currency in the form of tin blocks and was considered legal tender for taxes in Phuket, Thailand, until 1932. Tin is used in the manufacture of coatings for steel containers used to preserve food and beverages. Tin is also used in solder alloys, electroplating, ceramics, and in plastic. The world's major tin research and development laboratory, ITRI Ltd, is funded by companies that produce and consume tin. The focus of the research efforts have been on possible new uses for tin that would take advantage of tin's relative non-toxicity to replace other metals in various products. Some of the replacements could be lead-free solders, antimony-free flame-retardant chemicals, and lead-free shotgun pellets. No tin is currently mined in the U.S.

Tin futures and options trade on the London Metal Exchange (LME). Tin has traded on the LME since 1877 and the standard tin contract began in 1912. The futures contract calls for the delivery of 5 metric tons of tin ingots of at least 99.85% purity. The contract trades in terms of U.S. dollars per metric ton. Futures are also traded on the Multi Commodity Exchange of India (MCX).

Prices – The average monthly price of tin (straights) in New York in 2014 fell by -2.0% yr/yr to $13.36 per pound, which is below the 2011 record high of $15.86 per pound. The 2014 price was far above the 3-decade low of $2.83 per pound seen in 2002. The average monthly price of ex-dock tin in New York in 2014 fell -2.0% yr/yr to $10.20 per pound.

Supply – World mine production of tin in 2014 rose by +0.7% yr/yr to 296,000 metric tons, remaining below the 2007 record high of 303,000 metric tons. The world's largest mine producers of tin are China with 42.2% of world production in 2014, Indonesia with 28.4%, and Peru with 8.0%. World smelter production of tin in 2012 (latest data) fell -5.0% yr/yr to 304,000 metric tons, below the 2007 record high of 327,000 metric tons. The world's largest producers of smelted tin are China with 48.7% of world production in 2014, Indonesia with 13.8%, and Malaysia with 12.4%.

The U.S. does not mine tin, and therefore its supply consists only of scrap and imports. U.S. tin recovery in 2013 (latest data) fell -1.0% to 6,030 metric tons, a new record low.

Demand – U.S. consumption of tin (pig) in 2014 fell -18.3% to 24,752 metric tons (annualized through October), a new record low. The breakdown of U.S. consumption of tin by finished products in 2012 (latest data) shows that the largest consuming industry of tin is chemicals (with 35.6% of consumption), tinplate (22.0%), followed by solder (17.7%), and bronze and brass (8.9%).

Trade – The U.S. relied on imports for 74% of its tin consumption in 2014. U.S. imports of unwrought tin metal in 2013 (latest data) fell -0.8% to 36,600 metric tons, up from the 14-year low in 2009. The largest sources of U.S. imports in 2013 were Bolivia (16.6%), Malaysia (7.5%), and Brazil (6.9%). U.S. exports of tin in 2013 rose +3.6% yr/yr to 5,760 metric tons.

World Mine Production of Tin   In Metric Tons (Contained Tin)

Year	Australia	Bolivia	Brazil	China	Indo-nesia	Malaysia	Nigeria	Peru	Portugal	Russia	Thailand	Vietnam	World Total
2005	2,819	18,433	11,739	126,000	78,404	2,857	1,300	42,145	243	3,000	158	3,500	296,000
2006	1,478	18,444	9,528	126,000	80,933	2,398	1,400	38,470	25	3,000	190	5,400	293,000
2007	2,071	15,972	11,835	146,000	66,137	2,263	180	39,019	41	2,500	122	5,400	301,000
2008	1,783	17,320	13,899	110,000	53,228	2,605	185	39,037	29	400	215	5,400	260,000
2009	5,630	19,575	9,500	97,200	46,078	2,412	400	37,503	34	127	166	5,400	238,000
2010	6,600	20,190	10,400	115,000	43,258	2,668	520	33,848	22	144	291	5,500	255,000
2011	5,012	20,373	10,725	120,000	42,000	3,340	570	28,882	39	75	282	5,400	256,000
2012	5,849	19,702	13,667	110,000	41,000	3,726	570	26,105	42	100	124	5,400	243,000
2013[1]	6,470	19,300	12,000	110,000	95,200	3,700	570	23,700		420	200	5,400	294,000
2014[2]	6,100	18,000	12,000	125,000	84,000	3,500	500	23,700		600	200	5,400	296,000

[1] Preliminary.   [2] Estimate.   *Source: U.S. Geological Survey (USGS)*

World Smelter Production of Primary Tin   In Metric Tons

Year	Australia	Bolivia	Brazil	China	Indo-nesia	Japan	Malaysia	Mexico	Russia	South Africa	Spain	Thailand	World Total
2003	597	12,836	10,761	98,000	66,284	662	18,250	1,769	4,100	----	----	15,400	270,000
2004	467	13,627	11,512	115,000	49,872	707	33,914	25	4,570	----	----	20,800	295,000
2005	594	13,941	8,986	122,000	65,300	754	36,924	17	5,000	----	----	31,600	324,000
2006	572	14,089	8,780	132,000	65,357	854	22,850	25	4,980	----	----	27,540	320,000
2007	118	12,251	9,384	149,000	64,127	879	25,263	25	3,800	----	----	23,104	178,000
2008	170	12,667	11,020	140,000	53,417	956	31,691	15	1,425	----	----	21,860	316,000
2009	----	15,006	8,311	140,000	51,418	757	36,407	15	1,129	----	----	19,423	310,000
2010	----	15,003	9,098	150,000	43,832	841	38,737	----	1,081	----	----	20,000	318,000
2011	----	14,295	9,382	156,000	43,000	947	40,267	----	526	----	----	20,000	320,000
2012[1]	----	14,517	11,955	148,000	42,000	950	37,792	----	500	----	----	20,000	304,000

[1] Preliminary.   *Source: U.S. Geological Survey (USGS)*

United States Foreign Trade of Tin   In Metric Tons

Year	Exports (Metal)	Concentrates[2] (Ore) Total All Ore	Bolivia	Peru	Imports for Consumption — Unwrought Tin Metal Total All Metal	Bolivia	Brazil	China	Indo-nesia	Malaysia	Singa-pore	Thailand	Kingdom
2004	3,650	----	----	----	47,600	5,060	4,330	5,310	4,660	6,600	----	500	97
2005	4,330	----	----	----	37,500	5,400	2,150	4,510	5,220	1,530	194	45	67
2006	5,490	----	----	----	43,300	8,160	1,300	4,440	4,600	245	1,090	210	1,370
2007	6,410	----	----	----	34,600	4,340	2,600	4,230	1,680	14	1,730	15	881
2008	9,800	----	----	----	36,300	4,980	1,570	2,380	2,000	1,740	706	1,670	225
2009	3,170	----	----	----	33,000	6,300	1,050	1,210	3,220	169	451	15	----
2010	5,630	----	----	----	35,300	6,060	75	887	3,970	4,500	996	1,310	----
2011	5,450	----	----	----	34,200	5,680	676	1,490	4,930	3,980	645	2,310	----
2012	5,560	----	----	----	36,900	5,100	2,930	174	6,180	4,590	424	1,750	----
2013[1]	5,760	----	----	----	36,600	6,080	2,530	5	321	2,760	----	----	----

[1] Preliminary.   [2] Tin content.   *Source: U.S. Geological Survey (USGS)*

Consumption (Total) of Tin (Pig) in the United States   In Metric Tons

Year	Jan.	Feb.	Mar.	Apr.	May	June	July	Aug.	Sept.	Oct.	Nov.	Dec.	Total
2005	4,097	3,990	4,027	3,874	3,825	3,918	3,806	3,900	3,824	3,833	3,849	3,699	46,642
2006	3,877	3,694	3,508	3,439	3,447	3,580	3,475	3,420	3,456	3,442	3,407	3,356	42,101
2007	3,381	3,342	3,601	3,365	3,716	3,811	3,585	4,070	3,910	3,734	3,586	3,628	43,729
2008	2,653	2,626	2,630	2,693	2,639	2,641	2,665	2,697	2,687	2,607	2,662	2,653	31,853
2009	2,642	2,546	2,610	2,573	2,525	2,521	2,630	2,552	2,626	2,646	2,675	2,564	31,110
2010	2,678	2,673	2,689	2,698	2,666	2,655	2,706	2,740	2,724	2,730	2,599	2,951	32,509
2011	2,782	2,769	2,833	2,831	2,862	2,983	2,961	2,823	3,064	3,061	2,973	2,750	34,692
2012	2,718	2,748	2,868	2,829	2,908	2,775	2,735	2,745	2,696	2,724	2,684	2,725	33,155
2013	2,959	2,970	3,009	2,989	2,970	2,949	2,099	2,140	2,079	2,069	2,026	2,047	30,306
2014[1]	1,819	1,818	1,878	1,938	2,164	2,212	2,202	2,202	2,212	2,182	2,193	2,153	24,973

[1] Preliminary.   *Source: U.S. Geological Survey (USGS)*

Tin Stocks (Pig-Industrial) in the United States, on First of Month   In Metric Tons

Year	Jan.	Feb.	Mar.	Apr.	May	June	July	Aug.	Sept.	Oct.	Nov.	Dec.
2005	6,140	5,260	5,570	5,420	5,770	5,400	5,670	5,830	5,540	5,350	5,330	5,410
2006	5,400	5,380	5,330	5,350	5,400	5,380	5,420	5,400	5,740	5,650	5,650	5,830
2007	5,700	5,970	6,030	6,030	5,860	5,570	5,270	5,270	5,260	5,310	5,920	6,000
2008	6,140	8,070	8,280	8,020	8,000	7,970	7,930	7,960	7,980	7,960	7,990	7,940
2009	7,970	7,890	7,660	7,640	7,620	7,640	7,570	7,630	7,590	7,540	7,520	7,470
2010	7,450	7,030	7,080	7,060	7,080	7,180	7,270	7,220	7,130	7,060	7,090	7,090
2011	6,920	6,660	6,710	6,740	6,750	6,820	6,860	6,880	6,860	6,860	6,800	6,700
2012	5,230	6,810	6,860	6,780	6,710	6,750	6,790	7,290	7,280	7,340	7,310	6,360
2013	6,470	6,670	6,640	6,590	6,640	7,110	6,660	6,670	6,680	6,580	6,570	6,480
2014[1]	6,520	6,540	6,560	6,570	6,490	6,800	6,800	6,770	6,740	7,360	7,060	6,970

[1] Preliminary.   *Source: U.S. Geological Survey (USGS)*

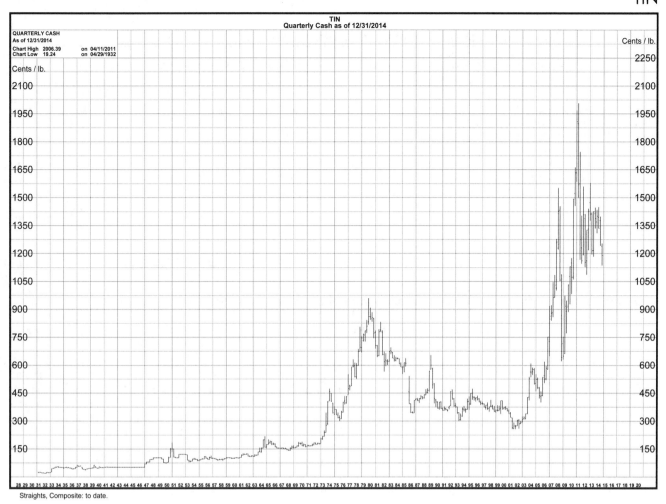

TIN
Quarterly Cash as of 12/31/2014

QUARTERLY CASH
As of 12/31/2014

Chart High 2006.39 on 04/11/2011
Chart Low 19.24 on 04/29/1932

Cents / lb.

Straights, Composite: to date.

Average Price of Ex-Dock Tin in New York[1]   In Cents Per Pound

Year	Jan.	Feb.	Mar.	Apr.	May	June	July	Aug.	Sept.	Oct.	Nov.	Dec.	Average
2005	376.37	393.05	408.41	395.40	394.68	367.81	347.78	347.96	331.01	313.73	300.96	323.43	358.38
2006	338.27	373.87	378.76	420.35	420.53	376.76	400.64	404.26	428.83	461.66	475.57	524.69	417.02
2007	535.46	604.14	648.82	656.53	661.04	659.63	689.99	705.01	700.45	748.39	777.74	756.89	678.67
2008	760.82	800.60	917.15	1,001.99	1,108.30	1,027.62	1,070.50	930.65	850.83	672.97	646.77	532.54	860.06
2009	539.32	523.68	508.12	554.44	646.09	702.56	657.47	694.15	695.88	701.13	698.44	721.79	636.92
2010	823.31	764.25	818.62	870.50	821.34	809.88	851.80	967.17	1,057.81	1,223.59	1,191.80	1,211.71	950.98
2011	1,274.29	1,456.60	1,422.69	1,501.64	1,339.50	1,188.91	1,271.42	1,137.37	1,055.80	1,019.31	998.78	913.27	1,214.96
2012	1,005.52	1,136.74	1,074.53	1,034.47	958.73	905.04	874.07	879.88	972.20	998.11	969.71	1,065.21	989.52
2013	1,147.61	1,132.62	1,088.32	1,016.82	968.64	946.60	914.64	1,008.50	1,062.18	1,076.08	1,064.68	1,061.89	1,040.71
2014	1,026.81	1,061.00	1,074.64	1,088.65	1,083.18	1,059.89	1,041.12	1,037.98	983.57	929.95	931.02	925.65	1,020.29

Source: American Metal Market (AMM)

Average Price of Tin (Straights) in New York   In Cents Per Pound

Year	Jan.	Feb.	Mar.	Apr.	May	June	July	Aug.	Sept.	Oct.	Nov.	Dec.	Average
2005	500.93	519.61	539.30	522.71	522.18	492.64	467.71	466.67	444.80	426.36	411.23	440.30	479.54
2006	464.54	509.45	519.31	574.53	575.57	517.52	548.29	552.06	583.57	623.07	644.19	705.62	568.14
2007	719.05	811.07	873.03	883.74	886.54	884.67	931.50	954.26	949.21	1,012.46	1,049.78	1,025.36	915.06
2008	1,025.05	1,071.97	1,224.20	1,325.79	1,461.85	1,357.22	1,410.60	1,229.27	1,124.02	887.70	841.86	694.41	1,137.83
2009	711.20	686.02	664.21	724.55	841.83	920.39	862.04	902.14	899.35	911.42	922.75	964.64	834.21
2010	1,090.89	1,011.26	1,082.71	1,149.23	1,084.11	1,067.12	1,117.84	1,268.74	1,386.44	1,597.89	1,552.75	1,588.29	1,249.77
2011	1,661.33	1,906.31	1,857.97	1,958.08	1,750.23	1,555.57	1,663.54	1,486.24	1,378.26	1,330.78	1,298.42	1,191.48	1,586.52
2012	1,312.08	1,481.62	1,404.14	1,351.56	1,251.34	1,180.70	1,142.08	1,148.33	1,269.91	1,300.73	1,264.64	1,393.41	1,291.71
2013	1,502.64	1,480.17	1,422.82	1,328.61	1,265.73	1,252.58	1,200.86	1,321.68	1,391.23	1,413.19	1,392.13	1,391.85	1,363.62
2014	1,345.40	1,388.75	1,406.24	1,423.40	1,416.15	1,388.17	1,365.31	1,362.21	1,289.78	1,219.57	1,223.03	1,211.06	1,336.59

Source: U.S. Geological Survey (USGS)

Tin Plate Production & Tin Recovered in the United States — In Metric Tons

	Tinplate Waste Gross Weight	Tinplate (All Forms) Gross Weight	Tin Content (Met. Ton)	Tin per Tonne of Plate (Kilograms)	Tin Metal	Bronze & Brass	Solder	Type Metal	Babbitt	Anti-monial Lead	Chemical Com-pounds	Misc.[2]	Grand Total
Year													
2004	W	2,550,000	7,700	3.0	----	----	----	----	----	----	----	----	----
2005	W	2,270,000	7,670	3.4	----	----	----	----	----	----	----	----	----
2006	56,400	2,130,000	6,810	3.2	----	----	----	----	----	----	----	----	----
2007	58,900	1,780,000	7,010	3.9	----	----	----	----	----	----	----	----	----
2008	30,900	2,280,000	6,690	2.9	----	----	----	----	----	----	----	----	----
2009	14,500	1,150,000	6,200	5.4	----	----	----	----	----	----	----	----	----
2010	18,163	1,416,758	6,920	4.9	----	----	----	----	----	----	----	----	----
2011	21,500	1,230,000	6,330	5.2	----	----	----	----	----	----	----	----	----
2012	16,300	1,160,000	6,090	5.2	----	----	----	----	----	----	----	----	----
2013[1]	20,800	1,090,000	6,030	5.5	----	----	----	----	----	----	----	----	----

[1] Preliminary. [2] Includes foil, terne metal, cable lead, and items indicated by symbol "W". W = Withheld. NA = Not available.
Source: U.S. Geological Survey (USGS)

Consumption of Primary and Secondary Tin in the United States — In Metric Tons

Year	Net Import Reliance as a % of Apparent Consump	Stocks, Jan. 1[2]	Primary	Secondary	Scrap	Total	Available Supply	Stocks, Dec. 31 (Total Available Less Total Processed)	Total Processed	Consumed in Manu-facturing Products
2003	89	8,220	32,400	1,380	3,440	37,300	45,500	7,770	37,700	37,400
2004	92	7,680	40,800	4,160	4,350	49,300	57,000	11,800	45,200	44,700
2005	78	8,060	32,500	5,790	3,840	42,200	50,200	9,120	41,000	40,600
2006	80	7,640	29,900	5,040	4,100	39,000	46,600	8,520	38,100	37,700
2007	72	7,230	25,600	4,950	3,030	33,600	40,800	8,980	31,700	31,100
2008	70	8,760	22,700	4,300	2,410	29,400	38,200	8,460	29,800	29,400
2009	74	8,940	26,200	5,930	2,170	34,300	43,200	10,300	32,900	32,600
2010	73	6,210	25,100	2,910	1,920	29,900	36,100	6,000	30,100	30,100
2011	73	5,830	25,200	2,840	916	29,000	34,800	5,880	28,900	28,500
2012[1]	74	5,800	24,800	2,810	879	28,500	34,300	6,140	28,200	27,700

[1] Preliminary. [2] Includes tin in transit in the U.S. NA = Not available. *Source: U.S. Geological Survey (USGS)*

Consumption of Tin in the United States, by Finished Products — In Metric Tons (Contained Tin)

Year	Tin-plate[2]	Solder	Babbitt	Bronze & Brass	Tinning	Chem-icals[3]	Tin Powder & Anodes	Bar Tin	White Metal	Other	Total	Total Primary	Total Secondary
2003	7,790	10,600	2,570	2,600	833	8,720	W	852	1,220	2,180	37,400	32,900	4,510
2004	7,700	19,000	728	3,070	798	9,120	W	680	937	2,630	44,700	36,700	7,990
2005	7,250	16,700	554	3,200	790	8,360	W	709	W	3,030	40,600	31,400	9,170
2006	7,110	12,800	484	3,300	696	9,290	W	698	W	1,040	37,700	29,200	8,480
2007	7,010	10,400	604	2,800	451	6,070	W	788	W	1,120	31,100	23,700	7,490
2008	6,840	5,110	604	2,460	395	5,440	227	767	W	5,370	29,200	23,100	6,250
2009	6,130	5,110	322	2,200	340	9,290	193	245	W	7,000	32,600	24,800	7,750
2010	6,920	7,340	288	2,460	387	9,470	192	W	W	811	30,100	25,300	4,820
2011	6,230	4,100	315	3,810	552	9,990	W	W	W	757	28,500	25,200	3,280
2012[1]	6,090	4,900	281	2,460	467	9,860	W	W	W	733	27,700	24,500	3,240

[1] Preliminary. [2] Includes small quantity of secondary pig tin and tin acquired in chemicals. [3] Including tin oxide.
W = Withheld proprietary data. *Source: U.S. Geological Survey (USGS)*

Salient Statistics of Recycling Tin in the United States

Year	New Scrap[1] (In Thousands of Metric Tons)	Old Scrap[2]	Recycled Metal[3]	Apparent Supply	Percent Recycled	New Scrap[1] (Value in Millions of Dollars)	Old Scrap[2]	Recycled Metal[3]	Apparent Supply
2005	2.3	11.7	14.0	46.3	30	24.3	125	150	495
2006	2.3	11.6	13.9	51.6	27	29.1	145	174	642
2007	2.9	12.2	15.1	44.5	31	56.7	242	298	882
2008	2.1	11.7	13.8	40.9	34	52.2	291	343	1,020
2009	2.3	11.1	13.4	44.7	30	42.5	204	247	825
2010	2.7	11.1	13.8	44.1	31	73.4	303	376	1,200
2011	2.5	11.0	13.6	42.8	32	87.9	383	470	1,490
2012	2.4	11.2	13.6	44.7	30	69.0	316	385	1,260

[1] Scrap that results from the manufacturing process. [2] Scrap that results from consumer products. [3] Metal recovered from new plus old scrap.
Source: U.S. Geological Survey (USGS)

Titanium

Titanium (atomic symbol Ti) is a silver-white, metallic element used primarily to make light, strong alloys. It ranks ninth in abundance among the elements in the crust of the earth but is never found in the pure state. It occurs as an oxide in various minerals. It was first discovered in 1791 by Rev. William Gregor and was first isolated as a basic element in 1910. Titanium was named after the mythological Greek god Titan for its strength.

Titanium is extremely brittle when cold, but is malleable and ductile at a low red heat, and thus easily fabricated. Due to its strength, low weight, and resistance to corrosion, titanium is used in metallic alloys and as a substitute for aluminum. It is used extensively in the aerospace industry, in desalinization plants, construction, medical implants, paints, pigments, and lacquers.

Supply – World production of titanium ilmenite concentrates in 2014 fell -0.7% yr/yr to 6.680 million metric tons, still well below the 2007 record high of 7.120 million metric tons. The world's largest producers of titanium ilmenite concentrates are Australia with 16.5% of world

production in 2014, China (15.0%), Norway (6.0%), Vietnam (7.5%), and India (5.1%) World production of titanium rutile concentrates in 2014 rose +15.4% yr/yr to 770,000 metric tons, which is a new record high. The world's largest producers are Australia with 62.3% of world production in 2014 followed by Sierra Leone with 15.6% and South Africa with 8.4%.

Demand – U.S. consumption of titanium dioxide pigment in 2012 rose +2.3% yr/yr to 722,000 metric tons, but remained well below 2004's record high of 1.170 million metric tons. U.S. consumption of ilmenite in 2005 (latest data available) fell −12.8% to 1.290 million metric tons, down from 2004's 8-year high of 1.480 million metric tons. U.S. consumption of rutile in 2005 (latest data) fell 4.7% yr/yr to a 7-year low of 424,000 metric tons.

Trade – U.S. imports of titanium dioxide pigment in 2012 (latest data) rose by +1.5% yr/yr to 203,000 metric tons, still below the 2005 record high of 341,000 metric tons. U.S. imports of ilmenite in 2012 rose +20.5% yr/yr to 618,000 metric tons.

World Produciton of Titanium Illmenite Concentrates   In Thousands of Metric Tons

Year	Australia[2]	Brazil	China	Egypt	India	Malaysia	Norway	Ukraine	United States	Vietnam	World Total	-- Titaniferous Slag[4] --- Canada	Africa
2005	2,080	82	900	----	686	38	810	375	500	523	6,050	860	1,020
2006	2,508	95	1,000	----	690	46	850	470	500	605	6,860	930	1,230
2007	2,503	100	1,100	----	700	60	882	500	400	643	7,140	960	1,270
2008	2,230	130	1,100	----	610	37	915	520	400	710	7,010	1,000	1,252
2009	1,611	53	900	----	700	16	671	500	300	699	6,260	765	1,084
2010	1,651	166	1,400	----	540	19	864	500	400	912	7,530	1,090	1,252
2011	1,501	166	1,700	----	550	29	870	261	400	841	7,570	878	1,346
2012	1,572	166	1,600	----	560	22	831	247	300	1,144	7,800	900	1,400
2013	960	100	1,020	----	340		498	150	200	720	6,730	770	1,190
2014[1]	1,100	70	1,000	----	340		400	210	100	500	6,680	900	1,100

[1] Preliminary.   [2] Includes leucoxene.   [3] Approximately 10% of total production is ilmenite. Beginning in 1988, 25% of Norway's ilmenite production was used to produce slag containing 75% TiO2.   NA = Not available.   *Source: U.S. Geological Survey (USGS)*

Salient Statistics of Titanium in the United States   In Metric Tons

Year	--- Titanium Dioxide Pigment --- Production	Imports[3]	Apparent Consumption	------ Ilmenite ------ Imports[3]	Consumption	-- Titanium Slag --- Imports[3]	Consumption	------ Rutile[4] -------- Imports[3]	Consumption	------ Exports of Titanium Products ------ Ores & Concentrates	Scrap	Dioxide & Pigments	Ingots, Billets, Etc.
2003	1,420,000	240,000	1,070,000	804,000	1,300,000	409,000	----	427,000	489,000	10,300	5,320	518,000	3,960
2004	1,540,000	264,000	1,170,000	701,000	1,480,000	457,000	----	360,000	445,000	8,690	9,760	576,000	4,990
2005	1,310,000	341,000	1,130,000	822,000	1,290,000	667,000	----	366,000	424,000	20,900	20,600	486,000	6,350
2006	1,370,000	288,000	1,080,000	187,000	----	693,000	----	355,000	----	32,800	10,800	513,000	7,900
2007	1,440,000	221,000	979,000	246,000	----	749,000	----	463,800	----	9,730	9,510	564,000	8,670
2008	1,350,000	183,000	800,000	433,000	----	461,000	----	487,000	----	14,900	8,180	668,000	10,500
2009	1,230,000	175,000	757,000	250,000	----	414,000	----	279,600	----	14,800	4,200	617,000	7,240
2010	1,320,000	204,000	767,000	377,000	----	475,000	----	351,000	----	18,900	3,480	717,000	8,450
2011[1]	1,290,000	200,000	706,000	377,000	----	513,000	----	381,000	----	26,600	5,150	741,000	15,600
2012[2]	1,140,000	203,000	722,000	374,000	----	618,000	----	436,000	----	43,000	8,760	587,000	138,000

[1] Preliminary.   [2] Estimate.   [3] For consumption.   [4] Natural and synthetic.   W = Withheld.   *Source: U.S. Geological Survey (USGS)*

World Production of Titanium Rutile Concentrates   In Metric Tons

Year	Australia	Brazil	India	Mada-gascar	Malaysia	Mozam-bique	Sierra Leone	South Africa	Sri Lanka	Thailand	Ukraine[2]	United States	World Total
2007	312,000	3,000	21,000	----	1,450	8,782	82,527	114,000	4,607	----	60,000	W	607,000
2008	325,000	2,309	21,000	----	1,834	6,552	78,908	134,000	11,335	----	60,000	W	641,000
2009	285,000	2,737	21,000	3,200	1,502	1,800	63,864	136,000	2,276	----	60,000	W	577,000
2010	429,000	2,331	24,000	5,700	7,567	4,700	68,198	130,000	2,568	----	60,000	W	734,000
2011	474,000	2,350	25,000	9,400	10,810	6,455	67,916	149,000	2,700	----	60,000	W	808,000
2012	439,000	1,881	26,000	13,000	20,008	3,713	94,493	150,000	2,800	----	58,000	W	809,000
2013	423,000	2,000	24,000	8,000	14,000	9,000	81,000	59,000		----	50,000	W	667,000
2014[1]	480,000		26,000	7,000	14,000		120,000	65,000		----	50,000	W	770,000

[1] Preliminary.   NA = Not available.   *Source: U.S. Geological Survey (USGS)*

World Production of Titanium Sponge Metal & U.S. Consumption of Titanium Concentrates

| | Production of Titanium (In Metric Tons) Sponge Metal[2] | | | | | | --- U.S. Consumption of Titanium Concentrates, by Products (In Metric Tons) --- Ilmenite (TiO$_2$ Content) | | | Rutile (TiO$_2$ Content) | | | |
Year	China	Japan	Russia	United Kingdom	United States	Total	Pigments	Misc.	Total	Welding Rod Coatings	Pigments	Misc.	Total
2006	18,000	37,800	32,000	----	W	121,000	----	----	1,510,000	----	----	----	----
2007	45,200	38,900	34,200	----	W	153,000	----	----	1,600,000	----	----	----	----
2008	49,600	40,900	29,500	----	W	155,000	----	----	1,440,000	----	----	----	----
2009	61,500	25,000	26,600	----	W	136,000	----	----	1,360,000	----	----	----	----
2010	57,800	31,600	25,800	----	W	137,000	----	----	1,520,000	----	----	----	----
2011	60,000	40,000	25,800	----	W	156,000	----	----	1,500,000	----	----	----	----
2012	80,000	40,000	44,000	----	W	200,000	----	----		----	----	----	----
2013[1]	100,000	40,000	45,000	----	W	222,000	----	----		----	----	----	----

[1] Preliminary.   [2] Unconsolidated metal in various forms.   [4] Included in Pigments.   NA = Not available.   W = Withheld.
Source: U.S. Geological Survey (USGS)

Average Prices of Titanium in the United States

Year	Ilmenite FOB Australian Ports[2]	Slag, 85% TiO2 FOB Richards Bay, South Africa	Rutile Large Lots Bulk, FOB U.S. East Coast[3]	Rutile Bagged FOB Australian Ports	Avg. Price of Grade A Titanium Sponge, FOB Shipping Point	Titanium Metal Sponge	Titanium Dioxide Pigments FOB US Plants Anatase	Titanium Dioxide Pigments FOB US Plants Rutile
	---------------------------- Dollars Per Metric Ton ----------------------------				--------------------- Dollars Per Pound ---------------------			
2005	$80.00	$390 - $555	$460 - $480	$550 - $650	----	$3.46 - $12.22	$0.95 - $1.00	$0.95 - $1.00
2006	$75 - $85	$402 - $454	$450 - $500	$570 - $700	----	$5.87 - $12.84	----	----
2007	$75 - $85	$418 - $457	$475 - $500	$650 - $700	----	$6.33 - $7.06	----	----
2008	$84 - $137	$393 - $407	$500 - $550	$675 - $725	----	$6.16 - $8.02	----	----
2009	$60 - $85	$401 - $439	$525 - $540	$700 - $800	----	$4.50 - $7.07	----	----
2010	$65 - $85	$367 - $433	$530 - $550	$760 - $805	----	$3.50 - $6.24	----	----
2011	$140 - $250	$468 - $494	$1,300-$1,400	$1,348-$1,600	----	$3.27 - $6.74	----	----
2012[1]	$250 - $350	$512 - $763	$2,050-$2,400	$2,500-$2,800	----	$3.53 - $6.95	----	----

[1] Preliminary.   NA = Not available.   *Source: U.S. Geological Survey (USGS)*

Average Price of Titanium[1] in United States   In Dollars Per Pound

Year	Jan.	Feb.	Mar.	Apr.	May	June	July	Aug.	Sept.	Oct.	Nov.	Dec.	Average
2009	12.93	12.50	10.50	9.93	9.20	9.00	9.00	9.00	8.92	8.75	8.75	8.75	9.77
2010	8.75	8.75	8.92	9.13	10.10	10.70	11.00	11.00	11.00	11.00	11.43	11.50	10.27
2011	11.50	11.76	12.00	12.00	12.00	12.00	12.00	12.00	12.23	12.25	12.25	12.25	12.02
2012	12.25	11.95	11.75	11.75	11.72	11.00	11.00	11.00	11.00	11.00	11.00	10.61	11.34
2013	10.40	10.25	10.25	10.25	10.25	10.25	10.25	9.80	9.55	9.09	8.76	8.59	9.81
2014	8.26	8.07	8.13	8.13	8.26	8.38	8.38	8.66	8.75	8.75	8.63	8.50	8.41

[1] Ingot, 6Al - 4V.   *Source: American Metal Market (AMM)*

Average Price of Titanium[1] in United States   In Dollars Per Pound

Year	Jan.	Feb.	Mar.	Apr.	May	June	July	Aug.	Sept.	Oct.	Nov.	Dec.	Average
2009	31.20	31.00	31.00	29.76	29.00	29.00	29.00	29.00	29.00	27.10	26.50	26.50	29.01
2010	26.50	25.55	24.50	25.50	26.50	26.50	28.50	28.50	28.50	28.50	30.20	30.50	27.48
2011	30.50	30.50	30.50	30.50	30.50	30.50	30.50	30.50	30.50	30.50	30.50	30.50	30.50
2012	30.50	29.90	29.50	30.36	30.50	30.50	30.50	30.50	30.50	30.50	30.50	30.31	30.34
2013	29.07	27.50	27.50	27.50	27.50	27.50	27.50	26.77	25.90	25.50	25.50	25.50	26.94
2014	25.50	25.50	25.50	25.50	25.76	26.00	26.00	26.00	26.00	26.00	25.75	25.50	25.75

[1] Plate, Alloy.   *Source: American Metal Market (AMM)*

Tobacco

Tobacco is a member of the nightshade family. It is commercially grown for its leaves and stems, which are rolled into cigars, shredded for use in cigarettes and pipes, processed for chewing, or ground into snuff. Christopher Columbus introduced tobacco cultivation and use to Spain after observing natives from the Americas smoking loosely rolled tobacco-stuffed tobacco leaves.

Tobacco is cured, or dried, after harvesting and then aged to improve its flavor. The four common methods of curing are: air cured, fire cured, sun cured, and flue cured. Flue curing is the fastest method of curing and requires only about a week compared with up to 10 weeks for other methods. Cured tobacco is tied into small bundles of about 20 leaves and aged one to three years.

Virginia tobacco is by far the most popular type used in pipe tobacco since it is the mildest of all blending tobaccos. Approximately 60% of the U.S. tobacco crop is Virginia-type tobacco. Burley tobacco is the next most popular tobacco. It is air-cured, burns slowly and provides a relatively cool smoke. Other tobacco varieties include Perique, Kentucky, Oriental, and Latakia.

Prices – U.S. tobacco farm prices in 2013 (latest data) rose +4.5% to 216.2 cents per pound, a new record high.

Supply – World production of tobacco in 2013 (latest data) rose +2.6% yr/yr to 7.435 million metric tons, a new record high. The world's largest producers of tobacco are China with 42.4% of world production, followed at a distance by Brazil (with 11.4% of world production), India (11.2%), and the U.S. (4.7%). U.S. production in 2013 remained unchanged yr/yr at 345,837 metric tons, where it was down by more than half from the 2-decade high of 810,750 metric tons posted in 1997. Tobacco in the U.S. is grown primarily in the Mid-Atlantic States and they account for the vast majority of U.S. production. Specifically, the largest tobacco producing states in the U.S. are North Carolina (with 51.8% of U.S. production in 2014), Kentucky (24.5%), Virginia (6.6%), Tennessee (6.0%), Georgia (3.9%), and South Carolina with (3.8%).

U.S. production of flue-cured tobacco (type 11-14), the most popular tobacco type grown in the U.S., rose by +26.1% yr/yr to 572.880 million pounds in 2014. The second most popular type is burley tobacco (type 31), which saw U.S. production in 2014 rose +10.5% to 217.860 million pounds.

Total U.S. production of tobacco in 2014 rose +21.1% yr/yr to 876.415 million pounds, which is less than half of the 2-decade high of 1.787 billion pounds posted in 1997. U.S. farmers have sharply reduced the planting acreage for tobacco. In 2014, harvested tobacco acreage rose +6.4% yr/yr to 378,360 acres, which is up from the 2005 record low of 297,080 but still far below the 25-year high of 836,230 posted in 1997. Yield in 2014 rose +13.9% to 2,316 down from a 15-year high of 2,325 pounds per acre in 2009. The farm value of the U.S. tobacco crop in 2013 (latest data) fell -0.8% yr/yr to $1.565 billion.

U.S. marketings of flue-cured tobacco (Types 11-14) in the 2006-07 (latest data) marketing year rose by +18.5% yr/yr to 454.7 million pounds. U.S. marketings of burley tobacco (Type 31) in the 2006-07 marketing year rose by +6.9% yr/yr to 224.6 million pounds.

U.S. production of cigarettes in 2009 (latest data) fell -14.6% to 338.1 billion cigarettes, which was far below the record high of 754.5 million posted in 1996. U.S. production of cigars rose by +65.2% yr/yr to 8.231 billion in 2009. U.S. production of chewing tobacco in 2009 fell by 9.8% to 29.3 million pounds, which was a record low.

Demand – U.S. per capita consumption of tobacco products in 2006 (latest data) was unchanged at 3.69 pounds per person but there appears to be a shifting from cigarettes to cigars. The 3.69 pounds per capita consumption of tobacco in 2006 is less than half the record high of 9.68 pounds per person that occurred at the beginning of the series in 1970. Per capita cigarette consumption in 2006 fell 1.5% yr/yr to 1,691 cigarettes per person, which was a record low. Per capita consumption of cigars in 2006 rose +1.9% yr/yr to a record high of 47.80 cigars per person. Per capita consumption of loose smoking tobacco in 2006 fell –6.3% yr/yr to 0.15 pounds.

Trade – U.S. tobacco exports in 2013 fell -0.8% yr/yr to 350.5 million pounds but remained above the record low of 325.8 million pounds seen in 2002. Meanwhile, U.S. tobacco imports in 2004 (latest data) fell –10.9% yr/yr to 561.7 million pounds from the 11-year high of 630.1 million pounds see in 2003. The U.S. exported 111.3 billion cigarettes and 180 million cigars in 2006.

World Production of Leaf Tobacco   In Metric Tons

Year	Brazil	Canada	China	Greece	India	Indo-nesia	Italy	Japan	Pakistan	Turkey	United States	Zim-babwe	World Total
2004	921,281	42,430	2,406,000	133,937	549,900	165,108	117,882	52,659	86,200	133,913	400,012	78,312	6,590,379
2005	889,426	43,000	2,683,000	124,351	549,100	153,470	115,983	46,800	100,500	135,247	292,574	83,230	6,757,733
2006	900,381	48,525	2,744,000	37,405	552,200	146,265	96,600	37,700	112,592	98,137	330,169	44,451	6,598,165
2007	908,679	44,000	2,395,480	29,370	520,000	164,851	110,000	37,800	103,240	74,584	357,273	79,000	6,186,873
2008	851,058	44,718	2,839,950	20,500	490,000	168,037	92,560	38,500	107,765	93,403	363,103	81,952	6,594,880
2009	863,079	45,951	3,067,930	27,098	622,830	176,510	97,860	36,600	104,996	85,000	373,117	85,085	7,056,890
2010	787,817	40,120	3,005,930	22,000	690,000	135,700	89,112	29,300	119,323	55,000	325,766	109,737	6,889,920
2011	951,933	33,575	3,158,740	23,900	830,000	214,600	70,130	23,600	102,834	45,000	271,363	111,570	7,448,830
2012[1]	810,550	34,500	3,127,870	24,000	820,000	260,800	50,620	19,700	97,878	75,000	345,837	115,000	7,248,320
2013[2]	850,673	34,500	3,150,200	24,000	830,000	260,200	49,770	19,700	108,307	90,000	345,837	150,000	7,435,070

[1] Preliminary.   [2] Estimate.   *Source: Food and Agriculture Organization of the United Nations (FAO-UN)*

TOBACCO

Production and Consumption of Tobacco Products in the United States

Year	Cigar- ettes - Billions -	Cigars[3] - Millions -	--- Chewing Tobacco --- Plug	Twist	Loose- leaf	Smoking Total Tobacco	Snuff[4]	Consumption[5] of Per Capita[6] Cigar- ettes ----- Number -----	Cigars[3]	Cigar- ettes	Cigars[3]	Smoking Tobacco	Chewing Tobacco	Total Products
			In Millions of Pounds							In Pounds				
2000	593.2	2,825	2.6	0.8	46.0	49.4	13.6	69.5	2,049	38.0	3.40	.62	.13	.48	4.10
2001	562.8	3,741	2.4	0.8	43.9	47.1	12.8	70.9	2,051	41.2	3.50	.68	.15	.47	4.30
2002	484.3	3,816	2.2	0.8	41.5	44.5	15.5	72.7	1,982	41.8	3.40	.68	.16	.43	4.16
2003	499.4	4,017	1.7	0.7	39.2	41.6	17.8	73.8	1,890	44.5	3.20	.73	.16	.40	3.97
2004	492.7	4,342	1.7	0.7	37.0	39.3	16.1	79.3	1,814	47.9	3.10	.79	.15	.37	3.87
2005	498.7	3,674	1.4	0.6	37.2	39.2	17.4	86.7	1,716	46.9	2.90	.77	.16	.36	3.69
2006	483.7	4,256	1.3	0.6	36.4	38.3	16.5	81.8	1,691	47.8	2.90	.78	.15	.37	3.69
2007	449.7	4,797	1.2	0.5	35.1	36.8	NA	NA	NA	NA	NA	NA	NA	NA	NA
2008[1]	396.1	4,984	1.1	0.5	30.9	32.5	----	----	----	----	----	----	----	----	----
2009[2]	338.1	8,232	0.9	0.5	28.0	29.3	----	----	----	----	----	----	----	----	----

[1] Preliminary. [2] Estimate. [3] Large cigars and cigarillos. [4] Includes loose-leaf. [5] Consumption of tax-paid tobacco products. Unstemmed rocessing weight. [6] 18 years and older. NA = Not available. *Source: Economic Research Service, U.S. Department of Agriculture (ERS-USDA)*

Production of Tobacco in the United States, by States In Thousands of Pounds

Year	Georgia	Kentucky	North Carolina	Ohio	Pennsyl- vania	South Carolina	Tennessee	Virginia	Total
2005	27,760	174,260	278,900	6,732	10,700	39,900	51,670	40,351	645,015
2006	30,090	186,780	330,580	7,000	16,790	48,300	49,135	47,322	727,897
2007	39,775	197,040	383,420	7,175	18,310	46,125	38,636	46,142	787,653
2008	33,600	205,850	390,360	6,970	17,630	39,900	52,380	45,970	800,504
2009	28,014	206,900	423,856	6,800	18,660	38,850	49,960	46,530	822,581
2010	26,790	181,760	352,625	5,125	19,965	36,000	45,740	44,299	718,190
2011	26,775	172,140	251,565	3,360	20,655	26,350	45,363	48,125	598,252
2012	22,500	195,800	381,190	3,990	22,985	25,200	53,000	53,599	762,709
2013	22,400	187,240	362,660	4,620	21,260	24,650	44,570	52,613	723,579
2014[1]	34,500	214,280	453,860	4,300	22,250	33,180	52,155	57,651	876,415

[1] Preliminary. *Source: Agricultural Statistics Board, U.S. Department of Agriculture (ASB-USDA)*

Salient Statistics of Tobacco in the United States

Year	Acres Harvested 1,000 Acres	Yield Per Acre Pounds	Pro- duction Million Pounds	Farm Price cents Lb.	Farm Value Million $	Tobacco (June - July) Exports[2]	Imports[3] - Million Pounds -	U. S. Exports of Cigar- ettes	Cigars & Cheroots ---- In Millions -----	All Tobacco	Smoking Tobacco[4]	Stocks of Tobacco[5] Various Types All Tobacco	Fire Cured[6]	Cigar Filler[7] In Millions of Pounds	Mary- land
2005	297.1	2,171	645	164.2	1,059	----	----	113,300	301	----	----	1,455	----	9.9	5.0
2006	339.0	2,144	728	166.5	1,211	----	----	111,317	180	----	----	1,167	----	10.8	0.8
2007	356.0	2,213	788	169.3	1,329	----	----	----	----	----	----	----	----	----	----
2008	354.5	2,258	801	185.9	1,488	----	----	----	----	----	----	----	----	----	----
2009	354.0	2,323	823	183.7	1,511	----	----	----	----	----	----	----	----	----	----
2010	337.5	2,128	718	178.2	1,280	----	----	----	----	----	----	----	----	----	----
2011	325.0	1,841	598	184.7	1,105	----	----	----	----	----	----	----	----	----	----
2012	336.2	2,268	763	207.2	1,580	----	----	----	----	----	----	----	----	----	----
2013	355.7	2,034	724	215.1	1,575	----	----	----	----	----	----	----	----	----	----
2014[1]	378.4	2,316	876	207.0	1,838	----	----	----	----	----	----	----	----	----	----

[1] Preliminary. [2] Domestic. [3] For consumption. [4] In bulk. [5] Flue-cured and cigar wrapper, year beginning July 1; for all other types, October 1. [6] Kentucky-Tennessee types 22-23. [7] Types 41-46. *Source: Economic Research Service, U.S. Department of Agriculture (ERS-USDA)*

Tobacco Production in the United States, by Types In Thousands of Pounds (Farm-Sale Weight)

Year	Class 1, Flue-cured (11-14)	Class 2, Fire-cured (21-23)	Class 3A, Light air-cured (31-32)	Class 3B, Dark air-cured (35-37)	Total Cigar types (41-61)	US Total
2005	380,850	37,631	206,383	11,530	8,621	645,015
2006	447,190	39,392	219,895	13,155	8,265	727,897
2007	503,760	40,888	218,507	13,056	11,442	787,653
2008	499,220	62,190	205,310	25,340	8,444	800,504
2009	525,414	52,990	219,726	17,040	7,411	822,581
2010	451,290	48,379	192,520	15,180	10,821	718,190
2011	344,610	51,721	178,265	16,082	7,574	598,252
2012	472,900	53,764	211,550	15,250	9,245	762,709
2013	454,350	50,388	197,165	13,790	7,886	723,579
2014[1]	572,880	59,164	217,860	17,490	9,715	876,415

[1] Preliminary. *Source: Agricultural Statistics Board, U.S. Department of Agriculture (ASB-USDA)*

U.S. Exports of Unmanufactured Tobacco   In Millions of Pounds (Declared Weight)

Year	Australia	Belgium-Luxem.	Denmark	France	Germany	Italy	Japan	Nether-lands	Sweden	Switzer-land	Thailand	United Kingdom	Total U.S. Exports
2005	2.9	12.7	8.4	10.7	55.3	5.8	21.7	25.4	.7	15.6	4.1	3.2	339.0
2006	4.9	16.8	8.4	7.5	81.2	3.2	3.9	37.0	.7	38.5	3.0	1.1	397.6
2007	3.5	18.0	9.7	13.2	63.1	.7	4.0	24.0	.3	41.7	1.8	.0	411.5
2008	1.3	3.9	6.5	7.0	39.2	.0	.0	46.3	.3	69.3	3.0	.1	372.3
2009	6.4	3.6	6.4	7.7	23.9	.4	.0	37.7	.3	59.1	2.8	.1	380.3
2010	5.2	44.6	4.5	8.3	20.8	.6	.0	44.7	.4	34.7	3.0	1.1	394.0
2011	.8	10.0	.7	8.9	25.9	.8	.0	27.2	.5	65.6	3.7	6.0	406.5
2012	.7	10.3	.8	11.8	20.2	.5	.2	29.6	.2	46.2	3.6	2.9	353.4
2013	.3	3.8	.7	6.5	20.1	1.5	.0	25.0	.5	62.2	2.7	1.4	349.6
2014[1]	.1	9.9	1.2	9.8	14.4	.5	.0	14.2	.4	63.5	3.2	3.2	330.3

[1] Preliminary.   *Source: Economic Research Service, U.S. Department of Agriculture (ERS-USDA)*

U.S. Salient Statistics for Flue-Cured Tobacco (Types 11-14) in the United States   In Millions of Pounds

Year	Acres Harvested 1,000	Yield Per Acre Pounds	Mar-ketings	Stocks Oct. 1	Total Supply	Exports	Domestic Disap-pearance	Total Disap-pearance	Farm Price cents/Lb.	Placed Under Gov't Loan (Mil. Lb.)	Price Support Level (cents/) Lb.	Loan Stocks Nov. 30	Loan Stocks Uncom-mitted
2004-05	228.4	2,283	499	823	1,322	189	338	526	184.5	94.9	169.0	108.2	128.5
2005-06	174.5	2,182	383	796	1,179	258	317	575	147.4	----	----	79.0	----
2006-07	213.1	2,095	455	604	1,058	270	248	518	149.6	----	----	----	----
2007-08	223.0	2,259	----	----	----	----	----	----	152.7	----	----	----	----
2008-09	223.0	2,239	----	----	----	----	----	----	175.7	----	----	----	----
2009-10	223.8	2,348	----	----	----	----	----	----	175.4	----	----	----	----
2010-11	210.9	2,140	----	----	----	----	----	----	----	----	----	----	----
2011-12	206.9	1,666	----	----	----	----	----	----	----	----	----	----	----
2012-13[1]	206.0	2,296	----	----	----	----	----	----	----	----	----	----	----
2013-14[2]	228.8	1,986	----	----	----	----	----	----	----	----	----	----	----

[1] Preliminary.   [2] Estimate.   NA = Not available.   *Source: Economic Research Service, U.S. Department of Agriculture (ERS-USDA)*

Salient Statistics for Burley Tobacco (Type 31) in the United States   In Millions of Pounds

Year	Acres Harvested 1,000	Yield Per Acre Pounds	Mar-ketings	Stocks Oct. 1	Total Supply	Exports	Domestic Disap-pearance	Total Disap-pearance	Farm Price cents/Lb.	Gross Sales[3]	Price Support Level cents/Lb.	Loan Stocks Nov. 30	Loan Stocks Uncom-mitted
2005-06	174.5	2,182	383	796	1,179	258	317	575	147.4	----	----	79.0	----
2006-07	213.1	2,095	455	604	1,058	270	248	518	149.6	----	----	----	----
2007-08	223.0	2,259	----	----	----	----	----	----	152.7	----	----	----	----
2008-09	223.0	2,239	----	----	----	----	----	----	175.7	----	----	----	----
2009-10	223.8	2,348	----	----	----	----	----	----	175.4	----	----	----	----
2010-11	210.9	2,140	----	----	----	----	----	----	----	----	----	----	----
2011-12	206.9	1,666	----	----	----	----	----	----	----	----	----	----	----
2012-13	206.0	2,296	----	----	----	----	----	----	----	----	----	----	----
2013-14[1]	228.8	1,986	----	----	----	----	----	----	----	----	----	----	----
2014-15[2]	245.3	2,335	----	----	----	----	----	----	----	----	----	----	----

[1] Preliminary.   [2] Estimate.   [3] Before Christmas holidays.   NA = Not available.
Source: Economic Research Service, U.S. Department of Agriculture (ERS-USDA)

Exports of Tobacco from the United States (Quantity and Value)   In Metric Tons

Year	Unmanufactured Flue-Cured	Value 1,000 USD	Burley	Value 1,000 USD	Total	Value 1,000 USD	Manu-factured	Value 1,000 USD
2005	62,779	420,532	61,606	412,588	153,762	989,588	19,364	1,301,834
2006	88,020	569,431	63,214	409,272	180,368	1,141,374	22,261	1,320,283
2007	82,093	541,816	75,905	498,168	186,643	1,207,945	17,552	1,122,176
2008	100,848	730,677	44,506	342,732	168,885	1,238,047	25,474	824,638
2009	86,429	659,772	37,395	300,744	172,504	1,158,970	4,654	489,480
2010	85,789	662,648	32,687	265,927	178,726	1,167,644	4,981	454,459
2011	88,876	643,946	33,385	256,006	184,369	1,148,991	7,472	489,454
2012	77,073	607,725	32,051	243,411	160,308	1,101,214	18,405	482,614
2013[1]	78,079	650,887	32,124	265,809	158,571	1,137,765	21,928	485,400
2014[2]	76,220	645,292	25,436	217,305	149,818	1,085,720	18,028	426,675

[1] Preliminary.   [2] Forecast.   *Source: Foreign Agricultural Service, U.S. Department of Agriculture (FAS-USDA)*

Tungsten

Tungsten (atomic symbol W) is a grayish-white, lustrous, metallic element. The atomic symbol for tungsten is W because of its former name of Wolfram. Tungsten has the highest melting point of any metal at about 3410 degrees Celsius and boils at about 5660 degrees Celsius. In 1781, the Swedish chemist Carl Wilhelm Scheele discovered tungsten.

Tungsten is never found in nature but is instead found in the minerals wolframite, scheelite, huebnertite, and ferberite. Tungsten has excellent corrosion resistance qualities and is resistant to most mineral acids. Tungsten is used as filaments in incandescent lamps, electron and television tubes, alloys of steel, spark plugs, electrical contact points, cutting tools, and in the chemical and tanning industries.

Prices – The average monthly price of tungsten at U.S. ports in 2014 fell by -3.8% yr/yr to $357.39 per short ton, below the 2012 record high of $375.16.

Supply – World concentrate production of tungsten in 2014 rose by +2.1% yr/yr to 82,400 metric tons, which is a new record high. The world's largest producer of tungsten by far is China with 68,000 metric tons of production in 2014, which was 82.5% of total world production. Russia is the next largest producer at 4.4% with miniscule production of only 3,600 metric tons.

Trade – The U.S. in 2014 relied on imports for 43% of its tungsten consumption. U.S. imports for consumption in 2014 rose by +11.1% yr/yr to 4,100 metric tons. U.S. exports in 2014 rose +41.5% yr/yr to 1,500 metric tons.

World Concentrate Production of Tungsten   In Metric Tons (Contained Tungsten[3])

Year	Austria	Bolivia	Brazil	Burma	Canada	China	Korea, North	Mongolia	Portugal	Russia	Rwanda	Thailand	Total
2007	1,117	1,107	537	183	2,305	41,000	230	245	846	3,400	920	477	53,600
2008	1,122	1,148	408	136	2,277	50,000	270	142	982	3,163	670	420	61,900
2009	887	1,023	192	87	1,964	51,000	100	39	823	2,665	450	190	61,200
2010	977	1,204	166	163	420	59,000	110	20	799	2,785	390	300	68,500
2011	706	1,124	300	140	1,967	61,800	110	13	819	3,314	640	160	73,900
2012	800	1,270	300	140	2,194	64,000	100	----	763	3,000	830	80	75,700
2013[1]	850	1,250			2,130	68,000			800	3,600	730		81,400
2014[2]	850	1,300			2,200	68,000				3,600	700		82,400

[1] Preliminary. [2] Estimate. [3] Conversion Factors: WO_3 to W, multiply by 0.7931; 60% WO_3 to W, multiply by 0.4758.
Source: U.S. Geological Survey (USGS)

Salient Statistics of Tungsten in the United States   In Metric Tons (Contained Tungsten)

Year	Net Import Reliance as a % Apparent Consump	Total Con- sumption	Steel — Tool	Stainless & Heat Assisting	Alloy Steel[3]	Super- alloys	Cutting & Wear Resistant Materials	Products Made From Metal Powder	Miscel- laneous	Chemical and Ceramic	Exports	Imports for Con- sumption	Concentrates — Con- sumers	Pro- ducers
2007	67	W	W	282	W	W	6,090	W	----	89	109	3,880	W	W
2008	60	W	W	283	W	W	6,650	W	----	80	496	3,990	W	W
2009	68	W	W	244	W	386	4,070	W	----	84	38	3,590	W	W
2010	63	4,820	W	71	W	W	5,990	W	----	99	276	2,740	W	W
2011	40	W	W	96	W	W	6,760	W	----	88	169	3,640	W	W
2012	39	W	W	123	W	W	6,800	W	----	88	203	3,650	W	W
2013[1]	41	W									1,060	3,690		
2014[2]	43	W									1,500	4,100		

[1] Preliminary. [2] Estimate. [3] Other than tool. [4] Included with stainless & heat assisting.   W = Withheld.
Source: U.S. Geological Survey (USGS)

Average Price of Tungsten at U.S. Ports (Including Duty)   In Dollars Per Short Ton

Year	Jan.	Feb.	Mar.	Apr.	May	June	July	Aug.	Sept.	Oct.	Nov.	Dec.	Average
2007	252.50	256.71	261.36	262.50	262.50	262.50	262.50	261.63	252.50	252.50	252.50	252.50	257.68
2008	252.50	252.50	252.50	252.50	252.50	252.50	252.50	252.50	252.50	252.50	252.50	252.50	252.50
2009	252.50	215.00	205.00	205.00	165.00	165.00	165.00	165.00	165.00	165.00	166.58	180.00	184.51
2010	173.95	175.00	175.65	177.50	177.50	177.50	175.12	169.46	217.50	238.21	240.00	240.00	194.78
2011	263.45	307.00	307.00	307.00	307.00	307.00	307.00	307.00	307.00	385.67	425.00	425.00	329.59
2012	420.50	395.00	393.64	389.64	382.84	402.50	402.50	390.00	360.00	346.96	320.50	297.78	375.16
2013	297.74	329.45	351.29	351.50	356.73	382.55	406.86	417.28	407.13	392.50	387.29	378.50	371.57
2014	374.39	368.18	367.12	363.64	368.81	376.00	369.60	363.57	353.81	345.00	329.31	309.19	357.39

U.S. Spot Quotations, 65% WO_3, Basis C.I.F.   *Source: U.S. Geological Survey (USGS)*

Turkeys

During the past three decades, the turkey industry has experienced tremendous growth in the U.S. Turkey production has more than tripled since 1970, with a current value of over $7 billion. Turkey was not a popular dish in Europe until a roast turkey was eaten on June 27, 1570, at the wedding feast of Charles XI of France and Elizabeth of Austria. The King was so impressed with the birds that the turkey subsequently became a popular dish at banquets held by French nobility.

The most popular turkey product continues to be the whole bird, with heavy demand at Thanksgiving and Christmas. The primary breeders maintain and develop the quality stock, concentrating on growth and conformation in males and fecundity in females, as well as characteristics important to general health and welfare. Turkey producers include large companies that produce turkeys all year-round and relatively small companies and farmers who produce turkeys primarily for the seasonal Thanksgiving market.

Prices – The average monthly price received by farmers for turkeys in the U.S. in 2014 rose +10.2% yr/yr to 73.2 cents per pound, a new record high. The monthly average retail price of turkeys (whole frozen) in the U.S. in 2014 fell -2.9% yr/yr to 160.1 cents per pound, below last year's record high of 164.9 cents per pound. Turkey prices have more than tripled from the low 40-cent area seen in the early 1970s.

Supply – World production of turkeys in 2014 fell -1.4% yr/yr to 5.288 million metric tons. World production of turkeys has grown by more than two and one-half times since 1980 when production was 2.090 million metric tons. The U.S. was the largest producer of turkeys by far with 2.600 million metric tons of production in 2014, which is 49.2% of world production. The value of U.S. turkey production in the U.S. in 2013 (latest data) was $4.839 billion.

Demand – World consumption of turkeys in 2014 fell -2.5% to 4.937 million metric tons. U.S. turkey consumption was 2.253 million metric tons in 2014, which accounts for 45.6% of world consumption. U.S. per capita consumption of turkeys in 2015 is forecasted to rise +0.6% yr/yr to 15.8 pounds per person per year. U.S. per capital consumption of turkeys has been in the range of 16-18 pounds since 1990, but the USDA is projecting that per capita consumption will drop somewhat.

Production of Turkey Meat, by Selected Countries   In Thousands of Metric Tons (RTC)

	Production							Consumption						
Year	Brazil	Canada	European Union	Mexico	Russia	United States	World Total	Brazil	Canada	European Union	Mexico	Russia	United States	World Total
2005	360	155	1,919	14	11	2,464	4,936	199	143	1,888	194	118	2,247	4,857
2006	353	163	1,858	14	16	2,543	4,960	197	144	1,841	197	107	2,297	4,866
2007	458	170	1,790	15	30	2,664	5,143	281	150	1,770	211	105	2,404	5,026
2008	465	180	1,830	15	39	2,796	5,337	261	163	1,836	212	107	2,434	5,101
2009	466	167	1,795	11	31	2,535	5,018	302	151	1,802	155	72	2,363	4,911
2010	485	159	1,946	11	70	2,527	5,212	327	143	1,913	163	105	2,306	5,023
2011	489	160	1,950	13	90	2,592	5,308	348	150	1,886	164	117	2,273	5,010
2012	510	161	2,010	14	100	2,671	5,480	340	142	1,953	173	120	2,282	5,105
2013[1]	520	168	1,950	10	100	2,599	5,361	359	150	1,893	166	112	2,291	5,063
2014[2]	470	170	1,920	9	105	2,600	5,288	350	152	1,848	158	115	2,253	4,937

[1] Preliminary.   [2] Forecast.   *Source: Foreign Agricultural Service, U.S. Department of Agriculture (FAS-USDA)*

Salient Statistics of Turkeys in the United States

| | | | Liveweight | | Value | | | Ready-to-Cook Basis | | | | Production | | Wholesale Ready-to-Cook | |
| | | | | | | | Be-ginning | Consumption | | | Costs | | | | |
Year	Poults Placed[3] In Thousands	Number Raised[4] In Thousands	Pro-duced Mil Lbs	Price cents Per Lb.	of Pro-duction Million $	Pro-duction	Stocks	Exports	Total	Per Capita Lbs.	Feed	Total	Pro-duction Costs	3-Region Weighted Avg Price[5]
2004	277,717	263,207	7,278.4	42.0	3,054.3	5,383	354	442	5,003	17.0	----	----	----	----
2005	293,683	252,053	7,096.0	44.9	3,182.8	5,432	288	570	4,952	16.7	----	----	----	----
2006	293,137	262,460	7,463.9	47.9	3,573.7	5,607	206	547	5,060	16.9	----	----	----	----
2007	308,402	266,828	7,566.3	52.3	3,954.5	5,873	218	547	5,294	17.5	----	----	----	----
2008	297,590	273,088	7,911.8	56.4	4,471.0	6,165	261	676	5,361	17.6	----	----	----	----
2009	273,974	247,359	7,149.3	49.9	3,573.3	5,588	396	535	5,201	16.9	----	----	----	----
2010	275,147	244,188	7,108.2	61.2	4,372.4	5,644	262	581		16.4	----	----	----	----
2011	278,044	248,500	7,313.2	68.0	4,987.6	5,791	192	703		16.1	----	----	----	----
2012[1]	284,148	253,500	7,561.9	71.9	5,452.1	5,967	211	797		16.0	----	----	----	----
2013[2]	284,195	240,000	7,276.8	66.4	4,839.1	5,959	296	759		16.0	----	----	----	----

[1] Preliminary.   [2] Estimate.   [3] Poults placed for slaughter by hatcheries.   [4] Turkeys place August 1-July 31.   [5] Regions include central, eastern and western. Central region receives twice the weight of the other regions in calculating the average.
Source: Economic Research Service, U.S. Department of Agriculture (ERS-USDA)

TURKEYS

Turkey-Feed Price Ratio in the United States   In Pounds[2]

Year	Jan.	Feb.	Mar.	Apr.	May	June	July	Aug.	Sept.	Oct.	Nov.	Dec.	Average
2005	6.9	6.9	6.6	6.7	6.9	7.0	7.3	8.0	9.0	9.5	10.0	9.5	7.9
2006	7.0	6.9	6.9	7.3	7.1	7.6	7.7	8.5	9.1	9.6	9.4	5.9	7.8
2007	5.6	5.3	5.5	5.8	5.9	6.1	6.6	6.7	6.6	6.4	6.1	4.9	6.0
2008	4.1	3.6	4.0	4.0	4.3	4.3	4.5	4.7	5.4	5.9	5.6	4.4	4.6
2009	4.1	4.6	4.8	4.7	4.7	4.8	5.1	5.2	5.3	5.6	5.7	5.6	5.0
2010	4.8	5.3	5.6	5.9	6.2	6.9	6.9	6.7	6.6	6.8	6.4	5.6	6.1
2011	4.6	4.2	4.4	4.5	4.6	4.8	4.7	4.7	5.2	5.8	5.9	5.4	4.9
2012	4.8	4.7	4.8	5.0	5.0	5.1	4.4	4.3	4.8	4.9	4.7	4.3	4.7
2013	4.0	3.9	4.1	4.2	4.1	4.1	4.3	4.6	5.0	5.8	5.3	5.5	4.6
2014[1]	5.2	5.4	5.3	5.1	5.4	5.6	6.2	6.8	7.6	8.3	8.1	7.1	6.3

[1] Preliminary.   [2] Pounds of feed equal in value to one pound of turkey, liveweight.   *Source: Economic Research Service, U.S. Department of Agriculture (ERS-USDA)*

Average Price Received by Farmers for Turkeys in the United States (Liveweight)   In Cents Per Pound

Year	Jan.	Feb.	Mar.	Apr.	May	June	July	Aug.	Sept.	Oct.	Nov.	Dec.	Average
2005	39.3	38.0	38.1	38.8	40.7	42.1	44.6	46.5	50.3	52.5	54.5	53.9	44.9
2006	40.8	39.6	40.3	42.5	43.3	45.4	45.9	48.6	53.3	62.7	66.3	42.7	47.6
2007	40.8	42.4	44.3	46.8	48.3	52.0	55.5	57.2	60.4	61.5	61.6	52.6	52.0
2008	44.8	47.5	52.9	55.1	58.1	59.8	60.9	63.2	66.4	64.6	58.6	44.5	56.4
2009	43.8	46.5	47.1	47.6	50.1	52.5	52.0	51.1	48.5	52.1	54.1	53.7	49.9
2010	46.5	49.1	52.2	53.7	56.1	61.7	64.7	66.8	69.0	73.4	73.6	67.7	61.2
2011	56.4	57.8	59.9	65.7	67.9	69.5	67.5	70.7	73.1	77.3	78.1	71.5	68.0
2012	65.7	65.0	69.0	73.7	72.7	73.9	72.9	74.4	76.2	76.9	75.1	67.4	71.9
2013	62.9	62.7	65.0	66.2	64.9	65.7	67.7	67.4	67.9	72.4	65.6	68.7	66.4
2014[1]	64.5	66.4	68.3	68.7	72.6	72.8	74.0	75.6	77.5	82.2	82.1	73.4	73.2

[1] Preliminary.   *Source: Economic Research Service, U.S. Department of Agriculture (ERS-USDA)*

Average Wholesale Price of Turkeys[1] (Hens, 8-16 Lbs.) in New York   In Cents Per Pound

Year	Jan.	Feb.	Mar.	Apr.	May	June	July	Aug.	Sept.	Oct.	Nov.	Dec.	Average
2005	67.63	65.34	64.68	65.86	67.69	69.50	72.56	75.98	80.90	82.40	85.75	82.60	73.41
2006	68.29	65.84	67.67	69.75	71.27	72.95	74.95	78.70	84.40	95.83	99.51	74.20	76.95
2007	67.63	69.84	71.66	74.45	76.98	82.12	86.89	89.70	93.12	95.20	94.71	82.47	82.06
2008	73.74	76.40	82.20	85.99	89.19	91.45	92.91	96.85	99.62	97.27	87.44	74.88	87.33
2009	71.20	74.32	75.22	76.59	78.71	82.00	82.68	81.33	80.26	82.52	84.96	83.95	79.48
2010	76.50	78.72	82.64	83.90	86.45	93.38	98.68	102.45	105.81	111.03	109.29	101.16	94.17
2011	88.14	89.97	92.38	96.68	99.75	103.14	104.00	105.39	109.79	114.83	113.57	106.54	102.02
2012	98.35	100.15	103.70	106.89	107.77	106.00	106.43	108.90	110.54	110.27	108.86	99.08	105.58
2013	96.27	95.00	96.58	97.30	97.59	98.18	100.40	NA	101.22	106.75	105.64	103.83	99.89
2014[2]	99.78	99.88	102.34	103.52	106.15	107.18	108.56	109.15	112.79	116.20	118.78	106.79	107.59

[1] Ready-to-cook.   [2] Preliminary.   *Source: Economic Research Service, U.S. Department of Agriculture (ERS-USDA)*

Certified Federally Inspected Turkey Slaughter in the U.S. (Ready-to-Cook Weights)   In Millions of Pounds

Year	Jan.	Feb.	Mar.	Apr.	May	June	July	Aug.	Sept.	Oct.	Nov.	Dec.	Total
2005	439.0	396.3	459.4	439.7	456.3	485.8	427.5	483.7	450.6	479.1	478.2	434.4	5,430
2006	443.0	412.4	487.9	430.3	492.8	504.4	453.5	493.6	456.5	535.8	499.7	423.5	5,633
2007	479.0	442.7	478.8	459.6	507.5	495.7	502.0	517.3	456.4	577.8	520.3	457.3	5,894
2008	544.6	504.0	484.5	515.9	517.9	519.7	544.1	503.8	511.5	570.1	507.9	488.2	6,212
2009	465.5	441.6	467.7	472.2	448.8	490.7	482.3	460.7	463.8	504.4	475.3	453.2	5,626
2010	421.1	423.3	488.0	452.8	437.5	487.0	463.9	478.2	464.1	521.7	518.0	458.6	5,614
2011	460.9	432.8	500.4	453.8	494.6	516.3	445.7	499.1	470.8	521.5	509.3	456.9	5,762
2012	474.5	464.8	499.9	475.2	516.9	504.1	494.9	526.3	450.7	576.3	512.9	438.5	5,935
2013	522.1	458.8	470.1	502.3	505.8	471.5	512.1	482.4	438.1	514.2	477.0	420.4	5,775
2014[1]	451.3	419.6	455.0	468.5	469.3	484.2	498.0	480.6	490.4	558.2	478.4	472.1	5,726

[1] Preliminary.   *Source: Economic Research Service, U.S. Department of Agriculture (ERS-USDA)*

Per Capita Consumption of Turkeys in the United States   In Pounds

Year	First Quarter	Second Quarter	Third Quarter	Fourth Quarter	Total	Year	First Quarter	Second Quarter	Third Quarter	Fourth Quarter	Total
2004	3.6	4.0	4.5	5.0	17.0	2010	3.5	3.6	4.1	5.2	16.4
2005	3.6	3.9	4.2	5.1	16.7	2011	3.5	3.5	4.0	5.0	16.1
2006	3.5	3.9	4.3	5.2	16.9	2012	3.5	3.6	4.1	4.9	16.0
2007	3.8	4.1	4.2	5.5	17.5	2013	3.7	3.6	4.0	4.8	16.0
2008	4.0	4.1	4.3	5.3	17.6	2014[1]	3.4	3.5	3.9	4.9	15.7
2009	3.7	3.9	4.0	5.3	16.9	2015[2]	3.2	3.5	4.2	4.9	15.8

[1] Preliminary.   [2] Estimate.   *Source: Economic Research Service, U.S. Department of Agriculture (ERS-USDA)*

Storage Stocks of Turkeys (Frozen) in the United States on First of Month   In Millions of Pounds

Year	Jan.	Feb.	Mar.	Apr.	May	June	July	Aug.	Sept.	Oct.	Nov.	Dec.
2005	288.4	332.9	379.4	414.2	440.1	465.9	506.3	518.9	523.1	477.8	417.6	194.7
2006	206.2	260.5	315.7	377.7	423.7	466.5	507.5	512.2	500.3	464.2	404.2	214.5
2007	218.4	293.4	312.9	346.8	360.2	398.0	448.4	503.5	524.4	504.9	417.0	206.9
2008	260.6	327.6	416.7	428.1	491.3	522.4	562.7	620.7	629.2	621.5	578.0	360.4
2009	396.1	446.2	462.4	513.4	571.7	585.7	594.7	641.1	653.5	613.9	517.5	244.5
2010	261.8	302.1	342.4	379.7	422.1	461.8	507.2	501.5	502.2	473.7	410.2	174.1
2011	191.6	253.5	289.0	325.7	364.5	447.9	508.7	524.8	528.4	509.7	406.9	194.2
2012	210.8	297.7	349.6	375.3	438.4	498.4	547.1	547.5	547.8	521.8	453.4	255.2
2013	296.5	360.0	394.8	401.2	457.6	521.6	566.5	581.4	580.1	541.2	434.5	221.2
2014[1]	237.4	275.8	310.8	336.4	375.0	422.5	462.6	489.8	494.8	484.5	390.7	187.6

[1] Preliminary.   Source: Economic Research Service, U.S. Department of Agriculture (ERS-USDA)

Average Retail Price of Turkeys (Whole frozen) in the United States   In Cents Per Pound

Year	Jan.	Feb.	Mar.	Apr.	May	June	July	Aug.	Sept.	Oct.	Nov.	Dec.	Average
2005	105.8	106.3	106.1	105.8	106.9	108.0	106.8	106.3	112.1	113.7	102.3	106.6	107.2
2006	106.9	119.7	120.9	111.1	108.4	112.8	113.0	110.6	115.1	114.9	97.3	99.1	110.8
2007	110.3	113.6	107.9	108.1	114.6	122.3	122.2	122.9	121.6	124.1	111.3	101.0	115.0
2008	120.7	123.0	115.1	117.0	125.8	123.8	127.0	128.8	132.0	122.2	130.9	133.2	125.0
2009	136.5	136.9	134.7	135.4	136.6	141.0	144.5	146.1	145.4	148.0	133.6	136.5	139.6
2010	139.8	137.5	142.5	147.9	146.4	147.4	155.4	152.1	156.6	167.7	140.7	138.0	147.7
2011	145.9	152.6	157.2	156.2	159.6	158.1	160.3	164.1	167.6	167.3	154.1	157.4	158.4
2012	167.1	167.1	181.2	179.1	160.8	155.7	156.1	158.6	162.1	166.1	148.8	143.3	162.2
2013	157.9	159.1	159.3	164.9	165.4	159.5	162.4	166.3	181.9	NA	172.1	165.0	164.9
2014[1]	171.3	169.9	173.3	161.0	160.2	160.6	164.1	160.4	158.4	166.7	142.5	133.1	160.1

[1] Preliminary.   *Source: Economic Research Service, U.S. Department of Agriculture (ERS-USDA)*

Average Retail-to-Consumer Price Spread of Turkeys (Whole) in the United States   In Cents Per Pound

Year	Jan.	Feb.	Mar.	Apr.	May	June	July	Aug.	Sept.	Oct.	Nov.	Dec.	Average
2005	31.3	33.4	33.3	31.5	30.9	29.4	25.6	22.4	24.1	22.9	8.7	16.8	25.9
2006	29.4	44.5	44.8	32.8	28.6	30.8	29.6	22.9	21.5	9.3	-11.3	15.9	24.9
2007	33.7	34.3	27.2	25.2	28.7	30.9	26.5	24.6	19.7	20.0	7.4	9.8	24.0
2008	38.0	37.5	23.7	21.6	27.3	23.4	25.1	23.0	23.4	18.0	33.9	48.8	28.6
2009	NA	NA	NA	NA	NA	51.0	53.9	56.0	56.2	56.3	39.4	43.7	50.9
2010	55.6	50.6	51.9	55.5	52.2	NA	NA	42.8	42.9	49.3	22.7	28.8	45.2
2011	48.8	NA	NA	NA	NA	NA	NA	49.7	48.8	43.5	31.5	41.9	44.0
2012	59.8	58.0	68.5	63.2	44.0	40.7	40.7	41.1	42.6	46.8	30.9	35.2	47.6
2013	52.6	55.1	53.7	58.6	58.8	52.3	54.3	58.0	71.7	NA	57.5	52.2	56.8
2014[1]	62.5	61.0	62.0	48.5	45.1	44.4	46.5	42.3	36.6	41.5	14.7	17.3	43.5

[1] Preliminary.   *Source: Economic Research Service, U.S. Department of Agriculture (ERS-USDA)*

Uranium

Uranium (atomic symbol U) is a chemically reactive, radioactive, steel-gray, metallic element and is the main fuel used in nuclear reactors. Uranium is the heaviest of all the natural elements. Traces of uranium have been found in archeological artifacts dating back to 79 AD. Uranium was discovered in pitchblende by German chemist Martin Heinrich Klaproth in 1789. Klaproth named it uranium after the recently discovered planet Uranus. French physicist Antoine Henri Becquerel discovered the radioactive properties of uranium in 1896 when he produced an image on a photographic plate covered with a light-absorbing substance. Following Becquerel's experiments, investigations of radioactivity led to the discovery of radium (atomic symbol Ra) and to new concepts of atomic organization.

The principal use for uranium is fuel in nuclear power plants. Demand for uranium concentrates is directly linked to the level of electricity generated by nuclear power plants. Uranium ores are widely distributed throughout the world and are primarily found in Canada, DRC (formerly Zaire), and the U.S. Uranium is obtained from primary mine production and secondary sources. Two Canadian companies, Cameco and Cogema Resources, are the primary producers of uranium from deposits in the Athabasca Basin of northern Saskatchewan. Secondary sources of uranium include excess inventories from utilities and other fuel cycle participants, used reactor fuel, and dismantled Russian nuclear weapons.

Prices – CME Uranium futures prices (Barchart.com symbol UX) rose above $140 per pound in early 2007 but then plunged in the following three years to post a low of $40 per pound in early 2010. Uranium prices recovered to a 6-year high of $73 in early 2011 but have since trended lower. Uranium prices in May 2014 fell to a record low of $28.00 per pound but then recovered moderately, closing the year of 2014 up +2.5% at $35.25 per pound.

Supply – World production of uranium oxide (U308) concentrate in 2003 (latest data available) rose +7.3% yr/yr to a 13-year high of 56,552 short tons; up from 2002's production of 52,709 short tons. The world's largest uranium producers in 2003 were Canada with 17,050 short tons of production in 2003 (30% of world production), the U.S. with 10,200 short tons of production (18% of world production), and Australia with 9,326 short tons of production (16% of world production).

U.S. uranium production in 2003 (latest data available) rose +64.4% yr/yr to a 20-year high of 10,200 short tons, up sharply from the record low of 1,315 short tons in 2001. U.S. production had reached a peak of 21,850 short tons in 1980 but then production fell steadily to the record low in 2001.

Trade – U.S. imports of uranium in 2013 (latest data) rose +2.0% yr/yr to 57.300 million pounds. The record high of 66.100 million pounds was posted in 2004. The U.S. has generally been forced to import more uranium as domestic production steadily declined. U.S. exports of uranium in 2013 rose +5.0% yr/yr to 18.900 million pounds, which is below the record high of 23.500 million pounds posted in 2009.

Uranium Industry Statistics in the United States   In Millions of Pounds U$_3$O$_8$

Year	Production — Mine	Production — Concentrate	Concentrate Shipments	Employment - Person Years — Exploration	Mining	Milling	Processing	Total[1]	Deliveries to U.S. Utilities[2]	Avg Price Delivered Uranium $/lb U$_3O_8$	Imports	Avg Price Delivered Uranium Imports $/lb U$_3O_8$	Exports
2007	4.5	4.534	4.050	375	378	107	216	1,231	51.0	32.78	54.1	34.18	14.8
2008	3.9	3.902	4.130	457	558	W	W	1,563	53.4	45.88	57.1	41.30	17.2
2009	4.1	3.708	3.620	175	441	W	W	1,096	49.8	45.86	58.9	41.23	23.5
2010	4.2	4.228	5.137	211	400	W	W	1,073	46.6	49.29	55.3	47.01	23.1
2011	4.1	3.991	4.000	208	462	W	W	1,191	54.8	55.64	54.4	54.00	16.7
2012	4.3	4.146	3.911	161	462	W	W	1,196	57.5	54.99	56.2	51.44	18.0
2013	4.6	4.659	4.655	149	392	W	W	1,156	57.4	51.99	57.3	48.24	18.9

[1] From suppliers under domestic purchases.   *Source: Energy Information Administration, U.S. Department of Energy (EIA-DOE)*

Commercial and U.S. Government Stocks of Uranium, End of Year   In Millions of Pounds U$_3$O$_8$ Equivalent

Year	Utility — Natural Uranium	Utility — Enriched Uranium[1]	Domestic Supplier — Natural Uranium	Domestic Supplier — Enriched Uranium[1]	Total Commercial Stocks	DOE Owned & USEC Held — Natural Uranium	DOE Owned & USEC Held — Enriched Uranium[1]
2004	27.9	29.8	[2]	37.5	95.2	W	W
2005	45.3	19.4	[2]	29.1	93.8	W	W
2006	54.3	23.2	[2]	29.1	106.6	W	W
2007	55.9	25.3	[2]	31.2	112.4	W	W
2008	58.8	24.2	[2]	27.0	110.0	W	W
2009	53.6	31.2	[2]	26.8	111.5	W	W
2010	48.8	37.7	[2]	24.7	111.3	W	W
2011	50.6	39.2	[2]	22.3	112.1	W	W
2012	45.0	52.6	[2]	23.3	120.9	W	W
2013	56.8	56.2	[2]	21.1	134.2	W	W

[1] Includes amount reported as UF$_6$ at enrichment suppliers.   DOE = Department of Energy   USEC = U.S. Energy Commission
Source: Energy Information Administration, U.S. Department of Energy (EIA-DOE)

Reported Average Price Settlements for Purchases by U.S. Utilities and Domestic Suppliers   In Dollars Per Pound

Year of Delivery	Purchased from Producers	Purchased from US Brokers/ Traders	Purchased from US Suppliers	Purchased from Foreign Suppliers	US Origin Uranium (weighted avg)	Foreign Origin (weighted avg)	Spot Contracts (weighted avg)	Short, Medium and Long-Term (weighted avg)
2007	----	34.10	W	32.36	28.89	33.05	88.25	24.45
2008	75.16	39.62	W	48.49	59.55	43.47	66.95	41.59
2009	W	41.88	W	46.68	48.92	45.35	46.45	45.74
2010	47.13	44.98	42.24	51.30	45.25	49.64	43.99	50.43
2011	58.12	53.29	52.50	56.60	52.12	55.98	54.69	55.90
2012	W	54.44	W	54.40	59.44	54.07	51.04	55.65
2013	W	50.44	W	51.93	56.37	51.13	43.83	54.00

[1] No floor.   Note: Price excludes uranium delivered under litigation settlements. Price is given in year-of-delivery dollars.   *Source: Energy Information Administration, U.S. Department of Energy (EIA-DOE)*

Total Production of Uranium Concentrate in the United States, by Quarters   In Pounds U_3O_8

Year	First Quarter	Second Quarter	Third Quarter	Fourth Quarter	Total	Year	First Quarter	Second Quarter	Third Quarter	Fourth Quarter	Total
2003	400,000	600,000	400,000	600,000	2,000,000	2009	880,036	982,760	956,657	888,905	3,708,358
2004	600,000	400,000	588,738	600,000	2,188,738	2010	876,084	1,055,102	1,150,725	1,153,104	4,235,015
2005	709,600	630,053	663,068	686,456	2,689,177	2011	1,063,047	1,189,083	846,624	892,013	3,990,767
2006	931,065	894,268	1,083,808	1,196,485	4,105,626	2012	1,078,404	1,061,289	1,048,018	957,936	4,145,647
2007	1,162,737	1,119,536	1,075,460	1,175,845	4,533,578	2013[1]	1,147,031	1,394,232	1,171,278	946,301	4,658,842
2008	810,189	1,073,315	980,933	1,037,946	3,902,383	2014[2]	1,242,179	1,095,011	1,468,608		5,074,397

[1] Preliminary.   [2] Estimate.   *Source: Energy Information Administration, U.S. Department of Energy (EIA-DOE)*

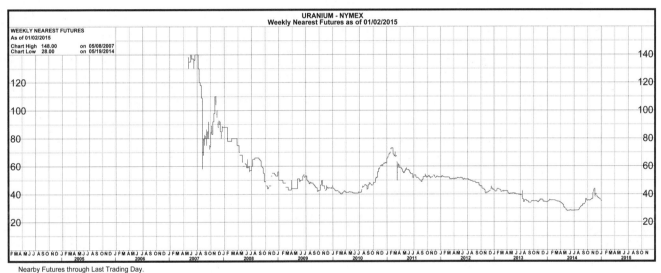

Nearby Futures through Last Trading Day.

Volume of Trading of Uranium Futures   In Contracts

Year	Jan.	Feb.	Mar.	Apr.	May	June	July	Aug.	Sept.	Oct.	Nov.	Dec.	Total
2008	157	22	719	617	511	14	1,617	10	7,553	2,000	30	41	13,291
2009	408	40	1,400	16	1	600	1,300	400	403	0	1,581	0	6,149
2010	152	2	101	2,031	4,024	1,743	4,728	330	750	2,933	7,619	1,684	26,097
2011	537	2,483	2,996	845	2,049	10,438	436	1,026	466	906	211	205	22,598
2012	421	1,109	400	817	306	12	1,000	202	965	976	400	1,505	8,113
2013	1,203	201	155	268	432	58	1,751	1,207	34	201	----	1,005	7,107
2014	564	7	181	77	0	200	825	0	224	821	186	368	4,144

Contract size = 250 pounds of U_3O_8.   *Source: CME Group; New York Mercantile Exchange (NYMEX)*

Month-End Open Interest of Uranium Futures   In Contracts

Year	Jan.	Feb.	Mar.	Apr.	May	June	July	Aug.	Sept.	Oct.	Nov.	Dec.
2008	552	508	1,158	1,479	1,949	1,912	2,200	2,206	2,644	2,604	2,544	2,343
2009	1,951	1,951	2,651	2,666	2,665	2,865	3,465	3,865	3,568	3,568	3,395	3,395
2010	3,277	3,279	2,980	4,710	8,013	9,753	11,742	11,649	12,274	13,534	15,154	15,622
2011	14,734	15,406	15,734	15,033	15,417	8,951	7,861	6,595	6,799	6,736	6,326	5,866
2012	5,214	4,767	4,567	3,767	3,665	3,367	4,001	4,134	5,009	5,159	5,559	5,620
2013	5,601	5,752	5,897	5,794	5,352	5,340	6,578	7,716	7,714	7,910	7,310	7,207
2014	7,132	6,503	6,604	6,601	6,251	6,301	6,642	6,527	6,260	6,004		

Contract size = 250 pounds of U_3O_8.   *Source: CME Group; New York Mercantile Exchange (NYMEX)*

URANIUM

Uranium Industry Statistics in the United States   In Millions of Pounds U₃O₈

Year	Total Operable Units[2/3] Number	Net Summer Capacity of Operable Units[3/4] Million Kilowatts	Nuclear Electricity Net Generation Million Kilowatthours	Nuclear Share of Electricity Net Gen. Percent	Capacity Factor Percent	Year	Total Operable Units[2/3] Number	Net Summer Capacity of Operable Units[3/4] Million Kilowatts	Nuclear Electricity Net Generation Million Kilowatthours	Nuclear Share of Electricity Net Gen. Percent	Capacity Factor Percent
2001	104.0	98.2	768,826	20.6	89.4	2008	104.0	100.8	806,208	19.6	91.1
2002	104.0	98.7	780,064	20.2	90.3	2009	104.0	101.0	798,855	20.2	90.3
2003	104.0	99.2	763,733	19.7	87.9	2010	104.0	101.2	806,968	19.6	91.1
2004	104.0	99.6	788,528	19.9	90.1	2011	104.0	101.4	790,204	19.3	89.1
2005	104.0	100.0	781,986	19.3	89.3	2012	104.0	101.9	769,331	19.0	86.1
2006	104.0	100.3	787,219	19.4	89.6	2013	100.0	99.1	789,017	19.4	90.1
2007	104.0	100.3	806,425	19.4	91.8	2014[1]	100.0	99.2	723,705	19.3	91.1

[1] Preliminary.   [2] Total of nuclear generating units holding full-power licenses, or equivalent permission to operate, at end of period.
[3] At end of period.   [4] Beginning in 2011, monthly capacity values are estimated in two steps: 1) uprates and derates reported on Form EIA-860M are added to specific months; and 2) the difference between the resulting year-end capacity and final capacity is allocated to the month of January.
purchases.   Source: Energy Information Administration, U.S. Department of Energy (EIA-DOE)

Nuclear Electricity Net Generation   In Million Kilowatthours

Year	Jan.	Feb.	Mar.	Apr.	May	June	July	Aug.	Sept.	Oct.	Nov.	Dec.	Total
2005	69,828	60,947	61,539	55,484	62,970	66,144	71,070	71,382	66,739	61,236	62,913	71,735	781,987
2006	71,912	62,616	63,721	57,567	62,776	68,391	72,186	72,016	66,642	57,509	61,392	70,490	787,218
2007	74,006	65,225	64,305	57,301	65,025	68,923	72,739	72,751	67,579	61,690	64,899	71,983	806,426
2008	70,735	65,130	64,716	57,333	64,826	70,319	74,318	72,617	67,054	62,820	63,408	72,931	806,207
2009	74,102	64,227	67,241	59,408	65,395	69,735	72,949	72,245	65,752	58,021	59,069	70,710	798,854
2010	72,569	65,245	64,635	57,611	66,658	68,301	71,913	71,574	69,371	62,751	62,655	73,683	806,966
2011	72,743	64,789	65,662	54,547	57,013	65,270	72,345	71,339	66,849	63,337	64,474	71,837	790,205
2012	72,381	63,847	61,729	55,871	62,081	65,140	69,129	69,602	64,511	59,743	56,713	68,584	769,331
2013	71,406	61,483	62,947	56,767	62,848	66,430	70,539	71,344	65,799	63,184	64,975	71,294	789,016
2014[1]	73,064	62,639	62,397	56,385	62,947	68,138	71,940	71,129	67,535	62,391	65,140		789,496

[1] Preliminary.   Source: Energy Information Administration, U.S. Department of Energy (EIA-DOE)

Nuclear Share of Electricity Net Generation   In Percent

Year	Jan.	Feb.	Mar.	Apr.	May	June	July	Aug.	Sept.	Oct.	Nov.	Dec.	Average
2005	20.4	20.4	19.4	19.2	20.0	18.2	17.7	17.6	19.1	19.4	20.6	20.6	19.4
2006	21.9	20.4	20.0	19.3	19.0	18.8	17.6	17.7	20.1	17.9	19.9	21.0	19.5
2007	20.9	20.2	20.1	18.9	19.7	19.0	18.5	17.2	19.0	18.5	20.7	20.8	19.5
2008	19.5	20.0	19.9	18.7	19.9	18.8	18.4	18.7	19.8	19.7	20.5	21.2	19.6
2009	20.9	21.3	21.6	20.5	21.0	20.1	19.6	19.0	20.1	18.9	19.9	20.2	20.3
2010	20.1	20.4	20.7	20.0	20.3	18.2	17.6	17.5	20.0	20.4	20.5	20.3	19.7
2011	20.0	20.7	20.6	18.0	17.6	17.7	17.3	17.5	19.8	20.5	21.2	21.4	19.4
2012	21.3	20.6	20.0	18.9	18.4	18.1	16.7	17.6	19.3	19.2	18.5	20.5	19.1
2013	20.5	19.9	19.4	19.0	19.5	18.6	17.9	18.6	19.3	20.1	20.7	20.2	19.4
2014[1]	19.4	19.4	18.8	19.0	19.4	19.1	18.7	18.5	19.9	19.9	20.5		19.3

[1] Preliminary.   Source: Energy Information Administration, U.S. Department of Energy (EIA-DOE)

Capacity Factor   In Percent

Year	Jan.	Feb.	Mar.	Apr.	May	June	July	Aug.	Sept.	Oct.	Nov.	Dec.	Average
2005	93.9	90.7	82.7	77.1	84.6	91.9	95.5	96.0	92.7	82.3	87.4	96.4	89.3
2006	96.3	92.9	85.4	79.7	84.1	94.7	96.7	96.5	92.3	77.0	85.0	94.4	89.6
2007	99.2	96.8	86.2	79.4	87.2	95.5	97.5	97.5	93.6	82.7	89.9	96.5	91.8
2008	94.4	92.9	86.3	79.0	86.5	96.9	99.1	96.9	92.4	83.8	87.4	97.3	91.1
2009	98.6	94.6	89.5	81.7	87.0	95.9	97.1	96.1	90.4	77.2	81.2	94.1	90.3
2010	96.4	96.0	85.9	79.1	88.6	93.8	95.5	95.1	95.2	83.4	86.0	97.9	91.1
2011	96.6	95.3	87.2	74.9	75.7	89.5	96.0	94.6	91.6	84.0	88.4	95.2	89.1
2012	95.8	90.3	81.7	76.4	82.1	89.0	91.3	91.8	88.0	78.8	77.3	90.5	86.1
2013	94.2	90.5	83.6	77.7	83.4	93.2	95.8	96.9	92.3	85.8	91.2	96.7	90.1
2014[1]	99.2	94.1	84.6	79.0	85.4	95.6	97.5	96.4	94.5	84.5	91.2		91.1

[1] Preliminary.   [2] Beginning in 2008, capacity factor data are calculated using a new methodology.   Source: Energy Information Administration, U.S. Department of Energy (EIA-DOE)

Vanadium

Vanadium (atomic symbol V) is a silvery-white, soft, ductile, metallic element. Discovered in 1801, but mistaken for chromium, vanadium was rediscovered in 1830 by Swedish chemist Nils Sefstrom, who named the element in honor of the Scandinavian goddess Vanadis.

Never found in the pure state, vanadium is found in about 65 different minerals such as carnotite, roscoelite, vanadinite, and patronite, as well as in phosphate rock, certain iron ores, some crude oils, and meteorites. Vanadium is one of the hardest of all metals. It melts at about 1890 degrees Celsius and boils at about 3380 degrees Celsius.

Vanadium has good structural strength and is used as an alloying agent with iron, steel, and titanium. It is used in aerospace applications, transmission gears, photography, as a reducing agent, and as a drying agent in various paints.

Prices – The price of vanadium in 2014 fell by -4.0% to $5.80 per pound, remaining well below the record high of $16.28 per pound in 2005.

Supply – Virtually all (99%) of vanadium is produced from ores, concentrates, and slag, with the remainder coming from petroleum residues, ash, and spent catalysts.

World production in 2014 from ore, concentrates and slag rose +0.5% yr/yr to 78,000 metric tons. World production of all vanadium in 2013 (latest data available) rose +5.0% yr/yr to 78,200 metric tons.

The world's largest producer of vanadium from ores, concentrates and slag is China with 41,000 metric tons of production in 2014 which was 52.6% of total world production. The two other major producers are South Africa with 21,000 metric tons of production in 2014, which was 26.9% of world production, and Russia with 15,000 metric tons of production which was 19.2% of world production. Production in Russia and South Africa has been relatively stable in recent years, while China's production grew sharply in the late 1990s. China's production level of 41,000 metric tons in 2014 is a new record high and more than four times the levels seen in the early 1990s.

Trade – U.S. exports of vanadium in 2014 were in the forms of vanadium pent-oxide, anhydride (120 metric tons, +55.8%yr/yr), ferro-vanadium (350 metric tons, +35.1%yr/yr), and oxides & hydroxides (280 metric tons, -21.8% yr/yr). U.S. imports of vanadium in 2014 were in the forms of ferro-vanadium (4,200 metric tons, +13.2% yr/yr), vanadium pent-oxide (3,400 metric tons, +66.7% yr/yr), ore, slag and residues (3,040 metric tons, +49.0% yr/yr); and oxides & hydroxides (200 metric tons, -2.4% yr/yr).

World Production of Vanadium   In Metric Tons (Contained Vanadium)

							From Petroleum Residues Ash, Spent Catalysts			
	------------------------- From Ores, Concentrates and Slag -------------------------									World
Year	Australia	China[3]	Kazak-hstan	Russia	South Africa	Total[4]	Japan[5]	United States[6]	Total	World Total
2009	----	29,000	----	14,500	14,353	58,200	560	----	560	58,800
2010	----	32,000	----	15,000	22,606	71,100	560	----	560	71,700
2011	----	36,000	----	12,860	21,652	71,500	560	----	560	72,100
2012	----	39,000	----	14,856	19,957	73,900	580	----	580	74,500
2013[1]	400	41,000	----	15,000	21,000	77,600	580	----	580	78,200
2014[2]	----	41,000	----	15,000	21,000	78,000				

[1] Preliminary.   [2] Estimate.   [3] In vanadiferous slag product.   [4] Excludes U.S. production.   [5] In vanadium pentoxide product.
[6] In vanadium pentoxide and ferrovanadium products.   Source: U.S. Geological Survey (USGS)

Salient Statistics of Vanadium in the United States   In Metric Tons (Contained Vanadium)

	Con-sumer & Producer Stocks, Dec. 31	-------- Vanadium Consumption by Uses in the U.S. ---------								Average $ Per Lb. V₂O₅	-------- Exports ---------			-------------- Imports --------------			
Year		Tool Steel	Cast Irons	High Strength, Low Alloy	Stainless & Heat Resisting	Super-alloys	Carbon	Full Alloy	Total		Vanadium Pent-oxide Anhydride	Oxides & Hydr-oxides	Ferro-Vana-dium	Ores, Slag, Residues	Vanadium Pent-oxide Anhydride	Oxides & Hydr-oxides	Ferro-Vana-dium
2009	295	W	W	1,540	119	12	832	1,920	4,690	5.43	401	506	672	791	1,120	25	353
2010	248	W	W	W	120	9	843	2,030	5,030	6.46	140	1,100	611	521	4,000	167	1,340
2011	193	W	W	W	62	16	815	1,530	4,140	6.76	98	254	314	1,420	2,810	886	2,220
2012	223	165	----	W	62	9	759	1,510	3,980	6.49	62	287	337	2,040	1,640	905	4,190
2013[1]	220	161	W	W	61	10	671	1,510	3,980	6.04	77	358	259	3,040	2,040	205	3,710
2014[2]	235								4,000	5.80	120	280	350		3,400	200	4,200

[1] Preliminary.   [2] Estimate.   W = Withheld.   Source: U.S. Geological Survey (USGS)

Average Price of Vanadium Pentoxide   In Dollars Per Pound

Year	Jan.	Feb.	Mar.	Apr.	May	June	July	Aug.	Sept.	Oct.	Nov.	Dec.	Average
2009	6.50	6.05	5.66	4.75	3.73	4.78	5.25	6.11	6.93	6.69	6.13	6.13	5.73
2010	6.97	7.25	7.72	8.00	7.85	6.96	6.23	6.41	6.75	6.63	6.63	6.63	7.00
2011	6.63	6.63	6.63	6.63	6.63	6.63	6.63	6.63	6.63	6.63	6.63	6.63	6.63
2012	6.65	6.75	6.75	6.75	6.39	5.87	5.69	5.53	5.37	5.30	5.30	5.63	6.00
2013	6.37	6.64	6.75	6.35	5.78	5.68	5.68	5.46	5.78	5.80	5.80	5.82	5.99
2014	5.83	5.82	5.80	5.79	5.39	5.54	5.31	5.30	5.27	5.25	5.24	5.10	5.47

Source: American Metal Market (AMM)

Vegetables

Vegetables are the edible products of herbaceous plants, which are plants with soft stems. Vegetables are grouped according to the edible part of each plant including leaves (e.g., lettuce), stalks (celery), roots (carrot), tubers (potato), bulbs (onion), fruits (tomato), seeds (pea), and flowers (broccoli). Each of these groups contributes to the human diet in its own way. Fleshy roots are high in energy value and good sources of the vitamin B group, seeds are relatively high in carbohydrates and proteins, while leaves, stalks, and fruits are excellent sources of minerals, vitamins, water, and roughage. Vegetables are an important food for the maintenance of health and prevention of disease. Higher intakes of vegetables have been shown to lower the risks of cancer and coronary heart disease.

Vegetables are best consumed fresh in their raw state in order to derive the maximum benefits from their nutrients. While canned and frozen vegetables are often thought to be inferior to fresh vegetables, they are sometimes nutritionally superior to fresh produce because they are usually processed immediately after harvest when nutrient content is at its peak. When cooking vegetables, aluminum utensils should not be used, because aluminum is a soft metal that is affected by food acids and alkalis. Scientific evidence shows that tiny particles of aluminum from foods cooked in aluminum utensils enter the stomach and can injure the sensitive lining of the stomach.

Prices – The monthly average index of fresh vegetable prices received by growers in the U.S. in 2014 fell -0.4% to 205.7, slightly below last year's new record high of 206.6.

Demand – The leading vegetable in terms of U.S. per capita consumption in 2013 (latest data) was the potato with 116.7 pounds of consumption. Runner-up vegetables were tomatoes (87.2 pounds), sweet corn (22.0 pounds), lettuce (23.8 pounds), and onions (18.7 pounds). Total U.S. per capita vegetable consumption in 2013 fell -2.0% to 385.7 pounds.

Index of Prices Received by Growers for Fresh Vegetables in the United States   (1990-92=100)

Year	Jan.	Feb.	Mar.	Apr.	May	June	July	Aug.	Sept.	Oct.	Nov.	Dec.	Average
2005	122.0	152.8	168.5	174.7	144.2	160.0	126.8	132.3	153.3	144.0	163.1	200.8	153.5
2006	207.6	138.8	137.6	174.4	147.9	128.7	134.1	179.5	193.1	167.7	138.3	178.4	160.5
2007	175.3	190.3	222.4	222.5	142.1	145.4	146.0	137.8	162.7	218.3	177.4	204.5	178.7
2008	200.2	158.3	194.1	179.3	170.7	191.7	168.3	146.1	158.7	185.1	200.3	155.9	175.7
2009	179.8	163.6	167.4	182.3	134.1	182.5	149.8	144.3	140.4	180.6	197.8	210.4	169.4
2010	178.6	190.6	310.4	274.1	215.4	158.6	177.1	157.3	171.2	153.7	156.0	186.7	194.1
2011	211.2	341.1	267.7	184.7	156.9	174.2	148.7	146.6	174.1	171.4	199.1	169.7	195.5
2012	146.9	129.5	150.2	133.7	144.2	156.2	147.1	159.4	163.7	143.2	164.7	154.0	149.4
2013	240.8	182.0	236.8	201.0	211.6	195.8	175.1	229.1	188.8	222.2	218.5	177.0	206.6
2014[1]	197.0	193.3	197.1	200.2	195.9	214.6	197.3	184.7	191.0	219.6	249.1	229.0	205.7

[1] Preliminary.   Not seasonally adjusted.   *Source: National Agricultural Statistics Service, U.S. Department of Agriculture (NASS-USDA)*

Producer Price Index of Canned[2] Processed Vegetables in the United States   (1982 = 100)

Year	Jan.	Feb.	Mar.	Apr.	May	June	July	Aug.	Sept.	Oct.	Nov.	Dec.	Average
2005	135.7	135.9	136.1	136.3	137.6	137.6	137.7	137.7	137.5	137.7	137.6	138.0	137.1
2006	138.0	136.8	137.1	137.3	138.8	140.2	140.0	140.5	141.4	141.5	142.2	142.2	139.7
2007	142.8	142.9	143.1	143.3	143.5	143.6	143.1	143.1	144.0	143.9	144.2	144.6	143.5
2008	147.8	148.4	149.6	151.2	150.2	151.3	153.3	158.6	162.5	163.0	164.2	167.8	155.7
2009	168.9	169.0	170.5	170.7	171.0	171.1	171.3	170.9	170.6	170.7	169.9	169.2	170.3
2010	169.8	167.3	167.2	167.0	166.7	166.0	164.1	164.6	161.6	161.1	162.0	161.7	164.9
2011	162.2	162.0	162.7	164.4	164.4	164.9	166.9	168.1	169.8	169.7	170.3	170.3	166.3
2012	171.3	171.1	171.7	171.5	170.7	172.9	172.4	175.6	175.0	175.3	174.2	174.3	173.0
2013	173.9	174.1	173.9	174.6	174.0	173.7	173.9	174.1	174.0	173.9	173.6	173.6	173.9
2014[1]	173.2	173.4	173.0	172.4	172.3	172.9	173.0	173.7	174.2	174.6	174.6	174.6	173.5

[1] Preliminary.   [2] Includes canned vegetables and juices, including hominy and mushrooms.   Not seasonally adjusted.   *Source: Bureau of Labor Statistics, U.S. Department of Labor (BLS)*

Producer Price Index of Frozen Processed Vegetables in the United States   (1982 = 100)

Year	Jan.	Feb.	Mar.	Apr.	May	June	July	Aug.	Sept.	Oct.	Nov.	Dec.	Average
2005	137.3	137.3	137.4	137.5	137.5	137.4	137.2	136.8	136.6	136.7	136.1	136.4	137.0
2006	137.3	137.7	138.7	138.6	138.8	139.5	139.4	139.3	139.9	142.0	142.7	142.6	139.7
2007	144.0	144.0	144.0	145.2	145.9	146.7	148.2	149.3	149.9	151.5	152.5	153.2	147.9
2008	153.3	153.8	155.6	156.5	156.7	157.1	158.8	161.1	163.9	170.6	172.7	177.9	161.5
2009	176.5	178.1	178.5	178.1	178.1	178.5	178.1	177.4	179.3	180.3	180.4	180.1	178.6
2010	179.9	180.3	180.8	180.2	180.5	180.3	179.6	179.8	179.0	174.9	175.5	175.9	178.9
2011	174.8	175.2	175.3	176.0	176.1	177.7	183.9	185.1	186.0	186.5	191.4	193.3	181.8
2012	193.8	193.7	193.7	194.1	194.1	194.5	194.5	194.1	193.6	193.6	193.9	193.9	194.0
2013	194.0	194.5	194.4	194.4	194.6	194.6	194.6	192.4	192.5	192.3	192.4	192.3	193.6
2014[1]	192.2	192.3	192.3	192.4	192.4	192.3	192.3	192.9	193.2	193.5	193.4	193.5	192.7

[1] Preliminary.   Not seasonally adjusted.   *Source: Bureau of Labor Statistics, U.S. Department of Labor (BLS)*

Per Capita Use of Selected Commercially Produced Fresh and Processing Vegetables and Melons in the United States   In Pounds, farm weight basis

Crop	2004	2005	2006	2007	2008	2009	2010	2011	2012[10]	2013[11]
Asparagus, All	1.4	1.4	1.4	1.4	1.5	1.5	1.6	1.7	1.7	1.6
Fresh	1.1	1.1	1.1	1.2	1.2	1.3	1.4	1.4	1.5	1.4
Canning	0.2	0.2	0.2	0.1	0.2	0.2	0.1	0.1	0.1	0.1
Freezing	0.1	0.1	0.1	0.1	0.1	0.1	0.1	0.1	0.1	0.1
Snap beans, All	7.6	7.6	7.9	7.8	7.4	7.2	7.6	6.8	6.7	6.7
Fresh	1.9	1.8	2.1	2.2	2.0	1.8	1.9	2.0	1.8	1.7
Canning	3.7	4.0	3.9	3.5	3.3	3.6	3.7	3.2	3.0	2.9
Freezing	1.9	1.8	1.9	2.1	2.1	1.9	2.0	1.6	2.0	2.1
Broccoli, All [1]	8.0	8.1	8.0	8.3	8.7	8.7	8.1	8.6	8.9	9.2
Fresh	5.3	5.3	5.8	5.6	6.0	6.2	5.6	5.9	6.3	6.8
Freezing	2.7	2.7	2.3	2.7	2.7	2.5	2.5	2.7	2.6	2.4
Cabbage, All	9.1	9.0	9.0	9.0	9.0	8.1	8.5	7.9	8.2	8.0
Fresh	8.0	7.8	7.8	8.0	8.1	7.3	7.5	6.9	7.1	7.1
Canning (kraut)	1.1	1.2	1.2	1.0	0.9	0.9	1.0	1.0	1.2	1.0
Carrots, All [2]	11.8	11.8	11.2	10.5	10.6	9.7	9.9	9.8	9.8	10.0
Fresh	8.7	8.7	8.1	8.1	8.1	7.4	7.8	7.5	7.9	7.6
Canning	1.1	1.1	1.0	0.9	1.0	0.9	0.7	0.8	0.8	0.8
Freezing	2.0	2.0	2.1	1.5	1.5	1.5	1.4	1.5	1.2	1.6
Cauliflower, All [1]	1.9	2.1	2.1	2.0	2.0	2.1	1.7	1.7	1.5	1.2
Fresh	1.6	1.8	1.7	1.7	1.6	1.7	1.3	1.3	1.2	1.2
Freezing	0.4	0.4	0.4	0.4	0.4	0.4	0.4	0.4	0.3	0.3
Celery	6.2	5.9	6.1	6.3	6.2	6.2	6.1	6.0	6.0	5.5
Sweet Corn, All [3]	26.2	26.7	26.1	26.1	25.1	25.8	24.7	24.3	25.2	22.0
Fresh	9.0	8.7	8.3	9.2	9.1	9.2	9.3	8.9	9.7	9.3
Canning	8.2	8.6	8.4	6.9	6.7	7.6	6.9	5.8	5.9	5.8
Freezing	9.1	9.5	9.4	10.0	9.3	9.1	8.5	9.5	9.7	7.0
Cucumbers, All	11.3	10.0	9.1	10.2	9.9	11.9	10.5	9.3	10.6	10.6
Fresh	6.4	6.2	6.2	6.4	6.4	6.8	6.7	6.5	7.6	7.4
Pickling	4.9	3.8	3.0	3.7	3.5	5.1	3.7	2.8	3.0	3.2
Melons	25.4	25.6	26.9	26.4	26.7	26.2	26.4	25.5	----	----
Watermelon	13.0	13.6	15.1	14.4	15.6	14.9	15.7	14.8	----	----
Cantaloupe	9.8	9.6	9.3	9.6	8.9	9.1	8.6	8.7	----	----
Honeydew	2.1	1.9	1.9	1.8	1.7	1.6	1.5	1.5	----	----
Other	0.5	0.6	0.6	0.6	0.5	0.6	0.6	0.5	----	----
Lettuce, All	33.2	30.6	32.0	29.9	27.3	26.1	27.9	27.5	25.8	23.8
Head lettuce	21.3	20.9	20.1	18.4	16.9	16.1	15.9	15.8	14.2	12.5
Romaine & Leaf	12.0	9.7	12.0	11.5	10.4	10.0	12.0	11.7	11.5	11.3
Onions, All	23.4	22.0	21.7	22.6	21.7	21.5	21.1	20.6	21.3	18.7
Fresh	21.9	20.9	19.9	21.6	20.2	19.6	19.6	19.1	19.8	18.7
Dehydrating	1.5	1.1	1.8	1.0	1.5	1.9	1.3	1.3	1.4	1.0
Green Peas, All [4]	2.8	2.7	2.8	3.0	2.9	3.0	2.6	2.2	2.6	2.4
Canning	1.2	1.1	1.2	1.2	1.1	1.3	1.1	0.8	0.8	0.9
Freezing	1.6	1.6	1.6	1.8	1.8	1.7	1.5	1.5	1.8	1.5
Peppers, All	14.8	15.3	15.8	15.2	15.8	16.4	16.9	17.2	18.6	17.3
Bell Peppers, All	8.6	9.2	9.5	9.4	9.6	9.8	10.3	10.6	11.4	10.3
Chile Peppers, All	6.1	6.1	6.4	5.9	6.2	6.6	6.6	6.6	7.2	6.9
Tomatoes, All	90.5	93.9	84.3	87.9	85.6	89.9	91.5	85.6	86.8	87.2
Fresh	20.0	20.2	19.8	19.2	18.5	19.6	20.6	20.4	20.3	19.6
Canning	70.5	73.7	64.5	68.7	67.1	70.3	71.1	65.9	66.5	67.6
Other, Fresh [5]	19.4	20.1	20.1	19.4	19.1	18.5	18.5	19.1	19.3	18.3
Other, Canning [6]	2.7	2.9	2.6	2.6	2.5	2.3	2.5	2.5	2.5	2.5
Other, Freezing [7]	3.8	4.1	4.1	4.1	4.0	4.3	4.9	4.7	4.5	4.3
Subtotal, All [8]	299.5	299.5	291.1	292.7	286.0	263.3	264.5	255.8	259.9	250.7
Fresh	176.8	173.7	175.2	174.5	170.0	141.4	144.4	142.9	145.5	138.8
Canning	99.7	102.7	92.3	94.5	92.6	98.7	97.4	89.6	90.9	91.6
Freezing	21.5	22.1	21.8	22.6	21.9	21.4	21.3	22.0	22.1	19.4
Potatoes, All	134.5	125.4	123.6	124.4	118.3	113.5	114.0	110.3	114.8	116.7
Fresh	45.8	41.3	38.6	38.7	37.8	36.7	36.8	34.1	34.4	36.1
Processing	88.7	84.1	85.0	85.7	80.5	76.8	77.2	76.3	80.4	80.6
Sweet Potatoes	4.6	4.5	4.6	5.1	5.1	5.3	6.7	7.5	7.3	6.7
Mushrooms	4.2	3.9	4.0	3.9	3.6	3.6	3.6	3.8	4.0	3.8
Dry Peas & Lentils [9]	0.7	0.8	1.2	0.7	0.4	0.9	2.3	1.3	1.2	2.3
Dry Edible Beans	6.0	6.1	6.5	6.4	6.5	6.1	7.0	5.6	6.4	5.5
Total, All Items	449.5	440.2	430.9	433.2	419.9	392.7	398.1	384.3	393.7	385.7

[1] All production for processing broccoli and cauliflower is for freezing.   [2] Industry allocation suggests that 27 percent of processing carrot production is for canning and 73 percent is for freezing.   [3] On-cob basis.   [4] In-shell basis.   [5] Includes artichokes, brussels sprouts, eggplant, endive/escarole, garlic, radishes, green limas, squash, and spinach. In 2000, okra, pumpkins, kale, collards, turnip greens and mustard greens added.   [6] Includes beets, green limas (1992-2003), spinach, and miscellaneous imports (1990-2001).   [7] Includes green limas, spinach, and miscellaneous freezing vegetables.   [8] Fresh, canning, and freezing data do not sum to the total because onions for dehydrating are included in the total.   [9] Production from new areas in upper midwest added in 1998. A portion of this is likely for feed use.   [10] Preliminary.   [11] Forecast.   NA = Not available.   *Source: Economic Research Service, U.S. Department of Agriculture (ERS-USDA)*

VEGETABLES

Average Price Received by Growers for Broccoli in the United States   In Dollars Per Cwt

Year	Jan.	Feb.	Mar.	Apr.	May	June	July	Aug.	Sept.	Oct.	Nov.	Dec.	Season Average
2007	69.80	25.40	27.60	36.90	26.70	24.80	28.80	38.20	41.80	61.00	38.10	40.70	36.70
2008	47.90	24.40	30.80	52.10	25.20	29.60	26.70	26.60	41.10	57.50	41.20	33.70	36.20
2009	44.60	29.50	46.90	41.90	32.80	31.00	26.50	29.70	31.60	64.60	57.10	53.50	37.80
2010	26.50	26.70	48.30	35.40	43.50	34.50	29.30	25.70	33.30	30.40	55.30	66.60	35.40
2011	57.10	45.40	40.80	33.90	40.20	55.70	28.70	35.60	33.60	33.10	42.90	51.60	41.55
2012	28.80	23.70	33.70	24.10	31.40	49.20	30.00	30.20	40.40	30.30	35.40	28.20	30.55
2013	80.40	38.10	30.60	NA	NA	NA	NA	NA	NA	NA	NA	NA	NA
2014[1]	NA	NA	NA	40.10	46.30	47.90	30.10	45.40	51.70	32.90	45.00	33.10	

[1]Preliminary.   NA = Not available.   *Source: National Agricultural Statistics Service, U.S. Department of Agriculture (NASS-USDA)*

Average Price Received by Growers for Carrots in the United States   In Dollars Per Cwt

Year	Jan.	Feb.	Mar.	Apr.	May	June	July	Aug.	Sept.	Oct.	Nov.	Dec.	Season Average
2007	21.00	28.10	28.30	29.60	32.00	25.90	19.70	17.10	16.10	15.80	15.80	16.20	22.10
2008	16.20	25.90	25.90	25.50	32.00	25.60	25.60	25.60	25.30	25.20	24.70	25.20	24.50
2009	25.20	25.20	25.20	25.20	25.50	25.80	25.60	24.00	25.20	25.30	27.20	27.80	25.20
2010	28.50	23.90	27.50	27.40	27.40	26.20	27.10	27.10	26.80	26.90	27.60	33.00	26.20
2011	38.00	40.70	44.60	46.20	44.80	35.10	28.40	20.40	17.30	14.80	14.10	25.50	30.83
2012	26.30	26.30	26.80	27.60	27.40	27.50	28.10	24.20	21.70	26.00	26.70	27.40	NA
2013	28.20	28.50	30.80	NA	NA	NA	NA	NA	NA	NA	NA	NA	NA
2014[1]	NA	NA	NA	28.20	27.20	25.50	25.10	23.10	21.00	26.80	28.00	33.40	

[1]Preliminary.   NA = Not available.   *Source: National Agricultural Statistics Service, U.S. Department of Agriculture (NASS-USDA)*

Average Price Received by Growers for Cauliflower in the United States   In Dollars Per Cwt

Year	Jan.	Feb.	Mar.	Apr.	May	June	July	Aug.	Sept.	Oct.	Nov.	Dec.	Season Average
2007	45.70	29.40	51.40	51.60	24.90	30.00	22.30	27.90	27.20	46.20	26.60	52.40	34.40
2008	51.80	30.00	41.70	63.80	24.90	53.90	38.20	43.20	29.50	48.50	29.50	43.90	40.70
2009	68.20	30.00	51.30	41.40	46.60	43.50	41.70	31.90	26.90	58.10	54.40	47.10	44.40
2010	33.20	36.70	50.40	58.00	68.60	32.90	31.20	26.30	27.70	31.50	52.60	66.40	39.60
2011	41.10	55.90	51.30	43.10	56.80	52.80	38.40	30.90	29.70	30.30	67.30	66.20	46.98
2012	31.90	32.10	39.00	28.50	35.40	38.90	27.90	29.60	39.20	29.40	47.70	40.00	NA
2013	69.90	43.30	46.00	NA	NA	NA	NA	NA	NA	NA	NA	NA	NA
2014[1]	NA	NA	NA	65.80	85.60	71.80	49.60	38.30	71.20	49.70	67.60	84.80	

[1]Preliminary.   NA = Not available.   *Source: National Agricultural Statistics Service, U.S. Department of Agriculture (NASS-USDA)*

Average Price Received by Growers for Celery in the United States   In Dollars Per Cwt

Year	Jan.	Feb.	Mar.	Apr.	May	June	July	Aug.	Sept.	Oct.	Nov.	Dec.	Season Average
2007	33.90	58.90	31.90	18.80	18.30	11.60	11.60	9.64	13.80	13.30	18.60	13.50	20.40
2008	16.20	13.20	13.40	14.00	37.40	30.10	22.10	12.40	11.90	17.10	16.90	20.30	18.50
2009	35.10	29.70	15.00	17.40	17.40	11.70	11.30	11.40	12.00	20.90	21.10	38.80	18.50
2010	37.40	21.60	25.70	17.10	20.00	15.80	16.00	13.90	15.10	15.00	14.30	20.20	19.70
2011	25.10	46.50	29.50	19.30	33.10	17.10	20.00	16.70	16.30	16.30	15.00	14.90	22.48
2012	20.10	12.60	12.50	12.70	15.80	13.50	23.60	22.10	24.80	19.10	20.30	21.20	NA
2013	39.70	47.00	29.20	NA	NA	NA	NA	NA	NA	NA	NA	NA	NA
2014[1]	NA	NA	NA	15.50	16.20	14.90	20.80	17.70	17.00	16.90	26.60	28.70	

[1]Preliminary.   NA = Not available.   *Source: National Agricultural Statistics Service, U.S. Department of Agriculture (NASS-USDA)*

Average Price Received by Growers for Sweet Corn in the United States   In Dollars Per Cwt

Year	Jan.	Feb.	Mar.	Apr.	May	June	July	Aug.	Sept.	Oct.	Nov.	Dec.	Season Average
2007	27.40	23.60	30.20	25.60	21.40	17.30	22.20	22.80	23.20	21.40	20.60	34.10	22.70
2008	30.80	23.00	28.60	20.50	21.90	19.90	28.50	27.20	27.10	23.70	30.80	22.20	25.90
2009	24.90	46.40	59.30	32.50	20.80	25.40	34.60	26.40	23.70	23.30	19.80	19.40	29.40
2010	37.80	58.50	62.70	40.10	25.10	16.00	20.20	23.10	24.00	28.00	20.60	31.60	25.70
2011	62.20	51.80	42.40	21.50	19.90	24.30	32.90	20.70	24.40	26.40	26.60	14.90	30.67
2012	37.30	31.00	33.70	22.90	21.10	22.80	25.60	16.60	22.70	25.60	26.60	27.80	NA
2013	30.40	36.70	33.30	NA	NA	NA	NA	NA	NA	NA	NA	NA	NA
2014[1]	NA	NA	NA	26.00	25.40	32.20	36.40	28.40	22.50	42.40	40.70	41.40	

[1]Preliminary.   NA = Not available.   *Source: National Agricultural Statistics Service, U.S. Department of Agriculture (NASS-USDA)*

Average Price Received by Growers for Head Lettuce in the United States   In Dollars Per Cwt

Year	Jan.	Feb.	Mar.	Apr.	May	June	July	Aug.	Sept.	Oct.	Nov.	Dec.	Season Average
2005	11.50	11.70	27.90	30.10	13.90	17.30	11.00	13.50	12.70	12.40	9.81	16.60	15.50
2006	10.50	12.00	19.10	22.40	33.70	11.80	12.20	20.70	16.30	11.80	12.50	22.40	16.90
2007	20.80	15.50	29.70	17.80	13.60	17.80	17.30	23.10	29.20	44.40	17.40	16.00	21.70
2008	17.60	13.40	14.70	21.60	15.50	17.70	17.30	17.20	31.90	32.90	18.80	23.50	20.10
2009	28.50	17.80	19.40	27.70	18.20	18.90	16.90	16.70	16.60	27.20	49.60	38.70	21.70
2010	17.30	14.10	20.80	19.00	24.30	25.70	26.00	23.30	17.20	20.20	35.40	17.50	23.80
2011	27.20	54.40	35.20	17.80	26.40	17.10	19.40	14.70	14.80	17.00	30.50	17.40	24.33
2012	13.40	12.60	12.00	17.90	19.00	19.00	19.10	19.20	20.50	17.70	20.10	12.80	NA
2013	44.80	31.70	46.90	NA	NA	NA	NA	NA	NA	NA	NA	NA	NA
2014[1]	NA	NA	NA	18.20	26.10	35.30	29.00	29.60	32.90	33.40	49.10	15.90	

[1] Preliminary.   NA = Not available.   *Source: National Agricultural Statistics Service, U.S. Department of Agriculture (NASS-USDA)*

Average Price Received by Growers for Tomatoes in the United States   In Dollars Per Cwt

Year	Jan.	Feb.	Mar.	Apr.	May	June	July	Aug.	Sept.	Oct.	Nov.	Dec.	Season Average
2005	15.40	40.90	40.70	65.10	49.40	40.00	28.00	26.10	46.10	37.30	36.50	96.80	41.80
2006	79.20	46.50	24.80	34.40	23.30	30.90	25.10	27.80	79.80	53.20	28.10	24.80	43.70
2007	35.60	31.20	26.30	52.60	35.60	29.60	26.70	28.60	33.10	41.60	58.70	81.20	34.80
2008	58.20	45.50	66.10	47.40	48.20	56.80	40.90	29.40	25.60	33.80	64.90	37.90	45.50
2009	29.30	32.70	41.50	45.40	33.20	67.20	31.70	35.90	34.40	40.20	73.70	65.00	40.60
2010	58.90	84.60	109.00	103.00	65.20	37.30	33.60	35.50	38.40	32.00	38.10	37.30	48.10
2011	51.90	108.00	98.70	67.60	49.10	44.60	33.10	30.30	35.50	26.60	42.40	26.50	51.19
2012	28.90	30.60	36.60	26.70	34.10	45.10	24.70	23.70	26.20	20.90	45.30	49.40	NA
2013	34.10	37.70	53.50	NA	NA	NA	NA	NA	NA	NA	NA	NA	NA
2014[1]	NA	NA	NA	45.20	39.10	57.60	25.00	31.80	33.50	53.90	71.80	66.70	

[1] Preliminary.   NA = Not available.   *Source: National Agricultural Statistics Service, U.S. Department of Agriculture (NASS-USDA)*

Frozen Vegetables: January 1 and July 1 Cold Storage Holdings in the United States   In Thousands of Pounds

Crop	2010 July 1	2011 Jan. 1	2011 July 1	2012 Jan. 1	2012 July 1	2013 Jan. 1	2013 July 1	2014 Jan. 1	2014 July 1	2015[1] Jan. 1
Asparagus	11,127	7,630	10,018	6,615	11,376	8,304	9,900	9,758	15,185	13,603
Limas, Fordhook	2,622	7,255	----	----	----	----	----	----	----	----
Limas, Baby	31,238	49,100	34,313	54,711	18,192	57,819	29,717	60,262	34,333	54,530
Green Beans, Reg. Cut	70,842	166,011	61,436	192,235	91,790	252,309	143,931	181,073	96,376	182,136
Green Beans, Fr. Style	13,169	19,028	8,220	22,509	11,019	15,761	8,749	14,248	8,194	14,754
Broccoli, Spears	35,163	20,851	32,338	25,164	39,251	27,652	27,359	21,705	34,093	27,108
Broccoli, Chopped & Cut	48,760	34,885	37,149	44,822	60,293	52,022	41,353	34,836	33,394	36,143
Brussels sprouts	13,813	17,845	10,510	11,135	10,466	13,663	10,675	13,612	12,480	15,960
Carrots, Diced	94,385	159,405	91,040	158,524	83,281	170,186	109,846	157,220	100,260	168,289
Carrots, Other	86,154	150,944	79,677	145,066	87,419	173,980	108,905	160,585	99,961	180,493
Cauliflower	19,977	23,524	16,707	23,433	21,877	26,249	21,738	23,139	16,497	20,567
Corn, Cut	305,686	571,012	216,687	458,788	189,031	465,827	249,147	550,708	250,726	529,586
Corn, Cob	102,824	249,387	101,891	249,459	85,464	235,766	100,019	238,575	101,087	223,053
Mixed vegetables	46,561	38,245	45,834	49,143	45,576	43,340	46,674	50,977	49,422	53,082
Okra	14,933	21,457	24,921	34,611	16,789	23,643	17,750	21,405	14,800	39,375
Onion Rings	5,382	4,955	5,611	4,435	7,197	8,214	12,287	9,889	11,141	9,057
Onions, Other	19,737	32,549	48,162	69,243	68,763	49,816	38,270	39,917	44,632	35,944
Blackeye Peas	2,757	2,764	2,447	1,756	1,818	1,597	1,693	1,386	1,655	1,565
Green Peas	298,995	276,587	234,439	238,909	288,133	219,559	240,208	228,586	284,293	243,251
Peas and Carrots Mixed	7,096	5,992	6,294	5,082	6,146	7,178	6,951	6,250	7,274	7,671
Spinach	96,542	52,103	84,296	49,062	75,117	48,781	55,678	39,053	52,579	38,024
Squash, Summer/Zucchini	39,685	64,783	39,010	73,109	49,364	64,510	49,657	61,133	42,958	62,828
Southern greens	16,742	13,507	20,022	15,084	17,194	12,432	17,240	11,043	14,873	11,253
Other Vegetables	280,686	360,009	264,367	372,890	294,654	387,366	298,588	425,010	281,639	381,070
Total	1,664,876	2,354,112	1,475,389	2,305,785	1,580,209	2,365,974	1,646,335	2,360,370	1,607,852	2,359,342
Potatoes, French Fries	899,847	820,872	866,965	802,278	924,433	905,662	1,009,457	902,139	807,376	842,464
Potatoes, Other Frozen	242,099	198,033	220,707	197,635	237,070	204,726	260,865	193,161	205,458	187,967
Potatoes, Total	1,141,946	1,018,905	1,087,672	999,913	1,161,503	1,110,388	1,270,322	1,095,300	1,012,834	1,030,431
Grand Total	2,806,822	3,373,017	2,563,061	3,305,698	2,741,712	3,476,362	2,916,657	3,455,670	2,620,686	3,389,773

VEGETABLES

Cold Storage Stocks of Frozen Green Beans[2] in the United States, on First of Month
In Thousands of Pounds

Year	Jan.	Feb.	Mar.	Apr.	May	June	July	Aug.	Sept.	Oct.	Nov.	Dec.
2009	211,997	188,915	169,346	147,596	126,359	116,493	95,706	139,967	197,238	240,107	211,003	194,184
2010	176,371	159,532	142,137	123,047	92,954	80,754	70,842	109,413	164,357	223,928	198,883	182,202
2011	166,011	139,152	124,368	105,607	86,575	76,704	61,436	94,272	168,094	233,617	208,185	195,833
2012	192,235	172,413	150,764	125,018	104,127	96,182	91,790	149,376	252,740	288,757	301,782	273,657
2013	252,309	203,122	201,608	179,446	164,526	152,338	143,931	166,636	237,400	252,315	224,385	200,790
2014[1]	181,073	162,305	149,444	139,195	125,882	109,855	96,376	147,470	225,135	253,066	235,830	205,861

[1] Preliminary.　[2] Regular cut.　*Source: Economic Research Service, U.S. Department of Agriculture (ERS-USDA)*

Cold Storage Stocks of Frozen Corn[2] in the United States, on First of Month
In Thousands of Pounds

Year	Jan.	Feb.	Mar.	Apr.	May	June	July	Aug.	Sept.	Oct.	Nov.	Dec.
2009	463,724	406,206	368,520	326,868	290,734	238,292	202,653	193,401	396,474	601,205	658,972	630,159
2010	584,048	547,232	497,712	448,133	401,942	343,136	305,686	291,404	472,963	629,274	676,527	617,660
2011	571,012	521,993	467,481	405,714	340,257	283,392	216,687	181,404	302,134	506,672	541,733	505,252
2012	458,788	440,071	390,574	334,802	293,211	242,158	189,031	195,078	349,927	478,194	529,202	490,123
2013	465,827	450,464	410,588	369,771	330,335	282,126	249,147	226,862	397,483	585,455	630,849	581,072
2014[1]	550,708	492,643	460,752	397,092	345,504	296,765	250,726	273,738	462,352	596,616	631,669	576,419

[1] Preliminary.　[2] Cut.　*Source: Economic Research Service, U.S. Department of Agriculture (ERS-USDA)*

Cold Storage Stocks of Frozen Corn[2] in the United States, on First of Month
In Thousands of Pounds

Year	Jan.	Feb.	Mar.	Apr.	May	June	July	Aug.	Sept.	Oct.	Nov.	Dec.
2009	264,562	247,402	218,649	192,534	169,269	131,665	98,389	107,043	181,263	292,652	293,967	265,665
2010	252,108	236,435	214,708	188,317	164,144	132,229	102,824	100,184	203,300	259,187	260,414	254,363
2011	249,387	230,771	210,381	180,463	156,146	132,393	101,891	89,845	181,470	270,417	261,853	254,979
2012	249,459	225,895	194,851	173,112	148,582	118,460	85,464	87,499	166,073	233,153	257,504	245,195
2013	235,766	219,301	202,672	173,684	150,267	123,501	100,019	83,647	151,447	244,077	271,819	251,382
2014[1]	238,575	225,426	200,562	174,569	156,311	121,262	101,087	108,477	175,199	258,604	268,087	240,784

[1] Preliminary .　[2] Cob.　*Source: Economic Research Service, U.S. Department of Agriculture (ERS-USDA)*

Cold Storage Stocks of Frozen Green Peas in the United States, on First of Month
In Thousands of Pounds

Year	Jan.	Feb.	Mar.	Apr.	May	June	July	Aug.	Sept.	Oct.	Nov.	Dec.
2009	255,471	232,757	199,313	167,606	143,908	121,027	252,937	437,572	403,023	376,205	335,817	303,632
2010	275,625	255,309	236,609	203,325	172,781	149,428	298,995	456,725	437,177	384,187	348,511	311,507
2011	276,587	234,314	209,119	178,577	147,077	126,467	234,439	440,127	392,908	345,682	321,545	275,665
2012	238,909	209,567	170,753	143,400	118,689	102,379	288,133	404,734	364,629	323,968	278,459	241,233
2013	219,559	195,388	165,683	138,449	112,263	99,542	240,208	392,588	349,572	305,131	285,313	256,457
2014[1]	228,586	192,134	168,608	136,081	111,179	95,529	284,293	427,634	395,401	354,716	314,577	285,406

[1] Preliminary.　*Source: Economic Research Service, U.S. Department of Agriculture (ERS-USDA)*

Cold Storage Stocks of Other Frozen Vegetables in the United States, on First of Month
In Thousands of lbs

Year	Jan.	Feb.	Mar.	Apr.	May	June	July	Aug.	Sept.	Oct.	Nov.	Dec.
2009	423,684	388,463	357,668	332,749	331,613	320,377	293,501	343,267	388,316	437,144	454,844	424,864
2010	408,829	374,017	357,202	326,698	327,483	302,126	280,686	313,144	387,885	395,523	417,899	385,495
2011	360,009	322,773	293,177	278,745	268,754	264,758	264,367	268,594	325,000	354,130	398,891	383,782
2012	372,890	329,313	314,884	319,645	308,607	308,273	294,654	325,156	396,862	428,486	445,035	426,539
2013	387,366	363,899	352,909	350,651	349,274	301,871	298,588	310,171	369,266	436,882	455,362	433,678
2014[1]	425,010	371,053	366,772	359,294	311,776	285,450	281,639	310,021	348,093	402,271	415,446	392,454

[1] Preliminary.　*Source: Economic Research Service, U.S. Department of Agriculture (ERS-USDA)*

Cold Storage Stocks of Total Frozen Vegetables in the United States, on First of Month
In Millions of Pounds

Year	Jan.	Feb.	Mar.	Apr.	May	June	July	Aug.	Sept.	Oct.	Nov.	Dec.
2009	2,366.0	2,172.1	1,984.1	1,830.5	1,716.8	1,572.1	1,564.0	1,832.2	2,186.4	2,624.7	2,724.6	2,603.6
2010	2,471.8	2,315.0	2,151.8	1,959.8	1,808.8	1,621.6	1,664.9	1,859.8	2,263.4	2,529.3	2,619.7	2,517.1
2011	2,354.1	2,117.0	1,934.9	1,751.2	1,602.4	1,503.7	1,475.4	1,654.6	1,984.8	2,372.8	2,493.6	2,422.9
2012	2,305.8	2,125.1	1,935.6	1,769.1	1,637.8	1,521.6	1,580.2	1,779.1	2,164.7	2,416.1	2,584.1	2,494.7
2013	2,366.0	2,203.9	2,046.3	1,874.4	1,760.8	1,581.4	1,646.3	1,763.7	2,090.0	2,431.0	2,578.5	2,480.2
2014[1]	2,360.4	2,157.4	2,025.0	1,842.1	1,660.2	1,519.9	1,607.9	1,863.8	2,232.8	2,530.6	2,663.6	2,546.1

[1] Preliminary.　*Source: Economic Research Service, U.S. Department of Agriculture (ERS-USDA)*

Wheat

Wheat is a cereal grass, but before cultivation it was a wild grass. It has been grown in temperate regions and cultivated for food since prehistoric times. Wheat is believed to have originated in southwestern Asia. Archeological research indicates that wheat was grown as a crop in the Nile Valley about 5,000 BC. Wheat is not native to the U.S. and was first grown here in 1602 near the Massachusetts coast. The common types of wheat grown in the U.S. are spring and winter wheat. Wheat planted in the spring for summer or autumn harvest is mostly red wheat. Wheat planted in the fall or winter for spring harvest is mostly white wheat. Winter wheat accounts for nearly three-fourths of total U.S. production. Wheat is used mainly as a human food and supplies about 20% of the food calories for the world's population. The primary use for wheat is flour, but it is also used for brewing and distilling, and for making oil, gluten, straw for livestock bedding, livestock feed, hay or silage, newsprint, and other products.

Wheat futures and options are traded at the CME Group, ICE Futures U.S., the Minneapolis Grain Exchange (MGEX), the Budapest Stock Exchange (BSE), the JSE Securities Exchange , the Mercado a Termino de Buenos Aires (MTBA), the NYSE LIFFE European Derivatives Market, and the Sydney Futures Exchange (SFE). The CME's wheat futures contract calls for the delivery of soft red wheat (No. 1 and 2), hard red winter wheat (No. 1 and 2), dark northern spring wheat (No. 1 and 2), No.1 northern spring at 3 cents/bushel premium, or No. 2 northern spring at par. Futures are also traded at ICE Futures Canada, the Moscow Exchange, the Multi Commodity Exchange of India (MCX), the National Commodity & Derivatives Exchange (NCDEX), the Rosario Futures Exchange, the Turkish Derivatives Exchange, and the Zhengzhou Commodity Exchange (ZCE).

Prices – CME wheat futures prices (Barchart.com electronic symbol ZW) started 2014 under pressure as they posted a 4-1/2 year low in January at $5.50 a bushel after the USDA in the January WASDE report raised its 2013/14 global wheat production estimate to a record 712.66 MMT. Wheat prices then rebounded sharply into Q2 and posted the high for 2014 in May at $7.35 a bushel, a 1-3/4 year high. Wheat prices surged on concern that escalation of tensions in Ukraine would disrupt wheat exports from Russia and Ukraine, the world's fifth and sixth biggest wheat exporters, respectively. Wheat prices trended lower in Q3 and posted a 4-1/2 year low in September at $4.66 a bushel on abundant global supplies. The USDA in the September WASDE report raised its 2014/15 global wheat production estimate to a record 719.95 MMT and raised its 2014/15 global wheat ending stocks estimate to a 4-year high of 196.38 MMT. Wheat prices in Q4 rallied sharply by $2.00 a bushel to $6.77 a bushel in December on global crop concerns after the driest weather in Russia in 5 years threatened its wheat output, while excessive rains in Australia hindered its wheat crop. Another positive for wheat prices was Russia's levy of a 15% tariff on its wheat exports. The tariff was designed to limit Russian wheat exports after the collapse of the ruble to a record low against the dollar gave Russian wheat exporters incentive to increase exports that were more profitable than domestic sales. Wheat prices finished 2014 down -2.6% at $5.90 a bushel. The USDA currently pegs the U.S. wheat 2014/15 stocks-to-use ratio at 30.5%, above the 10-year average of 28.7%, and the global 2014/54 stocks-to-use ratio at 27.4%, higher than the 10-year average of 25.7%.

Supply – World wheat production in the 2014-15 marketing year rose +1.1% to 723.384 million metric tons, a new record high. The world's largest wheat producers were the European Union with 21.5% of world production in 2014-15, China (17.4%), India (13.3%), Russia (8.2%), the U.S. (7.6%), and Pakistan (3.5%). China's wheat production in 2014-15 rose +3.3% yr/yr to 126.000 million metric tons, but is still below its record high of 123.289 million metric tons seen in 1997-98. India's wheat production rose +2.6% yr/yr to 95.910 million metric tons in 2014-15, a new record high. The world land area harvested with wheat in 2014-15 rose +0.5% yr/yr to 221.8 million hectares (1 hectare equals 10,000 square meters or 2.471 acres). World wheat yield in 2014-15 rose +3.1% to 3.30 metric tons per acre, a new record high.

U.S. wheat production in 2014-15 fell -5.1% yr/yr to 2.025 billion bushels, which was below the record crop of 2.785 billion bushels seen in 1981-82. Ending stocks for U.S. wheat for 2014-15 rose 17% to 691 million bushels. The U.S. winter wheat crop in 2014 fell -10.7% yr/yr to 1.377 billion bushels, which was well below the record winter wheat crop of 2.097 billion bushels seen in 1981. U.S. production of durum wheat in 2014 fell -8.4% yr/yr to 53.087 million bushels. U.S. production of other spring wheat in 2014 rose +11.4% yr/yr to 595.038 million bushels. The largest U.S. producing states of winter wheat in 2014 were Kansas with 17.9% of U.S. production, Montana with 6.7%, Colorado with 6.5%, and Washington with 6.2%. U.S. farmers planted 56.822 million acres of wheat in 2014, which was up +1.0% yr/yr. U.S. wheat yield in 2014-15 was 43.7 bushels per acre, a new record high.

Demand – World wheat utilization in 2014-15 rose +1.4% yr/yr to 714.1 million metric tons. U.S. consumption of wheat in 2014-15 fell -5.7% yr/yr to 1.183 billion bushels, below 2012-13 record high of 1.387 billion bushels. The consumption breakdown shows that 81.1% of U.S. wheat consumption in 2014-15 went for food, 12.7% for feed and residuals, and 6.2% for seed.

Trade – World trade in wheat in 2014-15 fell -3.4% yr/yr to 156.600 million metric tons, below last year's record high of 162.1 million metric tons. U.S. exports of wheat in 2014-15 fell -21.4% yr/yr to 925.000 million bushels, and remained below the record of 1.771 billion bushels of exports seen in 1981-82. U.S. imports of wheat in 2014-15 rose +6.8% to 180.0 million bushels, a new record high.

WHEAT

World Production of Wheat   In Thousands of Metric Tons

Crop Year	Argen-tina	Australia	Canada	China	European Union	India	Iran	Kazak-hstan	Pakistan	Russia	Turkey	United States	World Total
2005-06	13,800	25,173	25,748	97,445	132,856	68,640	14,308	11,197	21,612	47,615	18,500	57,243	618,875
2006-07	16,300	10,822	25,265	108,466	125,670	69,350	14,664	13,460	21,277	44,927	17,500	49,217	596,532
2007-08	18,600	13,569	20,090	109,298	120,833	75,810	15,887	16,466	23,295	49,368	15,500	55,821	612,651
2008-09	11,000	21,420	28,619	112,464	151,922	78,570	7,957	12,538	20,959	63,765	16,800	68,363	683,877
2009-10	12,000	21,834	26,950	115,120	139,720	80,680	13,485	17,051	24,000	61,770	18,450	60,117	686,805
2010-11	17,200	27,410	23,300	115,180	136,667	80,800	13,500	9,638	23,900	41,508	17,000	58,868	649,559
2011-12	15,500	29,905	25,288	117,400	138,182	86,870	12,400	22,732	25,000	56,240	18,800	54,244	695,773
2012-13[1]	9,300	22,856	27,205	121,023	133,949	94,880	13,800	9,841	23,300	37,720	15,500	61,298	658,041
2013-14[2]	10,500	27,009	37,530	121,930	143,513	93,510	14,500	13,941	24,000	52,091	18,000	58,105	715,359
2014-15[3]	12,000	24,000	29,300	126,000	155,505	95,910	13,000	12,500	25,000	59,000	15,000	55,129	723,384

[1] Preliminary.   [2] Estimate.   [3] Forecast.   *Source: Foreign Agricultural Service, U.S. Department of Agriculture (FAS-USDA)*

World Supply and Demand of Wheat   In Millions of Metric Tons/Hectares

Year	Area Harvested	Yield	Production	World Trade	Utilization Total	Ending Stocks	Stocks as a % of Utilization
2005-06	217.6	2.84	618.9	117.3	621.1	154.0	24.8
2006-07	211.6	2.82	596.5	111.7	616.5	134.1	21.8
2007-08	217.1	2.82	612.7	116.7	617.7	129.0	20.9
2008-09	224.2	3.05	683.9	144.2	644.3	168.6	26.2
2009-10	225.5	3.05	686.8	137.1	654.2	201.2	30.8
2010-11	216.7	3.00	649.6	132.8	653.4	197.4	30.2
2011-12	220.7	3.15	695.8	158.3	697.0	196.1	28.1
2012-13[1]	216.3	3.00	658.5	147.1	679.9	175.5	25.8
2013-14[2]	220.9	3.20	716.1	162.1	704.2	187.5	26.6
2014-15[3]	222.0	3.30	725.0	160.1	714.6	197.8	27.7

[1] Preliminary.   [2] Estimate.   [3] Forecast.   *Source: Foreign Agricultural Service, U.S. Department of Agriculture (FAS-USDA)*

Salient Statistics of Wheat in the United States

Year	Planting Intentions	Acreage Harvested — Winter	Acreage Harvested — Spring	Acreage Harvested — All	Average All Yield Per Acre in Bushels	Value of Production $1,000	Domestic Exports[2]	Imports[3]	Per Capita Consumption Flour	Per Capita Consumption Cereal
	--- 1,000 Acres ---						--- In Millions of Bushels ---		--- In Pounds ---	
2005-06	57,229	33,794	16,325	50,119	42.0	7,171,441	1,002.8	81.4	134.3	3.6
2006-07	57,344	31,117	16,769	46,810	38.7	7,694,734	908.5	121.9	135.7	----
2007-08	60,460	35,938	15,061	50,999	40.5	13,289,326	1,262.6	112.6	138.1	----
2008-09	63,193	39,608	16,091	55,699	44.9	16,625,759	1,015.4	127.0	136.5	----
2009-10	59,168	34,510	15,383	49,893	44.5	10,654,115	879.3	118.6	134.7	----
2010-11	53,593	31,741	15,878	47,619	46.3	12,827,254	1,291.4	96.9	135.0	----
2011-12	54,409	32,314	13,391	45,705	43.7	14,322,909	1,051.2	112.1	133.0	----
2012-13	55,294	34,609	14,149	48,758	46.2	17,383,149	1,012.1	122.8	134.0	----
2013-14	56,236	32,650	12,672	45,332	47.1	14,604,442	1,176.3	168.6		
2014-15[1]	56,822	32,304	14,077	46,381	43.7	11,923,931	900.0	160.0		

[1] Preliminary.   [2] Includes flour milled from imported wheat.   [3] Total wheat, flour & other products.   [4] Civilian only.   [5] Year beginning June.
Source: Economic Research Service, U.S. Department of Agriculture (ERS-USDA)

Supply and Distribution of Wheat in the United States   In Millions of Bushels

Crop Year Beginning June 1	Supply — Stocks, June 1 On Farms	Supply — Stocks, June 1 Mills, Elevators[3]	Supply — Stocks, June 1 Total Stocks	Supply — Production	Supply — Imports[4]	Supply — Total Supply	Domestic Disappearance — Food	Domestic Disappearance — Seed	Domestic Disappearance — Feed & Residual[5]	Domestic Disappearance — Total	Domestic Disappearance — Exports[4]	Total Disappearance
2005-06	161.3	378.8	540.1	2,104.7	81.4	2,724.8	917.1	77.1	156.6	1,150.8	1,002.8	2,153.6
2006-07	111.0	460.2	571.2	1,812.0	121.9	2,501.5	937.9	81.9	117.1	1,136.8	908.5	2,045.3
2007-08	73.2	383.0	456.2	2,051.1	112.6	2,619.9	947.9	87.6	16.0	1,051.4	1,262.6	2,314.1
2008-09	25.6	280.2	305.8	2,499.2	127.0	2,932.0	926.8	77.7	268.3	1,272.8	1,015.4	2,288.2
2009-10	140.7	515.8	656.5	2,218.1	118.6	2,993.2	918.9	68.0	142.2	1,129.1	879.3	2,008.4
2010-11	209.9	765.7	975.6	2,206.9	96.9	3,235.6	925.6	70.7	84.8	1,081.1	1,291.4	2,372.6
2011-12	130.9	731.3	862.2	1,999.3	112.1	2,968.2	941.4	75.6	157.4	1,174.4	1,051.2	2,225.6
2012-13	112.0	630.6	742.6	2,252.3	122.8	3,117.7	944.7	73.1	369.9	1,387.7	1,012.1	2,399.8
2013-14[1]	120.2	597.7	717.9	2,135.0	168.6	3,021.5	952.2	77.0	225.7	1,254.9	1,176.3	2,431.2
2014-15[2]	97.0	493.3	590.3	2,025.7	160.0	2,775.9	960.0	73.9	150.0	1,183.9	900.0	2,083.9

[1] Preliminary.   [2] Estimate.   [3] Also warehouses and all off-farm storage not otherwise designated, including flour mills.   [4] Imports & exports are for wheat, including flour & other products in terms of wheat.   [5] Mostly feed use.
Source: Economic Research Service, U.S. Department of Agriculture (ERS-USDA)

Stocks, Production and Exports of Wheat in the United States, by Class   In Millions of Bushels

	Hard Spring			Durum[2]			Hard Winter			Soft Red Winter			White		
Year	Stocks June 1	Pro-duction	Exports[3]	Stocks June 1	Pro-duction	Exports[3]	Stocks June 1	Pro-duction	Exports[3]	Stocks June 1	Pro-duction	Exports[3]	Stocks June 1	Pro-duction	Exports[3]
2005-06	159	467	282	38	101	47	193	930	430	88	309	76	63	298	175
2006-07	132	432	250	40	53	35	215	682	281	106	390	146	78	254	197
2007-08	117	450	305	21	72	42	165	956	538	109	352	209	44	221	170
2008-09	68	512	210	8	84	24	138	1,035	447	55	614	199	37	255	136
2009-10	142	548	214	25	109	44	254	920	370	171	404	109	64	237	143
2010-11	234	570	339	35	106	43	385	1,018	616	242	237	109	80	275	182
2011-12	185	398	242	35	50	27	386	780	397	171	458	165	85	314	218
2012-13	151	505	232	25	83	29	317	1,000	380	185	420	193	64	259	174
2013-14	165	490	246	23	58	31	343	747	446	124	568	283	63	271	171
2014-15[1]	169	556	295	22	53	30	237	738	285	113	455	140	50	224	150

[1] Preliminary.   [2] Includes "Red Durum."   [3] Includes four made from U.S. wheat & shipments to territories.
Source: Economic Research Service, U.S. Department of Agriculture (ERS-USDA)

Seeded Acreage, Yield and Production of all Wheat in the United States

	Seed Acreage - 1,000 Acres				Yield Per Harvested Acre (Bushels)				Production (Million Bushels)			
Year	Winter	Other Spring	Durum	All	Winter	Other Spring	Durum	All	Winter	Other Spring	Durum	All
2005	40,433	14,036	2,760	57,229	44.4	37.1	37.2	42.0	1,499.1	504.5	101.1	2,104.7
2006	40,575	14,899	1,870	57,344	41.7	33.2	29.5	38.7	1,298.1	460.5	53.5	1,812.0
2007	45,012	13,292	2,156	60,460	41.7	37.1	34.1	40.2	1,499.2	479.6	72.2	2,051.1
2008	46,307	14,165	2,721	63,193	47.1	40.5	32.6	44.9	1,867.3	548.0	83.8	2,499.2
2009	43,346	13,268	2,554	59,168	44.2	45.1	44.9	44.5	1,524.6	584.4	109.0	2,218.1
2010	37,335	13,698	2,560	53,593	46.8	46.1	42.1	46.3	1,484.9	616.0	106.1	2,206.9
2011	40,646	12,394	1,369	54,409	46.2	37.7	38.5	43.7	1,493.7	455.2	50.5	1,999.3
2012	40,897	12,259	2,138	55,294	47.1	44.9	38.4	46.2	1,630.4	540.4	81.5	2,252.3
2013	43,230	11,606	1,400	56,236	47.3	47.1	43.3	47.1	1,542.9	534.1	58.0	2,135.0
2014[1]	42,399	13,025	1,398	56,822	42.6	46.7	39.7	43.7	1,377.5	595.0	53.1	2,025.7

[1] Preliminary.   *Source: Economic Research Service, U.S. Department of Agriculture (ERS-USDA)*

Production of Winter Wheat in the United States, by State   In Thousands of Bushels

Year	Colorado	Idaho	Illinois	Kansas	Missouri	Montana	Nebraska	Ohio	Okla-homa	Oregon	Texas	Wash-ington	US Total
2005	52,800	66,430	36,600	380,000	29,160	94,500	68,640	58,930	128,000	47,580	96,000	120,600	1,499,129
2006	39,900	54,670	60,970	291,200	49,140	82,560	61,200	65,280	81,600	38,690	33,600	118,800	1,298,081
2007	91,650	51,830	48,950	283,800	37,840	83,220	84,280	44,530	98,000	38,160	140,600	104,780	1,499,241
2008	57,000	60,000	73,600	356,000	55,680	94,380	73,480	74,120	166,500	44,950	99,000	96,320	1,867,333
2009	98,000	56,700	45,920	369,600	34,310	89,540	76,800	70,560	77,000	42,000	61,250	96,760	1,524,608
2010	105,750	58,220	16,520	360,000	12,600	93,600	64,070	45,750	120,900	54,270	127,500	117,990	1,484,861
2011	78,000	63,140	46,665	276,500	34,000	89,790	65,250	49,300	70,400	63,525	49,400	129,750	1,493,677
2012	68,200	59,200	40,960	382,200	39,440	84,630	53,300	30,600	154,800	51,810	95,700	116,900	1,630,387
2013	40,750	63,640	56,280	321,100	56,145	81,700	39,900	44,800	105,400	48,360	68,150	115,230	1,542,902
2014[1]	89,300	58,400	44,890	246,400	42,920	91,840	71,050	40,330	47,600	40,700	67,500	85,280	1,377,526

[1] Preliminary.   *Source: Crop Reporting Board, U.S. Department of Agriculture (CRB-USDA)*

Official Winter Wheat Crop Production Reports in the United States   In Thousands of Bushels

Crop Year	May 1	June 1	July 1	August 1	September 1	Current December	Final
2005-06	1,590,862	1,545,971	1,525,302	1,520,848	----	----	1,499,129
2006-07	1,322,831	1,263,766	1,280,005	1,283,134	----	----	1,298,081
2007-08	1,615,613	1,609,679	1,561,907	1,537,262	----	----	1,499,241
2008-09	1,777,532	1,817,364	1,864,245	1,874,857	----	----	1,867,333
2009-10	1,502,074	1,491,769	1,524,771	1,537,348	----	----	1,524,608
2010-11	1,458,350	1,482,364	1,505,493	1,522,902	----	----	1,484,861
2011-12	1,424,357	1,450,115	1,491,739	1,497,429	----	----	1,493,677
2012-13	1,693,710	1,683,667	1,670,346	1,682,726	----	----	1,630,387
2013-14	1,485,757	1,509,142	1,543,095	1,542,605	----	----	1,542,902
2014-15[1]	1,402,505	1,381,060	1,367,432	1,396,742	----	----	1,377,526

[1] Preliminary.   *Source: Crop Reporting Board, U.S. Department of Agriculture (CRB-USDA)*

WHEAT

Production of All Spring Wheat in the United States, by State   In Thousands of Bushels

	-------------------- Durum Wheat -------------------						------------------------------ Other Spring Wheat ------------------------------							
Year	Arizona	Cali-fornia	Montana	North Dakota	South Dakota	Total	Idaho	Minne-sota	Montana	North Dakota	Oregon	South Dakota	Wash-ington	Total
2005	7,900	6,555	16,380	68,250	260	101,105	32,400	70,930	81,600	224,400	5,980	67,600	18,700	504,456
2006	7,400	6,435	6,715	31,500	90	53,475	34,310	77,550	63,800	212,350	5,750	42,600	21,250	460,480
2007	8,364	8,000	11,400	43,070	175	72,224	30,600	79,200	55,200	234,000	5,520	52,260	20,562	479,623
2008	14,602	15,225	10,830	42,250	190	83,827	37,440	100,800	59,520	246,400	7,650	68,400	22,470	548,004
2009	12,400	17,000	16,585	61,230	207	109,042	40,810	82,150	70,500	289,800	6,858	64,680	26,325	584,411
2010	9,085	10,450	18,020	66,750	555	106,080	47,970	85,250	103,740	277,200	9,316	59,220	29,900	615,975
2011	7,979	12,535	10,780	18,233	196	50,482	52,080	69,000	74,400	167,750	10,990	37,820	38,130	455,188
2012	9,880	12,720	15,260	42,720	115	81,501	37,240	74,670	95,700	256,500	5,766	41,410	27,775	540,419
2013	7,548	4,900	15,225	29,453	168	57,976	39,270	66,120	104,710	235,290	5,544	51,260	30,300	534,101
2014[1]	7,992	2,625	13,330	28,223	180	53,087	34,580	64,900	104,300	291,650	3,744	71,680	23,180	595,038

[1] Preliminary.   Source: Crop Reporting Board, U.S. Department of Agriculture (CRB-USDA)

Stocks of All Wheat in the United States   In Millions of Bushels

	------------------- On Farms -------------------				------------------- Off Farms -------------------				------------------- Total Stocks -------------------			
Year	Mar. 1	June 1	Sept. 1	Dec. 1	Mar. 1	June 1	Sept. 1	Dec. 1	Mar. 1	June 1	Sept. 1	Dec. 1
2005	304.7	161.3	721.4	513.0	679.7	378.8	1,201.9	916.4	984.4	540.1	1,923.3	1,429.4
2006	256.0	111.0	572.0	403.3	716.2	460.2	1,178.5	911.4	972.2	571.2	1,750.5	1,314.7
2007	192.5	73.2	495.0	289.5	664.3	383.0	1,221.9	842.4	856.7	456.2	1,716.9	1,131.9
2008	92.0	25.6	635.7	454.0	617.3	280.2	1,222.2	968.1	709.3	305.8	1,857.9	1,422.1
2009	280.4	140.7	836.0	558.8	759.7	515.8	1,373.3	1,222.9	1,040.1	656.5	2,209.3	1,781.7
2010	348.3	209.9	812.1	550.0	1,008.1	765.7	1,637.5	1,382.9	1,356.4	975.6	2,449.6	1,932.9
2011	288.0	130.9	633.0	405.4	1,137.3	731.3	1,513.7	1,257.3	1,425.3	862.2	2,146.7	1,662.7
2012	217.1	112.0	572.9	399.5	982.2	630.6	1,531.8	1,271.1	1,199.3	742.6	2,104.7	1,670.6
2013	237.0	120.2	555.0	398.4	997.9	597.7	1,314.6	1,076.5	1,234.8	717.9	1,869.6	1,474.9
2014[1]	237.5	97.0	713.5	472.6	819.4	493.3	1,193.8	1,052.0	1,057.0	590.3	1,907.2	1,524.6

[1] Preliminary.   Source: National Agricultural Statistics Service, U.S. Department of Agriculture (NASS-USDA)

Stocks of Durum Wheat in the United States   In Millions of Bushels

	------------------- On Farms -------------------				------------------- Off Farms -------------------				------------------- Total Stocks -------------------			
Year	Mar. 1	June 1	Sept. 1	Dec. 1	Mar. 1	June 1	Sept. 1	Dec. 1	Mar. 1	June 1	Sept. 1	Dec. 1
2005	35.2	24.1	70.2	57.7	20.5	13.5	31.1	24.4	55.7	37.6	101.3	82.1
2006	39.7	23.1	31.5	25.9	25.8	17.3	31.5	25.4	65.5	40.4	63.0	51.3
2007	17.1	9.0	34.7	17.6	21.7	12.4	35.8	22.2	38.8	21.4	70.5	39.8
2008	8.1	2.4	36.2	26.1	17.1	5.9	22.6	18.4	25.2	8.3	58.8	44.5
2009	18.7	13.3	74.1	50.6	13.6	11.8	27.7	25.2	32.3	25.1	101.8	75.8
2010	34.3	23.9	71.2	46.6	21.2	10.7	28.9	21.7	55.5	34.6	100.1	68.3
2011	35.7	22.1	34.9	24.5	20.7	13.4	28.8	24.0	56.4	35.5	63.7	48.5
2012	17.9	15.2	43.6	36.7	17.9	10.3	24.8	24.3	35.8	25.5	68.4	61.0
2013	21.4	13.6	42.9	32.8	21.1	9.5	23.5	21.2	42.5	23.1	66.4	54.0
2014[1]	20.7	12.8	38.7	22.0	17.4	8.7	19.1	20.0	38.1	21.5	57.8	42.0

[1] Preliminary.   Source: National Agricultural Statistics Service, U.S. Department of Agriculture (NASS-USDA)

Wheat Supply and Distribution in Canada, Australia and Argentina   In Millions of Metric Tons

	------ Canada (Year Beginning Aug. 1) ------					------ Australia (Year Beginning Oct. 1) ------					------ Argentina (Year Beginning Dec. 1) ------				
	--------- Supply ---------			-Disappearance -		--------- Supply ---------			-Disappearance -		--------- Supply ---------			-Disappearance -	
Crop Year	Stocks Aug. 1	New Crop	Total Supply	Domestic	Exports[3]	Stocks Oct. 1	New Crop	Total Supply	Domestic	Exports[3]	Stocks Dec. 1	New Crop	Total Supply	Domestic	Exports[3]
2005-06	7.9	25.7	33.6	8.2	16.0	6.7	25.2	31.9	6.6	16.0	1.3	13.8	15.1	5.1	9.6
2006-07	9.7	25.3	35.0	9.0	19.4	9.4	10.8	20.2	7.4	8.7	0.4	16.3	16.7	5.4	10.7
2007-08	6.9	20.1	27.0	6.9	16.1	4.2	13.6	17.8	6.6	7.5	0.6	18.6	19.2	5.7	11.2
2008-09	4.4	28.6	33.0	7.8	18.9	3.7	21.4	25.1	7.4	14.7	2.4	11.0	13.4	5.3	6.8
2009-10	6.6	27.0	33.6	7.2	19.0	3.1	21.8	24.9	5.2	14.8	1.3	12.0	13.3	5.8	5.1
2010-11	7.7	23.3	31.0	7.6	16.6	5.1	27.4	32.5	5.8	18.6	2.3	17.2	19.5	6.0	9.5
2011-12	7.4	25.3	32.7	9.9	17.4	8.2	29.9	38.1	6.5	24.7	4.1	15.5	19.6	6.0	12.9
2012-13	5.9	27.2	33.1	9.6	19.0	7.1	22.9	30.0	6.7	18.7	0.7	9.3	10.0	6.2	3.6
2013-14[1]	5.1	37.5	42.6	10.0	23.2	4.7	27.0	31.7	7.0	19.0	0.3	10.5	10.8	6.1	2.2
2014-15[2]	9.8	27.5	37.3	9.8	22.0	5.9	25.0	30.9	6.8	18.5	2.5	12.0	14.5	6.2	6.0

[1] Preliminary.   [2] Forecast.   [3] Including flour.   Source: Foreign Agricultural Service, U.S. Department of Agriculture (FAS-USDA)

Quarterly Supply and Disappearance of Wheat in the United States   In Millions of Bushels

Crop Year Beginning June 1	Supply				Disappearance					Total Disappearance	Ending Stocks		
					Domestic Use								
	Beginning Stocks	Production	Imports³	Total Supply	Food	Seed	Feed & Residual	Total	Exports³		Gov't Owned⁴	Privately Owned⁵	Total Stocks
2004-05	546.4	2,158.2	70.6	2,775.2	904.6	78.9	188.9	1,172.4	1,062.9	2,235.3	54.0	486.1	540.1
June-Aug.	546.4	2,158.2	17.4	2,722.1	227.5	4.1	265.2	496.8	286.8	783.6	61.9	1,876.5	1,938.4
Sept.-Nov.	1,938.4	----	18.7	1,957.1	235.6	48.2	-57.0	226.8	300.0	526.8	61.7	1,369.0	1,430.3
Dec.-Feb.	1,430.3	----	17.8	1,448.1	216.3	2.4	7.7	226.4	237.4	463.8	55.9	928.5	984.4
Mar.-May	984.4	----	16.7	1,001.1	225.2	24.2	-27.0	222.4	238.7	461.1	54.5	485.6	540.1
2005-06	2,105.0	2,104.7	81.0	4,290.7	914.0	78.0	154.0	1,146.0	1,009.0	2,155.0			571.0
June-Aug.	540.1	2,104.7	19.0	2,663.0	231.0	2.0	263.0	496.0	244.0	740.0	48.3	1,875.0	1,923.0
Sept.-Nov.	1,923.0	----	20.0	1,944.0	238.0	51.0	-61.0	228.0	286.0	514.0	44.1	1,385.4	1,429.0
Dec.-Feb.	1,429.0	----	20.0	1,450.0	219.0	1.0	1.0	221.0	257.0	478.0	----	----	972.0
Mar.-May	972.0	----	22.0	995.0	226.0	24.0	-49.0	201.0	222.0	423.0	----	----	571.0
2006-07	571.0	1,808.0	121.0	2,500.0	937.0	81.0	117.0	1,135.0	908.0	2,043.0	----	----	456.0
June-Aug.	571.0	1,808.0	26.0	2,406.0	235.0	2.0	205.0	442.0	214.0	656.0	----	----	1,751.0
Sept.-Nov.	1,751.0	----	29.0	1,780.0	243.0	56.0	-47.0	252.0	212.0	464.0	----	----	1,315.0
Dec.-Feb.	1,315.0	----	32.0	1,346.0	225.0	1.0	28.0	254.0	235.0	489.0	----	----	857.0
Mar.-May	857.0	----	34.0	891.0	234.0	22.0	-69.0	187.0	247.0	434.0	----	----	456.0
2007-08	456.0	2,051.0	112.0	2,619.0	947.0	88.0	16.0	1,051.0	1,262.0	2,313.0	----	----	306.0
June-Aug.	456.0	2,051.0	30.0	2,538.0	240.0	1.0	257.0	498.0	323.0	821.0	----	----	1,717.0
Sept.-Nov.	1,717.0	----	21.0	1,738.0	245.0	60.0	-120.0	185.0	421.0	606.0	----	----	1,132.0
Dec.-Feb.	1,132.0	----	24.0	1,156.0	227.0	2.0	-42.0	187.0	261.0	448.0	----	----	709.0
Mar.-May	709.0	----	37.0	746.0	235.0	25.0	-79.0	181.0	257.0	438.0	----	----	306.0
2008-09	306.0	2,499.0	127.0	2,932.0	924.0	75.0	256.0	1,255.0	1,016.0	2,271.0	----	----	657.0
June-Aug.	306.0	2,499.0	28.0	2,833.0	236.0	2.0	393.0	631.0	345.0	976.0	----	----	1,858.0
Sept.-Nov.	1,858.0	----	28.0	1,886.0	238.0	54.0	-124.0	168.0	295.0	463.0	----	----	1,422.0
Dec.-Feb.	1,422.0	----	36.0	1,459.0	219.0	1.0	28.0	248.0	170.0	418.0	----	----	1,040.0
Mar.-May	1,040.0	----	35.0	1,075.0	231.0	18.0	-41.0	208.0	206.0	414.0	----	----	657.0
2009-10	657.0	2,218.0	119.0	2,994.0	917.0	69.0	150.0	1,136.0	881.0	2,017.0	----	----	976.0
June-Aug.	657.0	2,218.0	28.0	2,902.0	231.0	1.0	261.0	493.0	200.0	693.0	----	----	2,209.0
Sept.-Nov.	2,209.0	----	24.0	2,234.0	237.0	46.0	-83.0	200.0	252.0	452.0	----	----	1,782.0
Dec.-Feb.	1,782.0	----	30.0	1,812.0	221.0	1.0	31.0	253.0	202.0	455.0	----	----	1,356.0
Mar.-May	1,356.0	----	37.0	1,393.0	228.0	21.0	-59.0	190.0	227.0	417.0	----	----	976.0
2010-11	976.0	2,207.0	96.0	3,279.0	930.0	80.0	170.0	1,180.0	1,288.0	2,468.0	----	----	862.0
June-Aug.	976.0	2,207.0	27.0	3,212.0	235.0	2.0	262.0	499.0	266.0	765.0	----	----	2,450.0
Sept.-Nov.	2,450.0	----	24.0	2,473.0	242.0	52.0	-63.0	231.0	310.0	541.0	----	----	1,933.0
Dec.-Feb.	1,933.0	----	23.0	1,956.0	221.0	1.0	-2.0	220.0	311.0	531.0	----	----	1,425.0
Mar.-May	1,425.0	----	22.0	1,448.0	233.0	73.0	-65.0	241.0	401.0	642.0	----	----	862.0
2011-12	862.0	1,999.3	112.1	2,968.2	941.4	75.6	157.4	1,174.4	1,051.2	2,225.6	----	----	742.6
June-Aug.	862.0	1,999.3	20.8	2,876.9	230.0	4.7	200.8	435.5	294.8	730.3	----	----	2,146.7
Sept.-Nov.	2,146.7	----	32.3	2,178.9	244.0	51.0	-16.4	278.5	237.9	516.4	----	----	1,662.5
Dec.-Feb.	1,662.5	----	30.1	1,692.6	230.9	1.4	43.5	275.9	217.4	493.3	----	----	1,199.3
Mar.-May	1,199.3	----	28.9	1,228.2	236.5	18.5	-70.5	184.5	301.1	485.6	----	----	742.6
2012-13	742.6	2,252.3	122.8	3,117.7	944.7	73.1	369.9	1,387.7	1,012.1	2,399.8	----	----	717.9
June-Aug.	742.6	2,252.3	25.1	3,020.0	237.6	1.4	402.2	641.2	263.7	904.9	----	----	2,115.1
Sept.-Nov.	2,115.1	----	32.8	2,147.9	246.6	55.4	-22.6	279.4	197.9	477.3	----	----	1,670.6
Dec.-Feb.	1,670.6	----	34.6	1,705.2	225.3	1.4	8.6	235.2	235.2	470.4	----	----	1,234.8
Mar.-May	1,234.8	----	30.3	1,265.1	235.2	15.0	-18.4	231.9	315.4	547.3	----	----	717.9
2013-14¹	717.9	2,135.0	168.6	3,021.5	952.2	77.0	225.7	1,254.9	1,176.3	2,431.2	----	----	590.3
June-Aug.	717.9	2,135.0	34.9	2,887.8	234.1	4.1	422.4	660.6	357.6	1,018.2	----	----	1,869.6
Sept.-Nov.	1,869.6	----	46.8	1,916.5	248.5	52.7	-169.6	131.6	310.1	441.6	----	----	1,474.9
Dec.-Feb.	1,474.9	----	40.3	1,515.1	230.4	1.9	-0.8	231.5	226.6	458.2	----	----	1,057.0
Mar.-May	1,057.0	----	46.5	1,103.5	239.2	18.3	-26.3	231.3	282.0	513.2	----	----	590.3
2014-15²	590.3	2,025.7	180.0	2,795.9	960.0	73.9	150.0	1,183.9	925.0	2,108.9	----	----	687.0
June-Aug.	590.3	2,025.7	43.2	2,659.2	237.6	3.3	256.1	497.0	255.0	751.9	----	----	1,907.2
Sept.-Nov.	1,907.2	----	32.5	1,939.7	252.8	48.5	-92.6	208.7	206.5	415.1	----	----	1,524.6

¹ Preliminary.   ² Forecast.   ³ Imports & exports include flour and other products expressed in wheat equivalent.   ⁴ Uncommitted, Government only.
⁵ Includes total loans.   ⁶ Includes alcoholic beverages.   *Source: Economic Research Service, U.S. Department of Agriculture (ERS-USDA)*

WHEAT

Exports of Wheat (Only)[2] from the United States   In Thousands of Bushels

Year	June	July	Aug.	Sept.	Oct.	Nov.	Dec.	Jan.	Feb.	Mar.	Apr.	May	Total
2005-06	64,553	90,760	83,173	102,761	103,423	77,164	91,531	84,659	71,175	74,420	69,050	72,209	984,878
2006-07	63,115	67,846	78,225	76,431	70,752	60,595	72,226	84,629	75,412	76,512	75,130	85,565	886,438
2007-08	73,088	80,285	153,223	149,168	158,064	116,504	82,343	87,539	84,414	92,251	82,781	79,725	1,239,385
2008-09	77,176	119,492	141,173	117,332	93,462	75,311	54,389	56,634	55,825	75,580	61,048	65,884	993,306
2009-10	63,851	58,627	68,321	100,213	77,627	68,117	54,438	65,060	76,522	73,780	76,958	68,473	851,987
2010-11	74,400	80,546	104,145	130,529	86,525	92,159	85,582	108,741	105,409	120,873	146,979	126,991	1,262,879
2011-12	107,349	83,260	100,294	99,523	71,073	61,287	72,639	71,447	68,957	86,770	103,778	102,576	1,028,953
2012-13	89,731	70,378	97,249	92,915	51,751	46,512	62,763	76,874	91,025	101,785	108,878	96,400	986,261
2013-14	98,174	113,731	141,038	151,309	94,466	63,040	74,469	77,203	70,973	78,911	103,942	93,715	1,160,971
2014-15[1]	76,739	72,407	100,573	94,279	59,095	47,047	59,842	54,751					847,100

[1] Preliminary.   [2] Grains.   *Source: Economic Research Service, U.S. Department of Agriculture (ERS-USDA)*

Wheat Government Loan Program Data in the United States   Loan Rates--Cents Per Bushel

Crop Year Beginning June 1	National Average[3]	Target Rate[4]	Corn Belt (Soft Red Winter)	Central & Southern Plains (Hard Winter)	Northern Plains (Spring & Durum)	Pacific Northwest (White)	Placed Under Loan	% of Production	Acquired by CCC Under Program	Total Stocks May 31	CCC Stocks May 31	CCC Loans	Farmer-Owned Reserve	"Free"
										In Millions of Bushels				
2002-03	280	386	NA	NA	NA	NA	120	7.5	2	491	66	55	0	425
2003-04	280	386	----	----	----	----	186	7.9	3	546	61	37	0	485
2004-05	275	392	----	----	----	----	178	8.3	10	540	55	58	0	486
2005-06	275	392	----	----	----	----	170	8.1	1	571	43	NA	0	528
2006-07	275	392	----	----	----	----	94	5.2	0	456	41	NA	0	437
2007-08	275	392	----	----	----	----	36	1.8	0	306	0	NA	NA	NA
2008-09	275	392	----	----	----	----	84	3.4	0	657	0	NA	NA	NA
2009-10	275	392	----	----	----	----	103	4.6	0	976	0	----	----	----
2010-11[1]	294	417	----	----	----	----	67	3.0	0	818	0	----	----	----
2011-12[2]	294	417	----	----	----	----	36	1.8	0		0	----	----	----

[1] Preliminary.   [2] Estimate.   [3] The national average loan rate at the farm as a percentage of the parity-priced wheat at the beginning of the marketing year.   [4] 1996-97 through 2001-02 marketing year, target prices not applicable.   NA = Not avaliable.
Source: Agricultural Marketing Service, U.S. Department of Agriculture (AMS-USDA)

United States Wheat and Wheat Flour Imports and Exports   In Thousands of Bushels

Crop Year Beginning June 1	Suitable for Milling	Wheat Unfit for Human Consump.	Grain	Flour & Products[2]	Total	P.L . 480	Sec. 416	Aid[3]	Total concessional	Export Credit	Export Enhancement Program	Total U.S. Wheat
			-- Wheat Equivalent --					In Thousands of Metric Tons				
2005-06	54,073	----	54,073	27,281	81,354	969	17	----	1,191	1,052	0	25,005
2006-07	92,928	----	92,928	21,752	121,870	767	0	----	961	1,008	0	29,636
2007-08	85,806	----	85,806	26,702	112,631	734	12	----	841	1,360	0	32,847
2008-09	101,964	----	101,964	22,356	126,970	722	12	----	965	2,691	0	22,545
2009-10	93,003	----	93,003	29,217	118,591	793	16	----	901	2,078	0	25,762
2010-11	69,053	----	69,053	23,434	96,919							
2011-12[1]	54,943	----	54,943	13,086	73,825							

[1] Preliminary.   [2] Includes macaroni, semolina & similar products.   [3] Shipment mostly under the Commodity Import Program, financed with foreign aid funds.   NA = Not available.   *Source: Economic Research Service, U.S. Department of Agriculture (ERS-USDA)*

Comparative Average Cash Wheat Prices   In Dollars Per Bushel

Crop Year June to May	Received by U.S. Farmers	No. 2 Soft Red Winter, Chicago	No 1 Hard Red Ordinary Protein, Kansas City	No 2 Soft Red Winter, St. Louis	No 1 Dark Northern Spring 14%	No 1 Hard Amber Durum	No 1 Soft White , Portland, Oregon	No 2 Western White Pacific Northwest	No 2 Soft White, Toledo	Australian Standard White	Canada Vancouver No 1 CWRS 13 1/2 %	Argentina F.O.B. B.A.	U.S. Gulf No. 2 Hard Winter	Rotterdam C.I.F. U.S. No 2 Hard Winter
2007-08	6.48	7.71	9.11	7.43	10.81	13.08	9.97	8.68	8.06	294	447	298	340	321
2008-09	6.78	5.04	7.03	4.86	8.53	----	6.25	6.62	4.98	217	350	244	292	----
2009-10	4.87	4.39	5.24	3.88	6.96	----	4.91	5.00	4.31	209	280	227	205	----
2010-11	5.70	6.60	7.55	7.01	9.93	----	6.77	4.63	6.62	273	394	302	284	----
2011-12	7.24	6.36	7.81	6.59	10.13	----	6.69	----	6.50	249	416	271	290	----
2012-13	7.77	7.82	8.95	7.91	9.61	----	8.34	----	7.71	324	359	330	332	----
2013-14	6.87	6.52	8.34	6.71	8.85	----	7.26	----	6.38	281	331	327	309	----
2014-15[1]	5.90-6.30	5.42	7.28	5.44	8.22	----	6.81	----	5.15		296	264		----

[1] Preliminary.   [2] Calendar year.   NA = Not available.   *Source: Economic Research Service, U.S. Department of Agriculture (ERS-USDA)*

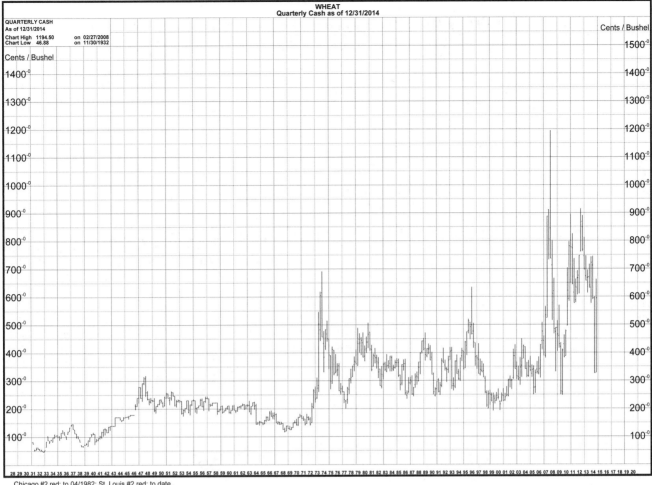

WHEAT
Quarterly Cash as of 12/31/2014

QUARTERLY CASH
As of 12/31/2014

Chart High 1194.50 on 02/27/2008
Chart Low 46.88 on 11/30/1932

Cents / Bushel

Chicago #2 red: to 04/1982; St. Louis #2 red: to date.

Average Price of No. 2 Soft Red Winter (30 Days) Wheat in Chicago   In Dollars Per Bushel

Year	June	July	Aug.	Sept.	Oct.	Nov.	Dec.	Jan.	Feb.	Mar.	Apr.	May	Average
2005-06	3.09	3.22	3.04	2.93	2.99	2.83	2.98	3.11	3.34	3.29	3.21	3.54	3.13
2006-07	3.26	3.43	3.20	3.39	4.40	4.35	4.49	4.19	4.20	4.07	4.25	4.50	3.98
2007-08	5.25	5.52	6.24	7.98	7.89	7.57	8.69	8.55	10.12	10.40	7.72	6.59	7.71
2008-09	7.20	6.87	6.77	5.45	3.76	3.68	4.01	4.62	4.28	4.40	4.43	4.96	5.04
2009-10	4.96	4.45	4.18	3.70	4.01	4.53	4.67	4.55	4.37	4.38	4.43	4.49	4.39
2010-11	4.26	5.38	6.29	6.43	5.97	6.20	7.20	7.55	7.99	6.95	7.56	7.44	6.60
2011-12	6.71	6.54	7.03	6.40	5.96	6.09	5.94	6.23	6.44	6.44	6.24	6.29	6.36
2012-13	6.56	8.57	8.70	8.62	8.49	8.58	8.03	7.69	7.40	7.18	6.97	7.01	7.82
2013-14	6.94	6.60	6.26	6.41	6.77	6.46	6.23	5.86	6.08	6.91	6.91	6.86	6.52
2014-15[1]	5.87	5.30	5.34	4.82	5.04	5.43	6.21	5.56	5.19				5.42

[1] Preliminary.   *Source: Economic Research Service, U.S. Department of Agriculture (ERS-USDA)*

Average Price Received by Farmers for All Wheat in the United States   In Dollars Per Bushel

Year	June	July	Aug.	Sept.	Oct.	Nov.	Dec.	Jan.	Feb.	Mar.	Apr.	May	Average
2005-06	3.23	3.20	3.24	3.36	3.43	3.45	3.53	3.52	3.66	3.79	3.81	4.09	3.53
2006-07	3.98	3.88	3.91	4.06	4.59	4.59	4.52	4.53	4.71	4.75	4.89	4.88	4.44
2007-08	5.03	5.17	5.64	6.76	7.65	7.39	7.71	7.96	10.10	10.50	10.10	8.87	7.74
2008-09	7.62	7.15	7.61	7.43	6.65	6.29	5.95	6.20	5.79	5.71	5.75	5.84	6.50
2009-10	5.72	5.17	4.85	4.48	4.47	4.79	4.87	4.90	4.73	4.70	4.41	4.33	4.79
2010-11	4.16	4.49	5.44	5.79	5.88	6.10	6.44	6.69	7.42	7.55	8.01	8.16	6.34
2011-12	7.41	7.10	7.59	7.54	7.27	7.30	7.20	7.05	7.10	7.20	7.11	6.67	7.21
2012-13	6.70	7.89	8.04	8.27	8.38	8.47	8.30	8.12	7.97	7.79	7.71	7.68	7.94
2013-14	7.37	6.95	6.88	6.80	6.94	6.85	6.73	6.65	6.49	6.75	6.82	7.08	6.86
2014-15[1]	6.49	6.16	5.98	5.74	5.71	6.05	6.11	6.14					6.05

[1] Preliminary.   *Source: Economic Research Service, U.S. Department of Agriculture (ERS-USDA)*

WHEAT

Average Price of No. 1 Hard Red Winter (Ordinary Protein) Wheat in Kansas City   In Dollars Per Bushel

Year	June	July	Aug.	Sept.	Oct.	Nov.	Dec.	Jan.	Feb.	Mar.	Apr.	May	Average
2005-06	3.87	3.83	3.96	4.30	4.57	4.53	4.52	4.46	4.72	4.62	4.86	5.21	4.45
2006-07	5.25	5.27	5.00	5.16	5.62	5.61	5.49	5.29	5.39	5.40	5.52	5.54	5.38
2007-08	6.22	6.28	6.84	8.52	8.89	8.62	9.80	9.97	12.28	12.29	10.29	9.33	9.11
2008-09	9.19	8.68	8.64	7.52	6.17	6.21	6.06	6.59	6.21	6.23	6.10	6.70	7.03
2009-10	6.63	5.58	5.15	4.56	5.06	5.58	5.37	5.24	5.10	4.99	4.86	4.78	5.24
2010-11	4.50	5.26	6.76	7.01	7.04	7.13	8.04	8.54	9.23	8.44	9.28	9.38	7.55
2011-12	8.61	8.03	8.63	8.30	7.77	7.74	7.46	7.69	7.59	7.52	7.11	7.24	7.81
2012-13	7.61	9.13	9.43	9.56	9.62	9.73	9.36	9.09	8.70	8.35	8.30	8.53	8.95
2013-14	8.32	8.14	8.12	8.00	8.70	8.44	8.03	7.56	8.04	8.87	8.81	9.01	8.34
2014-15[1]	8.23	7.61	7.33	7.11	7.35	7.20	7.54	6.75	6.44				7.28

[1] Preliminary.   *Source: Economic Research Service, U.S. Department of Agriculture (ERS-USDA)*

Average Price of No. 1 Dark Northern Spring (14% Protein) Wheat in Minneapolis   In Dollars Per Bushel

Year	June	July	Aug.	Sept.	Oct.	Nov.	Dec.	Jan.	Feb.	Mar.	Apr.	May	Average
2005-06	5.03	4.71	4.83	4.80	5.11	5.11	5.28	4.87	4.90	4.83	4.94	5.31	4.98
2006-07	5.59	5.65	4.94	4.86	5.36	5.55	5.44	5.27	5.40	5.55	5.65	5.64	5.41
2007-08	6.19	6.60	6.88	8.20	9.27	9.39	11.06	12.59	19.00	15.60	12.93	12.06	10.81
2008-09	11.46	11.46	9.87	8.51	7.37	6.80	7.78	8.02	7.64	7.57	7.72	8.13	8.53
2009-10	7.96	6.82	6.17	6.30	6.36	7.29	6.79	7.39	7.57	7.48	6.88	6.55	6.96
2010-11	6.90	6.89	7.92	8.35	8.61	8.67	10.14	11.24	12.22	12.36	12.76	13.04	9.93
2011-12	12.97	11.16	10.21	9.80	9.80	10.61	9.69	9.43	9.53	9.62	9.63	9.11	10.13
2012-13	9.31	10.12	9.71	9.82	10.17	10.15	9.83	9.43	9.33	9.17	9.11	9.15	9.61
2013-14	9.18	8.57	8.37	8.21	8.78	8.39	8.64	9.32	9.03	9.64	8.73	9.32	8.85
2014-15[1]	9.00	8.66	8.17	8.47	8.11	8.50	8.22	7.37	7.51				8.22

[1] Preliminary.   *Source: Economic Research Service, U.S. Department of Agriculture (ERS-USDA)*

Average Farm Prices of Winter Wheat in the United States   In Dollars Per Bushel

Year	June	July	Aug.	Sept.	Oct.	Nov.	Dec.	Jan.	Feb.	Mar.	Apr.	May	Average
2007-08	5.00	5.13	5.66	6.89	7.55	7.31	7.70	7.75	9.17	9.96	9.62	8.17	7.49
2008-09	7.51	7.10	7.30	6.99	6.03	5.65	5.40	5.70	5.26	5.27	5.26	5.52	6.08
2009-10	5.47	5.02	4.67	4.20	4.27	4.60	4.68	4.57	4.53	4.45	4.19	4.21	4.57
2010-11	4.05	4.47	5.47	5.76	5.83	6.02	6.40	6.35	7.03	7.02	7.37	7.80	6.13
2011-12	7.13	6.77	7.27	7.00	6.53	6.44	6.41	6.57	6.68	6.70	6.47	6.42	6.70
2012-13	6.55	7.76	7.92	8.25	8.33	8.38	8.15	8.01	7.85	7.63	7.52	7.49	7.82
2013-14	7.18	6.85	6.81	6.80	7.07	6.96	6.84	6.72	6.57	6.93	7.08	7.26	6.92
2014-15[1]	6.34	6.00	5.90	5.71	5.66	5.86	6.15	6.02					5.96

[1] Preliminary.   *Source: Economic Research Service, U.S. Department of Agriculture (ERS-USDA)*

Average Farm Prices of Durum Wheat in the United States   In Dollars Per Bushel

Year	June	July	Aug.	Sept.	Oct.	Nov.	Dec.	Jan.	Feb.	Mar.	Apr.	May	Average
2007-08	5.49	6.69	7.00	8.98	11.70	11.70	11.50	13.10	14.10	15.40	14.30	13.50	11.12
2008-09	8.48	11.70	12.60	11.90	11.50	8.93	8.40	8.26	7.53	7.40	7.18	7.05	9.24
2009-10	6.83	7.57	4.95	4.86	4.59	4.91	4.94	4.94	4.61	4.57	4.17	4.28	5.10
2010-11	4.58	4.44	4.45	4.89	5.07	5.55	5.71	7.09	8.45	8.09	8.60	7.86	6.23
2011-12	9.18	10.20	10.20	10.80	9.60	10.30	10.30	8.84	8.98	8.39	9.22	8.95	9.58
2012-13	8.31	8.67	7.76	7.77	7.61	8.11	8.31	8.24	8.19	8.12	8.01	8.06	8.10
2013-14	8.51	8.32	7.73	7.84	7.03	6.72	6.90	7.01	6.46	6.71	6.82	7.21	7.27
2014-15[1]	7.91	8.13	8.03	8.25	8.52	11.00	10.30	9.88					9.00

[1] Preliminary.   *Source: Economic Research Service, U.S. Department of Agriculture (ERS-USDA)*

Average Farm Prices of Other Spring Wheat in the United States   In Dollars Per Bushel

Year	June	July	Aug.	Sept.	Oct.	Nov.	Dec.	Jan.	Feb.	Mar.	Apr.	May	Average
2007-08	5.17	5.43	5.53	6.26	6.99	7.00	7.39	8.01	11.20	10.90	10.50	10.70	7.92
2008-09	10.10	9.52	8.18	7.76	7.20	7.10	6.89	7.02	6.61	6.50	6.49	6.76	7.51
2009-10	6.66	5.96	5.54	4.85	5.00	5.19	5.18	5.30	5.04	5.04	4.89	4.61	5.27
2010-11	4.58	4.71	5.47	5.97	6.14	6.35	6.60	7.14	7.68	8.07	8.67	8.85	6.69
2011-12	9.26	8.45	8.28	8.09	8.19	8.43	8.25	8.09	8.01	8.04	7.96	7.93	8.25
2012-13	7.78	8.39	8.27	8.38	8.56	8.65	8.48	8.34	8.11	7.95	7.90	7.84	8.22
2013-14	7.72	7.30	6.97	6.71	6.66	6.70	6.55	6.48	6.40	6.58	6.61	6.85	6.79
2014-15[1]	6.61	6.23	5.94	5.54	5.59	5.74	5.78	5.83					5.91

[1] Preliminary.   *Source: Economic Research Service, U.S. Department of Agriculture (ERS-USDA)*

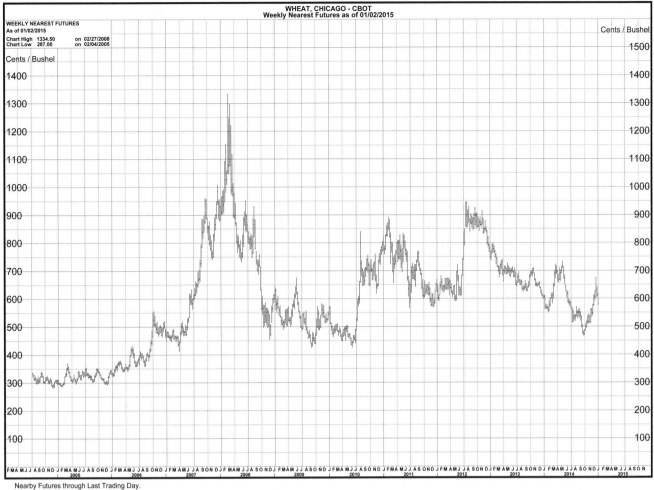

WHEAT, CHICAGO - CBOT
Weekly Nearest Futures as of 01/02/2015

WEEKLY NEAREST FUTURES
As of 01/02/2015

Chart High 1334.50 on 02/27/2008
Chart Low 287.00 on 02/04/2005

Nearby Futures through Last Trading Day.

Volume of Trading of Wheat Futures in Chicago   In Thousands of Contracts

Year	Jan.	Feb.	Mar.	Apr.	May	June	July	Aug.	Sept.	Oct.	Nov.	Dec.	Total
2005	613.0	1,053.6	827.8	937.5	694.7	1,088.0	690.3	1,024.8	660.0	717.4	1,164.5	642.4	10,114.1
2006	889.2	1,421.3	1,059.6	1,300.0	1,511.6	1,617.1	1,067.4	1,659.9	1,365.9	1,938.1	1,613.7	781.2	16,224.9
2007	1,346.2	1,506.0	1,148.0	2,082.5	1,170.5	2,343.7	1,514.4	2,111.3	1,320.3	1,648.4	2,109.7	1,281.8	19,582.7
2008	1,861.3	2,527.7	1,398.7	1,558.6	1,121.6	2,185.7	1,314.2	2,093.6	1,228.1	1,139.0	1,644.5	939.0	19,011.9
2009	986.9	1,505.7	1,213.8	1,747.8	1,300.1	2,350.9	1,298.1	1,926.4	1,040.0	1,451.2	1,952.5	904.2	17,677.5
2010	1,297.9	1,936.2	1,289.8	2,029.8	1,392.3	2,547.3	2,394.8	3,386.6	1,501.6	1,527.8	2,383.2	1,402.9	23,090.3
2011	1,651.7	2,601.4	2,131.8	2,475.9	2,095.9	2,857.2	1,699.9	2,301.0	1,470.5	1,594.4	2,217.0	1,186.8	24,283.3
2012	2,014.0	2,433.7	2,088.5	2,563.3	2,670.7	3,244.9	2,404.1	2,433.4	1,541.6	1,776.4	2,769.4	1,439.5	27,379.4
2013	2,006.5	2,679.0	1,937.3	2,888.9	1,872.7	2,488.8	1,872.6	2,487.0	1,323.5	1,741.4	2,312.0	1,235.7	24,845.5
2014	1,888.8	2,681.9	2,375.1	2,605.2	2,389.1	3,028.9	2,210.8	3,064.6	1,904.6	2,250.7	2,387.5	1,962.5	28,749.8

Contract size = 5,000 bu.   *Source: CME Group; Chicago Board of Trade (CBT)*

Average Open Interest of Wheat Futures in Chicago   In Contracts

Year	Jan.	Feb.	Mar.	Apr.	May	June	July	Aug.	Sept.	Oct.	Nov.	Dec.
2005	201,297	223,108	218,153	208,149	207,407	223,014	239,219	256,533	276,741	297,319	301,838	298,523
2006	320,974	380,405	389,284	385,698	466,013	491,343	473,749	459,650	455,755	476,906	435,059	426,976
2007	453,140	441,924	405,383	377,162	363,297	401,509	411,971	404,940	379,871	407,669	414,509	423,198
2008	443,193	440,137	400,426	375,845	362,835	359,429	332,360	331,301	294,696	279,041	283,832	250,914
2009	268,513	297,116	291,831	309,503	302,088	335,407	317,024	327,977	320,607	331,678	355,414	353,774
2010	388,660	431,434	427,821	457,548	469,103	490,351	477,461	504,547	487,184	516,982	507,512	480,059
2011	515,137	538,874	482,060	482,702	457,289	451,965	428,043	427,516	411,468	426,188	411,485	376,671
2012	435,379	458,289	446,242	462,078	431,133	425,379	450,423	456,537	450,653	462,690	478,767	444,929
2013	463,359	470,154	457,785	436,052	410,871	414,728	404,821	399,943	358,054	366,743	394,264	396,016
2014	429,507	413,808	350,290	371,767	371,689	389,610	407,989	417,932	400,815	419,886	403,348	372,284

Contract size = 5,000 bu.   *Source: CME Group; Chicago Board of Trade (CBT)*

WHEAT

Commercial Stocks of Domestic Wheat[1] in the United States, on First of Month   In Millions of Bushels

Year	July	Aug.	Sept.	Oct.	Nov.	Dec.	Jan.	Feb.	Mar.	Apr.	May	June
2005-06	127.5	138.6	159.9	163.5	158.5	147.8	137.9	130.9	128.8	122.9	116.7	126.2
2006-07	154.3	172.5	190.3	170.9	166.8	159.5	154.7	146.7	136.3	129.3	116.6	99.2
2007-08	108.6	155.9	173.1	185.7	164.8	151.2	148.3	138.9	123.5	112.3	87.1	78.7
2008-09	98.2	150.4	176.4	214.5	212.9	179.7	167.8	135.9	126.1	124.9	119.5	115.0
2009-10	152.4	198.2	221.3	224.5	219.8	208.8	199.8	192.9	184.1	177.1	181.2	174.8
2010-11	229.8	237.4	247.3	242.3	235.4	229.5	222.6	234.4	223.0	201.9	190.8	178.1
2011-12	202.9	220.3	232.6	236.2	219.9	203.8	193.4	184.6	172.1	160.4	154.3	159.5
2012-13	202.0	211.9	225.2	219.2	212.6	206.3	206.3	195.1	181.5	169.9	144.9	128.1
2013-14	136.1	159.5	168.3	167.9	157.0	145.3	136.3	121.6	106.0	95.9	89.4	84.9
2014-15	89.2	113.5	----	----	----	----	----	----	----	----	----	----

This report was discontinued as of August 26, 2014.   [1] Domestic wheat in storage in public and private elevators in 39 markets and wheat afloat in vessels or barges at lake and seaboard ports, the first Saturday of the month.   *Source: Livestock Division, U.S. Department of Agriculture (LD-USDA)*

Stocks of Wheat Flour Held by Mills in the United States   In Thousands of Sacks--100 Pounds

Year	Jan. 1	April 1	July 1	Oct. 1	Year	Jan. 1	April 1	July 1	Oct. 1
2000	5,099	5,217	5,062	5,244	2006	5,211	5,775	5,576	5,587
2001	5,241	5,506	5,178	5,393	2007	5,919	5,884	5,587	6,188
2002	5,377	5,164	4,632	4,184	2008	6,374	6,219	6,157	6,719
2003	4,265	4,707	4,622	4,554	2009	5,831	5,561	5,607	5,430
2004	4,764	4,666	4,700	4,868	2010	5,407	5,637	5,596	5,517
2005	5,085	4,268	4,637	4,781	2011[1]	5,660	5,680	NA	NA

[1] Preliminary.   *Source: Bureau of the Census, U.S. Department of Commerce*

Average Producer Price Index of Wheat Flour (Spring[2])   June 1983 = 100

Year	Jan.	Feb.	Mar.	Apr.	May	June	July	Aug.	Sept.	Oct.	Nov.	Dec.	Average
2005	128.5	130.4	130.8	127.6	129.6	130.8	130.3	129.7	130.6	131.4	133.6	131.8	130.4
2006	130.2	134.2	132.8	139.4	142.2	144.2	148.5	141.6	144.2	151.9	151.8	147.5	142.4
2007	144.8	144.6	148.2	153.2	154.3	161.9	167.4	174.0	196.2	209.4	207.1	229.5	174.2
2008	239.6	278.9	293.6	262.8	248.1	246.5	228.5	229.5	214.6	194.8	190.8	181.5	234.1
2009	187.4	185.3	186.5	183.4	185.0	196.2	176.4	171.1	165.2	168.0	169.2	168.5	178.5
2010	167.2	168.1	163.7	162.5	167.1	161.7	169.7	190.5	190.6	190.1	200.5	204.9	178.1
2011	212.0	228.4	211.8	226.5	225.2	219.5	217.0	224.1	224.8	216.1	216.5	207.8	219.1
2012	206.8	216.4	219.2	219.7	214.3	214.4	231.2	226.5	232.0	232.4	236.4	233.8	223.6
2013	231.0	223.5	219.6	220.6	229.1	230.2	226.0	219.8	218.4	225.5	220.1	218.4	223.5
2014[1]	223.3	224.9	235.6	229.5	234.8	225.5	225.7	218.8	231.5	225.3	225.6	230.3	227.6

[1] Preliminary.   [2] Standard patent.   *Source: Bureau of Labor Statistics, U.S. Department of Commerce (BLS) (0212-0301)*

World Wheat Flour Production (Monthly Average)   In Thousands of Metric Tons

Year	Australia	France	Germany	Hungary	India	Japan	Kazakhstan	Korea, South	Mexico	Poland	Russia	Turkey	United Kingdom
2005	NA	464.5	437.9	67.3	205.4	384.6	197.6	153.1	239.1	207.3	765.8	299.0	368.0
2006	NA	472.3	444.2	62.2	180.3	384.6	207.9	154.2	243.8	211.9	776.1	290.4	366.0
2007	NA	478.2	437.7	59.7	181.1	387.8	224.6	146.7	243.8	124.3	547.7	309.8	NA
2008	NA	477.8	453.0	57.6	178.6	387.3	242.0	140.1	244.1	109.8	762.4	327.8	NA
2009	NA	449.5	429.1	59.2	195.1	379.9	255.0	150.7	249.3	143.2	774.1	349.7	NA
2010	NA	461.9	458.0	NA	212.5	401.0	NA	160.5	257.5	122.6	746.7	371.4	NA
2011	NA	443.8	446.7	NA	215.0	408.9	NA	159.9	266.8	118.3	753.5	399.1	NA
2012	NA	NA	453.5	NA	NA	404.8	NA	161.9	266.5	124.5	735.1	374.6	NA
2013[1]	NA	NA	465.3	NA	NA	403.1	NA	156.9	277.2	125.4	759.4	407.5	NA
2014[2]	NA	NA		NA	NA	398.9	NA	159.2	273.8	122.7	713.8	453.1	NA

[1] Preliminary.   [2] Estimate.   NA = Not available.   *Source: United Nations (UN)*

Production of Wheat Flour in the United States   In Millions of Sacks--100 Pounds Each

Year	July	Aug.	Sept.	Oct.	Nov.	Dec.	Jan.	Feb.	Mar.	Apr.	May	June	Total
2002-03	-----	102.1	-----	-----	100.3	-----	-----	95.9	-----	-----	96.8	-----	395.0
2003-04	-----	103.1	-----	-----	100.5	-----	-----	96.6	-----	-----	96.8	-----	396.9
2004-05	-----	100.9	-----	-----	99.7	-----	-----	95.9	-----	-----	96.2	-----	392.7
2005-06	-----	102.5	-----	-----	100.3	-----	-----	98.1	-----	-----	98.0	-----	398.9
2006-07	-----	104.9	-----	-----	102.5	-----	-----	100.3	-----	-----	102.5	-----	410.1
2007-08	-----	109.0	-----	-----	107.1	-----	-----	101.4	-----	-----	102.5	-----	420.0
2008-09	-----	108.2	-----	-----	104.2	-----	-----	100.7	-----	-----	102.9	-----	416.0
2009-10	-----	107.4	-----	-----	103.7	-----	-----	102.5	-----	-----	101.5	-----	415.1
2010-11	-----	108.6	-----	-----	104.8	-----	-----	100.0	-----	-----	100.3	-----	413.7
2011-12[1]	-----	NA	-----	-----	NA	-----	-----		-----	-----		-----	

[1] Preliminary.   Source: Bureau of the Census, U.S. Department of Commerce

United States Wheat Flour Exports (Grain Equivalent[2])   In Thousands of Bushels

Year	June	July	Aug.	Sept.	Oct.	Nov.	Dec.	Jan.	Feb.	Mar.	Apr.	May	Total
2005-06	859	686	839	720	840	871	734	572	620	937	1,188	966	9,832
2006-07	720	488	780	610	532	754	756	786	999	941	1,425	2,711	11,502
2007-08	1,467	1,220	1,277	1,135	1,758	2,515	1,960	1,224	1,544	1,328	1,114	1,126	17,668
2008-09	1,417	1,052	1,093	1,053	856	1,055	958	969	858	750	687	793	11,541
2009-10	865	1,515	1,704	1,473	2,255	1,609	1,194	1,231	1,722	2,525	1,652	1,993	19,738
2010-11	1,158	915	898	1,005	1,727	988	1,130	1,638	1,641	1,239	1,982	1,116	15,437
2011-12	1,078	874	1,774	1,101	1,002	1,182	725	766	727	1,152	780	1,528	12,689
2012-13	1,264	1,883	1,616	1,790	1,236	1,021	1,023	1,077	1,112	928	785	1,506	15,241
2013-14	1,623	986	846	1,014	1,219	987	1,164	953	803	953	1,143	1,138	12,829
2014-15[1]	955	1,213	1,035	1,299	1,404	1,436	1,094	1,088					14,286

[1] Preliminary.   [2] Includes meal, groats and durum.   Source: Economic Research Service, U.S. Department of Agriculture (ERS-USDA)

Supply and Distribution of Wheat Flour in the United States

Year	Wheat Ground -- 1,000 Bu. --	Milfeed Production - 1,000 Tons -	Flour Production[3]	Flour & Product Imports[2]	Total Supply	Exports Flour	Exports Products	Domestic Disap-pearance	Total Population July 1 -- Millions --	Per Capita Disap-pearance -- Pounds --
					In 1,000 Cwt.					
2004	876,047	6,764	393,925	10,726	404,651	5,152	4,662	394,837	293.3	134.6
2005	884,101	6,826	394,973	11,262	406,235	3,747	4,741	397,748	296.0	134.4
2006	894,527	6,916	403,391	11,740	415,131	3,412	5,867	405,852	298.8	135.8
2007	923,756	7,103	418,836	11,511	430,347	6,707	6,486	417,155	301.7	138.3
2008	907,979	6,753	416,283	10,822	427,105	4,925	6,179	416,001	304.5	136.6
2009	896,060	6,460	414,658	10,313	424,971	5,911	5,338	413,722	307.2	134.7
2010	901,843	6,480	417,396	11,206	428,602	7,004	3,930	417,667	309.8	134.8
2011	895,255	6,402	411,745	11,698	423,443	6,309	3,615	413,519	312.0	132.5
2012	921,853	6,637	420,365	11,991	432,356	5,997	3,894	422,465	314.3	134.4
2013[1]	678,351	4,679	423,214	12,276	435,490	5,276	3,755	426,459	316.5	134.7

[1] Preliminary.   [2] Commercial production of wheat flour, whole wheat, industrial and durum flour and farina reported by Bureau of Census.
Source: Economic Research Service, U.S. Department of Agriculture (ERS-USDA)

Wheat and Flour Price Relationships at Milling Centers in the United States   In Dollars

	At Kansas City				At Minneapolis			
	Cost of Wheat to Produce 100 lb.	Wholesale Price of		Total Products	Cost of Wheat to Produce 100 lb.	Wholesale Price of		Total Products
Year	Flour[1]	Bakery Flour 100 lb. Flour[2]	By-Products Obtained 100 lb. Flour[3]	Actual	Over Cost of Wheat	Flour[1]	Bakery Flour 100 lb. Flour[2]	By-Products Obtained 100 lb. Flour[3]	Actual	Over Cost of Wheat
2007-08	22.67	22.83	2.00	24.83	2.16	24.66	24.94	2.03	26.98	2.32
2008-09	17.14	17.60	2.18	19.77	2.63	19.44	19.18	2.15	21.33	1.89
2009-10	13.29	14.13	1.51	15.64	2.35	16.16	15.90	1.55	17.45	1.29
2010-11	18.97	18.78	2.35	21.13	2.16	22.97	21.56	2.40	23.96	.99
2011-12	19.21	18.76	2.96	21.71	2.51	23.10	21.87	3.11	24.98	1.88
2012-13	21.29	19.92	3.62	23.53	2.25	21.91	19.46	4.06	23.52	1.61
2013-14	19.20	19.23	2.70	21.93	2.73	20.17	19.17	2.79	21.96	1.78
2014-15	17.17	18.44	1.56	20.24	2.62	19.35	20.02	1.90	21.00	1.37
June-Aug.	17.62	18.68	1.56	20.24	2.62	19.63	19.10	1.90	21.00	1.37
Sept.-Nov.	16.71	18.20				19.06	20.93			

[1] Based on 73% extraction rate, cost of 2.28 bushels: At Kansas City, No. 1 hard winter 13% protein; and at Minneapolis, No. 1 dark northern spring, 14% protein.   [2] quoted as mid-month bakers' standard patent at Kansas City and spring standard patent at Minneapolis, bulk basis.   [3] Assumed 50-50 millfeed distribution between bran and shorts or middlings, bulk basis.   Source: Agricultural Marketing Service, U.S. Department of Agriculture

Wool

Wool is light, warm, absorbs moisture, and is resistant to fire. Wool is also used for insulation in houses, for carpets and furnishing, and for bedding. Sheep are sheared once a year and produce about 4.3 kg of "greasy" wool per year.

Greasy wool is wool that has not been washed or cleaned. Wool fineness is determined by fiber diameter, which is measured in microns (one millionth of a meter). Fine wool is softer, lightweight, and produces fine clothing. Merino sheep produce the finest wool.

Greasy Wool futures are traded on the Sydney Futures Exchange (SFE). The SFE futures contract calls for the delivery of merino combing wool.

Prices – Average monthly wool prices at U.S. mills in 2014 (through November) rose by +1.1% yr/yr to $4.22 per pound, below the 2011 record high of $5.16 per pound. The value of U.S. wool production in 2014 fell -0.7% to $38.949 million, below the 2011 record high of $48.925 million.

Supply – World production of wool has been falling in the past decade due to the increased use of polyester fabrics. Greasy wool world production in 2013, the latest reporting year for the data series, rose +1.6% yr/yr to 2.126 million metric tons. The world's largest producers of greasy wool in 2013 were China with 22.2% of world production, followed by Australia (17.0%), and New Zealand (7.8%).

U.S. wool production of 14,000 metric tons in 2013 (latest data) accounted for only 0.7% of world production. U.S. production of wool goods rose +16.5% yr/yr in 2011 (9 months annualized) to 6.4 million yards, up from the 2009 record low of 4.8 million yards. That was less than 3% of the record high of 222.5 million yards of wool goods production seen in 1969.

Trade – U.S. exports of domestic wool in 2013 fell -17.2% yr/yr to 10.000 million pounds. U.S. imports in 2012 (latest data) rose +20.4% to 4.563 million pounds.

World Production of Wool, Greasy   In Metric Tons

Year	Argentina	Australia	China	Kazakhstan	New Zealand	Pakistan	Romania	Russia	South Africa	United Kingdom	United States	Uruguay	World Total
2004	60,000	467,580	373,902	28,499	217,700	39,900	17,505	47,111	44,000	60,000	17,046	37,271	2,158,877
2005	63,696	465,700	393,172	30,444	215,500	40,000	17,600	48,033	44,000	60,000	16,865	42,009	2,209,767
2006	67,794	472,530	388,777	32,389	224,700	40,100	19,378	50,276	44,000	57,552	16,284	46,709	2,213,761
2007	68,743	450,220	363,470	34,200	217,900	40,600	21,025	52,022	42,000	62,000	15,750	46,709	2,192,715
2008	65,000	407,880	367,687	35,200	157,500	41,000	22,051	53,491	41,583	63,290	14,952	45,085	2,091,810
2009	65,000	370,600	364,002	36,400	185,800	41,540	22,352	54,658	43,320	65,393	13,770	41,057	2,065,570
2010	54,000	352,740	386,768	37,600	176,300	42,000	20,457	53,521	41,091	67,000	13,776	34,700	2,020,030
2011	48,000	368,330	443,981	38,500	163,700	42,500	19,026	52,575	41,197	67,500	13,286	34,700	2,089,520
2012[1]	45,000	362,100	437,119	38,437	165,000	43,000	18,600	55,253	39,904	68,000	14,000	36,000	2,093,600
2013[2]	45,000	360,520	471,111	37,638	165,000	43,600	18,600	54,651	39,904	68,000	14,000	36,000	2,126,900

[1] Preliminary.   [2] Estimate.   NA = Not avaliable.   *Source: Food and Agriculture Organization of the United Nations (FAO-UN)*

Average Wool Prices[1] --Australian-- 64's, Type 62, Duty Paid--U.S. Mills   In Cents Per Pound

Year	Jan.	Feb.	Mar.	Apr.	May	June	July	Aug.	Sept.	Oct.	Nov.	Dec.	Average
2007	352	344	355	367	381	380	378	359	364	393	405	400	373
2008	416	411	407	404	378	376	386	346	317	257	226	239	347
2009	229	223	230	250	287	295	295	318	339	379	386	392	302
2010	423	404	412	404	381	379	381	381	390	419	450	479	409
2011	517	544	586	637	643	742	713	649	610	562	450	624	606
2012	635	667	668	635	607	576	578	536	517	533	542	589	590
2013	587	595	584	538	517	509	471	467	479	545	537	489	527
2014	518	506	486	492	504	498	502	486	479	471	468	456	489

[1] Raw, clean basis.   *Source: Economic Research Service, U.S. Department of Agriculture (ERS-USDA)*

United States Imports[2] of Unmanufactured Wool (Clean Yield)   In Thousands of Pounds

Year	Jan.	Feb.	Mar.	Apr.	May	June	July	Aug.	Sept.	Oct.	Nov.	Dec.	Total
2007	1,250.1	1,097.3	1,429.4	1,417.0	1,356.5	1,302.7	1,141.2	892.5	846.7	1,252.0	1,328.0	956.3	14,269.7
2008	1,753.3	888.8	1,405.6	1,090.1	1,269.2	1,100.0	1,259.0	825.6	1,231.3	980.6	706.8	671.5	13,181.8
2009	1,061.7	982.9	1,043.0	803.5	536.2	745.1	833.8	847.4	447.4	798.8	626.0	627.0	9,352.8
2010	705.5	340.8	663.7	757.1	424.3	576.4	1,183.0	702.2	652.4	607.1	594.8	385.4	7,592.7
2011	857.1	451.2	564.5	681.2	698.5	503.3	1,046.5	1,306.0	1,590.9	1,168.2	635.5	404.2	9,907.1
2012	711.7	968.1	1,018.9	880.7	919.9	944.7	715.9	536.0	779.2	693.8	610.2	416.4	9,195.5
2013	457.3	251.4	358.7	819.7	909.1	891.0	796.5	889.8	437.1	919.6	458.2	430.8	7,619.2
2014[1]	597.6	379.1	348.3	583.8	868.5	553.2	707.7	718.8	544.0	967.5	403.5	420.5	7,092.5

[1] Preliminary.   [2] Data are imports for consumption.   *Source: Economic Research Service, U.S. Department of Agriculture (ERS-USDA)*

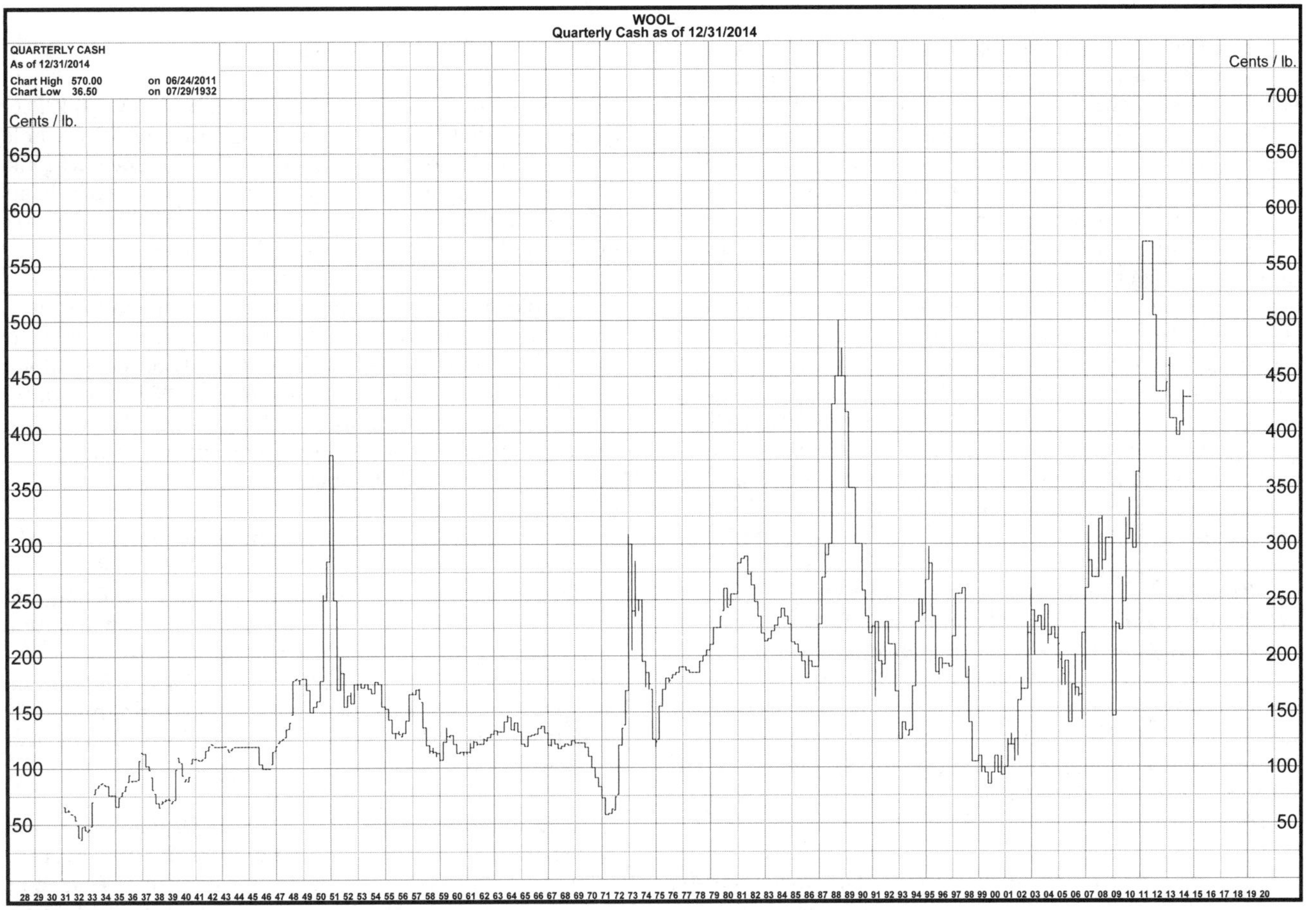
WOOL
Quarterly Cash as of 12/31/2014
QUARTERLY CASH
As of 12/31/2014
Chart High 570.00 on 06/24/2011
Chart Low 36.50 on 07/29/1932
Cents / lb.

Wool, 64's, Staple, Terr. Del: to date.

Salient Statistics of Wool in the United States

Year	Sheep & Lambs Shorn[4] -1,000's-	Weight per Fleece -In Lbs.-	Shorn Wool Production 1,000 Lbs.	Price per Lb.	Value of Production -$1,000-	Shorn Wool Support -- Cents Per Lb. --	Shorn Payment Rate	Raw Wool (Clean Content): Total Wool Production -- In Thousands of Pounds --	Domestic Production	Domestic Wool Exports	Dutiable Imports for Consumption[3] (48's & Finer)	Total New Supply[2]	Duty Free Raw Imports (Not Finer than 46's)	Mill Consumption: Apparel	Carpet
2007	4,657	7.50	34,723	87.0	30,242	100	40.0	34,723	18,334	17,077	5,245	15,527	9,025	NA	NA
2008	4,434	7.43	32,963	99.0	32,486	100	40.0	32,963	17,404	10,307	4,551	20,279	8,631	NA	NA
2009	4,195	7.40	38,060	79.0	24,337	100	40.0	30,860	16,294	10,207	3,306	15,439	6,046	NA	NA
2010	4,180	7.30	30,370	115.0	35,018	115	40.0	30,370	16,035	9,973	3,108	14,098	4,928	NA	NA
2011	4,030	7.30	29,290	167.0	48,925	115	40.0	29,290	15,465	9,349	3,791	14,601	4,694	NA	NA
2012	3,750	7.30	27,400	152.0	41,595	115	40.0	28,500	15,048	7,741	4,564	16,422	4,551	NA	NA
2013	3,700	7.30	26,990	145.0	39,209	115	40.0		15,000	10,000					
2014[1]	3,680	7.30	26,700	146.0	38,949										

[1] Preliminary. [2] Production minus exports plus imports; stocks not taken into consideration. [3] Apparel wool includes all dutiable wool; carpet wool includes all duty-free wool. [4] Includes sheep shorn at commercial feeding yards.
Source: Economic Research Service, U.S. Department of Agriculture (ERS-USDA)

Shorn Wool Prices In Dollars Per Pound

Year	US Farm Price Shorn Wool Greasy Basis[1] -- cents/Lb --	Australian Offering Price, Clean[2]: Grade 70's type 61 -- In Dollars Per Pound --	Grade 64's type 63	Grade 62's type 64	Grade 60/62's type 64A	Grade 58's-56's 433-34	Market Indicator[3] - Cents/Kg. -	Graded Territory Shorn Wool, Clean Basis[4]: 62's Staple 3"& up -- In Dollars Per Pound --	60's Staple 3"& up	58's Staple 3 1/4"& up	56's Staple 3 1/4"& up	54's Staple 3 1/2"& up
2006	68.0	3.17	2.65	2.75	2.47	2.26	NA	1.79	1.45	1.30	1.00	.94
2007	87.0	4.41	3.73	3.90	3.31	2.77	NA	2.65	2.24	1.82	1.32	1.04
2008	99.0	4.35	3.47	3.59	3.19	2.71	NA	3.09	2.45	2.25	1.82	1.20
2009	79.0	3.48	3.02	3.08	2.86	2.46	NA	2.27	1.89	1.73	1.36	1.34
2010	115.0	5.34	4.10	4.24	3.78	2.78	NA	3.27	2.54	2.15	1.89	1.48
2011	167.0	7.61	6.30	6.55	6.02	5.62	NA	4.25	4.36	4.07	3.40	NA
2012	152.0	5.77	5.90	5.98	5.78	5.66	NA	2.81	1.65	3.46	NA	NA
2013	145.0	5.59	5.34	5.39	5.24	3.69	1,073	4.23	3.36	3.01	2.17	NA

[1] Annual weighted average. [2] F.O.B. Australian Wool Corporation South Carolina warehouse in bond. [3] Index of prices of all wool sold in Australia for the crop year July-June. [4] Wool principally produced in Texas and the Rocky Mountain States.
Source: Economic Research Service, U.S. Department of Agriculture (ERS-USDA)

Zinc

Zinc (atomic symbol Zn) is a bluish-while metallic element that is the 24th most abundant element in the earth's crust. Zinc is never found in its pure state but rather in zinc oxide, zinc silicate, zinc carbonate, zinc sulfide, and in minerals such as zincite, hemimorphite, smithsonite, franklinite, and sphalerite. Zinc is utilized as a protective coating for other metals, such as iron and steel, in a process known as galvanizing. Zinc is used as an alloy with copper to make brass and also as an alloy with aluminum and magnesium. There are, however, a number of substitutes for zinc in chemicals, electronics, and pigments. For example, with aluminum, steel and plastics can substitute for galvanized sheets. Aluminum alloys can also replace brass. Zinc is used as the negative electrode in dry cell (flashlight) batteries and also in the zinc-mercuric-oxide battery cell, which is the round, flat battery typically used in watches, cameras, and other electronic devices. Zinc is also used in medicine as an antiseptic ointment.

Zinc futures and options are traded on the London Metals Exchange (LME). The LME zinc futures contract calls for the delivery of 25 metric tons of at least 99.995% purity zinc ingots (slabs and plates). The contract trades in terms of U.S. dollars per metric ton. Zinc first started trading on the LME in 1915. Futures are also traded on the Multi Commodity Exchange of India (MCX), the Shanghai Futures Exchange (SHFE), and the Singapore Exchange (SGX).

Prices – Zinc prices in 2014 rose +12.6% to a monthly average of 107.08 cents per pound, remaining below the 2006 record high of 158.44 cents per pound.

Supply – World smelter production of zinc in 2012 (latest data) fell -3.0% to 12.800 million metric tons, below last year's record high of 13.000 million metric tons. The world's largest producer of zinc in 2012 (latest data) was China with 37.7% of world smelter production, followed by Canada with 5.1%, Mexico with 2.5%, Australia with 3.9%, and Spain with 3.7%. China's production of 4.830 million metric tons in 2012 was almost ten times its production

level of 550,000 metric tons seen in 1990.

U.S. smelter production in 2012 rose by +5.2% to 261,000 metric tons. U.S. mine production of recoverable zinc in 2014 rose +4.2% yr/yr to 797,891 metric tons. U.S. production in 2014 of slab zinc on a primary basis rose +8.5% yr/yr to 115,000 metric tons, while secondary production fell -44.9% yr/yr to 70,000 metric tons.

Demand – U.S. consumption of slab zinc in 2014 rose by +5.3% yr/yr to 990,000 metric tons, up from the 29-year low of 893,000 metric tons seen in 2009. U.S. consumption of all classes of zinc fell by -16.4% yr/yr in 2007 (latest data) to 1.170 million metric tons, which was a new 16-year low. U.S. consumption of slab zinc by fabricators in 2014 rose by +3.5% yr/yr to 966,764 metric tons, a new record high.

The breakdown of consumption by industries for 2012 (latest data) showed that 85.0% of slab zinc consumption was for galvanizers, 6.2% for brass products, and the rest for other miscellaneous industries. The consumption breakdown by grades for 2012 showed that 44.4% for re-melt and other, 31.6% for high grade, 17.1% was for special high grade, and 6.9% for prime western. Within that grade breakdown, Prime Western consumption has fallen by over 80% since 2000.

Trade – The U.S. in 2014 relied on imports for 81% of its consumption of zinc, up sharply from the 35% average seen in the 1990s. U.S. imports for consumption of slab zinc rose by +13.6% yr/yr to 810,000 metric tons in 2014, while imports of zinc ore fell -51.1% yr/yr to 3,000 metric tons. The dollar value of U.S. zinc imports in 2012 (latest data) rose by +16.8% yr/yr to $1.684 billion, well below the 2007 record high $3.091 billion. The breakdown of imports in 2012 shows that most zinc is imported as blocks, pigs and slabs (655,000 metric tons); followed by dust, powder and flakes (28,200 metric tons); dross, ashes and fume (23,200 metric tons); waste and scrap (20,000 metric tons); ores (6,140 metric tons); and sheets, plates and other (2,920 metric tons).

Salient Statistics of Zinc in the United States   In Metric Tons

Year	Slab Zinc Production Primary	Secondary	Mine Production Recovered	Imports for Consumption Slab Zinc	Ore (Zinc Content)	Exports Slab Zinc	Ore (Zinc Content)	Consumption Slab Zinc	Consumed as Ore	All Classes[3]	Net Import Reliance As a % of Apparent Consump	High-Grade, Price -Cents/Lb.-
2005	195,000	156,000	748,000	700,000	156,000	784	786,000	1,080,000	----	1,290,000	67	67.11
2006	113,000	156,000	727,000	895,000	383,000	2,530	825,000	1,190,000	----	1,400,000	78	158.89
2007	121,000	157,000	803,000	758,000	271,000	8,070	816,000	1,040,000	----	1,170,000	73	154.40
2008	125,000	161,000	778,000	725,000	63,200	3,250	725,000	1,010,000	----	----	72	88.93
2009	94,000	109,000	736,000	686,000	74,200	2,960	785,000	893,000	----	----	77	77.91
2010	120,000	129,000	748,000	671,000	32,200	4,200	752,000	907,000	----	----	73	101.98
2011	110,000	138,000	769,000	716,000	26,700	19,000	653,000	939,000	----	----	74	106.24
2012	114,000	147,000	738,000	655,000	6,140	14,100	591,000	891,000	----	----	71	95.80
2013[1]	106,000	127,000	784,000	713,000	3,000	12,000	669,000	940,000	----	----	75	95.60
2014[2]	115,000	70,000	820,000	810,000	----	15,000	650,000	990,000	----	----	81	107.50

[1] Preliminary.   [2] Estimate.   [3] Based on apparent consumption of slab zinc plus zinc content of ores and concentrates and secondary materials used to make zinc dust and chemicals.   *Source: U.S. Geological Survey (USGS)*

World Smelter Production of Zinc[3]   In Thousands of Metric Tons

Year	Australia	Belgium	Canada	China	France	Germany	Italy	Japan	Kazakhstan	Mexico	Spain	United States	World Total
2003	613.0	244.0	761.2	2,320.0	268.0	388.1	123.0	686.1	316.7	320.4	519.0	351.0	10,100
2004	538.0	263.0	805.4	2,720.0	268.4	382.0	118.0	667.2	357.1	316.9	524.8	350.0	10,600
2005	463.3	257.0	724.0	2,780.0	267.5	344.9	121.0	675.2	364.8	327.2	506.2	351.0	10,300
2006	469.0	251.0	824.5	3,170.0	127.8	342.6	109.0	654.2	364.8	279.7	507.4	269.0	10,800
2007	508.0	241.3	802.1	3,740.0	129.1	294.7	109.0	638.7	358.2	321.9	494.1	278.0	11,400
2008	505.0	239.0	764.3	4,000.0	117.9	292.3	100.0	615.5	365.6	305.4	456.1	286.0	11,700
2009	531.0	14.0	685.5	4,280.0	161.0	153.0	100.0	540.6	327.9	385.4	500.8	203.0	11,400
2010	505.0	260.0	691.2	5,160.0	163.0	165.0	105.0	574.0	318.9	328.1	505.0	249.0	12,800
2011[1]	513.0	282.0	662.2	5,210.0	164.0	170.0	100.0	544.7	319.8	322.1	489.0	248.0	13,200
2012[2]	504.0	250.0	648.6	4,830.0	161.0	169.0	100.0	571.3	319.8	322.0	490.0	261.0	12,800

[1] Preliminary.   [2] Estimate.   [3] Secondary metal included.   *Source: U.S. Geological Survey (USGS)*

Consumption (Reported) of Slab Zinc in the United States, by Industries and Grades   In Metric Tons

Year	Total	By Industries Galvanizers	Brass Products	Zinc-Base Alloy[3]	Zinc Oxide	Other	By Grades Special High Grade	High Grade	Remelt and Other	Prime Western
2003	506,000	264,000	87,400	113,000	[4]	NA	310,000	60,000	27,600	109,000
2004	510,000	248,000	96,700	W	[4]	NA	321,000	58,800	33,600	96,200
2005	486,000	238,000	83,900	W	[4]	NA	316,000	62,100	40,300	68,000
2006	504,000	259,000	42,300	W	[4]	203,000	315,000	69,100	73,900	75,400
2007	484,000	304,000	39,700	W	[4]	141,000	242,000	80,700	92,700	69,000
2008	433,000	262,000	107,000	23,200	[4]	40,600	195,000	60,400	75,800	102,000
2009	306,000	226,000	45,500	17,900	[4]	17,200	170,000	46,600	55,000	34,600
2010	475,000	369,000	45,800	35,000	[4]	25,100	205,000	91,900	121,684	56,500
2011[1]	604,000	496,000	40,400	40,400	[4]	27,600	177,000	111,000	237,233	78,000
2012[2]	806,000	685,000	49,700	44,700	[4]	26,500	255,000	138,000	357,455	55,300

[1] Preliminary.   [2] Estimated.   [3] Die casters.   [4] Included in other.   W = Withheld.   NA = Not applicable.   *Source: U.S. Geological Survey (USGS)*

United States Foreign Trade of Zinc   In Metric Tons

Year	Imports for Consumption Ores[3]	Blocks, Pigs, Slabs	Sheets, Plates, Other	Waste & Scrap	Dross, Ashes, Fume	Dust, Powder & Flakes	Total Value $1,000	Zinc Ore & Manufactures Exported Blocks, Pigs, Anodes, etc. Unwrought	Wrought & Alloys Unwrought Alloys	Sheets, Plates & Strips	Angles, Bars, Rods, etc.	Waste & Scrap	Dust (Blue Powder)	Zinc Ore & Concentrates
2004	231,000	868,000	2,500	10,800	16,100	24,800	1,142,733	----	----	----	----	53,900	7,640	745,000
2005	156,000	700,000	3,630	9,580	15,800	23,400	1,198,040	----	----	----	----	56,000	9,310	786,000
2006	383,000	895,000	2,050	14,200	31,100	30,100	2,771,580	2,530	19,900	3,780	11,200	83,800	16,400	825,000
2007	271,000	758,000	2,160	21,800	18,600	31,300	3,090,910	8,070	22,500	4,310	26,700	102,000	19,400	816,000
2008	63,200	725,000	3,330	17,000	13,200	28,500	1,919,030	3,250	8,550	4,970	28,100	91,000	13,000	725,000
2009	74,200	686,000	3,010	9,100	8,610	20,400	1,336,134	2,960	6,280	6,160	16,600	47,100	12,100	785,000
2010	32,200	671,000	3,440	15,600	17,900	31,600	1,846,320	4,200	11,400	7,380	27,800	77,900	14,900	752,000
2011	26,700	716,000	3,650	18,500	14,400	30,100	2,023,910	19,000	13,500	8,730	25,700	85,600	15,600	660,000
2012[1]	6,140	655,000	2,920	20,000	23,200	28,200	1,684,190	14,100	17,900	6,040	17,700	90,500	14,200	592,000
2013[2]	2,550	713,000						11,500	23,200	6,500	8,580	87,500	10,700	670,000

[1] Preliminary.   [2] Estimate.   [3] Zinc content.   *Source: U.S. Geological Survey (USGS)*

Mine Production of Recoverable Zinc in the United States   In Thousands of Metric Tons

Year	Jan.	Feb.	Mar.	Apr.	May	June	July	Aug.	Sept.	Oct.	Nov.	Dec.	Total
2005	53.6	56.0	64.1	56.7	53.3	64.6	64.5	68.9	61.8	64.4	51.2	62.3	721.4
2006	58.1	51.4	61.5	54.2	54.3	59.8	64.7	62.3	65.8	66.3	51.5	47.4	697.3
2007	60.3	55.8	63.5	56.6	61.2	64.1	63.1	69.5	61.3	64.6	53.9	69.6	743.5
2008	72.4	67.3	72.1	65.6	67.8	72.5	72.4	61.6	58.7	52.2	52.8	64.7	780.1
2009	69.3	54.0	55.2	58.4	56.1	58.6	57.0	62.1	60.5	65.2	49.9	62.1	708.4
2010	59.4	56.5	63.5	61.6	62.6	57.4	64.8	60.3	60.0	66.0	50.0	63.2	725.3
2011	69.5	54.9	62.1	59.3	66.2	57.9	70.0	63.6	60.0	55.4	58.5	67.8	745.2
2012	58.0	57.5	58.4	60.4	60.2	54.7	58.4	56.8	60.2	55.8	65.1	68.2	713.7
2013	64.1	54.5	56.0	63.2	65.8	61.3	61.7	67.2	66.7	68.0	68.8	68.7	766.0
2014[1]	67.9	67.8	70.6	69.5	63.3	61.2	64.6	65.6	66.4	63.2	71.3		797.9

[1] Preliminary.   *Source: U.S. Geological Survey (USGS)*

ZINC

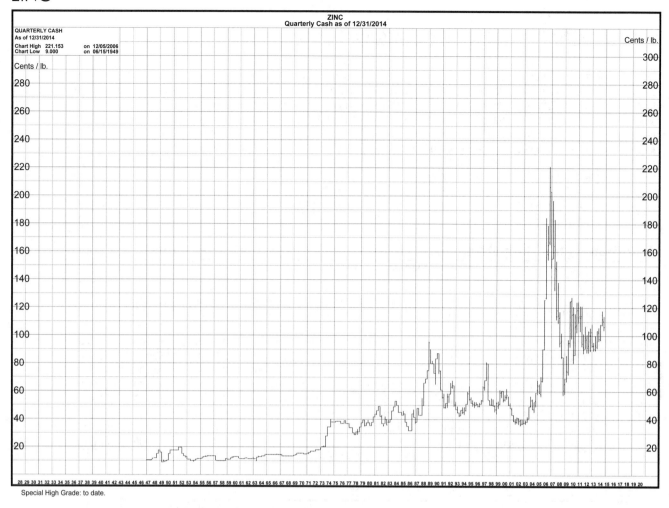

ZINC
Quarterly Cash as of 12/31/2014

QUARTERLY CASH
As of 12/31/2014

Chart High 221.153 on 12/05/2006
Chart Low 9.000 on 06/15/1949

Special High Grade: to date.

Average Price of Zinc, Prime Western Slab (Delivered U.S. Basis)   In Cents Per Pound

Year	Jan.	Feb.	Mar.	Apr.	May	June	July	Aug.	Sept.	Oct.	Nov.	Dec.	Average
2005	61.10	64.57	66.59	63.55	60.70	61.97	58.26	62.76	67.73	72.10	77.60	87.45	67.03
2006	100.02	106.57	116.10	147.28	170.57	158.11	163.89	164.23	166.56	185.80	210.32	211.82	158.44
2007	183.91	161.21	158.81	171.08	184.68	173.23	169.81	155.93	139.28	140.84	122.63	112.65	156.17
2008	111.49	115.37	117.27	107.07	102.59	89.16	87.44	81.53	81.83	62.25	55.26	53.22	88.71
2009	57.28	53.96	57.96	65.19	69.91	73.34	74.38	85.30	88.25	97.11	102.32	109.97	77.91
2010	113.30	100.72	106.15	110.33	93.02	83.34	88.25	97.11	102.16	112.55	109.67	108.04	102.05
2011	112.47	116.61	111.76	112.83	104.86	108.12	115.41	107.26	101.03	91.28	94.18	94.73	105.88
2012	97.62	101.31	99.99	98.01	95.19	91.62	91.32	89.77	98.67	94.43	94.32	100.33	96.05
2013	100.21	104.53	95.62	92.04	91.25	91.88	92.18	95.47	93.11	93.86	93.40	98.17	95.14
2014	101.35	101.41	100.58	101.54	102.75	105.78	113.91	114.56	112.82	112.02	111.17	107.09	107.08

Source: American Metal Market (AMM)

Consumption of Slab Zinc by Fabricators in the United States   In Thousands of Metric Tons

Year	Jan.	Feb.	Mar.	Apr.	May	June	July	Aug.	Sept.	Oct.	Nov.	Dec.	Total
2005	33.6	33.9	34.1	33.5	33.8	34.1	31.3	33.7	34.8	34.7	33.8	34.1	405.4
2006	34.8	34.5	34.8	34.0	33.1	34.2	32.4	33.4	31.4	32.8	32.0	32.4	399.8
2007	33.0	23.1	22.3	23.1	22.7	23.5	22.3	22.7	23.2	23.4	23.4	17.4	280.1
2008	19.7	19.8	21.0	18.6	24.8	23.3	21.5	21.5	22.1	20.2	19.5	19.4	251.4
2009	18.8	20.5	17.4	16.5	17.3	17.3	17.8	20.2	21.0	20.3	18.6	20.4	226.1
2010	19.7	19.1	20.4	20.8	18.3	18.8	19.1	18.3	16.4	14.9	14.0	13.1	212.9
2011	20.5	20.0	22.0	20.9	22.7	21.3	25.3	26.3	25.8	25.8	25.8	24.6	281.0
2012	35.6	35.5	37.5	36.2	38.3	37.5	37.2	37.0	36.7	37.3	36.7	35.6	441.1
2013	NA	NA	NA	NA	NA	NA	NA	NA	NA	NA	68.5	80.7	934.0
2014[1]	106.0	62.4	69.2	86.7	116.0	69.3	70.6	92.3	72.2	62.4	79.1		966.8

[1] Preliminary.   *Source: U.S. Geological Survey (USGS)*